COMPARATIVE CRIMINOLOGY

COMPARATIVE CRIMINOLOGY

by

HERMANN MANNHEIM

88379

HV6025
.M27c

HOUGHTON MIFFLIN COMPANY: BOSTON

NEW YORK – ATLANTA – GENEVA, ILL.

DALLAS – PALO ALTO

First published 1965

Reprinted 1967

© Hermann Mannheim 1965

Printed in Great Britain

To

Contents

CONTENTS

PART FOUR: THE SOCIOLOGY OF CRIME

Preface

It happened perhaps eleven years ago, not long before my retirement from the teaching of criminology in the University of London. One day, after I had just completed my first lecture of the new session and distributed copies of my, notoriously rather lengthy, reading list for the course, I was approached by a young girl student who, holding her copy in her hand, said in a voice which sounded polite but also rather determined: 'Sir, I am quite willing to read a book on criminology, but it must be only one, in which I can find everything required. Can you recommend such a book?' After some hesitation and with a strong feeling of guilt I replied that I could not comply with her request as there was no such book and she would probably have to read several of the items on my list, whereupon she silently and rather despondently withdrew.

As a university teacher of many years of experience in this field I could of course only too well understand that young people, confronted with ever-growing masses of material on a steadily multiplying number of subjects, were longing for a single, straightforward criminological Bible which could be trusted to relieve them of the need for an unending search in the darker corners of their university libraries. Some of these young beginners may not find it easy to grasp the plain truth that this endless search is a vital part of their academic education and they are inclined to hope for the coming of a 'textbook to end all other books'.

In the present book I have made no attempt to yield to such demands of that little student and others like her. I know that any such undertaking would be bound to fail. In fact, as the reader will see at once, in spite of its considerable length this book deals only with criminology in the narrower sense of the term, i.e., omitting penology. My original agreement with the publishers envisaged the writing of two textbooks, each of medium size, one on criminology and the other on penology, but in the course of my work I came to the conclusion that the real need now was for books which would deal far more fully with these subjects than could be done in two volumes of moderate size. Most American texts used in Britain and many other parts of the globe try to cope in one large volume with both subjects

ix

and, usually, in addition with the administration of criminal justice and the police. On a smaller scale and with the omission of these last-mentioned topics this has also been successfully done by my friend and former student Dr. Howard Jones in his *Crime and the Penal System*. In the circumstances, after a lengthy period of hesitation and heartsearching, I decided that instead of trying to copy what had already been well done in this field I should go my own way, i.e., set out to write a textbook on criminology only which would differ from its American and other predecessors in the following ways.

First, it would deal more fully than usual with such fundamental matters as the very concepts of crime and criminology and especially with the highly complex relationship between crime, the criminal law and certain burning moral issues of our time. This I have tried to do in Part One, especially in Chapter 2 of the first volume, which will, I expect, give rise to some controversy.

Secondly, this book would have several chapters on the methods of research used in criminological and penological investigations; chapters which, instead of the brief and scattered observations so far found in textbooks, would present a detailed and coherent picture of the various methods of approach, seen of course from the point of view of the statistical layman. I am fully aware of the many weaknesses and the rather elementary nature of this undertaking, which has been attempted with some diffidence mainly to fill an undeniable gap and *'pour encourager les autres'*. In addition to Part Two (Chapters 3 to 10), which deals exclusively with 'Research and Methodology', more space than customary has been given in several subsequent chapters to critical summaries of important researches carried out in various countries.

Thirdly, while in view of the dominant position held at present by American criminology much of the material presented in some of the sociological chapters of Part Four had to be taken from American sources, this does not apply to the book as a whole. It is the almost exclusive reliance on 'indigenous' material with only very few, not always systematic and well-balanced, glimpses at British and Continental European publications that diminishes the value of American textbooks to non-American readers. As the present writer has repeatedly stressed, especially in his *Group Problems in Crime and Punishment* (Part Three) and his Preface to *Pioneers in Criminology*, our indebtedness to American criminology is immense and lasting, but non-American countries possess not only their own crime problems but also their own criminological literature. No doubt, some of these problems can be brought considerably nearer to a solution or at least to a better understanding with the aid of American theories and experience. Others, however, have to be interpreted more independently and without a wholesale take-over of American ideas. Therefore, a special effort has been made in the present book to use not only British but also Continental criminological literature, especially German and to a smaller extent French and Italian, and occasionally also material neither European nor American. Naturally, limitations of space, language, and of access to the sources often created insurmountable obstacles, and it was for such reasons that the author had to concentrate mainly on those countries with which he is particularly familiar, i.e., Britain and Germany. Moreover, criminological literature has grown so enormously after the last World War that it is clearly impossible nowadays to be fully conversant with more than that of a few countries. It is with such important reservations that the present book is offered as a moderate contribution to international and comparative criminology and as an attempt to bridge some of the gaps between the various ways of approach. I realize that I may not have been very successful in this, but I regard the matter as important enough to justify the choice of the title. Many of us have been rightly impressed by Professor Sheldon Glueck's clarion call at the Hague Congress of 1960 for a 'Comparative Criminology' (now reproduced in *Ventures in Criminology*, Chapter 18). What he had in mind was something more ambitious and comprehensive than the comparative survey here carried out by one single worker: he understood by it the replication of researches 'designed to uncover etiologic *universals* operative as causal agents irrespective of cultural differences among the different countries'. In Professor Glueck's lecture several problems are mentioned as particularly suitable for, and in need of, a comparative approach by means of replication studies, e.g., the age curve of crime, the effect of growing industrialization and mobility, the somatotype study of young delinquents, and others. In the present book an attempt has been made to present some of the comparative material produced by research workers in various countries on a number of such topics, but so far usually without the co-ordinated teamwork and integration of research techniques which Sheldon Glueck had in mind and which is now slowly emerging from the work of the Gluecks, from that of Marshall B. Clinard, from the joint efforts of Marvin E. Wolfgang and Franco Ferracuti, and others. We non-Americans are likely to benefit from these efforts and we should clearly understand that, and why, our attitudes towards American criminology are—perhaps inevitably—ambivalent, i.e., a mixture of admiration, envy, inferiority feelings, criticism, and the unconscious desire to convince ourselves that, given the same opportunities, we could do just as well or possibly even better than our American colleagues. In 1963, the Assistant Director of the National Research and Information Center on Crime and Delinquency in New York, on his return from a study tour to a large number of European countries, reported how often he had been told in the course of his visits that American research workers were regarded as particularly fortunate, having at their disposal such lavish financial and other facilities for their work. While the comparative scarcity of research funds outside the U.S.A. may easily create a justifiable feeling of frustration, it is not the only source of that 'overly pessimistic attitude' encountered by this American observer. After all, any comparison of existing facilities for criminological research has to take into consideration the vastness of the American scene, the number and size of their universities and research organizations, the intensity and practical urgency of their crime problem, and their belief that they have a certain moral responsibility towards other countries, underdeveloped or not, to supply them with useful information. Perhaps equally important as the greater financial support and encouragement enjoyed by American research workers, though probably its natural consequence, is the more systematic nature of their research habits, which has no real counterpart in other countries. Once a plausible hypothesis has been put forward by responsible research workers in U.S.A. it is a matter of course that it should be tested and re-tested and the results be widely and critically discussed and wherever possible applied and applied again to the relevant practical problems. One has only to consider the systematic way in which prediction researches have been followed up in the United States as compared with similar investigations elsewhere. One of the few examples of cross-cultural re-testing of a criminological hypothesis outside the U.S.A. is the recent work on 'delinquent generations'. Now it is perfectly true that some of those carefully nursed problems and hypotheses of recent American criminological research may have hardly been worth the trouble taken with them, but even here one should not ignore the simple fact that the solution of the larger, more important and worthwhile problems can often be achieved, if at all, only by a piecemeal splitting up into smaller and smaller sub-problems. While, therefore, the sub- or sub-sub-problems in hand tend to appear less and less significant and the reports on the research done on them may become duller and duller, they may eventually constitute the basic material on which the structure of a new theory of real value to the progress of criminology can be erected.

In accordance with the existing 'distribution of powers' in our field most American textbooks on criminology, with a few important exceptions, have been written by sociologists, whereas elsewhere they have more often been the work of lawyers. The present writer has occasionally described himself as a cross between a lawyer and a 'sociological criminologist'; he is not a trained psychologist, psychiatrist, biologist, or statistician. From these limitations it follows that in the chapters of this book dealing with the last-mentioned subjects he has had to rely more than otherwise on the work of specialists in those disciplines. While this is a serious drawback, it is one which is shared by practically all other criminological writings. The criminologist who would be equally competent in every sector of his discipline does not yet exist, and most probably he will never exist. Perhaps the future will belong to teams of authors with different backgrounds of training, although this too may have its dangers.

Another problem exists for every writer of a textbook on criminology, whatever may be his credentials, i.e., how much space to give to certain legal aspects which have a close bearing on the subject. Many students of criminology, in Anglo-American countries even the majority, possess no legal training and cannot be expected to devote much time to matters of criminal law and procedure. On the other hand, there are certain criminological issues which cannot be properly treated without at least a modicum of knowledge of the corresponding legal aspects. This applies, for example, to the subject of mental abnormality, the legal implications of which have therefore been briefly discussed in a special Chapter 18; to the various forms of association in crime, where the legal side has at least been touched in Chapter 25. Moreover, as already indicated above, the relationships between the legal and the criminological concepts of crime and between the legal and the moral approach to criminological problems have been dealt with in Part One.

Our treatment of juvenile, including adolescent, delinquency, too, differs from that in most other textbooks, While the great significance of this subject is beyond doubt, the wisdom of separating it from that of adult crime by allocating it to a special section is less certain. The various criminological aspects involved are so closely related to those of their counterparts concerning adult crime that it is thought to be in the interest of the reader to treat both as far as possible together.

When deciding to concentrate in this book on criminology to the exclusion of penology two considerations have been in the mind of the author. First, criminology is not only the logical (though not historical) *prius*, it also provides the essential foundations without which the whole structure of penology would be left floating in mid-air. While this does not mean that each and every step in the field of penal reform should have to wait until all the mysteries of causation have been solved by criminological studies it does mean that the basic features of a future penal system cannot be sensibly mapped out before agreement has been reached on the nature of the fundamental criminogenic factors in our society, and the responsibility for them has been clearly established. To many this will seem postponing action until doomsday, but no action may occasionally be better than ill-conceived improvisation. This applies to legislation as well as to administration. Doctors have, of course, often to treat patients without being able to make a proper diagnosis of their illness, but this is nothing but a makeshift imposed upon the medical profession by sheer necessity and should not become the rule. While the legislator and the practical penologist may find themselves in the role of the medical practitioner more frequently than they would wish to, their theoretical advisers should leave nothing undone to supply them with the essential tools. Here again, however, a word of caution does not seem to be out of place, especially in view of what has been said before on the more fortunate position of American research workers. Nobody who has followed the development of criminology, as the present writer has, for the past fifty years or so can deny that its progress has been spectacular. In particular after the last World War publications, research projects, journals, societies, institutes, as shown in the Appendix, have greatly multiplied almost everywhere. International, regional, and national congresses and conferences abound. To a considerable extent, Britain has participated in all these developments, although compared with the expansion of similar disciplines criminology here, as in some other countries, has still remained under a cloud and is still regarded as a pseudo-science even by many of those who should know better. In the circumstances it is not surprising that criminology has had its regrettable share in the exodus of scholars of first-rate ability. However, the material side of scientific work, though of great importance, is not everything. More and higher grants for research, more Institutes, more senior posts are no doubt highly desirable for the future development of criminology, but they alone cannot be expected to solve all existing difficulties. Not long ago an English cancer expert issued a warning that in his field 'merely extending existing facilities without rethinking their aim' was likely 'to prove a great waste of money and a big disappointment' (Professor D. W. Smithers, *The Times*, 24.11.1964). The position is not likely to be different in the field of criminology. Here, too, research, in order to be useful, has not only to tackle the really crucial problems, but it has to do so in a spirit of resolution and realism. 'Parkinson's law' is lurking in *every* corner of the vast structure of scientific endeavour.

As to my second consideration, penology, it has been argued not entirely without reason, is so much in a state of flux at present, and there is so much uncertainty about the value of each of the existing methods of treatment, that the time is not yet ripe for an authoritative textbook which could provide the much-needed guidance to the practitioner. Nevertheless, just as the British Government has recently decided that the time is ripe for a 'fundamental review of the whole penal system' this may also be the moment for a comprehensive scholarly survey of the state of our knowledge on penal methods in Britain and abroad. It is my hope that a team of younger research workers may take up the torch and provide such a survey.

Every textbook writer can be expected to make it clear at once for whom his work is intended. In the present case I have in mind readers of widely differing qualifications and expectations. There is in the first place of course the serious research student wishing to familiarize himself with the existing literature and the principal methods of criminological research. I am addressing myself also, however, to the beginner who, bearing in mind what has been written earlier on in this Preface, is willing to devote more than the barest minimum of time and effort to the study of criminology. He may not wish to make full use of the documentation supplied in the Notes, but may prefer his own selection for which the Selected Reading Lists at the end of each volume will, I hope, be of some assistance, and he may also wish to skip the material printed in smaller type.

This book has, however, not been written only for university students and similar categories of predominantly academic users. The need for more than merely superficial information on a branch of knowledge struggling with problems of ever growing seriousness to the whole of modern society will be obvious to many members of legislative bodies, to judges, magistrates, lawyers, psychiatrists and psychologists engaged in work with criminals and juvenile delinquents, to penal administrators, probation officers and other social workers.

A few readers may object to the abundance of Notes, references and cross-references, and also perhaps to occasional repetitions. They should bear in mind that this is intended to be a textbook and a work of reference, and that it is often useful or indeed even essential to be reminded that the same problems may have to be treated from more than one angle. It should also be realized that the structure of the present book, containing as it does a separate methodological Part followed by the Sections dealing with the various 'Factors and Causes' necessitated a certain amount of repetition and cross-references. Moreover, it has been the wish of the author, as far as humanly possible, instead of trying to impose his personal views on the reader, rather to show how far these views were in agreement with those prevailing in the literature. All this requires much space.

I am most grateful to the publishers for having, ungrudgingly, given me all the space required for the purpose, and I wish to express my sincere thanks to them, especially to Mr. Norman Franklin who has been in charge of this publication, for their extraordinary patience and unfailing courtesy. The members of their staff who had to deal with my book have been most helpful, too.

Furthermore, I wish to acknowledge my indebtness to the librarian and staff of the British Library of Political and Economic Science in London, whose willing co-operation has made my task much easier, and to many friends and colleagues who, while watching the all-too-slow progress of my work, have through their interest and encouragement helped me to persist.

To University Secretarial Services and Research Publishers Limited, I am indebted for their valuable typing assistance.

Finally, my wife has, here as with all my previous books, given me her invaluable help and advice during the many years of preparing and writing this book.

HERMANN MANNHEIM

London, Spring 1965.

PART ONE
Introductory

Chapter 1

THE NATURE, SCOPE AND OBJECTS OF CRIMINOLOGY

By tradition, textbook writers are required first of all to define their subjects, but if they follow this tradition they are criticized for ignoring the fact that meaningful definitions cannot be produced without the knowledge which the textbook is expected to supply. In a way, such criticism is justified—our initial definition of 'Criminology', for example, will have to include words such as 'crime' and perhaps also 'punishment' whose real meaning can unfold itself only in the light of the material presented in later sections. It is generally agreed, however, that even with such limitations a preliminary working definition is indispensable as a provisional basis for further discussion.

I. NATURE AND OBJECTS OF CRIMINOLOGY

Criminology, in the narrower sense in which it is used in this book, means the study of crime. In its wider sense it also includes penology, the study of punishment and of similar methods of dealing with crime, and of the problem of preventing crime by non-punitive measures. Provisionally, we can define crime in legal terms as human behaviour which is punishable by the criminal law. The study of such behaviour can assume three basic forms:

1. *The Descriptive Approach*

It can be purely descriptive. Criminology in this sense means the observation and collection of facts about crime and criminals: the various forms of criminal behaviour; how crimes are committed; their frequency in different places and at different times; age, sex and many other characteristics of criminals; and the evolution of a criminal career. This might be called the *phenomenology* or *symptomatology* of crime.

'Description' should, however, not be taken in the narrow sense of

3

the word. Moreover, while it is essential as the first step, while it can furnish indispensable material and build the foundations for further enquiries, it should not remain the *only* object of criminological study. First of all, as will be pointed out in our later sections on methodology, 'facts' cannot be collected at random; they have to be selected on the basis of a scientific hypothesis or of a whole system of hypotheses.[1] The research worker, just as the judge who has to decide a case, finds himself surrounded by myriads of 'facts'. In order to make a reasonable and useful selection of the facts they wish to collect they have to define their objects. For the judge this is done by the formal indictment (the French *acte d'accusation*, the German *Anklageschrift*); for the research worker its place is taken by the hypothesis. Neither the judge nor the research worker can adopt the technique of a small schoolboy who spends a few hours trying to catch 'butterflies' at random. 'Science cannot start with observations, or with the "collection of data", as some students believe. Before we can collect data, our interest in *data of a certain kind* must be aroused; the *problem* always comes first', writes Popper.[2]

Secondly, 'facts' have no meaning without interpretation, evaluation and general understanding, and we may need a considerable knowledge of life in general and experience of certain specific sectors of life to arrive at a correct interpretation of the facts collected by observation. To the man from the moon who knows nothing about the institution of Parliament, or the structure of an orchestra, even the most careful observation of the happenings at a parliamentary session or a concert will convey not the slightest understanding of the real meaning of what is going on there. The fact that two people embrace and kiss each other, or that one of them puts a chain around the other's neck, may mean many different things, and the correct interpretation requires an intimate knowledge of the mores and traditions of a whole civilization.[3] This is what is meant by *verstehen* as opposed to a mere *beschreiben* or even *erklären* in German psychology and sociology. The general significance of this contrast has been explained mainly by Wilhelm Dilthey[4] and Max Weber,[5] and its specific meaning for criminology has been recognized by Franz Exner.[6] Whether it is the assassination of Julius Caesar or the outrages committed by Mau Mau or Eoka, or a complicated business fraud, the criminologist's task is not only to describe and, if possible, to give a reasoned explanation, but also to 'understand'. What such a wider interpretation of the descriptive function of criminology involves will be shown more fully below, especially in Part II.

2. *The Causal Approach*

(*a*) The approach can also be of a causal nature, i.e. the interpretation of the observed facts can be used to search for the causes of crime, either in general or in individual cases. Having observed, for example, that murder means very often the killing of women by men, or that in an individual case it meant poisoning of a husband by his wife, we wish to discover the causes of these phenomena. This aspect is called the etiology of crime. Whereas in former times it was regarded as the most important function of criminology, the role of causal research has recently become a more controversial issue. 'One can continue to write about "Causation and its place in modern Society" indefinitely, if one fails to notice how rarely the word "cause" appears in the writings of professional scientists', says Stephen Toulmin.[7] And Leslie Wilkins, who is altogether highly critical of the causal approach, writes: '. . . simple models of "cause" and "effect" will not be adequate to explain social phenomena' (p. 133 of his *Social Deviance* referred to below in Chapter 3, Note 2).

Causal research in criminology has, of course, functions different from the criminal lawyer's search for the causal connection between the behaviour of an individual and a specific crime. To obtain a conviction it must be proved that there was a causal nexus between an act (or in certain circumstances, an omission) of the accused and the prohibited result. Needless to say that more than such causal nexus, i.e. in particular *mens rea*, guilt, is usually required to establish criminal responsibility, and as, thanks to this requirement of guilt, unreasonable results can usually be avoided, the criminal law can safely use a very broad conception of causal nexus.[8] It is only in cases of so-called strict responsibility, where no guilt, or only a diluted form of guilt, is required, that the need for a narrower interpretation of 'causal nexus' may arise which tries to distinguish between different kinds of causes (see in particular the theory of 'adequate cause' in German literature).[9]

What interests us here is that whereas the criminal law, in order to establish the criminal responsibility of individuals (or in exceptional cases of a corporation), is concerned with the causal link between the forbidden act (or omission) and the result, the work of the criminologist begins at a later stage, i.e. when that causal link has already been established. For him, the question is not 'Has A committed this crime?' but '*Why* has he committed this crime?' or 'Why do persons of this kind commit crime in general or crimes of this kind?' The answers to such questions may be of considerable practical importance to the criminal court at the sentencing stage, but they will hardly affect the first stage of its work, which is concerned with criminal responsibility. In spite of this difference, certain basic problems of causality are, however, common to both criminal law and criminology, in particular that of how to define 'cause' itself.[10] Criminologists have, not without reason, been chided for employing an unscientific conception of causation,[11] and it is certainly true that more attention has been paid to the matter by criminal lawyers, especially on the Continent, than by criminologists.[12]

(b) What do we mean by 'cause'? Can criminologists, can social scientists in general borrow the concept of cause used by the natural sciences? Although still widely discussed by philosophers and the social sciences, this concept is, according to Bertrand Russell,[13] 'apparently not used in any advanced science', by which he means the natural sciences. One of the reasons may be that 'most empiricists have held that "cause" means nothing but "invariable antecedent" ' whereas 'for most philosophers "cause" means something different'. As Russell admits, 'invariable antecedents' are extremely rare, as something may always intervene to prevent the expected result, and it is this possibility that has led physics 'to state its laws in the form of differential equations, which may be regarded as stating what is tending to happen'.[14] There is, however, by no means unanimity even among modern physicists as to the role of causal laws in the natural sciences. While for Max Planck the law of causality was still 'a fundamental hypothesis', to many of his younger colleagues the dependence of statistical laws upon causal laws is no longer an unchallengeable truth, and a statistical law is not necessarily regarded as 'the sign that there is a causal law that has not yet been discovered'.[15]

Popper stresses the difference between the causal explanation of an 'individual or singular specific event' and that of some regularity or law,[16] adding that in the first case causal explanation requires some universal laws, well tested and corroborated, plus the 'specific initial conditions' usually called the 'cause'. In this he follows John Stuart Mill, making it clear, however, that the latter understands by 'cause' both universal laws and singular events. Popper further stresses that while the theoretical sciences (natural or social) are mainly concerned with the discovery and testing of universal laws, the historical sciences are mainly interested in singular events, in 'how and why' questions. Sociology and criminology are interested in both the universal laws and singular events, in other words, they are both nomothetic and idiographic disciplines.[17]

John Stuart Mill distinguishes sufficient and necessary causes. If B invariably follows A whatever else may or may not happen, A would be called a sufficient, but not always a necessary, cause.[18] If, however, B follows A only if A and certain other factors are present, then A is a necessary, but not a sufficient cause. If B invariably follows A without any other factors being required, and A cannot be replaced by any other alternative, then A is both a sufficient and a necessary cause. As pointed out above, the criminal law usually employs the widest possible conception, which is that of the necessary, but not sufficient cause, i.e. 'a man can be said to have caused the *actus reus* of a crime if that *actus* would not have occurred without his participation',[19] although many other factors were also necessary to produce the result. As far as the interpretation of individual cases is concerned, the same conception can be used in criminology, and here it can be done without any of the risks of injustice referred to above. A kills B with a knife, when he meets him in a pub. According to the judgment of the court, this would not have happened but for the presence of the following factors: (*a*) A was drunk; (*b*) he was a man of unstable and irritable temperament and low intelligence; (*c*) B was a Negro and a member of a rival gang; (*d*) A's attention was drawn to his presence by C; (*e*) D gave him a knife; (*f*) E locked the exit through which B was trying to escape, and (*g*) it was an exceptionally hot and sultry day. All or most of these, and many other known and unknown factors, may have been necessary causes; none of them in isolation was a sufficient cause. Obviously, the criminal court will be more or less interested in each of these seven factors to assess the guilt and responsibility of A, C, D and E. The criminologist will concentrate on the effect of alcohol on a person of A's temperament, and on the role played by alcohol, low intelligence and mental instability, gang rivalry, racial enmity and heat on such an individual. In their interpretation of A's actions, both the criminal court and the criminologist will be greatly dependent on the general body of scientific knowledge existing on these subjects. Indeed, the very selection of the five factors, drink, mental instability, gang rivalry, race conflict and heat, out of a multitude of possible explanations has very likely been the result of certain views about factors generally regarded as criminogenic. Every age has its preconceived ideas on the subject which determine at least the initial selection of criminogenic factors. If this kind of preliminary selection is done with an open mind and clearly recognized as merely a beginning, it can do little harm. Surrounded as we are by myriads of potential causes, we have to start somewhere in our unending search for causal explanations. The real danger arises when we are satisfied with our findings and abandon our search at too early a stage. It has occasionally been suggested that in the selection of causal factors criminal courts (and criminologists alike) have so far concentrated mainly on those phenomena which are regarded as capable of being altered more easily than others,[20] or those which are nearer to the prohibited effect, i.e. the crime, to the disadvantage of the more remote ones; and to simpler factors at the expense of more complicated ones. This has not always been so, and in particular under the influence of the anthropological-biological school the emphasis has been on more or less unalterable factors.[21]

(*c*) What are the consequences to be drawn by criminologists from these philosophical definitions and distinctions?

First of all, there is the very simple but fundamental insight that in criminology there are no causes of crime which are both sufficient and necessary. There are only factors which may be 'necessary' to produce crime in conjunction with other factors. Neither crime in general nor any specific crime can ever be due to one single factor which would invariably produce this result. This means a death blow to all one-factor theories of crime, such as Lombroso's, and leads straight to William Healy's and Cyril Burt's theory of the multiplicity of factors,[22] which might have become a commonplace by now had it not been for the determined opposition of Edwin H. Sutherland and his followers. It is interesting to note that the most influential pronouncement of the basic theories of the Sutherland school, his *Principles of Criminology*,[23] first appeared ten years after Healy's and one year before Burt's classic works. While a discussion of his theory of 'differential association' has to be left for a later stage (Chapter 23), it is here that his views on causation have to find their place. Thanks to the devoted work of some of his former colleagues and students they can now be more clearly seen in their historical evolution.[24]

Sutherland accepted the distinction of necessary and sufficient causes, but being dissatisfied with the multi-factor theory, this 'catalogue of disparate and unco-ordinated "causes"',[25] his ambition was to discover ' "the" sufficient and necessary cause'. He believed he had found it in differential association. No concrete condition, such as being a Negro or a male, can, he stated, be a cause of crime; rather should we try to abstract from the varying concrete conditions factors universally associated with it. The tests he applied to his own theory were very strict, 'the one thing being needed to disprove an hypothesis is a single exception'. Perhaps the best exposition of this rigid theory of causation in criminology has been given by Alfred R. Lindesmith, who rightly argues in its favour that it requires constant testing and reformulation, whereas the 'defeatist' multiple causation theory evades the real issue by admitting exceptions in advance.[26] It is true that the challenge of the Sutherland school has been a valuable stimulus to further thought, but the task which it has set itself has so far proved insoluble. As we can now read in a posthumously published paper, intended for private circulation only and originally entitled 'The Swan Song of Differential Association',[27] after twenty years of unremitting thought Sutherland himself seems to have become sincerely doubtful of the tenability of his single-factor theory. Other factors such as opportunities, intensity of need and available alternatives may, he indicates, play their part in the causation of crime in addition to differential association. This seems to mark the end, so far, of the search for a single cause, and the multiple factor approach, though only 'a makeshift to be tolerated' until something better has been found, now reigns supreme. Its eclectic nature is obvious. The longer the list of potentially causal factors which we have been able to collect in the course of our labours—whether it is Burt's 'more than 170 distinct conditions, every one conducive to childish misconduct',[28] or his 70 major factors, or his 'nine or ten subversive circumstances' operative in the case of each delinquent child, or whether it is Healy's more modest estimate of 3·5 factors per case—the picture seems to become less and less impressive with the growing thoroughness of our search. In the last resort, this was also the essence of Durkheim's criticism of Mill's theory which he regarded as 'a negation of the principle of causality'.[29] *Qui trop embrasse mal étreint*—is this true of the multiple theory of crime causation? Have we made much progress in our efforts first to isolate and then to combine the various causal factors? Perhaps the most conspicuous progress has been the negative one of excluding, by means of statistical techniques, a number of factors previously believed to have high causative value. The position is less satisfactory with regard to the positive side, i.e. obtaining scientifically more valuable evidence of the causative role of certain factors. We are here, at present, concerned not with the actual contents of such factors but with the current views on their causative nature. The customary technique—to be discussed more fully later on—is still to establish statistical correlations and then to assert that they prove cause and effect. It is this critical 'jump' from statistical correlation to causation which has been made hardly less hazardous through the research done in the course of this century. All we can claim is that we have perhaps become better aware of the existence and width of the gap. It would be presumptuous to assume that a master of research techniques such as Burt did not see the problem in all its ramifications when writing his *Young Delinquent*, but he gives at least the impression there that his statistical correlations are sufficient evidence of causal nexus. Writing fifteen years after Burt, McIver produced what is perhaps the clearest discussion of the processes which may gradually lead from mere correlation to the establishment of causal nexus,[30] but while leaving the details for later it should be stressed now that what these processes can achieve is merely to narrow, not to bridge, the gap. Correlations, as McIver says, are signposts, and as such of the greatest practical value,[31] but as far as causation is concerned we cannot argue that whatever the facts may be the signpost must be invariably right.

In *Unraveling Juvenile Delinquency* the Gluecks, consciously or not, have essentially followed McIver's prescriptions and, after throwing out factors showing no significant correlation, concentrate on those 'with probable causal significance'. While stressing that such correlations do not necessarily mean actual functional relationship, they nevertheless eventually produce their 'tentative causal formula or law of juvenile delinquency',[32] and one of these authors has in his otherwise masterly criticism of the theory of differential association only recently expressed his view that factors very frequently associated with delinquency make a 'very excessive' contribution to 'the causal scales'.[33] More cautious is the treatment in their *Physique and Delinquency*,[34] where the authors explain that they use terms such as 'causal' and 'criminogenic' not in the customary sense.

Perhaps the most obvious, but also the most important conclusion from the theory of multiple causation is the need to classify and bring some sort of meaningful order into the apparently chaotic lists of potentially causal factors found to bear a statistically significant correlation to crime. This can be done in a quantitative sense by classifying factors according to the degree of correlation, and, equally indispensable, in a qualitative sense by distinguishing primary and secondary or pre-disposing and precipitating factors and, finally, by attempting to combine various factors according to their nature. This recent search for a synthesis, for combinations, concatenations and permutations, is in fact the concession which the multiple causation theory has inevitably had to make to Sutherland and his followers, and it may eventually bridge the gap between the two extremes. Moreover, the more successful we are in our qualitative approach the more are we likely to 'understand'.[35] In passing, it may also be added that the controversy between the causal and the descriptive approach has, in recent years, become particularly acute in the field of prediction research (see below, Chapter 7).

In his recent book *Social Deviance* (see below, Chapter 3, Note 2) Wilkins has expressed the view that the theory of multiple causation 'can hardly be dignified by the term theory'; it 'does not facilitate the deduction of any hypotheses or practical consequences that are of any help whatsoever' (pp. 36–7). Rightly regarding it with Popper as an essential criterion of any theory that one should be able to disprove it he argues that the multiple causation theory cannot be proved wrong and is therefore no theory but 'at best an anti-theory which proposes that no theory can be formed regarding crime'. He further uses the argument that on the basis of the multiple causation theory crime preventing measures would have to be so all-embracing as to be

10

entirely impracticable (p. 126); moreover, it would be impossible to discover which of the many preventive measures put into operation had been effective (if any). The latter assertion is of course true if all, or several, of these measures would be put into operation at the same time; it is not correct, however, if one is tried out after the other. Moreover, Wilkins's assertion is not an argument against the scientific correctness of the multiple causation theory; it merely shows once more how utterly complicated and confusing the search for the causes of crime still is. Nor does Wilkins show why it should be theoretically impossible to prove that theory to be wrong; all one would have to do is to take one by one the alleged causal factors and prove that, with one exception, they are actually not causal factors, the only exception being of course the factor described by the differential association theory.—To sum up this part of our discussion: Why not admit, first, that the theory of multiple causation is a real theory, but not an ideal one, and that improvements—or if possible refutation—would be highly desirable, and, secondly, that differential association has to take its place side by side, not above, all other theories of criminological causation?

In conclusion, three final points should be made in this preliminary exploration of present-day views on crime causation:

First, as mentioned above, when building up our lists of factors statistically associated with crime and therefore potentially causative, we have to realize that our initial selection of factors for statistical analysis depends on our previous and almost inevitably preconceived notions about potentially causal factors.[36] This means that factors which do not fit into the picture painted by our personal bias will be more easily ignored and given less opportunity for further examination than those which appeal to us in view of our, perhaps unconscious, attitudes, our *Weltanschauung*. As Arnold Rose and others have pointed out, our personal value premises play an important, often even decisive, part in the very selection of our topics for research[37] (see below, Chapter 3).

Second, the question cannot be evaded of whether the time may not have come to discard the search for the causes of crime altogether and to replace the eclectic and to many scholars meaningless theory of multiple causation by some less ambitious but more practical formula such as statistical correlations, 'Decision theory',[38] 'Categoric risks'[39] and the like. In the present writer's view this step would be too radical. The search for causes has been an essential element of the work of social scientists for too long and still possesses an individual appeal too strong to dispense with it at a time when, except for certain limited practical purposes such as prediction techniques, those substitutes have not yet been adequately developed to fill the gap. 'The nature of a phenomenon'—wrote Durkheim sixty years ago[40]—'is much more profoundly got at by knowing its causes than by knowing its characteristics only, even the essential ones.' On the other hand, the practical penologist cannot be expected to wait with his preventive, predictive, protective and curative measures until the causes have been found,[41] just as medical practitioners may have to act before they are able properly to diagnose.[42] Moreover, we have to be aware not only of the difficulty of proving causal nexus but also of its limited practical value for treatment and prevention. An offence may have been due to certain specific and easily discoverable causes, but once it has been committed the latter may have spent their force, and the individual's future behaviour may be dominated by other factors (see below, Chapter 7). This is particularly likely in the case of juveniles whose personalities sometimes undergo rapid changes, and it may considerably affect the prognosis of recidivism.

Third, and arising from this, if statistics cannot prove causal relation, can this be done by the other extreme, the fullest possible individual case study? Or can we perhaps expect 'summit talks' between these two parties to lift the iron curtain still separating causation from correlation? The answer has to wait for the discussion of the various research techniques in Part II.

3. *The Normative Approach*

It has already been said elsewhere (*Group Problems*, pp. 261–4) that criminology is both an 'idiographic' discipline studying facts, causes and probabilities in individual cases and a 'nomothetic' discipline aiming at the discovery of universally valid scientific laws and uniformities or trends. The second part of this statement leads, naturally, to an examination of the nature of criminological 'laws' and trends. What is the difference between such 'laws' and mere trends, and between them and 'legal' or 'juridical' laws? Is criminology, in the same sense as jurisprudence, a 'normative' science? Or are we mistaken in assuming that legal laws are 'normative'? Closer scrutiny of the literature shows that not too much should be taken for granted in this field. On the one hand, with regard to the nature of juridical laws, the traditional view that such laws, in particular criminal law, are commands, rules, norms, imperatives, ordering the citizen to act or not to act in a certain way,[43] has been assailed from various quarters in the course of the present century. First, a distinction has often been made between a legal provision such as 'whoever steals will be punished', which, it has been argued, is nothing but a statement of fact, and the 'norm' behind it forbidding such an act (Binding's so-called *Normentheorie*). Secondly, even as far as the legal norm itself is concerned its

12

normative character has often been disputed. Emphasis has been placed upon the 'law shaping force of custom and habit' and the 'normative power of the factual' (Georg Jellinek's *Normative Kraft des Faktischen*),[44] i.e. what has been done over a long period of time will eventually be regarded as lawful. Moreover, important schools of legal philosophy, especially in the United States, such as the positivist and pragmatic schools, and the 'realist' movement, interpret law not as a body of norms but merely as a body of generalized predictions of what the courts will actually do in individual cases brought before them, which makes legal laws less different from the laws of the natural sciences than generally assumed.[45] Our criticism of this view is in brief that, while the function of law as a predictive instrument is of great practical importance, it is in no way incompatible with its equally important normative functions.

On the other hand, the difference between criminological laws, should they actually exist, and the laws of the natural, social and legal sciences is also in need of discussion. If, in opposition to the 'realist' view of law, we believe in the normative character of legal provisions, the contrast between the latter and any other kind of 'law' may seem to be clear. Criminology is not a normative, but a factual discipline. However, as the normative character of juridical laws has been questioned so has the non-normative character of criminology been doubted by other writers. H. Bianchi in particular has recently asserted that, since crime is a normative concept, this 'forces criminology to make a study of norms'[46] and it is therefore a normative discipline. This, however, seems to betray a confusion between the study of norms, which is in itself not normative, and the creation, establishment and use of norms, which characterize a normative discipline. It is a matter of opinion and terminology whether the scope of criminology should be widened so as to include *Kriminalpolitik*, *politique criminelle*, i.e. the questions of what *ought* to be done to reform the criminal law and the penal system. As the writer has already argued elsewhere[47] it is preferable to treat this as a separate discipline based upon the factual findings of the criminologist and penologist, whereas criminology should remain a non-policy-making discipline, 'piecemeal social engineering' which regards the 'ends' as beyond its province. This does, of course, not prevent the criminologist from advocating a certain measure of legal and administrative penal reform, but he has to do it as a politician or an ordinary citizen and voter rather than in his capacity of criminologist (see also below, Chapter 3, p. 78).

Having defined criminology as a factual, non-normative discipline we now have to examine the existence and nature of criminological 'laws'. Obviously, the position must be essentially the same here as in sociology or psychology. As we have already seen, most of these so-called criminological laws are attempts to formulate either a casual nexus or at least a statistical association between certain factors and crime. Take, for example, Adolphe Quetelet's 'thermic law of delinquency', according to which crimes against the person are more frequent in warm climates and seasons, whereas crimes against property are more prevalent in cold climates and in winter, or Prince Peter Kropotkin's even more ambitious formula using temperature and humidity to predict the exact number of future homicides in a given country,[48] or if we use Popper's way of formulating natural as well as sociological laws,[49] for example, 'You cannot have wars without an aftermath of crime'. It will be clear that Quetelet's thermic law is nothing but the precise formula asserting a high positive correlation between heat and crime against the person and, on the other hand, between a cold temperature and crime against property. In Chapter 11, an attempt will be made to interpret these correlations and to assess their significance, but they are not 'laws', but merely trends which could be manipulated and changed through a suitable administrative machinery.[50] If, for example, the police force were greatly strengthened and unemployment benefits and similar measures increased during the winter months, crime against property might easily become lower than in summer. It may be more difficult to devise effective crime-preventing counter-measures against the criminogenic after-effects of wars, unless we assume that future atomic wars will do their work so thoroughly that nobody will be left to commit crimes. As the whole of our discussion in the present book will show, criminology is not yet able to produce real 'laws'.

II. THE SCOPE OF CRIMINOLOGY

Should criminology, as suggested by Vouin-Léauté,[51] also include the study of the reaction of society against crime? It might be argued that this belongs, strictly speaking, to the domain of the sociology of the criminal law, but it has to be admitted that the reaction of society against crime is at least as important as the reaction of the state which is the subject-matter of penology. They are both strongly criminogenic forces and should therefore be studied by criminologists.

Even more controversial is the question whether criminology should confine itself to the study of crime in the legal sense or whether it should also cover anti-social behaviour which is legally not treated as a crime. The principal exponent of the broader view is Thorsten Sellin,[52] and it is shared by the present writer.[53] This view has been frequently criticized, among others recently by Vouin-Léauté[54] who argue that as all the more serious anti-social acts are anyhow legally crimes, the principle *de minimis non curat praetor* should be accepted

14

by criminologists, too, in order to avoid a serious discrepancy between criminal law and criminology. Moreover, they believe that criminology is so much dependent on the machinery of the criminal law to supply it with its material of study that the cases remaining outside that machinery would hardly be worth bothering about. These arguments are hardly valid, first because the present controversy is not concerned with acts which, though crimes, are not dealt with by the organs of the State—that such acts if they can be reached are the legitimate subject of criminological study has never been doubted—but with anti-social behaviour not punishable by the criminal law. Secondly, whether or not the current legal systems of all countries, or at least of the western world, actually cover all those forms of human behaviour which should be dealt with by the criminal law is an assumption which cannot be proved without thorough examinations of the whole field at present left outside. It is the scientific right of the criminologist to carry out such examinations that forms the object of the controversy. Clearly, the wider our concept of crime, the narrower the scope of this controversy; if we use a concept—as Bianchi does[55]—embracing violations not only of legal and social, but also of religious and moral norms, there will be hardly any need to extend the scope of criminology beyond the frontiers of this concept. There is still another point in favour of Sellin's view which seems so far to have escaped notice. Most systems of criminal law recognize —either explicitly as in most continental countries, or implicitly as in Anglo-American law—the principle *nullum crimen sine lege*, which means that behaviour no less blameworthy than behaviour falling under the criminal law can often not be dealt with as crime. In such cases it is for the criminologist, who is not bound by that principle, to supply the factual material required by the legislator to bring about a change in the law.

Even those who, keeping within the limits of the criminal law, prefer the narrower definition of criminology will agree that when studying a certain type of criminal behaviour it is not infrequently advisable to depart from the legal definition. In this way, not only greater uniformity of criminological studies can be achieved in spite of national differences in legal definitions, but the object of such studies can be more easily reached unfettered by perhaps antiquated legal formulations. It was for such reasons that Donald R. Cressey, in his *Other People's Money*, found it necessary to replace the concepts of 'embezzlement', 'forgery' and others, as used in American penal codes by a uniform, more sociological concept of 'criminal violation of financial trust'.[56] Similarly, the criminological study of murder should not follow too slavishly the definition of murder given in this or that particular penal code or statute (see p. 33 below).

Should criminology include the study of the technical processes applied by the police and criminal courts to obtain evidence of the commission of a certain crime by a certain individual or number of individuals, i.e. techniques such as dactyloscopy, photography, toxology, or the application of blood tests, 'lie detectors', hypnosis, narco-analysis? In brief, should it include criminalistics as the study of 'criminal identification'? Or should it be confined to the study of crime in general and of criminals after they have been found guilty or of those whose crimes are not in dispute although there has been no formal finding of guilt? Clearly, we are here concerned with two different aspects of the crime problem, both of equal importance, and no logical reasons can be adduced to exclude criminalistics, the French *Criminalistique*, the German *Kriminalistik*, from the work of the criminologist. To the man-in-the-street, those technical aspects which, all too narrowly, he relates mainly to detective work, or popularly 'Scotland Yard', are the only part of criminology of which he is aware, which he understands and respects. In one country, Austria, the study of criminalistics has for the past sixty years been regarded not only as an integral but even as the most important element of criminology. Hans Gross (1847–1915), first an examining magistrate, later a public prosecutor, a high court judge, and finally a professor of criminal law in various Austrian universities, was the founder of this school. His most important works were his *Handbuch für Untersuchungsrichter als System der Kriminalistik* (1st ed. 1893), later called *Handbuch der Kriminalistik* (8th ed. 1944 ff.) and his *Kriminalpsychologic* (1st ed. 1898, 2nd ed. 1905). In 1921 he founded the first Institute of Criminalistics (the K. K. Kriminalistische Universitätsinstitut) in Graz, and already in 1898 he published his periodical, the *Archiv für Kriminalanthropologic und Kriminalistik* (later called *Archiv für Kriminologie*), of which more than one hundred volumes have so far been published. His work has been continued at the universities of Graz and Vienna by his principal followers, the late Ernst Seelig, Roland Grassberger[57] and others. In Vienna, the University Institute for the Universal Penal Sciences and for Criminalistics was established in 1923, later called University Institute for Criminology. Both Institutes are administered by the faculties of law and political science and include criminalistics in their plans of studies.[58]

In several other countries, in particular Belgium,[59] Brazil,[60] France,[61] Italy,[62] and the United States (mainly in the School of Criminology of the University of California at Berkeley), the study of criminalistics is also to some extent included in the curriculum of the universities. It is different, as a rule, in Great Britain and Western Germany, perhaps not so much for reasons of principle, but because it is felt that this aspect of criminology is better left to the police colleges which possess the technical equipment needed.[63] Special care should of course be taken to uphold full scientific standards in the teaching of these subjects.

Other auxiliary disciplines, such as forensic medicine and the psychology of criminal procedure (judges and witnesses), are also treated in different ways in individual countries.[64]

In the textbooks of criminology, the auxiliary disciplines are, with few exceptions,[65] not included.

As most criminal acts, with the exception of very trivial cases, have to be interpreted in the light of the offender's personality and environment (see below, Part III) criminology has to depend on the findings of many other disciplines, notably anthropology, medicine, psychology, psychiatry, sociology, law, economics and statistics. As history shows, practically all contributions to its development have been made by scholars belonging to one or other of these disciplines, and this will to some extent no doubt also be true in the future. It may, therefore, quite legitimately be asked why it has been regarded as necessary to establish criminology as a new and independent branch of knowledge, and whether its representatives are real 'criminologists' or merely psychologists, sociologists, jurists, and so on, in disguise. The answer to the first question is simple; those other disciplines, important and indispensable as their contributions to the common pool have been, can in fairness be expected to pay only limited attention to the specific problems of crime. The psychology of crime will never form more than one section out of many in the whole of psychology, and the position is the same in other branches of knowledge. As long as the choice of subjects for research and the decisive voice in the preparation of syllabi and timetables for teaching purposes have to be left to the representatives of other disciplines, the field will be covered only partially and in a casual and badly balanced manner, especially as each of these various disciplines is really interested only in those aspects of crime nearest to it. The literature of criminology shows unmistakable traces of this lack of balance. Moreover, the methods of research and the scientific language employed, for example, by psychiatrists differ so greatly from those of sociologists and lawyers that without outside help they may not even fully comprehend each other's work.[66] It is not here suggested that criminologists will ever be able to acquire the all-round training needed to master all those different techniques and languages, nor would they even be wise to indulge in futile attempts to become 'Jacks of all trades'.[67] What they might possibly be capable of achieving is a more comprehensive understanding of the peculiarities and the mental climates of each of those disciplines than possessed by their average representatives, and by doing so they might eventually provide a neutral territory as a meeting place for the exchange of ideas on criminological issues. This is in fact the aim of certain existing organizations, such as the International Society of Criminology.

All this shows that the need for cross-disciplinary teamwork is particularly urgent in criminology.[68] In theory this has become universally accepted; in actual practice it still very often remains a distant ideal to which mere lip-service is paid at inter-disciplinary congresses and conferences.

Even more complicated is the relationship between criminology and the scientific study of the criminal law which, unlike those other disciplines, concentrates exclusively on the subject of crime and its punishment and treatment. In *Group Problems in Crime and Punishment* this relationship and also the line of demarcation between criminology, *Kriminalpolitik*, the sociology of the criminal law and sociological jurisprudence have been discussed at length,[69] and there is no need to go into the matter again. Reference may be made, however, to H. Bianchi's recent attempt to establish criminology as a 'metascience' to the criminal law,[70] i.e. a science of wider scope whose terminology can be used to clarify the conceptions and problems of the latter. Far from being a mere auxiliary to the criminal law it is therefore superior to it. Provided the distinction between criminology and *Kirminalpolitik* (see above) is preserved we can accept Bianchi's view.

One of the many fields where criminology can be used to widen the horizon of the criminal law is the international one. Being less restricted by national boundaries than the law, the criminologist can more easily work within an international framework.

So far the existence of criminology as an independent scientific discipline, with criminologists as its representatives, has been taken for granted. In fact, it has repeatedly been queried not only by outsiders but even by some of the most outstanding workers in this field. In his *General Report on the Sociological Aspects of Criminology* submitted to the Second International Congress of Criminology in Paris, 1950, Thorsten Sellin has coined the often-repeated phrase of criminologists as 'kings without a country', being nothing but sociologists, psychiatrists, jurists, and so on, with the courtesy title of criminologists. Against this, Van Bemmelen has however pointed out that, after all, no branch of science can nowadays thrive without the aid of others and also that criminology possesses a true king in the person of the judge, who decides the individual case.[72] While agreeing with his first argument, we are not convinced by the second. Scientific issues, unlike practical ones, cannot be settled by judicial decisions, which, moreover, can cover only comparatively small sections of the whole field. However, true as Sellin's phrase might have been in the

18

past, criminology has in recent years made considerable progress from colonial to 'dominion' status and further towards complete independence. No longer are we entitled, as Erwin Frey could still do in his remarkable critical survey of the work of the Paris Congress of 1950, to maintain that 'there exists at bottom no direct criminological research . . ., and criminology is in fact nothing but the scientific clearing house between the various other disciplines'.[73] With increasing facilities for criminological teaching and research, the latter can now often be done in the open, without having to use one of the back doors provided by other disciplines. The exceptions are largely due to the prejudices and guilt feelings of society which make it difficult for the average citizen squarely to face the existence of the crime problem within the community and to tackle it in a scientific spirit. However, this, as the whole idea of 'kings without a country', is after all only a passing phase without any future, and the criminologist, to stress his dependence on other disciplines and on public opinion, might rather be compared to the President of the United States. No such metaphors can, of course, decide the real issue whether or not criminology can already claim to be an independent branch of science. This is a difficulty in no way peculiar to it. Sociology, in particular, though slightly more consolidated and powerful, has still to contend with similar scruples. 'Has sociology in fact got a special contribution of its own to make, a body of knowledge, an angle of vision, a discipline and a method, or is it just a hotch-potch of fragments drawn from other fields?' asked T. H. Marshall in 1946.[74] In the case of both disciplines our answer can be re-assuring. On behalf of criminology it can even be claimed that in recent years it has not only been able to embark on research of a cross-disciplinary character making it less dependent on any single one of the participating disciplines, but is also beginning to repay old debts by producing control group material of direct value to the other social sciences. In spite of this on the whole optimistic tone of our discussion we have to admit that, in Great Britain at least, progress towards the formation of an independent profession of criminologists has been very erratic and generally unsatisfactory. As we wrote a few years ago (*Society*, London, 1962, p. 284), it is still 'too dangerous for young men to be branded as narrow specialists in a subject which may well turn out to be a "blind alley". . . . This is most unfortunate. Our discipline is still in too precarious a position to allow itself to become unduly crowded with, and dependent on, birds of passage finding temporary shelter within its territory but constantly longing for a warmer climate.'

The scientific character of criminology has further been doubted because, it has been claimed, the treatment of offenders is an art rather than a science. As pointed out in an earlier publication,[75] this argument is based upon a fallacy. In the treatment of offenders, as in that of physical or mental illnesses, both art and science have to play their part. It would even be mistaken to believe that the theoretical part of criminology is the exclusive domain of science and the practical treatment of offenders that of art. The two elements are inextricably mixed in both fields.

What makes a subject 'scientific' is far from clear and undisputed. Is it, as Malinowski thought, dependent upon 'the existence of general laws, a field for experiment or observation, . . . control of academic discourse by practical application'?[76] Is it the 'systematic collection of related facts' (Cantor)?[77] Is the emphasis on the availability and application of scientific method ('primacy of method') or on the existence of a worthwhile subject in need of independent study ('primacy of subject matter') even if adequate techniques of study are not yet available?[78] Or is it simply the fact 'that it has been . . . accepted into the scientific tradition'?[79] If this scientific tradition should not yet exist in this field, it is for the criminologist to build it up. Even in 1933 it was only with some exaggeration that Michael and Adler, in their devastating criticism of the scientific foundations of criminology, stated an empirical science of criminology to be impossible at the time because of the non-existence of psychology and sociology as empirical disciplines.[80] In the meantime, such a completely negative attitude has become still less justified.

Practical needs are particularly strong in the study of crime and punishment, and it is for this reason that criminology has sometimes been regarded as a technology rather than a scientific discipline. As Sellin has pointed out, there is here a 'clear-cut need for both', the work of the scientist aiming 'at the discovery of constants in the relationships among certain defined facts', and that of the technologist concerned with the 'adaptation of knowledge to the social needs of the moment'.[81] We cannot, however, accept his conclusion that the term 'criminology' should not include these technological aspects. Not only the study of criminalistics in the sense of the Viennese school might well be included but with even greater justification the study of the 'techniques required to apply scientific . . . knowledge to the treatment of criminals or the prevention of crime'. In fact, with the growing interest in more scientific methods now shown by many practical penologists it will often be difficult and invidious to distinguish between the scientific and the technological side of criminology, which latter stands much to gain from the closest contact with the practical application of criminal justice. 'Piecemeal social technology' (Popper)[82] presents the theoretical criminologist with many problems of which he would otherwise be unaware.

Being a non-legal discipline, criminology bears a stronger international flavour than the study of the criminal law which has often, especially in the past, tended to be parochial in its outlook. In the legal sphere, useful work has been done in the past quarter of a century, however, by the International Association of Penal Law and its journal, the *Revue internationale de Droit Pénal*. Criminology, unhampered by the limits of any national legislation, can afford to tackle its problems in a world-wide spirit. Actually, the opportunity has not always been taken, in part because of language difficulties, in part because of the varying nature of the problems concerned and the existing contrasts in approach and outlook. It is symptomatic of recent changes in the right direction that M. Jean Pinatel, the distinguished General Secretary of the International Society of Criminology, has in his text book *Criminologie* (Paris, 1963) deliberately and not without success attempted to give wider scope to international literature than had previously been customary in Continental criminological writings. As will be shown in subsequent chapters, different countries or regions have often been interested in different aspects of crime, have employed different methods of study and produced greatly differing answers. As a consequence, we are not seldom faced with the spectacle of several national or regional disciplines instead of one united body.[83] The work of the two international criminological organizations, the International Society of Criminology, founded before the Second World War, and the International Society of Social Defence, established in 1946, to some extent reflects these differences in emphasis.

Chapter 2

CRIME: ITS MEANING IN RELATION TO LAW, RELIGION, CUSTOM AND MORALS

Crime is, first of all, a legal conception, human behaviour punishable under the criminal law. It is, however, much more than only a legal phenomenon. The frontiers of criminology would not be so difficult to define as will have appeared from the previous chapter if there would not be so many doubts as to the meaning of its fundamental concept, crime. It is a dilemma confronting probably all scientific disciplines that they are engaged in an unending search for the definition of their basic concepts. Kant's famous dictum: *Noch suchen die Juristen eine Definition zu ihrem Begriffe vom Recht*[1] (Jurists are still trying to find their definition of 'law'), was, as the context shows, meant neither in a disparaging sense nor as pointing to a weakness peculiar to the science of law. The same lack of clear-cut definition characterizes such other basic concepts as health and disease, or electricity, or society, and it has even been maintained as a general proposition that it is not for the specialist but for the philosopher to provide all such definitions.[2] In this sense, too, criminologists may find their right challenged to be masters in their own house.

It is the object of this chapter to discuss and clarify the concept of crime in its relation to law and other forms of social control of human behaviour.

I. CRIME AND THE LAW

While the legal definition of crime as something punishable under the criminal law appears from the outside to be more precise, though less informative, than any other definition, closer scrutiny reveals certain weak spots even here.

1. *The legal term 'Crime' is too wide. Should 'Public Welfare Offences' or similar ones be excluded from it and if so what should be the legal consequences?*

22

(a) First, it has been argued that the notion of crime as covering everything punishable under the criminal law has become too wide, notably in legal systems which, as English law, make but little distinction in principle between serious crimes and petty offences. Felonies, misdemeanours and summary or petty offences, it is true, are distinguished in certain technical, especially procedural, respects, and there is also the division, now generally considered to be of little value, into indictable and non-indictable offences. This, however, does not alter the fact that 'the word "crime" is properly applicable to all these', even where the maximum penalty can be only a fine.[3] In the French and German Penal Codes so far a similar tripartite classification has been used, i.e. *crimes, délits, contraventions,* and *Verbrechen, Vergehen, Übertretungen* respectively, distinguished only according to the severity of the penalties which can be imposed, with the consequence that, apart from the question of punishment, there is very little difference in principle between the most serious and the most trivial violations of the criminal law. The widespread feeling that this lack of adequate differentiation is either unfair to those guilty of petty offences, or weakens the stigma of very serious crimes, has led to a number of attempts to classify violations of the criminal law according to various terminological or material criteria. The following are the most important of them. For crimes committed by juveniles the term 'delinquency' is now generally used to express the feeling among the community that altogether different considerations have to be applied to them than to those applied to adult offenders. The same, though to a lesser degree, is true with regard to 'female delinquency'. Regardless of the age and sex of the offenders and on a wider basis, there has been a tendency in several countries to split off from the main body of 'real' offences certain others mainly introduced into the penal codes in the course of the present century to serve the requirements of the modern industrial mass age and the Welfare State. In so far as the legal-philosophical and legislative-technical details of this development are concerned considerable differences can be noticed between the Anglo-American systems and those of the Continental and non-European countries concerned. It has to be admitted, though, that there is hardly any uniformity even within the latter group.[4] Some of these countries, notably Western Germany, Austria, and a number of Swiss Cantons,[5] Poland, Argentina, and Ethiopia (Code of 1957), possess separate codifications or at least separate statutes dealing with the so-called administrative offences, leaving the latter to the competence of administrative authorities. Other countries, while recognizing that certain categories of minor offences are in need of special treatment by the law, do not go so far as to hand them over to the administration. As an example of the first category, in Western

Germany a statute of the 25th March 1952[6] provides that acts which are punishable only by *Geldbussen*, i.e. non-criminal fines, are called *Ordnungswidrigkeiten* and have to be dealt with by administrative authorities. Their characteristic, it has been stated, is not that they are regarded as less important than criminal offences but that they are essentially different from them, violations not of norms for the protection of the fundamental values of society but of technical provisions useful in the interest of a well-ordered administration.[7] Punishment is therefore not necessarily dependent on guilt (§ 11 of the statute), but no *Geldbusse* can be imposed in case of excusable error (§ 12), and the offender has always the right of appeal to a judge (§ 54). Moreover, the same act may, according to circumstances, especially its gravity, be dealt with either by the ordinary court or by the administrative authority (§ 1). The German system therefore represents a compromise between judicial and administrative criminal justice. In view of the passing of the Act of 1952 the new Western German Draft Penal Code deals only with crimes and misdemeanours, not with contraventions.[8]

(*b*) In Anglo-American law attempts to distinguish a special category of 'strict (or absolute) liability offences' have been made for more than a century.[9] These offences have been largely identified as so-called *public welfare offences*, a name not very happily chosen since, as Glanville Williams has said, all offences are, in a sense, public welfare offences. In recent years the term 'regulatory offences' has therefore often been preferred. Their number and practical importance have immensely increased in recent years with the development of an administration grappling with the complicated problems of the modern mass-age and the Welfare State, their elephantine economy and the corresponding maze of laws and regulations. It has been argued, therefore, that this type of offence cannot be dealt with effectively in accordance with the traditional principles of criminal law and procedure which are still based on the ideas of moral guilt and *in dubio pro reo*. Their mass character, the pettiness of most of them if taken individually, contrasted with their dangerousness to society if considered in their totality, seem to make it impossible to apply to them those standards of thoroughness and fairness which we have come to expect from any civilized system of criminal justice. As Francis A. Allen has put it in a brilliant lecture on 'The Borderland of the Criminal Law':[10] 'It is more than poetic metaphor to suggest that the system of criminal justice may be viewed as a weary Atlas upon whose shoulders we have heaped a crushing burden of responsibilities relating to public policy in its various aspects. This we have done thoughtlessly without inquiring whether the burden can be effectively borne.' On the other hand, to ignore those traditional standards even in a limited field of criminal justice might easily undermine the whole fabric unless certain clearly defined criteria can be established which would show beyond doubt that the offences to which the principle of strict liability applies are different from all others not only in numbers but in fundamental issues. Various criteria have been suggested to distinguish the group of public welfare offences from the rest. First, according to Glanville Williams, they are mainly concerned with sale, possession, master and servant relations and road traffic.[11] There is, however, as Jerome Hall suggests,[12] also a 'great additional miscellany' that can hardly be brought under any classification. In fact, with regard to the characteristic features of this very important branch of legislation no further general formula can probably be used than that they owe their origin to the awakening concern of the modern State for the positive well-being of its members and to its growing realization that this well-being can be jeopardized in many ways not understood by former generations. It was only natural that this discovery should have led to the creation of a multitude of new criminal offences since, old-fashioned and clumsy as it was, the criminal law offered itself as one of the few instruments ready at hand to deal with such an emergency. No other body of systematic legal thinking was available to examine the possibilities of social control through alternative, in particular administrative, techniques. It was one of the principal recommendations in the present writer's *Criminal Justice and Social Reconstruction* that such administrative techniques should, in certain sectors, gradually relieve the criminal law of a burden which had become too heavy for it to be borne unaided.[13] This was argued mainly with reference to forms of anti-social behaviour, such as monopolistic conspiracies, too complex and powerful to be fought with the weapons of the criminal law alone. As we have seen, the corresponding problem arises at the other end of the scale with reference to offences often regarded as too trivial to be the concern of the criminal law, and here, too, it is only natural that attempts should have been made to shift the burden, which is here one of numbers rather than of complexity, on to the administration.

(c) This mass character of public welfare and similar offences, which have become far more frequent than all other offences put together, is another characteristic which, it has been said, justifies the demand for special treatment. The requirement of guilt, even in its milder form of criminal negligence, has often been regarded as obsolete by the legislator or the courts, and, as indicated above, it is here that the danger lies. No doubt, the large numbers of these offences impose a strain on criminal justice which might become intolerable if each case be treated 'according to rule', but from the point of view of the individual defendant any relaxation of standards would be a denial of justice just as a rise in certain other types of offence can be no real justification for the use of stiffer penalities for the sake of deterrence. If it is argued[14] that 'there would be little point in enacting that no one should break the defences against flood, and at the same time excusing anyone who did it innocently', the same argument could with the same justification be used even in cases of homicide. The utmost concession that can be made to ease the burden of the prosecution in certain offences is to shift the onus of proof to the accused, a device frequently used by the legislator.[15]

(d) The 'petty nature of the offences and of the penalties'—usually only fines—which can be imposed for them are usually mentioned as criteria of this category and also as justifying their special treatment. Here it is overlooked that the very fact of having to appear before a criminal court and of a criminal conviction with the acquisition of a criminal record are no mere trifles, and any attempt to treat them as such weakens the authority of the criminal law in the eyes of the public. For such reasons, the suggestion to regard public welfare offences as 'quasi-civil wrongs' or even as civil torts, is no solution as the stigma attached to a conviction would remain. Moreover, the idea that public welfare offences are by their very nature and without exception only trivial is in itself misleading; as in the case of many other offences, especially larceny, the potential harm done by them to society covers the whole scale from the minimum to the maximum.[16]

(e) The distinction of *mala per se* and *mala prohibita*, that 'ancient and revered theory' (Jerome Hall) with its underlying idea that there are certain offences which are at the same time moral wrongs and others which are not, has often been used as the criterion. As will be shown below, attempts to differentiate on such lines have so far failed, and it is inadvisable to try to narrow the scope of the concept of 'crime' by excluding the *mala prohibita*. What could be done is to select a number of minor offences, whether 'public welfare', petty traffic, or similar ones which show, as a rule, the characteristics listed above, and deal with them by way of some non-criminal, administrative procedure, but always leaving open recourse to the courts at the request of the prosecution or of the defendant.

2. *Crime and Torts*. Mala in se *and* mala prohibita. *Legal and Sociological Classifications of Crime*

Secondly, the difference between crime and *civil wrongs*, called *torts* in English law, is also far from clear. It is already controversial whether in primitive law such a distinction was known.[17] While Max Weber and many nineteenth-century legal writers denied its existence in primitive systems, more recent anthropological researches seem to have refuted their view. The distinction did exist, though it was one not of substance but merely of emphasis, according to whether it was the public or the private element that predominated.[18] In English law, it has been 'a commonplace for over seven hundred years', but one of procedure only.[19] Blackstone revived the old Roman distinction of *delicta publica* (crimes) and *delicta privata* (torts), or injury done to the community and injury done to individuals. In some ways, this reminds us of the contrast between 'public welfare' and other offences (see § 1 above), with the difference that Roman law and Blackstone regard the *delicta publica* as representing not the fringe, but the very heart of the concept of crime. As in the case of public welfare offences, however, it is now generally agreed that Blackstone's, or indeed any other distinction based on the differences in the contents of the specific act of wrong-doing is bound to fail.[20] The original idea of acts morally wrong *versus* acts merely prohibited by law is here as controversial as elsewhere (below, pp. 39 ff.). Nor would it be entirely correct to say that the commission of a crime, if detected and brought before a criminal court, must invariably lead to punishment—probation and absolute discharge are no penalties—whereas the commission of a civil wrong entails only the payment of damages or restitution—there are 'penal' or 'exemplary' damages in English law. It is true, however, that the latter go to the individual plaintiff, whereas fines imposed for criminal offences go to the State or another public agency. The best distinction so far is that referring to differences in procedure, but even here it is not invariably true that criminal proceedings, as opposed to civil ones, can be started only by the State. Kenny thought the way in which legal proceedings can be terminated, i.e. whether permission of a public authority is required for it, might be the crucial test, but as his editor, following Winfield, has pointed out,[21] this is a vicious circle since the decision as to whether such a permission is required in its turn depends on the question whether the wrong is a crime or only a tort.

To a very considerable extent, crimes and torts overlap, since most serious crimes, such as murder, arson, rape, robbery, are at the same time torts entitling the victim to claim civil damages. How far such damages can be claimed in the course of criminal proceedings varies from one country to another. English law has been comparatively reluctant in this respect,[22] but under the Criminal Justice Act, 1948, s. 11 (2), the court, when making a probation order or an order for conditional discharge, has power to order the offender to pay reasonable damages for injury or compensation for loss caused by him, the latter not exceeding £100 in all in the case of an order made by a court of summary jurisdiction. This reluctance may, to some extent,

27

reflect the historical development from the primitive stage when criminal proceedings were largely left to the initiative of the victim and his family or tribe to the present stage when this power is, on the whole, concentrated in the hands of the State. It is only recently that the part played by the victim of a crime and his interests have been receiving closer attention (see below, Chapter 25), and the proposal has been made that he should in suitable cases even be compensated by the State. This, together with the growing tendency in some countries to put less emphasis than before on the element of moral guilt in crime (below), represents a *rapprochement* between criminal and civil wrongs.

There is not only overlapping between crime and tort in the sense that the same wrong may be both and lead to punishment and to the payment of damages or compensation. In recent times, the idea, already mentioned, that the legislator can and should treat these two concepts as *alternatives*, with administrative action as the third possibility, has been playing an ever-increasing part in public policy. Not only in American anti-monopoly laws, but also in statutes dealing with the wartime black-market the American legislator provided a variety of remedies, and the Office of Price Administration (O.P.A.) in Washington was given authority to decide which of these remedies should be used in an individual case.[23] As a result, mainly for practical reasons of administrative convenience, but also because of the unwieldiness of Federal criminal procedure, less than 6 per cent of all O.P.A. cases were dealt with by way of criminal proceedings, and there was no evidence that those violations which were treated as criminal offences could be clearly distinguished from the rest.[24] Another important factor reducing the proportion of criminal prosecutions as against civil or administrative measures was the feeling of many officials, as well as non-officials, that these black-market offences were not really criminal in character and that the offenders were honest businessmen who had, more by accident than design, had the misfortune of falling foul of an over-strict law. This leads to the controversial question whether in particular 'white collar crime' (see Chapter 21) is crime, even when it is dealt with by non-criminal processes.[25]

It is this latter point, on which there has been a great deal of confused thinking, that concerns us at present, rather than the special problem of 'white collar crime'. The matter is closely connected with the contrast of *mala in se* and *mala prohibita* and also with the idea of 'natural crime', but it has a sociological rather than a moral and legal flavour.

The distinction of *mala in se* and *mala prohibita* has been popular in English law at least since the Middle Ages when it was held that the king, 'though he might deal with merely human laws and the offences created by them (*mala prohibita*) . . . could not deal with the offences created by these higher laws (*mala in se*)'. Coining, for example, belonged to the former, fornication to the latter category.[26] Blackstone taught that there were offences against 'those rights which God and nature have established', as compared with violations of 'laws which enjoin only positive duties and forbid any such things as are not *mala in se* . . . without any intermixture of moral guilt'.[27] It is an idea which, in a way, goes back to Aristotle's of φυςικὸν δίκαιον and νομικὸν δίκαιον or natural law and legal or positive law,[28] and the whole theory of the 'law of nature',[29] i.e. the idea that there is a body of law founded on the nature of man which is independent of time and place and of man-made laws; the idea that there are acts wrong 'by nature' and acts wrong only 'by convention'. This is not the place for any detailed discussion of the many different formulations of the concept of 'law of nature', its great merits and equally considerable dangers. On this see the 'historical sketch' below, pp. 42 ff. In the present connection it has to be stressed, however, that the fundamental object of that concept was not so much to exclude the positive law altogether from the definition of law as to establish the supremacy of the law of nature over the law of the State in cases where the two systems seemed to clash. The object of Blackstone's distinction between *mala per se* and *mala prohibita*, as that of the invention of the more recent category of 'public welfare offences', on the other hand, was not to establish supremacies in cases of conflict between two legal systems, of which one seemed to be superimposed on the other; rather was it to exclude certain offences altogether from the concept of 'crime' or at least from the applicability of certain provisions of the ordinary criminal law, in particular those concerning *mens rea*, or of certain forms of criminal procedure not regarded as suitable for them. The critics of Blackstone, however, have largely used the same argument as employed by the opponents of the natural law school, i.e. that there are no actions criminal in themselves regardless of time and place. While this is perfectly true, it does not entirely dispose of the claim of the natural law school that no such empirical differences can by themselves prove the futility of the search for universally valid formal categories.[30] This is the significance of Stammler's formal concept of 'natural law with varied content'.[31]

The distinction of *mala in se* and *mala prohibita* has recently been revived by the Dutch criminologist H. Bianchi who identifies the latter with his category of 'criminoid' behaviour, which is essentially not criminal, or immoral, but anti-social, 'not usually held blameworthy', a mere non-consideration of the demands of society and of 'living-together', a 'kind of behaviour which testifies to a person's degree of

29

'socialization', an indication of a 'dangerous state'.[32] What Bianchi has, apparently, in mind, seems to be more or less identical with the category of 'public welfare offences'. Whether or not they may properly be called 'criminoid', it cannot be admitted that they are usually not blameworthy and that a non-consideration of the demands of 'living-together' is usually a trifling matter.

In connection with Edwin H. Sutherland's discovery of the concept of 'white collar crime' an interesting controversy has arisen between lawyers and sociologists, between what is regarded as the legal and the sociological definition of crime. 'Is "White Collar crime" Crime?' is the title of one of Sutherland's best-known papers.[33] He was surprised to find that only in a very small proportion, 9 per cent of a sample of 547 cases, of violations of anti-trust, patent and similar statutes, the offenders had been punished by criminal courts, whereas the other cases had been dealt with by non-criminal agencies. Could it, in spite of this, still be maintained that all such violations were 'crimes'? His answer is in the affirmative as both legal requirements, the legal provision of a penalty and the socially injurious quality of these acts, were present, and the manner in which they had actually been dealt with by the State was indifferent. With regard to their gravity, such violations, he argues, may vary from *male in se* to mere *mala prohibita*. As mentioned above, a very similar situation was discovered by Marshall B. Clinard in his post-mortem investigation of the wartime activities of the American black-market and the O.P.A., and he follows Sutherland in regarding black-market violations as crimes regardless of the treatment received on the part of the authorities and of the fact that neither public opinion nor the offenders themselves had been willing to regard them as *mala in se*.[34] This view has been criticized from the sociological side because, it is argued, in view of the attitude of the public and the businessmen concerned their violations of the law cannot sociologically be regarded as crimes,[35] and from the legal side because to the lawyer 'only those are criminals who have been adjudicated as such by the courts'.[36] Paul W. Tappan, who has been the principal spokesman of this legalistic view, points out that, although unconvicted offenders are representative of important groups and the criminological study of these groups may be very desirable, these groups are still too vague and ill-defined and merely an expression of the 'desire to discover and study wrongs which are absolute and eternal rather than mere violations of a statutory and case law system which varies in time and place'. Tappan's criticisms are a mixture of truth and error. It is true that the sociological concepts of 'conduct norms' and 'socially injurious' are, in spite of the pioneer work of Sellin[37] and others, still in need of further clarification. It is mistaken, however, to think that sociologists in general here tried to include in their conception of crime mere violations of conduct norms which were not legally punishable. Sutherland in particular, as already stated, requires the legal provision of a penalty for the act, whereas Clinard seems to require merely 'a law outlawing certain behaviour' without making it entirely clear whether this must be a penal law in the strict sense. Our own view may be stated as follows: The whole controversy is partly, though not wholly, terminological, and it is essential to clarify the various issues involved.

Whether or not the *Oxford English Dictionary* is correct in giving the fourteenth century as the date of the earliest reference to the word 'crime'[38]—we might just as well go back to the Merovingian King Chlotar's Edict of 614 in which the term *causae criminales* is used[39]—in any case Bianchi is right when he stresses that 'the objective semantic function of the term "crime" is, as much as the phenomenon itself, independent of any legislative operation . . .' The term and the phenomenon are evidently pre-legislative. 'They exist independently of and in spite of any legislative use of the terms . . . On the contrary, the legislator takes it for granted that the term must have a previous sense'—this against Michael and Adler's 'disreputable sophism' that 'without a criminal code there would be no crime'.[40] And, long before Bianchi, Garofalo had opened his famous discourse on 'natural crime' and the sociological concept of crime (see below, p. 220) with the statement:

'*Le législateur n'a pas créé ce mot; il l'a emprunté au langage populaire; il ne l'a pas même défini, il n'a fait que rassembler un certain nombre d'actions, qui, selon lui, étaient des crimes*'[41] (on this see below, Chapter 12). Sociologists are, therefore, entirely free to use their own conception of crime. It does not necessarily follow, however, that they would always be wise to do so since they have not created the concept either and have so far, on the whole, not been able to define it more clearly than the jurists. What are in fact the reasons for their desire to establish a concept of crime independently of that of the criminal law or even of the civil law concept of wrong?

There are, it is suggested, mainly the following considerations:

There is the perfectly legitimate wish of lawyers and sociologists alike, indeed of everybody interested in the just and fair administration of the law, to know exactly what kind of human conduct has to be brought under the umbrella of the term 'crime' when the application of statutes is in question which attach certain disabilities to the commission of a crime, such as, for example, ineligibility to be admitted as an immigrant or to be naturalized, or of statutes which make a person eligible to be treated as a recidivist,[42] sentenced to preventive detention, corrective training, etc. It is clear, however, that these are matters to be decided in terms of the positive law, i.e. crime can here

31

be only an act regarded as such by the statute concerned. The latter may explicitly exclude certain criminal acts although they are legally crimes, for example those committed by juveniles. Sociological or moral considerations may here be introduced not as part of the conception of crime itself, but by making the operation of the statute dependent on the presence of certain additional requirements, such as 'moral turpitude', or of a penalty of a certain gravity such as imprisonment, thereby excluding minor offences which can be punished only by a fine. Whether or not a specific case of 'white collar crime' is a crime within the meaning of any such statute, thereby making the offender ineligible for immigration, naturalization, etc., or whether a white collar offender is a recidivist in the legal sense can be decided only in accordance with the wording of the statute concerned. In this connection it is interesting to note that those criminal statutes which provide loss of voting and other civil rights usually attach them not to the crime committed, but to the penalty imposed. While this may be regarded as unfair, the degrading character of former penal systems offers an explanation, though not an excuse.[43]

It would be a mistake, however, to push this legalistic view, with Tappan, so far as to maintain that 'only those are criminals who have been adjudicated as such by the courts'.[44] This is true for the application of statutes explicitly requiring a conviction, which most, if not all, the statutes just referred to do. It is not true, however, in any other way, and should in particular not be taken for granted where the question of stigma arises in a general, not legally stereotyped, sense, i.e. as social stigma rather than as legal disability or liability. Here a distinction has to be made between those 'unconvicted offenders' whose guilt has not been established by any legal tribunal and who should, therefore, not be stigmatized as 'criminals' and those who, though found guilty of an offence, have, for a variety of reasons, been dealt with by civil courts or administrative tribunals. It was this second group with which Sutherland was concerned, and seeing that, in the actual practice of the American anti-trust and similar statutes, the great majority of violators were spared a criminal conviction, his feeling of justice revolted against what he regarded as unfair discrimination in favour of the big 'white collar criminal'. An unlawful act, he rightly stated, 'is not defined as criminal by the fact that it is punished, but by the fact that it is punishable'.[45] He did not fail to see that in the case of non-criminal agencies the requirement of *mens rea* and the rules of evidence might be less strict than in criminal courts, but thought this argument could be refuted by referring to recent tendencies in favour of strict liability and the like.[46] It is here, however, that the real dilemma lies. Unless the separation of the criminal law from other branches of the law and unless the whole conception of crime are to be deprived of any meaning and function—a process in any case already too far advanced—criminal justice must preserve the full rigidity of its requirement of *mens rea* and of its rules of evidence. From this, it follows that where the law provides, or could provide, several alternatives of dealing with violators, the criminal law route should be chosen not merely for reasons of social prejudice or administrative convenience, but according to the merits of the individual case, which requires considerations not only of a legal but also of a sociological nature concerning the need to inflict a greater or lesser stigma or no stigma at all. The legalistic view, as represented by Tappan, is unsatisfactory in arguing that punishable acts are crimes only if actually dealt with by a criminal court, but the sociological view, as represented by Sutherland, is also questionable at present in maintaining that punishable acts are always crimes, even if dealt with by non-criminal agencies. What is needed is an injection of sociological thinking into the whole administration of criminal justice to ensure that the present incongruities between stigma and conviction will be reduced to the unavoidable minimum. This is a problem going beyond the scope of those specific phenomena which have given rise to the discussion.

While the divergence of views between criminal law and sociology so far discussed is one concerning the practical application of the former, the definition of crime has also caused difficulties in the field of theoretical criminology. It is not only the sociologist's feeling of justice that has been hurt by the legalistic definition of crime but his scientific conscience, too, has been dissatisfied by the rigid and often out-of-date classifications developed by the criminal law. It was found by Cressey, for example, that the concept of 'embezzlement' in American criminal codes did not cover a sociologically homogeneous form of behaviour, and for purposes of research it had to be replaced by the conception of accepting a position of trust in good faith and afterwards violating that trust by committing crimes such as embezzlement, larceny by bailee, or certain forms of forgery or confidence tricks. This sociological conception of 'criminal violation of financial trust', it was claimed, included all forms of criminal behaviour which are essentially similar from the economic and sociological point of view, but excluded cases essentially different, though covered by the legal terms of embezzlement, forgery, etc. In this way a sound criminological basis could be established for research into the socio-psychological characteristics of criminal violations of financial trust which, nevertheless, to some extent used the traditional legal concepts.[47] Another illustration could be drawn from the term 'manslaughter' which in English law has developed in a purely 'negative way' as being 'a homicide which for one reason or another did not amount to murder . . . even at the present day such is the confusion . . . that it is not possible to give an authoritative definition of manslaughter in plain terms'.[48] The fact that the same term manslaughter covers acts so different in character as voluntary and involuntary killing has particularly added to the present confusion. The scope of the concept of 'murder', too, differs so widely that criminologists might not be blamed for trying to study it as a socio-psychological entity rather than in strictly legal terms.[49] The immense variety of this crime has in fact been one of the arguments against establishing legal 'degrees' of murder: 'legal stereotyping and a doctrinaire approach would destroy the elasticity which today enables not three but many degrees of murder to be recognized', wrote Sir Norwood East.[50] Instead of any possible legal, and inevitably too rigid, classification criminologists lather distinguish murder according to its psychological and socio-rogical features, especially its motives, the age, sex, race, family status and other personal characteristics of the murderer, his relationship to the victim, etc.[51] H. C. Brearley even regards the legal distinction between premeditated murder and impulsive manslaughter as of little sociological significance.[52]

The essential points of this discussion are, first, that the term 'crime' should be used in technical language only with reference to conduct that is legally crime. Secondly, such conduct, if fully proved, is crime regardless of whether it actually leads to a conviction before a criminal court or whether it is dealt with by other agencies or not at all. Thirdly, the decision as to which of the available alternatives is to be used should depend entirely on the merits of the individual case. Lastly, criminology is in no way limited in the scope of its scientific investigation to what is legally crime in a given country at a given time, and it is free to use its own classifications.

II. THE RELATION OF CRIME TO RELIGION, CUSTOM AND MORALITY

From our premises that the term 'crime' should in technical language be used only with reference to conduct which is legally crime, but that criminology, on the other hand, should be free to pursue its studies unfettered by the legal conception of crime, it follows that criminologists and legal reformers have to be given at least a minimum of extra-legal guidance as to what *should* be treated as crime. It is only in this way that they can be provided with an approximate idea of where to look for potential problems. Otherwise their work would have no proper frame of reference, and they would be left to sail without a compass in an uncharted ocean of questionable 'facts' and untestable hypotheses. The guidance which we require can be obtained only if it is borne in mind that the law is nothing but one system of norms among other systems ordering human thoughts and behaviour, or in psycho-analytical language only one taboo among many. Where the law fails to provide the answer or where the answer it offers seems to be unsatisfactory we have to turn to religion, custom, morality, and other value systems operating in a given culture. This does not imply an undervaluation of the law as such and its relegation to a minor role as compared with those other controlling forces. It does not mean, for example, an uncritical acceptance of the orthodox Marxist view of the law as being a mere 'superstructure' created on a basis of economic factors, a mere 'function of economic processes without any independent existence' and independent history.[53] While fully admitting the strong influence which economic factors, throughout the course of history, have exercised on the contents and administration of the law we cannot ignore the reverse side of the picture: the law in its turn has also often affected the economic system and sometimes it has developed regardless of, or even contrary to, economic trends, which has usually meant that it has fallen behind the realities of economic life.[54] Nor is the position basically different in the non-economic sectors of cultural life: there has been mutual stimulation and cross-fertilization between the law, on the one hand, and religion, custom and social values and convictions, on the other, the law occasionally taking the lead, more often however lagging behind developments in other fields. In the following, the relationship between the criminal law and the most important of those other systems of social control will be briefly surveyed.

1. *The Relation of Crime to Religion*

Can we find in *religious* norms the guidance for which we are searching as to what should be treated as crime? Is crime identical with sin, and should the criminal law be a catalogue of sinful acts? Historically, the nineteenth-century theory of the religious origin of the law (Maine)[55] and the doctrine of crime as a pollution of the community have been abandoned by many modern writers. Diamond has been one of the most outspoken critics of Maine. There are, he writes, no rules in primitive religion for the conduct of man towards man, sanctioned by a regard for the will of supernatural beings, and 'the notion that homicide is wrongful made its appearance in the religion after it had appeared in the law, and it was derived from the legal notion'.[56] Other writers, such as David Daube and G. W. Paton, are more cautious. 'Is it safe', asks Daube, 'to argue that because the devout authors of the Bible see law as part of religion, law must have formed part of religion in the Hebrew State?' but he concludes that neither

35

view can be regarded as safely established.[57] Considering how difficult, and often impossible, it is to distinguish between religious and legal rules this conclusion is not surprising.[58] Regardless of this controversy as to the historical priority of religion or law, however, it is a fact that the norms of the criminal law have not throughout developed on the same lines as those of the main religions. Taking the Ten Commandments as an illustration, it is obvious that some of these have hardly ever been embodied in the provisions of any system of positive criminal law, probably because they are concerned with sentiments and desires rather than with actions or omissions which make them technically unsuitable for the work of the legislator. Modern legal systems have largely taken their cue from the secular conception of the State established after one of the most prolonged and painful struggles in history. Anthropologists, too, have found in primitive societies of today a legal order of some kind which they think was not based on religious beliefs.[59] As far as the problems of western civilization are concerned, all this means, however, only three things: in the first place, the renunciation of the old conception of the ecclesiastical law as being superior to, or taking the place of, secular criminal law, and the abolition of institutions arising from that conception, such as the 'Benefit of Clergy'.[60] Secondly, it means that most modern criminal codes contain provisions protecting not religion or the Churches as such but merely the religious feelings of individual citizens and the peaceful exercise of public or private worship.[61] Thirdly, it means that when trying to answer our question what kind of human conduct should be regarded as criminal we cannot borrow wholesale from the list of acts or omissions treated as sins by the various religions. Already the fact that different religions may have different views in the matter would make this impracticable. The discrepancy between religious principles or, perhaps more accurately, between the doctrines of some of the Churches and the criminal law of many countries has become particularly striking in the case of problems such as birth control, abortion, suicide, artificial insemination, although even here legal progress has often been hampered by ecclesiastical opposition.[62] Regarding homosexuality on the other hand, some of the Churches have recently expressed views more progressive than those still embodied in English criminal law. Regardless, however, of which system happens to be more progressive on a certain topic at a certain time in a certain place, generally speaking it should not be assumed that religious beliefs and values are, or should be, of no significance to the secular legislator, or to the criminologist, even an agnostic one. There are three very strong, though closely inter-related, arguments to the contrary. First, the decline in religious belief is often regarded as a potent cause of crime, and even if this view should be mistaken

36

or at least not provable (see below, Chapter 23) its existence cannot be altogether ignored. Secondly, religion plays an important part in the philosophy and psychology of punishment. Psychoanalysis and Christianity alike, although in different ways, are deeply concerned with the idea of guilt, which in its turn is closely related to the origin and institution of punishment (Chapter 17, below). Thirdly, and arising from this, religion can often play a therapeutic role in the process of punishment and treatment of offenders and in the prevention of crime. The ideas of reparation and confession are essential elements in both religion and penology.[63] In short, as Tappan writes, 'its potential role is tremendous', though the actual fulfilment of this potentiality depends 'on the vitality of a religion in the lives of its professants'.[64] That religion may be an important factor in our dealings with law-breakers is of course a highly controversial statement and one very difficult to prove or disprove by scientific methods, especially as any case material which might be produced is likely to come from persons rightly regarded as prejudiced. The history of penology knows of tragic mistakes committed by ardent believers in the name of religion, from the persecution of the early Christians to the burning of the witches and the Pennsylvanian system of solitary confinement.[65]

In the light of these considerations it goes without saying that we cannot accept the recent attempt of H. Bianchi to define crime as 'invariably an act against God',[66] even bearing in mind that his conception of crime excludes what he calls 'criminoid' behaviour.

2. *The Relation of Crime to Custom*

We have now to consider how far *custom, mores,* may be able to help the legislator in his search for the material contents of both the positive and the ideal criminal law. What we have in mind is not legal custom, which is itself law—though perhaps a primitive form of it—but social custom, *mœurs, coutumes,* in German *Sitte.* H. Kantorowicz, in his important posthumous work *The Definition of Law,*[67] has given a useful list of such rules of custom which are not law; he distinguishes rules concerning (*a*) good manners (at table, in the street); (*b*) the occasions for and the appropriateness of gifts; (*c*) forms of greetings and styles of address; (*d*) topics of conversation; (*e*) forms of letter-writing; (*f*) court and professional etiquette; (*g*) tact; (*h*) behaviour at ceremonies; (*i*) cleanliness of clothes; (*j*) degree of liberty allowed in social intercourse of the sexes; (*k*) comity of nations, and so on. As he admits, even this lengthy list is not exhaustive. The social class and caste system, for example, is almost exclusively based on custom and only in exceptional cases touched by law.[68] Evidently, many of these rules, in particular those under (*a*), (*b*), (*c*), (*f*), (*h*), (*i*), and (*j*), might in certain circumstances, in a given place and at a given time, become provisions of the criminal law. The rule which tells us not to jump a queue is usually only one of good manners, i.e. mere custom, but in periods of special emergency, for example in wartime, it may become a criminal offence to do so. The liberal distribution of gifts may be something entirely innocuous, but it may also be the subject of an official enquiry (e.g. that of the Lynskey Tribunal in 1949)[69] or even of a criminal charge of corruption. Violations of professional etiquette may be merely frowned upon by other members of the profession, or they may have serious disciplinary consequences or lead to a prison sentence, and similar considerations apply to misbehaviour at ceremonies (blasphemy) and towards the female sex (indecent assault). It would be a fascinating task to try to disentangle the respective contributions of law and custom to the 'American dilemma'[70] and to the treatment of minority groups in general (on the latter see below, Chapter 23), or to that of such social outcasts as ex-prisoners and homosexuals. Our present task is to find the discriminating criteria and to search for the lessons to be learnt from them by the legislator. One of the profoundest legal philosophers of the current century, Gustav Radbruch,[71] thought not only that all attempts to differentiate law and custom had so far been unsuccessful but that their futility could even be proved since these two institutions were so fundamentally different—law meaning cultural norm and value, custom having no relation to either—that no comparison was possible. On the other hand, he regarded custom as a kind of preparatory stage (*Vorschule*) to the law. This is often true, but occasionally the historical development takes the opposite course. As a rule, disabilities, prohibitions, privileges originate in custom (e.g. queueing, segregation), and are subsequently reinforced by the law either because custom proves too weak to achieve its objects without legal backing or because it proves so overwhelmingly strong that the legislator, *nolens volens*, has to yield to it. In the end, he may be able occasionally to abolish a bad custom, but it may also survive legal prohibition (duelling, segregation, customs supporting white collar crime, in some areas even blood-vengeance). Have we to conclude from this that 'custom is king', that 'mores can make anything appear right, even incest and cannibalism and the killing of the old'?[72] It certainly can do so for a period of time, but not for ever.

While these considerations are largely concerned with historical sequence and material strength of custom and law, we have now to turn to similarities and differences. Custom and law, it has been argued, both require only external compliance regardless of motive, which latter is the essential element in the moral sphere (see below, s. 3); and, against Radbruch who stresses the significance of internal compliance in the field of custom, it is true to say that in custom and law the emphasis is more on the external side,[73] though all this is very much a matter of degree. Those who act in accordance with custom will, except perhaps in a totalitarian regime, not be too closely questioned about their inner feelings.

An important difference between law and custom is that the latter is more often limited to certain geographical regions and social classes within the State, whereas the law with minor exceptions (local by-laws, ordinances) tends to be uniform for the whole country. It has also been said that while both law and custom are heteronomous, i.e. receive their norms from outside, only the law has at its disposal an organization to enforce its will. This is not altogether correct in the sense that enforceability is not a universal quality of the law and that, on the other hand, custom is also enforceable, though in a different way. As Max Weber has pointed out, the law can rely on a special staff whose task it is to take action in cases of transgression.[74] Custom possesses no such special staff; it is enforced by public opinion or, perhaps even more frequently, by the belief of the man in the street—however mistaken it may occasionally be—that this is what the majority wants.

Bad customs, for example in the field of racial discrimination, may breed actual crime, but even regardless of such acute potentialities it is the proper task of the criminologist to study them and to examine the case for and against criminal legislation in this field and the possibilities of crime prevention.

3. *The Relation of Crime to Morality*

Important as norms of religion and custom are to the criminal lawyer and criminologist, the problems presented by them are only preludes to those likely to arise from a potential clash between legal and *moral* rules. Here it is that our real battles are waged and only too often lost. Even if we should regard Jerome Hall's claim as slightly exaggerated that the 'moral quality of the criminal law . . . is the major issue of our times and permeates all the social disciplines',[75] there still remains ample reason for us to ponder and to worry about the matter, and it hardly needed the recent experience of the Wolfenden Report as a reminder.[76] If it is the business of criminologists to study crime and criminals and their treatment by law and society, the moral problems involved cannot possibly be set aside.

Of what kind are these problems? First and foremost, what is the true relation between the criminal law and the moral law; are they on identical or at least similar lines? Can we look to the moral law as the originator, interpreter, and protector of the criminal law of the State?

Can it be used as a guide by the legislator to use the weapon of the criminal law in order to enforce moral standards? Can we tell the offender, who is often disdainful of the whole machinery of criminal justice and regards his punishment as unfair, that he has broken not merely the law but the moral code, too, and that there is no higher authority left on earth to whom he could appeal? And the judge in sentencing and the penal administrator in carrying out the sentence—should they put into motion the full blast of moral indignation to make the greatest possible impact on the criminal and on the community? Considering that very few of those who are indifferent to religion and even willing to ignore the rules of custom would wish openly to defy the moral code, it might be of the greatest help to the upholders of law and order if the force of morality could be placed at their service without reservations. In fact, there are all too many such reservations.

The problem 'Law and Morality' has been unduly neglected by criminologists (in the narrower sense of the term), especially by those without a legal or philosophical background. Some of them, apparently, believe that it is not their problem at all. Penologists have shown slightly more interest and understanding because it so obviously goes to the roots of penal philosophy. Let us, before going into details, try to define the scope of the matter. All too often it has been regarded as something affecting only the field of legislation, and even here merely the question of whether a specific kind of human behaviour should, or should not, be punished as a crime. It was this aspect which was discussed by the Wolfenden Committee in connection with homosexuality and prostitution, but these two phenomena are by no means the only aspects of criminal legislation where the relationship between law and morals may play an important part. This relationship is of equally crucial importance for such matters as the attitude of the criminal law to birth control, artificial insemination, euthanasia, abortion, suicide, or the limits of the defence of 'superior orders' or of the legal right of an individual to sacrifice other innocent human beings in order to save his own life in a situation of common danger, such as shipwreck (the English *Mignonette* case and the American *Holmes* case).[77] In addition to such subjects, we can say that wherever the criminal law, rightly or wrongly, uses degrading penalties or makes the choice between different penalties, for example between penal servitude and imprisonment, dependent on the moral character of the offender or the moral quality of his offence—the *ehrlose Gesinnung* of the German Criminal Code (§ 20)—considerations of a moral nature become part and parcel of criminal justice. The same applies where the law contains directives for the sentencing policy of the criminal courts to treat certain moral qualities of the offender or of his action, especially his motives, as either aggravating or mitigating circumstances, or where, as for example certain American statutes do, the law makes the deportation of an alien dependent upon his conviction of a crime involving 'moral turpitude'.[78] Even in the absence of any such provisions judges and magistrates are often faced with similar questions within the limits left to their discretion.

As it is sometimes thought that homilies delivered by a judge or magistrate when passing sentence may influence an offender for good it is important to know how far moral exhortations should, as in fact they often are, be included on such occasions. Corresponding problems, only still more intricate and intense, arise for institutional staffs, after-care and probation officers in all their dealings with the offender after he has made his fleeting appearance in court. Twenty-five years ago the present writer was bold enough to assert, in no moralizing spirit: 'Only on a moral basis is it possible successfully to argue with the lawbreaker',[79] a formula now approved by the eminent American authority on criminal law and jurisprudence, Jerome Hall.[80] How far, and in what sense, is this still true in the light of more recent developments? And if it should be true in principle, can it be defended as a practical proposition in cases where the indispensable minimum requisites of such moral arguments may seem to be non-existent? To such questions an answer can be given only on the basis of an analysis of the personal qualities of individual offenders, which no doubt falls within the province of the criminologist.

Clearly, no solution can be attempted without considering at least a few of the milestones in the long history of the subject and of some of its vast literature—a history very closely bound up with that of the movement of 'natural law'.[81] As the present writer has pointed out before, it was the fundamental weakness of the Wolfenden Report, depriving it of much of its persuasive force, that it paid no attention to that history and literature. It is the fundamental idea behind the concept of a natural law that there exists an unwritten legal system, derived from the 'nature of man', side by side with, but independent of, and superior to, the positive law of the State. The natural law is thought to be immutable and eternal, valid regardless of time and place; it is of divine origin and in perfect harmony with nature itself and with justice. While these are the ideas which have given the natural law movement its immense driving force, closer scrutiny reveals many internal differences and sometimes almost imperceptible, but nevertheless profound, changes in its contents. 'The mere fact', writes d'Entrèves, 'that an identical expression recurs in different writers, is no proof of continuity of thought from one to the other. That Cicero and Locke should both have defined natural law in a very similar manner is no evidence of the uninterrupted acceptance of that

41

notion during the eighteen odd centuries which separate them.'[82] In fact, the history of the natural law movement has sometimes been over-simplified and condensed so as to conceal the truth that it presents a united front in its negative rather than in its positive aspects, i.e. in its negation of the monopolistic claims of the law of the State rather than in its own doctrines. Moreover, while its history is of the utmost importance for our present problem, the relationship of law and morals—d'Entrèves calls this the distinguishing mark of natural law history[83]—it also shows that the movement has, at least in its earlier stages, been concerned with the relationship between human and divine laws rather than between human law and morals. It is in particular Erik Wolf[84] who has closely examined the immense variety of possible and actual definitions of natural law and stressed that it has received its substance from the leading cultural values of the age, which may be of an individualistic or of a collective, social, political, economic, scientific, religious, or moral character.

4. *Historical Sketch of the Natural Law Movement*

According to the traditional interpretation of the history of the natural law, the problem did not arise in the earlier stages of ancient Greece since no distinction was then made between law, religion and morals; strictly speaking, there was no 'moral-free' sphere, nor could there be any criticism of the positive law on religious or moral grounds—there could be no 'unjust law'. As Welzel pointed out,[85] the idea of a natural law could originate only in a period of crisis, i.e. for Greece in the age of Pericles and the Sophists in the middle of the fifth century B.C. Even to Socrates, who appeared as the great questioner of all things human and divine, justice was, strangely enough, still identical with the rules of the positive law; having to fight against the attempts of some of the Sophists to undermine the force of law altogether, he preferred to be a rebel not against the positive law but merely against what seemed to him its mistaken application by the court.[86] Whether this was the opinion of Plato, too, appears somewhat doubtful, and this not merely in view of the many contrasts between the different periods of his writings. Considering his authoritarian leanings and his pragmatism; his maxim that the end justifies the means and that justice is what is useful to the State; his confession, through his mouthpiece Socrates, that he does not know the true nature of justice and that much further consideration would be needed to understand that nature, we may well be left with the impression that the idea of an eternal law of nature and of the possibility of an 'unjust' positive law was finally dismissed by Plato.[87] There are, however, also certain passages in his *Dialogues* which can be quoted for the contrary view (though not the dictum 'an evil decree cannot be law' in *Minos*, as the latter is a pseudo-Platonic, much later dialogue).[88]

Nor are Aristotle's writings on the subject free of inconsistencies.[89] While his starting point is the belief in the supremacy of the positive law (νόμος)

42

over justice (δίκαιον), while his idea of equality means equality according to the positive law, he also feels dissatisfied with the resulting identification of law and justice. He tries to construct a model of an ideal Constitution, but abandons this attempt because of the relative character of an ideal which would be different for different people. Here as in the case of Plato it is sometimes the emphasis on the positive and sometimes the emphasis on the ideal law that has been given pride of place by their various interpreters, but the final impression has usually been one of vacillation and doubt. It was the *Stoa* with its pantheistic and cosmopolitan philosophy (it 'took the step from the Polis to the Cosmopolis', Welzel); with its conception of reason as a universal force dominating the cosmos regardless of sex, nationality or race; its concentration on the internal side of human actions and on the conscience that promised a solution of the problem of natural law at a time of political and religious crises.[90] Obedience to the law of nature, based on reason, becomes a moral duty. Although the Stoics, too, had to make concessions to practical realities, their doctrines inspired the teachings of Cicero, the law of Justinian, and the early Christian thinkers. Previous attempts to fill the formal idea of natural law with contents of an objective character had failed. Aristotle's idea of equality, as part of the natural law, for example, remained sterile as long as no material formula, no yardstick, was provided to say which factors had to be considered and which others to be ignored when deciding whether two cases were in fact 'equal'. The same applies to the famous Roman formula *suum cuique* where it is not clear what this 'suum' is.[91] The Stoics provided an answer by basing the natural law on the moral convictions of the individual,[92] thereby strengthening its popular appeal but sacrificing its claim to objectivity.

Roman law has often been credited with having worked out a conception of natural law clearer than that of the Greek philosophers. Actually, modern historical jurisprudence stresses rather the many contradictions in the writings of classical Roman jurists. There was, it is true, their famous distinction between *jus civile*, *jus gentium*, and *jus naturale*, but the relationship thought to exist between these three systems is far from clear. To some writers the *jus naturale* is identical with the *jus gentium*, the law of nations, or even with the *jus civile*, to others it is their opposite;[93] and the whole trichotomy is nowadays often regarded as a later invention, although as d'Entrèves suggests it may well express the different stages in the evolution of Roman law. There is, however, unanimity on one important feature: on the fact that in the Roman view the law of nature was not superior to the positive law. If any proof were needed of this, the institution of slavery would provide it. Slavery was regarded as part of the *jus gentium* and therefore positive Roman law, although it was against one of the most fundamental notions of the law of nature, the Stoic ideal of equality of all men. It was under the influence of this ideal, however, that, although the institution itself was retained, at least some important improvements were gradually made in the legal and social position of slaves.[94]

It is this self-abdication of the Roman version of the law of nature that distinguishes it from the early Christian doctrine and medieval Canon law

43

from St. Augustine to St. Thomas Aquinas, nine hundred years later, neither of whom had any doubt that where positive law deviates from the law of nature it has no binding force, it is not *lex legalis* but merely a *legis corruptio*. 'St. Augustine says: "There is no law unless it be just". So the validity of law depends upon its justice. But in human affairs a thing is said to be just when it accords aright with the rule of reason, and . . . the first rule of reason is the natural law' (Thomas).[95] In Canon law the law of nature is derived from reason and from God, it is the source of all moral ideas, too; therefore it must be absolute and binding, and disobedience to unjust law becomes not only a right but also a duty. There are, however, several weak spots in this grandiose structure. First, according to Canon law the rules of natural law are of a very general kind only, such as 'Do the Good and avoid the Evil', and have therefore to be supplemented by the more specific provisions of the positive law of the State. With very few exceptions, all the adherents of the natural law school admit the necessity of such a system of positive law—a fact used by Kelsen and others to justify their rejection of the whole idea of natural law.[96] Secondly, to Thomas even the latter represents only one, not the final, step towards 'eternal blessedness'; and as new developments may require new institutions it is not altogether exempt from the general law that everything is subject to change.[97] Finally, Thomas shares with Plato and Augustine the tendency to ignore the rights of the individual and of minorities such as slaves and heretics.[98]

To Duns Scotus, too, the law of nature is founded on God's will alone, with the reservation that God himself is subject to what is logically possible. Moreover, a point of special importance to the theory of criminal law, there are for him no actions which are good or bad *per se*, and this view was shared by William of Ockham, according to whom acts such as larceny or adultery are not bad in themselves but only because they are prohibited.[99] A fundamental change could occur only at a later stage, in the seventeenth century, when the theological doctrines of natural law were replaced by the secular ones of Thomas Hobbes, Hugo Grotius, Samuel Pufendorf and their successors; when, in the words of Welzel,[100] the place of the theologians was taken by 'politically minded philosophers and philosophizing jurists'.

Whether Hobbes can be regarded as a member of any school of natural law seems to be very doubtful. His scepticism, imbued as it was with the teachings of natural science, was calculated to destroy rather than to rebuild that idea. As according to him man's nature, previously regarded as a positive and constructive force, is thoroughly bad and as good and evil are relative and subjective terms, salvation can come only from the sovereign State and its positive law. The latter can never clash with reason; therefore, it is for the State to decide what the law of nature requires, and the only function of the latter is to furnish the justification for the law of the State, which means 'the negation of natural law by natural law' (Kelsen).[101] The private conscience of the citizen has to be subordinated to the public conscience of the sovereign. Somewhat paradoxically, there remains, it is true, a private sphere where the individual is free to interpret the law of

44

nature for himself, though the boundaries of this sphere are uncertain and the contents of this law of nature very formal only.[102] On no account, however, can a violation of the positive law on the grounds of its divergence from the natural law be justified; the former may be bad, but it can never be 'unjust'. 'Every crime is a sinne', he wrote, 'but not every sinne a crime' (*Leviathan*), which in a way anticipates Georg Jellinek's theory of the law as the ethical minimum (see below).

Hugo Grotius (1583–1645) may not have been the 'founder of the natural law school' (Pufendorf), but his contributions to it have nevertheless been profound. It was he who, in his *De jure Belli ac pacis* (1625)—not for the first time and with cautious reservations—merely as a hypothetical possibility, but nevertheless with tremendous effect, put forward the view that the law of nature would be valid even if there were no God or if he would disinterest himself in human affairs; even God himself cannot change it.[103] This is so because the law of nature consists of eternal truths similar to mathematical principles. In his attempts to work out a detailed system of principles of natural law Grotius was eventually forced, however, to admit that the true quality of human actions was too difficult to determine and could not therefore provide the basis for a right of the citizen to disobey the positive law. In fact, he quotes Sophocles' Antigone: 'You must obey him whom the State has placed in power, in things unjust as well as just.'[104] He had begun by freeing the law of nature from its theological fetters, but he ended by subjecting it to the will of the sovereign State. Nor was he able to work out any new principles of natural law which would have added to Aristotle's formal principle of equality as the essence of justice.[105]

His successor Samuel Pufendorf (1632–94), too, in his *De jure naturae et gentium* (1672) had to admit that the law of nature provided no proof of the goodness or badness of specific forms of human behaviour. He rejected any claim that, for example, adultery or incest or larceny were morally bad *per se* (doctrine of *perseitas*); all one could say was that, for example, monogamy was probably the best way of regulating sexual relations, but even this could not be proved through the doctrines of natural law.[106] The real problem was to discover *why* certain acts were good and others bad. He found the basis of the natural law in the idea of *socialitas*, i.e. the human need to live closely together with other human beings, an idea which he used to develop his social system.[107] Concerning the relationship between natural law and positive law, while rejecting Hobbes' view that the State can do no wrong and his identification of natural law and the law of the State, he nevertheless established at least a presumption in favour of the latter, and the right of resistance to legal injustice was correspondingly restricted.[108]

One of the most important contributions which Pufendorf made to legal philosophy and ethics was to show the different role played by motives and other internal factors in human actions. While before the forum of ethics and theology such internal factors mattered even in acts which were externally irreproachable, the law—including natural law—enquired into the internal side only in the case of an illegal action. If an act was in

45

conformity with the law, its motives were of no interest to the latter. Here, Pufendorf 'anticipated Kant's distinction of legality and morality'.[109]

According to John Locke (1632–1704) resistance to the state is allowed, but only if the latter acts contrary to its own positive law as well as to natural law; the people, however, shall judge whether this has happened.[110] His doctrine of the natural liberty of the individual and the absolute right of the latter to be protected in his life, freedom and property became— together with the teachings of Pufendorf—the philosophical justification of the American Declaration of Independence.[111]

Christian Thomasius (1655–1728) further developed the distinction of law and morality on the lines laid down by his teacher Pufendorf. He tried to separate the law (*iustum*), which imposes only external duties and is based on compulsion, from morality (*honestum*) and mores (*decorum*) which are interested in the internal side of human behaviour. Natural law, using no compulsion and pronouncing recommendations rather than commands, is not really law, it is social ethics. On the other hand, it requires more than does the positive law: while the latter prescribes only that we should not do to others what we do not want others to do to us, the natural law requires that we should do to others what we want them to do to us. Thomasius 'was drawing the moral of two centuries of religious strife and persecution', writes d'Entrèves. 'His theory lays the foundations of the modern, secular, tolerant State. Its novelty, however, is practical rather than theoretical.'[112] But d'Entrèves, while stressing the fact that the difference between law and morality had been recognized long before Thomasius, makes it clear that the practical consequences of that insight, in particular regarding the exclusion of the State from the sphere of conscience, were sharply drawn only by writers such as Pufendorf and Thomasius.

As pointed out by most historians of the law of nature movement, its crucial testing time came towards the end of the eighteenth and the beginning of the nineteenth centuries, under the impact of the teachings of Immanuel Kant, on the one hand, and of the historical law school, on the other. While Kant's (1724–1804) philosophy of law has been called 'a typical application of the natural law doctrine'[113] it has also been regarded as its death-knell. The truth lies between these extreme views. If the doctrine of natural law 'is in fact nothing but an assertion that law is a part of ethics' (d'Entrèves),[114] Kant, whose *Einteilung der Moral* included the whole legal system,[115] might well be regarded as a member of the natural law school. At the same time, however, his emphatic distinction of legality (*Gesetzmässigkeit*), which he defines as the mere conformity of an act with the positive law regardless of its motives, and morality (*Sittlichkeit*), where the idea of a moral duty provides the only valid motive, shows him clearly as a follower of Pufendorf's doctrine (above).[116] Kant's concept of the 'good will' (*der gute Wille*) as the only criterion of a morally good act made it impossible of course to discover any objective basis for the natural law. On the political-practical side, he expressed himself strongly against any attempt to construct a right of resistance to the legislative power of the State.[117]

Nevertheless, 'lip-service continued to be paid to the idea of natural law' by great and influential lawyers such as Sir William Blackstone (1723–1780), who could write 'This law of nature being coeval with mankind and dictated by God himself is, of course, superior in obligation to any other' and at the same time maintain the absolute legislative power of Parliament.[118] It was the utilitarian school and the legal positivists and analysts, notably Bentham and Austin, who insisted again on a clear-cut distinction of the law as it is and the law as it ought to be and 'condemned the natural-law thinkers precisely because they had blurred this apparently simple but vital distinction'.[119]

Much more sharply than in Kant occurred the break with the whole conception of natural law in the writings of Hegel (1770–1831). In the first instance, in the period between the publication of Kant's and Hegel's main works, legal philosophy had undergone fundamental changes through the emergence of the powerful school of historical jurisprudence, led by Savigny, which stressed the ever-changing character of law and was averse to any attempt to deduce a universal system of law from reason and the nature of man, instead of studying the historical development and the collective *Volksgeist* (a term translated by d'Entrèves as 'particular genius of each nation').[120] Secondly, largely under the influence of political developments Hegel became the leading protagonist of a deified conception of the State.[121] If 'what is reasonable is real, and what is real is reasonable';[122] if the State is the realization of morality, then there is no room for the dualism of State law and natural law. Nor was there any place in his system for Kant's attempt to found morality on the subjective element of the 'good will'. The emphasis on the importance of the historical change and on the futility of working out any universal laws of reason and of nature was no doubt one of the merits of Hegel's philosophy, but even he could not finally destroy the idea of a law of nature as such.

Perhaps the most famous, though universally criticized, of the twentieth-century theories was Rudolf Stammler's compromising formula of the 'natural law with changing contents' which, while abandoning the hope of deriving any material rules of natural law from human nature and reason, tries to construct a few, supposedly only formal, principles of universal validity as part of the positive law itself. In this Stammler failed, and the prolific discussion provoked by his theory has shown that a purely formal version cannot satisfy the craving of men for some real yardstick of the validity of the positive law.[123]

Summing up the main lessons to be drawn from this age-old and tragic history of the natural law, we might make the following points.

(a) There is no single and unchanging concept of natural law. While its underlying idea is the longing of mankind for an absolute yardstick to measure the goodness or badness of human actions and the law of the State and to define their relations to religion and morality, the final lesson is that no such yardstick can be found.

(b) Starting from a condition where there was no clear distinction between the religious, the moral and the legal codes, the natural law school, without clearly defining the place of the natural law between these two systems, eventually at least succeeded in establishing certain distinguishing criteria between law and morality. The theological foundation of the natural law was almost entirely abandoned in the course of the seventeenth century.

(c) The natural law school, being incapable of working out any universally valid material criteria of natural law, could not prove in general terms why certain specific acts had to be regarded as bad in themselves (per se).

(d) Nor could it develop any universally accepted theory regarding the relationship between natural and positive law; but the latter came more and more to be regarded as indispensable even by adherents of the natural law school. In cases where the two systems clashed the medieval view of the superiority of the natural law was gradually abandoned; nor was any clearly defined right of the individual established to resist the application of 'unjust' positive laws. In the theories of Hobbes and Hegel the defeat of the original concept of natural law reached its climax through the more or less complete fusion of natural law and positive law and the absolute view of the rights of the State. Even the view that chronologically the natural law had emerged before the positive law has been challenged, and it has been suggested that the very existence of the latter may have stimulated criticism and thus led to the idea of a natural law.[124]

(e) In spite of this defeat of the natural law school its basic idea has survived in various shades, as has also the attempt to confine it to certain purely formal principles. It has become clear that we have here to deal with a certain attitude of mind rather than with a clearly definable theory. This is the peculiar strength and the weakness of the natural law, which has emerged from its long and complex history as the moral conscience of the positive law rather than as a second, independent, system of law.

(f) As we have seen, perhaps the greatest achievement of the natural law movement has been that, through the writings of both its adherents and its opponents, it has produced a better understanding of the relationship between law and morality. Let us now reconsider the principal criteria which have emerged in the course of this long discussion.[125]

(g) Going back to Pufendorf, Thomasius and Kant, there is the view that the law is concerned only with external conduct, morality only with the internal side of our conduct, with our motives and intentions.[126] On the surface, this is clearly unsatisfactory since the law, especially the criminal law, has to an ever-growing extent shown the tendency to pay attention to internal factors. The history of the criminal law is in part the history of this movement to exculpate offenders because of their general incapacity of acting with a 'guilty mind' (young children, low-grade mental defectives, certain categories of insane persons) or because in specific instances they did not act with the kind of intent required by the law (e.g. because of error, compulsion, etc.). The moral quality of the offender's motive, it is true, is generally not considered essential for the question of legal guilt itself, but it is usually taken into account in the choice of the penalty (see above, Note 78). In short, the courts 'are increasingly busy with ascertaining subjective mental states and with adjudging legal effects in accordance with them'.[127] Where, as in the cases of 'strict liability' (see above, p. 24), it is different, we feel that such provisions are not quite appropriate for inclusion in the criminal law, although they may be indispensable to other legal disciplines. If the criminal law would be entirely divorced from internal factors criminology, too, would be in danger of losing two of its most important branches, criminal psychology and forensic psychiatry.

Moreover, even the view that before the forum of morality it is only motive and intention that matter cannot be as fully accepted as it appears from Kant's rigoristic formula that nothing can be called morally good except a good will and an action done from a sense of moral duty. To quote only a few of the many philosophers who have opposed Kant on this point, Sir David Ross thinks that 'our (moral) duty is to do certain things, not to do them from the sense of duty',[128] admitting, however, that 'the moral worth of my doing it depends mainly on the worth of the motive', and Hocking writes: 'It is true that moral problems are matters of conscience and are referred to inner regions of motivation. But what are these hidden motives concerned with if not with decisions regarding behaviour?'[129] And a nineteenth-century legal philosopher, Georg Jellinek, concludes from the historical origin of both law and morality, which he finds in the *mores*, and in accordance with the emphasis he places on the social side of morality, that not only the legal, but also the moral norm requires for its fulfilment an action in accordance with that norm.[130] Another legal philosopher, Gustav Radbruch, distinguishes four different meanings of the contrast 'external-internal':[131] in addition to the one just mentioned, it could, he thinks, also mean that the law is concerned with the value of human actions to the community, and morality with the absolute value, from which it is sometimes concluded that in law there are not only duties but also corresponding rights of other persons whereas in morals there are only duties without corresponding rights.[132] The latter, however, can, as Radbruch and Kantorowicz have shown,[133] hardly be accepted in this generality. 'Mutual promises to be faithful to each other between lovers and friends are usually of a definitely non-legal, purely moral character, but they are felt to be contractually binding, as is shown by the violent reaction when they are broken' (Kantorowicz). More support has been given to a third interpretation of the distinction 'external-internal' as meaning that the law is 'heteronomous', morality 'autonomous'. But as Ginsberg points out, 'even in highly developed forms of morality the rules are in large measure heteronomous, since they come to the individual from the group and are maintained to a great extent by external sanctions'.[134] For this reason, it would be equally misleading to say that the law uses external force to safeguard its rules, whereas morality knows only the persuasive force of our own conscience. Although the law has often to resort to external force, there are legal provisions which dispense with the latter, and it can altogether be maintained that in the last resort the strength of the law, too, has to rest on something else than mere compulsion.[135]

Nevertheless, there is a great deal of truth in the view, which was first adumbrated by the great eighteenth-century teachers of natural law, Pufendorf and Thomasius, and then more clearly stated by Kant that the law 'never *prescribes* internal conduct' (Kantorowicz); it requires mere 'legality', external conformity. If only we conform to the requirements of the law, we are not questioned concerning our motives for doing so, whereas from the point of view of morality our conduct, though lawful, may have to be condemned. Because of our bad motives, Kantorowicz therefore calls this kind of 'legalistic justice' quasi-morality, and it is all, he thinks, that can be achieved by 'social reform, practical politics and the pressure of public opinion', although it may eventually lead to genuine morality (p. 49).

(*h*) Closely related to the points discussed under (*g*) is the generally held view that the criminal law does not, as a rule, prescribe positive action on the part of the citizen at all, but is rather satisfied with something negative, i.e. not to commit murder, rape, etc., whereas morality may well require us to do something to put our moral ideals into action. From this rule, however, there is a growing number of exceptions. It is obvious that the forces behind the development of the Welfare State are to some extent responsible for this trend. If it is an offence, for example, to make use of a vessel which is not seaworthy or a car which is not roadworthy, this means from the practical point of view in the last resort not merely that we should abstain from using such vessels or cars, but also that we should do something to improve their sea- or roadworthiness since mere passivity would lead to economic stagnation and the ultimate breakdown of communal life. Therefore, the shipowner commits a criminal offence if he does not provide his vessel with the lifeboats and other equipment needed for its safety. In other fields, too, the prohibition not to act in a certain way is supplemented by the legal command to do something. In his famous rhetorical question concerning the failure to save another person's life although it could have been done without any personal risk Jeremy Bentham regarded such omissions as clearly deserving legal punishment ('Who is there that in any of these cases would think punishment misapplied?').[136] English law has not yet accepted this view, provided of course that no specific duty to save life (such as, for example, in the case of parents towards their children) exists in which case omissions would be punishable.[137] The German Criminal Code, § 330c, however, establishes such a duty for cases of accidents or general communal danger and punishes contraventions with imprisonment up to one year or a fine, and the German Draft Code of 1962, § 232, proposes the same and points out[138] that the provision marks a break with the older conception of criminal law and means the inclusion within the latter of a sphere previously reserved to morality. The justification for this change is seen in the idea of the growing interdependence of all citizens and their increased responsibilities towards the community. Apart from this comparatively limited subject of mutual assistance in accidents, etc., there are certain instances where English law has provided penalties for mere inaction.[139] There is first the old common law misdemeanour 'misprision of felony', i.e. failure to reveal a felony to the authorities, and there is the case, referred to by Glanville Williams, of s. 22 of the Road Traffic Act, 1930, which punishes the driver of a vehicle for failing to report an accident, but in the latter case the driver is more than simply an onlooker; he has been somehow, though perhaps innocently, involved in the matter. The same applies to the case, also quoted by Williams, of the owner of a car convicted of abetting the driver in driving at dangerous speed although he had done nothing to encourage him. However, even without such doubtful examples there remains enough material to illustrate the growing tendency to punish mere omissions. The well-known legal tag 'Thou shalt not kill, but need not strive officiously to keep alive' is no longer as generally valid as it was in former times.

(*i*) One of the apparently simplest and therefore most popular distinctions has been Georg Jellinek's description of the law as the 'ethical minimum',[140] but it would be correct only if the criminal law would actually penalize all the worst cases of immoral behaviour. If this were so we could say that these cases form the minimum standard expected by the Moral Code, and all the less revolting cases of immorality would be excluded from the scope of the criminal law. However, neither of this is true. Once we realize that there are many cases of misbehaviour which are morally far worse than cases coming under the scope of the criminal law, Jellinek's formula falls to the ground. (It is of course a different matter to say that the ground covered by

51

the criminal law is narrower than that covered by moral rules.) To give only a few illustrations, bigamy is an offence in probably all countries possessing the institution of monogamous marriage, but provided there is no deception of the innocent spouse it is difficult to regard bigamy as morally worse than adultery, which is not punishable in most of those countries; actually adultery may often be far worse morally.[141] Or take the offence of false pretences: it is traditionally limited to false statements on 'existing facts', whereas mere promises for the future are as a rule not punishable, although such promises have occasionally been interpreted as implying a present intention to do something in the future, which would constitute an inner fact.[142] This limitation to false statements concerning the present may be wise jurisprudence, but its moral justification is more than doubtful. In the interesting case *R v. Dent* the Court of Criminal Appeal quashed a conviction on the ground that the accused had made only a promise as to his future conduct, Mr. Justice Devlin (as he then was) reading the judgment of the Court and the Lord Chief Justice addressing the appellant with the words: 'Do not think that we are doing it because we think you are an honest man because we do not.'[143] There is, we might add, of course common agreement that many highly immoral acts are committed every day which cannot, and should not, be legally punishable because of certain intrinsic limitations arising from the nature of law, some of which are mentioned below under (*k*).

Yet another view holds that law is 'standardized morality'. This is correct in its emphasis on the greater standardization needed by the law as compared with moral rules and on the fact that the latter distinguish more thoroughly between one type of conduct and another and that certain legal distinctions can be explained only by the need of the law to establish hard and fast lines of demarcation which may have no moral justification. The seduction of a girl of slightly over sixteen may be morally far worse in the light of the circumstances of the individual case than the seduction of a girl slightly under that age, but the criminal law treats only the latter as a crime.

(*k*) Certainty and predictability, 'provability', clarity and precision of definition are also regarded as essential attributes of the criminal law, whereas in the moral sphere, owing to the great individuality of moral decisions and the absence of specially trained legislators and interpreters, these qualities are even more difficult to achieve than in the legal field where, in fact, they are also more an ideal than reality.[144] Predictability, moreover, is a value hardly indispensable in moral decisions.

5. *The Present Dispute on Law and Morality*

The discussions of recent years, largely but not exclusively provoked by the Wolfenden Report of 1957, can here be considered only in their briefest outlines. Their main stages have been marked by the publication of a British Academy lecture on 'The Enforcement of Morals', delivered in 1959 by a judge of high repute, Sir Patrick (now Lord) Devlin, criticizing the Wolfenden Report and in its turn criticized by Professor H. L. A. Hart of Oxford in his Stanford University lectures on *Law, Liberty and Morality*, published in 1963, and already before in a B.B.C. broadcast of 1959 on 'Immorality and Treason'. These publications have been widely and thoughtfully reviewed both in Britain and the United States.[145] What are the principal points at issue in this controversy, which are likely to be of more than passing interest to the criminologist? Apart from its failure, already noted, adequately to consider the historical-philosophical literature on the problem the weakness of the Wolfenden Report was that it based its argument too strongly on the difference between crime and sin rather than on that between crime and immorality. 'Unless a deliberate attempt is to be made by society, acting through the agency of the law, to equate the sphere of crime with that of sin, there must remain a realm of private morality and immorality which is, in brief and crude terms, not the law's business' (para. 62).

This sentence can easily be interpreted as meaning complete identification of religious and moral concepts which should no longer be regarded as acceptable ever since Grotius had freed the law of nature of its theological fetters (see above). To base on it the principal, and highly creditable, recommendation of the Report, i.e. that homosexual conduct between consenting adults should no longer be a punishable offence, was a strategic mistake which has weakened the force of the Report. This has recently been admitted by Norman St. John Stevas, M.P., a Catholic lawyer and writer, who also takes issue with the Wolfenden Report on the ground that 'the distinction between crime and sin is not the appropriate one to draw. Sin, as such, is a theological concept.'[146]

Lord Devlin's attitude to this question of law and sin is not very clear, but after some hesitation he, too, reaches the conclusion that, while as a matter of history the moral principles which the law enforces have been derived from Christian teaching (a far too general statement which may be disputed in those very large parts of the world which do not adhere to the Christian religion), 'the law can no longer rely on doctrines in which citizens are entitled to disbelieve. It is necessary therefore to look for some other source' (p. 9).[147] This other source is what he calls 'public morality': 'Every society has a moral structure as well as a political one' (p. 11)—which may be true as an ideal but hardly as present-day reality—and every society has, he thinks, the right to pass judgment on matters of morals and to enforce its judgment by force of law. What, however, is 'public morality'? According to Lord Devlin immorality is 'what every right-minded person is presumed to consider to be immoral', or one can also say, what 'the man on the Clapham omnibus' or 'the man in the jury box' regards as immoral (p. 16). This 'right-minded' or 'reasonable' man is not necessarily identical with the 'rational' man: 'matters of this sort are not determined by rational argument. Every moral judgment, unless it claims a divine source, is simply a feeling that no right-minded man could behave in any other way without admitting that he was doing wrong. It is the power of a common sense and not the power of reason that is behind the judgments of society' (p. 18). Unfortunately, this last sentence is largely true, but such an abdication of reason on the part of society is highly regrettable and dangerous; it deserves no encouragement, and it is surprising that it should here be praised as an ideal state of affairs by a former judge of high authority who has no doubt always tried to base his own judgments not on vague feelings but on clear reasoning. Moreover, we cannot but note the use of an extremely hazy terminology in the formula just quoted, 'what every right-minded person is presumed to consider to be immoral': who decides whether a man is 'right-minded'? Probably the one who agrees with his views. Who 'presumes' that such a person 'considers' certain acts to be immoral? Again, presumably only the one who agrees with the views which that person is 'presumed' to have. This strange reasoning reaches its climax in the sentence: 'If the reasonable man believes that a practice is immoral and believes also—no matter whether the belief is right or wrong, so be it that it is honest and dispassionate—that no right-minded member of his society could think otherwise, then for the purpose of the law it is immoral' (p. 23). Surely, this constitutes a complete self-abdication of reason, law and ethics in favour of the views, however absurd and misguided, of the man whom the author regards as 'reasonable'.

However, we have now to proceed to the next stage of Lord Devlin's argument. According to him, in order to put the machinery of the criminal law into motion it is not enough for his right-minded man to harbour certain feelings; a balance has to be struck between the rights and interests of society and those of the individual. The latter has a *locus standi* too: 'he cannot be expected to surrender to the judgment of society the whole conduct of his life. . . . There must be toleration of the maximum individual freedom that is consistent with the integrity of society', although 'it cannot be said that this is a principle that runs all through the criminal law' (p. 17). Because of this need for toleration it is 'not nearly enough to say that a majority dislike a practice; there must be a real feeling of reprobation. . . . Not everything is to be tolerated. No society can do without intolerance, indignation, and disgust; they are the forces behind the moral law. . . .' After this trumpet-call for moral and legal judgments based on emotions rather than reasoning it comes almost as an anti-climax to be told that 'But before a society can put a practice beyond the limits of tolerance there must be a deliberate judgment that the practice is injurious to society' (p. 18). Moreover, while 'moral standards do not shift', the 'limits of tolerance' shift from generation to generation, and a time may come when the 'swell of indignation may have abated and the law left without the strong backing which it needs. But it is then difficult to alter the law without giving the impression that moral judgment is being weakened. This is now one of the factors that is strongly militating against any alteration to the law of homosexuality' (p. 19). While we can agree with much of this, especially with the emphasis on the need for a 'deliberate judgment that the practice is injurious to society'—this was in fact the *leitmotiv* of our *Criminal Justice* (p. 5)—we believe that not only the limits of tolerance but the underlying moral standards themselves do change. Moreover, while it is certainly a 'good working principle' that in any new matter of morals 'the law should be slow to act' (p. 19), it is difficult to understand the logic of the conclusion drawn by Lord Devlin that because the next generation may feel less indignation in matters of homosexuality, thus leaving the law without moral backing, this should be one of the reasons against changing the present law on the subject. The contrary should be true.

To sum up, the followers of Lord Devlin seem to be left with a criminal law founded not upon reason and a morality founded not on love, forgiveness and justice, but on the combination of three emotions which can scarcely be regarded as highly creditable: intolerance, indignation and disgust. Nor is Lord Devlin's concept of law and morality founded on Durkheim's theory of the 'collective conscience', which he ignores throughout.[148] One cannot help sympathizing with Professor Hart's comment:

If this is what morality is . . . we may well ask what justification there is for taking it, and turning it as such, into criminal law with all the misery which criminal punishment entails. . . . Why should we not summon all the resources of our reason, sympathetic understanding, as well as critical intelligence, and insist that before general moral feeling is turned into criminal law it is submitted to scrutiny of a different kind from Sir Patrick's? Surely, the legislator should ask whether the general morality is based on ignorance, superstition, or misunderstanding. . . . To any theory which, like this one, asserts that the criminal law may be used on the vague ground that the preservation of morality is essential to society and yet omits to stress the need for critical scrutiny, our reply should be: 'Morality, what crimes may be committed in thy name!'[149]

We have in fact already been reminded that 'we once burnt old women because, without giving our reasons, we felt in our hearts that witchcraft was intolerable', and Hitler's philosophy was also one of 'intolerance, indignation and disgust' as the forces behind his brand of the moral law.

Professor Ginsberg, too, though slightly less critical than Hart of Devlin's theory, concludes that the latter 'nowhere explains why he thinks society has the right to inflict pain or suffering on the offender other than that involved in the expression of public disapproval'. He also takes issue with Devlin's view that the value of an investigation such as that by the Wolfenden Committee lies in providing information on the question of how to balance the conflicting claims of society and the individual and how to find out whether a particular practice is regarded by society as sufficiently abhorrent to take penal action. In fact, as Ginsberg rightly remarks, the Wolfenden Report showed no way of how to discover an 'unequivocal public opinion' on the subjects of its enquiry nor, we have to add, did it even try to ascertain the state of such opinion.[150]

Turning now to Professor Hart's own views as far as they are not directly reflected in his criticism of Lord Devlin, he distinguishes four major questions concerning the relations between law and morality, each of them possibly to be sub-divided into several minor ones: First, has law been influenced in its development by morals? Second, has morality been influenced by law? In both cases the answer is 'yes'. Thirdly, is law open to moral criticism? Here, too, the answer is clearly in the affirmative. It is the fourth question, however, that is the real subject of Hart's Stanford lectures; it is the same as that of Lord Devlin's: the legal enforcement of morals. 'Ought immorality as such to be a crime?' Needless to say, Hart comes out strongly against this, taking his illustrative material mainly from the sphere of sexual morality, in particular from the topics of the Wolfenden Report and from the widely discussed case Shaw v. Director of Public Prosecutions.[151] In the latter, the House of Lords has, in Hart's words, 'fashioned a very formidable weapon for punishing immorality as such' (p. 10) by reviving the old 'exceedingly vague and indeed obscure' common law offence of 'conspiring to corrupt public morals'. In his view, there is a danger that the resuscitation of this antiquated concept might nullify the efforts of modern legislation such as the Obscene Publications Act, 1959, to restrict the powers of the criminal law to intrude into the realm of morals and to prevent the criminal courts from re-establishing themselves as *custodes morum*. Seen in conjunction with Lord Devlin's statement that 'in a number of crimes its function (i.e. that of the criminal law) is simply to enforce a moral principle and nothing else' (p. 9) and his views as to how to ascertain the existence of such principles and their hold on majority opinion, cases such as Shaw's do indeed seem to reveal the presence in the legal thinking of high judicial authorities of a tendency to play the role of sole arbiters in matters of morality, regardless of whether a particular brand of immorality causes real harm to the community.

Hart then goes on (pp. 17–25) to discuss the distinction between 'positive' and 'critical' morality, the former meaning the morality actually accepted by a given social group—this is the morality which Lord Devlin treats as the only one—whereas 'critical' morality embodies the 'general moral principles used in the criticism of actual social institutions including positive morality'. Here it seems we have a crucial distinction in the field of morality parallel to the one between positive law and natural law in the legal field, the natural law movement asking for the credentials of the positive law of the State and 'critical' morality asking for those of the 'positive' morality of society. Against Lord Devlin's thesis that 'society is justified in taking the same steps to preserve its moral code as it does to preserve its government and other essential institutions' (p. 15) Hart argues that this right depends on what sort of society it is and what the steps to be taken are: 'If the society were mainly devoted to the cruel persecution of a racial or religious minority, or if the steps to be taken included hideous tortures, it is arguable that what Lord Devlin terms the "disintegration" of such a society would be morally better than its continued existence, and steps ought not to be taken to preserve it' (p. 19).

Welcome as this restoration of a more critical attitude towards traditional morality is, it does not yet solve all our problems. We have already seen that the natural law school had failed in its prolonged efforts to produce a workable justification for the right of the individual to resist the application of 'unjust' positive laws. Closely allied to this is the corresponding question whether the courts have the right and the duty to treat as not binding statutes which they regard as violating the moral law. The matter assumed an unprecedented topicality and urgency in Germany after the Second World War in relation to laws made under the Nazi regime which were regarded as immoral after its downfall. In his Oliver Wendell Holmes lecture delivered in 1957 at the Harvard Law School, Hart discusses one of these cases, which is typical of many others.[152] In 1944, a German soldier was denounced by his wife, who wanted to get rid of him, for making insulting remarks on Hitler; he was sentenced to death under a Nazi statute, not however executed but sent to the front after a short spell in prison. In 1949 the wife was convicted of the offence of having, through the medium of the criminal courts, unlawfully deprived her husband of his liberty (§ 239 Criminal Code). The statute under which he had been sentenced was declared null and void as being 'contrary to the sound conscience and sense of justice of all decent human beings'. This sentence was representative of many similar ones passed on Nazi informers by German criminal courts at the time. Hart has some doubts as to whether the wife's conviction could be justified in this way; he would have preferred a retrospective law to the same effect; this would, he thinks, 'at least have had the merits of candour'. This is the logical consequence of his general view which is fundamentally in accord with that of the legal positivists and holds that law remains law even if it is evil, but if it is too evil it must not be obeyed. The opposite view, represented, for example, by the Harvard Professor of Jurisprudence Lon L. Fuller in his spirited reply to Hart and also by Gustav Radbruch in his later writings, claims that 'law' which is morally evil is not law at all. As far as the ultimate effect is concerned there is hardly any practical difference between these two points of view as they both agree that in certain extreme cases the law, or alleged 'law', ceases to be binding. They even agree, although for different reasons, that in the informer cases the passing of a retroactive statute might have been preferable to the alternative of leaving the decision to the courts.[153] The present writer shares this latter view, but mainly for the more practical than theoretical reason that if such matters are left to the judges their decisions may differ from court to court, whereas the legislator can achieve uniformity.[154] There is, however, one final point to be added to the Hart-Fuller debate of which these two brilliant exponents of Anglo-American legal philosophy have apparently been unaware: stimulated by the profoundly impressive experience of what Hart calls Gustav Radbruch's 'conversion' (p. 616), under the impact of the spectacle of the Nazi regime, from legal positivism to an attitude much closer to the teachings of the natural law school,[155] they reflect that the strongly positivist leanings of pre-Hitler German legal philosophy had undermined the sensitivity to moral issues and thus contributed to the success of the Nazi movement. Here it seems to have been ignored that already in the years before 1933 strong anti-positivist tendencies had come to the surface not only in parts of German legal literature but even in certain utterances of the Supreme Court of the Reich. Proof of this is, first, the support given in both theory and practice to the concept of *Ubergesetzlicher Notstand*, i.e. the idea that there are cases of acting under duress which, though not explicitly recognized by the positive law as grounds for justification or excuse, have nevertheless to be accepted as exempting the actor from punishment.[156] This was an idea

58

developed not *contra* but merely *praeter legem*, and, being in the interest of the accused, such exemptions were easily reconcilable with the general principles of the criminal law. First formulated as 'professorial' law, the concept soon became judicial law, and after the passing of the present German Draft Code (see Note 156 above) it will be promoted to the dignity of statutory law. It is a concept of great practical significance which tries to provide a legal solution for a wide variety of fundamental moral problems. Its essential features are briefly these: If a person can avert a present danger to his or another person's life, health, honour, liberty, property, etc., only by acting against the law such action is permissible if he has properly balanced the conflicting interests and if, in particular, the interests which he wishes to protect are of considerably higher value on the generally accepted scale of values than the interests he violates. This requires an assessment of conflicting interests and valuations which may force the acting person and, subsequently, the court to make moral judgments of the greatest complexity and responsibility. For a few typical constellations of this kind, such as abortions and operations performed without the patient's consent, the Draft Code provides detailed special regulations (§§ 152–62).[157] Compared with the Draft Code, the detailed analysis of the English case law of duress and necessity given by Glanville Williams (Chapters 17 and 18) shows that in the latter very similar considerations of how to balance the conflicting interests and evils have been used, with the main difference that according to the 'general, but not universal' view duress is not a defence against a charge of murder (see Note 77 above), whereas no general exception has been made for this crime in the Draft Code. Williams rightly concludes his analysis with the words: 'The solution may be that there is no general solution', and even the German formula can provide nothing but the abstract framework, within which the individuals and the courts will have to work out their own solutions as to the morality and legality of each individual case.

The second, far more extreme, illustration of natural law tendencies in recent German legal history occurred in the sphere not of criminal but of civil law when the judges of the Supreme Court in a public statement openly refused to apply a federal statute dealing with certain aspects of the German inflation because the judges regarded the way adopted by that statute as grossly unfair and therefore violating the moral law.[158] This was in the first place of course a striking symptom of the weakness of the Weimar Republic and of the scant respect for it on the part of some sections of the judiciary, but it was also an expression of the trend in favour of the ideas of the natural law school. How deeply the concern for problems of natural law and the relation of law to morality is felt in the present-day German literature on criminal law and legal philosophy is shown in such writings as the programmatical study by Thomas Würtenberger on *Die geistige Situation der deutschen Strafrechtswissenschaft*[159] (The Psychological Situation of the German Science of Criminal Law). While this author is somewhat critical towards the subject of natural law in view of the confusing variety of modern interpretations and opposes any attempts to replace careful legal reasoning on specific problems by premature appeals to natural law ideas, he nevertheless accepts the latter as an 'indispensable element of human existence' to which recourse has to be taken in cases of emergency and of the gravest attacks on human dignity (pp. 20–9), which is a clear reference to the Nazi outrages.

After these excursions into some of the historical, international and political aspects of the matter we now return to our starting point: Of what kind are the lessons to be drawn for our original question of how to argue with the lawbreaker on moral grounds? First, it has clearly emerged that the discussion stimulated by the Wolfenden Report has often been kept within the far too narrow boundaries of sexual morality, and even with the addition of certain border-line problems such as sterilization or artificial insemination by a donor and of such non-sexual matters as mercy-killing (the Liége Thalidomide Trial), abortion and other crimes against the person the discussion is on an inadequate basis. What we are here concerned with is lawbreaking in its entirety, i.e. the whole range of the social and economic problems behind the criminal law to be treated below in Part Four. Is it immoral to steal from the small owner, but moral to do so from a large one? Is the 'white collar criminal' morally in his right because he is backed by his peers and does not regard himself as a criminal? Or, for similar reasons, the traffic offender, who usually has most motorists, i.e. a very large part of the population, on his side? Is it true that '50,000 Frenchmen can do no wrong', and that the majority is morally justified in imposing its will on minority groups by means of violence? How far can a Michael Kohlhaas and the other social rebels go in their search for justice, or the worker who feels that he is denied the status which he thinks he can expect on account of his skill and performance? Have our 'angry young men' the right to break the law made for them by their elders and betters who, they argue, are incapable of understanding their peculiar problems, or have women this right in the interest of their families? Or what should be our moral judgment if in cases of swindling the victim's motives are as immoral as those of the swindler, i.e. if he is out to make high profits, to get rich quick? Should there be a squaring of accounts, with the guilt of the victim attenuating or entirely wiping out that of the offender? And what about the 'criminal from a sense of guilt' (Chapter 17) With him, it seems, we need hardly argue except to persuade him that he could perhaps get rid of his guilt feeling by means other than crime. But the psychopath (Chapter 15)? Has he no guilt feelings at all, is he not receptive to moral argument?

So far, neither our moral philosophers nor our philosophizing lawyers have given us entirely satisfactory answers to such highly practical questions. Nor can we be expected to supply them here, but the material presented below will perhaps encourage some of those better qualified to try again. In a previous book and in the earlier part of the present chapter we came to the conclusion that there is one moral argument that could possibly be used in our discussion with the lawbreaker—an argument in no way new and original, but for the time being apparently the only one at hand: As there is no system of natural law that could successfully compete with the specific provisions of the positive law of the state, the latter has to be obeyed even where in an individual case it seems to be unjust. And—to confine the argument for a moment to some aspects of economic crime—whoever wishes to expropriate the proprietor could do so, if at all, only in the interest of the community as a whole, not in his own selfish interest, and on condition that he does not claim for himself the protection of the same law which he has repudiated by his own action. Even then he has hardly at his disposal the technical means to undertake such a general redistribution of the wealth of the community more fairly than the latter with its greater resources of trained manpower and technical know-how. Therefore, he should better abstain from trying by means of criminal action to reform the world in which he wishes to live. In *Criminal Justice and Social Reconstruction* (especially Chapter 7) we have dealt with these matters at greater length and quoted (p. 107), among other references, what Friedrich Engels wrote in 1844 in his *Condition of the Working Class in England*: 'The workers soon realized that crime did not help matters . . . Besides, theft was the most primitive form of protest. . . . A new form of opposition had to be found . . .', i.e. the political. Since then, political and economic conditions have changed almost out of recognition, and it is more than ever true that breaking the law is, as a rule, not the best way of how to solve problems of inequality. Moreover, and this point will be obvious and accepted even by the least intelligent of the 'rebels', as in the case of Michael Kohlhaas's rebellion the damage done by crime usually falls on the innocent and poor far more than on the guilty ones. For other forms of economic crime, for example, white collar offences, the argument will of course have to be on different lines and probably more sophisticated.

To the general rule there is one exception, which has emerged from our survey of the history of the natural law movement up to the present time: only one, but it is fundamental: Where the State itself

61

is dominated by criminals, where an utterly brutal and callous form of dictatorship leaves no door open for legitimate political opposition, where its so-called law is only a pretence to make their crimes appear outwardly respectable and where its crimes are on a gigantic scale, resistance becomes a moral right and even a duty. This introduces a quantitative element into moral questions, but there often comes a point where quantity turns into quality. It is, moreover, the point where the criminal law merges into the law of revolution. 'The existence of heaven', wrote the historian Friedrich Meinecke,[160] 'made the existence of hell tolerable', which can only mean that with the weakening of religious beliefs the will to resist tyrannical governments on earth has been gaining strength and moral justification. Perhaps we have not, after all, made quite as much progress in our thinking as we often believe since the great Pufendorf wrote, three hundred years ago: 'individuals must endure the misuse of the State's authority as men endure storm and bad weather: they must go into exile themselves rather than expel the ruler; but they may be competent to resist if the worst comes to the worst and the fundamental contract itself is broken'.[161] And his perhaps even greater English contemporary John Locke—as we have seen, they were both born in the same year 1632—proclaimed essentially the same doctrine more cautiously in different words.[162] Long before them, however, another German thinker, Johannes Althusius (1557–1638), to whom Otto Gierke devoted his important monograph,[163] had developed his doctrine of the sovereignty of the people. Even so, the fundamental question of the existence and the scope of the *jus resistendi* and in particular whether such a right should be given to the people themselves or only to Parliament never received a clear and unambiguous answer in the literature of the natural law school. Nor was Luther, whose opposition was largely responsible for the defeat of the German Peasants' Revolt, more helpful in clarifying that doctrine, although he was inclined to affirm the existence of such a right whenever the vital interests of religion were at stake.[164]

The reader, whose patience will by now have become thoroughly exhausted, is likely to ask: 'Well and good, but what have these cogitations of sixteenth- and seventeenth-century philosophers, lawyers and theologians to do with the problem in hand?' Our answer is that all this is vital to our line of argument, and in fact no less so than the corresponding disputes between modern legal philosophers (Devlin–Hart–Fuller–Radbruch). But where, it will be asked, is the criminological significance of our discussion to be found? Is not criminology, as pointed out in Chapter 1, basically a 'fact'-finding, not a normative discipline? Has it not here become too deeply involved in moral disputes? We take the view that we are still keeping within the limits of

a discipline which tries to understand the causes of crime and the evolution of a criminal career. If it is true that the criminal from a sense
of injustice is an important criminological phenomenon we have to
understand the genesis of that sense just as the psycho-analyst keeps
within the boundaries of criminology when trying to understand the
genesis of the criminal from a sense of guilt. And if it should be said
that our explanations are unlikely to cut much ice with the modern
criminal, at least with the, still probably not very large, category of
the real professional, we might retort that even if this should be true
we have still to try to understand him regardless of his understanding
of our argument. Moreover, it is our contention that in spite of his
far greater sophistication and the vastly expanded range of his technical abilities, experience and know-how, the average lawbreaker of
today has not much advanced in his moral and social thinking beyond
that of his predecessor of three or four hundred years ago—it is mainly
the form in which he expresses his discontent that has changed—
and if he claims to have done nothing but defend his human rights
against an unjust government and system we may have to reply in
terms not very dissimilar from that of the writers of the natural law
school. This even more so since at that time there was, at least in some
of the countries of Western Europe where they worked, no Parliament worthy of the name; there was no 'Question Time', nor was
there an Ombudsman to help to redress well-founded grievances. On
the other hand, even Parliament and Ombudsman can only see to it
that the existing law is obeyed and faithfully applied; to change it in
essential points without a change in government is often impossible.
And if 'Robert Allerton' argues that, being less patient than his
father, he is not willing to wait a hundred years for changes in the
law and social system (Chapter 20, I (3)) we can again only point out
with Friedrich Engels that crime is only a primitive and purely individual response which cannot solve general social problems. To illustrate some of these points we can perhaps not do better than once
more to refer to the famous story of Michael Kohlhaas immortalized
by Heinrich von Kleist. Kohlhaas, a horsedealer and smallholder living in the middle of the sixteenth century in Saxony not far from
Brandenburg, is introduced by Kleist as 'one of the most honest but
at the same time most terrifying men of his time. Until he reached the
age of thirty he could be regarded as the model of a good citizen . . .
but then his sense of justice made him a robber and murderer.' It so
happened that he suffered grievous and entirely unprovoked ill-
treatment with humiliation and loss of property through the servants
of a nobleman of his district, a member of one of the most distinguished and influential families of the country. As all his efforts to
obtain redress by legal means had failed—his petitions were in fact

intercepted by relatives of the culprit who held high positions at the court of Saxony; therefore they never reached the tribunal and the prince to whom they were addressed—he disposed of the rest of his property and became a rebel against his sovereign. With the help of a quickly assembled gang he burned towns and villages, killing and robbing the inhabitants. When his rebellion had reached its peak, Martin Luther himself, who lived in the neighbourhood, issued a strongly worded appeal to him to come to his senses, pointing out that whatever injustice might have been done to him by subordinates the sovereign himself had had no part in it; but after hearing from Kohlhaas personally the details of his story he advised the sovereign not only to grant him safe conduct to enable him to bring his case before the competent tribunal but also to pardon him for his rebellion, thereby anticipating the provision made by Pufendorf a century later for cases where 'the worst comes to the worst and the fundamental contract itself is broken'. After a confused period of the usual court intrigues eventually only the first part of Luther's advice was accepted; Kohlhaas was given full and generous compensation for the losses and humiliation he had suffered; his enemy was severely punished, but he himself was executed for his crimes. There is something of the grandeur of Greek tragedy in this ending: having received belated satisfaction for the injustices done to him Kohlhaas willingly, in fact joyfully, accepts the penalty of death for his part in the tragedy—a rare example of successful legal and moral argument with the lawbreaker. There is one feature in this story, however, which somehow seems to detract from the stature of Kohlhaas as the perfect rebel and avenger of injustice: his all too complacent acceptance of the satisfaction offered to him without the slightest desire to understand his case as a mere symptom of the general misrule of class justice—he remains an individualist, without ever becoming a social and political reformer.

The modern state has put an end to rebellion of the Kohlhaas type, but it has not abolished the idea of social rebellion itself, and the criminal from a sense of injustice still remains, though in different forms, a criminological problem more frequent and more important than the psycho-analytical figure of the criminal from a sense of guilt (for example see below, Chapters 16 and 17).

6. *Summary and Conclusions*

It might be advisable for us now to look back and retrace at least some of our steps in the second part of this lengthy chapter.

(*a*) Searching for a workable definition of crime we had no doubt that any purely formal definition was inadequate and had to be supplemented by calling to our assistance the other, non-legal, forces of social control of human behaviour. If we think it unsatisfactory merely to say 'crime is what is punishable according to the criminal law', if we wish to enquire 'but *why* is just this kind of behaviour punishable and that one not?', we shall inevitably have to turn to the norms of religion, custom and morality. Thus we found that, while crime was not identical with conduct violating the norms of religion or custom, these two were often closely related to legal norms, either by inspiring the lawmaker or by being in their turn influenced by him (II, 1 and 2).

(*b*) Of even greater importance and complexity was, we found, the question of the relationship between the legal and the moral codes (II, 3). It is best described as two overlapping circles, with a large sector of each circle common to both, i.e. showing a large field of disapproved human behaviour as being both criminal and a violation of moral norms, but also showing considerable parts as remaining out-

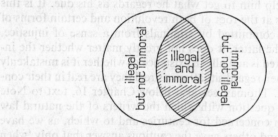

side the field covered by the two circles. In other words, there are many forms of human behaviour which are criminal without being against moral norms and also many forms which violate moral norms without being criminal. Such discrepancies had to be explained by reference to certain intrinsic differences between law and morality, their nature and objects; the law emphasizing more the external, morality more the internal side of human behaviour; the former stressing more the need not to commit disapproved acts than to do something positive, the latter expecting us not only to refrain but also to act; the law requiring of its norms and decisions a certain amount of standardization, precision and predictability, values which are less vital in the field of morality. Notwithstanding all such very important differences, however, it is imperative that law and morality should not be allowed to drift apart too often and too conspicuously, as otherwise the law would lose one of its strongest supports.

(*c*) These considerations led us first to a historical sketch of the teachings of the natural law school as the movement which, again and again, has tried to uphold the strength of the moral element in the law without, however, arriving at a clear conception of the actual relationship between the two sets of norms. Secondly, they led to a critical analysis of the present dispute on 'law and morality', largely stimulated by the Wolfenden *Report on Homosexuality and Prostitution* and continued in the writings of Lord Devlin, and Professors Hart and Fuller, and previously by Radbruch. Perhaps the most important of the many issues raised in these writings is this: whereas Devlin is content with a generally, i.e. by a vaguely defined majority, accepted brand of 'morality' as the basis for the criminal law, others, in particular Hart, ask for the moral credentials of that brand. Whether morally untenable laws have to be treated as null and void by the courts and citizens or whether they should be formally declared so by retrospective statute is also controversial. More important than this latter controversy, however, is the question of what the individual citizen is entitled to do when faced with an unjust system of law and government and when no court or statute or any other lawful way out is available to help him to get what he regards as his due. It is this situation that lies at the root of both revolution and certain forms of crime, i.e. those committed by criminals from a sense of injustice. With regard to the latter, it does not greatly matter whether the injustice to be averted is actually in existence or whether it is mistakenly felt to exist: 'If men regard situations as real they are real in their consequences' (W. I. Thomas, see also below Chapter 16, text to Note 108). This is the question with which the writers of the natural law school have been concerned for centuries and to which, as we have seen, Pufendorf and others gave the cautious answer that only 'when the worst comes to the worst and the fundamental contract is broken' can a right to revolution and to crime be recognized. Such an answer was in the end accepted by Michael Kohlhaas, but it will be of little comfort to professional criminals of the 'Robert Allerton' type, for whom the ordinary progress of social evolution is all too slow (Chapter 20 below). How large this latter group may be is a matter for speculation, but our discussion below in Chapters 19 ff. will show that it is not likely to be insignificant; moreover, for what it may be lacking in size it makes up in intensity. It is the task of the theoretical criminologist to try to give society an understanding of this human type and it is the task of the practical penologist to make him see that the alternative to what we might, for the sake of brevity, call 'Pufendorf's answer' would be injustice greater than that against which he fights, and that it may even mean utter chaos.

(*d*) So far, the discussions of this chapter have once more confirmed the truth that neither religion nor custom or morals can provide absolutely safe guides in our search for the definition of crime and the appropriate boundaries of the criminal law. This does not mean, however, that our findings have been wholly negative; quite the contrary: We have seen that, with all due reservations, those three great non-legal forces of controlling human behaviour can very often decisively determine not only the contents of criminal legislation but also the ways in which men act and react to the systems of law and society under which they have to live. This applies in particular to the crucial moral issues of our time: moral arguments with the law-breaker, of whatever kind they may be and at whatever level they may be carried on, simply cannot be altogether avoided, and criminal lawyers and judges, criminologists and penologists of all shades have to be aware of this.

Many years ago, in *Criminal Justice and Social Reconstruction* (pp. 5–6) we based our programme for the reform of the criminal law on the view that the guiding light of any such reform had to be the character of crime as *anti-social* (as contrasted to anti-religious or im-moral) behaviour: 'no form of human behaviour which is not anti-social should ever be treated as crime. . . . The reverse, however, is far from true. There are very many types of anti-social behaviour which are not, and many others which should not be, crimes', and we went on briefly to explain the reasons for this state of affairs. This formula has been widely accepted, but also occasionally misunder-stood. It was never intended as an extremist, 'out-and-out' socio-logical interpretation, but rather as a warning to the lawgiver not to penalize acts whose anti-social character could not be clearly seen. Our present discussion has a far wider scope, and its implications are in the last resort of a criminological rather than of a legal nature, i.e. we are concerned with the behaviour of actual or potential offenders more than with that of the lawgiver. Even in the present context, however, it is essential that crime should not be produced unneces-sarily and artificially by a body of criminal law which interferes with acts not clearly anti-social. It is in this sense that our previous dis-cussion links up with the points made in the present chapter.

PART TWO

Research and Methodology

Chapter 3

RESEARCH

I. ITS MEANING AND OBJECTS

Research can be defined as the use of standardized, systematic procedures in the search of knowledge.[1] The accent here is on 'standardized and systematic' as opposed to the casual accumulation of knowledge. The meaning of these adjectives will become clearer when the various methods of research are discussed below. Research has no monopoly in the search for knowledge; the latter may also be acquired by casual methods and by pure chance, but in this case it will usually be less reliable unless the casually acquired knowledge is confirmed by systematic research. Moreover, chance can as a rule lead to important discoveries only where it has been preceded by research as otherwise their significance will hardly be recognized. The role of chance in Sir Alexander Fleming's discovery of penicillin and Roentgen's discovery of the X-rays has often been described.

Although the term 'knowledge' includes far more than purely factual knowledge, research is primarily concerned with the discovery of facts, taken in the broadest sense of the word. If it can also lead to an improved understanding and evaluation of the facts observed all the better. Should it lead to the building up of generalizations, of theories, and to the discovery of scientific 'laws'? What is the relation between research and theory, and what is the place of the hypothesis in research? What are the principal pitfalls in research? These are fundamental questions so far hardly ever discussed in textbooks of criminology, with the partial exception of Vold's *Theoretical Criminology*, which tends, however, to over-estimate the role of a theory in this connection. In his chapter 'Theory as the Basis for Research'[2] he rightly stresses that criminological research has to be based on a theory of criminality and that it can find only what the theory underlying the project 'makes it possible to look for'. The results of research, he writes, may be 'pointless and meaningless' because the underlying theory is inappropriate and non-applicable to the problem in hand.[3] While all this is true, it does not fully explain the role of a

71

theory *vis-à-vis* a specific piece of research, and the theories used by Vold as illustrations tend to be too general and vague to form the basis for research. Theories suitable for research purposes have to be rather narrow and specific in order to be testable. There are of course also what Merton calls 'general sociological orientations',[4] which make it easier for the theorist to formulate his specific hypothesis. These general orientations which often stand behind a specific theory and are not necessarily sociological but may be psychological or biological as well, are themselves not testable and have first to be changed into the smaller coin of a specific theory. We are here using the terms 'specific theory' and 'hypothesis' as interchangeable,[5] and this is what they actually are. No general theory or 'orientation', such as, for example, the concept of anomie, can directly be used for research, and no specific theory should ever pretend to be more than a mere hypothesis, permanently liable to be tested by research.[6] Stephen Toulmin,[7] dealing mainly with the philosophy of the natural sciences, is inclined to reject the view that: '*all* empirical statements are hypotheses, which can, strictly speaking, never be called more than "highly probable" . . . For although all the statements we meet in science are such that one can conceive of their being reconsidered in the light of experience (i.e. empirical) only some of them can, in the present sense, be called "hypothetical" . . . One can distinguish, in any science, between the problems which are currently under discussion, and those earlier problems whose solutions have to be taken for granted if we are even to state our current problems.' 'Certainly', he writes, 'every statement in a science should conceivably be *capable* of being called in question, and of being shown empirically to be unjustified; for only so can the science be saved from dogmatism. But it is equally important that in any particular investigation many of these propositions should not actually be called in question, for by questioning some we deprive others of their very meaning. It is in this sense that the propositions of an exact science form a hierarchy and are built one upon another . . .' If we try to apply this to criminology, which is of course not an exact science, we might say, for example, that the statement that women are in general less likely to commit crime than men is a proposition which should not be called in question when we undertake to test the hypothesis that prostitution is an explanation for the lower female crime rate, but this immunity of our first proposition can be regarded only as temporary and never as final. There are important types of research which can, or even have to, be done without a hypothesis, i.e. mainly general surveys, for example, of the crime situation in a certain locality, or so-called action-research which has its origin in a general problem and will be discussed below (see Chapter 10). Even here it should not be overlooked, however, that where there is a general problem requiring investigation it can usually form the starting point for the formulation of a number of specific hypotheses. The latter, as a rule, have their origin in a broad and vaguely felt problem.[8]

The testing and retesting of hypotheses is an essential and the most obvious function of research, but not the only one. It helps to reformulate or radically to change hypotheses and to prepare for the next step in this never-ending process of readjustment which is going on between theory and hypothesis and research and the facts established by the latter.[9] It is a sign of progress in recent criminological research that it is becoming more and more used to the testing of specific hypotheses.[10]

A hypothesis has to be specific and precise, but otherwise it does not greatly matter how it is formulated, for example whether it asserts the existence of a certain correlation or whether it denies it, or whether we start from the hypothesis that there is a high positive correlation between the rate of crime against property in a certain district on the one hand and urbanism or the proportion of persons living on public assistance on the other, or whether we use the 'null' hypothesis that there is no such correlation.[11] It can safely be left to the research to find out whether the positive or the negative statement is correct. Moreover, a 'wrong' hypothesis can be as useful as a 'right' one.[12] The purpose of the hypothesis is merely to define the scope of the research, not to determine its result. It should, however, try to avoid bias (see II below).

Where does a specific hypothesis have its origin? To this vexed question Aubrey Lewis gives the answer that it 'is arrived at by divers routes, about which on the whole little is known',[13] and we might add that it is usually derived from our study of the relevant literature or from previous research or, as stated before, from a vaguely felt problem, a simple 'hunch'[14] and our experience of life. The latter may have given us the impression, for example, that certain family troubles produce juvenile delinquency.

Criminological research is most frequently concerned with the discovery of the causes of crime and the effect of various methods of treatment. Research into the frequency and distribution of crime according to age, sex, area and other social or psychological factors plays also an important role.

II. DIFFICULTIES AND DANGERS IN CRIMINOLOGICAL RESEARCH

(a) While, as we shall soon see, each of the research techniques discussed below has its specific difficulties and pitfalls, some of the latter are common to most of these techniques and might therefore be mentioned already at this stage. Some of the difficulties can be found in research in other disciplines as well, but a few are peculiar to criminology. Access to research material, for example, may be difficult to obtain in many disciplines, but the fact of penalization makes it almost impossible sometimes to obtain the material required because the fear of punishment and stigmatization deters offenders and others from giving information. This is particularly true of homosexual offences, abortion and all offences with a highly emotional flavour or offences where the police have to rely more than elsewhere on information from the public, but it also applies to the more commonplace types of offences, as the emotions connected with the fact of penalization easily falsify statistical information as well as case study material. Teachers and parents, for example, are notoriously disinclined to give truthful information about the delinquency of juveniles, unless their patience has reached breaking point. Occasionally, criminological research has to be disguised and done, for example, under the cloak of other, less stigmatizing, subjects such as housing, health or education. Access to criminological research material may be particularly difficult, moreover, because so much of it is in the possession of public authorities such as the prison administration or government departments or local authorities administering or controlling institutions for delinquent children. In some countries, including Great Britain and the United States, recent years have, however, seen considerable changes in the attitude of many authorities towards research which have removed some of the previously existing barriers. An outstanding illustration of the progress made is the study of Pentonville Prison in London, where the authors, Terence and Pauline Morris, acknowledge the 'virtually unlimited and hitherto unparalleled facilities for research' given them by the Prison Commission for England and Wales.[15]

As the fact of penalization affects the availability of case material criminological research is to some extent dependent on the contents of the criminal law; if certain penal sanctions are removed from the Statute Book access to relevant material should become easier and vice versa. It has to be borne in mind, however, that although the criminal law is strongly dependent upon public opinion legal changes may not invariably be accompanied by changes in the latter, and potential sources of information may therefore remain closed to research in spite of a relaxation in the law. The question of how far the law affects moral judgments has recently been experimentally studied by Nigel Walker and Michael Argyle (*Brit. J. Crim.*, Oct. 1964).

(b) The second difficulty arises from the existence of bias in the person of the research worker. Why should he be biased? Should not his scientific training enable him to recognize and exclude his own bias and to fight it wherever he encounters it in others? Is he not primarily concerned with the objective and dispassionate discovery of facts and facts alone? Moreover, are not his problems often selected for him by others, which should make it still easier for him to preserve an unprejudiced and unemotional attitude towards his work? To such questions the answer has to be 'yes and no'. Right from the beginning it has to be stated that our personalities and our work are dominated by certain values which determine our *Weltanschauung*.[16] We are not here concerned with their origin, we rather accept their existence as a fact from which we try to draw our conclusions, and we have also to accept the likelihood that of some of our values we are not even aware and that in our system of values—if one can here speak of a 'system' at all—conflict may be more conspicuous than consistency. A person who, whether consciously or not, holds certain values is likely to be prejudiced in a certain direction, and this may determine, first of all, the research worker's choice of his problem and his working hypothesis. There are, of course, as already indicated, cases where the choice is made for him, for example, by the foundation financing the research—although this will not often happen nowadays—or by the Government or university department which employs him. In other cases, however, the research worker is rightly left free to select the problem he wishes to study. He will choose one in which he is particularly interested, i.e. which has an emotional meaning to him, whereas other problems and hypotheses may be dismissed out of hand or may even entirely escape his attention. If he decides to work, say, in the field of capital punishment it is likely that he holds already certain views on the matter, and one might even venture to guess that if he works in a country still adhering to the death penalty he is likely to be an abolitionist who wishes to collect evidence in favour of abolition, and vice versa. In other words, the individual in question, before becoming a research worker in criminology or penology, is already a social or penal reformer of some sort, although he may not admit or even not know it. This conforms to the general development of criminology and penology which had their origin not in scientific but in humanitarian ideas.

While it is only right and proper to leave the research worker free to choose his own subject, completely unfettered freedom, too, may have its dangers. It is a common complaint in some disciplines, notably sociology, that too much research is wasted on entirely unimportant subjects, and with some slight exaggeration the sociologist has been called 'a man who spends fifty thousand dollars to find the way to a whorehouse', and 'what is worse is that with a team of collaborators, he then produces a book telling one exactly how it was done'.[17] Let criminologists beware lest they should be accused of telling us even less important things at still greater expense. Research 'should have both direction and purpose',[18] and especially the inexperienced worker has to be given both by his supervisors and the sponsoring bodies.

From the choice of the problem we proceed to that of the research technique to be employed, and here, too, personal bias may be decisive, although we should not forget that this is a choice largely predetermined by the worker's scientific training which, of course, may also depend on his special abilities and inclinations. On this we shall have more to say in Chapter 4.

Once the factual material collected by the research worker has been assembled he is faced with the question of how to present it—a task which almost inevitably means having to cut out masses of material regarded as less important or of doubtful quality. Into this process of selection an element of bias can also easily intrude.

Particular care is needed in the ultimate interpretation, classification and evaluation of the research findings. Statistics as well as case histories are often capable of contradictory interpretations, and unless we are aware of our hidden prejudices we may too rashly and exclusively accept those interpretations which fit in with our preconceived views.

Our research may not only be coloured by the values which we hold but also by our knowledge of criminological theories and literature. Case workers may be tempted to write their case records so as to fit into one of the theories encountered in their studies, not by falsifying the facts but unconsciously giving too much emphasis to some of them at the expense of others; and research workers using such records may uncritically employ them to buttress their own favourite theories.[19] Workers trained at one university department may therefore reach different conclusions from those trained at another.

Accepting the fact that our research may be coloured by our personal bias we have to ask whether anything can be done to counter the dangers threatening the integrity of our work from this quarter. As we cannot rid ourselves of our valuations and prejudices we have to live with them, but we can at least by making our own position clear protect others who may wish to avail themselves of our findings. 'There is no other device for excluding biases in the social sciences than to face the evaluations and to introduce them as explicitly stated, specific, and sufficiently concretized, value premises.'[20] Evidently, this protective device does not go very far as we can make our prejudices clear to others only if we are aware of them ourselves;[21]

in some cases others may spot them without our aid, but there will always remain a residuum of undiscovered prejudices.

(c) Criminology and penology are practical disciplines in the sense that they are generally expected to produce results likely to prevent or reduce crime and in particular to provide more effective methods of treatment. This is an important consideration in the choice of subjects for research. Projects which can have some immediate practical usefulness will often be preferred to more theoretical subjects whose practical value appears to be doubtful and in any case remote. Government departments in particular cannot be blamed if they expect something of value to the 'job in hand' to emerge from the research which they instigate and finance, and it can also be argued that 'fundamental knowledge will best be gained not by seeking it directly but as by-products of research which is designed first and only to be useful'.[22] All this is perfectly legitimate as long as it does not lead to a complete monopoly of purely 'practical' exercises. The physicist 'does not scorn to develop theoretical principles which have potential practical value', indeed he rightly assumes that 'all his theoretical findings will have ultimate practical value'.[23] The difference between criminology and certain other branches of the social sciences, for example sociology, is that whereas in the latter 'pure' research has always been given pride of place and applied practical research had to be artificially stimulated, the opposite holds true of criminology and specially penology which have too often been dominated by considerations of a too narrowly practical nature. Informed opinion is beginning to realize, however, that in the case of most criminological research projects, even if their character seems to be pre-eminently practical, no immediate practical results should be expected and research findings may have their value even if they cannot at once be exchanged into the ready cash of legislative or administrative reforms. The working out of a suitable technique for the construction of prediction tables is worth while although because of the inadequacy of the underlying case records, the tables cannot be offered for immediate use in the administration of criminal justice.

All this leads to a consideration of the attitude which the research worker should adopt and the role he should play with regard to his own findings. Clearly, the more he is engaged in research on practical problems the more strongly will he feel the urge to have penal policy shaped in accordance with the results of his research. On the other hand, it is the prevailing view among social scientists that the role of the research worker as such should be limited to the presentation of his findings, and that he has to leave it to others to struggle for their acceptance in the legislative and administrative fields. This does not exclude, however, the possibility of his entering the political arena in

77

his capacity of a citizen who has the same right as everybody else to fight for what he thinks right,[24] and in this fight he may join forces with political parties and propaganda organizations specializing in his subject.[25] Moreover, his role may differ according to the different character of the research projects and findings, which might be divided into three categories: First, those projects which produce results leading straight to the demand for certain action in the field of penal legislation or administration or court practice, for example abolition of capital or corporal punishment or of short prison sentences for certain categories of offenders, or greater use of pre-sentence enquiries. Secondly, findings which draw attention to certain specific social evils—real or alleged—outside the area of criminal justice proper, in the field of techniques of mass communication such as films or television, or of criminogenic business methods such as certain types of hire-purchase agreements. Thirdly, findings which seem to lay bare the criminogenic effect of certain more general aspects of our culture, for example in connection with the concepts of anomie or the 'criminal subculture'. The criminologist *qua* criminologist will be freer to express his views as to what should be done and to fight for their acceptance with regard to the first category than to the second and third categories, for the simple reasons that the two last-mentioned involve problems which are outside his own expert knowledge and that it is even more difficult here to produce convincing evidence than it is with regard to the first category.

The distinction between ends and means, to which Myrdal had given much thought,[26] also plays an important part in this problem. Criminological and especially penological research is usually concerned with questions of means rather than ends. The construction of tables trying to predict the future behaviour of offenders, for example, makes sense only if we expect the courts and penal administrators to react differently according to whether or not a person is likely to offend again and if they wish to adopt measures of crime prevention. If courts and administrators should adhere to a purely retributive policy such prediction tables would serve no purpose. The same applies to the whole of our present reformative efforts within the institutional and non-institutional penal systems of today; they would make no sense if the object were merely retribution. It is for the criminologist to produce evidence regarding the best means of crime prevention if this is what present-day society wants, and it is also his task as a penal historian and philosopher to produce evidence as to whether prevention is preferable to retribution, but to make the final choice between the various possible objects of punishment is not for him but for society through its appropriate organs.

III. THE AGENCIES OF CRIMINOLOGICAL RESEARCH

So far, we have referred to the criminological research worker without enquiring who he is, from where he comes, and how it is made
possible for him to do this kind of work. By and large, criminological
research has hitherto usually been done in one of the following
ways:

(*a*) by private individuals working alone: for example John
Howard, Jeremy Bentham, Henry Mayhew;

(*b*) by public officials having access to official material, but working in a private capacity, for example A. M. Guerry, Cesare Lombroso, Gabriel Tarde, Cyril Burt;

(*c*) by public officials working in an official capacity, e.g. Charles
Goring, Norwood East;

(*d*) by university departments or individual teachers, which is the
largest category;

(*e*) by Government departments or special research units, for
example in England the Home Office Research Unit established on
the financial basis provided by the Criminal Justice Act, 1948 (s.77),
which enables the Home Secretary and the Prison Commissioners to
spend money on 'research into the causes of delinquency and the
treatment of offenders, and matters connected therewith'. Under this
provision the *Studies in the Causes of Delinquency and the Treatment
of Offenders* are produced and published.[27] As can be seen from the
White Paper on *Penal Practice in a Changing Society*,[28] and more
recently still from the White Paper on *The War against Crime in
England and Wales 1959–1964*,[29] the activities of the Home Office
Research Unit cover a very wide range, consisting partly of projects
undertaken by the Unit itself and partly of projects wholly or in part
financed or otherwise assisted by it. As already indicated, the first
category includes mostly studies of a practical penological nature,
but it has to be regarded as an important step in the right direction
that these practical problems are now examined officially with
Government assistance. Many years ago, Professor Thorsten Sellin,
referring to the follow-up and prediction studies of the Gluecks,
expressed the view that to carry out such research was the duty of
properly organized prison and parole departments, and that it should
not be left to private organizations to keep the results of penal treatment under review.[30] In some countries this is now the accepted
policy. It might be objected, of course, that such work which could
lead to highly critical appraisals of the Government agencies involved
should better be left to impartial outsiders, but as the latter would in
any case be dependent on governmental good will and co-operation

79

their impartiality could always be doubted by sceptics. There are in fact cases on record where strongly critical surveys of the activities of courts or Government departments have been encouraged and their publication sanctioned by those criticized.[31] Even so, it has to be admitted that the most appropriate dividing line between govern-mental and private research in criminology has still to be worked out. In a penetrating short paper, one of our younger criminologists has recently published a well-balanced critical survey of the present policy of the principal grant-giving bodies in Britain, and we are in full agreement with his view that 'as a matter of principle it seems un-desirable for too much power to be concentrated in one body, because there is always a risk of inhibition of creativity and restriction of independence. In the last resort it should always be possible to launch a study which might substantially undermine official policy.'[32] It is only fair to add, however, that a few such studies have actually been financed or at least encouraged by the Home Office in recent years, but it has to be admitted that the crucial test may still have to come.

The emergence of the Home Office Research Unit does not mean that before its establishment no officially sponsored research had been done in Britain. Although such instances have not been numer-ous, reference can be made to four projects: Charles Goring's *The English Convict* (1919), Grace W. Pailthorpe's *Studies in the Psycho-logy of Delinquency* (1932), Norwood East's *The Adolescent Criminal* (1942), and A. M. Carr-Saunders, Hermann Mannheim and E. C. Rhodes' *The Young Offender* (1944).

Nor does the present easier availability of governmental research grants mean that there is no place any more in this field for the con-tributions of private foundations. On the contrary, most valuable grants have been made in recent years by the Nuffield Foundation, the Carnegie United Kingdom Trust, the Ford Foundation and others.

Criminological research projects undertaken since 1950 are listed in the section 'Research and Methodology' of the *British Journal of Delinquency* (since 1960 called *The British Journal of Criminology*) and for recent years in the White Papers mentioned before, but neither of these lists can be regarded as complete.[33] A few interna-tional compilations are listed in the Appendix.

(*f*) To some extent, Royal Commissions and Departmental or Inter-departmental Committees and more recently the Home Office Advisory Council on the Treatment of Offenders have also to be mentioned as potential research agencies. Some of the more important reports of these bodies up to the year 1939 have been listed else-where,[34] and there are also several post-war reports:

Royal Commission on Justices of the Peace 1946–48, July 1948, Cmd. 7463;

Royal Commission on Capital Punishment 1949–53, September 1953, Cmd. 8932;

Royal Commission on the law relating to Mental Illness and Mental Deficiency 1954–57, May 1857, Cmd. 169;

Committee on Homosexual Offences and Prostitution, September 1957, Cmd. 247;

Committee on Children and Young Persons, October 1960, Cmd. 1191;

Advisory Council on the Treatment of Offenders on Alternatives to Short Terms of Imprisonment, 1957;

On the Treatment of Young Offenders, 1959;

On Corporal Punishment, 1960, Cmd. 1213;

On Preventive Detention, 1963.

While much of the material collected by such bodies is of considerable value, their work can, as a rule, not be classified as research in the strict sense of the word. They start not with a hypothesis, but with the terms of reference received from the Government which usually ask not for the establishment of facts and correlations but for an expression of views on certain points of law reform, for example whether capital punishment should be abolished or corporal punishment be reintroduced or the law of homosexual offences and prostitution be amended. The terms of reference prescribed by the Government for these bodies are sometimes not the most suitable ones and may occasionally even try to evade the real issue, as in the case of the Royal Commission on Capital Punishment, which was not asked to deal with the question of abolition. Moreover, their techniques differ from those of the research worker in that they strongly rely on witnesses, individuals or organizations, giving oral or written evidence which is usually a mixture of facts and opinions. Statistics are often collected, but hardly ever on strictly scientific lines, experts may be heard, but they are sometimes allowed to submit masses of ill-assorted material and make biased statements without being required to produce scientifically admissible evidence. In only very exceptional cases has independent research been done or instigated by these Commissions or Committees.[35] An examination of their status and work and of their relationship to the growing body of research seems to be overdue. They are not likely to be completely superseded by research because they are regarded as indispensable mediators between the Government and public opinion as the latter is thought to be more inclined to listen to the views of these Commissions and Committees than to the conclusions of research bodies. Past experience shows, however, that it is usually more the attitude of the Government and Parliament than public opinion—whatever that may mean—which determines the fate of recommendations for changes in law and administration, from whatever quarter they may come.[36] It is true, however, that commissions, etc., consisting partly of interested laymen, may find it easier to reach the ear of the public and of Parliament, and a case can be made out for the existence side by side of Commissions of Enquiry and research provided both sides are aware of their different functions and techniques. An attempt to demonstrate this was made, though rather one-sidedly, in recent research on problems of short-term imprisonment.[37]

A close comparison between the report of the Home Office Advisory Council on the subject and a piece of research, undertaken by a psychologist and financed by the Home Office and the Nuffield Foundation at the request of the present writer, seems to be illuminating. The governmental body obtained written and oral evidence from a large number of official and other organizations and a few individuals, and statistics were supplied by the Home Office Statistical Adviser and the Scottish Home Department; but their report, valuable as it is in many ways, has of necessity remained on the surface. They realize that, in order to reach decisions on the merits or otherwise of short-term imprisonment and the question of its alternatives offenders have to be divided into categories, but these categories are largely based on the nature of the offence committed. When faced with the necessity of classifying according to personal traits of the offenders all they are able to say in the light of the evidence submitted to them is that, apart from the prisoner 'whose offence suggests that *prima facie* prison is unsuitable and useless'—they refer here among others to the fine defaulter and the chronic alcoholic—there is also the prisoner 'convicted of a criminal offence such as larceny, breaking or assault and given without the option of a fine a sentence of imprisonment which, it is said, will neither train nor deter but possibly contaminate him and for which there does not at present exist a suitable or adequate alternative. This is a much more elusive category. It would need the most extensive research to form even a tentative estimate of the numbers it contains. We have, however, formed the opinion that it exists in sufficient numbers to constitute a problem' (para. 8). No attempt is made further to define and sub-divide this category in a manner useful for practical purposes. The research worker, on the other hand, who began his work unaware of the evidence and findings of the Advisory Council, tackled his problem in an entirely different way. Following the suggestion made earlier on by the present writer[38] he interviewed a carefully selected sample of slightly over a hundred short-term prisoners in a London prison, collected further information from their files, and studied their post-release records over a short period to see which of them became recidivists and which did not. This, together with a factorial analysis of the data obtained, enabled him to divide his sample into various categories according to psychological traits for whose treatment he made tentative recommendations indicating which of them he regarded as in need of a prison sentence

and which should receive different treatment, the nature of which he outlined. Although, in view of the smallness of the sample and the shortness
of the follow-up period and other technical drawbacks, this can be
regarded only as a pilot study, it shows at least the direction which further
work on the subject should take.

Shortly after the last war the whole question of existing and
required facilities for social and economic research in Britain was
competently surveyed by two bodies, one of them official and one
private.[39] Although many changes and improvements have taken
place since these reports were published their comments and recommendations are still of interest, and while criminology had not yet
achieved sufficient status at the time to be regarded as worthy of
consideration as one of the branches of the social sciences some of the
facts collected and views expressed by the two committees are
directly applicable to criminological research of today. To mention
only a few basic points, we are still trying to clarify the relationship
between Government sponsored and university or private research;
we are still anxious to define the role of private foundations in the
provision of funds and to demonstrate the need for permanent rather
than casual financial provision for criminological research. Above all,
we are still suffering from a lack of sufficiently trained workers which
is at present perhaps a more serious impediment to research than
lack of finance.

In 1963, the then Home Secretary set up a 'Committee of Inquiry
into Research in the Social Sciences' under the Chairmanship of
Lord Heyworth. Its terms of reference are: 'to review the research at
present being done in the field of social studies in Government
departments, universities, and other institutions, and to advise
whether changes are needed in the arrangements for supporting and
co-ordinating this research'. It still has to be seen whether criminology will be included in this review, and if so, whether any useful
results will be forthcoming. In April 1964, however, another step was
taken by the British Government which is likely to give a stronger
and more specific stimulus to criminological research: the setting up
of a Royal Commission was announced by the Prime Minister with
terms of reference which include, among others, the following objects:
'In the light of modern knowledge of crime and its causes and of
modern penal practice here and abroad, to re-examine the concepts
and purposes which should underlie the punishment and treatment
of offenders in England and Wales . . .' (White Paper of 1964, p. 13).
The White Paper comments on this that while in 1959 it was, 'by
common consent', too early for such a fundamental re-examination,
in the light of more recent developments the time for it was now ripe
(p. 3). It may be doubted whether this change of attitude on the part

of the Government has really been due to such fresh developments or whether it had not become all too obvious in the meantime that the refusal to take the necessary steps already in 1959 had been too timid. In view of what has been said above on Royal Commissions in general there is no need here to stress again that the mere setting up of such a body is no guarantee that the right type of research and of practical reforms will result from it—it all depends on the quality and expert knowledge of its membership and the will and power of the Government to implement the Commission's recommendations. It will also depend on the right choice of subjects and the priority given to each of them: if the Commission should over-concentrate on all the milder and more easily tangible forms of deviant misbehaviour, including juvenile and adolescent delinquency—the then Home Secretary is reported to have already asked for an Interim Report on the latter—at the expense of the really serious problems of the affluent society, including the structure and extent of organized crime (see below, Chapter 25, IV), which are among the strongest factors behind the misbehaviour of the younger generation, it is not likely to reach its objects.

IV. GENERAL TRENDS IN CRIMINOLOGICAL RESEARCH

Assuming the correctness of our views about the need for a specific hypothesis as the usual, though not always essential, starting point of research we may roughly distinguish the following three stages in the historical development of criminological research over the past two hundred years:[40]

(a) The Pre-Scientific Stage

Here no hypothesis is formulated and tested, and no attempt is made to tackle the problem in hand without prejudice and to study the facts as they are found. This does not mean that such studies have no value. On the contrary, while most of the magnificent penological literature of the eighteenth and the first half of the nineteenth centuries belong to this category, the humanitarian progress in our penal systems is largely due to examples of this kind. They were highly emotional and biased, in the best sense of the word, but well adapted to the needs of the age and therefore often better able to reach their object than the detached work of the scholar. Even if Bentham's gentle reproach was justified that John Howard, his 'venerable friend', had collected 'a quarry of stones' rather than constructed a house, these stones could at least be used by his successors to demolish and replace the antiquated dungeons of the past. And even for present-day research we have already expressed the view that it can sometimes usefully be done without a hypothesis.

(b) The Semi-Scientific Stage

Work here starts from a hypothesis which may be explicit or implicit, but it is too wide and ambitious to be amenable to accurate testing. Moreover, no scientifically acceptable techniques of testing are available. Among mid-nineteenth-century penologists Captain Alexander Maconochie, in particular, comes to mind as an outstanding example. His system of marks and progressive stages and his idea of the indeterminate sentence clearly sprang from theories which could be formulated as hypotheses, and he tried to operate and validate them by what would nowadays be called operational techniques of research.[41] Cesare Lombroso, too, had a definite theory of the born criminal, theories of atavism, degeneration, epilepsy, etc., and various hypotheses which he tried to prove by careful observation of the clinical material at his disposal, but his techniques of examination, interpretation and validation were inadequate by present-day standards and his gift of enthusiastic intuition and imagination often got the better of him. Some more detailed criticisms will have to be made below when Lombroso's work will be discussed in Chapter 12.[42] Some of the mid-nineteenth-century European ecologists, such as Guerry (see below, Chapter 23), worked upon 'a series of *ad hoc* hypotheses', but without a 'specific body of theory'.[43]

(c) The Scientific Stage

To say that all the requirements so far outlined have been fulfilled at this stage would of course be to paint an ideal and entirely unrealistic picture: there would have to be a specific hypothesis originating in a general theory, tested by the correct application of one or several of the universally approved techniques, and the results would be subjected to careful and unprejudiced interpretation and validation. If necessary, the original hypothesis would be modified in the light of the research findings, and the whole process repeated with reference to this new hypothesis. Needless to say, there has never been such a perfect piece of research and we are not likely ever to see it; all we can do is to try in the light of previous experience to avoid the worst blunders.

Our criticism of Lombroso's excessive reliance on intuition[44] is not directed against the use of intuitive methods as such which have not only their legitimate place in criminological research but are often indispensable, especially in the formulation of a new hypothesis and in the interpretation of the findings.[45] It is only the unfettered, uncritical and uncontrolled use of intuitive methods that should be avoided, and 'our intuitions must be tested'.[46]

V. THE VALUE OF CRIMINOLOGICAL RESEARCH

Already in 1949, the present writer posed, but did not attempt to answer, the question: 'Has the research so far done been of any practical use to anybody . . . or has it simply been so much waste of effort and of paper?'[47] Today, our answer can be confidently given that criminological research had been of practical value in the following directions:

(a) It has destroyed or at least weakened many erroneous beliefs, mainly about alleged causes of crime and the efficiency of various methods of treatment. Illustrations will be given in the course of this book. This does not mean that such beliefs are no longer held any-where. There are inevitably individuals who do not care to find out whether and why they should change certain strongly held views which have a deep-seated emotional appeal to them, and there are others who stick to their views although on a rational level they are conscious of their unreasonableness. The existence of scientific refutation, however, forces them into a defensive attitude which weakens their position and makes them occasionally more amenable to compromise. This has happened in particular in the struggle for the abolition of capital punishment.[48]

(b) On the more positive side, it has been responsible for a number of improvements in penal treatment needed to fill the gaps left by the disappearance of outmoded methods. Although progress of this kind lies mainly in the penological field, the changes in attitudes thus produced have also affected the causative side by reducing the criminogenic effect of such methods. Moreover, outside the narrow field of the penal system proper the growing insight into the working of the human mind and of social institutions, due not only to socio-logical and psychological but also to criminological research, has given rise to a less timid and hide-bound approach to the whole problem of crime. The day is perhaps not too distant when crimino-logical research will take its place beside the press and the Royal Commissions and Departmental Committees 'as an equal partner among the public opinion forming bodies'.[49] Moreover, it is playing an increasing part in providing the factual basis for legislation (on 'experimental legislation' see 'experimental methods', Chapter 9, below).

On the other hand, criminologists would do well to take Gunnar Myrdal's[50] warning to heart that social scientists should not claim too much credit for their recent successes which are still greatly over-shadowed by their failures. They should be conscious, in particular, of the crudeness of most of their techniques, statistical and otherwise. To give only two illustrations out of many, it is sometimes pathetic to see how much reliance is placed on information derived from interviews which, at best, can produce a picture of the interviewee only at the moment of the interview without showing anything about the crucial process of his whole development over a period of years. It is equally pathetic to observe how many statistical refinements are wasted on utterly inadequate basic material.

(c) Criminology, for so long the debtor of other disciplines and their scientific discoveries, is now slowly and in a small way assuming the role of creditor as well, mainly through its control group and ecological researches which have provided general information pre-viously not available on non-delinquents and on localities of various characteristics.

Chapter 4

METHODOLOGY OF RESEARCH IN GENERAL

I. PROBLEM VERSUS METHOD

Once the hypothesis to be tested has been formulated, or if in exceptional cases we prefer to proceed without one, we have to decide on the methods to be used for a particular research project. A difference of opinion has arisen between the supporters of 'problem orientation' and those of 'methods orientation'.[1] Is it preferable in research to have a worthwhile subject for investigation, even if it can be studied only by second-rate methods, or to be able to apply first-rate methods to a subject of doubtful significance to the progress of criminology? Which of the two ways of thinking should dominate and which should have to adapt itself to the other? It is tempting enough for the enthusiastic methodologist to vote in favour of the second alternative, and it is here that our remarks on the subjective element in the selection of a suitable subject for research are also applicable (see above, Chapter 3, II(b)). Criminology has been suffering from such an abundance of research on important matters carried out with complete neglect of the most elementary methodological principles[2] that we might well be forgiven for preaching the gospel of the primacy of method. There is much to be said for the view that there should be no research on subjects which cannot be properly tackled with the methods or material at present available. 'Without an awl the cobbler's nobody.' On the other hand, to place all the emphasis on the perfection of methods at the expense of the quality of the subject to be investigated would lead to a mere *l'art pour l'art* mentality and to the building up of a secluded, highly abstract and sophisticated, methodology which would soon lose touch with reality and squander its resources on problems which interest nobody but its own high-priests and their acolytes. What we need is *both* worthwhile subjects and up-to-date methods of investigation, but if we find that with the material and the techniques at present at our disposal we cannot expect to obtain scientifically reliable results we should be self-denying and honest enough to postpone research on the problem in question, however interesting and pressing it may appear. Sometimes this will mean that in the interval we can profitably make arrangements for the training of staff and the collection of better material for future research.[3]

II. NATURAL OR SOCIAL SCIENCE METHODS IN CRIMINOLOGICAL RESEARCH?

Here we have to face two basic considerations:

(a) Although criminology is a branch of the social sciences, the causes of crime are physical as well as social (see the later chapters). Criminology, not unlike medicine, has its roots in both of these two camps, just as psychiatry, in the words of Aubrey Lewis,[4] is at the same time 'a form of applied social science' and of medicine. Moreover, as has been argued elsewhere,[5] criminology is at the same time a nomothetic discipline, aiming at the discovery of uniformities and general 'laws' in the sense explained in Chapter 1, and an idiographic discipline, concerned with the observation and systematic classification of facts about human behaviour in individual cases.

(b) Being a young discipline, not yet able to work out its own methods, criminology has still largely to use the methods employed by other, more fully developed branches of the natural and social sciences. This poses a serious dilemma because it means that criminology has to rely in part on the methods of the natural and in part on those of the social sciences and because these two are far from being identical. How can this dilemma be solved? Should we simply accept the fact that there is, and will always be, a dualism of methods in criminological research or should we try to overcome this dualism by attempting to reconcile the two methods?

First, are they actually so very different? No doubt, to mention only some of the most striking points, the social sciences are more complex, less accurate and less amenable to experimentation (see below, Chapter 9). The events they study are less likely to be repeatable in exactly the same way; mental factors, which can be ignored in the natural sciences, play a very important role in social causation; and it is also more difficult here to isolate the various causal factors. Moreover, the social researcher cannot 'put himself, as an impartial observer, outside of society'[6] because he is himself part of the society he observes, and inevitably he approves or disapproves much of what he sees, whereas the natural scientist can preserve a neutral attitude. In a way, medicine has to face a similar dilemma as criminology; it is concerned with individuals, but there is a 'social' medicine and, more specifically, a 'social' psychiatry as well. In the latter and in epidemiology, 'the study of the mass aspects of disease',[7] we find the closest parallels to the social science elements in criminology. There can be no doubt that the techniques of research used in the purely medical, psychiatric and in particular psycho-analytic sectors of criminology are different from those in the sociological and statistical ones. Should we conclude from this that, as Aubrey Lewis implies, once we accept the existence of those differences, a 'bewildering zig-zag' is likely to result, making the progress of criminology as of psychiatry 'a little indecisive and wobbly at times'? Or will a synthesis between these opposing disciplines eventually be achieved?[8] It would be claiming too much to say that such a synthesis is already in sight, but there are certain straws in the wind.[9] Even so, the student of criminology has to pay careful attention to the scientific background of the writers whose guidance he seeks because the writings of a natural scientist, his concept of causation, his views on experimentation, etc., may require a different interpretation from those of a sociologist or a lawyer.

III. THE NEED FOR TEAMWORK[10]

The conception of teamwork implies co-operation, but not necessarily between persons of different qualifications. Co-operation between workers of the same category is more and more needed as the size of research projects extends beyond the powers of one single person. In practice, however, we think of it mainly as co-operation between individuals possessing different abilities or training. From the fact that criminology is dependent upon the contributions of several other disciplines and from the multi-factor theory of crime causation follows the need for research in this field often to be planned and carried out by a team of scholars with widely differing backgrounds and interests. For prediction research at least a statistician and a penologist, for research of an ecological character a sociologist and a psychologist, both with criminological training, are required. The Bristol Social Project employed, at one stage or another, a sociologist, a psychiatric social worker, a group worker, a social worker, and, directing the whole operation, a criminologist with sociological training.[11] The Gluecks had on their staff for *Unraveling Juvenile Delinquency*[12] a large assortment of 'social investigators', psychologists, a 'psychiatrist-physician', two Rorschach Test specialists, physical anthropologists and statisticians, but no sociologist, an omission which has often been criticized.

This teamwork approach, essential as it is, entails considerable expenses and technical and psychological difficulties. First, unless one member of the team is obviously singled out as the leader by age and scientific eminence or has been appointed as such by the directing body, the question of who should lead has to be settled by the team itself, which may easily cause friction. It can be solved according to disciplines only if one of the latter is clearly of outstanding importance to the project. In Child Guidance work the leadership of the psychiatrist has so far usually been taken for granted, but his claims have recently been challenged by psychologists.[13] Secondly, in order to mould into one team workers of different scientific backgrounds, approaching the subject from different angles and accustomed to different research techniques, a great deal of tact and self-denial has to be expected from each member. It is not enough to have representatives of various disciplines employed on a project; there has also to be genuine co-operation and inter-action between them. Moreover, as Norbert Wiener writes in his *Cybernetics*,[14] each member should possess 'a thoroughly sound and trained acquaintance with the fields of his neighbours', and they should all know 'one another's intellectual customs'. This is an ideal often difficult to achieve, among other reasons because for the sake of economy they may have to be appointed for different stages of the project, which in fact often rules out the possibility of real teamwork, or if they are simultaneously employed they may be kept artificially separated because the project director may be afraid that they may influence one another's views and findings. In the project described in *Unraveling Juvenile Delinquency*, the Gluecks felt it necessary to 'curb the curiosity of their team members about the findings of those portions of the study in which they had no part . . . we were convinced that the data of each discipline should be gathered independently of all the others, not only to avoid circular reasoning and unconscious bias, but also ultimately to permit proper assessment of the contribution of each avenue of approach to the mosaic of crime causation'.[15] In the light of our previous remarks on the danger of bias in research this is a very serious consideration, but if driven to its logical conclusion it might mean the end of team research as it would rule out any kind of co-operation and discussion between members of a team. In fact, the Gluecks felt obliged to arrange occasional staff conferences with joint discussions.

There are still social scientists who believe in the unique value of individual as opposed to team research,[16] and it has to be admitted that most really great discoveries in the social sciences, including criminology, have so far been due to individuals rather than teams. Psycho-analysts, the most individualistic of all scholars, have been particularly sceptical of teamwork, but it is worthy of note that one of the most distinguished among them, Edward Glover, has at least seriously surveyed and delimited the possibilities and risks of team research on delinquency.[17] The sociologist, on the other hand, is probably the one most sympathetically inclined to the idea of team-work in research, and some of the most penetrating discussions of the subject can be found in John Spencer's report on the Bristol Social Project.[18] From the psychologist's point of view R. G. Andry's chapter in *Criminology in Transition* (1965) is also very valuable.

IV. THE NEED FOR REPLICATION AND PILOT STUDIES

Replication studies differ from teamwork in that here a project is carried out by the same or other workers as a replica of research already completed; and often it is done independently of the first. They are essential in order to increase the validity and reliability of research findings. Each single research project has to be regarded as one link in a chain of studies which combined are more likely to produce scientifically acceptable evidence than each of them would in isolation. One way of placing the individual project in the right per-spective is to study the literature of the subject and to examine how far the present enquiry, its scope, material, techniques and findings differ from those of its predecessors. This is an essential procedure which the individual research worker can neglect only at his peril— 'if it is true that "no man is an island", the same applies, in an increasing measure, to research in general and criminological re-search in particular'.[19] The second, and hitherto less customary, way is the replication study. Such studies should be undertaken in the same country or, as cross-cultural studies, elsewhere to see whether results produced in one country can be confirmed in another country, possibly one with a different culture. Two distinguished American sociologists, Arnold M. Rose in the field of the social sciences in general and Marshall B. Clinard for criminology, have given much thought to this subject,[20] and it also has been deplored by crimino-logists that consecutive studies on the same subject are so often not comparable because of the use of slightly different terms and tech-niques.[21] Comparability is needed in particular because criminological researches have, largely for financial reasons, hitherto often been using very small samples, and it has been one of the most common weaknesses to base conclusions on numbers of cases not suf-ficiently representative. On the other hand, Wilkins, *Social Deviance*, p. 155, has forcefully stressed the often superior value of small as against large samples. Moreover, research findings which may have been adequate to confirm a certain hypothesis for the country or culture of their origin are sometimes entirely beside the point else-where in a different social, economic or psychological atmosphere. It is for this reason that American scholars in particular, conscious of the unique features of their own culture, have felt the need to test some of their hypotheses not only within the United States but also abroad in order to make them usable as a basis of a general theory.

As Arnold M. Rose has pointed out, replication may mean either the repetition of a study with the same or similar techniques but different material or an effort to test the conclusions of a previous study with different techniques and different material. We are here mainly concerned with the first alternative which seems to be more fruitful for purposes of comparison and testing. It is often difficult, however, to apply the same methods of research with different material and in different surroundings. The research worker is sometimes forced to make concessions to the latter which may involve changes in the procedure as originally planned. Moreover, and this applies not only to cross-cultural but to all replication studies, the problem in question has to be formulated 'in generally meaningful terms' to provide the basis for fruitful replication.[22]

Replication studies are of course possible only if the study in question is actually 'repeatable', which will as a rule be the case if it employs objective rather than subjective criteria. Much depends of course on the question 'repeatable by whom?', i.e. by highly trained or semi- or untrained workers. As the matter is of particular importance to prediction studies it will be further discussed under that heading.

Validation studies are similar to replication studies, but validation can also be sought by means other than replication.[23] It may consist of the application of methods entirely different from those used in the study for which validation is required. As in criminological research validation, too, has mainly been tried for prediction studies the subject will also be further discussed below in connection with them.

Pilot studies, too, are of two different kinds. The usual meaning of the term refers to the preliminary stage of a larger project designed to try out the usefulness and accuracy of the methods to be applied to the project as a whole. The idea behind such studies is to spot at an early stage methodological errors or the suitability of the case material, of the area, or the questionnaire, etc., provisionally selected. No large-scale project should be undertaken without such a safety valve.[24]

Occasionally, however, we call a study a pilot study which was originally not intended to be one, because eventually it has been found that to achieve its objects the research should have been undertaken on a larger scale, for example with a larger sample or with a larger number of different groups to be used for the purpose of comparison. Myrdal has strongly criticized such procedures. 'Social scientists', he writes, 'have become accustomed to answer that "very much more detailed factual research is necessary before wise action can be planned upon the basis of scientific knowledge".' This statement, which, with few verbal variations, will be found so often in our literature, is an expression of scientific modesty. But it also expresses 'escape . . . practical action or inaction must be decided from day to day and cannot wait until eventually a lagging social science has collected enough detailed data for shouldering its part of the responsibility . . . [and] even with much more money and exertion spent on research, social science will, in this complicated and rapidly changing world, probably always be able to present this same excuse . . .'[25] There is, as experience shows, much truth in this. Research workers are often perfectionists and also too timid to offer the results of their small-scale studies as reliable foundations for responsible social action possibly determining the fate of many individuals. All too often, however, the fault is not theirs, and their attitude is due to their better insight into the small size and imperfect quality of their material and the doubtful value of existing techniques. The problem of 'subject versus method' may here be relevant (see s. 1 above).

Chapter 5

THE PLACE OF STATISTICS IN
CRIMINOLOGICAL RESEARCH I

In this and the following chapters a survey will be given of the functions of the various methods of criminological research. To put it in
a nutshell, such research can be done by means of any one of the
following methods, either alone or, more usually, in combination:

Principal methods: Statistical | Typological | Individual (psycho-
logical or psychiatric) Case Study

Secondary methods: Sociological (dealing with Institutions, Groups,
Areas) | Experimental | Prediction | Opera-
tional (action research)

The above scheme is intended to show, first, that the typological
method stands between the two extremes of the statistical method,
which is only concerned with the mass aspects of crime and punishment, and the case study method, which is solely concerned with the
individual case. Secondly, it is intended to show that each of the
secondary methods has to make use of one or several of the three
principal methods. The sociological method, for example, has to
employ either statistical, or typological, or case study methods or all
three combined, and the same applies to experimental, prediction and
operational methods.

General and Historical Considerations

The present chapter and Chapter 6 are concerned with the use of
statistical methods in criminology.[1] It is not their object to deal with
the matter from the point of view of the trained statistician; but
merely to explain what kinds of criminal statistics and statistical
methods are available or are needed, what has been their historical
development, what use can be made of them, and which pitfalls have
to be avoided in doing so.

Before going into details, a few remarks will not be out of place on the early beginnings of the scientific study of criminal statistics in the first decades of the nineteenth century, beginnings usually connected with the name of the famous Belgian statistician and Professor of Astronomy in Brussels, Adolphe Quetelet (1796–1874).[2] His main works are: *Sur l'homme et le développement de ses facultés, ou Essai de physique sociale* (Paris 1835, 2 vols.); *Recherches sur le penchant au crime aux différent ages* (1831); *Du système social et des lois qui le régissent* (1848). It was Quetelet who, aided by comprehensive statistical material drawn from French and Belgian sources, pointed out that, as many other social happenings such as marriage, divorce, suicide, birth and death, crime was more than something purely individual, that it was a mass phenomenon, and that the study of crime in the mass, i.e. criminal statistics, could therefore better than any other method lead to the discovery of important regularities and perhaps even social laws. The best-known of his observations was probably his assertion that the volume and kind of crime in a certain country need to remain strikingly constant, and that any fluctuations which may occur over a period of time were comparatively insignificant, provided the basic circumstances, economic, social, political, etc., did not substantially change. This proviso is, of course, of the greatest importance since, at least over longer periods of time, these circumstances will almost invariably undergo marked changes. It is significant that the statistical table first used by Quetelet to prove his thesis was one showing the number of murders committed in France in the years 1826–31, a period of six years only, also showing the weapons employed in these crimes. The figures are indeed fairly constant, varying only from a minimum of 205 in 1830 to a maximum of 266 in 1831 (see the table in Bonger, p. 51), and one wonders how far the revolution of July 1830 may have contributed to the sudden rise between these two years. If Quetelet had known the figures with their striking fluctuations presented in *Social Aspects of Crime in England between the Wars* for Germany (pp. 105–6) and for England (pp. 106–7) and for a later period below in this Chapter (p. 106), he would have rightly concluded that these must have been periods of profound economic, social and political upheavals. It is only in this sense and with such provisos that his famous dictum is correct that crime is '*un budget qu'on paie avec une régularité effrayante. . . . Triste condition de l'espèce humaine. . . . La société renferme en elle les germes de tous les crimes qui vont se commettre, en même temps que les facilités nécessaires à leur développement . . .*'—It is correct only if we bear in mind that other budgets, too, may undergo drastic changes.

Quetelet was not content to collect figures to demonstrate the con-

96

STATISTICS IN CRIMINOLOGICAL RESEARCH I

stancy of crime; he also tried to explain it scientifically. The distinguished Dutch criminologist J. M. van Bemmelen, who has made a special study of Quetelet's ideas, summarizes them roughly as follows (as has also been done briefly by Bonger in his *Introduction to Criminology*): The life of man, as that of all other creatures, is governed by certain laws of nature. This means that when we look at mankind as a whole, the individual faculties of men, physical, mental, social, are distributed in accordance with the law of individual variations as shown in the so-called Gaussian law, i.e. in the form of a bell-shaped curve, the largest numbers, about 70 per cent, are grouped in the middle, with the extremes, being the exceptions from the average, at both ends about 15 per cent each. For example, people with about average intelligence are much more frequent than geniuses or morons (Moroney, p. 110), and the same applies to height, weight and eventually also to what Quetelet, somewhat misleadingly, called the *penchant au crime*, the tendency to commit crime. What he meant was simply the statistical probability that of a given number of individuals in a certain country and at a certain time a certain number would commit a crime of a certain kind; it was likely to be a small minority, whereas the majority would remain law-abiding. Quetelet was conscious of the fact that this was a mere statistical probability, but by calling the *penchant au crime* a 'moral element' he introduced an element of value into it which was out of place.

When thus looking at crime as a mass phenomenon, which particular individual belongs to the criminal minority is of course irrelevant, and it was this consideration which led Quetelet, Bonger and others to the erroneous conclusion that psychological factors did not matter in the explanation of criminal behaviour. It all depends on the particular objectives that we have in mind, whether we happen to be more interested in the mass or in the individual aspects of crime. Quetelet's concept of the *homme moyen* was a useful tool when dealing with the mass aspects, but useless for the study of the individual aspects; it was, as he described it himself, 'a fiction, an imaginary creature to whom everything occurs in accordance with the average results obtained by the society in which he lives' (van Bemmelen, *Journal*, p. 224). In accordance with his general tendency to underestimate the importance of individual characteristics Quetelet's philosophy was rigidly deterministic, and there was no scope in it for the will of the individual.

While Quetelet was the most influential of the social statisticians of the early nineteenth century whose work determined the historical progress of criminological thought for several decades until the coming of the Lombrosian school, he was by no means the only one. Another important figure was his contemporary, the French statistician A. M. Guerry, who was mainly interested in the study of geographical areas of France and who, through the application of the cartographic technique, became the forerunner of the Chicago school of criminal ecology (see below, Chapter 23). His work has been described in some detail in Terence Morris's book *The Criminal Area* (pp. 44–52).

As in other fields of statistics, we can distinguish between officially produced criminal statistics and statistical information produced by private research workers. Although the distinction has become somewhat blurred in recent years through the emergence of a Government agency, the Home Office Research Unit, one of whose tasks it is to supply statistical information in much the same way and of the same quality as done by private workers, it is still useful to distinguish between the statistical material published by the various central and local authorities as a form of primitive accounting of the volume of crime and punishment and statistical research carried out privately. Sorokin's distinction between 'humble or book-keeping' and 'high-brow' statistics[3] or, for that matter, Bowley's distinction between administrative and scientific statistics are, however, no longer identical with that between official and private criminal statistics. The real distinction is now between statistical information presented more or less regularly on a certain minimum of items—usually the work of official agencies—and information collected irregularly on matters not included in the first category, usually but not necessarily by private workers in order to investigate a certain specific problem or to test a specific hypothesis, for example whether it is true that most juvenile delinquents come from 'broken' homes or from the working classes or are of subnormal intelligence. In other words, whereas the ordinary 'book-keeping' statistics are collected and published regardless of whether they are needed to solve a specific problem this is usually not done in the case of the 'scientific' statistics. Even regularity, however, is not invariably a characteristic of official statistics as shown by the very irregularly published reports of the Children's Branch of the Home Office.

ORDINARY 'BOOK-KEEPING' CRIMINAL STATISTICS

1. *Their General Object*

Their general object is as already indicated, to provide the interested Government departments, Parliament, the press and the public with a certain minimum of data concerning three broad categories of facts, i.e. relating to *offence*, *offender* and methods of *disposal*. This information usually refers to, first, the volume of, and changes in, crimes of various kinds and their local and seasonal distribution; secondly, the age and sex ratio of offenders, their previous convictions, sometimes their economic position, marital status, occupation, domicile, religious denomination and, very rarely, the offender's motive; thirdly, particulars of the sentences imposed or other forms of disposal used by different courts. However, this is only the average picture, and in some countries more, in others less information is actually provided.[4] In the present chapter, the position in Great Britain is described,[5] with only a few sidelights on other countries.

The object of this kind of simple book-keeping—the simplicity of which is in many ways deceptive—is to give the most elementary facts regarding the evolution and present position of crime in the mass, the main characteristics of those who commit it, again in the mass, and of the ways they are dealt with by the organs of the State. How far these objects are actually achieved by official criminal statistics will be discussed below.

Criminal statistics can be based upon the work of the police or on that of the courts. In the first case 'offences known to the police' (Police Statistics), in the second case 'offenders charged' or 'offenders found guilty' by the various courts (Court Statistics) are taken as the basis. The respective advantages and disadvantages of these two types will be discussed below (Chapter 6).

2. *Historical Sketch of Official Criminal Statistics*

Although occasional legislation, or legislative drafts such as the English Penitentiary Bill of 1778, provided for regular statistical returns on certain limited aspects of the matter, for example statistics of prisoners in individual penal institutions,[6] regular and systematic compilations in this field began only in the early nineteenth century with the publication of the first general censuses, which made it possible to relate the crime figures to those of the general population. Statistical material on crimes and penalties, usually from private sources, is of course available for much earlier periods, but it is mostly unreliable and unrelated to population and other social statistics.[7] In Britain the census was first established in 1801, and in the Parliamentary Papers of 1810[7a] we find *A Return of the Number of Persons, Male or Female, Committed to the Several Gaols in England and Wales for Trial at the Different Great Sessions, Assizes and Quarter Sessions. In the Years 1805, 1806, 1807, 1808.* In these returns the numbers are given of those convicted, acquitted or discharged, and also the sentences imposed. In 1805, for example, the totals amounted to 3,267 males and 1,338 females, of whom 1,962 and 768 respectively were convicted, 782 and 310 were acquitted and the others discharged. Death sentences were passed on 314 males and 36 females, of whom 62 males and 6 females were executed. In 146 and 15 cases the death sentences were commuted to transportation for life, whereas 29 and 5 received 14 years' and 434 and 127 7 years' transportation. The remaining offenders received sentences of imprisonment, whipping or fines. Gradually, these official statistics became more elaborate, and the *Report on Committals for the Years 1826-7*, for example, consists already of 18 pages.[8] These committals, divided according to districts, numbered 13,710 in 1820 and 16,147 in 1826, with 107 and 57 executions respectively.

Improvements were not infrequently made, and in 1895 the whole system was drastically revised in accordance with the report of a Departmental Committee published as an Appendix to *Judicial Statistics*, 1893.[9] Among other points this report recommended the complete separation of criminal and civil statistics; the transfer of certain tables from criminal statistics to the *Annual Reports of the Prison Commissioners and Inspectors of Reformatory and Industrial Schools*; the compilation of tables for calendar years instead of following the system used in the police returns which ended on the 29th September of each year; and the report also urged that tables using vague and unscientific terms such as 'suspicious character' or 'known thief' should be altogether abolished. Moreover, it proposed that wherever possible the proportions to population should be given and that much greater attention should be paid to comparisons with foreign criminal statistics. 'In France, Germany and Italy great improvements have in recent years been made in statistical methods, and we think that their annual volumes of judicial statistics should always be carefully studied by the Statistical Branch of the Home Office'; on the other hand, the report gives a warning that the 'extreme elaboration' which distinguished the German and Italian tables should not be imitated. Of considerable interest are the remarks of the report on the contents of the Introduction to the annual volumes. In addition to comparisons with foreign criminal statistics to be undertaken from time to time these Introductions, it was suggested, should contain 'not merely a repetition of what is contained in the tables'. Most readers 'will expect to find results and conclusions . . .' Regarding the arrangements of the tables, the report takes the view that this should not follow the chronological order of criminal proceedings, but the results of judicial proceedings, as the most important and accurate sources, should take precedence over the police returns although the latter are earlier in point of time—a recommendation which was followed for many years. The controversial question of how many details, apart from age and sex as the indispensable minimum, relating to the personal condition of criminals should be included is also discussed at some length. English criminal statistics at the time contained information on the birthplace, but not on the domicile, of criminals and on their occupation or profession. The committee was not in favour of going much beyond this: 'We cannot admit that this class of statistics has the pre-eminent value for the scientific study of crime which appears to be claimed for it.' Such personal data were regarded as interesting, but 'no deductions of practical utility have been obtained from them', and their object is 'mainly speculative'. Nevertheless, the report concludes, 'at some future time . . . a serious attempt should be made to obtain more precise and complete statistics on some of those subjects', but it should be restricted to prisoners (which was only natural at a time when the prison population was much more representative of the criminal population than it is now) and not necessarily presented every year or for the whole country. As items to be treated in this way the report mentions education, marital status, occupation, religion, nationality, domicile.[10] In accordance with the prevailing nineteenth-century tendency the report also recommended the publication of more maps and diagrams showing the regional distribution of crime.

One of the most important innovations made in the *Judicial Statistics* for 1893, published simultaneously with the report of 1895, is a table showing for the first time in detail the number of previous convictions of prisoners. It was found that 45 per cent of them had no such convictions, but it had to be admitted that the records were often too defective to give a reliable picture. An interesting attempt was also made in that volume to assess the effect of previous convictions on the length of sentences.

Among the recommendations of the report of 1893 taken up in subsequent volumes the following may be mentioned.[11]

(a) The Introductions were made more informative by providing material on the geographical distribution of crime (1899 and 1905), on the statistical relation between strikes and increases in crime (1908), on education (1928), on industrial depression (1929), on differences between the North and South of England (1929 and 1930), on the statistical results of different methods of penal treatment (1932 and 1938) and on corporal punishment (1935). Since 1950, a special analysis has annually been provided 'showing for all indictable offences combined the number of different persons in each age group found guilty during the year and the number of additional findings of guilt of indictable offences recorded at the same time as the principal findings of guilt'.[12] This is an important attempt to link the number of offences to that of individual offenders and at the same time to check the efficiency of the police. Moreover, a summary of the statistics of police cautions is now given.[13] The significance of these additions will be discussed below.

(b) As far as the 'Annual Tables' are concerned, it is worth mentioning that the bulk of the prison returns was transferred in 1928 to the *Annual Reports of the Prison Commissioners* and that the *Returns of the Reformatory and Industrial Schools* became, in 1923, part of a special publication, the *Reports of the Children's Branch of the Home Office*. On the other hand, probation statistics began to appear from 1908 as a consequence of the passing of the Probation of Offenders Act, 1907, and figures for sentences of Borstal and Preventive Detention commenced in 1909 after the passing of the Prevention of Crime Act, 1908. Many important tables had to be omitted in 1914 and 1915 because of the war, and while some of them were restored in 1918 or 1919, others re-appeared only several years after the coming of peace or not at all as a result of the economy drive.[14] In 1938, however, new tables were introduced containing more detailed information for the different age groups.

(c) From 1949 on, *Supplementary Statistics relating to Crime and Criminal Proceedings* have been published annually by the Home Office and distributed to a number of libraries, universities and organizations interested in the subject, and copies are also supplied to other organizations or individuals on application. They contain in part information which up to 1938 had been included in the published *Criminal Statistics*, in part they provide additional material. To the first category belong in particular the tables showing age, sex and offence of persons found guilty by magistrates' courts in each police district and by individual Assizes and Quarter Sessions, which makes it possible again to study the geographical distribution of crime. Additional material is provided especially on the numbers of persons found guilty of indictable offences, according to age, showing the numbers of such offences of either the same or other categories previously proved against the offender. In the year 1958, for example, of a total of 66,716 different persons aged 21 and over found guilty of indictable offences at all courts 42,701 had no previous proved indictable offences of the same category and 38,205 no previous proved indictable offences of all categories; 534 and 850 respectively had over 20 such previous offences. Information is also supplied in *Supplementary Statistics* on the numbers of indictable offences taken into consideration by the court when passing sentence and on the numbers of cautions administered by the police.[15] The material is thereby made available which enables some research to be done on such important matters as the extent of recidivism and the effect of the taking into account system and of police cautioning on the real statistical volume of detected crime.

102

3. *The Present Contents of English Criminal Statistics and Subsidiary Publications*

The following are the most important official publications.

(*a*) *Criminal Statistics England and Wales. Statistics relating to Crime and Criminal Proceedings.* This is a series published annually as a blue book, usually about six months after the close of the year to which it refers, which by international standards is very quick work. As the sub-title indicates, this publication is primarily concerned with crime and criminal proceedings, whereas data concerning the person of the criminal take second rank. 'Abstracts of Police Returns, which are laid before Parliament in accordance with the requirement of s.14 of the County and Borough Police Act, 1856' are also included. The report consists of an Introductory Note with Appendices; Comparative Tables comparing the figures of police and court statistics, related to the population, for the past thirty years; and of Annual Tables for the year in question.

The Introduction provides a short guide through the main body of the volume, summarizes the principal results in the light of previous years, illustrated by a number of graphs, gives percentages not to be found in the main body, highlights certain important findings, and draws attention to the contents of the *Supplementary Statistics*. It also includes an analysis of the number of persons against whom additional findings of guilt were recorded during the year. Very useful are the Appendices to this Note relating the number of persons found guilty of indictable offences to the estimated total number of persons of the same age and sex in the general population and showing, over a period of several years, the numbers of offenders per 100,000 of the population of the same sex in the particular age group, e.g. 2,313 males aged 14 and under 17 found guilty in 1959, as against 1,131 in 1938, per 100,000 of the male population in that age group. Another Appendix contains under 73 headings the 'List of Indictable Offences showing Classification Numbers', i.e. the number under which the offence in question can be found throughout the volume, for example, murder is No. 1, embezzlement No. 37, the various forms of larceny are Nos. 38–49. Occasionally, several offences of a different nature are lumped together under one number, with the consequence that no separate figures are obtainable for each offence, for example, No. 19 'Rape' includes also carnal knowledge of female idiots, lunatics or defectives, and No. 53 'Other Frauds' includes a great variety of fraudulent actions, and No. 49 'Other Simple and Minor Larcenies' a miscellaneous assortment of different kinds of stealing. The offences are further classified under six categories: Class I, Offences against the Person (which includes sex offences); Class II, Offences against

Property with Violence; Class III, Offences against Property without Violence; Class IV, Malicious Injuries to Property; Class V, Forgery and Offences against the Currency; Class VI, Other Offences (which is a mixed bag containing such heterogeneous offences as High Treason and other offences against the State, Libel, attempted Suicide and the more serious Motoring Offences). The non-indictable offences are listed under approximately 200 headings in the 'Magistrates' Courts Tables'.

No definition of the term 'indictable' offences is given in the volume. The whole distinction is largely obsolete, and the dividing line changes from time to time. In fact, 'all crimes are indictable unless by statute they are made triable summarily', i.e. without formal indictment. 'There are certain crimes which may only be tried upon indictment, but there is a large number of indictable offences which may, in certain circumstances, be tried summarily. Conversely, there are certain summary offences which may, if the accused so wishes, be tried upon indictment.'[16] A list of indictable offences is given in the Criminal Justice Act, 1925, but there have been several later amendments. The term 'offences' itself is also used very loosely, sometimes as a generic term to cover any kind of contravention of the criminal law, sometimes in a narrower sense so as to exclude the most serious crimes, i.e. meaning misdemeanours, not felonies. In English criminal statistics it is used in the wider sense and the only distinction according to seriousness is that between indictable and non-indictable offences.

The Comparative Tables go back over thirty years, showing at a glance the fluctuations of both police and court figures for individual offences per million of population, but as they usually lump together periods of five years important features may remain hidden and, as throughout the volume, the population figures can in the absence of an annual census be only estimated.

The Annual Tables now begin with the police returns of indictable offences known to the police with numbers 'cleared up', of persons proceeded against according to sex and the results of proceedings. According to the official definition,[17] 'offences cleared up include those for which a person is arrested or summoned or for which he is cautioned, those taken into consideration by a court when the offender is found guilty on another charge, and certain of those of which a person is known or suspected to be guilty but for which he cannot for some reason be prosecuted (e.g. because he had died)', a definition to which we shall have to return later on. Offences cleared up in this way amounted to 50·1 per cent of the total known to the police in 1938 and to 44·7 per cent in 1959, which figures refer to the whole country, with considerable variations for individual police districts[18] and different categories of offences. In the Metropolitan Police District, the percentage figure of crimes cleared up (for which a definition slightly different from that in *Criminal Statistics* is given) was in 1957 only 30·3 for all indictable offences, and only 20·8 for housebreaking, but 108·3 for manslaughter and infanticide, a figure which seems almost too good to be true and can only be due to the fact that more offences were cleared up than had become known to the police *during the year* in question. In Scotland the percentages of crimes cleared up is slightly lower than in England, but there the term 'crime' is distinguished from 'offences' for which the percentages are much higher.

The police returns give also the numbers of persons proceeded against for non-indictable offences, with results of proceedings. The police returns are followed by tables showing the numbers of persons tried at Assizes and Quarter Sessions, with nature of offence, and results of proceedings according to sex and age and also sex related to offence and length of sentence. The tables for Magistrates' Courts are given for indictable and non-indictable offences and also divided according to sex, age, offence and results of proceedings, and there are special tables for courts of appeal, for probation orders, public prosecutions, Broadmoor patients, legal aid and a few others.

It is thus a special feature of English criminal statistics that they present both police and court statistics, thereby enabling us to compare these two sets of figures, whereas many other countries concentrate on court statistics. Such comparisons, as will be seen later, lead to a number of interesting questions.

(*b*) Second in importance rank the annual *Reports of the Commissioners of Prisons*, also published one year after the period covered. (The Prison Commission has now been abolished, and its functions have been taken over by the Prison Department of the Home Office.) Although their principal interest lies not in the statistical material provided but in their general material on the administration of prisons, borstals and detention centres, they contain many tables of statistical interest on the characteristics of the population of these institutions, e.g. their age in relation to the length of the sentence (not shown in *Criminal Statistics*), on the daily average population of each institution, on the employment of inmates, on expenditure and many more. Together with these publications, the annual *Reports of the Council of the Central After-Care Association* (C.A.C.A.) should be studied, which provide information on the work of the various bodies forming the Association, especially related to recidivism.

(*c*) The annual *Reports of the Commissioner of Police of the Metropolis* provide information for the London area similar to that given in *Criminal Statistics* for the whole country, with special emphasis on matters of interest to the police such as arrests, motoring offences, drunkenness, percentages of offences cleared up.

(d) The, irregularly published, *Reports of the Children's Department, Home Office,* contain statistics on juvenile delinquency, the Approved School population, children in the care of local authorities, juvenile courts and similar matters. The most recent of these reports is the one for the years 1961-3, H.M.S.O., H.C. 155, London, 1964.

There are further several more specialized annual publications such as *Offences relating to Motor Vehicles* and *Offences of Drunkenness* and occasional papers such as *Papers relating to the Large Number of Crimes Accompanied by Violence Occurring in Large Cities* (House of Lords [121], July 1951). Attention may also be briefly drawn to *Criminal Statistics—Scotland,* published annually for the year before that of publication, giving statistics similar to that in *Criminal Statistics England and Wales,* but adapted to the different criminal law and procedure in Scotland and with informative notes on these legal differences in procedure.[19]

4. *Some Figures from 'English Criminal Statistics' and the Other Publications mentioned in Section 3*

To give an idea of the actual volume and development of crime and matters related to it, as reflected in these various publications, the following figures may be quoted:[20]

(a) Indictable offences known to the police

Year	Larceny	Breaking and entering	Frauds and false pretences	Sexual offences	Violence against the person	Total (which also includes receiving and other offences)
1938	199,951	49,184	16,097	5,018	2,721	283,220
1945	323,310	108,266	13,122	8,546	4,743	478,394
1952	341,512	97,941	27,230	14,967	6,997	513,559
1959	445,888	133,962	34,061	20,024	13,876	675,626
1963	635,627	219,138	45,823	20,518	20,083	978,076

Source: *Criminal Statistics England and Wales.*

106

(b) Persons found guilty of offences

Year	Indictable	Non-indictable	(Persons dealt with summarily)
1938	78,463	Annual averages 1935–39	797,026
1945	115,974	Annual averages 1945–49	583,913
1952	131,047	Annual averages 1950–54	731,654
1959	153,190	Annual averages 1959	1,049,946
		Number of persons found guilty in 1959	887,532
1963	211,718		1,107,429

Source: *Criminal Statistics England and Wales*, for the years concerned, Introductory Note, Chapter 6.

(c) Persons found guilty of traffic offences
(Nos. 122–138 of list of non-indictable offences)

1938	475,124	1959	635,366
1945	148,419	1963	820,780
1955	407,815		

Source: *Criminal Statistics England and Wales*, for the years concerned, Introductory Note, Chapter 4.

(d) Persons of different ages found guilty of indictable offences per 100,000 of population of the age or age group

Age or age group	1938		1959	
	Males	Females	Males	Females
8	220	9	270	15
9	451	27	635	35
10	703	37	967	57
11	931	62	1,257	89
12	1,111	66	1,539	135
13	1,315	73	2,236	218
14	1,141	84	2,855	291
15	1,145	97	2,025	210
16	1,110	91	2,048	220
17	867	99	2,163	224
18	740	106	2,214	231
19	766	108	1,988	194
20	665	94	1,752	156
21 and under 25	559	77	1,436	129
25 and under 30	431	62	960	103
30 and under 40	307	61	572	89
40 and under 50	182	50	313	77
50 and under 60	101	30	162	55
60 and over	51	10	60	21

Source: *Criminal Statistics England and Wales, 1959*, Introductory Note, Appendix III(a). The corresponding figures for 1962 are given below in Vol. II, p. 679.

(e) *Daily average population in prisons and Borstals*
(*men and women*)

1938	11,086	1951	20,787
1940	9,377	1959	25,453
1962	31,063 (incl. Detention Centres)		

Source: *Annual Reports of the Prison Commissioners* for the years 1939–41,
p. 27, 1959, p. 9, 1962, p. 1.

(f) *Indictable offences known to the police, and Persons arrested
for all offences in the Metropolitan Police District*

	Ind. offences known to police	Persons arrested for all offences
1938	95,280	
1955	95,262	76,416
1957	125,754	99,005
1962	214,120	

Source: *Reports of the Commissioner of Police of the Metropolis
for the years* 1957 and 1962.

Only a few comments are needed at this stage. First, the number of
indictable offences known to the police has risen between 1938 and
1959 more than that of persons found guilty of such offences, and the
number of persons dealt with for non-indictable offences has risen
even less than the corresponding number for indictable offences. Even
for traffic offences the rise was not as marked as often believed. When
we look at the various groups of indictable offences separately, we
find that sexual offences and offences of violence against the person
have risen more than the others. Moreover, non-indictable offences
do not invariably move in the same direction as indictable offences,
which can be seen particularly in the immediate post-war years. The
few figures presented under (a) and (b) may already suffice to indicate
that conclusions should never be drawn from the figures for all
offences taken together as each individual category of offence has its
own peculiar trends and problems. As far as the different age groups
are concerned, the increase per 100,000 of population of the same age
or age group was greatest for males aged 13, 14, 15, 16, 17, 18. The
total increase for all ages was only slightly greater for males than
females. The total volume of crime, however, was eight to nine times
as much for males as for females. In 1938, indictable offences known
to the police numbered approximately three and a half times the
figure for persons found guilty of such offences, whereas in 1959 the
proportion had risen to approximately four and a half.[21] As already

mentioned under 3(*a*), the overall percentage of crimes cleared up has slightly fallen in recent years, which may partly explain the changed proportion. Naturally, the proportion of crimes cleared up differs greatly for different categories of offences; in 1950, for example, the ratio of offences cleared up to offences known to the police was 100 for receiving, 93 for frauds and false pretences, 90 for violence against the person, 78 for sexual offences, 54 for robbery, 40 for larceny and 38 for breaking and entering.[22] Most, but not all, of these differences can be explained by the characteristics of each category of offences; the ratio for sexual offences, for example, appears surprisingly high.

Finally, the fluctuations of prison statistics should never be regarded as evidence for corresponding changes in the rate of crime; they reflect the sentencing policy of the courts rather than real movements of crime, and it is very doubtful whether increases in the latter produce, as a rule, a similar increase in prison sentences and vice versa. From 1938 to 1940, for example, there was a slight increase in the number of crimes known to the police, whereas the prison population declined, and its rise between 1940 and 1951 was much more marked than the rise in crime.

5. *The Interpretation of Official Criminal Statistics—Difficulties and Pitfalls*[23]

(*a*) *The Dark Figure.* The concepts 'crimes known to the police' and 'crimes cleared up' show already our awareness of one of the most fundamental limitations of crime statistics, the existence of crimes which remain either entirely unknown to the police or are at least not cleared up. This can be explained in various ways: First, the commission of an offence may remain altogether unknown, for example the disappearance of the murdered person may not be noticed, which can easily happen in the case of persons living alone and having no relations, neighbours or friends, or of tramps and vagrants or persons travelling abroad; or a theft may be committed without the owner noticing the loss or a fraud without the victim realizing that he has been cheated; or a child may be sexually assaulted without understanding the nature of the act or informing anybody. Secondly, the death of a person or the disappearance of an article may be noticed but explained in an innocuous way, for example murder may be cleverly disguised as death by accident or suicide. In this connection, special attention has lately been drawn by Havard to the low proportion of autopsies held by coroners in some districts.[24] Thirdly, the commission of an offence may become known to others or at least suspected by them, but the authorities are not informed and no official action is taken. This, too, may happen for a great variety of reasons, such as fear of reprisals or of public disapproval or shame, which latter feeling plays a large part in the case of rape and indecent assault; or to spare children the experience of having to appear in court as witnessess; or to shield the offender, which is often the case with incests or indecent assaults within the family; or because of the feeling that the lenient treatment which the offender is expected to get from the court would not justify the trouble of starting criminal proceedings; or because of disapproval of the law which has been violated, for example against homosexual or betting and gambling offences; or because of a generally anti-social attitude on the part of the person concerned who refuses on principle to co-operate with the authorities; or simply because of indifference and laziness. In an investigation made several years ago in Liverpool of losses incurred in foreign trade the author concluded: 'It is surprising how few of the thefts involving import or export goods appear to be reported to the authorities.' One explanation, he thinks, may be the lapse of time which frequently occurs before the theft is discovered.[25] Observations of this kind may in part help to explain the reluctance of some firms to enter the foreign market at all.

To the category of offences not brought to the notice of the police may be added that of offences classified as 'cleared up' where the offender is regarded as 'known' to the police because he has been charged or at least been suspected, but no prosecution has been possible or no conviction obtained because of insufficient evidence or for other reasons (see the official definition, 3(a) above). The dark figure resulting from these various causes not only explains the discrepancy between the numbers of crimes known to the police and persons found guilty, but must also throw some considerable doubt on the value of any official crime statistics. To deal first with the gap between police figures and court convictions, our immediate reaction to it will be to regard it as a reflection on the efficiency of the police, and to some extent this is correct. There are, however, also certain factors which have to be considered in favour of the police. Offences for which the offender is cautioned by the police, for example, necessarily reduce the number of persons found guilty without reflecting on the efficiency of the police; while such factors should always be considered, their numerical significance should, however, not be overrated.

Apart from such questions concerning the efficiency of the police we have to examine whether the existence of these dark figures of crime completely destroys the value of crime statistics or whether we can draw certain conclusions from the information at our disposal which may allow us at least to speculate as to the real size of the dark figures. Scientific work, after all, is largely an attempt to reduce the extent of the unknown by making the right use of the facts already known. Briefly, the information at our disposal comes mainly from three sources: it is, first, information derived from interviewing selected samples of persons on the number of offences which they had committed without being detected; secondly, information from persons or institutions unconnected with the police and the penal system who are in a position to hear about undetected offences; and, thirdly, information derived from our general knowledge of the nature of the offence concerned and the attitude of persons towards its detection and prosecution. As to the first, the literature on 'hidden delinquency', mostly American, is mainly concerned with juveniles or at least with offences reported by adults as committed in their youth. As the author wrote many years ago, 'when reading the autobiographies of criminals, one is usually struck by the immense number of petty offences they have committed as children before being caught'.[26] According to one of the most widely quoted of these studies, of a group of 337 Texas college students every one had committed, apart from traffic offences, illegal acts for which he could have been charged if they had become known.[27] A Swedish enquiry by Strahl and Nyquist among law students of the University of Uppsala showed that out of 75 male and 21 female students only 2 reported that they had never committed any of the offences listed in the questionnaire, and only about 20 per cent of them stated that at least one of their offences had become known to the police.[28] The questionnaire included various forms of stealing and fraud, drunken driving, etc., and 57·3 per cent of the male and 9·5 per cent of the female students confessed to offences of shoplifting. In an interesting Liverpool study by Mays of 80 boys, members of a club and interviewed by him as youth worker, the majority 'admitted having committed delinquent acts at some time or another during childhood and adolescence', i.e. acts for which they could have been charged.[29] 34 of them had been convicted and another 22 admitted criminal acts, some of them rather serious ones, without having ever appeared in court, one of them having committed as many as 12 undetected offences. One has to bear in mind that, mainly owing to the very low minimum age of criminal responsibility in this country, many people believe that in the case of very young children it is better to do nothing than to bring them before the juvenile court.

A few similar enquiries are concerned with adults, as for example a study by Wallerstein and Wyle which showed that of 1,698 persons in New York City who answered a questionnaire anonymously 91 per cent stated that they had committed crimes after the age of 16.[30]

It may be argued that such enquiries, notably those carried out merely by means of questionnaires, are not convincing as there is no guarantee whatsoever for the accuracy of the answers. There is, however, a certain amount of supporting evidence to be found not only in the above quoted percentages of crimes cleared up by the police, which show a considerable residue of undetected crime, but also evidence from other sources. An attempt was made by the author before the last war to discover the prosecuting policies of a number of large London stores with regard to thefts committed on their premises by their own employees and by strangers, both juveniles and adults. The result showed that these policies varied considerably in every direction, but the general impression was that big firms usually did not prosecute their own employees and that in the case of strangers there was a great variety of systems.[31] Similarly, Sellin found that in Philadelphia shoplifting, unless of a professional character, was rarely reported and that in the year 1933 more such thefts were known to the three large department stores investigated than the total known to the police for the whole of the city.[32]

Another example of an offence where some light on the extent of the dark figure can be thrown by outside agencies is abortion. The Inter-Departmental Committee on the subject, when trying to assess the frequency of this offence,[33] refers to an estimate of the British Medical Association of 1936, according to which from 16 to 20 per cent of all pregnancies ended in abortion. This estimate, which was supported by the records of various hospitals and clinics, led to a total of 110,000 to 150,000 abortions per year, of which about 40 per cent, i.e. 50–70,000, were regarded as criminal. In pre-war Germany the number of criminal abortions was for 1934–36 estimated at 200,000 per year.[34] On the other hand, the highest figure of abortion offences known to the police in England and Wales for the past thirty years was 347 as the annual average for 1940–4, usually the average annual figure is between 100 and 200.

For homosexual offences psycho-analysts and other experts maintain from their clinical observations that, while the number of detected offenders depends to some extent on the activities of the police, it is only a small proportion of cases that is detected.[35] For the most serious crimes, such as murder, we are tempted to minimize the size of the dark figure. 'The murderer', writes Hans von Hentig,[36] 'who, as every mass murderer does for years or even for ever, walks about in our midst without appearing in court and in the statistics, wounds our feeling of self-respect so deeply that we prefer to know nothing about the problem of the "unknown murderer". Police statistics try to comfort us with a rate of 89·3 per cent of cleared up murders, but the facts make us disbelieve this optimism, provided we use the word "cleared up" in its usual meaning.'

How far is it possible, in the light of the material so far presented and of our knowledge of the nature of specific categories of offences and of certain sociological and psychological factors relating to them, to make any positive statements regarding the dark figure of crime? To some extent, this question has already been answered. On the one hand, no such statements can be made regarding crime as such. On the other hand, however, our knowledge of the peculiar character- istics of individual categories of offences, the techniques of detection and the socio-psychological atmosphere surrounding them may en- able us to say that this or that category is likely to have a high or low dark figure. To some slight extent the percentages of crimes cleared up, as quoted above, may also serve as a guide, although the factors which determine the ease of clearing up an offence brought to the notice of the police may not necessarily be identical with the factors material for the question of whether an offence becomes known to the police. Once, for example, the commission of a homosexual offence has become known it is comparatively easy to clear it up—the diffi- culty lies before that stage. Of considerable assistance will be our knowledge of the attitudes of wide circles of the population to the type of offence in question. Abortion offences will, as a rule, only be detected if they result in death; and the reporting of rape will almost entirely depend on the willingness of the assaulted woman to inform others. In any case, it would be grossly misleading to treat the dark figures as representing a fixed proportion of the totals of the offences known in that particular category.[37] For some categories of offences these totals are likely to be higher, for others they are almost certain to be much lower than the dark figure, and the relationship between detected and undetected offences may differ not only according to type of offence, but also according to type of district, character and law-abidingness of population, popularity of local police and many other factors. Our conclusion, therefore, has to be that not much weight can be attached to the crime figures as such, as published in official criminal statistics. For juvenile delinquency, in particular, the author can only reiterate his conviction that 'statistics of juvenile delinquency can do little more than indicate the varying degree of willingness on the part of the public and the police to bring this cate- gory of delinquents before the juvenile courts'.[38] From all this it fol- lows that not too much weight should be attached by press and public to published figures and their movements unless they are carefully inter- preted. In short, it is the business of the police and the man in the street to reduce the size of the dark figures of crime, and it is the task of the criminologist to interpret them in the light of what is known to him.

(b) *Police Statistics and Court Statistics.* The report of 1893 (s. 2 above) regarded court statistics as more reliable than police statistics, and rightly so, but each of the two has its strong and its weak points. Police statistics cover a larger field and give the most comprehensive picture of the crime situation normally available to us, but the methods of recording employed by the various local or county police forces differ greatly and used in former years to be even 'purely discretionary', leading often to striking and unexplainable differences between neighbouring towns or counties. Technical changes in methods of police book-keeping may easily produce striking increases or decreases in police figures without any corresponding changes in the crime situation itself. The classical example is the abolition of the 'Suspected Stolen Book' in the Metropolitan area which resulted in a sudden 'rise' of property offences from 26,000 in 1931 to 83,000 in 1932.[39] Following the recommendations of a Departmental Committee of 1938 on Detective Work and Procedure there has been an improvement and greater uniformity since the last war,[40] but a number of other weaknesses still remain. Police statistics, as a rule, give no details concerning the person of the offender; they have to depend on possibly quite unreliable information from witnesses whose evidence can be evaluated only later in court; from the legal point of view they may classify reported offences differently from the classification ultimately decided by the court.[41] Moreover, police statistics reflect the activities of the police at any given time and place and are, therefore, greatly dependent on the interest taken by the police in a certain type of crime or certain classes of persons as also on the use made by the police of cautioning instead of formal charges, a factor the extent of which can now at least be ascertained from *Criminal Statistics*. The differential rates of arrest have been frequently discussed by American criminologists, and in a famous sociological study of an American community[42] the percentages of arrests are given as ranging from 0·43 for the 'upper-upper' class to 7·80 for the lower-middle class and 64·69 for the 'lower-lower class', the implication being that these wide differences in rates of arrest are not likely to be a true reflection of the actual crime situation. Moreover, the higher 'visibility' of certain minority groups, in particular Negroes, which makes them more liable to arrest and prosecution by the police, has often been commented on.[43]

Court statistics, while giving a more reliable picture not only of the crime but also of certain personal characteristics of the offender, are entirely dependent on the cases brought before the courts by the prosecution. While we can be reasonably sure that a person against whom a finding of guilt has been recorded in the court statistics was actually guilty of the offence there will be many others equally guilty but never appearing in court. Court statistics may be statistics of persons proceeded against (or persons for trial) or of persons found guilty. Both sets of figures are needed, the first because it includes the important categories of persons acquitted or 'charge withdrawn or dismissed', the latter because it contains only cases where the evidence has fully proved that this particular crime was committed by this particular person.

When all is said we have to conclude that both police and court statistics are needed, although for different purposes and each of them with many reservations. Moreover, the existence side by side of statistics of offences and statistics of offenders poses various specific problems. How can these two sets be brought into the most effective relationship, considering that very often one offence does not correspond to one offender and that one offence may be committed by several persons and, vice versa, one person may have committed several offences? With regard to the latter question, 'Surely', wrote the author in 1942, 'neither to society at large nor to the practical penologist can it be indifferent whether 100,000 offences "known to the police" have been committed by 100,000 first offenders or by a small group of perhaps 2,000 habitual law-breakers, each of whom is responsible for an average of fifty offences.'[44] To some extent, this information is now available in the *Introduction to Criminal Statistics* and in *Supplementary Statistics* (2(*c*) and 3(*a*) above). From the latter we can discover, for example, that in 1957 6,978 persons were found guilty of shopbreaking and that 10,500 offences against property without violence were recorded against them. While this is interesting it still leaves a number of questions unanswered.

On the question of how many crimes are committed by more than one person no information is at present available, except for some data in the, generally unpublished, *Annual Reports of Local Chief Constables*,[45] which refer to crimes committed by gangs, and except for those rare offences where the police returns show that the number of persons proceeded against was higher than that of crimes known to the police. This will, naturally be the case with offences such as rioting and unlawful assembly (Nos. 64 and 65 of classified list), but even here it does not help us very much to find, for example, that in 1959 crimes of the latter category numbered 8 as against 47 persons proceeded against.

Statistics of recidivism have nothing to do with the relationship between police and court statistics as previous offences committed by an individual may have been recorded as known to the police some years before he was found guilty by a court for his latest offence. *Criminal Statistics* at present gives no information on recidivism, but *Supplementary Statistics* (2(*c*) above) does and even more so the *Annual Reports of the Prison Commissioners* and of the C.A.C.A. (3(*b*) above).

(*c*) *Other Considerations concerning the Interpretation of Criminal Statistics.* So far we have drawn attention to certain weaknesses of the official figures arising from the existence of the 'dark figures' of undetected crime and from other deficiencies of police and court statistics. Now we have to consider various additional factors which may influence the interpretation of these official figures and occasionally even determine on paper the very extent of crime as reflected in *Criminal Statistics*. These factors are the criminal law, the law and practice of criminal procedure and of evidence, public opinion and, strangely enough, the criminal statistics.[46] First, the criminal law: if it is too strict it will often be disregarded by the public, the police and the jury, and the declining crime figures will mistakenly be taken as proof that its rigidity has had the deterrent effect desired; if it is lenient, those concerned may be more willing to co-operate with the law and to prosecute, which may give the impression that its leniency encourages crime; on the other hand, if it is too lenient, a prosecution may no longer appear to be worth while. Secondly, the law and practice of criminal procedure and of evidence: The strictness of certain rules of evidence, for example concerning previous convictions of the accused person, sometimes leads to an acquittal of offenders in spite of their guilt. Moreover, prosecutions by the police instead of being conducted, as abroad and in Scotland, by legally trained public prosecutors may occasionally have the same effect, and the lack of uniformity in prosecutions, due to the absence of a centralized system—the Director of Public Prosecutions intervenes only in serious cases[47]—may falsify the local crime picture, especially for minor offences. Whether lay magistrates are more inclined than professional lawyers to acquit or dismiss a case is impossible to judge on the strength of the available material. Less difficult to assess is the effect of certain changes in criminal procedure such as transfers of jurisdiction for an offence from a jury court to a court of summary jurisdiction where proceedings are less formal and costly. It has repeatedly been observed that as a result of such transfers the number of cases brought before the magistrates' courts greatly exceeded the decline in prosecutions for the offence in question before higher courts.[48]

While the effect of police methods on the official crime figures has already been discussed above, it may be mentioned in passing that the requirements of insurance companies of different kinds may greatly influence these figures by prescribing that police proceedings should be opened before claims can be acknowledged. Similar considerations apply to railway police regulations concerning thefts of goods in transit.[49]

Particularly high is the proportion of thefts of goods in transit which are not recorded in the official *Criminal Statistics*. 'Since the statistics are compiled by the Home Office from information supplied by each Police District there is a distinct possibility that "unplaced" thefts may not be counted at all. This applies particularly to thefts of goods in transit where there is no evidence to show where the thefts took place.'[50]

The influence on the volume of reported crime of public opinion, or rather of the views, attitudes and customs of various classes of the population, is quite immeasurable[51] and probably far exceeds even that of the police. We are not yet in a position, however, to give chapter and verse for this statement. Closely connected with it is the fact that the publication of official statistical figures in the field of crime and the way in which they are used by the press have a considerable effect upon subsequent changes in these figures. If a striking increase in crime of a certain type or in a certain district or for a certain age group is reported public opinion or the press take a special interest in the matter, as a result of which there is often an increase in cases reported to the police and therefore a further rise in official statistics. The figures 'gain momentum as a result of their own dead weight'.[52]

(d) *In Particular: the Relativity of Criminal Statistics and the Possibility of an 'Index of Criminality'*. Each single figure in *Criminal Statistics*, if taken in isolation, is almost meaningless. It conveys very little to us if we find, for example, that the number of murders of persons aged one year and over as known to the police in England and Wales during 1959 was 142 or the number of burglaries 4,627. We cannot even say that this is very much or very little. There is no objective way of defining the 'right' volume of crime of a certain type for a certain time or place. Such figures can acquire significance only if they are compared with others. Only if we know such facts as that the corresponding figures for the period 1930–4 were 103 for murder and 1,596 for burglary or that the number of male persons aged 14 found guilty of ind. offences was 1,141 in 1938 and 2,855 in 1959 per 100,000 of population of that age can our interest be aroused. Comparisons are the essence of criminal statistics and their interpretation, comparisons related to each of the various details published in these volumes: notably time, place, age, sex, type of offence and disposal. The factor perhaps most frequently used for such comparisons is time, but it is here that we have to face almost insuperable difficulties. The period of time used for our comparisons must be neither too short nor too long. If the periods are very short, for example a comparison of the murder rate over a period of three years, differences may mean very little because any changes observed may be due to chance. If we wish to study, for example, the influence of the Homicide Act, 1957, on the rate of murder we have to wait until a period of at least, say, five or ten years has elapsed so that any trends may become clearly marked. On the other hand, if we take very long periods, for example 30 or 50 years, we run the risk that within these years important factors such as the law, criminal

117

procedure, the population of the area, social and economic conditions and—last but not least—the structure of criminal statistics may all have changed so much that it is impossible to say which of these changes might have been responsible for the variations in the crime rate which we wish to explain. This, by the way, is an important consideration whenever changes in the structure of the tables of criminal statistics are contemplated; such changes should be made only when the advantages would greatly outweigh the drawbacks which inevitably arise for statistical research. There is no general rule for the optimum length of the period to be examined, and for each research the problem has to be solved independently in the light of the prevailing circumstances,

In view of the difficulties of interpreting and comparing the figures of criminal statistics criminologists have been trying for years to work out a reliable 'Index of Criminality' which could serve as a basis for further studies. The idea behind such an Index would be to select from the masses of published figures those which are most likely to present a true picture of the extent and movements of criminality in a certain country over a given period. Sellin, who has given much thought to the matter,[53] has established the following criteria to which such an Index would have to conform: it should be based on the rates of a few selected offences which are regarded as particularly dangerous to society, which are subject to public prosecution and where the greatest possible co-operation between the victim and the authorities can be expected. It is clear that such an Index should be formulated not in absolute figures, but related to 100,000 of the population at risk, i.e. preferably of the population liable to criminal prosecution. While an 'Index of Criminality' would have the advantage that it would present in a nutshell everything that is valuable in statistical figures it should not be interpreted as indicating what should be the normal volume of crime at a certain time in a certain place. The combing out of useless and misleading material is not enough to produce a norm.

6. *International and Foreign Criminal Statistics*

(*a*) Comparisons of the kind mentioned in Section 5(*d*) would seem to be particularly illuminating with regard to foreign criminal statistics, and many attempts have been made in the past to work out the foundation of an international body of criminal statistics which would make comparisons between the crime figures of different countries reliable and meaningful. As has been pointed out by one of the specialists in this field, Ernst Roesner,[54] already in 1838 work of this kind was undertaken by the French statistician Moreau de Jonnès in his *Statistique de la Grande Bretagne et de l'Irlande*, who thereby transferred to the international sphere some of the methods used some time before him by A. M. Guerry for France in his *Essay sur la Statistique morale de la France* (1833). While these studies were of a private character only, semi-official efforts began in 1853 when the first International Statistical Congress in Brussels, at the instigation of Quetelet, discussed the comparability of national criminal statistics. The International Penal and Penitentiary Congresses, too, repeatedly debated the subject;[55] for example, in 1872 in London the question was on the Agenda 'Is it desirable to establish international prison statistics? and if so, how may this be accomplished?' Similarly, the Stockholm Congress of 1878 and the St. Petersburg Congress of 1890 expressed themselves in favour of international penitentiary statistics, but for decades little progress was made even in this relatively limited field in spite of the appointment in 1932 of a mixed commission for the comparative study of criminal statistics which met several times until 1939. This lack of progress is not surprising, bearing in mind that criminal statistics are closely dependent on such national factors as criminal law, criminal procedure, the structure and functions of the prosecuting authorities, the composition of the criminal courts and the co-operation between the authorities and the public. Where even the definitions of murder, manslaughter, robbery, larceny and many other offences differ from country to country it is but little use comparing figures relating to them,[56] and statements of a comparative nature should be made, if at all, only by those who are thoroughly familiar not only with the whole system of law and penal administration but also with the social and economic structure and atmosphere of the countries concerned.

Some of the existing difficulties could possibly be, if not altogether removed, at least reduced if the recommendations adopted by the Conference of the International Statistical Institute[57] would be carried out that every country should include in its official criminal statistics an exposé of its penal legislation and judicial system, an account of the sources and methods used in collecting criminal statistics, and an explanation of the crime classification employed, and if certain general standards would be adopted for the tabulation of convictions according to age, sex, and other characteristics. It is exasperating to see how many unnecessary differences exist at present in the technique of recording simple facts, for example length of sentences.[58] However, even this, useful as it would be, would hardly penetrate beneath the surface of the problems of international criminal statistics.

(*b*) Concerning foreign criminal statistics in general, there are at present bewildering differences not only in the way of recording the same factors, but also in the selection of factors for recording. It is probably only sex and age of offenders that are universally recorded, and next in frequency come previous convictions, sentences received, place of conviction, occupation, residence, marital status. Rarer is the inclusion of data on religion, education, domicile, time and place of offence, economic position of offender, his alcoholic condition and motive.[59] It would be very difficult to draft minimum rules to which every country should be asked to adhere as the basic material may not be available everywhere. Moreover, one has to resist the temptation to ask more than is really needed; the warning given in the report of 1893 (s. 2 above) was not entirely unjustified, although the addition of two or three items to the present English criminal statistics might be welcome. What should be done internationally is to reach an agreement on the selection and tabulation of those comparatively few factors which are regarded not as merely desirable, but as indispensable for each of the countries concerned, with a set of simple rules for tabulation, which would imply that those countries where the basic material required is not yet in existence should take steps to produce it. For certain other factors, the regular collection of which is regarded as not essential, but desirable, the agreement should indicate that information should be collected and published officially at regular intervals for the whole country or in shorter intervals for various selected districts. For the rest, the collection of material should be left to the private research worker (see below, Chapter 6).

(c) A few data concerning some foreign countries:

France. French criminal statistics, *Compte général de l'administration de la justice criminelle,* which began in 1825, are usually regarded as the oldest regular official publication commenced after the creation of a census. This is true only if we disregard the *English Parliamentary Papers* of 1810 mentioned above (s. 2). French criminal statistics are combined in one volume with the *Compte général de l'administration de la justice civile et commerciale*; they are court, not police, statistics, distinguish between recidivists and first offenders and give, in addition to the usual data on age, sex, offence and sentence, detailed information on the departments where the offence is committed, on marital status, nationality and 'milieu social', i.e. occupation related to offence. There is a table 'Affaires concernant les Mineurs', which divides juvenile offenders into three groups, under 13, between 13 and 16, and over 16 years of age, showing the penalties and other measures ordered by the court (there are no penalties for those under 13). The French tables give only absolute figures, not related to population.

Western Germany. Considerable changes in the previous system were made when the regular publication of criminal statistics was resumed in 1948.[60] The various stages through which the new system

had to go until it reached its present form reflect the processes of upheaval and consolidation experienced in Western Germany after 1945.
For example, religion and occupation were excluded, the former because it had been introduced by the Nazi regime in connection with
its racial legislation, the latter because the social and economic
changes and the immigration from the East had introduced an element of instability which would have made the collection of reliable
data on the occupational structure of the criminal population too
hazardous. Data on occupation and marital status do not appear in
the published tables, but are collected by the Länder in case they
should at some future stage be required to fulfil international obligations. Often data have been collected in view of the likely requirements of the impending reform of the penal code and also as a consequence of amendments made in the old statutory law. The pre-war
classification according to the district of the provincial court of appeal
has been given up. The present official publications are 'Bevölkerung
und Kultur', No. 9: 'Rechtspflege' (Statistisches Bundesamt Wiesbaden)
und 'Polizeiliche Kriminalstatistik' (Bundeskriminalamt Wiesbaden).

The United States of America.[61] Considering the enormous extent
and high development of criminological studies in the United States
we should expect to find there an equally well-developed system of
federal and state criminal statistics. The actual position, however, is
disappointing; 'criminal statistics in the United States', writes Thorsten Sellin, one of the foremost authorities on the subject, 'usually
fall far short of reaching even modest standards. . . . The problem of
achieving national criminal statistics in the United States is somewhat
like the problem of establishing uniform statistics for Europe. Who is
to collect them and by what authority?' In fact, most of the difficulties
outlined above which stand in the way of achieving uniform international criminal statistics apply to the internal position in the
U.S.A., too. There are now fifty separate states, the Federal Government, and the District of Columbia, each with its own criminal law,
procedure and law enforcement agencies.[62] Attempts to produce
nation-wide judicial criminal statistics began in 1931, but were not
particularly successful and had to be given up in 1946. More important were the simultaneous efforts of the police organizations regularly to collect and publish Uniform Crime Reports. In 1930 this work
was taken over by the Federal Bureau of Investigation, United States
Department of Justice, and it has continued and grown ever since. It
depends on the voluntary co-operation of local police departments,
but even so according to Sellin in 1950 the departments filing regular
statistical reports with the Bureau numbered about 5,300 covering
over 72,000,000 inhabitants or nearly 50 per cent of the total population at the time, and the rate is steadily growing. Their drawbacks are

that they are limited to certain serious crimes—homicide, rape, robbery, aggravated assault, burglary, larceny and auto theft—that they unduly favour urban districts and provide inadequate interpretation of their data. A valuable feature is the division into 6 groups according to the size of cities and the classification according to geographical areas such as New England, Middle Atlantic, Pacific, etc.

In addition, there are juvenile court statistics, compiled by the United States Children's Bureau, and prison statistics. Moreover, most of the states and many municipalities and individual courts publish their own statistical accounts, some of which are of high quality, for example in New Jersey, New York, Massachusetts and Pennsylvania, and the city of Philadelphia.

Efforts have been made for some years to work out a Uniform Criminal Statistics Act providing for the establishment of a Federal Bureau of Criminal Statistics and to prevail on the states to adopt it.[63]

Chapter 6

THE PLACE OF STATISTICS IN
CRIMINOLOGICAL RESEARCH II:
RESEARCH STATISTICS

With the growing refinement of official 'book-keeping' statistics the dividing line between them and research statistics in the narrower sense is getting more and more difficult to draw. As we have seen (Chapter 5 under 'General Considerations'), it is no longer identical with the distinction between official and private collection of figures, although this distinction has not become entirely immaterial. Research statistics are, more often than official statistics, concerned with the solution of a specific problem; they are, therefore, but rarely published at regular intervals, and private research workers are more often than officials inclined to draw conclusions from their studies and use them as a basis and justification for critical appraisals of specific conditions and policies. Official statisticians are, naturally, reluctant to do so. This applies not only to regular official publications in the narrower sense, for example *Criminal Statistics for England and Wales*, where any such critical appraisals of, say, the work of the police or the courts would of course be entirely out of place, but also to official research statistics, such as, for example, the Report of the Home Office Research Unit on *Time Spent Awaiting Trial*[1] where certain figures are presented which could well have been used for criticisms of the police and the courts. It could be argued, however, that such criticisms should rather come from non-official quarters.

I. THE BASIC FORMS OF STATISTICAL RESEARCH IN CRIMINOLOGY

1. *Elementary Forms*

The criminologist who uses statistical techniques often limits himself to the most elementary of such techniques. Much of his work in this field merely consists in drawing fairly obvious, though often useful, conclusions from the published or unpublished official figures. In the

Report of 1893 (see Chapter 5) the view was expressed that the Introductions to *Criminal Statistics* might well provide the reader with 'results and conclusions'. In fact, this is, as a rule, not done, apart from the occasional adding of percentages to the absolute figures presented, which makes it easier for the reader to grasp the significance of the latter and to follow their movements over a period of time. Here, the researcher can do valuable work by further elaborating the picture given in the official volumes, for example by working out the age and sex ratios of crime over a period of years for specific offences and thereby laying the statistical foundations for further research into juvenile and female delinquency (see Chapter 26 below). Or, another important branch of simple statistical research, the crime statistics may be compared with other social statistics, for example the movements of the figures for property offences with national and local unemployment figures,[2] or the rates of juvenile delinquency related to the degree of urbanization.[3] It is of great importance that criminologists should constantly see their crime figures in the light of social, and occasionally also medical, statistics. The simple correlations worked out in this way should, however, not be regarded as showing cause and effect. Statistical correlations, needless to say, can never prove causal nexus, although they may serve as signposts to further research ultimately perhaps leading to causal explanations.[4]

The same simple statistical techniques are also often employed by workers collecting their own basic material in order to supplement the official figures. Such collections are frequently indispensable since official criminal statistics and their various supplements cannot be expected always to provide the material required to solve specific problems, either because the question to be examined, for example age or sex problems of crime, is not adequately treated in those regular publications or because it is entirely outside the scope of present official statistics, as for example, family, occupational, religious, educational or mental factors. In fact, the special collection of statistical material is one of the most common features of criminological research and it leads at once to more complicated matters of statistical technique, even if the ultimate analysis of the collected material should be on simpler lines.

2. *The Use of Samples*

Whereas to the user of official statistics his material is given, as a rule, for the whole country as the total volume of crime in general or, less frequently, in a certain area or of criminals of a certain age or sex, to the researcher who wishes to collect his own material the problem of *sampling* is the first to arise with all its pitfalls.[5] It cannot here be treated in an expert manner, but attention has to be drawn to certain difficulties as they have been found in criminological research. Some of these difficulties are especially related to control group research and will therefore be discussed later on.

The use of samples is often indispensable in the study of specific problems. If we wish to examine, for example, the incidence of 'broken homes' or mental defectives among juvenile delinquents or that of alcoholics or middle-class people among adults guilty of homosexual offences we cannot possibly make a study of every juvenile delinquent or every adult convicted of such an offence. Therefore we have to look around for a suitable, i.e. representative, sample, which would truly reflect all the characteristics of the total population we wish to study. Sample surveys are not necessarily to be regarded as makeshifts; they may in fact be more reliable than surveys of the total population from which the sample is drawn.[6]

The first question to be decided by the research worker is usually that of the size of the sample. It will often be decided by considerations of time and money available for the research. Within limits it may be said that the larger the sample the more likely will it be representative of the total population[7] and the more will it be able to withstand the strain of classifications and repeated sub-divisions to which the sample may have to be subjected in the course of the statistical analysis. It is sometimes frustrating to find that no further splitting-up of the sample is possible because the resulting fractions would become too small to be meaningful.

To illustrate some of the points so far made we might refer to the research described in *Prediction Methods in relation to Borstal Training*. The object of the research was to discover criteria facilitating the distinction between Borstal boys who were likely to be successes, i.e. not to recidivate after discharge, and those likely to be failures; and also to work out prediction tables which would present these criteria in statistical form. For this purpose a sample of Borstal boys was required that was representative of the total Borstal population and could be observed over an adequate follow-up period to enable us to distinguish successes from failures. At the crucial period, about 2,000 boys were received into English Borstal Institutions in the course of a year. 'Within the permitted sum allocated for this research project, it was calculated that about 700 cases would be studied.'[8] Thus, approximately one third of the total population could be covered, which was a comparatively large sample. It had now to be decided whether to take a complete intake for a third of a year, or rather to take every third case throughout a year. To exclude seasonal trends the second course was adopted. The cases were taken from registers of admissions kept at the two Reception Centres, but a small number of cases had to be rejected as mentally defective or because they were not properly included. Next, the most suitable period had to be considered. 'It had to be neither so recent as to allow for no adequate time for testing after discharge nor so remote as to be directly affected by the Second World War', which made the years 1946 and 1947 appear to be most suitable. A special pilot study was made to see whether there were any significant differences between the second half of 1946 and the first half of 1947, and as no such differences were found these two periods were finally selected. In the course of collecting these records, however, another significant difference emerged: cases of boys who had been sent to various prisons in previous years were often difficult to trace, and 'we found that there was a direct correlation between the time it took the Home Office staffs to trace the Borstal files and the proportion of successes in any batch. In total the success rate was 45 per cent, but in the first 300 files received the success rate was nearly 70 per cent. In the end we were 56 files short of the complete sample, and a search by Criminal Record Office revealed that 46 of these 56 cases were failures— a rate of 82 per cent. We cannot, therefore, regard the sample for which data were available from Borstal files as strictly representative of the Borstal intake in the year surveyed. This was a factor underlying and modifying a large proportion of our analysis', and certain statistical adjustments had to be made. Moreover, the completeness of the information recorded in the Borstal files differed from Institution to Institution, and it was found that 'the Institutions which were the better record-keepers also tended to have better success rates'.

In short, in this research project it could be demonstrated that an apparently simple process of sampling did not produce an unbiased sample as certain cases had a better chance than others of being included and were unrepresentative in their rate of success and other characteristics.

In any case it should be borne in mind that a sample can be representative only of the total population from which it has been drawn and not necessarily of other populations.[9] A study based on a sample taken from the whole population of Borstal boys of a certain year can be representative only of the total of boys of this particular vintage, not of Borstal boys in general, still less of delinquents as such. An exception would have to be made only in the case of human behaviour which is unmodifiable, but criminology is very rarely concerned with such behaviour.

To refer to a few comparatively recent sample surveys, Cyril Burt took 'two hundred consecutive cases of juvenile delinquency—all, in fact, for which I could get complete information for the particular conditions reviewed'.[10] This is a frequently used technique which may involve the risk of an unrepresentative selection if the cases for which full records are available differ from the rest. Maud A. Merrill, in her American post-war study, used '300 unselected run-of-the-mill cases . . . without reference to any selective factors';[11] in the English enquiry *Young Offenders* the first 1,000 cases used were brought before the juvenile courts in London after the 1st October 1938.[12] Gillin, in his study of inmates of the Wisconsin State Prison, distinguished according to the type of offence and of sentence: his study of the life prisoners, a small group, includes the entire prison population of lifers, and the same applied to the sodomists and rapists. Of the property offenders, however, only every third was included for most of the information collected, but for data easily available in the prison records all the offenders were included. Gillin adds: 'thus we were able to determine how representative our smaller sample was at least with respect to these categories'.[13] R. G. Andry, in his study of short-term prisoners,[14] employed a detailed questionnaire, but for reasons of time he used only some of the questions for a sub-sample of the prisoners.

Many other considerations may determine the selection of the sample. If, for example, it is intended to interview not only a group of delinquent and one of non-delinquent boys but also their parents, the choice of boys in an Institution such as an Approved School taking boys from a very large geographical area will, as a rule, be impracticable because it would involve undue expenditure of time and money in visiting the parents. Therefore, the choice of an Institution receiving only juveniles from a limited area may here be preferable.[15]

What has been said about the need for samples of adequate size does not exclude the use of smaller samples for *Pilot Studies*. The latter are often indispensable to check whether the problem in hand can successfully be investigated in the manner and with the kind of material envisaged, and which adjustments will have to be made. Such pilot studies will prevent avoidable mistakes being made on an unnecessarily large scale and at correspondingly high cost. A successful pilot study should, however, not be used as a pretext to abandon the large and more representative one. It sometimes happens, on the other hand, that a study not originally planned as a pilot study has eventually to be treated as such because its size proves inadequate to deal with all the problems which have emerged in the course of the work.[16] Moreover, as Glaser has recently pointed out, 'in many areas the accomplishment of a first research project can only be to determine the nature and dimensions of some problems, and not to provide solutions for the problems. Such knowledge may suggest solutions, but demonstration of the effectiveness of a proposed solution often requires a second research of a totally different sort.'[17]

3. *The Use of Case Records in Statistical Research*

Much statistical research in criminology has to be done by using case records, for example of probationers, prisoners, Borstal boys and so on. Here two possibilities arise: either records have to be used which are already in existence, having been written by probation officers, institutional staffs, etc., in the course of their ordinary duties, or the records are produced especially for the purposes of the research. The second alternative is extremely rare, and research workers have, as a rule, to be content with routine records not originally prepared with the objects of the research project in mind. This inevitably leads to many difficulties as the worker will often search in vain in such records for the kind of information he requires, and even where it is available it will often not be recorded in the specific form needed for the research. The matter has been treated at some length in *Prediction Methods in relation to Borstal Training*, from which the following points may be taken:[18] records compiled by different field workers are often written from different viewpoints, giving slightly different meanings to the same terms, introducing the individual bias of the recording officer, especially where an intuitive style of reporting is employed, giving perhaps a very vivid but highly subjective 'pen-picture' of the offender concerned and his environment. The Prediction Study concluded that for statistical purposes data should be recorded in a form which makes them capable of being reduced to numbers on Hollerith or similar cards, and that all the important items should be dealt with, even if the answer is negative or nothing is known about the item in question. Impressionistic, free style recording should not be discouraged, but it should be used only in addition to, not instead of, rigidly objective data and it should be done in a way which makes the meaning clearly understandable to other users of the records. Data for research purposes should be considered separately from data needed for administrative purposes, and a distinction should be made between data which are essential for every case and data which might be recorded only for certain cases. Reliable information is more useful than very detailed information. Continuous collaboration between the administrators in charge of the recording processes and the research workers making use of their records is essential, but obtainable in practice only in exceptional cases.[19]

The lack of information on certain data which the research worker frequently encounters poses for him the problem whether he should simply discard cases with incomplete data or whether he should rather exclude the factors concerned altogether in order to avoid bias.[20] Each of the two methods has its advantages and disadvantages.

The second possibility referred to above, i.e. that the research project is fortunate enough to collect its own records in accordance with its needs, can be found, for example, in the American Cambridge-Somerville Youth Study, where the forms were designed and filled in by the staff of the project.[21]

It is often regarded as a weakness of having to use existing records

128

that they are known by the research worker to refer to individuals who have committed offences, which knowledge may easily create prejudice and falsify the interpretation and evaluation of certain vague concepts such as 'good or bad family relations', 'bad neighbourhood', 'low intelligence', and many others. Wherever technically feasible, those who have to interpret the records should be unaware of the fact that they refer to a delinquent population. In control group studies this can occasionally be done if the records are privately collected for the special purposes of the research. Such cases, however, are very rare.[22]

4. *The Dangers of Post-factum Interpretation*

This leads to a problem of more general significance in social research. Merton[23] has drawn attention to the dangers involved in *post-factum* sociological interpretations, arising from the fact that often 'data are collected and only then subjected to interpretative comment'; an interpretation is introduced after the observations have been made instead of the more correct procedure of 'empirical testing of a predesignated hypothesis'. Merton uses as an example the observation that 'the unemployed tend to read fewer books than they did previously'. This can immediately be 'explained' by formulating the hypothesis that unemployment creates anxiety which makes concentrated thought difficult. If it had been observed, on the contrary, that the unemployed tended to read more, another *post-factum* hypothesis would have been ready at hand, i.e. that the unemployed have more leisure. In other words, it is usually not too difficult to produce a hypothesis which supports our observations. There is, however, also the opposite danger not mentioned by Merton that if we start with a 'predesignated hypothesis' this may prejudice our observations.

While the fallacy which Merton has in mind refers to the explanation of observed facts, the danger inherent in the use of existing records of criminal cases lies in the possibility of producing bias not in explaining but in interpreting the facts or in distorting them to fit into the general picture of a delinquent personality. To avoid such bias it has been suggested that criminological research should concentrate not on the collection and interpretation of criminal records but on the life histories of an unselected population, as it has been done in other branches of social research. Reckless, for example, recommends that information should be collected for an unselected group of 'every white boy enrolled in the fifth grade of the schools of a medium sized large city', that this group should be followed up over a number of years and their criminal conduct studied.[24] Similar suggestions were later made by Albert K. Cohen.[25] Such research would require larger numbers and be correspondingly more expensive, but its advantages are obvious. The Cambridge-Somerville Study did not begin with an unselected sample of the general population but with a mixture of ordinary and 'predelinquent' boys. Mays' Liverpool Study, which comes perhaps nearer than any other done, in this country at least, to the recommendation of Reckless and Cohen, used as the starting point an unselected group of members of a certain club and examined their delinquent habits.

We shall still have to return to the subject in connection with follow-up studies which are discussed later.

II. CONTROL GROUP STUDIES[26]

More refined statistical techniques may be used in control group (also called horizontal) or follow-up (vertical) studies. The idea of the control group is very old in medical and social research and fairly old in criminology. We cannot well make statements on the distinguishing characteristics of criminals unless we know something about non-criminals. Already the report of 1893 on criminal statistics (Chapter 5, I(2) above) stressed:[27] 'The proportion of prisoners possessing any feature or quality is of little value unless it can be compared with the corresponding proportion in the total general population, or in the general population of the same age and sex.' One of the main criticisms directed against Lombroso's theory of the born criminal (see below, Chapter 12) was the lack of an adequate control group.[28] Charles Goring, one of his principal opponents, used control groups, but they were also inadequate. One can safely say that modern criminological research largely depends on suitable control groups. One of the difficulties which in particular earlier criminologists had to face was the absence of reliable statistical information relating to the general population on many of the data on which they wished to base their comparisons. Even now some of these difficulties still remain, although the development of demography and of social statistics in the Census or elsewhere in the past hundred years has been of considerable assistance to criminological research.[29] It is easier now to find comparable statistics for the general population on such matters as unemployment, wages, housing, size of family, education and illiteracy, but criminologists who search for information, say, on the incidence of 'broken homes' or illegitimacy would have no easy task. It was a fortunate coincidence that the family structure and household size for the families of Borstal boys in the Borstal Prediction Study could be compared with the corresponding items in a sample of the general population which happened to be available.[30] Generally speaking, criminologists have to collect their own control samples to compare with their delinquent samples, and the same rules which apply to the selection of the latter also apply to that of the former, but certain additional difficulties may easily arise. First, whereas the records of the delinquent group are usually at the disposal of the researcher or can be collected with the help of the authorities concerned, the collection of corresponding data for a non-delinquent group, for example on family and home, income and similar private matters, often depends on the voluntary co-operation of the individuals concerned and their families. The difficulty does not arise in studies where the control group, as is sometimes the case, also consists of delinquents, but of a different category, for example first offenders who are to be compared with recidivists, mentally normal with psychopathic offenders, psychopaths with and without head injuries, etc. Secondly, especially where the control group consists of non-delinquents, the information available for them is often much less detailed than that for the delinquents as their contacts with the authorities have usually been less close.[31] Thirdly, we have to make sure that our 'non-delinquent' control group cases are really non-delinquents, which is not easy in view of the considerable volume of hidden delinquency. Fourthly, the two groups have to be matched in respect of as many factors as possible (technique of 'holding constant'), with the exception of the delinquency factor and those items the influence of which we wish to examine. It is for the research worker to select these latter items, but he must be careful not to expect his research to shed light on those factors on which the two groups have been matched. Ideally, the process of matching should produce two groups which are not merely approximately similar but as nearly equal as we can expect human beings to be. It is here that most investigations have so far failed. In their painstaking study *Unraveling Juvenile Delinquency*, the Gluecks matched their 500 delinquent boys committed to a State Correctional School in Massachusetts with 500 non-delinquent boys from public schools in Boston.[32] The eventual matching was done by pairs but when in the course of assembling the case material it was discovered that owing to the chosen method of selection the two groups were obviously dissimilar in certain factors which the researchers wished to hold constant suitable adjustments in the process of selecting were made. The matching of individuals on more than a few obvious factors such as sex and age is very difficult and requires a large original sample from which to choose. Even then exact matching on more refined factors can rarely be achieved.[33] 'At times it was like looking for a needle in a haystack to locate a boy meeting all the matching requirements', write the Gluecks. Not only were the losses very considerable—of 315 boys of one school listed for inclusion only 52 were found suitable—but the final result showed a great many dissimilarities between the two groups. As one reviewer wrote:

In spite of the endless care taken to ensure perfect equality of the two groups with regard to the four factors held constant, one gets the impression that, for reasons no doubt beyond the control of the investigators, this object was not completely achieved. Not only do the age composition and the I.Q.s show not inconsiderable differences (pp. 37–8 and Appendix B), the matching of the 'underprivileged neighbourhood' factor did not necessarily mean that the boys came from the same district, but only that they were selected from districts regarded as equally bad (pp. 30–32 and 40). With regard to ethnical origin Appendix B reveals that occasionally a boy of English origin was matched against one of Scottish ancestry, a Rumanian or Turk against a Syrian, a Lithuanian against a Russian, a Swede against a German or Dutch, a Greek against a Hungarian, and so on. All this only serves as just another illustration of the immense difficulties inherent in any such process of individual matching, difficulties to which attention has repeatedly been drawn in recent American sociological literature.[34]

For certain problems control group studies can be undertaken in two different ways, either by asking how many individuals possessing a certain characteristic, for example having no parents living, are present in a delinquent and in a matched non-delinquent group or by asking how many delinquents are present in a group of parentless and a matched group of other juveniles, how many immigrants and how many non-immigrants are delinquents or how many delinquents and how many non-delinquents are immigrants.[35]

When we said before that every research worker is free to select those items which he wishes to examine, this should not be taken to mean that he is equally free in the selection of those factors which he has to hold constant. Bearing in mind that the ultimate object of control group studies is to discover meaningful relations of cause and effect[36] we can leave uncontrolled those factors which can obviously have no effect on the result. Ernest Greenwood,[37] who refers to the need to identify the relevancy of factors 'through insight', concludes that control need not be absolute but only selective. He gives the example of goitre research where the object was to test the hypothesis that water from source X rather than Y was the cause of goitre, and all members of group A were therefore given water X to drink and all members of group B water Y. By chance it was discovered that the former were all Catholics and the latter all Protestants. Even so, it was obviously not necessary in this research to control the factor 'religion' by holding it constant since our insight tells us that it could not possibly affect the outcome. As Greenwood stresses, the research worker needs some preliminary knowledge of the whole field of his research to determine which factors could be left out of consideration altogether and which have to be controlled. Such knowledge may come from the acquaintance with a large material of individual cases which tells him in which direction to look for his problems. There are, however, many less obvious cases where the selection presents difficulties owing to the immense complexity of social data. Failure to control relevant factors, for example social class in research on physique or intelligence in their relation to delinquency, can have disastrous results.

The research worker, while free in the choice of his problems, is under a scientific obligation to make it clear that the exclusion of certain problems from the scope of his investigation is not intended to prejudge their significance. Moreover, it has to be borne in mind that because of the inter-connection which often exists between apparently very different factors the exclusion of some may closely affect other factors which are not excluded from the research. All this throws a heavy responsibility on the research worker. As an illustration the following may be used: Rubin[38] refers to control group research on American prisoners who had mutilated themselves 'in the institutions of certain states in which prison labor is imposed in an especially brutal way'. 'Obviously', he writes, 'such action calls for a study of the prison administration, and especially its methods of prison labor.' Instead, the research concerned itself with the characteristics of the individual prisoners and its findings were, in Rubin's view, totally irrelevant to the real problem. In other words, the institutional factors were held constant and thereby excluded from the investigation. 'The plain word for this', Rubin adds, 'is whitewash.' We agree with this verdict with the reservation that there might well have been two, not one, subjects for research, one into the conditions prevailing in the Institutions concerned and another into the characteristics of the mutilators as compared with those of the non-mutilators. If only the second study was undertaken, it should have been made clear that a crucial aspect of the problem was excluded from the research and the study actually done could not be expected to provide a complete answer.

Perhaps as a result of the criticisms levelled at the weaknesses of certain outstanding control group studies the general standard of control group research has greatly improved in recent years, and as a model of such more refined work William and Joan McCord's book *Origins of Crime* may be quoted (see Note 49). Even so, the story of control group research in criminology is still largely the story of compromise and concessions made to the inevitable weaknesses of this technique and also one of obvious mistakes in applying it.

Gillin,[39] whose controls consisted of the non-criminal brothers of his prisoners group, had to exclude all prisoners who had no criminal brother; if one of the criminal brothers was not available for interview another had to be taken, and as availability for interview often means greater stability there was 'a bias towards stability' in the control group. This factor, availability for interview, often introduces an element of unrepresentativeness into the control group. To choose siblings as controls, as was done by Healy and Bronner,[40] has the advantage of controlling, to some extent, the heredity factor, but it excludes all only children, an important section of the population; it also excludes what may well be the socially worst cases, i.e. those whose siblings are all delinquents, too, and may lead to an over-representation of psychologically disturbed cases.[41]

One of the principal concessions to be made in such studies is the admission that 'non-delinquency' can usually mean only absence of officially known delinquency. Matching with regard to geographical residence often means not the same area but one which to the researcher seems to possess the same characteristics, which leaves a wide field open to discretion. This in particular as we now know that under-privileged areas and even street-blocks which look identical to the superficial observer may actually be very different in their whole atmosphere.[42] This means that advancing sociological and psychological knowledge makes control group research more and more difficult as the scope of what can properly be 'matched' will be more and more reduced.

Particularly serious mistakes were made in older studies comparing the delinquency rates of American immigrants and native-born whites. Such comparisons often neglected important differences in the composition of the two groups: the typical European immigrant was, as a rule, a male adult city dweller and could therefore be compared not with an unselected group of white Americans, but only with a matched group of male adult white American city dwellers. If this was done it was found that the crime rate of the latter was, on the whole, higher than that of the former.[43]

Criminologists may find some comfort in the knowledge that other disciplines, especially medicine, encounter similar difficulties in their controlled researches. 'Without "control" comparisons', writes a well-known epidemiologist,[44] 'unbiased interpretation is impossible. It would be rash to assign significance to a finding that 40 per cent of patients gave a history of nail-biting in youth, without some knowledge of the frequency of such a habit in the population at large from which these patients are drawn. Yet this is a common error in clinical research.' Medical research workers find it easier, however, to use control groups in research on the effect of different methods of treatment, a field where criminologists are still much more restricted. In medicine, objections are less strong to giving experimental treatment to one only of two matched groups (see below, Chapter 9).

It means perhaps stretching the idea of controlled research slightly too far when Cressey calls each of the cases of 'trust-violators' whom he studied, 'his own "control" ' because in each case the psychological posi-

134

tion of the violator concerned at the time of the interview when a 'non-shareable problem' was present could be compared with his position at a previous stage when no such problem existed.[45]

It is one of the great merits of criminological control group research that it has collected a considerable amount of information on the characteristics of the non-delinquent population not otherwise available. On the other hand, it has been attacked, and sometimes even totally rejected, not only because of the faults in application to which attention has been drawn above but also because of certain inherent weaknesses. Durkheim did it because he thought it impossible to find properly matched control groups,[46] Stott because neither delinquents nor non-delinquents as such formed homogeneous groups which could be contrasted,[47] an objection which could probably be met by forming smaller comparable sub-groups. By far the strongest criticism is that control group research, by splitting the human personality and its environment into separate factors, particles, atoms, which are made the object of comparisons between the two groups, inevitably loses sight of the personality as a whole. We compare innumerable single characteristics and forget the unity behind them.[48] Moreover, control group techniques are usually static, i.e. they compare human beings and their environments only with respect to a single moment, without giving due consideration to the unending changes which they undergo in the course of their development. These are very real dangers which can be avoided only by combining the control group method with other methods which restore the balance by emphasizing the psychological, individual and dynamic aspects of criminological research. Control group methods have to be supplemented by individual case studies, and by typological and follow-up studies, and if this is properly done the criticism of 'atomization' loses much of its force. There are other, similar, processes used in scientific work, such as, for example, intelligence tests which are full of pitfalls when applied in isolation, but useful in conjunction with other, more individual, psychological methods.

III. FOLLOW-UP AND OTHER DESCRIPTIVE STUDIES OF CRIMINAL CAREERS[49]

1. *General Considerations*

These studies are different from control group studies in that they do not compare individual offenders with others, offenders or non-offenders, at a certain stage of their careers. Instead, they examine the evolution of criminal careers over a period of time; they are dynamic, not static. If they concentrate on the details of one individual life they are case history studies, which will be discussed later (Chapter 8); if they are rather interested in the fate of groups of offenders they are follow-up studies in the narrower sense. Often they are used as the basis for prediction research (see below, Chapter 7), but this is not necessarily so. They had their origin in the earlier part of the present century in the desire of penologists to check the results of institutional treatment. How much recidivism was there among offenders discharged from prisons and reformatories, and could one discover its causes? How far was it due to weaknesses in the penal methods applied and how far to other circumstances? This type of research was, therefore, closely connected with the phenomenon of recidivism which was as greatly worrying penal reformers at the turn of the century as it is now. Its value to the understanding of recidivism and of the effect of various treatment methods is, however, only one aspect of the follow-up study; it is equally indispensable to our efforts to understand, if not the causes, at least the evolution of criminal careers. If the latter are studied *en masse* a better appreciation of their structure and of the driving factors behind them can be achieved. While less detailed than individual case histories, such studies can provide valuable insight into the morphology and symptomatology of criminal behaviour. Descriptive studies in this more specific sense are distinct from follow-up studies in not being limited to the after-histories of criminals discharged from penal institutions or from a period of probation and to the study of the effect of such treatment, but rather examining the evolution of criminal careers of large numbers of individuals who may or may not have been subjected to penal treatment. Such descriptive studies are of criminological rather than of penological interest, and they deal with structure and patterns rather than with causes. If they can contribute to our understanding of the etiology of crime all the better, but even if they should not do so they retain their independent value. A beginning was made with such descriptive studies, with special reference to recidivism, at the Third International Congress of Criminology in London, 1955, but it has apparently not been followed up.[50]

2. *Follow-up Studies in Particular*

The technique and specific difficulties of follow-up studies have been so fully described in the various publications by the Gluecks (see Note 49) that it is hardly necessary to go into details. Moreover, we are in this chapter concerned with the techniques rather than with the findings of these follow-up studies.

Follow-up studies, as they have been developed mainly by the Gluecks, are greatly superior to the usual brand of official statistics

136

of recidivism as their material is far more detailed. Whereas official statistics give merely the percentage figures of recidivism, sometimes distinguished according to sex, age, offence, and the type of institution from which the offender has been discharged, follow-up studies supplement these scanty data by searching for information not merely on the presence or absence of reconvictions over periods of, say, from five to fifteen years, but also on changes in behaviour of a more subtle kind. 'While the basic aim of the peno-correctional system is to render men less criminalistic than they were before, any programme which relies on something more than just punishment calculated to frighten prisoners into being good citizens when returned to society must be designed to improve skills, means of recreational outlet, habits and attitudes generally.'[51] In a follow-up study of 1,000 persons placed on probation in 1937 in Essex County in the State of New Jersey, the authors examined the outcome over a period of eleven years in terms of personal adjustment in a number of 'basic areas of social life',[52] i.e. the physical, mental, familial and economic areas, and a lengthy list of criteria was drawn up by which adjustment or maladjustment was measured. To provide information of this kind, follow-up studies have to rely largely on sources outside the official records of prisons, probation and after-care officers, which latter can usually offer only a minimum of reliable information on the data required. Even if special investigations are conducted by the authorities concerned, they are, to quote the Gluecks again, 'while doubtless of some value, not likely to be as reliable as those made by neutral, outside investigators who have no special interest to protect, no axe to grind, no apologies to make, and who have achieved a degree of special competence in this type of research'.[53]

Obviously, research of this kind is expensive and time-consuming. It requires a staff of trained investigators and interviewers. Apart from a careful collection and verification of all the facts already known about the individuals concerned, the first task of a follow-up study is to locate the individuals selected for the follow-up. In the first study made by the Gluecks, that of 510 men released from the Massachusetts Reformatory at Concord, whose sentences expired in 1921 and 1922, a five-year post-parole test period was available to judge their success or failure. Over 90 per cent of this group were located at the end of that period, i.e. some eight or ten years after their discharge from the Reformatory, which must be regarded as a very high rate, especially when the great mobility of criminals and the absence of a centralized identification system in the United States are considered.[54] After being traced the men were interviewed by a highly experienced field worker,[55] and the information collected by him was then compared with the documentary material available. In this way a detailed and reliable body of knowledge about most of these 510 men and practically every aspect of their lives at various stages was assembled. Only in 27 cases no subsequent information was obtainable, and 55 men had died in the meantime. It was ascertained that of the men whose post-parole conduct could be ascertained 21·1 per cent had been successes, 16·8 per cent partial and 61·1 per cent total failures, a result totally different from the customary official picture publicized by the authorities at the time, which gave success rates of around 80 per cent. Among other weaknesses, the low standard of parole supervision was commented upon, though the proportion of failures was measurably lower during the parole than during the post-parole period with its total absence of control,[56] and it was stressed by the Gluecks that 'the aim of the criminal law is not merely to prevent offenders from further wrongdoing merely while they are still in the official toils, but to bring about a more or less permanent abandonment of criminal ways'.[57]

This group of ex-inmates of the Concord Reformatory was further followed up for two consecutive periods of five years each, the first of which is described in *Later Criminal Careers* and the second in *Criminal Careers in Retrospect*, so that altogether a follow-up period of at least fifteen years was available after their discharge from the Institution.[58] One of the most important results was the increase in the proportion of non-recidivists from about 20 per cent after the first period to 30 per cent after the second and 41 per cent after the third period. Considerable changes were also observed in the environmental and personal circumstances in the lives of these men, who had meanwhile reached an average age of 40 years. For example, the proportion of men who moved about excessively from one place of residence to another declined from 54 to 41 per cent, and the proportion of unmarried men from 45 to 32 per cent. Particular care was taken to separate the influence of the reformatory and the parole regime from factors independent of them, and the influence of the process of ageing and maturation was discussed in detail,[59] but we are at this stage concerned not with the substance of the findings, but only with the methodology. Corresponding methods were used by the Gluecks in the following-up of the group of one thousand juvenile delinquents appearing in the Boston Juvenile Court and examined in the Clinic of the Judge Baker Foundation during the years 1917–22.[60] Psychiatrists, too, have made follow-up studies to check the reconviction of various types of mentally abnormal offenders (see Gibbens *et al.*, Note 49). These and other similar studies have greatly contributed to our knowledge of the evolution of criminal careers and created a more realistic picture of the success or failure of correctional institutions.

With regard to European investigations, attention should be drawn in particular to the work of Erwin Frey and Walter Piecha (Note 49). While Frey's material consisted of a variety of follow-up material, Piecha made a detailed study of 66 male and 25 female juveniles discharged as 'uneducable' from the *Niedersächsische Landesjugendheim* Göttingen (an institution similar to Approved Schools and Reformatories) in the period 1945–50. His object was to see how far the unfavourable prognosis of being 'uneducable' was justified in the light of the subsequent careers of these young people. Concerning the yardstick of 'success', the criterion of reconviction is rejected as too narrow and replaced by the more comprehensive concepts of *Lebenserfolg* or *Lebensbewährung*, i.e. success in life. The author spent a year and a half in the institution to study conditions there and he was also able to visit most of the individuals in question. His over-all success rate of nearly 30 per cent is relatively high, considering that the case material consisted only of individuals labelled as uneducable. There were considerable differences in the success rates between different sociopsychological types (see below, Chapter 8, under 'Typology') and also between the sexes, but the numbers are too small for any conclusions to be drawn from these figures.

3. *Other Descriptive Studies*

Under this heading studies of the evolution of criminal careers may be briefly considered which are not follow-up studies in the specific sense of the term. As already said, such descriptive studies are not necessarily focused on the after-careers of offenders who have undergone one or the other form of correctional treatment, nor are they primarily concerned with the results of the latter. They are rather interested in the mass structure of criminal careers as important elements of social life and try to provide some of the flesh for the bare bones of criminal statistics. How, for example, does organized crime work as reflected in the histories of large numbers of individuals who play some part in such organizations? What is the pattern behind their evolution and their activities? Clearly, material of this kind would eventually form the basis for a typology of crime (on this see below, Chapter 8). Reckless has tried to construct certain patterns of recidivism, distinguishing primary and secondary components.[61] From his list of thirteen of the latter the following may be mentioned: age of onset of recidivism, socio-economic class origins of recidivists, degree of specificity (i.e. whether recidivists as a rule stick to the same type of crime or whether they are promiscuous in their choice of offences), the factor of maturation, prognosis and treatability. He also suggested that the degree of capacity or incapacity of individuals for socialization should be measured on a scale (Harrison G. Gough's 'De scale') which would determine an individual's tendency to delinquency as 'part of his incapacity to play socially acceptable roles in life'. Other points of interest for such descriptive studies are whether criminals as a rule advance from petty to more and more serious offences, whether persons who commit one type of crime, for example against property, are more inclined to become recidivists in this field than persons who commit another type, for example against life or sexual offences; whether members of minority groups in society are more likely to commit offences, and so on. Official criminal statistics can offer very little information on such matters because they are focused on crimes rather than on criminals and the statistical aspects of life histories are entirely outside their field of enquiry. Similarly, what Reckless has called 'categoric risks in crime'[62] requires in addition to the basic data provided by criminal statistics a great deal of supplementary material which can be derived only from large numbers of histories of criminal careers written according to a uniform pattern. Such studies might well be called 'exploratory rather than definitive', they are intended to 'open up ground for more careful investigation' and 'simply record what is observed and without any formal tests of hypothesis'.[63] In other words, such descriptive studies are a stage preliminary to the individual case history proper and to typological research.

Chapter 7

PREDICTION STUDIES[1]

I. THE OBJECTS OF PREDICTION

Prediction, while not the only object of scientific endeavour, is certainly among its most important ones. Without it, no planned human behaviour would be possible. In everyday life, men have to look into the future, trying to assess in advance how their environment and the physical forces on which they depend, how, in particular, their fellow beings are likely to behave in certain circumstances and how they will react to certain changes which may happen at some stage or another. Weather prediction and election polls, being more systematic and better organized and financed than other forms of prediction, have so far been most conspicuous in the public eye, but there have also been well-known prediction studies in the fields of marital adjustment, child development, vocational success and others.

All those concerned with the administration of criminal justice, judges and magistrates, practical and theoretical penologists and penal reformers, have been trying to predict throughout the ages, consciously or unconsciously, but it is only in the course of the present century that their efforts have been subjected to systematic and scientific scrutiny. Before going into details we should be clear in our minds what the philosophical premises of penological prediction studies are and in what directions predictive methods are required in the field of penology. First of all, it has to be stressed that the need for prediction work rests here largely on the assumption that we adhere to a non-retributive penal philosophy of prevention, deterrence and reformation. To some extent, prediction may be involved in a retributive penal system, too, because one of its objects is to create, at least as a by-product, a feeling of satisfaction in the minds of the victims and on-lookers of a crime, but the predictive element is far more conspicuous in a system where the practical effect to be achieved by penal measures is deterrence or reformation. Here the objects of predictive efforts are briefly these:

(*a*) The legislator has to consider the kind of penalties and other

141

measures most likely to achieve his aim of preventing or reducing future crime. Is, for example, the death penalty indispensable for murder or will long terms of imprisonment be equally or even more effective? Is probation likely to have a reformative, and at the same time deterrent, effect? Will Borstal training be preferable to a prison sentence for young offenders of a certain type? Predictive assessments of this nature are implied in legislative phraseology such as 'if the court is satisfied . . . that it is expedient for his reformation and the prevention of crime that he should undergo a period of training in a Borstal Institution' (Criminal Justice Act, 1948, s. 20; similarly s. 21(1) for corrective training) or 'that it is expedient for the protection of the public that he should be detained in custody for a substantial time . . .' (s. 21(2) for preventive detention). What the legislator does for offenders in general, the court has to do in relation to individual offenders. Any sentence or similar form of disposal passed by a criminal or juvenile court involves a predictive assessment of its effect on the future behaviour of the offender. Moreover, both legislators and courts have to try to anticipate the likely reaction of the public to their laws and sentences. Will public opinion be content with the abolition of capital punishment or with the de-penalization of homosexual activities or with the further replacement of prison sentences by probation, with a conditional discharge for this or a fine for that particular offender?

(b) Of equal importance is prediction for the penal administrator who has to assess the effect of innumerable decisions concerning the way he carries out the sentences of the courts, and the present tendency to leave more and more discretion in this field to the administration throws an ever growing burden of responsibility on him. Shall he concentrate on maximum security or rather on open institutions? what should be the ratio of staff to inmates? how should he operate his system of classification or his earning scheme? Should he release on licence at the earliest or at the latest possible moment? These and dozens of other decisions left to his discretion and his judgment of the effect of his actions on individual offenders and on society as a whole require a firm factual basis. To some extent, as in the case of legislators, judges and magistrates, this basis will be provided by their own experience.

Personal experience alone, however, may not be enough; it is subjective and varies in extent and quality according to the personality of those who have to make the decision. It is here that scientific methods of prediction enter the scene and offer not to supplant but to supplement the experience of the administrator or judge. Such methods try to provide a broader foundation for his judgment; they may show that certain measures which he is inclined to take are not likely to have the desired effect, and that certain individuals are likely to react differently from what he would expect in the light of his limited experience. The courts, proud of their judicial independence, may not be willing as yet to take advantage of predictive devices, but administrators, being less rigid and hide-bound, have been doing so to an increasing extent. In fact, most prediction studies in criminology have so far been done not for courts, but for administrators anxious to assess the future conduct of offenders to be discharged from penal or reformatory institutions and, occasionally, also of probationers. In exceptional cases, attempts have been made to predict what kind of persons, not yet delinquent, may be expected to become so.

Whereas follow-up studies are essentially backward looking, prediction, by its very nature, looks forward, but as will be pointed out below, it has to use the material supplied by follow-up work.

II. POSSIBLE MISUNDERSTANDINGS OF PREDICTION RESEARCH

Before going into the details of prediction techniques three possible misunderstandings might usefully be cleared away.[2]

(a) The first is related to the question: what exactly is the object of prediction work? Is it concerned with predicting the future behaviour of individuals or only that of whole groups, of categories of individuals? Are we here trying to predict how John Smith is going to behave after his discharge from Borstal or merely how a group of, say, a hundred ex-Borstal boys, of whom he is one, is likely to behave? The answer depends on the kind of prediction technique used, but before going into the matter we might well ask: for which of these two questions is an answer needed, for John Smith or for his group? Obviously, there are situations where an answer is needed to the first and situations where an answer is needed to the second of our questions. If, for example, the administration simply wishes to know for how many ex-Borstal boys reconvicted within six months after discharge they will be required to provide places in their institutions they are not interested in John Smith's fate as a person; it is not the individual but only the group that matters to them. If, however, and this is the more important aspect of the matter, they wish to know whether John Smith would do better when placed in an open rather than in a closed Borstal or at what stage he can be safely released then they will prefer an individual to a mass prediction. Needless to say, the courts are exclusively concerned with this individual side of the matter. The question has, therefore, to be faced: can prediction techniques forecast the behaviour of an individual? It is this problem which has given rise to many of the criticisms so far made of the technique

143

most frequently used in prediction research, i.e. the statistical. If it should really be true that statistical techniques are useless for the prediction of individual cases this would seriously impair their value. The main argument of the critics rests on the uniqueness of the individual as contrasted with statistics, which are concerned solely with multitudes. Statistical prediction can refer merely to the behaviour of groups of individuals of whom John Smith is only one. If the statistician finds that John belongs to a group with a failure rate of 80 per cent this tells us nothing about his actual performance after discharge as he may belong to the minority of 20 per cent who are destined to succeed, but the mere fact of his being included in a group with a high rate of failure may, it is argued, adversely influence those who have to deal with him; it may be very detrimental to his chances and contribute to his ultimate failure. In such a case we cannot say that the statistical prediction was 'wrong'; it was correct for the group, nor was it false for John Smith since it allowed for a minority of 20 per cent successes without pretending to make any statement about him personally. Nevertheless, it might easily be claimed that actuarial prediction is not only devoid of meaning as far as the individual is concerned, but actually unfair and dangerous to him. In this argumentation truth and falsehood are closely intermixed. It is certainly true that statistical prediction cannot, and does not pretend to, predict directly for the individual case. With individual prediction in this direct sense we shall be dealing below (v). On the other hand, statistical methods, by forcing us to see the individual as a member of a group, may bring to the surface features of his case which might be overlooked when dealing with him in isolation. Surprisingly enough, it has been found that mass prediction often produces better results than individual prediction.[3] Moreover, it may prepare the ground for the latter by offering a preliminary selection of predictive factors for the use of individual prediction (below, s. v). With regard to the danger of unfairly influencing the fate of an individual who belongs to the minority of 'incorrectly' predicted cases this could be a serious matter only if statistical prediction would be treated as absolutely conclusive.

(b) This brings us to the second of the three misapprehensions referred to above, i.e. that the fate of an individual offender should be decided solely on the strength of his classification under one of the statistical categories of success rates. No responsible worker in the field of prediction research has made such claims. Statistical prediction is nothing but one of many tools to be used in conjunction with others such as the personal impression made by the offender on those who have to deal with him, the experience of other cases within the knowledge of the judges, magistrates and administrators, and in suitable cases also the opinion of psychologists and psychiatrists. The statistical classification of an offender as a risk of 80 per cent failure provides nothing more than a warning to all those concerned with the case. As the Gluecks have repeatedly stressed, 'prediction tables should not be used mechanically and as a substitute for clinical judgment', nor, we might add, for any other well-considered judgment. 'They are intended to help him (the clinician, and we might add, the judge, magistrate, administrator and field worker) to see the individual in the perspective of organized experience with hundreds of other boys. . . .'[4] The name 'experience tables' is, therefore, preferable to that of prediction tables.

In addition to such close practical co-operation there is an equal need for constant interchange in the theoretical field between the statistician and the individual predicter to improve the reliability of the prediction tables. In particular those cases where the actual outcome differs from the statistical classification ('over-achievers' and 'under-achievers') should be closely examined to see which individual factors were responsible for the difference.[5]

(c) It is sometimes believed that the predictive factors used in statistical studies are assumed to be causal factors. If, for example, the factor 'poor working habits' is shown to have a high predictive value for future recidivism, does this mean that this factor was necessarily a strong cause of criminal behaviour in the past? If a bad family atmosphere was a causal factor in the past, will it necessarily have a high predictive value for the future? Obviously not, because with growing age the driving forces in an offender's life history may change his character, and what was of causal significance in the earlier stages of his career may not be so later on. Moreover, predictive factors are often rather broad and general and can be related to a variety of causes. On the other hand, it would be difficult to construct a prediction table on the basis of a multi-factor theory of crime causation; both sides have to be kept separate. Prediction tables are not intended to be catalogues of causal factors; they do not attempt to 'explain' and 'understand' criminal behaviour, or to reflect a certain typology (Chapter 8 below), but are merely practical devices to facilitate decision and action ('decision theory'). In so far, their objects are different from and less ambitious than those of the scientific criminologist. This self-imposed limitation does not mean that those engaged in prediction research should discard the idea of causation as a 'completely redundant concept';[6] it is merely unnecessary in this particular context, and even this only up to a point since in our original selection of potentially predictive factors, i.e. at the stage before the tables are constructed, we are consciously or unconsciously guided by certain views on causation.

III. THE CONSTRUCTION OF PREDICTION TABLES

The technical side of the matter and its historical development have been so often described in detail that only a summary will here have to be given.[7] The basic idea common to all the various systems is to select a sample of case records representative of the type of offender for whom the prediction is to be made, for example Borstal boys, and to abstract from them information on a number of factors—perhaps sixty or a hundred or more—which might have some bearing on their criminal conduct.[8] It is in the selection of these factors that we have to be guided by the results of previous research on causation or otherwise,[9] although we should, of course, not be entirely dependent upon them. The sample is then divided into two groups, those who have been 'successes' and those who have been 'failures' over a period after discharge from the Institution, and only the factors showing the highest correlations with success or failure are used for predicting future conduct.

In the first important prediction study, made by Professor Ernest W. Burgess in Chicago in the nineteen-twenties[10] and, as so many American studies of this kind, concerned with predicting the results of parole, information was extracted on 21 factors for 3,000 men paroled from three Illinois prisons. Each factor was divided into several sub-classes, for example according to types of offences, and it was found that for certain of these sub-classes the rate of parole violation was considerably higher and for others much lower than the overall rate. For example, for those with no previous work record the rate was 44·4 per cent, but for those with a record of regular work only 12·2 per cent. Burgess then proceeded to attribute to each of his 21 factors the same, arbitrary, weight of one point, so that a parolee whose violation rate was below average for, say, ten factors received ten favourable points. The cases were then scored, and a table was constructed for the various score classes showing, for example, a probable violation rate of 1·5 per cent for men with 16 to 21 good points and for men with only 2 to 4 good points a rate of 76 per cent. The principal weaknesses of this technique are that only material contained in the official records was used; that only conduct during the official period of parole was considered; that some of the categories and their sub-classes were over-lapping or too subjective; that no test was made of the reliability of the results; and that the same arbitrary weight of one point was attached to each factor, although some of them were more strongly correlated to the criterion than others. In spite of these weaknesses, the Burgess technique has been widely adopted, in particular in the well-known and influential work of Ohlin, based on his practical experience as research sociologist in the Division of Correction in the State of Illinois. While following Burgess in most points, for example absence of a weighting system and the use of highly subjective terms, he accepted the Glueck technique of using only a small number of factors (12 against 21 of Burgess).[11] An interesting feature of Ohlin's technique is that he includes 'psychiatric prognosis' in his list of predictive factors.

The distinguishing features of the various Glueck studies are the collection of basic information not contained in the official files, the extension of the testing time to periods of up to fifteen years after the completion of parole, the reduction of the predictive factors, finally used, to the five or six showing the highest correlations with the criterion, and the use of statistical techniques to attach different weight to each factor in accordance with the degree of its correlation with the criterion.[12] The scores of these zero order correlations are then added up and may result, for example, in the following table:[13]

Score	Success %	Partial failure %	Total failure %	Total %
244–295	75·0	20·0	5·0	100
296–345	34·6	11·5	53·9	100
346–395	26·2	19·1	54·7	100
396 and over	5·7	13·7	80·6	100
Total	20·0	15·6	64·4	100

Whereas most of the Glueck studies try to predict the future conduct of persons already delinquent, in *Unraveling Juvenile Delinquency* an attempt was made to predict the future delinquency of children aged 6 or 7. The great practical significance of this problem of spotting the danger signs at the onset of a criminal career is obvious, but the difficulties are formidable. The Gluecks realized that much of the information collected when the boys were already between $11\frac{1}{2}$ and nearly 17 years old had but little relevance to very young children and they decided to exclude from the predictive instruments constructed for this purpose all the physical and some of the psychological material collected in the course of this particular study. Therefore they utilized for their three tables (a) certain family factors, (b) character traits, determined by Rorschach tests, and (c) personality traits discovered in psychiatric interviews.[14] They found a fairly high rate of agreement between these three tables and concluded that the latter were ready for experimental application. Several validation studies

147

have since been made, and it is claimed that if the three tables had been applied to very young children in around 90 per cent of the cases their future delinquency or non-delinquency would have been correctly predicted.[15] These claims have been strongly questioned by several critics for various reasons, one of them being that the factor 'residence in an under-privileged neighbourhood' had been held constant and thereby excluded from the investigation,[16] and also because the proportion of delinquents in the Glueck sample was naturally far higher than that in the general population, which latter has to be considered when prediction tables are constructed for non-delinquents.[17]

The technique used for the English Borstal Prediction Study, which was based upon a sample of boys admitted between the 1st August 1946 and the 31st July 1947, was similar to that of the Gluecks, introducing, however, certain statistical improvements of which only a few can here be mentioned. It was thought, for example, that the Glueck technique of adding together the percentages for the factors showing the highest zero order correlations was not the most efficient way of dealing with the problem of possible overlaps between the various factors and that at least considerable overlap should be avoided because, where it occurs, the factors concerned taken together do not contribute substantially more to the result than does each factor separately. Moreover, it was decided to use for the construction of the tables only cases where information was available for all the selected factors.[18] Finally, a special effort was made to deal with the vexed problem of the 'centre group of "unpredictables"', i.e. those cases where the probabilities of success or failure are not very different, at least not different enough to justify a reasonably safe prediction.[19] While for the first equation, worked out for the total of cases, only the weightiest factors were used, dominated by the factor 'past criminal record', at a further stage a second equation was worked out for the centre group only which, using factors of a more personal nature such as intelligence and leisure activities, greatly reduced the number of 'unpredictable' cases.

In the Borstal Prediction Study a special effort was made to exclude predictive factors of a strongly subjective flavour, such as some of those used by Burgess and Ohlin, and to some extent also by the Gluecks. 'Statistics cannot deal with "intangibles"',[20] but outside the field of statistical methods there is no objection to the use of subjective terms. For statistical prediction, as here discussed, it is essential that those who will have to use the tables—possibly persons without statistical or other special training—should find them easy to operate. Repeatability is therefore important. The four basic requirements of such predictive work have been summed up as 'simplicity, efficiency, repeatability or reliability and validity'.[21] The inevitable consequence of such austerity is that the tables look distressingly primitive, and it is not surprising that their lack of refinement should fill psychologists and in particular psychiatrists with contempt and many non-statisticians with the feeling that a ridiculous little mouse has been born as a result of a disproportionately large outlay in money and brainpower. This state of affairs can be improved only if it is more generally appreciated that mathematical formulae cannot be expected to look like psycho-analytical case histories and that they are not meant to provide the final answer.

One problem which all predictive efforts have to face is how to make allowance for unforeseeable future developments affecting the lives of the individuals in the sample, including changes in the penal and after-care systems to which they are subjected. In the Borstal Prediction Study some indications have been given of how such changes might be taken care of by a system of continuous sampling.[22]

IV. VALIDATION OF PREDICTION TABLES[23]

It is generally agreed that no prediction table can be accepted as useful for practical purposes without validation by testing it on a group of cases different from the original one. For the Borstal Prediction Study the whole intake of one of the Reception Centres for the 6 months' period July to December 1948 was used for purposes of validation, making a total of 338 cases. No second equation was attempted for this group because the necessary information was not available, and no prediction was envisaged for the 'unpredictable' centre group. With these limitations, the validation proved satisfactory as far as success or failure within the Borstal system were concerned, but 'continuing validity is not assured because it has been once demonstrated'. In particular, it was stressed that subsequent changes in the Borstal and After-Care systems would necessitate corresponding alterations in the construction of the tables. As already mentioned, there have been several validation studies of the various Glueck tables, but their value has been controversial.

V. INDIVIDUAL PREDICTION[24]

Without anticipating the general discussion on the individual case history method (Chapter 8) a few remarks should here be added on the problem of predicting from and for the individual case direct which, as has been stressed before, is the essential supplement of statistical prediction. Case studies are not always made for purposes of prediction; often their object is simply to increase our understanding of present human behaviour.

The initial stages of individual prediction (also called 'idiographic' prediction) do not greatly differ from those of actuarial prediction. A certain amount of data is needed in both cases, but, whereas for actuarial prediction it is invariably obtained from factual material relating to a group of individuals, in the case of individual prediction it may be obtained from a variety of sources:[25] (*a*) either from other cases which show a similar 'configuration' of traits or situations, or (*b*) by 'typological reduction', or (*c*) by observing certain 'intra-individual' traits and trends of behaviour relating only to the individual for whom the prediction is to be made, i.e. the 'time sequence' of the 'unique' case.

(*a*): The life-history of the individual concerned is studied and a configuration of his essential traits is constructed for different periods of his life. This is compared with similar configurations obtained for other individuals whose success or failure in the field in question is already known. This, of course, is a combination of individual, typological, and statistical prediction, but whereas the latter is entirely concerned with the group to which the individual belongs we now place the emphasis on the individual case and look at its configuration in the light of other, similar ones.

(*b*): On the 'typological reduction', which means reducing the number of configurations to a smaller number of types, more will be said below in Chapter 8.

(*c*): The prediction is made on the basis of the 'time sequence' of the 'unique' case in the absence of corresponding information concerning similar cases. Here, as Stouffer suggests (see Note 1: Horst *et al.*), it would be essential to observe the behaviour of the individual in the past, his success or failure, under similar circumstances to see whether he was successful in the past in a life configuration similar to that for which the prediction is made. Even here, where the prediction uses, apparently, only material derived from the 'unique' case, Stouffer insists that the final test of accuracy must be a statistical one. Meehl, too, who deals very fairly with the merits and weaknesses of the two competing methods, thinks that the final word has always to rest with the actuary who has to study the ratio of accuracy in the clinician's guesses.[26]

Faced with this unending quarrel between statisticians and clinicians—to attach to them these over-simplifying labels, although many opponents of statistical prediction are not clinicians—we have to stress that both elements are equally indispensable to successful prediction. Individual techniques have the advantage that they are less rigid and that many more factors can be taken into consideration, especially those of a highly subjective nature such as motivation, insight, pathological states. Therefore, they will contribute far more to

the understanding of the individual case, although even here successful prediction is not necessarily dependent upon our understanding of
the causes of the individual's behaviour.[27]

In the existing literature cases of strictly individual prediction,
without any statistical ingredients, are rare. Usually the predictions
are made, although for each individual separately, in fact for a group
to which he is assigned, and statistical success rates are eventually
computed for the group and various sub-groups of it. A good example
is offered by a recent, non-criminological, study connected with the
Menninger Foundation in Topeka, Kansas, and fully reported by
Escalona and Heider.[28]

First a study was made in 1947–51 of a group of infants aged 4–32 weeks
(Infancy Study) who were followed up for some years to see how they
would cope with their problems, and a second study (Coping Project) was
made in 1953. Simultaneously with the latter, one of the original investigators who was not connected with the second study was asked to make
predictions of the subsequent developments of 31 of the infants in ignorance of the findings of the Coping Project. These predictions were made
for each individual child separately, using 16 to 55 predictive items for each,
altogether 1,003 items for the 31 cases and for 46 different content areas.
There were marked differences in the success rate of prediction for various
categories of the children, ranging from a maximum of 92 per cent to a
minimum of 33·3 per cent, with a median rate of 66·6 per cent, and the
predicter had to ask what accounted for the fact that predictions for some
children were more successful than for others. A high degree of interdependence of the predictive items used was observed, which meant that
if one prediction for the child concerned was correct most others were also
correct. Although the amount of statistical work was reduced to a minimum, the investigation had to use at least some statistical techniques to
bring order into what might otherwise have been chaos. Moreover, even in
this highly individualized study the danger was noted that the personality
of the child was lost sight of in the mass of single items, and often, even
where the prediction for each item was correct, 'yet the essence of the child
was missed'—'a personality description is in itself an artefact'.[29]

Granting that the two techniques are inextricably interwoven we
have to consider in what way they can be most profitably used side by
side. Some thought has been given to the matter in the Borstal Prediction Study.[30] There it has been pointed out that there is, first, the
general object of lending colour to the abstract statistical tables
through histories of concrete cases; with this we shall deal below in
Chapter 8. Secondly, in the special field of prediction studies the case
study has the function of illustrating the differences behind the various
statistical risk categories; for example how far do cases in the category of 80 per cent probability of success seem different from cases in
the category of 20 per cent? Here, it should be shown how great a

151

variety of cases can be accommodated in the same risk category, one case being a poor risk perhaps because of a bad family background, the other because of certain inherent weaknesses of personality, and so on, all this related to the predictive items used in the tables and with special emphasis on the multiplicity of possible combinations of factors which, taken together, may produce the same statistical result of, say, a failure score of 451 bad points. Moreover, special attention should be paid to atypical cases, especially to 'over- and under-achievers', to discover the reason why they deviate from the majority of cases in their risk category. Such individual case material may occasionally lead to a revision of the statistical tables, when it is found that important predictive factors have not been given adequate attention in the working out of the tables. On the other hand, the latter will often induce the individual predicter to reconsider his personal evaluation of a case, and in this way a continuous process of give and take will be achieved.

VI. TYPOLOGICAL PREDICTIONS

Typological predictions have also often been attempted, usually on the basis of constitutional or psychological typologies. The distinction between 'corrigible' and 'incorrigible' criminals which played such an important part in the teachings of the Continental crimino-biological school rested on the belief that, in Kretschmer's terminology, offenders of the pyknic type were mostly occasional and corrigible, whereas those belonging to the leptosome and athletic types were mostly habitual and incorrigible.[31] For the details reference may be made to Chapters 8, II, and 13.

Chapter 8

INDIVIDUAL CASE STUDIES AND
TYPOLOGICAL METHODS

I. INDIVIDUAL CASE STUDIES[1]

1. *General Considerations*

In Chapter 6, III(1), an attempt was made to draw the line of demarcation between, first, follow-up studies, which are mainly interested in the subsequent fate of groups of offenders who have undergone various forms of correctional treatment; secondly, descriptive studies of the evolution of criminal careers, which are also concerned with groups of offenders, but not necessarily in relation to their correctional experiences (of which there may be none); and, thirdly, individual case studies which concentrate on the life of one individual. There is, naturally, a great deal of overlapping between these three categories; the difference in emphasis, however, should be clear. As far as the object of individual case studies is prediction they have been dealt with in Chapter 7, v. Prediction, however, is by no means their only purpose; they are also indispensable to provide the basic material for a better understanding of motivation, causation, and of the place of the criminal in the world surrounding him. In the words of Earnest Hooton,[2] they are 'absolutely essential as the primary sources from which general deductions may be drawn'. He rightly objects, however, to the way in which the case study method has often been exploited, i.e. by producing highly selected and therefore unrepresentative illustrative cases in order to prove a particular point. The highly selective nature of case studies of homosexuals in particular has been stressed by Glover who writes:[3] 'The case-history, valuable as it undoubtedly is, constitutes merely a classroom diagram concerning such cases as have been indiscreet (or compulsive) enough to have brought detection and punishment on themselves or at most have felt that their homosexual organization is a distressing abnormality or handicap calling for treatment.'

Strictly speaking, there are only two legitimate ways of using this

153

technique: either by presenting the detailed and objective history of one individual, or at most a few, regardless of whether or not it supports a specific criminological theory, leaving it to the reader to draw his own conclusions from the facts and interpretations; or by making a statistically representative selection of the available material to illustrate the different types of cases emerging from the general discussion. The second alternative was recommended above (Chapter 7, v) for use in conjunction with statistical prediction, where it was stressed that only through case histories could the deviations from the statistical norm be explained. Moreover, two individuals may fall into the same statistical prediction group and, nevertheless, be different in essential characteristics which can be highlighted only through detailed study of their cases. William Sheldon's, otherwise not very illuminating, 200 short case studies, classified according to his system of somatotypes (see below, Chapter 13, p. 240), is another example of this technique of presenting case material.[4]

Very often, however, we find in criminological literature case histories, frequently taken from newspaper reports, used in a compromise manner standing somewhere between the two extremes, i.e. a number of 'illustrative' or 'typical' case histories are presented which are loosely related to some of the main points made by the author. No objections can be raised against this as it often helps us to a better understanding of those points, provided only not too much is claimed for the typicality and representativeness of the cases. The great danger of this technique is that, if not carefully handled, it may give undue weight to atypical cases without making the reader aware of it. Much will depend on the kind of readership to which the study is addressed.[5] Sometimes these histories are assembled in one special chapter, sometimes they are scattered over the whole book.[6] In Cressey's *Other People's Money*[7] more than 300 case histories of prisoners were obtained, of whom 133 were interviewed at length; for about one half of the latter short histories were presented, specifically related to some of the points made in the book. Where this can be done it greatly assists in our understanding and evaluation of the argument. The techniques used in the Glueck studies vary.[8] In *500 Delinquent Women*, for example, full histories of eleven women are given which, according to the authors, 'exemplify practically all the major problems of individual and social pathology', and various types are described in impressionistic terms, but it is stressed that these histories, while they may suggest hypotheses, can supply 'no reliable estimate of the extent and ramifications of the problems involved in delinquency'. In *One Thousand Juvenile Delinquents* ten histories were given, apparently not selected to illustrate different types or predictive probabilities, but mainly to demonstrate certain weak-

154

nesses in court and clinic procedure, which was the main object of that book.[9]

An interesting, entirely impressionistic, technique of using case histories to illustrate specific points has been developed by Hans von Hentig in his brilliant study *Der Gangster* and the several volumes of his series *Zur Psychologie der Einzeldelikte*.[10] From hundreds of cases a composite picture of the American gangster, or of the murderer, swindler, thief or blackmailer, emerges, but although the same individuals appear again and again in different connections no detailed and coherent case histories of them are presented. The information given is second-hand, taken from other books or from newspapers. While this technique has its merits, it should not be used excessively, and its results require careful checking.

Of a different character are those studies where the case history is not merely used to illustrate some of the theoretical points of the authors and to assist in bringing the typology to life but where, on the contrary, the case studies are the real essence of the book, and whatever theoretical argument may be presented is derived from the cases. As we shall see, the latter condition has only rarely been complied with. Such studies have been written mainly by psychotherapists, but also by sociologists. Some of them concentrate on one single case, for example in the U.S.A. Wertham's *Dark Legend* and more recently Helen Parkhurst's *Undertow*, and in Britain Tony Parker's outstanding books *The Courage of his Convictions* and *The Unknown Citizen*; others present a small number of very detailed histories, for example Bettelheim's *Truants from Life* or Karpman's *Case Studies in the Psychopathology of Crime*.[11] Wertham describes it as the object of his fascinating study of a case of matricide to make it useful not only to Gino, the murderer, but to others as well; it was to be 'his own detective case', and the end in view was to uncover the motive of the deed for which the best parallel seemed to be the story of Orestes. He studied reports of other cases of matricide[12] and found some 'startling similarities'. There was a pattern followed by Gino's and other 'typical' cases, which made it possible to recognize six characteristics of the 'Orestes complex' which Wertham decided to call 'Catathymic Crisis',[13] but although he derived some help from the few superficial data available for those other cases his real understanding and diagnosis of Gino's crime came not from any statistical correlations between them but from the intimate study of his 'unique' case.

An interesting discussion of the theory of case histories has been given by Bruno Bettelheim whose book *Truants from Life* contains four very detailed histories of children at the Sonia Shankman Orthogenic School of the University of Chicago.[14] His object was not 'to demonstrate the optimum that can be achieved for very disturbed

155

children' but rather to show on an unselected sample what this school could do 'on the average'. Therefore several histories were needed. On the other hand, a large number of brief accounts, 'so abundant in the clinical literature', would have been too superficial and could not have convinced the critical reader that the author had 'the correct or the only possible interpretation of complex life experiences that extended over or were separated by weeks—or perhaps years'; on the contrary, the author might have included in his narrative 'only those aspects that fitted the points he wanted to make'. A technique standing between these two extremes was therefore required.

2. *The Different Sources of Case Histories*

The most important sources of case histories, as used in criminological research, are the following: interviews, questionnaires, autobiographies, biographies, medical, psychological and psychiatric examinations, photographs,[15] written reports by those in charge of the case, accounts of participant observation and press reports. In actual practice, two or more of these sources are usually combined to form a 'life history'. In this country, the pre-war 'Mass-Observation' movement which, among others, also produced a volume on juvenile delinquency, had somewhat different objects and used different techniques. While for the details the reader has to be referred to the general literature on the subject[16] a few specifically criminological problems may be briefly discussed here.

Perhaps most of our criminological case histories have been reproduced from interviews conducted by research workers otherwise not connected with the case. The great pioneers in the use of personal documents in the study of the individual offender were the psychiatrist William Healy[17] and the sociologist Clifford R. Shaw, and the heyday for this line of approach was in the earlier part of this century. Healy's first major work in this field, *The Individual Delinquent*, published in 1915, was a landmark in criminological research almost comparable in its impact with Lombroso's *L'Uomo delinquente* nearly forty years earlier, but whereas Lombroso's main concern had been to use individual offenders for the construction of types Healy was primarily concerned with the individual as such. This does not mean that he rejected typology; on the contrary, in the part of the book headed 'Cases, Types, Causative Factors' he writes: 'Out of the chaos . . . we rejoice to see strongly marked causal types or classes emerging.' The book is based upon the study of 1,000 recidivists of an average age of 15–16; his case histories, a few hundred of them, are short and scattered through the book to illustrate specific points. Statistical methods are widely used, but 'statistics will never tell the whole story'. In *Delinquents and Criminals*, already published together with his future collaborator of many years, Augusta Bronner, a few 'fair and typical examples of careers' were used from a very extensive material. It can hardly be said that the case histories presented in these two earlier books were in any way remarkable; their merit was mainly that the technique was used at all. In two later collections, however, *New Light on Delinquency* and *The Roots of Crime*, the latter written jointly with the psycho-analyst Franz Alexander, the histories became more detailed and less superficial.

Rather different is the technique used by Clifford Shaw, especially in his two earlier books *The Jack-Roller* and *Natural History of a Delinquent Career*.[18] Stimulated by the example of Thomas and Znaniecki's great documentary study of *The Polish Peasant* (Note 16) and following the tradition of the Chicago school of sociology he concentrated on the life histories of delinquents as told by them in a long series of personal interviews stenographically recorded. Shaw's contact with these delinquents extended over periods as long as six years, in the case of the five 'brothers in crime' even over 16 years. He insisted that these personal stories had to be carefully checked and supplemented by other material such as interviews with relatives and friends and official records. This precaution has often been neglected, and we possess therefore a large number of books written by ex-prisoners or other ex-inmates of correctional institutions which have in no way been verified from other sources. This does not mean that such books are without any merit; even if their 'facts' are often distorted or entirely invented they can give important insights into the writer's attitudes and system of values, and, to quote W. I. Thomas' famous dictum: 'If men define situations as real, they are real in their consequences'. Their usefulness would be greatly enhanced, however, if the points where they deviate from the objective truth would be revealed.

Shaw's last life history study, *Brothers in Crime*, is distinguished, first, by the fact that here the criminal careers of five brothers are described in their similarities and differences and that in spite of existing personality differences these careers are regarded as typical illustrations of the relationship between delinquency and the culture conflicts in poor immigrant families in the United States. In the chapter on 'Personality Traits' contributed by Ernest Burgess the latter concludes that in the case of these brothers social factors were much more important than personality traits and that this seemed to be true of the vast majority of cases of crime and delinquency in American cities.

Sutherland, in his *Professional Thief*,[19] published the story of a representative of this class, called 'Chic Conwell', told in his own words and covering the period 1905–25. Sutherland started from the not improbable hypothesis that the professional thieves form a group which is in no sense pathological but possesses all the characteristics of other groups and that no one belongs to it unless he is recognized as a professional thief by other members of the group. Chic Conwell's story, he believed, served to confirm that hypothesis.

Many shorter extracts from essays written by prisoners have been published by Clemmer and others.[20] While the great merits of these life histories as presented by Thomas–Znaniecki, Shaw and Sutherland have been generally recognized, certain features have not escaped criticism, notably from Herbert Blumer and John Dollard.[21] Both stress the possible lack of representativeness of these histories and also the intrusion into their interpretation of the theories favoured by the editors. Dollard draws up a list of criteria to which every life history should conform and finds that Shaw's Jack Roller does not measure up to some of them. A personal document of this kind, he thinks, should not only reveal the existence of certain attitudes in the subject but also how they were formed; nor should it concentrate too exclusively on social and cultural factors, neglecting the biological ones. The early childhood of Stanley, the 'Jack Roller', he argues, is ignored: he 'simply appears at the age of 4 or 5 years and is taken for granted from then on'. This is an omission not seldom found in case studies, but easily explained by the difficulties encountered by both the subject and the editor in their attempts to unearth the happenings of these earliest years of childhood. Moreover, if sociologists are inclined to give too much prominence to social and cultural influences in their case histories, psycho-analysts may tend to play them down unduly.

In spite of such shortcomings Shaw's life histories are greatly superior to most of the material presented by certain other, less critical writers who, unconsciously, apply their own moral attitudes and the customs and prejudices of the social class to which they belong as yardsticks to measure and condemn the subjects of their histories.

A good example of this is Sir Leo Page's, otherwise in many ways valuable, study *The Young Lag*.[22] Twenty-three men, aged between 20 and 26 and selected by six prison governors 'as likely to become lifelong offenders', were interviewed in prison by the author with their consent once or twice for three hours or more, and their stories were checked by discussing them with the staffs of the prisons and the institutions in which the men had been before. Important aspects were, however, left unverified and, even more important, one hardly ever gets the impression that the stories obtained penetrate beneath the surface. The author, strongly opposed to any scientific interpretation, sociological or psychological, and unable to understand persons belonging to a class very different from his own, had to confess that many of these young men remained to him 'a saddening and baffling problem'. He particulary resented that some of them had told him lies, but it never occurred to him that lying might have been their most natural reaction in the circumstances.

Much better, though also open to criticism on account of its moralizing attitude, is Andreas Bjerre's *The Psychology of Murder*,[23] a study of three serious criminals in prison, on the lines of Adlerian psychology. Their stories are told in detail not by the subjects but by the author. He is at least capable of seeing the psychological problems of these three men and makes a serious attempt to understand their attitudes in the light of his scientific study of human problems, but, as Clifford Shaw took it for granted that these problems were primarily social ones, Bjerre approached his subjects armed with certain views on the psychology of the criminal. In conformity with Adlerian teachings he believed that the principal characteristics of the serious criminal, especially of the murderer, were weakness and self-deception. As a trained student of human behaviour he was aware that this theory may be an undue generalization and he also realized that the long periods of imprisonment which these men had already undergone at the time of the interviews were bound to influence their views on life, but the possibility that his theories may have coloured his accounts of his interviews cannot be excluded. Moreover, he had to admit that his openly expressed moral condemnation of the conduct of his subjects had the effect of making them gradually less frank in their own statements.

There is far less case material on the female side: One of the few pioneer studies in this field, a near-contemporary English counterpart to *500 Delinquent Women* by the Gluecks, is Grace W. Pailthorpe's study, undertaken on behalf of the Medical Research Council.[24] One hundred female prisoners, aged between 16 and 30, were interviewed in prison by the author, a medical psychologist, and invited to tell their stories which were received without any signs of moral condemnation. In contrast to Sir Leo Page's attitude, lying was regarded as a natural reaction. 'Some at first took the investigator for an official or lady-visitor, and it was of psychological interest to note how the story changed after the discovery was made that the investigator was unofficial and not a religious or moral adviser.' Mental tests were given, and the interviews were continued 'until all that was required had been obtained'. In addition, a group of a hundred girls in Preventive and Rescue Homes were also interviewed.

As in the case of prediction for a 'unique case' (see above, Chapter 7, v), attempts have occasionally been made to subject life histories to statistical treatment, for example, by asking several experts to interpret certain features in a number of such histories and to assess the degree of agreement.[25]

A few further remarks are finally needed on one of the most important and numerous categories of human documents in criminology, books written by prisoners or ex-prisoners. They are very uneven in quality; some of them, such as John Bunyan's *Pilgrim's Progress* or Dostoevsky's *Memoirs from a Dead House* or Silvio Pellico's *My Prisons*, are widely acclaimed masterpieces of world literature, others are poor, sensational stuff. Hans von Hentig, to whose excellent section and copious footnotes on the subject special reference should be made,[26] observes that while American and British books of this kind have been written mainly by confidence men, burglars and pickpockets, the Continental literature has been largely produced by political prisoners. This is an interesting reflection on the differences in the political climate. He also remarks that not much has been done in this field by murderers, sex offenders and blackmailers. The explanation may be that, while blackmailers have very little of interest to tell[27]—it is difficult to envisage the 'Memoirs of a Blackmailer'—murderers had in the past their careers too often cut short by execution. Nevertheless, we do possess a number of highly valuable books by murderers written either while awaiting execution or after reprieve, for example David Lamson, *We Who Are About to Die*, Nathan Leopold's *Life Plus 99 Years*, and Chessman's *Cell 2455*.[28] With regard to sex offenders there is at least one group of them, the homosexuals, who have produced a whole literature, though usually not written in prison. In recent years, Peter Wildeblood's *Against the Law*[29] has received much well-deserved attention. Dr. D. J. West's *Homosexuality*[30] contains a list of the better-known works of fiction concerned with the subject, including one of the most famous among them, Genet's *Notre-Dame des Fleurs*.

There can be little doubt that many of these books by prisoners, even the less reliable ones, have provided a useful stimulus for prison reform as they have been widely discussed in the daily press and professional journals and often forced the authorities to examine complaints and to take action.[31]

Fresh ground has recently been broken by William Clifford, Director of Welfare and Principal of the Oppenheimer College of Social Service in Northern Rhodesia, in collecting, by way of personal interview, ten case histories of African recidivist prisoners with the object 'to augment the meagre information which already exists on crime and criminals in Central Africa'. Though only short, these histories give a vivid picture of the lives of these African habitual offenders, their family ties, religious beliefs, attitudes to crime and punishment and many other aspects of crime among Africans in the Northern Rhodesian Copperbelt.[32]

Not only case histories of offenders but also biographies and autobiographies of non-offenders can be of great interest to criminologists. It is as important for our understanding of crime to study the personal documents of persons who, in spite of considerable handicaps and temptations, succeeded in remaining crime free as it is to speculate on the causes of failure in the case of those who succumbed.

II. THE TYPOLOGICAL METHOD

1. *Definition and General Application. What is a Type?*

As the idea of the type can be applied to a heterogeneous variety of phenomena, personal as well as impersonal, its definition has to be general and vague enough to accommodate all potential forms of application. We mean here by 'type' a combination of several factors regarded as characteristic of the phenomenon studied—usually a configuration of more factors than are capable of being easily correlated in statistical work, but considerably fewer than those emerging from the detailed study of one single unit of the phenomenon. There has to be a rational relationship between these individual factors which is capable of giving the impression that they 'belong' together, which may be entirely absent in the case of the factors in a prediction table. Often, though not always, we find a configuration of factors causally inter-related, mutually influencing each other and working in the same direction. From the point of view of multiple causation (see above, Chapter 1) only type-formations can be envisaged in which elements of each stream of causation are represented and combined. In this sense, our typology depends on our general views of crime causation.

The concept of type enables us to describe in a few words complex phenomena for which, without it, we would need many sentences. The phenomenon in question may be a group of persons, but it may also be wars, diseases, areas, communities, democracies, religions or offences. Typologies are unpopular in some scientific quarters, but they are indispensable. The bare bones of statistics are all too often disappointing and apparently meaningless; full case studies, on the other hand, are but rarely available and certainly not feasible for the masses of phenomena in need of scientific understanding. The typological method, standing somewhere between these two extremes, provides a compromise which may be acceptable at least for the initial stages of research and, *faute de mieux*, often perhaps even as the final answer.

The trend towards typological techniques is not confined to scientific research; writers in other fields, too, have noted, and sometimes regretted, its presence. 'Faced with the complexity almost every human being offers', writes André Gide, 'the eye tends inevitably, spontaneously, unconsciously almost, to simplify to some extent. Such is the French novelist's instinctive effort. He singles out the chief elements in a character, tries to discern clear-cut lines in a figure and reproduce the contours unbroken. Whether Balzac or another, no matter: the desire, the need even, for stylization is all-important. . . .

Woe betide the authors whose ideas refuse to be reduced to a formula!'[33] Or, to quote Edwin Muir: 'The type has become the mainstay of the professional novelist, the convenient counter which absolves him from deeper participation in human experience. . . . The whole tendency of our statistical civilization, with its need to enclose people in categories and its ravenous interest in the human machine as a machine, drives the writer to it.'[34] It may be questioned whether typological tendencies were not marked already in Shakespeare, for example, long before the coming of the 'statistical civilization'. C. G. Jung, in his famous book on *Psychological Types*, devotes a special chapter to 'The Problem of Types in Poetry'.[35]

It should not be too rashly assumed, however, that typology is nothing but a necessary evil, something which conveniently reduces the human personality to a mere figure within a larger unit without adding anything to our understanding of its essential characteristics. On the contrary, by searching for more and more refined typologies we may acquire an insight into complicated behavioural trends and reactions which neither the isolated study of individuals nor mere statistical correlations can supply (see also Chapter 7, v). On the other hand, even the creators of modern typologies, such as Kretschmer, did not claim for them anything like finality; the concept of type is for them rather a symbol for the point where a considerable number of important correlations meet—correlations which, as opposed to many statistical correlations, must be capable of being combined in a meaningful way.[36] A typology is usually developed by way of co-operation between intuitive, speculative thought, on the one hand, and the study of a number of individual cases, on the other.[37]

Complications may arise from the fact that cases belonging to the same type may otherwise exhibit different characteristics. Howard Jones,[38] for example, describes one of his types of drinkers as characterized by 'ego need', stressing that the individuals belonging to it differ otherwise in almost every possible way. 'It is in their general conformation that their fundamental identity with each other, as ego-need cases, is to be seen.' The main characteristics of this type are inferiority feeling, sense of inadequacy, insecurity, need to bolster up their ego-feeling by drink, all of which according to Jones provides strong support for the existence of 'ego-need' as a diagnostic category. Clearly, whatever phenomenon we may be concerned with, its various individual units will always differ in many ways and be identical only in a comparatively limited number of factors. Nevertheless, this may be sufficient to form a type, but exactly how many similarities are needed for it in an ocean of dissimilarities nobody can say with any degree of authority.

The comparative rarity of pure types has been stressed by Jung and

Kretschmer. According to Jung, every individual possesses both extravert and introvert traits; it depends only on their relative strength to which type he belongs, and it is the persistence of this relative strength that creates a type.

Eysenck[39] rightly defines a type as a group of correlated traits and a trait as a group of correlated behavioural acts or action tendencies. The difference between type and trait, therefore, lies in 'the greater inclusiveness' of the concept of type. He also refers to type as 'observed constellations or syndromes of traits' and to traits as 'observed constellations of individual action-tendencies'.

In a more recent book (*Crime and Personality*, pp. 8–19) Eysenck has taken up the interesting question of 'generality' versus 'specificity' of human conduct and character traits which was studied forty years ago by Hartshorne and May (*Studies in Deceit*; see also my *Group Problems*, p. 21). We are here concerned with the nature of such criminologically important traits as honesty and dishonesty: is an individual who is likely to be honest in one type of situation also likely to be honest in another, totally different, one? Hartshorne and May were inclined to decide in favour of the 'specificity' of certain character traits such as dishonesty, but of 'generality' of honesty. Eysenck stresses more the generality of conduct with its greater predictability. In this connection he refers to the recent researches of T. C. Willett on traffic offenders who, he found, were much more often than commonly believed also ordinary offenders.[40]

Modern scientific thought on the subject has received its impetus mainly from two different sources: on the one hand, from Max Weber's conception of the 'ideal type', and, on the other, from the growing popularity of empirical, especially biological-constitutional and psychological typologies. Max Weber has tried to explain his concept of the 'ideal type' briefly as follows:[41] An 'ideal picture' of a certain historical phenomenon, an institution such as 'state' or 'church' or 'sect' or 'capitalism', is constructed which excludes all merely casual elements and concentrates on essential characteristics. Although such an 'ideal type' is purely utopian and can never exist in real life it does not describe an ideal in the usual sense of the term, a model of what should be, which does not mean, however, that there has never been a historical relationship between ideal type and ideal. There are ideal types not only of morally and socially desirable but also of highly undesirable phenomena. In Weber's words, there may be an ideal type of brothels as well as religions. Nor is it a picture of the 'average' or a hypothesis, but it should be a guide to the construction of hypotheses. It is the task of scientific research to examine the relationship between the ideal type and reality. For criminological research Weber's concept might be useful in helping to bind statistical and individual techniques together. As Riemer expresses it, the ideal type is 'a construct for the purpose of guiding theoretical speculations and statistical control towards the end of more significant prediction units'. Its usefulness is, however, not limited to prediction research; because it stands between the innumerable varieties of real life and the unique ideal it can promote understanding of the essential characteristics of a phenomenon.

Empirical typologies have been useful as auxiliary techniques in case history studies where the material collected is often so bulky and unwieldy that it can be handled only by way of 'typological reductions' (Stouffer), i.e. the masses of factual material are classified according to similarities and traits, and the emerging configurations are then further reduced until we are left with something which can be presented as a type.[42] In a psychological investigation into the consistency of extravert-introvert tendencies among problem boys, Newcomb used for his observation a form with thirty items which had to be filled in each day over a period of time to discover the extent to which the boys tended to respond consistently. Some of them showed a consistency which justified the construction of certain traits and eventually an attempt was made to combine a number of these traits to form extravert or introvert 'types'. It was found that about one fifth of the boys were consistent in three to five traits, but no boy was consistent in more than five out of eight possible traits, and occasionally consistency occurred in opposite directions, i.e. in the same boy traits of consistent extraversion were found together with traits of consistent introversion. Therefore no types could be demonstrated.[43] Considering the great difficulty of establishing even single traits the obstacles standing in the way of consistent combinations of several traits to form a type or syndrome are often enormous.[44] Very often two types are needed, especially one personality type and one type of environment, to round off the picture and to produce jointly a certain effect.

It should be clearly understood that typological classifications are not necessarily of a causal character. Phenomena belonging to the same type have different causes, and, vice versa, the same cause may produce different types.[45]

2. *Typology in Criminological Research: General Considerations*

In criminological research, empirical typologies have been employed in every possible section, biological, psychological-psychiatric, sociological and prognostic. There is, moreover, the problem of classification of offences according to non-legal, criminologically useful typologies. While the details have to be reserved for later chapters, a few illustrations may be useful already now, but it should be understood that in accordance with the general design of this book, we are here concerned with the methods rather than with the contents and results of typological research.

It is notably the biological-anthropological school of criminology that has concentrated on the development of types, mainly constitutional types such as the born, the epileptic, the insane criminal in the writings of Lombroso,[46] and as that school has been more popular on the European Continent than in Anglo-American countries it is there that most research on typological lines has been done. It is only recently that through the work of W. H. Sheldon and the Gluecks attention has been drawn to constitutional types in American criminology.[47] As the Gluecks, whose typology is largely derived from that of Sheldon, have given a detailed description of their procedure, nothing more is needed here than a summary. Their starting point was Sheldon's 88 somato-types which are related to his three, more general, major constitutional components: endomorphy, mesomorphy, and ectomorphy,[48] to which a fourth, 'balanced' category is added in which none of the three components dominates. These four classes are then related by the Gluecks to 67 'traits' and 42 sociocultural factors, selected from the larger numbers used in *Unraveling*, to compare, for example, the influence of certain traits and factors on the constitutional types, and it was found that some of them had a stronger influence on one of these types than on the others and that traits atypical of the bodily type in question were particularly likely to lead to delinquency. The main result of this typological investigation was negative in the sense that from the correlation between bodily types, personality traits and socio-cultural factors no consistent combinations of physique, character, temperament and environment emerged which would have justified the assumption of a 'delinquent personality'. Nevertheless, the authors believe that there is enough evidence to show that different clusters of traits and sociocultural factors may have a selective effect on the delinquent behaviour of the various bodily types.[49] Whether or not this conclusion is justified, this research is an interesting example of the use of constitutional types to assess the potential effect of the interplay between physique and other factors involved in the causation of delinquency.

The Finnish criminologist Veli Verkkö, trying to explain the high rate of violent crime in his country in its relation to drink, refers to Kretschmer's typology and his contention that individuals of the athletic type display a particularly poor ability to carry liquor, while the leptosome (schizothyme) type is slightly better and the pyknic (cyclothyme) best of all.[50]

In the field of psychological, in particular characterological, and psychiatric typology mention might here be made, in addition to the extravert-introvert dichotomy, of the many different typological systems which dominate the researches on psychopaths. One writer on this subject, E. Kahn, even uses sixteen different types, another, Kurt Schneider, ten. A frequently used classification is that of Sir David Henderson into predominantly aggressive, inadequate and creative psychopaths.[51] Kurt Schneider's classification has, with certain modifications, been used in Erwin Frey's well-known study of the 'early recidivist'.[52]

On the subject of 'character types' Edward Glover has made a number of pertinent observations.[53] 'A useful classification', he writes, 'is one which avoids undue elaboration without being so simplified as to include under any one heading types that cry out for differentiation. This second condition is a stumbling block to most "type" classifications.' He compares Jung's typology of extraverts and introverts with the Freudian of oral, anal and genital characters, later subdivided according to whether any of these three types encountered gratification or frustration. The correlation of character groups with classical forms of mental disorder leads him to a division into hysterical, obsessional, depressive, alcoholic, hypochondriacal, paranoid, schizoid and psychopathic types, plus the addition of a number of 'special' mainly descriptive, not psychiatric types such as the miser, the gambler, the misanthrope, the moaner, the hypocrite, the egoist, etc. Of particular interest to the criminologist are the Freudian type of the 'criminal impelled by unconscious guilt' (see below, Chapter 17, II)[54] and also his classification of three 'libidinal types', the erotic, obsessional, and narcissistic, of which he regarded the latter, if exposed to frustration, as particularly liable to criminality, stressing that mixed types were much more frequent than pure ones.[55]

To this sketch of Freud's and Glover's psycho-analytic typology dozens of others could of course be added which have, directly or indirectly, played their part in criminological literature.[56]

On the sociological side typological systems outside the field of criminology, but with some bearing on it, have been presented, for example, by Riesman and Howard Becker. Riesman's distinction of three main types, the 'tradition-directed', the 'inner-directed' and the 'other-directed' types, with their sub-types and his attempt to link these different types of 'social character' to different types of society, social classes and population growth have become famous and widely accepted as characteristic not only of the American society to which he refers.[57] Howard Becker[58] distinguished the unsocialized, the desocialized or demoralized, the semi-socialized, the transitionally socialized, the uncritically socialized and other types, W. I. Thomas the 'Philistine', the 'Bohemian' and the 'creative' types.[59] By and large we have to agree with Kimball Young[60] that sociologists have not yet done as much work in this field as psychologists.

Criminological typologies, apart from the constitutional and psycho-analytical ones referred to before, have usually, and rightly, tried to combine the psychological and the sociological ways of approach. Clinard, following Lindesmith and Dunham,[61] uses a system based on social processes and behavioural differences, with the 'individual' type at one end and the 'career criminal' at the other. For the former type personality traits and role adjustment difficulties are decisive factors, for the latter attitudinal factors. At the one end he places the insane, the extreme sex deviate and most occasional offenders, at the other we find the organized and the professional types, with habitual petty offenders, white collar criminals and 'ordinary' criminal careers in the middle of the continuum. Clinard's distinguishing characteristics are the 'degree of development of criminal social roles and life organizations', identification with crime, the offender's conception of himself as a criminal, his patterns of association with others and his personality traits. Lindesmith and Dunham explain the 'individualized' criminal as one who is in his criminal activities 'not supported by a culture which prescribes them', whereas the 'social' criminal can rely on a group and a culture, a distinction particularly important for 'white collar criminals' (Chapter 21 below).

Seelig[62] has, more perhaps than any other criminologist, worked out a detailed typology and put it to the practical test by applying it to the population of 292 male prisoners received in the year 1940 at the prison of Graz. Excluding from his scheme etiological and prognostic elements as secondary in comparison with the phenomenological, descriptive, approach, he employs criteria relating to the offence, the offender and the environmental situation. Only through regular combinations of these three elements can, he thinks, types be formed. He distinguishes *Verhaltens- und Seins-typen*, i.e. types where the behaviour (*Verhalten*) of the offender is the essential factor and types where his personality (his *Sein*) matters most, admitting that in actual life both are closely related and that very often conclusions have to be drawn from the behaviour of an individual to his personality.[63] Seelig also underlines the logical difference between types and classes: whereas the latter are mutually exclusive, the former are not, and mixed types are in fact very frequent. Among his sample of 292 prisoners he found, however, 91·7 per cent pure and only 6·8 per cent mixed types, whereas 1·4 per cent were atypical cases, which seems a rather surprising result in view of the general observation that in real life mixed types appear to be at least as frequent as pure ones. Seelig's eight types are the following: (1) professional criminals who avoid work at any price; (2) property offenders lacking the power of resistance; (3) aggressive criminals; (4) sexually uncontrolled criminals; (5) offenders who in a crisis find only a criminal solution (*Krisenverbrecher*); (6) 'primitive-reacting' offenders; (7) offenders who follow their conviction; (8) offenders lacking in social discipline. This scheme, which on the surface seems rather too general and not without gaps, is supplemented by Seelig by detailed descriptions of sub-types and illustrative case material.

In a recent study of the files of 200 persons sentenced to preventive detention as dangerous habitual criminals under § 20a of the German Criminal Code types are distinguished according to the offence, heredity and family, criminal and other social antecedents and personality types. This may usefully be compared with a similar recent study of one hundred English preventive detainees.[64] In the field of juvenile delinquency attempts have repeatedly been made by the authors of typologies to relate their types of offenders to various types of childhood experiences. Jenkins,[65] for example, offers the following hypotheses for further research: (*a*) the aggressive delinquent was usually rejected from birth and has never known a normal child-parent relationship; (*b*) the loyal member of a delinquent gang is more likely to have enjoyed a normal relationship with his parents in early life, but later on lost it owing to lack of interest and control on the part of the parents and turned exclusively to his delinquent peer-group; (*c*) the 'con-man' type has grown up in an atmosphere of parental disharmony where he had to play off one parent against the other. Therefore he has taken to manipulating and exploiting other people.

One of the best known and most influential among these studies is John Bowlby's which was first developed in his analysis of forty-four juvenile thieves, where he writes:[66] 'statistics and conclusions regarding the cause of juvenile delinquency will remain unsatisfactory so long as no attempt is made to classify types of delinquents and to study each type separately'. His character types are the 'normal', the depressed, the circular, the hyperthymic, the affectionless and the schizoid. The case material consists of Child Guidance Clinic cases, i.e. a highly selected sample, of juvenile thieves, compared with the same number of children from the same source who did not steal. The classification is based on certain character disorders, mostly regarded as due to early childhood deprivations.

Parental rejection plays an important part in John Rich's typology of stealing which distinguishes marauding offences, comforting offences, secondary and other offences.[67]

Also based on differences in child-parent relationship, is the typology of D. H. Stott.[68] While disclaiming any intention to produce a

168

typology of persons he believes to have found in his group of 102 Approved School boys five different 'types of reaction or types of behaviour', but he acknowledges the existence of mixed types. His dominant types of reaction are: (a) 'avoidance excitement', leading the boy into delinquent escapades as a means of suppressing an anxiety with regard to his parents which is too strong for him to be faced; (b) feelings of spite, retaliation and resentment against the parents which drive the boy to commit spectacular offences in order to annoy his parents and force them to pay more attention to him ('delinquent attention'); (c) testing out the parents' loyalty by resorting to crime; (d) withdrawal reaction as a result of a final inability to establish affectionate relationships with the parents, leading eventually to misconduct of a sly and callous nature, possibly also to near-psychotic outbreaks of violence; (e) inferiority-compensation.

In sharp contrast to Jenkins, Bowlby, Rich and Stott, Whyte's well-known distinction of the corner boy and the college boy types has its roots not in diversities of family relations, but in the boys' attitudes to their gangs and their social aspirations.[69] Frankenstein stresses the 'configurational' approach in his case studies, trying to show that 'behaviour does not result from the quantitative combination of independently measurable factors but only from a specific causal constellation' and how the same factor may have different consequences, according to the specific constellation in which it operates.[70]

Of considerable practical importance are those typologies, constitutional, psychological or sociological, which try to relate their different types to differences in responses to treatment. The Continental pre-war crimino-biological school, as already mentioned above (Chapter 7, VI), took it almost for granted that criminals of the pyknic type were usually only occasional and corrigible ones, whereas those of the leptosome and, in particular, of the athletic type were mostly habituals and incorrigibles.[71] Post-war writers have become much more cautious in this respect. The Gluecks, in their *Physique and Delinquency*, admit that 'it is a far cry from diagnosis to therapy', although they express the hope that some of their findings might help to establish the vulnerability to delinquency of the various physical types even better than the prediction tables in *Unraveling Juvenile Delinquency*.[72] In some of their other works they have tried to demonstrate the different probabilities of response to various forms of treatment for individuals falling under their different prediction scores,[73] but the sum total of the latter, the 'prediction profile', often consisting of very heterogeneous factors, will usually not amount to a type in the sense outlined at the beginning of this section.

A Borstal Typological Survey was carried out by a Medical Officer,

Dr. Ogden, in Camp Hill Borstal Institution on 250 boys with the support of the Prison Commissioners and the active co-operation of the whole staff.[74] Its main object was the prediction of future conduct, making preventive action possible. Nine types were formed on the basis of certain medical and administrative criteria, to which an un-classified group and one consisting of abnormal individuals were added. Some of the types were: the adolescent immature, the emo-tionally unstable, the submissive, the shiftless, the egocentric, the aggressive, the hysterical swindler, the unethical. The assessments were checked against reconvictions after a four-year follow-up period, and considerable differences were found to exist not only be-tween some of these types but also between short- and long-term prospects, some types which failed badly and early being particularly good long-term prospects under proper after-care.

Another careful exercise in personality typing in relation to Borstal training has been made by A. G. Rose.[75] He distinguishes the follow-ing types: the apparently abnormal, subnormal, normal (sub-divided: weak, strong, immature, mature, well-adjusted) and the unapproach-able, and recommends a different emphasis for the training of each of these types. Here again, further progress in this direction would re-quire detailed comparisons of the types and the case material of such research workers as Ogden and Rose.

3. *Types of Offence and Conclusions*

For the typological classification of offences we have, of course, in the first place to rely on the guidance of the criminal law. In those coun-tries which possess Criminal Codes much thought has usually been given to this subject. The most commonly accepted classification is that of offences against the state, against the person, against property and against the public, leaving a miscellaneous group of unclassified offences. As universally admitted, this is still far too general and full of gaps and overlaps, and it has to be supplemented by a lengthy catalogue of individual offences such as murder, man-slaughter, theft, embezzlement and so on. Even this is often not sufficient, and the legislator, rather mistakenly, finds it advisable to create sub-types such as theft from dwelling-houses, public buildings, etc., or of electricity, cattle, dogs, etc. The long list of offences in *Criminal Statistics England and Wales* shows how far this tendency to form sub-types has gone. Legal typology of this kind, however, is often rather useless for purposes of criminological research, and occasionally attempts have been made by criminologists to replace it by other, sociologically or psychologically orientated, types. One of the best known of these attempts is that by Cressey[76] to substitute for

170

the many varieties of 'embezzlement' found in American legislations a uniform and more meaningful concept of 'criminal violation of financial trust'. It is particularly difficult to find a criminologically more meaningful typology of murder. The legal concepts have usually been framed in order to distinguish the most serious forms of unlawful killings from the less serious ones. Very few of these distinctions, however, have proved to be workable in practice.[77] This applies especially to the long history of 'degrees of murder', including the English Homicide Act of 1957 with its untenable line of distinctions of capital and non-capital murder. That the various categories of capital murder in that Act, most of them selected rather casually as a compromise between the two opposing views, do not represent types as understood in this chapter requires no further explanation. It can safely be said that as long as the death penalty is preserved no sensible line of demarcation will ever be drawn between cases for which the penalty is to be used and others. Criminologically, murder may be divided according to intent or motive into cases of murder committed for the sake or in the course of robbery or other property offences including arson, those committed for the sake or in the course of rape or other sex offences, murder committed out of revenge or jealousy and with political purposes or motives.[78] It might also be classified according to the role played by the victim. The latter aspect has been stressed in particular by Wolfgang, von Hentig, Gibbs[79] and recently also by T. P. Morris and Blom-Cooper.[80]

There is one offence—at least in those very few countries where it is still an offence—which has not been classified according to types by the legislator: attempted suicide. Durkheim, in his famous study,[81] established three types: egoistic, altruistic and anomic suicide. He did so not on the strength of individual case histories, which he apparently did not possess, but by way of largely statistical research into the different causes of suicide and by defining his types on the strength of his views on causation. 'We shall be able', he writes, 'to determine the social types of suicide by classifying them not directly by their preliminarily described characteristics, but by the causes which produce them . . . In a word, instead of being morphological, our classification will from the start be aetiological. Nor is this a sign of inferiority, for the nature of a phenomenon is much more profoundly got at by knowing its cause than by knowing its characteristics only, even the essential ones.' This method of establishing types differs, therefore, from that adopted by many other writers, such as Jenkins who draws conclusions from types to causes, not vice versa. Against Durkheim's method it can be objected that it is usually even more difficult to establish causes than types and possibly also that the same causes may produce different types.

The offence of shoplifting has been classified according to types as follows: shoplifting by professionals, by general delinquents, by offenders acting under unusual emotional strain, to whom the stolen goods have symbolic or practical value out of proportion to the risks taken, and by 'kleptomaniacs' who steal for the sake of stealing.[82]

Conclusion

From this survey a somewhat chaotic picture of typologies has emerged. Some of them are constitutionally oriented, others psychiatrically, psychologically or sociologically, again others according to offences, and within each of these groups there are many sub-groups and combinations. The Adlerian typology differs from the Freudian; juvenile delinquents are typed according to dominant personality patterns, childhood experiences and relations to parents, to peer-groups, social aspirations and so forth; murderers according to their objects and motives, relations to victims, etc. However confusing this picture may appear we have to realize that the chaos of existing typologies presents considerable progress if contrasted with the state of affairs which would prevail if there were no typologies at all. What is now needed is an attempt to bring order into this chaos by comparing and correlating these manifold typologies with one another and extracting the common denominators, always bearing in mind that each of the main groups of causal factors has to be represented and that the type of offence committed and the predictive aspect should not be unduly neglected. If this can be achieved it will be found that the typological approach is not only a step in the right direction, but essential for the progress of criminological research.

Note

After the completion of this chapter an important paper was published by Clarence Schrag[83] who presents a typological scheme which he regards as useful for purposes of prediction and the evaluation of treatment programmes. It is based on the concept of a criminal subculture and, more specifically, on the responses to questionnaire interviews given by inmates of penal institutions (apparently in the state of Washington). It tries to construct four sets of 'role alternatives' commonly recognized by the inmates and related to other aspects of life in a penal community. It was found that these four types—the 'pro-social', anti-social, pseudo-social and asocial, or in characteristic American prison slang the 'square John', the 'right guy', the 'con politician' and the 'outlaw'—were related to certain differences in criminal careers, patterns of offences, institutional adjustment, family and community experiences and attitudes to crime and society. The difference, already referred to above, between typologies and classification schemes, is rightly stressed by Schrag.

Two other American writers, Gibbons and Garrity, have also offered some 'tentative typologies of adult property offenders, along with tentative descriptions of possible causative factors', which have been described as 'a promising framework upon which future investigations may build'.[84]

These and some of the other researches mentioned in the present chapter make the somewhat disparaging reference to typology by Radzinowicz in his *In Search of Criminology*[85] appear to be rather ill-advised.

Chapter 9

EXPERIMENTAL METHODS[1]

I. DEFINITION

In a way, the whole of our penal system is one big experiment because we often call an experiment any kind of social action the ultimate effects of which are uncertain. In this sense, the legal provisions concerning the establishment of detention centres, the setting up of other new types of correctional institutions, the replacement of a prison sentence by a probation order or the earlier release of an offender on licence may be called experiments just as, in Popper's words, a grocer who opens a new shop is conducting a social experiment.[2] This, however, is not the meaning attached to the term in the present chapter, where it is throughout used in the narrower sense of a strictly controlled experiment which it has in the natural sciences and in experimental psychology. The criteria of such an experiment are as follows: It requires, first, two or more contrasting situations which are usually created by the experimenter (artificial or created experiment); in exceptional cases, however, they are already in existence without any interference on his part ('natural' experiment).[3] Greenwood[4] uses as an illustration the experiment which tries to discover the cause of goitre in certain communities by arranging the supply of water as a suspected cause in such a way that community A receives its supply from source X and community B from source Y (see Chapter 6, II, above). If this arrangement had been in existence by chance already before the experiment started no interference with the sources of supply would have been required. Secondly, two groups of people who drink the water have to be formed and carefully matched with regard to any variables which might possibly also be responsible for the causation of the disease such as age, sex, health, food, occupation, etc. The experimenter has now to make sure that group A uses only water from source X and group B only water from source Y, which is usually called the introduction of the stimulus. Thirdly, the incidence of goitre in the two groups has to be examined after a certain time has elapsed. In this example, which is an illustration of the experiment in its narrowest form, the water would be called the independent and the effect, the disease, the dependent variable or the criterion.[5] If this first experiment should be inconclusive, similar arrangements would have to be made with regard to other variables such as certain items of food, but 'the fundamental rule of the experimental method is to vary only one condition at a time' (Chapin). A statistical correlation has been discovered between the prevalence of dental caries in children and the fluoride content of their water supply. A controlled alteration in the fluoride content has produced a reduction in caries, and this experiment, while revealing nothing about the causal mechanism behind it, makes control and prevention possible.[6] As stressed by Greenwood and others, controlled experiments in this strictest sense of the word are rare in the social sciences, and many sociologists believe them even to be almost impossible. Moreover, where no serious attempt is made to control the situation and to keep the influence of variables out which are not the subject of the experiment it would be misleading to use this term at all. As will be pointed out below (IV) attempts have been made to fill the resulting gap by inventing certain 'quasi-experimental' techniques.

II. EXPERIMENTS IN OTHER DISCIPLINES

The criminologist who wishes to carry out experiments in his sphere of work will naturally look around, however cursorily, to see how this method has so far been applied by other branches of science. There is no need here to underline the vital importance of the experimental method in the natural sciences which owe most of their achievements to it, with the exception of astronomy where experimentation in the strictest sense of the word is not possible. Closely allied to this, general psychology, too, is largely dependent on the experiment, although it has recently been said that 'experimental psychology has not wholly justified the earlier confidence placed in it as a department of science . . . [and] the whole conception of experiment in psychology awaits clarification'.[7] Social psychology has been employing this method perhaps more fruitfully than any other branch of the social sciences, and much of its experimental work is of interest to the criminologist, too.[8] In medicine the position is not very different from that in penology as much of its work is experimental in the general sense of 'trial and error', but dissimilar in that the controlled medical experiment has here become much more willingly accepted by public opinion. Here it is possible to carry out the large-scale infection of volunteers to study, though not to find, the cause of the common cold. In 1955 it was reported that the South East Metropolitan Regional Hospital Board had authorized one of its hospitals to divide a group of one thousand children waiting to have their tonsils removed into two equal samples and to carry the operation out on members of the one sample, not however on the others, in order to study the effect of this differential treatment. While this procedure produced one indignant letter to *The Times*, its justification has apparently not been widely questioned.[9] Members of the medical profession will, however, try to restrict dangerous experiments to themselves and to volunteers aware of the risk,[10] and as far as vivisectional experiments are concerned the medical profession is still under heavy fire.

With regard to sociological experiments reference can here be made to the excellent treatment of the subject by Greenwood and Chapin (Note 1).

III. THE PRESENT POSITION IN CRIMINOLOGY

Criminology, being methodologically so much dependent on the work of those other disciplines which deal with human beings, shares their disadvantages, but has in addition to suffer certain disabilities peculiar to it. It has in common with them the extreme difficulty of producing two closely matched groups and of excluding changes in factors other than the one which is the subject of the experiment itself. Some of these difficulties, it is true, in particular that of matching, are inherent in any control-group research (see above, Chapter 6), but while the latter—unless combined with a follow-up study—is static, experimental research is dynamic with the additional pitfalls created by perpetual changes in the situations to be controlled. We might perhaps illustrate all this by taking the case of an experiment designed to study the effect of housing conditions on juvenile delinquency: A group of, say, two hundred families living in overcrowded conditions in a bad slum district is taken and divided into two groups, matched for economic conditions, numbers, sex and age of children, health, intelligence and other possibly relevant factors. One of them, the control group, is left in their slum dwellings, the other, the experimental group, chosen at random, is transferred by the housing authority to a new estate. Clearly, through this process of rehousing not only the independent variable, housing, the causal quality of which we wish to examine, but practically the whole conduct of life of these hundred experimental families will be affected: they will have to find new friends and enemies, new outlets for their leisure activities, new schools and clubs, possibly even new jobs; their fares may go up, furniture may be bought, which may upset their budgets, and so on. To control all these factors by correspondingly altering the circumstances of the families in the other group will be impossible. How, then, can we attribute any subsequent changes in the delinquency rates to the changed housing position? As the latter may have upset many other factors, for example the employment position, it might well be these other changes which have produced the changed rate of delinquency. It is certainly true that, as Popper points out,[11] perfect control is very difficult to achieve in the natural sciences, too, but it is even more so in the social sciences, including criminology. We agree with him, however, in our disapproval of the 'historicist' assertion that the experimental method is totally inapplicable to problems of society, although it is very difficult for the social scientist to vary his experimental conditions at will[12] or to secure strictly comparable control groups. Even natural scientists, for example the animal pathologist W. I. B. Beveridge,[13] complain that in certain fields experiments are often vitiated by compromise arrangements and therefore prove nothing. Beveridge also makes the point, which is pertinent to criminological experimentation too, that once 'an alleged remedy is released for use in human medicine, it is almost impossible subsequently to organise an experiment with untreated controls, and so the alleged remedy becomes adopted as a general practice without anyone knowing if it is really of any use at all'.[14] In criminological terms, this means that once a certain method of treating offenders, for example Borstal or Detention Centres or whatever else it may be, has become generally accepted in the mind of the public as the most promising way of dealing with that particular category it is very difficult to carry out real experiments with two matched groups. The idea of justice, meaning above anything else equal treatment of equal cases, clashes directly with the idea of experimentation which requires differential treatment of equal cases.[15] As an alternative, it requires equal treatment of unequal cases, and we shall see that this, too, has been tried experimentally. It is only if the idea of justice should in future become more treatment-orientated than equality-orientated—a process which cannot be carried beyond narrow limits—that it will be more amenable to experimentation. At present we can hardly expect the criminal courts to take an active part in penological experiments by deliberately treating equal cases as unequal or unequal cases as equal, though juvenile courts, whose main object is not justice but welfare (Children and Young Persons Act, 1933, s. 44), may be in a less fettered position. Not surprisingly, therefore, penological experiments have been undertaken so far not by the courts but by the administration and, in particular, by private agencies in charge of institutions for delinquent children. There is, however, a fairly large reservoir of cases where the courts unintentionally treat essentially equal cases in a different way or vice versa (see below, IV).

R. A. Fisher[16] and, following him, Beveridge have pointed out that we should not unnecessarily restrict the scope of our experimentation to changes in one single variable but could well test several of them at the same time. There are, however, practical limits to this procedure in the social sciences. Referring to our example of the rehousing experiment we might possibly include not only the housing factor but also the employment factor deliberately in our experiment, but the resulting picture is likely to be even more confusing. On the other hand, we might try to vary the employment conditions in the control group as well so as to correspond to the changes produced in the experimental group by rehousing and thereby keep the employment factor constant, but in actual life this would probably go beyond the limits of socially permissible and practicable experimentation.

In his study of the adolescent criminal, Sir Norwood East[17] quotes from a lecture by the first Lord Moynihan on 'The Advance of Medicine' the following sentences: 'We train the power of observation in our students; we neglect to teach the value of reason and relevant experiment. We teach the Hippocratic method; we neglect the Galenic. . . .' Sir Norwood adds: 'This investigation of the adolescent offender proceeded inevitably according to the Hippocratic method, for we were unable to control or experiment with the various facts that were collected.' He pleaded, however, as it were, mitigating circumstances by stressing that the Galenic method might well be served by an investigation on Hippocratic lines.

How far has the Galenic method hitherto been followed in criminological research? The list of the relevant projects is very short, and their achievements are extremely modest. It has to be headed by two large-scale projects, both of them American, the Cambridge-Somerville Youth Study[18] and the Highfields Experiment.[19] A detailed critical account of the former has previously been given by the present writer, to which reference can here be made.[20]

The project was initiated and financed by Dr. Richard Clarke Cabot, Professor of Social Ethics and Clinical Medicine at Harvard University, who wished to test the hypothesis that juvenile delinquency could be prevented by giving young boys heading for it the special services of a social worker, a counsellor and friend. 'A boy', he thought, 'should be early supplied with an ideal', for 'what is it that keeps any of us straight unless it is the contagion of the highest personalities we have known?' To carry out his experiment, which was expected to go on for ten years, a number of boys aged between six and twelve from two Massachusetts towns, Cambridge and Somerville, were to be selected by a committee of experts, one half of them to serve on the treatment group (T), the other as the matched control group (C). Of the 2,000 boys originally referred to the committee mostly by their school teachers, 782 were eventually selected; 46 per cent of them were thought to be 'pre-delinquent', 43 per cent 'normal' and 11 per cent were rated as 'zero'. The inclusion of not 'pre-delinquent' boys was regarded as advisable for reasons of public policy to avoid the project being labelled as only concerned with 'bad' boys. Of these 782, only 650 were retained, 325 for each group, including equal proportions of pre-delinquents, normals and zeros, and the matching was done by two psychologists for distribution into two equal groups. The details of the very complicated process of matching are fully described in the Powers–Witmer study, and the final allocation of the boys to the T and C groups was done by flipping coins. The T-boys were then assigned to their counsellors, each of whom was to have about 35 cases, pre-delinquents, normals and zeros, whereas the C-boys were left to their own and the ordinary community resources. The practical work began a few years before World War II and was seriously disrupted by it as many of the counsellors and older boys enlisted. The original plan to retain the close personal relationship between the worker and his boys throughout the experimental period had to be abandoned, and many other changes had to take place. A few hundred boys had to be prematurely 'retired', and when the practical side of the project was terminated in 1945 only 75 boys were left in it. Then the second major stage, that of evaluation, began, and it is greatly to the credit of the scheme that this was done by an outsider, Dr. Helen Witmer, on objective and scientifically sound lines. We are here concerned not with her findings as to the practical value of the help given to the T-boys—there was in fact very little difference between the two groups in the success rates with regard to delinquent behaviour. It is rather our object in this chapter to evaluate the experiment as a case study of the use of the experimental method in criminology, and here it has largely failed. For various reasons it cannot be regarded as a true experimental test of Dr. Cabot's hypothesis. This was in part due to the nature of the hypothesis itself, which was far too ambitious and vague to be amenable to experimental testing. According to the principles of this technique as outlined above, all other variables except the provision of counsellors should have been rigidly controlled to make sure that any subsequent developments in the behaviour of the T-boys were in fact due to no other influences but the work of the counsellors. No such control was attempted, nor was it possible in the circumstances. Moreover, even as far as the experimental stimulus, the help provided by the counsellors, was concerned, it was of a very different kind according to the personality of the individual counsellor and the changing circumstances of the time. The war, in particular, imposed so many alterations in the original design that the scheme as it emerged towards the end of the experimental period had but little in common with the project as planned by Dr. Cabot.

The Highfields Project has as its object to examine whether the long-term institutional treatment of adolescent offenders may in certain cases safely be replaced by probation coupled with short-term institutionalization with 'guided group interaction'.

The work at Highfields, a small Home in the State of New Jersey, begun in 1950, has taken the form of a comparison between the short-term treatment given there for up to four months and the long-term detention at the

State Reformatory at Annandale where the boys are kept for up to eighteen months, with an average stay of one year. This does not mean that the theoretical object of comparing the success rates of these two institutions was the main purpose behind the Highfields Study; as in the case of the Cambridge-Somerville Project it was in the first place established to achieve certain practical ends in helping young people. At the same time, however, it was a controlled penological experiment designed to test the hypothesis that adjustment can be achieved better and more cheaply by short- than by long-term methods of detention.

To obtain two matched groups for purposes of comparison, one group consisting of boys sent to Highfields and another of boys of the same type sent to Annandale, must have presented exceptional difficulties, greater even than those encountered in the Cambridge-Somerville Study. While the latter was an entirely private enterprise and no principles of public policy were involved in deciding which of the boys should receive the benefits of counselling and which of them should not, in the Highfields experiment it was for the courts to choose between the two institutions concerned. To some extent, the co-operation of the judges seems to have been secured, but even so the two groups were hardly comparable. Highfields took boys with no prior institutional experience, whereas Annandale received those with and without it. There is no evidence in the reports of Highfields to show that the judges tried to send the same type of boy to both institutions; on the contrary, it is admitted that committals were carried out on different lines. To counter this, it was claimed that only those Annandale boys were included in the study who would have been sent to Highfields by the courts if it had already been in existence at the time of their court appearance. This, however, meant that the Annandale group came from the 1946–50 vintages, whereas the Highfields boys were from the years 1950–4, a difference which the evaluators regarded as unimportant.[21] However: 'A common fallacy', writes Beveridge, 'is to compare groups separated by time . . . Evidence obtained in this way is never conclusive, though it may be usefully suggestive.'[22] There were other differences, too, not the least important among them when conduct after discharge was to be tested, arising from the fact that the Highfields boys were on probation, the Annandale boys however on parole, i.e. subjected to a different kind of supervision and control. Actually, the existence of considerable differences between the two groups has been admitted in the evaluation study.[23] The latter was done with great care and had the advantage over the Cambridge-Somerville Study that it had been planned and arranged right from the beginning and that a scientific Advising Committee, largely composed of outsiders, was established at an early stage.

To sum up, the Highfields experiment, though of great practical value, cannot be said so far to have produced convincing evidence of the superiority of its work over that of the traditional type of long-term institution.

As another example of controlled penological experimentation the California Intensive Parole Supervision Project may be briefly quoted,[24] designed to test whether lengthy periods on parole can be replaced by shorter, but more intensive, supervision.

Whereas in the examples so far given differential treatment is applied to 'equal' cases, now an experiment may be quoted where, in addition to this, identical treatment was applied to different types of cases.

In this experiment,[25] conducted under the auspices of the Social Research Laboratory in the Department of Sociology of the City College of New York, a group of 'problem' and one of normal children from the same schools were mingled in a natural way in recreational activities to see whether this form of non-segregative, but therapeutic treatment would have the same effect on members of the two categories. The problem children included chronic truants and delinquents who had committed arson and theft. There were 155 children in each category, but special treatment was given only to 120 of them. Experimental and control cases were individually matched, problem against problem, non-problem against non-problem, for sex, race, age, general intelligence, educational achievement and mechanical aptitude. To prevent publicity and stigma, the groups were not labelled as therapeutic, and the identity of the problem children was known only to the director of the experiment and his assistant, not however to the group work leaders, who in most cases were unsuccessful in identifying the members of the groups. The result was that 48 per cent of the experimental cases and 24 per cent of the control groups showed improvement in their behaviour. Another result was that the effect of treatment appeared to replace delinquency by causing emotional instability.

In another experiment, 'Reactions of Delinquent and Other Groups to Experimentally Induced Frustration' were tested by Brian Kay.[26] He applied to a group of delinquent and a matched one of reputedly non-delinquent children certain frustration tests and found that members of the control group showed a higher degree of frustration tolerance than the delinquents.

IV. QUASI-EXPERIMENTS

In view of the great obstacles standing in the way of genuine experimentation in the social sciences there has been a growing inclination on the part of statisticians, sociologists and others to pretend that social experiments can be carried out just as well without any active manipulation and interference on the part of the experimenter. The so-called *ex post facto* experiment can, it is believed, fully take the place of the real, the so-called projected, experiment. The idea behind the former is that just as the natural scientist may find that nature has created for him contrasting conditions which, without any manipulation on his part, enable him to carry out controlled comparisons of the two conditions, so may society occasionally perform the same service for the social scientists. As pointed out above (s. I), in the goitre experiment it might have happened that without the experimenter's manipulation community A already received its water-supply from source X and community B from source Y. Stuart Chapin has referred to the isolated life of the Eskimos as a natural experiment where many factors existing in other communities are absent. In the provinces of law and penology an illustration may be offered by two neighbouring states of the U.S.A., having similar social and economic conditions, but one of them retaining capital punishment which the other has abolished.[27] This appears to be a suitable setting for a study of the effect of capital punishment (see also below, s. v), and may be illuminating, but would it be an experiment in the narrower sense? Another illustration may be taken from the Borstal Prediction Study where the success rates of open and closed Borstal Institutions had to be compared. A real experiment would require that the experimenter would be given authority to select boys with the same characteristics randomly for the two types of institutions. This could not be done at the time, but the conditions were favourable to the carrying out of a 'natural' experiment because to some small extent at least the same types of boy were actually sent to open and closed institutions.[28] It was possible, therefore, without any manipulation on the part of the research workers to examine whether the same type of boy was more successful in an open than in a closed institution. In the case of the housing experiment (see above, s. III) the housing authority might already have done what the experimenter had in mind, i.e. divided the group of slum-dwellers randomly into two matched sub-groups and re-housed the one of them, leaving to the experimenter only the task of trying to exclude disturbing outside influences and to assess the possible delinquency-preventing effect of the rehousing scheme. The arguments for and against such *ex post facto* experiments have been admirably discussed by Ernest Greenwood,[29] and there is hardly anything of importance to be added to his views. The most serious weakness of the *ex post facto* experiment lies in the very fact that the experimenter has no power to supervise and control the allocation of cases to the two groups. In the housing experiment it might well have happened that the housing authority had left those families whom they regarded as hopeless failures in their old slum dwellings and rehoused only the more promising cases. To some slight extent, what Greenwood calls self-selection[30] of cases may occur in real experiments, too, but as he points out it is more likely to occur in *ex post facto* experiments. Another weakness of the latter is that the experimenter is here entirely dependent upon the existence of good records, whereas in real experiments he can delay the beginning until his requirements are met.[31] For these and other reasons the harshness of the criticisms sometimes levelled at *ex post facto* experiments[32] is understandable, but it has to be borne in mind that the use of such experiments may be well justified if only we are aware of their shortcomings; it might be better, however, to avoid using the word 'experiment' in such cases altogether.

V. EXPERIMENTS IN JURISPRUDENCE

Law and legal theory being very closely related to criminology some consideration should be given to recent literature on 'experimental jurisprudence'. As already indicated at the beginning of this chapter, in a way every new law is an experiment as its impact on the problem which it is supposed to tackle is more often than not mere guesswork. Even if its preparation, statistical and otherwise, should be more thorough than is usually the case,[33] the effect of a specific piece of legislation is, as a rule, far from predictable. Setting aside this popular usage of the concept of legal experiment the question arises whether some of the experimental techniques applied in the natural and social sciences have, perhaps with some modifications, their place in the theory and practice of legislation, too. The matter has recently been discussed by legal writers such as Wolfgang Friedmann,[34] Thomas A. Cowan,[35] and in particular by Frederick Beutel.[36] The latter has tried to show, with a wealth of material, that legislation should proceed on similar lines as experimental natural sciences and that in fact controlled legal experiments are possible. His argument suffers to some extent from a tendency to blur the lines between the 'natural' and *ex post facto* experiment, on the one hand, and the real experiment, on the other, and some of his illustrations have very little to do with the idea of experimentation, unless we regard the terms 'experimental' and 'scientific' as synonymous. He has provided no single example of legislation applied solely to one experimental group but withheld to a matched control group.

His major piece of research, described in great detail, concerns the offence of issuing bad cheques. He compares the state of affairs in his own state, Nebraska, with that of parts of the neighbouring state of Colorado where, he states, the physical and economic conditions are identical with those in Nebraska whereas the legislation differs in that the offence is technically a felony in Nebraska, with very heavy penalties, whereas it is only a misdemeanour in Colorado, with correspondingly milder penalties. The damage done to society, i.e. losses to business and costs of penal administration, was, according to Beutel, smaller in Colorado than in Nebraska, from which he concludes that the milder form of penalties was more effective than the harsher. Such comparisons between different types of legislation existing in similar surroundings, which are frequent in particular with regard to capital punishment laws,[37] come nearest to the idea of 'natural experiment'.

This type of research is sound provided the relevant conditions in the two legislations to be compared are really similar. Such similarity is more likely to be obtained if the legislator would be willing to arrange a real experiment by making statutes applicable only to certain districts, leaving other districts with identical conditions untouched, which is not often likely to happen because it may be against our ideas of justice=equality. It does occasionally happen that for reasons of economy the legislator or the administrator rightly decides to limit the application of certain measures to a few areas before extending them to the whole country. Normally, of course, the areas selected will be those where the need for such new measures is regarded as greatest, which again would make it more difficult to find suitably matched control areas. Possibilities for 'natural' experiments may arise where the administration provides certain types of institutions, such as detention and attendance centres or remand centres, only for part of the country, but here comparisons of results may be difficult because these centres may be available to offenders from other parts of the country as well.

Chapter 10

ACTION (OR OPERATIONAL) RESEARCH AND SOCIOLOGICAL METHODS

I. ACTION (OR OPERATIONAL) RESEARCH[1]

1. *Definition*

The terms action research and operational research are sometimes used as synonyms, and for our present purposes their meaning is in fact essentially the same, although the word 'operational' is sometimes used in a wider sense.[2] Sorokin calls it 'the experimental method *par excellence*', but defines it also as 'the substitution of collected opinions for scientific study of the facts', which would give it a meaning entirely different from that of action research.[3] Ferris F. Laune's technique of using the opinion of fellow-prisoners to predict the parolability of inmates might be an example of operational research in Sorokin's sense.[4] The latter term is, however, more often employed by natural scientists, technologists and mathematicians, whereas social scientists are more inclined to refer to action research. It means, first of all, the closest possible connection between theoretical research and practical action; it means research which is not, as other research, interested primarily in the promotion of knowledge but rather in the improvement of social conditions.[5] It is, however, mainly the emphasis that differs from that in other research (see above, Chapter 3). There is no need here for a formal hypothesis to be tested; control groups are usually dispensed with, and the research is not carried out in isolation, but in the closest collaboration with practical people concerned with practical problems. Action research would not simply try to examine, for example, the role of subnormal intelligence in juvenile delinquency by tests and statistical analysis but might open a club for subnormal youngsters in order to help them in their difficulties and at the same time study their delinquent behaviour, relate it to their subnormality and evaluate the work of the club.

Action research and experimental research (in the stricter sense of the word) have in common the fact that they interfere with the natural course of events, but the former is usually uncontrolled and altogether much less rigid than the latter. In the words of Morse and Kimball it is often observational rather than experimental. The two methods overlap to a considerable extent. Experimental research may involve close co-operation with the practical worker, but may also be carried out in isolation. Action research, on the other hand, may or may not be controlled and experimental.[6] Arnold M. Rose regards evaluation and incorporation into action as the two basic principles of action research, but the former is also needed for projects which are not action research. Some diversity of opinion exists with regard to the exact relationship between action and research: should the latter be itself involved in the action or should the research programme rather be 'built into the action project', or, in other words, should research and action be identical or should the latter have some independent status of its own? Spencer prefers the latter alternative. The answer may depend on the nature and scope of the action programme; if it is intended to go on after the research has come to an end it will have to be given an independent status.

Operational research had its origin in the needs of government departments, especially in time of war, and it is this aspect of the matter which is particularly stressed by natural scientists and technologists.[7] It can be equally useful, however, to communities and private agencies.

Projects applying the technique of participant observation (see also below, s. 2) cannot be action research because the participant observer should not intentionally interfere with the lives of the people whom he observes. Whyte, in his well-known study of Cornerville,[8] calls his own occasional and rather ill-fated attempt to do this 'a violation of the cardinal rule of participant observation', and he is right. One cannot have it both ways, being at the same time active and passive, and even if different members of the research team should be allocated to these opposing functions conflict is likely to ensue which may frustrate the object of the research.

2. The Use of Action Research Methods in Criminology

Opportunities for the application of such methods in criminology offer themselves mainly in the field of prevention. As far as treatment is concerned its direction lies to some extent in the hands of courts where there is only limited or no scope for action research techniques. Penal administrators, however, may occasionally be inclined to offer that close co-operation with research workers which is essential for action research, and this in particular in after-care work and in institutional or other activities with young delinquents. In these fields the action research approach may promise good results, especially as the line of demarcation between preventive and treatment schemes is here difficult to draw.

To give some illustrations, several of the preventive projects in the U.S.A. described in *Preventing Crime*, edited by the Gluecks,[9] and later in *The Problem of Delinquency*[10] and in *The Annals*[11] seem to have been combined with action research of some kind, although the latter aspect was probably far less conspicuous than the practical work. Without a more intimate knowledge of the way in which action and research were combined in each individual project it is impossible to decide whether it can be justly labelled action research. The best-known of American preventive programmes carried out with an eye on research are Clifford Shaw's Chicago Area Project and the Cambridge-Somerville Study, which has already been referred to in Chapter 9. While the Cambridge-Somerville Study was undoubtedly experimental, its status as a piece of action research is also clear. The members of the experimental group were supplied with the services of counsellors who were able, on a small scale, to dispense various social services, although they were not in a position to initiate larger community projects.[12] The group worked together with the other social services in the communities concerned, but its collaboration with the lay members of these communities seemed to have been limited to the parents of the boys.[13]

Community participation on the largest scale, so far, has been the key-note of the Chicago Area Project, initiated in the early nineteen-thirties, with its slogan 'the local neighbourhood can be organized to deal effectively with its own problems'.[14] In this chapter, we are concerned not with the substance of the Project or its results, but only with its methodology as an outstanding case of action research. It was research in that right from its inception it was closely related to a number of investigations, partly of an ecological character on the 'epidemiology' of delinquency areas[15] in large cities and partly of a socio-psychological character such as the individual case studies referred to above (Chapter 8, I, and Note 18), both of which supplied the ideas and the scientific knowledge from which the practical organization of the Project derived its shape and impetus.[16] And it was action in that it tried to put into practice the conviction that preventive work in juvenile delinquency areas has to work through the medium of suitable local people, who were given a specific active role to play in the programme. Under the supervision of the sociologists of the Illinois Institute for Juvenile Research as one of the sponsoring agencies, indigenous residents were employed to assist in the organization of the civic committees established in the various districts of Chicago in the course of two decades; qualified residents were appointed as staff members and 'the autonomy of the neighbourhood group was scrupulously respected'.[17] Reckless quotes the following statement which is a good summing up of this aspect of the Project: 'The primary and distinctive emphasis of the Project is upon the development of the fullest possible neighbourhood participation through active leadership of responsible residents . . . by providing them with facilities and professional guidance in planning *their own* program for the welfare of *their own* children.'[18]

As Kobrin points out, controlled experiments are hardly possible in projects such as the Chicago Area Project because identical areas for control purposes cannot be found and, if they would exist, it would be regarded as unfair to deny them the 'putative benefits' of the Project. Actually the latter difficulty may not always be present as such projects have an entirely unofficial character, which means that considerations of justice=equality do not arise in their full strength, and as the benefits of the Project may not always be recognized as such by the recipients.

In Britain action research on criminological subjects has been rare and small-scale beginnings which might have led to research of this kind have occasionally been abandoned because the funds and time at the disposal of the committee were inadequate.[19] The following post-war projects deserve to be mentioned.

(a) *The London Barge Boys' Club*.[20] It owed its origin to the widespread feeling among London social workers and social scientists that there were large numbers of delinquent or pre-delinquent boys who were not attached to any of the existing clubs or similar youth organization because none of the latter were capable of catering for the specific needs of these boys. They were therefore commonly labelled 'unclubbables', although the fault did not seem to be altogether on their side. A group, consisting of social workers and social scientists, was formed in 1947 to study the problem and after extensive preliminary discussions and case studies an organization was set up which bought and equipped a Thames sailing barge, *Normanhurst*, to be used as the headquarters of a new type of boys' club. It was intended exclusively for 'unclubbable' boys, defined as 'boys who should be in clubs, but are not; should be because otherwise they will be delinquent or unhappy', and no boy was admitted who could have become a member of one of the other clubs in the Wapping district of East London. A warden with quite exceptional qualifications for this kind of job was appointed. Among the first to join was a complete gang, and soon the practical work coupled with research into the activities of this small group could begin with a membership of twenty boys. Its object was, first, to help the boys and, secondly, in doing so to test the hypothesis that most of the so-called 'unclubbables' could actually become socially better adjusted if provided with an organization which would cater for their specific needs. For the details, reference has to be made to the description given by M. L.

Turner, the warden or 'worker' as he preferred to call himself. His book provides a detailed study of the history of this small group. In 1950 it became apparent to him that the experiment was succeeding and, as he had intended 'only to test the theories',[21] he left. Soon after his departure the older members joined a senior mixed club in the neighbourhood, thereby proving the correctness of the original hypothesis.

(b) *The Liverpool Dolphin Club*. This club for boys several years younger than the Barge boys (the minimum age on admission was eight), whose history over the first four years has been described in considerable detail by John B. Mays,[22] was founded in 1953 as 'a research project concerned with discovering new ways of treating juveniles whose delinquency could for the most part be attributed to environmental and social causes, or whose personal problems had not reached an intransigent phase for which the only hope of remedy is some type of institutional treatment or intensive psychotherapy'.[23] The characteristic feature of this club was a combination of individual case work with group work. While the experiment was to some extent inspired by the Cambridge-Somerville Study and while its type of case work was not fundamentally different from that provided by the latter, it differed from it by emphasizing the group work aspect which had been neglected in the American experiment. The primary purpose of the club was 'to see what could be done . . . to immunize children against delinquent infection',[24] which is, characteristically, a medical formula similar to the underlying idea of the Cambridge-Somerville Study. After the first four years a searching evaluation was undertaken, apparently not, however, as in the case of the American model, by an outsider. No control group was used, and the work, valuable as it was, makes no claim, therefore, to constitute a controlled experiment.

(c) *The Bristol Social Project*.[25] This is the most comprehensive and far-reaching piece of action research in the field of criminal sociology so far undertaken in this country. It has been fully described by its director, John C. Spencer, and his associates. Its scope was not limited to one particular club or other social groups; nor was it confined to delinquency problems, although the latter played an important part in it. Its breadth of design is best explained by reference to the proposals formulated by a 'committee of Bristol's leading citizens' as follows:[26] 'to investigate and take part in the life of a developing community in Bristol in an attempt to establish practical means of tackling those stresses and strains which arise in such a community in the form of delinquency and other disturbances. The main emphasis of the Project will be on encouraging local initiative and in getting local residents to take a greater degree of responsibility for their community life.'

Through its attempt to tackle the life of a whole community and to strengthen the sense of responsibility and self-reliance of its residents the Bristol Study has become the English counterpart of Clifford Shaw's Chicago Area Project. Three working-class areas of Bristol were selected for the research, two of them housing estates on the periphery of the city and one an old area in the centre. One had a population of 12,000, the other of 4,000 and the third of 11,000. Two of them possessed already local councils with and through whom the research team could do their work, concentrating mainly on one of the three areas which had a more than average share of 'stresses and strains'. The work took partly the form of local surveys of the existing community organizations and of certain symptoms of social disorganization; partly it consisted in providing new physical amenities such as a playground for children and a meeting place for small groups, and partly in work with such groups. In this last mentioned direction, groups were formed for toddlers, adolescents and mothers. Among the adolescent groups was an exceptionally difficult one consisting of twenty-six boys and girls, called 'Calypsos', most of them anti-social, destructive and disturbed. The most important features of the Project proved to be its work with the mothers (family research) and with the 'Calypsos', who proved to be the Project's biggest challenge and also the one with the greatest bearing on delinquency problems. There were in addition groups for teachers and social workers.

The Project was designed for a period of five years. Several important methodological conclusions emerged from it, for example:

(*aa*) Action research operating in specific local areas of a big city must be integrated to the whole pattern of civic policy prevailing in the centre of the city's local government;

(*bb*) As a starting point for action research the delinquency problem is of doubtful value because of the conflicting emotional attitudes and the stigma to which it gives rise;[27]

(*cc*) The scale of action projects should be small and its work intensive rather than extensive;

(*dd*) The local residents concerned should be sincerely anxious to participate and free to withdraw at any stage;

(*ee*) Action research, having no professional code as yet, has to evolve rules of its own, some of which closely approximate those regulating the relationship between doctor and patient.

Only a few of the substantive findings of the report can here be mentioned. It is stressed that no stereotyped picture of a uniform 'subcultural' area had emerged, and there seemed to be rather a variety of standards existing side by side within the same locality. In its attempt to explain the high rate of juvenile and adolescent delinquency in some new housing estates the Report states that the latter had suffered the worst of both worlds, lacking the amenities of suburbia without the compensating advantages of a really urban environment. With regard to the alternatives open to official housing policy, one of dispersal of difficult tenants is not regarded as practicable in view of the strong tendency of low status families to come to live together in close proximity. The fact of concentration of such families in one area has to be accepted, and to counter the resulting undesirable features such areas should be given priority in the provision of health and welfare services.

1. *General Considerations*

It might be doubtful whether we are really justified in speaking of a separate sociological method in criminological research, bearing in mind that sociology itself does not claim to have evolved a method of its own. A small, though valuable, literature on sociological methods does exist, but as pointed out in one of the best existing surveys of the subject, methodology is usually not 'bound up with sociological problems *per se* . . . Most of its problems are in common to a number of disciplines . . .'[28] Sociological criminology, as biological or psychological criminology, has to make use of the generally available methods such as statistical, typological, case study, predictive, experimental or operational methods, and its distinguishing features can be seen only in its specific objects of study and have to be closely related to them. Even some of the techniques which seem predominantly to belong to the sociological sphere, such as general surveys, have their place in psychiatric research, too, and on the other hand personal interview techniques, though in a form somewhat different from those used by the psychiatrist, are also needed in sociological studies. There is, however, a certain process of interaction between problem and method, and the one influences the other (see above, Chapter 4, s. 1). It is not entirely beside the point, therefore, briefly to consider the main problems of sociological criminology as they affect the methods of research.

These problems are roughly threefold, concerned, first, with social *institutions* such as social class, the family, property, church and State; secondly, with the *interrelation* between *individuals* as such and as members of social *groups* as formed by whole communities, youth organizations, schools, prisons and many more; thirdly, with geographical *areas*. Obviously, there is here a great deal of overlapping, the family, for example, constituting an institution as well as a group, or the community constituting a group as well as a geographical area, and social class being an institution as well as a 'quasi-group' (Chapters 20 and 24 below).

(*a*) Research on the criminological significance of specific institutions has been largely limited to the role of the various kinds of property where the differences between the position of the large and the small property owner have been studied.[29] The technique adopted in this field has usually been that of the interview by outsiders, in exceptional cases such as that of Dr. N. Muller of Amsterdam, examination by a judge professionally concerned with the matter. As there exist competent and detailed descriptions of interview techniques in the social sciences,[30] there is no need here for their description; they are, moreover, better developed in psychology and psychiatry than in sociological research, and the objects of interviewing are somewhat different according to the professional status of the interviewer.[31] Naturally, interviewing techniques will also show considerable differences according to the specific characteristics of the interviewee, and the same applies to questionnaire techniques. Clemmer[32] rightly stresses the incongruity of applying to a primitive prison population the refined distinctions of a psychological questionnaire on moral values or social attitudes.

In crimino-sociological research into property violations the emphasis has usually been on the interviewee's attitudes towards different types of property and his motives for its violation. Cressey, for example, in his study of embezzlers[33] fashioned his interviews in accordance with his hypothesis about the typical characteristics of the violation of financial trust. As this is an offence almost invariably committed by individuals acting in isolation, the research and interview can be confined to the study of individuals as such, whereas in certain types of stealing the individual offender may be greatly influenced by his group, and the research worker would have to pay attention to group attitudes. Interviews limited to individual offenders would therefore hardly be enough to secure a full understanding of the attitudes, values and motives behind the offence.

G. W. Lynch[34] studied the extent of dishonesty in London industries, individual and group reactions to the risks involved in stealing by employees, the psychological effects of depersonalized ownership, the psychological effects of bulk production on concepts of values, etc. He endeavoured to obtain a sample of employees, whose identity was to remain unknown to him apart from the fact that it had to be representative of the employees in that area. Interviewing men and women who appeared to be representative of the sample required and whom he stopped in the streets, he formulated his questions so as to be acceptable to them, for example he asked not whether the interviewee personally used to take from his place of work goods which did not belong to him, but whether he thought that the 'average person' would take them, how often, in what quantities, which risks he would be willing to run, etc. Moreover, words which were likely to give offence, such as 'stealing' had to be replaced by 'taking goods', 'winning', 'fiddling', etc. The answers indicated personal actions and attitudes or those observed by friends and workmates or were of an entirely general nature.

Criminological research into problems of class has, as will be shown below in Chapters 19 ff., been either statistical (for example Preben Wolf in Denmark) or it has taken the form of investigations into the effect on criminal behaviour of specific patterns of living such as 'deferred gratification' (Chapter 20), or of typological studies (Chapters 20 and 22).

(b) The emphasis on techniques trying to integrate the individual into his group is even more strongly expressed in research of the second category, i.e. on the interrelations between individuals and on the relations between individuals and groups. Individual interviewing will often be necessary, but observation, whether or not in the role of a participant observer, or in some cases action research will be equally important. On observational techniques, too, a considerable literature is available,[35] and only a few brief remarks will be required to show how it has been used by criminologists. Generally speaking, the techniques of (participant or simple) observation have to be used in cases where action research is not feasible, because the research workers are not permitted or have not got the resources needed to take an active and constructive part in solving the problems under examination.

Observational techniques, including the participant form, show many variations. The observer may be concealed or he may be known to his object, but his role as an observer may be disguised. Ackoff seems to regard 'disguised' observation as identical with 'participant', but there is no reason for such usage.[36] It is more natural to call participant observer the person who takes an active part in the life of the group which he is observing. This differs from action research in that the participant observer has scrupulously to refrain from any attempt to influence and to change what he observes. In practice, the dividing line may often be difficult to draw, but it has to be done.[37] One of the most interesting examples of participant observation in penological research is that of the prison reformer Thomas Mott Osborne. Anxious to introduce radical changes in American prison administration in the early years of the present century, he entered Auburn prison for a short period in the disguise of a convict, Tom Brown, in order to study the life of the inmates. His identity was known only to the Warden. After leaving the prison, he described his impressions in his famous book *Within Prison Walls*[38] and began his campaign for prison reform, becoming Warden of Auburn and founding his Mutual Welfare League. This shows that Osborne was somehow aware of the need for keeping action separate from participant observation.

Research on the life of a prison community has been more frequently done by means of simple observation plus interviewing and, above all, informal contacts, for example Sykes' work in the Trenton Penitentiary, New Jersey, or that of T. P. and Pauline Morris in Pentonville Prison.[39] In the latter case, some attempts were occasionally made by a member of the team, a psychiatric social worker, to assist individual prisoners to cope with their personal problems, and in the early stages of the research the principal research worker participated actively in the daily work of the inmates of Maidstone Prison, where a preliminary pilot study was made. This did not, however, alter the essential nature of this research. As these authors write (p. 7), 'It must be emphasized that this study has in no way been an example of "action research", that is to say the research workers did not involve themselves deliberately in activities which are an integral part of the prison's life for the purpose of initiating change. Although the aim throughout has been to observe, inevitably there have been situations of involvement . . .'

Interesting attempts have been made in the United States to let prisoners participate in specific research projects, for example by Donald P. Wilson in his much discussed book *My Six Convicts*[40] and by J. Douglas Grant[41] at Camp Elliot in California. The latter stresses that prisoners can make a useful contribution to society by being given some share in research as subjects, participating observers or clerical workers and he also thinks that prison staffs can play a useful role in it. The example of Nathan Leopold is even better known.[42] On the other hand, John James (Note 44 below) has drawn attention to the dangers which might arise from the use of inmate participant observers.

John C. Spencer's and Norval Morris' researches[43] in various English penal institutions were not intended as general surveys of the institutions concerned but as examinations of a specific criminological problem, i.e. military service as cause of crime and the forms and causes of certain types of recidivism respectively, which could best be done in various penal institutions with inmates who, in the case of the first-mentioned research, had experienced a period of military service or, in the case of the second, were recidivists with repeated experiences of institutionalization. It was the problem, not the institution, that represented here the frame of reference.

In a valuable discussion of 'The Application of the Small Group Concept to the Study of the Prison Community',[44] John James suggests that prison administrators should make use of the knowledge of the theory of small groups which has been accumulated in recent years and indicates the kind of information on the group life of prisoners required for the use of the practical administrator. It goes without saying and is apparent from studies such as those of Clemmer, Sykes and Morris, that prominent among the features to be studied is the complex inter-group structure of the prison community, i.e. relations between prisoners, between staff members, and between prisoners and staffs, and that this involves among others the observation of the working of the underground code of inmates as opposed to the official code.

The Nottingham University study of 'Radby',[45] a mining town of slightly over 20,000 inhabitants in the English Midlands, offers a good example of community research in the open, similar to the Bristol Social Project, but not designed as action research. The methods used were mainly interviewing and participant observation in clubs, pubs, dancing classes, community centre and similar places. In order further to facilitate contact a play room for some of the local children was obtained by the female member of the team, but in contrast to Bristol this was not done consciously to improve social conditions but merely to obtain information and to help explaining the worker's frequent presence in one particular street. The male member of the team worked for some time as an unskilled labourer in one of the local factories. For further details on this research see below, Chapter 22, s. 4.

As already indicated, many community studies are at the same time studies of the area over which the community is distributed, and it is often difficult to decide whether the socio-criminological study of the groups within that community or the study of the local distribution of crime within the area is the primary object of the research. In the cases of the Bristol Social Project and of 'Radby' it was obviously the community and group aspect that prevailed, but in many other cases this is doubtful, and where the aspect of local distribution seems to predominate such studies have here been classified as area research.

There are, in addition, studies of delinquency in certain areas which are, however, neither sociological community nor area studies in the true sense, but contain merely statistical information of a local character.

Sociometric techniques have occasionally been employed in criminological research, and it is worth mentioning that Moreno's original work was done in an institution for delinquent girls at Hudson, New York.[46] Such techniques are of value in the study of small groups, clubs, school classes, open and closed institutions, where isolated and frustrated individuals or sub-groups, pre-delinquents and likely absconders, leaders and easily led can be spotted. In this country sociometric studies in the field of delinquency have been made by Piercy, Rose, Grygier and Croft.[47]

(c) As will be explained below (Chapter 23) *Area Studies* have been done since the early decades of the nineteenth century, roughly following the same pattern. The socio-economic characteristics of the area are closely surveyed and related to the distribution and character of crime and delinquency and the offenders in it. The techniques are those of social surveys, often supplemented by detailed statistical analysis and by case material. The literature is very extensive and will be discussed below.

2. *The Role of the Research Worker*

Although the question of what kind of role the research worker should assume in criminological investigations may arise in connection with other techniques, too, in particular in the field of individual case studies, it is perhaps most acute in research of the sociological type. When doing community research in a group setting, whether in a large community of the 'Cornerville', Bristol or 'Radby' type or with gangs or in a prison, the research worker will immediately arouse suspicion, and sooner or later he will have to give reasons for his presence and his activities. Should he tell the truth, the whole truth, or only part of it or should he altogether disguise himself and pretend to be what he is not? The answers given in different projects cover a very wide range from one extreme to the other, according to the circumstances of the research and the personality of the worker. In criminology the dilemma is more acute than elsewhere. Very few communities or other groups, very few prisoners have any particular desire to see their criminal activities closely scrutinized by an outsider without any obvious benefit to themselves, nor are they likely to take kindly to the intruding scientist. The temptation is strong, therefore, to disguise the object of the enquiry and the role played in it by the research worker. Where the latter—as was the case with Clemmer—is at the same time already on the staff of the prison or club, etc., and therefore generally known in that capacity, the solution is comparatively easy, but this does not happen very often. The frankest explanation, and in most cases the only true one, is that the worker wants 'to write a book' about things he observes and that he hopes its publication will help to improve conditions. Whyte started his research at Cornerville introduced by 'Doc', one of the boys there, as 'his friend', but after a while this explanation no longer satisfied their curiosity; he then pretended to study the social history of the place, but soon this, too, was not plausible enough to justify his activities, and people developed the theory that he was writing a book. Eventually, he came to the conclusion that his acceptance in the locality depended far more on the personal relationships he was able to establish than on the explanation he could offer.[48] While this may have been true in Whyte's case it is not likely to apply in general as the possibility of establishing good personal relations may not arise if the observer has no plausible explanation to start with. If the book eventually appears other difficulties are likely to arise. Whyte is one of the very few research workers who, in the Appendix to the second edition, has something to say about the reception of his book by those directly concerned. Apparently very few of them read it at all, and Doc, the man who had helped him most in his research, realizing the embarrassment it might cause, did his best to discourage the others from reading it.

In the case of the Barge Boys' Club, although a book was eventually written on it this was certainly not the main object of the experiment. According to the explanation given by the worker to the club members his object was 'to test his theories' about the true nature of 'unclubbability', and no deception was involved.

Where some form of disguise is regarded as indispensable—and it should be used only where it is really indispensable—it will assume different forms, depending on the nature of the research, the publicity it has already received, and other factors, and it would be unwise to deviate from the truth more than absolutely necessary. If the worker should tell stories which can easily be disproved he would completely spoil his chances of success. In another direction, too, great caution has to be exercised. Most research workers are sincerely convinced that their work will, at least in the long run, help to improve our understanding of the problems involved and the conditions in our society, and it is tempting enough to paint an over-optimistic picture of the likely results when trying to persuade people to give information. The subsequent disappointment may be very severe and breed cynicism and contempt for the whole idea of research. If the research is done under the auspices of a university or similar institution of universally recognized status reference to it will often be enough to dispel suspicion without any exaggerated statements on the immediate practical value of the research. If the worker and those whose co-operation and confidence he tries to gain have something real in common, all the better. When Grygier,[49] after the war, wished to interview and test Polish displaced persons in Germany, some of them former inmates of concentration camps, he told them truthfully that he was himself a displaced Pole, but had been deported 'to another part of the world'. This proved to be effective with groups where Poles were in the majority. Grygier, while making much use of the Rosenzweig Picture Frustration Test, disapproves of the advice given by Rosenzweig that the tester should deliberately mislead his subjects by making false statements on the object of his testing.

One of the most difficult research situations arises in prisons, in particular in maximum security prisons with a hardened recidivist population. Not only may the role of the worker differ in different prisons, but even without that role his behaviour, attitudes and contacts will have to assume a different colour according to the general atmosphere of the place. Spencer, who deals with the problem very fully,[50] points out that at Dartmoor, as contrasted with Maidstone, it was essential for him not to be identified with the disciplinary staff, and as the Prison Chaplain there was universally accepted as a person to whom prisoners could give confidential information without fear of indiscretion he decided to assume the role of a worker who had come to help the Chaplain in the running of his classes. This also gave him the pretext for moving around the prison and helped him to observe the men in a group situation. Terence and Pauline Morris, on the other hand, in their study of Pentonville, made it clear that they were making 'an independent study of the prison to see how it worked, so that we might be able to assist those responsible for making changes. We hoped that it would eventually appear in book form.' Appendix A contains a discussion on the methodological aspects of the research, such as availability of the material, attitudes of staff and prisoners to the research, the role of a woman research worker in a men's prison, and the 'creation of a research role'.[51] It has to be stressed that in the period of approximately ten years which lies between these two researches, people in general have become more research-minded, and even prisoners seem more willing now to accept research workers inside closed institutions.

In researches which take place in the open, such as the Bristol and Nottingham ('Radby') studies, it has still been found advisable not to disclose crime and delinquency as the main objects of study.

PART THREE

Factors and Causes Related to Crime

In view of what has been said in Chapter 1 (I, 2(b)) we intend to deal in this part with 'Factors and Causes', a neutral phrase which may mean a real cause here and a mere 'factor' there. To single out for closer attention a large number of such phenomena in their relation to crime is one of the principal objects of criminology. In our methodological chapters the need for such a procedure has become apparent. In researches of a statistical nature and in the building up of official criminal statistics we have to make a preliminary, and often hazardous decision on which of the very many facets potentially connected with crime statistical material should be collected and which statistical facts can safely be ignored as having no conceivable relation to the subject. The same applies to the construction of prediction tables. Nor can those who assemble the information needed for individual case histories indiscriminately write down whatever facts they may be able to gather from records, personal documents, interviews and so on; they have to be selective, and their technique of selection will be determined by certain preconceived ideas about potential relevance, causal or otherwise. Or the action researcher whose object it is to reduce crime by relieving certain 'stresses and strains': he, too, cannot approach his problem with a completely blank mind. In short, whatever method of research is used in criminology it cannot start from nothing.

For the following chapters no originality is claimed regarding the preliminary selection of these factors or for their classification, and we shall be content to follow the traditional lines. It has become customary to divide these factors into three major spheres, the physical-anthropological-biological, the psychological-psychiatric, and the social-economic. Consequently, we shall deal with these three spheres in three sections, each of them divided into a number of chapters. This is in accordance with the theory of multiple causation which, with certain reservations, we have accepted above (Chapter 1, I, 2(c)).

This customary division into three groups of factors or causes is somewhat artificial, however, because of the high degree of overlapping between them. As a distinguished biologist has written,[1] cultural influences on the human organism are so strong and begin so early in life that 'they become incorporated in the tissues of those who have been exposed to such influence'. Cultural factors are not merely 'added to, or superimposed upon, the physical organism', but actually incorporated into it and an inseparable part of it. Equally close is the interrelationship between psychological and social factors. Physical

201

shortcomings may produce psychological handicaps, and the two together may lead to social inabilities. The latter, in their turn, may account for physical neglect, which may complete the vicious circle. For purposes of clearer presentation and in the interest of easier discussion, however, it is advisable to retain the tripartite scheme. The question arises whether the three groups are, generally speaking, of equal significance for the study of crime, whether they stand on the same level or whether certain distinctions have to be made. That such distinctions will be inevitable for each individual case is obvious as the weight of the factors will differ from case to case. From a general point of view, however, only one distinction can be made which follows from our view that the physical-anthropological-biological as well as the social and economic factors can become operative only by going through the 'transformator' of a psychological or psychiatric factor. This might be shown in the following diagram:

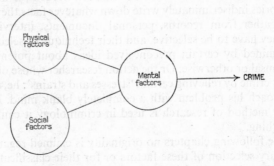

Only by producing a certain state of mind can any of the other factors lead to crime. This has been well expressed in Bernard Glueck's formula: 'a factor is not a cause unless and until it becomes a motive'.[2] A relationship of this kind does not necessarily mean the invariable pre-eminence of the psychological-psychiatric aspects. The pressure of the other factors may be so overwhelmingly strong in an individual case that the addition of a very small psychological dose may be sufficient to produce crime. It does mean, however, that in the absence of such a dose no crime could happen. On the other hand, a large dose of psychological-psychiatric factors may suffice without the addition of any physical or social factors of a criminogenic nature.

THE PHYSICAL SIDE OF CRIME

Chapter 11

PHYSICAL-ANTHROPOLOGICAL-BIOLOGICAL ASPECTS I: GEOGRAPHY AND PHYSICAL HEALTH

The discussion has to be divided into two main aspects: physical factors affecting human environment, from which the individual can escape by changing his environment, and those affecting man himself. The former are the subject of *physical geography*, while the latter belong to human *anthropology* and *biology*. As far as the physical characteristics of delinquents are concerned, it is sometimes overlooked that here, too, we have to deal with two different, though related, problems: first, the question how far the physical health of an individual may be a factor in his criminal behaviour, and, second, whether criminals belong to distinct physical types. It is the first of these questions which will be discussed in the present chapter (II), whereas the typological problem will be treated in Chapter 12.

I. PHYSICAL GEOGRAPHY

Physical geography as contrasted with the social aspects of the spatial distribution of the population, or in other words the physical, non-social aspects of biology, has been neglected in modern criminology in spite of various publications on the subject at the beginning of the present century. Older writers had perhaps been inclined to overrate their importance as causes of criminal behaviour, and the present tendency may simply restore the balance. Bonger has briefly reviewed the historical development, from Herodotus via Montesquieu and Quetelet to Roesner.[1] The criminological significance of the physical environment has been studied chiefly with reference to the climate of a country, to the weather and the seasons.[2] Quetelet, Guerry de Champneuf, Lombroso, Ferri, Aschaffenburg and others tried to show statistically that in France, Italy and Germany respectively crimes against the person were more frequent in hot climates and in the summer months, whereas crimes against property prevailed in cold climates and in winter. Lombroso regarded the subject as important enough to devote the first chapter of his *Crime: its Causes and*

Remedies to it; he quotes some figures from Guerry and Ferri, adding some of his own, but admits that the statistics do not always seem to be associated with differences in climate. Quetelet even went so far as to deduce from such statistics his 'thermic law of delinquency' (Chapter 1 above), and Prince Peter Kropotkin added to this his even more extravagant formula claiming a fixed correlation between average temperature, the degree of humidity and the volume of crime, especially the number of homicides,[3] a formula which, as Barnes and Teeters point out, is absurd as no allowance is made in it for the size of population of the country concerned. Some of the other statistical material presented in older publications is of a primitive character, too, and open to criticism.[4] As far as international comparisons, in particular, are concerned previous writers have not always been aware of the dangers in comparing homicide rates between countries possessing different legal conceptions of murder and manslaughter and different systems of police and criminal procedure (Chapter 5 above). National comparisons between northern and southern regions of the same country are on safer ground, although even here differences in public attitudes, in police and procedure may play an important part in accounting for variations apparently due to the climate, and the latter, where it influences the activities of offenders, may well have some bearing on those of the forces of law and order, too.

In this country, obviously under the impact of nineteenth-century literature, the Introduction of *Criminal Statistics* of 1893 (see Chapter 5 above) paid special attention to the subject, producing much material to show that crimes against the person were highest in summer and lowest in winter and property crimes had the opposite tendency.[5]

Cyril Burt,[6] in his *Young Delinquent*, criticizes English writers for simply quoting figures from other countries as if they were applicable everywhere regardless of latitude or climate. His own data for juvenile offenders in London show two maxima, June and December, and two minima, February and August, and some small amount of concordance between juvenile delinquency and the length of daylight. He, too, found that offences against the person reached their climax in summer and property offences in winter, but he relates the latter fact to the temptations of Christmas shop windows rather than to the climate. Malicious injury had its maximum in November, which he regards as due to Guy Fawkes day.

For the United States very few studies are available comparing states with different climatic conditions. Dexter made a comparison between New York City and Denver, Colorado,[7] without any conclusive results. He did show, however, that in New York arrests for assaults and battery in the months May to September were much more frequent than in the colder months (in July 24 per cent above, in January 22 per cent below average). Brearley's study of seasonal variations in homicide in South Carolina showed no consistent pattern.[8] He concludes that the months with heavy agricultural work produced less violence than months of leisure, and this regardless of temperature, December and July having the highest figures as months of increased social life and festivities. This he regarded as an illustration of the interrelationship of meteorological and cultural factors.

Wolfgang, in his study of homicide in Philadelphia for the years 1948 to 1952, found no statistically significant differences between hot and cold months, which forced him to reject any hypothesis of a relationship between monthly or seasonal changes and rates of homicide.

One gets the impression that the more recent studies, being less prejudiced and using more refined statistical techniques, fail to corroborate the findings of the more enthusiastic and less critical studies of the nineteenth and early twentieth centuries. This does not necessarily force us completely to deny the influence of climatic conditions on criminal behaviour. The assumption which lay behind the work of those earlier writers that human emotions, sexual or otherwise, are more intense in hot weather and material human needs more acute in a cold climate may well be true. All we can say for the time being is that the expression of such emotions and material needs in criminal acts has not yet been clearly and unequivocally demonstrated in the available statistics. Nor has that assumption been refuted by this negative fact. The reason for this state of affairs may be, as usual, the complexity of the problem and the corresponding difficulty of establishing trends which are not masked by contrary trends:

Not only may the climatic influences be obscured by those of learning but the cultural influences may be so numerous and so powerful as to make the effect of climatic change quite negligible. Climate and geographical location may stimulate physiological functioning and also cultural achievements, provided the culture does not otherwise change and is the same from region to region. But such is never the case. Cultures vary from region to region, and are nearly everywhere in a state of change. Hence the effect of climatic stimulation is small or even infinitesimal compared to the cultural stimulation.[9]

Mutatis mutandis, we can agree with this conclusion. As we have seen, the more penetrating studies all show that fluctuations which, superficially, seemed to be due to the climate were in fact more likely to be related to certain cultural events such as Christmas, Guy Fawkes, which happen to occur at certain times of the year and have various complex social and economic repercussions. Strict evidence for this assumption, however, is not available either.

II. PHYSICAL HEALTH[10]

As already pointed out before, we are in this chapter concerned exclusively with the physical health of delinquents, regardless of whether or not any evidence of ill health, any deviation from what is regarded as 'normal' in this field, may be characteristic of a certain anthropological type.

Evidence on the incidence of ill health among delinquents has been collected partly from statistical samples and partly from individual cases. It is somewhat more plentiful for juveniles than for adults, but there is, regrettably, no routine check of the physical health of every juvenile delinquent appearing before a juvenile court in this country. According to the Children and Young Persons Act, 1933, s. 35(2), it is the duty of the police when bringing a child or young person before the court to notify the local authority, which then has in all cases, except those appearing to be trivial, to make investigations into, among other matters, his health, and the information obtained shall be rendered available to the court. Various studies made of samples of juvenile court cases have shown, however, that medical examinations of physical health are in fact not made as a matter of routine and that the magistrates often rely on the results of out-of-date school medical inspections.[11] Nor does the position appear to be much more favourable in juvenile courts in the United States.[12] On the physical health of offenders above juvenile court age there exists even less general information.

As far as prisoners are concerned, it is provided in the *Statutory Rules for English Prisons* that the Medical Officer has to examine every prisoner on reception, record the state of his health and that he has the care of the physical health of the prisoner throughout his stay in prison.[13] The *Annual Reports of the Prison Commissioners* contain some information on the physical health of the prison population; in the years 1955-9, for example, the daily percentage of prisoners treated in and out of hospitals ranged from 14·6 to 15·6 per cent of the daily population.[14] While this seems to be a fairly high figure, it gives no complete picture of the health of the population, in particular not of the seriousness and length of the illnesses and on the question whether the latter had already existed on reception and at the time of the offence or whether they were contracted subsequently in prison.

In the circumstances we have to rely on whatever scanty information is available from special private investigations into the subject. For juvenile delinquents, what appears to have been the first attempt in Britain to study some physical characteristics of delinquent as compared with non-delinquent children was made in 1883 when a report was published by the Anthropometric Committee of the British Association for the Advancement of Science which had been appointed 'for the purpose of collecting observations on the systematic examination of the height, weight, and other physical characters of the inhabitants of the British Isles'.[15] The approximately 53,000 individuals measured by the Committee included a group of 1,273 boys and 601 girls from Industrial Schools, and comparisons with the general population showed that these delinquent children from Industrial Schools were considerably shorter and lighter in weight than children of the same age in the general population. For children aged 13 years, for example, the following figures were given:

Average Weight (including clothes) in lb.

General Population	Professional Class	Labouring Class	Industrial Schools Boys	Industrial Schools Girls
87·2	89·8	84·0	72·31	72·76

Average Height (without shoes) in inches

General Population Boys	General Population Girls	Industrial Schools Boys	Industrial Schools Girls
56·91	57·77	53·23	52·98

While, on the one hand, the figures for Industrial Schools could at the time be regarded as more representative of juvenile delinquents than Approved School figures would be now, the usefulness of these data suffers from the lack of information how long the children had been in the institution at the time when they were measured.

Soon afterwards a well-known nineteenth-century writer on the subject, the Rev. W. D. Morrison, in his book *Juvenile Offenders*, while complaining about the lack of data, ventured the statement that 'among the many causes which produce a criminal life the physical inferiority of the offender is one of the most important'.[16] More substantial evidence was produced by Cyril Burt, whose chapter on the subject ranks among the best sources of information available.[17] In his samples of delinquent and control cases he found that defective physical conditions were about one and a quarter times as frequent among the former as they were among the latter. Actually, he found an average of 119·3 pathological factors among his delinquent group as against 78·5 among the non-delinquents. With regard to the question of causal nexus he stresses that 'poor health means poor control; and even a temporary physical weakness may be the occasion of a passing criminal lapse', and also that misconduct may appear after the illness has passed, sometimes because of undue pampering while it lasted. 'With most young convalescents, it is character rather than

207

physique that remains permanently enfeebled by the circumstances of their disease'—a good illustration of the truth of our previous remarks on the mental factor as the great 'transformator'. Therefore, he adds, one should not expect too much from a purely medical approach. It is not only true that 'the mere presence in a young thief of a swollen gland or joint does not prove it was the swelling that forced him into theft', but also that the mere removal of a physical defect does not invariably remove its criminogenic effects because in the meantime 'a mental habit may have been formed'. This dependence of the physical factor on the mental transformator does not prove, of course, that the former is of no importance in the chain of causation, and Burt fully endorses the demand that 'every child charged should be carefully examined by an experienced medical practitioner before being brought before the courts'—a demand which, as we have seen, has remained largely unfulfilled in the period of forty years since Burt's book was first published.

Probably under the influence of this study by its eminent psychologist the London County Council produced a full medical account in 1931 on 696 boys and 107 girls admitted to the Ponton-Road Place of Detention.[18] This report showed 'a very marked inferiority in respect of nutritional state and physical make up' when compared with average London children. 22·2 per cent of the Ponton-Road children were estimated to be poorly nourished against the 4·5 per cent of the average London children.

Eilenberg[19] contrasts groups of London Remand Home boys for the years 1935 and 1955 and also compares them with L.C.C. figures for 1954. He concludes that the present higher standard of living in this country has resulted in a generation characterized by an increase in both height and weight and that up to the age of 14 there is little difference in this between the Remand Home boys and those in the general population. There was also noticeable an increased physical well-being and absence of illnesses in the 1955 child compared with the 1930 child.

For Glasgow, Ferguson[20] compared the convictions of a group of 1,349 ordinary boys who had left school in 1947 with those of a group of 489 physically handicapped boys. He found a very slightly higher rate of convictions per head among the latter; only for a few types of physical handicap, those due to injuries and respiratory diseases, the rate was much higher. In the light of his figures his conclusion is hardly justified that 'there seems to be some evidence that poor physique does itself exert an adverse influence on the incidence of juvenile delinquency, particularly where conditions in the home are unsatisfactory'.[21]

With regard to Borstal cases, the present writer found among the

208

files of 606 boys and 411 girls examined before the last war only 37 cases of boys—6·1 per cent—and 14 cases of girls—3·4 per cent—listed as showing 'physical defects and unprepossessing appearance'. The records were, however, rather scanty at the time (the files referred to boys discharged between 1922 and 1936 and to girls discharged between 1916 and 1935), and many cases of this kind may have been overlooked.[22] For a sub-sample of 44 cases of Borstal boys received in 1946–7, whose files were examined in connection with the Borstal Prediction Study,[23] 19 cases were found to be below normal physically and a 'surprisingly high proportion of cases with serious physical defects' was encountered.

The comprehensive investigation made by Norwood East and his associates into the characteristics of 4,000 Borstal boys[24] was handicapped by the lack of an external control group. Therefore, comparisons could be made only within the Borstal sample by distinguishing according to type and frequency of the offences committed. Where, in exceptional cases, comparisons with a corresponding sample of non-criminals were possible, as for height and weight, no significant differences were found.

With regard to adult criminals, Goring's famous investigation,[25] which will be more fully discussed below (Chapter 13), came to the conclusion that the Parkhurst prisoners whom he studied, except for an inferiority in stature and weight, were equal in physique to the general population.

Norval Morris's analysis of his groups of 32 preventive detainees and two hundred and seventy 'confirmed recidivists', studied in English prisons in 1948,[26] includes many details concerning their physical condition. 6 of the 32 he regarded as 'precluded by their physical condition from living for more than a short time outside an institution', while 6 others were seriously hindered by bad health 'from pursuing extra-mural occupations suitable to their mental abilities'. The remaining 20, 'though not necessarily good specimens physically', were at least not in need of frequent medical attention. The average age of this group was 50 years 9 months, with a standard deviation of 8 years 1 month. Of the second group of 270 'confirmed recidivists' the health of 78 is given as fair, of 31 as indifferent and 29 as poor, and 51 were either precluded by bad health from living for more than a short time outside an institution or seriously hindered in pursuing extra-mural occupations in keeping with their mental abilities. The average age of this group when last sentenced was 41 years 6 months, with a standard deviation of 8 years 6 months. The material does not allow any guesses how far these physical abilities had been present at the beginning of the criminal careers of these men, how far they had been responsible for their criminal activities and how far the heavy sentences served had contributed to their physical deterioration. Nor do the case histories add sufficient details on the early condition of these men to permit any guesses in this respect. One has to bear in mind that their criminal histories go back over four decades or more to a time when even less attention than today was paid in court and prison files to the health of offenders.

Approximately ten to twelve years after Norval Morris's observations, Terence and Pauline Morris, in their Pentonville Study, came to the conclusion that the physical health of the prisoners was probably no better and no worse than that of a population of comparable social and economic status outside, whereas the matter was very different for their mental health. At roughly the same time, D. J. West stated that, in his group of Wandsworth prisoners, 'although only a minority were physically afflicted, the incidence of physical illness and handicap was higher than might be expected among a population of working men of similar age', and his interviews gave him the impression that 'an undue proportion of the men were prematurely ageing'. Here again, the position was strikingly more unfavourable with regard to mental health.[27]

In the United States a painstaking enquiry into the subject was conducted by the Gluecks in their *Unraveling Juvenile Delinquency*.[28] In view of the large size of their samples, 500 delinquent and 500 non-delinquent boys, the physical examinations had to be limited to 20–30 minutes per case, and it may be open to doubt whether they could do full justice to all the items mentioned: developmental health history, immunity from contagion, height, weight, dynamometric strength of grip, skeleton and palate, teeth, nose and throat, eyes and ears, heart and lungs, abdomen and genitalia, skin, glands and nervous system. With this important reservation in mind, we note that the findings did not support the view that the health of the delinquents was worse than that of the non-delinquents. Certain minor differences were found, but they are too insignificant to be mentioned. The researchers were asked to consider whether the fact that their delinquents were all selected from inmates of institutions might not have affected their physical condition, but they took the view that the periods of institutionalization had been too short to have any influence.

In an earlier Glueck study *One Thousand Juvenile Delinquents*[29] the percentage of children in poor health had been very high, but as there was no control group no conclusions could be drawn from this. In the follow-up study *Juvenile Delinquents Grown Up*, no difference was found in health between those who had reformed and the recidivists.[30]

The evidence from most other American studies of juvenile delinquency is similarly negative. Typical in this respect are statements by William Healy, the McCords and the Cambridge-Somerville Study.[31]

210

The authors of the latter stress, in particular, that, as pointed out by Burt long before, the removal of physical handicaps does not necessarily lead to a cessation of delinquent behaviour—a fact which has but little to do with the question of how far such behaviour may have been originally caused or at least precipitated or aggravated by that handicap.

Far more positive is the English study of Pearce[32] who, writing soon after the last war as a psychiatrist with personal experience of several thousands of London juvenile delinquents, endorses the finding of the London County Council's report of twenty years before that the delinquents showed an inferiority both in nutritional state and physical make-up. He disagrees with the conclusion of that report that physical inferiority had little direct bearing on delinquency, but stresses even more its indirect psychological influence and disabilities resulting from absence from school during illness and undue spoiling afterwards.[33]

To sum up: while the statistical evidence of physical ill-health leading to delinquency is, at least for more recent years, not impressive, those with personal knowledge of large numbers of cases are inclined to regard it as an indirectly important factor in the causation of delinquent behaviour. More direct is the effect of certain affections of the brain, such as encephalitis lethargica, which will be discussed in Chapter 14 below.

Chapter 12

ANTHROPOLOGICAL-BIOLOGICAL ASPECTS II:
THE POSITIVIST SCHOOL

In the present chapter we have to deal not as in the previous one with physical disabilities of any conceivable kind, but with certain types of physical irregularities or stigmata which have been regarded as being characteristic of the criminal. The principal method used by the anthropological-biological school of criminology is the typological one. This school has derived its immense strength largely from the support received through the widespread popular belief that, first, criminals are born, not made, and secondly, that they conform to certain physical characteristics which make them look different and easily distinguishable from ordinary human beings. This belief is strongly reflected not only in popular writings but also in several well-known figures in great works of world literature such as Homer's *Thersites* or Shakespeare's *Richard III* or in part also in *Julius Caesar*:

> Let me have men about me that are fat,
> Sleek-headed men, and such as sleep o' nights;
> Yond Cassius has a lean and hungry look,
> He thinks too much; such men are dangerous.

From here it is only one further step to the conviction expressed in *The Times* of the 11th October 1935: 'The fat, says a judge, do not write anonymous letters ... It is the lean bodies that sit at writing tables, and bony fingers that dip pens in vitriol and build up bombshells for harmless postmen to deliver.'

I. THE PHRENOLOGISTS

The scientific study of the matter goes back to the eighteenth and early nineteenth century phrenologists, especially to Franz Joseph Gall (1758–1828), John Gaspar Spurzheim (1776–1832), and the American Charles Caldwell (1772–1853),[1] and to a smaller extent to the physiognomic work of J. K. Lavater (1741–1801). While the impact of the latter, i.e. of the idea that the human physiognomy provides the key to an understanding of the human personality, was insignificant in the field of criminology—Norwood East refers to an English Statute of 1743 which made all persons pretending to have skill in physiognomy liable to be whipped as rogues and vagabonds[2] —phrenology, i.e. the corresponding search for relations between the skull, the brain and social behaviour, aroused somewhat greater interest at least until the middle of the nineteenth century. Gall and his supporters maintained that there was a close correspondence between the exterior shape of the skull, unusual cranial protuberances or other abnormalities of the cranium and the structure of the brain; moreover, the different regions of the latter were related to certain psychological characters, propensities and sentiments, of which phrenologists identified a large number, up to thirty-five. Each of these psychological characters had a specific cerebral organ allocated to it which produced certain abnormalities of the brain causing specific criminal tendencies. This causal nexus was, however, not regarded as inevitable as the so-called lower propensities could well be overcome by the influence of the higher sentiments. This theory led to a number of phrenological studies of the skulls of prisoners, notably in the United States, but any anatomical abnormalities which were discovered might as well have been exhibited by the non-criminal population of which there was no control group. Moreover, as Fink writes, the essential weakness of phrenology was its failure to understand that no single part of the skull and the brain can be held solely responsible for the very complex variations of human behaviour. However, it was the merit of this school, as that of its successor, the anthropological-biological school, that it drew attention to this need for the close examination of individual criminals instead of the vague general theorizing on crime which, with a few exceptions, had monopolized the field up to the beginning of the nineteenth century. In some cases, for example in the Annual Reports of the famous Eastern State Penitentiary of Pennsylvania, phrenological ideas and terms were used for the classification of the prisoners even up to the beginning of the present century.[3] In Europe, the work of the phrenologists was carried on by a number of scholars, especially Lauvergne, Broca, Thomson and others mentioned by Bonger and Wolfgang.[4]

In spite of the stir which the phrenologists and their immediate successors had caused, the immense popularity of the anthropological interpretation of crime was due not so much to them as to Lombroso,[5] whose theories and writings have influenced the course of thinking more deeply than those of any other criminologists.

213

II. LOMBROSO'S PERSONALITY AND WORK

Cesare Lombroso was born of Italian-Jewish parents on the 6th November 1835 in Verona, which was at the time still under Austrian rule, and died in 1909.[6] He studied medicine at Pavia and other Italian universities and also at Vienna where he became interested in psychiatry. Philosophically, he was influenced, as Wolfgang writes, 'by the French positivists, the German materialists, and the English evolutionists', and he strongly disagreed with the indeterministic views dominant among contemporary Italian philosophers and jurists. Apart from the phrenologists, Darwin and Comte, as also the French psychiatrists Esquirol and Morel, the German pathologist Virchow and the French anthropologist Broca were among his most important spiritual ancestors.[7] His earliest researches were concerned with cretinism and pellagra, particularly rampant in Italy at the time, and, after becoming an Army physician, he carried out the anthropometric measurement of 3,000 soldiers in order to observe the physical differences existing between the inhabitants of the different regions of Italy. This was followed by work in mental hospitals, leading among other publications to a lecture on *Genio e follia* (1864), a forerunner of one of his best-known later works *L'Uomo di genio* and *Genio e degenerazione* (1897). In 1874 he became a lecturer in legal medicine and public hygiene at the University of Turin, where he later became a professor of psychiatry and of criminal anthropology. In 1880, assisted by his pupils Ferri and Garofalo, he founded the *Archivio di Psichiatria e Anthropologia criminale* and in 1906 the Museum of Criminal Anthropology. In the intervening years he had published many papers on brain pathology and psychiatry, such as the *Antropometria di 400 delinquenti veneti* (1872) and *Affetti e passioni dei delinquenti* (1874).[8] These last papers prepared the ground for his most famous work, *L'Uomo delinquente*, which was first published in 1876 and soon translated into French and German and other languages, but surprisingly enough never into English. In the course of the five Italian editions of this book, covering a period of twenty years, Lombroso expanded it from its original size of 252 pages to a three-volume work of over 1,900 pages (5th ed. 1896–7), modifying and adding continuously under the impact of external criticisms and of the researches of his supporters and his own. In his later work *Le Crime, causes et remèdes* (1899), translated into English as *Crime: its Causes and Remedies*,[9] he once more gave expression to certain changes in his scientific views by underlining the significance of the socio-economic factors, which had been comparatively neglected in most of his previous writings. Together with the husband of

214

one of his daughters, Ferrero, he published a study of *The Female Offender* in 1893, translated into English in 1895.[10] Towards the end of his life he developed an interest in hypnotism and spiritualism, on which he published a book rendered into English as *After Death— What ?*[11] The story of his life and work was told by the same daughter Gina after his death.[12]

As far as Lombroso's working techniques are concerned, he firmly believed in the need for first-hand observation and measurement of individual cases instead of philosophical-logical-juridical speculation and abstraction. First through his studies of Italian soldiers and later by examining inmates of Italian prisons he was able to collect a very large body of anthropometric material, some of it relating to the skulls of notorious Italian brigands. Notwithstanding his devotion to facts, however, his style and his basic approach to his problems were often highly intuitive, not to say fanciful. While imagination and inspiration are truly indispensable elements of scientific research, the flashes of insight which they produce have to be rigidly controlled to guard against the danger that unconscious bias may lead to imaginary discoveries not borne out by the facts.[13] Lombroso's scientific method has been characterized by Aschaffenburg, who in spite of many criticisms was favourably disposed towards him, as 'mehr genial schauend als sorgfältig prüfend' (i.e. perceiving with the intuition of genius rather than examining with care).[14] Characteristic of this is his famous description of how he was once standing with the skull of a notorious brigand in his hand and pondering over the problem of crime when suddenly the sun broke through the clouds and the sun-rays fell on the skull. Then, he said, it suddenly dawned on him that this skull and its anatomical structure provided the answer. In contrast to the phrenologists, however, Lombroso did not limit his study of the relation between crime and the human physique to the anatomy of the skull and the brain, but tried to take into consideration the other parts of the body, too. According to him, there exists a distinct anthropological type,[15] the born criminal, *delinquente nato* (a name invented by Ferri), an individual likely, or even bound, to commit crime. This type is characterized by certain malformations of the skeleton and the skull, in particular cranial and facial asymmetry, as well as by other physical stigmata of degeneration: an under- or oversized brain, a receding forehead, high cheek-bones, squinting eyes, bushy and prominent eyebrows, a twisted nose, big ears, a projecting or receding jaw, scanty beard as contrasted with the general hairiness of the body and overdeveloped arms. In addition to these physical stigmata, he noted a lack of moral sense, vanity, cruelty, idleness, the use of a criminal argot, a specific nervous insensibility to pain with contempt of death and suffering, and, finally, an inclination for tattooing which he had first observed among the soldiers. This congenital criminal, this moral imbecile, is an atavistic type, i.e. he represents a reversion to earlier, primitive, human types or even to pre-human ancestors of mankind with cannibalistic instincts. He 'reproduces in his person the ferocious instincts of primitive humanity and the inferior animals', a clear expression of Darwinian ideas. Under the influence of criticisms of this theory Lombroso tried to find a broader basis for it and added to the conception of atavism another explanation, that of epilepsy. While not every epileptic was a born criminal, the latter, according to Lombroso, was always an epileptic. Moreover, this type was an international one, i.e. the Italian born criminal showed the same characteristics as, say, the Chinese or English.

As has already been noted, in the course of his writings Lombroso was quite prepared to compromise on some of his ideas. From the third edition of his *L'Uomo delinquente* on, for example, he restricted the category of the born criminal to about 35 per cent of all criminals, recognizing in addition the existence of the insane and, in particular, the occasional criminal. This latter group, the largest of all, was divided into pseudo-criminals, who commit crimes without evil intent and without seriously harming society; the criminaloids, in whose cases adverse environmental circumstances are mostly to blame, criminals out of passion and, somewhat paradoxically, the habitual criminals who, without showing any of the stigmata, were driven into persistent criminal activities by their upbringing and associations. Another important concession, which greatly facilitated the numerical reduction of the born criminal type to 35 per cent, was Lombroso's insistence that, to fall under this category, an individual had to exhibit at least five of the physical stigmata. It is noteworthy, too, that he opened his late work *Crime: its Causes and Remedies* with the words: 'Every crime has its origin in a multiplicity of causes. . . .'

In making the born criminal, in spite of such reservations, the most important figure in his system Lombroso had powerful allies not only among his predecessors, the phrenologists, but also among his contemporaries. The famous English psychiatrist Henry Maudsley (1835–1918) wrote: 'Of the true thief as of the true poet it may be indeed said that he is born not made.'[16] The question arises: what is here meant by 'true'? In any case Maudsley, too, modified his views with advancing years.[17]

III. LOMBROSO'S CRITICS AND SUPPORTERS

Criticism of Lombroso's theories began early and became very widespread. His conceptions of atavism and degeneracy as applied to primitive men were not in keeping with the changing views even of the immediate post-Darwinian period which did no longer believe in 'evolution along a single line' or expect 'all evolution to be progressive'.[18]

Moreover, 'a psychological and logical analysis of the processes involved in the thought and behaviour of primitive man as he is described by modern anthropologists shows that in form or structure his mentality does not differ radically from that of civilized man'.[19] As Bertrand Russell writes:[20] ' "Evolution" is a word which is often used with an ethical flavour, but science is not improved by an admixture of ethics' and 'the particular motive force which Darwin suggested, namely the struggle for existence and the survival of the fittest, is not nearly so popular among biologists as it was fifty years ago'. In addition, it has been stressed by a writer otherwise not unsympathetic towards Lombroso, Earnest Hooton, that the ideas of atavism and degeneration do not go well together as the latter is a concept of pathology, which the former is not.[21] To make matters worse, Lombroso used the term 'atavism' wrongly. Meaning the reappearance in a present-day individual of signs of an earlier trait which may have remained dormant for many generations, it can be applied exclusively to hereditary qualities. Lombroso, however, used that term also to explain certain non-hereditary phenomena such as the frequency of tattooing, and he seems to have believed in the possible inheritance of acquired characters.[22]

Apart from criticism of the doubtful quality of some of Lombroso's most fundamental general conceptions, scepticism regarding the accuracy of his anthropometric measurements of individual criminals became also widespread. In the first place, he approached the individual physique not as a dynamic and changing but as a static phenomenon and was not interested in the observation of morbid processes.[23] Secondly, he often relied on measurements carried out by others, of whose techniques he had no first-hand knowledge; thirdly, in the statistical handling of his material he was not yet able to use the more advanced methods developed only some decades later by Karl Pearson at University College, London; and, fourthly—with the exception of his study of female offenders[24]—he had no control groups and could not, therefore, prove that the criminals whom he measured showed physical abnormalities more frequently than noncriminals. Hooton regards as the most serious objections to Lombroso's claims in the field of craniology the numerical inadequacy and ethnic and racial heterogeneity of the case material assembled by him and his students and the absence of any scientific statistical analysis.[25] He calls the belief that the born criminal presented always the same anthropological type regardless of ethnic and racial differences

217

rightly as 'almost too fantastic for serious consideration',[26] and it should indeed be obvious without further evidence that the physical differences between the different races are, generally speaking, far more important than those between criminals and non-criminals of the same race. In spite of such grave shortcomings, however, Hooton maintains that Lombroso's principal ideas, though not proved, have so far not been disproved either.

Outstanding among Lombroso's contemporary critics were A. Lacassagne (1843–1924) who, although a professor of medicine, became the head of the French environmental sociological school of criminology and who coined the famous phrase 'every society gets the criminals it deserves'; the anthropologists L. Manouvrier[27] and Topinard and, in particular, the lawyer and sociologist Gabriel Tarde (1843–1904). In his *La criminalité comparée*[28] Tarde stressed the ever-changing character of crime and the criminal law throughout the ages, the social origins of crime, and the various contradictions in Lombroso's theories. If, for example, one explains crime as atavism one cannot at the same time regard it as a form of insanity which is a product of civilization rather than of savagery. Tarde was interested in the phenomenon of criminal societies such as the Mafia, and in the professional character of crime in general.[29] If one would examine judges, advocates, musicians or labourers in the same way as Lombroso had examined his criminals one might, Tarde suggested, also find born judges, advocates, musicians, etc., among these occupational groups.[30] Lombroso's born criminal was, therefore, perhaps only one professional type of many. Among other arguments against the anthropological theory of crime he refers to the fact that women, although showing the same stigmata, have a much smaller crime rate than men which, he thought, could not be explained, as Lombroso had suggested in his book *La donna delinquente*, by maintaining that prostitution was the female substitute for crime (on this see Chapter 26 below).[31]

On the other hand, Lombroso was able to build up a very large and powerful following, chiefly in his native country. The most important figures among his friends and students were Ferri and Garofalo.[32]

Enrico Ferri (1856–1929) has rightly been called by Sellin[33] 'one of the most colourful and influential figures in the history of criminology . . . the acknowledged leader of the so-called positive school of criminal science, a highly successful trial lawyer, Member of Parliament, editor of the socialist newspaper *Avanti*, indefatigable public lecturer, university professor, author of highly esteemed scholarly works, founder of a great legal journal, and a tireless polemicist in defence of his ideas'. The principal stages of his development may be sketched as follows: Born of poor parents in the province of

ANTHROPOLOGICAL-BIOLOGICAL ASPECTS II

Mantua, he studied law at the University of Bologna. At the end of these studies he wrote a thesis in which he formulated already one of his principal ideas, i.e. that the criminal law should not be based upon free will and moral responsibility, which he regarded as mere fictions.[34] Greatly attracted by Lombroso's *L'Uomo delinquente*, which had appeared a few years earlier, he went to Turin in 1879 to study with the master and to lay the foundations of a lasting, though on his part not entirely uncritical, friendship. Soon, however, he proceeded to Paris where, in an attempt to widen the factual basis of his studies, he embarked on a large-scale analysis of French criminal statistics between 1828 and 1878, in which particular emphasis was placed upon the social factors as the only ones capable of explaining the great increase of crime in France during that period. He was thus able to show that members of the Lombrosian school were not, as commonly believed, exclusively interested in the anthropological side of crime. Ferri, in fact, was a strong advocate of the theory of multiple causation, paying special attention also to such physical factors as race, soil and climate.[35] At the same time, as his examination of several hundred prisoners and a control group of soldiers and his studies of homicide show,[36] he did not neglect his anthropological interests. After several years of teaching at the Universities of Bologna, Siena, Rome and Pisa his academic career suffered a setback when in 1893, because of his socialist activities—he had been a Member of Parliament already for several years—he was deprived of his professorship. It was only in 1906 that he was appointed professor of criminal law in Rome. In the intervening years, he had published, among many other works, his most famous book *Sociologia criminale*.[37] In the legal field he became known as an opponent of the jury, except for political trials, and of the death penalty, and in 1892 he founded a journal which became the centre and mouthpiece of the positive school of criminology, *La scuola positiva*. His influence in Italy and abroad grew steadily, in particular as the result of two brilliantly successful lecture tours to South America in 1908 and 1910. Perhaps nowhere else have his ideas been so enthusiastically acclaimed as in the South American republics, many of whose new Penal Codes purported to be written in accordance with positivist principles, although in some cases mere lip service was paid to them.[38] In Italy, his influence on the reform of the old Penal Code of 1889 was less lasting than originally expected. While a Draft Code published in 1921 was so strongly inspired by him that it became generally known under his name, the final Code of 1930, worked out under the Fascist regime with which, superficially, he had come to terms,[39] shows various important deviations from Ferri's ideas, notably in the field of penalties where the death penalty has been more widely

219

applied in the Code than Ferri could have sincerely approved. A summary of his theories will be given below under IV.

Second in importance among Lombroso's followers ranks Raffaele Garofalo (1852–1934), but the attention paid to his personality and work has never equalled the fascination aroused in wide circles by the other two members of the famous trio. Garofalo, born in Naples, was a lawyer and became a magistrate and professor of criminal law in his native city, but his career lacked the brilliance and the vicissitudes of that of Ferri. Although he produced several books, among them one on reparation for the victims of crime, he has become mainly known through his *Criminologia*, first published in 1885 and usually regarded as the first book to bear this name.[40] Although a leading member of the positivist school, he disagreed in important points with Lombroso and especially with Ferri, whose socialism did not appeal to him, and it has been doubted whether his emphasis on moral conceptions was at all compatible with the main trends of positivist thought. This applies in particular to his theory of 'natural crime' (see Chapter 2 above). With the natural law movement he shared the endeavour to find an extra-legal definition of crime, which he thought should be a sociological one. He realized the impossibility of reaching a material conception of crime which would be valid independent of time and space, but believed that two criteria could be discovered applicable to crime in general: the violation of feelings of pity and probity. One could establish natural crimes by means of the inductive method, 'the only one which the positive school can use'. He explicitly refused to ask whether all that was crime in his age and society had always been so as this would be a childish question. Instead of actions one should analyse sentiments. Although these, too, are changeable, each race possesses, he thought, a nucleus of inborn moral instincts, transmitted by heredity, just as it possesses a physical type. After discussing a number of moral instincts which he regards as fundamental, such as patriotism, religion, honour, shame, he concludes that the idea of crime is associated with actions which are not merely harmful and immoral but violate the fundamental sentiments of pity (crimes of violence) and probity (crimes against property). This, he thinks, is not in violation of the theory of evolution, but his whole line of argument becomes rather tortuous and unconvincing and he has to make a number of exceptions for actions provoked by religious or political commands or social or traditional institutions. Moreover, he writes, if one considers the extreme tolerance usually exercised towards acts of industrial improbity one begins to query the existence of a sentiment of probity in the majority of the population. Mere police contraventions, too, are not crimes, but actions not yet regarded as crimes might

acquire this character at a later stage because of the growing refinement of our moral sentiments—a point later to be more fully elab-
orated by Durkheim. In some of the examples he gave he was right,
for example cruelty to animals, and in others, for example exploitation of labour in various forms, he was wrong only because social
legislation has stepped in and to some extent taken over the functions
of the criminal law. To the criticism that the moral sense cannot be a
valid criterion because it, and public opinion with it, are to some
considerable extent shaped by the fact and effect of punishment so
that it would be a vicious circle to use it as a criterion to decide
which acts should be punished he replied that the mere existence of
penalties was not enough to give a criminal character to acts otherwise not regarded as such.

As Allen points out,[41] this theory created for Garofalo the formidable task of reconciling the moral concept of crime with the
positivist rejection of moral responsibility. Moreover, in spite of
important reservations and the concessions which he made to the
ever-changing character of crime it was, as Tarde wrote,[42] not easy
for an evolutionist 'to attach himself to some fixed point' in the process of evolution. Actually, there is no insurmountable difference in
this respect between Garofalo and the evolutionists. Spencer, for
example, although an opponent of the idea of a universal moral sense
and believing that every society creates for itself the system of morals
needed for its survival, thought it possible to reach an 'absolute
Ethics' with certain fundamental principles.[43] Ginsberg, too, thinks
there is a certain 'relative constancy' in moral rules, and elementary
moral duties are widely recognized.[44] The real difficulties arise only
when we try to define these duties more specifically and to use them,
as Garofalo intended, as the basis for criminal legislation.

It is easy to find the link between Garofalo's legal philosophy and
his concept of natural crime, on the one hand, and Lombroso's
criminological theory, on the other: the born criminal is an individual
particularly lacking in the sentiments of pity and probity.

IV. THE SYSTEM OF THE POSITIVE SCHOOL

In spite of the considerable differences between the views of its
leaders it is possible to sum up the essential features of the positive
school.[45] Although it came into being largely in opposition to the
classical school it is in fact the first coherent system of criminological
thought ever constructed. The classical school, as represented by such
great figures as Beccaria, Romilly, Feuerbach and, with many reservations, Bentham, was mainly interested in the reform of criminal
law, of criminal procedure and of the system of penalties. It was

opposed to the arbitrary and cruel character of the contemporary administration of criminal justice, to the lawmaking powers of the judiciary, to torture, capital punishment and transportation; it favoured equality before the law, trial by jury, fixed penalties and an objective equation between crime and punishment.[46] With the study of the individual offender it was but little concerned, and it did hardly anything to provide the scientific tools for such study; even the very idea of it was premature at the time. The 'statistician-sociologists'— to use Bonger's label—who followed them in the middle of the nineteenth century tried to create a scientific criminology, but only for the study of crime as a mass phenomenon. Jeffery has recently made a strong attack on the positivist school for having shifted the whole trend of scientific criminology from crime to the criminal;[47] but he does not pay sufficient attention to the historical fact that this shifting of the emphasis was nothing but a defensive action against the equally one-sided trends which had made their appearance before. It is our task today to restore the balance between these conflicting schools of thought and action.

The principal views, achievements and weaknesses of the positive school can be summarized as follows, and this summary may be read in conjunction with the present writer's analysis of positivism in the Introduction to *Pioneers in Criminology*. It will be clear that the theoretical system of the positivists is far more comprehensive than their specifically anthropological-biological doctrines and that positivists can be found among criminologists who do not support these doctrines.

In the field of criminology proper, (a) the positivists took over Comte's idea of the progress of scientific thought from the theological to the metaphysical stage, and from there to the scientific or positive stage. This implied the complete divorce of science and law from morals; the priority of science; the repudiation of free will and moral responsibility, which latter had to be replaced by the legal and social responsibility of the criminal, as the idea of guilt had to be replaced by that of dangerousness (*pericolosità* and its subjective elements, *temibilità*); (b) the attempt of the classical school to construct an equation between crime and punishment had to be replaced by an equation between the individual criminal and his treatment; (c) therefore, the individual criminal had to be studied by means of scientific quantitative observation of facts, and the effect of treatment by way of experimentation. The legal nature of the crime committed was comparatively unimportant. The classical school, Ferri wrote,[48] wanted to reduce punishment, the positive school wanted to reduce crime by effective treatment of the offender in accordance with his needs.

In the fields of penology and criminal law, it follows (a) that the moralizing concept of punishment had to be replaced by a morally neutral system of measures of security, protecting society against the criminal, and of reform and rehabilitation. Such measures might, in individual cases, be much more severe than the old-fashioned penalties of the classical school as the limiting principle of the just equation between crime and punishment was no longer valid; (b) that, in particular, the system of penalties fixed by the court had to be replaced by indeterminate sentences, the length of which was to be decided in the course of their application in accordance with the needs of treatment; (c) that, if the idea of replacing the concept of guilt by that of dangerousness is to be taken seriously, measures of security and reform should be applied not only to those who have already committed crime, but also preventively to those whose dangerous state (*état dangereux*) makes it likely that they will do so in future (predelinquents). This—one of the most controversial points in the positive programme—would imply the abandonment of the fundamental principle of the criminal law: no punishment without crime, which would be justified, however, in the eyes of the positivists because of the sharp distinction which they made between the moralizing idea of punishment and morally neutral measures of security and reform. In doing so they initiated the long and drawn-out legislative struggle between the compromising double-track system, which tried to keep penalties and measures of security and reforms side by side (e.g. the previous system of preventive detention in the Prevention of Crime Act, 1908), and the more extreme single-track system, which combines both in a uniform sentence (e.g. the new system of preventive detention and corrective training in the Criminal Justice Act, 1948).[49]

Altogether, notwithstanding certain deep-seated differences between individual members of the positivist school,[50] the main outlines of their programme were distinct enough to enable them to exercise a profound practical influence on the criminological and legislative thought of the late nineteenth and early twentieth centuries. Naturally, a criminological theory based upon the idea of a born criminal, of the strength of hereditary biological factors in crime, is bound to be of a pessimistic, negative character as there seems to be very little that can be constructively done to improve these factors, except perhaps through far-reaching eugenic measures. Nevertheless, Lombroso, especially in his later writings, and his friends tried very hard to devise a system of constructive, in particular preventive, measures. To give a few illustrations: Lombroso's very detailed discussion of the alleged dangers of education, especially in penal institutions,[51] bears no doubt a heavy responsibility for the very slow progress of the educational system in prisons, but in spite of all his misgivings Lombroso was most anxious to explain that he was not against education as such. Whilst 'schools in prison' should be suppressed as only serving to multiply recidivism, children in elementary schools found to exhibit the stigmata of the born criminal should be segregated and given some special training designed to strengthen the inhibitory factors and suppress criminal tendencies. Penalties for children should be milder, and imprisonment should not be used for them. Adult offenders should be isolated in cellular prisons and treated under a graded system (Lombroso favoured the Irish system of Sir Walter Crofton). Deportation should be used for criminals by passion; probation he regarded as the best preventive measure for minor and occasional offenders. On the other hand, adult born criminals should be kept in perpetual confinement already for their first crime, if serious, and so should also be recidivists, although they should be subjected to less severe discipline. For incorrigibles special penal institutions and agricultural colonies should be established where they could live under a comparatively relaxed regime, only exceptionally in cellular confinement, but in strict isolation from the outside world. As already indicated, this opened the way to the subsequent building up of non-punitive preventive detention. The death penalty was to be retained—here Lombroso and Garofalo differed from Ferri—but limited to the most hopeless cases of incorrigibility.

In conclusion, it may be said that the ideas of the positive school contain a mixture of truth and falsehood, of progress and deviation, a fact which fully explains the heat of the controversies to which they have given rise. That an up-to-date scientific discipline has to make full use of the methods of factual observation and experimentation and that they should be applied to the study of the individual criminal is incontestably true. There is no reason, however, why such methods should not equally be applied to the less personal aspects of crime in society, and the positivists, though with less originality, did try to include this, too, in their programme. In both fields, however, their scientific tools were not equal to the task. Moreover, while a purely moralizing view of crime is incompatible with the insights of modern criminology and penology, the complete rejection of moral considerations in the interpretation of crime and the treatment of criminals, as favoured by some positivists, went far beyond the limits of what could be tolerated by public opinion (see also Chapter 2 above). The same is true of the slogan that only the criminal, not the kind and gravity of crime committed should be taken into consideration. Some of their most important practical recommendations, such as the use of entirely indeterminate sentences and the replacement of punishment by measures of security and re-form, while following logically from their theoretical promises, have had to be watered down by the legislation of most countries to make them generally acceptable.

Chapter 13

POST-LOMBROSIAN DEVELOPMENTS. HEREDITY. TWINS AND GLANDS. THE CRIMINO-BIOLOGICAL SCHOOL

I. POST-LOMBROSIAN DEVELOPMENTS

In the history of criminology there is hardly any chapter more fascinating and thought-provoking than the twentieth-century developments following the death of Lombroso. As already indicated, the influence of his ideas was very different in different countries.[1] Strongest in Italy and South America, weaker in France and Spain, almost completely absent in Russia. In Germany and Austria, after a great deal of original opposition there was a revival, whereas a different historical process took place somewhat later in the United States.[2] In England the two opposing trends are best represented by Havelock Ellis as leader of the pro-Lombrosian party, Charles Goring as his opponent, with Henry Maudsley standing in the middle. Ellis, while not pretending to produce any original material on the subject, made a conscientious and painstaking attempt 'to present to the English reader a critical summary of the results of the science now commonly called criminal anthropology'. In this he was highly successful. By no means uncritical, he opposed Lombroso's use of the concept of atavism; he stressed that there was no uniform 'school' of criminal anthropology and no real type of born criminal, preferring the phrase 'moral insensibility' of the instinctive and habitual criminal.[3] Much of his material is anecdotal and naïve, but he possessed a fairly comprehensive knowledge of the contemporary literature and presented it well. He protests against the accusatorial Anglo-American system of criminal procedure, which heralds 'the barbaric notion of the duel', and asks that on questions of insanity at least two experts should be heard, appointed by the judge. He adopts Ferri's concept of 'social reaction' in the place of punishment and calls for social reforms instead of mere repression, for education 'in the true sense' and for sterilization of the unfit. Like Ellis, Henry Maudsley (1835–1918), the great psychiatrist, was also strongly influenced by the idea of moral insanity as developed earlier in the nineteenth century by James C. Prichard and others.[4] Without completely sub-scribing to Lombroso's theories he believed in the existence of individuals who, because of congenital or acquired characteristics, are entirely lacking in the capacity for moral feeling and for comprehending moral ideas. This condition, however, was not, as Lombroso thought, a morbid entity, a distinct disease, but could arise from a variety of causes. Crime and madness were both 'antisocial products of degeneracy', but crime, he wrote later, was not necessarily a symptom of degeneracy. Similarly to Lombroso, however, he linked epilepsy with physical stigmata of degeneration and with crime.[5]

It is interesting to observe that in spite of many differences in criminological outlook the practical reform programmes of Ellis, Maudsley and Goring bear a striking similarity. All three pin their faith in the triad of better education in the moral sense, segregation of the dangerous criminals, and, at least Ellis and Goring, sterilization of the unfit.

Passing now to Charles B. Goring (1870–1919), he was a solitary figure, belonging to no criminological 'school', but devoting his considerable gifts and energies to the one object of testing and refuting the claims made by Lombroso and his followers. A prison medical officer, a physician with an exceptional mastery of statistical and biometrical techniques, he was appointed by the English Prison Commissioners in 1902 to continue and complete the work begun shortly before by his colleague Dr. Griffiths in Parkhurst Prison. He enjoyed the full support of the Government and the advice of Karl Pearson and his staff at University College, London. The resulting book *The English Convict*,[6] remained, with only a few exceptions, practically unchallenged as the refutation of Lombroso for a quarter of a century until strongly attacked by Hooton in 1939. It was based upon a painstaking biometric examination of 3,000 English convicts. Those measurements were compared internally, i.e. by contrasting the data for different offences, and externally—with a motley group of controls: Oxford and Cambridge undergraduates, inmates of a General Hospital, Royal Engineers, etc. He started with the idea that there existed in every person what he called a 'criminal diathesis', a 'hypothetical character of some kind, a constitutional proclivity', an 'inward potentiality' to commit crime, which if Lombroso's theories were correct, should differ according to physical type. He did find certain physical differences, which were partly related to the type of crime committed—thieves and burglars were smaller in stature than other offenders and also than members of his control groups—and partly to the social class to which the offenders belonged. Accordingly, he arranged his material in four social and seven occupational classes. Among his final conclusions are the following: 'When a sample of criminals and a sample of non-criminals are similarly constructed with regard to the proportional numbers of professional men, shop-keepers, labourers, artisans, etc., . . . criminals, on the average, are seen to be 1·7 inches less in stature than the law-abiding population', and a similar inferiority was shown in body weight. In addition, he found criminals, with the possible exception of those convicted of certain kinds of fraud, to be markedly inferior in intelligence: 'In every class and occupation of life it is feeble mind and the inferior forms of physique which tend to be selected for a criminal career' (p. 261). The following dictum has become rather famous, however: 'From a knowledge only of an undergraduate's cephalic measurements, a better judgment could be given as to whether he were studying at an English or Scottish university than a prediction could be made as to whether he would eventually become a university professor or a convicted felon' (p. 145). Although he found insanity and epilepsy to be more frequent in prison than outside the difference was hardly sufficient to support Lombroso's claims. In the controversy 'heredity or environment', however, he was on Lombroso's side, and perhaps even more than the latter he was inclined to underrate environmental influences: 'Crime is only to a trifling extent (if to any) the product of social inequalities, of adverse environment or of other manifestations of . . . the force of circumstances' (p. 371). To support this theory, he uses, among others, the following strange argument: 'The earlier a child commits a criminal offence and is consequently removed from his home, the more a criminal does he become; and, accordingly, we conclude that criminal proclivities are more bred in the home than inoculated there' (p. 368). Apart from the concept of the criminal type, there were indeed many similarities between Goring and the anthropological school against which he fought.

Hooton, notwithstanding his profound admiration for Goring's 'statistical genius', accused him of a strong preconceived emotional bias against Lombroso's work and even of twisting the results of his investigation to make them conform to his bias. Among other grounds for criticism are the unrepresentative nature of Goring's control groups, the reliance upon insignificantly small coefficients of correlation to prove his points, his crude technique of measuring intelligence, his failure to divide his English convicts according to their social origins. According to Hooton Goring left the problem of the physique of the criminal unsolved.

II. HEREDITY. THE 'CRIMINAL FAMILIES'. TWIN RESEARCH. GLANDS.

(a) Heredity and the Criminal Families

Before continuing our historical sketch of the aftermath of Lombrosianism it seems advisable to deal more specifically with what was, after all, one of its main features: the part played by heredity in the causation of crime. It was the period around the turn of the century when this question was most heatedly discussed. Lombroso himself devoted to it a chapter of his *Crime: its Causes and Remedies*, in which he presented a collection of vague and questionable statistical data purporting to show the frequency of crime, alcoholism, physical illnesses, insanity, suicide and other undesirable features among the ancestors of criminals. American nineteenth-century literature betrays, according to Fink,[7] a strong belief in the inheritance of crime, but disagreement as to what exactly it is that is inherited and how the transmission takes place: is it crime itself or merely a propensity, a predisposition to it? The latter view prevailed and received strong support eventually through the work of William Healy. Strangely enough, it was in the long run also supported by the publication of several books on the so-called 'criminal families'. The first of them, Richard Dugdale's *The Jukes* (1877),[8] the study of a family with a striking number of criminal or otherwise socially deviant members, has often been misinterpreted as if purporting to prove the hereditarian theory. Actually, as pointed out by Fink, Dugdale was anxious to stress the tentative nature of this work and to do justice to both hereditary and environmental influences. Much later, in 1912, two similar studies of criminal pedigrees were published in the U.S.A.: *The Nam Family* by Estabrook and Davenport and Henry H. Goddard's *The Kallikaks*, and Estabrook also published in 1916 a further follow-up study of the Jukes. They were, however, studies of the heredity of feeble-mindedness rather than of crime, and Goddard in particular queried the direct inheritance of criminal tendencies.[9] Family histories of this type are not convincing evidence because the families selected are entirely unrepresentative and because the material collected is incomplete and not tested in accordance with modern scientific methods. At the crucial time when the founders of these families lived, reliable information on their biological constitution was not available, and the research done at some later period could not satisfactorily fill the original gaps. It is therefore mere guesswork to maintain, as Exner does in spite of his critical attitude towards these researches, that the accumulation of criminality in those families was much too long to be explainable by

229

environmental influence alone.[10] Exner agrees, however, that research into the question of heredity can successfully be done not by singling out individual family pedigrees, but only by the collection of statistical material on large numbers of cases. He quotes several German and Austrian investigations of this kind on the frequency of insanity, psychopathy, drunkenness, and criminality among the parents and other relatives of criminals, which show especially for criminality very high percentage figures for the parents of recidivists. Here again, Exner rightly stresses that such figures alone cannot prove the strength of hereditary factors as the children of criminals are, as a rule, naturally exposed to very unfavourable environmental influences. He also quotes, however, an investigation by Kuttner into the criminality of several hundred children and stepchildren of Bavarian preventive detainees which shows that approximately 50 per cent of these children had been convicted whereas the corresponding figures for the stepchildren were much lower. Exner regards this difference as proving the strength of heredity against environment. This conclusion would be justified only if it would be shown that the stepchildren had been under the influence of their stepfathers for as long as the own children of these detainees; moreover, the frequent antagonism between stepfathers and stepchildren will often militate against a willing acceptance by the latter of the criminal habits of the stepfathers and identification with them.

In England, research into the problem of hereditary criminal tendencies has used statistics rather than selected pedigrees. Cyril Burt[11] found major or minor unfavourable congenital factors more than three times as often recorded among delinquent children than among the controls, and in between one third and rather less than one half of the delinquents some 'deep constitutional failing' seemed to be the primary source of the misconduct. Of the hereditary conditions which he lists most are either physical or 'temperamental (with moral symptoms)', fewer are intellectual. His conclusion is that, while the share of innate conditions in the causation of juvenile delinquency is considerable, it would be a gross distortion to regard every criminal as the helpless victim of his inborn nature—a distortion, we may add, which is nowadays hardly ever encountered among responsible writers.

In the next large-scale English study, East's *Adolescent Criminal*, no attempt was made to determine the relative share of endogenous and external factors, but some figures are given to show the connection between inherited and familial defects and the offences committed. A criminal history of the father was recorded in 9 per 1,000 and of the mother in 3 per 1,000 of the Borstal lads, and from both sides in 1·5 per 1,000, and a family history of sexual immorality, epilepsy and insanity in somewhat higher proportions, but there is no material on the question of hereditary transmission,[12] and in a later work the same writer states explicitly that neither this research nor his other experiences have given him any reason to regard criminality 'as such' as transmissible.[13]

(b) Twin Research

Of greater interest than the rather obsolete attempts to trace the pedigrees of criminal families are the more recent researches into the criminal behaviour of twins.[14] Their main value lies in the methodological field. If we compare the life histories of criminals with different hereditary endowment and different environment it will be difficult or even impossible to decide how far their criminal behaviour has been due to the one or to the other. If we should be able, however, to eliminate one set of differences by keeping it constant our task would be easier. If, for example, all hereditary differences could be eliminated it would be clear that any contrasts in the criminal behaviour of the individuals concerned must be due to environmental differences, and, on the other hand, if in spite of such differences their criminal behaviour should be identical then the conclusion would seem inevitable that it is heredity that matters in the causation of crime. Nature, by creating the so-called identical, also called uniovular or monozygotic twins, has apparently provided us with favourable conditions for researches where hereditary differences are eliminated. Whereas dizygotic, also called fraternal, binovular or ordinary, twins come from two separate eggs, which have been simultaneously fertilized, and therefore carry separate sets of genes, monozygotic or identical twins, who are always of the same sex, are born as the result of the splitting of one egg after fertilization and carry the same set of genes. Accordingly, it can be assumed that identical twins have the same hereditary endowment and should provide the ideal material for research into crime causation. It was probably Sir Francis Galton who first recognized that there were two kinds of twins and collected data on a large number, one hundred pairs of twins. In the twentieth century twin research has been done in several countries, including the United States, Soviet Russia, Holland, Japan, Germany[15] and in Britain.[16] While much of it has been unconnected with criminology, there have also been a number of investigations of criminal twins. The first and most widely discussed of them is that by the German psychiatrist Johannes Lange, who examined all male inmates of Bavarian prisons who were twins and also such inmates of the German Psychiatric Institute in Munich who were criminals and twins. Wherever possible, the non-institutionalized twin was traced and physically and mentally examined. In this way, he obtained information on 30 pairs of twins. Of them, 13 pairs were monozygotic, and in 10 of these cases the other twin had also been in prison (which is called 'concordant behaviour'), whereas of the 17 dizygotic pairs the other twin had been imprisoned in only 2 cases. From these figures and from the whole life histories of these twins Lange concluded that, as far as crime is concerned, monozygotic twins on the whole react in a similar manner, whereas dizygotic ones often behave differently ('discordant'), although their upbringing and environment had been just as much alike as those of the monozygotic twins. It is surprising how widely these findings, especially in the years following publication, were accepted as convincing proof of the hereditary nature of crime. Eventually, however, the critical voices have prevailed. Among the objections brought forward against Lange are the following: First, the number of his cases was too small for sweeping generalizations; secondly, some of the cases were taken from a psychiatric clinic, presumably showing some mental abnormality, and their criminal behaviour might therefore have been determined more by this abnormality than by heredity; thirdly, most of the identical twins had been brought up in the same environment, which makes it impossible to say with any certainty how far they had both been likewise affected by this environment and also by each other; thus all the more because of their exceptional likeness in appearance the environmental responses to which they are subjected are probably much more similar than in the case of ordinary twins, who can easily be distinguished;[17] fourthly, the similarities in the behaviour of identical twins observed by Lange are often not at all impressive and could easily occur without the existence of identical heredity—especially as Lange took only imprisonment, not criminality as such, as his criterion; fifthly, in view of the difficulties, pointed out by some biologists, of diagnosing identity in twins,[18] Lange's diagnosis, too, may occasionally have been wrong; sixthly, important congenital differences have been reported even in identical twins, for example congenital syphilis is one of them,[19] which shatters the fundamental assumption of equal heredity; seventhly, it has been argued, for example by Reckless, that if heredity were really the determining factor discordant identical twins should be impossible, whereas Lange's figures showed their existence in three out of thirteen cases.

While later investigations, especially the American one by Rosanoff, have considerably added to the size of Lange's case material and made certain improvements in his methods, some of the criticisms listed above have remained. Ashley Montagu[20] summarizes the five best-known studies as showing together among the identical twins

67·3 per cent concordant and 32·7 per cent discordant behaviour, among the fraternal twins 33·0 per cent concordant and 67·0 per cent discordant behaviour, in other words a considerable minority of discordant cases even among the identical ones. Stumpfl[21] criticizes the superficial way in which Lange dealt with his dizygotic cases and his method of finding concordant behaviour among monozygotic twins in cases where it hardly existed. He estimates that there is discordant behaviour in the latter in 37·40 per cent and in the former in 54·59 per cent, a difference which is far from impressive. He himself tries to give more precise definitions of the concept concordant behaviour by distinguishing degrees of it according to the degree of similarity of criminal activities and in other respects. He stresses that concordant behaviour in identical twins is largely limited to serious criminals with hereditary psychopathic tendencies. For them, he thinks, the hereditary factor is decisive, whereas environmental influences are material only for less serious criminals.[22]

In an investigation of 8 pairs of monozygotic and 16 pairs of dizygotic twins, it was found that only one twin of each pair of monozygotics had committed suicide and that the behaviour of the dizygotics had also been discordant in this respect. It was concluded that suicide could not be simply explained by a certain type of genetic constitution and personality.[23] On the other hand, Kallmann claims not to have found in his researches a single pair of monozygotic twins, reared together or apart, who did not exhibit the same kind of homosexuality, whereas in dizygotics the situation was quite different.[24]

Of an entirely different character is the investigation into behavioural differences of brothers made at the same time by William Healy and Augusta Bronner.[25] Among their material was no pair of identical twins, and the differences in the behaviour of the children from the same families whom they studied—including several pairs of fraternal twins—are entirely traced back to inner stresses in their parental relations from which the delinquent, not however the control cases, suffered. They dismiss Lange's material as proving merely the identical behaviour of mentally abnormal, not of criminal, personalities.

An important contribution to criminological twin research has been made in Japan, where Shûfu Yoshimasu, Professor of Criminal Psychology and Forensic Psychiatry in Tokyo, has published the results of his follow-up studies between 1941 and 1961 of 28 uniovular and 18 binovular pairs.[26] He, too, found far more concordant criminal behaviour in the former than in the latter sample, but it is interesting to note that up to the end of the last war the concordance rates of both groups were much lower than found elsewhere, only 50 per cent for uniovular and 0 per cent for binovular twins. After the war, however, the rates went up to 60·6 per cent and 11·1 per cent respectively, an increase which Yoshimasu relates to the general postwar increase in crime in Japan: if the crime rate for the whole population greatly increases, the likelihood that there will be more crime and therefore concordant criminal behaviour among twins will also increase. Of the other results of this study the observation may be mentioned that most of the criminals among the discordant uniovular twins were first offenders and late starters, whereas almost all the concordant uniovulars committed a crime before the age of 25 and repeated it many times. The author also presents two case histories of uniovular twins separated and brought up in different families soon after birth—thus constituting what he calls, not without justification, the most interesting problem in criminology. In one of these cases the author concludes that both twins, though reared in different families from birth, had 'in the long run the same outcome in criminal career'; one might point out, however, that these twins went to the same elementary school. In the other case, the contrast in social behaviour was profound and could be explained only 'through the striking difference of their environments from the time of birth'. There were also differences in basic personality traits and in health, although both suffered from pulmonary tuberculosis, an illness from which their mother had died when they were 14 years of age. In short, inconclusive as these two case histories are they have the great merit of underlining the immense variety of factors which come together to produce the life history of an individual, a variety which makes the factor 'uni- or bi-ovular' birth almost insignificant as compared with the sum total of all the other happenings in human life.

In conclusion it may be said that the view prevailing thirty years ago in many quarters of the convincing nature of the evidence in favour of heredity produced by the twin researchers has been replaced by sober criticism of their material. They have been able to present only very few cases where, owing to very early separation, environmental influences on identical twins have been so different as to be safely ignored. In fact, most of the twin researchers, notably Lange himself (in spite of the sensational title of his book), and Rosanoff, have frankly admitted that the question 'heredity or environment' is misleading because it over-simplifies a very complex problem. After presenting a model investigation of one pair of identical twins with different life histories Dr. Wheelan concludes by emphasizing 'the difficulties of drawing unequivocal conclusions from twin research'.[27] We are again thrown back to our original question: what is it that can be inherited? Crime as such, it is clear, being not a biological but a legal and social phenomenon, cannot be transmitted by heredity, but can character? 'Environment', writes Martin

Turnell in a reference to Stendhal's *Le Rouge et le Noir*,[28] 'does not determine a man's character, but it does determine his fate.' On the other hand, 'characters are not and cannot be inherited in the sense in which inheritance is used by the geneticist,' says Julian Huxley, 'what are inherited are genes, factors, genetic outfit. Any character whatsoever can only be a resultant between genes and environment . . . the old question whether nature or nurture is the more important is meaningless . . .'[29] This being so, it is hardly surprising that Exner, who among modern textbook-writers has paid particular attention to these problems, concludes his discussion with the not very startling statement that there are individuals who become criminals because of their environment and others who do so because of their heredity.[30] Even less enlightening is the treatment of the matter by Olof Kinberg who, in his *Basic Principles of Criminology*, while maintaining that much knowledge has been accumulated on the way that predispositions are transmitted fails to give any further information.[31] Kretschmer stresses the highly complicated ways in which temperamental traits are transmitted from ancestors to descendants.

The practical significance of the whole controversy lies only in part in the differences in treatment proposed by the followers of the opposing camps. It is clear that the environmentalists will put their faith more in the manipulation of the living conditions of the potential or actual criminal, while the believers in hereditary transmission will recommend eugenic programmes. Perhaps more important than this are the dangers of a fatalistic attitude so easily assumed by members of the public who are always ready to regard an offender as incorrigible because 'it is in his blood'.

(c) *Endocrinology*

Almost simultaneously with Lange's *Crime as Destiny* a book was published in the United States which partly supported and partly contested Lombroso's theories: *The New Criminology* by Schlapp and Smith.[32] In this highly controversial publication it was claimed that individuals suffering from endocrine disturbances were the typical born criminals 'with their destiny largely determined'. It is interesting that the authors used this theory in order to explain what was at that time regarded as an indisputable fact, i.e. the particularly high crime rate among the first American born generation of foreign immigrants: they believed to have found the cause in glandular disturbances of the mothers who, on their voyage and after arrival in the foreign country, had to undergo a period of great physical and mental strain coupled with economic worries and transmitted the resulting glandular imbalance to their next-born children. The difference between this theory and that of Lombroso is that, while emphasizing the overwhelming importance of the inheritance of physical, especially endocrinological factors in the causation of crime, these authors did not regard hereditary endowment as unchangeable. The same immigrant mother might a few years later, with improved living conditions, give birth to a healthy child. This theory offers, therefore, a convenient explanation of the fact that so often only one child of a family becomes a criminal. Moreover, while Lombroso had no medical cure for unfavourable hereditary factors the endocrinologists regard a cure as possible, although some of them are more optimistic than others. Many cases of endocrine disturbances are not due to inheritance at all.[33] Apart from the special case of certain sex offenders, the prevailing view explains the possible connection between glandular imbalance and criminal conduct as an indirect, psychological, one in that the feeling of abnormality and inadequacy caused by disorders of the pituitary or other glands may give rise to aggressiveness and other compensatory emotional reactions leading to crime.[34] Especially in cases of sex offenders hormone treatment is sometimes believed to be successful. In this country it has been cautiously advocated, mainly by Golla and Hodge.[35]

III. THE MODERN CRIMINO-BIOLOGICAL SCHOOL

This school originated in the nineteen-twenties in Germany, Austria and Italy. Its scientific value has at times greatly suffered from the exaggerated claims made on its behalf by the totalitarian regimes at the time in power in these countries. Its leading ideas and literature can best be studied in the writings of one of its most prominent legal exponents, Eduard Mezger,[36] and of the famous German psychiatrist Ernst Kretschmer. It is the latter in particular who has done the fundamental typological spadework on which the whole structure of that school has been erected. In his book *Körperbau and Charakter* which, slowly expanded over a period of more than thirty years and running into more than twenty editions, has become one of the international classics of psychiatry, he did not at the outset deal with criminological problems, and in the English translation of 1936 there is only one insignificant reference to criminals.[37] In contrast, the most recent German editions contain a full-sized chapter on 'constitution and crime'.[38] Kretschmer's original object was to examine the complex relationships between the various types of physique, character and mental abnormality. He distinguished three major constitutional types which, as he stressed, were not 'ideal types' but empirical ones:

(a) the *leptosome* or *asthenic* type, characterized by long and thin limbs, narrow shoulders, lean arms with under-developed muscles and

236

by a tendency to premature ageing. 'In extreme cases,' Kretschmer writes, 'I found men of between 35 and 40 years already quite senile.' While the term leptosome is used for the whole range covered by this type, the term asthenic is reserved for the more extreme cases approaching the morbid. Leptosomes are frigid, reserved, unsociable and cold.

(b) the *athletic* type, roughly the opposite of the first, with strongly developed skeleton and musculature. To describe their temperament, Kretschmer uses the term '*viscös*', which he defines as stable, heavy, not nervous, but occasionally explosive.[39]

(c) the *pyknic* type, small and round, with a pronounced development of the body cavities and a tendency to a distribution of fat around the trunk. They are friendly and sociable.

Mixed types he regarded as very frequent.

In addition, he established a number of so-called 'dysplastic' special types, the members of which differed greatly from any of the three main types and were characterized in particular by certain glandular disturbances.[40]

In working out this typology, which is here only very roughly reproduced, Kretschmer tried to take account of every single feature of the biological personality instead of limiting himself to a comparatively few selected characteristics. He stressed that his three main types were meant to be '*wertfrei*', i.e. neither 'normal' nor 'abnormal' in the usual sense, but normal in that they referred to the most frequently met anthropological phenomena and abnormal in that they reflected certain dispositions towards potential pathological conditions.[41] His next step was to see whether there was a clear relation between these constitutional types and specific forms of mental disease or at least dispositions towards them. His answer was in the affirmative, i.e. he found a strong positive correlation, a biological affinity between leptosomes, athletics and certain dysplastics, on the one hand, and schizophrenia on the other, and also between the pyknic type and manic-depressive, circular forms of insanity. There was very little affinity between the pyknic type and schizophrenia or between the leptosomes and athletics and manic-depressive insanity.[42] Kretschmer quotes statistical material for several thousand cases to prove these correlations, which have by now been commonly accepted.

The scope of Kretschmer's theory is however not limited to the relation between biological constitution and the various forms of mental illness. As already indicated, he regards the two forms of psychosis with which he is mainly concerned only as extreme forms of psychological dispositions, traces of which can also be found in normal individuals. The great masses of normal human beings constitute reservoirs from which these two forms of psychosis are recruited. He calls the members of that large constitutional class who, *if* they should ever become insane, are most likely to develop schizophrenia *schizothymes* and those normal people who, *if* they should become insane, are likely to become manic-depressive *cyclothymes*.[43] And, finally, there is a third pair of types, the *schizoids* and the *cycloids*, consisting of individuals who stand between health and sickness and exhibit the psychological symptoms of the corresponding abnormal types to a slighter degree.[44] Kretschmer offers a wealth of psychological observations and some case material to characterize these two intermediate types. They are sometimes related to the Jungian typology as the schizoids are extreme introverts and the cycloids extreme extraverts.[45]

The final task is now to relate these Kretschmerian types to different forms of criminality. On this, a considerable literature has grown up, mainly in the Continental countries primarily devoted to Kretschmer's typology and the ideas of the crimino-biological school,[46] and Kretschmer himself has now dealt with the matter fairly fully on the basis of material derived from 4,414 cases. He stresses from the outset that the kind and gravity of social failure are no necessary indication of the abnormality of personality structure, which latter has to be measured according to entirely different yardsticks, such as physical constitution and heredity. He also points out that a person may be a serious psychopath 'in the sociological sense' without possessing a seriously morbid constitution and heredity. Legal concepts such as 'murderer' cannot be taken as the starting point for the formation of constitutional and hereditary typology; they cannot show any specific physical characteristics. All we can say in this respect is that certain groups of serious habitual criminals show the signs of serious hereditary degeneration and a higher proportion of dysplastics than the normal population. These dysplastic abnormalities of criminals are, however, not exclusively peculiar to them, but can also be found in mental defectives and serious hereditary illnesses. This higher proportion of dysplastic abnormalities is not to be found among criminals in general, but only among serious habituals—a fact which Kretschmer thinks is difficult to reconcile with Lombroso's doctrine of the accumulation of physical stigmata. Here Kretschmer seems to forget that Lombroso, too, restricted his theory of the stigmata to one type, the born criminal.

The most important points in Kretschmer's system of criminal biology are these: On the whole, criminals show roughly the same proportional distribution of constitutional types as the general population, i.e. approximately 20 per cent pyknics, 40–50 per cent leptosomes and athletics, 5–10 per cent dysplastics, and less than

30 per cent mixed types, except that there are somewhat fewer pyknics among criminals than among the whole population. Pyknics are socially better adaptable, their criminality begins later, and they recidivate much less than the other types. The 'life curve' of criminality of leptosomes has its peak very early, that of pyknics has it very late, between 40 and 50, when that of the leptosomes is already very low. Athletics show a fairly stable degree of criminality up to the age of 55. Regarding the offences committed by members of the different types, the leptosomes are very strongly represented among thieves and swindlers, athletics among offences against the person, sexual and others. Pyknics tend to commit frauds, dysplastics commit sexual offences. Throughout it has to be borne in mind, however, that even if members of different constitutional types commit crimes of the same legal classification, for example murder, the criminological characteristics of that crime would be entirely different in accordance with their different biological and temperamental features.[47] Mezger, while quoting further material in support of Kretschmer's theory, points out[48] that the claims of the crimino-biological school are much more modest than those of Lombroso: one does no longer pretend to be able to predict whether an individual will become a criminal, but only which forms his criminal activities are likely to assume *if* he should become one. The latter question can, he admits, often not be answered on the strength of the individual's biological constitution regardless of environmental factors. Even with such reservations, however, it can hardly be denied that the work of the Continental boards of crimino-biological investigation, established in the nineteen-twenties in order to draw the practical conclusions from the theoretical studies of this school, placed the emphasis mainly on the biological aspects of crime.[49] The same was true of the Crimino-Biological Society, founded in 1927 by Adolf Lenz in Graz, whose work has, however, in recent years been placed on a more comprehensive basis.[50] One of the most important criticisms voiced against the work of the boards and of the Society was that the theory of the likely incorrigibility of offenders of the leptosome and athletic types was insufficiently supported by the available scientific facts and could easily lead to a sterile and reactionary system of penal administration,[51] a danger which became soon reality under the Nazi regime.

While the crimino-biological school had practically no following in Britain, its ideas aroused much interest in the United States. It is doubtful, though, how far Earnest Hooton[52] was influenced by them as his published work shows no awareness of post-Goring developments. His major opus, *The American Criminal*, of which he could complete only the first volume, has been so widely criticized that it is hardly worth while to summarize it.[53] His principal findings were that criminals were biologically inferior and that their inferiority was largely hereditary.

Far more influential have been the writings of William H. Sheldon, especially his *Varieties of Delinquent Youth*,[54] whose classification and technique of somatotyping have been accepted, among others, by the Gluecks (see below). There exists a clear connection between Sheldon and Kretschmer, the former acknowledging a certain indebtedness to Kretschmer, whose work he studied on the spot, and the latter referring repeatedly and approvingly to Sheldon's typology—if it can be called a typology at all—which, he thinks, has reached essentially similar results from a different methodological angle.[55] Sheldon's main criticism of Kretschmer is that the latter was satisfied with mere verbal descriptions of his somatotypes and disliked the idea of making his descriptions more exact by quantification.

Sheldon's very complicated terminology[56] differs from that of Kretschmer. Instead of leptosomes he speaks of ectomorphs, instead of athletics of mesomorphs, and instead of pyknics of endomorphs. Their physical characteristics are, however, essentially the same as those described by Kretschmer. He uses a statistical technique which enables him to describe the constitution of an individual by using a 3-digit number indicating the strength of each of those three components, with 1 as the minimum and 7 as the maximum. An extreme mesomorph, for example, would be described as 1–7–1, an extreme ectomorph as 1–1–7. The term dysplastic is used differently from Kretschmer to describe disharmonious mixtures of the three components in different parts of the body. Sheldon used his classification for a minute morphological description of two hundred delinquent boys from the Hayden Goodwill Inn, a rehabilitation home in Boston. They showed a preponderance of mesomorphs and very few ectomorphs, with the endomorph type standing between. A previously collected group of 4,000 college boys showed a more balanced distribution between mesomorphs and ectomorphs. Sheldon tries, as Kretschmer did, to relate his somatotypes to temperamental and psychiatric types, for which relationships he has coined several odd-sounding terms. This part of his investigation, too, shows results very similar to those of Kretschmer. His work has been widely criticized, most vehemently by Sutherland who regards it as useless.[57] His technique of somatotyping has, however, been widely accepted by research workers of various disciplines. Especially his careful collection of standardized photographs of each subject in his series has been useful, and he himself described the omission of this technique in Hooton's study as 'criminal' since no measurements and verbal descriptions of physical types could be a substitute for photographs.[58] As far as criminological research is concerned, his influence has been mainly indirect, through the adoption of his basic ideas and typology by the Gluecks.

The Gluecks had made use of Sheldon's somatotypes already in their *Unraveling Juvenile Delinquency*, when each boy in their series was photographed in accordance with Sheldon's technique.[59] Appendix C of that book consists of a very detailed study by a physical anthropologist, Dr. Carl C. Seltzer, of the morphological characteristics of the 500 delinquents and the 500 non-delinquents in the series, showing—as in Sheldon's own work—an excess of mesomorphs and a deficiency of ectomorphs and extreme endomorphs among the delinquents. These findings provide the starting point for the subsequent study *Physique and Delinquency*,[60] not, as the authors are careful to point out, because of any belief in the preponderant criminogenic role of the bodily structure, but only as one of several studies to follow up the results of *Unraveling*. One of these findings was that 60 per cent of the delinquent boys were mesomorphs against only 30 per cent in the control group. It was, however, an isolated discovery not related to the other findings regarding the two groups. An attempt was therefore made in the second study to search for certain syndromes by correlating various other factors to Sheldon's somatotypes. Correlations were worked out between the latter and a selection of sixty-seven traits and forty-two socio-cultural factors to compare the delinquent and non-delinquent groups. The technique used is to show, first, the statistical significance of a trait or factor in the total group of delinquents as compared with the total group of non-delinquents and, secondly, the same for each somatotype separately. The object was to see which trait or factor had a stronger or weaker influence on the delinquency of one somatotype than on that of another. The results are very complicated and not always revealing. Only a minority of the traits and factors thus examined were found to vary in their relationships to the different somatotypes. To give but one example of difference in these relationships, the factors 'broken home' and 'incompatibility of parents' were found to distinguish more sharply between delinquents and non-delinquents of the sensitive ectomorph type than in the other somatotypes. In the view of the authors, the material thus collected seems to explain the higher delinquency potential of the mesomorphs and also which particular traits or factors are likely to make them actual delinquents. On the other hand, unfavourable socio-cultural factors seem to produce delinquency in mesomorphs less often than they do in the other somatotypes. The final conclusion is, however, that there is no specific combination of physique, character and temperament to be found which would determine whether an individual becomes a delinquent.

PSYCHOLOGICAL AND PSYCHIATRIC
ASPECTS OF CRIME

Chapter 14

MENTAL DISORDERS I: PSYCHOSES,
ALCOHOLISM AND DRUG ADDICTION

When dealing with the psychological and psychiatric aspects of crime it seems advisable to take a course which may seem contrary to common sense and natural expectation, i.e. to begin with the psychiatric, pathological part of the subject and to leave the psychology of the normal lawbreaker to the end. Our justification lies in the regrettable fact that the concept of mental health is so very difficult to define[1] and that it is therefore largely limited to what remains after deducting all those cases where mental ill health is generally assumed. This, as should be stressed already now, does not mean that we regard the pathological section of offenders as numerically stronger than the normal one—the opposite is true. Within the field of the pathological, we shall also deal first with the most seriously abnormal group, that of the psychotics, and proceed from there via the less extreme groups of neurotics and psychopaths to the mental defectives, of whom there are many classes of varying degree of abnormality. This procedure is, of course, again the reverse of the statistical picture since cases of psychosis are very rare among the general population as well as among criminals, whilst neuroses and psychopathic states are more frequent and the great majority of criminals can be regarded as mentally normal.

Our presentation of the subject, which has to be made from the point of view of the interested and, to some extent, informed psychiatric layman, has to overcome certain formidable obstacles arising from the existing lack of a generally accepted terminology and from the innumerable controversies encountered in present psychiatric literature.[2] The Royal Commission on the Law relating to Mental Illness and Mental Deficiency 1954–7, which reported in 1957,[3] and, following its recommendations, the Mental Health Act, 1959, s. 4, have tried to bring order into the existing confusion. The Act, avoiding the discredited word 'insanity', introduces the general term 'mental disorder' to cover 'mental illness, arrested or incomplete development of mind, psychopathic disorder, and any other disorder or disability of mind'. It is clear from the Act and, in particular, from the report of the Royal Commission that the term 'mental illness' is here used in a much narrower sense than 'mental disorder' and that it is largely confined to the various forms of psychosis. It is further clear that the Act upholds the previous distinction between insanity and mental deficiency by defining the latter as a state of 'arrested or incomplete development of mind', whereas it is the characteristic of mental illness (insanity or psychosis) that it occurs in persons 'whose minds have previously functioned normally and have become affected by some disorder, usually in adult life'.[4] It goes without saying that a mentally defective person may also develop a form of mental illness.

We have now to give a brief survey of the various forms of *mental illness* in relation to crime. The classification used is in all essentials similar to that in the well-known psychiatric standard works,[5] but the reader has to bear in mind that there is frequent disagreement between psychiatrists with regard to the details. The essential feature of this classification is the distinction between those forms of psychosis which are of an organic origin and those which are functional, i.e. not due to any physical illness.

I. ORGANIC PSYCHOSES

For our purposes the most important organic psychoses are the general paralysis of the insane (or dementia paralytica), due to syphilitic infection, encephalitis lethargica, traumatic psychoses caused by accidents, the various forms of intoxication and senile dementia.[6]

(a) *The general paralysis of the insane*[7] is characterized by a progressive deterioration of the whole personality. In its initial stages criminal acts such as thefts, frauds, forgeries, may be committed with astonishing openness and silliness. In a case reported by East the accused had carried away some table knives in the presence of several witnesses; in another case he had smashed a window and waited to be arrested. In the later stages of the illness the patient is usually confined in an institution where his opportunities to commit offences are very limited.

In this as in other forms of psychosis the offences are nearly always committed without accomplices as the psychotic is too deeply withdrawn into his own world to wish to enlist, and too abnormal in his behaviour to attract, associates.

(b) *Traumatic psychoses* due to injuries to the brain caused by accidents, may also produce profound personality changes leading to criminality and/or vagabondage and may make the injured person particularly susceptible to the effect of alcohol.[8] The so-called Korsakoff syndrome may be present in such cases.[9] Patients may easily become excited and prone to crimes of violence. The case has been reported[10] of a child of eight who breaks his skull and receives a serious concussion. The consequence was feeble-mindedness coupled with persistent criminal tendencies, but twenty years later another complete change occurs and his behaviour becomes again normal.

(c) A form of organic psychosis which was particularly frequent among children in this country after the First World War is *encephalitis lethargica*, popularly called sleepy sickness.[11] It is an acute infectious fever producing an inflammation of the brain, usually followed by serious and lasting after-effects and changes in physique, intelligence and character. 'The younger the patient the more likely is it that he will develop disagreeable anomalies of personality.... Many children and adolescents after their acute attack become social problems...' (Mapother and Lewis).[12] Highly anti-social acts, often of an explosive or sexual nature, may easily happen in the post-encephalitic period.

(d) *Senile dementia*[13] is another organic form of mental illness. East[14] and others distinguish between senile and arteriosclerotic dementia, but the difference is not clear and there is said to be an occasional overlap of symptoms. The impairment of the physical and mental faculties, emotional disturbances and the loss of control over sexual urges, coupled with growing suspicion of other people, may provoke acts of violence or sexual assaults on children. The nature of the crimes committed may vary according to whether the dementia takes a depressive, manic or paranoid form.[15] In a case quoted by East a man of sixty-eight killed his wife under the delusion that she had incestuous relation with her son and was pregnant. Silly acts of petty theft may also occur, as in the case of a company director of means and excellent character who stole three eggs from a shop.[16]

(e) While encephalitis lethargica affects the young and senile dementia the old, *puerperal insanity* is the illness of the pregnant and post-pregnant mother. It is a form of exhaustion psychosis occurring in women in a condition of extreme anxiety due, for example, to the birth of an illegitimate child, economic stress plus physical fatigue.[17] English law has a special provision for such cases, the Infanticide Act, 1938, which provides that when a woman by any wilful act or omission causes the death of her child, being a child under the age of twelve months, but at the time of the act or omission the balance of her mind was disturbed by reason of her not having fully recovered from the effect of giving birth to the child, or by reason of the effect of lactation consequent upon the birth of the child, then she is treated as being guilty not of murder but of infanticide and punishable for manslaughter.[18] Apart from child-killing, other offences, such as theft, may also be committed by women suffering from this form of transitory psychosis.

(*f*) *Epilepsy*, one of the most widely known types of mental disorder, is at the same time among the most difficult ones to grasp, not only for the layman but apparently for the specialist, too.[19] Because of the different forms which it can assume many psychiatrists refer to 'epilepsies' rather than to epilepsy. The attention of criminologists was drawn to it mainly by Lombroso who exaggerated its criminological significance by maintaining that all born criminals were epileptics and that among occasional criminals there was at least one class, the epileptoids, in whom a trace of epilepsy was the origin of their criminal tendencies.[20] Actually, reliable estimates of the frequency of epilepsy among criminals are very difficult to obtain, and most of the more recent ones are very low,[21] partly perhaps because of the great difficulties often encountered in the diagnosis of this illness. The electro-encephalogram (E.E.G.) has somewhat reduced, but by no means resolved these difficulties since 'some persons who are clinically known to be epileptic do not show the characteristic E.E.G. abnormality and its absence does not therefore conclusively disprove the absence of epilepsy'. This was the conclusion of the Royal Commission on Capital Punishment, following the evidence of Dr. Denis Hill.[22] The latter has also stressed that abnormal E.E.G.s are found in only 60–70 per cent of epileptics and that, while the E.E.G. is a most valuable diagnostic aid, taken alone it can provide proof of epilepsy in only 15–20 per cent of all cases.[23] If it is often difficult, therefore, to diagnose epilepsy, evidence that a crime is actually caused by it is sometimes also not easy to obtain.[24] It is commonly believed, however, that epileptics are prone to sudden outbreaks of apparently motiveless violence and to develop strongly anti-social attitudes. In fact, the feeling of the epileptic to be at a permanent disadvantage in his employment and in many other ways, which is likely to have a depressing and irritating effect on him, may be responsible.[25] Apart from this, it is mainly the so-called epileptic equivalents, i.e. states of delirium, unconsciousness and epileptic furor, or post-epileptic automatism, in which crimes are committed. In post-epileptic automatism originally harmless actions may be continued, for example cutting sandwiches, which had begun before the fit, but are now carried on in such a way as to injure other persons.[26]

With the ever-increasing volume of motor traffic the epileptic motorist who endangers the life and health of others is becoming a real problem. Not long ago a man aged 39, charged with causing the death of two others by dangerous driving, was found not guilty at Stafford Assizes because since the age of ten he had been suffering from epilepsy and committed the offence in a state of automatism during an attack of *petit mal* with a total loss of reasoning. It was stated on his behalf that he had never been told by his doctors that he was an epileptic and should not drive. All the court could do was to send a request to the licensing authority that his licence should be withdrawn.[27] This ignorance of the nature of his illness had saved him from punishment. In similar cases of traffic accidents reported by Brousseau in his valuable paper on the subject[28] this excuse was not available. Brousseau also draws attention to the grave danger of acts of violence being committed during the periods of a few hours to two or three days preceding the *paroxysme épileptique* with their profound changes in the temper, character and conduct of the patient.

Sleep-walking and the so-called 'blackout' may also be forms of epileptic automatism.[29]

In the much discussed case of Lees-Smith in 1943, hypoglycaemia (abnormally low blood sugar content) was believed to be an important factor in the killing of his mother by an epileptic. Before the act he had taken four pints of mild beer, but was in no state of drunkenness; the same quantity of water would, it was stated, have had the same effect of producing an abnormal state of mind.[30]

In the state of so-called epileptic Fugue patients may become disorientated, wander about aimlessly for long periods and commit minor offences.

(*g*) *Intoxication psychosis, especially alcoholic disorders.* As morphinism, cocainism and similar forms of intoxication[31] are not very frequent in this country,[32] we are first concentrating on alcoholism.[33] The part played by alcoholic intoxication as a potential cause of crime has for many years been a favourite subject in criminology, but drink has important social as well as psychological and psychiatric causes and consequences, and only comparatively few cases of alcoholic intoxication lead to a psychosis. It seems to be advisable, however, to deal with the whole subject—including some of its social aspects—briefly in this chapter. There is no suggestion, of course, that drunkenness invariably produces a psychosis, see below (*cc*). The following questions have to be asked: (*aa*) How far is drunkenness itself an offence? (*bb*) How far is it a cause of crime? (*cc*) What is its psychiatric significance? (*dd*) How does the criminal law deal with crimes committed in the various stages of drunkenness? This last question will be dealt with later in Chapter 18 in connection with our discussion of the other legal problems of mental illness.

(*aa*) According to the Licensing Act of 1872, every person found drunk in a highway or other public place, or on licensed premises, is punishable with a fine up to 40s. This is the non-indictable offence of so-called simple drunkenness. Moreover, every person guilty while drunk of riotous or disorderly behaviour in a highway or public place, or who is drunk and in charge of any carriage or of a child, etc., is punishable either by a fine of up to 40s. or by imprisonment up to one month or, in certain cases, for a longer period. This is the offence of drunkenness with aggravations. Drunkenness as such is, therefore, not an offence. Taken as a whole, the number of such convictions has gone down very markedly in this country in the present century, from an annual average of about 200–220,000 to roughly one quarter.[34] However, there has been a steep upward movement, in the past twenty years, especially among young people, and in 1962 the number was over 80,000, or, according to *The Times* fo 9.5.1963, even 92,000, where the results of the Licensing Act of 1961 have been called disastrous. Convictions per 10,000 males aged 14 to 16 in England and Wales increased from 1·5 in 1946 to 4·0 in 1954.[35] Penalties have changed, too. In the *Annual Report of the Prison Commissioners for 1919* we read: 'It is almost inconceivable that fifteen years ago 70,000 persons were committed to prison on a charge of drunkenness . . . The numbers committed last year were actually no more than 671 males and 999 females.' In 1959, 963 persons were committed to prison without the option of a fine. On the sex ratio of convictions and prison sentences something will have to be said later in Chapter 26, II(3).

Local differences in the frequency of these convictions are often very considerable, but it is doubtful how far they are due to real differences in the drunkenness rate and how far merely to different police methods.[36] Apart from this difficulty of making local comparisons, it is certain, however, that the decline in convictions reflects a real fall in drunkenness in this country, due to a great variety of reasons, such as changes in drinking habits brought about by the world wars, by higher social and educational standards reached by the great masses, changes in licensing hours, the higher price of alcoholic drinks, their weaker alcohol content, the habit of drinking in closed clubs, etc., and especially the availability of other media of mass entertainment, such as cinema, radio and television.

(*bb*) Of greater interest than the number of these minor drunkenness offences is the question how far drunkenness has to be regarded as a cause of other, possibly much more serious, offences.[37] The official *Criminal Statistics* gives no information on this subject, although the previous system, under which in the case of several convictions for different offences only the offence was tabulated in our *Criminal Statistics* for which the heaviest punishment was awarded, has now been given up for cases where a person is convicted for an indictable and a non-indictable offence.[38] While this means that the recording of drunkenness offences is now less incomplete than before, even the present system gives no indication of how often drunkenness offences are committed together with other offences—a gap which is filled by the *Licensing Statistics*. Table VI. A mere coincidence of this kind, however, does not imply cause and effect, and it has to be borne in mind that it is not the object of statistical tables to indicate causal relations. The proportion of these other offences is small, between 3 and 5 per cent of drunkenness offences for men and around 2 per cent for women. Most of them are likely to be of a less serious character as in the case of serious crimes there will hardly be a separate charge for drunkenness. Views on the criminogenic effect of drink differ greatly according to time, place and the type of offence. For the various forms of non-indictable assault, for example, the decline from an annual average of 55,000 in 1900–9 to 18,000 in 1938 and about 16,000 in 1962 can be explained by the fall in drunkenness.[39]

Far more complex is the relationship between drink and motoring offences. For the successful execution of payroll, mail or bank robberies and similar carefully planned crimes abstention from alcohol is almost essential, and alcoholic members of the gang will soon be got rid of as unsuitable by their colleagues. Of greater interest in the present connection is the offence of driving under the influence of drink or drug. Convictions for it number about 5,000 per year. Road accidents attributed to drivers under the influence of alcohol are regarded as responsible for about 500 deaths and 2,000–3,000 injuries annually.[40] In the view of an experienced Chief Constable, the task of proving this offence is so difficult that the prospect of a conviction has become too remote to act as a deterrent.[41] In other countries the tests for drunkenness are said to be much stricter,[42] and the penalties more severe. The matter is at present under active consideration in this country.

With regard to homicide, Wolfgang made a detailed study of the relationship between alcohol and his Philadelphia sample, regretting the absence of a record in the police files of the amount of alcohol in the blood, liver, brain or urine of the offender and his victim.[43] The files contained sufficient information, however, to record whether either of them had been drinking directly before the crime and whether the drinking had been excessive and over a prolonged period. He found that in 36 per cent of his 588 cases alcohol had been entirely absent; in 44 per cent it had been present in both the offender and the victim, and in the remaining 20 per cent either in the one or in the other. A number of other correlations were worked out, and a review of the literature is given. The part played by drunkenness of the victim has been frequently discussed by other writers, too.[44]

Dr. Glatt, a psychiatrist specializing in the treatment of alcoholics, has made a study of the relationship between alcoholism and crime in this country.[45] His material shows that, while the great majority of alcoholics do not get into serious conflicts with the law, inebriety by releasing aggressive tendencies is a contributing factor to crime in a substantial minority of cases. This estimate is borne out by a number of studies. In certain other countries, notably Sweden and Finland, the part played by drink is more important. Veli Verkkö (Note 33) has shown that in his country the connection between crimes of violence and alcohol is very close; he concludes: 'a feature of the Finnish national character is the Finn's poor capacity to hold his liquor', trying to explain this characteristic by reference to Kretschmer's theory of the 'viscous' temperament of the athletic type common in Finland.[46]

The criminality of the children of alcoholic parents, too, has often been discussed. Burt found parental alcoholism to be three times as frequent among his delinquents as among his control group, but he rightly stresses that its effect on descendants may be environmental as well as hereditary.[47] In Dr. Young's series of 2,217 consecutive cases of youths aged 16 to 21 in Wormwood Scrubs Prison parental drunkenness occurred only in 4·51 per cent of the cases.[48] Norwood East found little definite evidence in his group of Borstal boys that the offspring of drunkards are themselves predisposed to become alcoholics, but he regards alcoholism as an indication of a psychopathic inheritance.[49] Case histories of notorious criminals often contain references to alcoholism of the father,[50] but most of them are unchecked.

(*cc*) Passing now to the psychological and psychiatric significance of drink, we have to distinguish between different types of drinking, with very different psychological origins and effects and possibly also different criminological consequences. First, as Exner, Verkkö, Howard Jones and other writers have pointed out and as every traveller in foreign lands can easily discover for himself through personal observation, the consumption of alcohol and alcoholism do not have the same meaning everywhere. 'The alcohol addict in France may be a psychologically more normal person, and the Jew who becomes an alcoholic is likely to be even more deviant than his counterpart in Anglo-Saxon culture' (Jones, p. 155). Secondly, even within the same culture one has to distinguish between the mere drunkard who 'still has the ability to decide for himself at what times he will drink and how much he will take at any particular time' and the true alcoholic addict who has no such freedom of choice any more. According to Howard Jones, there were an estimated number of over 350,000 such addicts in England and Wales in 1961.[51]

From the psychiatric and criminological points of view, three types may have to be distinguished: First, the normal type of drunkenness which occurs from time to time in the average, healthy person and may produce a transitory form of dementia, leading to more or less serious disturbances of the physical and mental capacities of the individual. Crimes of violence, though usually not very serious in character, sexual offences, arson or malicious damage may occasionally be the result. The second, less common but potentially more dangerous, type is the so-called pathological drunkenness occurring in mentally unstable persons, people who have suffered some head injury or heatstroke or who are epileptics or mental defectives, psychopaths or psychotics. Such persons may become violent even under the influence of very small doses of alcohol.[52] The third group is that of chronic alcoholism which may lead to delirium tremens with its hallucinations—there is here an overlap with paranoia (see below)—sleeplessness and over-excitement. 'There is usually a state of extreme terror, and assaults on persons entering the room are not infrequent.'[53] Suspicions of marital infidelity may result in murder or suicide.

II. FUNCTIONAL PSYCHOSES

The most important forms of functional psychosis are paranoia and paraphrenia, schizophrenia and manic-depressive psychosis.

(a) The characteristics of *paranoia*[54]—in many ways highly controversial—are well systematized and unshakable delusions with little or no visible impairment of other mental functions, and no definite external factor such as alcohol present. The alcoholic psychosis is thereby excluded from this narrow definition which roughly conforms to that given by Emil Kraepelin, the great nineteenth-century psychiatrist on whose researches the original conception of paranoia was mainly based.[55] Other writers have expressed doubts as to whether it is worth while to retain so narrow a syndrome as an independent unit, especially as some of the cases previously regarded as paranoic are now brought under the umbrella of schizophrenia. In forensic psychiatry, however, the concept of paranoia, though usually interpreted in a somewhat broader sense than by the followers of Kraepelin, continues to play an important role, especially in murder cases. In modern writings on the subject the importance of environmental factors in the aetiology of criminal paranoia has been underlined, in particular by Milner who points out that it may sometimes be a reaction to, and indeed the only escape from, an intolerable and seemingly inescapable situation and that the further removed a case of paranoia is from the schizophrenic syndrome the more obvious is the

250

role of such external factors.[56] Among the various forms of paranoia are the persecution and the religious forms, according to the contents of the delusions. The sufferer may imagine himself to be so mercilessly persecuted by his enemies that the only way out is to kill them in self-defence, or he may be so firmly convinced of the misery of this world that it is his religious duty to kill his whole family. In other cases the main feature is extreme quarrelsomeness leading to interminable, costly and hopeless lawsuits, or amorous delusions resulting in very inappropriate attempts at one-sided courtship and love-making.[57] Another well-known symptom complex in paranoid and schizophrenic disorders is morbid jealousy with delusions of marital infidelity, but it may also occur in neurotic, non-psychotic, cases.[58]

Paraphrenia is closely related to paranoia, the difference being that the delusions are less completely systematized and any crimes committed by the paraphrenic may be unplanned sudden reactions to hallucinations.[59]

(b) The characteristic feature of the *manic-depressive psychosis*,[60] a form of affective disorder, is the alternating of moods of elation and excitement (periods of mania) and of depression and melancholia. Each phase may last for days or weeks or even longer, and there may be periods of apparent normality occurring between them. Kretschmer's view that manic-depressives usually belong to the pyknic somatotype and that their criminality is usually less serious has been mentioned before (Chapter 13, III). Crimes, especially of violence, and suicide will occur mainly in the depressive phase, whereas in the manic phase petty stealing, swindling and drunkenness offences are more frequent.[61] Most homicidal attacks are made on members of the sufferer's own family for reasons basically similar to those of the religious paranoiac. In 1941, a professor of linguistics was charged at the Central Criminal Court in London with the murder of his wife and found guilty but insane, suffering from manic-depressive insanity. He had been under the impression that he could no longer cope with his work and rather than expect his wife to face what he thought to be a bleak future he had decided to kill her.[62] Particularly severe attacks of depression and agitation occur in cases of so-called involutional melancholia, especially in women at or after the menopause and, though less often, in men in their fifties.[63] In 1937, a woman of 44 was charged, also at the Central Criminal Court, with the murder of her daughter, aged 15, and found guilty but insane, suffering from involutional melancholia. Because the daughter, who had otherwise done well at school, had failed in an examination owing to ill health, the mother had decided to strangle her.[64] Several other cases of crimes due to depression have been reported by Dr.

G. M. Woddis, with special reference to the preventative role of psychiatry and the possibility of predicting the development of homicidal tendencies in such persons.[65] The same author has found among 91 offenders examined by him 14 cases of reactive and 15 cases of endogenous depression, of whom 14 cases were cases of murder.[66]

(c) *Schizophrenia*[67] is generally regarded in forensic psychiatry as the most frequent and important form of functional psychosis.[68] Kraepelin called it *dementia praecox*, regarding its onset in adolescence and its inevitable termination in complete dementia as essential features. Since the writings of E. Bleuler, the Swiss psychiatrist, in the early decades of the present century the term schizophrenia, popularly called split-mindedness, has superseded the older one,[69] but the nature and causes of this illness are still controversial. While Kraepelin, Kretschmer, Lange, Mapother-Lewis and many others stress its constitutional and heredity character,[70] the opposite view of a psychic origin has also strong support. Endocrine disturbances have been held responsible, too. The essential features are a complete withdrawal of the patient's personality into himself ('shut-in' type) with a progressive deterioration and disorder of thought, emotions and conduct, flight into phantasy life, defects of judgment, peculiar mannerisms, delusions and hallucinations. 'Thinking is incoherent, rambling and jumbled. He brings together the most far-fetched topics . . . The usual logical sequences are ignored . . .'[71] Contact with reality is eventually completely lost. 'Often the patient complains that people work on his mind, hypnotize him, influence him for his own good, set about to drive him mad or ruin him.'[72] In most cases the illness begins between the ages of 15 and 25, but it has been argued, by Stern for example, that phantasy life is a normal feature of the child's life and is therefore recognized as pathological only later in adolescence.

It goes without saying that a mental disorder of this kind makes the patient a potentially dangerous person, and it may in fact lead to almost any crime, notably homicide. Kretschmer's picture of the schizophrenic as belonging usually to the athletic or, more often, to the leptosome types has been mentioned above (Chapter 13, III).

To give a few illustrations, a theological student aged 21 was found guilty but insane on a charge of murdering a pantry boy of 16. He was described as 'intensely and narrowly religious and by nature unsociable and reserved, living in two worlds, one described as a world of phantasy and the other of dissociation'. His attitude at his first interview with the psychiatric expert was described as 'comparable to a child who has been brought in from his solitary play to listen to the polite conversation in a drawing room of grown-ups. He was mildly bored and not in the slightest interested. . . . He played with the idea of dismembering the victim—taking off his arms and legs . . . He still thinks that it could be done without the death of the victim, and he would then keep the trunk and play with it.'

The psychiatric expert found him to be a schizophrenic, and he was sentenced to be detained during His Majesty's pleasure.[73] The same verdict was returned for similar reasons in the case of a soldier of 20 who had killed his father by blowing him up with a land mine which he had placed in his father's invalid chair.[74]

A phenomenon may once more be briefly mentioned here which, although in itself constituting neither a psychosis nor a neurosis, might be a symptom of mental disorder: *amnesia*. It indicates 'an alleged interruption of consciousness, complete or partial, with alleged inability of the accused to recall his actions' during the time when he committed a crime. A psychiatrist, Brian A. O'Connell, in a study of fifty murderers, found that twenty of them had 'claimed at one time or another to have no memory, or at best only the haziest recollection of the actions that had led to their arrest'.[75] He discovered certain differences in personality between the amnesic and the non-amnesic cases, in particular a far higher percentage of dullards and hysterics in the former group; there was however a higher percentage of abnormal E.E.G.s in the non-amnesic group. He concluded that, 'excluding the possible contribution of alcoholic intoxication, amnesia for a criminal act is likely to be of emotional rather than organic origin' and that 'epileptic features seemed to be of little aetiological significance'. Hypoglycaemia, however, is regarded as potentially leading to a state of confusion with subsequent amnesia, and a case of this kind is quoted where a young married man, 'following an enforced starvation of three days, murdered, for no reason, one of his children, with whom he had been on the best of terms. . . . The abnormality of his E.E.G. became more marked as his blood sugar fell and was associated with confusion.' He had no memory of his action, but 'recalled waking up to find himself covered in sweat'.

NOTE ON DRUG ADDICTION[76]

Similarly to alcoholism, drug addiction is a social as well as a psychological and psychiatric problem, and, as alcoholism, it may lead to psychotic and neurotic disorders or itself be caused by the latter. Therefore, the same difficulties of placing it correctly in a criminological system arise as in the case of alcoholism. As compared with the latter, the extent of drug addiction in Britain is believed to be small, certainly much smaller than in the United States, where it has become one of the major social problems, especially for young people. Whereas the volume of British literature on it is correspondingly inconsiderable, the American output has been huge and is steadily growing. One of the aspects of the matter which has been attracting the special attention of American students in recent years is the question why the position should appear to be so much more favourable in Britain, and to this question Edwin M. Schur in particular has devoted a painstaking study, based on prolonged first-hand observations of the British system of dealing with drug addicts. He finds the answer essentially in the fact that, in contrast to the U.S.A., drug addiction as such is not an offence in Britain; that the addict commits an offence only if he obtains drugs illegally; that there is no compulsory treatment of drug addicts in Britain, and that the Government gives the medical profession 'almost complete professional autonomy in deciding whether an addict needs and should receive drugs for health reasons'. If the doctor regards this as necessary the patient may obtain the prescribed drugs under the National Health Service, which makes it unnecessary for him to pay excessive prices in the black market; therefore, there is but little incentive for the latter to operate extensively in Britain. So far so good, but in this country as in many other countries, there are two sides to the matter: drug addiction as a problem of the individual sufferer and illicit traffic in drugs, but the latter need not always be the supplier for the home market only: it may mainly cater for an international market and therefore have little bearing on the internal position. Whereas drug addiction is a medical and possibly a psychiatric problem, trafficking in drugs is an economic crime, with which we are not primarily concerned in the present chapter. Nevertheless, a few cases may be quoted.

In July, 1962, three Chinese members of the crew of the cruiser H.M.S. *Belfast* were sentenced at the Central Criminal Court in London to terms of imprisonment ranging from 12 months to five years for unlawfully possessing opium and heroin. It was stated that, while the ordinary value of these drugs was £670, their illicit value on the black market was approximately £325,000, the 'biggest single haul of illicit drugs that has ever been made' and far in excess of what could reasonably be sold in Britain. It was clear, therefore, that most of this quantity was destined for abroad, notably for North or South America. (*The Times*, 26.7.1962.)

Five years before, a quantity of Indian hemp, 175 lb in weight, had been seized in the Port of London, valued at £100,000 in the black market and destined to be smoked as 'reefers' in cafés, night clubs, and so on, in London or other places (*The Times*, 15.7.1957). It was stated at the time that of the persons convicted of dealing in Indian hemp seven out of eight were coloured men, mainly West Indians. In their Pentonville study, T. and P. Morris found 13 cases of offences against the Dangerous Drugs Act, 1951, among the prisoners there, all non-white men sentenced for possessing marijuana (p. 59). The total of prosecutions for these offences was 727 in 1962 (*Criminal Statistics England and Wales 1962*, p. 29), but no distinction is here possible according to colour and origin. Modern music club and dance band leaders are said to be particularly prominent among these offenders, but white girls who are friendly with West Indians are also introduced to hemp smoking. The Denning Report[77] contains some references to this. Opium, on the other hand, is said to be largely confined to the Chinese population of London and since the war in particular Liverpool, but even here it is believed to be declining in favour of other pastimes. Recently, a drug drinamyl, popularly known as 'purple heart' tablets, has been named in the House of Commons as being addictive and very widely used among young people in London (*Hansard*, 30.1.1964).

Gasoline smelling among juvenile delinquents in the United States has been the subject of an interesting case study by two American medical experts.[78]

From the sociological side Cloward and Ohlin (Chapter 22, below) have dealt with the problem of drug addiction as a special type of the delinquent subculture, the 'retreatist'. Its characteristic features are cultural and social isolation and exclusion from the dominant streams of society. Feelings of frustration and discontent are particularly noticeable among these addicts, and the high proportion of adolescent Negroes among them is therefore not surprising. While these observations are no doubt correct it is less convincing to treat the drug addicts as a sub-type of the delinquent subculture, on a par with the other types worked out by these authors and responsible for gang formation; and in fact Cloward and Ohlin admit that the ties among addicts are not as close as those uniting members of the other forms of subculture (p. 179).

The psychiatric effect of drug-taking differs greatly according to the type and quantity of the drug and the personality involved. Reckless, after a detailed examination of the available evidence, concludes that one can only assume that there is a strong relation between mental abnormality and drug addiction, but one does not know 'how much connection actually exists' (p. 366).

The criminological significance of drug-taking is twofold: first, law-breaking as a concomitant of the process of obtaining the drug, including the forgery of prescriptions and the stealing of money to purchase the drugs; and, secondly, lawbreaking unconnected with this process but rather a consequence of taking the drug. The first aspect, as already indicated, depends greatly on the state of the law, which is stricter in the U.S.A. than in some other countries. Regarding the second aspect, the evidence is not very impressive. Reckless (p. 356) believes that stealing and drug peddling are the two major realities of the relation between drug addiction and crime and that any other connections are comparatively minor. Bloch and Geis are similarly sceptical, pointing out how difficult it is to determine how much crime the individual would have committed if he had not become a drug addict and that the latter usually do not commit serious crimes of violence (pp. 238 and 356). Valuable as such case studies as that on gasoline smelling are psychologically and psychiatrically, they shed hardly any light on the specifically criminological effect of this phenomenon. Clearly, much more research on the subject will have to be done particularly in this country, before any meaningful statements can be made on the extent and the criminological aspects of drug addiction.

After this note was written, public anxiety over the growing illicit possession of and traffic in 'pep pills' among young persons and in particular over their alleged, though not proved, use to stimulate offences of the 'Clacton' type (Chapter 25 below) reached such dimensions that the Home Secretary felt compelled, in March 1964, to introduce a Bill, the Drugs (Prevention of Misuse) Bill, to make the unauthorized possession of a specified number of these pills or their importation without licence an offence punishable with a fine of up to £200 and/or six months' imprisonment. This Bill would give the police power to deal with these pep pills in a similar way as with heroin, morphine and Indian hemp, and would strengthen the penal element in the English law on drugs. For this reason the Bill has been not unanimously welcomed by doctors and social workers.[79] At the Committee stage of the House of Commons debate on the Bill the Government was criticized for not having sufficiently studied the 'Soho nerve centre' of the 'purple heart' racket, and reference was made to certain clubs which were alleged to be involved in this racket (*Evening Standard*, 9.6.1964).

After this had been written, the Bill became law on the 31.7.64.

Chapter 15

MENTAL DISORDERS II:
NEUROSES AND PSYCHOPATHY.
MENTAL DEFICIENCY AND ITS OPPOSITE

I. NEUROSES AND PSYCHOPATHY

1. *Neuroses and Psycho-neuroses*

The nature of the difference between psychosis, neurosis and psycho-neurosis is controversial.[1] While some authorities regard it as merely quantitative in the sense that the psychosis represents a more severe form or stage of the neurosis or psycho-neurosis, others make a qualitative distinction: the psychotic, they say, lives in a world of phantasy no longer subject to the ordinary laws of nature and has completely lost contact with reality; the neurotic still lives in the real world but cannot any longer cope with its difficulties. According to this second view, a neurosis may in certain cases be a more serious disturbance of the personality than a psychosis. Whichever view we may prefer, it is generally accepted that in practice the dividing line is often very difficult to draw and that a neurosis or psycho-neurosis may eventually lead to a psychosis, for example a depression to a manic-depressive psychosis.[2] Again, the terms neurosis and psycho-neurosis are often used indiscriminately by psychiatrists, whereas others distinguish between them.[3] The meaning of the distinction is that neuroses can have a somatic origin, psycho-neuroses not. Glover agrees to call certain 'instinctual and affective disturbances of somatic function *organ-neuroses*; so long as it is remembered that they have no psychic *content* and are not therefore psycho-neuroses'.[4] In the following, the term neurosis will be used for the sake of simplicity to cover both categories.

The incidence of the various forms of neurosis in the general population is very high. In a survey, sponsored by the Medical Research Council, on the incidence of neurosis among factory workers it was found that in a sample of over 3,000 male and female workers in engineering factories 10 per cent had suffered from 'definite and disabling neurotic illness and a further 20 per cent from minor forms of neurosis, during the course of six months'.[5] Admittedly, this enquiry was concerned with 'stabilized wartime conditions', but peacetime investigations had shown similar figures.[6] Among delinquents, too, neurosis is far more frequent than psychosis. A survey made of all cases seen at the Institute for the Study and Treatment of Delinquency in London (I.S.T.D.) in the years 1937–41 showed the following significant figures: 2 per cent psychotic, 4½ per cent borderline psychotic, 1 per cent alcoholic, 25 per cent sexual disorders, 29 per cent psycho-neurotic, 5 per cent behaviour problems, 5 per cent cases of organic origin. This excludes 3 per cent mentally defective, 8 per cent borderline mentally defective and 13 per cent psychopathic personality—categories with which we are not concerned at present. For juveniles only, the figures were much higher for psycho-neurosis, 37 per cent, character cases (including behaviour problems) 22 per cent, mentally defectives 5 per cent and borderline mentally defectives 11 per cent.[7] It has to be borne in mind that the cases sent to the I.S.T.D. (now The Portman Clinic) are carefully selected and therefore hardly representative. With the exception of the psychopath, who will be discussed below and who should preferably not be regarded as a neurotic at all, the relationship between neurosis and delinquency is less close than frequently assumed. To some extent it is even believed that this relationship is of an alternative rather than of a cumulative character, i.e. rather than being both neurotic and delinquent people tend to be either the one or the other. 'Neurosis is uncommon in the prison population', writes a prison medical officer of very long experience.[8] The explanation lies in the nature of the neurotic illness, which is rooted in inner conflict. If the individual has, unconsciously, to choose between neurosis and delinquency, his choice may depend on the source of the conflict responsible for his difficulties. If they are rooted in himself, he is likely to develop a neurosis; if, however, they are caused by other people, he is more likely to commit delinquent acts,[9] but he may also take refuge in a neurosis as a defence against his aggressive impulses.[10] The delinquent who is somehow deprived of his delinquent outlets may occasionally develop neurotic symptoms,[11] especially if his victory over his delinquent tendencies was achieved through overgreat self-control.

According to Freudian teachings on which the dominant theory of the neurosis is largely based (see also Chapter 17 below), the latter arise from an unconscious inner conflict between the ego and the instinctive, mainly sexual (in an 'extended sense') desires which have to be repressed because they are incompatible with the demands of the outside world, the ego and especially the super-ego.[12] According to Freud, the Oedipus complex is 'the nuclear complex of the neurosis'.[13] Such conflicts may also exist in the mind of the normal person, but here they are usually suppressed without creating special difficulties. In certain cases, however, the process of repressing them requires an excessive effort and thereby produces an unconscious feeling of guilt and the need for self-punishment, i.e. a neurosis. The neurotic, who is in most cases highly moral, tends to turn against himself to satisfy his need for punishment (see also Chapter 17 below) instead of hurting others. The delinquent, however, 'deals with his guilt by the mechanism of punishing the environment'.[14] 'The delinquent usually does not suffer.'[15] If all this were universally true there could be no neurotic delinquents, whereas their existence is beyond doubt; what is doubtful is merely the size of this group. We may take as an example of neurotic delinquency Franz Alexander's 'neurotic character', an individual who, different from the true neurotic, lives out his impulses which are often asocial, who is active whereas the true neurotic is inactive. Nevertheless, the neurotic character is not a 'real' criminal as at least one part of his personality condemns his anti-social actions. As there is, therefore, a split in his personality the inner conflict characteristic of the true neurotic does exist here as well.[16] Apart from this controversial category, the neurotic character, there are other, though limited, possibilities too of combining neurosis and delinquency.[17] This might be illustrated by briefly reviewing a few of the most important forms of neurosis:

(a) *Anxiety Neurosis and Phobias*.[18] This condition is characterized by a morbid, excessive and largely unjustified fear of dangers from within or without. If associated with a specific object or idea and entirely unjustified it is called phobia. One of the most frequent forms of neurosis, it has very little criminological significance. East gives the example of a young man who embezzles money because he is afraid that he may lose his girl unless he spends more money on her than he can afford. Anxiety may also be a cause of suicide.

(b) *Hysteria*. A term which has different connotations to the layman and the medical expert.[19] The latter distinguishes between conversion hysteria and anxiety hysteria; according to whether the pathogenic energies are discharged 'primarily through somatic or through ideational and affective channels' (Glover). Hysterics may 'almost unwittingly manufacture some situation . . . and enter into it emotionally with a rapidity and fervour impossible for more stable people. Egotism and untruthfulness (pseudologia phantastica) may be pushed to the point of delinquency. The emotional attitude of a hysteric towards other people is often influenced by sexual factors' (Mapother and Lewis). Hysteria is more common in women than in men. Offences such as writing anonymous libellous letters or wrongly

259

accusing men of indecent assaults may be committed by hysterical women.[20]

(c) *Obsessional and Compulsive Neurosis*.[21] One might distinguish between obsessional thoughts, actions, doubts, ruminations and rituals (Glover, *Psycho-Analysis*). Neurotics of this type are seldom aggressive—although they may feel an urge to push another person over a cliff or in front of a train they will but rarely act it out—but many sexual perversions contain obsessive elements, for example exhibitionism, fetishism and also kleptomania and pyromania, both of which will be discussed separately below. Freud was, at one time at least, inclined to regard the neuroses as 'the negative of perversions', but as Schmideberg points out, both neurotic and perverse symptoms have a similar aetiology, although the pervert is more anti-social than the neurotic and normally turns his abnormal urges against others instead of himself.[22] It is certainly true that only a comparatively small proportion of perverts are obsessional neurotics.[23] To take, for example, exhibitionism, one of the most frequent sexual offences, it can be found in persons of very different mental make-up, acting with a great variety of motives, including cases of obsessional neurosis as probably one of the smallest groups.[24] East found only five psycho-neurotics in a series of 150 exhibitionists, and in the East-de Hubert Report it is also stated that very few exhibitionists show symptoms of a long-standing obsessional personality.[25]

Two forms of criminality are often regarded as particularly clear expressions of obsessional-compulsive neurosis: the so-called kleptomania and pyromania. Both terms are ill-chosen because they give the impression of referring to forms of mania in the sense of monomania, i.e. the old idea of a mental illness which affects only one small sector of the mind, leaving the personality as a whole totally unaffected. This would mean that a kleptomaniac is a mentally normal person whose only weakness is an obsessional urge to steal, a pyromaniac the same with a corresponding urge to commit arson, etc. Modern psychiatry has abandoned this idea, realizing that an individual who suffers from obsessional urges of this kind cannot be regarded as 'otherwise normal'. 'All mental symptoms, whether major or minor, always involve the total personality', writes Bowlby.[26] Another misconception encouraged by the term kleptomania is its frequent use to describe any kind of excessive, repetitive and apparently unreasonable stealing, especially from shops. The misuse of the word to provide an easy defence for habitual shoplifters belonging to the middle classes has recently led to a reaction, and the man-in-the-street now believes that the idea of kleptomania is nothing but a trick invented by psychiatrists and defence counsel to provide well-to-do people with an easy excuse. 'What is called pilfering east of

Temple Bar is called kleptomania in the West-end.' The truth lies somewhere between these extremes. Recent investigations into shoplifting, especially by Gibbens,[27] distinguish four overlapping types of shoplifters: (a) the professional who steals, often in collaboration with receivers, in order to sell the goods; (b) the ordinary offender who wants the goods for himself; (c) people, mostly women of good character, who act under an emotional stress, anxiety and depression because the stolen goods, regardless of their practical value, have a symbolic significance for them which forces them to disregard the social risk they run; (d) kleptomaniacs who steal for the sake of stealing in a repetitive, compulsive manner. The act of touching and handling the goods gives them sexual excitement, and it is often committed during or after menstruation or at the onset of the menopause. The thefts are carried out in a clumsy way, sometimes without any attempt at concealment; shining, glittering things are preferred, and they are often hoarded without ever being used. As Gibbens writes, 'There is no doubt that such cases exist, but they are relatively rare.' Fetishism may be connected with, or a preliminary stage to, kleptomania.[28] Glover[29] regards kleptomania as 'essentially obsessional in type', but distinguishes it from 'compulsive delinquencies of a psychopathic type', in which some degree of satisfaction is obtained, whereas in true kleptomania the stealing is often followed by some action of an expiatory nature such as a donation to charity. This requirement, too, shows how restricted the use of the term kleptomania is in modern psychiatric and psycho-analytical literature.

While pyromania also shows obsessive-compulsive features, with a similar background of inner conflict, often of a sexual nature, its object is destruction rather than acquisition, and it occurs more frequently in the younger age groups, notably among adolescent girls.[30] Epileptics seem to be fairly well represented among them,[31] which is not surprising in view of their well-known difficulties (see Chapter 14 above). Young people, deprived of a happy home life and feeling sexually frustrated and generally unhappy, may become obsessed with the urge to set fire to external objects which are to them symbols of a hostile and wicked world only fit to be destroyed and replaced by a better one. A soldier aged 20 was tried in 1939 by Nottinghamshire Assizes on a charge of setting fire to stores at a Royal Ordnance Depot and causing £36,000 of damage because 'he felt that the social system of the country was not as it should be and he decided to register a protest against it'. The police were satisfied that he was not connected with any subversive movement nor influenced by other people.[32] The prison medical officer thought he was a schizophrenic, but the same offence might have been committed by an obsessional-compulsive neurotic.

'There is a strong similarity', writes Schmideberg,[33] 'between the arsonist and the sex offender, both etiologically and symptomatically, and in the reaction they elicit from the community, justice, and our law-enforcing agencies.' She stresses in particular the sadistic element in many pathological firesetters and also the absence of any emotion or feeling of guilt relating to the crime. In an older German investigation covering 100 cases Többen[34] found the following main motives of arson: revenge and hatred in 38 cases, alcohol in 6, poverty or greed in 22, homesickness in 7, to cover up other crimes in 4, to get away from a reformatory or from military service in 7, the pleasure of firesetting or naughtiness in 5, motives connected with mental disorder in 11. He refers to an early publication of Karl Jaspers who stresses the importance of loneliness and homesickness in young girls. Loneliness may have similar effects also on individuals who are not so very young any more. A single woman clerk aged 29 was charged with setting fire to the local Church Hall because, as a member of the church council, she was disappointed to hear that the vicar, from whom she had received some pastoral attention because of her loneliness, was moving to another district. Soon afterwards, she set fire to the vicarage to which he had moved (*The Times*, 23.3.1962).

Occasionally, an element of financial gain may be present which, at least to the superficial observer, may be difficult to separate from the deeper, emotional, subconscious ones. On the 15th March 1962, a part-time fireman, aged 32, married with four young children, was sentenced at Winchester Assizes to seven years imprisonment for sixteen crimes of arson. Soon after he had taken up his employment with the fire brigade he caused 'a reign of terror' in his district by starting on an average one fire a week and causing over £27,000 of damage. He was stated to have received nearly £2 a week for turning out and fighting the fires he had raised. He told the police: 'I don't know what I do it for, only that I feel good in uniform and it gives me some sense of importance.' The psychiatric expert thought he could be helped by psychological treatment.[35]

A similar case was reported soon afterwards from Breconshire where a grocer, aged 39, a former leading fireman, was committed for trial to Assizes for setting fire to four buildings. He was alleged to have made a confession, saying: 'After each fire I decided it would be the last, but found myself carrying on again . . . it always seems to be on a sudden impulse.' The offences were stated to have occurred between 24th March and 8th September 1962 (*The Times*, 20.9.1962), i.e. starting approximately a week after the two previously mentioned cases had been reported in the press.

The accused, a married man with four children, who was said to

262

have been very helpful to the police on a number of occasions and had received recommendations from the Chief Constable, asked for five similar cases to be taken into consideration. A medical report stated that he was not insane in the legal sense, but was suffering from an anxiety state, worried over his business and had started the fires to relieve his anxieties. The case was adjourned for a further medical report (*The Times*, 20.11.1962).

Although this brief discussion of a few types of neurosis may have shown that the latter is less important than often believed as a causal factor in delinquency this does not necessarily mean that very few delinquents are neurotics. It does mean, however, that they may have become delinquents for reasons other than their neurosis. In his survey of the Wakefield Prison population, Roper who, as we have seen (Note 8), regards neurosis and criminality as 'in many ways the reverse of each other', notes that 'neurosis in prison consists largely of somatized anxiety and comes out mainly in fear of disease and in exaggerated reaction to simple ailments',[36] i.e. neurosis does exist among prisoners, but it is not necessarily the cause of their delinquency.

2. *Psychopathy*[37]

The term psychopath has changed its meaning many times since it was first introduced, apparently in 1888 by Koch whose 'psychopathic inferiority' was a very broad conception including much of what would now be called neurosis.[38] Historically, its forerunner was Prichard's 'moral insanity', and the description of this condition given by the latter as early as 1834 is still regarded as containing much of the essence of the modern term psychopath.[39] In 1870, Isaac Ray, the great American psychiatrist, quoting Prichard, spoke of moral mania.[40] The main characteristic of this condition was that it was a morbid perversion of feelings, temper, habit and moral disposition without any notable impairment of the intellectual faculties. Apart from this emphasis on moral, as opposed to intellectual, defect there was in the older literature on the subject also a strong tendency to use the term as a convenient pigeon-hole where any form of mental abnormality which did not seem to fall under any other recognized form of mental illness could be accommodated. The modern trend is opposed to this, and psychiatrists have made great—though not always successful—efforts to limit the concept to certain clearly definable types and to underline in particular the differences rather than the similarities between the psychopath and the neurotic.

The emphasis on moral weaknesses led, understandably, to the temptation to over-estimate the closeness of the relationship between psychopathy and crime, in other words to regard, if not every criminal as a psychopath, at least every psychopath as a criminal. Present-day psychiatrists, however, have worked out typologies in which the criminal psychopath is only one of many types of psychopathic personality.[41] Among the most influential of these typologies are those by Kurt Schneider, who has many followers especially on the Continent, and by Sir David Henderson. While Schneider distinguishes ten different types of psychopaths,[42] Henderson is content with three. It should be borne in mind, however, that Schneider's typology is intended as an empirical description of certain combinations of characteristic qualities rather than as a theoretical typology.[43] His definition of psychopaths as abnormal personalities 'who suffer from their abnormality or produce suffering in their environment' has been widely quoted; the two parts of this definition should, however, not be interpreted as being mutually exclusive as it is quite possible for a person to suffer himself and to cause suffering to others. It is one of the merits of Schneider's definition to make it clear that the psychopath is not a person who suffers from an illness called psychopathy, but that the term characterizes the personality as a whole.[44]

Henderson's three types are (a) the predominantly aggressive, (b) the predominantly inadequate, and (c) the predominantly creative. It will be noted that he has no special type of criminal psychopath, but divides the latter between his first two groups. Glover[45] suggests a division into two subgroups, 'a condition of "private" and (in the social sense) "benign" psychopathy in which the condition affects the individual's private life and character and a (again socially speaking) "malignant" or "criminal" psychopathy where the condition gives rise to serious and persistent anti-social manifestations', or 'masochistic' and 'sadistic' psychopathy.

The Chief Characteristics and Aetiology of the Psychopath. A recent writer, after surveying two hundred publications on the subject, produced the following list of 'signs attributed to psychopathic syndromes', in order of frequency:[46] (a) affectionlessness or lack of relation to others; (b) disregard of community or group standards with antisocial behaviour on a verbal, acquisitive, personal or sexual plane; (c) apparent absence of guilt feeling and failure to learn by punishment; (d) emotional liability and immaturity, leading to short-circuit reactions with immediate pleasure, satisfaction or unpremeditated violence; (e) a lack of foresight; (f) continued sexual experimentation, immaturity or aberration; (g) undue dependence on others.

The element under (a), lack of ability to establish warm personal relations with others, has been underlined perhaps more often than anything else. Another psychiatrist, Anthony Storr, has recently described it well as the inability 'to put himself in other people's shoes and . . . to appreciate their feelings. It is probably our capacity for identification which makes us behave relatively decently. If this is absent we treat people as things rather than as human beings' (*New Statesman*, 27.4.1962, p. 572).

This list, while highlighting the principal characteristics of the psychopath as discussed in the literature, has of course to be interpreted critically, and checked against and supplemented in the light of the results of more detailed studies of the problem such as those by Glover and others. To mention only one recent study, it has been suggested by members of the Eysenck school of psychology, notably by Franks,[47] that extraverts condition very poorly and that, as the psychopath is usually an extravert, he too is unable to condition, to profit from experience, and that this explains his high rate of recidivism. As we shall see below (Chapter 17) this characteristic plays an important part in other studies too.

Barbara Wootton's criticism of the whole concept, while a useful antidote to the enthusiasm of certain over-credulous adherents of modern psychiatry, goes too far in its equally exaggerated scepticism. It culminates in the sentence: 'He [i.e. the psychopath] is, in fact, *par excellence*, and without shame or qualification, the model of the circular process by which mental abnormality is inferred from anti-social behaviour while anti-social behaviour is explained by mental abnormality.'[48] She rightly insists that the mental abnormality of the psychopath should be deducible from criteria other than his anti-social conduct, but she ignores the fact that this very requirement has to some extent been met by modern psychiatric research and she has therefore thrown out the baby with the bathwater. An investigation of a group of 104 prisoners in three London prisons, all of them clinically classified by the prison medical officers as psychopaths, with 61 non-psychopathic controls,[49] for example, has shown that the psychopath can be distinguished from non-psychopaths in many ways quite *apart* from his anti-social tendencies: he shows abnormalities in the electrophysiological, constitutional, and psychological fields which make his criminal behaviour appear 'almost irrelevant. Certainly criminality *per se* seems to add little to our knowledge of this particular form of character disorder': failure to mature and inability to accept authority in any form are the most outstanding characterological qualities emerging from this study,[50] but in addition to them the electrophysiological examination showed a significant positive correlation with abnormality on the part of the psychopaths as compared with the controls. Moreover, capillaroscopy—a newly developed diagnostic procedure—suggested 'developmental anomalies and dysplasias at the morphological level' in 81 per cent of the psychopaths against only 19 per cent of the controls. As part of the clinical study the response of the prisoners to punishment was examined under four headings: (a) punishment accepted and alteration of conduct displayed; (b) punishment apparently accepted, but no alteration of conduct; (c) punishment resented but an attempt made to avoid trouble; (d) punishment resented with the response of rebellion and a determination to get even with society. The results showed that 'the majority of the psychopaths fell under the last three categories, whereas the majority of the controls fell under the first category, and this socio-psychological criterion, attitude to punishment, agreed with the clinical diagnosis of psychopathy in 89·3 per cent.[51]' This was regarded by the authors as the nearest sociometric method for providing objective confirmation of a clinical impression.[52]

It is this negative response to punishment on the part of the psychopath—explained by Franks as part of his extraversion and poor ability to condition and learn from experience—that has been selected by the Danish Penal Code of 1930 as the guiding criterion for the choice of treatment on the part of the criminal court. Section 17(1) of the Code provides that, 'if at the time of committing the punishable act the permanent condition of the perpetrator involved defective development, or impairment or disturbance of his mental facilities, including sexual abnormality, of a nature other than indicated in § 16 of this Act (which deals with insanity and pronounced mental deficiency), the court shall decide, on the basis of a medical report and all other available evidence, whether he may be considered susceptible to punishment'.[53] As a definition of psychopathy this is of course just as inadequate as the equally negative formula in s. 4(1) of the English Criminal Justice Act, 1948, but the courts in both Denmark and England have interpreted it as referring to the various forms of neurosis and psychopathy. A survey published in 1948 by the Danish psychiatrist and Director of the Asylum for Psychopathic Criminals at Herstedvester, Dr. Georg Stürup,[54] shows that § 17 had been applied to considerable numbers of psychopaths. Similarly, Grünhut found in an examination of the manner in which s. 4(1) of the Act of 1948 had been applied,[55] that out of 414 offenders placed on probation with a condition of mental treatment 154 were labelled constitutional and 41 environmental psychopaths. With regard to the criterion of susceptibility to punishment, §§ 17 and 70 of the Danish Penal Code provide, in short, that those who are regarded as possessing this susceptibility may be committed to penal institutions, especially to a so-called psychopathics prison, whereas the others may be sent to the asylum at Herstedvester. A great deal of discretion is, however, left to the courts, and susceptibility to punishment is not the only criterion to be considered by them. For this reason and also because of the great difficulty of establishing the presence or absence of the criterion in individual cases the dividing line between the inmates of penal institutions and of Herstedvester is far from clear.[56]

Whereas the Danish Code uses 'susceptibility to punishment' as an important criterion, s. 4 of the Criminal Justice Act, 1948, uses susceptibility to treatment as a requirement for a probation order with condition of mental treatment, and the definition now given in the Mental Health Act, 1959, s. 4(4), does the same: 'In this Act "psychopathic disorder" means a persistent disorder or disability of mind (whether or not including subnormality of intelligence) which results in abnormally aggressive or seriously irresponsible conduct on the part of the patient, and requires or is susceptible to medical treatment.' By stressing the possibility that psychopaths, while not responding constructively to punishment, may be amenable to treatment, modern legislators and psychiatrists show a more positive approach to the problem than some of their predecessors. It is also of special significance in this respect that the Mental Health Act, 1959, provides in s. 4(5) that a person should not be treated as suffering from mental disorder 'by reason only of promiscuity or other immoral conduct'. A provision of this kind was needed in particular because of the experiences met with in the American so-called psychopathic sex offenders laws. While no detailed analysis of this type of legislation can here be given,[57] it has to be said that one of its main weaknesses lies in its failure to provide a reasonably clear definition of the term 'sexual psychopath', in its over-emphasis on the sexual aspects of psychopathy and its tendency to permit dangerous inroads into the liberty of the individual without providing in exchange scientifically sound measures of treatment. More recent American legislation, for example in California and Maryland, tries to remedy at least some of these defects, and the Maryland Defective Delinquency Law of 1951[58] does no longer single out the sexual psychopath for special treatment, but provides indeterminate confinement coupled with treatment for the 'defective' delinquent whom it defines as 'an individual who, by the demonstration of persistent aggravated anti-social or criminal behaviour, evidences a propensity toward criminal activity, and who is found to have either such intellectual deficiency or emotional unbalance, or both, as to clearly demonstrate an actual danger to society so as to require confinement and treatment under an indeterminate sentence . . .' Those responsible for the administration of this Act admit that, although tests for the assessment of the degree of emotional unbalance are available, they are not sufficiently precise to enable them to decide whether an individual is so unbalanced emotionally as to justify the application of the Act, and case histories and clinical impressions will have to supplement the picture. It is clear, however, that it is the object of the Maryland Act to protect society against the dangerous psychopath. The English Mental Health Act of 1959, sects. 60, 65, 66, contains provisions for detention and treatment of psychopaths and other mentally abnormal persons which are not very dissimilar to those of the Maryland Act, and it remains to be seen whether its definitions provide greater protection for the individuals concerned.

All the statutory definitions of psychopathy so far mentioned wisely abstain from including any statements about the *aetiology* of psychopathic disorders. This issue is still much too controversial to be suitable for legislative formulation. Here as in many other fields we can observe a certain difference of views between Continental and Anglo-American writers, the emphasis on constitutional and inherited factors being slightly stronger among the former and that on environmental factors slightly stronger among the latter. On the whole, however, we find here too a growing willingness on both sides to admit the complexity of the interplay of constitution and environment, although most attempts to arrive at a face-saving formula have to be hedged around with many reservations and exceptions from the rule. Lange, for example, writes:

Psychopathies are abnormal permanent states which we regard mostly as inborn. . . . On the other hand there is no doubt that many of these childhood neuroses can be favourably influenced or even cured by changes in the milieu or very simple medical treatment . . . and there are schools of psychotherapy which put the main emphasis regarding the causes of the psychopathies on external influences and experiences. Against this we have to stress that certain forms of psychopathy are definitely hereditary or exist at least as inherited anomalies. . . . We have to assume that, apart from certain permanent psychopathies which are transmitted wholly by heredity . . ., the other psychopathies are again and again revived in the course of inherited transmission by force of the unfortunate coincidence of qualities which are not unfavourable as such but incompatible.[59]

He adds that one occasionally sees the coming into existence of psychopathies which look similar to the inherited ones but are in fact the consequence of serious external damage, for example the injuries due to encephalitis epidemica or other serious brain damage. In his survey of recent research on aetiology Craft[60] notes three general syndromes as emerging from his review: (*a*) syndromes due predominantly to brain damage; (*b*) syndromes which are predominantly affectionless, usually due to 'a deprivation of essential parental figures or a lack of training of affective bonds'; (*c*) syndromes consisting predominantly of emotional immaturity or instability, 'the result of erratic training by antagonistic or variable parent figures'. It is also interesting that, according to the *Report of the Royal Commission on Mental Illness and Mental Deficiency, 1954–7*: 'most of our witnesses who spoke to us about psychopaths emphasized that psychopathy usually seems to have its origins in the social environment in which the patient grew up.'[61]

In accordance with the different emphasis given to constitutional and environmental factors respectively, expert views on the chances of treatment differ. Glover[62] stresses that the previously assumed incorrigibility of the psychopath meant merely incorrigibility by the penal methods then employed, lack of response to punishment, admitting however that 'until comparatively recently the psychotherapeutic methods employed were not specially designed for the psychopathic criminal; they were methods that had been found useful in a number of psycho-pathological states (neuroses, character disorders and sexual disabilities) in which as a rule no special antisocial features are present'. 'The prerequisite of any therapy of the psychopath is a capacity to endure repeated disappointment . . .' 'The criminal psychopath begins treatment in a state of hostile defence . . . he persists in trying to exploit his analyst . . . there is in fact no end to the crises . . . that the psychopath may engineer . . .' In spite of all this, Glover concludes that given the right treatment the criminal psychopath is not so refractory as generally supposed, and this conclusion seems also to be borne out by the results of special treatment centres such as Herstedvester, Utrecht, or Belmont in this country.[63] Eysenck, too, comes to similar results from the entirely different angle of learning theory. As already mentioned above, in his view the psychopath conditions poorly, but 'he does condition'.[64] It is therefore fairly generally agreed that psychopaths usually become socially more or less adjusted by the age of forty or even earlier.[65] In this connection, a follow-up study of the psychopathic prisoners in various London prisons, to which reference was made above, is also of interest. It was found that eight years after the original investigation their rate of recidivism was not as high as expected, and while the rate was higher than that of the control cases, 24 per cent of them had only one or no reconvictions. 'Clearly,' the authors conclude, 'the diagnosis of psychopathic personality, even in severe cases, does not inevitably portend as hopeless a prognosis as is usually implied.'[66]

The legal responsibility of neurotic and psychopathic offenders will be discussed below in Chapter 18.

An interesting attempt has recently been made by a prison psychologist, Paul de Berker, to contrast the psychopath and the inadequate personality, although the latter, as will be remembered, is one of

Henderson's three types of psychopaths.[67] In de Berker's view the differences are chiefly as follows: While the psychopath shows a certain exuberance and determination in the pursuit of his short-term goals, this is lacking in the inadequate: 'the psychopath has at least invested in himself; the inadequate has invested nothing.' It is this 'lack of drive and general purpose that permeates the whole of the life picture'. He is not a neurotic either, because inner conflict and his response to stress are not, as in the case of the latter, specific, there is 'no symptom-like neurotic pattern', perhaps with one exception: marriage breakdown seems to be a specific symptom amongst inadequate personalities. Considering that prison psychologists and doctors are inclined to regard a very high proportion of prisoners, in particular of preventive detainees and corrective trainees, as falling into this category,[68] the practical significance of this classification is evident. What is not yet clear is, however, how far these inadequate personalities have to be treated as 'abnormal'. This leads to the question of how to define 'normality', which will be discussed below (Chapter 16, II).

II. MENTAL DEFICIENCY (SUBNORMALITY) AND ITS OPPOSITE[69]

1. *Definitions*

The same question of how to define normality is also at the bottom of the problems of mental deficiency, but with the emphasis on intelligence rather than on character and personality defects. Moreover, while attempts to produce legal definitions of psychopathy and to provide a privileged legal position for it are of very recent date, all this has been done in the case of mental defectives already for many centuries. English legal history of the subject is said to go back to the reign of Edward I, when a distinction was already drawn between the 'born fool' or idiot and the 'lunatick', i.e. a person who 'at birth hath had understanding, but by disease, grief, or other accident, hath lost the use of his reason'.[70] In later centuries, the distinction became blurred and cases of *dementia* ('lunatics') and *amentia* ('idiots') were often dealt with indiscriminately until in the later decades of the last century the special needs of the latter and the existence of various grades of amentia were more clearly recognized by the law. Nor were psychiatrists much more advanced than the lawyers, and it was only in 1838 that the French psychiatrist Esquirol and the American Isaac Ray produced a clear distinction between amentia and dementia.[71] In English law, it was the Idiots Act of 1886 which used the terms 'idiot' and 'lunatic' as mutually exclusive and the Mental Deficiency Act of 1913, based on the *Report of the Royal Commission on the*

Care and Control of the Feeble-minded of 1908, defined four classes of defectives, i.e. idiots, imbeciles, feeble-minded persons and moral imbeciles. The amending Act of 1927 re-defined these classes and replaced the term 'moral imbecile' by 'moral defective'. The overall definition of mental defectiveness given in this Act was 'a condition of arrested or incomplete development of mind existing before the age of eighteen years, whether arising from inherent causes or in-duced by disease or injury'. Therefore, the concept of mental de-ficiency was no longer exclusively confined to 'born fools'; it also included those whose defect had been caused by disease or injury provided it had happened before the age of eighteen. Nevertheless, it is the prevailing view that 'mental deficiency due solely to post-natal factors . . . is comparatively rare . . . In the majority of cases the chief factor, as a detailed study unquestionably shows, is heredity', which does not, however, necessarily imply that the majority of mental defectives are born of mentally defective parents.[72]

There is no need any more to reproduce here the definitions of the four classes given in the Act of 1927 as the whole Act has been repealed by the Mental Health Act, 1959, which replaces the term mental deficiency altogether by two new terms, 'subnormality' and 'severe subnormality', defined as follows (s. 4): ' "Severe subnormal-ity" means a state of arrested or incomplete development of mind which includes subnormality of intelligence and is of such a nature or degree that the patient is incapable of living an independent life or of guarding himself against serious exploitation, or will be so incapable when of an age to do so.' 'Subnormality' means the same, but with the difference that it 'requires or is susceptible to medical treatment or other special care or training of the patient'. The main innovations are the following: The four terms used in the previous Acts have been abolished as offensive or unnecessary. The former applies in particular to the terms 'idiot' and 'imbecile', the latter—for reasons to be given below—to the term 'moral defective'. The term 'mental defective' itself is no longer used because in the previous legislation it was made to cover mental abnormalities of a range too wide to be brought under the same term. It was argued in the report of the Royal Commission of 1957, for example, that there was far more similarity between some feeble-minded persons and psychopaths than between the former and idiots and imbeciles.[73] Moreover, the new classification, by having only two categories instead of the previous four, is more flexible, the former age limit of eighteen years has been given up as causing unnecessary practical difficulties, and there is now an explicit reference to subnormality of 'intelligence', which was missing in the previous Acts. The reason for its absence was probably the fact that previously mental deficiency included 'moral defectives', defined as 'persons in whose case there exists mental defectiveness coupled with strongly vicious or criminal propensities and who require care, supervision and control for the protection of others'. The definition given in the Act of 1913 referred to 'permanent mental defect' and lack of response to punishment, and there is little doubt that the whole idea goes back to Prichard, Ray and Maudsley, with an additional indebtedness to Lombroso.[74] Among more recent psychiatrists, in particular Mercier and Tredgold favoured the idea of an inborn lack of moral sense, whereas many others maintained that the latter was either acquired through adverse circumstances or due to inferior intelligence. One of the most outspoken critics of the concept, the late prison doctor M. Hamblin Smith, wrote in his *Psychology of the Criminal*:[75]

Is there such a thing as a 'moral sense', apart from the intellect? The author has already stated his view that there is no such sense. What we call our 'moral sense', our ideas of 'right and wrong', seems to him indissolubly bound up with our social judgments, and with the gradual growth of our social relationships. Intelligence and experience (which depends upon intelligence) enter into the problem. . . . Many cases have arisen in which moral imbecility has been advanced as a solution. But, upon investigation, they have all been found to be insane, or to be intellectually defective, or to be the subjects of some mental conflict. . . .

While there is much truth in these statements, especially in their emphasis on the importance of upbringing and other social factors, we now realize that they tend to over-simplify a very complex issue and to identify morality too much with intelligence. In any case, considering the highly controversial nature of such questions as the meaning and origin of moral sense[76] it is clearly improper for the legislator to brand certain individuals as 'moral defectives'. In its practical application, this part of the Acts of 1913 and 1927 was almost useless since medical experts refused or were at least very reluctant to certify a person under it. In an often quoted study by Sir Norwood East a group of 283 convicted defectives were classified as consisting of 33 imbeciles, 244 feeble-minded and 6 moral defectives.[77] The Mental Health Act of 1959 has merely underwritten this development by altogether dropping any reference to morality in its definition of subnormality and leaving it to the expert to deal with cases of apparent 'moral deficiency' either as cases of subnormality or of psychopathic disorder. In the latter case it is at least no longer necessary, as it was under the previous Acts, to prove or at least pretend that the individual concerned was not only morally but also mentally deficient, and psychiatrists who have to diagnose a case of psychopathy can do so without having to commit themselves to any rigid statement regarding 'moral obliquity'.

In spite of the absence of rigid classification in the Mental Health Act of 1959 it is fairly certain that intelligence tests will still play some part in helping to answer the question of whether a particular delinquent has to be classified as 'subnormal' or 'severely subnormal'. Although with the abolition of formal certification and growing scepticism regarding the practical value of such tests the former dependence on them may gradually weaken, the material presented below (2) shows that within limits psychiatrists and psychologists cannot be expected altogether to dispense with the use of intelligence tests and the yardstick of the I.Q. As the Gluecks say, intelligence 'still forms an important part of the protocol'.[78] This is not the place to deal with the concept of intelligence itself or with the various intelligence tests, and reference may be made to the extensive literature on these subjects.[79]

It is mainly in deference to the older criminological literature which was largely dependent on lines of demarcation using intelligence tests and I.Q.s that the following data may be given:

As 'idiots' persons were classified showing a mental age of under 3 years and an I.Q. of under 25; as 'imbeciles' persons of a mental age of 3 and under 6 years and an I.Q. of 25–50; as 'feeble-minded' persons of a mental age of 6 and under 10 years and an I.Q. of 50–70.[80] In addition, there was a category of persons who, though of subnormal intelligence, did not fall under the Mental Deficiency Act: the mentally dull or educationally backward children with an I.Q. of over 70 but below 85; whereas the former term referred to subnormal intelligence, backwardness was an educational concept.[81] As far as the frequency of these different states was concerned, an investigation made for the Committee on Mental Deficiency of 1929 estimated that in every 100 mental defectives there were roughly 5 idiots, 20 imbeciles, and 75 feeble-minded, whereas dullness and backwardness was estimated at about 6 times the size of the feeble-minded group. According to older estimates, still reproduced by Burt in 1955, at least 10 per cent of the London school population were 'educationally backward'.[82]

Mental defectives may, as any other person, become psychotics or they may at least undergo psychotic episodes such as paranoid hallucinations.[83]

2. *Mental Deficiency (Subnormality) and Crime*

This subject can be examined by means of the statistical and of the case study methods. It can be approached from the delinquency and from the mental deficiency angles, i.e. we can ask either how many mental defectives there are among offenders as compared with the non-delinquent population, or we can ask how many delinquents there are among mental defectives. As usual, the first way of approach has been more frequently used than the second.

CCI—T

273

The history of the subject over the past fifty years shows a steady decline in the belief in the importance of mental deficiency as a causal factor in crime. This belief reached its highest point in the first decades of the present century[84] with the publication of the American psychiatrist H. H. Goddard's book *Feeble-mindedness; its Causes and Consequences* (1914). Goddard, already known to us through his book on the Kallikak family, who introduced the Binet-Simon test to the United States and did much mental testing of delinquent children, claimed to have discovered percentages as high as sixty-six of feeble-minded cases in a sample of juvenile delinquents in the Juvenile Court of Newark, and surveying a number of other studies of inmates of Reformatories he found their percentage ranging from 28 to 89. For adult criminals his estimate was at least 25, but possibly 50, per cent. In most of the studies which he surveyed no tests had been used, nor had Goddard himself any control material for the general population. A few years later Charles Goring, as mentioned above (Chapter 13), giving an estimate of between 10 and 20 per cent mental deficiency among adult criminals, also regarded inferior intelligence as one of the most important characteristics of criminals and destined to replace Lombroso's physical stigmata.[85] He did not use intelligence tests, but relied on the subjective opinion of prison officials. On the other hand, he had at his disposal the estimates of mental deficiency among the general population produced by the Royal Commission of 1908 which believed less than half per cent of the general population of England and Wales to be mentally defective. Among a sample of over 2,000 inmates of local prisons, casual wards and shelters, etc., however, the Commission found more than 10 per cent defectives. These figures are misleading. First, the extent of mental deficiency in the general population is difficult to assess. In a report of the Mental Deficiency Committee of 1929, a slightly higher estimate was made than in 1908, i.e. over 0·6 per cent for urban and over 1 per cent for rural districts as persons requiring the type of care provided by the Mental Deficiency Acts. As pointed out in the Report of the Royal Commission of 1957:[86]

. . . any estimate of the number of persons who may require care from the special mental health services is affected by the extent to which general social conditions, such as full employment and general social welfare services, make it possible for persons suffering from mild degrees of mental disability to manage in the general population without special care, and by the degree of administrative separation or integration of mental health services and other social services which is thought desirable at any period. An estimate made in 1929 might not be equally applicable in 1956.

Similarly open to criticism is the figure of over 10 per cent defec-
274

tives given in the Report of 1908 as an estimate of mental deficiency among criminals. Their sample did not even distinguish between prisoners and inmates of casual wards, nor are prisoners representative of the criminal population as a whole, but even so the estimate of the Report of 1908 was far lower than that of Goring shortly afterwards. Cyril Burt's figure for his sample of juvenile delinquents was 8 per cent mental defectives as tested with the Binet-Simon test, which was five times as much as among the school population at large. From this he concluded that 'mental defect, beyond all controversy, is a notable factor in the production of crime'.[87]

Norwood East, in his study of Borstal boys, also found the proportion of mental defectives, about 3·5 per cent, 'very much higher than would be expected in a random sample of lads from the general population', but it was lower among the recidivists than among the first offenders, probably, he suggests, because many defectives are placed under control, instead of being brought before a criminal court, after their first offence.[88] Dr. Grace Pailthorpe, who about ten years earlier examined a group of 100 female prisoners aged between 16 and 30 in Holloway Prison, found a much higher proportion, 15 per cent, to be mentally defective and another 21 per cent subnormal.[89]

In his survey of 350 American psychometric studies of the subject Sutherland showed that between 1910 and 1928, if the median study is taken as representative of the period, the proportion of feeble-minded persons among delinquents decreased from 50 to 20 per cent.[90] If he had repeated his survey thirty years later, he would have found that, with improved tests, the proportion of marked defective delinquents had further declined. The McCords, for example, in their study of 1959 maintain that their sample of Cambridge-Somerville boys showed no correlation between low intelligence and convictions, but none of the boys of high intelligence had been sent to a penal institution. Superior intelligence, they conclude, might influence judicial policy.[91] Mary Woodward, in a table summarizing a number of American studies between 1931 and 1950, shows that the mean I.Q. had increased from 71 to over 92. From her review of British studies she concludes that, while the average intelligence of detected delinquents in Great Britain is not known, it might well be the same as in U.S.A., i.e. somewhat over 90.[92] This still leaves a difference of nearly 10 points in favour of non-delinquents. To some extent, the more cautious attitude towards mental deficiency as a causal factor in crime may have been due not only to the growing refinement of the techniques of mental testing but also to the increased understanding of the role played in the process of testing by cultural factors associated with both low intelligence and delinquency. Attempts have been made, therefore, to match such cultural factors so as to keep them identical for both groups to be tested, delinquents and non-delinquents. None of these attempts have so far succeeded in eliminating all these cultural differences.[93]

Changing views regarding the intelligence of the general population have also contributed to the present, more favourable, view of the intelligence of criminals. The results of tests applied during the First World War to several millions of American Army recruits may have been primarily responsible for these changes. In earlier enquiries the lower limits of normality seem to have been much too high.[94] These American experiences caused Professor Murchison, who was professionally connected with them, even to proclaim the superior intelligence of the criminal.[95]

Besides the technical weaknesses already mentioned, all these comparisons of the intelligence of criminals and non-criminals which consist of counting the percentages of mental defectives in the two groups, suffer from two major defects: First, there is the unavoidable defect that we can deal with the intelligence of the criminal only if he is detected, and there is a probability that detection is positively correlated with inferior intelligence. In *Prediction Methods in relation to Borstal Training*[96] it was found that the more intelligent Borstal boys—with the exception of the most superior ones—had more crimes taken into account at their request when sentenced, i.e. they had probably been more successful in evading arrest for some time than the duller boys. Criminals who are even more intelligent than those in the higher classes of the Borstal study might have been able to evade detection altogether.

Secondly, as all statements or questions referring to 'the criminal' in general terms are beside the point, it is equally senseless to examine the intelligence of this mysterious figure. The least we can do—inadequate though it is—is to distinguish between the various types of crime. Obviously, there are offences which can be successfully planned and carried through only by individuals possessing certain intellectual abilities. Already Goring[97] gave a list of the various types of crimes committed by his group of convicts together with the percentages of crimes committed by mental defectives. While for all types together this percentage was 14·4, it was 55·2 for setting fire to haystacks, 39·5 for indecent assault, 8·8 for murder, 6·3 for embezzling, 2·3 for coining and 2·1 for fraud. Similar lists could probably be produced from other samples of the criminal population.[98] This does not, of course, exclude the possibility that a mental defective may occasionally commit an apparently clever offence or a person of high intelligence do something stupid. Moreover, success in carrying out an offence should not be confused with intelligence as it may be due to stupidity, daring or the inability to see the dangers in a given situation.

However divergent may be the views on the delinquency of mental defectives, it is beyond doubt that the dull and backward group of subnormals has a far higher delinquency rate than persons of average intelligence.[99]

While the material so far presented has been mainly concerned with the incidence of mental deficiency among criminals, we may now turn to the other way of approach to the problem, i.e. the incidence of criminality among mental defectives. We owe most of our knowledge of this side of the picture to psychiatrists working in institutions for mental defectives. For example Dr. R. G. Blake Marsh, Medical Superintendent, Bromham House Colony near Bedford,[100] looking at the matter from the point of view of a psychiatrist charged with the institutional care of mental defectives, distinguishes sharply between the low-grade and the high-grade defectives. The former, feeling themselves at a disadvantage on account of their low earnings, resort to petty thefts or commit sexual offences against young children as normal girls of their own age will have nothing to do with them. Their offences are spontaneous and but rarely planned, and in institutions, where they find themselves with others of the same disability, they give little trouble and usually do well. It is the high-grade defective inmate who is likely to cause trouble. He commits offences, sometimes with cunning and some evidence of planning, to gain prestige and publicity, and he may also induce others of lower mentality to commit offences for him. Another psychiatrist, Dr. K. O. Milner, Medical Superintendent of the Aston Hall Mental Deficiency Institution, near Derby,[101] stresses the great preponderance of sexual crimes and crimes of violence among mental defectives. He refers to a report of the Board of Control (now dissolved under the Mental Health Act, 1959, s. 2) for 1934–6, according to which 26 per cent of the offences committed by mental defectives were sexual offences, and to an investigation by Norwood East who had found 22·6 per cent of such offences in a sample of 283 mental defectives. From this he concludes that sex offences are nearly ten times as common among defectives as in ordinary criminals, whereas crimes of violence are two or three times as frequent. Sadistic acts, too, are not uncommon among them. Milner also mentions the very high proportion of acts of violence among female patients of institutions for mental defectives, due mainly to the feeling of sexual frustration or homosexual or heterosexual jealousy. A non-psychiatrist, Ferguson, in his study of a sample of 301 mentally handicapped Glasgow boys,[102] also found the proportion of boys convicted and of recidivists far higher among those mentally handicapped than among the other groups he examined, and the proportion of sex offences, although not particularly high in absolute figures, far exceeded that for ordinary school-leavers and physically handicapped boys.

In conclusion we might say that the uncertainty still prevailing in this field is reflected in the fact that one of the most recent students of the subject, Mary Woodward, reaches two slightly contradictory conclusions in her simultaneous publications: on the one hand, that 'low intelligence plays little or no part in delinquency', and on the other that it 'cannot be regarded as an important causal factor' in it.[103] We are inclined to prefer the second formula to the first. Here as in many other fields of criminology there is a danger that insight into the exaggerations and shortcomings of previous generations may lead to errors of the opposite kind: over-estimation of the role of subnormality may be replaced by under-valuation.

Finally, passing to a discussion of the reasons why mental subnormality may be a cause of delinquency we are running the risk of trying to explain a phenomenon whose very existence is still in dispute. It is in fact much easier to find reasons for a likely causal relationship between subnormality and delinquency than to establish the relationship itself. Explanations can be found in the intellectual, in the economic and the emotional spheres. In the intellectual sphere: The mental defective may occasionally not grasp the full significance of his actions. Although he knows that stealing and similarly simple offences are forbidden and punishable by law, he may not understand the legal implications of more sophisticated acts such as forgery, embezzlement, stealing by finding and of sexual misbehaviour. Because of the ease with which defectives can be persuaded to take part in criminal exploits they may be used as tools by older and more experienced persons. Naturally, such considerations will lose in weight for the higher grades of deficiency where their place will be taken by emotional difficulties. 'With sufficient intelligence to realize how far they are left behind, they feel they belong nowhere and to nobody . . . what wonder that at times they become violent . . . or act recklessly so that they may obtain some notice. If not credit why not notoriety?'[104] Mistakes made by parents, who may drive them too hard,[105] or by unsympathetic teachers[106] may make things worse. Unlike the physically handicapped, the mental defective is unable to make up for his defects by his achievements in other spheres. Especially if he is of the self-assertive type, he has to shine somehow, and the only way may be delinquency.[107] If detained in closed institutions, where he may have to mix with low-grade defectives, the borderline case may feel particularly humiliated and frustrated. At least as obvious are the economic causes of misbehaviour. Unless specific protective measures are taken on his behalf, the defective will often be the last to get a job and the first to be sacked. Bearing all this in mind we have to agree with Weber who writes: 'It is indeed remarkable that the association of mental backwardness with delinquency is not more frequent than it is.' In any case, it will greatly depend on the social environment whether a mental defective becomes a delinquent. For females Lombroso's view that prostitution often takes the place of crime can hardly be disputed. Most studies of prostitutes draw attention to the high proportion of defectives and in particular of dull girls among them.[108] In an investigation into the causes of sex-delinquency in girls, Burt gives the following figures for his sample: 12 per cent mentally defective, 27·4 per cent definitely dull and 53·2 per cent educationally backward. Here, as always, we have to bear in mind that the prostitute studied by psychologists and social workers is probably even less representative of the *genus* prostitute than the prisoner or probationer is of the criminal.

3. *Genius and Crime*

Having treated mental deficiency at some length we should devote at least a few pages to the opposite side of the matter. By including them in a chapter on 'mental disorders' we do not of course imply that geniuses are always mentally ill. The following text will make this clear. It is only as a deviation from the average mental make-up of human beings that this category can legitimately find its place in the present chapter. 'Genius' is not defined by law, it is no mass phenomenon, nor can it easily be investigated statistically, although this has repeatedly been attempted, by Sir Francis Galton for example.[109] Nevertheless, its relation to crime has attracted the attention of criminologists for a long time and mainly for two reasons: first, the alleged affinity of genius and insanity and, secondly, the belief that men of genius are likely to be anti-social, or at least too individualistic and unconventional to be capable of submitting to society's rules. To define the meaning of genius is no easy task. Rejecting the subjective definition of Lange-Eichbaum[110] as genius being something entirely dependent on the recognition by mankind at large we might perhaps accept Kretschmer's formula, 'the ability to create special values bearing a personal stamp . . . novel ideas and forms of expression and the production of factors which initiate new historical epochs'.[111]

The idea that highly creative and original minds are apt to hover on the verge of insanity is very old, as old perhaps as the idea that the personality finds its external expression in the face and bodily structure of man. Kretschmer[112] quotes Aristotle's statement: 'Famous poets, artists and statesmen frequently suffer from melancholia or madness', and in Shakespeare's *Midsummer Night's Dream*, we read (V i): 'the poet's eye, in a fine frenzy rolling'. These are only expressions of an assumed very general association between the two phenomena. Attempts to explain it in more specific psychiatric terms were made much later, notably by Lombroso, Lange-Eichbaum and Kretschmer. The latter, in his brilliant treatment of the subject, strongly attacks the generally held view that mentally sound individuals are always superior to less normal ones and that it would therefore be disparaging to men of genius to state, as Kretschmer does, that among them mental diseases, and especially psychopathic conditions, are 'decidedly more frequent' than among the general population. While it would be difficult to prove this statistically, the general impression given by the material presented by the above-mentioned writers supports Kretschmer's view. If Tredgold disputes the existence of this relationship he may be too much inclined to identify genius with 'outstanding ability' and to ignore the qualitative difference between these two concepts. From these premises, there is only one further step to the conclusion that there is also an over-average rate of crime among men of genius. Havelock Ellis[113] maintained in his *Study of British Genius* that 'at least 160, or over 16 per cent, of our 975 eminent men were imprisoned, once or oftener, for periods of varying lengths, while many others only escaped imprisonment by voluntary exile', a statement which is of little use without a careful distinction between political and common offences. Among men of genius who committed ordinary crimes the most frequently quoted names are François Villon, Veit Stoss, Benvenuto Cellini, the Borgias and Rousseau. Of Cellini, Jacob Burckhardt has said 'he is a man who can do everything, risks everything, and bears his measure within himself'.[114]

Turning now to the younger age groups, it seems to be generally agreed that there are comparatively few offenders among children of super-normal ability and vice versa. In Cyril Burt's group a high degree of super-normality was 'conspicuously rare'.[115] According to Leta Hollingworth,[116] such children are, as a rule, more stable emotionally, more adaptable and better able to resist temptations than normal or subnormal ones. Any difficulties which they may experience arise when there is too great a disproportion between their superior intelligence and their general level of maturity, their inability to suffer fools gladly, their inner isolation and sexual imbalance.

In his profoundly stimulating discussion of what he calls the 'great character'—a concept which probably differs from that of genius in stressing more the moral than the intellectual superiority of the person—Martin Buber stresses that the great character is not beyond the acceptance of norms, 'no responsible person remains a stranger to norms', but in a reference to Ibsen he adds: 'Today the great characters are still "enemies of the people", they who love their society, yet wish not only to preserve it but to raise it to a higher level.'[117] However, not all men of genius are 'great characters' in Buber's sense. Some of them live in that large territory between good and evil where it often depends only on chance whether or not they stray in that part of it which we call crime. Of Tchaikovsky, for example, Gerald Abraham writes[118] that 'in everyday life . . . he seems never to have shrunk from a convenient lie . . . and it is hardly too much to say that his whole outward life was a façade . . . to give the world a certain impression and conceal his true nature'. There is little doubt that he was a 'creative psychopath' of genius who may have been saved from crime by his good fortune of meeting a woman benefactor whose financial help protected him from the cold blasts of ordinary life.

281

Chapter 16

THE PSYCHOLOGY OF THE NORMAL OFFENDER

I. HISTORICAL INTRODUCTION

The treatment of this subject has long been suffering from two handicaps: it has been neglected in favour of criminal anthropology and biology, and it has been too much identified with the study of criminal pathology, i.e. of the mentally abnormal offender. It is only from the early decades of the present century on, with the gradual weakening of the influence of the Lombrosian school, with the coming of psycho-analysis and the growing awareness that there is no hard and fast line of demarcation between the normal and the abnormal, that the psychology of the normal offender has come into its own. A brief, but valuable sketch of the history of the subject, to which special reference may here be made, has been given by Bonger.[1] Among the first to collect a volume of case material on the matter was the French lawyer F. G. de Pitaval in his *Causes célèbres et intéressantes* (1734 ff. in 20 volumes), followed by a German work *Der Neue Pitaval* (1842 ff.) and several new editions (1742–95), one of them with a preface by no less a person than Friedrich Schiller, whose intense interest in the subject is well known. The nineteenth century saw the publication of Anselm von Feuerbach's *Merkwürdige Kriminalrechtsfälle* (1808–11) and his *Aktenmässige Darstellung merkwürdiger Verbrechen* (1827–9), as of several other works which had this in common with their famous predecessor that they were collections of interesting criminal cases, especially of sensational trials.[2] While these collections have greatly increased our knowledge of individual crimes and criminals, most of them suffered from the weakness that they concentrated too much on the 'interesting', i.e. the sensational, case to the exclusion of the great masses of ordinary 'run of the mill' cases and that they paid too much attention to criminal trials to the exclusion of crimes not brought before the courts. Moreover, their psychology was often primitive, in accordance with the backward state of the scientific study of psychology at the time when the earlier of these publications appeared. More recent collections, such as the 'Notable

British Trials Series',[3] usually consist of verbatim reproductions of the trial with introductions which often attempt to break through the barriers and formalities of English criminal procedure and to make at least a brief assessment of the psychological and psychiatric factors at work.

Apart from the collections of case histories there are also several theoretical works by criminologists entirely or partly devoted to criminal psychology. While Lombroso produced in this field mostly platitudes and unwarranted generalizations such as remarks on the vanity, cruelty and cowardice of 'the' criminal, Goring tried to measure the association between criminality and certain psychological factors such as temperament, suicidal tendencies, egotism and in particular intellectual inferiority.[4] Of far greater value was the material published in the volumes of Hans Gross' *Archiv für Kriminalanthropologie und Kriminalistik* (since 1898), of Aschaffenburg's *Monatsschrift für Kriminalpsychologie und Strafrechtsreform* (since 1904, now called *Monatsschrift für Kriminologie und Strafrechtsreform*) and of the *Abhandlungen aus dem Gesamtgebiete der Kriminalpsychologie* (published in Heidelberg irregularly since 1912). Although there are several books, especially in German, called *Kriminalpsychologie* or *Psychologie des Verbrechers* (e.g. by Gross, Sommer and Wulffen), Hans W. Gruhle, himself the author of various excellent monographs and articles on the subject, was not altogether wrong when he stated as late as 1933 that a textbook of criminal psychology did not yet exist.[5] It is mainly the immense stimulus received from the work of Freud and his successors that has advanced the study of the subject in the present century. In spite of this and of the existence of a vast literature it is still true to say that we do not yet seem to possess any single publication dealing satisfactorily with the psychology of the 'normal' offender in all its aspects.[6] In fact, most writers still tend to neglect the normal in favour of the abnormal.

Of immeasurable value to the study of criminal psychology have, of course, throughout been the great masterworks of world literature, to think only of Shakespeare, Schiller, Dostoevsky, Balzac (of whom it has been said that only his criminals were really alive), Victor Hugo, Dickens, Stendhal, Gorki, Thomas Mann and many others. This, however, is a subject too vast to be treated within the framework of the present chapter.[7] While the contributions of psychoanalysis will be dealt with separately in Chapter 17, certain other issues will here be treated beforehand.

II. THE CONCEPT OF NORMALITY

We have repeatedly stressed the difficulty of drawing the line between the mentally normal and the abnormal offender. Moreover, the meaning of *'normality'* has so far remained an open question, and the course hitherto followed has been to deal with the various forms of abnormality first. Normality could then be defined as a condition of mind to which neither of these concepts can be applied, i.e. the normal offender would be one who is neither psychotic nor neurotic or psychopathic or mentally defective. It is only natural that we should be inclined to take this easy course. However, as Barbara Wootton rightly points out,[8] the existing difficulties are not altogether avoided by adopting such a negative formula. Is it impossible to find a positive definition of normality or mental health, or, for that matter, of mental illness? Is there a common element in these terms which goes beyond a mere assortment of negations?[9] Wootton and others have shown the existing confusion. To the many quotations given in her book we would only add Durkheim's famous discussion of the concept of normality.[10] To him, crime itself was 'normal' because a society without it was inconceivable; therefore it was an integral element of every healthy society.[11] This did not mean to him that the individual criminal, too, was necessarily healthy and sane; there was a great difference in this respect, he stressed, between sociological and psychological facts. Durkheim admits, moreover, that an excessive rise in crime would be no longer normal but morbid,[12] an admission which, although it leads to the unanswerable question of what is 'excessive' at a given time and a given place,[13] is nothing but a consequence of the fact that in the sociological field, too, there is an imperceptible transition from the normal to the abnormal. The dilemma remains, though, that, according to Durkheim, on the one hand, the normality of crime has nothing to do with the frequency of its occurrence and, on the other hand, the greater its frequency the more likely is it to be regarded as abnormal.

As far as the individual offender and his mental condition are concerned, the concept of normality will usually be considered in relation to the mental condition of the 'average' person of that particular type, which inevitably introduces the statistical element of frequency.[14] In addition, considerations of 'norm' and of behaviour which is sanctioned and approved cannot be altogether avoided, which introduces the element of value.[15] In fact, much of Wootton's discussion is intended to show that most definitions of mental health are permeated with the value concepts of the writers concerned and that in particular the capacity of adjusting oneself to the values of a given society plays a dominant part in those definitions, 'adjustment to a particular culture or to a particular set of institutions', the ability to achieve such adjustment being regarded as the criterion of mental health and normality.[16] It has to be admitted that the literature on criminal psychology is not free from this kind of reasoning and only in extreme cases, such as Nazism, has the desirability of an adjustment to the existing 'culture' been seriously questioned.[17] With this very important proviso, however, the ability to adjust one's conduct to the standards of the majority cannot be altogether ignored in our definition of normality. If the factor 'majority' is properly underlined, the frequent objection falls to the ground that adjustment may also include compliance with criminal norms.[18] It is true, of course, that, as Fromm points out,[19] this is only one aspect of normality or mental health, i.e. the one seen 'from the standpoint of a functioning society', and that there is also another possible point of view, i.e. the happiness of the individual, which may lead to different results. The Mental Health Act, 1959, uses, as we have seen (Chapter 15, II), the formula 'incapable of living an independent life or of guarding himself against serious exploitation', but this 'independence' of the life of the mentally normal person is obviously not meant to imply being independent of the standards of ordinary society.

Granting that normality is closely connected with adaptability to the requirements of life in society, the further question arises whether the degree of normality necessarily corresponds to the ease and completeness of adaptation and adjustment to these requirements. This is likely to be the case, and the neurotic who has to go through serious inner conflicts to achieve that state of external peace with society is clearly less 'normal' than the philistine to whom adjustment comes naturally without any struggle. From this it follows that for our purposes normality can be defined operationally as a condition of mind where no special efforts, no extraordinary measures of a psychiatric nature are required on the part of the criminal law and the penal system to deal satisfactorily with the case. This implies that the dividing line has to be kept very flexible and that it may have to be moved forward or backward from time to time in accordance with our changing views on the matter,[20] and that it also depends on such factors as age, sex and social class. There is no absolute definition of normality, mental health or illness, 'the "normal" mind . . . is obviously impossible to describe'.[21]

III. PSYCHOLOGICAL AND SOCIOLOGICAL
APPROACHES TO THE 'NORMAL' OFFENDER.
EXTRA-, INTRA-, AND IM-PUNITY

When trying to describe the normal offender and to explain his behaviour we are inevitably driven towards the direction of what used to be that vast no-man's-land between psychology and sociology, now to a large extent occupied by the new discipline of social psychology. Bearing in mind what was said in our 'Preliminary Observations' to Part III, i.e. that a mental element has always to be present in criminal behaviour, we might be tempted to accommodate the whole sociology of crime under the heading of 'criminal psychology', and there is indeed no rigid line of demarcation between the two branches. The differences are merely such of degree and emphasis. If we find the ultimate explanation of a crime predominantly in the environment of the offender the problem will be classified as one for the sociologist; if, on balance, we find it more in the individual himself the matter is one for the psychologist. In the words of Dr. Ernest G. Schachtel, the Rorschach Test expert employed by the Gluecks in *Unraveling*,[22] when trying to decide whether or not a boy was likely to be a delinquent, 'I asked myself whether his character structure, as I saw it on the basis of the Rorschach Test, was of a type likely to resist the inducements toward becoming delinquent offered by poor socio-economic circumstances and by the neighborhood.' Sociology tells us that there are certain factors in the individual's environment which might possibly produce crime. Psychology describes the kind of individual personality likely to incline towards crime if exposed to such a challenge. For example, given a frustrating environment, a 'criminal subculture', or conflicting systems of norms and values as to be described below, it is for the psychologist to say which type of person can be expected to overcome such difficulties and which is likely to be overwhelmed by them.

All this means that a great deal of uncertainty and controversy is unavoidable in determining whether an individual case belongs more to the domain of the psychologist or that of the sociologist, and that in our discussion of criminal psychology and sociology there is bound to occur much overlapping and repetition, but these shortcomings are preferable to the superficial appearance of simplicity and to the drawing of artificial lines of demarcation which have no basis in reality. Moreover, as Glaser has said,[23] 'the "great debates" between sociology and psychology have lost some of their former fervor. The disputes ultimately led to concessions on both sides, or, more accurately, to reformulations on both sides.' It still remains true, however, that there are certain considerable differences in the main interests and outlook of the two disciplines.[24] In a forthcoming book by Franco Ferracuti and Marvin E. Wolfgang on the *Subculture of Violence*, Ch. 1, much valuable material is presented on these and kindred problems concerning the object of full 'integration' between different scientific disciplines, in particular sociology, psychology and biology.

Much of the progress that may have been made in recent decades towards a clearer understanding of the psychological characteristics of normal offenders as compared with non-offenders has been due to better classification, less sweeping generalizations and greater scepticism. Senseless statements such as Lombroso's on the psychology of 'the criminal' have become rarer, although they have by no means altogether disappeared. As an illustration of the growing scepticism, not to say complete despair of the possibility of finding any psychological differences between the personality make-up of offenders and non-offenders, an often-quoted article by Schuessler and Cressey may be referred to.[25] These authors made a survey of all American studies published up to 1950, 113 altogether, in which the personality characteristics of delinquents or criminals and non-delinquents or non-criminals were compared, with the result that, in their view, while in a minority of 42 per cent differences in favour of the latter group had been found, in a majority of 58 per cent of the studies no such differences had emerged. Their conclusion was that from these studies, in view of 'the doubtful validity of many of the obtained differences, as well as the lack of consistency in the combined results', no significant association between criminality and personality elements had emerged. While this conclusion has been unreservedly accepted by Wootton,[26] another sociologist, Marshall B. Clinard,[27] has criticized it for two reasons: first, because personality traits are more likely to be significant for certain types of crime than for crime in general, and, secondly, because the researches included in the survey had been made too early to benefit fully from the just constructed Minnesota Multiphasic Personality Inventory (MMPI). With regard to the first point it has to be noted that Schuessler and Cressey themselves criticize the studies included in their survey for lumping all types of crime together. Moreover, they pay attention to the fact that practically all these studies had been done on prisoners, i.e. an unrepresentative group of offenders, and—closely linked with this—that it could not be stated whether crime had to be regarded as the result of a certain personality trait or whether the latter was itself the product of criminal experience, i.e. whether the trait had already existed at the beginning of a criminal career or had developed only later as the result of imprisonment, etc. In short, what the Schuessler-Cressey survey has been able to demonstrate is not the final impossibility of distinguishing the personality of delinquents and non-delinquents, but merely the inadequacy of the studies surveyed by these writers. This is its significance and its limitation.

In view of Clinard's second criticism the question has to be faced whether the MMPI has, more than other projective tests, succeeded in discriminating between the personality traits of delinquents and non-delinquents. The literature on the application of the MMPI in this field is considerable, and one recent American writer refers already to the 'demonstrated capacity of this instrument to discriminate between delinquents and non-delinquents'.[28] Barbara Wootton is more sceptical,[29] and even some of the principal workers on the MMPI have recently expressed themselves with the greatest possible reserve. Summing up the results of a large piece of research they write:[30]

Surely we cannot say that these data put us far ahead either in prediction or understanding. . . . Although the 550 items of the MMPI are probably adequate to explore the maximum relationships between the personality the children put into the patterns of their answers and their behaviour, it is not likely that the scales of the MMPI, as now used, are developing the maximum relationship. In spite of the great amount known about delinquency, we have no way available to sharpen the test tool . . . The facts suggested by the data are not pretentious. They do seem to provide a foundation for the continuing analysis . . . data not presented here show that these various personality traits have environmental correlates, such as with the broken home, but it is a significant finding that the personalities are also partly independent of obvious environmental influence. . . . We suggest that the adolescent himself is a contributing factor both to his environment and his behavior.

In another recent Minnesota study[31] only those children of a previously tested larger group were included who had achieved 'invalid protocols on the basis of high scores on the L and/or F scales or high scores in the "Cannot say" category'.[32] Subsequent follow-up studies showed that delinquency was most frequent among this 'invalid' group, and the central hypothesis of the study was, therefore, that high scores on these three scales might be useful predictors of delinquency. Generally speaking, it cannot be said, however, that this or any other study using the MMPI has produced a workable synthesis of the delinquent personality as such. Moreover, it has to be borne in mind that the scales of the MMPI have been constructed from abnormal clinical cases and that it is expected to spot juvenile delinquents just because delinquency is believed to exhibit the same symptoms as a neurosis or psychosis.[33] The question arises, therefore, how far the usefulness of the MMPI would be reduced if this belief is disputed as an unwarranted generalization. Special attention has here been given to the MMPI because it is widely regarded as one of the most promising modern projection techniques. A modification of the MMPI has been developed by another American psychologist, Harrison G. Gough, to whose work attention has been drawn by Reckless and Clinard and who claims that his scale provides a reliable measurement of an individual's tendency towards delinquency 'as a part of his incapacity to play socially acceptable roles in life'.[34]

The present writer cannot be expected to pass judgment on the extremely complicated question of the value of projective techniques in general; most readers will be familiar with the negative views expressed by Eysenck which leave no doubt about the wide differences of opinion even among professional psychologists.[35]

The criminologist, looking to the latter for help in his efforts to build up, with the aid of projective tests, an image of the personality of the normal offender will find much interesting material in T. Grygier's brilliant study *Oppression*.[36] It is the main object of this book 'to examine the changes in the psychological aspect of culture under oppression', and, more specifically, whether there is a positive association between oppression and an extrapunitive attitude and crime and between crime and the tendency to direct aggression outwards. Grygier's main hypothesis was that 'an oppressive environment brings about certain measurable changes in personality'. The method used was an examination of samples of persons, mostly Poles, discharged after the last war from German concentration camps, some of them kept in prison for common offences committed after the liberation, while others were not. Care was taken to match the concentration camp and the offenders' groups by individual pairing, and large numbers of both groups were then given intelligence (Otis) and personality tests, the latter consisting of the Thematic Apperception Test (T.A.T.) and Rosenzweig's Picture-Frustration Study (P-F.S.) The latter was mainly employed to establish the rate of extrapunitive, intrapunitive, and impunitive attitudes, i.e. whether a subject was more inclined to blame aggressively other persons or external objects for his feeling of frustration (extrapunitive), or rather to blame himself (intra- or self-punitive) or to blame nobody (impunitive). As already stated, the hypothesis was that delinquency was associated with extrapunitiveness. No personality questionnaires were used, 'as the weaknesses of this technique were considered too great for it to be practicable', nor were any attitude scales applied because of the difficulty of measuring directly 'anything that is merely potential'.[37] While Grygier is much more favourably inclined towards the Rorschach Test than Eysenck, for example, he did not use it in this study because it 'presents a picture of the total personality', whereas he was interested only in certain aspects of it. Moreover, the T.A.T. seemed more useful when the object was to trace major differences between whole groups of people. 'By using both the P-F.S. and the T.A.T. we could not only measure the tendency to direct aggression in a certain direction, but could also trace the psychological mechanism underlying this tendency' (p. 58).

The material used by Grygier for the P-F.S. tests was limited to 15 Polish delinquents with a background of forced labour in industry or agriculture and a control group of non-delinquent Polish displaced persons with a similar background, matched for sex, citizenship, nationality and religion and coming from similar types of community (p. 124). They were not matched for education, intelligence and age—but it was not considered that this invalidated the results. The statistical data suggested that the delinquents were more extra-punitive than the non-delinquents, i.e. they showed a stronger tendency than the others to perceive ambiguous social situations as frustrating to themselves, with the emphasis on the frustrating obstacle, while minimizing the frustration caused by them to others; they also showed a reluctance to admit guilt and blame themselves. 'They rarely express the impunitive type of optimism, but rather tend to think that something must be done to satisfy their needs' (p. 127). Grygier stresses that there may be nothing wrong or antisocial in certain occasional extrapunitive attitudes; what is symptomatic is rather the persistence of this type of response and the tendency to expect that *all* problems will be solved by somebody else (p. 73). Moreover, he admits that on certain aspects of the extrapunitive character his findings were merely suggestive, not conclusive (p. 132), but he regards them as being in line with observations made in the practical administration of criminal justice. He also found that the rate of extrapunitive responses was higher for those who had undergone particularly severe forms of oppression in concentration camps and that these latter forms had produced a particularly high rate of crime, in fact approximately forty-five times greater than for groups who had experienced less severe forms of oppression (p. 108); in other words, the association between degrees of oppression and the rate of crime was proved.

While the P-F.S. measures 'the more superficial level of action', the T.A.T. is 'considered to reveal a deeper level of personality', the level of phantasy, 'the underlying inhibited tendencies which the subject is not willing to admit, or can not admit because he is unconscious of them'.[38] Only a few more of the complicated findings of the Grygier study can here be mentioned: the delinquents showed more abasement and guilt feelings than the non-delinquents, which 'supports the view that delinquency may be associated with unconscious guilt feelings, although in real conflict situations (or in the quasi-real situations of the P-F.S.) the delinquents deny guilt and accuse others' (p. 203), which shows that the results of the T.A.T., reflecting the unconscious level of personality, may differ from the more superficial picture presented by the P-F.S. 'At the level of action the delinquent is aggressive . . . , but at the level of fantasy he is the victim.'[39] Other findings of the T.A.T. were that the heroes of the delinquents live in a more hostile world than those of the non-delinquents, the delinquents tell more stories about rejection by the mother, and there is less family affiliation among them. They are more pessimistic and regard themselves more often as inadequate. 'Their whole perception appears to be coloured by a feeling of the overwhelming power of an inimical Press.'[40] ' "Normal delinquents" show particularly strong feelings of personal inadequacy', 'the delinquent has a different perception of the world around him and of his own role in this world; that general trend of thought changes his perception of social events in which he is involved and affects his actions' (p. 208). Although these statements are formulated in a general way as if they would apply to all delinquents anywhere they are, as the context shows, meant to apply only to the limited sample used for these tests. In fact, researches such as Grygier's, and those of the Minnesota school, show quite clearly how greatly methods of studying the psychology of the criminal have changed from the rather primitive generalizations of many nineteenth-century criminologists. The change in methods has not necessarily produced a wholesale revolution in our views on the subject; some of the factors now regularly quoted as characteristic of criminals were mentioned already seventy or a hundred years ago, for example frustration and the feeling of being teased and irritated was stressed by Maudsley and the absence of repentance and remorse by Lombroso.[41] What the greater sophistication of modern research techniques has done is rather to produce a picture of the criminal personality far more complex than available before and less suitable for general verdicts.

After making a penetrating survey of some of the modern literature on the subject, Grygier concludes that 'all extrapunitive traits are found by observers among psychopathic and delinquent subjects. . . . Our research gives experimental evidence and a conceptual scheme in support of these observations' (p. 244). He admits, however, that 'delinquents as a class seem to vary among themselves much more than they differ from non-delinquents' (p. 240), and this is a point which has to be stressed above anything else. Present-day research, while rightly trying to discover certain traits common to all criminals, should never ignore the fact that the differences are probably more profound than the similarities. Whether the observer notices more the former or the latter may to some extent depend on his own personality.

Another attempt to compare the psychological characteristics of delinquents and non-delinquents by means of personality tests was made by Dr. Ernest Schachtel, a Rorschach expert, as part of the Glueck study *Unraveling Juvenile Delinquency*. The main differences in character and personality structure found by the application of Rorschach tests were as follows:[42] the delinquent boys were much more assertive, defiant, ambivalent to authority, resentful to others, hostile, suspicious, destructive, impulsive and more extravert; they suffered less from fear of failure and defeat, were less co-operative, less conventional and self-controlled. (Here it may be noted that in about one half of the studies surveyed by Schuessler and Cressey the delinquents were found to be slightly more introverted.) In addition to being given the Rorschach test these boys were also interviewed by a psychiatrist who found the delinquents to differ from the non-delinquents in a number of traits characteristic of the 'dynamics of temperament'.[43] It is stressed by the Gluecks that the Rorschach analyst and the psychiatrist were not given access to each other's findings and that their terminology and even the meaning of the terms employed by them were often so different that comparisons were difficult. Nevertheless, with regard to some traits a high measure of agreement was discovered, for example, where the Rorschach analyst had labelled the delinquents as more 'assertive' and 'defiant', the psychiatrist called them more 'stubborn' than the others.[44]

Only one more of the many comparative findings of *Unraveling* may here be mentioned because it contradicts one of the most common assumptions in criminological literature: the delinquents were found to show a slightly lower incidence of feelings of insecurity and anxiety and of not being loved or wanted.

While, as already mentioned above (Chapter 1, I(2c)), the Gluecks in 1950 still believed that from the wealth of data accumulated in *Unraveling* a tentative causal formula or 'law' seemed to emerge which enabled them to construct not only a physical and socio-cultural but also a psychological picture of delinquents as a mass (p. 281), six years later they had to admit that from the evidence available 'we cannot conclude that there is a "delinquent personality" as a relatively constant and stable combination of physique, character, and temperament'.[45] However, if we compare the picture presented in *Unraveling* with the results of other studies using case material of a different kind we find on balance slightly more agreement than disagreement. Certain features such as aggressiveness or the feeling of personal inadequacy are widely regarded as characteristics of the delinquent personality, whereas on others, such as extraversion or insecurity, the views tend to differ.[46] Even where there is a certain measure of agreement that a given trait is more frequent among the delinquents than the non-delinquents the difference, though perhaps statistically significant, is often still small enough to make us wonder whether it really contributes much to our understanding of the delinquent. Added to this, it is the principal weakness of all such statistical comparisons of individual traits that they ignore the personality as a whole. It may be a matter of some interest to us to know that 80 per cent of a group of offenders were found to be aggressive, inadequate and frustrated against, say, only 60 per cent of a group of non-offenders, but this still does not tell us whether these traits have all been present in 80 or 60 per cent respectively of the individual members of these two groups or whether some of those found to be aggressive were not inadequate and frustrated and vice versa. It is here that the typological studies referred to above (Chapter 8, II(2)), with their attempts to work out configurations of several factors, are of value, and recent research designed to show certain relationships between a variety of phenomena by means of factorial analysis may also be mentioned. Through factorial analysis a large number of variables can be correlated with each other in the expectation that 'from this mass of correlations a few factors can be extracted which are themselves independent of each other . . . and if we are lucky we finish up with an explanation of *why* these variables are correlated with each other'.[47] B. Marcus, psychologist at Wakefield Prison, believes he has extracted in this way a factor which distinguishes, sociologically and psychologically, middle-class criminals, for example false pretenders and homosexuals, from working-class criminals, i.e. mainly thieves and housebreakers. Further research on similar lines may produce further concatenations of psychological traits. The latest volume of the Glueck studies, *Family Environment and Delinquency*, published after the completion of the present chapter,[48] in fact provides many illustrations of the complex ways in which psychological, sociological and biological factors may combine in one individual to produce delinquency. To single out a few of these combinations may give a misleading picture; the reader will have to study the book as a whole to appreciate the extreme complexity of this work and the equally great caution with which—as the authors are fully aware—the results have to be interpreted.[49]

IV. PSYCHOLOGICAL PROBLEMS OF DIFFERENT TYPES OF CRIME AND CRIMINALS, WITH SPECIAL REFERENCE TO MURDER

To make a complete survey of the psychological factors which might potentially lie behind criminal behaviour a systematic analysis would be needed of the main types of both the human personality and the motives which stimulate it into action and then show which of the psychological features of the personality and which motives have been encountered with particular frequency among criminals. Personality—a term of which Allport listed no fewer than 48 definitions already in 1937[50]—could be defined in this connection with Eysenck as 'the more or less stable and enduring organization of a person: character, temperament, intellect, and physique, which determines his unique adjustment to the environment'.[51] In this chapter we are concerned with character and temperament rather than with intellect and physique. Cattell, whose preliminary definition of personality is simply 'that which determines behaviour in a defined situation', distinguishes dynamic traits concerned with 'motivation, action and purpose', temperamental traits concerned with 'pervasive, unchanging qualities and tempos of our actions', and ability.[52] The studies referred to above under III and in Chapter 8, II, have produced some material on various character and temperamental traits of offenders, but, as already stated, it is far from adequate to give a complete picture, and the psychological study of some of the most common types of offenders is still in its infancy or, possibly, in its early adolescence. Whether the legal typology of offences is the most suitable basis for psychological differentiation may be open to doubt, but it has at least the practical advantage that it offers the easiest access to the case material.

Because of its gravity and the fascination which it invariably exerts, more psychological work has been done on homicide than on any other crime, except sexual offences, and the occasional attempts on the part of legislators to use psychological factors, especially motives, in order to distinguish murder from manslaughter[53] have also helped to swell the volume of literature on the subject. It is not surprising that the legislator, if he wishes to introduce in this field psychological factors other than the usual ones such as intent, negligence, malice, should prefer the distinction according to motives, which can be defined comparatively easily, rather than personality types which are more difficult to describe. It should be remembered, however, that with very few exceptions such as the one just mentioned the motive of a crime is irrelevant to the question of legal responsibility and becomes important only for the sentence and for the criminological understanding of the criminal act.

Out of the literature on motives of murder the following deserve special mention: Wolfgang, von Hentig, Bjerre, F. Tennyson Jesse, Roesner, Brearley, Norwood East, Abrahamsen, Ferracuti and Frederic Wertham, to whose study of a case of matricide attention was drawn above (Chapter 8).[54] In addition, there are the E.E.G. studies (Chapter 51 above), which deal mostly, but not exclusively, with abnormal cases, and a few attempts have also been made to assess the motives of murder statistically.[55] Unfortunately, the concept of motive is not always used in the same sense and occasionally confused with intention or cause in general; nor is the terminology on which the statistics are based always identical. Moreover, the frequency of the various motives depends to some extent on the legal definition of murder to which the statistical figures refer, for example if that definition requires certain motives it is obvious that the latter will appear more frequently here than in legislations which do not distinguish murder from manslaughter according to motive. With these important reservations the following statistical data may be reproduced: For 551 cases of murders committed in England and Wales during the 20 years ending 1905 (*Criminal Statistics for England and Wales, 1905*, p. 52, reproduced in *Report on Capital Punishment, 1953*, p. 329) 'quarrels or violent rage' were regarded as the 'motive or cause' in 68 cases, 'jealousy and intrigues' in 92, 'revenge' in 77, robbery in 50, extreme poverty in 39, sexual passion in 26 cases. For 465 persons charged with murder in 1957–60 Morris and Blom-Cooper give as 'motive or reason', theft in 33, sex in 23, quarrel and/or fight in 87, public brawl in 34, fit of temper/desperation in 33, mental disorder in 105, jealousy, etc., in 54, mercy or despair, etc., in 33, revenge or intrigue, etc., in 18 cases. In the figures for 1955–60 in the Home Office Research Unit report, quarrels or violent rage and jealousy and intrigue account for about one half of the cases, with robbery or financial gain and sex accounting together for about 30 per cent. This shows that the picture has not greatly changed in the past seventy years in this country, the emotional type of murder remaining most prominent. In Germany, where the conception of murder has been, both before and after the legal changes of recent decades, narrower than in English law, and where emotional killings are therefore more likely to be treated as manslaughter, a higher proportion of murder cases is due to economic motives, although this applies, naturally, more to murders of men than to murders of women.[56] In the United States, the picture is not so clear, but Wolfgang's recent figures for Philadelphia show a great preponderance of emotional over economic motives. Finally, in accordance with the Egyptian idea of revenge and retaliation as the basis of justice the motive of murder in Egypt is given in the official statistics as revenge, quarrels and disputes in roughly 50 per cent.[57]

Admittedly, all these attempts to classify the motives of murder statistically are bound to remain on the surface as they are by necessity often based on a superficial knowledge of both external and internal facts. For further knowledge we have to turn to more detailed studies of individual cases which will at once demonstrate the utter complexity of the motives sometimes working together in one single murder case, making any generalization very hazardous. There may be a layer of motives, and the one nearest to the deed may be entirely different from the more remote and actually decisive ones. Murder committed for financial gain may have ulterior sexual or political motives, and what seems to be a sexual murder may in fact have been due to financial considerations. Hentig has stressed the dynamic nature of a motive which may have to pass through many environmental changes and stimuli, some of them reinforcing, others weakening the strength of the motive. In many cases, especially of murder for the sake of robbery, the motive seems entirely inadequate in any rational way to explain the crime; the murderer himself is certainly unable to do so, and we have to search for unconscious motives, which means a psycho-analytic explanation (Chapter 17).[58]

This lack of a rational, adequate motive, which would be clearly understood by judges and the public, explains the not infrequent tendency to speak of a *motiveless* crime. A girl of fifteen is found murdered in the lavatory of a train. She has not been sexually assaulted, nor are any of her belongings missing: consequently, according to the prosecution this was 'apparently a crime without motive' (*The Times*, 15.9.1964). Stafford-Clark and F. H. Taylor, in the paper annexed to the *Minutes of the Royal Commission on Capital Punishment*, 1953 (p. 330), include in one of their five groups of cases of murder with different E.E.G.s those cases 'in which the crimes were apparently motiveless or in which the motive was very slight' and in many of which the E.E.G. was slightly or severely abnormal. We are not here concerned, however, with crimes committed by mentally abnormal persons whose motives are often so remote from the understanding of ordinary persons that their actions seem unmotivated to them. Even here, although we find it impossible to accept Cressey's extreme sociological theory of criminal motivation in its entirety he is right in stating that most behaviour traditionally labelled 'compulsive' is in fact motivated.[59] Of André Gide we are told that the idea of the 'unmotivated crime' committed by a normal person had constantly occupied his mind and that he treated it most thoroughly in his novel *The Vatican Cellars*. Has he succeeded in bringing the problem nearer to a solution? Lafcadio, his hero, pushes a man with whom he was travelling, a complete stranger to him, out of the fast moving train to his death. Certainly, no motive in the traditional sense was present in the case of this murder, and we are rather faced with a crime committed with the motive to kill without any of the traditional motives. What Gide has done in this novel is, therefore, not to demonstrate the possibility of a motiveless crime but to add to the catalogue of traditional motives, and this is essentially what he puts into the mouth of his frustrated novelist, Julius de Baraglioul. 'I don't want a motive for the crime—all I want is an explanation of the criminal. Yes! I mean to lead him into committing a crime gratuitously—into wanting to commit a crime without any motive at all. . . . His very reason for committing the crime is just to commit it without any reason.'[60] But, as Gide tries to show, Lafcadio's motive is also to find out whether he is a man capable of doing this: 'It's not so much about events that I'm curious, as about myself. There's many a man thinks he's capable of anything who draws back when it comes to the point. . . . What a gulf between the imagination and the deed!' (p. 185). In other words, we are here faced with yet another motive which we shall soon meet again in Dostoevsky's Raskolnikov: to prove to himself that he is a man capable of translating his imagination into action. In his interesting article on *Liberté et gratuité du crime dans l'œuvre d'André Gide*[61] the Spanish lawyer and writer Antonio Quintano Ripollès argues that Lafcadio shows the most obvious characteristics of the leptosome type (see above, Chapter 13), i.e. poor physique, coldness and egocentricity. He admits that from Gide's description no evidence emerges of mental disorder; on the contrary, he thinks Gide has proved the possibility of a 'motiveless' crime committed by a sane person. Nevertheless, he suggests that Lafcadio may show symptoms of latent schizophrenia or psychopathy, and the latter concept may indeed offer the most likely interpretation of Lafcadio's behaviour.

Motives can become operative only when they are joined together with a certain personality; a motive that will easily drive this particular person into this particular crime may utterly fail if working on another person. This, too, is demonstrated in Gide's novel. This 'motiveless' murder could be committed only by a man to whom human life had no intrinsic moral value: 'I felt as though I could have clasped the whole of mankind to my heart in my single embrace—or strangle it, for that matter. Human life! What a paltry thing! . . .' (p. 177). One can distinguish between crimes which are an expression of the offender's personality (*persönlichkeits-eigen*) and crimes which seem to be a deviation from it, an 'acting out of character' (*persönlichkeits-fremd*).[62] The same applies to the offender's motives, which may or may not be in line with his personality. If a motive is in harmony with the personality of the actor it need not be particularly strong, whereas if it is entirely out of keeping with the latter it will have to be of great force in order to drive a person into crime. The supreme difficulty which this distinction has to overcome lies in the problem to determine whether an act is 'in harmony' with the personality as a whole and whether it is therefore something easily to be expected of a certain individual. It is here that individual prediction will so often go astray (see Chapter 7 above) and it is here, too, that the idea of the *état dangereux*, so widely discussed in recent decades in Continental criminology, encounters one of its major stumbling blocks.[63] This concept, first formulated by Garofalo, has been defined in different ways; its object is to describe a human condition which justifies the expectation that the individual concerned is likely to commit a crime or crimes because of his biological and psychological characteristics, his *perversité constante*, his inability to adapt himself to his social environment. In the Italian Penal Code of 1930, art. 108, the 'delinquent tendency' is mentioned which is regarded as being caused by the particularly mischievous disposition of the offender, and according to art. 133 the judges, in sentencing the offender, have to consider, among other factors, his motives and character as indices of his capacity for wrongdoing. All this reminds us rather ominously of Lombroso and his followers, but it has to be admitted that modern criminology has taken considerable pains to produce a less biased and unscientific picture of the criminal personality. It has, for example, been shown that there are two different types of *état dangereux*, the permanent condition which the Lombrosians had especially in mind and a merely transitory state of mind through which many delinquents have to pass before they commit the criminal act and during which phase much can be done to divert them from it. As Pinatel rightly says[64] it was this second type which has been greatly clarified through the writings of the late Belgian psychiatrist and criminologist Etienne de Greeff, notably in relation to homicides committed out of jealousy or sexual passion.[65] de Greeff describes in detail the phenomena of what he calls *désengagement* and *révalorisation*, taking place in the case of individuals who have suffered an acute disillusionment and betrayal, feelings which lead to a sudden and complete reversal of all their beliefs and values and are the frequent cause of murder and/or suicide. The road to the final catastrophe may be very short or very long, but if those observers who can foresee the seemingly inevitable outcome are able to secure a postponement of the fatal action with some helpful psychological intervention in the interval, that action may sometimes be averted for good. Although both personality and motive may strongly favour the commission of the crime it also requires a certain atmosphere, a mood, a congenial situation and an opportunity, and once they have passed the crime may appear senseless. Othello might have been an example of this type. In striking contrast to such cases there are those where no outside interference short of physical force is capable of creating an effective diversion because of the principal actor's unbending determination to commit the murder. This is mainly the field of the family tragedy or the homicide committed for political ends or for revenge where, for example, a man sentenced to a long period of imprisonment for a crime of which he regards himself to be innocent kills, after his discharge, the principal witness for the prosecution. Here the hope to be able to take revenge has supported him throughout his years in prison, and no force on earth can make him change his mind once he is free.

With such cases we have already entered the field where a distinction is made between crimes with an intense 'ego involvement' and others where the actor's ego is not deeply involved.[66] Although this is very close to the previously mentioned distinction between *persönlichkeits-eigen* and *persönlichkeits-fremd*, it is not identical with it. While the latter is concerned with the question of whether a particular deed is in harmony with the total personality of the actor, the former is more specifically interested in the relationship between this personality and the victim or object of the crime. If the murderer wants to kill just this particular person or the thief to possess just this particular picture, book, stamp or piece of jewellery; if the murderer feels that his own life depends on the death of this person and the thief that he cannot exist without this article, which is still missing in his collection, then we would say that his ego is deeply involved in the matter.[67] As already indicated, this is the field of many family tragedies, the long drawn-out blood feuds or political murders. Homicides committed as the seemingly only way out of an impossible marital impasse have repeatedly been studied by psychiatrists and psychologists. In a short, but penetrating, Canadian study by Cormier[68] observations are reported on eight men who had killed their wives or women with whom they had stood in an equivalent relationship. They were seen in prison some years after they had been sentenced to imprisonment either for life or for shorter periods. Although these men were very different in personality, attainment, social position and in many other ways, a 'repetitive pattern' emerged from these studies, and eventually the observing psychiatrist 'began to have the sensation that we were listening to the same story'. There had been strong ties between these men and the women, 'a realization from the start that they were in some way interlocked and that they needed one another not only for their well-being, but for the reverse, because of their problems'. In the course of their relationship, distrust, jealousy, violence, separations and reconciliations occurred, but in spite of a growing awareness of the dangers involved in their living together, a 'kind of foreknowledge that it might end in tragedy', neither party was willing or able to make a final break, until the murder occurs 'at a point of intense emotion and a feeling that to continue is inconceivable and to give up impossible'. It is only after the trial that the men begin to understand why the relationship had broken down and in what way each of the partners had been guilty.[69]

A type of murder which was *persönlichkeits-eigen* and in which the ego was also deeply involved, is the case of 'Gunnarsson' discussed by Bjerre.[70] Here, the crime arose without the clash of two incompatible personalities but in a one-sided fashion, if we accept Bjerre's Adlerian interpretation—entirely out of the various defects in the actor's character, his insecurity, inferiority feeling, fear of life, inner isolation, hatred of other people and dependence on his mother.

The opposite extreme is represented by murders, which occur from time to time, of persons who are complete strangers to the actor and who are killed, not as in the case of Gide's Lafcadio, in order deliberately to demonstrate the characteristics of a 'motiveless' crime, but because the actor has the real urge to kill, to kill *in abstracte*, one might say, while the person of his victim is entirely indifferent and uninteresting to him. A prostitute was murdered in London in this way some years ago, not as usual in such cases for sadistic reasons by mentally abnormal persons or for financial gain by a very ordinary customer, but as the killer explained, because 'she would not be missed'. Here, the crime was probably wholly in line with the total personality structure (*persönlichkeits-eigen*), but there was no 'ego-involvement' in this particular murder; the latter concept is therefore narrower than the former.

The Report of the Warren Commission established in 1964 by President Johnson to investigate the circumstances of the assassination of President Kennedy cautiously concluded that, on the strength of the available evidence, no definite analysis could be made of Oswald's personality and motives. Even so, certain driving forces seem to emerge from the facts assembled by the Commission: resentment of any kind of authority; inability to establish meaningful relationships with other persons; an urge 'to try to find a place in history' (which is reminiscent of the 'destroyer' of the Library of Alexandria??); all this combined with the despair over the failure of his various attempts to achieve his object, with his communist indoctrination and his tendency to use violence (*The Times*, 29.9.1964). One might perhaps argue that such a case, as many other political assassinations, stands somewhere between those crimes which are clearly *persönlichkeits-eigen* with ego-involvement and those where, as in the case of the prostitute, there is no ego-involvement. In the Kennedy murder case the ego of the murderer was deeply involved, and the person of the victim was of the greatest significance to him, but not really as an individual but merely as the highest representative of authority (on political crimes see also below, Chapter 21, i).

The so-called 'short-circuit' actions (*Kurzschluss-Handlungen*) will usually, but not always, be out of harmony with the total personality. This name has been given to crimes where an intensely emotional

300

situation suddenly triggers off an impulsive action, usually homicide.[71] Here, the intense stimulus due to an unexpected, highly affective, external event, such as the discovery of marital infidelity, an insulting word, the unforeseen resistance of the victim of robbery or rape, easily releases acts such as murder by shooting, stabbing or strangling. Lenz describes such cases as reactions to an overwhelmingly strong outside stimulus where the impact of the latter does not 'run through' the whole of the personality, but shows its effect immediately in impulsive action. He mentions as illustrations the 'smash ups' in prisons with furious attacks on officers and furniture and also family murders, which latter may however be of a very different kind.[72]

As an example of a 'short-circuit' murder the case of a man of 21 may be quoted who stabbed to death a 'complete stranger' for, as the prosecution thought, no apparent motive. He gave himself up to the police, stating: 'There was an argument because he bumped into me. I lost my temper and let fly at him with my knife.' According to the psychiatric evidence he had been rejected for the Army because of 'anti-social trends of long standing'. Moreover, the accused had stated that the murdered man had called him a name inferring that he was illegitimate, and to him 'the word was like a spark to gunpowder'.[73] He was sentenced to death, as this happened several years before the Homicide Act of 1957.

Or, another, more recent, case:[74]

While two brothers were watching television a dispute arose between them over whether the dining room door should be shut or open. A scuffle arose, in the course of which the elder brother, aged 16, stabbed and killed the younger, aged 14. He was said to be a well-behaved boy who had never shown any violent temper, and the prison medical officer expressed the view that he was suffering from some emotional immaturity which would probably right itself in the future; there was no need for special treatment. The boy was placed on probation for manslaughter.

Cyril Burt,[75] discussing a similar case, uses it to stress the importance of deep unconscious motives and suspects that 'some long-drawn-out situation has been secretly playing on his (the offender's) deeper emotions, until at last the exasperation has grown too great for his powers to control. In short . . . to understand such exceptional actions, we have to assume, not an exceptional class of persons, but merely the persistence of rough, irrational and emotional springs of action which come into play when, not the person, but his situation becomes exceptional. . . .' Of course, in the above case of the two brothers this does not apply as the situation was hardly exceptional.

Lange[76] draws attention to the close relationship of these short-circuit actions and those committed by schizophrenics and people suffering from chorea.

In the famous case of Albert Camus' *Outsider* (*L'Etranger*) there was the factor of sultry, oppressive heat that provided an additional stimulus to the actor's feeling of intense anxiety as to whether the Arab would attack him with his knife. 'A few hundred miles farther south', writes Cyril Connolly,[77] 'and a touch of the sun would have been readily recognized, no doubt, as a cause for acquittal in the case of a white man accused of murdering a native' (this was written in 1946). Here, the hero, Meursault, shows none of the conventional emotions throughout the whole narrative, neither before or after the shooting incident, nor during or after the trial, until right at the end he explodes. The same impassivity, though in entirely different circumstances, we find in Adolf Eichmann who, however, defended himself to the best of his ability at the trial, whereas Meursault showed no interest in his fate.

The *crime passionnel* has been brilliantly discussed by Marc Ancel[78] from the point of view of the criminologically oriented lawyer and mainly, though not exclusively, within the framework of French law and court practice. Ancel, speaking of the 'new conception of *crimes passionnels* emerging in modern penal legislation', points out that these crimes may be of a very different character psychologically and committed with very different motives, often 'a curious mixture of cupidity, egoism and a warped sense of justice', but likewise the result of violent emotions which paralyse all the forces of self-control. As he rightly says, all this is increasingly taken into account in modern criminal legislation and court practice (see also Chapter 18 below), but, on the other hand, French juries who used to be over-lenient in such cases have of late adopted a sterner attitude. In English law and practice, as the Brighton homicide and other cases show, the opposite trend has become apparent.

The number of homicides committed in Britain between 1957 and 1960 in a 'fit of sudden temper or desperation' has been estimated at 33.[79]

The close connection between murder and suicide, so often stressed in criminological literature, offers very valuable insights into the psychology of the murderer. While it is a wild exaggeration to regard every homicide as a veiled form of suicide there is no doubt that in many cases, especially those with strong ego-involvement, either the homicide is followed by suicide, or at least attempted suicide, or stands psychologically in the place of the latter.[80] In England and Wales between 1955 and 1960, murderers committed suicide in about 20–27 per cent (men who had killed women over 16) and 8–15 per cent (women who had killed men over 16).[81] The fundamental psychological drive is here aggression which is sometimes turned against other persons and sometimes against the individual himself, but in the former case, too, it may happen that this aggression seems only to the superficial observer to be turned against somebody else; indirectly and on a deeper level it is meant to be directed against the actor himself. In the widely discussed Loeb-Leopold case of 1924, according to Abrahamsen[82] the killing of the boy at least for Loeb was 'a psychic killing of himself' and an expression of his desire for punishment. Others are more inclined to think it was done 'for a kick' or to carry out the 'perfect' crime which would defy detection.

On the other hand, a suicide may in fact be nothing but the 'introjected' killing of another person.[83] Here again, however, we enter the realm of psycho-analytical explanations. Where the homicide does not stand in the place of suicide but is combined with it, often as a so-called suicide-pact, the circumstances and motives may show a considerable variety. Where the suicide remains at the stage of attempt intricate questions may arise for the criminal law and its reform,[84] but more because of the difficulty of proving the seriousness of the attempt than because of the other psychological problems involved (the latter have been psycho-analytically explored by Ernest Jones and others).[85]

When all is said about the psychology of murder and the murderer one will have to agree with the Report of the Royal Commission of 1953, referring to their sample of fifty cases (Appendix 4), that this crime 'may be human and understandable, calling more for pity than for censure, or brutal and callous to an almost unbelievable degree. . . . The motives . . . show some of the basest and some of the better emotions of mankind, cupidity, revenge, lust, jealousy, anger, fear, pity, despair, duty, self-righteousness, political fanaticism, or there may be no intelligible motive at all.'[86]

For many crimes other than homicide the range of personality factors, motives, psychological situations, emotions, sentiments, attitudes, drives, etc., which may be regarded as connected with criminal behaviour, is not much less wide. In view of the somewhat uncertain state of modern psychological terminology it is not easy to find generally accepted descriptions of the psychological factors involved. McDougall[87] distinguished between a sentiment which he described as 'an enduring structure within the total structure of the mind or mental organization', and an emotion which was 'a passing phase or, more strictly, an aspect of a phase of mental process'. Nowadays one is more inclined to speak of attitudes than of sentiments. To W. I. Thomas[88] the terms temperament and character were merely concepts to express the fact that 'there are always a few organized groups of attitudes in a personality which play a predominant part in its activity . . .'

303

V. VARIOUS SPECIFIC PERSONALITY TRAITS: IN PARTICULAR: INADEQUACY AND IMMATURITY. THE FRUSTRATION-AGGRESSION THEORY. THE 'FOUR WISHES'. THE SENSE OF INJUSTICE. THE 'EXTRAORDINARY MAN'. RATIONALIZATION

In addition to the material already presented in this chapter, attention may also be drawn to the following:

As already mentioned (Chapter 15) the 'inadequate' personality of many criminals is an experience which impresses in particular psychologists working in prisons. In Dr. Roper's masterly analysis of 1,100 inmates of Wakefield Prison 1948-9 (all 'stars' with a sentence of at least one year) 51 per cent were classified as inadequate, meaning a 'rather vague and ineffective personality'.[89] Obviously, this is not much different from what Bjerre regards as 'the determining factor in all crime', i.e. weakness or general unfitness, to which he adds self-deception, escape from the realities of life.[90] Moreover, at the end of Chapter 15, I (2), the view of de Berker was mentioned that a large percentage of 'normal' prisoners fall under the category of 'inadequate' personality, and to some extent this was confirmed by Grygier's T.A.T. research.

Roper also stresses the *immaturity* of most criminals. He estimates that in addition to the 'inadequates' another 20 per cent of his sample, schizoids, hysteroids and aggressives, had to be regarded as 'immature' personalities, making a total of 71 per cent. He even suggests that immaturity and criminality may be much the same thing and that, as we all start as immature beings, criminality may be the 'natural' condition of man. 'Crime', he writes, 'is essentially the solution of personal problems at childlike level of conduct either because basic attitudes have never developed beyond that level or because there has been regression to childish attitudes as a result of frustration.'[91] In this, without mentioning Freud, he refers of course to essentially psycho-analytical ideas; see for example Glover's dictum: 'judged by adult social standards the normal baby is for all practical purposes a born criminal'.[92] While this theory, apart from its intrinsic merits, is well in keeping with the statistical age curve of crime (below, Chapter 26) it cannot explain the behaviour of the minority of late starters,[93] whose problems are often quite different from those of the bulk of criminal cases.

An interesting attempt has been made by the Gluecks to work out a theory of *maturation* and to explain why the factor of ageing plays such an important role in the reformative process. Among those who continued their criminal careers after what was regarded as the crucial age of 35 there was, in addition to several unfavourable environ-

mental factors, a markedly higher proportion of 'emotionally unstable' persons.[94] For them, the passage of time which socializes the
environmentally conditioned offender, only tends to aggravate their
maladjustment. The Gluecks suggested the establishment of a 'maturation quotient' (M.Q.) to measure the degree of deviation from the
maturation norm.[95] In their subsequent publications, however, the
matter has not been taken up again.

While, as mentioned above, the Gluecks, in *Unraveling*, did not find
that the delinquents in their sample felt more insecure than the non-
delinquents, the feeling of insecurity has been regarded by other
writers as an important factor in the interpretation of delinquency.
T. R. Fyvel, for example, entitles a book, to be discussed further
below, *The Insecure Offenders*.[96]

The *frustration-aggression theory*, too, has a wide following,
especially since its comprehensive treatment by Dollard.[97] In his very
influential book the assumption is used as the point of departure
that aggression is always a consequence of frustration, although
frustrating situations do not inevitably produce overt aggression.
After briefly discussing the place of the frustration-aggression thesis
in the Freudian and Marxist systems he surveys in his criminological
chapter a large number of factors, such as economic conditions,
occupation, physique, age, sex, in their relation to frustration and the
anticipation of punishment (in its widest sense). His assumption here
is that criminals show 'higher-than-average frustration and lower-
than-average anticipation of punishment', i.e. they are more easily
frustrated and less easily deterred by the expectancy of punishment.
Frustration is of course the all-pervading feeling in our western
civilization at present,[98] but criminals suffer even more from it than
others. Grygier's research has produced some further evidence to
support the frustration-aggression hypothesis. Roper, too, writes:
'crime starts, as I have seen it, as a reaction to frustration . . .' but he
admits that 'special determinants are usually necessary before a
frustration reaction will take the form of crime'. In fact, we might
perhaps say, frustration, especially repeated and prolonged frustration, will express itself somehow, very probably in an anti-social feeling which may take the form of aggression in its widest sense, for example in strikes, 'working to rule', unkindnesses and discourtesies of
all sorts, chicane and so on. If other essential personal and environmental conditions are present it may take the form of crime. For
children Brian Kay found that delinquents and neurotics had a lower
frustration tolerance than the members of his control group, but that
it varied according to frequency, intensity and type of frustration.[99]
An impressive illustration of the psychological effects of persistent
and complete frustration in a primitive setting is given in one of

Maxim Gorki's *Short Stories* in the following dialogue between two Russian peasants of the Tsarist epoch:[100]

'You may have many reasons for it, but it's not your wife's temper that causes you to treat her so unwisely. The cause is your own unenlightened condition.' 'That's just so,' exclaimed Yakoff—'We do indeed live in darkness as black as pitch'—'The conditions of your life irritate you, and your wife has to suffer from it. . . . She is always there ready to your hand, she can't get away from you.' Thereupon Yakoff turns to the other man and says: 'Stop! You beat your wife also, don't you?' 'I'm not saying I don't, because I do. How can I help it? I can't beat the wall with my fists when I feel I must beat something.' 'That's just how I feel,' says Yakoff.

Mutatis mutandis, this will go a long way to explain seemingly senseless or psychotic acts of violence.

In his long experience as a prison medical officer Roper found that the anti-social reaction caused by frustration, unless stopped at once by the 'crisis of discovery', might take ten or twenty years to 'burn itself out'—which is probably only another name for the maturation concept of the Gluecks—'partly because crime can be made profitable, and partly because the original frustration situation, if unresolved, is apt to become worse as disgrace and punishment accumulate'. Each of these two considerations helps to explain the making of a persistent criminal career, the one of a successful, the other of an unsuccessful one.

As frustration is largely due to social and economic conditions more will have to be said on it below (Chapters 19 ff.).

In the field of juvenile delinquency it may be useful to classify the various potential sources of frustration by adopting W. I. Thomas's list of the 'four wishes', which if remaining unsatisfied easily lead to anti-social conduct. Although Thomas changed his classification many times,[101] the following four wishes seem to have remained essential components: the desire for security, (conflicting with it) for new experience, for response and for recognition. Other psychologically important classifications of the various types of juvenile delinquency have been mentioned above in Chapter 8 (text to Notes 46–7). In popular language, they can perhaps be summed up as follows. Why does a child steal? Because he wants (*a*) to use the article for his own enjoyment, which seems the most 'normal' case; or (*b*) because he wants to hoard it, which betrays some complications; or (*c*) because he wants to give it away to buy with it love, security, response, recognition; or (*d*) for the thrill of stealing (new experience); or (*e*) because he wishes to test somebody's affection, notably that of his parents (Stott's 'delinquency attention'); or (*f*) because he has given up hope and only wishes to spite and hurt (see also Stott). A subsidiary of (*f*) may be the wish to be removed from home (also Stott). While no list of this kind can be exhaustive, this one seems to contain most of the essential possibilities.

This scheme is, however, applicable not only to juveniles. Adults, too, are liable to similar emotions. Their need for recognition, for example, may be responsible for economic offences committed to 'buy' status. While more on this will have to be said below (Chapter 20) as an illustration the following case may here be quoted:

A single woman aged 53, with many previous convictions, had been discharged from prison in 1955 and settled down in a village in South England where she led a blameless life for about five years, attaining a position of trust in the community and becoming a parish councillor and president of the local women's institute. She then began to give expensive parties, to arrange flower shows, etc., for which the money had to be obtained by false pretences. The defence pleaded that she had not acted for personal gain and that there was 'absolutely no motive' for her offences. She was sentenced to 21 months' imprisonment. There was of course a strong motive present, the need for social recognition and rehabilitation, particularly active in a person with her criminal background.

As a more specific form of frustration the *sense of injustice* has to be especially mentioned. As Freud has said, 'the first requisite of culture is justice',[102] and if the individual's sense of justice is outraged his feeling of frustration may drive him to particularly violent acts of aggression. The present writer has in previous publications referred to famous instances of this type of criminal in world literature, such as Karl Moor in Schiller's *The Robbers* and Michael Kohlhaas in Heinrich von Kleist's great novel[103] (above, Chapter 2 at the end). Etienne de Greeff made a special study of this psychological factor, *le sentiment d'injustice subie*, which he regards of supreme importance for the understanding of normal as well as of mentally disordered criminals.[104] According to him, nobody acts in matters of any importance without having first established an at least preliminary harmony with his own conscience, and it is through the medium of his feeling of unjust treatment, be it actually suffered or only imagined, that the criminal brings his action into harmony with his own moral code. Normally, de Greeff thinks, which is probably too sweeping a generalization, no case can be found where the criminal has acted without this mechanism of justifying his conduct through his sense of having suffered some injustice. He links this with the human tendency to suspect an evil intent behind every unhappy experience, and here his reasoning is reminiscent of the discovery of modern anthropology that primitive man tries to explain all happenings, especially those painful to himself, as the result of the sinister machinations of evil spirits.[105] All this shows that what de Greeff had in mind is a somewhat wider concept of injustice than the usual one; almost any kind

307

of unpleasant experience coming from whatever source. His criminal suffering from a sense of injustice resembles the one who tries to rationalize his motives so as to make them acceptable to himself and others (see also below, p. 310).

Rosenzweig and Grygier's extrapunitive type 'aggressively attributes his frustration to other persons or objects', whereas we are here concerned only with cases where the criminal has experienced some specific treatment which he regards as unjust, be it from a court or other official source, or from an employer or teacher or similar authoritative figure. Naturally, the penal system and the criminal courts are particularly conspicuous and frequent sources of this feeling of injustice. Especially the very harsh sentences imposed in former days even for minor offences, the inequality of sentences or sentences on mere suspicion as being a 'suspected person', coupled with the rigours of imprisonment and the inadequacy of the aftercare services, have been major factors in the growing rate of recidivism. Recidivists sentenced to long terms of preventive detention for comparatively minor offences often fail to understand the reasoning behind the system; others sentenced to corrective training who fail to receive the 'training' to which they think they are entitled—all these easily develop a deep-rooted grudge against society and its representatives.[106]

A distinction not apparent in de Greeff's discussion but important for our purposes is that between the sense of injustice (a) as the original factor in the commission of a crime; (b) as something conveniently exploited to fortify an already existing criminal intent; and (c) as an instrument to justify the crime afterwards.[107] Probably in the majority of cases the sense of injustice is nothing very real, but merely a pretence which, in the course of time, may of course become something very real and the criminal's only support. Let us never forget W. I. Thomas's famous doctrine: 'If men define situations as real, they are real in their consequences,'[108] i.e. men act as if they were real.

A factor which detracts somewhat from the moral value of the sense of injustice as a point in favour of the criminal, is the experience of certain investigators that prisoners are in no way sympathetic towards their fellow prisoners. There is but little loyalty between thieves. This has been stressed by Donald Clemmer in his *Prison Community*[109] and in the Californian study of the *Authoritarian Personality*.[110] The latter, which presents the results of questionnaire research on a sample of 110 inmates of San Quentin Prison, concludes that criminals are not to be regarded as genuine rebels with a feeling of real sympathy for the underdog; on the contrary, they are unable to identify with other outcasts and try to make 'moralistic distinctions' between themselves and their fellow prisoners, each inmate tending to be 'an island in itself'. We may not be prepared to accept the San Quentin example as wholly representative of the prison population, still less of the criminal as such. The picture may get somewhat blurred if we consider such special cases as the code of honour which binds the prisoner population together and, if violated, provokes the most violent reactions against informers,[111] or loyalty among members of a gang of adolescents. As will be pointed out below, teenager delinquency is actuated not so much by a feeling of injustice experienced in individual cases, done to and by specific individuals or agencies, as by a general sense of disillusionment directed against society as a whole. This and the whole problem of sociological interpretation of the rebel will be treated below in Chapters 20 ff.

Inadequacy and immaturity are basically negative phenomena, leading mostly to offences of the 'drifting' type, asocial rather than anti-social. Frustration with its potential sequel, aggression and the feeling of injustice, occupy the middle range, i.e. a person smarting under a feeling of frustration or injustice may drift into petty crime or he may indulge in serious acts of violence. The latter are even more likely as the outcome of jealousy.[112] There is a certain psychological affinity between the sense of injustice and jealousy as in both cases the individual feels aggrieved because he cannot get or loses something which he thinks he has a right to possess.[113] Therefore, he sometimes not only kills but also mutilates and dismembers his victim so that nobody else should 'possess' her.[114] André Gide contrasts the behaviour of Othello with that of some of Dostoevsky's jealous characters, in most of whom he thinks the feeling of suffering is stronger than the urge to take violent action, nor is it accompanied by hatred of the rival—on the contrary there may even be some sort of affection for him.[115] McDougall[116] quotes Tolstoy's *Kreutzer Sonata* as a study in jealousy where the anger of the jealous husband turns not against the person of the intruder but against the beloved object. However, the matter is not so clear as McDougall seems to assume. In the first place, it is very doubtful here—and this is one of the crucial issues of that great novel—whether Pozdnishev had ever really loved his wife; according to his own story he did not. And, secondly, as the reader of that terrific murder scene will immediately notice, he might have killed the lover if the latter had not managed to escape and if—to mix a comic element with the general horror—Pozdnishev had not felt that 'it was comic to rush after my wife's lover in my stocking feet, and I wanted to be terrifying and not comic'. In short, there are no fixed rules to decide who will be the victim in such cases; it all depends on chance and on the character of the principal actors and their relations to one another.

Glover confirms the view that the feeling of jealousy is stronger in homosexual than in heterosexual relationships.[117]

Perhaps the most strongly anti-social emotions are lust for power, be it political or economic power, covetousness, greed and vanity. In *War and Crime*[118] attention has been drawn to criminal types of this kind, to a Horatio Bottomley, a Kreuger, in the world of big business, or in the realm of world literature to Ibsen's John Gabriel Borkman, and in that of world politics to a Hitler. Dostoevsky's Raskolnikov commits his murder not, as Gide's Lafcadio did, in order to experience a 'motiveless' murder and to find out whether he was capable of performing it, but to demonstrate the right of an 'extraordinary' man to commit any crime he liked. However, another, psycho-analytical, interpretation—more fully to be discussed below in Chapter 17 II(*b*) —regards Raskolnikov as a severe neurotic with a profound feeling of guilt who kills in order to be punished.[119]

To Colin Wilson,[120] Raskolnikov is a perfect example of the 'outsider' who 'hates his own weakness, he hates human weakness and misery' and thinks that in order to overcome it he has to 'arouse his will to some important purpose, to find *a definite act*', a 'gesture of defiance' which would 'give his future life a settled purpose'. Why did he fail? Wilson rejects the moral explanation that 'our neighbour is more precious than any abstract notion', but is not his own explanation that Raskolnikov is 'over-sensitive and over-estimates his own callousness' in the last resort also a moral one?

An important motivational technique employed to overcome the individual's inner resistance to the commission of crime is *rationalization* (also implied in de Greeff's interpretation of the sense of injustice). As its significance has been stressed by sociologists and psychoanalysts alike it might be mentioned in the present, more neutral, chapter instead of the next, to which it really belongs as a technique of unconscious concealment.[121] Not only criminal acts are rationalized but many others as well. Of one of the leading British politicians of our time it has been said: 'He has the gift—which Gladstone had and Macmillan had to a certain extent—of making a decision for political purposes and then believing in it, with sincerity and even with passion' (*Evening Standard*, 15.2.1962). In short, rationalization is 'constantly employed to cover the minor and major conflicts of everyday life' and has to be distinguished from deliberate lying (Glover). It may appear as a *post facto* justification of behaviour which the actor feels to be wrong, but it may also play its part before the commission of a forbidden act, in which latter case it has some motivational force. Cressey[122] has shown how this technique has worked in a number of cases of trust violation (embezzlers) studied by him. He regards it as an illustration of Sutherland's theory of differential association since it is only through frequent contacts with a culture which justifies trust violation that the would-be offender can acquire the most useful set of rationalizations. It does not seem necessary, however, to resort to Sutherland's theory; rationalization can operate independently of it. As indicated above, the sense of injustice may be closely related to it, and while it may in some cases be caused or at least strengthened by a comparison of the offender's experiences with those of others, it may also come into existence as the result of highly individual disappointments.

Imitation, which, although different from rationalization, has certain features in common with it, will be treated in Chapters 20 and 23 as it bears a particularly strong sociological connotation.

Chapter 17

THE CONTRIBUTIONS OF PSYCHO-ANALYSIS.[1]
FREUD, ADLER, JUNG

I. BASIC IDEAS OF PSYCHO-ANALYSIS

Considering the vastness and complexity of psycho-analytical litera-ture, it is clear that no complete and original account can here be given of even the essential features of this branch of psychology as represented mainly by Sigmund Freud (1856–1939), but a brief sum-mary will be presented as an introduction to the assessment of the specifically criminological contributions of psycho-analysis. Details and changes which the system has undergone in the course of its development will largely have to be ignored, and the same applies even to essential features such as the theory of dreams, or the mech-anism of transference, or the whole question of treatment, which have no direct bearing on criminological problems. Nor can any critical evaluation of the whole doctrine be attempted as it would go far beyond the scope of this book and the author would not be qualified to undertake it. All that has to be said here by way of introduction is that in the present writer's view some of the many aspects of psycho-analytical thought are of the greatest value to the understanding of crime and punishment, while others can be accepted only with im-portant reservations or not at all.

(a) Probably the best known of these basic ideas is the emphasis placed on the part played in our mental processes by the *Unconscious*, the 'submerged, invisible part of the iceberg' which forms the largest, and in many ways most powerful, sector of our mind.[2] It is distinct from the 'pre-conscious' which, although unconscious now, can be recalled to consciousness. The unconscious contains 'our instinctive urges and our repressed memories', originating to a considerable part from traumatic experiences in early childhood, some of which may have been suffered consciously, whereas others had remained un-conscious. This means that in our thoughts, emotions and actions we are governed by forces which are largely hidden and can be brought to our knowledge, if at all, only through a special technique called psycho-analysis.

(b) Considerably later than this fundamental, though not altogether original, emphasis on the significance and dynamic power of the unconscious, came the comprehensive Freudian picture of the personality structure as being divided into three layers, the *Ego*, the *Super-Ego*, and the *Id*. In this system of 'mental topography' (Foulkes) the *Id*, so called because of its impersonal, primitive, 'unorganized' quality, represents the lowest level, the 'inherited reservoir of drastic, instinctual demands', illogical and immoral, subject only to the 'Pleasure Principle', seeking immediate gratification of those demands and standing 'at the border between the somatic and the psychic . . . it supplies both the ego and the super-ego with the energies with which they operate. It is permanently unconscious' (Glover, *Psycho-Analysis*, p. 64).

The *Ego* is the largely conscious part of the human personality, but it has also a deeper, unconscious part. It does not yet exist in early childhood; the infant possesses no conscious personality, but slowly an awareness of itself is developed. Gradually, the ego becomes stronger and modifies and controls, at least to some extent, the instinctual and anti-social urges of the id. Although not sharply distinguished from the latter, the ego strives to be moral and to conform to the demands of the external world and the 'Reality Principle', which latter is supposed to govern the mature, adult person.

Finally, the *Super-Ego*, which corresponds essentially to the traditional idea of the conscience. It, too, is largely an unconscious agency. 'Conscious conscience is not the main regulator of moral and ethical behaviour. Morality and social behaviour depend primarily on the smooth operation of unconscious codes, which have been laid down during the process of upbringing.'[3] This super-ego, according to Freudian doctrine, has various sources. Flugel,[4] for example, distinguishes four of them, the most obvious of which is derived from 'the process of "introjection" or incorporation into one's own mind of the precepts and moral attitudes of others, particularly of one's parents or of other persons *in loco parentis* in one's youth'. This is also brought out in Freud's own definition, quoted by Flugel, of the ego-ideal or super-ego as 'the representative of our relation to our parents. When we were little children we knew these higher natures, we admired them and feared them; and later we took them into ourselves' (*The Ego and the Id*). In short, the basis of the super-ego is the internalized authority of the father or father-substitute. The super-ego is, however, as Flugel points out, 'no direct copy of the moral standards of the community'; it often tends to be more severe because the child, frustrated by external circumstances and too weak to turn its aggression outwards, but also because the frustrating agents are often the parents whom he loves, has to turn its aggression against the self, so shat 'the inward recoiling aggression also becomes attached to the super-ego'. 'The conscience thus contains a double dose of aggression, the aggression of the father and that towards the father' (Ginsberg, who criticizes the too exclusive concentration of Freud's doctrine on the negative, repressive side of moral life).[5] Therefore, the super-ego may become hyper-moral and tyrannical towards the ego. This and the attempts of the super-ego to control the aggressive tendencies of the ego create conflict and a sense of guilt.

Foulkes compares these three layers of the human personality to another trio: criminal–society–judge, the ordinary citizen standing between the first and the third.

From this very brief and superficial outline of the role played by the three sectors of the personality it follows that the ego is exposed to attacks from two hostile and incompatible powers, the instinctual urges of the id and the 'censorship' exercised by the super-ego. Naturally the ego tries to compromise between the two by shaping the wishes of the id so as to make them more acceptable to the super-ego, which is done by a process of *sublimation*. In the normal person some sort of sublimation will, possibly after many failures, be achieved and with it a more or less satisfactory conciliation of the two opposing forces leading to relative stability within the individual. The little boy learns in time, for example, that instead of hurting other children or pulling off spiders' legs he might better take his toys to pieces and put them together again. 'The instinct has been diverted from its original aim—inflicting pain—to a new social aim, investigation and construction.'[6] In those, very frequent, cases, however, where sublimation is impossible its place has to be taken by forcible *repression*, i.e. the aggressive or otherwise undesirable instincts are not constructively resolved, but pushed back into the unconscious where they have to remain until they break through whenever the opportunity arises. This process of repression prevents those undesirable tendencies from becoming conscious, but it may shape the future development of the personality. If, for example, the first sexual desires of the child are too forcibly repressed this may establish a general pattern of sexual repression for the rest of its life. What kind of instinctual wishes we have to repress depends largely on the kind of culture in which we live.

The struggle between the repressing and the repressed forces leads to the so-called *reaction-formation*. 'In general, reaction-formations are directed against infantile pregenital forms of love and hate. They are built up from about the age of two onwards . . . [and] constitute some of the most permanent and recognizable features of normal character, and, when they are excessive, a number of pathological character traits. Excessive scrupulosity, for example, is a typical response of the obsessional character.'[7] Exaggerated prudery as a defence against sexual urges and exaggerated brusqueness as a defence against shyness and inferiority feelings are some of the classical examples of reaction-formation.[8]

(c) The two great drives which dominate the personality are self-preservation and procreation (subsequently replaced in Freud's writings by the Life and Death instincts, Eros and Thanatos). While the first requires hardly any explanation, the second, which is identical with the Freudian concepts of *libido* and *sex*, has been the subject of much doubt and misinterpretation. Although Freud did not hold that sex was the only instinct that mattered, his extremely wide conception of the term which was in no way restricted to the genitals was bound to cause misunderstanding and dislike. We are here only concerned with the great emphasis placed by psycho-analysts on the sex-instinct as dominating human life from earliest childhood and with the resulting doctrine that infantile sexuality consists of three components or zones which, although all of them exist from birth, exercise their primacy during different phases of the child's development: first, the *oral* or suckling phase, followed by an *anal* phase, and, lastly, the *phallic* or *genital* phase.[9] There is much overlapping between the three, but generally speaking each of them has its proper time, and the way in which a child passes through them, i.e. with or without difficulties, profoundly influences its adult behaviour. If, for example, the individual experiences too much satisfaction or frustration at any one of these stages he will turn from the point of frustration to that of satisfaction, and if the latter occurred in childhood he will as an adult go back to the sexual impressions of his childhood (*fixation*).[10] Fixation, thus, is one aspect of the more general phenomenon of *regression*, the falling back upon earlier and more primitive stages in human development when greater happiness had been experienced. This process is regarded as the cause of neurosis and of sexual perversions. The latter are 'indications of conflict over earlier (infantile) forms of sexuality' (Glover, p. 35).

The period between infantile and pubertal forms of sexuality is called the *latency* period, characterized by a comparative quietening down of the sexual urges.

Another important concept is that of *identification*, which can be 'good' or 'bad', according to its objects. If the boy sublimates his feelings of hatred towards his father by trying to identify himself with the latter and to accept him as his model, or if he identifies himself with his mother by trying to comply with her reasonable wishes, this would be all to the good.

(d) So far, no reference has been made to one of the best-known concepts of Freudian theory, the *Oedipus complex*. This complex, called after the King of Thebes in Sophocles' tragedy who killed his

315

father and married his mother without identifying them as such, develops according to Freud at the time of the phallic or genital phase, roughly at the age of three, as the wish to have sexual relations with the parent of the opposite sex accompanied by a feeling of hatred and rebellion against the parent of the same sex. (In the Greek legend Freud saw 'childhood experience reproduced in the guise of adult dramatic action'.) For the boy this incestuous complex is normally resolved by the processes of identification and sublimation, but also by the castration complex and the resulting castration fear,[11] whereas for the girl its place is taken by the Electra complex, also derived from the Greek legend (Electra contributing to the murder of her mother Clytemnestra who had killed her husband Agamemnon).[12] The Oedipus complex will normally die down roughly at the age of four or five and, as Freud expressed it, its heir will be the super-ego and the conscience,[13] but on the other hand the Oedipus complex is also the 'nuclear complex of the neuroses'.[14] As usual in psycho-analytical literature, the details of all these processes are extremely complicated and controversial, but in spite of this Foulkes probably expresses the view prevailing among psycho-analysts that the Oedipus complex is no peculiarity of neurotics but 'universal and inevitable . . . a phase of crucial importance in the life of the individual', and that 'all the deeper conflicts which arise in later life can be traced back to it'.[15]

Not surprisingly, our inborn feelings of aggression and hatred and our incestuous desires create an intense sense of *guilt*. The latter is described as some sort of fear or anxiety, mainly due to the Oedipus complex, to the eventual internalization of the child's primitive impulses and the inevitable deviation from the moral standards of conduct expected by the super-ego.[16] This feeling of guilt, which exists in greatly differing strength in different individuals, is one of the fundamental concepts in the psycho-analytical interpretation of crime (see below).

Another conception of criminological significance arising from psycho-analytical theory is that of *ambivalence*. The feelings of love and hatred existing in the child towards its parents and other persons alternate so often and so rapidly as to create a 'permanent mixed attitude' of simultaneous opposing feelings towards the same object, i.e. ambivalence.[17]

The concepts of *displacement* and *symbolism* are also to be mentioned. Displacement, closely related to transference and symbolism, means the 'unconscious transfer of an interest from an earlier and more primitive object to a later substitute'; it can be a socializing process, but can also be the opposite if, for example, 'hostility is transferred from infantile objects to persons or institutions in the present day'.[18]

Symbolism is a 'primitive thought-system' in which an idea becomes the substitute for another, unconscious, one. Symbols represent mainly the love and hate relations of the child to its parents and consist of objects somehow related to the genitals, such as a dagger or knife and the serpent as representing the male and a house or bag as representing the female genitals.[19] Money or sweets are symbols of love. One object or person stands for another object or person, which latter have to be excluded from the conscious mind. 'The symbol is one of the means whereby forbidden wishes from the unconscious id are allowed to manifest themselves in disguised form in consciousness.'[20] 'Although the number of symbols runs into thousands', writes Glover,[21] 'the unconscious ideas represented in symbols are confined to a small number of primitive interests concerning the subject's own body, family figures and the phenomena of birth, sexuality and death. By far the greatest number are sexual. . . . Contrary to the views held by Jung, the symbol is regarded not as a concrete representation of an abstract idea but as a concrete representation of a more inaccessible idea, i.e. the snake represents the phallus, not just power, virility or sexuality.'

Finally, there is the mechanism of *projection*.[22] This is an unconscious process intended to enable the individual 'to identify pleasure with the self and unpleasure with the non-self'; it is therefore 'a manifestation of Freud's pleasure-principle' (Flugel). In other words, the child, and the adult as well, projects his painful experiences and aggressive desires on to other persons who become the bogies, a process which may lead to phobias, i.e. morbid fears of objects, persons or situations. Projection is one of the methods by which guilt can be diverted from ourselves to somebody else, the scapegoat. Flugel[23] has given a particularly clear analysis of this phenomenon which, with the institution of 'vicarious punishment', presents, as he says, one of the constantly recurring themes in human history. The projection of guilt on to another human group has become a convenient way of dealing with our own aggression or other anti-social instincts.

II. THE BEARING OF PSYCHO-ANALYTICAL THEORY ON CRIMINOLOGY

Even these few remarks will be sufficient to illustrate the implications of psycho-analytical theory for the understanding of crime and punishment.

(*a*) Above all, it has to be stressed that to the orthodox psycho-analyst man is by nature anti-social. 'Judged by adult social standards the normal baby is for all practical purposes a born criminal.'[24] This makes it necessary from the beginning to enquire into the relationship of Freud to *Lombroso*. One fundamental difference obviously lies

317

in the fact that to Freud all human beings alike enter life with immoral and anti-social instincts, whereas Lombroso distinguishes between the born criminal type and the rest of mankind. The third view, forcibly expressed by Martin Buber, is that 'man is not good, man is not evil. He is, in a pre-eminent sense, good and evil together.'[25] Moreover, Lombroso, at least in his earlier writings, attaches the greatest importance to inborn hereditary, or at least congenital, factors, whereas Freud recognizes the import of external experiences. Not that he ignored the force of the individual's biological and inherited endowment—far from it.[26] It was even one of the major sources of disagreement between Freud and some of the 'Neo-Freudians' whether, as he believed, 'personality is based on biological drives mainly sexual in nature which, rooted in the body with its unalterable hereditary constitution pass inexorably through certain stages of development during the first five years and then cease to develop but continue to influence behaviour throughout life',[27] or whether, as in particular his American successors maintained, the human personality is largely shaped by its social environment. 'We have reason to believe that the extent to which an individual is able to sublimate instinctive urges is dependent on constitutional, that is, inherited factors', writes the Freudian Kate Friedlander.[28] But, contrary to Lombroso, Freud, although he, too, took a too static view of society, was at least fully aware of the developmental factors in human personality, distinguishing them from the constitutional and environmental ones.[29] In addition to the succession of the oral, anal and genital phases already referred to above there is his distinction of three stages of psycho-sexual development: the Infancy period, lasting to the age of approximately five, i.e. to the dying down of the Oedipus complex, the Latency period up to the age of twelve and the Pubertal period to about eighteen. It is also interesting to note that psycho-analysts regard Lombroso's attempt to draw a hard-and-fast line of distinction between the criminal and the non-criminal as 'a narcissistic wish of the scholar to separate himself and his fellows from the criminal'.[30] On the other hand, Freud's interest in evolution brings him in some respects near to the ideas of the Lombrosian school. In his view, the unconscious psychic life of the child seems to recapitulate the evolution of the species. As in the development of the child it became necessary to suppress primitive and even cannibalistic urges, the same happened in the development of civilization as a whole. Especially the anthropologically trained psycho-analysts, Róheim and others, have tried to amalgamate their findings relating to primitive societies with Freudian theories on the development of the individual.[31] Freud himself was profoundly interested in anthropology, but in a way entirely different from Lombroso. While the latter concentrated on the anthropometric measurements of individual criminals in order to demonstrate their atavistic physical characteristics (Chapter 12 above), Freud studied the evolution of the human race to explain such phenomena as totem and taboo, the origin of social institutions, and, what is of special interest to criminal lawyers and criminologists, the sociological and psychological factors behind such crimes as parricide and behind the prohibition of incest. In his books *Totem and Taboo*[32] and *Group Psychology and Analysis of the Ego*[33] Freud, who was sceptical of the existence of a 'herd instinct',[34] tried to explain the origin of human group formation by going back to Darwin's 'primal horde', held together by the absolute power of the tyrannical father. When the sons finally rose in revolt against him and his monopoly over all the females of the horde he was killed, but this first case of parricide led to the creation of the 'two fundamental taboos of totemism out of the sense of guilt of the sons', i.e. murder of the father and incest. The sons—an illustration of their ambivalent attitude to the father, mixed of love and hatred—denounced the fruits of their deed by denying themselves the liberated women. In this way the first two crimes known to mankind were established which the community as such recognized and which forced it to take penal action. In this connection the famous controversy about the explanation of the incest taboo deserves to be mentioned, where we find Sir James Frazer and Freud on one side and Westermarck and Havelock Ellis on the other.[35] They were all interested in the question: Why do we punish incest? Is it because sexual intercourse between near blood relations is, either through instinct or through the fact of joint upbringing in the same household, something so disgusting to the normal person that he demands heavy punishment for it? Or is it because incest is so tempting to us that such punishment is needed as a deterrent? Whereas Westermarck and Ellis preferred the first alternative, Frazer and Freud came down decisively in favour of the second.[36] In their view, the essential object of the criminal law is not merely to make a solemn declaration of those actions of which the community profoundly disapproves, but to reinforce our fight against the strongest temptations in ourselves. 'Every prohibition must conceal a desire' (Freud).

Frazer argued that, far from there being a natural aversion to incest there was rather a natural instinct in its favour, and Freud reinforced his argument by making use of psycho-analytic experience and doctrine which, in his view, proved that the first sexual impulses of children were of an incestuous nature. Obviously, this controversy concerns not only those interested in the *raison d'être* behind our criminal laws, but also criminologists trying to discover the mainspring of criminal behaviour, and psycho-analysis has greatly contributed to the understanding of this problem.

All this has, of course, only a very tenuous connection with our original question of how Freud's theories are related to those of Lombroso. It shows, however, how very different was the use made by these two men of their anthropological studies.

(b) The psycho-analytic *classification*[37] of the criminal population does not basically deviate from others, and often one gets the impression that it is the scientific jargon rather than the substance that makes it sound different from the rest. The usual distinction is made of neurotic, psychotic, physically handicapped, intoxicated, normal and accidental criminals, but the numerical distribution between the various categories is different from the usual one and the interpretation is in accordance with psycho-analytical theories. With regard to the *neurotic* criminal it has to be borne in mind that the Freudian explanation of the origin of the neurosis as an unresolved conflict, on a sexual basis, between the three layers of the personality (see also Chapter 15, I) is still predominant and that psycho-analysts have shown a far greater interest in specifically criminological problems than their principal opponents, for example those of the Eysenckian school. Not surprisingly, this psycho-analytical theory of neurosis attributes to the latter a more important role in the understanding of criminal behaviour than do the followers of other psychological schools, whether they may be Jungian, Eysenckians, etc. While enough has been said in the present chapter and in Chapter 15 on the general subject of neurosis and crime, some further attention has still to be paid to what is perhaps the most fascinating and valuable of Freud's discoveries in our field, the *criminal from a sense of guilt*. He is the opposite extreme to the criminal from a sense of injustice who also may or may not be a neurotic (Chapter 16, v). Whereas the latter suffers from a real or imaginary wrong done to him or others, this Freudian figure is troubled by something he has, or believes he has, done himself, or would have liked to do. As we have seen, this feeling of guilt is attributed by Freudians mainly to the Oedipus complex and the infantile sexual urges related to it. This feeling of guilt, of course, has, as psycho-analysts admit, not been altogether invented by them out of nothing. 'All religion', writes Ernest Jones,[38] 'is founded on the idea of sin, i.e. the sense of guilt at not reaching a prescribed standard', adding however, 'The precise relation of the sin of religion to the psycho-analytical conception of feeling of guilt is too delicate a question for the answer to be given in a word.' In any case, it seems to be clear that the origins of sin in the religious sense are different from those responsible for the feeling of guilt of psycho-analysis. However, as Flugel, summarizing an article by a German theologian, points out,[39] both Christianity and psycho-analysis aim at reducing the sense of guilt, and in both there is a tendency 'to look upon suffering as a punishment for infringing the commands of some stern authority (God and the super-ego respectively)'. In both cases this stern, punishing authority is later replaced by a milder father figure and finally by the moral autonomy of the individual, although as Flugel hints Christianity and, we might add, psycho-analysis too have failed to eliminate altogether 'internal guilt and external aggression'.

According to psycho-analytical theory this feeling of guilt even positively stimulates the commission of crime, because the individual suffering from an excessive and intolerable sense of guilt looks at punishment as a possible relief. He unconsciously wants to be punished because in this way he hopes to atone not only for his new crime but also for his forbidden desires of the earlier past. His actual transgressions are usually of a comparatively minor nature: in any case, his super-ego regards them as less serious than his unconscious wishes. He feels, therefore, that the punishment he receives from the court is too severe, and a surplus remains which can be used to pay for those desires. As Alexander writes,[40] this is a mechanism betraying a primitive theory of justice, but 'latent in the depths of the personality'. It is the theory that any crime can be paid off by punishment or other suffering. Even in the normal criminal it very often leads to recidivism, in particular where in his view the penalty undergone by him has been too severe for the crime actually committed; in the criminal from a sense of guilt it is still more likely to do so because of the psychic relief which the punishment gives him. In a very interesting discourse, Flugel has linked the psycho-analytical concepts of feeling of guilt and consequent need for punishment to the old Greek idea of *Hubris* which, he thinks, has greatly retarded human progress throughout the ages.[41] Pioneers in any field have usually been accused of Hubris, and they and their achievements have been sacrificed in order to forestall divine punishment. 'It is only in so far as this fear of Hubris is diminished that rapid human progress becomes possible.' Flugel calls this fear the *Polycrates complex*, after the tyrant of Samos mentioned by Herodotus whose story is the subject of Schiller's famous poem *Der Ring des Polycrates*. While there is some truth in Flugel's interpretation of the fear of Hubris as a progress blocking force, the latter may, however, also act as a necessary and socially welcome brake which prevents the all-too-reckless exploitation of individual success to the detriment of society at large. Occasionally, this feeling of guilt may operate neither as a progress blocking force nor as a brake, but may be used as a protection against the envy of others. The Swiss psychiatrist André Repond has told the story of highly successful fathers who exploit the criminal activities of their sons to arouse pity for themselves by exhibiting their family misfortunes quite openly and, protected by the sympathetic feelings of the public, continue their own doubtful business practices.[42]

From the Freudian theory of guilt we can draw the following conclusions: First, the normal order of cause and effect between crime and guilt becomes reversed in such cases: instead of the usual sequel of events, i.e. (a) various causal factors leading to crime, (b) guilt, (c) punishment, we find: (a) guilt feelings, (b) crime, (c) punishment, (d) crime, (e) punishment, and so on, the feeling of guilt taking the place of other causal factors. Secondly, the commission of crime can lead to punishment and psychic relief only if the crime is detected. This explains why such criminals so often commit their crimes in a manner designed to lead to discovery and why they frequently show a distinct craving to make a confession, even a wrong one. This craving has been made the subject of a brilliant book by one of the ablest Freudians, Theodor Reik,[43] who, among other points, draws attention to the many indirect ways, for example by apparent slips of the tongue, in which the offender gives his secret away. A classic illustration of the unconscious urge to confess has been given by Dostoevsky in his *Crime and Punishment* to which we referred earlier on as an example of the man who commits murder because he feels himself a superman above the rules of common morality (Chapter 16, v). Raskolnikov's behaviour shows, however, that this feeling was probably only superficial, whereas the deeper, unconscious roots of his crime were his feeling of guilt and desire for punishment.[44] Perhaps the most important sections of that great novel are those which describe the many devious ways by which Raskolnikov's urge for self-betrayal expressed itself, leading to his final open confession and gladly accepted punishment. This urge to confess and to beg for forgiveness is often regarded as a peculiarly Russian characteristic which played its part in some of the notorious political trials of the Stalin regime.[45]

On the other hand, if the feeling of guilt and the desire for punishment are too strong, the offender will not confess since he does not want to be relieved of his guilt in this simple way which may lead to an undesirable mitigation of his punishment. In most cases it is clear, however, that the criminal from a sense of guilt cannot be deterred by punishment. On the contrary, punishment and pain of any kind, for example, in physical illness, may become positively attractive and satisfy latent masochistic tendencies.[46] In psycho-analytical literature cases have been reported of such offenders whose conduct was clearly designed to bring them into conflict with the criminal law, for example the case of 'Bruno' in Alexander and Staub's book, some of the cases in Alexander and Healy's *Roots of Crime*, and the case of 'Dorothy' reported by Hedwig Schwarz (see Note 1). How frequent this type of offender is cannot be ascertained statistically. Sceptics will be inclined to suspect that the sense of guilt and the wish to be punished have been read into the case history by the analyst. Occasionally, this may have happened, but in fairness it has to be stressed that even hard-boiled prison doctors have told the writer of cases where they could find no other explanation of the prisoner's conduct than the psycho-analytical one.

Moreover, it has to be borne in mind that at least some psycho-analysts are conscious that neither the feeling of guilt nor any other of their explanations are in themselves sufficient to serve as causal factors. In particular, Alexander and Healy[47] have been careful to stress the 'interplay of social and psychological factors' and certain features of American life, such as 'the heroic exhibitionist evaluation of criminal deeds' and the adoration of material success as criminogenic phenomena leading to 'over-compensatory reactions' on the part of the unsuccessful. In doing so they express views reminiscent of Adler on the psychological ((d) below) and Merton on the sociological side (see Chapter 22).

Observers are unanimous in ascribing to sex offenders, especially to homosexuals, a particularly intense feeling of guilt.[48] Among white-collar criminals, on the other hand, it is usually regarded as completely lacking, but the absence of adequate case studies may have helped to establish this view.

In his later writings, in particular in *Civilization and its Discontents*,[49] Freud placed the whole phenomenon on a broader basis than the Oedipus complex by explaining guilt as 'the expression of the conflict of ambivalence, the eternal struggle between Eros and the destructive or death instinct', a conflict which arises first within the family, later in wider forms of communal life. The sense of guilt, he writes, is 'the most important problem in the evolution of culture . . . the price of progress in civilization is paid in forfeiting happiness through the heightening of the sense of guilt'. He refers to Goethe's *Lied des Harfners*:

> *Ihr lasst den Armen schuldig werden*
> *Dann überlässt ihr ihn der Pein;*
> *Denn alle Schuld rächt sich auf Erden.*

To existentialist philosophy, too, guilt is a basic problem, but here it arises from man's responsibility for his actions. Existentialists do not accept Freud's theory of the unconscious and of the origin of guilt. To them, the sense of guilt of certain individuals stems not so much from specific acts or omissions as from a much more instinctive sense of badness or worthlessness which attacks their 'very right to be in any respect'.[50] The psychiatrist R. D. Laing, in his case history of 'Peter', relates the latter's guilt feeling to 'being in the world' and 'occupying space' although his parents had not wanted him.[51]

Another potential relationship between guilt and repeated crime may arise from the sense of shame originating from a previous crime. Shame, it is true, normally 'reinforces guilt in the control of non-conformity',[52] but occasionally, just as guilt itself, if it is too strong and threatens to undermine the essential self-respect of the personality, it may also work in the opposite direction. The offender may try to get rid of his feeling of shame by reassuring himself that what he has actually done is not evil, and in order to persuade himself and others that he is right, he commits other crimes which he tries to justify in the same way.

Resuming our description of the psycho-analytical classification of criminals we now pass on to the *normal* criminal. He is naturally much less interesting to psycho-analysts than his neurotic counterpart, and reference is usually made to him only to make it clear how uncertain the line of demarcation is between the two categories. To the psycho-analyst the main criterion of the normal criminal is that his super-ego is criminal, too: there is consequently no friction between it and the other sectors of the personality. Their whole personality identifies itself with the crime, which is of course only a different way of saying that the normal criminal, through his upbringing and environment, has been so thoroughly conditioned to a life of crime that he regards it as natural and has no qualms about it. This definition of 'normality' differs from that adopted in Chapter 16 above, where reference was made to Emanuel Miller's 'operational standard of the normal person as one who is able to meet the requirements of social life without anxiety or a tendency to withdraw . . . and meet fearlessly the inevitable obstacles of life'.[53]

Alexander and Staub include in this category not only many habitual criminals but also persistent minor offenders of the beggar and vagabond type, but in addition they mention as a borderline type the 'genuine' criminal who is socially altogether unadapted and whom they describe in a way reminiscent of Lombroso's born criminal.

While there is nothing worth mentioning in the psycho-analytic description of the physically handicapped and the alcoholic type of criminal, psycho-analysis has made an important contribution to our understanding of the *accidental or occasional* type of offence, and especially of offences due to negligence. This type of offence is subdivided into what Freud called the *Fehlleistungen*, usually translated as 'faulty acts', and the situational offence. With the first Freud dealt in two of his most widely known books, his *Psychopathology of Everyday Life*[54] and his *Introductory Lectures in Psycho-analysis*, Part I.[55] His basic idea was that such 'faulty acts', for example the forgetting of names or words, mistakes in speech, reading or writing, and similar lapses such as the losing or misplacing of articles, are not mere accidents but have a deeper meaning. He formulated the following 'principle': 'Certain inadequacies of our psychic capacities . . . and certain performances which are apparently unintentional prove to be well motivated when subjected to the psycho-analytic investigation and are determined through the consciousness of unknown motives.'[56] Although some of Freud's explanations of such faulty acts may seem rather far-fetched and although, apart from their obvious forensic implications,[57] he pays hardly any attention to the criminological significance of his discovery its importance for the understanding of offences due to negligence is very considerable. Already in my *Criminal Justice and Social Reconstruction* (p. 57) I wrote: 'it [i.e. English criminal law] has not yet grasped the profundity of the revolution which Freudian psychology has brought about in our interpretation of the idea of "negligence". Formerly a Cinderella of the criminal law, negligence has become one of its pivotal conceptions which modern legislative technique can no longer afford to neglect. . . . The reckless motorist is only the most frequent and most familiar representative of that new type of offender.' In the intervening years legislators have been trying, no doubt unconsciously, to draw certain practical conclusions from Freud's discovery of the symptomatic character of offences due to negligence, for example, by stiffening the penalties for careless driving, but the old idea that no 'real' guilt or blame attaches to such acts, which are seemingly unconnected with the personality, still lingers on in the unconscious minds of legislators, magistrates and juries alike (see also below, Chapter 21). It is, however, not only the careless motorist whose behaviour can be explained in the psychoanalytical way. The girl who is unconsciously jealous of her baby sister and, in spite of her ostensible love and care for her, lets her fall to the ground three times and nearly kills her, is another example of negligence deeply rooted in the unconscious.

The psycho-analytic explanation of the 'situational' type of occasional offender is that here the feeling of justice has been so badly hurt as to make the power of a usually well-functioning super-ego inoperative. On this type enough has been said above in Chapter 16 in non-psycho-analytical terms.

(c) For all types of criminals, the emphasis on unconscious motivation means that the teachings of psycho-analysis make us less disinclined to believe the offender when he tells us that he does not know himself 'why he did it'. When pressed for an explanation he often produces something which, although it may sound quite plausible, is nothing but a rationalization which occurs to him after the event. In a different field, too, we have been told that certain politicians 'possess the gift of making a decision for political purposes and then believing in it with sincerity and even with passion' (above, p. 310).[58]

This sceptical attitude which we owe to psycho-analysis will not only make us less angry with the offender but also more willing to search for his real motives which may be entirely different from the conscious ones. Without it we are in danger of repeating in another sphere the mistake made by medieval judges who insisted on a confession because they were sure that the accused person must have been the guilty one. In a similar way we are tempted to believe that the guilty person, because he had committed the crime, must know his motives. Moreover, the sceptical attitude which we owe to psycho-analysis—regardless of whether or not we accept its other teachings—will further help us to understand that the real motives of a crime may not only be different from the apparent ones but may even be of a character far removed from that of the crime. If in former times it was taken for granted that theft, robbery or any other economic crime must have been committed for economic reasons we now realize that the reasons may have been sexual or political. There is no inherent homogeneity between the type of crime and its motives. Kleptomania, which has already been discussed before (Chapter 15, I, 1(c)), is the best known, but not the only example of this kind.

All this is closely related to the psycho-analytical theory of *Symbolism* (see s. 1 above). Since according to it every object, every action and every person may have an unconscious symbolic value and stand for something else, this may fundamentally affect the real meaning of a crime as well. The object stolen may represent love, and the person injured may represent another person who somehow reminds the offender of the one he actually wishes to hurt. As most examples of this kind are generally known only a few typical ones may here be mentioned. Alexander and Staub[59] tell the case of a girl who stole a cheap edition of Goethe's *Faust*, worthless pictures representing a mother and child and some dresses which she could not wear. Her explanation that she hoped to become an actress and make use of the things stolen was brushed aside by the authors in favour of the psycho-analytical one that the *Faust* represented for her masculinity, the pictures stood for motherhood and the theft of dresses was an act of revenge against her mother who had neglected her. In short, all her thefts had the object of undoing the wrongs which she believed life had inflicted on her. Or there is Glover's case[60] of the girl who, shortly after the birth of a brother, began to steal cucumbers and later on pencils; these symbolic actions represented 'the desire to deprive the rival of his sexual organ and . . . to compensate herself for what she took to be a sign of girlish inferiority'. Glover adds further details to defend himself against the 'considerable scepticism among lay readers' which, he admits, would be only natural. Hedwig Schwarz's Dorothy (Note 1 above) stole always from a woman, and 'almost in-

variably a woman in a superior or enviable position (mother figure)',
i.e. all her thefts were unconsciously directed against her mother although the actual victims were other female persons. Articles of clothing are symbols of something with which to 'cover up', and hiding
clothing becomes an irresistible urge in certain persons. Abrahamsen[61]
regards robbery in certain cases 'psychiatrically speaking' as a symbolic expression of rape.

Of special interest is the application of symbolism to *political
crimes*. Its starting point is the equation of the State with the father
figure; hatred of the latter, therefore, develops into political rebellion
in later life. 'There can be little doubt', writes Flugel in an earlier
book,[62] 'that much of the general resistance to . . . authority that may
be exhibited by certain individuals, or at times by whole sections of a
community . . . derives its motive power from a persistence in the
Unconscious of parent hatred.' The political offender, it has been
said, builds up a political theory that would enable him to give vent
to his father-hatred without feeling guilty. It has also been suggested
that displaced father-hatred may often be responsible for strikes as
the tyranny of the father is, or used to be in the past, particularly oppressive among the working classes. John Gunther, in *Inside Europe*,[63]
refers to the work of another Freudian, Wilhelm Stekel, according to
whom 'an attentat is a displacement of a small personal conflict into
the life of nations'. 'Perhaps Booth was beaten by a drunken father.
So Lincoln died. Perhaps Princip had an unhappy childhood. So the
World War came.' While this referred to the First World War, the
explorers of Hitler's childhood may be able to draw similar conclusions for the second one. Generally speaking, however, it has to
be stressed that, while the revolutionary actions of certain individuals
may occasionally be explainable in psycho-analytical terms, political
mass movements cannot easily be reduced to this individualistic level.
Max Eastman has tried to give a probably over-simplified answer to
such attempts from the Marxian point of view: 'Doctors are . . . petty
bourgeois, and these Freudian doctors are driven on, in their attempts
to explain away revolution, by unconscious motives of mass loyalty
and pecuniary self-defence.'[64] While this answer is obviously not quite
convincing, it seems clear that psycho-analysis has here arrived at a
point where it is in danger of over-reaching itself and of ignoring
some of the real driving forces in history. Psycho-analysts may retort,
however, that their explanation refers merely to the individual side of
the problem and does not pretend to deal with its mass-aspects, perhaps also that the distinction between predisposing and precipitating
factors of crime, which they frequently stress,[65] may here be applied
in a way different from the usual one, treating the mass aspects as
predisposing and the individual ones as precipitating factors.

The abortive attempt made in 1936 by a man called MacMahon upon the life of King Edward VIII has been quoted by Bowlby as an example of the ambivalent love-hate mechanism noticeable in some political as well as in non-political crimes.[66] MacMahon's attitude, it is pointed out, was 'a perfect compromise between attacking and protecting' the king. Before the attempt he phoned the police and warned them that an attack would be made, and his attempt consisted not in shooting but in throwing a revolver at the king. Similarly, according to Bowlby, the man who later actually murdered President Doumer of France gave himself up to a policeman and told him that he was going to shoot the president, but the policeman did not take this seriously.

In this connection a case may be mentioned with which the present writer had to deal as a judge. A young man who often quarrelled with his father one day accompanied his friend, a soldier, to the barracks. On leaving he took his friend's service revolver with him, and after wandering aimlessly about for a few days he went to a pawnshop and pawned the revolver, but left the money behind. At his trial he told the court that he had stolen the revolver to commit suicide, but his courage had failed him. The pawnbroker reported that he had made a very distressed and confused impression. The psycho-analyst called by the defence took the view that the prisoner had committed the theft because he identified the State with his father and had taken the revolver as an unconscious act of revenge on the latter. However, in this case the explanation offered by the prisoner may have been the correct one, and it was quite in accordance with the distress he had shown at the pawnshop.

Occasionally the analogy father–state has been extended to explain the great masses of offences against big impersonal bodies within the State, such as nationalized industries, insurance companies, large department stores, etc., and in some cases there may indeed be a feeling of displaced authority-hatred behind such acts. More convincing, however, is the reference to the belief, so frequent among ordinary people, that there is nothing dishonest in robbing or cheating these overgrown bodies because they can afford such small losses and because they rob or cheat you as well.[67]

While we are here not concerned with the psycho-analytical treatment of criminals, a few points have to be made in passing. First, from what has so far been said, it will have become clear that the psycho-analytical interpretation of crime is of great practical relevance to penologists. It has sometimes been asserted that psychoanalysis wants altogether to 'abolish' such concepts as guilt and responsibility, and the institution of punishment. It is true that, while the idea of guilt plays a dominant part in the Freudian system, the scope of free will is considerably limited in it, but, as Ginsberg has said,[68] the object of psycho-analytical treatment being to enable the patient to face realities and to become a responsible person such treatment would be futile if it is assumed at the outset that he could not be helped to help himself. In the case of the girl who stole *Faust*, etc., quoted above from Alexander and Staub, Ginsberg rightly argues that her treatment consisted in bringing her unconscious motives to light and helping her to seek her gratifications in real life instead of living on the 'substitute gratifications of a neurotic'. Likewise, the institution of punishment has not been eliminated by psycho-analysis, but what the latter has done is to produce a far better understanding of the motives behind the penal system and, even more important, behind our own need for self-punishment and the use of scapegoats. It has also shown how very difficult it is to use punishment in the right way, i.e. without creating that sense of injustice and of having 'paid' for one's crimes which we have already diagnosed as one of the strongest incentives to recidivism.

While this is not the place to deal with the many serious obstacles which stand in the way of applying psycho-analytical techniques to the treatment of offenders, one or two points may be briefly made in conclusion. First, some analysts, especially Melitta Schmideberg,[69] have claimed good results for shorter periods of treatment than usually required, which would make the application of such techniques within the penal system at least a practical possibility. Secondly, psycho-analytical methods should never be applied to find out whether a certain crime has been committed by a certain person; they should never play the role of the detective. This was made clear approximately thirty-five or forty years ago on the occasion of the famous Halsmann murder trial in Austria.

(*d*) Of the many followers of Freud who later parted company with him and founded their own schools or at least systems, Adler and Jung have to be briefly mentioned as the psychologists whose writings had probably the strongest impact, second to Freud's own, on criminological thought.

Alfred Adler (1870–1937) became famous as the founder of the school of individual psychology and as the inventor of the inferiority complex.[70] Whereas Freud's system is mainly based on the idea of sex (in its broadest sense), that of Adler rests on the 'will to power', the original sense of inferiority and the consequent struggle for superiority, and it has therefore been compared to the power-philosophy of Friedrich Nietzsche, with which it has otherwise not much in common. While Nietzsche is mainly attracted by the strong superman, Adler rather concentrates on human weakness. When the individual becomes aware of his frailty he tries to compensate for it, and these attempts often lead to over-compensation, i.e. to excesses in the direction opposite to the one where the inferiority is most conspicuous. Demosthenes, the stammerer, by devoting all his energy to the fight against this handicap, becomes a great orator; Beethoven, over-coming his growing deafness, rises to the greatest heights as a com-poser; but these are very rare exceptions. As Wexberg says, the 'law of compensation' has been recognized in nature for many years, and it is of course closely related to Freud's concept of sublimation.

This concept of the inferiority complex has become one of the most convenient devices for the interpretation of human behaviour, especi-ally as it is a complex which can be attributed to practically everyone. Inferiority is a relative concept, and there will be a sector in the life of every individual when he is, or at least feels, inferior to others, be it his age, sex, physique, intelligence, race, social class or education. Naturally, if an inferiority is shared with very many other persons, its effect will be less harmful than if it is peculiar to only a few. This should apply, for example, to the Freudian penis-envy of the female sex, if one should be permitted to transfer psycho-analytical doctrines to Adlerian concepts. The object of psychological treatment should be, according to Adler, to discover the patient's 'style of life', his specific pattern of compensatory drives.

On this basis, it is easy to understand the practical significance of Adler's teachings in the field of criminology. An inferiority complex can lead to the commission of crime because this is one of the best ways of drawing attention to oneself, of becoming the centre of in-terest and thereby compensating for one's inferiority. For many people this may be their only chance in life of standing in the lime-light which they so fervently desire to bolster up their self-esteem. In the modern machine-age, the feeling of inferiority is, as Adler rightly stressed, deepened by the soulless and mechanical tech-niques employed in industrial work, which leave very little free-dom of self-expression and individual pride in the product of one's labours.

In addition to the sense of weakness and inferiority which to Adler were the main characteristics of the criminal, he found in him a conspicuous lack of co-operation,[71] which he traced back to an un-happy childhood. He particularly mentioned the feeling of frustration aroused in a first-born child who, after the birth of the younger ones, imagines himself to be deprived of his parents' love and attention.

To quote but a few case histories where, apart from Bjerre's murder cases, Adlerian concepts have been used as an explanation, East and Hubert[72] tell the story of a youth, disabled through long illness, who murdered a girl who 'did not refuse him intercourse, but made it clear to him that it would be unwelcome'. They regard the killing as, in Adlerian terminology, 'the masculine protest' of a person unable to accept further evidence of failure and due to an inferiority feeling rather than to sexual excitement.

Or, in a probation record we find the story of a girl of fifteen, between her mother's two marriages, who tries to make up for her inferior status in the family by committing incest with her three half-brothers.

The general impression left by Adler's writings is that, while his emphasis on inferiority, weakness and lack of co-operation with others has been of considerable value to our understanding of crime, he is inclined to over-simplify matters and to generalize too readily. In contrast to psycho-analytical theory which often strikes the outsider as over-sophisticated and artificially complicated, Adler's opposition tended to 'throw out much of the rich insight into the complexities of mental life that psycho-analysis had won'.[73] As Erich Fromm writes,[74] Adler sees only the rational side of the psychological phenomena he describes, he 'cannot see beyond purposeful and rational determinations of human behaviour', whereas—one might add—Freud concentrated perhaps too much on the irrational side. Nevertheless, Adler's greater willingness to acknowledge the important role of social factors in the causation of crime makes it sometimes easier for sociologists to reach a common basis with the Adlerian than with the orthodox Freudian school. On the whole, however, again apart from a few exceptions such as Bjerre (Chapter 8, I, above) and frequent references in case histories to some of his concepts, Adler's influence on modern criminology has not been significant.

Carl Gustav Jung (1875–1960) and his system of analytical psychology play an important role in the history of criminology mainly through his theory of psychological types and his concepts introvert and extravert, both of which have been mentioned above (Chapters 8, II, and 16).[75] Even after his defection Jung's theories had many points in common with those of Freud, but the points of difference are very numerous and significant. Only very few of them can here be mentioned. Like Adler he disapproved of what he regarded as Freud's excessive emphasis on the sexual instinct, but unlike Adler he regarded it as a mistake to assume 'the continuous operation of a single instinct, as though it were a chemical constituent, always there and always of the same quantity. . . . If that were the case, certainly man would be sexual, as Freud says he is, and intent upon power, as Adler describes him . . . we can easily reconcile Freud with Adler when we consider the psyche not as a rigid and unalterable system.'[76] Consequently, he thought that for purposes of treatment, too, Freudian and Adlerian techniques could be reconciled: 'In the neurosis of a youthful introvert the psychological theory of Adler seldom fails, and in the treatment of the young extravert it is always advisable, indispensable indeed, to take full account of the Freudian standpoint.'[77] Such and similar remarks, however, should not be taken as indicating his agreement with Freud and Adler on other fundamental issues. As Brown writes, 'like Adler, Jung is more concerned with future goals than past history, and he sees the present situation as the key to neurosis',[78] which is in direct opposition to Freud's theory of the latter. He uses the concept of inferiority, but qualifies this by saying that 'to have complexes (a term also introduced by Jung) does not necessarily indicate inferiority'.[79]

The theory that there is 'a continuance from extraversion to introversion on which all human beings could be placed' was not discovered by Jung—according to Eysenck[80] these terms go even back as far as the sixteenth century—but he popularized it and drew important clinical conclusions from it which have recently become the starting point for a number of investigations into the psychological basis of recidivism. One of these conclusions was that hysteric conditions are more likely to develop in extraverts than in introverts, whereas for anxiety states and obsessive-compulsive neuroses the opposite is true. Moreover, according to Eysenck, the introversion-extraversion continuance is one of the basic dimensions of the personality, and, developing Pavlovian ideas, he has hypothesized that extraverts, including in particular psychopaths, are more difficult to condition than introverts and therefore more likely to become recidivists. Reviewing the literature on the subject with special reference to the problems of psychopathy and recidivism, Franks[81] has concluded that there are two kinds of recidivists: first, the introverted ones who can easily be conditioned, but whose environment is so anti-social that their ease in conditioning makes them relapse again and again; and, secondly, the extraverted ones, mostly psychopaths, who are unable to learn the norms of conduct prevailing in their, perhaps socially favourable, environment. In other words, ease of conditioning had the same bad effect on the first group as difficulty in conditioning on the second. Further research done on the subject by Bartholomew has failed to substantiate this hypothesis.[82] Moreover, Alan Little[83] applied the Short Maudsley Personality Inventory to 290 Borstal boys in three institutions receiving boys of various degrees of criminality to test Eysenck's theory as expanded by Franks; none of the predictions based upon this theory could be confirmed, nor was any relationship found between the extraversion and neuroticism scores of the boys and their probability of recidivism as measured by the Mannheim-Wilkins recidivism rates for the different institutions. Little leaves it open, however, whether the Eysenck theory might be useful for adult recidivists. In his latest book *Crime and Personality*[84] Eysenck admits that the evidence for his conditioning theory has not yet been adequately tested and is anyhow not intended to apply indiscriminately to all criminals. For his theory of the extravert character of most recidivists, however, there exists in his view already more evidence, and in this he is probably justified.

It is not without interest to remember that a typically extravert psychopath, Neville Heath, wrote on the eve of his execution in 1946 to his former Approved School headmaster, Mr. C. A. Joyce: 'It is a great pity I did not remember the many lessons I learnt there, but unfortunately my memory has always been abominably short, and I have usually paid dearly for it. However, all that is my fault and my fault alone.'[85]

Whereas Jung's fundamental concepts of extravert-introvert have thus been taken up and used by present-day psychological research workers, the same cannot be said of Freudian theories. On the contrary, it is here that the contrasts and controversies between psychiatric and psychological methods show themselves more strongly than anywhere else.[86]

Chapter 18

THE CRIMINAL LAW AND THE MENTALLY ABNORMAL OFFENDER[1]

It is a debatable point whether, and to what extent, purely legal matters should be included in a book on criminology. Certainly, their treatment should not be too detailed, but an outline of the manner in which the criminal law deals with mentally abnormal offenders would seem to be not out of place.

I. GENERAL AND HISTORICAL REFLECTIONS

1. *The Relationship between Criminal Law and Psychiatry*

On general grounds it would have to be expected that the legal treatment of mentally abnormal offenders should provide a fertile soil for clashes between law and psychiatry. If we look at it from an abstract and dogmatic point of view we have to admit the existence of the following contrasts:

(*a*) The law is concerned with the well-being and protection of society rather than with those of the individual, whose treatment and care are the main interest of the psychiatrist. It is only in recent times that the administration of criminal justice has accepted the reformation and rehabilitation of the offender as one of its objects, but even nowadays they are hardly accepted as equals with deterrence and retribution, which in their turn are tolerated only as perhaps necessary evils by the psychiatrist. The very conception of 'success' has a different colour to each of these two disciplines; to the law it means absence of reconvictions, to the psychiatrist cure of the particular abnormality which he is called upon to diagnose and treat. On the other hand, the criminal law is primarily concerned with one particular action of an individual and widens its interest only at the sentencing stage so as to permit a consideration of the offender's motive and whole personality, whereas the latter is from beginning to end the crucial problem for the psychiatrist.[2]

(*b*) The criminal law is a normative discipline; it contains norms of

334

conduct to be complied with in the interest of society. Psychiatry, as any other branch of medicine, does not evaluate; its norms of conduct are practical rather than moral ones, and it issues only prescriptions which have to be carried out by the patient for his own sake.

(c) The criminal law requires clear-cut terms which provide the individual citizen with well-defined directions; otherwise its effect becomes unpredictable and it cannot act as a deterrent. (That this is only an ideal but rarely realized in legislative practice has been pointed out elsewhere.)[3]

Therefore, the criminal law, even at the risk of being unjust in an individual case, has to use standardized concepts, since only they can, it is believed, ensure certainty and predictability of judicial decisions. Important legal distinctions will, for example, depend on the chronological age of the offender which may in fact be much less important than his mental and emotional age (see above, Chapter 2).

The psychiatrist, on the other hand, delights in the twilight of an often ambiguous terminology and classification, and he tries to base his decisions entirely on the special characteristics of the individual case, although in actual practice he may not always stick to this principle.

(d) The criminal law, as law in general, is a conservative force. As a distinguished American jurist writes, 'the function of the criminal law ... is not to anticipate but to reflect and implement the consensus already achieved in the community'.[4] While this was written with special reference to offences against property in the United States and in opposition to the present writer's views as expressed in *Criminal Justice and Social Reconstruction*, it reflects the still prevailing general view of lawyers anywhere. Psychiatry, as a much younger discipline and as one which, not unlike criminology, has often been forced into ideological and practical conflict with legal dogmatism, has fewer vested interests and can, therefore, move more freely.

(e) It has often been maintained that the criminal law is based on the dogma of indeterminism, whereas the psychiatrist is wholly opposed to it, and that the law assumes our full responsibility for all our actions, whereas the psychiatrist denies it altogether. Without going here into the ancient problem of free will it can be said that neither of these two extreme positions has many followers any more nowadays. Concessions have been made from both sides. Naturally, the extent of these concessions differs greatly in accordance with the particular brand of criminal law and of psychiatry with which we are concerned, and we may even find lawyers who are more uncompromising determinists than many psychiatrists, and vice versa. While freedom of will was one of the fundamental principles of the classical school of criminal law,[5] it was completely denied by the positivists,

335

notably by Ferri, whose obsession with his fight against any assumption of moral responsibility for criminal acts had gained him the nickname of 'freewill Ferri'.[6] In the half-century or more which has elapsed since these controversies were at their height much water has been poured on to the fire from both sides. Jerome Hall, otherwise a bitter opponent of positivism, admits that while 'some degree of autonomy' is necessary if we have to evaluate human conduct, determinism is an equally necessary postulate for the psychiatrist who wishes to understand rather than evaluate such conduct.[7] Psychoanalytical discoveries, it is true, have, perhaps more than anything else, contributed to a further weakening of our belief in free will by demonstrating that apparently casual and accidental actions were in fact clearly determined, but even Freud was occasionally forced to admit that there were certain limits to his psychic determinism and that, if we follow the development of an individual case from the beginning, instead of tracing it backwards, we may have to admit that there is 'no longer the impression of an inevitable sequence of events which could not be otherwise determined. We notice at once that there might have been another result, and that we might have been just as well able to understand and explain the latter.'[8] This is a reflection which reminds us of what was said in Chapter 7, v, on the difficulties standing in the way of predicting for the individual case.

(f) In the field of criminal procedure the conflict between law and psychiatry centres mainly on the position of the expert witness and of the jury. Lawyers, especially in Britain, are inclined to place too much faith in the latter and to make inadequate and often inapt use of the former by putting him into a procedural strait-jacket which makes it often impossible for him to apply his knowledge to the fullest advantage. Naturally, the psychiatric expert has more than any other to suffer from this handicap.[9] He should at least be given the right first of all to present his views fully and coherently, instead of being forced to take part in a play of questions and answers which is often nonsensical and occasionally even designed not to elicit but to hide the truth and to make the expert appear ridiculous in the eyes of the jury. Having presented his views, he should of course be subjected to examination and cross-examination. Giving fuller scope to the psychiatric expert does not mean, however, that he should be allowed to decide the case, nor does he wish to be given this responsibility. It is a distortion of the truth to maintain that psychiatrists as a body are anxious to take the place of judge and jury. Even the treatment tribunals which have been established in different parts of the U.S.A. are bodies composed of penological rather than psychiatric experts.[10]

2. *The Existing Possibilities*

We are now in a position to appreciate that the problems under discussion can be approached from two different angles. From an extreme psychiatric view one might argue that every person who is mentally disordered, or at least every psychotic, should be exempt from responsibility and punishment by the criminal law. In support of this one would have to maintain that neither the concepts of guilt and responsibility nor any of the various objects of punishment apply to mentally disordered lawbreakers. They cannot be deterred by it because they do not react to punishment in the ordinary and generally expected manner; nor can they be reformed by the measures at the disposal of the criminal law; nor does the community, including the victim, insist on punishing them for the sake of retribution. This extreme position, which would make the psychiatric expert the final arbiter in the matter, is, however, taken only by a minority of psychiatrists, whereas most of them—including, as we have seen, many psycho-analysts—would not go so far as completely to deny guilt and responsibility of the mentally abnormal offender nor his potential responsiveness to penal measures; rather would they wish to distinguish according to individual personality and symptoms, and to the extent and seriousness of the disorder.

The lawyer, on the other hand, will argue that the criminal responsibility of a lawbreaker is, after all, a legal problem, and that it is primarily a matter for the law to decide who should be held responsible and how the offender should be punished. While this, too, leads to a distinction according to the nature and seriousness of the abnormality it inevitably makes the proportion of cases in which responsibility is entirely or in part denied smaller than it would be from the psychiatric angle. Lawyers are often prone to assume that even mentally disordered persons can be deterred by punishment and open to educative measures in the same way as normal individuals. Moreover, they are very reluctant to forgo the deterrent effect which, they believe, the punishment of offenders must have on the community at large. The history of the criminal law in most civilized countries shows, however, a continuous inclination to depart from the orthodox legal point of view in favour of greater concessions to psychiatry.

3. *Historical Developments*

The history of the subject forms an important part of the general evolution of the criminal law from its primitive stage, when punishment was imposed for the commission of a criminal act regardless of the mental condition of the actor, to the present age which regards the internal side of a crime as of an importance equal to the external facts. This evolution, tardy and often interrupted by periods of regression, forms one of the truly significant achievements of the human mind. To it we owe the more humane treatment of juvenile lawbreakers and the admission of such legal defences as mistake of fact or duress, and the working out of an elaborate doctrine of *mens rea*.

With regard to the special problem of mental abnormality, the change was very slow and, here as elsewhere, it was brought about at first not so much by considering each individual case on its merits but by exempting from punishment certain standardized situations as such. Moreover, anthropologists have shown that among primitive peoples mental disorder is ascribed not to deficiencies or changes within the individual personality but rather to external causes.[11] This is in conformity with the general refusal of primitives to think in terms of natural causes and with their habit of substituting for them explanations derived from their belief in witchcraft and a system of taboos. Mental illness, as any other disease, is therefore regarded as the work of evil spirits or as retribution for, perhaps unconsciously committed, crimes against divinity. Nowhere has this been more cogently demonstrated, with a wealth of material from anthropological sources, than in Kelsen's *Society and Nature*.[12] In spite of this basically different approach, primitive communities do recognize that mentally ill lawbreakers should not be treated in the same way as normal persons, and their behaviour is often tolerated unless it oversteps the limits of possible toleration.[13] In Ashanti law, for example, a madman was not executed, but was chained to a tree to prevent further crimes, and it was left to his relatives to feed him and keep him alive. At a later period, however, the defence of insanity was abolished because mental illness was no longer regarded as completely and necessarily excluding understanding.[14] Roman law was among the first to admit that *furiosus non intelligit quid agit*, therefore he cannot act with *mens rea*. English law, it is stated, even in its harshest days, recognized insanity as a possible defence, 'but only insanity of a particular and appropriate kind will produce exemption' (Kenny-Turner with reference to a source dated 1313).[15] In the old laws of Iceland and Norway the insane wrongdoer was punished with outlawry, just as the normal one.[16] In the German regional statutes (*Volksrechte*) of the eleventh and twelfth centuries madness, whatever the degree, was not admitted as a mitigating factor in cases of homicide unless the guilty person had clearly demonstrated his madness by inflicting grievous injuries on himself at the time of the murder; and whatever minor concessions were made in the direction towards a more 'guilt-orientated' criminal law were mainly due to the influence of the Church. For Bracton it was only the raving type of madman who was excused; the melancholic type was discovered much later. Even as late as 1724 in the often quoted English case *R. v. Arnold* (16 St. Tr. 695) Tracey, J., instructed the jury that unless a man 'is totally deprived of his understanding and reasoning and does not know what he is doing, any more than an infant, or a wild beast, he was to be punished as any sane person'.[17] At the beginning of the nineteenth century, through the case *R. v. Hadfield* in 1800 (27 St. Tr. 1281), this 'wild beast' test was, however, abandoned in favour of a more progressive attitude. Hadfield,[18] who had sustained very serious head injuries in war, suffered from the delusion that the world was coming to an end and that he had been destined by God to sacrifice himself to save mankind. Not wishing to commit suicide he decided to shoot King George III in order to be hanged (homicide, as we have seen above, not infrequently being an alternative to suicide). He was acquitted on the ground of insanity although neither the wild beast test nor the subsequent M'Naghten Rules would have supported this decision, and in fact when the famous case arose which led to the formulation of these Rules in 1843 English law reverted to far greater rigidity. A man called Daniel M'Naghten had killed a Mr. Drummond, private secretary to the then Prime Minister, Sir Robert Peel, mistaking him for the latter. He suffered from a form of paranoia which made him feel that he was being persecuted by enemies, of whom Peel was one, and he had to kill him in self-defence (4 St. Tr. N.S. 847).[19] He was acquitted, as Hadfield and others had been before him, but this acquittal aroused so much dissatisfaction, shared in particular by Queen Victoria, that after a debate in the House of Lords certain abstract questions on the law concerning insane offenders were submitted by the Lords to the High Court judges—a somewhat unusual procedure considering that it is normally not the function of judges to answer abstract questions of law. The judges, however, complied and gave full written replies, the context of which is through constant application by the courts over a hundred and twenty years still regarded as binding and enforced not only in Great Britain and most parts of the Commonwealth but also in most states of the U.S.A. In some states of Australia and in fourteen states of the U.S.A. they have been modified by the addition of the so-called test of irresistible impulse.[20]

4. *The Present English Law: The M'Naghten Rules*

There is no need here to reproduce the full text of these Rules[21] as they are not all of equal significance nowadays. Their essence is the so-called 'right and wrong test', contained in the judges' answers II and III:

to establish a defence on the ground of insanity it must be clearly proved that, at the time of committing the act the accused was labouring under such a defect of reason, from disease of the mind, as not to know the nature and quality of the act he was doing, or, if he did know it, that he did not know he was doing what was wrong.

For a detailed analysis and criticism of these Rules the reader has to be referred to the literature quoted in Notes 2, 19 and 20. Here only the following points may be made: The 'right and wrong' test concerns itself too exclusively with the rational elements of knowledge, neglecting the equally important element of will and emotion and the unconsciousness. To the psychiatrist this test means very little, and a trial and cross-examination limited to it force him to deal with, to him at least, immaterial aspects at the expense of far more essential features of the case.

It is also open to doubt and in fact controversial whether the words 'quality' and 'wrong' refer to the moral or merely to the legal side of the act. While English courts prefer the second interpretation,[22] which is unfavourable to the accused, the High Court of Australia has adopted the first and decided that the criminal liability of the accused 'depends on his ability to reason about the wrongness of his act with a moderate degree of sense and composure'.[23] Moreover, the Rules deal only with the more extreme cases of insanity, excluding the less obvious ones, in particular the 'non-sane non-insane' cases. It has often been maintained by supporters of the Rules that English judges and juries tend to interpret them very broadly and that therefore no injustice is actually done. While this may be true in quite a number of cases it is, as among others the evidence submitted to the Royal Commission of 1953 shows, certainly not true in general. Clear-cut cases of schizophrenia, general paralysis of the insane, paranoia and of similar forms of psychosis will always stand a good chance of being somehow covered by the Rules. What, however, may happen to the others, which probably form a considerable majority? The British Medical Association, in their evidence before the Commission:

gave the following examples of abnormal mental states in which, although the prisoner knew the nature and wrongfulness of his act, responsibility for the crime of murder might in their view be either absent or diminished as a result of emotional disorder.[24]

  (a) aggressive psychopathic states;
  (b) states associated with organic damage to the brain (epilepsy, epidemic encephalitis, etc.);
  (c) depressive states with desire for self-destruction or self-punishment;
  (d) early schizophrenia;
  (e) paranoia and paraphrenia.

Ignoring for the moment the categories (a) and (c), this list shows that in the view of the British Medical Association certain cases of psychosis are in danger of being left outside the scope of the Rules, even if the latter are fairly liberally interpreted. The paranoiac who kills his wife and children in obedience to what he believes to be a command from God to relieve them from their earthly sufferings and who is firmly convinced that his action, though illegal, was in accordance with his religious and moral duties, is still not entirely out of danger of being convicted of murder. With regard to epilepsy the Royal Commission merely recommended that in murder cases where the offender could not be held to be wholly irresponsible on the ground of insanity the question whether the death penalty should be carried out should be approached 'with the presumption that, if not the epilepsy itself, then the underlying abnormality of the brain may have provided a link in the chain of reaction which led to the crime' (p. 276, also pp. 134–5). The problem of murder committed by psychopaths was also treated by way of a recommendation that, although not amounting to insanity, this form of mental abnormality should be given due weight in deciding whether the death penalty should be carried out (p. 276). All this makes it clear that the Rules exclude the less obvious cases of insanity as well as the 'non-sane non-insane' groups. Controversial is the position of the mental defective who is not at the same time insane according to the narrower interpretation of the M'Naghten Rules. The high-grade mental defective Straffen was found guilty of murder and sentenced to death, though later reprieved. This case gives rise to a number of interesting legal, psychiatric and criminological problems.[25]

Other weaknesses of the Rules are that they place the onus of proof on the defence[26] and that, by restricting their application to the jury courts, they sanction a dual system of justice. Because they are unduly narrow they hand the final decision over to the Home Secretary and his advisers who are thereby established as the supreme arbiters, which gives the court proceedings an air of unreality.

In the circumstances, it is only natural that there should have been frequent attempts to make the Rules less rigid and extend them beyond their present narrow limits, for example by adding the defence of *irresistible impulse* and making special provision for the 'non-sane non-insane' groups. The objection can be raised against the first-mentioned defence that it is often impossible for an expert to state whether an impulse is 'irresistible'[27] and, in the words of the Royal Commission, it 'carries the implication that ... [the crime] must have been suddenly and impulsively committed after a sharp internal conflict', which is not true, for example, in cases of melancholia where the act may be coolly and carefully prepared, but nevertheless bear all the marks of insanity. The Commission therefore preferred the phrase that the accused 'did not know that it was wrong or was incapable of preventing himself from committing it', which would bring English law closer to most Continental Codes using the formula 'inability to recognize the wrongness of his action or to act in accordance with his insight'.[28] In any case, as Norval Morris points out, in view of the narrow interpretation of the words 'nature and quality' and 'wrong' by the English courts the need for the statutory adoption of a formula of this kind is greater than in countries where, as in Australia, these words receive a more liberal interpretation. Moreover, the Privy Council in the recent Australian case *South Australia v. Brown* agrees with the High Court of Australia that 'irresistible impulse' can be a symptom of 'M'Naghten insanity' (Morris 291), but how tortuous and artificial is the Council's whole reasoning!

Among the many other proposals for the legislative reform of the Rules the following deserve special mention. The Royal Commission of 1953 recommended in the first place to abrogate the Rules altogether and to leave the jury free to determine whether the accused was suffering from disease of the mind (or mental deficiency) to such a degree that he ought not to be held responsible. Failing this, they recommended the formula quoted above in the place of the test of irresistible impulse (paras. 317 and 333). The first recommendation cannot be approved as it would leave the jury without any guidance and result in haphazard and amateurish verdicts; the second would mean an improvement of the present position, but might not go far enough. The emphasis on the inability of the offender to control himself or to prevent himself from committing the act may also, if pronounced publicly at the trial, have an undesirable effect on the offender's future conduct.[29] The formula used by the Danish Criminal Code of 1930, arts. 17 and 70: 'persons unable to be influenced by ordinary punishment' and therefore to be subjected to other measures, might perhaps avoid these dangers. In the U.S.A. two other solutions have been tried out in a small area outside that following the M'Naghten Rules: The New Hampshire Rule, adopted in that state already in 1870, and the Durham Rule, in force in the District of Columbia since 1954.[30] The former, which has repeatedly been revised, was the model for the recommendation of the Royal Commission to leave the issue to the jury whether the accused suffered from a mental disease which had taken away his capacity to form a criminal intent. The Durham Rule, so called after the case *Durham v. United States*, [1954] 214 F. 2d 862 of the Court of Appeal for the District of Columbia, states that an accused is not criminally responsible 'if his unlawful act was the product of mental disease or mental defect', therefore called the 'product-rule'. Finally, the American Law Institute's Draft No. 7 of a Model Code proposes a formula which is in essence a return to the

European Codes referred to above, excluding, however, the psychopath. This is not the appropriate place for a detailed discussion of the merits or otherwise of these various American attempts to solve the legislative problem, and the author can only reiterate his view that more important than an ideal formula, which is in any case out of reach, is 'the harmonious co-operation between well-trained lawyers and psychiatrists, each of them willing to listen to reason and to play his own part instead of trespassing on the field of the other'.[31] And of perhaps equal importance is the manner in which the onus of proof of insanity is distributed since in a high proportion of cases the crucial issue remains in doubt. It is an anomaly contrary to the general principles of the criminal procedure to throw the burden of proof, as the M'Naghten Rules do, entirely on the defence.

If an accused person is found by the jury to be falling under the McNaghten Rules their 'special' verdict under the Criminal Procedure (Insanity) Act 1964 (s. 1) is 'not guilty by reason of insanity', with the consequence that 'the court shall make an order that the accused be admitted to such hospital as may be specified by the Secretary of State' (s. 5(1)). Detention now takes place in a special institution at Broadmoor in Berkshire (established in 1863), which under the Criminal Justice Act, 1948, s. 62, was transferred from the prison authorities to the Board of Control and is now, as the latter was dissolved by the Mental Health Act, 1959, s. 2, under the Ministry of Health. The inmates, called at first 'criminal lunatics', later under the Criminal Justice Act, 1948, s. 62, promoted to 'Broadmoor patients', are now, as the Mental Health Act, 1959, repeals that section, simply patients detained under H.M.'s pleasure. Instead of Broadmoor, mental hospitals provided by the National Health Service may be used for less dangerous persons. For mental defectives the Rampton or the Moss Side State Institutions are available.

Of greater practical importance than the legal technicalities arising from the M'Naghten Rules is the right of the Home Secretary under the Criminal Lunatics Act, 1884, s. 2, even in cases where the jury has found the prisoner to be outside the Rules and he has been convicted and sentenced in the ordinary way, to order an enquiry into his mental condition.[32] The Act, though establishing certain technical differentiations between prisoners under sentence of death and others, applies to both categories, and in both cases the Home Secretary has to appoint experts who are not bound in their judgment to apply the M'Naghten Rules with their narrow definition of insanity and their wrong distribution of the burden of proof. If as a result of this statutory enquiry the prisoner is found insane he is removed to Broadmoor 'until further signification of Her Majesty's pleasure' and if he had been under sentence of death the latter is 'respited'. The same applies if the prisoner was actually sane at the time of the crime and the trial, but became insane afterwards.

According to statistics published in the Report of the Royal Commission (p. 311) the number of persons found guilty but insane in proceedings for murder in England and Wales during 1900–49 was 798, that of persons convicted and sentenced to death 1,210, and that of persons certified insane after medical enquiry 48. The number of those death sentences 'respited and commuted to penal servitude for life wholly or partly on grounds of mental condition' after medical enquiry was 37 and without medical enquiry 40. Detention in Broadmoor, if not actually for life, is often for a very long time. As the then Superintendent of Broadmoor told the Royal Commission of 1953, 'as a rule, if a man does not get out within 10 years, he probably does not get out at all'.[33] When the present writer visited it in 1947 he was told that in most cases of homicide the minimum period was 6 years. *Criminal Statistics for England and Wales* provides annual tables of receptions and discharges (at present Tables XIXA and B and XX). On the 31st October 1960 there were 114 male and 50 female patients in Broadmoor who had been detained for 20 years and over (*Criminal Statistics for 1960*, Table XX).

5. *The Post-M'Naghten Law*

The impact of the shortcomings of the M'Naghten Rules has in recent years also been greatly reduced in England by two important statutes, the Homicide Act, 1957, and the Mental Health Act, 1959. It is their special merit that they deal with cases of the 'non-sane non-insane' category and of mental deficiency in a more progressive way than do the Rules for cases of insanity.[34] Under the Homicide Act, 1957, s. 2, 'where a person kills or is a party to the killing of another, he shall not be convicted of murder if he was suffering from such abnormality of mind (whether arising from a condition of arrested or retarded development of mind or any inherent causes or induced by disease or injury) as substantially impaired his mental responsibility for his acts and omissions in doing or being a party to the killing'; instead he is liable to be convicted of manslaughter, but the burden of proof is on the defence. This section introduces the legal concept, for a fairly long period already familiar to Continental and Scottish law, of diminished responsibility, and thereby remedies the rigid attitude of the M'Naghten Rules according to which an offender could only be either completely sane or completely insane. Attempts to let the 'knowledge of right and wrong' test enter by the backdoor have been unsuccessful so far. Unfortunately in the last resort the section is unsatisfactory, however, in containing no provisions for psychiatric treatment, except for the facilities already existing for offenders sentenced in the ordinary way to imprisonment, Borstal, etc., or placed on probation. In actual court practice, until 1961, most of those so far found guilty of manslaughter under s. 2, i.e. 45 out of 85, have been sentenced to fixed terms of imprisonment ranging from one to ten years, another 5 to more than 10 years, while 30 received life sentences and 5 were placed on probation with a condition of mental treatment under Criminal Justice Act, 1948, s. 4.[35] It has to be borne in mind that a life sentence is in fact an indeterminate sentence which has to be reviewed periodically and enables the Home Secretary to release a prisoner when he is regarded as a fit person to return to society; it is more elastic, therefore, than a fixed prison term. Apart from this advantage, however, it is equally lacking in treatment facilities. It is somewhat paradoxical that while those found insane under the Rules should be sent to Broadmoor where they can receive appropriate treatment, those found to be of diminished responsibility should often receive nothing but ordinary imprisonment. The position is likely to improve, however, as soon as the new 'psychiatric prison', to be known as H.M. Prison Grendon (in Buckinghamshire), but often referred to as the East-Hubert Institution, will be fully available.[36] This is a maximum security prison for up to 350 inmates to be divided into groups 'to facilitate treatment according to their attitudes and needs'.[37]

Concerning the special care of criminal psychopaths, the courts have recently resisted attempts to exclude them altogether from the operation of s. 2 and rejected the argument that the latter referred only to 'abnormality of the mind', not to emotional abnormalities of the personality. It can be regarded as established, therefore, that a psychopath may, in appropriate cases, be brought under the scope of s. 2.[38] The question when this should be done is, naturally, one of the most difficult ones to confront the criminal courts and the psychiatric experts.

In one of the most recent cases of this kind, *R. v. McCrorey* (*The Times*, 31.7.1962), diminished responsibility was assumed and a life sentence imposed in a case where a psychopath had killed a woman in the furtherance of theft. The psychiatric experts had testified that if the killing had been done on the spur of the moment by a man taken by surprise it was likely that the prisoner had acted in a state of substantial impairment of his faculties, whereas if the killing had been premeditated this would lead to the opposite conclusion. So far, it cannot be said that a clear line of policy has emerged from the literature or from court decisions. One thing is certain, however, i.e. that the problem can be brought nearer to a solution not by adopting the superficially perhaps plausible view of Lady Wootton that the more horrible the crime the more likely a finding of diminished responsibility, but only by further research as indicated above (Chapter 15).

The weaknesses of the present system are still further aggravated by the principle of English criminal procedure that insanity and diminished responsibility are defences which have to be raised by the accused in person or on his behalf with his consent, and that they cannot be raised at all if the accused pleads innocence, especially mistaken identity. The latter point was recently discussed in connection with the Hanratty trial. Here after the prisoner's execution a psychiatrist pointed out that, although the case had shown various circumstances which strongly indicated abnormality of mind, none of those defences could be raised in court because the accused had to the last maintained that he had not been the killer.[39] This attitude of the law is unreasonable; it is difficult to understand why the defence should not have the right to argue that the accused was innocent of the act, but if the court should regard him as guilty of the facts of the offence, the plea would be changed to one of insanity or diminished responsibility.[40]

The value of the contribution made by the Mental Health Act, 1959, is that it has not only given new statutory definitions of mental disorder and for the first time attempted a definition of psychopathy (Chapter 15, above), but that it has also made court decisions and administrative action in such cases more flexible. Under s. 60 the court has discretionary power in all criminal cases except capital murder to authorize the admission of the offender to and his detention in a mental hospital or place him under guardianship, provided the mental disorder is of a nature or degree which warrants such a decision.[41] As rightly stressed by Edwards against Wootton, the Act of 1959, differently from the Homicide Act, is concerned not with the question of criminal responsibility but only with that of treatment; it does not, therefore, eliminate responsibility.

The Act empowers the criminal courts if a person is convicted of any offence except a capital or a very trivial one and they are satisfied on the written or oral evidence of two medical practitioners

(1) that the offender is suffering from mental illness, psychopathic disorder, subnormality or severe subnormality; and
(2) that the mental disorder is of a nature or degree which warrants the detention of the patient in a hospital for medical treatment, or the reception of a patient to guardianship under this Act; and the court is of opinion, having regard to all the circumstances including the nature of the offence and the character and antecedents of the offender, and to the available methods of dealing with him, that the

most suitable method of disposing of the case is by means of an order under this section,

by order to authorize his admission to and detention in a specified hospital or place him under the guardianship of a local health authority or of a person approved by the latter (s. 60). Where a hospital order is made by a court of assize or quarter sessions, and it appears to the court, having regard to the nature of the offence, the antecedents of the offender and the risk of his committing further offences if set at large, that it is necessary for the protection of the public so to do, the court may further order that the offender shall be subject to certain special restrictions, either without limit of time or during a specified period (s. 65(1)). The nature of these restrictions is defined in s. 65 (3); they are related mainly to the duration of the detention, leave of absence, transfer, discharge, and recall, and give very extensive powers to the Home Secretary in all these matters. There are also provisions giving the Home Secretary power to transfer to specified hospitals persons already serving sentences of imprisonment and falling under the categories defined in s. 60 (sects. 72–75), and in such cases he may also impose restrictions of the kind defined in s. 65 (s. 74).

Without going too much into the details of the highly complicated provisions of the Act the following few observations may be made. First, as already stated, s. 60 does not apply to capital murder, where, therefore, the M'Naghten Rules still apply. Moreover, it is left entirely to the discretion of the courts whether in cases falling under s. 60 they wish to make a hospital or guardianship order or whether they prefer to impose, for example, an ordinary prison sentence, and for this reason the powers given in s. 72 to the Home Secretary are of great practical importance. Furthermore, even if an order is made by a court of assize or quarter sessions there has first to be a conviction, although the offender may be insane. Magistrates' courts may make an order without convicting (s. 60 (2)). In spite of certain defects, it is clear, however, that the Mental Health Act provides a procedure far superior to that of the M'Naghten Rules and that its definition of the various forms of mental disorder makes it much easier to conform with modern psychiatric ideas. It is still too early to state how far the courts are, and shall be, ready to exercise their powers under the Act. According to *Criminal Statistics for 1960*, Table XIXB, which covers only a very short period, 50 persons were detained in psychiatric hospitals under restriction orders, but the kind of restriction is not specified. For 1961 (Tables XIX and XX) the number of restriction orders has already risen to 153, and some information is given on the duration of the restriction: 86 were without limit of time, ten for 10 years or more, and the remainder for shorter periods. For 1962 the figures were slightly lower. To give two illustrations from newspaper reports, in the case of a man aged 30 convicted of manslaughter a 40-year restriction order was made, in the case of another, aged 23, sentenced to two years' imprisonment for causing grievous bodily harm, the Court of Criminal Appeal substituted for it a restriction order for three years as the offender had possibly been suffering from an epileptic attack.[42]

There are some special provisions for psychopathic and subnormal persons. While such patients, if not found guilty of an offence, can be detained in hospital or kept under guardianship beyond the age of 25 only if they are found to be dangerous to others or themselves (s. 44), this does not apply to them if they fall under s. 60 (see s. 63 (31)).

An order committing the offender to hospital cannot be combined with imprisonment, detention, a fine or probation, nor shall it be made for the purpose of punishing him, but only for treatment and the safety of society.[43] As Glanville Williams points out, offenders are more likely to have confidence in the disciplinary powers of the judges under the new procedure than in those of the Home Secretary's unknown advisers under the Criminal Lunatics Act, 1884. It has to be borne in mind, however, that within the limits imposed by a judicial restricting order the Home Secretary's powers are still very wide indeed.

For reasons of space, such special points of procedure as insanity on arraignment or during trial ('unfit to plead') are not dealt with in this chapter, and the reader is referred to the detailed discussion by Glanville Williams, *op. cit.*, 2nd ed. (§ 143). Attention should be drawn, however, to the particularly interesting case *R. v. Podola* (autumn 1959), in which, it is believed, the plea of unfitness to plead on the ground of amnesia was for the first time raised in England. In spite of the extreme thoroughness in which the matter was treated by the courts, this case has led to some just criticisms of the manner such pleas are handled at present in English law (see also p. 253 above).[44]

6. *The Law Concerning Offences committed in a State of Drunkenness*[45]

Such offenders have for a long time presented the criminal law with particularly difficult problems. On the one hand, it can be argued that drunkenness might well produce an abnormal condition of mind which should be legally treated in the same way as any other form of mental disorder. On the other hand, the fact that drunkenness is usually self-induced cannot be entirely ignored. (That 'involuntary' drunkenness, occurring for example when a person does not know that he is drinking a heavily intoxicating beverage, is a complete defence is beyond dispute.) While the first argument may in certain cases

348

lead to a denial of criminal responsibility, the second serves as a warn-ing not to be over-generous with such exceptions. This explains the dilemma confronting the law and the criminal courts. Glanville Williams opens his admirable discussion of the matter with the statement that 'there is, in general, no special law on the subject of drunkenness', but is immediately forced to admit a number of signifi-cant exceptions to this rule.

If we apply the existing law to the three categories outlined above in Chapter 14, p. 250, the result would be as follows:

(a) The 'normal' drunkenness occurring in an otherwise mentally sane person and being so heavy as to produce a state of mind which amounts to temporary insanity is no defence in law, unless—and this is a very important proviso—it 'negatives' the specific intent or know-ledge required for the crime in question or, where not intent but reck-lessness is required, it negatives the necessary foresight of the likely consequences. For example, if the offender is so drunk as not to real-ize that he is killing another person he is not guilty of murder, though he may be guilty of manslaughter. Under the Homicide Act, 1957, his responsibility may be regarded as 'diminished', although there has been some doubt as to whether drunkenness can be brought under s. 2(1) of the Act.[46] Or, somebody who hits his victim with a stick may because of his drunkenness, be found not guilty of causing grievous bodily harm, but only of the less serious offence of common assault if he did not have the intent needed for the former, but only that needed for the latter offence. Or a person who, in his drunkenness, walks off with another person's umbrella probably does so without the intent to deprive the owner permanently of his property. Killing in the course of rape, however, has been treated as murder in the fam-ous case of Beard, [1920] A.C. 479 because the intent required to com-mit rape could not be negatived by drunkenness. Apart from such special cases, ordinary drunkenness, which 'merely removed the brakes' (Goodhart), is no defence. It may, however, affect the penalty. While the Italian Penal Code of 1930, § 92, provides that ordinary drunkenness is not to be treated as a mitigating circumstance, else-where the matter is usually left to the discretion of the courts,[47] which means that personal inclinations and prejudices may occasion-ally decide. Against undue leniency it may be argued that offenders may intentionally get drunk before committing a crime (the *actio libera in causa* of Continental legal doctrine), but such cases are not very frequent (the Gallagher case discussed by Goodhart may be one as the offender had told the police: 'I made up my mind to kill her about a fortnight or three weeks ago').

(b) The pathological drunkenness occurring in mentally unstable or abnormal persons, often caused by very small quantities of alcohol.

349

In such cases where the two factors of mental abnormality and drunkenness are combined there will usually be no difficulty either in finding the accused 'guilty but insane' or of diminished responsibility or in non-capital offences of imposing a comparatively lenient penalty or making an order under the Mental Health Act. The latter may be advisable particularly in cases where there is need for prolonged medical treatment.

(c) Chronic alcoholism may lead to pathological changes in the brain affecting the whole personality. The result may be delirium tremens and an alcoholic psychosis, and in epileptics a seizure. There is no reason why insanity produced by chronic alcoholism should be excluded from the M'Naghten Rules or the appropriate provisions of the Homicide Act and Mental Health Act.

The real problem in many cases of categories (b) and (c) is not the question of punishment but that of treatment. The regrettable failure of the Inebriates legislation of the last century has not yet led to a more resolute tackling of the institutional side of the matter, although a number of voluntary inebriates' homes are available.[48]

For cases of category (a), where the drunkenness is of such a kind as to provide a defence against charges of manslaughter, wounding, etc., some Continental legislations have provided a new and, it seems, satisfactory solution. The Danish Penal Code of 1930, art. 138, and the German Penal Code, § 330a, have established a special offence of committing a crime while in a condition of wilfully or negligently induced drunkenness excluding normal responsibility for the crime. In other words, while the offender cannot be punished for the crime he happens to commit in such a condition he can be punished for this special offence; the penalty is normally milder than the one which would be imposed if criminal responsibility had not been excluded.[49] These provisions do not apply to cases of *an actio libera in causa*, where the offender got drunk with the intent to commit the crime under the protection of drunkenness; here he may in clear cases be punished for the crime actually committed, unless it seems doubtful whether it was really the outcome of that intent or rather the result of a mere inner resolve to commit it.

Selected Reading Lists*

Most of the abbreviations in the following Selected Reading Lists and Notes in Vols. I and II are taken from *Excerpta Medica*, 'List of Journals abstracted', 1964, Excerpta Medica Foundation, Amsterdam–New York–London–Milan–Tokyo, with grateful acknowledgments for their permission.

CHAPTER 1

H. Mannheim, *Group Problems in Crime and Punishment*, London, 1955, Ch. 12.

Karl R. Popper, *The Poverty of Historicism*, London, 1957.

L. Susan Stebbing, *Philosophy and the Physicist*, Harmondsworth, 1944, Ch. 9.

The Sutherland Papers, ed. by Albert Cohen, Alfred Lindesmith, and Karl Schuessler, Bloomington, 1956, Part 1.

(On causality): Karl R. Popper, *The Logic of Scientific Discovery*, 1959, pp. 59 ff. and *passim*.

R. M. McIver, *Social Causation*, Boston, 1940.

Sheldon and Eleanor Glueck, *Ventures in Criminology*, London, 1964, Ch. 16.

Arnold M. Rose, *Theory and Method in the Social Sciences*, Minneapolis, 1954.

Hermann Mannheim and Leslie Wilkins, *Prediction Methods in relation to Borstal Training*, H.M.S.O., London, 1955.

W. Friedmann, *Legal Theory*, 3rd ed., London, 1953.

Pioneers of Criminology, ed. by H. Mannheim, London, 1960, Ch. 11.

UNESCO, *The University Teaching of Social Sciences: Criminology*, Paris, 1957.

CHAPTER 2

Kenny's *Outlines of Criminal Law*, an entirely new ed. by J. W. Cecil Turner, Cambridge, 1952.

---

* The publications have been listed here neither in alphabetical order nor according to their importance or date of publication, but in the order in which they appear in the Notes. As the general textbooks of criminology have been listed separately in the Appendix they are not here included. There is inevitably some overlapping, and consequently some publications appear in several lists. Only English language publications have here been included, and the accessibility of the material has also been a consideration.

351

Glanville Williams, *Criminal Law: The General Part*, London, 1953, Ch. 7.
Jerome Hall, *General Principles of Criminal Law*, Minneapolis, 1947, Ch. 10.
Jerome Hall, *Studies in Jurisprudence and Criminal Theory*, New York, 1958.
H. Mannheim, *The Dilemma of Penal Reform*, London, 1939, Ch. 4.
H. Mannheim, *Criminal Justice and Social Reconstruction*, London, 1946.
Morris Ginsberg, *Essays in Sociology and Social Philosophy*, London, 1956.
Thorsten Sellin, *Culture Conflict and Crime*, New York, 1938.
E. Bodenheimer, *Jurisprudence*, New York and London, 1940.
B. Malinowski, *Crime and Custom in Savage Society*, London, 1932.
H. Kantorowicz, *The Definition of Law*, Cambridge, 1958, Ch. 5.
A. P. d'Entrèves, *Natural Law*, London, 4th imp., 1957.
Hans Kelsen, *What is Justice?*, Berkeley and Los Angeles, 1957.
H. L. A. Hart, *Law, Liberty and Morality*, London, Oxford Univ. Press, 1963.
Lon L. Fuller, *The Morality of Law*, New Haven, 1964.
Glanville Williams, *Sanctity of Life and the Criminal Law*, London, 1957.
Norman St. John Stevas, *Life, Death, and the Law*, London, 1961.

CHAPTER 3

Robert K. Merton, *Social Theory and Social Structure*, Glencoe, Ill., 1957.
Gunnar Myrdal, *Value in Social Theory*, London, 1958.
Leslie Wilkins, *Social Deviance*, London, 1964.
Claire Selltiz *et al.*, *Research Methods in Social Relations*, London, 1959.
Arnold M. Rose, *Theory and Method in the Social Sciences*, Minneapolis, 1954.
Hermann Mannheim, Foreword to R. G. Andry, *The Short-Term Prisoner*, Library of Criminology, London, 1963.
Stephen Toulmin, *The Philosophy of Science*, London, 1953.

On the methodology of social research in general see Karl R. Popper, *The Logic of Scientific Discovery*, London, 1959.

CHAPTER 4

Arnold M. Rose, *Theory and Method in the Social Sciences*, Minneapolis, 1954.
H. Bianchi, *Position and Subject-Matter of Criminology*, Amsterdam, 1956.
Morris Ginsberg, 'Social Change', *Brit. J. Sociol.*, Vol. 9, No. 3, 1958.
Wilson Gee, *Social Science Research Methods*, New York, 1950.
Edward Glover, *The Roots of Crime*, London, 1960, Sect. 6, 272 ff.
John C. Spencer, *Stress and Release in an Urban Estate. A Study in Action Research*, London, 1964.
Marshall B. Clinard, 'Research Frontiers in Criminology', *Brit. J. Delinq.*, Vol. 7, No. 2, 1956.
Sheldon and Eleanor Glueck, *Ventures in Criminology*, London, International Library of Criminology, Vol. 9, 1964, Ch. 19.
Hermann Mannheim, *Group Problems in Crime and Punishment*, Ch. 6.
Barbara Wootton, *Social Science and Social Pathology*, London, 1959, Ch. 3.

CHAPTER 5

Thorsten Sellin and Marvin E. Wolfgang, *The Measurement of Delinquency*, New York, London, Sydney, 1964.

J. M. van Bemmelen, 'The Constancy of Crime', *Brit. J. Delinq.*, Vol. 2, No. 3, 1952.

Hermann Mannheim, *Social Aspects of Crime in England between the Wars*, London, 1940, Part 1.

M. Grünhut, 'Statistics in Criminology', *J. roy. statist. Soc.*, Vol. 114, Part 2, 1952.

Barbara Wootton, *Social Science and Social Pathology*, London, 1959, Ch. 1.

Lord Pakenham, *Causes of Crime*, London, 1958.

Mabel Elliott, *Crime in Modern Society*, 1952.

Ronald H. Beattie, 'The Sources of Criminal Statistics', *Ann. Amer. Acad. Polit. Soc. Sci.*, Vol. 217, 1941.

Gunnar Fredriksson, *Kriminal-Statistiken och Kriminologien*, Stockholm, Göteborg-Uppsala, with English summary 1962 (to be published in an Eng. translation).

CHAPTER 6

H. Mannheim, *Social Aspects of Crime*, London, 1940, Ch. 5.

M. Grünhut, *Juvenile Offenders before the Courts*, Oxford, 1956.

M. J. Moroney, *Facts from Figures*, Harmondsworth, 1951.

C. A. Moser, *Survey Methods in Social Investigation*, London, 1958.

H. Mannheim and T. Wilkins, *Prediction Methods in relation to Borstal Training*, London, 1955.

(On Control Groups): E. Greenwood, *Experimental Sociology*, 5th imp., New York, 1949, Ch. 6.

Claire Selltiz et al., *Research Methods in Social Relations*, London, 1959.

Sheldon and Eleanor Glueck, *Unraveling Juvenile Delinquency*, New York, 1950.

Sol Rubin, *Crime and Juvenile Delinquency*, 2nd ed., New York, 1961, Ch. 1.

William McCord and Joan McCord et al., *Origins of Crime*, New York, 1959.

(On Follow-up Studies): Sheldon and Eleanor Glueck, *After-Conduct of Discharged Offenders*, London, 1945; the same: *500 Criminal Careers*, New York, 1930.

Jay Rumney and Joseph P. Murphy, *Probation and Social Adjustment*, New Brunswick, 1952.

Walter C. Reckless and C. H. Andersen, *Summary of Proceedings of the Third International Congress of Criminology London 1955*, London, 1957.

A. G. Rose, *Five Hundred Borstal Boys*, Oxford, 1954.

CHAPTER 7

H. Mannheim and Leslie Wilkins, *Prediction Methods in relation to Borstal Training*. London, 1955, 2nd imp. 1965.

Lloyd E. Ohlin, *Selection for Parole*, New York, 1951.

Paul Horst *et al.*, *The Prediction of Personal Adjustment*, Soc. Sci. Res. Counc. Bull. No. 48, New York, 1941.

Brit. J. Delinq., Vol. 6, No. 2, Sept. 1955: Special Number on Prediction and Recidivism.

S. and E. Glueck, *Predicting Delinquency and Crime*, Cambridge, Mass., 1959.

S. and E. Glueck, *Ventures in Criminology*, London, 1964.

Sol Rubin, *Crime and Juvenile Delinquency*, 2nd ed., New York, 1961, Part 6.

Paul E. Meehl, *Clinical v. Statistical Prediction*, Minnesota and London, 2nd imp. 1956.

CHAPTER 8

(On Individual Case Studies): John Madge, *The Tools of Social Science*, London, 1953, Chs. 2 and 4.

Gordon W. Allport, *The Use of Personal Documents in Psychological Science*, Soc. Sci. Res. Counc. Bull. 49, New York, 1942.

Claire Selltiz *et al.*, *Research Methods in Social Relations*, Chs. 6–9.

Frederic Wertham, *Dark Legend: A Study in Murder*, London, 1947.

William Healy and Augusta Bronner, *New Light on Delinquency*, New Haven, 1936.

Franz Alexander and William Healy, *The Roots of Crime*, New York, 1935.

Clifford R. Shaw, *The Natural History of a Delinquent Career*, Chicago, 1930.

Clifford R. Shaw *et al.*, *Brothers in Crime*, Chicago, 1938.

E. H. Sutherland, *The Professional Thief*, Chicago, 1937.

Grace W. Pailthorpe, *Studies in the Psychology of Delinquency*, London, H.M.S.O., 1932.

Nathan Leopold, *Life plus 99 Years*, London, 1958.

William Clifford, *Profiles in Crime*, Lusaka, 1964.

(On Typological Methods): C. G. Jung, *Psychological Types*, London, 1923.

Ernst Kretschmer, *Physique and Character*, London, 1925.

H. J. Eysenck, *The Structure of Human Personality*, 2nd ed., London, 1960.

Jack B. Gibbs, 'Needed: Analytical Typologies in Criminology', *Southwestern Social Science Quarterly*, Vol. 40, March 1960.

William H. Sheldon, *Varieties of Delinquent Youths*, New York, 1949.

S. and E. Glueck, *Physique and Delinquency*, New York, 1956.

S. and E. Glueck, 'Varieties of Delinquent Types', *Brit. J. Crim.*, Vol. 5, Nos. 4 and 5, 1965.

T. C. N. Gibbens, *Psychiatric Studies of Borstal Lads*, London, 1963.

R. S. Taylor, 'The Habitual Criminal', *Brit. J. Crim.*, Vol. 1, No. 1, July 1960.

John Bowlby, 'Forty-four Juvenile Thieves', *Int. J. Psycho-Anal.*, Vol. 25, 1944.

D. A. Ogden, 'A Borstal Typological Survey (Camp Hill)', *Brit. J. Delinq.* Vol. 5, No. 2, Oct. 1954.

A. G. Rose, *500 Borstal Boys*, Oxford, 1954, Ch. 7.

D. H. Stott, *Delinquency and Human Nature*, Dunfermline, 1950, esp. Ch. 14.

Marvin E. Wolfgang, *Patterns in Criminal Homicide*, Philadelphia, 1958, esp. Ch. 10.

CHAPTER 9

Ernest Greenwood, *Experimental Sociology*, New York, 1945, 5th imp., 1949.

Stuart Chapin, *Experimental Designs in Sociological Research*, 2nd ed., New York, 1956.

John Madge, *The Tools of Social Science*, London, 1953, Ch. 5.

W I. B. Beveridge, *The Art of Scientific Investigation*, London, 1950, Ch. 2.

Edwin Powers and Helen Witmer, *An Experiment in the Prevention of Delinquency*, New York, 1951.

H. Ashley Weeks *et al.*, *Youthful Offenders at Highfields*, Ann Arbor, Michigan, 1958.

Lloyd McCorkle *et al.*, *The Highfields Story*, New York, 1958.

Hermann Mannheim, *Group Problems in Crime and Punishment*, London, 1955, Ch. 6, III.

Brian Kay, 'Reactions of Delinquents and Other Groups to Experimentally Induced Frustration', *Brit. J. Delinq.*, Vol. 4, No. 4, April 1954.

Frederick K. Beutel, *Some Potentialities of Experimental Jurisprudence*, Lincoln, Nebraska, 1957.

(On experiments see also Karl R. Popper, *The Logic of Scientific Discovery*, pp. 106 ff. and 207 fn.)

CHAPTER 10

(On Action or Operational Research): John C. Spencer, *Stress and Release in an Urban Estate. A Study in Action Research*, London, 1964.

Arnold M. Rose, *Theory and Method in the Social Sciences*, Minneapolis, 1954, Ch. 8.

Claire Selltiz *et al.*, *Research Methods in Social Relations*, Ch. 13.

Sheldon Glueck, *The Problem of Delinquency*, Boston, 1959, Sects. 174–186.

Solomon Kobrin, 'The Chicago Area Project, a 25-year Assessment', *Ann. Amer. Acad. Polit. Soc. Sci.*, Vol. 322, March 1959.

M. L. Turner, *Ship without Sails*, London, 1953.

John B. Mays, *On the Threshold of Delinquency*, Liverpool, 1959.

(On Sociological Methods): John C. McKinney, in *Modern Sociological Theory*, ed. by Howard Becker and Alvin Boskoff, New York, 1957.

George A. Lundberg, *Social Research*, 2nd ed., London–New York, Toronto, 1942.

Donald Clemmer, *The Prison Community*, Boston, 1940.

Donald R. Cressey, *Other People's Money*, Glencoe, Illinois, 1953.

John C. Spencer, *Crime and the Services*, London, 1954.

Norval Morris, *The Habitual Criminal*, London, 1951.

John James, 'The Application of the Small Group Concept to the Study of the Prison Community', *Brit. J. Delinq.*, Vol. 5, No. 4, April 1955.

The Social Background of Delinquency, Univ. of Nottingham, Rockefeller Research 1952–54 (unpublished).

Gordon Rose, 'Sociometric Analysis and Observation in a Borstal Institution', *Brit. J. Delinq.*, Vol. 6, Nos. 3 and 4.

Terence and Pauline Morris, *Pentonville*, London, 1963.

CHAPTER 11

(On Physical Geography): W. A. Bonger, *An Introduction to Criminology*, London, 1936, Sect. 20.

Joseph Cohen, 'The Geography of Crime', *Ann. Amer. Acad. Pol. Soc. Sci.*, Vol. 217, Sept. 1941.

(On Physical Health): Sir Cyril Burt, *The Young Delinquent*, 4th ed., 1944, Ch. 6.

T. Ferguson, *The Young Delinquent in his Social Setting*, Oxford, 1952, Ch. 3.

M. D. Eilenberg, 'Remand Boys 1930 to 1955', *Brit. J. Crim.*, Vol. 2, No. 2, Oct. 1961.

Terence and Pauline Morris, *Pentonville*, London, 1963, Ch. 9.

Sheldon and Eleanor Glueck, *Physique and Delinquency*, New York and London, 1956.

T. C. N. Gibbens, *Psychiatric Studies of Borstal Lads*, Oxford, 1963, Ch. 9.

CHAPTER 12

(On the Phrenological School): Arthur E. Fink, *Causes of Crime*, Philadelphia, 1938, Ch. 1.

W. Norwood East, *Society and the Criminal*, London, H.M.S.O., 1949, Ch. 7.

(On Lombroso and his School): Marvin E. Wolfgang in *Pioneers in Criminology*, ed. by H. Mannheim, London, 1960, Ch. 9.

Hermann Mannheim, *Group Problems in Crime and Punishment*, London, 1955, Ch. 4.

T. Sellin, in *Pioneers in Criminology*, Ch. 13, and Francis Allen, *ibid.*, Ch. 10.

CHAPTER 13

(On Post-Lombrosian Developments in general): Hermann Mannheim, Introduction to *Pioneers in Criminology*.

Edwin D. Driver, in *Pioneers in Criminology*, Ch. 17.

(On Heredity and Crime): Arthur E. Fink, *Causes of Crime*, Philadelphia, 1938, Ch. 7.

Cyril Burt, *The Young Delinquent*, 4th ed., 1944, Chs. 2 and 14.

(On Twin Research): H. H. Newman, *Twins and Super-Twins*, London, 1942.

Johannes Lange, *Crime as Destiny*, London, 1931.

Ashley Montagu, 'The Biologist looks at Crime', *Ann. Amer. Acad. Polit. Soc. Sci.*, Vol. 217, Sept. 1941.

William Healy and Augusta Bronner, *New Light on Delinquency*, New Haven, 1936.

Lorna Whelan, 'Aggressive Psychopathy in One of a Pair of Uniovular Twins', *Brit. J. Delinq.*, Vol. 2, No. 2, Oct. 1951.

(On the Crimino-biological School): Ernst Kretschmer, *Physique and Character*, trans. by Sprott, London, 1936.

Hermann Mannheim, *Group Problems in Crime and Punishment*, London, 1955, pp. 75 ff.

William H. Sheldon, *Varieties of Delinquent Youth*, New York, 1949.

T. C. N. Gibbens, *Psychiatric Studies of Borstal Lads*, Oxford, 1963, Ch. 14 (on somato-typing).

CHAPTER 14

Barbara Wootton, *Social Science and Social Pathology*, London, 1959, Ch. 7.

Michael Hakeem, 'A Critique of the Psychiatric Approach to Crime and Correction in "Crime and Correction" ', *Law and Contemporary Problems*, Vol. 23, No. 4, 1958.

Edward Mapother and Aubrey Lewis, 'Psychological Medicine' in F. W. Price, *Textbook of the Practice of Medicine*, 5th ed., 1937.

Sir D. K. Henderson and R. D. Gillespie, *A Textbook of Psychiatry*, 8th ed., 1960.

David Stafford-Clark, *Psychiatry To-day*, 1st ed., 1952.

East and de Hubert, *Psychological Treatment of Crime*, H.M.S.O., 1939.

W. Norwood East, *Introduction to Forensic Psychiatry in the Criminal Courts*, London, 1927; the same, *Society and the Criminal*, London, H.M.S.O., 1949.

Angus MacNiven, in *Mental Abnormality and Crime*, London, 1944.

A. M. Lorentz de Haas, 'Epilepsy and Criminality', *Brit. J. Crim.*, Vol. 3, No. 3, 1963.

(On Alcoholism): H. Mannheim, *Social Aspects of Crime*, London, 1940, Ch. 6.

G. M. Scott, in *Mental Abnormality and Crime*, London, 1944, Ch. 8.

Howard Jones, *Alcoholic Addiction*, London, 1963.

M. M. Glatt, 'Alcoholism, Crime and Juvenile Delinquency', *The Brit. J. Delinq.*, Vol. 9, No. 2, 1958.

(On Schizophrenia): Don D. Jackson (ed.), *The Etiology of Schizophrenia*, New York, 1962.

(On Drug Addiction): Alfred R. Lindesmith, *Opiate Addiction*, Bloomington, 1952.

Edwin M. Schur, *Narcotic Addiction in Britain and America*, Bloomington, Indiana, London, 1964; the same, 'British Narcotics Policies', *J. crim. Law Criminol. Police Sci.*, Vol. 51, No. 6, 1961.

CHAPTER 15

(On Neuroses): Kate Friedlander, *The Psycho-analytical Approach to Juvenile Delinquency*, 1st ed., London, 1947.

Edward Glover, *The Roots of Crime*, London, 1960.

Franz Alexander and Hugo Staub, *The Criminal, the Judge, and the Public*, London, 1931.

Gillespie and MacCalman, in *Mental Abnormality and Crime*, London, 1944.

Edward Mapother and Aubrey Lewis, 'Psychological Medicine' in F. W. Price, *Textbook of the Practice of Medicine*, 5th ed., 1937.

Sigmund Freud, *Collected Papers*, Vol. 5, 1950.

David T. Maclay, *Brit. J. Delinq.*, Vol. 3, No. 1, July 1952.

T. C. N. Gibbens and Joyce Prince, *Shoplifting*, London, 1962.

Melitta Schmideberg, 'Pathological Firesetters', *J. crim. Law Criminol. Police Sci.*, Vol. 44, No. 1, 1953.

(On Psychopathy): D. K. Henderson, *Psychopathic States*, New York, 1939.

Brit. J. Delinq., Vol. 2, No. 2, October 1951: special number on Psychopathy.

Edward Glover, *The Roots of Crime*, London, 1960, Sect. 4.

Michael Craft, *Brit. J. Crim.*, Vol. 1, No. 3, January 1961.

William and Joan McCord, *Psychopathy and Delinquency*, New York and London, 1956.

T. C. N. Gibbens, D. A. Pond, and D. Stafford-Clark, *J. Ment. Sci.*, Vol. 105, No. 438, January 1959.

(On Mental Deficiency): A. F. Tredgold, *Mental Deficiency*, 9th ed., London, 1956.

Mary Woodward, *Low Intelligence and Crime*, London, I.S.T.D., 1955.

Cyril Burt, *The Young Delinquent*, 4th ed., London, 1944, Ch. 7.

Hilda Weber, 'The Borderline Defective Delinquent', *Brit. J. Delinq.*, Vol. 3, No. 3, January 1953.

K. O. Milner, 'Delinquent Types of Mentally Defective Persons', *J. Ment. Sci.*, Vol. 95, No. 401, Oct. 1949.

(On Genius): Ernst Kretschmer, *Psychology of Men of Genius*, London, 1931.

W. Lange-Eichbaum, *The Problem of Genius*, London, 1931.

Leta S. Hollingworth, *Children above 160 I.Q.*, New York, 1942.

CHAPTER 16

David Abrahamsen, *The Psychology of Crime*, London and New York, 1961.

Barbara Wootton, *Social Science and Social Pathology*, London, 1959.

Emanuel Miller, *Brit. J. Delinq.*, Vol. 10, No. 3, January 1960.

Karl F. Schuessler and Donald R. Cressey, 'Personality Characteristics of Criminals', *Amer. J. Sociol.*, Vol. 50, March 1950.

Tadeusz Grygier, *Oppression*, London, 1954.

S. and E. Glueck, *Unraveling Juvenile Delinquency*, New York, 1950, Ch. 18.

H. J. Eysenck, *The Structure of Human Personality*, London and New York, 1953.

Marvin E. Wolfgang, *Patterns of Homicide*, Philadelphia, 1959, Ch. 10.

W. Norwood East, *Society and the Criminal*, London, 1949, Ch. 17.

Franco Ferracuti, 'The Psychology of the Criminal Homicide', *Rev. Jur. Univ. Puerto Rico*, Vol. 32, No. 4, 1963.

Jackson Toby, 'Criminal Motivation', *Brit. J. Crim.*, Vol. 2, No. 4, April 1962.

Leonard Berkowitz, *Aggression: A Social Psychological Analysis*, New York, 1962.

Andreas Bjerre, *The Psychology of Murder*, London, 1927.

CHAPTER 17

Sigmund Freud, *Collected Papers*, Vol. 4, London, 1925.

Edward Glover, *Psycho-Analysis*, 2nd ed., London, 1949; the same, *Roots of Crime*, London, 1960.

Franz Alexander and William Healy, *The Roots of Crime*, New York, 1935.

Franz Alexander and Hugo Staub, *The Criminal, the Judge, and the Public*, New York, 1931.

S. H. Foulkes, *Psycho-Analysis and Crime*, Cambridge and Toronto, 1944.

Kate Friedlander, *The Psycho-Analytical Approach to Juvenile Delinquency*, 1st ed., London, 1947.

Robert M. Lindner, *Rebel without a Cause*, New York, 1944.

G. W. Elles, 'The Closed Circuit', *Brit. J. Crim.*, Vol. 2, No. 1, July 1961.

J. A. C. Brown, *Freud and the Post-Freudians*, Harmondsworth, 1961.

CHAPTER 18

Glanville Williams, *Criminal Law: The General Part*, 2nd ed., London, 1961 Ch. 10.

Sheldon Glueck, *Law and Psychiatry: Cold War or Entente Cordiale?* Baltimore, 1962, and London, 1963.

Hermann Mannheim, *Brit. J. Crim.*, Vol. 1, No. 3, January 1961.

Henry Weihofen, *The Urge to Punish*, London, 1957.

Jerome Hall, *Studies in Jurisprudence and Criminal Theory*, New York, 1958, Ch. 15.

G. W. Keeton, *Guilty but Insane*, London, 1961.

Barbara Wootton, *Crime and the Criminal Law*, London, 1963.

Hermann Mannheim, *Group Problems in Crime and Punishment*, London, 1955, Ch. 13.

Notes

CHAPTER 1

[1] H. Mannheim, 'Über einige neuere Entwicklungstendenzen in der Kriminologischen Forschung', *Mschr. Kriminol. Strafrechtsreform*, Vol. 40, Feb. 1957 reproduced in *Deutsche Strafrechtsreform in englischer Sicht*, München-Berlin, 1960, Ch. 4.

[2] Karl R. Popper, *The Poverty of Historicism*, London, 1957, pp. 121, 134.

[3] See H. Mannheim, 'Beiträge zur Lehre von der Revision', *Abhandlungen aus der Berliner Juristischen Fakultät*, Vol. 3, Berlin, 1925, pp. 51 ff., 41 ff., where a detailed discussion of the definition of *Tatsache* (fact) is given.

[4] Wilhelm Dilthey, 'Ideen über eine beschreibende und zergliedernde Psychologie 1894', *Gesammelte Schriften*, Vol. 5, Leipzig–Berlin, 1924, pp. 139 ff., esp. p. 172; H. A. Hodges, *The Philosophy of Wilhelm Dilthey*, London, 1952, Ch. 5.

[5] Max Weber 'Über einige Kategorien der verstehenden Soziologie, 1913', *Gesammelte Aufsätze zur Wissenschaftslehre*, Tübingen, 1922, pp. 403 ff.; see also Popper, *op. cit.*, pp. 20 ff., who regards this view as 'very closely related to historicism, although it is not invariably combined with it'. McIver, Foreword to B. Lander, *Towards an Understanding of Juvenile Delinquency*, New York, 1954, p.viii, writes 'the end of science is comprehension . . . to comprehend human relations is to make them understandable in the light of human responses to conditions'.

[6] Franz Exner, *Kriminologie*, esp. 3rd ed., Berlin–Göttingen–Heidelberg, 1949, p. 6.

[7] Stephen Toulmin, *The Philosophy of Science*, London, 1953, p. 10.

[8] Glanville L. Williams, *Criminal Law: The General Part*, London, 1953, Chs. 4–7.

[9] See the most recent discussions in the *Leipziger Kommentar* on the German Penal Code, Berlin, 1956, pp. 19–30.

[10] Kenny's *Outlines of Criminal Law*. An entirely new edition by T. W. Cecil Turner, Cambridge, 1952. The problem of causality, previously rather neglected by English and American writers on criminal law, has been very fully discussed in Continental literature. This previous deficiency of Anglo-American legal literature has, however, recently been made good by several important publications, especially H. L. A. Hart and A. M. Honoré, *Causation in the Law*, London, 1959; Gerhard O. W. Mueller, 'Causing Criminal Harm' in *Essays in Criminal Science*, ed. by him, London–Hackensack, 1961, Ch. 7; Jerome Hall, *Studies in Jurisprudence and Criminal Theory*, New York, 1958, Ch. 10.

[11] Peter Lejins, *Soc. Forces*, Vol. 29, No. 3, March 1951.

[12] There are a few notable exceptions: Walter C. Reckless, *Criminal Behavior*, New York, 1940, p. 2, and Ch. 9; the same, *The Crime Problem*, 2nd ed., New York, 1955, esp. Ch. 5; Paul W. Tappan, *Juvenile Delinquency*, New York–Toronto–London, 1949, pp. 55 ff.; Sheldon and Eleanor Glueck, *Unraveling Juvenile Delinquency*, New York, 1950, pp. 4, 281; Franz Exner, *op. cit.*, p. 9; Ernst Seelig, *Lehrbuch der Kriminologie*, 1st ed., Graz, 1951, pp. 4, 118.

[13] Bertrand Russell, *Human Knowledge, Its Scope and Limits*, London, 1948, p. 471; also Sir A. S. Eddington, *The Nature of the Physical World*, Cambridge, 1927, pp. 297–8: 'the great laws hitherto accepted as causal appear on minute examination to be of statistical character'.

[14] Bertrand Russell, *op. cit.*, pp. 332 ff.

[15] The text is largely based upon the admirable discussion in the late Professor L. Susan Stebbing's *Philosophy and the Physicists*, Harmondsworth, 1944, Ch. 9. See also John O. Wisdom, *Causation and the Foundation of Science*, Paris, 1946, according to whom 'natural laws are causal laws, scientific laws apparently are not' (p. 7), but the 'concept of scientific laws presupposes that of causation' (p. 20).

[16] K. Popper, *op. cit.*, pp. 122 ff., 143 ff.

[17] H. Mannheim, *Group Problems in Crime and Punishment*, London, 1955, pp. 261–3, with bibliog.

[18] Karl Britton, *John Stuart Mill*, Harmondsworth, 1953, pp. 152 ff.

[19] Kenny-Turner, *op. cit.*, § 13.

[20] So Lejins, *loc. cit.*; see also Lewis S. Feuer, 'Symposium on Causality in the Social Sciences', *J. Philos.* Vol. 51, No. 23, 11.11.1954, pp. 681–94.

[21] See below, Chs. 12/13.

[22] Sir Cyril Burt, *The Young Delinquent*, London, 1st ed., 1925, 4th ed. 1948, p. 599; William Healy, *The Individual Delinquent*, Boston, 1914.

[23] Edwin H. Sutherland, *Principles of Criminology*, 1st ed., Philadelphia, 1927; 5th ed. edited by D. R. Cressey, London, 1955.

[24] See *The Sutherland Papers*, ed. by Albert Cohen, Alfred Lindesmith, and Karl Schuessler, Bloomington, 1956.

[25] Editorial Note in *The Sutherland Papers*, p. 6, see also pp. 19, 31.

[26] Alfred R. Lindesmith, *Opiate Addiction*, Bloomington, 1947, pp. 17–20.

[27] Edwin H. Sutherland, *op. cit.*, pp. 30 ff.

[28] Cyril Burt, *op. cit.*, pp. 600 ff. The same impression is given by Burt's more recent discussion in *The Subnormal Mind*, 3rd ed., London, 1955, p. 163.

[29] Emile Durkheim, *Les Règles de la méthode sociologique*, pp. 125 ff., Eng. ed., Chicago, 1938, pp. 126 ff.

[30] R. M. McIver, *Social Causation*, Boston, 1940.

[31] See also my paper 'Why Delinquency?', reproduced in *Group Problems in Crime and Punishment*, London, 1955, p. 134.

[32] Sheldon and Eleanor Glueck, *Unraveling Juvenile Delinquency*, pp. 272, 281.

[33] Sheldon Glueck, 'Theory and Fact in Criminology', *Brit. J. Delinq.*, Vol. 7, No. 2, Oct. 1956, p. 106, now reproduced in Sheldon and Eleanor Glueck, *Ventures in Criminology*, London, 1964, Ch. 16, on p. 257. In his General Report to the Third International Congress of Criminology, 1955, too, he writes that statistical correlation indicates 'a high probability of a functional relationship . . . even though one cannot as yet trace the specific and subtle links in the chain of causation', see *Summary of the Congress*, London, 1957, p. 163.

[34] Sheldon and Eleanor Glueck, *Physique and Delinquency*, New York, 1956, pp. 40, 43.

[35] Max Weber, *op. cit.*, pp. 412–13.

[36] See W. I. Thomas in *Social Behavior and Personality*, ed. by Edmund H. Volkart, New York, 1951, p. 66.

[37] Arnold M. Rose, *Theory and Method in the Social Sciences*, Minneapolis, 1954, p. 165, and the Review in *Brit. J. Delinq.* Vol. 7, No. 2., Oct. 1956, p. 154; Walter A. Reckless, *Criminal Behavior*, p. 176.

[38] Hermann Mannheim and Leslie T. Wilkins, *Prediction Methods in relation to Borstal Training*, H.M.S.O., London, 1955, pp. 40, 43–5, 217.

[39] Walter A. Reckless, *The Crime Problem*, 2nd ed., New York, 1955, Ch. 3.

[40] Emile Durkheim, *Suicide*, Eng. trans. George Simpson, London, 1952, p. 147.

[41] No more than this has been maintained in Mannheim–Wilkins, *op. cit.*, p. 216, where it is stated: 'research on decisions rather than on finding out things (particularly "causes") is certainly likely to take us much further much faster. . . . Indeed "cause" is an unnecessary concept in the whole *of this part, at least*, of the criminological field' (italics mine).

[42] The medical analogy has been stressed by Dr. R. C. Cabot, as quoted by Edwin Powers and Helen Witmer, *Prevention of Delinquency, The Cambridge-Somerville Youth Study*, New York, 1951, p. 112.

[43] The literature on this subject is enormous. Only a few references can here be given. See, e.g., W. Friedmann, *Legal Theory*, 3rd ed., London, 1953, pp. 192, 196 ff., also 112 ff. on Kelsen and 151 ff. on Austin.

[44] Edgar Bodenheimer, *Jurisprudence*, New York–London, 1940, pp. 208 ff.

[45] See the excellent discussion on 'The Concepts of Juridical and Scientific Law' by Morris Ginsberg in *Reason and Unreason in Society*, London, 1947, Ch. 12; also Bodenheimer, *op. cit.*, pp. 310 ff.

[46] H. Bianchi, *Position and Subject-matter of Criminology*, Amsterdam, 1956, p. 121.

[47] See H. Mannheim, *Group Problems in Crime and Punishment*, London, 1955, pp. 271 ff., also Popper, *op. cit.*, p. 64.

[48] Quoted from Bernaldo de Quiros, *Modern Theories of Criminality*, Boston, 1911.

[49] Karl R. Popper, *op. cit.*, p. 61.

[50] On the difference between laws and trends see Popper, *op. cit.*, pp. 115, 128.

[51] Robert Vouin and Jacques Léauté, *Droit pénal et criminologie*, Paris, 1956, pp. 22, 57.

[52] Thorsten Sellin, *Culture Conflict and Crime*, Soc. Sci. Res. Counc. Bull. 41, New York, 1938, pp. 19 ff., 30 ff.

[53] See *Group Problems*, pp. 136, 262.

[54] Vouin-Léauté, *op. cit.*, pp. 34 ff.

[55] H. Bianchi, *op. cit.*, p. 110.

[56] Donald R. Cressey, *Other People's Money*, Glencoe, Ill., 1953, pp. 19 ff.

[57] See on Hans Gross, esp. Roland Grassberger, *J. crim. Law Criminol. Police Sci.*, Vol. 47, No. 4., Nov.–Dec., 1956, pp. 397 ff. (reproduced in *Pioneers of Criminology*, ed. by H. Mannheim, London, 1960, Ch. 11); Ernst Seelig, *Lehrbuch der Kriminologie*, 1st ed., Graz, 1951, pp. 27 ff., 1952 ff. English translations of Hans Gross's principal works are available.

[58] See the details given by R. Grassberger in *The University Teaching of Social Sciences: Criminology*, Paris, UNESCO, 1957, p. 62. On the Vienna Institute see the details given by W. Gleispach in *Z. ges. Strafrechtwiss.*, Vol. 49, 1929, pp. 586 ff.

[59] UNESCO Report, pp. 70 ff.

[60] *Ibid.*, p. 84.

[61] *Ibid.*, pp. 93 ff. According to Vouin-Léauté, *op. cit.*, p. 21, 'Criminalistics should remain outside Criminology'.

[62] UNESCO Report, pp. 102, 105.

[63] *Ibid.*, p. 131 for Great Britain.

[64] *Ibid.*, pp. 37, 39.

[65] One of the exceptions is Barnes and Teeters, *New Horizons in Criminology*, New York, 1943, where 'scientific methods of detecting and apprehending criminals' are very briefly treated.

[66] See also Thorsten Sellin, 'L'Etude sociologique de la Criminalité', General

Report to the Second International Congress on Criminology, *Proceedings*, Vol. 5, Paris, 1953, p. 113 (also published in English in *J. crim. Law Criminol.*, Vol. 41, 1950).

[67] So rightly H. Bianchi, *op. cit.*, p. 208.

[68] On teamwork in criminology see below, Ch. 4, s. 3.

[69] Hermann Mannheim, *Group Problems*, Ch. 12.

[70] H. Bianchi, *op. cit.*, pp. 16 ff.

[71] Thorsten Sellin, *op. cit.*

[72] J. M. Van Bemmelen, *Juridical Rev.*, Vol. 63, No. 1., April 1951, pp. 24 ff.

[73] Erwin Frey, 'Kriminologie: Programm und Wirklichkeit', *Schweiz. Z. Strafrecht*, Vol. 66, 1951, p. 67.

[74] T. H. Marshall, *Sociology at the Crossroads*, London, 1947, p. 10. See also David Lockwood, *Brit. J. Sociol.*, Vol. 7, No. 2, June 1956, p. 142.

[75] Hermann Mannheim, *Group Problems in Crime and Punishment*, pp. 155–6. See also Max Weber, 'Wissenschaft als Beruf', *Ges. Aufsätze zur Wissenschaftslehre*, pp. 531–2.

[76] Bronislaw Malinowski, *A Scientific Theory of Culture*, New Haven, 1944, pp. 8–11.

[77] Nathaniel Cantor, *Crime and Society*, New York, 1939, p. 10.

[78] Arnold M. Rose, *Theory and Method in the Social Sciences*, Minneapolis, 1954, pp. 246–7.

[79] W. B. Gallie, *Brit. J. Phil. Sci.*, Vol. 8, No. 30, Aug. 1957, pp. 118, 126. See now also L. T. Wilkins, *Social Deviance* (Ch. 3, note 2 below), pp. 1–2.

[80] Jerome Michael and Mortimer J. Adler, *Crime, Law and Social Science*, London, 1933, p. 85.

[81] Thorsten Sellin, *Culture Conflict and Crime*, New York, 1938, p. 3.

[82] Karl R. Popper, *The Poverty of Historicism*, p. 59.

[83] See *Group Problems in Crime and Punishment*, pp. 209–10.

CHAPTER 2

[1] Immanuel Kant, *Kritik der reinen Vernunft*, Cassirer ed., Vol. 3, p. 495.

[2] See, e.g., Julius Binder, *Philosophie des Rechts*, Berlin, 1925, p. 213.

[3] Kenny's *Outlines of Criminal Law*, an entirely new ed. by J. W. Cecil Turner, Cambridge, 1952; Glanville Williams, 'The Definition of Crime' in *Current Legal Problems*, London, 1955, p. 111.

[4] See the full details in *Materialien zur Strafrechtsreform*, Vol. 1, 1954, pp. 11 ff., and Vol. 2, 1955, pp. 499 ff., and for the legal-philosophical basis of this development Erik Wolf in *Festgabe für R. von Frank*, Tübingen, 1930, Vol. 2, pp. 516 ff.

[5] On the historical development of Swiss legislation on this point see the detailed account of Jean Graven, 'La Classification des Infractions du Code Pénal et ses Effets', *Revue pénale Suisse*, Vol. 73, 1958, pp. 3 ff. Graven was also the redactor of the Ethiopian Penal Code of 1957.

[6] *Gesetz über die Ordnungswidrigkeiten.* For details see the Commentary by H. E. Rotberg, Berlin, 1952, and on the wider theoretical and practical significance of this Act especially the important lecture by H. H. Jescheck in *Juristen Zeitung*, No. 15–16, 14 August 1959.

[7] Rotberg, *op. cit.*, p. 24.

[8] *Entwurf des Allgemeinen Teils eines Strafgesetzbuchs*, Bonn, 1958, 'Begründung', p. 5. The same applies to the Draft Code of 1962; see pp. 98, 121.

[9] For the following text see the illuminating discussions by Jerome Hall, *General Principles of Criminal Law*, Minneapolis, 1947, Ch. 10, and Glanville

Williams, *Criminal Law: The General Part*, London, 1953, Ch. 7. Important also F. B. Sayre, 'Public Welfare Offences', *Columbia Law Rev.*, Vol. 33, 1933, pp. 55 ff., and more recently Colin Howard, *Strict Responsibility*, London, 1954; the same in Norval Morris and Colin Howard, *Studies in Criminal Law*, London, 1964, Ch. 6; James E. Starrs, 'The Regulatory Offence in Historical Perspective', in *Essays in Criminal Science*, ed. by Gerhard O. W. Mueller, London–South Hackensack, 1961, Ch. 9.

[10] Francis A. Allen, 'The Borderland of the Criminal Law: Problems of "Socializing" Criminal Justice', *Soc. Serv. Rev.*, Vol. 32, No. 2, June 1958, pp. 107 ff.

[11] Glanville Williams, *op. cit.*, p. 240.

[12] Jerome Hall, *op. cit.*, p. 285.

[13] Hermann Mannheim, *Criminal Justice and Social Reconstruction*, 2nd imp., London, 1949, pp. 127, 169 ff., 196 ff. and *passim*.

[14] A. L. Goodhart in an Editorial Note, *Law Quart. Rev.*, Vol. 74, July 1958, pp. 342–3, supporting a judgment of the Court of Criminal Appeal in *R. v. St. Margaret's Trust Ltd.*, [1958] 1 W.L.R. 522.

[15] On this see Jerome Hall, *General Principles*, p. 310; Glanville Williams, *Criminal Law*, p. 707. For traffic offences in particular such measures have frequently been suggested to make the police and the courts better equipped to deal with this mass problem of our time; see, e.g., the important essay by Erwin R. Frey, 'Reobjektivierung des Strafrechts im Zeitalter der Technik', in *Die Rechtsordnung im technischen Zeitalter*, Zurich, 1961, which, although based on Swiss law and traffic conditions, is of general interest too.

[16] So rightly Erik Wolf, *loc. cit.*, p. 581.

[17] A. S. Diamond, *Primitive Law*, London, 1935, pp. 277 ff., believes it to have been universal.

[18] See in particular the material quoted by Gerhard O. W. Mueller, 'Tort, Crime and the Primitive', *J. crim. Law Criminol. Police Sci.*, Vol. 46, No. 3, 1955, pp. 303–332.

[19] Theodore F. T. Plucknett, *A Concise History of the Common Law*, 5th ed., London, 1956, p. 421.

[20] For criticisms of Blackstone, see Kenny, *Outlines of Criminal Law*, 1952 ed., App. I, pp. 531 ff; Jerome Hall, *General Principles*, Ch. 7, pp. 188 ff. On the differences between civil and criminal law see also Richard C. Donnelly *et al.*, *Criminal Law*, Glencoe Free Press, New York, 1962, Ch. II, Part 1, and on the 'Requisites of a Crime', Part 4.

[21] P. H. Winfield, *The Province of the Law of Tort*, Cambridge, 1931, pp. 196–8; Turner in Kenny, *op. cit.*, p. 547.

[22] See Stephen Schafer, *Restitution to Victims of Crime*, London, 1960.

[23] On the following see the detailed account by Marshall B. Clinard, *The Black Market*, New York, 1952, Ch. 9.

[24] Clinard, *op. cit.*, pp. 234, 238.

[25] See Clinard, *op. cit.*, pp. 227 ff.

[26] Sir William Holdsworth, *History of English Law*, Vol. 6, 3rd ed., London, 1922–23, p. 218; also Vol. 2, 3rd ed., 1923, p. 444.

[27] Sir William Blackstone, *Commentaries on the Laws of England*, Vol. I, p. 53. Against him J. W. C. Turner in Kenny, *Outlines*, 1952 ed., p. 22, and in *The Modern Approach to Criminal Law*, London, 1945, pp. 220 ff., 240.

[28] On this see Julius Binder, *Philosophie des Rechts*, pp. 753 ff.

[29] On the history of the Law of Nature, see below, notes 81 ff.

[30] See Gustav Radbruch, *Rechtsphilosophie*, 4th ed., Stuttgart, 1950, ed. by Erik Wolf, p. 107.

[31] Morris Ginsberg, *Essays in Sociology and Social Philosophy*, Vol. 1: 'On the Diversity of Morals', London, 1956, p. 115, and on Stammler in general Vol. 2, Ch. 11.

[32] H. Bianchi, *Position and Subject-Matter of Criminology*, Amsterdam, 1956, Ch. 17.

[33] *Amer. sociol. Rev.*, Vol. 10, 1945, pp. 132 ff.; reprinted in *The Sutherland Papers*, ed. by Albert Cohen, Alfred Lindesmith, Karl Schuessler, Bloomington, 1956, and also in an expanded version as Ch. 3 of Sutherland's book *White-Collar Crime*, New York, 1949.

[34] Clinard, *op. cit.*, p. 236, and the whole of Ch. 9; also his *Sociology of Deviant Behavior*, New York, 1957, pp. 159 ff.

[35] Ernest W. Burgess, *Amer. J. Sociol.*, Vol. 56, 1950, pp. 32–3.

[36] Paul W. Tappan, *Amer. sociol. Rev.*, Vol. 12, 1947, pp. 98 ff.; *Federal Probation*, Vol. 11, 1947, p. 44.

[37] Thorsten Sellin, *Culture Conflict and Crime*, New York, 1938, pp. 25 ff.

[38] This is accepted by Kenny, *Outlines*, 1952 ed., p. 2.

[39] Julius Goebel, *Felony and Misdemeanor*, New York, 1937, pp. 146 ff.

[40] H. Bianchi, *op. cit.*, pp. 95 ff.

[41] R. Garofalo, *La Criminologie*, 2nd French ed., Paris, 1890, p. 2.

[42] For a general survey of provisions dealing with recidivism, see *Summary of Proceedings*, Third International Congress on Criminology, 1955, London, 1957, General Reports, Section 1, by Norval Morris and Roland Grassberger.

[43] On the whole subject, see H. Mannheim, *The Dilemma of Penal Reform*, London, 1939, Ch. 4, esp. p. 117. On the present French law see Vouin-Léauté, *op. cit.*, pp. 585 ff.

[44] Tappan, *Amer. sociol. Rev.*, Vol. 12, p. 100.

[45] Sutherland, *White-Collar Crime*, p. 35.

[46] *Ibid.*, p. 40.

[47] For further details see Donald R. Cressey, *Other People's Money*, Glencoe, Ill., 1953, Introduction.

[48] Kenny, *Outlines of Criminal Law*, 1952 ed., § 129.

[49] See, e.g., Andreas Bjerre, *The Psychology of Murder*, Eng. trans. London, 1927; John Lewis Gillin, *The Wisconsin Prisoner*, Madison, 1946; Hans v. Hentig, *Zur Psychologie der Einzeldelikte* II: *Der Mord*, Tübingen, 1956; Veli Verkkö, *Homicides and Suicides in Finland and their Dependence on National Character*, Copenhagen, 1951; Austin L. Porterfield and Robert H. Talbert, *Mid-Century Crime in our Culture*, Fort Worth, 1954; Marshall B. Clinard, *Sociology of Deviant Behavior*, New York, 1957, pp. 210 ff. Also see below, Ch. 16.

[50] Sir Norwood East, *Society and the Criminal*, London, 1949, p. 254. See also *Report of the Royal Commission on Capital Punishment*, Cmd. 8932, paras. 498 ff.

[51] Ernst Roesner, *Z. ges. Strafrechtwiss.*, Vol. 56, 1936, pp. 336 ff.

[52] H. C. Brearley, *Homicide in the United States*, Chapel Hill, 1932, p. 64.

[53] See E. Bodenheimer, *Jurisprudence*, p. 216; G. Radbruch, *Rechtsphilosophie*, 4th ed., pp. 111, 185. Both writers stress that even Marxism was eventually forced to accept the independence of cultural and especially legal forms (Radbruch). On this subject, see more fully below, Ch. 20.

[54] Hermann Mannheim, *Criminal Justice and Social Reconstruction*, Sections 3, 4; the same, *The Dilemma of Penal Reform*, London, 1939, esp. Parts 1 and 2.

[55] Sir Henry Sumner Maine, *Ancient Law*, London, 1861.

[56] Diamond, *Primitive Law*, pp. 49, 124, 153, 164. William Seagle, *In Quest of Law*, New York, 1941, p. 125, agrees with him and regards Maine's view as representative of the Victorian age.

[57] David Daube, *Studies in Biblical Law*, Cambridge, 1947, Ch. 1; G. W. Paton, *Textbook of Jurisprudence*, Oxford, 1946, p. 44.

[58] 'There is probably no subject in the world about which opinions differ so much as the nature of religion', writes Sir James Fraser, 'Magic and Religion', Ch. 4 of the *Golden Bough*, The Thinker's Library ed., Vol. 100, p. 81. See also K. N. Llewellyn and E. Adamson Hoebel, *The Cheyenne Way*, Norman, Okla., 1941, pp. 55 ff., 132 ff.; Joachim Wach, *Sociology of Religion*, London, 1944, pp. 290 ff.

[59] See, e.g., Bronislaw Malinowski, *Crime and Custom in Savage Society*, London, 1932, p. 51.

[60] On the Benefit of Clergy, see the references in Hermann Mannheim, *Criminal Justice and Social Reconstruction*, p. 94, fn. 2.

[61] See, e.g., the following Criminal Codes: German, §§ 166; Italian, arts. 402 ff.; Swiss, art. 261; Danish, arts. 139–40. In England, the law of blasphemy is part of the law of criminal libel: Rupert Cross and T. Asterley Jones, *An Introduction to Criminal Law*, London, 1948, p. 253. The Soviet Criminal Code penalizes 'any interference with the celebration of any religions, in so far as such rite does not disturb public order and is not accompanied by any attempt to encroach on the rights of any citizen' (art. 127).

[62] For details see Hermann Mannheim, *Criminal Justice and Social Reconstruction*, Ch. 2–5; Glanville Williams, *The Sanctity of Life and the Criminal Law*, London, 1957.

[63] See in particular J. C. Flugel, *Man, Morals and Society*, London, 1945, Ch. 17: 'The Problem of Religion', esp. pp. 271 ff., 146 ff., 164 ff.

[64] Paul W. Tappan, *Juvenile Delinquency*, New York, 1949, p. 514. See also Arthur Kielholz, in *Die Prophylaxe des Verbrechens*, ed. by Heinrich Meng, Basel, 1948, pp. 360 ff. For one of the best discussions on the place of religion in the treatment of juvenile delinquents see W. David Wills, *The Barns Experiment*, London, 1945, Ch. 8.

[65] On the Pennsylvanian system see Negley K. Teeters, *They Were in Prison*, Chicago, 1937; Harry Elmer Barnes and Negley K. Teeters, *New Horizons in Criminology*, New York, 1943, Ch. 23.

[66] H. Bianchi, *Position and Subject-Matter of Criminology*, pp. 110, 128. Against the identification of crime and sin also Sir Walter Moberly, *Responsibility*, Oxford, 1950, p. 36.

[67] H. Kantorowicz, *The Definition of Law*, ed. by A. H. Campbell, with an Introduction by A. L. Goodhart, Cambridge, 1958, Ch. 5, p. 52.

[68] William F. Ogburn and Meyer F. Nimkoff, *A Handbook of Sociology*, London, 1947, pp. 215 ff.

[69] See the details in *Group Problems in Crime and Punishment*, pp. 276 ff.

[70] Gunnar Myrdal *et al.*, *An American Dilemma*, New York; also his *Value in Social Theory*, ed. by Paul Streeten, London, 1958, pp. 78, 99, 139, 180.

[71] Gustav Radbruch, *op. cit.*, pp. 142 ff.

[72] Ogburn-Nimkoff, *op. cit.*, p. 33.

[73] Kantorowicz, *op. cit.*, p. 54.

[74] On Max Weber's view see, e.g., Max Rheinstein in his and E. Shils's Introduction to Max Weber on *Law in Economics and Society*, Cambridge, Mass., 1954, p. lxvii.

[75] Jerome Hall, *Studies in Jurisprudence and Criminal Theory*, New York, 1958, p. 244.

[76] See *Report of the Committee on Homosexual Offences and Prostitution*, H.M.S.O., Cmd. 247, London, 1957, pp. 9, 80; and my contribution to *Law and Opinion in England in the Twentieth Century*, ed. by M. Ginsberg, London, 1959, pp. 274–5.

⁷⁷ On these cases see Glanville Williams, *Criminal Law: General Principles*, p. 176; Edmond Cahn, *The Moral Decision*, pp. 61 ff.

⁷⁸ On legislation explicitly introducing moral factors and considerations into the process of sentencing see my lecture 'Some Aspects of Judicial Sentencing Policy', *Yale Law J.*, Vol. 67, No. 6, May 1958, esp. p. 963, and on 'moral turpitude' Edmond Cahn, *op. cit.*, p. 166.

⁷⁹ *The Dilemma of Penal Reform*, London, 1939, p. 21.

⁸⁰ Jerome Hall, 'The Purpose of a System for the Administration of Criminal Justice'. Lecture delivered 9.10.1963, Georgetown University Law Centre, Washington, D.C., p. 17, fn. 41.

⁸¹ The literature on natural law is immense, and any selection is bound to be arbitrary. In addition to the books referred to below (n. 125), which deal more specifically with the relation of law to morality, the following may be mentioned: As an admirable introduction to the subject, with excellent bibliographical notes, A. P. d'Entrèves, *Natural Law. An Introduction to Legal Philosophy*, 4th imp., London, 1957. Also Otto Gierke, *Natural Law and the Theory of Society*, trans. with an Introduction by Ernest Barker, 2 vols., Cambridge, 1934; Gierke, *Johannes Althusius*, 3rd ed., Breslau, 1913; W. Friedmann, *Legal Theory*, 4th ed., London, 1960; Erik Wolf, *Das Problem der Naturrechtslehre*, Karlsruhe, 1955; Hans Welzel, *Naturrecht und materielle Gerechtigkeit*, Göttingen, 1951; Julius Binder, *Philosophie des Rechts*, Berlin, 1925, pp. 751 ff.; Roscoe Pound, *Law and Morals*, 2nd ed., Chapel Hill, 1926; Edgar Bodenheimer, *Jurisprudence*, New York-London, 1940, Part 2, esp. pp. 73, 103, 156; Hans Kelsen, *What is Justice?*, Berkeley and Los Angeles, 1957, pp. 139 ff.; Carlo Antoni, *From History to Sociology*, trans. from the Italian, Detroit, 1959. Thomas Würtenberger, *Archiv für Rechts und Sozialphilosophie*, Vol. 41, No. 1, 1954, pp. 58-87, gives an account of German contributions since 1948 to the history of natural law.

⁸² d'Entrèves, *op. cit.*, p. 9.

⁸³ *Ibid.*, p. 80.

⁸⁴ Erik Wolf (*op. cit.* at note 81), p. 87.

⁸⁵ Hans Welzel (*op. cit.* at note 81), p. 9.

⁸⁶ *Ibid.*, p. 21.

⁸⁷ This is the impression given by Hans Kelsen, *What is Justice?*, Ch. 3.

⁸⁸ See Jerome Hall, *Studies* (cited at note 75), Ch. 3, esp. pp. 74 ff.; Welzel, *op. cit.*, p. 21.

⁸⁹ On Aristotle's views on natural law see Kelsen, *op. cit.*, Ch. 4; Welzel, Ch. 5.

⁹⁰ On the Stoa see Bodenheimer, *op. cit.*, pp. 107 ff.; Welzel, *op. cit.*, Ch. 6; Friedmann, *op. cit.*, p. 22.

⁹¹ Wolf, *op. cit.*, p. 89.

⁹² Welzel, *op. cit.*, p. 47.

⁹³ Bodenheimer, *op. cit.*, p. 111; d'Entrèves, *op. cit.*, p. 22.

⁹⁴ Bodenheimer, *op. cit.*, p. 113; d'Entrèves, *op. cit.*, p. 30.

⁹⁵ This quotation from St. Thomas's *Summa Theologica* is taken from d'Entrèves, *op. cit.*, p. 43. On St. Thomas see also Welzel, *op. cit.*, Part 2, Ch. 2, and Norman St. John Stevas, *Life, Death, and the Law*, London, 1961, pp. 19-22.

⁹⁶ Kelsen, *op. cit.*, p. 142; Bodenheimer, *op. cit.*, p. 124.

⁹⁷ d'Entrèves, *op. cit.*, pp. 43, 45.

⁹⁸ Welzel, *op. cit.*, pp. 65-6.

⁹⁹ *Ibid.*, pp. 76, 83.

¹⁰⁰ *Ibid.*, p. 108.

¹⁰¹ On Hobbes see Kelsen, *op. cit.*, pp. 142 ff.; Welzel, *op. cit.*, p. 112; Wolf, *op. cit.*, p. 100.

[102] See Howard Warrender, *The Political Philosophy of Hobbes*, Oxford, 1957, esp. pp. 322 ff.

[103] d'Entrèves, *op. cit.*, pp. 52, 70; Welzel, *op. cit.*, p. 130.

[104] Kelsen, *op. cit.*, p. 148; Welzel, *op. cit.*, p. 133.

[105] Welzel, *op. cit.*, p. 144.

[106] *Ibid.*, p. 152.

[107] Wolf, *op. cit.*, p. 64; Welzel, *op. cit.*, p. 154.

[108] Kelsen, *op. cit.*, pp. 148-9.

[109] Welzel, *op. cit.*, p. 161.

[110] Kelsen, *op. cit.*, pp. 149-50.

[111] Friedmann, *op. cit.*, p. 42.

[112] d'Entrèves, *op. cit.*, p. 87; Welzel, *op. cit.*, p. 162; Wolf, *op. cit.*, p. 65.

[113] Kelsen, *op. cit.*, p. 150.

[114] d'Entrèves, *op. cit.*, p. 103. On p. 93, however, he warns us 'not to speak of natural law as a confusion between law and morals'.

[115] Kant, *Einteilung der Rechtslehre, Immanuel Kant's Werke*, Berlin, Vol. 7, p. 44.

[116] Kant, *Einleitung in die Metaphysik der Sitten, Werke*, Berlin, Vol. 7, pp. 19 ff.

[117] Kelsen, *op. cit.*, p. 150.

[118] Friedmann, *Legal Theory*, p. 50.

[119] H. L. A. Hart, 'Positivism and the Separation of Law and Morals', *Harv. Law Rev.*, Vol. 71, No. 4, Feb. 1958, pp. 593 ff.

[120] Friedmann, *op. cit.*, pp. 119 ff.; d'Entrèves, *op. cit.*, p. 98.

[121] Welzel, *op. cit.*, p. 177, points out that Hegel's state was not merely organized power, but a spiritual force.

[122] Hegel, *Rechtsphilosophie, Vorrede*, p. 33, *Sämtliche Werke*, ed. Hermann Glockner, Stuttgart, 1928, Vol. 7.

[123] See Friedmann, *op. cit.*, pp. 87 ff. For more general criticisms of Stammler see Ginsberg, *Reason and Unreason in Society*, Ch. 11; Max Weber, *Gesammelte Aufsätze zur Wissenschaftslehre*, pp. 291 ff. More specifically on his theory of natural law: Max Ernst Mayer, *Rechtsphilosophie*, Berlin, 1922, pp. 20-1.

[124] See, e.g., Jerome Hall, *Studies in Jurisprudence and Criminal Theory*, pp. 28-9.

[125] For the following text see, in addition to the literature in notes 81 ff., H. Kantorowicz, *The Definition of Law*, pp. 41 ff.; M. Ginsberg, *Essays in Sociology and Social Philosophy*, Vol. 2, pp. 16 ff.; Edmond Cahn, *The Moral Decision*, pp. 38 ff.; A. L. Goodhart, *The Nature of Law and Morals*, London, 1955; Sir Patrick Devlin, *The Enforcement of Morals*, Oxford, 1959; H. L. A. Hart, *Law, Liberty and Morality*, Oxford, 1963; Lon L. Fuller, 'Positivism and Fidelity to Law—A Reply to Professor Hart', *Harv. Law Rev.*, Vol. 71, No. 4, Feb. 1958, pp. 630-72; M. Ginsberg's review of Hart in *Brit. J. Crim.*, Vol. 4, No. 3., Jan. 1964, pp. 283-90; Kurt Baier, *The Moral Point of View*, Ithaca, 1958. Now Devlin, *The Enforcement of Morals*, Oxford, 1965.

[126] See the literature quoted by Bodenheimer, *op. cit.*, pp. 73, 158 ff.

[127] Cahn, *op. cit.*, p. 45.

[128] Sir David Ross, *Foundations of Ethics*, London, 1939, p. 122.

[129] William Ernest Hocking, 'Ways of Thinking about Rights', in *Law. A Century of Progress, 1835–1935, Contributions in Celebration of the 100th Anniversary of the Founding of the School of Law of New York University*, Vol. 2, 1937, pp. 242 ff.

[130] Georg Jellinek, *Die sozialethische Bedeutung von Recht, Unrecht, Strafe*, 1878, p. 49.

[131] G. Radbruch, *Grundzüge der Rechtsphilosophie*, 1st ed., 1914, p. 43 ff.

[132] This is the view of Leon Petrazycki, *Law and Morality*, Eng. trans., London–Cambridge, Mass., 1955.

[133] H. Kantorowicz, *The Definition of Law*, p. 51.

[134] M. Ginsberg, *op. cit.*, p. 16.

[135] In his discussion of this point Kelsen, *op. cit.*, p. 236, seems to over-estimate the role of compulsion in the law.

[136] See my *Dilemma of Penal Reform*, p. 24.

[137] See Glanville Williams, *op. cit.*, § 69. The German Draft Code of 1962, § 13, tries to define the conditions required for the punishment of omissions and deals very fully with the theory of the matter, pp. 124–6. One of the difficulties is to decide whether omissions should be treated exactly like the corresponding commissions or whether they should be punished as special offences.

[138] Draft Code 1962, p. 396.

[139] Glanville Williams, *op. cit.*, §§ 56, 69.

[140] Jellinek (*op. cit.* at note 130), p. 42.

[141] Hart, *Law, Liberty and Morality*, pp. 38–43.

[142] Kenny-Turner, *op. cit.*, p. 346, and for the German law the commentary by Dreher, note Ac to § 263.

[143] *The Times*, 5.7.1955. Goodhart's view that 'English Law and the moral law are rarely in conflict' (p. 37) is perhaps slightly over-optimistic.

[144] See *Criminal Justice and Social Reconstruction*, Ch. 10, III.

[145] See, e.g., Morris Ginsberg, *Brit. J. Crim.*, Vol. 4, No. 3, Jan. 1964, pp. 284–90; Robert S. Summers, *N.Y. Univ. Law Rev.*, Vol. 38, Dec. 1963, pp. 1201–13.

[146] Norman St. John Stevas, *op. cit.*, p. 35; also in *The Times*, 24.3.1961.

[147] As our historical survey of the development of the natural law has shown, Lord Devlin is not quite correct in thinking that 'up till a century or so ago no one thought it worth distinguishing between religion and morals' (p. 12).

[148] On Durkheim see Walter A. Lunden in *Pioneers of Criminology*, Ch. 14, and briefly my *Dilemma*, pp. 213 ff.

[149] *The Listener*, 30.7.1959, p. 163.

[150] See my article in *Law and Opinion* (*op. cit.* above at note 76), p. 273.

[151] [1961] 2 A.E.R. 446; [1962] A.C. 223.

[152] *Harv. Law Rev.*, Vol. 71, pp. 618–19.

[153] Fuller, *op. cit.*, p. 661.

[154] Wolfgang Friedmann, *Legal Theory*, 4th ed., London, 1960, p. 313, is also inclined to regard the conflict between Hart and Fuller as 'perhaps more verbal than real'.

[155] Compare Radbruch's *Grundzüge der Rechtsphilosophie*, 1st ed., 1914, p. 170, and 4th ed. 1950, p. 336.

[156] This concept has now been incorporated, and thereby deprived of its former status as being *praeter legem*, in the German Draft Code of 1962; see §§ 39, 40, and pp. 158–62 and for the present German law the commentary by Dreher, note 7 to § 54. For English law see Glanville Williams, *op. cit.*, Ch. 18.

[157] See *The Acquittals at Liège*. An account of the trial and correspondence reprinted from *The Times*, London, 1962. Moreover see my *Criminal Justice and Social Reconstruction*, pp. 13–17, and now the admirable discussion by Prof. Jean Graven, 'Le Procès de l'Euthanasie', *Revue pénale Suisse*, Vol. 80, Nos. 2 et 3, 1964, pp. 121–258.

[158] See the statement of the judges of the former Supreme Court of the Reich, published in *Juristische Wochenschrift*, 1924, p. 90, and the famous comment on it by Prof. James Goldschmidt of Berlin University on pp. 245–7: *Gesetzesdämmerung?*

[159] Karlsruhe, 1957, Ch. 2, with many further references.

[160] *Die Idee der Staatsraison*, Munich–Berlin, 1924, p. 532.

[161] See Otto von Gierke, *Natural Law and the Theory of Society* (*op. cit.* above at note 81), Vol. 2, p. 337.

[162] John Locke, *Two Treatises on Government*, ed. by Morley, 1884, Book 2, Ch. 19, §§ 221–2; Bodenheimer, *Jurisprudence*, p. 144. Sir Ernest Barker, in his *Notes to Gierke*, Vol. 2, p. 349, corrects the latter and states Locke's position as follows: 'Locke is arguing that if a controversy arises between the prince and some of the people on a matter on which law is silent or doubtful, the proper umpire is the body of the people who have given him his power as a trust and can therefore decide upon his use or abuse of that power. If the prince, however, declines that way of determination "the appeal then lies nowhere but to Heaven", i.e. the case is carried in the last resort to the divine ordeal of battle in civil war.' On the whole problem of the *jus resistendi* see the German monograph by Kurt Wolzendorff, *Staatsrecht und Naturrecht in der Lehre vom Widerstandsrecht des Volkes, etc.*, Breslau, 1916.

[163] Otto von Gierke, *Johannes Althusius*, 3rd ed., Breslau, 1913, pp. 145 ff.

[164] *Ibid.*, pp. 149, fn. 80 and 308.

CHAPTER 3

[1] Ernest Greenwood, 'Social Work Research: A Decade of Reappraisal', *Soc, Serv. Rev.*, Vol. 31, No. 3, Sept. 1957, p. 312.

[2] George B. Vold, *Theoretical Criminology*, New York, 1958, Ch. 14, p. 265 Ch. 16, p. 310; Marshall B. Clinard, *Sociology of Deviant Behavior*, New York, 1957, pp. 54 ff., also refers to methodological problems. In German: Armand Mergen, *Methodik kriminalbiologischer Untersuchungen*, Stuttgart, 1953; *ibid.*, *Die Wissenschaft vom Verbrechen*, Part IV: 'Die Methoden', Hamburg, Kriminal-istik, 1961.

Leslie T. Wilkins's important new book *Social Deviance*, London, 1964, arrived too late to be fully considered. Its scope is far wider than criminology, and it 'attempts to draw together the needs of social action and the techniques of social research, and to define some of the basic problems of social policy.' He also tries to develop a general, value-free, theory of deviance and to measure the degree of the latter. Moreover, he offers some observations on the definition of science and the scientific approach; on pure and applied research, on the need for 'research into research' and on the relationship between science and ethics, and on the technique of matching.

[3] Vold, *op. cit.*, p. 274.

[4] Robert K. Merton, *Social Theory and Social Structure* (revised and enlarged ed.), Glencoe, Ill., 1957, pp. 87–8.

[5] R. B. Braithwaite, *Scientific Explanation*, Cambridge, 1955, p. 22, gives a somewhat different definition.

[6] See the excellent discussion by Gunnar Myrdal, *Value in Social Theory*, London, 1958, pp. 232 ff.

[7] Stephen Toulmin, *The Philosophy of Science*, London, 1953, pp. 80–1. The view that research can begin without a hypothesis is also expressed in Claire Selltiz, Marie Jahoda, Morton Deutsch and Stuart W. Cook, *Research Methods in Social Relations*, London, 1959, p. 35. There are excellent sections in this book on the formulation of a hypothesis and on research and theory.

[8] J. P. Martin, *Social Aspects of Prescribing*, London, 1957, p. 141, states that as the correlations he was able to calculate in order to substantiate his hypotheses were relatively low he had to adopt 'an approach rather different from the tradi-

tional scientific method of verifying specific hypotheses. It was not that we had no hypotheses nor that the correlations discovered were without significance, rather it was that individually they did not tell us very much. Our approach was to collect as much information as possible that had any conceivable relevance whatsoever. Once this was assembled it was subjected to a series of statistical analyses in an attempt to discover the nature of the influences underlying the behaviour in which we were interested. The specific hypotheses, in fact, gave way to a more generalized assumption that a consistent pattern of influences existed and underlay this behaviour. It became our prime concern to discover the nature of this pattern . . .'.

[9] Merton, op. cit., p. 12, also p. 225: 'there is two-way traffic between social theory and empirical research'; also Myrdal, op. cit., p. 233.

[10] See, e.g., Clinard, 'A Cross-cultural Replication of the relation of Urbanism to Criminal Behavior', Amer. Sociol. Rev., Vol. 25, No. 2, April 1960, pp. 253 ff.; ibid. in Burgess and Bogue, Contributions to Urban Sociology, Chicago, 1964, pp. 541–58; Robert G. Andry, Delinquency and Parental Pathology, London, 1960, pp. 17, and passim.

[11] On 'null hypothesis' see M. J. Moroney, Facts from Figures, Harmondsworth, 1951, p. 217.

[12] Aubrey Lewis, 'Between Guesswork and Certainty in Psychiatry', The Lancet, 25.1.1958 and 1.2.1958, with interesting historical material on the subject in general. Also Morris R. Cohen and Ernest Nagel, An Introduction to Logic and Scientific Method, London, 1934, p. 208, who quote De Morgan's dictum: 'Wrong hypotheses, rightly worked, have produced more useful results than unguided observation.'

[13] Loc. cit.

[14] In his valuable discussion of some of these points Gordon Trasler, The Explanation of Criminality, London, 1962, p. 15, rightly says 'hunches are not theories', but they can well become the source of a hypothesis and a theory.

[15] Terence and Pauline Morris, Pentonville, London, 1963, p. 13.

[16] On the following text see in particular Gunnar Myrdal, op. cit., esp. Ch. 5 and pp. 128 ff., and in The American Dilemma, New York–London, 1944. Arnold M. Rose, Theory and Method in the Social Sciences, Minneapolis, 1954, esp. Section 2, and Rose, 'Sociology and the Study of Values', Brit. J. Sociol., Vol. 7, No. 1, March 1956, pp. 1–17, are also indispensable contributions to these problems. See, moreover, Hermann Mannheim, Deutsche Strafrechtsreform in englischer Sicht, München, 1960, pp. 113 ff., and Brit. J. Delinq., Vol. 7, No. 2, Oct. 1956, pp. 154 ff.; and G. D. H. Cole, Brit. J. Sociol., Vol. 8, No. 2, June 1957, p. 161.

[17] Donald G. MacRae, 'Between Science and the Arts', Twentieth Century, May 1960, p. 435.

[18] The Times, 6.6.1960, in a leader on 'Research without Direction'.

[19] See also John Madge, The Tools of Social Science, London, 1953, p. 102, fn. 1.

[20] Myrdal, op. cit., p. 132. See also Rose, Theory and Method, pp. 163 ff.

[21] In so far the criticism of James Vander Zanden, Soc. Forces, Vol. 39, No. 2, Dec. 1960, pp. 192–3, is justified.

[22] Hermann Mannheim and Leslie T. Wilkins, Prediction Methods in relation to Borstal Training, H.M.S.O., London, 1955, pp. 217, 223.

[23] Rose, Theory and Method, pp. 154 ff.; also Karl R. Popper, The Poverty of Historicism, London, 1957, pp. 55 ff.

[24] See Hermann Mannheim, Group Problems in Crime and Punishment, London, 1955, pp. 273, 277.

[25] On the work of the Howard League for Penal Reform and other 'pressure groups' see A. Gordon Rose, *The Struggle for Penal Reform*, London, 1961.

[26] Myrdal, *op. cit.*, pp. 48 ff., 206 ff.

[27] No. 1: Hermann Mannheim and Leslie T. Wilkins, *Prediction Methods in relation to Borstal Training*, H.M.S.O., London, 1955; No. 2: Evelyn Gibson, *Time Spent Awaiting Trial*, H.M.S.O., London, 1960; No. 3: Leslie T. Wilkins, *Delinquent Generations*, London, 1960; No. 4: *Murder*, H.M.S.O., London, 1961; No. 5: W. H. Hammond and Edna Chayen, *Persistent Criminals*, H.M.S.O., London, 1963.

[28] London, H.M.S.O., 1959, Cmd. 645, App. B.

[29] London, H.M.S.O., Cmd. 2296, April 1964, Apps. A, B.

[30] Thorsten Sellin, *J. crim. Law Criminol.*, Vol. 35, No. 4, Nov.–Dec. 1944, p. 224.

[31] E.g. Alfred J. Kahn, *A Court for Children*, New York, 1953; Sheldon and Eleanor Glueck, *One Thousand Juvenile Delinquents*, Cambridge, Mass., 1934.

[32] John P. Martin, 'On Beginning Criminological Research', *Cambridge Opinion: Criminology*, Autumn 1960, pp. 35 ff.

[33] There is in fact a regrettable omission in the White Paper of 1964 in that the important study by T. P. and P. Morris on Pentonville is not included. Moreover, the publications in App. B. under Nos. 2, 5 and 6 are listed as 'Library of Criminology' (L.S.E.) whereas that 'Library' is in fact published under the auspices not of the London School of Economics but of the Institute for the Study and Treatment of Delinquency (I.S.T.D.).

[34] Hermann Mannheim, *Social Aspects of Crime in England between the Wars*, London, 1940, pp. 16 ff.; and on juvenile delinquency, Ch. 1 of *Young Offenders*, Cambridge, 1944.

[35] See Hermann Mannheim, *Social Aspects*, p. 20, and *Group Problems in Crime and Punishment*, pp. 235 ff. See also O. R. McGregor, *Divorce in England*, London, 1957, pp. 177–8, for some strong criticisms of the work of the Royal Commission on Divorce; A. G. Rose, *Five Hundred Borstal Boys*, Oxford, 1954, p. 173.

[36] See Hermann Mannheim in *Law and Opinion*, London, 1959, pp. 264 ff., 272–3.

[37] See the *Report on Alternatives to Short Terms of Imprisonment 1957*, on the one hand, and Robert G. Andry, *The Short-Term Prisoner*, London, 1963, with my Introduction, on the other.

[38] *Group Problems*, pp. 253–4.

[39] *Report of the Committee on the Provision for Social and Economic Research*— so-called Clapham Report, H.M.S.O., London, 1946, Cmd. 6868, and Social and Economic Research and Government Departments, Nat. Inst. of Economic and Social Research, London, 1947.

[40] The substance of the following text has been taken from Hermann Mannheim, *Deutsche Strafrechtsreform in englischer Sicht* (cited at note 16 above), pp. 115 ff.

[41] On Maconochie see John Vincent Barry, *Alexander Maconochie of Norfolk Island*, Melbourne, 1958, esp. Chs. 5, 9; also in *Pioneers in Criminology*, ed. by Hermann Mannheim, London, 1960, Ch. 4; Max Grünhut, *Penal Reform*, Oxford, 1948, pp. 78 ff.

[42] On Lombroso see Marvin E. Wolfgang, Ch. 9 in *Pioneers in Criminology*, esp. pp. 182 ff., and on Lombroso's methods of research, pp. 193 ff.

[43] Terence Morris, *The Criminal Area*, London, 1957, p. 42.

[44] See also Hermann Mannheim, *Group Problems in Crime and Punishment*, p. 72.

[45] See Mannheim and Wilkins, *op. cit.*, pp. 37–8.

[46] Wilson Gee, *Social Science Research Methods*, New York, 1950, p. 158.

[47] 'Why Delinquency? The Limits of Present Knowledge', reprinted in *Group Problems*, p. 138. For a spirited discussion of the value of criminological research from the lawyer's point of view see Norval Morris and Cynthia Turner, 'The Lawyer and Criminological Research', *Virginia Law Rev.*, Vol. 44, No. 2, 1958, pp. 163–83.

[48] See *Law and Opinion in England in the Twentieth Century*, pp. 278–9.

[49] *Ibid.*, p. 285.

[50] Gunnar Myrdal, *op. cit.*, p. 28.

CHAPTER 4

[1] For the following text see the excellent discussions in Arnold M. Rose, *op. cit.*, Ch. 14, and H. Bianchi, *Position and Subject-Matter of Criminology*, Amsterdam, 1956, pp. 8 ff.

[2] See Hermann Mannheim, *Group Problems*, Ch. 6; Barbara Wootton, *Social Science and Social Pathology*, London, 1959, Chs. 3–6, 10, 11.

[3] This is the method adopted in the Borstal Prediction Study; see Mannheim and Wilkins (*op. cit.*, Ch. 3, note 27), pp. 214 ff., 58 ff., 175, 209. There it is stressed that the prediction tables so far constructed were not suitable for immediate practical application and recommendations were made for the improvement of the methods of recording.

[4] Aubrey Lewis, *loc. cit.*, p. 18.

[5] *Group Problems*, p. 263.

[6] Allyn A. Young, quoted from Wilson Gee, *Social Science Research Methods*, New York, 1950, p. 133. On the whole problem see Morris Ginsberg, 'Social Change', *Brit. J. Sociol.*, Vol. 9, No. 3, Sept. 1958, pp. 205 ff.

[7] This definition by Major Greenwood is quoted by D. D. Reid, 'Epidemiological Methods in the Study of Mental Disorders', W.H.O., Geneva, 1960, p. 8. See also Michael Shepherd, 'The Epidemiology of Neurosis', *Int. J. soc. Psychiat.*, Vol. 5, No. 4, Spring 1960, p. 276.

[8] Thomas Würtenberger, *Die geistige Situation der deutschen Strafrechtswissenschaft*, Karlsruhe, 1957, pp. 44–5.

[9] Karl L. Popper, *The Poverty of Historicism*, pp. 130 ff., stresses the 'unity of method' in spite of all those differences, and Ginsberg, *loc. cit.*, p. 220, also acknowledges a fundamental similarity. Moreover see now Wilkins, *Social Deviance*, p. 113.

[10] Hermann Mannheim, 'Teamwork in the Administration of Criminal Justice', *Proc. Canad. Congress Correct.*, Montreal, 1957, pp. 241 ff., reprinted in the (Indian) *J. correct. Wk*, 6th issue, 1959, pp. 1 ff., is mainly concerned with teamwork in correctional practice.

[11] See John C. Spencer, *Stress and Release in an Urban Estate: A Study in Action Research*, London, 1964.

[12] Sheldon and Eleanor Glueck, *Unraveling Juvenile Delinquency*, New York, 1950, p. viii.

[13] See my Teamwork lecture (cited at note 10), p. 7.

[14] Norbert Wiener, *Cybernetics*, New York, 1948, p. 9.

[15] *Unraveling Juvenile Delinquency*, pp. 25–6. On similar dangers of bias see my lecture on Teamwork, p. 8.

[16] On this see, e.g., Wilson Gee (*op. cit.* at note 6), pp. 361 ff.

[17] Edward Glover, *The Roots of Crime*, London, 1960, Section 6, pp. 272 ff.

[18] John C. Spencer, *op. cit.*, Part 1, pp. 61 ff., Part III, pp. 288 ff.

[19] See my review of the Cambridge Study on 'Sex Offences', *Brit. J. Delinq.*, Vol. 9, No. 1, July 1959, p. 70.

[20] See especially the illuminating discussion by Arnold M. Rose, *op. cit.*, pp. 262 ff., where a list of replicated studies is given; also Marshall B. Clinard, 'Research Frontiers in Criminology', *Brit. J. Delinq.*, Vol. 7, No. 2, Oct. 1956, pp. 113 ff.; *ibid.*, 'A Cross-cultural Replication of the Relation of Urbanism to Criminal Behavior', *Amer. Sociol. Rev.*, Vol. 25, No. 2, April 1960, pp. 253 ff. The importance of the matter has also been stressed by Sheldon Glueck, 'Wanted: A Comparative Criminology', *Ventures in Criminology* (cited at Ch. 7, note 2), Ch. 19. On the difficulties of retesting a particular hypothesis see Ronald L. Akers, 'Socio-Economic Status and Delinquent Behavior: A Retest', *J. Res. Crime Delinq.*, Vol. 1, No. 1, Jan. 1964, pp. 38–46.

[21] Hermann Mannheim, *Group Problems*, p. 135; Barbara Wootton, *Social Science and Social Pathology*, London, 1959, Ch. 3, 10.

[22] Selltiz *et al.* (*op. cit.* at Ch. 3, note 7), p. 46.

[23] *Ibid.*, pp. 311 ff., and *passim*.

[24] For examples of such pilot studies see Mannheim and Wilkins, *op. cit.*, p. 53, IV, 5.

[25] Myrdal, *op. cit.*, pp. 132–3.

CHAPTER 5

[1] Thorsten Sellin and Marvin E. Wolfgang's book *The Measurement of Delinquency*, New York–London–Sydney, 1964, was published too late to be fully considered. Its main object is the construction of 'an index of delinquency that rests on juvenile offences against criminal law but is not dependent on the specific labels given by the law to such offences'. Its significance is, however, wider than the mere construction of such an index, and it has to be regarded as one of the most important modern contributions to the statistical study of crime in general. Similar considerations apply to the Swedish study by Gunnar Fredriksson, *Kriminalstatistiken och Kriminologien*, Stockholm, 1962, which will soon appear in an Eng. trans.

[2] On Quetelet see J. M. van Bemmelen, *Criminologie*, 3rd ed., Zwolle, 1952, pp. 46 ff., 226 ff.; also, 'The Constancy of Crime,' *Brit. J. Delinq.*, Vol. 2, No. 3, Jan. 1952, pp. 208–28; W. A. Bonger, *An Introduction to Criminology*, London, 1936, pp. 50–3, 121–6; E. Roesner in *Handwörterbuch der Kriminologie*, Vol. 2, Berlin–Leipzig, 1933, pp. 28–9; M. Halbwachs, *La théorie de l'homme moyen*, Paris, 1913; T. P. Morris, *The Criminal Area*, London, 1958, p. 51; Jean Pinatel, *Criminologie*, Paris, 1963, pp. 81–2. On the Gaussian Law M. J. Moroney, *Facts from Figures*, Harmondsworth, 1951, pp. 108 ff., 57.

[3] Pitirim Sorokin, *Fads and Foibles in Modern Sociology and Related Sciences*, Chicago, 1956, pp. 139 ff.

[4] Perhaps the best international survey of the contents of official criminal statistics is given by Ernst Roesner in *Handwörterbuch der Kriminologie* (cited at note 2), Vol. 2, pp. 48–9, but some details have changed in the meantime.

[5] A detailed critical analysis of the structure, interpretation and contents of English criminal statistics has been given in the present writer's *Social Aspects of Crime in England between the Wars*, London, 1940, Part 1. In the following text the most important changes are mentioned which have occurred since that book was published.

[6] M. Grünhut, 'Statistics in Criminology', *J. roy. statist. Soc.*, Series A (general), Vol. 114, Part 2, 1951, pp. 139 ff.

[7] Some material of this kind may be found in Hans von Hentig, 'Kriminalstatistische Daten aus früheren Jahrhunderten', *Schweiz. Z. Strafrecht*, Vol. 72, No. 3, 1957, pp. 276 ff. See also Gustav Radbruch and Heinrich Gwinner,

Geschichte des Verbrechens, Stuttgart, 1951, p. 7, who stress that in the absence of reliable statistical data the history of crime has to be written with the assistance of other contemporary sources. Thorsten Sellin, 'Two Myths in the History of Capital Punishment', *J. crim. Law Criminol. Police Sci.*, Vol. 50, No. 2, July–August 1959, pp. 114 ff., shows how these two myths, one of them the widespread belief that there were 72,000 hangings in England during the reign of Henry VIII, had originated and quotes, among other critical voices, James Fitzjames Stephens' statement that it was difficult to discover how Tudor justice worked in practice as 'no statistics as to either convictions or executions were kept then, or till long afterwards' and all that was available were 'a few vague generalities, with here and there a piece of positive evidence'.

[7a] *Accounts and Papers*, Session 23.1—21.6.1810, Vol. 14, pp. 549 ff.

[8] *Accounts and Papers*, 1826–7, Vol. 19, pp. 183 ff.: 'Committals. Summary Statements of the Number of Persons charged with Criminal Offences who were Committed to the Different Gaols in England and Wales, 28.3.1827.'

[9] *Judicial Statistics—England and Wales*, 1893, Part I, 'Criminal Statistics'; 'Statistics relating to Criminal Proceedings, Police, Coroners, Prisons, Reformatory and Industrial Schools, and Criminal Lunatics for the year 1893', *Accounts and Papers*, 1895, Vol. 108, pp. 1 ff.

[10] Similar recommendations were made in the excellent Memorandum by Sir John Macdonell which was appended to the report.

[11] For the following see *Social Aspects of Crime*, pp. 90 ff.

[12] See, e.g., *Introduction to Criminal Statistics*, 1959, paras. 7, 15–18. On the system used up to 1938 see *Social Aspects of Crime*, pp. 32–3.

[13] *Introduction*, paras. 7, 48.

[14] The resulting gaps are discussed in *Social Aspects of Crime*, pp. 94 ff.

[15] The *Supplementary Statistics* go a long way, therefore, towards fulfilling the requirements postulated by the present writer in *Social Aspects of Crime*, pp. 30, 33, 44–5, 74 ff.

[16] Rupert Cross and P. Asterley Jones, *An Introduction to Criminal Law*, London, 1948, art. 10.

[17] *Criminal Statistics—England and Wales*, 1959, p. viii.

[18] See also Lord Pakenham, *Causes of Crime*, London, 1958, p. 25.

[19] Comparisons between English and Scottish crime figures may be found in T. S. Lodge, *Brit. J. Delinq.*, Vol. 7, 1956, pp. 50 ff.; A. M. Struthers, *Measuring Bad Behaviour*, N.C.S.S., London, 1950.

[20] By permission of the Comptroller of H.M.S.O.

[21] On developments before 1938 see the detailed discussion *Social Aspects of Crime*, pp. 40–6.

[22] See T. S. Lodge, *J. roy. statist. Soc.*, Series A (General), Vol. 116, Part 3, 1953, p. 287.

[23] See the details in *Social Aspects of Crime*, Ch. 3.

[24] See in particular on cases of homicide J. D. J. Havard, *The Detection of Secret Homicide*, London. 1960, and on the general problem Bernd Wehner, 'Die Latenz der Straftaten (Die nicht entdeckte Kriminalität)', *Schriftenreihe des Bundeskriminalamtes*, Wiesbaden, 1957, with literature and case material. Also Hans von Hentig, *Crime: Causes and Conditions*, New York, 1947, pp. 58 ff., and in particular Hentig, *Der Mord*, Tübingen, 1956, pp. 19 ff., and *Diebstahl, Einbruch, Raub*, Tübingen, 1956, pp. 18 ff.

[25] H. Silcock, *The Increase in Crimes of Theft 1938–1947*, Liverpool, 1949, p. 27.

[26] *Social Aspects of Crime*, p. 8.

[27] Austin L. Porterfield, *Youth in Trouble*, Fort Worth, 1946, pp. 32–5. Other

American investigations are reported in Marshall B. Clinard, *Sociology of Deviant Behavior*, New York, 1957, p. 165.

[28] See Ola Nyquist, *Juvenile Justice*, London, 1960, pp. 107–8, who also draws attention to a similar Norwegian study.

[29] John B. Mays, *Growing up in the City*, Liverpool, 1954, pp. 76 ff., 32.

[30] James S. Wallerstein and Clement J. Wyle, 'Our Law-abiding Law-breakers', *Probation*, March–April, 1947. pp. 102 ff., quoted from Clinard, *op. cit.*, p. 165.

[31] *Social Aspects of Crime*, pp. 82 ff.

[32] Thorsten Sellin, *Crime in the Depression*, Soc. Sci. Res. Counc. Bull. 27, 1937, p. 69. See also T. C. N. Gibbens, *Thefts from Department Stores*, General Report for the Fourth International Criminological Congress, The Hague, 1960, and C. N. Peijster, *Preparatory Paper for the Congress*.

[33] H.M.S.O., 1939, Ch. 2.

[34] Wehner (*op. cit.* at note 24), p. 37.

[35] Edward Glover, *The Roots of Crime*, London, 1960, p. 204 fn.

[36] Hentig, *Der Mord*, p. 19.

[37] See also T. S. Lodge (*op. cit.* at note 22), p. 491; Thorsten Sellin, *J. crim. Law Criminol.*, Vol. 22, 1931, pp. 335 ff., and *Law Quart. Rev.*, Vol. 67, 1951, p. 489; Georg von Mayr, *Statistik und Cesellschaftslehre*, Vol. 3, 1917, Tübingen, pp. 414 ff. The most recent discussions of the representative character of the 'dark figure' are to be found in Sellin and Wolfgang (*op. cit.* above, note 1), Ch. 8, and more briefly in Wilkins, *Social Deviance*, pp. 140 ff.

[38] *Social Aspects of Crime*, p. 80.

[39] See the discussion in *Social Aspects of Crime*, pp. 35 ff. with bibliog.

[40] See Lodge, *loc. cit.*, p. 288.

[41] *Social Aspects of Crime*, p. 72.

[42] W. Lloyd Warner and Paul S. Lunt, quoted from Barnes and Teeters, *New Horizons in Criminology*, 1st ed., New York, 1943, p. 86. See also Walter C. Reckless, *The Crime Problem*, 2nd ed., New York, 1955, pp. 28 ff.

[43] Marshall B. Clinard, *Deviant Social Behavior*, pp. 23–4; William M. Kephart, 'Negro Visibility', *Amer. Sociol. Rev.*, Vol. 19, No. 4, Aug. 1954, pp. 462 ff. For Liverpool see John B. Mays, *Growing up in the City*, App. B: A Study of a Police Division.

[44] Reprinted in *Group Problems in Crime and Punishment*, p. 102.

[45] *Social Aspects of Crime*, p. 32.

[46] The following text follows closely the more detailed discussion in *Social Aspects of Crime*, p. 48 ff.

[47] According to *Criminal Statistics 1959*, Table 16, the total of prosecutions undertaken by his office in that year was 1,698.

[48] *Social Aspects of Crime*, pp. 63 ff., where the effect of other procedural changes on the figures in criminal statistics is also discussed.

[49] See H. Silcock (*op. cit.* at note 25).

[50] *Ibid.*, p. 21.

[51] On public opinion in general see the references in *Law and Opinion*, pp. 264 ff.

[52] *Social Aspects of Crime*, p. 79.

[53] Thorsten Sellin, *J. crim. Law Criminol.*, Vol. 22, 1931, pp. 335 ff.

[54] *Handwörterbuch der Kriminologie*, Vol. 2, pp. 50 ff.

[55] See Negley Teeters, *Deliberations of the International Penal and Penitentiary Congresses*, Philadelphia (no date).

[56] *Social Aspects of Crime*, p. 48.

[57] 'Directives pour l'élaboration des statistiques criminelles dans les divers pays', *Bulletin de l'Institut International de Statistique*, Vol. 29, No. 3 (Session d'Athènes 1936), The Hague, 1937. See also 'United Nations Survey of Social

Statistics', *Statistical Papers*, Series K, No. 1, Dec. 1954, Ch. 17, and *Transactions of the Third International Congress of Criminology*, London, 1955, published 1957, Conclusions of s. 1, p. 218 (the committee which was recommended in the Resolution has not been formed). An international group of experts, convened by United Nations in 1950, requested the Secretary General to prepare a manual which would establish minimum standards for national criminal statistics and determine the ultimate practicability of international statistics on homicide, aggravated assault, robbery and burglary.

[58] See my article on 'Sentencing' in *Law and Contemporary Problems*, *Symposium on Sentencing*, Summer 1958, pp. 557 ff.

[59] See the table in Ernst Roesner, *Handwörterbuch der Kriminologie*, Vol. 2, pp. 48–9.

[60] See the detailed account by Hans Bartz in *Mschr. Kriminol. Strafrechtsreform*, Vol. 40, Nos. 1–2, Feb. 1957, pp. 22 ff., on which the following text is largely based.

[61] Principal literature on American Criminal Statistics: Thorsten Sellin, 'The Uniform Criminal Statistics Act', *J. crim. Law Criminol.*, Vol. 40, No. 6, March–April 1950, pp. 679 ff.; also, *Status and Prospects of Criminal Statistics in the United States*, Stockholm, 1949, pp. 290 ff.; Ronald H. Beattie, 'The Sources of Criminal Statistics', *Ann. Amer. Acad. Polit. Soc. Sci.*, Vol. 217, Sept. 1941, pp. 19 ff.; Emil Frankel, *Encyclopedia of Criminology*, ed. by Vernon C. Branham and Samuel B. Kutash, New York, 1949, pp. 478 ff.; National Commission on Law Observance and Enforcement (so-called Wickersham Commission), *Report on Criminal Statistics*, Washington, D.C., 1931; Mabel A. Elliott, *Crime in Modern Society*, 1952, pp. 49 ff.

[62] On a smaller scale, similar problems exist in other Federal States, e.g. in Switzerland.

[63] See, e.g., the draft published by Sellin in the article quoted in note 61 and John G. Yeager, 'Criminal and Correctional Statistics in Pennsylvania', *Prison J.*, Vol. 40, No. 2., pp. 63 ff.

CHAPTER 6

[1] See Ch. 3, note 27.

[2] This was done in *Social Aspects of Crime*, Ch. 5. See also M. Grünhut, *Juvenile Offenders before the Courts*, Oxford, 1956, p. 47, and the material quoted in Thorsten Sellin, *Crime in the Depression*, Ch. 3.

[3] E. C. Rhodes, *J. roy. statist. Soc.*, Vol. 52, Part 3, 1939, pp. 384 ff.; briefly also A. M. Carr-Saunders, Hermann Mannheim, and E. C. Rhodes, *Young Offenders*, Cambridge, 1944, pp. 48 ff.

[4] See the references in *Group Problems in Crime and Punishment*, pp. 118, 134; also Mannheim and Wilkins, *Prediction Methods in relation to Borstal Training*, pp. 59, 79 and *passim*.

[5] On the subject of sampling see the textbooks on statistics. In addition reference may be made to John Madge, *op. cit.*, pp. 205 ff., Selltiz *et al.*, *op. cit.*, App. B; M. J. Moroney, *Facts from Figures*, Harmondsworth, 1951, pp. 120, 173 ff.; C. A. Moser, *Survey Methods in Social Investigation*, London, 1959; Yon Poh Seng, 'Historical Survey of the Development of Sampling Theories and Practice', *J. roy statist. Soc.*, Series A, Vol. 110, No. 4, Part 2, 1951, pp. 214 ff.

[6] See Madge, *op. cit.*, p. 207 fn.; Selltiz, *op. cit.*, p. 514, and now also Wilkins, *Social Deviance*, p. 155.

[7] Selltiz, *op. cit.*, p. 422, fn. 18; Madge, *op. cit.*, p. 213; A. G. Rose, *Five Hundred Borstal Boys*, Oxford, 1954, p. 170.

[8] Mannheim and Wilkins, *op. cit.*, p. 52.

[9] Arnold M. Rose, *op. cit.*, p. 258.

[10] Cyril Burt, *The Young Delinquent*, 4th ed., London, 1944, p. 12.

[11] Maud A. Merrill, *Problems of Child Delinquency*, London, 1947, p. 15.

[12] A. M. Carr-Saunders, Hermann Mannheim, E. C. Rhodes, *Young Offenders*, p. 55.

[13] John Lewis Gillin, *The Wisconsin Prisoner*, Madison, 1947, pp. 4–5.

[14] R. G. Andry, *The Short-term Prisoner*, London, 1961.

[15] See. e.g., Andry, *Delinquency and Parental Pathology*, London, 1960, p. 10. D. H. Stott, *Delinquency and Human Nature*, Dunfermline, 1950, was able to visit the parents of his group of Approved School Boys.

[16] E.g. Andry, *Delinquency and Parental Pathology*, p. 129. On Pilot studies in general see Russell L. Ackoff, *The Design of Social Research*, Chicago, 1953, pp. 336 ff.

[17] Daniel Glaser, *Prison J.*, Vol. 40, No. 2, Autumn 1960, p. 61.

[18] See *Prediction Methods in relation to Borstal Training*, pp. 54–62, 214–16. Also John Madge, *op. cit.*, p. 101. On the use of existing records see also Selltiz *et al.*, *op. cit.*, pp. 316 ff.

[19] The need for continuous discussions between academic researchers and the leading correctional officials on research plans, policies and progress is also stressed by Glaser, *op. cit.*, p. 52.

[20] *Prediction Methods in relation to Borstal Training*, p. 56.

[21] Edwin Powers and Helen Witmer, *An Experiment in the Prevention of Delinquency. The Cambridge-Somerville Youth Study*, New York, 1951, Ch. 4.

[22] Examples are the Cambridge-Somerville Study and its follow-up by the McCords. See William and Joan McCord with Irving Kenneth Zola, *Origins of Crime*, New York, 1959, pp. vii, 17, 62, 167. According to these writers, the basic information for their work was collected before the onset of criminality.

[23] Robert K. Merton, *Social Theory and Social Structure*, 2nd ed., pp. 93–5, 99.

[24] Walter C. Reckless, *The Etiology of Delinquent and Criminal Behavior*, Soc. Sci. Res. Counc. Bull. 50, 1943, pp. 81–2.

[25] Albert K. Cohen, *Delinquent Boys*, Glencoe, Ill., 1955, p. 170.

[26] For the following text see *Group Problems in Crime and Punishment*, pp. 120 ff., 147 ff., and for more general discussions of the problems involved Ernest Greenwood, *Experimental Sociology*, 5th imp., New York, 1949, esp. p. 23 and Ch. 6: *The Technique of Control in Experimental Sociology*, and Selltiz *et al.*, *op. cit.*, pp. 98 ff.

[27] Report 1893, p. 42.

[28] Marvin E. Wolfgang, chapter on Lombroso in Hermann Mannheim (ed.), *Pioneers in Criminology*, London, 1960, p. 200.

[29] For a brief international account see the UNO Survey of Social Statistics (cited above at Ch. 5, note 57).

[30] See *Prediction Methods in relation to Borstal Training*, pp. 84 ff.

[31] For an example of this see Christian Debuyst, *Criminels et valeurs vécues*, Louvain-Paris, 1960.

[32] The details of this process are described in *Unraveling Juvenile Delinquency* (cited above at Ch. 4, note 12), pp. 33–9.

[33] Selltiz, *op. cit.*, p. 105.

[34] From my 'Critical Notice', *Brit. J. Delinq.*, Vol. 2, No. 3, Jan. 1952, p. 260. On the difficulties of matching now also Wilkins, *Social Deviance*, App. II.

[35] See also Greenwood, *op. cit.*, p. 24.

[36] This is true in spite of what has been said earlier on the place of causal research in criminology.

[37] *Experimental Sociology*, pp. 73 ff.

[38] Sol Rubin, *Crime and Juvenile Delinquency*, New York, 1958, 2nd ed., 1961, p. 23 ff.

[39] J. L. Gillin (*op. cit.* at note 13), pp. 19 ff.

[40] William Healy and Augusta Bronner, *New Light on Delinquency*, New Haven, 1936. Siri Naess, 'Mother–Child Separation and Delinquency', *Brit. J. Delinq.*, Vol. 10, No. 1, July 1959, p. 32, excludes boys who had no brothers born between 1939 and 1947.

[41] Sybil Clement Brown in a review of Healy-Bronner in the *Howard J.*, 1937, p. 392.

[42] On this see esp. the well-known Nottingham University Study 'The Social Background of Delinquency', ed. by W. J. H. Sprott (1954, not published).

[43] Among others, see H. C. Brearley, *Homicide in the United States*, Chapel Hill, 1932, p. 41; Donald R. Taft, *Criminology*, 3rd ed., New York, 1956, pp. 154 ff.; Mabel A. Elliott, *Crime in Modern Society*, New York, 1952, pp. 289 ff.

[44] D. D. Reid, *Epidemiological Methods in the Study of Mental Disorder*, WHO, Geneva, 1960, p. 50, with further illustrations. The history of cancer research is also relevant.

[45] Donald R. Cressey, *Other People's Money*, Glencoe, Ill., 1953, p. 70.

[46] Emile Durkheim, *Les Règles de la Méthode sociologique*, 11th ed., p. 129.

[47] D. H. Stott, *op. cit.*, p. 416.

[48] This is the essence of some of the criticisms of modern criminology by G. Th. Kempe, *Vers une criminologie mieux fondée* in *Une nouvelle Ecole de Science criminelle—l'Ecole d'Utrecht*, presentée par Jacques Léauté, Paris, 1959, esp. pp. 83 ff. See also my *Group Problems*, p. 122, and my review of Kempe, *Brit. J. Crim.*, Vol. 1, No. 3, Jan. 1961, pp. 281 ff.

[49] On the subject see the following literature: Sheldon and Eleanor Glueck, *After-Conduct of Discharged Offenders*, London, 1945; the same, *Five Hundred Criminal Careers*, New York, 1930; the same, *Later Criminal Careers*, New York, 1937; the same, *Criminal Careers in Retrospect*, New York, 1943; the same, *Five Hundred Delinquent Women*, New York, 1934; the same, *One Thousand Juvenile Delinquents*, Cambridge, Mass., 1934; the same, *Juvenile Delinquents Grown Up*, New York, 1940; the same, 'Follow-up Studies', in *Encyclopedia of Criminology*, pp. 167 ff.; the same, *Unraveling Juvenile Delinquency*, New York, 1950, Ch. 20; the same, *Predicting Delinquency and Crime*, Cambridge, Mass., 1959 (with Supplementary Bibliography, 1955–58); Mannheim and Wilkins, *Prediction Methods in relation to Borstal Training*, H.M.S.O., 1955 (with Bibliography up to 1955); A. G. Rose, *Five Hundred Borstal Boys*, Oxford, 1954; the same, 'Follow-up and/or Prediction?' *Brit. J. Delinq.*, Vol. 7, No. 3, April 1957, pp. 309 ff.; Erwin Frey, *Der Frühkriminelle Rückfallsverbrecher*, Basel, 1951, and my review of it reproduced in *Group Problems*, pp. 139 ff.; Edwin Powers and Helen Witmer, *An Experiment in the Prevention of Delinquency. The Cambridge-Somerville Youth Study*; T. C. N. Gibbens, D. A. Pond, and D. Stafford-Clark, 'Follow-up Study of Criminal Psychopaths', *Brit. J. Delinq.*, Vol. 6, No. 2, Sept. 1955, pp. 126 ff.; William and Joan McCord, *The Origins of Crime*, New York, 1959; Jay Rumney and Joseph P. Murphy, *Probation and Social Adjustment*, New Brunswick, 1952; Walter Piecha, *Die Lebensbewährung der als 'unerziehbar' entlassenen Fürsorgezöglinge*, Göttingen, 1959.

[50] See the General Reports by Walter C. Reckless and C. H. Andersen in the *Summary of Proceedings of the Congress*, London, 1957, pp. 88 ff., 100 ff.

[51] Sheldon and Eleanor Glueck, *After-Conduct of Discharged Prisoners*, p. 22.

[52] Rumney and Murphy, *op. cit.*, pp. 12, 84 ff.

[53] Sheldon and Eleanor Glueck, *op. cit.*, pp. 2–3. See also Ch. 3 under III above.

[54] *Five Hundred Criminal Careers*, pp. 7–8, 89 ff.

[55] Sheldon and Eleanor Glueck, *op. cit.*, pp. 101 ff.

[56] For other findings reference may be made to the summary in *Five Hundred Criminal Careers*, pp. 306 ff., and to *After-Conduct of Discharged Prisoners*, pp. 23 ff.

[57] *After-Conduct*, p. 21.

[58] For the detailed findings reference is made to these two books and the summary in *After-Conduct*, pp. 31 ff.

[59] On maturation see, e.g., *Later Criminal Careers*, pp. 105 ff.; *After-Conduct*, pp. 80 ff.; *Juvenile Delinquents Grown Up*, pp. 90 ff., 267 ff.

[60] See *One Thousand Juvenile Delinquents* and *Juvenile Delinquents Grown Up*.

[61] Walter C. Reckless, *Summary of Proceedings*, Third International Congress of Criminology, 1955, London, 1957, p. 94.

[62] *The Crime Problem*, 2nd ed., 1955, Ch. 3.

[63] Thomas C. McCormick and Roy G. Francis, *Methods of Research in the Behavioral Sciences*, New York, 1958, pp. 24 ff.

CHAPTER 7

[1] See the literature to Ch. 6, note 49, and in addition: Paul Horst, Paul Wallin, Louis Guttmann *et al.*, *The Prediction of Personal Adjustment*, Soc. Sci. Res. Counc. Bull. 48, New York, 1941; Sibylle Escalona and Grace Moore Heider, *Prediction and Outcome. A Study in Child Development*, London, 1959; Lloyd E. Ohlin, *Selection for Parole: A Manual of Parole Prediction*, New York, 1951; Walter F. Dearborn and John W. M. Rothney, *Predicting the Child's Development*, Cambridge, Mass., 1941; Samuel A. Stouffer *et al.*, *Measurement and Prediction*, Princeton, 1950; *Brit. J. Delinq.*, Vol. 6, No. 2, Sept. 1955: Special Number on Prediction and Recidivism. From it: D. R. L. Morrison, 'Prediction Research'; Edward Glover, 'Prognosis or Prediction'. Also A. Walters, 'A Note on Statistical Methods of Predicting Delinquency', *Brit. J. Delinq.*, Vol. 6, No. 4, April 1956, pp. 297 ff.; George Benson, 'Prediction Methods and Young Prisoners', *Brit. J. Delinq.*, Vol. 9, No. 3, Jan. 1959, pp. 192 ff.; D. H. Stott, 'The Prediction of Delinquency from Non-delinquent Behaviour', *Brit. J. Delinq.*, Vol. 10, No. 3, Jan. 1960, pp. 195 ff.; Bernard C. Kirby, 'Parole Prediction Using Multiple Correlation', *Amer. J. Sociol.*, Vol. 49, May 1954, pp. 539 ff.; Hermann Mannheim, *Deutsche Strafrechtsreform in englischer Sicht*, München–Berlin, 1960, pp. 33 ff., 123–7; Wolf Middendorff, 'Die Prognose im Strafrecht und in der Kriminologie', *Z. ges. Strafrechtswiss.*, Vol. 72, Nos. 1–2, pp. 108 ff.; Friedrich Geerds, 'Zur kriminellen Prognose', *Mschr. Kriminol. Strafrechtsreform*, Vol. 43, Nos. 3–4, Oct. 1960, pp. 92 ff.; Fritz Meyer, *Der kriminologische Wert von Prognosetafeln*, *ibid.*, 1959, pp. 214 ff.; Helga Daniela Spieler, *Die vorbeugende Verwahrung*, Bonn, 1960.

[2] For the following text see in particular Mannheim and Wilkins, *op. cit.*, pp. 41 ff.; S. and E. Glueck, *Predicting Delinquency and Crime*, pp. 144 ff.; *Summ. Proc. Third Int. Congress Criminol.*, London, 1955, published 1957, pp. 18, 155 ff. Manuel Lopez-Rey in *Essays in Criminal Science*, ed. by Gerhard O. W. Mueller, London, 1959, pp. 16 ff., repeats most of the usual misconceptions. On this see Mannheim, *Brit. J. Crim.*, Vol. 3, No. 1, July 1962, pp. 94–5, and Wilkins, *ibid.*, Vol. 4, No. 1, July 1963, pp. 74–6. Most of the scattered recent papers by the Gluecks on prediction and other subjects have now been republished with a complete bibliog. of their writings as *Ventures in Criminology*, London, 1964.

[3] See Theodore R. Sarbin in Arthur H. Brayfield (ed.), *Readings in Modern Methods of Counselling*, New York, 1950, pp. 83 ff.; Mannheim and Wilkins, *op. cit.*, pp. 57, 248 ff.

[4] *Unraveling Juvenile Delinquency*, p. 269.

[5] Mannheim and Wilkins, *op. cit.*, p. 174.

[6] See Wilkins, *Brit. J. Delinq.*, Vol. 6, No. 2, p. 83; against him see the other contributions to the Symposium.

[7] See the various writings of the Gluecks and Mannheim-Wilkins, Chs. 4-6 and the historical sketch in Ch. 1.

[8] For the Borstal Prediction Study see the list of factors in App. 1.

[9] See also Ohlin, *op. cit.*, p. 48.

[10] Bruce, Burgess and Harno, *The Working of the Indeterminate Sentence Law and the Parole System in Illinois*, 1928.

[11] Ohlin, *op. cit.*, pp. 51 ff.

[12] See, e.g., *Predicting Delinquency and Crime*, p. 25.

[13] Taken from *After-Conduct of Discharged Offenders*, p. 67.

[14] *Unraveling Juvenile Delinquency*, Ch. 20.

[15] *Ibid.*, Ch. 10, and *J. crim. Law Criminol. Police Sci.*, Vol. 51, No. 3, Sept.-Oct. 1960, pp. 303 ff., and now the Gluecks in *Brit. J. Crim.* Vol. 4, No. 3, Jan. 1964.

[16] Rubin, *Crime and Delinquency*, pp. 225 ff.

[17] A. Walters, *Brit. J. Delinq.*, Vol. 6, No. 4, April 1956, pp. 297 ff.; D. H. Stott, *The Prediction of Delinquency from Non-Delinquent Behaviour*, Vol. 10, No. 3, Jan. 1960, pp. 195 ff.

[18] *Prediction Methods in relation to Borstal Training*, pp. 143 ff.

[19] *Ibid.*, pp. 153 ff. (the reference under VI. 62 should be to Table 81, not 86).

[20] *Ibid.*, pp. 39, 56 ff.

[21] *Ibid.*, pp. 137 ff.

[22] *Ibid.*, pp. 219 ff.

[23] *Ibid.*, Ch. 7; S. and E. Glueck, *Predicting Delinquency and Crime*, pp. 47-60, 126-36.

[24] See, in particular, Horst *et al.*, *op. cit.*, pp. 26 ff., 99, 117, 181-249; Mannheim and Wilkins, *op. cit.*, Ch. 8; Stouffer *et al.*, *op. cit.*, pp. 573 ff.; Escalona and Heider, *op. cit.*; Gordon W. Allport, *The Use of Personal Documents in Psychological Science*, Soc. Sci. Res. Counc. Bull. 49, 1942, pp. 148, 154 ff.; Paul E. Meehl, *Clinical versus Statistical Prediction*, Minneapolis, 1954; John D. Benjamin in *Dynamic Psychopathology in Childhood*, by Lucie Jessner and Eleanor Pavenstedt, New York-London, 1959, Ch. 2; T. R. Sarbin, 'A Contribution to the Study of Actuarial and Individual Methods of Prediction', *Amer. J. Sociol.*, Vol. 48, 1942-3, pp. 593 ff.

[25] For the following text see Horst *et al.*, *op. cit.*, pp. 209 ff., 240 ff.; Allport, *op. cit.*, pp. 154 ff.

[26] Meehl, *op. cit.*, p. 137.

[27] This is also admitted by Allport, *op. cit.*, p. 149.

[28] Note 1 above.

[29] Escalona and Heider, *op. cit.*, pp. 107 ff.

[30] *Op. cit.*, Ch. 8, esp. pp. 173 ff.

[31] See *Group Problems in Crime and Punishment*, p. 79.

CHAPTER 8

[1] On the general principles of individual case studies in criminology see, e.g., Walter C. Reckless, *Criminal Behavior*, London, 1940, pp. 173 ff.; Sheldon Glueck, *The Problem of Delinquency*, Boston, 1959, pp. 237 ff.; Howard Jones, *Crime and the Penal System*, London, 1956, pp. 18 ff.; Arthur Evans Wood, 'Difficulties of Statistical Interpretation of Case Records of Delinquency', *Amer.*

J. Sociol., Vol. 39, 1933–4, pp. 204 ff. On life histories in social science John Madge, *The Tools of Social Science*, London, 1953, pp. 81 ff.; Cavan, Hauser and Stouffer, 'Note on the Statistical Treatment of Life-History Material', *Soc. Forces*, Vol. 9, 1930, pp. 200 ff.

[2] Earnest Albert Hooton, *The American Criminal*, Cambridge, Mass., 1939, 16.

[3] Edward Glover, *The Roots of Crime*, London, 1960, p. 390.

[4] William H. Sheldon, *Varieties of Delinquent Youth*, New York, 1949.

[5] So rightly Thomas C. McCormick and Roy G. Francis, *Methods of Research in the Behavioral Sciences*, New York, 1958, p. 28.

[6] As examples of this technique the following may be quoted out of many: Cyril Burt, *The Young Delinquent*, 4th ed., London, 1944; S. and E. Glueck, *Five Hundred Criminal Careers*, New York, 1930; D. J. West, *Homosexuality*, London, 1955; Howard Jones, *Reluctant Rebels*, London, 1960; Kate Friedlander, *The Psycho-analytical Approach to Juvenile Delinquency*, 1st ed., London, 1947; Norval Morris, *The Habitual Criminal*, London, 1951.

[7] Donald R. Cressey, *Other People's Money*, Glencoe, Ill., 1953.

[8] For a few details see the Borstal Prediction Study, pp. 173–4.

[9] *One Thousand Juvenile Delinquents*, p. 191.

[10] See the titles quoted in my review, *Brit. J. Delinq.*, Vol. 10, No. 2, Oct. 1959, p. 154.

[11] Frederic Wertham, *Dark Legend: A Study in Murder*, London, 1947; Bruno Bettelheim, *Truants from Life*, Glencoe, Ill., 1955; Helen Parkhurst, *Undertow*, New York, 1959, Eng. ed., London, 1964; Tony Parker and Robert Allerton, *The Courage of his Convictions*, London, 1962; Tony Parker, *The Unknown Citizen*, 1963, and on the latter my Critical Notice *Brit. J. Crim.*, Vol. 4, No. 4, April 1964, pp. 395–9; Ben Karpman, *Case Studies in the Psychopathology of Crime*, Vol. 2, Washington, 1944. For psycho-analytical, non-criminal, case studies see Freud's *Collected Papers*, Vol. 3, London, 1925.

[12] For the description of one case of matricide and patricide see Kenneth H. Raizen, *Brit. J. Delinq.*, Vol. 10, No. 4, April 1960. See also Freud's famous essay 'Dostoevsky and Parricide', in his *Collected Papers*, Vol. 5, London, 1950, pp. 222 ff.

[13] Wertham, *op. cit.*, pp. 15, 95 ff.

[14] Bettelheim, *op. cit.*, pp. 4 ff., 473 ff. ('On writing case histories').

[15] Sheldon (*op. cit.* at note 4 above), p. 752, thinks that no amount of measurement and description can be a substitute for photographs.

[16] Horst *et al.* (*op. cit.* above at note 1, Ch. 7), pp. 187 ff.; John Madge, *The Tools of Social Science*, pp. 81 ff., Ch. 4; Selltiz *et al.* (*op. cit.* above at note 7, Ch. 3), esp. Chs. 6–9; Gordon W. Allport (*op. cit.* above at note 24, Ch. 7), Part 2; 'Social Behavior and Personality': Contributions of W. I. Thomas to *Theory and Social Research*, ed. by Edmund H. Volkart, New York, Soc. Sci. Res Counc., 1951, pp. 297 ff., 145 ff.; W. I. Thomas and F. Znaniecki, *The Polish Peasant in Europe and America*, Boston, 1918–20; Gardner Murphy, L. B. Murphy and Theodore M. Newcomb, *Experimental Social Psychology*, New York–London, 1937, pp. 838 ff.; A. Vexliard, *Le Clochard*, Bruges, 1957; Christian Debuyst, *Criminels et valeurs vécues*, Louvain–Paris, 1960.

[17] William Healy, *The Individual Delinquent*, Boston, 1916; William Healy and Augusta F. Bronner, *Delinquents and Criminals. Their Making and Unmaking*, New York, 1926; the same, *New Light on Delinquency*, New Haven, 1936; Franz Alexander and William Healy, *The Roots of Crime*, New York, 1935 (psycho-analytical).

[18] Clifford R. Shaw, *The Jack-Roller*, Chicago, 1930; *The Natural History of a*

Delinquent Career, Chicago, 1931; Shaw *et al.*, *Brothers in Crime*, Chicago, 1938.

[19] *The Professional Thief, by a Professional Thief.* Annotated and interpreted by E. H. Sutherland, Chicago, 1937.

[20] Donald Clemmer, *The Prison Community*, Boston, 1940.

[21] On Thomas and Znaniecki see Herbert Blumer, *Critiques of Research in the Social Sciences*, Vol. 1, Soc. Sci. Res. Counc. Bull. 44, 1939; on Shaw's *Jack-Roller* see John Dollard, *Criteria for the Life History*, New Haven, 1935.

[22] Sir Leo Page, *The Young Lag*, London, 1950.

[23] The German original *Zur Psychologie des Mordes* was published in Heidelberg, 1925, the Eng. trans. *The Psychology of Murder*, London, 1927.

[24] *Studies in the Psychology of Delinquency*, H.M.S.O., London, 1932 (reprinted 1934). It is strange that Barbara Wootton who complains so strongly about the neglect of the female delinquent in criminological literature (see Ch. 26 below) does not even mention Dr. Pailthorpe's work.

[25] Cavan, Hauser and Stouffer, *Soc. Forces*, Vol. 9, 1930, pp. 200 ff.

[26] Hans von Hentig, *Crime: Causes and Conditions*, New York–London, 1947, pp. 82 ff.

[27] This does not imply that the crime of blackmail itself is of no interest. v. Hentig has in fact written a fascinating book on it: *Die Erpressung*, Tübingen, 1959.

[28] David Lamson, *We Who Are about to Die*, New York, 1935; Nathan Leopold, *Life plus Ninety-nine Years*, London, 1958; Caryl Chessman, *Cell 2455 Death Row*, London, 1956. On the Chessman case see T. A. Joyce, *The Right to Life*, London, 1962, Ch. 1.

[29] First published London, 1935; Harmondsworth, 1957.

[30] D. J. West, *Homosexuality*, London, 1955, pp. 136–7. On Genet see John Croft, *Brit. J. Delinq.*, Vol. 6, No. 3, Jan. 1956, pp. 236 ff.

[31] The volumes of the *Howard Journal* contain informative reviews of most of these books, and some of the more recent ones are listed in D. L. Howard, *The English Prison*, London, 1960, pp. 164–5, to which may be added Mark Benney's *Low Company*, London, 1936, and Brendan Behan's *Borstal Boy*, London, 1958.

[32] W. Clifford, *Profiles in Crime*, Soc. Wel. Res. Mono. No. 3, published by the Ministry of Housing and Social Development, Northern Rhodesia, 1964.

[33] André Gide, *Dostoevsky*, 2nd ed., London, pp. 107, 119.

[34] Edwin Muir in *The Observer* of 13.5.1951.

[35] C. G. Jung, *Psychological Types*, Eng. trans., London, 1923, Ch. 5. Jung defines a type rather narrowly as 'a characteristic model of a general attitude occurring in many individual forms', adding 'in so far as such an attitude is habitual . . . I speak of a psychological type' (p. 612).

[36] On this see in particular Johannes Hirschmann in *Kriminalbiologische Gegenwartsfragen* (cited at note 47 below), pp. 23 ff., 28.

[37] McCormick and Francis (*op. cit* at note 5 above), p. 26.

[38] Howard Jones, *Alcoholic Addiction*, London, 1963, p. 53.

[39] H. J. Eysenck, *The Structure of Human Personality*, 2nd ed., London–New York, 1960, pp. 10 ff.; *Dimensions of Personality*, London, 1947, pp. 25 ff.; *Crime and Personality*, London, 1964, p. 31.

[40] T. C. Willett, *Criminal on the Road*, London, 1964.

[41] See, e.g., Max Weber, *Gesammelte Aufsätze zur Wissenschafts-Lehre*, Tübingen, 1922, pp. 190 ff.; also Max Rheinstein in his and E. Shils's edition of *Max Weber on Law in Economy and Society*, Cambridge, Mass., 1954, p. xxxvii; Carlo Antoni, *Vom Historizismus zur Soziologie*, 1951, pp. 235 ff.; Morris Ginsberg, *Evolution and Progress*, London, 1961, p. 263; W. J. H. Sprott, *Sociology*,

London, 1956, pp. 37–8. Svend Riemer in Walter C. Reckless, *Etiology of Delinquent and Criminal Behavior*, pp. 138 ff.

[42] Allport, *op. cit.*, p. 146; Paul Wallin in Horst *et al.*, *op. cit.*, pp. 215 ff.

[43] Murphy and Newcomb (*op. cit.* at note 16), pp. 274 ff.

[44] These difficulties are also stressed by W. I. Thomas (*op. cit.* at note 16), pp. 148 ff., 159 ff.

[45] As Howard Jones, *Alcoholic Addiction*, Ch. 7, points out, the type of drinker characterized by maternal dependence may arise out of a great variety of situations, e.g., over-protective or over-domineering maternal attitudes.

[46] On the older literature see, e.g., Arthur Fink, *Causes of Crime*, Philadelphia, 1938; on Lombroso Marvin E. Wolfgang in *Pioneers of Criminology*, ed. by Hermann Mannheim, London, 1960, Ch. 9; on the more recent literature S. and E. Glueck, *Physique and Delinquency*, New York, 1956, pp. 15 ff.

[47] Some of the principal publications on typological research in criminology are: W. A. Willemse, *Constitution Types in Delinquency*, London, 1932; William H. Sheldon, *Varieties of Delinquent Youths*, New York, 1949; S. and E. Glueck (*op. cit.* at note 46; Franz Exner, *Kriminologie*, 3rd ed., Berlin 1949, pp. 203 ff.; Ernst Kretschmer, *Physique and Character*, Eng. trans. by Sprott, London, 1925; in German under the title *Körperbau und Character*, 21st/22nd ed., Hamburg, 1955; Ernst Seelig, *Lehrbuch der Kriminologie*, Graz, 1950; Seelig and Weindler, *Die Typen der Kriminellen*, Munich, 1949; *Kriminalbiologische Gegenwartsfragen*, No. 2, Stuttgart, 1955 (esp. the chapters by Hirschmann and Seelig); René Resten, *Caractérologie du Criminel*, Paris, 1959; on the typology of Borstal boys: D. A. Ogden, 'A Borstal Typological Survey', *Brit. J. Delinq.*, Vol. 5, No. 2, Oct. 1954, pp. 99 ff., and *Annual Report of the Prison Commissioners for 1949*, p. 68; A. G. Rose, *Five Hundred Borstal Boys*, Ch. 7; Peter Scott in *The Roots of Crime*, ed. by Norwood East, London, 1954, Ch. 3; Jack P. Gibbs, 'Needed: Analytical Typologies in Criminology', *Southwest. Soc. Sci. Quart.*, Vol. 40, No. 4, March 1960, pp. 321 ff.

[48] *Physique and Delinquency*, pp. 7 ff.; and also *Unraveling Juvenile Delinquency*, pp. 192 ff. For Sheldon's definition of the 'somato-type' see his *Varieties of Delinquent Youths*, p. 14.

[49] *Op. cit.*, p. 250.

[50] Veli Verkkö, *Homicides and Suicides in Finland and their Dependence on National Character*, Copenhagen, 1951, pp. 87, 142.

[51] See Edward Glover, *The Roots of Crime*, London, 1960, s. 4, esp. pp. 120 ff.; Milton Gurwitz, 'Developments in the Concept of Psychopathic Personality 1900–1950', *Brit. J. Delinq.*, Vol. 2, No. 2, Oct. 1951, pp. 88 ff.; Michael Craft, *Brit. J. Delinq.*, Vol. 2, No. 2, Oct. 1951, pp. 88 ff.; Michael Craft, *Brit. J. Crim.*, Vol. 1, No. 3, pp. 237 ff., both with extensive bibliographies. Craft concludes that three general syndromes emerge from his review of the literature: syndromes due predominantly to brain damage, syndromes which are predominantly affectionless, and syndromes consisting predominantly of emotional immaturity or instability. On Schneider's typology see his classic work *Die psychopathischen Persönlichkeiten*, 9th ed., Vienna, 1950.

[52] Erwin Frey, *Der frühkriminelle Rückfallsverbrecher*, Basel, 1951, pp. 116 ff. On this see *Group Problems*, p. 143.

[53] Edward Glover, *Freud or Jung*, London, 1950, pp. 90 ff.

[54] See, e.g., his *Collected Papers*, Vol. 4, pp. 342 ff.

[55] *Collected Papers*, Vol. 5, pp. 247 ff.

[56] See, e.g., F. Alexander and H. Staub, *The Criminal, The Judge and The Public*, New York, 1931, pp. 145 ff.; Kate Friedländer, *The Psychoanalytical Approach to Juvenile Delinquency*.

[57] David Riesman, Nathan Glazer and Reuel Denney, *The Lonely Crowd*, New Haven, 1950.

[58] Howard Becker, *Through Values to Social Interpretation*, Chapel Hill, 1950, pp. 79 ff.

[59] See Volkart, *op. cit.*, pp. 126, 159.

[60] Kimball Young, *Handbook of Social Psychology*, 2nd ed., London, 1957, pp. 153 ff.

[61] Marshall B. Clinard, *Sociology of Deviant Behavior*, New York, 1957, p. 201; also in *Sociology Today*, New York, 1953, p. 521; Lindesmith and Dunham, 'Some Principles of Criminal Typology', *Soc. Forces*, Vol. 19, March 1941, pp. 307 ff.

[62] See literature cited in note 47.

[63] This is also stressed by Mezger in *Kriminalbiologische Gegenwartsfragen* (cited at note 47), p. 4.

[64] Joachim Hellmer, *Mschr. Kriminol. Strafrechtsreform*, Vol. 43, Nov. 1960, pp. 136 ff.; R. S. Taylor, 'The Habitual Criminal', *Brit. J. Crim.*, Vol. 1, No. 1, July 1960, pp. 21 ff.

[65] Richard L. Jenkins in Reckless, *Etiology of Delinquent and Criminal Behavior*, pp. 144 ff. See also Jenkins and Hewitt, *Amer. J. Orthopsychiat.*, Vol. 14, 1944, pp. 84–9.

[66] John Bowlby, 'Forty-four Juvenile Thieves: their Characters and Home-Life', *Int. J. Psycho-Anal.*, Vol. 25, Parts 1–4, 1944, pp. 6 ff.

[67] John Rich, 'Types of Stealing', *The Lancet*, 21.4.1956, pp. 496 ff.

[68] D. H. Stott, *Delinquency and Human Nature*, Dunfermline, 1950, esp. pp. 328 ff.

[69] William Foote Whyte, *Street Corner Society*, 2nd ed., Chicago, 1955.

[70] Carl Frankenstein, 'The Configurational Approach to Causation in the Study of Juvenile Delinquents', *Arch. crim. Psychodyn.*, 1957, pp. 572 ff.

[71] See *Group Problems*, p. 79.

[72] *Unraveling Juvenile Delinquency*, pp. 264, 258.

[73] See, e.g., their *Predicting Delinquency and Crime*, p. 100 ff.

[74] D. A. Ogden, *Brit. J. Delinq.*, Vol. 5, No. 2, Oct. 1954, pp. 99 ff.

[75] A. G. Rose, *op. cit.*, Ch. 7. For a typology of 'uneducable' inmates of a correctional institution in Germany see Walter Piecha, *Die Lebensbewährung der als 'unerziehbar' entlassenen Fürsorgezöglinge*, Göttingen, 1959, pp. 39 ff.

[76] Donald R. Cressey, *Other People's Money*, Glencoe, Ill., 1953, pp. 19 ff.

[77] On this see the *Report of the Royal Commission on Capital Punishment*, Cmd. 8932, 1953–55, pp. 167 ff.; *Group Problems*, pp. 229 ff.; and Marvin E. Wolfgang, *Patterns in Criminal Homicide*, Philadelphia, 1958.

[78] Wolfgang, *op. cit.*, Ch. 10.

[79] *Ibid.*, Parts 2, 3; von Hentig, *The Criminal and his Victim*, New Haven, 1948; Jack P. Gibbs (*op. cit.* at note 31).

[80] T. P. Morris and Louis Blom-Cooper, *A Calendar of Murder*, London, 1964.

[81] Emile Durkheim, *Suicide*, Eng. trans. ed. by George Simpson, London, 1952, pp. 146–7.

[82] T. C. N. Gibbens, *Thefts from Departmental Stores*, General Report to Fourth International Congress of Criminology, The Hague, 1960, and Gibbens and Prince, *Shoplifting*, London, 1962.

[83] Clarence Schrag, 'A Preliminary Criminal Typology', *Pacific Sociol. Rev.*, Vol. 4, No. 1, Spring 1961, with many references to literature. The same issue contains two other papers on typology.

[84] Don C. Gibbons and Donald L. Garrity, 'Definition and Analysis of Certain Criminal Types', *Amer. J. crim. Law Criminol. Police Sci.*, Vol. 53, No. 1, March

1962, pp. 27-35, and the criticism by Julian B. Roebuck, in the same Journal Vol. 54, No. 4, Dec. 1963, pp. 476-8.

[85] Leon Radzinowicz, *In Search of Criminology*, London, 1961, p. 38.

CHAPTER 9

[1] The general literature on social experiments is fairly comprehensive. The following books are of special importance: Ernest Greenwood, *Experimental Sociology*, New York, 1945, with excellent bibliography; Arnold M. Rose (*op. cit.* above at Ch. 3, note 16), Chs. 14, 16; F. Stuart Chapin, *Experimental Designs in Sociological Reseach*, 2nd ed., New York, 1956; John Madge (*op. cit.* above at Ch. 3, note 19), Ch. 5; Murphy, Gardner, Newcomb, *Experimental Psychology*; Selltiz *et al.* (*op. cit.* above at Ch. 3, note 7), pp. 94 ff.; Gee (*op. cit.* at Ch. 3, note 46), Ch. 11; *Handbook of Research Methods in Child Development*, ed. by Paul H. Mussen, New York–London, 1960; George A. Lundberg, *Social Research*, 2nd ed., New York, 1942, pp. 54 ff. On experiments in general: R. A. Fisher, *The Design of Experiments*, 4th ed., Edinburgh, 1947.

[2] Karl R. Popper, *The Poverty of Historicism*, London, 1957, p. 86.

[3] On natural experiments see Greenwood, *op. cit.*, pp. 10, 25 and *passim*; Selltiz *et al.*, *op. cit.*, p. 92; Madge, *op. cit.*, p. 279 (on Moreno).

[4] Greenwood, *op. cit.*, pp. 22 ff.

[5] Selltiz *et al.*, *op. cit.*, p. 20; *Handbook of Research Methods*, p. 140.

[6] Sir Charles Goodeve, *Proc. First Int. Conf. Operat. Res.*, Oxford, 1957, Engl. Univ. Press Ltd., London, pp. 13 ff.

[7] O. L. Zangwill in *The New Outline of Modern Knowledge*, ed. by Alan Pryce-Jones, London, 1956, pp. 182-3.

[8] The best survey is given in Murphy and Newcomb, *op. cit.*

[9] See *The Times* of 26.4, 7.6, and 16.6.1955.

[10] On the position in psychiatry and epidemiology see Reid (*op. cit.* at Ch. 4, note 7), p. 14. See also A. V. Hill, *The Ethical Dilemma of Science*, Oxford, 1960, pp. 27 ff.

[11] Popper, *op. cit.*, p. 93.

[12] *Ibid.*, p. 96.

[13] See W. I. B. Beveridge, *The Art of Scientific Investigation*, London, 1950, p. 17. The whole of Ch. 2, on 'Experimentation', is worth studying.

[14] *Ibid.*, p. 18.

[15] See already my *Group Problems in Crime and Punishment*, p. 128. Norval Morris and Cynthia Turner, 'The Lawyer and Criminological Research', *Virginian Law Review*, Vol. 44, No. 2, 1958, pp. 178 ff., are strongly in favour of judicial experiments as 'a heroic measure to bring knowledge into the chaos of our correctional methods'.

[16] R. A. Fisher, *The Design of Experiments*.

[17] W. Norwood East, *The Adolescent Criminal*, London, 1942, pp. 6-7.

[18] Edwin Powers and Helen Witmer, *An Experiment in the Prevention of Delinquency: The Cambridge-Somerville Youth Study*, New York, 1951.

[19] H. Ashley Weeks *et al.*, *Youthful Offenders at Highfields*, Ann Arbor, 1958; Lloyd McCorkle *et al.*, *The Highfields Story*, New York, 1958. See the review of these two books by T. P. Morris, *Brit. J. Crim.*, Vol. I, No. 1, July 1960, pp. 80 ff., and briefly my *Group Problems*, pp. 217-19.

[20] *Group Problems*, pp. 146 ff.

[21] Weeks *et al.*, *op. cit.*, p. 140.

[22] Beveridge, *op. cit.*, p. 19.

[23] See also Morris, *loc. cit.*, p. 81.

[24] *Group Problems*, p. 219; *Brit. J. Delinq.*, Vol. 5, pp. 67–8.

[25] Harry Manuel Shulman, 'Delinquency Treatment in the Controlled Activity Group', *Amer. Sociol. Rev.*, Vol. 10, 1945, pp. 405 ff.

[26] Brian Kay, *Brit. J. Delinq.*, Vol. 4, No. 4, April 1954, pp. 245 ff.

[27] See *Report of Royal Commission on Capital Punishment*, 1953, pp. 365 ff.

[28] Mannheim and Wilkins, *op. cit.*, pp. 111–12, 122.

[29] Greenwood, *op. cit.*, *passim*, esp. Chs. 4 and 8.

[30] *Ibid.*, pp. 97 ff., 126 ff.

[31] *Ibid.*, p. 135.

[32] See, e.g., Howard Becker, *Through Values to Social Interpretation*, pp. 102 ff.

[33] 'Even in the second half of the twentieth century, the statistical basis of major legislation can be extraordinarily primitive', wrote *The Times* on 22.12.1960.

[34] Wolfgang Friedmann, *Legal Theory*, 4th ed., 1960.

[35] Thomas A. Cowan, 'Experience and Experiment', *Philosophy and Science*, Vol. 26, No. 2, April 1959, pp. 77 ff.; *Archiv für Rechts- und Sozialphilosophie*, Vol. 44, No. 4, 1958, pp. 465 ff.

[36] Frederick K. Beutel, *Some Potentialities of Experimental Jurisprudence as a new Branch of Social Science*, Lincoln, Nebraska, 1957.

[37] See for a recent example the *Massachusetts Report of the Special Commission, established for the Purpose of Investigating and Studying the Abolition of Death Penalty in Capital Cases*, Boston, No. 2575, 30.12.1958.

CHAPTER 10

[1] The first part of this chapter is particularly indebted to John C. Spencer's report on the Bristol Social Project, the first volume of which has now been published under the title *Stress and Release in an Urban Estate. A Study in Action Research*, London, 1964. In addition, the following may be consulted: Philip M. Morse and George E. Kimball, *Methods of Operations Research*, New York-London, 1951; *Proc. Second Int. Conf. Operat. Res.*, 1960, ed. by J. Banbury and J. Maitland, London, 1961; Arnold M. Rose, *Theory and Method in the Social Sciences*, Ch. 8; Selltiz *et al.*, *op. cit.*, Ch. 13; John Madge, *op. cit.*, pp. 46 ff., 136; John B. Mays, *On the Threshold of Delinquency*, Liverpool, 1959, esp. pp. 22 ff.

[2] Hornell Hart, *Amer. Soc. Rev.*, Vol. 18, 1953, pp. 612 ff., lists four definitions of 'operational', of which only one is 'action' research. According to John C. McKinney in *Modern Sociological Theory*, ed. by Howard Becker and Alvin Boskoff, New York, 1957, p. 207, the doctrine of 'operationalism' was established in physics by Bridgeman in 1927 and taken over by some of the 'more pragmatically inclined' sociologists, such as Lundberg, in the thirties. It means that concepts are nothing more than sets of operations, e.g. 'intelligence is what intelligence tests test', which would imply that there are as many kinds of intelligence as tests. The operational definition of justice, we might add, is 'what is done by the courts in their administration of the law' which is in fact the view of the legal pragmatists. As McKinney writes, this would make any systematic theory impossible. In the following text the term 'operational' is not used in this purely pragmatic sense. A less extreme definition is also given by P. M. S. Blackett who writes (*Operat. Res. Quart.*, Vol. 1, No. 1, March 1950, p. 3): 'the element of relative novelty lies . . . in the comparative freedom of the investigators to seek out their own problems and in the direct relation of the work to the possibilities of executive action'. He also quotes the following definition: 'A scientific method for providing executives with a quantitative basis for decisions'.

[3] Pitirim A. Sorokin, *Facts and Foibles in Modern Sociology and Related Sciences*, Chicago, 1956, Ch. 3, 'The Illusion of Operationalism'.

[4] Ferris F. Laune, 'Predicting Criminality', *Northw. Univ. Stud. Soc. Sci.*, No. 1, Chicago, 1936.

[5] Michael Argyle, *The Scientific Study of Social Behaviour*, London, 1957, p. 13, is for this reason perhaps unduly critical of action research.

[6] Rose, *op. cit.*, p. 169, seems to regard the two methods as identical.

[7] E.g. Morse and Kimball, *op. cit.*, p. 1.

[8] William Foote Whyte, *Street Corner Society*, 2nd ed., Chicago, 1955, pp. 309 ff., 325, 335-6.

[9] *Preventing Crime*. A Symposium ed. by Sheldon and Eleanor Glueck, New York-London, 1936. See, e.g., p. 53 on the research connected with one of these projects.

[10] *The Problem of Delinquency*, ed. by Sheldon Glueck, Boston, 1959, esp. §§ 174-86.

[11] 'Prevention of Juvenile Delinquency', *Ann. Amer. Acad. Polit. Soc. Sci.*, Vol. 322, March 1960. See, e.g., the description of the research for the Boston Delinquency Project by Walter N. Miller, pp. 99 ff., and the contribution by Eva Rosenfeld, pp. 136 ff.

[12] Powers and Witmer (*op. cit.* at Ch. 9, note 18), pp. 99, 154, and Chs. 8, 9, 23.

[13] *Ibid.*, pp. 106 ff., 118, 147 ff.

[14] The literature on the Chicago Area Project will be quoted in Chapter 23, note 1.

[15] See the excellent assessment of the Project by one closely connected with it: Solomon Kobrin, 'The Chicago Area Project—A 25-year Assessment', *Ann. Amer. Acad.* (see note 11), pp. 19 ff.

[16] As Taft writes, the Project was 'an experiment to test the soundness of principles derived from the research which preceded it' and it was also 'a continuation of that research', Donald R. Taft, *Criminology*, 3rd ed., New York, 1956, p. 716.

[17] Kobrin, *op. cit.*, p. 25.

[18] Clifford R. Shaw and Jesse A. Jacobs, quoted by Walter Reckless, *The Crime Problem*, 2nd ed., New York, 1955, p. 69.

[19] See, e.g., M. L. Turner and J. C. Spencer in *Spontaneous Youth Groups*, ed. by P. H. K. Kuenstler, London, 1955, pp. 52 ff.

[20] M. L. Turner, *Ship without Sails*, London, 1953.

[21] *Op. cit.*, p. 131.

[22] John B. Mays, *On the Threshold of Delinquency*, Liverpool, 1959. See also the Review by Herschel Prins, *Brit. J. Crim.*, Vol. 1, No. 1, July 1960, p. 84.

[23] *Op. cit.*, p. 9.

[24] *Op. cit.*, p. 29.

[25] John C. Spencer *et al.* (*op. cit.* at note 1).

[26] Spencer, *op. cit.*, p. 3.

[27] For similar reasons the Cambridge-Somerville Study had to include non pre-delinquent children in its programme (see Ch. 9 under III).

[28] John C. McKinney in *Modern Sociological Theory*, p. 185. Other useful works on sociological methods, in addition to those by Merton, Selltiz *et al.*, and Madge, Rose, Sorokin, Gee, and Greenwood, are Stuart A. Rice (ed.), *Methods in Social Science*, New York, 1931; George A. Lundberg, *Social Research*, 2nd ed., London-New York-Toronto, 1942; R. M. MacIver, *Social Causation*, Boston, 1942; L. L. Bernard, *The Fields and Methods of Sociology*, 2nd ed., New York, 1934 (with a short chapter by Sellin on Criminology); and S. and B. Webb, *Methods of Social Study*, London, 1932. On the use of sociological methods in criminology see my *Group Problems in Crime and Punishment*, Ch. 1, and

my *Deutsche Strafrechtsreform in englischer Sicht*, München–Berlin, 1960, pp. 128 ff.

[29] See *Criminal Justice and Social Reconstruction*, Chs. 6, 7, esp. pp. 103 ff.; *Group Problems*, Ch. 2(i); W. J. H. Sprott, 'Psychology and the Moral Problems of our Time', *Philosophy*, July 1948; J. A. Waites, *Brit. J. Psychol.* (Gen. Sect.), Sept. 1945.

[30] E.g. Madge, *op. cit.*, Ch. 4; Selltiz, *op. cit.*, Ch. 7 and App. C.

[31] *Group Problems*, p. 10.

[32] Donald Clemmer, *The Prison Community*, Boston, 1940, p. 322, which also contains many valuable remarks on interviewing in criminological research.

[33] Donald R. Cressey, *Other People's Money*, Glencoe, Ill., 1953, pp. 23 ff.

[34] G. W. Lynch, 'An Estimate of the Extent of Larceny in Industry', unpublished London M.Sc.(Econ.) thesis, 1954.

[35] E.g. Selltiz, *op. cit.*, Ch. 6; Madge, *op. cit.*, p. 130.

[36] Russell L. Ackoff, *The Design of Social Research*, Chicago, 1953, p. 292.

[37] See note 8 above.

[38] *Within Prison Walls*, New York, 1914.

[39] Gresham M. Sykes, *The Society of Captives*, Princeton, 1958, App. A; Terence and Pauline Morris, *Pentonville*, London, 1963.

[40] Donald P. Wilson, *My Six Convicts*, New York, 1951.

[41] J. Douglas Grant, *Brit. J. Delinq.*, Vol. 7, No. 4, April 1957, pp. 301 ff.

[42] Nathan Leopold (*op. cit.* at Ch. 8, note 28).

[43] John C. Spencer, *Crime and the Services*, London, 1954; Norval Morris, *The Habitual Criminal*, London, 1951.

[44] John James, *Brit. J. Delinq.*, Vol. 5, No. 4, April 1955, pp. 269 ff.

[45] 'The Social Background of Delinquency', University of Nottingham, Rockefeller research 1952–4, Director: Prof. W. J. H. Sprott (unpublished, privately circulated). See note in *Brit. J. Delinq.*, Vol. 5, April 1955, p. 307, and T. P. Morris, *The Criminal Area*, London, 1957, p. 104.

[46] Ludwig Moreno, *Who shall survive?*, Nerv. Ment. Dis. Monogr., Ser., No. 58, Washington, 1954.

[47] E. F. Piercy, 'Boys' Clubs and their Social Patterns', *Brit. J. Delinq.*, Vol. 2, No. 3, 1952, pp. 229 ff.; Gordon Rose, *Sociometric Analysis and Observation in a Borstal Institution*, ib., Vol. 6, No. 4, April 1956, pp. 285 ff.; the same, ib., Vol. 6, No. 3, Jan. 1956, pp. 202 ff.; J. Croft and T. Grygier, 'Sociometric Study of Truancy and Delinquency in a Secondary School', *Human Relations*, Vol. 9, 1956, pp. 439–66.

[48] Whyte (*op. cit.* at note 8), p. 300.

[49] Tadeusz Grygier, *Oppression. A Study in Social and Criminal Psychology*, London, 1954, pp. 87 ff.

[50] Spencer (*op. cit.* at note 43), pp. 274 ff.

[51] Terence and Pauline Morris, *Pentonville*, p. 9, and App. A.

PRELIMINARY OBSERVATIONS TO PART THREE

[1] M. F. Ashley Montagu, 'The Biologist looks at Crime', *Ann. Amer. Acad. Polit. Soc. Sci.*, Vol. 217, Sept. 1941, p. 46. See also Marshall B. Clinard, *Sociology of Deviant Behaviour*, New York, 1957, p. 32.

[2] Quoted from S. and E. Glueck, *Physique and Delinquency*, New York, 1956, p. 16. On the inter-relationships between psychiatric and social factors see now also T. C. N. Gibbens, *Psychiatric Studies of Borstal Lads*, Inst. Psychiat.

Maudsley Mono. No. 11, London, 1963. This important work should also be consulted in connection with the subjects of Chapters 11–15.

CHAPTER 11

[1] W. A. Bonger, *An Introduction to Criminology*, transl. from the Dutch by Emil van Loo, London, 1936, pp. 106 ff. See also the revised Dutch ed. by G. Th. Kempe, Haarlem, 1954, pp. 135 ff.

[2] Esp. Ernst Roesner in *Handwörterbuch der Kriminologie*, Berlin–Leipzig, 1933, pp. 688 ff., with full bibliography; Joseph Cohen, 'The Geography of Crime', *Ann. Amer. Acad. Polit. Soc. Sci.*, Vol. 217, Sept. 1941, pp. 29 ff.; Barnes and Teeters, *New Horizons in Criminology*, New York, 1943, pp. 132 ff.; H. C. Brearley, *Homicide in the United States*, Chapel Hill, 1932, Ch. 9; Marvin E. Wolfgang, *Patterns in Criminal Homicide*, Philadelphia, 1958, Ch. 6; Edwin Dexter, *Weather Influences*, New York, 1904; Franz Exner, *Kriminologie*, 3rd ed., Berlin–Göttingen–Heidelberg, 1949, pp. 56 ff.; J. M. van Bemmelen, *Criminologie*, 3rd ed., Zwolle, 1952, pp. 101 ff.; Howard Jones, *Crime and the Penal System*, London, 1956, pp. 112–13.

[3] Quoted by Cohen, *op. cit.*, p. 31.

[4] See, e.g., Wolfgang, *op. cit.*, p. 98, and Cohen, *op. cit.*, p. 31, on Dexter.

[5] Introduction, pp. 92 ff.

[6] Cyril Burt, *The Young Delinquent*, 4th ed., 1944, pp. 161 ff.

[7] See the full account by Brearley, *op. cit.*, pp. 168 ff.

[8] *Ibid.*, p. 177.

[9] William F. Ogburn and Meyer F. Nimkoff, *A Handbook of Sociology*, 4th ed., London, 1960, pp. 73–4.

[10] Useful comparative material for the general population is contained in W. J. Martin, *The Physique of Young Adult Males*, H.M.S.O., 1949 (Medical Research Council Memorandum, No. 20).

[11] See Hermann Mannheim, *Juvenile Delinquency in an English Middletown*, London, 1948, pp. 50, 110.

[12] Teeters and Reinemann, *The Challenge of Delinquency*, New York, 1950, p. 268.

[13] For the details see Lionel Fox, *The English Prison and Borstal Systems*, London, 1952, Ch. 14.

[14] *Annual Report for 1959*, H.M.S.O., London, 1960, p. 101.

[15] British Association for the Advancement of Science, *Annual Report 1883*, pp. 253 ff. See also A. M. Carr-Saunders, Hermann Mannheim, E. C. Rhodes, *Young Offenders*, Cambridge, 1944, pp. 8–9.

[16] W. D. Morrison, *Juvenile Offenders*, London, 1895, p. 102.

[17] Cyril Burt, *op. cit.*, Ch. 6.

[18] *L.C.C. School Medical Officer*, Vol. 3, Part 2, 1930, published May 1931, pp. 76 ff. The investigation was carried out by Dr. Verner Wiley. See also *Young Offenders*, pp. 23–5, for further details.

[19] M. D. Eilenberg, *Brit. J. Crim.*, Vol. 2, No. 2, Oct. 1961, pp. 116–18.

[20] T. Ferguson, *The Young Delinquent in his Social Setting*, Oxford, 1952, Ch. 3.

[21] *Ibid.*, p. 116.

[22] Hermann Mannheim, *Social Aspects of Crime in England between the Wars*, 1940, pp. 250 ff., 262.

[23] Hermann Mannheim and Leslie T. Wilkins, *Prediction Methods in relation to Borstal Training*, p. 209.

[24] Norwood East *et al.*, *The Adolescent Criminal*, London, 1942, pp. 175 ff., 186 ff.; also his *Society and the Individual*, Ch. 6, pp. 87 ff.

[25] Charles Goring, *The English Convict*, H.M.S.O., London, 1913, pp. 200–1.

[26] Norval Morris, *The Habitual Criminal*, London, 1951, pp. 310, 354.

[27] Terence and Pauline Morris, *Pentonville*, Ch. 9; D. J. West, *The Habitual Prisoner*, p. 51.

[28] S. and E. Glueck, *Unraveling Juvenile Delinquency*, pp. 55–6, and Ch. 14.

[29] See Ch. 6, note 49 above.

[30] *Juvenile Delinquents Grown Up*, pp. 109, 179, 182, 194.

[31] William Healy, *Mental Conflicts and Misconduct*, Boston, 1936, p. 321; William and Joan McCord with Irving Kenneth Zola, *Origins of Crime*, New York, 1959, p. 66; Powers and Witmer (*op. cit.* at Ch. 9, note 18), pp. 45 ff.

[32] J. D. W. Pearce, *Juvenile Delinquency*, London, 1952, pp. 34 ff.

[33] See also the case history in Maud A. Merrill, *Problems of Child Delinquency*, London, 1947, p. 200.

CHAPTER 12

[1] On the history of phrenology see Arthur E. Fink, *Causes of Crime*, Philadelphia, 1938, Ch. 1; also Bonger, *An Introduction to Criminology* (cited at Ch. 11, note 1), pp. 44–6; W. Norwood East, *Medical Aspects of Crime*, London, 1936, Ch. 7; George B. Vold, *Theoretical Criminology*, New York, 1958, pp. 44–9. Fink is mainly concerned with the influence of phrenology on American criminology. The following text is largely based upon his work.

[2] W. Norwood East, *Society and the Criminal*, H.M.S.O., London, 1949, p. 70.

[3] Fink, *op. cit.*, pp. 152 ff.; Vold, *op. cit.*

[4] Bonger, *op. cit.*, p. 78; Wolfgang in *Pioneers in Criminology*, pp. 180–1.

[5] The literature on Lombroso and his school is immense. Only the following references can here be given: Marvin A. Wolfgang in *Pioneers in Crimonology*, ed. by Hermann Mannheim, London, 1960, Ch. 9 (with extensive bibliog.), to which the following text is particularly indebted; Hermann Mannheim, *Group Problems in Crime and Punishment*, Ch. 4: 'Lombroso and his Place in Modern Criminology'; W. Norwood East, *op. cit.*, Ch. 6; M. F. Ashley Montagu, 'The Biologist looks at Crime', *Ann. Amer. Acad. Polit. Soc. Sci.*, Vol. 217, Sept. 1941, pp. 46 ff.; Vold (*op. cit.* at note 1); A. E. Hooton, *The American Criminal*, Cambridge, Mass., 1939; Gustav Aschaffenburg, *Crime and its Repression*, Amer. ed., Boston, 1913; the same in *Handwörterbuch der Kriminologie*, Berlin, 1933, Vol. 1, pp. 825 ff.; Edmund Mezger, *Kriminalpolitik*, 1st ed., Stuttgart, 1934.

[6] There are differences of opinion regarding date and place of Lombroso's birth; see Wolfgang, *op. cit.*, p. 169, fn. 2. Vold, p. 28, gives Venice as his place of birth.

[7] Many details on the various scientific influences which helped to shape Lombroso's basic ideas are given by Wolfgang, *op. cit.*, pp. 177 ff. Hooton, *op. cit.*, p. 17, disputes the widely held view that Lombroso's theories had something in common with those of the phrenologists.

[8] See the details given by Wolfgang, *op. cit.*, pp. 171 ff.

[9] Cesare Lombroso, *Crime: Its Causes and Remedies*, Boston, 1913.

[10] Cesare Lombroso and Guglielmo Ferrero, *The Female Offender*, London, 1895.

[11] Cesare Lombroso, *After Death—What?* Boston, 1909.

[12] Gina Lombroso–Ferrero, *Cesare Lombroso*, 2nd ed., Bologna, 1921.

[13] Austin L. Porterfield, *Creative Factors in Scientific Research*, Durham,

N.C., 1941, esp. Parts 2 and 3, has made a special study of this problem. Also Sorokin, *Facts and Foibles*.

[14] *Handwörterbuch der Kriminologie*, Vol. 1, p. 834.

[15] Havelock Ellis, *The Criminal*, London–New York, 1st ed., 1890, 4th ed. 1910, stresses that Lombroso himself did not regard the 'born criminal' as a real type, but 'emphatically asserted that all that can be asserted is a greater frequency of anomalies' (4th ed., p. 58).

[16] Henry Maudsley, *Insanity and Crime*, London, 1964, p. 29.

[17] See Peter Scott in *Pioneers in Criminology*, Ch. 8.

[18] Morris Ginsberg, *Reason and Unreason in Society*, London, 1947, p. 31. Also Karl Popper, *The Poverty of Historicism*, pp. 127, fn. 1, 108, fn. 1.

[19] Ginsberg, *Evolution and Progress*, London, 1961, p. 245.

[20] Bertrand Russell, *Human Knowledge*, London, 1948, pp. 45, 48.

[21] Hooton, *op. cit.*, p. 11.

[22] See Karl Murchison, *Criminal Intelligence*, Worcester, Mass., 1926, p. 28. Against the lamarckian view of such inheritance see Julian Huxley, *Evolution*, London, 1942, pp. 457 ff., and on atavism and degeneration, pp. 20, 567.

[23] Wolfgang, *op. cit.*, p. 194, quoting Kurella, p. 136.

[24] *Ibid.*, p. 202.

[25] Hooton, *op. cit.*, p. 13.

[26] *Ibid.*, p. 15.

[27] On Lacassagne and Manouvrier see Bonger, *Introduction*, pp. 78 ff.

[28] Gabriel Tarde, *La criminalité comparée*, 1st ed. Paris, 1886, 2nd ed., 1890, Ch. 1.

[29] *Op. cit.*, pp. 40 ff. Also M. S. Wilson Vine in *Pioneers in Criminology*, Ch. 10.

[30] Tarde, *op. cit.*, p. 52.

[31] *Op. cit.*, 2nd ed., p. 49, fn. 1.

[32] On Ferri see Thorsten Sellin, *Pioneers*, Ch. 13; on Garofalo Francis A. Allen, *Pioneers*, Ch. 12. The following text is greatly indebted to these two articles.

[33] *Pioneers*, p. 277.

[34] Published in 1878 in an enlarged form as *La negazione de libero arbitrio e la teórica dell' imputabilita*.

[35] Sellin, *op. cit.*, p. 283.

[36] *Ibid.*, pp. 285–7.

[37] The 3rd ed., the first to bear this title, was published in 1892, the 5th and last after his death in 1929-30. A full American translation of the 4th ed. appeared in 1917 as *Criminal Sociology*, Boston. The English edition of 1896 is greatly abridged.

[38] See *Pioneers*, pp. 21–2.

[39] *Ibid.*, p. 293.

[40] The American edition was published in 1914 in Boston in the Modern Criminal Science Series where also works by Lombroso and Ferri appeared (see *Pioneers*, p. ix).

[41] Allen, *Pioneers*, p. 268.

[42] Gabriel Tarde, *Penal Philosophy*, Eng. trans. Boston, 1912, p. 72.

[43] See Morris Ginsberg, *On the Diversity of Morals*, London, 1956, p. 99.

[44] *Reason and Unreason in Society*, London, 1947, p. 320.

[45] See my Introduction to *Pioneers in Criminology*, pp. 9 ff., 14 ff.

[46] See the chapters on Beccaria, Bentham, and Maconochie in *Pioneers*.

[47] Clarence Ray Jeffery in *Pioneers*, Ch. 19.

[48] Enrico Ferri, *The Positive School of Criminology*, 1901, Eng. ed., Chicago, 1908, pp. 9, 23, 96.

[49] For the details see Max Grünhut, *Penal Reform*, Oxford, 1948, pp. 391 ff., and in particular Norval Morris, *The Habitual Criminal*, London, 1951, pp. 201 ff., and *passim*.

[50] See *Pioneers*, pp. 23 ff.

[51] Lombroso, *Crime: Its Causes and Remedies*, pp. 114 ff., and the whole of Ch. 6.

CHAPTER 13

[1] See my Introduction to *Pioneers in Criminology*, pp. 17-23, and Wolfgang, *op. cit.*

[2] On U.S.A. see Arthur E. Fink, *op. cit.*, Chs. 5, 6.

[3] See note 15 to Ch. 12.

[4] On Prichard and his successors see Fink, *op. cit.*, Ch. 3.

[5] See Peter Scott in *Pioneers in Criminology*, Ch. 8, and Maurice Parmelee's Introduction to the English version of Lombroso's *Crime: Its Causes and Remedies*, p. xxi.

[6] H.M.S.O., London, 1913. There exists an abridged edition of 1919. On Goring see Edwin D. Driver in *Pioneers*, Ch. 17, the critical Summary in Walter C. Reckless, *Criminal Behavior*, New York-London, 1940, pp. 170-3, and the full-scale criticism by Earnest A. Hooton, *The American Criminal*, Cambridge, Mass., 1939, pp. 18-31.

[7] Fink, *op. cit.*, Ch. 7, p. 176.

[8] New York, 1877. On it see Fink, *op. cit.*, Ch. 8; Barnes and Teeters, *New Horizons in Criminology*, 1st ed., New York, 1943, pp. 175-6.

[9] Henry H. Goddard, *The Kallikak Family*, New York, 1912; see Fink, *op. cit.*, p. 220, Barnes-Teeters, *op. cit.*, pp. 176 ff.

[10] Franz Exner, *Kriminologie*, 3rd ed., Hamburg, 1949, p. 114.

[11] *The Young Delinquent*, pp. 49 ff., 602 ff.

[12] W. Norwood East, *op. cit.*, pp. 37 ff.

[13] Sir Norwood East, *Society and the Criminal*, H.M.S.O., London, 1949, p. 85.

[14] From the extensive literature the following may be quoted: Johannes Lange, *Verbrechen als Schicksal*, Leipzig, 1929, Eng. trans. by Charlotte Haldane, as *Crime and Destiny*, New York, 1930, London, 1931; Friedrich Stumpfl, *Die Ursprünge des Verbrechens*, Leipzig, 1936; A. J. Rosanoff and others, *J. crim. Law Criminol.*, Vol. 24, 1934, pp. 923 ff.; H. H. Newman, *Twins and Super-Twins*, London, 1942; the same, *Evolution, Genetics and Eugenics*, Chicago, 1930; Walter C. Reckless, *Criminal Behavior*, pp. 185 ff.; R. S. Woodworth, *Heredity and Environment*, New York, Soc. Sci. Res. Counc., 1941.

[15] On Russian twin research see S. G. Levit in *Character and Personality*, Vol. 3, No. 3, March 1935, pp. 188 ff.

[16] James Shields, *Monozygotic Twins*, London, 1962, has hardly anything of criminological interest.

[17] Exner, *Kriminologie*, 3rd ed., p. 125, thinks this argument can be neither proved nor disproved. Newman, however, in *Twins and Super-Twins*, p. 123, regards this as the only serious criticism of the twin method of studying crime causation; here, he thinks, we encounter a 'lack of control features' in Nature's scientific experiments as we can hardly assume that the social environment of ordinary twins will be as similar as that of identical ones. Cases have been reported where identical twins were made to share automatically all the punishments at school incurred by either of them because the masters could not distinguish them; see Sir W. Beveridge, *Changes in Family Life*, 1932, p. 59.

[18] See H. H. Newman, *Evolution, Genetics and Eugenics*, p. 535, who even

speaks of 'reasoning in a vicious circle with a vengeance', i.e. if two twins correspond to our preconceived ideas of identical twins we classify them as such. In his *Twins and Super-Twins*, Ch. 7, however, he is confident that safe distinctions can be made.

[19] Lionel Penrose, *Mental Defect*, London, 1933, p. 23. Ernst Kretschmer, *Körperbau und Charakter*, 21st/22nd ed., Hamburg, 1955, pp. 157 ff., quotes cases of identical twins with entirely opposite temperamental personalities.

[20] *Ann. Amer. Acad. Polit. Soc. Sci.*, Vol. 217, Sept. 1941, p. 53.

[21] Stumpfl, *op. cit.*, pp. 21-2.

[22] *Ibid.*, pp. 159-60, 171 ff.

[23] Abstract from a study by F. J. Kallmann *et al.*, in the *Eugenics Review*, Oct. 1950, p. 173.

[24] Quoted from M. Guttmacher, *Sex Offences*, 1951, p. 38.

[25] *New Light on Delinquency*, New Haven, 1936.

[26] Shûfu Yoshimasu, 'The Criminological Significance of the Family in the Light of the Study of Criminal Twins', *Acta Criminologiae et Medicinae legalis Japonica*, Vol 27, No. 4, 1961, pp. 117-41.

[27] Lorna Whelan, *Brit. J. Delinq.*, Vol. 2, No. 2, Oct. 1951, pp. 130 ff.

[28] Martin Turnell, *The Novel in France*, London, 1950, p. 146.

[29] Julian Huxley, *The Uniqueness of Man*, London, 1931, p. 42.

[30] Exner, *op. cit.*, p. 133.

[31] Olof Kinberg, revised French ed. of the English original, Copenhagen, 1935, under the title *Les Problèmes fondamentaux de la Criminologie*, Paris, 1960, p. 239.

[32] Max Schlapp and E. H. Smith, *The New Criminology*, New York, 1928. For other discussions of the effect of the glands on crime see Montagu, *op. cit.*, p. 55, Reckless, *op. cit.*, pp. 197 ff., and on endocrinology in general R. G. Hoskins, *The Tides of Life*, London, 1933, and his *Endocrinology*, London, 1941; V. H. Mottram, *The Physical Basis of Personality*, Harmondsworth, 1944.

[33] Mottram, *op. cit.*, p. 61.

[34] Mottram, *op. cit.*, p. 57; Gordon-Harris-Rees, *Introduction to Psychological Medicine*, London, 1936, p. 197; Hoskins, *The Tides of Life*, p. 165; William Wolf, 'The Role of the Endocrine Glands', *J. clin. Psychopath*, Jan. 1946, p. 540.

[35] See F. L. Golla and S. Hodge, *The Lancet*, 2, 1949, pp. 1006-7; also P. A. H. Baan in *Beiträge zur Sexualforschung*, Vol. 2, Stuttgart, 1952, p. 33; Käte Friedländer, *The Psychoanalytical Approach to Juvenile Delinquency*, London, 1947, p. 155; David Abrahamsen, *The Psychology of Crime*, New York, 1961, p. 234, recommends the matter for special investigation by a Research Institute.

[36] Eduard Mezger, *Kriminalpolitik auf kriminologischer Grundlage*, 1st ed., Stuttgart, 1934, with comprehensive bibliographical notes.

[37] *Physique and Character*, trans. by Sprott, London, 1936. A detailed analysis of Kretschmer's theory and its practical application has now been given in German by the Spanish lawyer and theologian Carlos Maria de Landecho, S.J., *Körperbau, Charakter und Kriminalität*, Bonn, 1964 (*Kriminologische Untersuchungen*, No. 13, editors H. von Weber and Thomas Würtenberger).

[38] See, e.g., the 21st/22nd ed. of 1955 (cited at note 19).

[39] pp. 237 ff.

[40] pp. 77 ff.

[41] See 21st/22nd ed., p. 31.

[42] *Op. cit.*, pp. 38 ff.

[43] pp. 218 ff.

[44] pp. 163, 179.

[45] See, e.g., H. T. P. Young, *J. ment. Sci.*, May 1937, p. 282.

[46] See my *Group Problems in Crime and Punishment*, pp. 78–80; Mezger, *op. cit.*, pp. 95 ff.

[47] pp. 350 ff.

[48] Mezger, *op. cit.*, p. 103.

[49] On the work of these boards see Mezger, *op. cit.*, pp. 111 ff.; Ernst Seelig, *Kriminologie*, Graz, 1951, pp. 276 ff.

[50] See *Kriminalbiologische Gegenwartsfragen*, No. 2, 1955; No. 4, 1960, Stuttgart, with several important contributions.

[51] Such criticisms were expressed early by Rudolf Sieverts, *Mschr. Kriminalpsychologie u, Strafrechtsreform*, Vol. 23, 1932, pp. 588 ff. Mezger's reply, *op. cit.*, pp. 128 ff., is hardly convincing.

[52] See note 6 above. A popular edition was simultaneously published under the title *Crime and the Man*, Cambridge, Mass., 1939.

[53] A good summary is given by Richard M. Snodgrasse, *J. crim. Law Criminol. Police Sci.*, Vol. 42, No. 1, May–June 1951, pp. 20 ff. See also my review in the *Law Quart.*, July 1941, Vol. 57, pp. 435 ff. A rather inconclusive attempt to apply Sheldon's somatotypes to a group of hospital patients was made by Leopold Ballak and Robert R. Holt, *Amer. J. Psychiat.*, Vol. 104, No. 11, May 1948, pp. 713 ff.

[54] New York, 1949.

[55] Kretschmer, *op. cit.*, 21st/22nd ed., pp. 19 ff., 242.

[56] On this see the summary by Snodgrasse (cited at note 53), pp. 29 ff.

[57] Edwin H. Sutherland, *Amer. Sociol. Rev.*, Vol. 18, 1951, pp. 142 ff., reproduced in *The Sutherland Papers*, 1956, pp. 279 ff.

[58] Sheldon, *Varieties of Delinquent Youth*, p. 752. F. D. Klingender, 'A Victorian Rogues' Gallery', in *Pilot Papers*, ed. by Charles Madge, Vol. 1, No. 1, Jan. 1946, pp. 55 ff., reproduces a large number of photographs taken by Mr. William Garbutt, a former deputy governor of Derby Gaol in the middle of the last century.

[59] *Unraveling*, p. 55, and Ch. 15.

[60] Sheldon and Eleanor Glueck, *Physique and Delinquency*, New York, 1956. See my review in *Int. J. soc. Psychiat.*, Vol. 3, pp. 72–5, from which some of the following text is taken and to which reference may be made.

CHAPTER 14

[1] On this see Barbara Wootton, *Social Science and Social Pathology*, London, 1959, Ch. 7.

[2] The existing chaos has been described in detail by Michael Hakeem, 'A Critique of the Psychiatric Approach to Crime and Correction', in *Crime and Correction, Law and Contemporary Problems*, Vol. 23, No. 4, Autumn 1958, pp. 650 ff.

[3] May 1957, Cmd. 169, pp. 24–7, 46 ff., where the complicated historical development is described.

[4] *Report of Royal Commission on the Law relating to Mental Illness and Mental Deficiency*, 1954–7, p. 25.

[5] See, e.g., Edward Mapother and Aubrey Lewis, 'Psychological Medicine' in F. W. Price, *Textbook of the Practice of Medicine*, 5th ed., London, 1937, pp. 1798 ff.; also David Stafford-Clark, *Psychiatry Today*, Harmondsworth, 1952, pp. 82 ff. Sir D. K. Henderson and R. D. Gillespie, *A Textbook of Psychiatry*, 8th ed., London, 1960, pp. 20 ff., reproduce the British and American and also their own systems of classification. East and de Hubert, *Psychological Treatment of Crime*, H.M.S.O., 1939, pp. 5–6, use the scheme of the Prison Commission.

[6] On the criminological issues involved see W. Norwood East, *Introduction to Forensic Psychiatry in the Criminal Courts*, London, 1927; the same, *Medical Aspects of Crime*, London, 1939; the same, *Society and the Criminal*, H.M.S.O., London, 1949; Friedrich Leppmann, *Forensische Psychiatrie*, and Hans Gruhle, 'Geisteskranke Verbrecher und verbrecherische Geisteskranke', *Handwörterbuch der Kriminologie*, Vol. 1, 1932, pp. 456 ff., 559 ff.

[7] Angus MacNiven in *Mental Abnormality and Crime*, London, 1944, pp. 40 ff.

[8] Leppmann, *op. cit.*, p. 462, and the case briefly reported in my *Group Problems*, pp. 293–4.

[9] Henderson–Gillespie, *op. cit.*, p. 527.

[10] *Mschr. Kriminalbiologie*, 1939, pp. 89 ff.

[11] See Cyril Burt, *The Young Delinquent*, pp. 269 ff.; Mapother and Lewis, *op. cit.*, pp. 1826 ff.; F. C. Shrubsall, *J. med. Psychol.*, Vol. 7, 1927, pp. 210 ff.; Lionel Penrose, *Mental Defect*, pp. 116, 177.

[12] See the case described by East and de Hubert (*op. cit.* at note 5), p. 118, No. 60.

[13] Mapother and Lewis, *op. cit.*, pp. 1819 ff.; East, *Introduction to Forensic Psychiatry*, pp. 217 ff.

[14] East, *Crime, Senescence and Senility*, in *Society and the Criminal*, p. 65.

[15] Mapother and Lewis, *op. cit.*, p. 1820.

[16] *The Times*, 3.9.1938.

[17] J. C. M. Matheson, *Medico-legal Rev.*, Vol. 9, Part 3, July 1941; W. S. Craig and Beaton, *Psychological Medicine*, 4th ed., 1926, p. 232.

[18] See D. Seaborne Davies in *The Modern Approach to Criminal Law*, London, 1945, Ch. 17.

[19] Of the very extensive literature the following may be quoted: A. M. Lorentz de Haas, 'Epilepsy and Criminality', *Brit. J. Crim.*, Vol. 3, No. 3, Jan. 1963, pp. 248–56; Cyril Burt, *op. cit.*, pp. 269 ff.; MacNiven (*op. cit.* at note 7), p. 46 ff.; East, *Introduction*, pp. 282, 299; Tylor Fox in R. G. Gordon (ed.), *Survey of Child Psychiatry*, London, 1939, pp. 10, 48 ff.; D. K. Henderson, *Psychopathic States*, New York, 1939, pp. 71 ff.; Matheson and Hill, *Medico-legal Rev.*, Oct.–Dec. 1943, pp. 173 ff.

[20] Wolfgang, in *Pioneers*, pp. 188–9.

[21] See, e.g., East, *The Adolescent Criminal*, pp. 229 ff.; MacNiven, *op. cit.*, p. 48; Burt, *op. cit.*, pp. 268–9, who found only 1 per cent of his cases suffering from *grand mal* and another 3 per cent as being suspected epileptics. In 1946, out of a total prison population of nearly 15,000, only 62 were considered by the medical officers to be undoubted epileptics; see *Report of Prison Commissioners for 1946*, pp. 66–7, where post-war changes in the treatment of epileptic prisoners are also described. Gibbens and Prince, *Shoplifting*, 1962, p. 64, found only 3 cases of epileptics in their sample, and there was no connection between the offence and a fit.

[22] Report of 1953, p. 134, fn. 3; Denis Hill, *Minutes of Evidence*, No. 13, pp. 297 ff.

[23] *Medico-legal Rev.*, 1943, pp. 173 ff.

[24] See esp. de Haas, *op. cit.*, p. 255.

[25] Fox, *op. cit.*, note 19, p. 52.

[26] East, *Introduction*, pp. 281–2; Fox, *op. cit.*, p. 48.

[27] *The Times*, 15.12.1961.

[28] A. Brousseau, 'L'Etat dangereux dans les Epilepsies', in *Le Problème de l'Etat dangereux*, Deuxième Cours International de Criminologie, organisé par la Société Internationale de Criminologie, Paris, 1953, pp. 206 ff.

[29] See Glanville Williams in *Essays in Crimina Science*, ed. by G. O. W.

Mueller, Ch. 12, and in *Criminal Law, General Part*, 2nd ed., 1961, § 156. Also Rupert Cross, *The Listener*, 7.12.1961, p. 967.

[30] On hypoglycaemia see W. Lindesay Neustatter, *Psychological Disorder and Crime*, London, 1953, pp. 169, 192–4; Glanville Williams in *Essays*, p. 352, and *General Part*, § 157; David Abrahamsen, *Psychology of Crime*, p. 219; T. C. N. Gibbens and Joyce Prince, *op. cit.*, p. 77; Brian A. O'Connell, 'Amnesia and Homicide', *Brit. J. Delinq.*, Vol. 10, No. 7, April 1960, pp. 269–70; Sanford J. Fox, 'Delinquency and Biology', *Univ. Miami Law Rev.*, Vol. 16, 1961, pp. 65 ff.

[31] Mapother and Lewis, *op. cit.*, pp. 1833–5; MacNiven, *op. cit.*, p. 43.

[32] Edwin M. Schur, *J. crim. Law Criminol. Police Sci.*, Vol. 51, No. 6, 1961, p. 623. On American law and practice see M. Ploscowe in *Essays in Criminal Science*, ed. by G. O. W. Mueller, London–South Hackensack, N.J., 1961, Ch. 13.

[33] The literature is very large. The following may be mentioned: W. Norwood East, *Society and the Criminal*, Ch. 18; G. M. Scott in *Mental Abnormality and Crime*, Ch. 8; Mapother and Lewis, *op. cit.*, pp. 1830 ff.; on the social aspects Veli Verkkö, *Homicides and Suicides in Finland and their Dependence on National Character*, Copenhagen, 1951, esp. Chs. 8 to 10; Hermann Mannheim, *Social Aspects of Crime in England*, London, 1940, Ch. 6; Exner, *Kriminologie*, 3rd ed., pp. 197 ff.; Donald R. Taft, *Criminology*, 3rd ed., New York, 1956, Ch. 16. On the drink problem in general see Marshall B. Clinard, *The Sociology of Deviant Behavior*, 1957, Ch. 11; Mabel A. Elliott and Francis E. Merrill, *Social Disorganization*, 4th ed., New York, 1961, Ch. 7; Howard Jones, *Alcoholic Addiction*, London, 1943, with extensive bibliog.

[34] See Table XXVII in *Social Aspects*, p. 165.

[35] *Social Problems of Post War Youth*, London, Economic Research Council, Jan. 1956, p. 11.

[36] See my *Social Aspects of Crime*, pp. 169 ff.; *New Survey of London Life and Labour*, Vol. 9, London, 1935, Ch. 9. In 1960, the number of persons prosecuted for drunkenness offences in Liverpool was still more than twice as much as that in Manchester with its larger population.

[37] On this see *Social Aspects*, pp. 175 ff.; Veli Verkkö, *op. cit.*; Marvin E. Wolfgang, *Patterns in Criminal Homicide*, 1958, Ch. 8.

[38] See, e.g., note 6 in *Criminal Statistics for 1959*, p. vii.

[39] A diagram in *Handwörterbuch der Kriminologie*, Vol. 2, 1936, p. 1108, shows the parallel movements of beer consumption and certain crimes of violence in Germany between 1882 and 1931. Such parallel movements have, however, not been found everywhere; for Greece, e.g., the parallelism has been disputed by Gardikas, *Mschr. Kriminologie*, 1935, p. 465.

[40] See the *Observer* of 6.10.1959, referring to a report by the Medical Research Council on the effect of small doses of alcohol on driving.

[41] *The Times* of 7.10.1959.

[42] See an article 'Drinking and Driving' in *The Magistrate* of Nov. 1957, where the view is expressed that 'there is an alcoholic factor in about 40,000 annual road accidents and in 50 per cent of accidents occurring after 10 p.m.'

[43] Marvin E. Wolfgang, *Patterns in Criminal Homicide*, Ch. 8.

[44] See, e.g., Hans v. Hentig, *The Criminal and his Victim*, pp. 156 ff., 412; Margery Fry *et al.*, *Howard J.*, 1938, p. 14; Clifford Shaw, *The Jack-Roller*. Also see below, Ch. 25: Victimology.

[45] M. M. Glatt, *Brit. J. Delinq.*, Vol. 9, No. 2, Oct. 1958, pp. 84 ff.

[46] Veli Verkkö, *op. cit.*, pp. 83, 87 ff.

[47] Burt, *op. cit.*, p. 99. See also the Gluecks, *Unraveling*, pp. 95, 98, 110; Glatt, *op. cit.*, pp. 88 ff.

[48] Dr. H. T. P. Young, *Brit. J. Inebriety*, Vol. 35, Jan. 1938, pp. 93 ff.

[49] East, *The Adolescent Criminal*, pp. 55 ff.

[50] E.g., George Godwin, *Peter Kürten*, London, 1938, p. 26.

[51] Howard Jones in *New Society*, No. 25, 21.3.1963, p. 16.

[52] See Scott, *op. cit.*, p. 168; East, *Introduction to Forensic Psychiatry*; Mapother and Lewis, *op. cit.*, p. 1830. Also the case reported in *Group Problems*, pp. 293–4.

[53] Scott, *op. cit.*, p. 170; Mapother and Lewis, *op. cit.*, p. 1830; East, *op. cit.*, p. 260.

[54] Mapother and Lewis, *op. cit.*, p. 1869; MacNiven, *op. cit.*, pp. 26 ff.; K. O. Milner, *J. ment. Sci.*, Vol. 95, No. 398, Jan. 1949, pp. 124–32; Henderson and Gillespie, *op. cit.*, Ch. 11; East, *Introduction*, pp. 193 ff.

[55] See Johannes Lange, *Lehrbuch der Psychiatrie*, 2nd ed., Leipzig, 1936, p. 228.

[56] Milner, *loc. cit.*; also MacNiven, *op. cit.*, p. 27.

[57] Illustrative cases are given by East, *op. cit.*

[58] On morbid jealousy see the valuable discussion, with many case histories, by Michael Shepherd, *J. Ment. Sci.*, Vol. 107, No. 449, July 1961, pp. 687 ff.

[59] East, *op. cit.*, p. 193; MacNiven, *op. cit.*, p. 34, Henderson–Gillespie, *op. cit.*, p. 345, regard the term paraphrenia as useless.

[60] Mapother and Lewis, *op. cit.*, pp. 1844 ff.; MacNiven, *op. cit.* pp. 9 ff.; East, *Introduction*, pp. 315 ff.; East and de Hubert, *Report on the Psychological Treatment of Crime* (cited at note 5), p. 30; Stafford-Clark, *op. cit.*, pp. 97 ff.

[61] See the list in East, *op. cit.*, p. 317.

[62] *The Times* of 11.2.1941.

[63] Mapother and Lewis, *op. cit.*, p. 1845; Stafford-Clark, *op. cit.*, p. 98. See also Chapter 26 below, text to note 41.

[64] *The Times* of 15.12.1937. See also the case described by MacNiven, *op. cit.*, p. 17.

[65] G. M. Woddis, 'Depression and Crime', *Brit. J. Delinq.*, Vol. 8, No. 2, Oct. 1957, pp. 85–94.

[66] *Ibid.*, 'Clinical Psychiatry and Crime', *Brit. J. Crim.*, Vol. 4, No. 5, July 1964, pp. 443–60.

[67] The literature of schizophrenia is immense. See McNiven, *op. cit.*, pp. 18 ff.; Mapother and Lewis, *op. cit.*, pp. 1856 ff.; Stafford-Clark, *op. cit.*, pp. 56, 100 ff.; Lange, *op. cit.*, pp. 164 ff.; Edward S. Stern, 'The Aetiology and Mechanism of Dementia Praecox', *Brit. J. med. Psychol.*, Vol. 19, Part 1, 1941; East, *Introduction*, pp. 164 ff.; H. Warren Dunham, *Amer. Sociol. Rev.*, Vol. 4, 1939, pp. 352 ff.; several articles in *J. ment. Sci.*, Vol. 80, Jan. 1935; Gregory Zilboorg, *Amer. J. Psychiat.*, Vol. 113, No. 6, pp. 519 ff.; R. O. Laing, *Int. J. soc. Psychiat.*, Summer 1964, pp. 184–93; Don D. Jackson (ed.), *The Etiology of Schizophrenia*, New York, 1962.

[68] In a broadcast of 1958 the late Prof. Alexander Kennedy stated that 'of the 150,000 patients in the mental hospitals of this country at the moment more than three-quarters are schizophrenics of one kind or another'; *The Listener*, 13.2.1958, p. 277: 'The Unsolved Problem of Schizophrenia'.

[69] On Bleuler see, e.g., Gregory Zilboorg and G. W. Henry, *History of Medical Psychology*, New York, 1941, pp. 501–2.

[70] Kennedy, too, giving the history of two identical twins, stresses the hereditary side, but also the possibility of treatment in certain cases.

[71] Mapother and Lewis, *op. cit.*, p. 1859.

[72] *Ibid.*, p. 1861.

[73] *The Times* of 7.4 and 8.4.1938.

[74] *Ibid.*, 5.11.1943.

[75] Brian A. O'Connell, 'Amnesia and Homicide' (cited at note 30 above where other literature on hypoglycaemia is also quoted).

[76] Literature on Drug Addiction: Alfred R. Lindesmith, *Opiate Addiction*, Bloomington, 1952; Edwin M. Schur, *Narcotic Addiction in Britain and America*, Bloomington-London, 1964; the same, 'British Narcotics Policies', *J. crim. Law Criminol. Police Sci.*, Vol. 51, No. 6, March–April 1961, pp. 619–29; Morris Ploscowe, 'Methods of Treatment of Drug Addiction', in *Essays in Criminal Science*, ed. by Gerhard O. W. Mueller, London–South Hackensack, 1961; Fritz A. Freyhan (ed.), *Drug Addiction, A Symposium*, New York, 1963; David Sternberg, 'Synanon House', *J. crim. Law Criminol. Police Sci.*, Vol. 54, No. 4, Dec. 1963; Walter C. Reckless, *The Crime Problem*, 2nd ed., Ch. 16; Herbert A. Bloch and Gilbert Geis, *Man, Crime and Society*, New York, 1962, pp. 236–40, 355–61; Richard A. Cloward and Lloyd E. Ohlin, *Delinquency and Opportunity*, London, 1961, pp. 25–7, 89, 178–86; Isidor Chein *et al.*, *Narcotics, Delinquency and Social Policy*, London, 1964, published in the U.S.A. as *The Road to H*.

[77] Lord Denning's Report, H.M.S.O., London, 1963, pp. 8, 19.

[78] G. E. Voegele and H. J. Dietze, 'Addiction to Gasoline Smelling in Juvenile Delinquents', *Brit. J. Crim.*, Vol. 4, No. 1, July 1963, pp. 43–60.

[79] See, e.g., *The Times*, 31.3., 1.4., 20.4., and 1.5.1964. One London doctor stated at an inquest that in the past year she had treated 70 Canadian drug addicts, some of whom had come to Britain mainly to get drugs, some of which they sold on the black market. On prescription the cost was about 15s. per 100, whereas on the black market it was £1 for four to six pills.

CHAPTER 15

[1] Aubrey Lewis writes (*The Lancet*, 15.8.1942, pp. 175 ff.): 'The common distinction between neurosis and insanity is at bottom so arbitrary and vague, except for legal and administrative purposes, that many cases fall equally well into either category.'

[2] See, e.g., Stafford-Clark, *Psychiatry Today*, p. 92; Freud, *Collected Papers*, Vol. 2, pp. 250 ff., 277 ff., Vol. 5, pp. 202–3; John Bowlby, *Personality and Mental Illness*, London, 1940, pp. 127 ff.

[3] Edward Glover, *Psycho-analysis*, 2nd ed., London, 1949, p. 130.

[4] *Op. cit.*, p. 173.

[5] Russell Fraser, *The Incidence of Neurosis among Factory Workers*, H.M.S.O., London, 1947, p. 4.

[6] *Op. cit.*, p. 6.

[7] Edward Glover, *The Roots of Crime*, London, 1960, pp. 90–1.

[8] W. F. Roper, *Brit. J. Delinq.*, Vol. I, p. 23.

[9] For other explanations of the 'choice' see Friedländer (*op. cit.* below at note 12), p. 116.

[10] David Abrahamsen, *The Psychology of Crime*, New York, 1960, p. 127.

[11] Healy and Bronner, *New Light on Delinquency*, 1936, p. 194.

[12] See, e.g., Freud, *Collected Papers*, Vol. 5, p. 84, and often; Käte Friedländer, *The Psychoanalytical Approach to Juvenile Delinquency*, London, 1947, pp. 116 ff.

[13] Glover, *Psychoanalysis*, p. 147.

[14] Glover, *The Roots of Crime*, p. 302.

[15] Friedländer, *op. cit.*, p. 223.

[16] Franz Alexander and Hugo Staub, *Der Verbrecher und seine Richter*, Vienna, 1929, pp. 68–9 (Eng. ed., *The Criminal, The Judge, and The Public*, London, 1931); critical E. Glover, *The Roots of Crime*, p. 135.

[17] Some of the cases referred to by Melitta Schmideberg, *Brit. J. Delinq.*, Vol. 4, No. 4, April 1954, pp. 272 ff., are probably neurotics.

[18] Gillespie and MacCalman in *Mental Abnormality and Crime*, pp. 73, 127; Stafford-Clark, *op. cit.*, pp. 93 ff.; Mapother and Lewis, *op. cit.*, pp. 1878–9; Norwood East, *Society and the Criminal*, p. 232; Glover, *Psycho-Analysis*, pp. 47, 149 ff., and *passim*.

[19] Gillespie, *op. cit.*, p. 74; Mapother and Lewis, *op. cit.*, pp. 1870 ff.; Stafford-Clark, *op. cit.*, pp. 113 ff.; Glover, *Psycho-Analysis*, pp. 140 ff.

[20] East in *Mental Abnormality and Crime*, p. 189.

[21] Stafford-Clark, *op. cit.*, 110 ff.; Mapother and Lewis, *op. cit.*, pp. 1879 ff.; Glover, *The Roots of Crime*, pp. 184 ff.; Glover, *Psycho-Analysis*, pp. 157 ff.

[22] Melitta Schmideberg, *Brit. J. Delinq.*, Vol. 7, No. 1, July 1956, pp. 44 ff. Also Glover, *Psycho-Analysis*, p. 254.

[23] Mapother and Lewis, *op. cit.*, p. 1882. Friedländer, *op. cit.*, p. 161, also admits the possibility of a combination of perversion and neurosis.

[24] See David T. Maclay, *Brit. J. Delinq.*, Vol. 3, No. 1, July 1952, p. 34 ff.; Glover, *Roots of Crime*, p. 387.

[25] *Report on The Psychological Treatment of Crime*, 1939, p. 108.

[26] John Bowlby, *Personality and Mental Illness*, p. 4.

[27] T. C. N. Gibbens, *Theft from Department Stores*, General Report to the Fourth International Criminological Congress, The Hague, 1960, and more detailed the same in *Shoplifting* by Gibbens and Joyce Prince, an I.S.T.D. Publication, London, 1962. For a valuable German discussion of the subject see Werner F. J. Krause, 'Ladendiebstahl und Zurechnungsfähigkeit' (Shoplifting and Responsibility), *Mschr. Kriminol. Strafrechtsreform*, Vol. 46, No. 2, April 1963, pp. 49–73. For Belgium Chr. Debuyst, G. Lejour, and A. Racine, *Petits voleurs de grands magasins*, Bruxelles, Centre d'Etude de la délinquance juvenile, 1960. On kleptomania in the case of children, Cyril Burt, *The Young Delinquent*, pp. 585 ff.

[28] Emanuel Miller, *Brit. J. Delinq.*, Vol. 10, No. 3, 1960, p. 170.

[29] *Psycho-Analysis*, pp. 163, 275. Abrahamsen (*op. cit.* above at note 10) regards the kleptomaniac and pyromaniac as prototypes of the obsessive-compulsive offender. W. Lindesay Neustatter, *Psychological Disorder and Crime*, London, 1953, p. 48, doubts whether kleptomania is an obsessive-compulsive state as the clear-cut repetitiveness of thought and action characteristic of it is, he thinks, absent.

[30] Helen Yarnell, *Amer. J. Orthopsychiat.*, April 1940, pp. 272 ff.; Ernst Seelig, *Kriminologie*, pp. 106–7.

[31] J. Clarke, *Brit. J. Crim.*, Vol. 3, No. 2, Oct. 1962, p. 156.

[32] *The Times*, 27.6.1939.

[33] Melitta Schmideberg, 'Pathological Firesetters', *J. crim. Law Criminol. Police Sci.*, Vol. 44, No. 1, May–June, 1953, pp. 30 ff.

[34] Heinrich Többen, *Beiträge zur Psychologie und Psychopathologie der Brandstifter*, Berlin, 1917, pp. 54, 85 ff.

[35] *The Times*, 16.3.1962.

[36] Roper, *Brit. J. Delinq.*, Vol. 1, No. 4, April, 1951, p. 261.

[37] The following is a selection from an enormous literature (most of the publications included here contain full bibliographies): D. K. Henderson, *Psychopathic States*, New York, 1939; H. Cleckley, *The Mask of Sanity*, St. Louis, 1941; *Brit. J. Delinq.*, Vol. 2, No. 2, October 1951 (Special Number): 'Papers on Psychopathy'; Edward Glover, *The Roots of Crime*, Section 4; Norwood East, *Society and The Criminal*, Chs. 8, 14; Michael Craft, *Brit. J. Crim.*, Vol. I, No. 3, Jan. 1961, pp. 237 ff.; Abrahamsen (*op. cit.* above at note 10), pp. 134 ff.; C. M. Franks, *Brit. J. Delinq.*, Vol. 6, No. 3, Jan. 1956, pp. 192 ff.; D. K. Henderson in *Mental*

Abnormality and Crime, Ch. 5; Barbara Wootton, *Social Science and Social Pathology*, Ch. 8; William and Joan McCord, *Psychopathy and Delinquency*, New York–London, 1951; *Report of the Royal Commission on Capital Punishment*, 1953, pp. 135 ff.; Peter Scott, *Howard J.*, Vol. 10, No. 1, 1958, pp. 6 ff.; Seymour Parker, *Brit. J. Delinq.*, Vol. 7, No. 4, April 1957, pp. 285–300.

[38] Milton Gurwitz in 'Papers on Psychopathy' (see note 37), p. 88, where a historical survey of developments since 1900 is given.

[39] See, Glover, *op. cit.*, p. 120; Sir David Henderson, *Brit. J. Delinq.*, Vol. 6, No. 1, July 1955, pp. 5 ff.; East, *op. cit.*, p. 128.

[40] Winfred Overholser, in *Pioneers in Criminology*, p. 120.

[41] A short survey of the most important classifications is given by Gurwitz, *loc. cit.*

[42] Schneider's famous book, *Die psychopathischen Persönlichkeiten*, which has gone through many editions, has only very belatedly been translated into English: *Psychopathic Personalities*, London, 1958, which may account for its neglect in this country. On Schneider's typology much of Erwin Frey's *Der Frühkriminelle Rückfallsverbrecher*, Basel, 1951, is based; see esp. pp. 116 ff., also my *Group Problems*, p. 143, Exner, *Kriminologie*, 3rd ed., pp. 185 ff., and Mezger and Leferenz in *Kriminalbiologische Gegenwartsfragen*, Heft 2, Stuttgart, 1955, pp. 6–7, 13 ff.

[43] See Mezger, *loc. cit.*, Exner, *op. cit.*, and Gurwitz, *loc. cit.*, p. 91.

[44] Leferenz, *loc. cit.*, p. 16.

[45] *The Roots of Crime*, pp. 122–3.

[46] Michael Craft (*loc. cit.* above at note 37). See also the description given by witnesses to the Royal Commission in the *Report on Mental Illness and Mental Deficiency*, 1954–7, pp. 52 ff.

[47] C. M. Franks, *Brit. J. Delinq.*, Vol. 6, No. 3., Jan. 1956, p. 192 ff.

[48] Wootton (*op. cit.* at note 37), p. 250.

[49] D. Stafford-Clark, Desmond Pond, and J. W. Lovett Doust, *Brit. J. Delinq.*, Vol. 2, No. 2, 'Papers on Psychopathy', pp. 117 ff.

[50] *loc. cit.*, p. 126.

[51] This part of the investigation has been criticized by William and Joan McCord (*op. cit.* above at note 37), p. 46, on the ground that the selection of prisoners had been made on the basis of Henderson's definition which includes lack of responsiveness to treatment, but they admit that this was not the only important result of the research.

[52] In other studies attention is drawn to the close relationship between the aggressive psychopath and epilepsy, which is also a feature independent of anti-social conduct. See, e.g., the references given by Wheelan, *Brit. J. Delinq.*, Vol. 2, No. 2, p. 141.

[53] See the English translation, Copenhagen, 1958.

[54] Georg Stürup, 'Treatment of Criminal Psychopaths', *Acta psychiat. neurol.*, 1948, pp. 21 ff.

[55] Max Grünhut, *Probation and Mental Treatment*, London, 1963, p. 24.

[56] See Stürup, *loc. cit.* and in *Acta Psychiat. neurol.*, 1946, pp. 781 ff.

[57] See my *Group Problems*, p. 205 ff., with further references.

[58] See Boslow *et al.*, *Brit. J. Delinq.*, Vol. 10, No. 1, July 1959, pp. 5 ff., and the Editorial, p. 1. See, e.g., the survey of literature in William and Joan McCord, *op. cit.*, Ch. 4.

[59] Johannes Lange, *Kurzgefasstes Lehrbuch der Psychiatrie*, 2nd ed., Leipzig, 1936, p. 210 (my translation).

[60] Craft (*loc. cit.* above at note 37), pp. 243–4

[61] Report 1957, p. 57.

[62] *The Roots of Crime*, pp. 148 ff.

[63] On some of the institutions see T. C. N. Gibbens, 'Papers on Psychopathy' (see note 37), pp. 103 ff.; W. J. Gray, *Howard J.*, Vol. 10, No. 2, 1959, pp. 96 ff.

[64] H. J. Eysenck, 'Learning Theory and Behaviour Therapy', *J. ment. Sci.*, Vol. 105, No. 438, Jan. 1959, pp. 61 ff. and elsewhere.

[65] Eysenck, *loc. cit.*, p. 64; Glover, *op. cit.*, p. 161; André Repond in *Die Prophylaxe des Verbrechens*, ed. by Heinrich Meng, Basel, 1948, p. 2. Repond presents a particularly interesting collection of cases of young thieves and swindlers, many of them psychopaths, and shows how, in addition to the usual characteristics of the criminal psychopath, their behaviour had to be explained as a reaction to their domineering fathers and as an inheritance of traits which were also present in the latter, but had there been sublimated and adapted to the requirements of society. See also p. 321.

[66] T. C. N. Gibbens, D. A. Pond and D. Stafford-Clark, *J. ment. Sci.*, Vol. 105, No. 438, Jan. 1959, pp. 108 ff.

[67] P. de Berker, *Brit. J. Crim.*, Vol. 1, No. 1, July, 1960, pp. 6 ff.

[68] In the *Report of the Prison Commissioners for 1956*, p. 166, the proportion of 'inadequate or ineffectual personalities' among preventive detainees is estimated at probably 80 per cent. Roper (*loc. cit.* at note 36), p. 265, regards half the population of his Wakefield prison survey as inadequate. See also the *Report of the Prison Commissioners for 1946*, p. 64.

[69] Literature on Mental Deficiency and Crime: A. F. Tredgold, *Mental Deficiency*, 5th ed. 1929, 9th ed. 1956, London; L. S. Penrose, *Mental Defect*, London, 1953; Cyril Burt, *The Subnormal Mind*, 3rd ed., London, 1955; the same, *The Young Delinquent*, Ch. 7; E. O. Lewis in *Mental Abnormality and Crime*, Ch. 4; Mary Woodward, *Low Intelligence and Crime*, London, I.S.T.D., 1955 (with bibliog.), also in *Brit. J. Delinq.*, Vol. 5, No. 4, April 1955, pp. 281 ff.; Mapother and Lewis, *op. cit.*, pp. 1839 ff.; Howard Jones, *op. cit.*, pp. 29–33; *Report of the Departmental Committee on Sterilisation*, H.M.S.O., Cmd. 4485, 1934; *Report of Royal Commission on Mental Illness and Mental Deficiency* (see above, note 46); Hilda Weber, 'The Borderline Defective Delinquent', *Brit. J. Delinq.*, Vol. 3, No. 3, Jan. 1953, pp. 173 ff.; B. Marcus, *ibid.*, Vol. 6, No. 2, Sept. 1955, pp. 147 ff.; John E. Tong and G. W. Mackay, *ibid.*, Vol. 9, No. 4, April 1959, pp. 276 ff.; Eirk Goldkuhl, *Psychische Insuffizienzzustände bei Oligophrenien leichteren Grades*, Copenhagen, 1938; of the large amount of American literature only the following can here be mentioned: H. H. Goddard, *Feeble-mindedness: its Causes and Consequences*, New York, 1914; Carl Murchison, *Criminal Intelligence*, Worcester, Mass., 1926; S. H. Tulchin, *Intelligence and Crime*, Chicago, 1939; E. H. Sutherland, in *Social Attitudes*, ed. by Kimball Young, New York, 1931, reprinted in *The Sutherland Papers*, Bloomington, 1956, pp. 308 ff.

[70] Burt, *The Subnormal Mind*, p. 63; Penrose, *op. cit.*, p. 8; on these historical developments, esp. Report of Royal Commission 1957, pp. 44–6.

[71] See Fink, *Causes of Crime*, p. 211.

[72] Burt, *The Subnormal Mind*, p. 79. See also *Report on Sterilisation*, Ch. 2.

[73] Report of the Royal Commission 1957, p. 60.

[74] See *Pioneers in Criminology*, pp. 119, 149, 187; Burt, *The Young Delinquent*, pp. 35 ff.; *The Subnormal Mind*, p. 68.

[75] 1st ed., London, 1922, pp. 153 ff.

[76] See, e.g., Morris Ginsberg, *On the Diversity of Morals*, London, 1956, Ch. 7 and *passim*; *Reason and Unreason in Society*, 1947, pp. 18 ff.; J. C. Flugel, *Man, Morals and Society*, London, 1945, pp. 200–1; Burt, *The Subnormal Mind*, p. 69.

[77] E. O. Lewis in *Mental Abnormality and Crime*, p. 98.

[78] *Unraveling Juvenile Delinquency*, p. 14.

[79] Apart from the well-known textbooks of psychology and the books by Burt quoted above, see H. J. Eysenck's *Uses and Abuses of Psychology*, Harmondsworth, 1953, and *Sense and Nonsense in Psychology*, Harmondsworth, 1957; D. R. Price-Williams, *Introductory Psychology*, London, 1958, Ch. 6, and in particular Cyril Burt, *Intelligence and Fertility*, London, 1946, appendix on the Meaning of Intelligence.

[80] Slightly different, E. O. Lewis, *loc. cit.*, p. 98.

[81] Burt, *The Subnormal Mind*, p. 179.

[82] Mapother and Lewis, *op. cit.*, p. 1842.

[83] Burt, *op. cit.*, p. 119.

[84] On the history in U.S.A. and on other American studies see Arthur E. Fink, *Causes of Crime*, Ch. 10.

[85] Charles Goring, *The English Convict*, London, 1919, pp. 179, 184, 247.

[86] Cmd. 169, p. 310.

[87] Burt, *The Young Delinquent*, p. 300.

[88] East, *The Adolescent Criminal*, p. 234.

[89] Grace W. Pailthorpe, *Studies in the Psychology of Delinquency*, H.M.S.O., London, 1932, p. 16; Woodward, *loc. cit.*

[90] Sutherland (*op. cit.* at note 69), p. 309.

[91] William and Joan McCord, *Origins of Crime*, 1959, pp. 64–6.

[92] Woodward, *Brit. J. Delinq.*, pp. 285–6 (see above, note 69).

[93] *Ibid.*, pp. 287 ff.

[94] Morris Ginsberg, *Studies in Sociology.*, London 1932, p. 148.

[95] Murchison (*op. cit.* at note 69).

[96] Mannheim and Wilkins, *Prediction Methods in relation to Borstal Training*, pp. 81, 98–9.

[97] *The English Convict*, pp. 256–7.

[98] See also Sutherland, *loc. cit.*, p. 324. In the Cambridge Survey of sex offenders, only 3 in 100 of those convicted were mentally defective; *Sexual Offences, English Studies in Criminal Science*, London, 1957, p. 128.

[99] Cyril Burt, *The Young Delinquent*, p. 321.

[100] *Annual Report of the Mental Hospitals Association for 1945.*

[101] K. O. Milner, 'Delinquent Types of Mentally Defective Persons', *J. ment. Sci.*, Vol. 95, No. 401, Oct. 1949, pp. 842 ff.

[102] T. Ferguson, *The Young Delinquent in his Social Setting*, London, 1952, Chs. 4, 6.

[103] Mary Woodward (*loc. cit.* at note 69), under 'Summary and Conclusions'.

[104] Hilda Weber (*loc. cit.* at note 69), p. 174.

[105] See, e.g., the Borstal case in my *Social Aspects of Crime*, p. 316, No. 102.

[106] See the case in Weber, *loc. cit.*, p. 177. She also presents several other cases to show the special importance of sympathetic handling for borderline defectives.

[107] See Berry in R. G. Gordon (ed.), *Survey of Child Psychiatry*, London, 1939, pp. 100 ff.

[108] Glover, *Roots of Crime*, p. 252.

[109] See Lewis M. Terman, *Psychological Approaches to the Biography of Genius*, London, 1947, p. 4, where he criticizes certain studies inspired by Galton as 'stereotyped along statistical lines'. See, moreover, Wolfgang in *Pioneers in Criminology*, p. 198, on Lombroso's *L'Uomo di genio* and W. Lange-Eichbaum, *The Problem of Genius*, translated from the German by Eden and Cedar Paul, London, 1931.

[110] *Op. cit.*, p. x.

[111] Ernst Kretschmer, *Textbook of Medical Psychology*, Eng. trans. by E. B. Strauss, London, 1934, p. 160.

[112] Ernst Kretschmer, *Psychology of Men of Genius*, trans. by R. B. Cattell London, 1931, pp. 3 ff.

[113] *A Study of British Genius*, London, 1922.

[114] Burckhardt, *Kultur der Renaissance*, Vol. 2, Ch. 5. On Villon, see, e.g., Henry T. F. Rhodes, *Genius and Criminals*, London, 1932, pp. 65 ff. Rhodes's view that 'the genius and the criminal type are fundamentally one and the same thing' (p. 37) is clearly unjustified. Criminals, as a rule, are not creative, men of genius usually are.

[115] *The Young Delinquent*, p. 354.

[116] Leta S. Hollingworth, *Children above 180 I.Q.*, New York, 1942, pp. 254 ff.

[117] Martin Buber, *Between Man and Man*, Paperback ed., London, 1961, pp. 143 ff. (first published London, 1947).

[118] Gerald Abraham, *Tchaikovsky*, London 1944, p. 11.

CHAPTER 16

[1] W. A. Bonger, *An Introduction to Criminology*, London, 1936, Ch. 8.

[2] See the titles given by Paul Englisch in the *Handwörterbuch der Kriminologie*, Vol. 2, 1934, pp. 301 ff.

[3] London–Edinburgh–Glasgow.

[4] Driver in *Pioneers in Criminology*, p. 341.

[5] Article 'Kriminalpsychologie' in *Handwörterbuch der Kriminologie*, Vol. 1, p. 914.

[6] One of the most recent attempts in this field is David Abrahamsen, *The Psychology of Crime*, London–New York, 1961.

[7] See, e.g., Gerhard Ledig, *Philosophie der Strafe bei Dante und Dostojewski*, Weimar, 1935; Thomas Würtenberger, *Die deutsche Kriminalerzählung*, Erlangen, 1941, with bibliogr.; Hermann Mannheim, 'Rechtsgefühl und Dichtung', *Z.f. Rechtsphilosophie*, Vol. 3, 1920, pp. 251 ff.; on Victor Hugo: Paul Savey-Casard, 'Le Crime dans l'œuvre de Victor Hugo', *Études internationales de Psycho-Sociologie criminelle*, No. 3, Jan.-March, 1957, pp. 16–21; on Dickens: Philip Collins, *Dickens and Crime*, Cambridge Studies in Criminology, Vol. 17, 1962. On Dostoievsky see the literature quoted at the end of the Chapter.

[8] *Social Science and Social Pathology*, pp. 221 ff.

[9] Naturally, the term 'mental disease' and corresponding terms in other languages are commonly used in Criminal Codes, e.g., in § 51 of the German Criminal Code and §§ 24, 25 of the German Draft Code of 1960. This has been criticized, e.g., by the German psychologist Thomae on account of the impossibility of defining the concept of disease (*Krankheit*); see *Mschr. Kriminol, Strafrechtsreform*, August 1961, pp. 117 ff.

[10] Emile Durkheim, *Les règles de la methode sociologique*, 11th ed. Paris, 1950, p. viii and Chs. 3 and 4.

[11] *Op. cit.*, pp. 64 ff.

[12] *Op. cit.*, p. 75, fn. 1, and *Suicide* (Eng. trans., London, 1952), p. 363.

[13] See, however, the illuminating discussion by J. G. Peristiany in his Introduction to Durkheim's *Sociology and Philosophy*, London, 1953, pp. x, xvii ff.: 'The phenomena and the rate of their occurrence are healthy and normal when they reflect conditions of existence which are associated with the average society of this type'.

[14] Against this standard Norwood East, *Society and The Criminal*, p. 232.

[15] For Durkheim, see Peristiany, p. xx.

[16] Wootton, *op. cit.*, p. 218.

[17] The danger that social workers might too easily expect 'the whole process of

social adjustment to come from the client' has been mentioned in my lecture on 'The Unified Approach to the Administration of Criminal Justice', *Proc. Canad. Congress Correct., 1957*, p. 260.

[18] Ginsberg, *Essays in Sociology and Social Philosophy*, Vol. 1, p. 70 ff.

[19] Erich Fromm, *The Fear of Freedom*, London, 1942, p. 118.

[20] See also Emanuel Miller, *Brit. J. Delinq.*, Vol. 10, No. 3, Jan. 1960, p. 168, who refers to an 'operational standard of the normal person' and to Nietzsche's dictum 'What appears as health in one person might appear as contrary to health in another' (p. 165).

[21] Sir Maurice Craig and Thomas Beaton, *Psychological Medicine*, 4th ed., London, 1926, pp. 64-5. See also David Abrahamsen, *The Psychology of Crime*, New York, 1960, p. 209.

[22] *Unraveling Juvenile Delinquency*, p. 216.

[23] Daniel Glaser, in 'Crime and Correction', *Law and Contemporary Problems*, Vol. 23, No. 4, Autumn 1958, p. 687.

[24] On this see Arnold M. Rose, *Theory and Method in the Social Sciences*, 1954, Ch. 12.

[25] Karl F. Schuessler and Donald R. Cressey, 'Personality Characteristics of Criminals', *Amer. J. Sociol.*, Vol. 50, March 1950, pp. 476 ff.

[26] Wootton, *op. cit.*, p. 301.

[27] Marshall B. Clinard, *Sociology of Deviant Behavior*, New York, 1957, p. 206.

[28] Morris G. Caldwell, 'Personality Trends in the Youthful Male Offender', *J. crim. Law Criminol. Police Sci.*, Vol. 49, No. 5, Jan.-Feb. 1959, pp. 405 ff. with bibliog.

[29] Wootton, *op. cit.*, pp. 181, 196.

[30] Hathaway, Monachesi and Young, *J. crim. Law Criminol. Police Sci.*, Vol. 50, No. 5, Jan.-Feb. 1960, pp. 439-40.

[31] Clara Kanun and Elio D. Monachesi, in the same Journal, Vol. 50, No. 6, March-April 1960, pp. 525 ff.

[32] The L scale or score of the MMPI 'consists of a series of items indicating whether the subject falsified his score by consistently choosing responses which place him in a socially approved position', whereas big F scores 'may indicate that the subject was either careless in responding and/or did not comprehend the meaning of the items', Monachesi, *J. crim. Law Criminol. Police Sci.*, Vol. 41, No. 2, July-August 1950, p. 168.

[33] Starke R. Hathaway and Elio D. Monachesi (ed.) *Analysing and Predicting Juvenile Delinquency with the M M P I*, Minneapolis, 1953, p. 9.

[34] Walter C. Reckless in *Summ. Proc. Third Int. Congress Criminol.*, London; 1957, pp. 95-6; Marshall B. Clinard, *Sociology of Deviant Behavior*, pp. 206-7, Harrison G. Gough and Donald R. Peterson, *J. cons. Psychol.*, Vol. 16, April 1952, pp. 207 ff.

[35] H. J. Eysenck, *Sense and Nonsense in Psychology*, Ch. 5, esp. pp. 218 ff.

[36] Tadeusz Grygier, *Oppression*, London, 1954 (with extensive bibliog.).

[37] Grygier, *op. cit.*, pp. 48, 52 ff.

[38] *Ibid.*, p. 189, quoting H. A. Murray, *Thematic-Apperception Test Manual*, Cambridge, Mass., 1943.

[39] *Op. cit.*, p. 207.

[40] The term 'Press' (in T.A.T. literature) 'designates a directional tendency in an object . . . or situation which is perceived as able to harm or benefit the subject', Grygier, pp. 79-80. It usually implies the existence of a hero, p. 81.

[41] See *Pioneers in Criminology*: Peter Scott, p. 152, on Maudsley, and Wolfgang, p. 187, on Lombroso.

[42] *Unraveling Juvenile Delinquency*, Ch. 18 with Summary, p. 240.

[43] *Ibid.*, Ch. 19 with Summary, p. 251.

[44] *Ibid.*, pp. 221–2, 275.

[45] *Physique and Delinquency*, New York, 1956, p. 269.

[46] See, e.g., Grygier, *op. cit.*, pp. 12–13, on the one hand, and *Unraveling*, p. 275, on the other.

[47] B. Marcus, 'A Dimensional Study of a Prison Population', *Brit. J. Crim.*, Vol. 1, No. 2, Oct. 1960, pp. 130 ff.

[48] London, 1962.

[49] See my review in the *Int. J. soc. Psychiat.*, Vol. 8, No. 4, Autumn 1962, pp. 309–11.

[50] G. W. Allport, *Personality*, New York, 1937; see also D. R. Price-Williams, *Introductory Psychology*, London, 1958, p. 149.

[51] H. J. Eysenck, *The Structure of Human Personality*, London–New York, 1953, p. 2.

[52] Raymond Cattell, *An Introduction to Personality Study*, London, 1950, pp. 21, 222.

[53] See in particular § 211 of the West German Penal Code as amended in 1941 where 'murderous lust, satisfaction of sexual lust, greed or other mean motives' are enumerated as criteria of murder (similarly § 135 of the West German Draft Code of 1960). In the English Homicide Act, 1957, certain motives such as the commission of theft or the avoidance of arrest are also mentioned as characteristics of capital murder.

[54] Marvin E. Wolfgang, *Patterns of Homicide*, Ch. 10; H. von Hentig, *Zur Psychologie der Einzeldelikte*, Vol. 2: *Der Mord*, Tübingen, 1956, esp. Chs. 3, 5; Andreas Bjerre, *The Psychology of Murder*, Eng. trans., London, 1927; F. Tennyson Jesse, *Murder and its Motives*, London, 1924; Ernst Roesner, *Z. ges. Strafrechtwiss.*, Vol. 56, 1936, pp. 336 ff.; Norwood East, *Society and the Criminal*, 1949, Ch. 17; H. C. Brearley, *Homicide in the United States*, 1932; David Abrahamsen, *Crime and the Human Mind*, New York, 1944; Franco Ferracuti, 'La personalità dell'omicida', *Quad. Criminol. clin.*, Oct.-Dec. 1961 (with an excellent bibliog.), now also in English: 'The Psychology of the Criminal Homicide', *Rev. Jur. Univ. Puerto Rico*, Vol. 32, No. 4, 1963; also Wolf Middendorff, *Soziologie des Verbrechens*, Düsseldorf–Köln, 1959, pp. 165 ff.

[55] See *Murder: A Home Office Research Unit Report*, H.M.S.O., London, 1961, pp. 23, 32 ff.; Terence Morris and Louis Blom-Cooper, 'Murder in Microcosm', the *Observer*, London, 1961, pp. 8 ff.; Royal Commission on Capital Punishment, 1953, p. 329.

[56] Roesner, *op. cit.*, p. 339; Ernst Gennat, *Handwörterbuch der Kriminologie*, Vol. 2, p. 197; *Deutsche Kriminalstatistik für das Jahr 1931*, Berlin, 1934, p. 35.

[57] From an unpublished London Ph.D. Thesis by Hassan El-Saaty, 'Juvenile Delinquency in Egypt', 1946, pp. 122–3.

[58] On 'criminal motivation' see now Jackson Toby, *Brit. J. Crim.*, Vol. 2, No. 4, April 1962, pp. 317–36, and on motivation in general, R. S. Peters, *The Concept of Motivation*, London, 1960.

[59] Donald Cressey, 'The Differential Association Theory and Compulsive Crimes', *J. crim. Law Criminol. Police Sci.*, Vol. 45, No. 1, May-June, 1954, pp. 29 ff. (now Ch. 6 of his *Crime, Delinquency and Differential Association*, The Hague, 1964).

[60] Paperback ed., Harmondsworth, pp. 195–6, trans. by Dorothy Bussy.

[61] *Rev. int. Criminol. Police tech.*, Vol. 11, No. 4, Oct.-Dec. 1957, pp. 246–54.

[62] Norwood East, *Society and the Criminal*, pp. 273 ff., gives a few brief case

histories to illustrate this distinction. Ernst Seelig, *Schuld, Lüge, Sexualität*, Stuttgart, 1955, pp. 46 ff. and 86, presents a detailed critical analysis of the distinction, especially of its implications for problems of guilt and sentencing. He doubts whether it is generally true that crimes which are '*persönlichkeits-fremd*' deserve to be treated more leniently than those which are '*persönlichkeits-eigen*'.

[63] On this see in particular 'Le Problème de l'Etat dangereux', Deuxième Cours International de Criminologie organisé par la Société Internationale de Criminologie, Paris, 1953.

[64] See Jean Pinatel, *La Criminologie*, Paris, 1960, pp. 130 ff.

[65] Etienne de Greeff, *Introduction à la Criminologie*, Vol. 1, Bruxelles, 2nd ed. 1946, pp. 310 ff.; *Le Problème de L'Etat dangereux*, pp. 194 ff.

[66] On this distinction see, e.g., Irwin August Berg and Vernon Fox, *J. Soc. Psychol.* August 1947, pp. 109 ff.

[67] The case described by Robert M. Lindner, *Rebel without a Cause*, New York, 1944, p. 215, of the boy who wanted to kill his father, but as the latter was needed to support the family killed a stranger instead and was quite content, is probably exceptional, but this boy was a psychopath.

[68] Bruno M. Cormier, 'Psychodynamics of Homicide committed in a Marital Relationship', paper read at the Third World Congress of Psychiatry, Montreal, June 1961.

[69] J. L. Gillin, *The Wisconsin Prisoner*, Madison, 1946, p. 70, concludes from his American material that marital disharmony is a potential cause of murder only for persons whose emotional stability is greatly below the average.

[70] Andreas Bjerre, *The Psychology of Murder*, Ch. 2.

[71] See, e.g., Norwood East, *Society and the Criminal*, p. 275; v. Hentig, *Der Mord*, p. 211; Lenz, *Handwörterbuch der Kriminologie*, Vol. 2, p. 266. Glover's 'trigger impulse' has probably a similar meaning, see *Brit. J. Crim.*, Vol. 3, No. 1, July 1962, p. 68, fn. 4.

[72] See, e.g., the Case of Angerstein recounted by Paul Reiwald, *Society and its Criminals*, Eng. trans. by T. E. James, London, 1949, pp. 27 ff. The constant interplay between situation and personality is also stressed by Stephan Quensel, *Sozialpsychologische Aspekte der Kriminologie*, No. 1 of the new series '*Kriminologie. Abhandlungen über abwegiges Sozialverhalten*', ed. by Thomas Würtenberger, Stuttgart, 1964, Ch. 5, who (p. 82) presents an interesting illustration from Jean Genet's *Notre Dame des Fleurs*.

[73] *The Times*, 4.6.1952.

[74] *Ibid.*, 9.1.1962.

[75] Introduction to Foulkes, *Psycho-Analysis and Crime* (cited below at Ch. 17, note 1), p. 3.

[76] Johannes Lange, *Lehrbuch der Psychiatrie*, Leipzig, 1936, p. 169.

[77] Introduction to *The Outsider*, Eng. ed. London, 1946, p. 10.

[78] Marc Ancel, *Law Quart. Rev.*, Vol. 73, Jan. 1957, pp. 36–47.

[79] Morris and Blom-Cooper, *loc. cit.*, p. 9.

[80] On the history of this problem see Veli Verkkö, *Homicides and Suicides in Finland*, Ch. 15.

[81] *Murder: A Home Office Research Unit Report*, p. 23.

[82] David Abrahamsen, *The Psychology of Crime*, New York, 1960, p. 200. On the Leopold–Loeb case see also Nathan Leopold's book, *Life plus 99 Years*, London, 1960, and the review by T. P. Morris in *Brit. J. Delinq.*, Vol. 9, No. 4, p. 303.

[83] Alexander and Staub (see below, Ch. 17, note 1), German ed., p. 104, with reference to Freud.

[84] The Royal Commission on Capital Punishment, 1953, recommended no

change in the present law according to which the survivor of a suicide pact is guilty of murder; Report, pp. 63, 275.

[85] Ernest Jones, *Essays in Applied Psycho-Analysis*, London, 1923, Chs. 2, 3.

[86] Report, p. 6.

[87] William McDougall, *An Introduction to Social Psychology*, 29th ed., London, 1948, pp. 435 ff.

[88] See *Social Behavior and Personality*, ed. by Edmund H. Volkart, New York, 1951, esp. Ch. 9.

[89] W. F. Roper, *Brit. J. Delinq.*, Vol. 1, No. 4, April 1951, pp. 243 ff., 265.

[90] Bjerre, *op. cit.*, pp. 4 ff.

[91] Roper, *loc. cit.*, Vol. 1, No. 1, p. 18.

[92] Edward Glover, *The Roots of Crime*, p. 8.

[93] See Wootton, *Social Science and Social Pathology*, pp. 159 ff., and her references.

[94] S. and E. Glueck, *Later Criminal Careers*, New York, 1937, pp. 120, 205.

[95] *Juvenile Delinquents Grown Up*, New York, 1940, p. 270.

[96] London, 1961.

[97] John Dollard *et al.*, *Frustration and Aggression*, New Haven, 1939, esp. Ch. 6. On the subject of aggression and crime, see also Leonard Berkowitz, *Aggression: A Social Psychological Analysis*, New York, 1962; Arnold Buss, *The Psychology of Aggression*, New York, 1961.

[98] Not only at present! H. V. Morton, *A Traveller in Rome*, London, 1957, p. 121, refers to the writings of the great Russian historian Rostovtzeff who early in this century mentions the 'disenchantment' which afflicts our civilization, the feeling that the future is not worth while.

[99] Brian Kay, 'Reactions to Experimentally Induced Frustration', *Brit. J. Delinq.*, Vol. 4, No. 4, April, 1954, pp. 245 ff. See also Maud A. Merrill, *Problems of Child Delinquency*, Boston–London, 1947, p. 188.

[100] Quoted from Margaret Kornitzer, *The Modern Woman and Herself*, London, 1932, p. 45.

[101] See Volkart (*op. cit.* at note 88), Ch. 8.

[102] Sigmund Freud, *Civilization and its Discontents*, London, 1939, p. 59.

[103] See my *War and Crime*, London, 1941, p. 56, and my article 'Rechtsgefühl und Dichtung' (cited at note 7), p. 279.

[104] Etienne de Greeff, *Introduction à la Criminologie*, Vol. 1, 2nd ed., Bruxelles, 1946, pp. 258 ff.

[105] On this see in particular Hans Kelsen, *Society and Nature*, London, 1946, Part I.

[106] This has again been confirmed by recent research such as T. P. and Pauline Morris' study of Pentonville.

[107] Edmond N. Cahn, *The Sense of Injustice*, New York, 1949, deals with the subject in another sense, especially with our feeling of sympathy with those who have suffered from actual injustice.

[108] See Volkart (*op. cit.* at note 88), pp. 5, 14.

[109] Donald Clemmer, *The Prison Community*, Boston, 1940, p. 147.

[110] *The Authoritarian Personality* by T. W. Adorno *et al.*, New York, 1940, Ch. 21.

[111] Gresham M. Sykes, *The Society of Captives*, Princeton, 1958, Ch. 5.

[112] On jealousy in the psychotic person see Ch. 14, II.

[113] See de Greeff (*op. cit.* at note 104), p. 267. On jealousy murders see also E. Seelig, *Kriminologie*, pp. 100–1.

[114] David Abrahamsen, *Crime and the Human Mind*, New York, 1944, pp. 162 ff.; the same, *The Psychology of Crime*, p. 197.

[115] André Gide, *Dostoevsky*, Eng. ed., London, 1949, pp. 111–12.
[116] McDougall (*op. cit.* at note 87), p. 120.
[117] Edward Glover, *The Roots of Crime*, p. 210.
[118] *War and Crime*, pp. 41 ff.
[119] Abrahamsen, *op. cit.*, p. 155.
[120] Colin Wilson, *The Outsider*, London, 1956, pp. 163 ff., 250.
[121] Edward Glover, *Psycho-Analysis*, pp. 87–8.
[122] Donald R. Cressey, *Other People's Money*, Glencoe, Ill., 1953, esp. Chs. 4. 5.

CHAPTER 17

[1] *A Selection of basic publications on Psycho-Analysis and Crime*: August Aichhorn, *Wayward Youth*, revised Eng. ed., London, 1951; Franz Alexander and William Healy, *Roots of Crime*, New York, 1935; Franz Alexander and Hugo Staub, *Der Verbrecher und seine Richter*, Wien, 1929, Eng. trans., *The Criminal, The Judge and the Public*, New York, 1931; Franz Alexander, 'The Development of the Ego-Psychology', in Sandor Lorand, ed., *Psycho-Analysis Today*, London, 1948; J. C. Flugel, *Man, Morals and Society*, London, 1945 (also in a paperback ed.); S. H. Foulkes *Psycho-Analysis and Crime*, English Studies in Crim. Science, Cambridge, and *Canadian Bar Rev.*, Toronto, 1944; *Psycho-analysis and Social Science*, ed. by Hendrik M. Ruitenbeek, New York, 1962 (esp. chapters by Lasswell and Erikson); Sigmund Freud, 'Some Character-Types met with in Psycho-Analytical Work', *Collected Papers*, Vol. 4, pp. 318 ff., London, 1925 (first published in German in 1915). Freud's other contributions to the subject are too numerous and scattered to be mentioned here. A useful bibliography of his writings and of other publications on psycho-analysis can be found in the Appendix to Walter Hollitscher, *Sigmund Freud: An Introduction*, London, 1947. Kate Friedlander, *The Psycho-analytical Approach to Juvenile Delinquency*, London, 1947; Edward Glover, *Psycho-Analysis*, 2nd ed., London, 1949; the same, *The Roots of Crime*, London, 1960; William Healy, Augusta Bronner, and A. M. Bowers, *The Structure and Meaning of Psycho-Analysis*, New York, 1930; A. C. MacIntyre, *The Unconscious*, London, 1961; Paul Reiwald, *Society and its Criminals*, London, 1949; *Proc. Second Int. Congress Criminol.*, Vol. 3, Paris, 1952, pp. 133–92, contributions by various authors; *Searchlights on Delinquency*, dedicated to August Aichhorn, London, 1949. On the further development of Freud's theories see J. A. C. Brown, *Freud and the Post-Freudians*, Harmondsworth, 1961; Martin Birnbach, *Neo-Freudian Social Philosophy*, Stanford, California, 1961.

Critical of certain aspects of psycho-analytical theory Morris Ginsberg, *Essays in Sociology and Social Philosophy*, Vol. 1, Ch. 5, Vol. 2, pp. 24, 190. Critical also William Sheldon, *Varieties of Delinquent Youth*, New York, 1949, Ch. 6, pp. 854 ff.; H. J. Eysenck, *Uses and Abuses of Psychology*, Harmondsworth, 1953, Ch. 12.

Detailed psycho-analytical case histories of delinquents are given, e.g., by Ben Karpman, *Case Studies in the Psychopathology of Crime*, Washington, Vol. 1, 1935, Vol, 2, 1944; Hedwig Schwarz, 'Dorothy: The Psycho-Analysis of a Case of Stealing', *Brit. J. Delinq.*, Vol. 1, July 1950, pp. 29 ff.; Werner O. Lippmann, 'Psychoanalytic Study of a Thief', *Arch. crim. Psychodyn.*, Vol. 2, No. 4, 1957, pp. 782 ff.; Robert M. Lindner, *Rebel Without a Cause*; Frederic Wertham, *Dark Legend*; Bruno Bettelheim, *Truants from Life*, Part 5 (Harry); G. W. Elles, 'The Closed Circuit', *Brit. J. Crim.*, Vol. 2, No. 1, July 1961, pp. 23 ff.; Ethel Perry, *The Psycho-Analysis of a Delinquent*, ed. by Melitta Schmideberg and Marjorie E. Franklin, London, 1946; David Forsyth, *The Case of a Middle-aged Embezzler*,

409

I.S.T.D. Publication, London, 1938; Karl Abraham, *Geschichte eines Hochstaplers*, Imago, Vol. 10, 1924.

Most textbooks of criminology treat the subject of psycho-analysis very briefly or ignore it altogether. An exception is Clinard's *Sociology of Deviant Behavior*, pp. 125 ff., which of course deals not merely with criminology. See also the brief treatment by Vold, *Theoretical Criminology*, pp. 114 ff.

On the legal side see Helen Silving, 'Psychoanalysis and the Criminal Law', *J. crim. Law Criminol. Police Sci.*, Vol. 51, No. 1, May-June 1960.

[2] Hollitscher, *op. cit.*, pp. 9 ff.; MacIntyre, *op. cit.*

[3] Glover, *Roots of Crime*, p. 12.

[4] Flugel, *op. cit.*, Chs. 3, 6, 7.

[5] Ginsberg, *op. cit.*, Vol. 1, p. 58.

[6] Friedlander, *op. cit.*, pp. 31–2.

Glover, *Psycho-Analysis*, p. 73.

[8] Flugel, *op. cit.*, p. 69.

[9] See, e.g., Glover, *op. cit.*, p. 35; Friedlander, *op. cit.*, pp. 17 ff.; Hollitscher, *op. cit.*, pp. 30 ff.; Brown, *op. cit.*, pp. 20 ff.

[10] Glover, *op. cit.*, p. 82; Friedlander, *op. cit.*, p. 33.

[11] Hollitscher, *op. cit.*, p. 35.

[12] Brown, *op. cit.*, p. 25.

[13] Gregory Zilboorg, art. 'Psychoanalysis and Criminology', in the *Encycl. of Criminol.*, New York, 1949, p. 403, complains that the Super-Ego has too often been confused with the conscience, but fails to make the difference clear.

[14] On all this, see Glover, *op. cit.*, pp. 36, 145; Friedlander, *op. cit.*, p. 42; Flugel, *op. cit.*, p. 106; Brown, *op. cit.*, p. 24; on the Oedipus complex and homosexuality, Glover, *Roots of Crime*, p. 222.

[15] Foulkes, *op. cit.*, p. 21.

[16] Glover, *Psycho-Analysis*, pp. 23, 27, 49; Friedlander, *op. cit.*, p. 48; Flugel, *op. cit.*, pp. 143 ff.

[17] Glover, *op. cit.*, p. 43.

[18] Glover, *Roots of Crime*, p. 13, and more detailed in *Psycho-Analysis*, p. 74. On the theory of symbolism see also Ernest Jones, *Papers on Psycho-Analysis*, 3rd ed., London, 1923, Ch. 8.

[19] Glover, *Psycho-Analysis*, p. 114.

[20] Brown, *op. cit.*, p. 108.

[21] Glover, *Freud or Jung*, London, 1950, p. 42.

[22] Flugel, *op. cit.*, pp. 111 ff., 164 ff., 209 ff.; Glover, *Psycho-Analysis*, pp. 80 ff.

[23] Flugel, *op. cit.*, Ch. 12, See also Reiwald, *op. cit.*, pp. 91 ff.

[24] Glover, *Roots of Crime*, p. 8.

[25] Martin Buber, *Between Man and Man*, London, 1947, Paperback ed. London, 1961, p. 103.

[26] See, e.g., Flugel, *op. cit.*, p. 192; Brown, *op. cit.*, pp. 11 ff., 130.

[27] Brown, *op. cit.*, p. 12.

[28] Friedlander, *op. cit.*, pp. 103–4.

[29] Glover, *Roots of Crime*, p. 133.

[30] Alexander and Staub, *op. cit.*, German ed. p. 25.

[31] Flugel, *op. cit.*, p. 113, and Brown, *op. cit.*, 109 ff.

[32] First published in German in 1912, Eng. translation, Harmondsworth, 1938, pp. 217 ff.

[33] 2nd German ed. 1923, in English 1922, Ch. 10.

[34] See, e.g., Ginsberg, *Essays in Sociology and Social Philosophy*, Vol. 1, p. 301.

[35] See Freud, *Totem and Taboo*, pp. 189 ff. On the incest taboo see also Talcott Parsons, *Brit. J. Sociol.*, Vol. 5, No. 2, June 1954, p. 101, and the references to the

literature in my *Criminal Justice and Social Reconstruction*, p. 77, fn. 2; also Brenda Seligman, *Brit. J. Psychol.*, Vol. 22, 1932, pp. 250 ff.

[36] Freud, *Totem and Taboo*, Paperback ed., pp. 189 ff., 35 ff., p. 116.

[37] See, e.g., Alexander and Staub, *op. cit.*, at the end of their Part I.

[38] Jones in Lorand, *op. cit.*, pp. 322–3. On the problem of guilt in general see now John G. McKenzie, *Guilt*, London, 1962.

[39] Flugel, *op. cit.*, p. 272.

[40] Franz Alexander, *The Medical Value of Psycho-Analysis*, London, 1932, p. 108.

[41] Flugel, *op. cit.*, pp. 151 ff. On the idea of retribution in Greek religion see Hans Kelsen, *Society and Nature*, London, 1946, Ch. 4.

[42] Repond in Heinrich Meng (ed.), *Die Prophylaxe des Verbrechens*, Basel, 1948, p. 4. See also above p. 402, note 65.

[43] Theodor Reik, *Strafbedürfnis und Geständniszwang*, Vienna, 1925; also *The Unknown Murderer*, London, 1936, and Reiwald, *op. cit.*, *passim.*

[44] David Abrahamsen, *The Psychology of Crime*, pp. 186–7, and earlier in his *Crime and the Human Mind*, p. 155.

[45] See, e.g., Sir John Maynard, *The Russian Peasant*, London, 1947, pp. 193, 267–70.

[46] The literature on sadism and masochism is very large; see, e.g., Flugel, Ch. 8; Glover, *Roots of Crime*, p. 180 and *passim.*

[47] Glover, *Roots of Crime*, Ch. 10.

[48] *Roots of Crime*, Ch. 5., Fitch, *Brit. J. Crim.*, Vol. 3, No. 1, July 1962, p. 29.

[49] *Civilization and its Discontents*, Eng. trans. London, 1939, pp. 105 ff.

[50] See, e.g., Maurice Cranston, *Sartre*, Edinburgh–London, 1962, pp. 17–18, 50, 74.

[51] R. D. Laing, *The Divided Self*, London, 1961, pp. 131, 141, 171.

[52] See Jackson Toby, 'Criminal Motivation', *Brit. J. Crim.*, Vol. 2, No. 4, April 1962, p. 324.

[53] Emanuel Miller, *Brit. J. Delinq.*, Vol. 10, No. 3, Jan. 1960, p. 168.

[54] First published in German and English in 1914, Paperback ed. Harmondsworth, 1938.

[55] First published in German in 1917, Eng. ed., London, 1922.

[56] *Psychopathology of Every-day Life*, Paperback ed., p. 174. On these 'symptomatic acts' see also Glover, *Psycho-Analysis*, pp. 117 ff.

[57] See, e.g., *Psychopathology*, Paperback ed., pp. 102, 191, fn. 1.

[58] *Evening Standard*, 15.2.1962, p. 8.

[59] *Op. cit.*, German ed. p. 65. For another case of symbolic stealing see Hans Zullinger, *Brit. J. Delinq.*, Vol. 1, No. 3, Jan. 1951, pp. 198–204.

[60] *The Roots of Crime*, p. 14.

[61] David Abrahamsen, *Who are the Guilty?*, London, 1954, p. 174.

[62] *The Psycho-Analytical Study of the Family*, London, 1921, pp. 119-20.

[63] *Inside Europe*, London, p. 380.

[64] *Marxism: is it a Science?* London, 1941, p. 108.

[65] E.g., Glover, *Roots of Crime*, pp. 85 ff., 304.

[66] Bowlby in E. Durbin and C. Catlin, *War and Democracy*, London, 1938.

[67] See *Criminal Justice and Social Reconstruction*, pp. 109 ff.

[68] Ginsberg (*op. cit.* at note 1), Vol. 1, pp. 82–3.

[69] Melitta Schmideberg, *Short-Analytical Therapy in The Nervous Child*, ed. by Ernest Harms, 1950, and *Amer. J. Orthopsychiat.*, Vol. 23, No. 1, Jan. 1953, pp. 13 ff. See also Glover, *Roots of Crime*, pp. 52, 107, on the techniques applied at the Portman Clinic (I.S.T.D.), London.

[70] On Alfred Adler see Hertha Orgler, *Alfred Adler, The Man and his Work*, 3rd rev. ed., London, 1963; Brown, *op. cit.*, pp. 38–41; Flugel, *op. cit.*, pp. 45 ff., and *A Hundred Years of Psychology 1833–1933*, 2nd ed., London, 1951, pp. 294 ff.; Lewis Way, *Alfred Adler*; Erwin Wexberg, *Individual Psychology*, Eng. trans. by W. Beran Wolfe, London, 1929. Of the many books by Adler only the following can be mentioned: *What Life Should Mean to You*, London, 1932; *The Practice and Theory of Individual Psychology*, Eng. trans., by P. Radin, London, 1924; *Social Interest*, London, 1938.

[71] *What Life Should Mean to You*, pp. 201, 205–6.

[72] *The Psychological Treatment of Crime*, London, 1939, p. 13.

[73] Flugel, *A Hundred Years of Psychology*, Ch. 9.

[74] Fromm, *The Fear of Freedom*, p. 129.

[75] Most of Jung's works have been published in English translations in the International Library of Psychology, Psychiatry and Scientific Method, London, in addition to his *Psychological Types*, e.g., his *Contributions to Analytical Psychology*, 1928; *Modern Man in Search of a Soul*, 1933, Eng. trans. London, 1947 (Paperback ed. 1961); *Essays on Contemporary Events*, 1948. Books on Jung: Jolan Jacobi, *The Psychology of C. G. Jung*, London, 1942, trans. by K. W. Bash; Frieda Fordham, *An Introduction to Jung's Psychology* (Paperback ed.). Highly critical Edward Glover, *Freud or Jung*, London, 1950. See also Brown, *op. cit.*, pp. 42 ff.

[76] *Contributions*, p. 344.

[77] *Two Essays on Analytical Psychology*, London, 1928, p. 62.

[78] Brown, *op. cit.*, p. 49.

[79] *Modern Man in Search of a Soul*, p. 91.

[80] Eysenck, *Sense and Nonsense in Psychology*, Paperback ed., pp. 256–7.

[81] C. M. Franks, *Brit. J. Delinq.*, Vol. 6, No. 3, Jan. 1956, pp. 192 ff.

[82] Allen A. Bartholomew, *ibid.*, Vol. 10, No. 2, Oct. 1959, pp. 120 ff. Already before the War, a prison medical officer, Dr. H. T. P. Young, *J. ment. Sci.*, May 1937, pp. 268 ff., had made an assessment of the distribution of extraversion and introversion among a group of 1,000 young offenders aged 16 to 21 in Wormwood Scrubs Prison, with the result that 130 were classified as extraverts, 344 as introverts, whereas the remaining 526 had to be placed at some indefinite point between them. Young was aware of the fact that these two terms did not necessarily describe permanent states, but that conditions varied from time to time in the life of an individual.

[83] Alan Little, *Brit. J. Crim.*, Vol. 4, No. 2, Oct. 1963, pp. 152–63.

[84] H. J. Eysenck, *Crime and Personality*, London, 1964, p. 122.

[85] Quoted by Dr. J. A. Waycott, in the *Magistrate*, Nov. 1960, p. 128. On the Heath case see also Macdonald Critchley, *Med. legal J.*, Vol. 26, I, 1958, 14–24.

[86] See, e.g., Gardner Lindzey, *Assessment of Human Motives*, New York, 1958; E. R. Hilgard in *Psychoanalysis as Science*, ed. by E. Pumpian-Mindlin; Gordon Trasler, *The Explanation of Criminality*, London, 1962, pp. 32 ff.

CHAPTER 18

[1] From the vast literature only the following can be quoted here:

(a) *General*

Glanville Williams, *Criminal Law: The General Part*, 2nd ed., London, 1961, Ch. 10 (particularly detailed and valuable); *Report of the Royal Commission on Capital Punishment*, 1953, Chs. 4–6; Hermann Mannheim, 'The Criminal Law and Mentally Abnormal Offenders', *Brit. J. Crim.*, Vol. 1, No. 3, Jan. 1961, pp. 203 ff.

(Hague Congress lecture); Sheldon Glueck, *Mental Disorder and the Criminal Law*, Boston, 1925; the same, *Law and Psychiatry: Cold War or Entente Cordiale?*, Baltimore, 1962, and London, 1963; Jerome Hall, *Studies in Jurisprudence and Criminal Theory*, New York, 1958, Ch. 15; Philip Q. Roche, *The Criminal Mind*, New York, 1958; Henry Weihofen, *The Urge to Punish*, London, 1957; Barbara Wootton, *Crime and the Criminal Law*, London, 1963 (15th Hamlyn Lecture).

(b) *Historical*

Sir William Holdsworth, *History of English Law*, Vol. 3, 3rd ed., London, 1923, pp. 372 ff., Vol. 8, 1925, pp. 439 ff.; Sir James Fitzjames Stephen, *A History of the Criminal Law of England*, 3 vols., London, 1883. Very brief on the historical side the *Report of the Royal Commission on Capital Punishment*, 1953, p. 397.

(c) *Comparative*

American: *American Law Institute Tentative Draft Model Penal Code*, No. 4 Philadelphia, 1955; Jerome Hall, *op. cit.*; John Reid, *Yale Law J.*, Vol. 69, No. 3 Jan. 1960.

French: *Les délinquents anormaux mentaux. Ouvrage publié sous la direction de Georges Levasseur. Introduction comparative de Marc Ancel*, Paris, 1959.

German: H. H. Heldmann in *Materialien zur Strafrechtsreform*, Vol. 2, *Allgemeiner Teil*, Bonn, 1954, pp. 345–65; *Entwurf des Allgemeinen Teils eines Strafgesetzbuchs mit Begründung*, Bonn, 1958.

In general: H. Mannheim, *Group Problems*, Ch. 13; the same, *Brit. J. Crim.* (cited under (a) above); *Vergleichende Darstellung des Deutschen und Ausländischen Strafrechts*, Berlin, Allgemeiner Teil, 1908, Vol. I, pp. 1 ff. (Kahl), Vol. 5, pp. 1 ff. (v. Lilienthal).

[2] Modern criminal law does no longer 'virtually disregard the criminal', as Ben Karpman asserts, *J. crim. Law Criminol. Police Sci.*, Vol. 48, No. 2, July-August 1957, pp. 164 ff.

[3] H. Mannheim, *Criminal Justice*, pp. 202 ff.

[4] Francis A. Allen, *Ann. Amer. Acad. Polit. Soc. Sci.*, Vol. 339, Jan. 1962, p. 76.

[5] For the following see *Pioneers in Criminology*, Index under 'Free Will'.

[6] Sellin in *Pioneers*, p. 279.

[7] Hall, *op. cit.*, p. 271.

[8] Quoted from D. Stafford-Clark, *Psychiatry Today*, p. 289. Glover, *Freud or Jung*, p. 193, too, thinks that even if the amount of 'freed-will' is only marginal, 'it at any rate allows man the freedom to decide to continue the struggle'. See on Freud's psychic determinism Brown, *op. cit.*, pp. 3–4, and Ginsberg (*op. cit.*, at Ch. 17, note 68); on determinism in history Isaiah Berlin, *Historical Inevitability*, London, 1954; on the penological side of the problem Barbara Wootton, *Social Science and Social Pathology*, pp. 245 ff.

[9] On all this see my *Criminal Justice and Social Reconstruction* (Index under 'Experts') and *Group Problems*, pp. 298–9.

[10] On treatment tribunals see *Criminal Justice*, pp. 228 ff., also my *Dilemma of Penal Reform*, London, 1939, pp. 201 ff.

[11] B. J. F. Laubscher, *Sex, Custom and Psychopathology*, London, 1937, contains an excellent chapter on mental disorder among natives.

[12] London, 1946.

[13] See, e.g., Laubscher, *op. cit.*, p. 226.

[14] E. Adamson Hoebel, *The Law of Primitive Man*, Cambridge, Mass., 1954, pp. 237–8.

[15] Kenny-Turner, *Outlines of Criminal Law*, 16th ed., Cambridge, 1952, p. 68.

[16] Rudolf His, *Deutsches Strafrecht bis zur Carolina*, Berlin, 1928, p. 8.

[17] Kenny-Turner, *op. cit.*, p. 68.

[18] See Glanville Williams, *op. cit.*, p. 328; Weihofen, *op. cit.*, p. 175.

[19] On this case and the Rules see, e.g., Royal Commission, p. 79; Williams, *op. cit.*, p. 291; Kenny-Turner, *op. cit.*, p. 68; Roche, *op. cit.*, p. 90; Weihofen, *op. cit.*, Ch. 2; Mannheim, *op. cit.*, p. 209.

[20] On Australia see in particular Norval Morris in *Essays in Criminal Science*, ed. by Gerhard O. W. Mueller, London, 1961, Ch. 10; also, *Med. J. Austr.*, 8.3.1958; J. E. Hall Williams, *Brit. J. Delinq.*, Vol. 5, No. 1, July 1954, pp. 72 ff.

[21] The full text can be found in Appendix 8(a) of the *Report of the Royal Commission on Capital Punishment, 1953*, and in App. A of the *Report of the Committee on Insanity and Crime* (Lord Atkin Report), Cmd. 2005, 1924. Summaries are given by Kenny-Turner, *op. cit.*, p. 69, and Williams, *op. cit.*,

[22] *R. v. Windle*, [1952] 36 Cr. App. R. 85.

[23] *Stapleton v. The Queen*, [1952] 86 C.L.R. 358; Norval Morris, *op. cit.*, p. 283.

[24] *Report of Royal Commission*, p. 88.

[25] See Straffen case, [1952] 36 Crim. App. R. 132; *Report of Royal Commission*, pp. 84, 119, 265; Norval Morris (*op. cit.* at note 14), p. 279; *The Trial of John Thomas Straffen*, ed. by Letitia Fairfield and Eric P. Fullbrook, Notable British Trial Series, London, 1954; *Brit. J. Delinq.*, Vol. 5, No. 4, April 1955, pp. 303–9.

[26] On this see *Group Problems*, p. 297, and Glanville Williams, *Criminal Law*, §§ 102, 224–5, also his contribution to *Essays in Criminal Science*, pp. 348–50.

[27] That the question whether an impulse was 'irresistible' is not always unanswerable is shown by Karl Jaspers in the examples given in his *Allgemeine Psychopathologie*, 4th ed., Berlin–Heidelberg, 1946, p. 98. In one of his cases a schizophrenic (non-criminal) patient reports that one day he was suddenly seized with an overwhelming and to him inexplicable impulse to jump, fully clothed, into a river, and he became aware of the folly of his action only when he was already in the water.

[28] *Report of Royal Commission*, pp. 110, 276; Morris, *op. cit.*, p. 286–98; Mannheim, *op. cit.*, pp. 212–13.

[29] See my Hague lecture (cited at note 1(a)), p. 214.

[30] *Ibid.*, p. 215.

[31] *Ibid.*, p. 216.

[32] *Report of Royal Commission*, p. 157; Glanville Williams, *op. cit.*, General Part, sect. 92.

[33] *Minutes of Evidence*, p. 360, Q. 4388. On life in Broadmoor see C. H. Rolph, *New Statesman*, 24.2.1951.

[34] See on the Homicide Act Glanville Williams, *Howard J.*, Vol. 10, No. 4, 1961; J. E. Hall Williams, *Mod. Law Rev.*, July 1957, pp. 381 ff.; J. Ll. J. Edwards, *Brit. J. Delinq.*, Vol. 8, No. 1, July 1957, pp. 49 ff.; and more recently on diminished responsibility under the Homicide Act and the Mental Health Act, Edwards, *Essays in Criminal Science*, Ch. 11; Glanville Williams in *Medicine, Science and Law*, Vol. 1, No. 1, Oct. 1960; T. P. Morris and Louis Blom-Cooper, 'Murder in Microcosm', *Observer*, 1961, p. 11; W. Lindesay Neustatter, *Medico-Legal J.*, 1960, pp. 92 ff. See, e.g., the decision of the Judicial Committee of the Privy Council in Rose v. The Queen, *The Times*, 6.3.1961.

[35] T. P. Morris and L. Blom-Cooper, *op. cit.*, p. 11. On the practical results of sect. 4 see Max Grünhut, *Probation and Mental Treatment*, London, 1963.

[36] See *Prison Commissioners' Annual Report* for 1960, p. 75; and for 1962, pp. 59–60.

[37] A. W. Peterson, *Brit. J. Crim.*, Vol. 1, No. 4, April 1961, p. 315. The 'three primary tasks' of Grendon have now been described officially as being '(a) the

investigation and treatment of mental disorders generally recognised as responsive to treatment in suitable cases; (b) the investigation of offenders whose offences in themselves suggest mental morbidity; (c) and exploration of the problems of dealing with the psychopath' (*Report of the Commissioners of Prisons, 1962*, pp. 59-60). See also the paper by Dr H. K. Snell, Director of Prison Medical Services, in the *Medico-Legal J.*, Vol. 31, Part 4, 1963, pp. 175 ff., with discussion.

[38] Edwards, *op. cit.*, pp. 320-1; Glanville Williams, *op. cit.*, *General Part*, 2nd ed., §§ 173-7.

[40] It has recently been suggested that this course could have been followed even under the present law: *Brit. J. Crim.*, Vol. 4, No. 4, April 1964, pp. 415-6.

[41] On the impact of the Act of 1959 on English criminal law see Edwards, *Essays*, pp. 327 ff.

[42] *The Times*, 31.10.1961.

[43] Glanville Williams, *op. cit.*, *General Part*, 2nd ed., § 152.

[44] On this case see G. W. Keeton, *Guilty but Insane*, London, 1961, Ch. 4; Rupert Furneaux, *Guenther Podola*, London, 1961; C. D. L. Clark, *Brit. J. Delinq.*, Vol. 10, No. 4, April 1960, pp. 302-4, and the full reports in *The Times*, 15, 16, 21.10.1959.

[45] Glanville Williams, *op. cit.*, §§ 178-83; my *Group Problems*, pp. 292-9; A. L. Goodhart, *The Listener*, 28.12.1961, mainly on the case *Attorney General for Northern Ireland v. Gallagher*, [1961] 3 W.L.R. 619.

[46] Edwards, *op. cit.*, pp. 323-4.

[47] *Group Problems*, pp. 292-3.

[48] See G. M. Scott in *Mental Abnormality and Crime*, p. 175; Williams, *op. cit.*, § 179; my *Social Aspects of Crime*, p. 184.

[49] See *Group Problems*, pp. 297-9. Williams, too, seems to favour this solution.

PART FOUR
The Sociology of Crime

Chapter 19

OUR CRIMINOGENIC SOCIETY I:
A PRELIMINARY SURVEY

I. A FEW BASIC CONCEPTS

The sociology of crime[1] has as its main object the relationships between society and its individual or corporate members as far as these relationships may have some bearing on crime. Moreover, as mentioned in our methodological chapters, the criminological significance of certain social institutions, of certain areas, and of the age and sex factors are also within the scope of the sociological approach to crime, although age and sex have important biological and psychological implications and areas have important physical aspects, too. Before going into the details of all these problems certain preliminary observations are, however, not out of place. The sociological interpretation of crime is, perhaps even more than its biological and psychological counterparts, affected by the subjective value judgments of the individual observer.

A society can be understood and judged only against the background of its own peculiar culture, its norms and values. Whether this culture, these norms and values are good or bad, how far they and the many conflicts between one norm of conduct and another, between one value and others can be regarded as generating criminal behaviour, or at least contributing to it—all such questions are likely to be answered in different ways by different observers. We have already pointed out in Chapter 3, II(*b*), that it is not the business of the criminologist as such to pronounce value judgments and that this rule should be observed especially with regard to 'findings which seem to lay bare the criminogenic effect of certain more general aspects of our culture'.

We have now reached the stage in our discussion where those previous remarks are of immediate practical significance. We should not allow our personal views and prejudices on the great moral, political, cultural, social and economic issues of our time unduly to colour our interpretation of the socio-criminological scene; and as far as it is humanly impossible to prevent the intrusion of those views and prejudices they should at least be made clear to the reader; moreover, a moralizing attitude should be avoided even where the temptation is strong to disapprove of certain features of our society. It is our task to explain rather than to accuse. This is a platitude, but it needs saying more than once. Sweeping generalizations based on limited factual material are likewise a mistake, and, finally, no concepts should be used which have not been clearly defined or, where no such clear definition can be given, the reasons should at least be indicated.

(a) Crime is only one, and certainly not the most important of the many problems confronting a particular society, and it can be understood only against its whole cultural background. *What do we mean by 'culture'?* Philosophers, cultural anthropologists, sociologists, and many others, including some criminologists, have tried to define it, the philosophers mostly in general terms, the others in more concrete ways, either by working out the characteristics of a specific, for example American, culture or by comparing the different features of primitive and more advanced, or of aristocratic, bourgeois and working-class cultures. In recent years special attention has been paid to the evil effects of an inferior type of mass-culture and of the delinquent subculture. With the exception of these two phenomena, which have been subject to strong criticism and will be discussed later on, definitions of culture in general tend to be framed in objective, neutral terms, i.e. accepting its existence as a social fact without expressing any criticisms of the good or bad qualities of a specific culture. This applies especially to the anthropologists who have given so much thought to, and collected so much material on, the 'diffusion of culture', i.e. the 'transference of culture traits from one area to another, or from one part of culture to another part',[2] and for this reason this objective interpretation is sometimes called the anthropological view of culture. It is only natural that those who are familiar with several, possibly very different, cultures should find it easier to adopt such a neutral attitude than those whose knowledge is limited to one. Raymond Williams, in his *Culture and Society 1780–1950*,[3] traces the development of the idea of culture over the whole period under discussion with special emphasis on the many changes which this idea has undergone as 'a record of a number of important and continuing reactions to the changes in our social, economic and political life'. Particularly popular and widely adopted is the definition of Primitive Culture by E. B. Tylor, as 'that complex whole which includes knowledge, belief, art, morals, law, custom and any other capabilities acquired by man as a member of society', or, shorter, as 'the mode of life created by man' (Gittler). In certain

countries and at certain periods this mode of life is comparatively stagnant, in other areas and at other times it is subject to rapid changes.

One of the most stimulating, but also most controversial discussions of
the subject of culture is T. S. Eliot's book *Notes towards the Definition of
Culture*.[4] It has often been criticized as merely pretending to be objective
and detached, be doing nothing more than 'define', while in fact being
reactionary and subjective, prejudiced in favour of an aristocratic, conservative, and religious view of society.[5] While this bias is certainly clear
enough for everybody to see, some of Eliot's observations, though un-
palatable to many readers, are nevertheless profoundly true. He was perhaps deceiving himself, however, in thinking that a writer with his strongly
felt convictions on the subject could honestly limit himself to mere 'definitions'. As it is, the reader constantly finds himself sitting between two
stools. There is on the one hand Eliot's well-known catalogue of all those
'characteristic activities and interests of a people' which, he maintains, are
embraced by the term culture: 'Derby Day, Henley Regatta, Cowes, the
twelfth of August, a cup final, the dog races, the pin table, the dartboard,
Wensleydale cheese, boiled cabbage cut into sections, beetroot in vinegar,
nineteenth century Gothic churches and the music of Elgar. The reader can
make his own list' (p. 31). While this is presented as an objective, 'anthropological', statement of facts—actually it is of course bitingly sarcastic—the
book as a whole contains an abundance of strongly felt value-judgments.
Another of Eliot's recent critics, Richard Wollheim, whose able pamphlet
'Socialism and Culture'[6] we shall have to consider again below in Chapter
22, attacks mainly Eliot's contention that culture is essentially a minority
phenomenon. Wollheim, too, uses a non-anthropological, subjective interpretation of culture, arguing, probably too optimistically, that mass culture
possesses certain elements which raise it 'above the level of a mere anthropological phenomenon: in coherence, that is, though not, of course, necessarily in quality' (p. 8). His main problems: 'What is wrong' with mass
culture, with middle-class culture, with the structure of culture in general?
are quite clearly problems of evaluation.

The culture of a society moulds, to a large extent, the personality
of its individual members as far as personality is the product of
childhood experiences more or less common to most of them. However, even within the same culture, unless it is a very primitive one—
there exist many profound differences and shades, giving rise to the
formation of various subcultures. These, coupled with physical and
mental differences existing between individual members, lead to the
innumerable variations in human personality observable within the
same culture.[7]

It has been the main object of this discourse to illustrate the
scintillating and well-nigh indefinable meaning of the word 'culture'
with its inevitable repercussions in the field of criminal sociology.
Crime is rightly regarded as one of the manifold ways in which the

culture of an age and a nation expresses itself. If, however, the concept of culture itself remains so vague and ill-defined there is a danger that the light it can shed on crime may not always be as clear as we might wish, but this warning should not provide an excuse for those who would rather shirk the many hazards involved in facing the sociological problems of crime.

The interdependence between the culture of a society and its crime has been the principal tenet of the sociological school of criminology for approximately a century and a quarter, and it is rather surprising to read in Taft's otherwise excellent chapter on 'Law Making and Law Breaking in the American Setting' the statement: 'The fact that crime and its treatment are rooted in the general culture seems to have been somewhat neglected.'[8] Already in his *Physique sociale* of 1835 Adolphe Quetelet had coined the famous phrase that society 'contains in itself the germs of all future crimes'.[9] Together with A. Lacassagne's equally famous dictum of 1885: 'The social milieu is the culture-medium of criminality (*le milieu est le bouillon de culture de la criminalité*); the microbe is the criminal element which has no importance until the day when it finds the culture which sets it multiplying . . . *Societies have the criminals they deserve*'—that phrase has become the *leitmotiv* of criminal sociology. In accordance with our insistence that unnecessary moralizing should be avoided we would instead of Lacassagne's strongly loaded term 'deserve' rather use the more neutral formula: *every society possesses the type of crime and of criminals which fits into its cultural, moral, social, religious and economic conditions.*

The *history of crime*, as distinct from the history of the criminal law and that of punishment, has been comparatively neglected, especially in its earlier stages and outside the field of the so-called primitive societies where much work has been done by social anthropologists. The historians of culture, such as Jacob Burckhardt in his *Civilization of the Renaissance in Italy*,[10] or Gustav Freytag in *Bilder aus der deutschen Vergangenheit*, G. M. Trevelyan in *English Social History* or W. E. H. Lecky in his *History of European Morals*, have taken the criminological aspects of their subject more or less in their stride. Historical studies exclusively devoted to the history of crime are few and far between. For England, Luke Owen Pike has done excellent pioneer work in his *History of Crime in England*,[11] and so has Henry Mayhew in his *London Labour and the London Poor*,[12] but their techniques are probably not quite up to the requirements of modern historical scholarship, and Mayhew was concerned with contemporary conditions in the Metropolitan area rather than with historical developments in general. Pike was a lawyer, and his book deals at the same time with the history of crime, of the criminal law, and of penal methods. He assembled considerable masses of material and treated them in a comprehensive manner against the background of the social and economic conditions of the period. Characteristic of this is the concluding remark of his Chapter 5 which leads up to the year of the Black Death: 'The object of the present chapter has been attained if it shows with sufficient clearness what was the actual condition of our forefathers in the year 1348, how insecure were their lives and property, and how vast is the difference between them and us in manners, in sentiments, and in knowledge.'

Germany, too, possesses two outstanding works on the history of crime, the one, Avé-Lallement's famous *Das deutsche Gaunertum*[13] preceding Pike by 15–20 years, the other, modern one, Gustav Radbruch and Heinrich Gwinner's masterly *Geschichte des Verbrechens*.[14] Avé-Lallement's great work is nowadays usually quoted as of importance only to students of criminal argot; in fact it is far more comprehensive: the first part of its first volume deals with the history, the second part with the literature of criminals, the second volume with the contemporary position, and the remainder with the linguistic aspects. It is worthy of note that the book begins with the following sentence. 'Crime is a secondary malady affecting the ailing body of bourgeois society; it can be stamped out only by healing that body, but the steadily growing materialistic tendency of our age makes the prospects of achieving this object more and more doubtful' (my translation). This, it will be remembered, was written in the period between the publication of Quetelet's and Lacassagne's similar dicta and shortly before the appearance of Lombroso's main work. Avé-Lallement was strongly opposed to any attempts to proclaim the existence of a specific physiognomy of the criminal, while on the other hand stressing that there was no conceivable political movement, no change in social conditions that did not give the criminal his chance (I, 16). Criminality to him was a profession which recruited itself from all classes of the population (I, 3). Referring to the strong Hebrew element in criminal argot, this remarkable author calls it 'a sad monument of the inhuman persecution and humiliation of this ancient people of God' (Part III, p. viii).[15]

Radbruch and Gwinner's book, though limited to the history of crime in Germany, is of general interest, too, because of its wealth of references to cultural trends of universal significance. 'It is the task of historical criminology to compare the criminological physiognomy of different cultural periods and to show how the atmosphere and the conditions of the time influence its criminality, thereby making us aware of the fact that the criminality of our age is also dependent on its historical setting' (p. 6, translated by the present writer). Of particular interest in this connection are the occasional attempts made by

Radbruch-Gwinner to compare, for example, the German criminality of the time of the Reformation with that of the Italian Renaissance as depicted by Burckhardt (pp. 101 and 123).

In addition to such comprehensive publications covering the developments of criminality in a certain country over many centuries there are also several less ambitious, but more specific, studies focused on limited periods of time, especially on the two world wars and their aftermath, and in a few cases even here restricted to certain forms of criminality.

The following may here be mentioned:

Franz Exner, *Krieg und Kriminalität in Österreich*, Vienna, 1927; Moritz Liepmann, *Krieg und Kriminalität in Deutschland*, Stuttgart and New Haven, Conn., 1930; Hermann Mannheim, *Social Aspects of Crime in England between the Wars*, London, 1940; also, *War and Crime*, London, 1941; also, *Three Contributions to the History of Crime in the Second World War* and after, in *Group Problems in Crime and Punishment*, London, 1955, Chapter 5; International Penal and Penitentiary Commission, 'The Effect of the War on Criminality', *Recueil de Documents en matière pénale et pénitentiaire*, Vol. 15, Nov. 1951; Marshall B. Clinard, *The Black Market*, New York, 1952; Estes Kefauver, *Crime in America*, London, 1952.

Jerome Hall's *Theft, Law and Society*, 2nd. ed., Indianapolis, 1952, although primarily a study in legal history, is also an important contribution to the history of crime in medieval England through its detailed analysis of the famous Carrier's Case of 1473, one of the milestones in the development of the English law of theft, in its political, economic and social setting.

(*b*) In most human societies there is in operation a system of *norms* and *values* as the focal point of their respective cultures. It is one of the main tasks of a culture to provide such norms and values, related to which there are certain human *attitudes* towards them and towards other people and to social institutions, etc. The definitions of these three basic terms differ, unfortunately, from one writer to another not less than the definition of culture. Value, for example, has been defined in the following way: 'those individual personal qualities which are considered to be desirable in a given culture', such as bravery, strength, perseverance, self-control, aggressiveness;[16] or as 'a conception of the essential rightness or wrongness of a certain kind of activity or of the desirability of a certain kind of goal, held in common by members of a social group ... values ... represent the association of an emotion (of approval, respect, aversion) to an idea or conception.'[17] To another writer, values are 'general standards', but elsewhere he states that 'a beefsteak is a value'.[18] Similarly, Murphy and Newcomb refer to a value as an object, but also as 'a statement of preparation for a response'.[19] These obvious contradictions reflect a general inconsistency and woolliness of thought which has already been exposed by Myrdal. 'The term "value" has, in its prevalent usage, a loose meaning,' he writes. 'When tightened it is generally taken to refer to the object of valuations rather than to the valuations themselves,'[20] i.e. to the beefsteak rather than to our like or dislike of it. Myrdal, therefore, prefers to call the standards, our 'ideas about how it (i.e. reality) ought to be', our valuations (pp. 71 ff.), and in the following we shall adopt this usage by calling the beefsteak a value and our feelings about it a valuation.

This leads to the question of how values and valuations are related to norms and which of them can claim priority. Bianchi,[21] reviewing some of the philosophical literature on the subject, concludes that 'The theory of criminology badly needs the priority of norms to value.' Priority of value to norm, he argues, 'leads easily to the un-scrupulous view that ends might justify means; the higher value justi-fying the violation of lower values.'

In this connection, he also criticizes the view that 'culture or society are the sole providers of value' (p. 134). To him, the norm is 'The rule of our action, determining what value must be strived after and what phenomena pertain to positive or negative value. It is only the norm that in case of conflict of values points out the value that has to be realized', and it makes no difference whether norms are 'conceived to lie in some eternal law' or whether they are given by God. This view is logically consistent with Bianchi's conception of crime as identical with sin and of a supernatural origin of norms. If, however, we believe in the secular nature and origin of our norms we shall be more inclined to regard them partly as creators of values and partly created by them. Norms, whether moral, legal or social ones, deter-mine behaviour and values, but actual behaviour and strongly felt values may also crystallize into norms; in other words, there is a constant give and take between them. 'Conduct norms are the pro-ducts of social life—A conduct norm is originally an *ex post facto* rule. Generally speaking, "breach is the mother of law" and equally a mother of conduct norms.'[22]

Another important concept to be mentioned in this brief termino-logical note is that of *attitudes*; they are of particular interest to social psychologists, whereas sociologists tend to concentrate more on an analysis of norms and values. Attitudes are formed by the indi-vidual's subjective awareness of certain basic norms and values of his society or group; they are tendencies 'to respond in a particular fashion in given circumstances'; 'they are learned and become habi-tual or characteristic of the individual'.[23] Our use of the words 'The individual's awareness' is, however, not intended to exclude the possibility of attitudes common to whole groups—they are in fact the more important ones—or of those which exist only in the unconscious but find their expression in the behaviour of the individual or group. Murphy and Newcomb regard attitudes as being in most cases of a verbal nature, as 'verbalized or verbalizable tendencies, dispositions, or adjustments toward certain acts' (p. 889), and as they are mainly concerned with the measurement of attitudes this is understandable, but they admit that attitudes may also be inferred from other forms of overt behaviour, for example, belonging to certain extremist groups (p. 896). Research has often been done on the measurement of attitudes, for example towards certain races and occasionally also towards certain crimes to ascertain the views of individuals or groups on the relative seriousness of various crimes (Murphy, p. 901).

The relationship between norms and values (or valuations), on the one hand, and attitudes, on the other, may be defined as representing two stages, the individual acquiring first certain valuations, for example about the dignity and sacredness of human life, and secondly, as a consequence of this, developing the corresponding attitudes towards its preservation and protection against attacks; or workers acquire certain valuations regarding the respective value of their own and their employers' contributions to the common good in relation to their respective rewards and, consequently, develop certain attitudes towards work and the integrity of their firm's property. Myrdal, by using the term 'attitude' simply as a 'convenient synonym for valuation' (p. 78), seems to oversimplify the relationship.

Although attitudes are to some extent related to the whole personality[24] and although the latter is characterized by a certain consistency, attitudes can change and have occasionally been changed experimentally.[25] However, Murphy and Newcomb, after surveying several of these experiments, rightly express their dissatisfaction with the outcome and their unreal character (pp. 971–2). Trasler maintains that group values and standards change more slowly than individual attitudes and that the task of the psychologist, who has to reconstruct the latter long after the event, for example, the crime, is therefore more difficult than that of the sociologist whose interest is focused on more permanent group phenomena.[26]

II. OUR CRIMINOGENIC SOCIETY

Having tried to clarify a few basic concepts, it is now our task to examine the impact on present-day crime of the culture, the norms, values, valuations and attitudes prevailing in our society. It is easy enough to draw up a long list of the sins of commission and omission within this society, of its follies and iniquities. Many of them will have to be given their proper places in the chapters which are to follow. Any such catalogue can make sense, however, only if founded on a certain generally accepted system of norms, values and valuations, and here it is equally true of the criminologist what has been said of the psychologist, i.e. that 'he is only as wise or ignorant as the next man in the street concerning what religious, ethical, artistic or other values are better than others'.[27]

Anglo-American society—the use of this phrase does not imply an even approximate identification of the two parts—has ever since the end of the First World War been called many different and usually rather unflattering names by social philosophers, economists, and sociologists. R. H. Tawney's *Acquisitive Society* of 1921, perhaps the only critical study of real stature in this series published between the two great wars, has been followed, after a lengthy interval, by J. K. Galbraith's *Affluent Society* of 1958, by Richard M. Titmuss's *Irresponsible Society* of 1959, Michael Shanks's *Stagnant Society* of 1961, and by the 'distorted materialist society without purpose' of T. R. Fyvel's teenagers.[28] Very rarely does one encounter a laudatory title such as McClelland's *Achieving Society*,[29] and even he does not claim that ours is an 'achieving' society, but is merely trying to discover the driving force behind economic growth in general. To these few publications which put their cards openly on the table could, of course, be added many dozens which, though equally critical in substance, hide their true contents behind a neutral façade or relegate it at least to the sub-title, such as David Riesman's *Lonely Crowd* or Daniel J. Boorstin's *The Image. Or What Happened to the American Dream*. And apart from these rather academic sociological studies there are the whole of the 'angry young man' literature and the incessant critical comments of the left-wing periodicals.

What are the principal grievances of these critics? We can here select only a few of the most obvious and most frequent ones and only those which are most likely to have a bearing on our problems, although even here their actual responsibility for the state of crime in our society cannot often be clearly proved, and we have to be content with mere probabilities. Naturally, different writers deal with different facets, but taken together they present a fairly coherent picture of a deep-seated malaise of our society. Official and officially inspired statements and researches, though perhaps vaguely aware of it, persistently refuse to face the real issues and are therefore often reduced to mere shadow-boxing. The opening paragraph of the widely quoted and influential Home Office White Paper *Penal Practice in a Changing Society* (1959) is characteristic of this attitude:

It is a disquieting feature of our society that, in the years since the war, rising standards in material prosperity, education and social welfare have

427

brought no decrease in the high rate of crime reached during the war: on the contrary, crime has increased and is still increasing. The purpose of this paper is first to give the facts about this situation, then to set out proposals of the Government for dealing with some of its aspects. This Paper does not seek to deal with those deep-seated causes which, even were they fully understood, would be largely beyond the reach of Government action (p. 1).

It is of course only too true that these 'deep-seated causes' are largely beyond the reach of Government action, but even action on a modest scale without an attempt to understand them can only make confusion worse confounded. However, as matters stand, criminological research into these fundamentals is hardly to be expected under Government guidance, and perhaps altogether incompatible with it.

What is disturbing is that the White Paper 'looks forward to the possibility of a fundamental re-examination of penal philosophy *on the basis of the knowledge to be gained in this* way' (p. iv, italics mine), whereas it should be clear that nothing fundamental can be achieved without that investigation of those deep-seated causes which the Paper excludes from its deliberations.

It is only in line with this self-abdicating policy that so much modern criminological writing in this country has, on the whole, kept meticulously aloof from 'dangerous thoughts'. It is encouraging, however, that the more recent Home Office White Paper *The War against Crime in England and Wales 1959–1964* (H.M.S.O. 1964, Cmnd. 2296) takes a less limited view.

Obviously, no original and comprehensive survey of the principal causes of the malaise of present-day society can be expected within the framework of a textbook on criminology, but a cursory glimpse at them cannot be avoided in anticipation of their more factual treatment in subsequent chapters. To classify them according to their predominantly political, economic, social and cultural character might be possible, but would at this stage be of little practical value because of the large extent of overlapping. In the following we shall as much as possible rely on the expressed views of widely accepted and unsuspected experts rather than try to impose our own views on the reader, and we can hardly do better than begin with a few extracts from the remarkable 'Postscript' which Lord (now Viscount) Radcliffe, a Lord of Appeal in Ordinary, in 1958 added to his Reith Memorial Lectures of 1951[30] and which reflect the thoughts of a man of wide experience who is a conservative by temperament and training without being a reactionary. There is in this country at present, he writes, 'no coherent public philosophy', and 'our present phase of egalitarian sentiment varies between a self-righteous rejection of all distinctions of value between one person and another and an indifferentism, amounting to boredom, which obliterates both the distinction and the value'. With regard to the latter, it may become necessary 'to reassess the system of values which commends itself to the "silent people" who "have not spoken yet". Such an analysis may yield some startling results', and one of the most startling of these results is that 'we seem to be losing at an alarming rate the power of independent judgment, the independent sense of value'. Lord Radcliffe, who is primarily concerned in his book with 'the problem of power', draws an interesting comparison between bloody revolutions and the kind of bloodless, 'legal, social revolution which this country has undergone in the past decades. While the former are normally brought to an end by the revolutionary leader himself and while it can therefore be said that they carry within themselves their 'own controlling mechanism', this is not true of the bloodless revolution of our time which possesses no such leaders and no such controlling mechanism of its own and may therefore not only last longer, but may also produce a more complete break with the past. It can be left open whether this contrast really applies to revolutions everywhere, but there seems to be some measure of truth in Lord Radcliffe's observation that the social revolution which has been transforming this country in the past thirty years or so may eventually equal those other revolutions in the profundity of its social import. Faced with it, our leaders are helpless and powerless: 'our governors, though plainly conscious of the fact that we are going somewhere, do not possess in themselves or convey to others any clear sense of what it is that we are intended to reach.' It is only too tempting to take the easy way out: 'the whole pressure of the democratic state is in favour of giving them (the public) what they want.' What do they want? 'It seems to be the fate of the member of contemporary society that he should be invited to participate in everything and to experience nothing.' When men are perpetually exposed to the impact of mass-fabricated emotions at second hand by radio, television and cinema, or—as Lord Radcliffe expresses it—'when the full range of Pity and Terror can be travelled two or three nights a week, at stated hours, in all the comfort of the home', this must necessarily lead to a flattening of these emotions, to indifference and boredom. The greater the crowds of spectators at football matches and the louder they shout, the larger the television audiences and the readerships of popular magazines, the less do they care about the true values of human life, about political issues as far as they do not involve their own pockets and about moral or religious values, though occasional lip-service may be paid to them. All this, and much more besides, has been expressed by Lord Radcliffe in a few memorable phrases, of which only a few more can here be quoted:

429

In the curious half-world of shadows which is created by the arts of publicity, advertising, public relations, promotion and popular entertainment in general, these (i.e. political) ideas, though more and more often invoked, become more and more dim and blurred in meaning. The majority of people do not want to understand them . . . What they must not believe is that they will be saved by their institutions if they are not saved by themselves . . . Constitutional forms and legal systems are very well in their way, but they are the costumes for the men who wear them.

And he concludes with the very unpopular observation that 'It does not matter at all that people should become more and more comfortable or that they should travel faster and faster, or that they should visit more and more places,' but he thinks it does matter that they 'should not "sleep before evening" '. Contrasted with Lord Radcliffe's austerity, how much more pleasing is the politician's assurance that we have never had it so good, and his cheerful prophecy that 'within the next twenty-five years the standard of living in this country will be doubled'. Let us not misunderstand all this, however, and it is all too easy to misinterpret Lord Radcliffe's remarks. There is no reason at all why we should not wish people to become more comfortable and to travel faster and travel more, why life should not become easier for 'Mrs. Average' (*Britain, An Official Handbook*, H.M.S.O. 1961); what can be dangerous is only excess, lack of moderation and of understanding of the meaning and purpose of comfort and travel, and this is what we are observing in every sphere at present. Television sets, washing machines and glamorous cars are certainly not evil in themselves, but they become a very mixed blessing if, as they do today, they completely crush all the higher values in most people's lives and minds and if one has to discover marked negative correlation between the size of a car and the intelligence, maturity and sense of social responsibility of its possessor. And to take up another of Lord Radcliffe's points, it is all to the good that travelling, including travel abroad, has become a mass phenomenon, but many of the present 'package tours' are planned for cheap amusement rather than for any broadening of the mind through contact with the cultural values of the countries visited. Great centres of art are sometimes visited without giving the tourist the slightest inkling of what he could see if he only knew and cared about their treasures.

Another eminent public figure, Lord Shawcross, Attorney General in the Labour Government of 1945, but now politically independent, in a speech to the Royal Society of St. George in London criticized the British people for 'playing for safety, looking for salaried jobs with pensions, shirking responsibility and trying to get more by giving less and less' (*The Times*, 4.5.1962). He preferred to talk of 'blood, toil, tears and sweat' rather than of 'never having it so good'. To him, the outstandingly successful barrister, the idea of a salaried job with a pension obviously did not appeal, but it is not certain whether his harangue will cut much ice with people in the lower income brackets exposed to the threats of sudden redundancy and unemployment. Galbraith has rather severely criticized those who cherish economic insecurity for others (p. 77), and Fyvel (p. 195) calls 'this sort of moral lecturing pretty pointless'.

In the field of high international politics it can hardly be claimed that recent developments in atomic testing or Governmental attitudes to reactionary colonial powers and the like have been able to strengthen the public sense of moral values and to guide the man in the street in his attempts to distinguish between right and wrong.

The distorted sense of values has been deplored not only by distinguished lawyers standing politically fairly to the right or at least not too close to the left, but also by many others in responsible positions, whether members of the Labour party or of unknown political affiliations. To give only a few examples out of many, Mr. Frank Allaun, Labour M.P. for Salford East, in a letter to *The Times* (23.4.1962), and in the House of Commons, denounces the fact that there are nearly five million households, i.e. approximately fifteen million people, in this country without a bath of their own: 'In an age of automation, atomic energy and space travel, we cannot provide families with a bath in their house. This is a wrong sense of values.' While this fact, if it should be one, is universally deplored, members of different parties differ, of course, in their views on causes and remedies concerning the absence and provision of these five million baths. Or, another example: At the annual Conference of the National Union of Teachers of 1962 the president disapproved of what he called 'the pursuit of novelty for its own sake' and the showing of photographs of the now invisible side of the moon in schools which still possess 'sanitary and heating systems that would have been condemned years ago if the Factory Acts had been applied to educational buildings . . .' 'Sanitation before space travel' was his slogan (*The Times*, 23.7.1962). A psychiatrist, writing to *The Times* at approximately the same time (5.4.1962) about the incidence of mental breakdowns in new towns such as Crawley, in Sussex, reveals the existence of a strong sense of guilt 'in a world where two thirds of the population are below subsistence level and the richer third spend their substance on better methods of atomic annihilation'. Such international comparisons between the under- and over-nourished sections of the world population easily lead to similar juxtapositions of the pecuniary rewards offered to different groups of persons in this country: The five-months dispute between the commercial television companies and 'Equity', the Actors' Trade Union, was happily brought to an end in the same month of April, 1962, to which, as the reader will have noticed, most of our quotations so far refer (any other month of perhaps any other post-war year might have produced a similar collection of material). Under this settlement, 'for pronouncing the words "Dinner is served, milady" a fee of twenty-eight guineas will be offered if the show is flashed all over the country; and if an actor's contribution consists of more than ten words his minimum payment will be thirty-six guineas' (*The Times*, 4.4.1962). The modest increases in the salaries of probation officers recommended by the Morison Committee of 1962 were contrasted with the attitude of a television actor portraying a probation officer who was reported to have demanded a fee of £850 for an appearance instead of the £450 so far paid (*Hansard*, 10.5.1962, col. 670). Footballers are 'sold' for up to £150,000 by one club to another (the *Observer*, 13.5.1962), and the adulation freely afforded to them, to cricketers, ballet dancers, film and television stars and the like makes our present society look ridiculous, if not downright imbecile. During the Post Office workers' period of 'working to rule' in early 1962 it was claimed that Football Pool coupons were receiving preferential treatment. One can understand the feelings of a 'civil servant' who writing to the *New Statesman* (6.4.1962), regards the pay of £1 9s. less deductions, received by his daughter, a staff midwife at a local hospital, for ten hours' work delivering two babies, as unsatisfactory, and we are indeed tempted to compare this with the fee now payable to the members of 'Equity'. Obviously, two live babies are worth far, far less than four words on television, although the acquittal at the Liége thalidomide trial provoked the most indignant moral outcries and protestations of the dignity and inviolability of human life (see the daily and Sunday papers from 11th November 1962 onwards). On the other hand, the workers of the Ford Company at Dagenham and others were severely criticized for staging a one-hour strike in sympathy with the nurses' pay claim because this was endangering production and therefore the wrong means towards a laudable end.

Some of these cases lead us straight to the heart of what are some of the top problems of our present society, that of production and that of the relationship between the public and the private sectors of the economy. On both of them much light has recently been shed by Galbraith's widely quoted *Affluent Society*. As far as production is concerned he courageously attacks the tendency prevalent in western society to make a fetish of production regardless of the nature of the goods produced, and thereby to 'divorce economics from any judgement on the goods with which it was concerned' (p. 115). Whereas in former days more production meant more food for the hungry, more clothing for the cold, it now means satisfying the craving for more luxury goods. 'When man has satisfied his physical needs, then psychologically grounded desires take over,' which can never be fully satisfied (p. 112). In this Galbraith followed Keynes' distinction between needs which are absolute and those the satisfaction of which only serves to make us 'feel superior to our fellows' (p. 118), just as Keynes may have followed Durkheim (see Chapter 22, s.1). And as many of the needs of the second category have only been artificially created by those who produce such goods these needs cannot be used to justify production. There is—as Galbraith admits—perhaps not much that is novel in all this and in the emphasis on the peculiar role played in the creation of such wants by modern advertising and salesmanship (p. 121), but it is useful to have it so emphatically stated by an economist of great authority. What he may not sufficiently take into consideration is the position of a country such as Britain which more than the United States depends on its exports of goods, whether they may be essential or luxury goods. Moreover, and of this he is only too well aware, the matter looks quite different from the point of view of the worker who would lose his job if society would give up the production of unnecessary goods. To satisfy his own essential needs he may be dependent on such production, but does this necessarily imply that he is entirely unconscious of its wasteful and parasitic character? And, after all, a high proportion of these luxury goods —among them those giant cars which Galbraith regards with particular disfavour—finds its way not into the export trade but into the home market. Workers engaged in their production would be less than human if their reaction to the bewildering abundance of mass production would not also be one of bewilderment and ambivalence. While their attitude may be one of admiration and gratitude for the chance of full employment which it provides, it may be mixed with envy as many of the goods produced are out of their reach and there may also be the vague feeling that having to spend their lives producing what is not really needed for the good of society is in fact misusing their labour and skill for the wrong purpose. One of the many effects of this feeling is their ever-increasing readiness to strike or to use restrictive practices, although it is of course not the only cause.

The second criticism, so forcefully made by Galbraith, extravagant spending on luxury goods in the private sector of the economy at the expense of a half-starved public sector (pp. 104, 155 ff.), is probably not applicable in quite the same strength to conditions in Britain. Private consumption is always justified, Galbraith complains, whereas public spending is, at its best, a necessary evil. As every visitor to the United States knows, this contrast between private opulence of a few and public squalor as affecting the lives of the masses is far more striking over there than it is in post-war Britain, but nobody can contend that it has here been completely eradicated. Fyvel (pp. 208–210 and after) has already presented some evidence on this, and it would be easy to add to it. 'Expenditure by local authorities on welfare services for the aged, the handicapped and the homeless . . . recognized as one of the most under-staffed and impoverished services in 1949, has risen at a slower rate than almost all categories of private and public expenditure', wrote Titmuss in 1960 (p. 2).

The incessant struggle between the public and the private sectors of society for a larger share of the available wealth and power has recently found a clear expression in the House of Lords' debates on commercial television and the influence of the 'pressure groups' working for its further expansion (9.5.1962). It was significant that the passionate attack on the promoters of commercial television made by Lord Reith, a former Minister and Director General of the B.B.C. and often regarded as the father of British broadcasting, found the strong support of *The Times* who wrote that 'No amount of protestation about the evils of monopoly . . . can get round the facts of what happened . . . it was not immorality that the opponents of commercial television feared. It was the inanity that can now be heard and seen for hours on end. The commercial programmes had . . . to make the running, and the B.B.C. could not or did not ignore them. The loss to true values is irreparable in the sense that for some years now a public that would have taken happily to better fare has been fed largely on chaff' (11.5.1962). These are strong words, but perhaps not even strong enough. It may only be added that, according to Lord Francis-Williams in the same debate, commercial television advertising revenue had risen from 42 million pounds in 1955 to 293 million in 1961.

After this had been written, the *Report of the Pilkington Committee on Broadcasting* (H.M.S.O., Cmd. 1753, June 1962) was published which condemns commercial television in the strongest terms, but is much too lenient as far as the B.B.C. is concerned, large parts of whose programmes are equally deplorable. It is symptomatic of this low standard that *The Times* (14.11.1962) could 'welcome' the promised extension of broadcasting hours with a leader headed 'More and More of Less and Less'. The Pilkington Report rightly criticizes the well-worn excuse used by all the agencies of mass entertainment that it is their duty 'to give the public what it wants'; this phrase, questioned already by Lord Radcliffe, is, the Report says, 'patronizing and arrogant, in that it claims to know what the public is, but defines it as no more than the mass audience; and in that it claims to know what it wants, but limits its choice to the average of experience'. Unfortunately, that excuse conforms to general Government practice. All too often, Government spokesmen have used that phrase to defend the failure of the legislation to implement progressive proposals to which they were opposed on grounds of party politics.[31]

It can hardly be denied that the malaise of British post-war society has been greatly mitigated by the growing impact of the Welfare State with its increased spending on the social services. Together with full employment and rising wages it has prevented at least some of the most dangerous effects of our crisis in values. Taken as a whole, a physically much healthier and far better nourished generation has made its appearance as compared with its predecessors, a generation also far better aware of the need for proper medical care and making higher demands on it.[32] As mentioned earlier on, these improvements have also been visible in the physical conditions of juvenile delinquents (Chapter 11, II, Note 19). On the other hand, the idea of the Welfare State has been subjected to bitter attack as unduly favouring the working classes at the expense of the others and as fostering the lack of individual responsibility, the tendency to expect too much from the State and encouraging a 'wanting everything for nothing' attitude. For such reasons it has often been suspected of leading to an increase in crime and juvenile delinquency. A former Chief Metropolitan Magistrate, Sir Laurence Dunne, for example is reported as having said: 'I put it down very largely to the Welfare State. That removed a lot of responsibility from people. And wages have gone up out of all recognition. In the vernacular, a very large section of the population have tasted meat for the first time, and they want bigger helpings. They have developed expensive tastes and they go to any length to get the necessary money.'[33] Some of these charges are probably well-founded, although exact evidence is difficult to obtain.

Social services requiring an enormous administrative apparatus can easily be abused and exploited by the less conscientious members of the community, and, unavoidably, they lead to a weakening of the individual citizen's sense of responsibility for himself and his dependants. Those whose business it is to prevent and discover abuses are not throughout sufficiently well trained and alert to cope with the problem. Speaking generally, however, it seems to be clear that the Welfare State has produced vastly more good than evil. Moreover, as Titmuss and his fellow-workers have shown, the widespread belief that the Welfare State favours one-sidedly the working classes at the expense of the others has little foundation in the facts if the concept of the 'social services' is defined widely enough so as to include, for example, taxation reliefs and many 'fringe' benefits which favour mainly the middle classes.[34] As he points out, the terms 'needs' and 'social services' have a different meaning today from fifty years ago, and in particular man's 'culturally determined dependencies' have grown in range and importance in accordance with Durkheim's observation that such dependency increases with the increasing in-dividualization and specialization of labour.[35]

The existing gaps in the services provided by the Welfare State have been exposed by such writers as Audrey Harvey and Peter Townsend who maintain that, while the British working classes as a whole have become much more prosperous in the post-war period and it is very difficult to assess the real extent of present-day 'residual' poverty the latter seems to be far greater than generally assumed.[36] Of course, those who belong to this minority of perhaps a few million people, most of them 'retired, sick, unemployed and widowed persons and their dependants' (Townsend), carry little weight politically, nor are they likely to be of any direct criminological significance, but their presence is a reminder that the Welfare State has not been able to resolve all the economic and social problems of the community which it serves—a reminder only too necessary in a society where, in the words of the London correspondent of the *Corriere della Sera*, it is 'unfashionable to talk of poverty' (*The Times*, 12.4.1962). Nor has the Welfare State so far succeeded in solving its psychological diffi-culties and anxieties. Fyvel has called his book *The Insecure Offenders*, implying that the feeling of insecurity is largely responsible for the misconduct of teenagers—a point to be further discussed at a later stage. Here we are concerned with the wider issues of how insecurity and inequality affect the social and moral climate of society as a whole.

In an important speech delivered at a New York banquet of the American Publishers' Association, the then Prime Minister Mac-millan seems to have dealt with some of these issues (*The Times*, 27.4.1962). Referring to Disraeli's *Two Nations* he said: 'That has gone. We are one nation now': unemployment and poverty have been obliterated, and 'as a result, the class war, as we used to call it, is dead or nearly dead'. Of course, 'we have plenty of problems . . . but at least they spring from buoyancy and not from stagnation'. Was this perhaps a reply to Shanks's book *The Stagnant Society*? *The Times* was not quite convinced by the Prime Minister's statement: Is the class war in Britain, for example, 'dead or nearly dead'? Do all our problems 'spring from buoyancy not stagnation'? Let us consult the experts. We have already found that they do not regard poverty as having been completely obliterated in Britain, but it might perhaps be added that according to Galbraith—whose remarks on this point are borne out by our personal observations, however scanty—even in the United States 'poverty survives', though no longer 'as a uni-versal or massive affliction'.[37] It survives if only because it is a relative conception which constantly changes with the changing standard of living of the people as a whole. If, as he states, in the mid-fifties one American family in thirteen had a cash income of less than a thousand dollars, this is poverty on a fairly substantial scale, but, as he rightly observes, as the very poor are no longer in the majority they no longer interest the politicians.

While Galbraith's views on the American affluent society have so far seemed to be, *mutatis mutandis*, applicable to Britain, too, there is one point, a very important one, where this is not true: his often repeated thesis that in modern western society the interest of the masses in equality and security is fading away, being replaced by the overriding interest in production (pp. 64 ff., 93, 244). His explanation is, in part, the changing distribution of wealth and income in favour of the poorer sections (p. 67). That considerable changes in the same direction have occurred in this country, too, is a commonplace observation. For example, while in 1911–13, 1 per cent of the adult population owned 70 per cent of the total capital, and in 1924–30 still 60 per cent, at present the figure is only 35 per cent.[38] But even so, the distribution is still 'fantastically unequal', with 2·5 per cent of the adult population owning 52·2 per cent, i.e. more than half of the total (Brittan). To understand why this and the feeling of insecurity are still burning issues in Britain one has only to turn to the recent book of an economist whose political views seem to be moderate rather than on the extreme left, Michael Shanks's *Stagnant Society*. Apparently he has had far fewer and less glamorous reviews here than Galbraith, probably because criticism of the U.S.A. is more popular and attractive in this country than self-criticism and many reviewers may not have realized that some of Galbraith's strictures are applicable outside the U.S.A. as well. Shanks's main points, as far as they are relevant in the present context, may be summarized as follows: Contrary to what Prime Minister Macmillan said a year after the book had been published, in the author's view the class war does still exist in Britain, 'in cold, if not in hot form' (pp. 59 ff.); there is an almost complete lack of mutual understanding and confidence between the middle and the working classes, and many of the older working-class communities still live in a world of 'we' and 'they'. He admits that modern Britain is no longer divided into 'rigid mutually exclusive social classes', and that the class structure is rather a continuance where it is hard to tell where one class ends and the other begins, but the old conflict in basic attitudes is still the same, with the working classes looking at some basic economic and moral problems in a way entirely different from that of the middle classes. Industrialists and managers may well argue that, because of their small numbers, their aggregate share of the cake, though substantial for each individual, is, as far as the community as a whole is concerned, insignificant—the worker, 'with his worm's eye view', sees things differently and does not understand the fuss made by employers

437

about a few shillings' rise in his weekly wage packet. Nor has he, in present circumstances, any incentive to work harder and to increase production. On the contrary, the old fear of 'working oneself out of a job' and the preference for overtime work are still very strong. While there are certain signs that 'the old working class is dying' it takes a very long time in doing so, and there may be a danger that its traditional attitudes may be carried over to the new society. A mixture of old and newly acquired attitudes may exist within the same person, which may be 'either beneficent or explosive' (p. 68). This particular subject is taken up by the author in a later chapter (pp. 139 ff.), where he tries to show that the new prosperity so evident in industrial boom towns such as Coventry and Nottingham has produced neither greater happiness nor more security. The contrary is true he thinks: there is among these workers earning very high wages a strong sense of guilt for two conflicting reasons: because they have it so much better than their parents and because all this is too good to last—feelings and apprehensions which are in part responsible for their often excessive spending, much of it of course on the 'never-never'. Moreover, under the present system of unemployment benefit the latter declines in proportion as wages rise, while on the other hand, greater prosperity heightens the aspirations and makes sudden deprivations even less tolerable.[39] All this justifies the paradox 'the higher the income the greater the insecurity'. Whether in the depressed mining areas of pre-war Britain or in comparatively prosperous towns, twenty years of full employment have not been long enough to wipe out the scars of the 'hungry thirties'. All this confirms the view expressed by the present writer nearly a quarter of a century ago[40] that 'long-term unemployment may show its effect even many years after being brought to an end, and it is capable of changing permanently the whole attitude of a family towards society. Such a change may express itself in actions at a time when its external cause has already disappeared.'

In times of recurring sudden and prolonged unemployment or short-time work the effect may be disastrous as some of those boom towns experienced a few years ago when work in the motor industry became slack and there was a great deal of redundancy. In this connection Shanks refers to the less insecure position of American motor workers who now receive up to 60 per cent of their normal pay for the first six months of unemployment. The lack of security which hangs like a dark cloud over the British working population is highlighted by the changing fate of the miners and dockers who move uneasily from a state of hectic over-employment to the opposite extreme and back again without even fully comprehending the reason why.

With regard to the dockers, attention was drawn in my *Social*

Aspects (p. 140) to the 'unduly large proportion of casual labour' in Liverpool between the wars and its effects, and it is interesting to read in the Devlin Report of 1955 on 'Port Transport Industry' the following:[41]

In 1939 the dockers were still struggling for jobs; by 1949 they were in a position—even a minority of them—to paralyse the life of the nation and to bring about a State of Emergency . . . their sufferings before 1939 were more severe than most; all bitter memories have not gone; many men take longer than the dockers are doing to learn the lesson that there can be no power without responsibility . . . The fear of ostracism is especially great, for they form a tightly knit community and still live to a large extent . . . in a close neighbourhood round the docks . . . Conditions in the industry have never permitted the creation of an ordinary human relationship between employer and employed which perhaps more than anything else makes for peace in industry.

'The biggest nightmare for many of the weekly wage-earners is redundancy,' writes a Company Chairman (*The Times*, 7.6.1962), 'after all this time we have not yet implemented the Workers' Charter which was advocated several years ago', and he suggests that a percentage of the Profits Tax should be set aside for security purposes. It was only in the Queen's Speech of the 29th October 1962, at the re-opening of Parliament, that the Government promised a Bill providing a Workers' Charter to alleviate some of the hardships of redundancy (see *The Times*, 30.10.1962, also Geoffrey Goodman, *Redundancy in the Affluent Society*, Fabian Society Pamphlet, 1962). The Contracts of Employment Bill, introduced in November 1962, provides that employers will be required to give two weeks' notice of termination of employment to those who have been continuously employed by them for two years and four weeks to those who have been employed for five years. This 'Belated Charter' fails, however, in the words of *The Times*, 'to give security to those most in need of it, the men in casual industries like building and shipbuilding who may be sacked on two hours' or a day's notice and seldom work for the same employer continuously for two years . . . The . . . Bill must be seen as a beginning, not as a last word.' (13.12.1962.) It became law on the 31.7.63.

It is interesting to compare Shanks's picture with that presented simultaneously by Ferdynand Zweig in his study *The Worker in an Affluent Society*[42] which, differently from Shanks's general survey of the whole field, is based on 672 interviews with samples of workers in five British factories. The whole tone of Zweig's book and his way of looking at the situation are somewhat more rosy, and the reader gets the impression that he is doing his utmost to be as positive and optimistic as his material permits, but his patent intellectual honesty as a scholar forces him to stress the darker sides as well. Moreover, it is doubtful—and the author himself shares this doubt (p. xi)—whether his case material is really representative of the British working population as a whole since it was obtained from prosperous and expanding industries where rates of pay and earnings tended to be above average (p. xi). Moreover, unskilled labourers numbered only 11 per cent of the sample, whereas there were 53·7 per cent semi-skilled, 29·1 per cent skilled workers and 6 per cent supervisors in the sample. One might perhaps say, therefore, that the book should have been called 'the Affluent Worker in an Affluent Society'. Even so, Zweig concludes that, while the 'Two Nations' may be a thing of the past in terms of economics, they are not so in terms of education and culture. 'One cannot help feeling deeply disturbed at the apparent waste of human intelligence amongst manual workers' (p. 95), but he expresses the hope that the rise in cultural standards will come in due course, with the significant proviso, however, that the worker 'is not deflected by vested interests into the marshlands of the candyfloss world'. 'The intensity of class consciousness and class sub-conscious-ness seem to be on the decline', he thinks (p. 135), but the latter 'sometimes lingers in the dim recesses of man's mind, primarily fed by past unemployment, starvation wages, unfair treatment, class dis-crimination, by a common struggle against injustice . . . it often comes to life when a man is confronted by some acts which forcibly bring home his status to him.' And 'those conceptions which deny the existence of a conflict between capital and labour are false to life. No amount of sermons on the theme of social solidarity will do away with the basic conflict between capital and labour. But the conflict is also not the whole truth' (p. 204), and the worker 'wants little things rather than big things. The class struggle interests him less and less' (p. 209).

The confidence of the workers in the honesty and reliability of the business world is further undermined by the goings-on on the stock market, by successful or unsuccessful take-over bids, by the all-too conspicuous, apparently effortless, and socially undesirable accumu-lation of vast fortunes in the hands of a very few individuals and companies. While some of these transactions may be economically sound, many of them have but little justification and do not contribute to the common good. The growth of monopolies, regardless of the interests of the industries concerned, continues practically unchecked by the existing legislation which, different from its American counter-part,[43] has proved to be entirely inadequate for the objects it is sup-posed to achieve. 'A basic philosophy of values', writes Wolfgang Friedmann (p. 285), 'must underlie any legal approach to the problem of excessive concentration of economic power and other restrictive practices and situations.' This basic philosophy of values does not exist at present, and most observers when watching the battles of the 'giants', such as the recent one between I.C.I. and Courtaulds,[44] find themselves in a position equally bewildering as that of Sir Norman Angell's little niece: on entering a cinema where 'a thrilling drama was half-way through, with one group of men belabouring another, after a few moments of watching she asked her companion in tones of agony: "Do tell me whether these men are the good men or the bad men. I cannot go on any longer not knowing whether to be glad or sorry".'[45] The difference is, however, that the bewildered members of the public watching these events have no wise uncle to turn to. The Government is hardly in a position to advise them, having themselves 'no firm principles by which it is judging moves in the industrial field' (*The Times*, 13.3.1962). It is not surprising, therefore, to read that a large group of Conservative backbenchers, feeling that 'the party image has been damaged by the failure to act against monopolistic tendencies', even in a case (concerning the Imperial Tobacco Company) where the Monopolies Commission had decided that the relationship under investigation was 'not in the public interest', opened 'what promises to be a determined campaign to persuade the Government to act against monopolies' (the Political Correspondent of *The Times*, 31.5.1962). To this and similar points which can be only briefly referred to in this preliminary *al fresco* survey we shall have to return at some greater detail in the subsequent chapters.

Take-over cases such as the Grunwald, Jasper Group and State Building Society affair of 1959–60 or the I.C.I.–Courtaulds struggle of 1961, or the disappearance of the *News Chronicle* in 1961 resulting in the loss of employment for many clerical and manual workers; sudden slumps on the American and European Stock Exchanges such as the one of the 28th May 1962, which, as the booms of the years before, seem to serve mainly to enrich a small group of professional speculators, amply demonstrate to the great masses of the population the weaknesses of the present economic and legal structure. Especially at a time when great efforts are made to spread the idea of share ownership among circles previously untouched by it, slumps for which no obvious reasons can be produced can easily arouse the suspicion that the 'share owning democracy' is only an additional device to concentrate the wealth of the nation even more in the hands of a few; and it matters very little whether or not such suspicions are justified or even reasonable—the essential fact is that they exist and may well exist in the minds of men who are perhaps not particularly well informed but not necessarily fools. Moreover, as *The Times* complained (23.5.1962), the long-promised statute to protect small investors against 'fly-by-night' firms has not yet seen the light of day. Already in March 1960 several Conservative M.P.s, supported by *The Times*, had introduced a Bill to 'stop certain un-scrupulous financial manipulators from trying to get money under false pretences', but the Government doubted 'whether it was appro-priate to deal with a subject of such complexity in a private member's Bill', although 'there was no doubt that a most valuable service had been performed in focussing attention on the surprising fact that a company which published no accounts should be free to solicit deposits from the public' (House of Commons debate, 18.3.1960, *The Times*, 19.3.1960); but it was not before the 10th July 1963 that a rather narrow 'Protection of Depositors Act' was formally placed on the Statute Book. How far the so-called Capital Gains Tax—some writers dispute its right to this proud name—and any of the measures which may be taken to implement the rather timid recommendations of the Jenkins Committee on the reform of the Company Law (see the *Observer*, 24.6.1962) will ensure greater fairness and honesty in business matters remains to be seen and the same applies to the measures of the present Government.

It is, however, not merely these anomalies in the economic field that are undermining the confidence of the masses but, as writers such as Shanks and Titmuss have shown,[46] the equally profound dis-crepancies in status and opportunities between employers and em-ployees, conspicuously present in matters small and large: from the different hours of work (the earlier you have—with the emphasis on the 'have'—to start work in the morning the lower is your status) to the differences in dress, in the description of your pay, in the length of your holidays, the notice of dismissal required and dozens of other items. 'Nobody deliberately planned it,' writes Shanks, but it is 'always there, invisible but all-pervasive', the distinction between 'we' and 'they'. Moreover, the increasing mechanization of modern in-dustry leads to a down-grading of old manual skills and subsequent loss of status which 'can be a serious injury to the personality. It can lead to less dependable behaviour. It is thus closely linked to what is called a "sense of responsibility" ' (Titmuss). Shanks (p. 167), who is in no way concerned with the criminological aspects of the matter, nevertheless has a reference here to 'the able man whose ambitions are frustrated through lack of opportunity' and what he rightly regards as one of the greatest dangers to society: 'Such men are only too apt to become embittered. In extreme cases they become master criminals. In less extreme cases they will become political rebels and extremists.' From his personal experience he refers to a number of 'highly militant and in some cases deliberately obstructionist shop stewards' who felt, he thinks rightly, that they could have done a better job than their managers if they had been given the same opportunities. He is objective enough to add that the cases where men felt like that without justification were rather more frequent and that there are men who would be rebels in any society. But, as we have seen already before, 'if men define a situation as real it *is* real in its consequences' (W. I. Thomas). We shall come back to the subject in the next chapters; here we have only to point out that a sociological-economic discussion such as that presented by Shanks has, by way of an objective analysis of important aspects of our society, led to much the same result as was reached in one of our psychological chapters: the emphasis on the key position of the 'feeling of injustice'.

Moreover, industrial sociologists and psychologists have shown in a large number of recent studies that technological and managerial changes have given rise to new forms of conflict between management and labour.[47]

In the non-criminological field the consequences are, among others, a more or less complete absence of a feeling of loyalty towards their employers on the part of the workers, constantly recurring unofficial strikes, and shoddy workmanship damaging the reputation of industry at home and abroad.

To interpret this chapter or the following as a criticism of individual persons or even groups of persons would mean a misunderstanding of its objects which are solely concerned with the structure of our contemporary society as such. There can be no indictment of individuals where 'all are guilty'. Value judgments are, of course, present everywhere, but as pointed out before (Chapter 3) they are made by the writer as a citizen, not as a criminologist, and no special expert knowledge is claimed for them. Moreover, the picture presented is one-sided in placing the emphasis almost exclusively on the darker side of our society; obviously, there are many brighter spots as well, otherwise this society would no longer be able to function. As it is not altogether affluent, so it is not throughout stagnant or criminogenic either. It is in the nature of a criminological enquiry that in its endeavour to explain crime it has to draw special attention to those darker sides. In the valuable series of discussions presented by the B.B.C. in summer 1962 under such headings as 'What is wrong with Britain' and in some of the articles published in *The Times* at the same time under the title 'The Pulse of England: People in Need of a New Outlook' all these points were made once more in a concise form by a number of responsible people, and some of the hostile reactions which these publications received showed, with very few exceptions, merely the truth of the charges made.[48] In our following chapters we have to examine how far the picture is further darkened by the class character of our society.

Chapter 20

OUR CRIMINOGENIC SOCIETY II: SOCIAL CLASS AND CLASS CONFLICT: THEIR CRIMINOLOGICAL IMPLICATIONS

I. SOCIAL CLASS AND CLASS CONFLICT[1]

In our previous chapter the problem of social class has been touched upon mainly with reference to the relationship between worker and employer in factories, but it has of course a much wider significance and dominates the whole of British society and, perhaps to a lesser degree, some other parts of the western world too. And as most criminals are believed to belong to the lower social classes the subject presents us with one of the most important issues of the sociology of crime. In spite of the existence of an immense sociological literature on class, basic questions such as the definition of class; the dividing line between the various social classes; the extent, directions and effect of social mobility which has taken place in the post-war years; the forms of social conflict engendered by the existence of different classes, and many others are still far from settled. They have been studied by sociologists, social anthropologists, journalists, novelists and playwrights alike. Criminologists have up to the last ten or fifteen years lagged somewhat behind, but, mainly thanks to the work of Edwin H. Sutherland and his school, they are beginning to make up for past omissions. For us the basic problems are these: how far does the pattern of crime depend on the class structure of society? how far do changes in this structure, therefore, lead to corresponding changes in the pattern of crime? and how far are class conflicts responsible for crime? Before dealing with these criminological implications of the problem we have to consider the attempts made by sociologists and others to clarify the general issues.[2]

1. Historical Remarks and Definitions

Even today, a hundred years after the publication of the major works of Karl Marx (1818–83), it seems impossible to discuss the meaning of class and class conflict without referring to him. Such a reference is unavoidable at least in order to show where his prophecies of things to come have been refuted by subsequent developments. Marx was wrong in thinking:

(a) that there could be only two classes in a capitalist society, the exploiting capitalists and the exploited proletariat, the former growing ever richer and richer, the latter getting more and more miserable and also more uniform in their *misère*, so that a violent explosion would become inevitable and the victorious proletariat would finally take over.[3] He underestimated the importance and force of the middle classes which he thought would eventually be wiped out altogether;

(b) that this class struggle was entirely concerned with the question of private property in the means of production;

(c) that the only way in which fundamental social changes could be effected was by violent social revolution;

(d) that all conflicts were class conflicts and all social changes could be explained in terms of class conflicts; and that there was a predetermined course which every such conflict had to take. In other words, he was wrong in his belief in the historical inevitability of a specific form of class conflict, and in looking at society too narrowly in terms of the specific capitalist society of his period.

Actually, there has occurred not a reduction but a proliferation of social classes. In the first place, as a consequence of the invention of joint-stock companies, of co-operative and state-managed enterprises and the 'managerial revolution' with its separation of ownership and control, the capitalists of Marx's system have split at least into the two classes of the owner-managers and the non-owning managers with their new inter-group conflicts in which the working classes are not involved—a development which has been called the 'decomposition of capital'.[4] Secondly, the working classes of today bear but little resemblance to the unskilled and impoverished masses whom Marx had in mind. There has been a steady and ever-growing tendency for industrial workers to become semi-skilled and highly skilled, with a corresponding decline in the proportion of unskilled labourers.[5]

This latter decline has been observed in the U.S.A. (from 30 per cent of the total labour force in 1910 to 20 per cent in 1950) and in Britain (from 16·5 per cent in 1931 to 12·5 per cent in 1951). Dahrendorf estimates that the clerical group of workers, which may have numbered one out of twenty of the total at the time of Marx's death, is now one in five and in some industries even one in three. In any case, 'white collar' workers have multiplied by leaps and bounds, and the very complex question arises how many of them actually belong to the working and how many to the middle classes. Of course, to do

Marx justice, he had also written: 'the stratification of classes does not appear in its pure form even here [i.e. in England]. Middle and transitional stages obliterate even here all definite boundaries, although much less in the rural districts than in the cities' (*Capital*, Vol. 3, quoted from Grant, *op. cit.*, p. 23). But he did apparently not expect the differences within the working class to become so great and 'the uniting force so precarious' (Dahrendorf, *op cit.*, p. 51). And, finally, the middle class: here the process of differentiation has gone so far that most writers on the subject have to apologize for using this term at all because it has lost so much of its original meaning. Standing between the two other groups it has continuously been losing members to and also gaining some from them. In short, to do justice to the present, extremely diversified and frequently changing, class system in western society one has to split those original two or three classes into at least five or even nine. Danish sociologists use the latter system by dividing each of the three original classes, the upper, middle and lower, again into upper, middle and lower.[6] The American writer Vance Packard[7] uses five classes: the real upper, semi-upper, limited-success, working, and real lower class, but in addition there are in his system the 'horizontal' and 'vertical' layers which distinguish the minority groups such as Negroes, Jews, and certain immigrant groups, from the rest.

The criteria most commonly employed in the definition of 'class' are wealth, education, occupation, speech and accent,[8] family background, housing and 'address', child rearing habits,[9] and level of aspirations, interest in serious arts, literature, music and similar cultural pursuits, but it is invariably stressed that neither of them is necessarily decisive, and that there may be considerable national and regional variations. Some of the criteria used in American studies, for example, may have little meaning in other countries, and vice versa, and even within country and region the emphasis changes according to personal prejudices. 'Of all the signs an Englishman registers in socially "placing" his fellow man, speech remains the most flagrantly decisive', writes John Coleman, but this excludes of course the foreigner whose accent places him outside the pale anyhow. Or take matters of food: 'If you eat salad for lunch or dinner you are probably upper class. Raw tomatoes and carrots are the mark of a high social class. But serve potatoes only with vegetables—and your lower-class origins are showing' (*New Statesman*, 1.3.1963, quotation from *Daily Express* in 'This England').

One might be tempted to say that all these criteria make sense only against the background of a certain, almost indefinable, cultural atmosphere, and that 'class' is nothing but an abbreviation to describe a way of living, thinking and feeling. One can observe very

446

many families nowadays who, although middle-middle class in matters of property, income, housing, a minimum of formal education and so on, share, secretly at least, most working-class tastes and have no interest whatsoever in 'culture'. To them, their middle-class aspirations are entirely limited to matters concerning their material well-being.

In the U.S.A. much research has been done in recent years on the concept of 'deferred gratification' which was introduced to describe the phenomenon of 'impulse-renunciation' or 'self-imposed postponement of gratification or satisfaction'.[10] The object has been to test the, by no means new, hypothesis that this phenomenon is a typically middle-class pattern designed to facilitate upward social mobility into the middle class or to maintain already existing middle-class status. While this hypothesis has not invariably been confirmed by the available statistical investigations of a local character,[11] general impressions seem to indicate that we have in fact to regard the 'deferred gratification pattern' as one of the elements peculiar to middle-class and aspiring middle-class culture and closely linked to the idea of upward social mobility (below, s. 2). In the Nottingham University study of 'Radby' this has been well described as one of the characteristics distinguishing the respectable working-class 'Gladstone Road' from the also working class but less respectable and more delinquency-prone 'Dyke Street' people: 'Dyke Street will give the children anything they ask if possible because they had such a rough childhood themselves. Gladstone Road sees a danger in this. It wants long distance benefits rather than immediate pleasures for their children. Their children have got to rise educationally and financially.'[12] All this is nothing but a consequence of the splitting-up of the working class into several sub-classes: what used to be one of the dividing lines between working and middle class has now been transferred to a lower point on the continuum so as to form a barrier between the various divisions of the working class. The picture is similar to that found in recent American research (see Note 11).

Dahrendorf differs from most other writers in regarding the criteria mentioned before as factors determining not class but stratum (p. 76). To him, the most important characteristic of class is authority and power: 'the fundamental inequality of social structure, and the lasting determinant of social conflict, is the inequality of power and authority which inevitably accompanies social organization . . . classes are social conflict groups the determinant of which can be found in the participation in or exclusion from the exercise of authority . . .' (pp. 64, 138, and *passim*).

Private property in the means of production, regarded as all important by Marx, is only one of many forms of authority (p. 136). In his complete rejection of the economic factor as a criterion of class Dahrendorf goes perhaps too far, although he concedes that there is an 'empirical tendency' for authority to be, to some extent, accompanied by high income.

Each of the comprehensive factors involved in the extremely complicated definition of class consists of innumerable smaller items, all of them subject to more or less frequent changes with changing fashions in the struggle to keep up with either the 'Joneses' or, in the higher ranges of society, with the 'Cecils and Cavendishes'. Large cars and conspicuous television aerials are status symbols today; tomorrow they may be replaced by more expensive houses and indoor aerials because it will then be fashionable not to let people know that you have 'so degraded yourself as to admit to watching the telly' (letter to *The Times*, 6.6.1960). For the great majority of working- and lower middle-class families, however, the possession of a telly and a big motor car are still among the most important status symbols,[13] with washing machines and telephones taking second or third rank. In some cases, the 'six seater' assumes a status symbol of tragi-comic intensity; if its claims can be legitimately met, well and good; otherwise, the stage is set for the conflicts described in Chapter 22 below, and not only in the case of adolescents, but occasionally of adults as well.

In a short, but closely argued article Goldthorpe and Lockwood[14] have recently challenged the view that 'with the coming of the affluent society the old conception of a distinctive working class is being fast outmoded; and that today many manual wage earners and their families are becoming in most respects socially indistinguishable from various other groups . . . generally regarded as middle class'. As they point out, in spite of economic prosperity (which is only too often not identical with economic stability and security), certain characteristic patterns of middle-class social behaviour, which they call the normative and relational aspects (i.e. values, perspectives and modes of behaviour, on the one hand, and acceptance on equal terms by middle-class people, on the other), are still absent even among many higher working-class families. They conclude that, although there may be a converging of the two classes, there is no swallowing up of the one by the other.

There is an important difference of opinion as to whether 'class' can be defined by objective criteria at all or whether all we have to do is to ask how individuals classify themselves. Naturally, the subjective approach is preferred by psychologists such as Centers in U.S.A. and Eysenck[15] in Britain, the latter using the term 'social class' as measuring something entirely subjective, the term 'status' as meaning something entirely objective. Dahrendorf (pp. 145 ff.) is critical of the distinction objective-subjective, but the main points of his criticism seem to be reducible to differences in emphasis. There can be no doubt that subjective elements play an important role in the definition of class, but it would be a mistake altogether to deny the significance of objective elements. Before people can express any views as to the particular class to which they think they belong they must have an at least vague conception of the objective characteristics of the various classes in existence. Even so, Zweig[16] was right in asking the men in his sample how they placed themselves on the social scale, and their answers were revealing as demonstrating, often unconsciously, the great importance attached to class by the British working population. As mentioned above (Chapter 19) in Zweig's view the intensity of class-consciousness seemed to decline, but does not the very fact that of 346 workers who were asked how they placed themselves only 229 answered working class, whereas 54 thought they were middle class, 17 were indefinite, and 46 refused to answer, in itself prove the intensity of their feelings?

2. Social Mobility

(a) There are two socio-psychological mechanisms which greatly affect the existing class system. Social mobility, i.e. the frequency, facility and direction of the changing-over of individuals from one social class to another, is one of them, imitation the other. Social mobility has been studied in Britain mainly by D. V. Glass and his associates. Without going into details it can be said that the picture emerging from this study, carried out shortly after the war, is, in Barbara Wootton's words, 'on the whole, discouraging to the complacent equalitarian'; there is less upward mobility than one might have expected, and downward mobility is far from negligible.[17]

Simey, quoting a slightly later study by Prais, confirms this result: 'Though there is evidently a great deal of mobility in our society, and it is wrong to regard the class structure as rigid, there is room for much more than exists at the present time' (p. 842). Matters may have slightly improved in recent years. Zweig (pp. 139 ff.) found that of the sons of the workers in his sample one quarter were reaching middle-class level, but here again we have to bear in mind that his is not a truly representative sample. Simey poses the question whether lack of mobility creates conflict or whether, on the contrary, mobility itself may be a cause of conflict, and he may be right in thinking that there is something to be said for each of these opposing views (p. 840). On the one hand, 'class distinctions may be easier to tolerate if it is obvious that there is no "damned merit" in them', and if the individual victim of such distinctions can persuade himself and others that it is the rigidity of social barriers rather than his personal inadequacy that is to blame for his failure to climb the social ladder. On the other hand, where social mobility does to some extent exist, but the individual is through no fault of his own excluded from its advantages, for example because his parents cannot, or do not want to, provide the means for an extended education, he is likely to become embittered, and, as Simey points out, the number of such persons is substantial. Or the individual who has failed may blame himself and become disheartened and stop trying altogether.[18] It seems that absence and presence of social mobility are both capable of creating psychological problems, but probably in different ways and for different types of people. All we possess at present are 'crude hypotheses' (Simey), but even so we shall have to return to them later on (Chapter 22) as the matter is of crucial importance to the criminologist. American writers stress that in their society the era of limitless opportunities has come to an end, that social mobility is now relatively insignificant in the United States, that even the growing availability of college education has proved a rather illusory blessing to students from poor homes lacking the advantages of family background and connections, without which education cannot secure the expected success.[19]

In this country, too, a few sociological studies have been published after the war on the effect of educational reform on social mobility, the most recent of them being by Jean Floud, A. H. Halsey, and F. M. Martin, *Social Class and Educational Opportunity*,[20] and Brian Jackson and Dennis Marsden, *Education and the Working Class*.[21] The latter in particular is of considerable interest to the student of social mobility because it takes up in greater detail one of the subjects of Richard Hoggart's *The Uses of Literacy*, i.e. the fate of the scholarship boy.[22] Like Hoggart, these two authors came themselves from the working classes in the North of England, had worked their way through grammar school and university and possessed, therefore, some personal experience and understanding of the human and social problems they were examining. They are grateful for the chances of a higher education given them by the Welfare State; had they been born fifty years earlier they would probably have spent their lives as weavers in northern mills (p. 13), but they are naturally anxious to see the picture as a whole instead of resting on their own personal laurels.

The place of their research was 'Marburton', a prosperous industrial city of medium size in the North where they had spent their youth, with a working-class population (skilled, semi-skilled and unskilled) of 78 per cent against an average of 74 per cent for Great

Britain, with (at the time) little unemployment and a slightly over-average successful educational system. Thanks to the Education Act of 1944 and the abolition of school fees, here as elsewhere the number of working-class children going to grammar school had increased, but even so in the period 1949–52, which was taken as an example, only 36 per cent of its pupils who passed had working-class fathers, whereas 64 per cent were of middle-class origin (p. 11).[23] Moreover, the impressions of the authors confirmed the statement of the Crowther Report of 1959[24] that nearly one half of the young men with an I.Q. of over 120 left school at the age of 16 and that for those with an I.Q. between 108 and 120 the figure was 87 per cent; that those who left without taking the full course were predominantly working class and that this wastage of talent was largely a class wastage (pp. 13 and 210). In other words, 'very many able working-class children either do not reach grammar school at all, or they leave without taking the full course'. The same conclusion was reached by Jean Floud and her co-authors. Not satisfied with these statistical findings, Jackson and Marsden interviewed ten middle-class and eighty-eight working-class children and their parents to discover why so many more middle-class children were able successfully to complete their grammar school course; and what kind of difficulties the working-class children, whether successful or not, encountered; what were the outstanding characteristics of those who succeeded and of those who did not; and what was the effect of higher education on the successful ones. Only a few of their findings and impressions can here be mentioned. A high proportion, more than one-third, of the successful working-class children came from what the authors call 'sunken middle-class' families, i.e. those who had originally been middle class and had come down in the world, but tried 'to re-invest their energies in the education of their children' (pp. 54–5). This means a further reduction in the numbers of successful working-class children, most of whom, by the way, came from small families.

Among them, there were some who, at the bottom of their hearts, refused to 'accept' the grammar school with all the conflicts it produced between their previous ways of living and thinking and those of their families, on the one hand, and the middle-class values of the grammar school on the other. However, more important than this comparatively small group were those, in the authors' view, very large numbers of gifted working-class children who left the school prematurely because of such conflicts. 'The rebels left' (p. 103). Even for those who conformed and stayed on, 'the picture of social mobility was not as easy and triumphant as all that, when examined closely' (p. 158). Many found themselves socially and psychologically sitting between two stools or rather two classes and belonging to neither of them; only 58 per cent of them considered themselves as middle class when interviewed later in life, and over half of the parents thought their children were still working class (pp. 171–2). From this the authors conclude that ' "class" could be something in the blood, in the very fibre of a man or woman . . . not something to be shuffled off with new possessions, new prospects, new surroundings . . .' However, this feeling of loyalty to their class of origin was not often found, and the authors stress that for very many of the successful ones 'the most vital connections between the child and his working-class home were atrophied or severed' (p. 173), but they were also aware that some of these psychological difficulties may arise in the case of non-working-class families, too (p. 186).

In short, Jackson and Marsden's excellent study shows that 'the crudest economic barriers [to higher education] have been removed, only to reveal subtler ones at work. It is now clearer to see the many small ways in which money and power in society prepare early for a competitive situation' (p. 210). Their book has provoked a great deal of both applause and criticism. Critics have been quick to point out, for example, that the psychological and social problems which working-class grammar school children have to face are negligible as compared with the frustration suffered by those gifted children who because of their origin fail to obtain a better education. Headmasters have also claimed that in view of the rapidly changing social climate of our time the picture painted by the authors, based upon early post-war conditions, is already getting out-of-date.[25] While it is difficult to accept the latter claim, it is certainly true that the fate of the few grammar school successes, interesting as it is, should not be allowed to obscure the more tragic and from the point of view of society more important situation of those, apparently far more numerous, failures. They provide a fertile recruiting ground for the army of able men to whom Shanks refers as 'one of the greatest dangers to society' (p. 167; see Chapter 19, text to Note 39) and representing one of the most obvious illustrations of sociologically explainable frustration (see Chapter 22 below).

In the present chapter we are, of course, concerned with education only as far as it affects social mobility; its more specifically criminological aspects will be treated in Chapter 24.

At this stage it might be apposite to refer again to Dahrendorf's theory of class and class conflict and his insistence that the recent improvements in the economic position of the masses in western society do not touch the problems of class conflict, because the essence of the latter lies in the distribution of authority rather than of wealth. 'Even if every worker owns a car, a house and whatever other comforts of civilization there are, the root of industrial class conflict is not only not eliminated, but hardly touched' (pp. 64 and 254). Although modern society has been able to 'institutionalize class conflict', i.e. to develop a number of institutional devices such as collective bargaining and organs of conciliation and arbitration designed to eliminate conflict, 'they may, indeed, actually increase the violence of conflict by redirecting it' (p. 66). Dahrendorf is, therefore, critical of those writers who, like Mayo and Drucker, believe that class conflict will be eliminated by proper organization (p. 109 ff.). To him, 'societies create out of their structure with predictable certainty the conditions of social antagonism . . . therefore society is . . . at best a relatively integrated system of conflicting structural forces', and 'conflict is an essential element of the structure of every society' . . . 'Psychological factors are a secondary characteristic, not the cause of social conflict.' What distinguishes this theory from that of Marx is that for Dahrendorf class conflict does *not* mean an 'inevitable process of intensification leading up to a revolutionary explosion', and there is no 'predetermined course of class conflict' (pp. 132–3). While we can agree with most of these statements, there seems to be insufficient evidence as yet for the claim that institutionalization may actually increase the violence of class conflict, and the author himself admits at a later stage (p. 277) that the violence and intensity of industrial conflict have actually declined. Moreover, the power of the psychological forces involved seems to be somewhat underrated by Dahrendorf. With regard to strikes, for example, the present writer tried to show in an earlier book[26] how much their conduct depends on national and individual characteristics. Another point where we differ from Dahrendorf is his view that the lowest strata of society, Marx's *Lumpenproletariat*, are excluded from conflict group formation because they are largely recruited in 'structurally irrelevant ways', for example by delinquency (p. 187).

3. *Imitation and Rebellion*[27]

The significance of imitation, formerly often overrated, has been somewhat neglected by modern academic writers. One of its strongest nineteenth-century protagonists, Gabriel Tarde (1843–1904),[28] is nowadays usually ignored by psychologists, sociologists and criminologists alike. The reasons are not far to seek. For all his wealth of fruitful ideas, Tarde was perhaps, as Miller and Dollard point out (p. 246), 'not actually very important as a theorist in regard to the imitative mechanism. He was quite properly willing to leave this problem to the social psychologists.' Moreover, he was inclined to oversimplify the issue and to use it in too broad a sense so as 'to explain everything (which was decidedly over-working the trick)'.[29]

He formulated three 'laws of imitation': first, men imitate others in proportion to the closeness of their contacts and, therefore, they do so more in cities and other places where crowds assemble than elsewhere. Secondly, the social trend of imitation goes from the lower to the higher social classes, i.e. the former tend to imitate the latter. Thirdly, where there is a clash between two opposing fashions one can become the substitute for the other. We are here mainly interested in the second of these 'laws', all of which are of course nothing but mere trends.

The work of modern theorists has mainly consisted in certain refinements of that general idea of imitation, based upon observations of animal and child behaviour. Social psychologists have made use of imitation as one of the starting points for their theory of learning as opposed to the previous tendency to regard it as an instinctive, non-learned process. They distinguish between the various forms of behaviour which had formerly been indiscriminately called imitation, such as 'a kind of conditioned reflex imitation', on the one hand, and the 'conscious and deliberate copying of the behaviour of another' (Allport, p. 155); or between 'matched-dependent behaviour', where the imitator 'does not need to be keenly aware that his act is matched', and deliberate copying (Miller and Dollard, p. 9). The Freudians[30] place the main emphasis on the idea of identification as the basis of imitation; to them identification rather than mere imitation becomes one of the principal factors in the formation of the super-ego, but as Mowrer writes (p. 590), the exact nature of the relationship between identification and imitation is not quite clear. While the work of leading theorists and psycho-analysts has thus led to greater discernment and sophistication in our views on imitation (in its widest sense), it has so far remained on too abstract a level to be of much practical use to the solution of criminological problems.

While the present chapter is focused on the subjects of social class and mobility it should be made clear that the processes of imitation are operative not only in this field but in various others as well. Miller and Dollard, for example (Chapter 12), distinguish four classes of persons who are imitated by others, and 'superiors in a hierarchy of social status' form only one of these classes; 'superiors in an age-grade hierarchy' form another, very important, one.

In the present context, attention has to be drawn to the fact that there are important differences between imitation and social mobility, although they are both concerned with the relationship between the various social classes. Those who are successful in the process of upward mobility desert their original class and acquire membership in another. As we have seen in connection with the study of educational mobility such a desertion may in some cases not be complete, and the individual may be left sitting between two stools, but even so it amounts to a real transfer from one class to another. Mere imitation can never have this far-reaching effect; it remains more on the surface, and the individual who imitates certain aspects of the behaviour of members of a superior class hardly ever leaves his own, although imitation may occasionally act as a preparatory stage to upward mobility. 'Copying from below upward is likely to be fragmentary and transitory' (Miller–Dollard, p. 159). One might conclude, therefore, that while there are examples of completely successful social mobility, there can never be equally complete cases of mere imitation, and for this reason imitation, too, creates its own sources of discontent and frustration.

In his two books *The Hidden Persuaders* and *The Status Seekers* Vance Packard has given an abundance of illustrations of how the process of imitating higher social classes works in the U.S.A., although efficient persuaders operate, of course, through other processes as well such as 'image building', 'symbol selling', etc. It has also been discovered by market researchers that in certain situations and with certain types of people imitation may not work, and advertisers have occasionally run into trouble by too easily assuming that lower-class people would simply copy what, they were told, were the tastes of classes above them. Sometimes people want to be able to 'identify' themselves rather than to imitate, and where they find such identification impossible or where they fear to be humiliated by attempting to imitate they may altogether refuse to play the advertiser's game.[31] More often, however, copying the behaviour and fashions of other people such as film stars believed to belong to a higher social level tends to become exaggerated and farcical.

The extreme opposite of the imitator is the *rebel*; he is interested in the behaviour of other individuals or classes mainly because he is determined to behave and act in a different way to demonstrate his opposition and to exhibit his class consciousness or simply his 'otherness'. In Freudian terms this uncompromising and lasting opposition to authority is easily explainable by reference to an unresolved Oedipus complex. Mowrer describes such rebels as individuals whose 'inner personality structure remains relatively little differentiated, whose ego is almost indistinguishable from the id and whose total energies are directed towards attacking, exploiting and resisting the social order . . .' (Mowrer, p. 523). He admits that this is an oversimplification which does not do full justice to the complexities of criminal psychology. However, examples of this type are well-known in criminological literature, although it may be difficult, if not impossible, to decide in individual cases whether the psychological origins of the rebellion go back to an unresolved Oedipus complex or to later experiences, possibly outside the family, creating an overwhelming sense of injustice (see also Chapter 16, V, and Chapter 17, 'political crimes'). If we can accept as true the interesting self-analysis of 'Robert Allerton',[32] his early differences with his father were not due to any lack of sympathy for, and antagonism to, the latter but rather to a fundamental, and rather impersonal, conflict of two opposing social philosophies: while the father, notwithstanding all his bitter disappointments, pinned his faith in evolution and a gradual improvement of the social system, the son preferred to better himself by a highly personal form of revolution, i.e. crime: 'I believed the system was wrong, but I knew it wouldn't ever be changed by our sort. I didn't want to wait two hundred years for the day when everyone had fair shares' (p. 21). His fundamental attitude towards society was one of mistrust and suspicion (p. 112). To him, rebelliousness was 'almost like a natural instinct' (p. 72); so he became what his interviewer and co-author calls 'a well-integrated personality' (p. 13), but the careful reader of this challenging book may well doubt whether it is already the last word in the evolution of this, possibly not so well integrated, rebel.

One of the profoundest discussions of the problem of the rebel is that presented in Camus's *L'Homme révolté*.[33] He uses the concept in a far more comprehensive sense than has here been done and approaches it from the metaphysical and philosophical, from the historical, religious and literary angles. Even so, one of the focal points of his book is the comparison between the rebel and the criminal, in particular the murderer, but his concept of crime is as vague as that of rebellion. Logically, he concludes (pp. 245 ff.), murder and rebellion are contradictory because rebellion, as he sees it, is a constructive force; when it 'emerges into destruction' it is illogical. 'Its most profound logic is not the logic of destruction; it is the logic of creation . . . the logic of the rebel is to want to serve justice so as not to add to the injustice of the human condition.' He has to do evil, but he has to do it despite himself. Is Camus's rebel a rebel against the injustice of class distinctions? Occasionally, it seems so, as for example when he writes: 'The spirit of revolt can only exist in a society where a theoretical equality conceals great factual inequalities' (p. 26), which seems to express ideas very similar to those of Merton (see below, Chapter 22).

Far less ambiguous than that of Camus is Merton's socio-psychological interpretation of the rebel. He treats rebellion as one of his five modes of individual adaptation, the other being conformity, innovation, ritualism and retreatism (see also Chapter 22). Its distinguishing feature is that it combines the rejection of the prevailing values of society with the desire to substitute new values for the old ones. Ready candidates for rebellion are those who find the source of their personal failure in the structure of society rather than in themselves. The rebel regards the prevailing goals and standards as purely arbitrary, not commanding his allegiance. His object is to produce a closer correspondence between merit, effort and reward. Rebellion differs from *ressentiment* in that the latter aims at no genuine change in values; its pattern is rather that of sour grapes—one condemns what one secretly cherishes and craves, whereas the rebel condemns the craving itself (see also Cohen's use of the concept of ambivalence, Chapter 22 below).

The *tramp* or *vagrant*[34] has this in common with the rebel that he refuses to fit into society, to belong to any of its social classes, and to imitate the one or the other. He differs from the rebel in possessing no positive ideal or cause for which to fight society; his antagonism is purely negative and passive (see also below, Chapter 22, on Merton's 'retreatism'). In Britain, vagrancy as a mass-problem has practically disappeared in the course of the present century as the result of full employment and the changes produced by the Welfare State. The end of full employment might revive it. In other countries the phenomenon still remains under various names; research is done on it, and there exists a valuable literature, of which the work of A. Vexliard in France and of John C. Spencer in Canada deserves special mention. Of the great novelists who were fascinated by the subject, Maxim Gorki perhaps deserves pride of place. The Russian tramp of the pre-Soviet period was the hero of several of his novels and of his play *The Lower Depths*. In the words of his most recent biographer, Richard Hare, Gorki 'brilliantly distinguished that internal temperamental urge to vagrancy (deep-seated in many Russians and nomad Asiatics) from the involuntary vagabondage imposed by unstable employment and the threat of hunger'.[35]

To go back to the subject of imitation, in Britain it means not only copying the behaviour of higher social classes, but also that of Americans; the class problem, however, is never far removed even here because of the dominating role played by class in this process of copying members of other nations who, on account of their greater wealth, may also be regarded as socially superior. People who have little experience in dealing with foreigners sometimes find it difficult correctly to determine the social class to which the latter belong in their own countries and are therefore easily misled by a display of wealth, especially as they are as a rule unable to classify foreigners by their accents.

The American Invasion (Francis Williams) has become a favourite topic of discussion, and many observers of the contemporary scene are profoundly alarmed by this wholesale absorption of American films, popular singers and comedians, fashions, gadgets, pills and ideas.[36] British critics have found ample confirmation of their anxieties in the work of such well-known American writers as Riesman, Packard and, still more recently, Boorstin,[37] all of them denouncing with a wealth of material the sickness of modern American society, the unreal nature of some of its foundations, some of its false values and exaggerations. Mistakes in the upbringing of children are among the most dangerous of these exaggerations.

It is certainly true that, as an American critic of Francis Williams' book puts it, 'each country chooses for itself the way in which it wants to obliterate the national soul; if it happens in Britain, it won't be because of chewing gum and supermarkets'.[38] It is also tragically true, however, that this fateful choice has been, and is being, made all too easy by the blandishments of American big business and its powerful British allies. This country, as are many others, is deeply indebted to the United States not only for its material help in war and post-war years but also for its great contributions in the scientific fields. Modern criminology, too, as the present writer has repeatedly pointed out and the present book bears witness,[39] owes much of its recent progress to the stimulus received from American scholars, and it can safely be said that they are no less disturbed than Europeans by the manifestations of the cultural 'diffusion' which we are witnessing. And, as J. B. Priestley has recently written, 'remember, we mostly borrow what thoughtful Americans have been condemning for years' (*New Statesman*, 26.10.1962, p. 564).

II. CRIMINOLOGICAL IMPLICATIONS

Some readers of this chapter and of the preceding one may have been wondering whether this discussion, or at least part of it, really belongs to a textbook on criminology. Is it necessary, is it tactful to touch on these sore points, to rub in certain painful truths which should better be left to politicians, journalists and sociologists? Our answer is that without such discussions criminology has no right to claim its place as a branch of the social sciences. We have tried to reproduce the facts of the situation; and the feelings of members of different social classes as reflected in our quotations are important socio-psychological facts which cannot be ignored.

To the criminologist, as already stated, the class problem has a twofold significance. He is interested first in the statistical class distribution of offenders, and, secondly, in the question of whether and how class differences and conflict may be actually responsible for crime. As according to the plan of this book class is one of the pivotal concepts in our discussion of criminological problems many

458

subjects will, wholly or in part, be treated in this context which in other textbooks are dealt with under entirely different headings. This applies in particular to the subject of juvenile delinquency, various aspects of which are treated here (see, e.g., Chapter 22) instead of being reserved for Chapter 26 which deals with the subject of age.

In parenthesis, it may be noted that the concept of class has occasionally also been used in criminal legislation. The German Penal Code contained, until 1960, a provision (§ 130), which threatened with a fine or imprisonment up to two years 'any person who publicly in a manner which could endanger the peace of the community incited different classes of the population to acts of violence against one another'. 'Class' in this section was, according to a decision of the former Supreme Court of the Reich, to be defined as 'the natural limbs of the organism of the nation, grown out of the soil of its society and differentiated according to property and calling, occupation and trade, education and ancestry'.[40] However, the concept of 'class' has in the present version of the Code (Act of 30.6.1960) been replaced as 'sociologically out-of-date'[41] by the more neutral and comprehensive phrase 'parts of the population', which is intended to cover any groups within the population which can, in some way or another, be distinguished from others, provided they have a certain size and significance. Commentators of the Act have mentioned as examples the workers, peasants, civil servants, Catholics, Protestants, Jews, Bavarians, and political parties (Schwarz-Dreher). The maximum penalty has now been raised to five years' imprisonment, in addition to which a fine can be imposed.

In English law, one of the forms of sedition, which is a common law misdemeanour, consists of an attempt to promote feelings of ill-will and hostility between different classes of Her Majesty's subjects,[42] and an Act dealing with racial hatred is in preparation.

This kind of law has, of course, no bearing on the criminological problems of the present section.

1. *Class Distribution of Offenders in General*

There is a conspicuous lack of information on this subject. In Britain, neither criminal statistics nor prison statistics contain anything on it; even such potential indices of class as occupation and educational standard of offenders are not recorded, although several foreign countries include them in their official statistics.[43] We are, therefore, left with little more than the widespread general impression that crime is most prevalent among the members of the lower social classes, and for further information we have to rely on certain limited private studies of specific samples or categories of offenders. For Denmark,

459

Preben Wolf has recently made a study of the class distribution of a sample of over 3,000 Danish males aged 21 and over.[44] Of this sample 10 per cent had been at least once found guilty of an offence against the Penal Code and another 9 per cent of an offence against the special laws outside the Code. Using the Danish sociologist Svalas-toga's scheme of nine social classes, Wolf found that there was a difference between offenders against the Penal Code and offenders against special laws such as traffic-laws, by-laws, and laws mainly violated by white collar criminals. For offenders against the Penal Code the distribution was as follows (the percentage figures for offenders against the special laws will be given in brackets): Of the total number of persons in the sample belonging to the 4 upper classes 2 per cent (11 per cent) were offenders, of the total in class 5, 4 per cent (8 per cent), in class 6, 5 per cent (10 per cent), in class 7, 11 per cent (9 per cent), in class 8, 15 per cent (7 per cent), in class 9 and unknown, 16 per cent (26 per cent). There is, thus, a steady *increase* in the percentage of offenders against the Penal Code as we move down the social scale, whereas for other offenders the movement is rather irregular. Moreover, the number of registered offences per person also increased fairly steadily in the same direction. Wolf leaves it open how far these results may have been influenced by the likelihood of the offender's subsequent decline in social class as a consequence of his conviction; and he also discusses the view that most penal legislations are biased in favour of the groups in power and that, therefore, the criminal law is written 'primarily with reference to the types of crime committed by people of lower economic levels'. As the present writer has pointed out elsewhere,[45] there is much truth in this contention. The history of criminal legislation, in England and many other countries, shows that excessive prominence was given by the law to the protection of property against comparatively minor depredations, which of course means that the types of offences likely to be committed by members of the lower social classes figure more predominantly than others in criminal statutes and, therefore, also in the criminal courts and criminal statistics. On the other hand, there was a marked reluctance to treat the various forms of fraud as criminal offences. For the details reference may be made to that earlier discussion of the subject. It is only in comparatively recent times that those forms of anti-social behaviour more congenial to the position, ways of life, and mentality of the higher social classes have been seriously considered for inclusion in the penal codes and statutes. The differences in class distribution between offenders against the Danish Penal Code and other statutes, as discovered by Wolf, are here significant. It is, however, not only the fact that so much of penal legislation is aimed at the misbehaviour of the lower classes that explains their predominance in criminal statistics; it is also their higher 'visibility', i.e. 'the extent to which they come to the attention of people within a society'.[46] While this phenomenon has been discussed mainly in the U.S.A. in connection with the high Negro crime rate,[47] it has important bearings upon the differential class crime rate in general. This does not mean that offences, once they have been brought before the criminal courts, are given less publicity if the person charged belongs to a higher social class; usually the contrary is true. If, for example, a member of the peerage or another 'titled' person appears in court accused of a motoring or a homosexual offence the case is often reported more prominently and at greater length because of its publicity value,[48] whereas it may remain unnoticed if a lower-class offender is concerned. Nor does it mean that the sentences imposed betray any signs of 'class justice' in favour of the higher classes; again, the opposite may be true because judges or magistrates may 'lean over backwards' to guard themselves against the slightest suspicion of class bias. Certain exceptions have been tentatively noted in the recent study of magisterial sentencing policy by Roger G. Hood[49] who found it likely that the percentage of prison sentences, as contrasted with more lenient forms of disposal such as fines, differed according to the social composition of the community and the magisterial bench. It seemed to him, on the strength of his statistical material and his on-the-spot observations, that the working-class offender may be more severely dealt with in a community with a strong middle-class element and that the social composition of the bench when combined with certain community characteristics might be an additional factor in affecting the prison rate. While the material on which Hood's tentative conclusions are based is too limited to warrant any more definite statements his hypothesis is important enough to be followed up by further research on a larger scale. However, in our present context we are concerned with class differences not in sentencing policy but in the actual crime rate.

The real meaning of the concept of differential social 'visibility' is that our whole approach to, and our interpretation of, social misbehaviour may right from the beginning be coloured by unconscious distinctions related to class. To give but one, admittedly trivial, illustration: according to a report in *The Times* (19.5.1962) 'rockets were fired from the rooftops, bottles were hurled from windows and fire extinguishers were let off when the ancient feud between Jesus and Exeter Colleges broke out again in Oxford tonight (May 18). The city police had to intervene after the narrow street which separates the two colleges had become a litter of broken glass . . . But no undergraduates were arrested.' This report probably aroused only

461

some mild amusement in the minds of the readers of *The Times*, but what might have been their reaction if something similar had been reported of a fight between two juvenile gangs in East or South London or Glasgow? No wonder that we suspect this differential approach of ours to have some influence on the official crime rates of classes and of areas.

Exact statistical evidence is difficult to obtain. In one of the few recent investigations of the crime problem in this country where attention is paid to class differences, Terence Morris's study of Croydon,[50] the author states that among his group of persons charged the descriptions 'labourer', 'dealer' and 'no gainful occupation' occurred 'with monotonous regularity'. Among his group of probation and Approved School cases no child came from the two upper classes I and II, although in the total population of Croydon these classes were larger than the lowest classes IV and V; and for boys and girls together the distribution of delinquent cases was: class III: 1 case per 3,003; class IV: 1 per 380; class V: 1 per 187. Rejecting the hypothesis that this may merely reflect partiality on the part of police and prosecution Morris concludes that '*legally defined* delinquency is a social characteristic of the working classes in general and the family of the unskilled worker in particular. The behaviour of individuals in other social classes is so organized that departure from established norms is far less likely to bring the non-conformist into collision with the criminal law' (p. 167).

Albert K. Cohen has shown that in the United States, too, most juvenile offenders come from the lower classes (see below, Chapter 22, 2(*b*), pp. 507–12). Researches carried out by Austin L. Porterfield in Texas, which showed that all of 337 college students interviewed confessed to having committed unreported offences, are interesting, but hardly sufficient in scope to warrant different conclusions.[51]

As far as 'visibility' in the juvenile courts is concerned, Lady Wootton, a London juvenile court chairman of long experience, writes: 'Until the age of criminal responsibility is raised for all children, the present social discrimination will continue by which the misdeeds of public school children are dealt with (as they should be) between home and school while offenders from less favoured circles are made the subject of criminal charges' (*The Times*, 13.2.1963).

2. *Class Distribution for Specific Offences*

It goes without saying that class distribution varies greatly according to type of offence. In English social history, poaching and vagrancy used to stand out as typically lower-class offences. Trevelyan writes:[52] 'Poaching was not only the livelihood of outlaws, but the passion of men of all classes', but the crucial difference was that the law discriminated between them and made the passion of the gentry legal and that of the others criminal. Radbruch and Gwinner, who devote an illuminating chapter of their *History of Crime* to the corresponding position in Germany, quote the word of Ernst Landsberg, the historian of German jurisprudence, that poaching 'was a privileged field of the activities of a mischievous class legislation'.[53] The dominating part played by vagrancy in the development of professional crime is too well-known to need any elaboration (see also Radbruch-Gwinner, Chapter 9).

Turning to the present time, Wolf's study (above, s. 1) shows the differential class distribution of offences in his Danish material. Otherwise, evidence is available only for a few categories of offences, mostly for *sex offenders*. According to the Cambridge study,[54] of its total sample of nearly 2,000 sex offenders 11 per cent had more than an elementary education, which is probably higher than the rate for the general male population, and the proportion was higher (14·8 per cent) in the homosexual than in the heterosexual (4·3 per cent) and the indecent exposure (9·6 per cent) groups. The occupational distribution, too, showed a preponderance of professional and other higher occupations among the homosexuals (11·7 per cent against 4·6 per cent for the heterosexuals and 3·2 per cent for exhibitionists). In Fitch's group of 139 men convicted of sex offences against children,[55] also, the homosexuals came from a higher social level than the heterosexuals. Neither of these investigations, however, compares the class level of sex offenders with that of other categories of offenders or of the general population. In addition to their class distribution there is another peculiarity which characterizes certain sex offences, especially rape: their dependence on social attitudes towards sexual behaviour, which in their turn are greatly affected by national, regional and class morality—although here, too, a great deal of levelling has taken place in recent years.[56] Whether certain sexual activities are regarded as rape or indecent exposure and whether they are made the subject of court proceedings and lead to convictions will, at least in certain borderline cases, depend upon the social class of all those concerned.[57]

Offences which require a certain level of educational and cultural refinement, or can be committed only by persons in positions of trust and have therefore, as a rule, middle-class rather than working-class character, are *art forgeries* and *embezzlement*. The former can be successful only if the forger possesses some genuine understanding of the style of the artist whom he copies; in his case the process of imitation often rises to the level of a real art, and it may show some of the qualities of artistic creation. It is only when the imitator exploits his specific gifts in order to deceive and defraud others that his activities enter the field of crime. The psychological, sociological and artistic problems involved have been brilliantly analysed in several publications by Thomas Würtenberger.[58] As he points out, art forgeries were practically unknown and pointless in the Christian Middle Ages because the person of the artist was of little interest to the public compared with the religious value of the painting: 'The world admired the religious content of the altarpiece more than the person of the generally anonymous artist.' It was only in the Renaissance, when individualism and the idea of the unique originality of a work of art arose, that art forgeries began to make sense at all. The latter became really profitable, however, only with the coming into existence of a class of wealthy patrons, first the princes and great aristocrats, later the bourgeois capitalists and *nouveaux riches*. Especially the latter, blessed with plenty of money and the burning desire to emulate aristocratic traditions but little understanding of art, are indispensable for large scale forgeries to flourish. Würtenberger refers in particular to the post-war West German *Wirtschaftswunder*, but similar conditions have been noticeable for nearly a century to an ever growing extent in the whole Western world, led by the United States. The modern multi-millionaire, partly to impress his friends and competitors, partly to find a 'safe' investment for his fortune or to re-sell with great profit or to buy a title, spends enormous sums on genuine or faked works of art either to keep them in his own home or to present them to a museum (for which he can, at least in the United States, obtain some considerable tax benefits). The ingenious manner in which the snobbery or greed of such men has been exploited by highly skilled forgers is common knowledge. We are here faced with an interesting illustration of the part played in crime causation by social class problems on the side of the victim (see also below, Chapter 25). As further pointed out by Würtenberger, while painters and sculptors may belong to a variety of social classes, a strikingly large number of forgers are sons of famous artists and many of them are highly qualified technically and artistically.[59] Radbruch and Gwinner, too, have stressed the great varieties of social class among artists (at the end of the Renaissance): 'in addition to such princely figures as Titian, Rubens or Michelangelo, and the financially secure middle class of painters there existed an artistic proletariat, due largely to over-production and the fact that the Church had ceased to commission works of art . . . The consequence . . . was the growth of art forgeries on a large scale . . .' (p. 83).

Embezzlers are often bank clerks or other white collar employees or solicitors,[60] in short, middle-class people who, for various reasons, have lived beyond their means or incurred gambling losses too heavy for them to bear. Working-class persons have comparatively fewer opportunities to dispose of 'other people's money'; from the legal point of view, their offences in this sphere will rather be classified as 'larceny by a servant'. Cressey's case material[61] provides good illustrations of the principal types involved. Jerome Hall,[62] on the other hand, thinks that embezzlers are to be found among all classes, but his long list of cases which, taken from newspaper reports, is of course not representative, hardly bears this out. He offers, however, some other interesting observations on the subject. Whereas, according to him, the moral and social values held by thieves are opposed to those of the community and the latter is in no doubt that larcenies have to be prosecuted and punished, it is, according to Hall, different with embezzlers. They are very often not prosecuted, and their employers are inclined to hush matters up. This is true, but what is the explanation? Is it that embezzling is regarded as something less serious than stealing? Considering that it involves a breach of trust absent in ordinary cases of theft the opposite should be true. The real explanation may be, first, that employers may feel that they are themselves to blame for having selected their employees badly; secondly, that embezzlers and their employers often belong to the same middle class, although probably to different subdivisions, which creates certain social links between them; and, thirdly, closely connected with this, that, as Hall points out, the embezzler presents no real challenge to the values of the community which he himself shares. The professional thief or burglar has no counterpart in this field. There are very few professional embezzlers, partly because the mentality and position of embezzlers usually go against the ideology of professional crime and partly, of course, because the embezzler, once convicted, will as a rule find it difficult to obtain another position of trust. All this, however, is an indication of the fundamentally middle-class character of this type of offence.

Abortionists may be middle-class doctors, but probably in the majority of cases they are more or less unqualified quacks.

For *shoplifting* children it has been found by Gibbens and Prince that there was a very slight preponderance of the professional-teacher-clerical workers group among their fathers as compared with the general population; the difference is too slight, however, to be statistically significant.[63]

It has occasionally been suggested that *auto thieves* tend to come from 'favoured' middle-class families, but here too the evidence seems very slender.[64] The motives behind auto theft cover such a wide range from mere pleasure to robbery that one can hardly expect to find any similarity of social types among these offenders. Scotland Yard distinguishes three such types: adolescents wishing to have a joy ride; professional thieves who need another person's car to do a job, after which the vehicle is abandoned; and professional car dealers who take the stolen cars to pieces (*The Times*, 31.10.1960).

This leads to the closely allied subject of *motoring offences*, closely allied not only because motor cars are used in both auto theft and motoring offences but also because the former very often leads to the latter. From the quantitative point of view, motoring offences have become the most important of all. In 1961, they numbered 712,584 (persons found guilty) out of 970,180 persons found guilty of all non-indictable offences in England and Wales (*Criminal Statistics*, 1961, p. xxvi), and in addition there are some indictable offences committed by motorists in the course of driving. Barbara Wootton has severely censured criminologists for ignoring this revolution in the traditional crime structure 'to a degree that really queers all criminological discussion'; and, she thinks, 'Apparently on the Marxian principle that the law is made and operated in the interests of the well-to-do, motoring offences ... are not ordinarily thought to "count" as crimes at all.'[65]

This underlines a point made by the present writer many years before, in the course of his discussion of the whole subject of criminal negligence referred to above in Chapter 17, II(*b*).[66] It is certainly true that criminological research in this field, though by no means as completely non-existent as Wootton thinks,[67] is not yet of the comprehensive and systematic nature required for this many-sided subject, but this failure is not primarily due to the indifference and incompetence of criminologists but to the popular misconceptions still apparent in this field. It is only very recently that a comprehensive study of the subject, with some first-hand research, has been made in this country: T. C. Willett's *Criminal on the Road*.[68]

Our present discussion is not concerned with motoring offences in general, but merely with one, admittedly important, aspect; their class character. Here again, exact statistical information on the class distribution of offending motorists is lacking, and we can only try to draw a few tentative conclusions from our general impressions and from scattered foreign material. There can be no doubt that after the last war a wholesale revolution has taken place in the class distribution of motorists. Previously the privilege of the well-to-do, the possession of a motor car has now become one of the status symbols of the working and lower middle classes. In Zweig's samples the percentages of factory workers who owned a car varied from 12 to 40, though the latter figure, referring to Vauxhall, was not regarded as representative.[69] The question arises how far this extension of car-ownership has affected the class distribution of those who are found guilty of motoring offences. It has to be borne in mind that committing such offences does not necessarily imply car-ownership, and that even in pre-war times many lorry or taxi drivers and similar non-owners appeared in court on these charges. Nevertheless, the image created in the minds of magistrates and wide circles of the public was that of the motoring offender as a 'nice man' who was not a criminal and found himself in court largely through a combination of circumstances for which he was only mildly, if at all, to blame. Today when most magistrates and perhaps the majority of people over 17 are motorists, traffic offences are no longer status symbols or even characteristic of certain occupations but have become a phenomenon common to all classes.

For the special category of motorists found guilty of driving under the influence of drink Middendorff, the German criminologist and traffic judge, had previously expressed the view that they often belonged to the 'so-called better strata', but in a more recent study he suggests that this group has been declining because of the effect of the publicity campaign against drunken drivers which, he thinks, has been more effective with middle-class people than with the newcomers from the working classes.[70] Whether this applies to conditions in Britain may be doubtful, and in particular, the frequency with which doctors are charged with drunken driving is remarkable.

After this had been written, Willett's careful examination of the class distribution of motoring offenders was published (Ch. 8). In his Surrey sample, which is admittedly not entirely representative of the national distribution, he found no evidence for Barbara Wootton's view that motoring offenders come mainly from the upper social classes. In fact, the two lowest classes were over-represented in his sample, although the skilled manual workers were under-represented. The class distribution differed, however, in an interesting way according to the type of motoring offences; for example there was a particularly high proportion of manual workers among those convicted of driving while disqualified and failing to insure, while the highest proportion of non-manuals was found in the group convicted of driving under the influence of drink, a disparity for which Willett produces some plausible explanations. Of considerable interest are also Willett's findings (a) that even serious motoring offenders did not, as a rule, regard themselves as 'criminals' but were, when more closely questioned, rather confused about the meaning of this term which they vaguely associated only with offences showing dishonesty and malice; a minority of those interviewed, however, regarded driving under the influence of drink and failing to stop after an accident as 'criminal'. Women drivers had a stronger feeling of guilt than men; (b) that motoring offenders were treated by the

467

police and the courts in a way very different from other offenders, and most of them were regarded as 'highly respectable'.

Although we are in this book not concerned with penological questions attention should be drawn to the fact that class differences play their part and often hamper the treatment of offenders, be it in institutions such as Borstals or in probation and aftercare work. The idea of Borstal treatment has been taken from the English public school system, and its atmosphere and ideology are therefore largely incomprehensible to the young urban toughs with whom it has to deal. Borstal and Approved School housemasters, as probation officers and other social workers, often come from middle-class families whose ways of thinking may be fundamentally different from those of their charges, and the same applies to the voluntary worker in prison aftercare.

Chapter 21

OUR CRIMINOGENIC SOCIETY III: WHITE COLLAR AND OTHER 'NON-WORKING-CLASS' CRIMES[1]

I. INTRODUCTORY

Notwithstanding the clear statistical association between certain property offences, especially larceny, and lower social class it cannot be said that to any of the offences so far discussed, or indeed to any other category of offences, the idea of social class conflict is essential. Although it will but rarely happen, an act of stealing or house-breaking can be committed by a person of high social standing as well. White collar crime (WCC) is different: here the very fact of the offender's membership of a certain social class is an inherent, built-in, element. No doubt, many offenders steal because stealing is to them a natural expression of the feeling of belonging to an under-privileged social class (see below, Chapter 22), but there are many others who have no such feelings or whom it does at least not drive to larceny. And it is similar with acts of violence which may or may not be motivated by class conflict. This applies even to political assassinations as political conflict may be due to causes other than class differences, especially to nationalistic or racial fanaticism. Cases such as that of the man, described as a 'general labourer', who not long ago stabbed a Conservative Member of Parliament, Sir Walter Bromley-Davenport, 'because of his title—no one should have a title' (*The Times*, 19 and 28.6.1962), are rather exceptional. The details published in the press were too scanty to allow us to judge whether this was the act of a mentally disordered individual or a political crime in the traditional sense of the term, but it has to be borne in mind that, generally speaking, political crimes are committed in order to further the objects of political movements, large or small, not the idiosyncrasies of isolated individuals.[2] In the present case, the attacker seems to have acted as a lone wolf, an 'outsider'. Whether he would conform to Camus's conception of the rebel (Chapter 20 above) is impossible to decide on the basis of the facts so far known, but it seems unlikely.

The white collar criminal is neither a political offender nor a rebel. He exploits the weaknesses of society rather than rebelling against its iniquities, and his interest in the reform of the legal, political and social system is normally confined to changes which might enable him to make more and more money and to get more and more influence in order to exert increasing pressure to obtain his selfish objects.

The concept of WCC will always, and rightly, be connected with the writings of the late Edwin H. Sutherland of the University of Indiana. There is no Nobel Prize as yet for criminologists, and probably there never will be one, but if it had been available, Sutherland would have been one of the most deserving candidates for his work on WCC. It is certainly true that similar ideas had been expressed before him. Merton,[3] for example, draws attention to the otherwise little-known writings of Ambrose Bierre who at the beginning of the century 'described the ways in which the successful rogue achieves social legitimacy' and anatomized the 'discrepancies between cultural values and social relations'. Bloch and Geis (p. 381) quote some relevant passages from the far better-known textbook of criminology by Albert Morris, published in 1934, and Terstegen (p. 82) refers to an English book, Edwin Hill's *Criminal Capitalists* of 1872.

The present writer included a chapter on 'Methods of Business Administration' in his study of Crime in England between the two World Wars (1940), trying to show that 'certain methods of large-scale business administration are bound to produce corresponding types of lawbreaking' and stressing that these methods 'may cover the whole range of activities from the manifestly criminal ones to those that, in themselves, are not only perfectly honest and useful, but even indispensable for the well-being of the community at large' (p. 186). Among other matters, he dealt with the criminological effects of various forms of insurance and with hire purchase. In *War and Crime*, published in 1941, the emphasis was on the psychology of great businessmen criminals, such as Kreuger and Bottomley, and their driving motives, vanity and greed, and a comparison was made between them and great war criminals such as Hitler.

The main difference between the study of business methods in *Social Aspects* and Sutherland's work was that, whereas the former was concerned with what were regarded as inevitable by-products of certain legitimate business activities, Sutherland described, defined, and attacked some of these activities themselves as white collar crimes. Moreover, he produced a comprehensive theory of this phenomenon which he tried to fix into his general explanation of criminal behaviour. While much of his work in this field is of lasting value and deserves to be regarded as one of the most important

470

discoveries in the history of criminology, some of it suffers from weaknesses which have been detrimental to the progress and general acceptance of his ideas. In the following a brief summary of both the credit and the debit side will be given within the framework of our general discussion of the subject.

Considerable progress has been made in this field since Sutherland's principal contributions were published, in part through the collection of case material, mainly, however, through the growing clarification of the theoretical concepts involved. In both directions we are still primarily indebted to American writers. Case material has been presented by Clinard, Cressey, Hartung, Newman (see Note 1), and in particular in the Report on the United States Senate Hearings in the 'General Electric' cases of 1961.[4] Theoretical clarification and refinement have been effected by Geis, Geis-Bloch, Newman, Clinard, Tappan and others. The almost inevitable result of this near-monopoly of American thinking, case material and writing on the subject has been, however, that its discussion has become too extensively concentrated on American conditions, American big business, American Anti-Trust law and similar legislation, and on American judicial and administrative procedure. The very term 'white collar', though common to all parts of the English-speaking world, has if used in conjunction with the word 'crime' assumed a very specific meaning bestowed on it by Sutherland, but—as will be pointed out immediately—differing from common usage. It has been adopted by most non-English-speaking writers as well; Terstegen, for example, in his highly perceptive contribution translates it into German as *Weisse Kragen-Kriminalität* but abandons the latter at once in favour of the American term.

II. DEFINITIONS

Although Sutherland stressed that his definition of WCC was merely 'approximate' and nothing definitive it has been generally accepted; it had five elements: (*a*) it was a crime; (*b*) committed by a person of *respectability* and (*c*) of *high social status*; (*d*) in the course of his *occupation*.[5]

Moreover, fifthly, it is usually a *violation of trust*. The first of these five elements, i.e. that a 'crime' must have been committed, is of fundamental importance. Sutherland has often been accused of trying to extend his concept of WCC beyond the limits of actions punishable under the criminal law, in particular by including wrongs generally dealt with not as crimes but by the civil or administrative law, and thereby making it even less concise and useful for scientific purposes. It is true that some of his many pronouncements on the

471

subject seem to justify such charges; basically, however, as already stated above (Chapter 2, I), he tried to keep WCC strictly within the scope of the criminal law (see, e.g., *Annals*, p. 112: 'a white collar crime is defined as a violation of the criminal law . . .'). He was right in doing so, but here as elsewhere we have to distinguish between things as they are and things as they might and should be. Here as elsewhere it is the right and the duty of the criminologist to collect material concerning the territory which surrounds the inner zone of conduct violating the existing criminal law, material which might in suitable cases be used for recommendations for its reform (see above, pp. 13 and 77–8).

The fourth element in Sutherland's definition is entirely non-controversial; nobody would call a murder committed by a director of a large company for reasons of jealousy or the manslaughter of a pedestrian committed by him on a holiday excursion or a homosexual offence by a member of the Peerage a WCC. The second and third elements, however, are more doubtful. What does 'respectability' mean in this connection? Probably absence of previous convictions; or did Sutherland mean only absence of convictions of offences of the traditional type such as stealing? In any case, it differs from the third element, 'high social status', in being less closely related to social class; an illiterate and unskilled labourer can be highly respectable, but not of 'high social status'.[6] On the other hand, how far does the latter concept imply respectability? According to Sutherland, apparently not necessarily, and there can indeed be persons of high social status who are not respectable. The latter quality may depend more on the judgment of the public at large, whereas the former may rather reflect the views and prejudices of certain sections.

Whatever may be our views on such matters of detail, even a radical opponent of the whole concept of WCC such as Tappan admitted that Sutherland's original attempts to define it were a 'fruitful beginning', pointing to 'the significant and difficult problems of enforcement in the areas of business crimes . . .'[7]

In fact, this original definition, vague and inadequate as it was, had at least the merit of clarifying Sutherland's scientific objective, which was, in his words, not 'muckraking' but 'to call attention to a vast area of criminal behaviour which is generally overlooked . . .' (*Annals*, p. 112). Even if limited to his original category of persons of 'high social status' this would have amounted to a Copernican revolution in criminology; if backed by adequate case material it would have represented the perfect antidote to the one-sided preoccupation of traditional criminology with lower-class crime and delinquency. 'It made articulate the vague feeling of some of us that much of our work so far had been lop-sided and our conclusions misleading,'[8] and it was a serious attempt to give the right balance to criminological thinking. As Newman rightly says, 'interest in WCC [is] a sign of maturity of both theory and method' (p. 736). Unfortunately, Sutherland committed two definitional mistakes which made his concept even more vulnerable to attack than it had been from the outset on account of its vagueness and unorthodoxy: on the one hand, he limited it to crimes of corporations—his most comprehensive work on the subject is in fact little more than an analysis of the offences committed by seventy of the largest American business corporations—and, on the other, rather illogically he included in it crimes by persons who could in no way be classified as of 'high social status'. The present writer can hardly be suspected of underestimating the importance of the big corporation in modern life[9]—there are now about 331,000 registered companies in this country, eleven times as many as in 1900[10]—and there is little doubt that in the field of WCC, if it is really confined to the 'big fish', the practical problem will largely be one of the corporation. This, however, is no adequate reason for ignoring the—admittedly rare—white collar offender who conducts his business as an individual or who, while conducting his business through a corporation, nevertheless commits certain offences closely connected with it (e.g. tax evasions in his own or his wife's income declarations) in his private capacity. Some of the legal difficulties arising from crimes committed by corporations will be dealt with below in section IV(b).

On the other hand, in his references to illustrative case material Sutherland himself went, quite consciously, beyond the realm of large corporations and offenders of 'high social status' by including frauds or thefts by middle-class, even lower-middle-class, people such as poorly paid bank clerks, owners of small car, watch, radio and typewriter repair shops and salesmen.[11] This use of the term 'white collar' is perfectly in line with the general usage in the U.S.A. as well as in Britain. C. Wright Mills, for example, in his monograph devoted to the sociological, non-criminological, aspects of the matter —it is characteristic of the lack of interest in criminological problems shown by sociologists who are not criminologists themselves that the name of Sutherland does not appear in the index of his lengthy book first published in 1951—deals in it with practically every type of work except manual labour.[12] Similarly Vance Packard who shows, moreover, that there has been in recent years 'a revolutionary blurring of the boundary line between white- and blue-collared people' mainly by downgrading the former (*The Status Seekers*, p. 36). In Britain, the existence of large and powerful 'white collar' trade unions with hundreds of thousands of members demonstrates convincingly that the term is used here in a far wider sense than Sutherland's.

From the point of view of Sutherland's definition, the inclusion in his case material of the masses of comparatively humble people was inconsequent[13] and, as Geis observes, seems to point to the dearth of his material on 'high-status' crime. In our view *the right way out of this impasse is either to use the phrase 'white collar' in accordance with common parlance by admitting to it the whole of the middle classes not, as Sutherland did, by the backdoor but quite openly or to restrict it to the 'high status' class and to deal with crimes committed by members of the 'non high status' middle classes separately.* The present writer would prefer the second alternative. The decision may be of terminological rather than practical importance as long as we make sure that no section of the non-working-class population is excluded from our criminological investigations. It is clear, however, that significant features of WCC would be obscured if the first alternative should be adopted and the difference between higher- and lower-class WCC be altogether obliterated. In any case, we have to take account of the fundamental changes in class structure which have occurred in the course of this century (see above, Chapter 20). Sutherland's concept of 'high social status' is far too vague to be of much use within a social system as complicated as that of the modern western world; he never gave a clear definition of the criteria which he regarded as essential elements of this concept. Not every 'company director' or 'executive' is necessarily a person of 'high social status'. If, very legitimately, we wish to relate crime to the various social classes we have to give a clear account of how we intend to draw the lines between them. This having been done, we should try to show how the characteristics of certain types of crime differ according to social class. Sutherland, by indiscriminately lumping together offenders of very different social classes, failed to reach this objective.

As already indicated, Sutherland's insistence that the concept of WCC requires a close relationship between the crime and the offender's occupation has given rise to no controversy. It is true, however, that many non-white collar offenders also commit offences closely connected with their occupations, for example, to name only a few, domestic servants, postmen, or window cleaners (on this occupational element see below, Chapter 23), and it has to be borne in mind that this factor is only one of at least five elements in Sutherland's definition.

There is also a close relationship between the factor 'persons of high social status' and the emphasis on *violation of trust* as the fifth element in Sutherland's definition, this notwithstanding the obvious fact that such violations can also be committed by offenders lacking such status, such as domestic servants and other minor employees placed in positions where they are able to dispose of their employers' property. Sutherland described seven methods of trust violations in the field of WCC, adding that there were doubtless many others as well.[14] Among those which he specially mentioned were the securing by executives of corporations of positions which offered them opportunities to violate the trust which had been placed in them or, as he expressed it in an earlier paper (*Annals*, p. 112), the holding of 'two or more incompatible and conflicting positions of trust' by businessmen; the payment of huge salaries and bonuses to directors at a time when their corporations had net losses; the 'looting of a subsidiary by a parent corporation' by purchasing the former's assets at too low a price; and public misrepresentation of the financial affairs of the corporation. Most of the seventy large corporations which he studied in his book had, he found, at times been guilty of some of these violations of trust. He regarded the financial losses from WCCs, vast as they were, as far less damaging to society than the resulting undermining of the community's confidence in its leaders. Moreover, 'leadership against white-collar crime is generally lacking since most leaders come from the upper socio-economic class and since the persons in this class who do not participate in white-collar crimes are generally reluctant to attack other members of their own class' (*Annals*, p. 113). There is loyalty not only between thieves. These observations are profoundly true, but *mutatis mutandis* we find much the same obstacles to an effective and impartial administration of criminal justice in the field of some non-WCC as well. Unless personally injured many working-class people are equally reluctant to appear in court as witnesses against their fellow workers. The difference lies mainly in the far greater power of higher-class persons imperceptibly to influence the course of justice right from the start.

Terstegen makes the valuable point that one has to distinguish between violations of confidence which is given not only after careful consideration but also because it *had* to be given as there was no other choice and, on the other hand, violations of confidence arbitrarily and foolishly placed in undeserving individuals or corporations (p. 91). He rightly stresses that modern society is of necessity based upon mutual trust and that its economic life has become far too hectic and complex to enable its individual members to do business with one another only after painstaking and lengthy examination of their respective trustworthiness. 'Who buys from a dispensing chemist's shop *has* to trust that he will be well served; who buys drugs from a pedlar trusts foolishly.' In this connection he argues that there are certain differences from one country to another regarding the trustworthiness of businessmen and their customers: for example in the United States it is throughout safe, he thinks, to accept payment by cheque, whereas in Germany this is not yet the case. This is a subject which has recently been studied for some parts of the United States by Frederick K. Beutel who regards the popular estimate of total annual losses to American business by bad cheques to the amount of $500–600,000,000 as exaggerated; in his own state of Nebraska he found the extent of the phenomenon to be insignificant.[15] The issuing of bad cheques is of course WCC as a rule only in a wider than the Sutherlandian sense since very few of such offenders will be persons of 'high social status'.

It would be going too far, however, if we would limit the concept of WCC to cases where a trust is violated which *nolens volens had* to be given because of lack of any other alternative. This is true for large sections of our economic life, where the consumer in order to acquire food, shelter, clothing, and the other necessities of life, has to place his trust in producers and distributors some of whom are not worthy of it. Up to recently, the law and the courts gave no or entirely inadequate protection against exploitations and deceptions in the name of 'freedom of trade', that 'perhaps most ambiguous and most elusive of all the basic ideals of modern liberal democracy'.[16] It is only in the course of the present century that in some of the legal systems of the western world the need for consumer protection by the civil, administrative and criminal law has slowly been recognized, and even more recently that the great masses of consumers, those most unorganized and long-suffering of all human animals, have come together to build up a system of self-defence. Growing public anxiety about the sharp practices of certain sections of industry and trade led to the setting up of private organizations such as the Consumers' Association Ltd. with its publication *Which?* and the Consumer Advisory Council which published the *Shopper's Guide* and also to the appointment in 1959 of the Molony Committee on consumer protection, which reported in 1962. The recommendations of this report have not yet produced all the desirable legislative changes. Generally speaking, however, it can be said that the revolt of the consumer coupled with the growing strength of the Welfare State has in the course of the present century led to a multiplication of 'public welfare' statutes (see above, Chapter 2, I) which, as they are invariably backed by penal provisions, have resulted in a considerable widening of the scope of offences of the WCC type. While it has to be borne in mind that certain forms of WCC bear all the characteristics of these public welfare offences it would be a grave mistake to establish without careful enquiry a presumption that *all* WCC belong to this category and should enjoy the legal privileges connected with it.

476

III. FURTHER ANALYSIS OF SUTHERLAND'S THEORY

In addition to the two points of definition where we disagree with Sutherland, there are certain other aspects of his theory which seem to be unacceptable or acceptable only with reservations.

(a) He, quite naturally, tried to use his discovery of WCC as an important illustration and justification of his pet theory of differential association. While the case for and against this theory will be discussed in more general terms below (Chapter 23, E) a few brief remarks are here needed regarding its specific value for the explanation of WCC. Here, as elsewhere, we are ready to admit the value of the theory in linking criminological thought to the modern psychological literature on learning. Sutherland performed this task in a rather primitive fashion by submitting what he regarded as 'two types of documentary evidence,' i.e. biographical or autobiographical material illustrating the careers of businessmen and, secondly, 'descriptions of the diffusion of criminal practices from one situation to another' (*White Collar Crime*, Chapter 14). As he admits, all his documents come from young men in subordinate positions and are in no way representative of the WC criminals whom he has in mind, and he rightly complains that 'unfortunately similar documents . . . are not available for the managers of large industries' (p. 240) and that no first-hand research on the subject has ever been published. Even books demonstrating that 'many of the large American fortunes originated in illegal practices' fail, he thinks, to explain 'the process by which illegal behaviour develops in the person'. True as this may be, the material presented by Sutherland is not sufficient to fill the gap and to demonstrate the validity of his theory of differential association. The examples he gives of the 'diffusion of illegal practices' (pp. 241 ff.) are in fact examples of the imitative effect of competition: if one company makes profit by illegal business practices its competitors are forced to do the same; no special theory of the kind formulated by Sutherland is needed to explain this simple process.

(b) Secondly, Sutherland, who was led astray by his conviction that 'crime' must always show essentially the same pattern regardless of type of offence and varieties of offenders, insisted that through his studies of WCC he had proved the insignificant role played by poverty in the causation of criminal acts. 'The general theories of criminal behaviour which take their data from poverty and the conditions related to it', he wrote, 'are inadequate and invalid.'[17] If by 'inadequate' he meant 'incomplete' we could agree with him; no single explanation of criminal behaviour can ever be complete. But why 'invalid'? For large numbers of offenders the economic explanation, together with other factors, is entirely valid (see below, Chapter 23); for others it has but little meaning; should we, therefore, discard it altogether?

(c) One of the most frequent criticisms of Sutherland's work on WCC—as of his theory of differential association in general—refers to his treatment of the psychological aspects of the matter. His tendency to minimize the significance of the latter culminated in the often-quoted sentences:

Business leaders are capable, emotionally balanced, and in no sense pathological. We have no reason to think that General Motors has an inferiority complex or that the Aluminium Company of America has a frustration-aggression complex or that U.S. Steel has an Oedipus complex, or that the Armour Company has a death wish or that Du Ponts desire to return to the womb. The assumption that an offender must have some such pathological distortion of the intellect or the emotions seems to me absurd, and if it is absurd regarding the crimes of businessmen, it is equally absurd regarding the crimes of persons in the lower economic class.[18]

These sentences, which, by the way, were contained in a lecture published only after his death, exhibit a strange mixture of truth and falsehood, of self-evident and entirely unproven statements. Significantly, they occur in a paper on 'Crime of Corporations' and in their most striking formulation (second sentence of quotation) contain nothing but the platitude that a corporation as such can have no *mens rea*, no feelings, no sense of guilt, etc., and it required no scholar of Sutherland's stature to tell us that. In the preceding and the subsequent sentences, however, he makes certain statements concerning the mentality of the individual businessmen standing behind the corporations for which he had no confirming evidence whatsoever. As mentioned before under (a), Sutherland himself deplored the absence of adequate research or biographical material on such questions as how 'illegal behaviour develops in the person' of individual white collar offenders, and we are in fact largely dependent on speculations as to their mental make-up, their attitudes and the motives behind their actions. Occasional glimpses may be cast on all this through whatever case histories might be available or through works of literature such as Ibsen's *John Gabriel Borkman*.[19]

Neither on the strength of the available evidence nor on general grounds is there any justification for Sutherland's assumption that big business tycoons have no psychological problems, that there are among them no psychopaths or neurotics or men with a strong feeling of guilt or people plagued and spurred on by an inferiority complex—just as there is but little evidence for the opposite assumption. This dearth of material on the psychological side of the subject

478

is not surprising, considering that the courts when dealing with such cases are often not interested in it beyond the usual questions of knowledge and intent, as far as the statute in question requires positive answers to the latter. Psychoanalysts who might be privately consulted by such offenders may know more about their problems, but professional etiquette imposes silence. Even so, it does occasionally happen that in the course of prolonged criminal trials or U.S. Senate Hearings in anti-trust cases (see below, s. V(*b*)) some light is shed on the mentality of the businessmen involved.

Sutherland, we are told by Cressey,[20] took the criticisms of his alleged neglect of 'personality factors' seriously, but he believed that his theory of differential association did sufficiently explain why some persons with certain personality traits committed crimes whereas others possessing the same traits did not. As Cressey's further observations show, the theory was in fact not capable of adequately answering this question and similar ones concerning the personality structure of the WC criminal.

Sutherland's critics have also gone astray on a few important points. First, the contention that 'only those are criminals who have been adjudicated as such by the courts' (Tappan) is not only sociologically but also legally mistaken since it confuses issues of substantive and of procedural law: according to the former—the only one that interests us in the present context—a person is a criminal who has violated one of its provisions, regardless of whether he has been found guilty in accordance with the rules of criminal procedure.

Secondly, the sociological objections raised by Burgess are equally mistaken. Burgess[21] has argued that WC offenders should not be regarded as criminals because they do not conceive of themselves as such. The answer to this argument is that while the 'image' which the offender has of himself is of very considerable, often even of crucial, significance psychologically for such matters as crime causation and the prevention of recidivism, it cannot be the decisive factor for our judgment whether or not he should be legally or sociologically classified as an offender. The criminal law cannot be made completely dependent on the offender's own view of whether or not he has violated the law and should be punished. As we have seen above, many motoring offenders, too, are disinclined to regard themselves as criminals; in spite of this, they are properly punished, although often all too leniently.

Thirdly, and closely connected with the foregoing, there is what may perhaps seem to be the most important objection: Vold,[22] under the heading: 'The Paradox: Reputable Persons as Criminals', argues that 'an obvious and basic incongruity' is involved in Sutherland's contention that the responsible leaders of a community can also be its criminals. Even if corporations may commit violations of regulations concerning such matters as labour practices, trade and marketing agreements, advertising, and so on, yet 'it raises some very serious questions of both logical and theoretical consistency' to label the individuals involved as 'criminals'. What makes a person a criminal is, Vold emphasizes, dependent on the 'community definition' just as much as on the actual behaviour of the individual. Moreover, no law can be enforced, he rightly states, that does not have 'overwhelming popular support' (p. 257), and such support is not likely to be forthcoming in the United States with its 'glorification of the "free market"'. In these, on the surface very persuasive, arguments, truths and falsehoods are again closely interlocked. Big business tycoons are not necessarily and automatically, as Vold seems to assume, 'leaders of the community' as far as moral and social leadership is concerned. Sutherland's view that WC offences committed by such men are likely to undermine the confidence of the community in its leaders is correct as, even if not every big businessman can be accepted as a moral and social leader, the power and authority he wields in his own particular sphere as a large-scale employer of labour and a large-scale buyer and seller of goods makes him at least an important figure in the economic and social life of the place. Whether or not he deserves it, he will as a matter of course be given honorary posts in local government and all sorts of private organizations, as a lay magistrate, church warden, etc., and if he commits offences this will cause a considerable shock to the community. To use this as an argument against the possibility of WCC is, however, a misconceived idea which does not do justice to the complexity and many-sidedness of modern social life. Moreover, while it is true that no law can in the long run be effectively enforced against public opinion Vold seems to assume too rashly that the public as a whole are here on the side of the WC offender against the law-enforcing agencies. As the present writer has said elsewhere, 'there is a very strong temptation in our field to base action or, more often still, inaction on the alleged state of public opinion, without knowing exactly what public opinion really wants and whether it wants anything at all'.[23] Vold's argument is principally based on his knowledge of the 'traditional American view' with its strong opposition to government interference in business affairs, and so far we are not competent to question his thesis; but granting all this, has there not been, in spite of all traditional preference for *laissez-faire*, a 'New Deal' even in the United States and has there not been a critical reassessment of the role played by big business in America, Britain and elsewhere? A process of eye-opening has been taking place since Sutherland's first publications on the subject, a process which may

eventually make 'public opinion' more willing to support the authorities in their fight against WCC.

Bloch and Geis, while fully acknowledging the importance of
Sutherland's work, regard his concept of WCC as too vague and all-
embracing to be of real scientific value.[24] He has failed, they think,
to 'delineate clearly homogeneous types of offences', and their solution is to concentrate on specific, well-definable forms of WCC such
as advertising frauds or violations of the anti-trust laws. While their
criticism is well-founded in particular on account of Sutherland's
tendency to include a mixed bag of offences by lower-class persons,
the proposed solution can be accepted only as far as individual
researches are concerned, not, however, if it is intended to involve a
delimitation of the basic concept as such. Just as there is a comprehensive legal concept of false pretences, which embraces defraudations of the most diversified characteristics, so can very heterogeneous
forms of WCC be included in this sociological concept provided its
fundamental elements are preserved—a proviso which was unfortunately ignored by its originator. Under the umbrella of this
comprehensive sociological concept can very easily be brought violations of penal statutes dealing with a large number of anti-social
actions.

In his foreword to the second edition of Sutherland's *White Collar
Crime* Cressey makes the point that future research on WCC should
try to determine the structural conditions of society which are
responsible for the existing differences in crime reporting: i.e. to
explain why in a given society certain crimes are noticed, whereas
others are ignored. To some extent, this is what we have been
attempting in the present and the immediately preceding chapters.

IV. LEGAL ASPECTS

The difficulties arising in the legal sphere from the introduction of the
sociological concept of WCC should not be under-rated. They are
mainly to be found in three directions: concerning (*a*) the legal structure and philosophy of 'public welfare offences', (*b*) the criminal law
of corporations, (*c*) the various problems of specific WC offences, such
as violations of anti-trust laws, statutes against the adulteration of
food, the sale of dangerous drugs, fraudulent advertising, tax evasions,
licensing offences, etc. There is, of course, much overlapping between
these three sets of subjects.

(*a*) Public welfare offences have been dealt with above in Chapter 2,
and all we have to do at present is to draw attention to the following
points: The origin of the modern tendency to create a new category
of illegal acts or omissions, loosely held together as 'public welfare

offences', lies in the growth of modern society with its gradual abandonment of the old *laissez-faire* economy and philosophy; in the increasing political and economic power of the previously underprivileged parts of the population and in their insistence on adequate legal and penal protection against exploitation. As pointed out in that chapter, the mass-character of these newly created offences, 'the pettiness of most of them if taken individually, contrasted with their dangerousness to society if considered in their totality', led to the impression, widely held among lawyers, that the traditional standards of criminal justice with all the slowly and painfully evolved safeguards of the rights of the accused could not be upheld in this special field. Particularly strong is the tendency, among legislators as well as among theoretical jurists, to water down or altogether to abandon the requirement of individual guilt which has to be proved to the accused. Moreover, it has been argued with a great deal of justification that the administration of criminal justice has been dangerously overloaded to near-breaking point with matters which should better be dealt with by administrative agencies. With much of this the present writer is in sympathy—with some important reservations. The process of shifting society's reaction against anti-social behaviour from, say, the field of penal to that of administrative reaction requires the utmost caution and subtle discrimination, and it should be limited to cases where the advantages of administrative over criminal proceedings can be clearly seen and understood by the public at large. The changeover has to be in the interest of society as a whole, not merely of certain classes, and it may have to be confined to certain sections of the social problem involved. Not enough thought has so far been given to the technicalities of the matter for which a satisfactory solution can be found not by wholesale regulation but only by careful examination of each legislative problem separately. One of the major points here to be considered is that within each category of public welfare offences contraventions of very diverse types and degrees of gravity are likely to exist which may make differential treatment necessary. For some of the less serious types the requirement of *mens rea* might safely be relaxed and administrative action be preferable to penal sanctions; for others such changes might be intolerable. All this applies to many WC offences as much as to other public welfare offences, not however to those forms of WCC which are not covered by the latter term, such as ordinary business frauds, which have to be treated in the same way as other frauds even if committed by members of the higher social classes.

(*b*) While Sutherland went too far in restricting the scope of WCC to the anti-social conduct of corporations, it has already been stressed that the latter do play an extremely important role in this field. The legal treatment of WCC is, therefore, largely dependent on a satisfactory solution of that very old problem, the criminal liability of corporations.[25] It is true, the criminal law can do very little to assist in the attempts to overcome the economic and social difficulties which constantly arise in this field, but even such modest contributions as it has so far been able to make are not entirely without significance.

Corporations differ from individuals, for whom the criminal law has, by tradition, been primarily intended, in that they have neither a physical body on which the pain of punishment could be inflicted nor a mind which can be guilty of a criminal intent. Both of these two deficiencies can, however, to some extent be overcome. Those who used to stress the obvious truth that corporations cannot be hanged, flogged or imprisoned, have had to concede that corporations are not insensitive to heavy fines and to loss of face. As W. Friedmann and Glanville Williams have rightly stressed, the latter, i.e. the diminution of respectability, the stigma, is the real penalty of a corporation, and this factor provides one of the weightiest arguments in favour of punishing not, or not only, the director or manager who has acted for it but also the corporation itself. 'The offence should be linked in the public mind with the name of the company, and not merely with the name of directors or managers who may be nonentities' (Williams, § 221). From this Williams draws, however, the conclusion that only a declaratory judgment is justified against the corporation, not a fine which would penalize the shareholders who are not responsible for the crime. His objections are important, but not really decisive, for two reasons: First, if the real punishment lies in the stigma, the shareholders are not punished since the stigma does not extend to them, and the financial loss resulting from a heavy fine has to be borne by them in the same way as they have to bear other financial losses due to bad management. It often happens that the penalties imposed on an offender injure other persons, especially his family, more than himself; the innocent wife and children have to suffer when the breadwinner goes to prison. Why should shareholders be privileged? Secondly, a mere declaratory judgment condemning the conduct of a corporation would fail to convey to the general public the gravity of the offence and the degree of the condemnation which it deserves in the opinion of the court. The man in the street usually assesses the gravity of a crime mainly according to the length of imprisonment or the amount of the fine imposed, and this essential yardstick would be missing in a merely declaratory judgment. The social function of punishment, therefore, requires something more than a mere declaration of guilt. Where an offence cannot be punished by a fine no penalty can of course be imposed, but apart from serious crimes against the person, such as murder or rape, of which a corporation cannot be guilty anyway, such offences are now very rare, and it is always possible for the legislator to provide for a fine as an alternative.

Having accepted the legal principle of bringing the corporation as such within the competence of the criminal law we now have to examine, first, for whose actions the corporation should be made criminally responsible and, secondly, whether the persons acting for it should be punished. The answer to the first question is to be found in the so-called *alter ego* doctrine, according to which a corporation is responsible for the activities of its organs, i.e. of those who are in control of its business affairs, managing directors and similar high executives. It is for the court to draw the line in each individual case.[26] The second question has been answered in different ways by the various Statutes concerned. From the detailed analysis given by Glanville Williams (§ 222) it appears that the English legislator employs one of the following two main solutions: either the directors, managers, secretaries or other officers with whose consent or connivance the offence has been committed are held co-responsible together with the corporation, but the burden of proving their guilt falls on the prosecution. Or this burden is shifted to the person concerned who has to prove his innocence—a form of legislation greatly disliked in the world of business. As Friedmann writes, the actual decision whether to impose criminal liability in a given case on an individual acting for the corporation must 'in large measure depend on the wisdom, and the sense of practical realities, of the court'.

V. CASE MATERIAL ON WCC

The existing case material on WCC, while not particularly extensive, is not as limited as Sutherland thought twenty years ago. A number of recent court cases, especially in the United States and Britain, with the public discussions arising from them, have in fact greatly contributed to our understanding of this category of offences. We can here deal only with the most significant types and the most flagrant of individual cases. They show, however, that there is no reason to restrict our examination, as some recent writers have suggested (see above), to anti-trust law violations and similar offences, although they form no doubt one of the most important groups.

A particularly valuable contribution to some of the problems discussed in the present chapter and the previous one has recently been presented in the September 1962 issue of *The Annals of the American Academy of Political and Social Science* (Vol. 343), devoted to 'The Ethics of Business Enterprise'. Although it is mainly concerned with the ethical rather than the legal aspects of the matter, the latter are by no means neglected, and the shadow of the 'Philadelphia Electrical

Equipment Cases' (see below, s. (*b*)) is visible in a number of contributions. While the contributors and their material are, without exception, American their conclusions are of general interest.

Very significantly, the symposium opens with a quotation from an article by Peter F. Drucker in the *Harvard Business Review* of March–April 1962:

There is evolving a new concept of the role of the big-business enterprise in our society. 'Big business' is 'private' and accepted as such—in the sense in which a big university is 'private' . . . But it is not a 'private affair' and the concern only of its stockholders, executives and employees. In the pursuit of its everyday 'private business', and in performing its economic job, big business is therefore expected to further human values, and to serve national purpose. This . . . is at the core of big-business ethics.

To which the editor of the issue, Arthur S. Miller, Professor of Law, George Washington University, Washington, D.C., adds:

In other words, the ethical question of business enterprise is not so much that of the personal peccadilloes of a few errant businessmen. It is the larger matter of the relationships that the dominating corporations have with other segments of the nation . . . It is the social obligation of the corporate giant that is the subject of scrutiny in this symposium. (Pp. 9–10.)

True as it is that we are concerned with the general picture, with the problem as a whole rather than with certain more obvious and possibly exceptional malpractices, it is equally true that the general picture provides the background, the atmosphere, against which these malpractices have to be seen and judged. As another contributor points out (p. 2), 'profit maximization' is no longer universally regarded as the only goal of the large corporation, but it is much less obvious what could take the place of this greatly over-simplified concept, bearing in mind that a corporation consists of so many different people with different roles and interests. And, as a third contributor asks, 'what is a businessman's moral duty when there is real uncertainty whether a contemplated action will be held legal or illegal?' (p. 33). A great deal of heart-searching may have been going on in recent years within the large firms, but the results of this process are summed up in one of these essays as 'too little, too late and too superficial, directed at the wrong objects' and not leading to 'an exercise of responsibility commensurate with the size and importance of the modern corporation' (p. 67).

Let us now turn to a few matters of detail.

(*a*) *WCC Connected with 'Take-over Bids'*

A 'take-over' has been defined by a legal journal as 'merely a technical procedure by which the control of a company passes from one group

THE SOCIOLOGY OF CRIME

of shareholders to another, with or without amalgamation of the acquiring and the acquired company. A take-over which may assume many legal forms is an entirely neutral procedure; it is neither intrinsically "good" nor "bad".[27] However, as the same journal admits, the technique of take-over bids, this 'legitimate instrument of business activity', is liable to very serious abuses unless certain precautionary measures are strictly observed. For example, the shareholders to whom a bid is made should be informed 'adequately and independently' of the true value of their shares and should be consulted before the decision. Moreover, attention is drawn in the same journal to 'a type of take-over bid which is rarely justifiable and often pernicious', i.e. the one 'intended to be financed out of the assets of the company which the bidder wants to take over'. The attempt of the Companies Act, 1948, s. 54, to cope with such abuses by making it unlawful for a company to give financial assistance for the purchase of its own shares, is described as 'wholly inadequate' and easily evaded. An interesting debate took place in the House of Commons on the 29th June 1959 on a motion of Labour M.P.s:

that this House, in view of undesirable developments in private industry, including take-over bids, excessive speculation in share and property values and practices designed to avoid taxes, calls upon Her Majesty's Government to take steps to prevent these and other abuses and to ensure that private industry is carried on in accordance with the national interest. (*Hansard*, 29.6.1959, cols. 34–163.)

The motion was lost, with 254 votes for and 316 against, but the debate produced some valuable material on, among other points, our subject of take-over bids. In spite of fundamental differences in outlook, members of both the Government and the Opposition agreed that 'it would be wrong to condemn all take-over bids out of hand'. Labour spokesmen were willing to admit that 'If we accept, as we do, the continuance of a substantial private sector, we must accept that there is a case for greater industrial concentration, whether by private negotiations or under mechanisms of take-over bidding', provided the result of the latter was greater efficiency and not merely a quick and tax-free profit by the bidder who has no other interest in the fate of the company to be taken over (cols. 37–8, 84, 130, 147). 'Take-over bids are not made to secure the stability of British industry, but to create values on the Stock Exchange and force up share values . . .' (col. 110). One particular, unsuccessful, bid was said to have increased by over £9 million the value of the shares of the company for which the bid was made (col. 122) and to have brought a profit of £500,000 to the unsuccessful bidder (col. 39). Reference was also made to a 'new technique . . . spiv bidding', which means that shares are bought and the rumour is spread that a take-over bid is imminent, with the result that the share values are pushed up although no such bid is intended (col. 147). Although many of these charges were disputed by Conservative M.P.s, at least one of them, with a special knowledge of problems of modern industry, admitted that 'sometimes there is an anti-social tendency in private enterprise' (col. 84). No doubt, abuses of the kind mentioned in that debate are not very frequent, but those which do occur are usually not brought before a court or other competent tribunal, and those few which lead to criminal proceedings present, in all probability, only a tiny fraction of those which actually happen and contain certain violations of the criminal law. The dark figure is here, as always, not ascertainable, but it may be very high. Those who regard this statement as mere speculation should bear in mind that similar speculations are frequently made with regard to other types of offences without provoking indignant protests.

This is the background which has to be borne in mind if we wish to understand the full significance of the sensational trial of Friedrich Grunwald and Herbert Hugh Murray, which was held at the Central Criminal Court in London on 28 days in June and July 1960—apparently one of the longest and most complicated trials in the sphere of commercial fraud ever held before an English court.[28] 'When I started to work out my summing-up I almost despaired of getting it into a simple form easily understood,' the presiding judge told the jury. Both Grunwald and Murray were found guilty of 'fraudulently converting to their own use and benefit proceeds of 32 cheques worth £3,255,500 received for or on account of the State Building Society' and of other similar offences, and each of them was sentenced to five years' imprisonment. What, in a nutshell, were the essential facts of this case?

Murray, aged 67, was managing director and secretary of the State Building Society in London; Grunwald, aged 34, was a solicitor acting for that Society, and also a company director. Murray's salary was stated to be £16,000, and a few years before the trial he had been President of the Faculty of Architects and Surveyors (*The Times*, 16.6.1960). The essence of the charges against them was that, after having used the moneys of the State Building Society to finance various take-over bids and acquire the companies concerned for themselves, they had tried to use the same technique in order to take over the Lintang Investments Ltd., which, besides other property, owned the shares of Dolphin Square, one of the largest blocks of flats in London. The sum required for this operation was stated to be approximately £7m. or 8m., of which Grunwald obtained from the State Building Society, through the good offices of Murray, about £3,250,000. This was, as they knew, against the rules of the Society, whose object was 'to provide a safe and secure investment for the small man' (*The*

Times, 9.7.1960), and it was especially reprehensible as the Society received no security whatsoever for the large sum lent to finance the Murray–Grunwald take-over (*The Times*, 8.7.1960). As the remaining sum required could not be obtained, the whole transaction broke down, and the money lent by the Society was, at least temporarily, lost.[29] One of the defences put up by the accused Grunwald was that he had hoped the shares of Lintang would, as the result of the take-over, go up, and he would have no difficulty in repaying the 'loan'; he also maintained that, in spite of his legal training, he had not known that the funds of a Building Society could not lawfully be used for loans to finance risky take-over bids without any security. If the deal had been successful, both Murray and Grunwald would have made very big profits for themselves through the expected rise of the Lintang shares. As it was, Grunwald was accused by one of counsel acting in the case of having been driven to his reckless manipulations by *folie de grandeur*, to have been 'intoxicated with success' and to have felt nothing would be too much for him (*The Times*, 8.7.1960)—which again reminds us of Ibsen's John Gabriel Borkman. Apart from this we have on the personal side only the information supplied by Grunwald himself for a series of articles on 'Grunwald—Take-over King' in the *News of the World* (beginning 31st July 1960). After his release from prison—if not before—we shall no doubt get his memoirs which may shed more light on his state of mind. On that of Murray we have no information beyond a few interesting remarks in the Faulks Report (see Note 28) which try briefly to sum up these two men (p. 4):

'Mr. Murray is a valuer of property whose astuteness is quite remarkable. He was elderly, unscrupulous and rich: Mr. Grunwald was and is an extremely astute lawyer, who was young, unscrupulous and poor . . . Both Mr. Murray and Mr. Grunwald were greedy for money, although it may be said on Mr. Grunwald's behalf that he used a large part of his moneys improperly obtained for charitable purposes . . . and when in difficulty over Lintang called on "my wife's last £55,000".'

This case shows all the typical features of a WCC. The offenders were persons apparently regarded as highly respectable and of considerable influence in the business circles in which they moved, and they regarded themselves not as 'criminals' but only as 'unlucky'. While Murray professed to have been completely ignorant of the use made of the money by Grunwald, the latter used the well-worn rationalization that he had merely 'borrowed' it with Murray's consent to repay it after the successful completion of the take-over bid.

It will also be observed that, once the external and internal facts of the offence had been proved there were no legal difficulties in finding the accused guilty of fraudulent conversion (Larceny Act, 1916, s. 20).

Many further details concerning the transactions leading to the Grunwald-Murray trial are given in the report made into the affairs of H. Jasper and Co. Ltd., by Mr. Neville Faulks, Q.C., for the Board of Trade. This report made it clear, for example, that breaches of s. 54

of the Companies Act, 1948 (see above) were regarded by many take-over bidders and even by their banks as merely technical offences which would not invalidate the transactions concerned, and unless the breaches were too flagrant to be ignored the banks were willing to connive at them. Mr. Faulks recommended a steep increase in the maximum penalty of £100 (!) which had led to a state of affairs where s. 54 was honoured more in the breach than in the observance (pp. 6–7, 17).

As pictured in the Faulks Report we see on the stage, in addition to the two principal actors, a number of other figures, some of them engaged in a mad scramble for extravagant profits to be gained through 'business' activities of no conceivable social value or even clearly anti-social. It was only a matter of chance that Grunwald and Murray were finally caught in one of the traps they had so cleverly set, and it was also nothing but chance that only these two were caught and punished for doing what, in divers forms, apparently others had also been doing with excessive profits for themselves and harm to society at large.

(b) Monopolistic and Other Restrictive Practices

Between take-over bids and monopolistic practices there is, obviously, a close connection, but they may be regarded as two overlapping circles rather than as identical. Take-over bids, if successful, may or may not produce a monopoly in the branch of trade or industry concerned; in the Grunwald–Murray case it was unlikely that the operation would have created a monopolistic domination of the London property market, whereas an I.C.I.–Courtaulds merger would have led to a 96 per cent monopoly in synthetic fibres (Hansard, 16.2.1962). Anxiety was also expressed in the press and in Parliament regarding the proposed merger between Odhams Press and Thomson Newspapers and certain activities in the boot and shoe and tobacco trades (Hansard, 14.2.1962).

In the present writer's Criminal Justice and Social Reconstruction (pp. 152–73) an analysis of the problems of monopolies was made for the time up to the end of the last war from the point of view of the sociology and reform of the criminal law. This story has been brought up-to-date by Sir David Cairns, Professor John C. Spencer, Sir Henry Clay, Laisley P. Wragg et al.[30] Their writings have been supplemented by various Government Reports, such as that of 1955 on Collective Discrimination.[31] Although the latter, in a majority opinion, recommended legislation to create a new criminal offence to deal with certain monopolistic tendencies (p. 86), this has so far not been implemented, and altogether, in the words of Spencer, 'Great Britain has moved away from the use of criminal sanctions as a means of control of restrictive practices.' Nothing that has occurred in the past twenty years has convinced the present writer that he was wrong in allocating to the criminal law a modest, but nevertheless essential, role in this field, provided certain important conditions were fulfilled (see esp. pp. 169 ff.). The various attempts of the Government to cope with the matter without recourse to penal sanctions have apparently proved ineffective. The measures provided by the Monopolies and Restrictive Practices (Inquiry and Control) Act, 1948, i.e. setting up a 'Commission' with no real authority, and in particular by the Restrictive Trade Practices Act, 1956, i.e. establishing a 'Restrictive Practices Court', have, up to a point, been useful (see Cairns) in fighting such practices as were found to be against the 'public interest', and *The Times* (1.2.1961), reviewing the first annual report on the work of the new Court, thought it had been working 'at an almost breathless pace'. Nevertheless, there have been rather critical assessments, too (see, for example, Wragg, *loc. cit.*), and it was not without significance that in spite of the existence of the Commission and the Court in spring 1962 a group of about 50 Conservative backbenchers 'opened what promises to be a determined campaign to persuade the Government to act against monopolies': it was feared that 'the party image has been damaged by the failure to act against monopolistic tendencies' (*The Times*, 31.5.1962). It is only now (March 1965) that the Labour Government has introduced a 'Monopolies and Mergers Bill'.

The picture is different in the United States, where after a long period of comparative inactivity the penal provisions of the Sherman Act of 1890 have been vigorously enforced in the now famous Philadelphia Electrical Equipment cases of 1961. Already in 1959 'more anti-trust cases (sixty-three) were filed than at any time since 1943' (Spencer). The following brief analysis of the Philadelphia cases is based on the accounts given in the *Annals of the American Academy of Political and Social Science* (esp. pp. 77 ff.), and by Geis, Spencer (see Note 1) and Fortas.[32]

Twenty-nine corporations, including some of the biggest American firms such as the General Electric Company and the Westinghouse Electric Corporation, and forty-six individuals were convicted of violating § 1 of the Sherman Act by fixing prices on various types of electrical equipment. All defendants pleaded eventually guilty or *nolo contendere*. Fines totalling nearly two million dollars were imposed and prison sentences were passed on thirty individual defendants, of whom seven had to serve 30 days each, whereas in the cases of the others the sentences were suspended. In addition, there came 'a deluge of private treble damage actions' (Fortas); the Federal Government itself, as a large-scale purchaser of the heavy electric equipment concerned, and the Tennessee Valley Authority settled their damage claims against one of the defendant firms for a sum of seven and a half million dollars, and it was estimated that the damages to be paid to the victims might altogether amount to 500 million dollars (Fortas).[33] 'American public opinion', wrote the correspondent of *The Times* (21.2.1961), 'is exercised about the implications of what President Kennedy has called "the effort made by large electrical companies to defraud the Government",' and the Judge said: 'The conduct of the corporate and individual defendants alike . . . has flagrantly mocked the image of that economic system of free enterprise which we profess, and has destroyed the model which we offer today as a free-world alternative to state control and eventual dictatorship' (*The Times*).

Apart from its economic and political implications the Philadelphia case is interesting for the following reasons:

(*aa*) This is said to be the first time that high-ranking representatives of the U.S.A. big business have actually served prison sentences for anti-trust law violations (Fortas, p. 31).

(*bb*) The proceedings are believed to have demonstrated convincingly the bad faith of those convicted, i.e. they were fully aware of the illegal and criminal character of their activities. As Fortas writes:

Forty-five executives of the leading electrical companies met for a period of many years in plush resorts and motor hotels to eliminate competition among them, to split up the electrical equipment business in proportion to the size of each company, to eliminate 'outsiders', to engage in contrived and fictitious 'bidding' and to 'maintain' prices. To avoid detection, they used public telephones rather than their office equipment. They used only blank stationery and omitted names . . . they used code numbers to refer to the members of the team. They never gathered together in public dining rooms or hotels lobbies . . . Expense accounts were often altered to hide the location of the meetings . . .

Surely, these are tactics almost reminiscent of those of professional criminals. As Geis (pp. 166–7) has shown on the strength of his analysis of the *Hearings of the Senate Subcommittee on Anti-trust and Monopoly*, these offenders did regard themselves as law violators both before and after their convictions; their 'self-image was as "criminalistic" as that of amateur shoplifters' (Geis).

(*cc*) An important feature of the proceedings is that, although the presidents of a few smaller companies and five vice-presidents of two of the largest of them were indicted in addition to the slightly less prominent officials, the Government did not charge any members of the top management, the 'highest echelons' of the corporations involved. The trial judge commented, however, that the latter, too, bore a grave responsibility as it would be 'most naïve indeed' to believe that such persistent violations of the law could have remained unknown to them. Senator Kefauver, the Chairman of the Senate Committee investigating the case, took the same view (*Annals*, pp. 78–9), and some of the witnesses had testified under oath that the top management had not only known of these activities but had actually ordered them to be carried out.

(*dd*) Some of the offending corporations were 'recidivists'; they had often been involved in anti-trust litigation and had in fact issued written orders to their employees strictly to avoid anti-trust law violations, but their subordinates felt that this was not to be taken seriously and the general maxim was 'Don't tell the lawyers' (*Annals*, pp. 79–80).

(*ee*) The heavy treble damages payable as a side-effect of the criminal case might, as Fortas points out, so greatly weaken the smaller firms as to eliminate them as competitors, while the largest firms are likely to survive; in consequence, competition, which the prosecution had intended to revive, may well suffer through the case: 'Anti-trust is not without its paradox.' However, against this it might be argued that it was not so much the criminal case but the treble damages that had this effect.

(*ff*) As far as 'public opinion' was concerned it seemed to have been overwhelmingly on the side of the Government, and 'on the whole, business opinion condemned the guilty' (*Annals*, p. 116). This contradicts Vold's contention that penal anti-trust legislation cannot be enforced because it lacks the support of public opinion (above, III). If it can be convincingly shown to the man in the street that certain big business practices are against his interests he will back even strong legal action.

(c) *Tax Frauds*

Tax defraudations are not necessarily WCC; they are often committed by working-class people and small traders. PAYE makes it more difficult for some of them, but it does not affect their part-time earnings and similar forms of income which are never brought to the notice of the tax inspector. Even so, most really serious tax evasions are committed by offenders who fall under the category of WCC.

In *Criminal Justice and Social Reconstruction* (pp. 145–52) the position up to 1945 and the difficulties arising from the distinction between illegal tax evasion and lawful, though often immoral and anti-social, tax avoidance were briefly discussed. In the present context we are not concerned with the innumerable legal niceties of the subject which have been engaging the attention of successive Chancellors of the Exchequer year after year when faced with the well-nigh impossible task of devising in the annual Finance Act a general formula to reduce to a tolerable minimum the scope of anti-social tax avoidance. The trend of recent legislation has been to cover as many of these anti-social activities as can be done without arousing too strong opposition on the part of the business world. The crux of the problem lies in the almost limitless and undefinable concept of 'avoidance'. As a correspondent wrote in *The Times* (16.4.1960), the man who cuts down his cigarette smoking because of the tax increase commits an act of 'tax avoidance' as much as the millionaire who disposes of his estate 'lawfully' in order to escape the death duties. In an instructive article in *The Times* (12.4.1960), a tax law specialist, Professor G. S. A. Wheatcroft, points out that against two of the most notorious devices, bond washing and dividend stripping, the British legislator has been fighting for years with very little success: 'as fast as one loophole has been stopped another has been found and used. The existence of high taxpayers side by side with tax exempt bodies, with dealers and tax loss companies near at hand, enables innumerable favourable tax situations to be created which are indistinguishable by legislation from genuine business transactions.' Wheatcroft indicates various ways of how the legislator might possibly cope with these and other acts of tax avoidance. One of them is to introduce retrospective legislation at frequent intervals between Budgets, a technique which would be effective but is politically hardly feasible because of 'the natural antipathy of most citizens to retrospective legislation'.

In the financial year 1959–60, investigations into fraud and evasion of taxes brought to light 13,734 cases involving over £19 million (*The Times*, 30.11.1960, quoting from Revenue Departments, Appropriation Accounts, H.M.S.O., 1959–60). High as these figures may seem, they are in fact insignificant considering the real scope of tax evasion. As a responsible and knowledgeable financial writer, Andrew Shonfield, then Economic Editor of the *Observer*, has pointed out (*Observer*, 27.3.1960), according to statistics compiled from the tax returns for 1957–58, '115,000 incorporated businesses engaged in trade earned less than £250 a year. . . . The average "net true income" per company in this group was £31.' Shonfield comments drily that 'on the face of it a lot of people are going to a lot of trouble in order to earn extraordinarily little money'. As far as individual businessmen are concerned, nearly 500,000 of them had a 'net true income' of less than £250 a year, and another 484,000 had incomes of between £250 and £500 a year. Shonfield quotes from an article by an official of the Inland Revenue Staff Federation: 'Is it really the case that nearly a million go-ahead self-employed people remain satisfied every year . . . with less than a railway porter or an agricultural worker can earn? . . . For my part I remain convinced that there is substantial evasion of income tax.'

Discussing the various techniques by which 'the rich can arrange to shift their resources between wealth and income over a period of years and between various members of the same family', Professor Titmuss concludes that it is a fallacy to think that there has been a trend to greater equality of income in post-war Britain.[34]

For West Germany, Terstegen states that a ten-year's collection of cases has supplied ample evidence for the existence of tax-evasions in all classes of WCC (Note 1 above, p. 86).

(d) Other Forms of WCC

In addition to the three types of WCC so far discussed there is a great variety of other forms, too diversified to be covered here *in toto*. In fact, every day cases of WCC are reported in the press with the same regularity as bank robberies and pay bag snatches. Obviously, the so-called 'Shoddy Goods Inquiry' (*The Times*, 19.1.1960), which produced the Molony Report, originated in the widespread feeling that in many branches of industry and trade customers were induced by dishonest methods to pay 'inflated prices for inferior articles and also to buy goods which they neither wanted nor needed'. The notion of 'built-in obsolescence', i.e. the business practice of systematically producing goods of inferior quality which have to be replaced much more quickly than would be needed if the goods would be satisfactory, is characteristic of the whole matter (see *The Times*, 11.2.1963). In his book *The Waste Makers*[35] Vance Packard has produced overwhelming masses of American material on this and similar abuses. A corresponding British investigation might be worth while; it would hardly suffer from lack of evidence. The Molony Report accepted the widespread view that the Merchandise Acts had not been adequately enforced and that the number of prosecutions undertaken bore no relation to the number of offences committed.

Offences connected with hire-purchase transactions[36] are to a large extent not WCC, i.e. when committed by purchasers of small means who, when in financial straits, unlawfully dispose of the goods before the full price has been paid. The extent of hire-purchase sales depends largely on the often changing laws regulating the size of the deposit to be paid; for example, they were said to have risen from £760m. in 1957 to £1,070m. in 1959 (*The Times*, 24.2.1960). Failure to keep up instalment payments depends greatly on the fluctuations of the labour market. The finance companies operating mainly, but not exclusively, in the car hire-purchase field have also been occasionally blamed for facilitating such offences by giving excessive h.p. credit to untrustworthy people without adequate enquiries (see also Spencer's study mentioned below). In cases before the Birmingham magistrates, for example, it was claimed that 'an organized ring in Birmingham had

494

obtained more than £4,000 worth of goods on hire purchase and had sold them' (*The Times*, 30.11.1960). The *Sunday Express* (15.11.1959) reported that police and finance companies were fighting 'a wave of hire-purchase frauds involving millions of pounds', that there were markets in fraudulent sales of TV sets and radios, and that one finance company had lost £250,000 through such frauds. How far any of these offences were WCC is impossible to say because of lack of detailed information. No such doubts can exist with regard to certain 'car hire' or 'contract hire' arrangements, allegedly used by a few hire purchase finance companies, which were in fact disguised hire purchase agreements framed in this way in order to avoid the legal requirements regarding minimum deposits, etc. 'No deposit—you pay only three months' rental in advance. . . . A new car every one or two years'—it is stated in one of these advertisements, and the Finance Houses Association had to issue a warning that anyone participating in such agreements might be prosecuted (*The Times*, 2.6.1960).

In the American television quiz cases, as far as they involved breaches of the criminal law, those participants who admittedly had been coached for the notorious '$64,000 Question' before each show had not acted within their normal occupations. The organizers of these quiz programmes, however, did act in their professional capacity. It was even alleged that some producers had tried to persuade contestants to give perjured testimony to a grand jury. How far other offences were involved under existing American law is not quite clear; efforts were made, however, to make it a criminal offence 'with intent to deceive the public to engage in "rigged" television contests' (*The Times*, 3, 4, 5.11.1959, 8.2.1960).

Bribery and corruption are often WCC. In 1962, a former Alderman was committed for trial on the charge that, being a member of the Staffordshire County Council, he had corruptly received £3,400 in 15 months for supplying information to a building company about planning applications (*The Times*, 31.10 and 1.11.1962). The American case of Goldfine, the Boston business man, and Sherman Adams, former Governor of New Hampshire and one-time right-hand man of President Eisenhower, is interesting because of its political repercussions. As Adams has convincingly shown in his book *First-hand Report*, on his part nothing more had occurred than 'mistakes of judgment not of intent', but the line between such mere mistakes and the offence of passive bribery is often a very delicate one to draw with certainty, and because of this Adams had to resign from his office.[37]

A former Sheriff of the City of London was fined a total of £20,000 at Bow Street Magistrates' Court for offences against the Exchange Control Act, 1947 (*The Times*, 17.3.1960). The Principal of a College of Further Education, 'a man said to be held in the highest repute everywhere', was sentenced to nine months' imprisonment on six charges of embezzlement, some of which involved tuition fees (*The Times*, 1.11.1962). A 'wealthy property owner whose companies controlled premises worth £3 million' was fined £25,000 at the Central Criminal Court after pleading guilty to living wholly or in part on the earnings of prostitution in respect of premises in Soho between 1959 and 1961. He had charged rents of £20 per week from prostitutes, stated to be far in excess of the ordinary residential rents (*The Times*, 12.10.1962). This list could be continued *ad infinitum* since similar cases of WCC are reported almost daily in the press.

Further valuable material from English sources, particularly interesting on account of the data given on individual personalities, has been presented by John C. Spencer (Note 1 above). Only a few of the facts collected in this pioneer study can here be reproduced.

Spencer collected the cases of 30 prisoners from the open prison at Leyhill in Gloucestershire; his criterion of WCC was, in accordance with Sutherland's definition, 'an offence committed by a person of high status in the course of his occupation', and, considering the classification system used at the time in the English prison administration, it was obvious that such persons if at all sent to prison could be found mainly in Leyhill. The offences were mostly fraud in its various forms, but persons who 'deliberately set out to make money by fraud' were excluded. Twenty-four of the thirty men were personally interviewed, some of them twice, and as far as circumstances permitted an attempt was made to study their personalities, in particular in relation to their capacity 'to handle the conflict of norms presented by membership in different social groups'. In spite of the criterion 'persons of high social status' the prisoners came in fact from a heterogeneous group of occupations and very different social backgrounds. They were predominantly middle-aged or elderly, and judging by previous convictions they were latecomers to crime. Their sentences ranged from 3 to 8 years. From their occupational records it became clear that 'no sample of top businessmen from large corporations would be available at Leyhill', although it might perhaps contain some of their 'lesser followers' (it has to be remembered that this investigation was carried out before Murray and Grunwald were sent to prison). On the Hall-Jones occupational scale[38] the sample could be classified under the three highest classes as Class 1: 6 men; Class 2: 13 men; Class 3: 11 men. A great deal of upward mobility was discovered: whereas their fathers belonged mainly to Classes 4 and 5, many of the sons had worked their way up from skilled manual workers to important positions, but there were among them no executives of well-known firms. Only two had been to a university. Spencer comments that he had expected to find many more men in leading positions and with superior social and educational backgrounds. We may have to seek the explanation to some extent in the tendency to exclude monopolistic and similarly large-scale anti-social activities from the scope of English criminal law. Marital relationships seemed to be reasonably stable, in contrast to those of most habitual offenders. There was a noticeable contrast in temperaments between the offenders and their non-criminal brothers whom they regarded as less ambitious and ruthless, stabler, and less willing to take risks. Even so, the adventurous and ruthless gambler type was not typical of this group of men; they amounted to no more than about one-third of the sample, and there was an equally large group of mere muddlers and drifters. There was a striking conflict of norms of behaviour apparent in the behaviour of the prisoners; several of them referred to their 'two lives', one set of norms ruling their business activities, the other their private existence, in particular within their families. To some of them such conflicts caused intense strain and feelings of guilt, while others tried to solve them extra-punitively by blaming the authorities for their conviction and sentence. All of them, however, rationalized their conduct, mostly by pointing out that everybody behaved as they had done. Professional men seemed to show stronger feelings of guilt than business men, perhaps because of the disciplinary trials which meant to them exclusion from their profession. Spencer stresses the prevalence of bankruptcy in his sample and urges a criminological study of this phenomenon. He also criticizes the absence of adequate public control over the activities of hire-purchase finance corporations and over dealings in property and real estate—two types of business which accounted for nearly half of his cases. He supports the view that the criminal law should be more closely related to administrative methods of business control and that for certain forms of anti-social behaviour 'neither internal regulation alone nor government control *unsupported by criminal sanctions* is enough. The proper decision as to the appropriate method of control can only be made on a foundation of social research.'

In the Soviet Union, with its entirely different social and legal systems, the concept of WCC must inevitably be on lines quite different from those used in non-communist countries. While in the latter an important aspect of WCC is, for example, to be found in the monopolistic and anti-competitive character of free enterprise, competition and free enterprise, even the very possibility of setting up in private business, are almost non-existent in Soviet Russia. The Russian white collar criminals are not those who try to restrict free competition but those who try to compete with the economic activities of the monopolistic state. As Beermann writes,[39] 'the bottlenecks which still exist in the supply of some consumer goods, tools and raw materials are a constant inducement to act as manufacturer, distributor or purveyor by illicit means'. As the collective farmers and others who produce surplus food can legally sell them only at artificially reduced prices, black markets are bound to flourish. Moreover, there are frequent reports in the press of 'underground capitalism' and illicit factories. Those who operate them and their auxiliaries are the Soviet white collar criminals, and the so-called 'Parasite Law' of May 1961 represents the latest effort of the Government to deal with them.

Beermann traces the history of this piece of legislation back to 1957 and shows that in recent years the types of offenders against whom the parasite laws have been directed have changed: while previously the law had been concerned mainly with the tramp, beggar, and other workshy elements of low calibre, the Act of 1961 is mainly aimed at the more prosperous categories, those 'who are exploring the new regions of freedom' of the post-Stalin era. Against these entrepreneurs proceedings may be taken under the Parasite Law even if there is not sufficient evidence for criminal proceedings. Evidence of 'conspicuous consumption' unexplained by lawful means and earnings would be enough, and according to Beermann reports in the Russian press and legal periodicals indicate that prosecutions under the Parasite Law for extensive speculations in currency and goods, for illicit trading and underground manufacturing may have led to the detection of criminal offences, such as bribery and large-scale embezzlement of State property. It is as if in this country in the Vassall spy case of 1962 proceedings opened merely on account of Vassall's 'conspicuous consumption' such as living in an expensive flat in spite of a very low salary would have led to the disclosure of his treasonable activities. The legal safeguards essential to criminal procedure are circumvented by the simple device of calling parasite proceedings mere administrative measures—a device reminding us of similarly doubtful manipulations used in the earlier American sexual psychopath legislation. According to Beermann the parasite legislation does not, however, as those American statutes did, even require the courts to explore the personal circumstances of the offender.

In a subsequent article Beermann traces 'The Further Development of the Anti-Parasite Laws' (*Brit. J. Crim.*, Vol. 5, No. 2, April 1965).

Chapter 22

CLASS-ORIENTED THEORIES OF CRIMINAL SOCIOLOGY. IN PARTICULAR: ANOMIE AND THE CRIMINAL SUBCULTURE

After sketching the sociological and potentially criminogenic background of a class-dominated society and presenting some of the material which shows the significance of class differences in crime, especially with reference to the phenomenon of white collar crime, we can now pass on to the discussion of a variety of socio-criminological theories to examine how far they reflect the class factor in crime.

It is not our ambition in this chapter and the following to deal with the total body of socio-criminological theories—there have been too many of them in recent decades, each of them claiming to be original and stressing the differences from its predecessors rather than the similarities, whereas the actual differences are often too slight to justify the space and publicity so readily offered to them. On the other hand, some of the theories here to be discussed have greatly enriched our understanding and even fundamentally changed our views of the sociological and socio-psychological factors in crime. In accordance with the general orientation of the preceding chapters of this volume we shall distinguish between theories which are essentially class-oriented and those not so oriented. Our presentation will therefore not always be on strictly chronological lines. What do we here mean by 'class-oriented'? Obviously, not every theory which stresses the undisputed prevalence of delinquency of the traditional type in the lower social strata can be called 'class-oriented'—otherwise nearly all theories of delinquency would come under this heading. This label can be attached only to those explanations which are based on certain characteristic features of the different social classes, on the existing conflicts between the latter and between the subcultures created by them.

CLASS-ORIENTED THEORIES

By far the most important, comprehensive and influential of the class-oriented theories of crime and delinquency are those based upon the concepts of the criminal subculture and anomie. Above in Chapter 19 (s. I(*a*)) we have briefly surveyed the different views on the concept of 'culture' and its significance for the sociological interpretation of crime. We have also referred to the fact that, while under the influence of the cultural anthropologists that concept has more and more been interpreted in an objective, neutral, *wertfrei* sense, this does not invariably apply to the terms mass-culture and criminal subculture which are often used with undertones of strong moral condemnation. In sharp contrast to such undertones recent decades have seen the development of a comprehensive and consistent concept of the criminal subculture capable of interpreting in detached scientific language certainly not the whole but at least considerable sections of adolescent and even adult criminality. While, with one important exception, most of the theoretical spadework has been done in the United States, some significant contributions of a mainly factual nature have also been made in Britain.

Before describing the external forms and the various types of the criminal subculture we have to trace the historical development of its theoretical basis.

Human society is divided into groups: the more advanced, complex and sophisticated it becomes the larger will be the number of groups which it contains. With some of these groups we shall have to deal below in Chapter 24. Groups are not classes; they may—as in the case of schools or religious communities—consist of members of different social classes, but the latter may with Ginsberg be called quasi-groups.[1] In a criminal subculture we find groups, such as gangs, as well as classes, but its most characteristic feature are the problems arising from class conflict. When searching for the historical roots of the connection between class conflict and crime we have to remember that, while for Marx economic conditions were responsible for crime, he made no important contribution to the sociological analysis of crime and the criminal subculture. His closest collaborator Friedrich Engels, too, dismissed crime as a futile and primitive form of individual protest against the iniquities of society; therefore, it 'never became the universal expression of the public opinion of the working man, however much they might approve of it in silence', and a new form of opposition, i.e. the political, had to be found instead.[2] Ferri, for much of his life an enthusiastic Marxist,[3] was also more concerned with the economic causes of crime than with its sociological analysis. We have to turn to a non-Marxist sociologist, Emile Durkheim, for the beginnings of such an analysis of the sources of the criminal subculture.

1. *The Theory of Anomie: Durkheim and Merton*

We have to be careful in our use of the vital but often too vaguely defined and too generously applied term anomie. As Merton points out,[4] it can be found already in the late sixteenth century in roughly the same sense in which it was revived three centuries later by Durkheim, notably in his *Division of Labour* and his *Suicide*.[5] At a first glance, the connection between anomie and the criminal subculture seems far from clear. The literal translation of anomie is normlessness; in a criminal subculture there may, as we shall see, well exist strong norms of conduct, but they are at variance with those of the dominant larger culture. Durkheim opens his discussion of anomic suicide with the statement: 'No living being can be happy or even exist unless his needs are sufficiently proportioned to his means.'[6] While there are obvious limits to the physical needs of man, the 'quantity of well-being, comfort or luxury legitimately to be craved by a human being' cannot be defined and limited in objective terms; such desires are insatiable, and 'insatiability is rightly considered a sign of morbidity'. The only force which could possibly regulate such desires is a moral one provided by society and public opinion. There are certain accepted ideas in society of, for example, the upper and lower limits of the standard of living for workmen or for the different categories of workmen, just as for members of other social classes, but these ideas and limits are subject to change according to changing economic and moral standards. In times of economic disasters or of an abrupt growth of power and wealth those standards are suddenly and violently upset, and it takes a long time to find new ones. Disorientation of appetites, no longer controlled by public opinion, and a state of deregulation or anomie is the result; no established classes exist any more, and a race begins for unattainable goals. 'The less limited one feels, the more intolerable all limitation appears.' Under such conditions, religion loses most of its influence, and the government which should regulate the economy becomes its servant. Suicide, anomic suicide, is one of the consequences of this state of affairs, homicide may be another. In fact, Durkheim used his analysis of the general phenomenon of anomie to examine, among other problems, the statistical relationship between suicide and homicide and tried to prove that while what he called the egoistic form of suicide moved in the opposite direction to homicide, anomic suicide was likely to move in the same direction, in other words in an anomie-ridden society we are likely to find a high rate of both suicide and homicide.[7]

'Sociologists cannot be allowed to go on for ever clinging to the coat-tails of Durkheim and Weber', writes a political philosopher,

Stuart Hampshire. One can hardly criticize Robert K. Merton for 'clinging to the coat-tails of Durkheim'—what he did in his *Social Theory and Social Structure*[8] was immeasurably to enrich and deepen the ideas of his predecessor. If, *mutatis mutandis*, we would use an—admittedly rather far-fetched—analogy from musical history we might compare the relationship between Durkheim's and Merton's concepts of anomie with the relationship between Beethoven's earlier and, say, Mahler's later symphonies. In the words of one of his biographers,[9] 'from Beethoven . . . Mahler inherited his conception of the symphony as a work concretely expressive of aspects of human life', but Mahler expanded the Beethoven symphony to express 'a whole world of feeling'—which, of course, does not mean that Mahler was a greater composer than Beethoven, but merely that he was able to draw upon the lessons of another century of musical history and creative experience. Like Durkheim, Merton bases his analysis on the dangers inherent in any sort of discrepancy between human needs and the means available to satisfy them, but while Durkheim's discussion remains somewhat abstract, almost independent of time and place and remote from the realities of life, Merton uses a wealth of observations drawn from the contemporary American scene to demonstrate in a far more concrete way the consequences of a conflict between 'cultural goals and institutional norms' and to work out a typology of different responses to this conflict. Moreover, while Durkheim emphasized—and perhaps even over-emphasized—the basically limitless nature of certain human needs and ambitions as one of the main sources of anomie, Merton shows that dangerous discrepancies can also arise in a society and in circumstances where those needs and ambitions are not at all unlimited but merely go beyond what can be satisfied in socially acceptable ways.[10] Far more clearly than Durkheim and with much greater sophistication he deals with the problems created by the lack of proper balance between, on the one hand, the values dominating a given society and the cultural goals which, in accordance with those values,[11] are held out as justifiable objects to all members of that society, and, on the other hand, the approved 'institutional norms' and opportunities of reaching those goals. If there is no equilibrium between these fundamental elements of the social structure the conditions are created for anomie to become widespread. Neither the relationship between goals and norms nor the emphasis placed upon them are static; at times the emphasis is mainly on the goals to be reached at all costs, whereas there is but little interest in the ways in which they could be legitimately reached. On the other hand, where sacrifices are required in consequence of conformity to institutional norms social rewards should be offered as compensation, and positive incentives to conformity should be given to members of all classes. In contemporary

502

American culture, Merton believes, a stage has been reached where the emphasis is overwhelmingly on the achievement of certain objectives without due regard to the question of whether they can be achieved by legally approved means. The 'American Dream' knows of no limitations on the road to success (p. 136), a statement which reminds us of the stress placed by Durkheim on the limitless nature of human ambitions. In this 'American Dream' monetary success plays the predominant role, and there exists an immense amount of 'exhortational literature' to keep up intense pressure on individuals to strive for such success, with correspondingly strong condemnation of those who fail in this rat race. While the striving for monetary success is not peculiar to American society it is not its only theme (p. 166), and Merton makes it clear that there are also other forms of imbalance between cultural goals and the approved means of reaching them which may equally well produce anomie (p. 166).

It is of crucial significance for the understanding of Merton's theory to bear in mind that he does not regard the discrepancy between cultural values and goals and approved ways of achieving them as in itself sufficient to produce anomie and deviant behaviour; in other words, lack of opportunity is not enough unless it occurs in a society with an egalitarian ideology which preaches the gospel of equal opportunity for all comers. It is this irreconcilable contrast between the prevailing ideology and the actual state of affairs that causes the trouble and explains why there may be a higher correlation occasionally between unfavourable economic and social conditions and crime in American society than in far poorer countries where a 'rigidified class structure' exists side by side with 'differential class symbols of success', i.e. where the ideology of desired achievements is suitably adapted to the diverse opportunities open to the various social classes (pp. 146–7). It is here that, as we observed above in Chapter 20, I(3), Merton's theory may remind us of Albert Camus's statement: 'The spirit of revolt can only exist in a society where a theoretical equality conceals great factual inequalities', and already there we mentioned Merton's five types of individual adaptation (some of which may rather mean maladaptation) to those incongruities within society.

It is this insistence on the fateful role played by the egalitarian ideology in a world of factual inequality that makes Merton's theory of anomie a class-oriented theory of society and of crime, especially as he tries to relate his types of adaptation (or maladaptation) to the general characteristics of the different social classes. His first type is conformity, where no discrepancy exists between goals and opportunities and which is probably the most common type among all classes—otherwise society would break down. It is different with his second type, perhaps not quite appropriately called innovation: here the cultural goals and ambitions exist in the same way as in the conforming cases, but the approved institutional means of achieving them are rejected in favour of more effective, though officially proscribed, techniques for which Merton uses the term innovation. While from the point of view of individual psychology this solution is not unlikely to be encountered in all classes of the community there are sociologically good reasons to believe that it is particularly frequent among lower-class Americans, because the American stigmatization of manual labour and the inferior status of the minor white collar workers exclude the possibility of success comparable to that of organized vice, rackets and crime. One might add that, as far as manual labour is concerned, it is not only its stigmatization and lower rewards, but also its narrowing scope which means reduced opportunities and growing frustration. With regard to the latter, it was also discussed above (Chapter 16, V) in connection with the 'frustration-aggression' hypothesis as a potential cause of crime within the framework of individual psychology. Merton explains, however, that he is not concerned with individual character or personality types but with 'general modes of adaptation' to general sociological situations arising within a certain cultural and social structure (p. 152), and he is critical of individualistic psychologies such as the Freudian which pay insufficient attention to the fact that different social classes are likely to produce different forms of frustration (p. 140, Note 12).

Passing to his other types of adaptation Merton hypothesizes that what he calls 'ritualism' should be characteristic of the American lower-middle class, i.e. the type of adaptation which implies resignation, abandonment of any more ambitious social and pecuniary goals coupled with an almost compulsive adherence to social norms, i.e. the 'playing safe' philosophy (p. 150). Here he rightly pauses to ask himself whether this can really be treated as a form of 'deviant' behaviour as it is not generally regarded as a social problem. Although potentially leading to suppressed frustration, anxiety neuroses, and guilt feelings this mechanism of lower-middle-class family discipline is, Merton believes, not likely to be a frequent factor in crime, but he admits that further research is needed on it.

The least frequent form of adaptation is what Merton calls 'retreatism', i.e. the rejection of both high cultural goals and socially approved techniques of achieving them (p. 153). Such persons are sociologically speaking aliens; they do not really belong any more to the society in which they seem to live. Here we enter the world of the bum, the vagrant, drunkard and drug addict (see also above, Chapter 20, I, 3). Retreatism is not, however, restricted to them; it may equally affect certain other classes of persons socially greatly under-privileged for reasons of race, religion, nationality, etc.

As Merton briefly discusses white collar crime under the heading of 'innovation' it seems that he makes no fundamental distinction between the white collar crimes of prosperous business men and the general run of offences committed by lower-class persons as a result of the conflict between goals and lawful opportunities. This is surprising in view of the obvious sociological and psychological differences between these two categories.

Merton's theory of anomie has had a profound impact on criminological thought, especially in the U.S.A., but it has had its critics, too. We will deal with the latter first. Tappan, in the excellent chapter on 'Social-cultural Theory' of his recent textbook,[12] points out that, while American society is in some parts criminogenic, this should not be taken as meaning that Americans live altogether in a 'criminal culture' or in a 'sick society'. However, it was Merton himself who stressed that anomie should not be regarded as an all-pervading phenomenon. Tappan regards Merton's theory as a generalization which is becoming increasingly less accurate in the middle of the twentieth century since the rigidity of the present class structure is more generally accepted now by the lower and lower-middle classes. The Welfare State together with a powerful trade unionism and the growth of the civil service have, he thinks, made the common man willing to accept the fact that he is common and that he would be well advised to make no effort to be more. All this reduces the frustration felt by the growing lower-middle classes and is likely to reduce the volume of crime and other forms of discontent within this group. It is different with the middle-middle and upper-middle classes, 'a diminishing though still significant part of the population'; here the scars left by their failure to achieve the desired success may explain some unexpected middle-class crimes. Finally, Tappan regards Merton's emphasis on the normless character of American culture as exaggerated; in this culture there are still certain firmly fixed standards, and in particular the values attached to human life and personal liberties are no less strong than in the last century.

Our criticism of this analysis is briefly this: Tappan's view seems to be far too optimistic and hardly justified in the face of the constant increase in crime. The U.S.A. Federal Bureau of Investigation reports for 1962 an increase in arrests for crime of 7 per cent over 1961, and for teenagers alone it was even 9 per cent (*The Times*, 4.3.1963)—increases which are in conformity with the general trend over the years. To assume that the growing prosperity of recent decades has brought with it growing contentment and a feeling of resignation overlooks the fact, to which attention has been drawn above in Chapter 19, that with improved economic and cultural conditions aspirations usually rise accordingly; people do not always accept their limitations as easily as Tappan imagines. A certain measure of support for his views may be derived from the findings of a British investigator, Ferdynand Zweig (see above, Chapter 19), but as already stressed the latter's working-class material does not seem to be representative. If there would be nothing else to show how little many working and lower-middle class persons have in fact accepted their present lot and given up hope to 'better themselves', the enormous volume of betting in every form—13,000 or 14,000 betting shops have been opened in Britain in the past few years since this form of betting was made lawful—should provide food for thought. Generally speaking, gambling and especially a gambling fever of the kind the western world has been witnessing for years are a symptom not of contentedness but of the opposite frame of mind.[13] In the strike-ridden Ford factory town of Dagenham, Essex, where, an investigator asks, do its interests lie? 'In football pools, betting shops, television, bingo, cars and public houses' (report in *The Times*, 5.2.1963).

Bloch and Geis,[14] in their criticism of Merton's theory, question among other points his view that there are hardly any lawful opportunities for upward mobility among lower-class male adolescents. This is a factual issue on which opinions can be divided, and Bloch and Geis write of course only with American conditions in mind, but as mentioned above (Chapter 20, I(2)) the view seems to be widespread among American writers and certainly not limited to Merton that the era of truly substantial opportunities for social betterment has vanished in the United States.

2. *The Theory of the Delinquent Subculture*

We can now turn to those, also mainly American, writers who have further enlarged and enriched the basic elements of the Durkheim–Merton theory of anomie in order to strengthen the foundations of the theory of a criminal subculture. They are almost exclusively interested in the implications of this theory for the criminal behaviour of American lower-class male juveniles and adolescents, while the corresponding implications for adult crime are often neglected. In the present chapter we are following this line of thought only in so far as the problems of juvenile and adolescent delinquency will here be discussed from the angle of social class. In Chapter 26 they will be treated independently of class as phenomena of physiological and psychological development and maturation, while Chapter 24 looks at them in connection with family, school, and other social groups.

(*a*) There is, first, Bernard Lander's statistical study of 8,464 cases of juvenile delinquents in Baltimore.[15] One of the hypotheses in his research, in particular in the section based on factorial analysis, is that anomie is the most important factor in the analysis. The delinquency rate is a measure of the degree of anomie; another measure is the percentage of house ownership, i.e. the latter is an index of social stability, and so is the percentage of Negroes in an area, i.e. the higher this percentage the higher the likelihood of anomie. The second factor in Lander's analysis is a socio-economic one, measured by rent and education. Lander's interpretation of the results of his factorial analysis is that juvenile delinquency in Baltimore is 'fundamentally related to the *stability* or *anomie* of an area' (p. 59). While the districts of the city which are characterized by poor economic conditions such as bad housing, low rents and overcrowding are often identical with those showing instability and anomie, the relationship that really matters in our search for the causes of juvenile delinquency in the city is anomie. On the other hand, it alone is not sufficient 'to account for a complex matrix of social inter-relationships'; it has to be supplemented by the socio-economic factor (p. 88). While Lander's work is valuable on account of the sophistication of its statistical techniques and also because of its understanding of the non-economic aspects of the problem it cannot be regarded as a substantial contribution to the anomic theory of delinquency. It stresses the close association between anomie and certain economic factors and postulates the supremacy of the former, but how the two sets of factors have to co-operate in order to produce delinquency is not altogether clear. Merton, while expressing appreciation of Lander's 'ingenious effort' to define the meaning of anomie in objective terms, is also doubtful whether anomie can really be measured by the factors used in his analysis. The fortuitous availability of certain variables in the Baltimore census records cannot, he points out, make adequate substitutes for data directly reflecting the rates of disrupted social relationships (p. 165).

(*b*) Far more influential than Lander's mainly statistical work has been the almost simultaneous sociological study of the criminal subculture in Albert K. Cohen's *Delinquent Boys*.[16] Although Durkheim and the concept of anomie are not mentioned in this book and there is only a short and perfunctory reference to Merton's 'illicit means' theory, the influence on Cohen's ideas of these two great predecessors is probably far deeper than he seems to realize. In his view that theory may offer a plausible explanation of adult professional crime and of certain types of adolescent and juvenile delinquency, i.e. of utilitarian offences against property, not however of the non-utilitarian offences which are, he argues, the real characteristic of the criminal subculture with which his book is primarily concerned (p. 36). However, as already stressed in our review of Cohen's book and also underlined by Merton, there is no reason why the conflict between culturally prescribed goals and the limitations imposed by the narrowing of lawful

507

opportunities should not be capable of leading also to offences of a non-utilitarian character.[17] What Cohen does not seem to take sufficiently into account is the lasting and all-pervading effect which frustration may have on the whole personality of the individual and the potential irrationality of his reactions (see above, Chapter 16).

Leaving aside this point where the difference between Cohen's and Merton's theories can easily be resolved we now have to examine the similarities between them and consider how far Cohen has proceeded farther in the direction indicated by Merton. First and foremost, his theory is also strongly class-oriented. The whole of his theory has as its basis the overwhelming strength of class differences, and one of the central chapters of his book is entitled 'Growing Up in a Class System'. It is not his view that only the working-class child has problems, but that the latter are different from those of middle-class children and more likely to lead to delinquency. The family plays an important role in this, not, however—as psychological and psycho-analytical case studies try to show—because of its internal structure (broken homes, etc.) but because of its specific position within the larger social structure, i.e. as a unit in a class system. What he has to say about the characteristics of this system is more or less on the lines of the comprehensive American literature on the subject, and reference can be made to our discussion in Chapter 20. For him, the salient point here is the child's growing awareness of the existence and the strength of class differences as they affect his family and himself. Cohen admits that in a democratic society such as that of the U.S.A. status, as inherited from his family membership, is not everything—personal qualities do also matter—but it is nevertheless of profound significance. Moreover, middle-class ethics—partly derived from Protestant capitalism (Tawney)—and working-class standards and values differ in important aspects. Much more weight is attached by middle-class families to such qualities as ambition, personal responsibility and achievement, rational planning and the ability to postpone the gratification of desires, to control of aggression and respect for property. The lives of middle-class children are less restricted to narrow primary group relationships, and they tend to cultivate wider, secondary group associations extending beyond the family circle. In one way or another these middle-class values are also imposed upon the working-class child, and this co-existence of two different status and value systems in the working-class child's life and that of his family inevitably leads, in the author's view, to conflict and confusion, especially as— and this is the point where Cohen's analysis has met with much criticism—working-class boys are by no means all inclined in a wholesale fashion to reject those middle-class values and standards in favour of their own. There are too many strong pressures working in the

508

opposite direction, and in practice the cleavage between middle- and working-class standards is often far less marked than might be expected from the theoretical distinction. Not only are many working-class parents to some extent, perhaps subconsciously, attracted to the middle-class way of life, but the educational system of American society is wholly devoted to the preaching of middle-class ideals and the development of middle-class personalities (p. 113). The working-class boy, who is subject to these influences and to some extent internalizes the middle-class standards with all their attractions, but is nevertheless aware of his many handicaps in the competitive game, will develop ambivalent attitudes towards the two social classes which dominate his life and has to face a difficult problem of adjustment. Basically, there are three ways of solving this problem, and in describing them Cohen makes use of W. F. Whyte's classic distinction between college boys and corner boys.[18] Both types hail from the working classes of a poor Italian district of Boston, but their solutions differ widely. The college boy deserts his original way of life in favour of middle-class education and standards, and his career bears close similarity to the English grammar school boy of working-class origin as described by Jackson and Marsden (see above, Chapter 20). The second, and most common, solution open to the working-class boy is what Cohen calls the 'stable corner boy response' (p. 128), i.e. an acceptance of his limitations and an effort to make the best of whatever legitimate chances are offered to him within his working-class life. It is essentially the type of adjustment which Merton calls conformity and it avoids the efforts, risks and potential disappointments attached to the college boy's solution, on the one hand, and the radical break with traditional values inherent in the third, the delinquent, solution.

What are the characteristics of this delinquent solution? They have to be explained in terms of Cohen's theory of the criminal subculture which plays a crucial role in his book, and it is here in particular that he claims to have advanced beyond the explanations of juvenile delinquency given by other, similar, theories. Whereas the latter have merely tried to show how a criminal subculture is transmitted from one individual to another he tries to explain its specific content and the reasons for its existence (p. 18). This claim is not quite justified as other writers before Cohen have also described the essential features of a criminal subculture and why it exists in certain surroundings. It has to be admitted, however, that Cohen's analysis, while producing no further factual evidence, has added important new considerations to our theoretical understanding of the phenomenon, and it has done so mainly through the light it has shed on the significance of class conflicts. The idea that there are cultural variations, subcultures, within a common culture is certainly not a new one in sociological and anthropological literature.[19] In fact, it might be said that most social groups, institutions, professions and classes have their own specific subcultures, although their members also share a common culture within the nation and may have some part in the subcultures of groups outside their own. There is no reason why the concept of a subculture should be limited to geographical areas: it might well be extended to groups, occupational and others, scattered throughout the whole country. Criminologists have turned their attention to the problems of a criminal subculture comparatively late, and probably first in relation to its existence within the narrow confines of penal institutions, although the work of the ecological school (Chapter 23, below) had no doubt prepared the way. It is only in the past ten or fifteen years, however, that the matter has been tackled systematically and on a broader basis, although—as already indicated—mainly with reference to juvenile delinquency and usually ignoring its implications for adult crime. As Cohen rightly stresses, even if confined to juvenile delinquency in the United States there are many variants of the criminal subculture, but certain traits are, he thinks, common to all of them (p. 23). The most striking of them is its negativistic character (p. 28), largely caused by the ambivalent attitude, mentioned before, of many working-class boys towards the norms and values of middle-class culture. It means that the delinquent subculture is not really different from, or in conflict with, those dominant norms and values but rather shows a 'negative polarity', i.e. certain forms of behaviour are considered right for the only reason that they are held to be wrong by the dominant culture. In this way, by accepting middle-class standards but 'turning them upside down' in his actual behaviour, can the delinquent type of 'corner-boy' build up for himself a subculture and acquire status in terms which he is able to meet (p. 121). Whereas the ordinary, conforming, type of 'corner-boy' is willing to 'temporize with middle-class morality', the member of a delinquent subculture rejects any such compromise (p. 130). Utterly contemptuous of that morality, this subculture glorifies acts such as stealing, vandalism, and violence because they are the very antithesis of middle-class values. In psycho-analytical terms, the mechanism of 'reaction-formation' comes here into play (p. 132; see on it Chapter 17, I(*b*)). Cohen does not claim that this emphasis on the distinctly negativistic contents of the delinquent subculture applies to the whole range of working-class delinquency (p. 155); it applies only to those for whom wholesale participation in that subculture is achieved through effective interaction with others who are in the same position with similar problems of adjustment—interaction leading to group solidarity and the emergence of common standards (pp. 59 ff.). Only by sharing these standards with others can the participants acquire the status

510

denied to them in the middle-class culture, which leads to the conclusion that the delinquent subculture is a gang culture. The solution has to be 'a group and not a private solution' (p. 66), which explains the subtitle of the book 'The Culture of the Gang'. Altogether, as Cohen repeatedly stresses (for example pp. 148 ff.), his book does not try to answer questions concerning individuals, i.e. why a certain boy becomes a delinquent and a member of a gang and of its delinquent subculture; it is rather concerned with the general, sociological, question why this subculture comes into existence in a certain section of the community and its working class. On the other hand, he acknowledges our debt to the psycho-analysts for their often illuminating studies of individual cases (p. 183); he is also willing to concede that there may be two or more different types of juvenile delinquents, some of them mainly subculturally and others mainly psychogenically determined (p. 17), and there is even the possibility that in most cases these two sets of factors 'blend in a single causal process'. Looked at in this way, there is no doubt that Cohen was justified in concentrating on one of these sets, leaving the study of the individual side to psychologists and psycho-analysts, but the reader of his book will often find himself asking why it is that, for example, some of the 'corner-boys' remain conformists and non-delinquents, whereas others in the same sociological category join the delinquent subculture and the gang. The answer can be given only by reference to psychological and psycho-sociological, in particular temperamental and family, factors. Cohen explains that his own approach, far from minimizing the importance of the family in all this, rather magnifies it (p. 75), but as mentioned before, he is interested not in the internal structure of the family but in its role in the social structure as a whole.

When trying to evaluate Cohen's work we have to bear in mind that it is based on the author's general impressions, apparently derived mainly from his work as Director of Orientation at the Indiana State Institution for juvenile delinquents, rather than on exact field study. As Trasler points out,[20] Cohen uses certain fundamental notions as 'constructs', i.e. as convenient assumptions and not as descriptions of processes that have been actually observed. Cohen is aware of this limitation and underlines the need for further research on such debatable points in his argument as the question whether working-class boys are in fact as ambivalent in their attitudes towards middle-class norms and values as he suggests (for example pp. 123 and 169–74). That such feelings of ambivalence do in fact exist is shown, for example, in Jackson and Marsden's analysis of the, of course entirely different, psychological situation of British lower-class 'college boys' who have made their way into the middle classes without being able wholly to discard their loyalties towards their original class (see above Chapter 20, I, 2(*a*)). Another point where Cohen's theory has been questioned is his insistence upon the irrational, negative, non-utilitarian nature of working-class gang delinquency,[21] but here too we have to remember that he does not regard this as applicable to the whole of working-class delinquency. It is in fact most likely that Cohen's characterization is true only for some sectors even of American juvenile gang delinquency, whereas its other sectors show strongly rational, utilitarian features. It is even likely that within the same sector and the same gang delinquent acts may occur of both a utilitarian and a non-utilitarian nature and that even the same individual may indulge today in acts of the first and tomorrow in acts of the second type, according to his mood and the specific situation in which he finds himself. It is also a matter of regret that Cohen has made no attempt to relate his theory of the negativistic content of the delinquent subculture to the observations of Merton and Camus on the rebel (see above, Chapter 20, I(3)), which latter seems to bear the closest resemblance to the type which Cohen has in mind. With such reservations, his book has the merit of drawing attention to, and offering plausible explanations of, the great significance of the class factor in this field.

(*c*) The years after the appearance of Cohen's book have seen the publication of several American studies also wrestling with the problems of class as a decisive factor in delinquency. The most important of them is Cloward and Ohlin's highly perceptive and influential *Delinquency and Opportunity*.[22] Similarly to Cohen, these authors do not here present the results of first-hand field work, and their book is also limited to the theoretical analysis of one particular feature of American juvenile delinquency, i.e. the delinquent gang. They, too, claim to be filling a gap in delinquency theory by searching for the origins of the delinquent subculture, which concept they define as one in which certain delinquent acts are required from the members as gestures essential for the performance of dominant roles within the subculture (p. 7). This definition is believed to cover the most important forms of serious and persistent delinquency because only by frequent repetition of such acts can the coveted reputation for toughness be acquired and maintained. Unlike Cohen, these authors explicitly acknowledge their indebtedness to Merton and Durkheim (in Cohen's book the latter is not even mentioned). While their theory is strongly class-oriented, they are inclined to attach greater significance than Cohen does to inequalities arising from economic factors. To do justice to this book it seems advisable to separate, as far as possible, those points which merely constitute criticisms of the preceding literature from those where the authors make their own positive, and to some extent original, contribution. Much overlapping between these

512

two sides of the book is, however, bound to occur. To take the former aspect first, the strongly class-oriented character of their theory emerges with particular clarity in their detailed criticism of the view, expressed by Bloch and Niederhoffer,[23] that delinquency, although much more common among lower-class youths, is basically due to the general difficulties of adolescence which are similar everywhere irrespective of social class, race and culture. For the lower-class boy there are, these authors admit, the additional problems of adjustment to middle-class status; their dilemma is therefore a twofold one, but their delinquencies, while more frequent, are basically of the same kind and have the same causes as those of middle-class boys. More recently, Herbert A. Bloch, in his spirited contribution to *Organized Crime*,[24] has repeated his view that the 'intergenerational' tensions between young and old are far more important as an explanation of gang delinquency than conflicts between the social classes. It seems doubtful, however, whether these eternal tensions between the generations, important as they will remain (see below, Chapter 24, I), are as serious and bitter nowadays as they used to be in the past. The growing economic strength and consequent independence of the working-class adolescent together with the increasing indifference and apathy of their parents make it appear to be more likely that the previous struggle for power is getting more and more replaced by a silent submission of the older generation. Moreover, it is argued by Cloward and Ohlin that, while delinquent acts do occur among adolescents of all classes, middle-class youths involved in them do not belong to delinquent subcultures, nor do they receive any support and approval from the non-delinquent members of their class and from the conventional norms predominant in it. For this reason alone middle-class delinquency is not only rarer but also less dangerous than its lower-class counterpart. This touches what seems to us one of the most fundamental issues of the whole problem discussed in the present chapters. It is an issue which writers such as Dahrendorf or Hoggart have in mind when they ask 'how people see society' and find the answer in the everlasting dichotomy of 'them' and 'us' and its correlates in other languages.[25] It was also one of the fundamental issues in our chapters on 'Economic Crime' in *Criminal Justice and Social Reconstruction*, where we dwelt on the attitudes of different sections of the community towards certain legal enactments and different types of property,[26] and in *Group Problems in Crime and Punishment* where the conclusion was drawn from various observations that 'there are groups within society, probably much larger and more deeply affecting its well-being than the small stage-army of professionals: people neither downright anti-social nor altogether honest, but honest in certain situations and dishonest in others. There is no such thing as "honesty" or "dishonesty" in general.'[27] The inevitable consequence for our present discussion is this: while there are many subdivisions nowadays within that all-embracing term 'the working classes' with a great deal of differentiation according to income, standards of living and education, aspirations, and the like, that old dichotomy—which is far older than Marxism (Dahrendorf, p. 287)—still remains, and with it remain many of the old differences in attitudes towards the legality, morality and binding force of the official code of lawful behaviour. In particular, a sceptical and ambivalent attitude towards the law and its administration and towards authority in general, as the latter present themselves today, is probably far more widespread than commonly believed in official and upper- and middle-class circles. What is nowadays called the criminal, or if limited to juveniles, the delinquent, subculture is only the visible part of the iceberg, consisting of the minority of those who actually break the criminal law for the reasons given by Cohen and Cloward–Ohlin, but behind it stands a much larger, invisible or only dimly visible section of the population, drawn from the same social class and the same subculture, which, openly or by implication, encourages and supports them in the same way as white collar criminals are encouraged and supported by their peculiar subculture.

There exists, however, a criminal subculture not only in certain sections of the working or lower-working classes, but *mutatis mutandis* also in the higher social classes. This seems to be the inescapable conclusion to be drawn from our discussion of white collar crime. The difference may be—but this is only speculative—that the subculture of big business is limited to certain sectors of social life, encourages and supports only the lawbreaking activities of its adult members, and probably has in fact mainly adult members, whereas the lower-class subculture embraces with equal strength juveniles and in particular adolescents. There are also middle-middle and lower-middle class subcultures in which lawbreaking activities of types different from those of the lower class are encouraged and supported. It may be doubtful whether all these subcultures are in fact formed within certain social classes or rather within certain occupational or professional groups whose memberships are drawn mainly from the same social class. Subcultures can exist in groups as well as in areas (see above). For example, there may be subcultures of lower-middle-class coal-merchants or greengrocers or small builders respectively, each of them with certain specific ways of thinking and acting, with specific attitudes concerning the way their business should be conducted, most of them appearing perfectly respectable (or nearly so) to the world outside but nevertheless condoning or even supporting the unlawful activities, the fiddling and diddling of a minority, maintaining by way of rationalization that without such practices their particular branch of business could not survive. The attitude of deeply hurt innocence, the complete lack of comprehension of the other fellow's view we may encounter when politely rejecting, for example, the well-intentioned proposition of a builder, carrying out repairs for which an insurance company is ultimately responsible, to pay him a sum lower than shown on his estimate and receipt and to 'split the difference', or of a business man selling a new luxury article liable to a high purchase tax and proposing to give us a declaration that the article was second-hand and therefore free of tax—all this has to be seen to be believed. There are, in short, plenty of widely employed illegal techniques and usages of conducting business, in short, lower-middle-class white collar offences, which are to all those concerned known to be clear violations of the criminal law, but rationalized as a matter of course and without any signs of compunction. Very rarely will they come to the notice of the authorities and be punished.

The main points arising from this digression are, first, that we agree with Cloward and Ohlin, against Bloch and Niederhoffer, that the delinquencies of lower-class adolescents have to be explained in the first place as the natural outcome of a delinquent subculture sup-porting them and that the difficulties stemming from the general prob-lem of adolescents everywhere how to achieve adult status, though important, play a secondary role only. We also agree that for this reason middle-class delinquency is likely to assume a different charac-ter from that prevailing among lower-class groups. We regard it as essential, however, that the present abundance of studies limited to the subject of the delinquent subculture of lower-class gangs should be supplemented by similar studies of other criminal subcultures exist-ing in different social classes among adults rather than adolescents. That the practical difficulties will be very substantial cannot be denied.

Of some importance is also Cloward and Ohlin's criticism of Cohen's over-emphasis on the ambivalent and negativistic outlook of the lower-class delinquent adolescent, with their consequent greater emphasis on economic factors (pp. 91 ff.). There are in their view many such youths who do not aspire to middle-class status and are content to remain in their own class, but feel dissatisfied with their economic prospects and are all out to improve them by legal or illegal means. In this connection the authors suggest a more refined typology of aspirations, according to whether or not aspiration is directed towards change of social class, and try to relate it to four different types of adolescents. The most serious type of delinquent is, they think, likely to be the one who does not aspire to middle-class status but feels frustrated in his effort to achieve better living standards within his own class. Cloward and Ohlin are somewhat critical of

Cohen's assumption of a strong feeling of ambivalence towards middle-class norms and values on the part of lower-class gang members—an ambivalence leading to an equally strong reaction-formation, with a violent but in reality only superficial rejection of middle-class culture. This assumption of ambivalent feelings has also been to some extent questioned in a widely quoted article by Sykes and Matza[28] who claim that many lower-class juvenile delinquents are in fact willing to admit both the legitimacy and the moral rightness of the dominant, i.e. middle-class, social order and are therefore in no way ambivalent towards it. If such boys commit offences they assuage their guilt feelings not by the psychological device of reaction-formation but rather by that of 'neutralization', a term which these authors prefer to the more commonly used 'rationalization' (see above, Chapter 16), i.e. they work out a 'system of defences to crime' analogous to the generally accepted legal defences of insanity, necessity, etc. This system may mean, for example, a denial of responsibility because the injury inflicted was due to an 'accident', or in maintaining that the victim alone was to blame or that he could well afford the loss.

The solution of this controversy concerning the ambivalent nature of lower-class delinquency will probably have to be found partly in individual differences and partly in differences concerning the depth of the criminal subculture to which the individual belongs and the intensity of its anti-social tendencies. Too much generalization will be futile. As Mays points out in one of his studies of a Liverpool slum district.[29]

What we are probably faced with in these inner city areas is not so much a well-integrated community whose standards and values are in sharp conflict with the wider society, but a very loosely related population which as a whole is less intolerant of ways of behaving that would give offence in other areas, and where the mechanisms of social control are less rigidly applied . . . Buried within this generally tolerant and unambitious mass are a number of smaller groups which are more closely knit together and which in many respects accept a deviant, even defiant, way of life, and these smaller groups have a pervasive influence which to some extent infects the whole population to a sufficient degree to produce a pattern of life which is so unusual that it may be termed a subculture.

Mays expresses some doubts as to whether the term subculture should be applied to the whole inner urban area or whether it should be confined to the more closely knit pockets of resistance, but he concludes this part of his discussion by admitting that so far insufficient data are available and 'our conceptual categories are too blurred' to give a satisfactory answer. We would suggest, for the time being at least, that we might accept the likelihood of a criminal sub-subculture existing within the larger subculture, implying that feelings of ambiguity towards middle-class norms and values may be traceable in the latter but hardly in the former.

In an able analysis of the theories so far discussed David Bordua[30] finds a contradiction between the theories of Cohen and Cloward–Ohlin in the fact that the former believes the members of delinquent gangs to be recruited mainly from those who, unable to cope with the demands of middle-class society, turn their backs to it, whereas according to Cloward–Ohlin that category comes from the ranks of those who feel well equipped to reach middle-class status, but are prevented from it through the handicaps of their social background. This contradiction, however, is apparent rather than real since the different interpretations may well fit different types of individuals. As stressed above in Chapter 20, I(2), both the presence as well as the absence of opportunities for upward social mobility may create their own peculiar psychological traumata, but of different kinds and for different individuals. Even in a society where such opportunities do exist they are likely to be restricted to the very gifted or lucky few, and many members of the excluded majority will become embittered. Where no such opportunities exist, some of the underprivileged will draw comfort from the thought that their misfortune is nobody's fault, whereas others will, as 'Robert Allerton' did, turn against society (see Chapter 20, I(3)). Some of these grievances are justified, others are not, again others are perhaps justified only to some extent. To the psychologist the question of justification does not really matter since in W. I. Thomas's famous phrase, which cannot be often enough repeated, 'if men define a situation as real it is real for them' (see above at the end of Chapter 2, and Chapter 16, next to Note 108). His interests lie elsewhere: *why* does this particular person 'define this particular situation as real', whereas others do not? To the sociologist, as to the political reformer, however, that question of whether certain grievances are, from the viewpoint of an impartial observer, justified, does matter.

In a rigidly sociological study such as that of Cloward and Ohlin we cannot expect too many concessions to the psychological and psycho-analytical ways of thinking, but as Cohen had to borrow from the latter the concept of reaction-formation, Cloward and Ohlin have to resort to that of extrapunitiveness (Rosenzweig, see above, Chapter 16, III). They are aware of the great practical significance of Rosenzweig's classification of individual reactions to frustration, but refer to his work only in a short footnote (p. 112 f. 4) and complain about the scarcity of our knowledge about the conditions that produce an extrapunitive rather than an intrapunitive or impunitive frame of mind. The rigid limitation of their book to American publications prevents any reference to Grygier's study with its important combination of original hypotheses and factual material (above, Chapter 16), and their own lengthy discussion of the subject (pp. 112–24) hardly advances our knowledge. It might have been worthwhile, for example, further to consider the relationship between the impunitive type of Rosenzweig and Grygier and Merton's retreatist type and drug addiction, or between the extrapunitive type and their criminal or conflict subcultures. Similarly to Cohen's explanation of gang delinquency Cloward and Ohlin make it clear, however, that the, for all practical purposes most important, sub-species of the extrapunitive type, i.e. the one who puts all the blame for his failure on the injustice of the social system, is also the one who is mostly in need of collective support and finds it in the gang (pp. 124–7). Of the more original features of Cloward and Ohlin's treatise two deserve to be mentioned. There is first their attempt to divide the varieties of delinquent subculture into three major types, the 'criminal', the 'conflict', and the 'retreatist' respectively (pp. 20 ff.), the first of them striving mainly after material gain and committing property offences, the second seeking status through force and committing acts of violence, the third—reminiscent of Merton's retreatism—characterized by a withdrawal from conventional roles and goals and therefore seeking refuge in drug addiction and liable to commit the kind of offences connected with it. Each of them presents its own peculiar problems of control, but while conflict and retreatist groups seem to predominate in Negro and Puerto Rican districts the exact distribution of the three types in lower-class areas cannot as yet be ascertained. Nevertheless, the authors make an interesting, though largely speculative, attempt to relate their three types to the specific milieu of the neighbourhood and the opportunities it offers for criminal activities of a particular brand (for the details see their Chapters 6 and 7). This emphasis on the opportunities for crime existing in different areas is closely bound up with the second, and probably most original, contribution of Cloward and Ohlin to the sociological analysis of delinquency, especially collective, i.e. gang, delinquency, i.e. their attempt to link the Durkheim–Merton line of thought to that of the Chicago ecological school of Clifford Shaw and Sutherland's theory of differential association. While these latter theories will, as not class-oriented, be more fully discussed below in Chapter 23, the following brief remarks have to find their place in the present discussion of Cloward and Ohlin's work. The link between those two, in many ways so dissimilar, lines of thought is found by the authors in this: while both stress the profound discrepancy existing in the opportunities available to under-privileged youths of American city slums, the kind of opportunities which they have in mind is not the same: while Merton means opportunities for lawful aspirations and success, Shaw and Sutherland are mainly interested in the fact that the opportunities of committing crime differ according to the type of area (Shaw) and according to frequency and intimacy of contacts with criminals (Sutherland). Shaw and his school stress, in their 'cultural transmission' theory, that certain areas breed a criminal tradition with its peculiar, anti-social value system, passed on from one generation of residents to the next (see below, Chapter 23); Sutherland, in his theory of differential association (also see below, Chapter 23), concentrates upon the learning processes which enable the beginner to acquire criminal habits through his relationships with established criminals. The combination of these two kinds of opportunities, the one for lawful success and the other for crime, i.e. Merton *plus* Shaw and Sutherland, leads to what Cloward and Ohlin call their theory of 'differential opportunity systems' (pp. x and 145 ff.). To them, each individual occupies a certain position in both the 'legitimate and the illegitimate opportunity structures' (p. 150). Merton's theory of anomie describes the differentials in the availability of legitimate ways to success, Shaw and Sutherland those in illegitimate opportunities; each of the two opposing approaches ignores the fact that both sets of differentials are significant and have to be correlated. To refer more concretely to the three types of delinquent subculture presented by Cloward and Ohlin, the 'criminal' type can develop only where opportunities for stealing and where fences exist, the 'conflict' type only where there are opportunities for violence, the 'retreatist' only where drugs can be obtained. This fairly obvious point is further developed at some considerable detail by the authors who, in their concluding chapter, try to make use of their theory to predict the future trends in the American crime pattern. In what is perhaps the most thought-provoking and 'down-to-earth' section of the book they foresee a further growth in aggressive and violent crime as a consequence of the growing 'disintegration of slum organization' (p. 203). As Merton, W. F. Whyte and Daniel Bell before them,[31] they explain this phenomenon in the first place by referring to the, in recent years greatly improved, centralized and modernized organization of American crime. While this development, being outside the subject of the present chapter on class-oriented theories, will be further discussed below in Chapter 25, it has to be mentioned here because of the relevance which, according to Cloward and Ohlin, it has to their theory of the three subcultures. To them it means that, with adult crime becoming technically more complicated and refined, with its control and organization becoming more centrally directed, its techniques are getting too difficult to acquire for adolescent gang members, and the delinquent subculture of this type of gang is no longer regarded as an adequate apprenticeship for organized adult crime. This has the effect of driving more and more youngsters away from the 'criminal' type of subculture, which as we remember is concerned with crimes against property, towards the 'conflict' and 'retreatist' types, i.e. to violence and drug addiction. The latter conclusion does not seem to be entirely convincing as even in the modern, centralized and highly organized world of adult crime there will be many opportunities left for youngsters to commit their less sophisticated offences of stealing, housebreaking, etc. It seems more likely, therefore, that the effect of the changes outlined by the authors and of the growing complexity of modern life will be an all-round growth of subcultural delinquency.

Other factors which Cloward and Ohlin regard as further contributing to the 'disintegration of slum organization' are the growth of the Welfare State and the consequent decline of the political machine, the racket, in its previous form, a process already well described by Merton, Bell, and Whyte. In the view of these writers, with whom Cloward and Ohlin are in substantial agreement, the Welfare State has taken over many, but by no means all, of the socially useful functions of the American political machine which provided valuable services to the slum population and was better integrated and in closer touch with the lower classes than the socially too distant, too respectable and therefore impersonal organs of the Welfare State, i.e. the professional social workers, can ever be. The latter, hemmed in by official regulations and without influence on the political machine, are not in a position to offer those necessary services to the lower-class population which, in the past, the political boss could provide. All this, together with large-scale slum clearance which destroys the close social coherence of the old slum (on this see below, Chapter 23), has led to a breakdown of its organization.

Non-American readers of these concluding reflections may be left wondering how far they might be applicable to their own respective countries, in which the American-type political machine either does not exist or has developed on different lines. One of the issues to be borne in mind is that in its origin and characteristics that machine owes much to the influence of the Mafia (Chapter 25, below).

3. *Middle-class Crime and Delinquency* (see also above, pp. 459–68)

The middle-class offender has often been ignored by criminologists as hardly worth studying. White collar criminals, in the narrower sense suggested here in Chapter 21, II, i.e. limited to big corporations, their top executives, and other big business men, are not only more interesting but also more dangerous because of their powerful position in society, and the same applies to lower-class criminals because of their numbers and recidivist tendencies. Middle-class criminality is discussed mainly against this background to illustrate the discriminatory character of criminal statistics in which a particularly large proportion of offences committed by middle-class persons remains unreported, and also because the norms and values of middle-class culture have to be contrasted with those of the lower class to bring into high relief the peculiar characteristics of the latter. Cohen, who presents a detailed comparison of these two cultures, nevertheless admits (p. 160) that the section of his book in which he tries to explore the causes of middle-class delinquency, is 'frankly a speculative toying with possibilities', and he expresses the view, which is similar to our own (above, p. 514), that each social class possesses its own criminal subculture, but that in spite of a certain kinship there are important differences between them. What are these differences? In accordance with those advantages, already referred to, in status, opportunities, education, parental supervision and training, there is the belief in the value of delayed gratification, and, consequently, a higher level of aspirations for the future. Middle-class youths find it easier to control their aggressive tendencies; violence is as a rule disapproved of and largely replaced by canalized inoffensive activities such as sport, or in a few countries by organized duelling. On the other hand, there are aspects of middle-class culture which seem to work in the opposite direction, i.e. to the disadvantage of middle-class youths, and therefore to provide temptation of an anti-social nature. In both Cohen's and Cloward–Ohlin's books much attention has been paid to Talcott Parsons' theory of the boy's masculine protest against his feminine upbringing.[32] Without introducing any class distinctions Parsons points out that in the typical American urban family the child's training rests mainly in the hands of the mother which leads to early feminine identification. While this may be desirable for girls it seems unnatural to the boy and leads him to an attitude of masculine protest with consequent aggressive and anti-social behaviour.[33] This is of course an old problem and one which can hardly be solved here in passing or without recourse to psycho-analytical theories (see above, Chapter 17). In the present chapter we are merely concerned with any potential class differences in the prevalence and intensity of this 'masculine protest'. Cohen suggests that the phenomenon is 'accentuated in the social world of the middle-class child' because the latter has less opportunity than his working-class contemporary to see his father at home in his occupational role or to establish contacts with other adult males who could act as father-substitutes. The ensuing conflicts are further aggravated by the middle-class boy's prolonged economic dependence upon his parents. If all this were true, it would help to explain a higher rate of delinquency among middle-class than among working-class adolescent males, which is contrary to the prevailing views about the actual class distribution of delinquency. Until far more specific research is done on the points raised by Parsons we have to regard any explanation of middle-class delinquency on the lines indicated by him and Cohen as mere guesswork. It is more than doubtful, for example, whether the urban working-class child has nowadays much opportunity of 'seeing his father at home in his occupational role'—usually, according to the routine of city life, when fathers work they are not at home and when at home they do not work, at least not in their normal occupations. Exact investigations of the subject of identification with and domination by parents such as carried out by the Gluecks and R. G. Andry have used almost exclusively case material from working-class families and give, therefore, no information on class distinctions.[34]

A few writers have recently, following Thorstein Veblen, expressed the view that there is in fact hardly any difference in the values and the behaviour of the so-called 'leisured', i.e. upper and upper-middle, and the working classes and they quote Veblen's dictum: 'The ideal pecuniary man is like the ideal delinquent in his unscrupulous conversion of goods and services to his own ends and in a callous disregard for the feelings and wishes of others and of the remoter effects of his action.' The only difference, they argue, lies in the way the state and society react against criminal acts committed by members of the upper and middle classes, which leads one of these writers, Shoham, to pose the question: 'whose normative barriers are more injured by this type of conflict situation, those of the lower classes or of the upper classes youths?'[35] His hypothesis is that the situation is likely to be more injurious to the upper- and middle-class youths because they realize that it is easier for them than for the others to get away with criminal actions, whereas the lower-class boy is generally 'too far removed both geographically and socially from the upper-middle-class youths' to realize fully that the latter can get away with behaviour which would get him into trouble. Whether this hypothesis is correct will probably depend on many factors such as, apart from individual differences, the possibility of making such comparisons as indicated by Shoham on the part of the under-privileged and the likelihood of growing out of their anti-social leanings and of replacing them by more constructive activities on the part of the over-privileged youths.

Ralph W. England[36] finds certain differences between middle- and working-class subcultures in their contents as well as in the duration of their impact on the lives of their members, i.e. for working-class youths participation in their subculture ends earlier, he thinks, because of their lower age of marriage with its responsibilities. Another often quoted American writer, Walter B. Miller, while also upholding the usual distinction of middle- and lower-class value systems, maintains, in opposition to the prevailing view, that the working-class gang subculture is not, as Cohen assumes, merely a negative reaction to middle-class values.[37] Miller regards it rather as an independent system generating positive values of its own. In this his writings bear some resemblance to Richard Wollheim's Fabian pamphlet (see above, Chapter 19, Note 6), who believes in the emergence of a really independent culture of the English working classes. This view rests on a slightly over-idealized conception of working-class standards, but there seems to be nothing in it which would inevitably contradict Cohen's interpretation. In spite of the existence of a positive working-class culture some delinquent members of a gang might nevertheless be driven by an urge to 'turn middle-class values upside down' as a protest against their assumed superiority.

English writers of working-class origin, such as Raymond Williams (see above, Chapter 19, Note 3), are more reserved on the subject. Williams (pp. 307 ff.) thinks that what has remained of working-class culture after the Industrial Revolution commands respect but is in no sense an alternative to middle-class culture. His concept of culture, however, is here rather restricted to 'intellectual and imaginative work', i.e. largely to art and literature, although he also stresses that present-day working-class culture is social rather than individual, i.e. it has produced important social institutions of its own and been sympathetic towards education, learning and art. It is interesting that, no doubt entirely unaware of the controversy existing between American criminologists, he maintains (p. 311) that English working-class people are by no means anxious to become middle-class: 'The great majority of English working people want only the middle-class material standard and for the rest want to go on being themselves', which corresponds to Cloward and Ohlin's rather than to Cohen's views.

It is clear that on many decisive points raised in this chapter further research is needed. There are at present several projects on various aspects of class in relation to crime in progress or at least contemplated which might produce some further clarification: two of them in England, i.e. one 'to test recent American theorization on delinquency and opportunity', the other on the problems 'facing the middle-class offender upon and after his discharge from prison'; one in the United States on the subculture of violence,[38] and one on middle- and upper-class delinquency in Israel.[39] The American research by Wolfgang and Ferracuti, to be carried out with Puerto Rican case material, postulates that the dominant upper- and middle-class culture and also a large portion of the lower class are non-violent in character, but that the other portion of the latter accepts violence in its normative system. The hypothesis to be tested is that those violent offenders who come from a non-violent type of culture show a more pronounced abnormality in their personalities than the violent offenders coming from a violent subculture.

4. *British Material*

British studies on the subject are not numerous and mainly of a practical rather than theoretical interest, presenting the results of, usually first-hand, observations made in certain geographical areas and therefore closely linked to the ecological aspects discussed in Chapter 23 below. The work of Jephcott and Carter in Nottinghamshire, the various Liverpool studies of Mays, T. P. Morris's research in Croydon, and Fyvel's book, which concentrates primarily on London, have here to be mentioned.[40] They are, of course, also relevant to the discussion of the ecological theory of delinquency but as they provide much material on the relationship between class and delinquency in Britain their place is here, too.

(*a*) The Nottingham University study of 'Radby', the fictitious name for an English Midland mining town of 23,000 people, is, as far as class differences are concerned, perhaps the most detailed and systematic.[41] Completed in the year in which Cohen's book was published it could not benefit from his discussion, but it did refer to the writings of the Chicago school and to Merton's first edition. On account of its importance and because it is not easily accessible,[42] it will here be described more fully than the others. From the American studies on class differences mentioned so far it differs in many important respects: although intended to be an investigation of juvenile delinquency in a small town it became, from the outset, an attempt to draw a detailed picture of local working-class life differentiated according to sub-divisions within that class. Its hypotheses were that 'within working-class areas different standards are upheld, and that the differences between the norms of behaviour contribute to the differential rates of delinquency distribution', or more specifically, that 'contiguous and similar-looking working-class streets might live by different codes and have different habits' (pp. 14, 275 and 122). This is only another way of claiming that there are different sub-subcultures within the working-class subculture. The study does not concentrate on the way in which this is reflected in the lives of adolescents, be it as creating college-boys and stable or delinquent corner-boys or a criminal or violent or retreatist subculture. It is interested not in the origin and character of adolescent gangs, but in the way lower-class families of different shades live, act and feel. Various techniques of collecting the factual material required were employed: participant or passive observation by the two field workers in Men's Clubs, Youth Clubs, Pubs, Dance Halls, Children's Play Rooms, the

Community Centre, a Factory; house-to-house interviewing of families or officials and social workers, and others. While most contemporary American studies concentrate perhaps too exclusively on the adolescent boy and his gang, the Nottingham enquiry, in its concern for the working-class family as a whole, has perhaps tended to neglect the specific problems of the teenager. The existence of five 'delinquency areas' was ascertained, but also the fact that within them there were 'white' and 'black' streets and that in some instances streets materially comparable with the bad ones seemed to be free of trouble. Eventually, two streets in the same bad area, within two minutes' walk of each other, were selected for more detailed investigation and comparison, the 'white' Gladstone Road and the 'black' Dyke Street (pp. 122 ff.), the first on the whole artisan, the other labouring class, with incomes 'probably higher in the latter'. Material was further collected on two other streets, but here the contrasts were not so clear-cut, and therefore individual households were compared rather than streets (pp. 157–67). There were 104 households in Gladstone Road and 115 in Dyke Street. A five-point scale was used to classify the different families, with two grades (IV and V) of 'white', two of 'black' (I and II) families, and one intermediate grade III, the latter type being content to live alongside the 'blacks' but maintaining a different set of standards more in accord with that of the 'whites'. The criteria used for this classification are explained in detail, and 23 statistical tables are presented to show their distribution among the 5 grades (pp. 184 ff.). In the concluding chapter another detailed comparison is made, using 10 factors (pp. 278–86). If we now ask how far these grades and factors tally with the classification in, say, Cohen's list of qualities characteristic of the American middle- and working-classes respectively, we have first to bear in mind that the Radby families included in the Nottingham survey were all working class, though with different standards. The contrasts emerging from this study are therefore differences within the working classes rather than between the latter and the middle classes, which may be taken as just another symptom of the growing transformation of many upper-working-class people into members of the lower-middle class. Nevertheless, the same or very similar points of contrast emerge in both, the American and the English, value systems: for example, ambitions, postponement of gratification, conscious planning for upward mobility, disciplining of children, street play, control of aggression, respect for other people's property, appear on Cohen's list as characteristics of the middle class, and on the Radby list as characteristics of the 'white' working-class families (grades IV and V). Many more details are, however, given in the Nottingham enquiry than in Cohen's more abstract scheme, and many more aspects of working-class life are used to complete the picture, such as the constant contact between the inhabitants of the 'black' subculture, instability of their family relationships, their lack of independence, privacy, and co-operation with external authority, whether represented by the Church, the school, or the police, etc., and the over-riding interest in gambling. There are, of course, differences in the degree to which all those values of the 'white' families are actually cherished and acted upon. Moreover, it is clearly the view of the research workers that there are no sharp dividing lines between these two subcultures within the working classes or, for that matter, between them and the middle classes, but that everything could rather be plotted on a continuum. This is true in particular because of the growing corrosion of middle-class values which recently prompted *The Times* to write in a leading article (18.3.1963) of a 'middle class that, either through comparative affluence, weariness or disgust, has thrown in its hand or lost sight of its responsibilities'. The hypothesis that very different codes of values, habits and standards of behaviour existed even within the Radby working classes and that they found their reflection in the delinquency pattern was amply confirmed. No case of official delinquency was encountered from the high-grade families IV and V (p. 286), and delinquency was concentrated in the families of grades I and II (p. 182), but even here the figures are not high. 'Unofficial' delinquency was also found almost exclusively in the households I and II. There was no direct evidence of that negativistic or ambivalent attitude towards middle-class values so much underlined by Cohen; the position is rather that for some members of the lowest-class households delinquency, in particular theft, 'does not constitute a problem'—they 'see nothing wrong with it'. It is a 'legitimate social activity, unassociated with any feeling of guilt' (p. 288). Discussing Clifford Shaw's proposition that in delinquency areas preventive measures can succeed only through the fullest active co-operation of the local residents (see below, Chapter 23, A 4), the authors take the pessimistic but realistic view that, while certain possibilities for collective action may well exist in 'black' areas, this does not apply to delinquency prevention:

. . . it would be very difficult, if not impossible, to persuade the citizens of Dyke Street that they have a collective duty to restrain each other from delinquent behaviour. Their whole life is tied up with such behaviour in many ways . . . The Dyke Street code of conduct, and that of the lower grades, does not represent just an obstinate refusal to accept the laws of the larger society . . . [but] the people see no reason for accepting the principle that 'thou shalt not steal' whether it be because they are informed that God said so or because the law of the land said so (p. 292).

This in particular as they consider that there is 'abundant justification for them to lead the sort of life which they do lead'. This means

526

that 'they tend to base their behaviour upon practical tests . . . how about the boss working a fiddle? Is not the boss accorded status by society, and yet is not the only difference between you and he that "you steal in farthings and he steals in pounds"?' . . . The belief derived from such facts as these, linked perhaps with previous experience of unemployment and low incomes, is widely held, namely that 'there is no justice in this world' . . . (pp. 293–4).

Inevitably, the authors of the Nottingham enquiry are therefore drawn to Merton's analysis of the situation and its problems. Of course they have to make the usual reservations: not everything relating to American society is applicable to contemporary Britain, but there are at least 'some parallels in his description of the various modes of adaptation with some features of the "black" and "white" people' (p. 296), especially as far as his modes of 'adaptation' and 'ritualism' —and, we might add, 'retreatism'—are concerned. This leads to the interesting question of the level of aspirations among members of the working classes to which so much attention has been paid by authors such as Cloward and Ohlin. There is no clear-cut evidence in the Nottingham report on the statistical distribution of the existence or absence of higher aspirations among the various grades of the working classes in Radby, but not only the 'black' but also many of the 'white' families seem to be conspicuously lacking in ambition for themselves and their children. Of course, the 'whites' want their children to have 'just a little bit more than we had' (p. 286), but the wisdom of 'Don't aim high and you won't be disappointed' also plays an important role in their philosophy (p. 297). This bears out Zweig's view that 'the worker wants little things rather than big things' (Chapter 19, above) and Hoggart's blunt statement that there is 'lack of scope for the growth of ambition . . . Once at work there is for most no sense of career . . . life is not seen as a climb . . .'[43] As far as delinquency is concerned, this attitude may occasionally encourage the commission, or support, of minor dishonesties to make up for the absence of legitimate opportunities. In the case of the minority of rebels, however, this absence may, as pointed out above (Chapter 19), lead to far more serious and persistent crime. The Nottingham study presents hardly any material on these crucial issues. Instead it concludes its work with some thought-provoking references to Professor Sprott's pertinent observations of Chinese prisons and society.[44] In China, it is claimed, there are very few prisoners, very few persistent criminals, and there is very little juvenile delinquency, largely because of the 'wave of moral enthusiasm', which sweeps the country and makes everybody concerned with the part he is playing in the new society, and because of the weight of public opinion which regulates the behaviour of the individual and forces him to respect the law of the land—a factor which, the report concludes, 'does not operate to anything like the same extent in English society, or apparently in that of the U.S.A.'. Those who had been criminals under the old regime in China—their numbers must be dwindling rapidly—are greatly helped in their rehabilitation efforts by the thought that it was all the fault of the pre-revolutionary system, which promptly takes the stigma off their shoulders. Moreover, to revert to Merton's phraseology, there is in contemporary China, the authors think, no cleavage between culturally prescribed aspirations and socially structured avenues for realizing these aspirations; everyone is 'capable of attaining the status to which he is encouraged to aspire'. How far the picture thus painted reflects the reality of Chinese society we find impossible to judge, but for our present discussion this hardly matters. What does matter is the fact that these students of delinquency in 'Radby' find the cause of the anti-social attitudes and activities of certain classes of its population in the absence of those features which they believe make for law-abidingness in modern China.

Even the black spots in 'Radby', however, do not seem to be so very black and their crime pattern seems to be relatively harmless as compared with that in the largest American and British cities. Is the explanation to be found in the real facts of life in 'Radby' or in the way of looking at them, i.e. were the Nottingham investigators by the way their study was focused on the families precluded from discovering those blackest of the blackest spots which are outside the lives of even the 'problem families'? Or was it merely the difference in size, i.e. an ecological factor, that explains the contrast? If so, we should find an entirely different picture in Britain's large cities.

(b) This brings us naturally to the various writings on the subject of the delinquent subculture in Liverpool by J. B. Mays. In his first book, *Growing up in the City*, which appeared in the same year as the Nottingham report and Cohen's book, he gives a very detailed picture of an underprivileged area in that city with special emphasis on the material which emerged from his intimate knowledge of the lives of eighty boys, members of a youth club, who were interviewed individually over a period of months (p. 29). Although he refers already to the existence of a criminal subculture (p. 83) and stresses the function of the gang in generating delinquency he is not yet concerned with class problems as such. He discovers the existence of important differences in the adjustment of these boys to the subculture of the area and distinguishes between the 'delinquents', who form the majority of juvenile offenders, and go only temporarily through a delinquent period, and the 'criminals', few in numbers, whose anti-social behaviour is 'a form of protest against and an escape from an emotionally unbearable situation within the family circle' (p. 148). Similarly, in an earlier discussion of outbreaks of more serious violence by adolescent gangs (p. 113), Mays writes: 'Not a few boys, brought up on an arbitrary and affectionless regime of parental blows, seem to transfer their resentment to the outside world and seek to get their own back on society at large.' In other words, more serious gang delinquency is explained as in many cases due to particularly unsatisfactory family conditions in a subcultural area rather than as a reaction to class conflict.

Five years later, in his *On the Threshold of Delinquency*, which describes his group work with members of the Dolphin Club in a similarly underprivileged Liverpool district, he also stresses the existence of a 'discernible delinquent subculture' (p. 27). Many of these boys come from families with all the characteristics of the 'problem family'; they have no social ambitions and an 'inward sense of failure'. The gangs of adolescents who roam the streets at evening are 'frightening'. Many of them have developed 'a chip on the shoulder' as a result of their unhappy relationships with their parents (p. 161), and their attitudes towards authority are ambivalent. When called up for the Forces they are resentful of military authority and may refuse to take a stripe because they do not want to be different from their fellows and to rise above them. 'Big-headedness' is disapproved (p. 164). There is 'a sharp division between those who hold themselves to be superior to their neighbours . . . and those who assume no such status', between the 'respectables' and the 'roughs', with the former striving towards middle-class values and only rarely producing delinquents (pp. 28–9, 169–70). Between them stand the marginal families who are probably in the majority. We are thus reminded of the Nottingham classification of Gladstone Road and Dyke Street and their five grades, with the lowest grade in Mays's words (p. 171) perhaps representing no longer a subcultural, but rather a sub-subcultural type and diminishing in numbers in each generation. Similar doubts regarding the scope of this hardest core of the delinquent subculture are expressed in Mays's most recent treatment of the subject.[45] Although there are many facts and observations in Mays's surveys of the Liverpool slums which seem to provide ample material to build up a class-oriented theory of delinquency, the author himself has in his larger studies refrained from explicitly declaring his approval of the Merton–Cohen–Cloward and Ohlin line of theoretical reasoning. It is only in his recent 'Re-assessment' of the delinquency area theory that he takes a step in this direction by acknowledging our indebtedness to their writings (pp. 224–5) and by stressing that in a society such as ours certain disadvantageously placed classes will feel themselves 'debarred from enjoying their share of the rewards of industrial productivity' and that the resulting frustration will in certain cases lead to crime.[46] In his latest important book *Crime and the Social Structure*,[47] which was published after this chapter had been completed and can therefore be only briefly referred to, Mays explains more fully his view that the concepts of criminal subculture as developed by Cohen, Cloward and Ohlin and other American writers are only of limited value to our understanding of crime in Britain. He finds here 'not so much a hostile, negativistic and resentful reaction against higher income group ways of life as the development of an indigenous culture which met their own peculiar and social needs in a fairly satisfactory way' (p. 96). Moreover, he believes that 'curiously enough, the differential class structure has itself probably helped towards creating sufficient stability in the social structure to preclude the development of excessively criminalistic and violent sub-groups' (p. 97). This view, coming from a research sociologist with an unsurpassed knowledge of working-class life in one of Britain's largest cities, deserves to be taken very seriously, and if it should be correct it would disprove the validity of our tentative criticism of parts of the 'Radby' study (see above at the end of (*a*)). Is it correct, however? It was probably so not many years ago when Mays collected the case material for his earlier books, but things have been moving very fast in this country after the war, and they seem to be moving in the direction of more and more Americanization with all its consequences here as in so many other fields.

Although Mays frequently stresses the very important role played by the working-class mother in the lives of the family he makes no attempt to use this factor to produce a theory of 'masculine' protest'.[48]

(*c*) The picture which Fyvel presents in his book *The Insecure Offenders* is of course painted in many different colours. There are the feelings of emptiness, boredom, insecurity, of being excluded, of having no real prospects, which haunt the teenagers in our present society. Behind it all, however, looms the ghost of the class problem. While Fyvel knows his Galbraith and his Barbara Wootton, he may not know Merton and Cohen, but he hits on explanations which are practically identical with theirs, though formulated in less abstract-theoretical language. In the last resort, he sees the causes of the glaring deficiencies in the lives of working-class teenagers in the 'historic division of England into two nations which has enabled the middle classes to look after their own leisure time . . . while anything in crude or commercial entertainment was thought good enough for the working class' (p. 96). The educational reforms produced by the 1944 Act simply mean that the talent found among working-class children is drained away and those who are left behind, the 'also-rans', feel all the more strongly that they are second-class citizens (pp. 26, 227). The schools, the youth clubs are all inclined towards the old middle-class culture with its sharp distinctions (p. 22), whereas in reality we are witnessing the 'passing of the Bourgeois Age' (Chapter 15): 'It is this exclusive bourgeois class system and culture which is today cracking up', with its own classic concepts of right and wrong (p. 190). Seen from this angle, and with some further glimpses at the blessings of mass-advertising, there is no need for any other explanations of the present rise in teenager delinquency.

(*d*) Reference has already been made in Chapter 20 to T. P. Morris's *The Criminal Area* which, though primarily a study in social and criminal ecology, is also of some importance in the present context as it strongly underlines the class-oriented character of crime. For some purposes, he writes, class may represent 'the most meaningful frame of reference' (p. 165), and he maintains that, while what he calls 'psychiatric' delinquency occurs in all social classes, 'social' delinquency flourishes in working-class districts because of the support it finds in working-class culture (p. 176).

Chapter 23

NON-CLASS-ORIENTED THEORIES. IN PARTICULAR: THE ECOLOGICAL THEORY. CULTURE CONFLICT. RACIAL AND OTHER MINORITIES. ECONOMIC FACTORS. THE EFFECT OF WARS AND OTHER CRISES. DIFFERENTIAL ASSOCIATION

Most of the sociological theories discussed in the present chapter have got rather out of fashion nowadays, having been pushed into the background by the class-oriented theories of the previous chapter. To some extent this has been nothing but part of the usual process of a more up-to-date and refined theory succeeding one that has become slightly stale and failed to keep up with the trend of modern scientific ideas in general. In some cases, however, these very grown-up babies have been thrown out rather brusquely with the bath water. To do them justice it has to be borne in mind that most of the theories in this chapter are not only closely inter-related with one another, but have also helped to prepare the ground for the class-oriented theories of Chapter 22.

A. THE ECOLOGICAL THEORY[1]

This is true in particular of the ecological theory which, after arousing a great deal of interest already in the middle of the nineteenth century, reached the peak of its popularity in the period between the two world wars, but has gradually retreated into the background in the decades after 1945. It is striking to compare its full treatment in the slightly older American textbooks such as Barnes–Teeters, Taft or Reckless's *Criminal Behavior*, with its neglect in those first published a few years ago; often the words 'ecology' and 'delinquency area' do not even appear in the index. Even Tappan, to mention only one of the best of them, can spare no more than two pages for it, much of which is taken up by a reproduction of one of Shaw's diagrams of Chicago. Vold, too, has only two pages.[2] *Sic transit gloria mundi.* Clearly, every theory has its proper life span and climate, and thirty to forty years seems to be the average period allotted to most of them where they can flourish and dominate the scene. After that, people begin to get tired of them and bored. In contrast, the leading post-war Continental textbooks, such as van Bemmelen, Exner, and Hurwitz, give more space to the subject; and so does the pre-war edition of the German *Handwörterbuch der Kriminologie*.[3]

Whereas in Chapter 11 the potential criminogenic influence of a few geographical factors, such as the climate, were briefly discussed, we are now concerned with the role played by certain aspects of human or social ecology such as the density and mobility of the population, in particular migration, urbanization and urbanism, and the problem of the 'delinquency area'. Some overlapping between the physical-geographical and the ecological-sociological ways of approach is, of course, inevitable. Moreover, writers on human ecology, including students of delinquency areas, have occasionally borrowed concepts and theories from physiological ecology; for example, the idea that cities grow in successive zones from the centre to the outskirts (see below, s. 4) seems to have been taken from the physiological-biological theory that biological organisms develop in this way, with certain organs such as the brain forming the centre of nervous activity and sending its waves to the periphery. As with most of such analogies, this one proves confusing rather than illuminating.[4]

In this connection, the comparisons attempted by various writers between the different regions of a country have also to be mentioned. Reference has already been made previously to the attempts of some nineteenth-century criminologists such as Lombroso to explain differences in crime rates between North and South in terms of climate (see above, Chapter 11). Exner,[5] who studied such regional differences for Germany, considered the potential effect of the differential consumption of alcohol and also of the mixing of races through successive waves of immigration and invasion, with particular emphasis on racial characteristics. His tentative conclusion was that the lower crime rates of the north-western provinces of Germany had largely, though not exclusively, to be explained in terms of such racial and temperamental characteristics, formed in the course of centuries through the mixing of races.

I. POPULATION DENSITY AND MOBILITY. MIGRATION AND IMMIGRATION. TOWN AND COUNTRY: URBANIZATION AND URBANISM

We are here concerned with at least three different, but closely inter-related problems: How far does (1) the density, and (2) the mobility of the population, and (3) its distribution over communities of different size affect the adult and juvenile crime rates? And what are the explanations of the existing variations? The main reason why, after nearly a century of detailed study, these subjects are now attracting so much less attention is probably the greater scepticism and sophistication of present-day criminologists, who are better aware of the unsatisfactory statistical material usually at their disposal and of the danger of reducing very complex subjects to over-simplified causal explanations. The theory of multiple causation, with its readiness to admit the potential causality of many factors, thereby inevitably reduces the importance of each single one of them and in particular of those factors which are most closely inter-related with, and dependent on, others.

In addition to the three major general problems referred to above, there exists a variety of more specific aspects, often of a national or even regional character only, which have, in certain periods and certain countries, been regarded as particularly important, such as, for example, that of the frontier criminality[6] and especially of the crime rate among foreign immigrants.

1. *Density*

Of all the problems so far mentioned, that of the relationship between crime and the density of the population has been studied least systematically. At first glance, it seemed attractive and plausible to assume that greater density, with its consequent intensity of friction, would mean greater criminality. The statistical evidence for this assumption, however, is particularly difficult to produce. Density has to be studied mainly in relation to larger areas such as whole countries or at least provinces, and such overall pictures are likely to hide profound internal differences within the areas concerned. It is not surprising, therefore, that the work devoted to this particular aspect in the nineteenth century in Britain and on the Continent now appears to have been largely wasted. This conclusion emerges, for example, from the historical details given in T. P. Morris's book *The Criminal Area*.[7] In his discussion of A. M. Querry's work Morris criticizes as not altogether convincing Querry's rejection of the hypothesis that increases in population density lead to increases in crime, but he has to admit that the truth is often more complex than might appear from the casual collection of a few statistical figures such as usually presented in nineteenth and early twentieth century publications. In Britain and France comparisons between the densely populated 'manufacturing' districts and the sparsely populated agricultural areas were frequently made, throughout showing the same trend in favour of the latter.

In Professor Leone Levi's detailed survey of offences committed in England and Wales between 1857 and 1878[8] the relation between density and crime is regarded as very intimate, 'closer probably than to any other cause whatever'. To illustrate this he produces figures, at the extremes of which we find the rural counties of Wiltshire, Dorset, Devon, Cornwall and Somerset with a density of 238 persons to the square mile (1871 Census) and 0·59 crimes and the suburban counties of Middlesex and Surrey with 3,490 density and a crime rate of 1·15.

In *Criminal Statistics England and Wales* for the year 1893 (pp. 88 ff.) a comparison is made between the figure of 48 crimes against property per 100,000 of population in Cornwall, 184 in England and Wales and 343 in Monmouthshire. A warning is given there, however, that comparisons of whole counties may be misleading since crime may not be equally distributed over the whole area. In *Criminal Statistics England and Wales* for the year 1908, the following figures are given for crimes per 100,000 of population: (1) above 250: London, Glamorgan, Monmouthshire; (2) 201–250: Durham, Northumberland, Lancashire, Staffordshire, Worcestershire; (3) 151–200: Kent, Middlesex, Nottinghamshire, North and East Riding, Northamptonshire, Cheshire, and so on, down to (7) 50–75: Caernarvon, Merioneth, Cardigan, Pembroke, Carmarthen, and (8) under 50: Cornwall. Similar trends emerge from the figures quoted by Bonger from *Criminal Statistics England and Wales*[9] for 1905. Glamorgan used to be the subject of special attention on the part of criminologists, and in the *Howard Journal* of 1932 (pp. 3–4) it is pointed out that that county, with only twice as many inhabitants as the rest of Wales (which meant of course a far greater density of population), had four times as much crime, but that the very high rate of emigration was gradually reducing the difference (see also *Criminal Statistics* for 1930, p. viii). However, here as elsewhere it was probably not so much the high population density as such but the rate of unemployment, closely related to it, that was to blame, although here, too, generalizations are risky.[10] It may be noted, though, that in a very careful recent study of French crime statistics Szabo found a high positive correlation between density and crime or, as he expresses it, '*délinquance et population éparse*'.[11]

The exceptional difficulties of drawing reasonably safe conclusions from density figures may explain the shift of criminological interest to the apparently more tangible subjects of town versus country and of migration, and eventually to that of delinquency areas within cities.

2. *Mobility and Immigration*

(*a*) *In General.* We are here concerned not with social or vertical mobility (see above, Chapter 20), but with physical or horizontal mobility. That the latter has vastly increased in the course of the present century is a commonplace observation, and the explanation, improved transport facilities combined with greater restlessness, is also obvious. The almost universal availability of motor cars and the expansion of air traffic have provided the opportunities for easier mobility and with them the stimulus. People have got used to frequent changes of their places of residence and work and to travelling wider distances for work and pleasure. In addition there are large-scale movements in certain directions, such as in Britain from the periodically distressed North and from South Wales to the prosperous South-East and the Midlands, in the United States from East to West and from South to North. For California the present writer could report already in 1955[12] a population increase from less than seven million in 1940 to nearly thirteen million in 1953, and the state seems now to have reached seventeen million. Of the 1940–53 increase, four million immigrated from outside the state. For American Negroes the mobility rate is particularly high. In an interesting table in Elliott and Merrill's *Social Disorganization*[13] it is shown that within the period March 1957–8, 19·2 per cent of whites and 25·1 per cent of non-whites had moved to a different house in the United States, which involved the movement of thirty-three million persons. How many of them had moved to different communities or states is not stated, however. The Second World War was a period of perhaps unprecedented population movements within Britain, caused partly by the needs of war industries and partly by mass evacuation from the most vulnerable towns to safer places.[14] It was, therefore, a migration in an unusual direction.

As, with such exceptions, migrations go mostly from rural to urban areas the subject is closely related to that of urbanization. However, even in normal times not all migrants move in this direction; people also leave the towns for the country or they migrate from one area to another of a similar type. The location of industries may be a determining factor, and the present efforts of the British Government to move people and industries from the over-populated areas and the coming into existence of new towns may, in the end, to some extent counteract the prevailing trend. To give only one example, the most recent venture in this field, the town of Dawley, between Wolverhampton and Shrewsbury, with a planned population of 90,000 is intended to provide housing and employment for some 50,000 people from the Black Country and Birmingham (*The Times*, 9.4.1963). Moreover, efforts are made to move large numbers of civil servants from the London area to smaller towns. Migration, in other words, has features of its own in addition to those resulting from its major tendency to make large cities even larger.

How far is mobility associated with crime and delinquency? It has often been taken for granted that people who move, and in particular those who move frequently, are more likely to commit offences, which leaves it open what is here cause and what is effect. It may well happen that those who have already become offenders find it advisable to change their abode, partly in order to avoid detection and partly because of the stigma incurred after detection and punishment. Occasionally, two adjoining districts have been contrasted to show that the one with a stable population is more law-abiding than that with a fluctuating one; the high rate of juvenile delinquency in the London Borough of Shoreditch with high mobility has been compared with the low rate of the neighbouring Borough of Bethnal Green with its stabler population, but one has to bear in mind that there are many other factors, too, which show the former to be more under-privileged than the latter.[15] In short, mobility may be one criminogenic factor of many and, especially where it is often repeated, it may be merely a symptom of general instability and a restless disposition. Moreover, it has to be borne in mind that migrants are very often young unmarried males, i.e. a category with a particularly high crime rate.

In Italy an investigation is in progress[16] to study the criminological effect of the internal immigration from the South to the North, in particular to Lombardy. Its preliminary findings have been summarized as follows: 'At least as far as adults are concerned, migration does not appear to represent a criminogenic factor of social importance. There has been no significant growth of crime parallel to the migratory movement. . . . The only things that have been observed with greater frequency are patterns of criminal behaviour whose origin is to be found in the ethnical and cultural tenets the immigrants bring with them to their new homes.'

In the City of Philadelphia, Leonard Savitz, who has made a special study of the subject, found, in spite of various reservations due to the nature of his material, that for the Negro children of that city migration did not have the criminogenic effect usually attributed to it;[17] in fact, 'the Negro migrant population was considerably less delinquent than the Negro Philadelphia born population' (meaning the juvenile population). Among the explanations tentatively put forward by Savitz is the possibility that the acquisition of the local subcultural norms may be thwarted by a barrier isolating the migrants from the non-migrants; he also regards it as possible that the crimino-genic features of migration come into play only where the number of migrants is small so that they are unable to create their own ghetto-like community. In the area which he studied 44 per cent of the entire population in question were migrants. This seems to be in line with the finding of other American investigators that the Negro crime rate is negatively associated with the proportion of Negroes in the population, i.e. the higher the latter the lower the former.[18]

In the Borstal Prediction Study it was found that those Borstal boys who had lived at the same address since childhood were better 'risks' than those who had moved about frequently, but the value of this finding was somewhat reduced through the large numbers of cases where no information was available on this factor.[19]

The criminogenic effect of the wartime migrations within Britain, referred to above, is also difficult to assess with any degree of accuracy as the available material is too scanty and imprecise.[20]

(b) *Immigration of Foreigners in Particular*.[21] The criminological significance of large-scale immigration movements of foreigners has been studied especially in the United States as the principal receiving country. It is now followed, on a much smaller scale, by Israel. In Britain, the subject aroused considerable interest in the earlier part of the century, mainly in relation to the Irish immigrants, and more recently it has been revived in connection with the increased rate of immigration from Commonwealth countries such as the West Indies and Pakistan. The latter was preceded by the influx of refugees from Nazi persecution which was, however, rather reminiscent in charac-ter to the Huguenot emigration from France in the seventeenth cen-tury. Neither the immigration of the nineteen thirties nor that of Russian Jews to the East End of London around 1900 seem to have been widely discussed from the criminological angle.

Some interesting material on the last-mentioned wave is given, however, in a study by an American writer, Lloyd P. Gartner,[22] where it is stated that, although the terms 'peaceful' and 'law-abiding' were consistently applied to this particular immigrant community of the East End of London, nevertheless 'it had its criminal offenders'. No comparative statistics are given, and reference is made to the difficulty of sorting out Jewish aliens from aliens in general. Crimes of violence were absent, and the offences committed were, as had to be expected, mostly of a commercial character. By far the most alarming aspect of the matter was the 'decorously termed social evil' of prosti-tution and, closely connected with it, the 'white slave traffic'. While the number of Jewish girls who became victims of this traffic is regarded by Gartner as entire guesswork, there was apparently no doubt about the participation of Jewish immigrants in it. As far as the size of this particular wave of immigration is concerned, Gartner estimates that in the 40 years after 1880 the population of Russian Jews in East London had approximately quintupled from its original 60,000, partly by direct immigration and partly by a high birth rate.

The whole matter is in any case closely related to racial, religious, and political factors, and also to the theory of culture conflict to be discussed below (B, 1). Here we shall confine ourselves mainly to the statistical side of the subject.

With the gradual diminution of mass immigration from Europe to the U.S.A. the subject has nowadays lost most of its practical interest to American criminologists and has become rather old-fashioned. To the theoretical and historical criminologist and to the student of human prejudices and errors in general it is still important, however, as demonstrating the many pitfalls of criminal statistics, especially when influenced by differential penal treatment, and also the danger of trying to provide plausible explanations for phenomena the existence of which still remains to be proved. This danger is particularly acute where, as in the case of the U.S.A., those errors were eagerly seized upon to produce an increasingly restrictive anti-immigration legislation.[23] It is one of the lasting merits of modern American criminologists to have destroyed the old anti-immigrant myth, although full success was achieved only after the flood of immigrants had already been brought to a halt by that legislation.

Only rarely have these criminological studies been related to the corresponding work done by psychiatrists. The latter have been mainly concerned with the apparently high incidence of schizophrenic disorders among immigrants, sometimes explained by selective immigration, i.e. the theory that pre-schizophrenic individuals, inadequately integrated within their environment, may seek a solution of their difficulties in emigration.[24]

As will be pointed out later, the concept of culture conflicts covers a field much wider than the conflicts likely to arise through migration from one country to another with possibly very different language, mores and laws. In fact, however, it has been studied mainly in relation to the foreign immigrant, where it provided a welcome, ready made, opportunity to blame the immigrant for the increasing American crime rate. One of the best surveys of the literature up to 1938 is provided in Sellin's classic volume *Culture Conflict and Crime*, where it is pointed out that ever since 1910 investigations had shown the immigrant crime rate to be slightly lower than that of native white Americans. This in spite of the 'differential', i.e. unfavourable, treatment by the forces of law and order suffered by the immigrant on account of his origin and his inferior economic and political status (Sellin, pp. 73-4). Soon it was discovered that the term 'foreign-born' was far too general, that if the statistical figures were to make sense at all distinctions were essential according to age, sex, country of origin, marital status, length of stay in the new country, whether the immigration had been from village life at home to city life in the U.S.A., and so forth, and that a classification had to be made according to types of crime. It had to be taken into account, for example, that immigrants included a particularly high proportion of young, single, impecunious males of little education and skill, in other words, of a section of the population always showing a higher crime rate than others. Another point frequently ignored in earlier statistical studies of immigrant crime was that many of these offences were simple passport contraventions;[25] nor was sufficient attention paid to the great diversity of the factors which were responsible for the immigrant's decision to leave his native country. Moreover, American criminal statistics, by considering not the racial, ethnic and cultural background but merely the previous nationality of immigrants, had lumped together groups as different as Russians and Russian Jews, Slavs and Czechs, Italians and Sicilians.[26] These weaknesses have to be taken into account also when the striking contrasts between immigrants from different countries are compared.[27]

When some years later the searchlights were switched from the immigrants themselves to their American-born children it was believed by many investigators that it was this second generation that produced the highest crime rate.[28] In his famous study of the American juvenile gang Thrasher stated that this phenomenon was, in Chicago at least, largely one of the immigrant community of the poorer type, mostly concerning American-born children of immigrant parents.[29] Eleanor Glueck found that the social and economic conditions of these second generation children were not more unfavourable than those of their parents, and she concluded that their higher crime rate could, therefore, be due only to their more intense culture conflict.[30] In fact, their crime rates were higher than those of their parents, but slightly lower than those of the native-born, i.e. they had become more Americanized than the first generation.[31]

Another interesting finding was that certain changes appeared in the type of crime in that, for example, the American-born children of Italian immigrants committed mostly property offences, whereas their fathers had mostly committed crimes of violence—a clear example, it was thought, of the operation of an 'acculturation process'.[32] However, changes in the type of crime committed were observed not only between the first and second generation of immigrants but also within the first generation itself. Thomas and Znaniecki in their study of the Polish peasant immigration to the U.S.A. maintained that, whereas those peasants who had committed murder at home usually killed members of their families or other people near to them, those who became murderers in America mostly killed strangers. Their explanation of this phenomenon, if it should be borne out by the facts, is interesting and seems also quite convincing; it is not so much based on the concept of culture conflict —unless taken in a very general sense—as on the contrast between rural and city life. As one writer quoted by Sellin (p. 89) puts it: 'It is not simply that a Pole or an Italian has come to America, but rather that a villager has come to the great city.' As long as the peasant remains in his native village his contacts with strangers are very limited and his emotions and frictions are almost exclusively concerned with his own family. Once he is plunged into the abyss of city life his contacts with outsiders widen; while his emotional life becomes less intense, he is full of suspicions and fears of the unknown people around him, and, whereas now his wife and family are on his side, every stranger is an enemy.[33] In short, we may conclude from this, that Maxim Gorki's Russian peasant who in his village had to beat his wife to give vent to his frustration (see above, Chapter 16, V) will instead assault strangers after his emigration to New York. Another important distinction affecting the crime rate of immigrants was made by E. D. Beynon in a study of Hungarian immigrants in Detroit,[34] i.e. between immigrants living in closed colonies and those living in mixed communities. The delinquency rate of the former is usually lower, an observation also made in other studies reported by Sellin (e.g. on Japanese immigrants). The explanation is that people living together in closed national communities are less inclined to report delinquencies to the police and that there is closer group control and solidarity among them which favours the internal settlement of conflicts.[35]

As far as countries outside the U.S.A. are concerned, for France Gabriel Tarde refers already to an investigation of 1876 which had shown a crime rate of 8 per 100,000 for Frenchmen against one of 41 for foreigners resident in France, which he explains as the result of their separation from their home country and their families.[36] For a period approximately eighty years later, Denis Szabo reports that while in the big cities the crime rate of the foreigners exceeded that of the natives it was lower in the small towns and rural areas, but he adds that the high proportion of foreigners residing illegally in Paris explains to some extent their high crime rate.[37]

The large-scale immigration of Irish labourers into certain parts of Britain has for many years attracted attention as a social problem and occasionally been blamed for the exceptionally high crime rate of Liverpool and the whole of Merseyside. Before the First World War the main stream of Irish migration went to the U.S.A. and the

British Dominions, but after that war these countries became practically closed to them, and Britain, especially Lancashire and the Glasgow area of Scotland, was the only alternative. According to the report presented in December, 1937, by an inter-departmental committee the figures of migration from the Irish Free State to the United Kingdom rose from 11,300 in 1934 to 24,000 in 1946, which was however not regarded as a complete picture (*The Times*, 6.12.1937). Some material on this subject was also published in 1934 in the Social Survey of Merseyside[38] where it is stated that the Irish population there was not quite as large as often estimated. Taken together with the fact that the official crime rate of Liverpool had for a long time been very high[39]—although there has been some recent improvement[40]—it was tempting to blame the Irish immigrant for it. While reliable figures do not seem to be available to form a definite judgment, it is likely that the Irish rate is in fact higher, possibly much higher, than the non-Irish one. The explanation would be in many ways similar to that provided by American criminologists for their own immigration crime problem, with the difference that language difficulties do not play the role here which they may have played in the U.S.A. It is rather unemployment and the system of casual dock labour that are to blame as they hit the poor Irish immigrant even harder than the native. According to the Merseyside Survey (p. 202) 56·8 per cent of the Irish immigrants were unskilled labourers. More recently, attention has been drawn to the subject of crime among Irish people in London by the Cambridge survey *Robbery in London*.[41] The authors are very fair, however, in stressing that taking into account the high proportion of young single men among these immigrants it did not appear that in 1951, for which year the figures were collected, the numbers of Irish involved in robbery were disproportionately high. (Figures for 1957, the year which otherwise served as a basis for comparisons, were not available.) They conclude: 'It cannot be assumed without further evidence that Irishmen are more likely to commit robbery with violence than Londoners when like is compared with like . . .'[42] Another important finding was the unusually high proportion of first offenders among those born in the Irish Republic, a finding which was regarded as reliable in view of the great care taken to verify it (p. 65).

No other wave of immigration to Britain has created so many difficulties and aroused so much passion as that of coloured people, mainly West Indians, Pakistanis and Indians, in the last ten or fifteen years. The literature on it is already fairly substantial,[43] and the subject is of interest to criminologists from three angles: first, the aspect dealt with in the present chapter, i.e. immigration and crime; secondly, as an important contribution to the phenomenon of crowd behaviour, notably in connection with race riots (Chapter 25 below); and, thirdly, from the point of view of victimology (Chapter 25 below). It is, of course, almost impossible to keep the discussion of these various aspects strictly separate since as soon as we deal with the criminological significance of this particular wave of immigration the second and third of these topics are immediately involved, too. An accurate estimate of the size of this particular immigrant population is difficult to obtain. According to Ruth Glass (p. 32), it was not known for example how many West Indians lived in London in 1960, but the figure of about 40,000 was accepted in 1958, at the time of the notorious disturbances, 'by virtue of mere repetition'.[44] The bulk of the statistical information presented in her book refers not to total numbers but to a selected sample only. Nor are apparently any figures available which would enable us to compare the crime rate of these immigrants with that of the white residents for the country as a whole or for individual areas. The tools for any statistical investigations of this kind are, therefore, missing and wherever there are references to offences committed by West Indian immigrants they usually occur in the course of discussion of the racial disturbances in order to explain or justify the latter. On the other hand, interesting information is given, particularly in Ruth Glass's book, on the local distribution and housing problems of these immigrants in London, matters which are indirectly of great criminological significance as explaining both the offences committed by and against them. It is the well-known vicious circle of colour prejudice, high rents and overcrowding, a way of living not yet adapted to the strange new surroundings creating further prejudice and more intense friction.[45] Added to this are 'the folklore of the coloured man's sexual behaviour, and of the white man's reactions to it' (Glass, p. 85) to make the whole picture a most depressing one. However, in view of the close inter-relationship between offences by and against the immigrants and the scarcity of material available on the first category the whole subject will be left for later discussion in connection with the phenomenon of crowd behaviour in general and race riots in particular (Chapter 25 below).

Interesting sidelights on the criminality of foreigners, whether or not classed as 'immigrants', have been thrown by a recent study of shoplifters by Gibbens and Prince.[46] Of their 1959 sample of 532 London women shoplifters 150 (29 per cent) were born abroad, whereas according to the 1951 Census only 7·1 per cent of the London population were foreign born. This large proportion was mainly concentrated in the younger age groups, which was explained by the prevalence of foreign au pair girls and students. Most of the foreign women had been in England only for short periods, and most of them (70 per cent) were Europeans, only 16 per cent Asians and

4·6 per cent each were Americans and white or coloured 'dominions'. The authors suggest that the 'Europeans', for language and other reasons, feel more foreign here than, for example, the coloured immigrants; moreover, they feel less constrained in their conduct here since if things go wrong they can more easily return home than the immigrants from Commonwealth countries, many of whom intend to settle here. It was only in rare cases, therefore, that West Indians, although under greater economic pressure than most Europeans, were involved in shoplifting. The authors mention as additional reasons for the high shoplifting rate of European women resentfulness about conditions of their employment—a factor widely discussed in recent years in the English press—and the consequent wish to take revenge in some form or another; moreover, social isolation and detachment were regarded as an important factor too. We might add that in some instances this may be a somewhat milder reaction to pressures which in their more severe and lasting forms lead to arson and other serious crimes (see above, Chapter 15, I(c).

The high share of persons from certain Commonwealth countries of convictions of being in possession of dangerous drugs and of living on the immoral earnings of prostitutes has often been noted. Between July 1, 1962, and April, 1963, it was 272 out of 416 (drugs) and 52 out of 123 (living on immoral earnings) for the metropolitan police district only.[47]

3. Town and Country: Urbanization and Urbanism[48]

To get the exact meaning of these two terms clear, by urbanization we understand the trend of migration from rural areas to towns, by urbanism the specific way of life resulting from this trend. In a report on the work of a committee on urbanization set up by the American Social Science Research Council,[49] the author, Philip M. Hauser, points out that the fairly voluminous literature on the subject is concerned more with the consequences of this phenomenon, i.e. urbanism, than with a 'consideration of the city as a dependent variable'. Many of the generalizations presented in that literature were, the committee thought, drawn from samples inadequate in time and space in order to produce 'ideal-type constructs as tools of research' rather than being themselves products of research, and 'as western scholars have had increasing opportunity to live in and to observe urban areas in other parts of the world, they have recognized more and more clearly that the process of urbanization is far from a unitary one: that, on the contrary, there are various types of urbanization . . .' A similarly sceptical attitude towards the whole subject of 'urban sociology', urbanization and urbanism can be found in Ruth Glass's stimulating chapter on it in *Society*.[50] One of her main points is that, while most countries have become more and more urbanized, the previous distinctions between urban and rural characteristics have become rather faint, and any clear-cut dichotomy in terms of 'urban versus rural' is out of place (pp. 487-8). Instead, there is growing interaction, or even fusion, of urban and rural influences, and to define 'urban' is even more difficult than to define 'sociology'. Moreover, the very attempts to escape from urbanism have contributed to its further spread as large numbers of people who used to live and work in cities are now dispersed and live in suburbs or new towns. New 'configurations of settlements' are emerging in the metropolitan regions of Tokyo, London, Los Angeles and elsewhere, vast and featureless, neither towns nor country. The resulting evils have been blamed on urbanism, but is it 'the culprit or the scapegoat? Is it not the social system that has created cities in its own image . . .?' (p. 493). In Britain, where in the past hundred years the proportion of the urban population rose from 50 per cent in 1851 to 80 per cent in 1931, but has remained stable since then, 'urban diffusion' and the consequent fusion of urban and rural elements have become more advanced than elsewhere in their physical, occupational and cultural aspects (p. 487).

The implications of these developments on criminological thought are obvious. In periods less sophisticated and confused than the present, when most social phenomena were more clearly definable, criminologists could proclaim as an undisputable truth the dogma that there was far more crime in cities than in the country, with the exception of crimes against the person where the relationship was reversed. Two hundred years ago Adam Smith could explain this phenomenon in the following words, impressive in their simplicity and also interesting in view of our previous discussion on the class problem:[51]

A man of rank and fortune is the distinguished member of a great society who attend to every part of his conduct, and thereby oblige him to attend to every part of it himself . . . A man of low condition, on the contrary, is far from being a distinguished member of any great society. While he remains in a country village his conduct may be attended to, and he may be obliged to attend to it himself. In this situation, and in this situation only, he may have what is called a character to lose. But as soon as he comes into a great city he is sunk in obscurity and darkness . . . and he is very likely to . . . abandon himself to every sort of low profligacy and vice.

In a similar vein, Disraeli wrote in 1845 in his *Sybil*: 'There is no community . . . there is aggregation . . . Christianity teaches us to love our neighbours . . . but modern society acknowledges no neighbours.'[52]

Similar ideas have more recently been expressed by Robert Sinclair in his *Metropolitan Man*, who writes, 'virtue needs the power of devils wherever there are so many people that nobody is anybody's neighbour'.[53] And indeed, what was true two hundred or a hundred years ago is true today in a far more serious sense. It is this anonymity of modern city life that, together with its greater temptations and opportunities, may well be used to explain the criminogenic effect of urbanization.

It is not inconsistent with this anonymity that many inhabitants of the modern city are, to use Riesman's terminology, 'other-directed'.[54] This type loses its own individuality and depends entirely on others as the source of direction, but this does not necessarily mean that because of this dependence such persons will readily accept their control as a stabilizing force. Moreover, the guidance they receive from these other persons will very often have an anti-social bias or at least be socially and morally indifferent.

For the period of a generation ago which he had in mind and for some parts of the world even nowadays Clifford Shaw[55] was probably right when he wrote that in a small village community every member is considered as a total person in the total role he plays in the life of the community. In the city, except for family and other small primary groups, this is not so; individuals are either totally unknown to one another or they deal with their fellow men only at some narrowly circumscribed point, for example as the milkman, ticket collector, newsboy or grocer. The prostitute, Shaw thought, was the exemplification of city life as the woman in whom people were interested only as a sexual object.

On the other hand, while the social control exercised by the neighbours is a crime reducing factor of country life, in towns the police will usually be stronger and more efficient than in villages, and city dwellers may also be more ready to report offences than country folk. Vold,[56] who discusses the 'two basic hypotheses' on which, he thinks, the explanation of the higher crime rate of cities mainly rests, i.e. selective migration and the criminogenic effect of city life as such, dismisses the first of them. There is no reliable information available, he maintains, to enable us to state with certainty that those who migrate from rural to urban areas are more inclined to commit offences than are those who stay behind; they may rather be the more intelligent and active ones. Generally speaking, views on selective migration are divided; some writers believe that the better elements tend to migrate, others maintain the contrary,[57] but all this will probably depend on the circumstances and causes of migration.

The second hypothesis, based on the cultural differences between city and rural life, still remains as the most plausible one, but with the growth of 'urban diffusion' (see above) these differences are steadily diminishing. Lastly, Bernard Shaw's view may be mentioned, who claimed that the quarrels which 'make country life so very unarcadian are picked mostly because the quarrelers have not enough friction in their lives to keep them goodhumoured'.[58]

Statistical investigations of the problem have to contend with several difficulties: First, when comparing the crime rates of urban and rural areas we have to consider whether we wish to study them in relation to the residence of the offender or to the place where the crime has been committed: the first would be significant as revealing potential breeding grounds of crime, i.e. the place where the offender lives presumably helps to shape his personality and conduct; the second would indicate the regions which possess certain features attractive to lawbreakers. To gain a complete picture both sets of information would be essential, although especially in an age of very high mobility the place where the offender happens to live may often mean very little, at least for adults. Referring to a period which nowadays may seem to be the age of innocence, i.e. the years after the First World War, the present writer[59] quoted from the Introduction to *Criminal Statistics England and Wales*, 1928 (p. xiii), certain figures to show how greatly crimes against property with violence, i.e. mainly burglary and housebreaking, had increased in the country districts outside the great towns, increases therefore probably due to increased motor traffic; while the numbers of crimes recorded per million of population had remained steady in the Metropolitan District and the inner parts of the Home Counties (457 in 1911, 465 in 1928), they had risen from 116 in 1911 to 519 in 1928 in the outer parts of these Counties. Nowadays distance does not greatly matter to the criminal any more. In 1940, it could still be stated that 'street robberies and smash-and-grab raids are not frequent in this country, but whenever they occur they are made possible only by the utilization of the motor car'.[60] Nowadays, the number of these crimes has alarmingly risen, and it does not matter to the type of criminal responsible for them whether he operates from a city or a country district and whether a particular bank robbery or pay-roll raid is committed inside or outside the city boundaries, if only the essential requirements of success are likely to be present. The same applies to the thefts of lorries with valuable goods on transit; they are often committed in rural districts by criminals operating from a city. Statistics showing only the district where these crimes are committed —including those published by the Commissioner of Police of the Metropolis which can, of course, only give the figures for crimes

547

committed within the Metropolitan district—are, therefore, of limited value within the framework of the town versus country problem, although the technical details of the *modus operandi* are of great interest to the police. In cases of larceny of goods in transit it is often quite impossible and even immaterial to find out whether they have been committed in an urban or a rural district. The great Buckinghamshire train robbery of August, 1963 (Chapter 25 below), was the work of criminals from the Greater London area operating in a rural district. In this sense, John Mack is perfectly right in saying: 'There are in fact no *criminal* areas left, i.e. areas in which known criminals are known to reside in sizeable groups. But there are in every conurbation a number of *delinquent* neighbourhoods.'[61] Criminologists are more concerned with the general trends showing themselves in the commission of these crimes, their sociological background, the organization which makes them possible (see below, Chapter 25) and the psychological and social characteristics of the individuals behind them. Very little information on these essential aspects of the matter is given in the Cambridge publication *Robbery in London*.[62] The records of Scotland Yard, in particular, contain a wealth of material on travelling professional criminals to whom local and regional boundaries mean nothing, but no systematic study of it has so far been published.

Having made all these reservations we can now present a small selection of the statistical material published in various countries. Older statistics, which are often of doubtful reliability, will be omitted. For the United States, Vold (*Annals*, p. 39) presents a table showing the offences per 100,000 of population known to the police in 1940, adapted from the *Uniform Crime Reports* which do not, of course, cover the whole country, but are usually regarded as fairly representative. According to this table the proportion of offences of all types, including rape, increased with the size of the town. There were a few minor variations from the general pattern, however; in particular, cities of more than 250,000 inhabitants had for some categories of crime slightly lower rates than those between 100 and 250,000. Clinard presents more recent American figures[63] which show that in 1954 the rates for robbery, aggravated assault, burglary, larceny, and automobile theft were far higher in urban than in rural areas, whereas for murder and rape they were the same.

A detailed international survey was published in 1936 in German by Burchardt.[64] While most of his figures have become out-of-date, some of his methodological observations and his conclusions are still valid. He criticizes in particular the differences in the basic structure existing in the national crime statistics which make international comparisons impossible. The dividing line between 'urban' and 'rural' crime, for example, is far from uniform. In some countries only the residence of the offender is shown, in others only the location of the sentencing court, which may not be identical with his residence or the place of the crime. Burchardt's conclusions follow more or less the traditional line, i.e. confirming the great preponderance of crime in urban districts, with frequent exceptions for crime of violence. Twenty-five years later another comparative study was published in French by Szabo[65] which, though in the main limited to two countries, France and Belgium, is more thorough and sophisticated in its statistical techniques. Moreover, as Jean Pinatel observes in his Introduction,[66] Szabo has gone beyond the statistical evidence and tried to correlate it to broader sociological aspects. As Ruth Glass does in her almost simultaneous analysis (see above), he stresses the growing assimilation of town and country life and the consequently diminishing importance of his subject. In his historical chapter he shows that, whereas neither Guerry nor Quetelet had attached much significance to the matter, it was, at least in France, only towards the end of the nineteenth century that with growing industrialization the towns were labelled as criminogenic; but even then Tarde maintained that this label could be applied only to the new, not yet properly integrated, urban communities. In his statistical work Szabo, in order to make his comparisons more meaningful and specific, makes use of a special urbanization index (pp. 23–30), but he is somewhat handicapped by the fact that in France, as in many other countries, the *arrondissements judiciaires* are not identical with the *arrondissements administratifs* (p. 65). With important exceptions, his findings confirm those of most other investigators: crimes against property are more frequent in urban areas. but the preponderance of crimes of violence in rural districts has been exaggerated and it is further declining with the growing urbanization of the villages (p. 121). In short, urbanization is only one criminogenic factor among many (p. 223).

To cast a glimpse at one of the Iron Curtain countries, in the first volume of a Polish criminological journal, the *Archiwum Kryminologii*,[67] the English Summary gives the following information: In post-war Poland, with a population of 29,000,000, of whom 13,500,000 lived in towns and 15,500,000 in villages, the highest crime rates were observed in the western and most industrialized regions and the large cities of Warsaw, Lodz and Katowice. In fact, nearly one-third of all offences known to the police were committed within three voivodeships containing only over one-fifth of the population. For property offences, the coefficients rose in accordance with the size of the towns; for robbery, for example, 46 per 100,000 were committed in the country against 138 in the towns.

Some rates for India, with special reference to the state of Bombay, are given in Perin C. Kerawalla's book *A Study in Indian Crime*.[68] Bombay state has, according to her, an urbanization rate of 30·8 per cent, almost twice as high as that for the rest of the Indian Union, and over 44 per cent of its urban population live in cities with over 1,000,000, against 37 per cent in the rest of the country. Consequently, the author points out, the crime situation there is more of an urban problem than in India as a whole, although she is reluctant to ascribe the greater incidence of crime in the state of Bombay and its city exclusively to its greater urbanization. She shows, however, that in the city of Bombay the crime rates are higher than in the rest of the state, for certain offences even very much higher. With regard to specific types of crime the picture is not throughout uniform. Even dacoities, which are essentially a rural phenomenon of the Indian scene, are rare in some of the most rural districts. On the other hand, crimes of violence connected with rioting and blood feuds, often due to land disputes, are frequent in Indian villages.[69]

For Britain, Dr. E. C. Rhodes published detailed figures in 1939[70] to show the correlation between the size of the English counties, their percentage of urbanization, and the incidence of juvenile delinquency and adult crime. Although no consistent trend emerged he found an unmistakable association between these three sets of figures, for example,

Group I (Urbanization Index of less than 90) had crime rates of 80 (juv.) and 94 (adult);

Group II (Urbanization Index of 90–109) had crime rates of 106 and 103;

Group III (Urbanization Index of 110 and more) had crime rates of 113 and 114.

The smallest county, Rutland, with an urbanization rate of 18 per cent had the crime rates of 0·19 (juv.) and 0·49 (adults), against Lancashire, one of the largest, with urbanization rate of 87 per cent and crime rates of 0·45 (juv.) and 0·84 (adults). There was also proportionally more crime in the largest cities (over 400,000) than in those of 40–50,000 people, but otherwise mere size was not throughout decisive.

From present-day *Criminal Statistics for England and Wales* it is not easy to construct a clear picture. Local and regional figures are no longer given in the published annual volumes but have to be gathered from the *Supplementary Statistics* distributed by the Home Office to libraries, universities and interested persons (see above, Chapter 5), and the population of individual districts is no longer shown. To quote a few figures for 1961 (Table 4: Police Returns of Indictable

550

Offences known to Police), the county of Cornwall had a total of 4,575 against 8,556 of the city of Newcastle with roughly the same population. Lancaster county, with about twice the population of Liverpool or Manchester, had 28,096 against 20,909 and 24,804 of these two cities, but the picture is not throughout as unfavourable for the big cities, for example Gloucester county and the city of Bristol, with roughly the same population, have also similar totals (6,410 against 6,210). There are big differences between cities.

In the Borstal Prediction Study it was found that, although about 20 per cent of the population of England live in rural areas, less than 10 per cent of the boys in the sample lived in such areas at the time of their crimes; but it was left open whether this was evidence of the greater prevalence of crime in towns or whether rural boys who commit offences tend to migrate to towns. A slight, but statistically not significant, positive association was also found between the index of industrialization and the rate of failure after Borstal treatment.[71]

An informative comparison between town and country delinquency in Leicestershire was made by Howard Jones.[72] Because of the lower detection rate for the country (in 1954 it was 55 per cent in the county of Leicestershire against 71 per cent in the city of Leicester) he estimates the official court figures for the former as by 15–20 per cent too low. Disregarding this source of error, the findings are on the traditional lines, with the additional observation that new housing development is in both rural areas and towns associated with higher delinquency rates. There are more gangs, but fewer delinquent girls in country districts.

Finally, a research project undertaken by Marshall B. Clinard should be mentioned.[73] In accordance with the emphasis he places on replication and cross-cultured studies (see above, Chapter 3) he presents the results of his work on samples taken in the early nineteen forties in Iowa, with replications carried out ten years later in the same state and in Sweden; and he also tries to work out a typology of rural and urban offenders. His first two hypotheses, i.e. that the rates of property offences increase with the degree of urbanism and that offenders from rural areas and small towns are more characteristic of urban than of rural persons, more mobile and impersonal and less well integrated in their communities, were confirmed in both Iowa and Sweden. His third hypothesis, i.e. that rural offenders attempt to gain the anonymity of the city by committing their offences outside their own communities, was not throughout confirmed, but the fourth hypothesis, that rural offenders are of the individual rather than of the group type, was again confirmed.

4. *Delinquency Areas*[74] *and Housing*

This aspect of the ecological theory is concerned with the differential distribution of crime and especially juvenile delinquency within the area of a city or town. It was only natural that it should have attracted attention many years later than the allied problems of urbanization and urbanism. While the latter deal with the antithesis of town versus country, our present subject regards the town no longer as a uniform entity to be contrasted with the surrounding countryside, but distinguishes within the former a great variety of sectors of a diverse criminogenic nature. It therefore belongs to a later era.

Extremely popular in the period between the two world wars, this problem, too, has for the reasons indicated at the beginning of this chapter gradually receded into the background of criminological interest. As T. P. Morris and others have shown, its history goes back to the middle of the last century. To quote only a few of those earlier writers, Henry Mayhew pointed out that, in the period 1841–50, two of the Metropolitan Police Divisions, those including Hoxton and Westminster, had produced 65 per cent of all London's criminals. Interesting is also the observation made to a Select Committee of 1852 by Matthew Davenport Hill, the famous Recorder of Birmingham, that among the leading causes of juvenile delinquency in his time was 'the gradual separation of classes which takes place in towns by a custom which has gradually grown up, that every person who can afford it lives out of the town', whereas before 'rich and poor lived in proximity, and the superior classes exercised that species of silent but very efficient control over their neighbours to which I have already referred. . . .'[75] It will be noted that Hill seems to have in mind a period prior to the age of Adam Smith who regarded that 'silent but very efficient control' exercised by the superior classes over their low-class neighbours in big cities already as a thing of the past. In any case, however, what Hill regards as criminogenic is the crowding together of masses of poor people in certain city districts abandoned by the wealthy.

The modern study of delinquency areas begins with Cyril Burt's work in this country,[76] limited to London, and, above all, with the far more detailed American studies of Clifford R. Shaw.[77] The latter have been so widely discussed in textbooks, monographs and articles that a brief summary may here suffice.[78] Shaw was fortunate or, in some respects at least, unfortunate in having at his disposal, and being influenced by, the impressive ecological work of the Chicago school of sociology, famous through the writings of Robert E. Park, R. W. McKenzie, Ernest W. Burgess, Harvey Zorbaugh, Frederic M.

Thrasher and others.[79] It was one of the basic contentions of that school that a big city develops in concentric circles through a number of zones radiating from the centre. As shown in a 'schematic design of the ecology of Chicago',[80] the first and most central of these zones or rings, in Chicago the famous 'Loop', contains the central business area with its big banks, department stores and the most expensive shops, the city administration, the main railway terminals, etc. The second zone is one of transition, an 'interstitial' area in the throes of a change-over from residential to business and industrial life, containing rooming houses, brothels and in Chicago the Ghetto, Chinatown and 'Little Sicily'. In the third zone there are the workmen's homes, but also the 'second immigrant's' settlements. The fourth and fifth zones are respectable residential and commuters' districts of typical suburbia. It was Clifford Shaw's contention in his first major publication *Delinquency Areas*, based on very detailed statistical studies of many thousands of cases of juvenile and adult offenders in Chicago, altogether about 55,000, that there was a distinct positive correlation between the location of the residence of people within those five zones and the delinquency rate of the area. In fact, the delinquency rates for boys brought before the Chicago juvenile court differed in 1926 from nil in the best to 26·6 per cent in the worst areas. Taking as the basis for his calculations the seven-year period of juvenile court eligibility, Kobrin concluded from this that 65·9 per cent could be regarded as the official delinquency rate in the worst areas, i.e. almost two out of three of these boys had engaged in behaviour serious enough to lead to a police record.[81]

Shaw emphasized that it was not his intention to prove that delinquency was *caused* by the 'simple external fact of location', but merely that it tended 'to occur in a characteristic type of area' (*Delinquency Areas*, p. 21). Moreover, he stated that, generally speaking, delinquency rates were higher the nearer to the centre a given locality was and in areas of declining population, but he admitted that this 'radial pattern' may not be characteristic of all cities, although marked differences in concentration between local areas could be found everywhere (p. 202). There was a higher rate of recidivism in areas having the greatest proportion of delinquents, and the latter tended to have also as a rule the highest proportion of adult crime (pp. 186, 202).[82] These findings were linked to the fact that the most recent immigrants settled first in the districts of worst deterioration, from where they pushed the previous inhabitants out into areas of less obvious neglect, i.e. the second zone (p. 18). And, finally, Shaw contended that, while over a period of thirty years immigrants of very different races and nationalities had lived in these localities and after a while been replaced by other, even poorer, newcomers,[83] the delinquency rates of the area had remained more or less unchanged in spite of all these changes in the composition of its population; in other words, it was not race, colour, or nationality, but the area itself that was in a certain way consistently associated with crime and delinquency. At the first glance, this may give the impression that Shaw wanted to propagate the idea of something like a 'born' delinquency area, i.e. an area which inevitably, regardless of the characteristics of, and changes in, its inhabitants, was doomed to produce a fixed rate of crime, delinquency and recidivism. Such a conception would have been the complete opposite in the socio-logical field to Lombroso's earlier theory of the born criminal in the biological field, entirely rigid and uncompromisingly deterministic. In fact, Shaw never went as far as that. He was, to some extent at least, aware of the rather doubtful quality of the statistical material on which his theory and his conclusions had to be based. He did not claim that even in the worst areas the delinquency rate was anything like 100 per cent or that the underlying conditions were unchange-able; he realized that many other factors beside the character of the area could determine the final outcome in each individual case (see, e.g., Shaw and McKay, p. 440); but he did perhaps not sufficiently appreciate certain other weaknesses of his work. For example, it has been argued not without reason that even for Chicago the concentric zone theory was rather unrealistic and that in most American cities, with the main streets running east to west and north to south, development tended to be along these streets rather than radiating from a central business district (Morris, p. 15). For Baltimore Lander in his very careful investigation concluded that the city did not con-form to the zonal hypothesis and that in fact the most important concentrations of industry were located not in the centre but the outlying districts.[84] Moreover, the statistical basis of Shaw's conten-tion that the delinquency rate of the area concerned had remained constant in spite of wholesale population changes has been hotly disputed by Christian T. Jonasson.[85] In spite of all this, Shaw and his fellow workers tried to demonstrate that, with a few exceptions, their theory was also applicable to the other cities which they had studied.[86] Another weakness of this type of research is that it was based on the statistical distribution of the places where the delinquents lived ('breeding areas'), neglecting the location of the places where they committed their offences ('attracting areas'). The need to consider both aspects has been stressed above (s. 3), as it had already been in the (unpublished) Cairo study by El-Saaty and in the present writer's study of Cambridge, where the nature of the available material and the wish to compare the results with those of Shaw and Cyril Burt made it necessary to concentrate on the 'breeding' areas.[87] The

practical difference between 'breeding' and 'attracting' areas of
delinquency varies, of course, greatly in accordance with the character of the community and the way in which residential and business
districts are separated. Where in line with modern ideas of town
planning these two are widely apart there will be very little overlapping,[88] whereas in older, unplanned communities they will be
largely identical. What 'Robert Allerton' tells us about his London
childhood in Shoreditch[89] characterizes the latter type of district:
'The street [in which his family lived] had a market at the top and
a Mission Hall near the bottom, an old church in the middle,
and a crossroads with a pub on one corner and a shop that sold everything on the other. . . . The kids wriggled in and out like fishes,
pinching to their heart's content because everyone was too busy to
notice. . . .' Obviously, not much difference here between 'breeding'
and 'attracting' areas.

Another of the inner districts of London, Soho, has for many years
had a reputation for being 'the villain's natural home', the 'inevitable
capital city of the underworld',[90] an environment breeding a plethora
of serious crimes, protection rackets, prostitution, and drug peddling.
Many of the crimes planned in that district are, of course, carried out
elsewhere, 'just as a take-over bid hatched in the City will ultimately
manifest itself far away from Threadneedle Street', to use the parallel
drawn by a writer in the *Evening Standard*. In the House of Lords,
Lord Morrison of Lambeth maintained that in the view of many
Continental and some British people 'this part of London was the
most disreputable place to be found in Europe', and on behalf of the
Government it was stated that the London County Council had in
1963 initiated 51 successful prosecutions of Soho clubs where objec-
tionable forms of entertainment were practised (*The Times*, 29.5.1963).
The borough of Stepney was described in 1963 as 'plagued with vice
. . . fights included bottle fights' (from a libel action reported in *The
Times*, 9.5.1963).

With partial slum clearance and the multiplication of new housing
estates, often near the outskirts, the problem of the delinquency area
has to some extent changed its character. Already in the Cambridge
study, undertaken more than twenty years ago, it was found that,
contrary to the observations of the Chicago school, and in this
country by Burt for London and Bagot for Liverpool, the delinquency
rates for the central wards of the city were far lower than those of
some of the residential suburbs.[91] Various explanations were suggested, among them the small size of Cambridge and the presence of
open spaces and playing fields near the centre. One of the most significant findings, however, was the high delinquency rate of some of
the new housing estates in the outer wards, in this respect confirming

the data presented by Bagot and others. In fact, to some extent at least the problems of the delinquency area of thirty years ago have been replaced by those of the 'difficult housing estate', which have recently been lucidly analysed by Roger Wilson on the basis of the comprehensive material collected by the Bristol Social Project under the leadership of John C. Spencer.[92] This material makes it clear that the accent is no longer on the topographical location of an area but, almost regardless of it, rather on the atmosphere of the neighbourhood as it is often shaped not, as in Shaw's Chicago, by successive waves of foreign immigrants but by the rehousing policy of the local authority. This brings us to one of the crucial aspects of the present situation. Slum clearance and the large-scale transfer of the slum population to new housing estates were an important feature of social policy already between the two world wars. The further deterioration of these old slums, together with war-time destruction of many houses through bombing and the increased need for better and larger accommodation on account of the rising birthrate in an affluent society and higher levels of expectation in the field of housing as elsewhere, have accelerated this process of rehousing, although very much is still left to be desired. Moreover, with increasing geographical and social mobility the 'area' or 'neighbourhood' to many people means much less nowadays than in previous days. 'The focus of people's human interest is no longer, of necessity, where they live . . . They are far freer to follow their own inclinations and to make their own choices' (Wilson, pp. 11 and 23). However, as Wilson would be the first to admit and as clearly emerges from his own analysis, this happy state of freedom of choice and movement applies by no means to everybody; the poorer strata of the community are more or less excluded from its blessings. For them, 'the housing manager or his agent, the rent collector, acts as a kind of status registrar, locating the family on the estate and even in the street which he considers to be most appropriate . . . The delinquency area is, as it were, the extreme case', as John C. Spencer, foreshadowing the results of his Bristol study, wrote already in 1956.[93] To a considerable extent, we should expect the rehousing policy of the local authorities to be responsible for the formation of delinquency areas or the prevention of their coming into existence. Spencer is anxious not to put all the blame on the shoulders of housing managers; the tenants' own preferences, especially their wish to move their children away from notorious delinquency areas, and selective migration to and from such areas, are very important factors, too: 'Once estates have been established for some time, and have begun to acquire a "tone" and a tradition, transfers and changes will accelerate the process of self-selection . . . The team was forced to the conclusion that it is quite inevitable over a period of time that there will be some pockets on some estates with a quite disproportionate number of tenants whose behaviour lowers the tone of the neighbourhood' (Wilson, p. 14). Something of this kind of negative selection may already have played its part in the separation of the Gladstone Road from the Dyke Street families in the 'Radby' research (see above, Chapter 22, 4(a)). Wilson (pp. 16 ff. and 7) divides the tenants of such new housing estates into three groups, the solids, the brittles, and the difficults, largely on characteristics not purely economic but rather 'according to their skill in managing their internal family life harmoniously in relation to the pressures and demands of outside society'. Leaving aside the details of this classification, which might well be compared with that of the 'Radby' study, the distribution of delinquency within these three groups varies greatly in that there is apparently none in the first group; if it occurs in the second one it seems to outside observers to happen out of a blue sky, whereas the third type of families more or less flouts conventional standards and adheres to its own subcultural pattern of living. No statistics are given to show the size of each group, but Wilson (pp. 18–19) makes the important observation, which conforms to the view of Mays regarding the Liverpool area (see above, Chapter 22), that while the reputation of a district or housing estate depends on the proportion of respectable to disreputable residents, it is not entirely a question of numbers but also of the social class to which the majority belongs: 'a blacksheep accountant who lives in a road with a dozen solicitors will not give the road as bad a name as will a rogue scrap-metal dealer living in a road with a dozen honest unskilled labourers.' In other words, it is not so much honesty as status, class, and occupation of the majority that make or mar the good name of an area.

Another interesting contribution to the study of the post-war delinquency area in British cities, with special reference to the situation on new housing estates, has been made by Howard Jones in his ecological investigation of juvenile delinquency in Leicester.[94] Using both the home addresses of young offenders found guilty by the juvenile court and the place of the offence, and distinguishing between 'real', i.e. more serious, and other cases, he found the highest rates of the former in the old city-centre areas, but also in areas comprising newer housing estates on the outskirts. Comparing the years 1946 and 1953, the rates for the old areas were found to have remained stable, whereas a marked contrast had developed between two of the housing estates which, on the surface, appeared to be very similar: one had strikingly improved, the other greatly deteriorated. The explanation seemed to be the higher mobility in the latter, due partly to the smaller size of its houses and partly to the moving out of the more respectable tenants, thus creating the well-known vicious circle. One of Jones's conclusions is that rehousing is no cure-all; it has to be accompanied by measures designed to stabilize community life. The same conclusion had emerged from the Cambridge study where the absence of special community services on most housing estates was noted.[95] Comparisons of 'breeding' and 'attracting' areas of Leicester showed that within the comparatively small, central shopping area 28 per cent of all offences were committed against only 18 per cent within all the new housing estates combined which covered a far larger area. Many offenders living on the latter had committed their offences in the centre.

Thomas Ferguson's statistical study of Glasgow boys suffers from its neglect of the broader sociological background factors and of the literature. He conveys no real picture of the distribution of delinquency over the different areas of the city—which might have been particularly valuable for a community such as Glasgow—but he distinguishes different types of new housing estates, concluding—as had to be expected—that those used to rehouse slum-dwellers had a much higher incidence of juvenile delinquency than the other estates, in fact as high as the rate for those who had remained in the slums.[96]

Of recent investigations carried out outside the Anglo-American countries one of Tokyo might be mentioned.[97] One of the largest and most rapidly growing cities (at present approx. 9,000,000 inhabitants), Tokyo is obviously a very suitable object of ecological research. One of the features of the brief summary so far published is that the results are not in agreement with the Chicago theory. Delinquency is particularly frequent in the intermediate areas between the centre and the outskirts where there are many amusements districts to which juveniles flock. Tokyo, it is stated, differs in structure from that of Chicago.

On the other hand, a detailed study of Gross Berlin, published in 1950 (see Note 1), confirmed the gradient theory at least in its very general outlines, showing however increasing delinquency rates around the large suburbs such as Neukölln and Charlottenburg which tended to form independent centres from which new zones seemed to radiate. Moreover, within the various zones there were great variations with high rates around the railway termini, on allotments and new housing estates. In his practical conclusions, the author of the survey stresses the need to avoid the concentrating on new housing estates of 'problem families' and altogether of families belonging to one social class only.

It would mean doing Clifford Shaw and his many followers a serious injustice if their work were to be judged only on the strength of its significance for the ecological theory of crime. Their object was, after all, the practical one of utilizing their results, gained through statistical investigation or detailed case studies (see above, Chapter 8), for the designing of improved techniques of prevention. Interpreting their theoretical work as the study of the epidemiology of delinquency[98] they proceeded to establish their famous Chicago Area Project, based upon the, to them crucial, assumption that 'a delinquency prevention programme could hardly hope to be effective unless and until the aims of such a programme became the aims of the local populations'. In his '25-Year Assessment' of the Project, Kobrin, who acted for eighteen years as its supervising sociologist, expressed the optimistic view, which characterized its whole work and was essential for its success, that while the residents of such under-privileged areas could not be expected to support the established welfare agencies[99] they might perhaps be persuaded to take con-structive action themselves. Making use of the existence of a rudi-mentary communal life even in areas of social disorganization and apathy they gained the co-operation of many residents 'involved in the basic socializing experiences of youngsters' to help the 'unreached boys . . . to find their way back to acceptable norms of conduct' (Kobrin). This 'do it yourself' programme was, of course, not left entirely to its own resources; Shaw's Chicago Area Project, a private corporation founded in 1934, assisted it financially and through con-stant advice and moral support. In 1941 it established the South Side Community Committee in a district with a Negro population of more than 100,000; its report for 1954-5—one of the last issued while Clifford Shaw was still alive—could already list ten similar organiza-tions in other districts of Chicago.[100] Can the practical effect of this pioneering work be measured in statistical success rates? Kobrin is modest enough to admit that the reduction in delinquency rates which he regards as probable 'is not subject to precise measure-ment', and the report for 1954-5, too, places the main emphasis on the 'new attitudes' formed as a result of the banding together of the residents of an area and working collectively in a community welfare programme. It is interesting to compare the optimism pervading the writings of Shaw and his co-workers with the more pessimistic tone of the Radby Report and of Roger Wilson's analysis of the Bristol Project who stresses 'how little the estate neighbours could actively contribute to the leadership required, and the consequent unreality of any expectation that . . . there could be any substantial "degree of responsibility for their community life"' (p. 38) and 'on difficult estates the residents themselves can have little direct influence in socializing this difficult minority' (p. 40). The recent publication of the full Bristol Report makes it possible to compare the material on which the Bristol team had to work and their techniques with the material and techniques of the Chicago team in order to judge whether the former was too pessimistic or the latter too optimistic or whether the differences between them were so considerable as to make any such comparisons futile.

Housing Conditions. Closely related to the question of slum clearance and the criminological significance of the new housing estates is the role played by housing conditions in general and overcrowding in particular as a causative factor in delinquency. Here as on so many similar problems the unsophisticated assuredness shown by earlier writers has given way to doubts and scepticism. Matthew Davenport Hill, in his evidence to the Committee of 1852, to which reference has already been made (Note 75), still listed 'the state of the dwellings of the poor' as one of the leading causes of juvenile crime. Seventy years later, Cyril Burt was no longer satisfied with such generalizations; he worked out a precise standard of overcrowding as meaning more than two adult occupants per room, with two children under ten counting as the equivalent of one adult. Using this yardstick he found that 21 per cent of his delinquents lived in such overcrowded tenements, as against 16 per cent in the control group and 11 per cent in the whole of the county of London.[101] The latter figure presented the correlation of 0·77 between overcrowding and delinquency, a correlation higher than any other which Burt was able to obtain for the social factors he studied. Burt stressed, however, that if only juveniles from the same social class were compared the contrast was much less striking, overcrowding being only 1·32 times as frequent among the delinquents.

Next in chronological order comes the investigation published in 1942 as *Young Offenders*,[102] where both type and condition of homes and also overcrowding were examined for delinquent and control group boys. On the whole, the position was found to be more favourable for the controls, especially regarding the condition of the home, but the differences were not very considerable. Overcrowding was examined separately for day and night, and here too the proportion of unfavourable home conditions was higher for the delinquent group, for example overcrowding by day and night occurred in London in 16·3 per cent of delinquents against 5·4 per cent of the controls. No control group figures were available in the study of Cambridge, but a comparison with the Census of 1931 showed that the families of the delinquents had an average of about six persons against only 3·3 in the same number of rooms in the general population of Cambridge.[103] This underlines the close connection between overcrowding and the size of the families of delinquents (see Chapter 24 below).

Ferguson, in his Glasgow study, also presents some figures on the association of overcrowding and delinquency (pp. 45–54) and he rightly attempts to combine the overcrowding factor with various other environmental factors, but the resulting picture is confusing rather than illuminating. The survey of Gross Berlin (p. 23), too, concludes that the relationship between housing conditions and social problems is far from clear; good housing may well go hand in hand with symptoms of social deterioration. The Institute of Community Studies in London is inclined to take a similar view, contrasting for example the good atmosphere prevailing in overcrowded and slummy Bethnal Green with the 'housing estate neurosis' often to be found on the new estates. All this is of course not an argument against better housing, but merely a reminder that improvements in this field are needed for their own sake, not just as a means of delinquency prevention. The three and a half million new homes which the British Government is said to have built between 1951 and 1963, resulting among other benefits in the rehousing of over a million slum dwellers and a 50 per cent increase in home ownership, are good in themselves, not only as a means to some other end.

American studies of the connection between housing and delinquency seem to be equally inconclusive.[104] Lander, who paid special attention to it in his Baltimore investigation,[105] concludes that, although high delinquency areas often showed a frequency of bad housing and overcrowding this in itself did not prove a causal nexus any more than the equally high frequency of tuberculosis and child mortality proved the responsibility of these social evils in the causation of delinquency. The analogy is perhaps not quite convincing as there are features in bad housing and overcrowding which are *prima facie* more likely to produce delinquency than can be said of tuberculosis, etc. Bad housing and overcrowding may easily aggravate friction in families and with their neighbours, drive husbands and children out into pubs and streets, and facilitate sexual offences such as incest and assaults on children. In the *Report of a Departmental Committee on Sexual Offences against Young Persons* (H.M.S.O., 1925, p. 80) this aspect of the matter was strongly underlined.

Lander also deals with house-ownership as a measure of community stability and anomie.[106] Whereas he regards the association between delinquency and such factors as poverty, bad housing, population density and nearness to the city centre as mere surface relationships, he takes the proportion of house-ownership and high Negro concentration as more serious symptoms, at least in Baltimore; it may be different in New York with its many apartment house areas. In Britain, too, it can be argued that house-ownership may in future lose its place as an index of stability on account of the growing popularity of flat blocks. Twenty-five years ago the present writer tried to compare English and Continental habits of housing in large cities and discussed their potential effect on female delinquency.[107] ('Vertical slums abroad, horizontal slums in England' (Elizabeth Denby).) Since then, these differences have slowly been getting smaller, but it is too early yet to assess the criminological significance of all these developments.

The present section on housing was written before the Profumo–Ward case broke upon Britain early in 1963 and, quite accidentally, led to the revelations on 'Rachmanism' with which it had no intrinsic connections. In the present chapter we are concerned only with what has, for want of a better name, been labelled the 'techniques of Rachmanism'. What many of those with inside knowledge of conditions in Paddington, Kensington and neighbouring parts of the Metropolis had been saying for years became now common knowledge. In the light of these revelations much of what has been written above on conditions in Soho or Stepney and on the connection between bad housing and crime seems to be somewhat academic. Judging from the House of Commons debates and the simultaneous press and television comments and ignoring one-sided and tendentious statements and charges, the following points seem to stand out quite clearly:

(a) The still extreme shortage of decent and reasonably priced accommodation in many districts of inner London (as in other large cities of Britain) has somewhat been aggravated through the influx of coloured immigrants.

(b) The partial de-control of housing through the Housing Act, 1957, has made it even more profitable to landlords to get rid of old tenants still protected by legislation and to let instead at far higher rents to new tenants not so protected. This has been done by legal and by illegal means, the latter involving threats of eviction or direct violence, so-called 'strong-arm methods'.

(c) The legal remedies against such acts given to local authorities and tenants have, for a variety of reasons, often proved inadequate, and the result has been a series of criminal acts committed against tenants, which shows that bad conditions in the field of housing may lead to crime not only on the part of tenants but also of landlords. The new Labour Government is preparing strong measures against these evils.

B. CULTURE CONFLICT. RACIAL, RELIGIOUS, AND OTHER MINORITY GROUPS

1. As pointed out above in Section I, 2(b), the term 'culture conflict' and the criminological theory based on it cover a field much wider and more important than merely the problems arising from the

physical migration of individuals, although it cannot be denied that the various forms of such migrations have provided some of the most obvious examples of these conflicts. Clashes between different cultures can arise without local changes in the composition and structure of the population and, on the other hand, such changes may occur without causing culture conflicts. In particular cases, such conflicts may persist and give rise to deep-seated antagonisms and serious outbreaks of crime decades or even centuries after the physical migration or immigration had taken place. Perhaps Sellin had something of this kind in mind when he wrote:[108] 'all "culture conflicts" are conflicts of *meanings*: social values, interests, norms. There can be no clashes between the material objects of culture.' As he further points out, such conflicts are sometimes regarded as by-products of the growth of civilization and studied as mental conflicts or as clashes of cultural codes. They may arise through the introduction of alien customs, norms and values into a closed system, but also without it on account of the inevitable changes due to the, real or imagined, progress of civilization and to social change within the system. As Sellin maintains, clashes of cultures may occur without corresponding mental conflict in the individuals concerned, i.e. where the latter are so firmly and uncompromisingly convinced of the rightness of their own cultural norms and values that nothing can make them doubt. Sellin refers to the model case of the Sicilian immigrant in New Jersey who killed the 16-year-old seducer of his daughter in defence of his family honour. Such cases may occur even now in remote areas, but with the growing diffusion and intermingling of different cultures, with growing scepticism and the weakening of our beliefs in absolute values, they will become rarer and rarer, and it will be more usual now for the individual to be caught in a mental conflict between two cultural systems, to both of which he consciously owes allegiance and between which he has to make a, more or less agonizing, choice. This will often be the position of political, national, racial, linguistic or religious minority groups. Minorities are not social classes—within each of them members of very different classes can be found—but their problems may be very similar to those of underprivileged classes in the field of social discrimination. Many of them are not immigrants but rather the old inhabitants of the region who have been invaded or otherwise taken over by newcomers, who now form the majority, as the result of conquests, peace treaties, or frontier regulations. Most of them have become more or less assimilated, but culture conflicts often remain simmering under the surface and give rise to large-scale armed revolts of substantial sections of the whole group or smaller outbreaks of violence on the part of a lunatic fringe. We may think in this connection of a great variety of such minorities, large or small, for example, the Kurds in Iraq, the German-speaking population of South Tirol after the First and Second World Wars, the French-Canadians, the Doukhobors in British Columbia,[109] the Welsh in Britain, most of whom have at times in order to achieve their political ends produced political extremists inclined to resort to violence. Outrages have, of course, been committed not only *by* minorities but more often also against them; disregarding the persecution of religious minorities in previous centuries such as that of the Protestants in France or the Catholics in England, slaughter of Armenians in the former Turkish Empire is one of the outstanding examples; the anti-Jewish pogroms in Tsarist Russia, the communal riots in India at the time of partition in 1946–7, those in Ceylon in 1958 and previously and, though on a smaller scale, the lynchings of Negroes in the American South provide other examples. The communal disorders in India before and after the establishment of the present states of India and Pakistan have been briefly described by Rao[110] who writes: 'The extraordinary uprooting of population, the exodus, the heights of frenzy, and the breakdown of the agencies of law and order in both the countries struggling to survive, are matters of history and have no place in a book on crime. But it is also a history of crime—of murder, loot, arson, rape and vandalism.'

For Ceylon, the relations between the Sinhalese (Buddhist) majority and the Tamil (Hindu) and Muslim minorities have been fully discussed in their socio-criminological significance by Arthur Lewis Wood who has also made a careful study of criminological minority problems in general.[111] Mainly statistical material on the Ceylon riot is provided in the *Report of the Commission of Inquiry on Capital Punishment* of 1959.[112] Faced with the question whether the suspension of capital punishment in 1958 had produced an increase in homicide, the Commission, led by Professor Norval Morris, then of Adelaide University, concluded that for their assessment of the evidence it would be desirable but impossible to exclude homicides committed as part of communal rioting, in particular as the effect of such riots was to:

increase grossly the level of insecurity in the community, they embitter personal relationships, consolidate and inflame personal hatreds, greatly intensify individual fear and, in consequence, tend most strongly to raise the level of violence and homicide in the community. The man who fears tends to be aggressive, violent and lethal; nothing more obviously increases fear than riots of the nature experienced in Ceylon in April, May and June of 1958 (p. 28).

The lynchings of Negroes in the U.S.A. are a subject rather

neglected in American textbooks, with a few notable exceptions such as Barnes–Teeters.[113]

All these phenomena, of course, pale into insignificance when compared with the killing of six million Jews by the Nazis. It has occasionally been said that crimes against minorities of so vast a scale are, as events of world history, outside the scope of criminology (see also Rao above), but mere size and numbers cannot alter the legal and criminological nature of such happenings, a view which is further confirmed by the verdict of the International War Crimes Tribunal at Nuremberg and the many sentences imposed on war criminals afterwards.[114]

To some of the issues here discussed we shall have to return below in connection with the behaviour of crowds (Chapter 25).

2. Turning now from the crimes committed against minority groups to their own criminality it is here that the changed face of criminology is perhaps more clearly visible than anywhere else. The bias in favour of the biological and ethnical explanation in terms of race, strong already in the writings of some members of the Lombrosian school and reaching its climax during the Nazi regime, has been replaced by a sociological-psychological interpretation based on the peculiar position of minority groups. This does not mean that modern criminologists regard racial differences as entirely immaterial, but merely that they are more clearly aware of the inadequacy of the anthropological and statistical material at their disposal and of the impossibility of separating racial from sociological-economic factors. While a few of these writers have attempted fairly ambitious and comprehensive surveys of the whole relationship between race and crime (especially Bonger, von Hentig, and Exner)[115] others have been content with a discussion of the problems of those racial minorities who happened to be most conspicuous in the public eye, i.e. notably American Negroes and Jews.

The very high statistical crime rate of the *Negro* in U.S.A.[116] has for several decades been a matter of deep concern to American criminologists, sociologists and politicians alike. According to E. Franklin Frazier, the distinguished Negro sociologist, studies on Negro crime began to appear towards the end of the nineteenth century,[117] and most textbooks give detailed information on it. In my *Group Problems* I tried to present a picture of the situation as I saw it in 1953. Alexis de Tocqueville maintained that 'twelve years are more in America than half a century in Europe'.[118] It may appear doubtful whether the past twelve years have seen changes in the Negro situation in the U.S.A. comparable with certain developments in other fields during the same period in Europe. There have been considerable improvements in various respects—in Washington Negroes are stated to have one out of every four federal jobs, and in federal, state and local governments together they are said to hold nearly one out of every ten jobs, which would almost correspond to their proportion in the general population[119]—but the struggle for de-segregation of schools and universities is still going on in spite of the, now ten years old, decision of the Federal Supreme Court and the recent efforts of the Federal Government. Violent clashes are still frequent, and feelings are running higher than ever on both sides, which cannot well make for a reduction in the statistical Negro crime rate.

The inadequacy of existing criminal statistics in the field of race has often been stressed. Firstly, the vagueness of anthropological terminology makes it unsafe as a basis of statistical classification, and there are in fact very few countries outside the U.S.A. where information on race is included in criminal statistics.[120] Public authorities are often reluctant to disclose information which they possess because it might be misused to aggravate racial feelings.[121] Secondly, information on Negro criminality in U.S.A. rests on the figures of arrests in the *Uniform Crime Reports* and on prison and other institutional statistics. Arrest figures, as v. Hentig has pointed out,[122] are unsafe as many of those arrested by the police are subsequently found not guilty. Prison figures are equally unreliable as Negroes may be more likely than whites to be sent to prison and receive longer sentences. The significance of the racial factor in American prison sentences has recently been examined by H. A. Bullock,[123] with the result that ' "being black" generally means one type of sentence while "being white" means another', although the bias was not invariably against the Negro; for example, Negroes seemed to get shorter sentences than whites for murder, whereas for burglary the opposite was true. As, however, burglary is numerically far more important than murder this would help to explain the high proportion of Negroes in prisons. Altogether there is reason to believe that the difference between the Negro and white crime rates is in fact less striking than the figures seem to indicate. However, the statistical differences are too great to be entirely explained away by stressing the above weaknesses. For the year 1960, for example, the total of arrests in the 2,446 communities included in *Uniform Crime Reports* was 2,320,635 whites against 1,064,814 Negroes, i.e. nearly 30 per cent of all those arrested were Negroes while they comprise only about 10 or 11 per cent of the total population.[124] It is generally agreed that there is a real excess of Negro crime behind these figures which can be explained only in terms of the unfavourable economic and housing conditions, and the social friction and discrimination, to which this minority group is still exposed. v. Hentig draws further attention to the preponderance of certain illnesses among them which he thinks may also explain their greater irritability and aggressiveness (pp. 164–5). The further discovery that the Negro crime rate is lower in districts with a very high Negro population indicates that crime is here mainly an expression of social tension and insecurity rather than of race as such.[125]

Reference has already been made above to the Negro crime problem in Britain, certain aspects of which—in particular the riots of 1958—will be dealt with below (Chapter 25).

With regard to the criminality of *Jews* the position is different in so far as it has never appeared to be very high in general. On the contrary, most writers stress their low crime rate as illustrating the universal experience that strong family ties and close internal cohesion within a minority group—such as also found among Chinese and Japanese immigrants in the U.S.A.—tend to diminish its criminality. Against this generally favourable background, especially for crimes against the person, it is pointed out, however, that Jewish criminality is exceptionally high for the so-called commercial offences such as frauds, fraudulent bankruptcy, forgery and embezzlement. Details for a number of countries referring to the late nineteenth and early twentieth centuries have been given by Bonger,[126] who observes that the subject of Jewish criminality has been mostly treated by Jewish writers, which is not entirely correct, especially of course for the Nazi period. He notes the considerable agreement existing between Jewish and non-Jewish writers, which is also true only with the exception of Nazi extremists. It might be safer to say that there has been substantial agreement with regard to the facts, not however concerning their interpretation. In the following reference will mainly be made to the views of non-Jewish authors. Exner deals with the subject in his first edition, published in 1939,[127] whereas the third edition, which appeared in 1949, ignores it. In 1939 Exner presented two tables based on the *German Criminal Statistics* for 1892–1902, showing the offences for which the percentages of Jews convicted were higher and those offences where they were lower than for non-Jews. The offences with a substantially higher Jewish crime rate include, in addition to those mentioned before, usury, gambling, perjury, bribery, blackmail. Although Bonger's and Exner's figures are rather old they are likely to present a fairly accurate picture of present-day Jewish criminality in most Western European countries.

Regarding the explanations offered for the differential Jewish crime rate we find that, again with the exception of Nazi extremists, most writers are careful not to fall into the trap of a purely biological-racialist explanation. An outspokenly anti-Nazi author such as Bonger refers exclusively to the social milieu, i.e. the Jews, who had once been an agrarian people and have recently returned to the land

567

again in Israel, became city dwellers and perforce established a commercial tradition; moreover they were a persecuted minority with a strong family feeling. Most German writers whose contributions were published during the Nazi period leave it more or less open whether the explanation has to be sought in terms of race or occupation or both. Hagemann[128] considers that, while the choice of an occupation is likely to depend on racial factors, the specific conditions prevailing within a given occupation cannot be disregarded, especially in the case of Jews doing heavy manual labour. E. Mezger regards the matter as not yet sufficiently clear and in need of further examination.[129] Exner, in his first edition, was more outspoken in his view that the specific features of Jewish criminality were due to racial rather than occupational characteristics, but he too had to admit that very little is actually known about it and that Jewish criminality was of a different kind in former centuries when the Jews were mostly occupied outside the field of commerce.

Far more interesting than Exner's speculations is the wealth of factual material presented in Radbruch and Gwinner's *History of Crime*[130] to which attention has already been drawn above in Chapter 19 (Note 14). They refer, among other historical documents, to the *Reichsabschied* of 1497 to show that usury was at the time common in Germany among Christians and Jews alike. They show how the medieval persecutions and the undermining of their social status forced the Jews again and again to search for new ways of how to make a living and in the process to establish close contact with groups of outlaws and criminal elements. This explains their frequent membership of the gangs of robbers towards the end of the eighteenth century. By exempting them from the law which prohibited the taking of interest the state forced them into an ambiguous position which proved morally disastrous to both parties: it was convenient to the authorities first to allow the Jews to take excessive rates of interest and afterwards to confiscate their profit. Equally demoralizing was the privileged legal position of the Jews with regard to the acquisition of stolen goods, which they had to return to the lawful owner only against payment of the price they had paid to the thief. This 'privilege of the receiver' made them the confederates of criminals. All this was brought to an end through the emancipation of the Jews in the second half of the eighteenth and the beginning of the nineteenth centuries.[131]

The eminent early twentieth-century German economist Werner Sombart, in his widely discussed and controversial book on the subject,[132] makes a distinction between the role played by the Jews in the early and in the later periods of the capitalist age. In the early days of capitalism the accusations against the Jews were, he thought, on the whole not unfounded. From this verdict he explicitly excluded the commission of such universally accepted crimes as stealing and receiving which were disapproved by Jews and non-Jews alike. There were, however, certain commercial practices which went against law and custom, but were not regarded as wrong by Jewish business men, and it was here that Sombart thought to have found the symptoms of a specifically Jewish outlook. As time went on, this, he argues, became the universally adopted 'modern' outlook, and the observer who would examine the catalogue of 'sins' laid at the door of the Jews in the seventeenth and eighteenth centuries would, according to Sombart, find nothing in it that would not be treated as a matter of course in every business.

In the light of the foregoing it is of a special interest to examine the criminality of Jews in the newly founded State of Israel. In the context of the present chapter, developments there have to be considered from various angles: there is, first, the fact that Israel has, in particular in the past fifteen years, become one of the principal receiving countries for Jewish immigrants[133] and that it can, therefore, supply important information on the criminality of immigrants. While in 1948, when the new State came into being, its Jewish population numbered approximately 650,000, in the nine years up to the end of 1957 many more, i.e. nearly 900,000, new immigrants arrived from various countries and continents. In cultural background, in language, education and practically every other respect there were vast differences between these groups, and their crime rates, too, showed considerable differences. The rates were the lowest where the cultural background of the immigrants was similar to that of the old Palestinian settlers; they were higher where, as in the case of newcomers from North African and Asian countries, their background was entirely alien to that of the old residents and where a lengthy and painful process of assimilation was, therefore, required. Secondly, as the occupational structure of the Jews in Israel differs from that in the *Diaspora*, with a far larger proportion living in rural districts and working on the land, the question arose whether this change in occupational structure would be reflected in the crime statistics and whether the proportion of crimes against the person would be higher and of commercial crimes lower than among Jews outside Israel. The material at our disposal is not yet sufficiently detailed to give a clear picture, but the following figures, taken from Shoham,[134] seem to confirm the hypothesis that a change in the expected direction has indeed occurred. The percentages of serious offences are shown overleaf.

Moreover, the rates per 1,000 immigrants were from Africa 13, from Asia 10, from Europe and America 5.

	For Immigrants from		
	Europe and America	Africa	Asia
Offences against the Person	26	30	27
Offences against Property	25	27	26
Especially Arson and Damage to Property	6	10	9
Forgery and Embezzlement	2	1	1

These figures show, first, that offences against the person were as numerous in Israel as offences against property, which differs from the usual pattern of Jewish criminality, and, secondly, that criminality was higher among African and Asian immigrants than among those from Europe and America. How far these differences are due to economic factors and how far to broader cultural conflicts has to remain unanswered, but it is likely that both of them play their part. The official *Criminal Statistics in Israel*, 1949–58, in which the figures for Jews and non-Jews are separately given, also shows no appreciable difference between crimes against the person and crimes against property.[135]

Even where it is not further aggravated by racial strife religious antagonism is one of the most dangerous forms of cultural conflict. The influence of *religion* on crime has been often discussed, notably by Dutch criminologists,[136] but also in some American, German and other textbooks and monographs.[137] The results of such discussions, however, have generally been found to be unsatisfactory, mainly because, as Bianchi has rightly stressed, they have approached this intricate subject from the wrong angle. Religion has too closely been identified with the Churches and with the professed denominations of individuals, from which it was, quite naturally, the next step to look for statistical correlations between denomination and crime, between the decline of churchgoing and the increase in the number of prisoners, and similar external indices. Clearly, the matter is not as simple as that. In the first place, even the statistical approach is beset with pitfalls. Scholars who write on the subject will usually know to which denomination, if any, they belong; inmates of penal institutions may not be so sure or may adjust their statements to the receiving officer according to the privileges or disadvantages to be expected from alleged membership of this or that Church. It has also been hinted that the known religious affiliations of the members of the Parole Board, which decides on the date of release on parole, may influence the statements of American prisoners (Taft, p. 275).[138] When the present writer was searching in the files of the Cambridge Juvenile Court for the denominations of the boys who had appeared before it, he found that the percentage of those who had professed to be 'Church of England' had declined from 75 per cent in the pre-war group to 41 per cent in the wartime group, whereas the number of those who declared to belong to no denomination had increased from 1 to 55. Soon he found out, however, that during the war the probation officer responsible for these entries had listed all those whose membership appeared to be purely nominal as belonging to no religious community even if they had described themselves as 'C. of E.'. If the same method had been adopted before the war the change in the percentages might have been negligible.[139] Experiences such as this may make us somewhat sceptical of the value of statistical data in this field. Moreover, even if the crude figures should correctly reflect the religious denominations of offenders what else would they prove? The statistician Moroney[140] has referred to an American investigation by the sociologist William F. Ogburn who had found a correlation of -0.14 between the crime rate and the rate of church membership, which would have indicated that such membership was associated with a lower crime rate. However, when such factors as the numbers of young children and of foreign immigrants were excluded the relation between church membership and the crime rate became positive, i.e. the more church members, the more crime. It now seemed that it was rather the foreign immigrant with a large family who had a low crime rate, whereas the native-born church member with a smaller family had a higher rate. Moroney thinks it may be a good thing that the Church should attract not only the respectable citizen but also some of those who really need it, which seems to be not unreasonable.

We are now armed with an adequate dose of scepticism to look at some of the figures which claim to offer us information on the differential crime rate of the religious denominations. van Bemmelen, who deals with the subject in a careful and detached manner, begins with the statement that in most countries the crime rate of Catholics is higher than that of Protestants. He refers to the explanations of this fact given by Kempe and van Rooy who interpret it as a consequence of the different attitude of these two denominations to human activities in the economic sphere, which is bound to place the Catholics in a worse economic, social and cultural position. Protestantism, they believe, has a different, more favourable, conception of gainful business activities than Catholicism. Kempe bases his view on the famous writings of Max Weber on this subject,[141] whereas Tawney in his equally renowned *Religion and the Rise of Capitalism*[142] expresses some doubts and regards Weber's thesis, though 'one of the most fruitful examinations of the relations between religion and social theory', as at several points 'one-sided and over-strained'. van Bemmelen, too, is critical and finds it particularly paradoxical that in van

Rooy's view the greater morality of the Catholics should bring them more easily into conflict with the criminal law; he rather believes in a multiplicity of causal factors (p. 302). This latter view is also confirmed by Hacker's investigation of the position in Hungary before the Second World War. As pointed out by Mannzen in his analysis of Hacker's figures there are hardly any substantial differences left today between the socio-ethical beliefs of the various denominations and their ways of living, and the strength of religious feelings is inaccessible to statistical examination. It is not the denomination as such but certain socio-economic and cultural factors, possibly associated with it, which influence criminality.[143] This is a conclusion with which writers such as Kempe may in the last resort also agree. It would certainly be too rash to maintain that minorities, other factors being equal, are as such likely to produce higher crime rates, and as these 'other factors' will never be entirely equal, it is a hypothesis which cannot be reliably tested.

One of the most recent and most original contributions to the subject has been made by the Dutch criminologist W. H. Nagel, who after a penetrating analysis of the literature describes three cases of manslaughter committed in Holland in the present century under the influence of mystical religious ideas by mentally deeply disturbed people. Nagel concludes by changing William James's dictum: 'Religion, whatever it is, is a man's total reaction to life' to 'criminality, whatever it is, has a religious character', which—unless the word 'religious' is here used in an extremely wide sense—seems to be an all too sweeping generalization.[144]

In his study of Ceylon, Wood has made an attempt to test the assumption that 'religious beliefs and practices serve to prevent criminal activity' by interviewing Ceylonese villagers. The results seem to be inconclusive.[145]

C. ECONOMIC FACTORS AND CRIME[146]

I. GENERAL AND HISTORICAL CONSIDERATIONS

The consideration of the potential effect on crime of economic conditions and changes is closely related to that of class, on the one hand, and of ecological factors, on the other. Although, as pointed out in Chapter 20, class distinctions are in no way exclusively based on wealth, the well-to-do are more likely than the poor to belong to, or work their way to, the higher social classes. Moreover, as shown in Chapter 22, it is often difficult to decide whether social frustration, especially among the younger age groups, is due more to lack of opportunities for upward social mobility or to the absence of opportunities for economic betterment or to both. And as far as white collar criminals are concerned they are a category not only socially but also economically apart from other offenders (Chapter 21). The ecological theory of crime, too, has close links with economic factors as clearly emerges from the examination of such subjects as town-country, immigration, and the delinquency area. In the present discussion, however, the main emphasis is, as far as possible, on economic factors *per se* regardless of class and ecological aspects. Such a discussion has in recent years become rather unfashionable, for a variety of reasons: first, because of the greater attention paid to class problems; secondly, as a reaction to the over-emphasis placed on economic aspects by the older school of crimino-sociology; and, lastly, because this over-emphasis seemed to be particularly mistaken in the light of the experiences of the past twenty years or so. While that older school could easily point to crime as the natural consequence of the misery of the great masses, the new affluent society had, it was believed, every right to expect a wholesale reduction in economic crime as the result of the universally improved standard of living. When such a reduction failed to appear the only conclusion to be drawn was, it seemed, that economic factors did not matter or, in more popular terms, that poverty was not a cause of crime. In the opening paragraph, already quoted in Chapter 19, II, of the Home Office White Paper on *Penal Practice in a Changing Society*—a paragraph highly characteristic of this whole line of thought—this failure of material prosperity, better education and improved social welfare is called 'a disquieting feature of our society'. As a rule, people find disquieting those developments which they could not foresee and are unable to understand and to explain in causal terms. Was this failure really unpredictable and inexplicable? The answer is 'yes' and 'no'; it depends on our interpretation of the economic theory of crime, on the way in which we formulate the questions to be asked, on the quality of the factual material at our disposal when we try to answer these questions, and on our evaluation of these facts.

The following are, in brief, the mistakes most frequently encountered in popular, and occasionally also in learned, discussions of the subject:

(*a*) The 'economic' factor in crime has often been interpreted in the narrow sense of meaning solely poverty;

(*b*) The meaning of 'poverty' has been interpreted too narrowly;

(*c*) One-sided political theories have prejudiced the issue;

(*d*) The matter has been treated too exclusively with reference to western European and American conditions;

(*e*) It has been treated in a manner static rather than dynamic; and

573

(*f*) In terms of a 'single cause' instead of a multi-factor theory.

(*g*) As far as statistical techniques have been used, the periods of investigation have often been too short, but where they have been long the totality of the changes which occur within such periods has not been and often could not be adequately considered;

(*h*) Competent individual case studies have been rare, and their authors and interpreters have not always realized that certain economic factors such as unemployment present in one case at one time may show their effects not in the same but in other cases or at a different time.

In the subsequent discussion these points will be taken up in some greater detail, but, as they are closely interrelated, not necessarily in the same order or separately.

The history of criminological thought shows that the effect of economic factors in the broadest, though often only vaguely defined, sense has frequently attracted the attention of writers widely apart in time and approach. Both van Kan and Bonger have presented admirable historical surveys to which hardly anything of importance could be added. Aristotle already put some of the crucial points in a nutshell when he wrote:[147] 'The greatest crimes are caused by excess and not by necessity . . . There are crimes of which the motive is want . . . But want is not the sole incentive to crime; men desire to gratify some passion which preys upon them . . .' Bonger begins his historical chapters with a long quotation from Sir Thomas More's First Book of *Utopia* (1516) with its vivid description and grave condemnation of the sins of the English upper classes of his time, the early sixteenth century. There More shows how the great landowners, by persistently replacing wide stretches of arable land by pastures, deprived the masses of the common people of their lawful means of livelihood and forced them to steal or rob or beg.[148] The writers of the Age of Enlightenment, too, such as Rousseau, Montesquieu, Beccaria and many others, expressed, *mutatis mutandis*, similar views. It was, however, only the nineteenth century which, with the gradual development of modern scientific thought and social theories, slowly produced a more systematic discussion of the subject. Quetelet questioned the traditional conception of poverty and stressed the criminogenic significance of sudden changes from economic well-being to distress. Edouard Ducpétiaux in Belgium tried to prove the close statistical correlation between the numbers of indigent persons and those of prisoners.[149] W. Russell and J. Fletcher in England produced similar material, the latter underlining already the close connection between the price of food and the number of criminal commitments.[150] There is no need here to stress the enormous influence which the writings of Karl Marx and Friedrich Engels had on contemporary thinking on the subject; it is a matter of political and economic history rather than of criminological history in particular (see also above, Chapter 20); but those interested in it can find many details in Bonger's monograph (pp. 27-9, 246 ff., 338, and *passim*), although Bonger admitted that even a book of the size of his could not deal adequately with the matter. Generally speaking, it can be said that the progress of nineteenth-century criminological theory and research has been promoted by specialist workers rather than by Marxist philosophers, for whom crime could be only a sideline.

Henry Mayhew, writing at approximately the same time, was rather out of step with the general trend in rejecting the idea that crime was due to poverty, illiteracy, and the growth of towns; instead he stressed the professional and traditional character of crime,[151] thereby in some ways anticipating Sutherland's theory of differential association. The anthropological school, including even Lombroso, paid more attention to economic factors than might have been expected. Lombroso,[152] while admitting that a rise in the price of food had a marked effect on the number of thefts, tried to minimize the weight of this observation by pointing out that the theft of food-stuffs played only a very small part in the statistics of larceny—a remark which Bonger rightly calls naïve because it ignores the fact that modern society is based on exchange, on barter, and that practically every article stolen, particularly money, can easily be turned into food (Bonger, p. 89). The material which Lombroso presented showed that the wealthier provinces of Italy had more frauds than the poorer ones, whereas for homicides the reverse was true and for thefts and sex offences the figures were not consistent. Lombroso's final conclusion was that both poverty and wealth, especially however the latter, had a considerable influence on crime, but that their effects were frequently neutralized by race and climate.

Whereas Garofalo's contribution to our present subject seems to be negligible, we should expect to find in the writings of Ferri, the outspoken Marxist and historical materialist, particularly valuable, though possibly controversial, material and ideas. Bonger, whose political outlook was to some extent similar, devotes 36 pages to his analysis of Ferri, especially of the latter's book *Socialismo e criminalità* (1883), but much of it is merely an attempt to disprove Ferri's view that physical-anthropological factors play an important part in the causation of crime besides the social ones. Bonger was in fact a far more one-sided and radical environmentalist and socialist than Ferri; he was the enemy of any form of compromise and he regarded Ferri's brand of Marxism as based on inadequate knowledge and misunderstanding (Bonger, p. 128). In his famous study of the movements of the French criminality between 1826 and 1878[153] Ferri had

575

shown that the French crime rates for practically all categories of offences had enormously increased in spite of the great improvements in the economic conditions of all classes. How could this be explained? With better nutrition man's organic powers are more strongly developed; there follows greater activity which expresses itself in lawful as well as in unlawful acts. While there is a great deal of truth in this it is certainly not the whole truth. Here as in the case of many other, similar, statistical studies the inescapable dilemma has to be faced, that as stressed above figures for short periods mean very little and figures for long periods can never adequately reflect the complex changes which have taken place in the society concerned. It may well be doubted whether even Ferri, with all his knowledge and brilliance of mind, was in a position to do full justice to all that had happened in France between 1826 and 1878, a period distinguished by several wars, revolutions and other major changes in government and social structure.

A few decades before Ferri, the eminent German social statistician Georg von Mayr (1841–1925) had already published his famous study of the relation between thefts and the price of grain in Bavaria for the period 1835–61.[154] Illustrating his findings with the help of several diagrams, one of which has been frequently reproduced,[155] he showed that a fairly high statistical correlation existed for that period between the movements of the following four variables: crimes against property—begging—emigration—and the price of rye, which latter was the most important staple food for the masses of the German population at the time. von Mayr went so far as to say that—translated into English currency—almost every half-penny of increase in the price of rye caused a corresponding increase of one theft per 100,000 of the population and a decline in the number of offences against the person, and vice versa. von Mayr's views were opposed by many contemporary writers such as W. D. Morrison in England, Tugan-Baranowski in Germany (using English material), and Tarde in France, to mention only a few of those best-known at the time,[156] but von Mayr was also widely acclaimed and supported by further statistical material collected and analysed by way of more up-to-date statistical techniques.[157] It may be left open whether von Mayr's statistical picture was correct for the period under examination; in any case now, after the passing of a century, his technique would certainly be regarded as far too one-sided and failing to do justice to the complexity of the modern problem. No single commodity can nowadays be selected as providing an accurate index of the economic condition of the population of a given country, especially in the over-developed western world. There are, it is true, still areas where the majority of the inhabitants derive their means of livelihood from one single industry, be it cotton in parts of Lancashire or motor cars in Coventry or Dagenham,[158] dock labour in Liverpool or Bootle, but even here determined efforts have been made to widen the range and thereby to insure against sudden slumps in the predominating industry. Cotton may still have the monopoly in Egypt and cocoa in Ghana, but with growing industrialization the picture will soon be changing there too. Moreover, even within one particular community changes in the condition of the prevailing industry or trade may affect the members of different groups and classes in different ways. Already against von Mayr it was argued that the agricultural population was likely to benefit from an increased price of rye which was detrimental to the townspeople.

All this was recognized by research workers in the decades after von Mayr, and attempts were made to work out more representative economic indices. The most painstaking and statistically refined of these attempts was made by an economic statistician, Dorothy S. Thomas, in her often quoted *Social Aspects of the Business Cycle*, 1927 (see Note 146), which examines the correlations between business cycles and various social phenomena, such as marriages, births, deaths, emigration, pauperism, alcoholism, and crime. One of the merits of this study was the construction of a composite index of the business cycle comprising data on the value of British exports, pig iron production, coal production, railway freights, bank clearings, unemployed trade union members (see her Chapter I). This index was no doubt superior to von Mayr's, but its construction was by no means the end of the researcher's difficulties.[159] First, a representative crime index was also needed, which opens up the controversial question of whether statistics of crimes known to the police or of persons found guilty by the courts or, standing somewhere between these extremes, the figures of prosecutions are most likely to be representative of the real volume of crime (see above, Chapter 5, 5(*b*)).[160] Thomas preferred the prosecution figures (p. 207). Secondly, there was the question of the time lag; should the economic index figures be compared with the prosecution figures for the same or the following year or the year after that? It is here that this kind of research encounters some of its most serious difficulties, and the door is wide open to the subjective discretion of the individual research worker. The present writer can only repeat his warning that human beings are not likely to react to stress as promptly as lower animals or electric machines react to various cleverly designed stimuli and that changes in the economic fortunes of men may show their criminological effects possibly at once, but equally possibly after some years and only at a time when the economic cycle may already have taken a different turn.[161] Bonger, too, has stressed that the whole past of an individual plays its part in producing the motives of his behaviour (p. 103). What has actually happened may be discovered in individual cases through careful psychological examination, but there seems to be no safe way of dealing with the problem statistically. Dorothy Thomas saw this difficulty without discussing it at length. All she has to say on it is: 'frequently the response of a social phenomena [sic] to the business cycle is delayed several years' (p. 19), but at least she calculated her correlations for time lags of various length, reaching very different results according to the time lag on which the calculation was based. Vold has recently used this difficulty of the time lag to show how ambiguous Thomas's findings are and how one can base on them conclusions of an opposite nature, according to which time lag is actually used. He criticizes Sutherland–Cressey for ignoring this point.[162]

Almost simultaneously with Dorothy Thomas, Cyril Burt published his findings on the effect of poverty on juvenile delinquency in London.[163] He, too, begins with the search for a definition, not however of the economic conditions of the country in general, as was done by those trying to construct an economic index, but merely for a definition of poverty. Being essentially a psychologist interested in individuals, he was not concerned in this research with the economic condition of the country as a whole but merely with the position of the families from which his delinquents came. His classification of the various categories of economic status was based on the work of Charles Booth in his *Life and Labour in London* and of Seebohm Rowntree,[164] and on this basis he found that over one-half of his sample of London juvenile delinquents came from homes poor or very poor, 19 per cent of them from very poor ones, whereas of the general population of London only 8 per cent came from such homes. On the other hand, 42 per cent came from homes ranking under Booth's classification as 'comfortable', from which figure Burt concluded that poverty could hardly be the sole or the most influential cause. In only 3 per cent of his male delinquents could poverty be called the *prime* contributory factor (p. 92). Interesting is his Table V (p. 77), which shows the incidence of poverty and delinquency in the various London boroughs and gives the high overall correlation of 0·67 between these two factors.

The next large-scale statistical survey of juvenile delinquency in certain English cities[165] produced no general yardstick of poverty, but limited itself to various economic factors, such as the regularity of the father's employment, type and condition of home. For all these factors the position of the delinquent cases was found to be less favourable than for the control group, but nowhere could the differences be described as very remarkable.

One of the best modern investigations of the subject which, since it was published in Germany in 1933, has remained largely unknown, was made by Renger for the period 1882–1929 and limited to Saxony.[166] He used as his economic index what he called the 'real wage', i.e. a figure reflecting the relationship between nominal wages and prices (p. 20), and he found a strong dependence of economic crimes on the movements of these real wages, whereas for crimes of violence there was no such dependence (pp. 42, 46). The time lag was of no significance for the workers, for whom changes in real wages showed their effect immediately, but it was different for business people (p. 35).

II. SPECIFIC PROBLEMS

We can now proceed to a further discussion of several specific points, some of which have already been touched upon in the previous section and in earlier chapters.

1. *The Techniques of Study*

It has been seen that the influence of economic factors can be studied in at least three ways. First, by examining the economic position of groups of offenders, preferably contrasting it with the position of a control group of non-offenders. Secondly, by constructing an economic index reflecting the economic condition of a country or region and comparing its fluctuations with those of crime. Such comparisons can be extended to several countries or regions. Thirdly, individual case studies can be made to illustrate the effect of the economic condition of individuals on their criminal behaviour. The results of all such studies have differed widely, but most of them have clearly confirmed the theory of the multiplicity of causes, i.e. the view that however strong the influence of economic factors may be they can hardly ever operate without the support of other factors, and in particular they have to pass through the 'psychological transformator.' (See above, Preliminary Observations to Part III).

Even Bonger, who is inclined to proclaim the sovereign influence of economic factors and especially of the mode of production—capitalist or communist—and its consequences, admits that most of the authors mentioned in his historical survey recognize that other factors are at work, too (pp. 244–5).

Moreover, the scope of scientific thought on the subject, all too often limited to enquiries into the effect of poverty, has gradually widened to a full-scale, though still imperfect, searching into the impact on crime of the whole economic structure of a given society.

This widening opened the door to the idea, vaguely understood already by Aristotle, that prosperity was of an importance equal to poverty in the field of criminology—an idea which has provided further support to the study of white collar crime, although the latter, as explained above, has rightly been defined in terms not only of economic wealth but also of social class.

2. Poverty and Prosperity: definitions and effect; can we have it both ways?

As indicated above (Chapter 20), our definition of poverty has considerably changed since the days of Booth and Rowntree, and the absolute and static conception has been replaced by a relative and dynamic one. Man's material needs rise with a general rise in well-being, and what was enough ten or twenty years ago is no longer adequate today. In recent years, this has been a recurrent theme in the writings of some of our younger social scientists.[167] The concept of a universally valid 'level of subsistence' has been attacked, 'as if a fixed yardstick could be applied whether the date is 1900 or 1950, or the place York or Calcutta. But poverty is a dynamic, not a static, concept. Man . . . lives in a complex of changing pressures to which he must respond—as much in his consumption of goods and services as any other aspect of his behaviour. . . . In failing to appreciate this fact we have lost sight of social injustices which prevail today,' and 'Judgments of one social class on another are notoriously untrustworthy, and things which are treated as necessary by one group may not be so regarded by another' (Peter Townsend). But not only in our fight against social injustices has this to be borne in mind; it is also crucial for our understanding of the role of poverty in the causation of crime. This relativistic interpretation of poverty not only necessitates a broader definition of the concept; it makes the latter also far more subjective and more difficult to handle with statistical techniques. If a person is poor only when he feels himself to be so in his 'response to changing pressures' then the possibility of ascertaining objectively the number of poor people at a given time and place becomes rather remote, and all one can say with a fair degree of probability is that certain fluctuations of the business cycle are not unlikely to lead to similar fluctuations in the number of those who regard themselves as poor. The same is, *mutatis mutandis*, also true of the statistical coverage of the well-to-do classes as they are well-to-do only if they feel to be so and are content with their position; otherwise they will always try to better themselves, sometimes by lawful and sometimes by unlawful methods. Attitudes and feelings are more important here than statistical figures.

We are now in a position to assert, without fear of too much contradiction, that both poverty and affluence can lead to crime because both are relative conditions in which men, rightly or wrongly, may suffer from dissatisfaction and crave for something better. Vold, in his otherwise admirable chapter on the subject, is one of those who still refuse to accept this truth; to him it is proof of muddled thinking to maintain that these two opposites—economic distress and economic affluence—can have similar effects on crime. Would he equally accuse the heart specialist of muddled thinking who maintains that heart diseases may be due to too much physical exertion as well as to physical inactivity or, for that matter, the economist who claims that the same economic effect—accumulation of a certain capital sum—may be achieved by earning more or by spending less? Different or even opposite causes may indeed have the same effect although of course the causal chain will run on very different tracks. At the bottom of Vold's view seems to lurk the single-cause theory of Sutherland to which reference was made above (Chapter 1, I, 2(c))[168] and which led him to the astonishing view that, as white collar offenders were not poor, poverty had to be ruled out altogether as a possible cause of crime (Chapter 21 above). In a previous discussion of the same problem, originally published in 1942, the present author wrote: 'the same factor can affect different types of people in a different way, and if other factors change, it may even affect individuals of the same type in a different manner ... events which, as a rule have a crime-preventing effect may lose this character under special circumstances ...'[169] This was written early in the last war to explain why at the time so many people earning unusually high wages appeared in court on charges of offences against property. While this phenomenon may easily have puzzled many observers at the time it is more difficult to understand that so many fail to grasp it even nowadays.

3. *Various Other Aspects of the Problem*

(*a*) To the statement that poverty and prosperity may both lead to crime the important qualification has to be added that there will often be a difference in the *type of crime*. This has been recognized by many writers, and von Mayr's work, for example, was remarkable for his distinction between crimes against property which, he thought, fluctuated directly according to the price of rye, and crimes against the person where the relationship was more complex. Dorothy Thomas, who makes a similar distinction, found that the inverse correlation between the business cycle and offences against property without violence was neither strong nor constant. For such offences committed with violence, however, the inverse correlation was both

THE SOCIOLOGY OF CRIME

significant and constant. She concluded that for the former category the picture might have been blurred by changes in law and procedure —changes which, we would have to add, are less likely to have influenced the trend of the more serious second category. For offences against the person there was a certain tendency to increase with growing prosperity, but it was neither significantly high nor constant. For drunkenness prosecutions, however, the positive correlation with the business cycle was high, especially for earlier years. This tendency for such prosecutions to increase with growing prosperity has also been noticeable in this country after the war (see above, Chapter 14, I(g), but remembering the far higher figures of the beginning of the century when the economic position of the masses was incomparably worse one might venture the apparent paradox that drunkenness prosecutions increase with misery because of despair and with prosperity because of *hubris* or insecurity.

(b) The statistical picture may become blurred not only through changes in law and procedure but also through other forms of governmental interference with the ordinary working of the business cycle and the free market, particularly through the many forms of public assistance in its broadest sense as developed in the Welfare State. This is a factor which had not, or not to the same extent, affected the work of previous researchers. In present circumstances, through controlled rents, council houses, unemployment pay, national assistance and similar measures, the worst forms of poverty are reduced in quantity and severity and can no longer be sensibly correlated to the crime figures.

(c) There is, moreover, yet another aspect of the matter which may also deprive statistical researches in this field of much of their value. On the one hand, even in our present affluent society the number of indigent people is still large; according to the various possible yardsticks applied, figures such as four or even six million persons have been quoted for Britain. On the other hand, these are mainly elderly, retired, sick, widowed, or unemployed persons who are not likely to commit offences, except perhaps for some occasional shoplifting or insurance frauds. Many of those who commit more persistent and more serious offences are not really poor and some of them are, as we have seen (see above, Chapter 22), actuated by factors other than their personal poverty. This, however, does not necessarily rule out the possibility that the poverty of others may be a motivating force for them, since the existence of fairly widespread and undeserved poverty among certain sections of the population in the midst of plenty for those who are for the most part equally undeserving poisons the general atmosphere and offends the sense of justice and decency which is one of the strongest crime-preventing elements in

582

society. In any case, it can serve as a good excuse for crime. Very few of those who come under this category are probably rebels against society of the Robin Hood type (see above, Chapter 20, I, 3). Maurice Keen, in his attractive monograph on *The Outlaws of Medieval Legend*,[170] points out that Robin Hood or the rebellious peasants of the English peasants' revolt of 1381 and the German peasants' war of 1525 were 'God's avengers of injustice'; they ravaged and burned, but they did not steal. To some extent, this is also true of Kleist's Michael Kohlhaas.[171]

(*d*) In this connection, attention has once more to be drawn to the different *attitudes to property offences* exhibited by different people. The matter has been dealt with at some length in the present writer's earlier books,[172] and afterwards a systematic enquiry into it was made by G. W. Lynch by means of comprehensive interviewing.[173] It has become clear beyond reasonable doubt that for such offences as stealing there is in the minds of very many people all the difference in the world between public and private property and, within the latter category, between the property of the small man and that of the rich, especially of the large company. It is in fact for many a tenet of natural law that only the small man's property deserves to be respected, whereas the other categories of property are the legitimate objects of occasional or persistent predatory attacks. There are, of course, many nuances, which have been well described in Lynch's, unfortunately unpublished, study. This aspect has, not surprisingly, been somewhat neglected in psychiatric studies of shop-lifting, and it will not often happen that a shoplifter when caught will openly plead in his (or her) defence what was in fact foremost in his (or her) mind, i.e. that such small losses meant nothing to a big store. This impression is, moreover, sometimes unintentionally, encouraged by non-shoplifters. There was, for example, the much discussed announcement of the Chief Constable of a well-known seaside resort that he would in future prosecute only selected cases of shoplifting, coupled with the statement of managers of supermarkets that, with a weekly turnover of many thousands of pounds, the amount lost through shoplifting was comparatively insignificant.[174] No wonder, then, that a Metropolitan Magistrate had to complain that shoplifting from self-service stores in his district (East London) was 'an absolute scourge and had reached its limit' (*The Times*, 3.6.1963).

That the attitudes of many people towards crimes against property have been greatly influenced for the worse by the expansion of the insurance business needs no further explanation.[175] Thefts and burglaries have been rationalized and made to look almost respectable by the thought that it is only 'the insurance' that suffers; arson, frauds and even an occasional murder are committed to get the insurance money; and property owners tend to become careless when insured.

Moreover, people, especially children, who possess no or very little property of their own are not likely to respect that of others. This became noticeable during the wartime evacuation period in the case of some of the children from certain public institutions billeted with private families.[176] Respect for other people's property can be developed only through training, in which instruction in the value and handling of individual property plays an important part; otherwise pilfering and wanton destructiveness may be the consequence.[177] This does not mean, of course, that pilfering and vandalism on the part of children and adolescents are usually due to poverty and lack of spending money; on the contrary, with increasing prosperity other factors, to which attention was drawn in Chapter 22, have become far more important. Fyvel[178] gives a vivid impression of the mixture of primitive emotions, the crowd stimulus, the feeling of frustration and the suspicion of being excluded from something, which may lead to senseless outbursts of violence. The railways, especially when transporting large crowds of football fans and on similar occasions, have to suffer great losses from the destruction of their property. (Not long ago the total annual cost of acts of vandalism to British Railways was given by a Government spokesman as £500,000, *The Times*, 16.5.1964.) All this is often the work of adolescents with high earnings and ample spending money. A recent report by a market research organization has calculated that in contemporary Britain unmarried young people between the ages of 15 and 24 have a disposable weekly income (after paying tax, insurance, rent and keep) of £3.14.6 (for the males alone it was £4.6.6).[179] Commenting on these figures, the General Secretary of the National Association of Boys' Clubs pointed out, however, that it was misleading to lump together boys of 15 and adults of 24 and that the figures for the younger age groups would be much lower.[180] This was confirmed in a survey made on behalf of the University of Durham for a town in that county, where the average wages for boys of 15 and 17 were found to be 70*s*. and 94*s*. respectively and for girls 67*s*. and 79*s*.[181] Teenage prosperity was believed to be due not to high wages but to excessive spoiling by the parents who, having themselves been brought up the hard way, were inclined to make things too easy for their children, and there was also 'an element of keeping up with the Jones's'. While all this seems to rule out poverty as a factor in most cases of juvenile crime, it shows the need for training in the proper use of money; as a probation officer told Fyvel (p. 226): 'There's a shocking failure of society to prepare them for the first phase when they have money.'

Further interesting sidelights on the attitudes of people towards property and stealing were thrown by an examination of press reports on 424 wartime cases of looting.[182] Going through these press cuttings and analysing the excuses put forward by those brought before the courts on charges of looting, the present writer found 'utter bewilderment and perplexity rather than moral wickedness', for which the best cure, at least in the case of first offenders, would be 'education and guidance rather than severe punishment and stigmatization'.

(e) A point sometimes overlooked in the discussion is that considerable differences may exist between countries of different economic conditions and development, i.e. economic factors may have more effect on crime in poorer than in wealthier countries. It is only in recent years that under the auspices of the United Nations Secretariat, Section on Social Defence, closer attention has been paid to the impact of poverty on crime in the economically underdeveloped countries of Asia and Africa. The reports for the UNO Congress of 1960 referred to in Note 1 deal with the situation, though only briefly and in very general terms, and the same applies to the discussions at the Twelfth International Course in Criminology on 'The Causation and Prevention of Crime in Developing Countries', held at the Hebrew University of Jerusalem in October, 1963 (Publications of the Hebrew Institute of Criminology No. 5).

The contrast may not always be as clear-cut, however, as might be expected. Already Bonger referred to the 'fact'—if it was one—that England, a much richer country, had more crimes against property than Italy, and also to the comparatively lower rate of criminality in Ireland, at the time also one of the poorest countries (p. 225). He offered the explanation that it was not the total wealth of a country that mattered, but rather the way in which its wealth was distributed, and 'in no country is the difference between rich and poor more pronounced' than in England at the turn of the century. The manner in which the resources of a country are distributed is no doubt of great influence on its crime rate; where everyone is poor there is little incentive to steal, and in the England of fifty or a hundred years ago the contrasts between very rich and very poor districts and individuals were indeed particularly striking. Such considerations may help to explain the reticence of recent Indian writers, for example, to regard the poverty of their country as the strongest criminogenic factor.[183] The position in contemporary Italy, with its growing over-all prosperity, is also somewhat obscured by the great contrast between the booming North and the economically backward provinces of the South and Sicily. Whereas the former shows already some traces of the adolescent delinquency typical of an affluent society, in the latter crime is still largely determined by poverty. Smuggling, for example,

585

is said to be a necessary occupation on the Neapolitan coast as a means by which large sections of the population could find enough to eat. The demonstrative funeral celebrations on the death of a smuggler who lost his life in a clash with the coastguards were symptomatic of the feelings and needs of the people.[184] For Sicily, Danilo Dolci and Carlo Levi[185] have given impressive descriptions of the abject poverty of some of the villages and its physical and social consequences, including the support given to the Mafia (Chapter 25 below).

(f) The dangers arising from sudden and usually unexpected changes in the economic fortunes of men are well-known. Such changes may happen to a whole people, mostly as a consequence of a lost war, or to special sections, as for example in the case of widespread unemployment in one industry or of inflation hitting with particular severity the elderly and those living on a fixed income, or they may be confined to certain families or individuals as a result of the death of the breadwinner, of illness or a criminal conviction, etc. Such sudden economic changes are, however, not invariably for the worse, and reference has just been made to the effect which unaccustomed prosperity may have on young people.

The criminogenic significance of a general economic depression has been studied for the U.S.A. by Sellin, who explained the technical difficulties encountered by the research worker and insisted on the need for further research (Note 146). Taft (pp. 170 ff.) stresses that as vast sums were spent in the U.S.A. on relief the depression of 1930–5 did not show its full criminogenic effects there. He summarizes the results of several American studies of the subject, which were largely inconclusive. To examine the problem in its whole nakedness one has to turn to countries lacking the material resources to temper the wind to the shorn lamb. The movements of the crime figures during the German inflation of 1920–4 provide perhaps the most impressive evidence for the havoc played by a wholesale destruction of a country's currency. The present writer had ample opportunity to observe this phenomenon on the spot in the courts, the administration, and in actual life. The statistical repercussions can be seen in the material provided by Exner.[186] He shows that what happened was not simply a considerable increase in convictions but a wholesale and profound revolution in the structure of German criminality. As the currency had completely lost its value, and everybody was interested not in money, but only in goods (Sachwerte), those offences, such as larceny and breakings, which aim at the acquisition of goods, rose to three times their previous figures, receiving even to six times, whereas frauds, especially insurance frauds, and arson, which aim at the acquisition of money, declined in the same way. The stabilization of the

586

German currency in 1924 brought the figures back in 1925 to the pre-inflation standard. Exner concluded from this that economic fluctuations of such vehemence have a profound effect on the character of criminality. In this he was right, but what he did not sufficiently examine was the corresponding change in the composition of the criminal population. It is only natural that anti-social elements had to revise their techniques of committing crime on account of the inflation and subsequent deflation; what has still to be examined is whether and how far these events affected the numbers and characteristics of offenders as opposed to offences; whether and to what extent previously law-abiding citizens had succumbed to the excessive pressure of a mad world. This question of changes in the proportion of first offenders to recidivists is one of special significance in times of economic crises and war. 'Surely, neither to society at large nor to the practical penologist can it be indifferent whether 100,000 offences "known to the police" have been committed by 100,000 first offenders or by a small group of perhaps 2,000 habitual law-breakers, each of whom is responsible for an average of fifty offences.'[187] Most official criminal statistics are of little assistance on this point. It might be guessed, however, that periods of crisis tend to swell the ranks of first offenders and to reduce those of recidivists. The large increase in certain offences observed during the inflation probably meant, therefore, an increase in the number of previously unconvicted persons. We shall have to return to this aspect below in connection with wartime criminality.

(g) *Unemployment* as one of the most widespread causes of economic distress has repeatedly been studied by criminologists.[188] The results of statistical investigations in the U.S.A. and Britain have not been consistent enough to warrant any sweeping conclusions. As an illustration, the difficulties may be quoted which were encountered by the present writer in his detailed review of the position in Britain between the two world wars to which reference may here be made. The coverage provided by official unemployment statistics was found to be incomplete; no clear distinction was often made between short- and long-term unemployment; there were important local differences blurring the national or regional picture, and unemployment pay and other welfare work seemed to have an important crime-preventing effect, interfering with the simple chain of cause and effect. Statements by prisoners on their employment position were misleading, and comparisons between different communities often showed contrasts in the crime rates for which no explanation could be found in the unemployment figures. The conclusion was that unemployment seemed to play a widely varying role in different areas and also for different age groups, and that subtle psychological factors had to be taken into account which did not become so easily visible in statistical investigations. Juveniles seemed at the time to be particularly liable to commit offences when out of work, but Cloward and Ohlin report that in the U.S.A. the position is different. Glaser and Rice, too, found that whereas the adult crime rates varied directly with unemployment the picture was not so clear for juveniles.[189] On the other hand, John Morgan, presenting an impressionistic picture of the impact of mass unemployment in Kentucky and neighbouring states of the Union as a result of automation, indicates that this is one of the factors responsible for juvenile crime in those districts.[190]

Certain changes in the nature of offences may occur at times of high unemployment, i.e. unemployment insurance frauds may to some extent take the place of the more usual offences against property.

(h) *Occupation*.[191] Criminology is, however, not only interested in those out of work. People in employment, too, may have their occupational problems which are of concern to criminologists, whether they may be of an economic, social or psychological nature. There are obvious links in particular between occupational psychology and criminology, and the decision to discuss the subject in the present context, i.e. as part of the sociology of crime, may be open to criticism, but any other choice would have been equally controversial.

Information on the occupational status of criminals is available only for certain sections. As mentioned in previous chapters, it is known that the working classes, especially unskilled labourers, supply far more than their proportional share to the total figure of persons convicted of such offences as stealing, house-breaking, etc., and the same applies to juvenile delinquents. Most white collar criminals, on the other hand, naturally belong to the middle classes. Apart from this, there is very little reliable statistical material on the occupations of offenders in Britain, whereas in a number of foreign countries this is included in their criminal statistics.[192] Even the tables on the subject previously included in the *Annual Reports of the Prison Commission for England and Wales* were discontinued soon after the last war. It is doubtful whether this is a serious loss since the tables were based on information supplied by the prisoners themselves who are notoriously unreliable when interviewed on this subject. This applies in particular to professional criminals and most other recidivists. T. and P. Morris have collected valuable material on this in their recent Pentonville study (*Pentonville*, pp. 65-7).

The significance of an individual's occupation for his well-being and social behaviour can be briefly summed up by saying that the job, including the treatment received by mates and superiors, has to fit the man and his peculiar abilities, inclinations and susceptibilities. It must not be too difficult or too easy, nor should it be more monotonous than he can bear. Moreover, it should not be a blind-alley job but offer reasonable prospects for the future. The conflict between the desire for high earnings in early life and better training (apprenticeship) with delayed gratification has to be solved in the best interests of the individual. Any discrepancy on any of these points may cause a grievance and contribute to anti-social attitudes. The dangers arising to young people in the past from blind-alley jobs and other unskilled work have been described in *Social Aspects of Crime*; *mutatis mutandis*, many of them are still in existence, and with expanding automation the position is likely further to deteriorate.

With more specific reference to the criminogenic significance of the various types of work the following points may be made:

(*aa*) As far as the individual is at all in a position to choose his calling his personal characteristics, likes and dislikes will to some extent determine the choice. From this it has sometimes been concluded that persons with certain criminal tendencies will select occupations which offer good opportunities of living out those tendencies either criminally or by way of sublimation. Homosexuals, it has been argued, may become teachers or priests, sadists will be butchers or surgeons or soldiers,[193] nymphomanic girls will join the oldest profession, pyromaniacs the fire brigade, and so on. The emphasis here is almost equally on the crime-facilitating as on the crime-preventing, sublimating, canalizing qualities of the occupations concerned, but in either direction what we have got so far are hunches and possibilities rather than actual evidence.

(*bb*) Certain occupations, while not consciously or unconsciously chosen because of any innate criminal tendencies, may be dangerous to some individuals because of the special opportunities and temptations which they offer for wrong-doing: for example occupations giving easy access to poison or to other people's property. Doctors, druggists, nurses, domestic servants, window cleaners, solicitors, bank clerks, locksmiths, and many more entirely respectable professions and occupations have here been listed and as any others they have their occasional black sheep. There is little doubt that many large-scale thefts or burglaries could not have been successfully carried out without the complicity of domestic servants, or pay-roll hold-ups without that of chauffeurs or other employees of the firms concerned. An assessor to insurance companies has described the dangers inherent in his profession through the contacts with fraudulent clients.[194] To Cressey's detailed sociological and psychological analysis of the defrauding bank clerk reference has already been made before; it supplies ample evidence of the specific temptations arising from such a position. In other cases the relation of cause and effect may be more complicated, and we are in danger of over-simplifying it. With regard to homosexuality, for example, Hans Walder has asked whether it is really the 'cause' of the selection of a certain calling or whether it is the latter which leads to homosexuality or whether there may be a common causative factor behind both of them.[195]

(*cc*) On the other hand, there are a few occupations to which protective, crime-preventing qualities are sometimes ascribed. In addition to some of those mentioned under (*aa*), going to sea used to be regarded as one because of its psychological effects and the possibility it provides to cut unhelpful family bonds. The life of a seaman may, however, also involve the risk of committing offences connected with drink and prostitution.

Providing useful work and training in prisons and other correctional institutions has always been regarded as one of the strongest crime-preventing forces available, and a considerable literature exists on this aspect of the subject. The recent Report on 'Work for Prisoners' tries to give an outline of 'suitable work for prisoners and its availability' and the corresponding Report on Borstals does the same. There is, of course, the danger that the facilities made available may be exploited by some inmates for criminal purposes; as Mark Benney writes: 'I chose work in the engineer's shop to fit me for safebreaking' (*Low Company*, p. 239), but his expectations came to nothing, and generally speaking one should not use the bad intentions of some to deprive all of the potential benefits of industrial training in institutions.

(*dd*) Naturally, the offender's occupation or previous occupation plays an important role not only in providing him with the techniques and opportunities required for his offences, but it may determine his whole outlook and way of behaviour and thereby influence the shape of his offences. The army officer or diplomat, after being dismissed for misconduct, may still pose as such and use his perfect manners to help him in his confidence tricks. Mark Benney paints a picture of the work of the coal miner (before nationalization) to show how it influences his character and may lead to aggressive behaviour.[196]

(*ee*) To deal adequately with the part played by the monotony of modern labour as a potential cause of criminality one would have to digress more fully than space permits into the literature on occupational psychology and kindred subjects. Monotony, it is true, is only one source of the widespread dissatisfaction with modern conditions of labour; moreover, it is felt in very different ways by different people. There are some workers who are capable of introducing into the apparently most soulless types of work an element of variety which captures their imagination and gives them pleasure, whereas others complain of the monotony of potentially highly interesting occupations.[197] Many manual workers envy the academic and office workers not only for their higher earnings—if any—and their higher social status, but also for what they regard as their less monotonous work. Actually, office work can also be monotonous, but generally speaking there is indeed a scale of monotony which rises in a direction opposite to that of earnings and status. C. Wright Mills, in his thought-provoking chapter on work, refers to American enquiries showing that of a national cross-section of clerical and sales employees 64 per cent found their work interesting and enjoyable against 85 per cent of professional and executive people and 41 per cent of the factory workers.[198] He admits that such figures prove very little; nevertheless, they may vaguely reflect the prevailing feeling in most industrialized countries. Dealing with the criminogenic effects of modern mass production techniques, Paul Reiwald stresses that one of the most important functions of work, the sublimation of libidinal and aggressive energy, is entirely ignored today, and he expresses views very similar to those of Alexander and Healy and of Adler to which we referred above in Chapter 17. In *Social Aspects of Crime* (p. 292) reference was also made to the monotony of the jobs many of the Borstal boys in the sample had to do. Even in the case of a dull boy who 'does not resent monotony', the Medical Officer gives the warning that 'his instinctive energies had not been sufficiently utilized'.

Closely connected with the monotony factor is that of frequent job-changing, that has some psychological affinity with truancy at school, the 'Kindergarten' of juvenile delinquency (William Healy). It is common knowledge that these two phenomena are particularly prevalent among delinquents. Both have deep-rooted emotional causes which are still further strengthened by certain unsatisfactory features of some jobs and schools. Various control-group enquiries have shown the much higher rate of job-changing among delinquents.[199] Work habits of offenders, a term of which the steadiness of employment and the frequency of job-changing are important elements, have been essential factors in practically all systems of crime prediction, i.e. the worse the work habits and the higher the rate of job-changing the more likely is future relapse into crime.

D. THE EFFECT OF WARS[200]

1. In the whole field of criminology there is hardly a subject of greater interest than this. Of all the crises which can befall a nation war causes perhaps the most profound and lasting changes, and it is only a natural consideration that the present spectacle of an unusually large increase in the volume and seriousness of crime witnessed in many

countries should often be ascribed to the effect of the two world wars. At the same time, this is a subject on which it is extremely hazardous to generalize. Each war, or at least each type of war, produces its own effects on crime, which may be different in different countries, and the material so far collected on wars of the past may have very little bearing on the nuclear war of the future. Even for the past, the information available for many countries is very scanty. Whereas for a few, notably Germany and Austria, thanks to the support of the Carnegie Foundation, very detailed and careful studies have been published concerning the First World War, for Britain the position is far less favourable for the First as well as the Second World War. The official War History largely ignored the criminological aspects, and when the present author republished three essays written on the subject during or soon after the second war he had to explain that this was done mainly to illustrate the scarcity of the existing information. More surprisingly, not even the U.S.A. seems to possess a comprehensive official criminological history of the two world wars, and here too we are dependent on the sporadic efforts of private scholars. The existing gaps have to some extent been filled by the symposium produced and published under the auspices of the International Penal and Penitentiary Commission (I.P.P.C.), which covers eight European countries and the U.S.A., but even this useful work is of very uneven quality and leaves several regrettable gaps, notably for Germany, Italy, Russia and the whole of the Balkan countries, all of which have been omitted. The contributions are written by individual scholars or officials of the countries concerned, with the exception of England and Wales, the chapter on which is the work of the Home Office Advisory Council on the Treatment of Offenders. This corporate and anonymous authorship has resulted in a rather dull and impersonal piece of work, in which excessive attention is paid to institutional, especially prison, developments, in short to administration, at the expense of the more important and lasting causative aspects of the crime problem. It is also characteristic of this type of governmental survey that it is admittedly not based on any kind of 'intensive research or the analysis of detailed statistics', but rather on 'expressions of opinion by some of those best qualified to express an opinion' (p. 113). It was not even found necessary, for example, to examine the files of a sample of cases, prisoners or probationers, to analyse the principal causal factors involved, as was done, for example, in Belgium.

Of the countries covered by the I.P.P.C. symposium one, Sweden, was neutral, two, U.S.A. and England and Wales, remained unoccupied by the enemy, whereas, of the remaining six, five, France, Denmark, Norway, Holland and Belgium, were occupied and one, Austria, was in a somewhat doubtful position between belligerent, neutral and occupied. It will be interesting to examine the criminological differences between these categories. As already stated, the contributions to the I.P.P.C. symposium vary greatly in value and in length: whereas, for example, Austria and Belgium have only 5 to 10 pages each, Denmark has 38 and Sweden nearly a hundred pages. This may have been due in part to the varying extent to which information was available in individual countries—neutral Sweden was probably in a much better position than Austria or Belgium, but greater uniformity might possibly have been imposed from a centre, and the absence of a concluding chapter, summing up the individual results and comparing them with those of the First World War, is also to be regretted. The difficulties which this study, in common with most other researches on the subject, had to face should not be underestimated. There was not only the general scarcity of reliable information especially in the belligerent and, in particular, in the occupied countries, but in the latter also the difficulty of distinguishing between real offences and acts committed as part of the resistance movement, such as sabotage, destruction of property, and even violence (pp. 8, 14, for Belgium and pp. 145, 150, for Holland). As a consequence the general sense of right and wrong became blurred, and 'group resistance towards crime was reduced'. Christiansen, who reports this for Denmark, regards it as a case of culture conflict (p. 40), and it might indeed pass as such if we treat the matter as a conflict between the norms imposed by the occupying power and the traditional ones which the individuals concerned had been taught to respect and which prescribed resistance to a foreign invader. These latter norms were certainly not legal ones since the law, while forbidding active collaboration, does as a rule not demand active resistance to the enemy on the part of civilians. However, such problems connected with the resistance movements are merely part and parcel of the far larger, legal and psychological, embarrassments resulting from the need to switch our thoughts and actions rapidly from peacetime to wartime requirements and back again.[201]

Another difficulty to be faced by criminal statistics for the war years arises from the fact that a large, but undefinable, number of young and middle-aged men were either in the Forces or, as in the case of the occupied countries during the last war, deported or had gone underground (p. 63 for France). Here again this is only one aspect of the wholesale movement of populations characteristic of the world wars and even of some smaller ones. Equally deceptive are, for some countries, the wartime figures of prison inmates which were, in part at least, dependent on political rather than penological factors (e.g. p. 138 for Holland).

There are many other changes, too, which make the picture

presented by wartime criminal statistics unsafe as a basis for our conclusions, for example changes in the fields of the criminal law, which
usually requires various modifications and additions to suit the needs
of wartime security and economy; of criminal procedure which has
to be simplified and speeded up; and of police work where the shortage of personnel makes the proportion of crimes cleared up still lower
than usual. The recruitment needs of the Armed Forces often have to
take preference over the requirements of criminal justice. In some
countries, notably Nazi Germany, the statistical crime figures were
artificially reduced by means of large-scale political amnesties.[202]
Moreover, the collection and analysis of the statistical material had
to be reduced to a minimum or altogether abandoned because of lack
of manpower.

2. 'It is true', writes Hurwitz,[203] 'that the effects of war are an
object-lesson in the capacity of environmental factors to induce
criminality in normally law-abiding populations; however, the matter
is not so simple as is sometimes assumed.' Both parts of this statement
are correct: there is evidence to show that war is one of the strongest
of all those environmental factors likely to produce substantial
changes in the structure of crime, but it is also true that the general
pattern of these changes is far from clear and uniform. 'War' is in fact
one of those broad concepts which include a great variety of types
having certain elements in common side by side with many other elements present in only a limited number of cases. For the two world
wars, for example, one has only to compare their effects in Germany,
Austria and Russia, on the one hand, and the United States, on the
other, with Britain standing somewhere between these two extremes,
to understand that war and belligerency may mean very different
things in every respect, including crime. This partly explains the detached attitude adopted, for example, by most American criminologists towards the subject and the very limited space allotted to it in
their textbooks; partly, however, the reason may also be found in the
extraordinary difficulties confronting those who are bold enough to
search for the facts and their meaning in terms of causality:

Scientific investigations into causal connections require the presence of at
least a certain minimum of all those factors which war practically excludes:
stability of the external conditions, an observer with an easy, undisturbed
mind, and the necessary technical prerequisites to the assessments of those
factors . . . Should the world fall to pieces, Archimedes can still draw his
circles on the sands; not so the criminologist . . .[204]

In the circumstances, is it at all possible to pinpoint certain patterns
which seem to be common experience in many countries during the
two world wars? The material presented in the author's previous

publications for Britain, by Exner for Austria, Liepmann for Germany and in the I.P.P.C. volume shows how cautious we have to be in our interpretations of the available statistics. Attempts have been made to divide the periods of war into different stages, each of them showing its own peculiar criminological characteristics and requiring its own interpretations. Moreover, within these stages distinctions are needed according to country, age, sex, and type of offence.

With all such reservations, there is a fairly widespread tendency to regard the initial stage of a war as one of general enthusiasm, a wave of patriotic sentiments, and a consequent decline in crime.[205] John Galsworthy's juryman, in his moral indignation at having to attend a criminal trial in that early period, expressed this feeling in the characteristic words: 'There oughtn't to *be* any crime in these days.'[206] Even here, though, exceptions are not altogether missing concerning people who, through the wartime dislocation of the economy, had suddenly lost their means of livelihood without receiving any kind of substitute in the Forces or as civilians. After a few months of elation much of that wave of enthusiasm disappears, and the crime figures begin to rise. This happened at the beginning of the First as well as of the Second World War, and in neutral Sweden no less than in the belligerent countries. There are sceptics, however, who do not believe in the existence of that wave of moral uplift and ascribe the initial decline in criminality to the shifts in the structure of the population, and the general improvement in economic conditions and occupational opportunities.[207] If there are any emotional factors at all responsible for the improvement in crime figures they are more likely to be found in the new outlets for legalized violence or depredations offered by the exceptional conditions of war.[208] Moreover, the initial decline did not occur in all those countries,[209] nor did it affect women and children. In any case, it was soon brought to a halt, although even then distinctions have to be made according to sex, age, type of offence and the military fortunes of the country concerned. It is not surprising that the position develops on more favourable lines in victorious than in defeated countries,[210] and it is equally natural that in the latter the years following the war should show a further serious deterioration, whereas at least in some of the victorious powers conditions should tend to return to normal. For Germany after the last war no statistical figures of crime existed for the years up to 1948, and the historian of that period, Karl S. Bader, had to collect the material for his interesting picture from a great variety of sources. What emerges as one of its most striking features is the primitivity of early post-war crime in Germany, with the predominance of robbery, murder, and rape. It was a repetition of the experiences had after the First World War, and together with a decline of the more sophisticated types of economic offences such as frauds in favour of black-marketeering, together also with the changes in the numerical distribution of crime between the different categories of the population, it lent force to the view expressed by both Bader and Exner that the transformation of the crime picture by the war proves, as hardly anything else, the environmentally conditioned nature of crime as a mass phenomenon.[211] This is particularly significant in view of the strong tendency in pre-war German criminology to overstress the role of biological factors. Outside Germany and Austria these trends, though also unmistakably present, have shown themselves in perhaps less striking forms.

For England and Wales, for example, the gradual rise in indictable offences known to the police from 303,771 in 1939 or 305,114 in 1940 to 415,010 in 1944 or 478,394 in 1945 or 498,576 in 1947 means comparatively little when compared with the near-doubling of the numbers in peacetime to 806,900 in 1961. The proportion per 100,000 of population aged 17 and over found guilty of indictable offences fell from 162·5 in 1938 to 149 in 1939 and 150 in 1940, but increased to 201 in 1941, 214 in 1942, 206 in 1943, 204 in 1944, 223 in 1945.

3. Among the special aspects of the subject none is perhaps more important in its lasting effects than the wartime redistribution of the criminal population. There is first the increase in first offenders as against recidivists; a point on which the available material is not as full as the matter deserves. Moreover, the trends are to some extent conflicting. On the strength of the information existing for the First World War and the initial stages of the Second, the present writer[212] expressed the view that in wartime recidivism tended to decline; the old lag, usually given well-paid work with no questions asked or even accepted for the Forces, seemed to keep straight, whereas large numbers of newcomers appeared in court and went to prison. To a large extent, this is in fact true. English prison statistics show a decline in the percentage of men with previous convictions received in prison from over 50 per cent before the war to the lowest figure of 35·9 per cent in 1942.[213] Similar declines have been reported for France and Holland.[214] The reason given for France was the absence of middle-aged men, likely candidates for recidivism, who were in the resistance or deported. In Sweden and the U.S.A., however, both countries less affected by the war, increases in recidivism seem to have occurred.[215] To know why this has happened one would require much more detailed information.

Closely connected with this decline in recidivism among adult men is the large increase in female and juvenile delinquency. For women of all ages the number of those found guilty of indictable offences in England and Wales rose from 9,784 in 1938 to 13,248 in 1940, and reached its peak in 1943 with 18,855, which meant a near-doubling.

In most of the countries covered by the I.P.P.C. survey the position was similar or even worse. For example in Denmark, the numbers rose from 520 in 1937 to 2,097 in 1943; in Holland the proportion of convictions increased from 10·8 in 1938 to 16·6 in 1943, and in Sweden it was worse.[216] For Germany, Bader has tried to compensate for the absence of statistical material for the country as a whole by presenting a wealth of significant detail which shows not only a great increase in economic offences but also one of aggressive crimes by women.[217]

The following explanations have been offered for this wholesale deterioration of female criminality: In the early stages of the two world wars many women lost their jobs;[218] many hasty marriages were concluded merely to get the family allowances,[219] leading to unhappiness, adultery, desertion, with their aftermath in the field of crime. The increasing shortages of consumer goods in conjunction with the greater family responsibilities of married women produced a flood of economic, including rationing, offences, stealing and receiving. The disruption of family life through enlistment and other forms of war work, shelter life and evacuation added to the mental and financial strain.

The same factors were responsible for the wartime darkening of the picture as far as juveniles were concerned. For many reasons this was only natural. For juveniles war offers no constructive alternative to their usual occupation, which for most of them means attending school. They cannot evade the net of criminal statistics by taking cover in the Armed Forces, nor can they take advantage of the many lawful opportunities of exploiting the economic machinery created by the war. If their families are broken up and their schools closed they have to suffer and are exposed to additional temptations. At the end of 1940 there were still about 80,000 school children left in London in spite of the large-scale wave of evacuation, and in other big cities the position was similar, but the schools were closed partly because the buildings were needed for other purposes and partly because there were no teachers.[220] For adolescents the closing of most of their clubs, hostels, playing fields and evening institutes was almost equally detrimental. Shelter life and black-out together with many empty houses offered ideal opportunities for pilfering and sexual misconduct. Those who were evacuated to country districts had to face the inevitable culture conflicts, but only few of those who offended were brought before the local courts as it was so much simpler to send them home. That in the rather chaotic conditions prevailing in large parts of Britain during the blitz the official picture of juvenile delinquency could be only fragmentary is obvious. According to *Criminal Statistics for England and Wales* the proportion of offenders per 100,000 of the population in each age group increased by roughly 60–70 per cent for boys and by 100–120 per cent for girls between 1938 and 1944. These figures are probably nothing but a faint reflection of the actual state of affairs. Moreover, they refer only to those aged between 8 and 17 at the time, and can reveal nothing about the criminogenic effect of the war on children below the age of criminal responsibility. Nor do they cover the far wider problem of the after-effect on persons who grew up under wartime conditions. When D. H. Stott made his study of 102 Approved School boys a few years after 1945 he estimated that in 19 of them the war had been the direct cause of their delinquencies in the sense that they were unlikely to have offended without it.[221] Some of these wider aspects have recently been analysed statistically by Leslie T. Wilkins in his *Delinquent Generations*,[222] who believes to have found in the official figures some support for the hypothesis that 'children born in certain years (for example, during war-time) are more likely to commit offences than others, and that this tendency remains from childhood to early adult life'. More specifically, Wilkins found the greatest 'crime-proneness' to be associated with that birth group who passed through their fifth year during the war, and he regards it as a likely hypothesis that 'disturbed social conditions have their major impact on children between the age of four and five'. Whatever may be the merits of Wilkins's able and painstaking analysis, which has been questioned by other statisticians,[223] it has to be borne in mind that even the post-war official statistics of juvenile delinquency, on which Wilkins's study depends, may not present an accurate picture of the actual movements. What is important, however, is the fact, rightly stressed by Wilkins, that the criminogenic effects of war, as of other social upheavals, may make themselves felt many years after its end. It is interesting to note in this connection that when the crime rate in France rose after the year 1851 among middle-aged and elderly men it was argued that this might have been the consequence of their having been born during the Napoleonic Wars or the Revolution. Although there was hardly any statistical evidence available at the time in support of this conjecture it might serve as an illustration of our general thesis.[224] A few individual cases illustrating the long-term psychological effects of war are given in *War and Crime* (pp. 72–4).

After this digression we might cast a glance at the wartime development of juvenile delinquency in some other countries. In France the number of those under 18 charged in juvenile courts rose from 20,475 in 1938 to a peak of 53,466 in 1942, after which it declined to 29,476 in 1945.[225] In Belgium, too, as in Sweden, the figures more than doubled between 1938 and 1942/1943, after which there was also a sharp decline.[226] For Holland figures are available only up to 1943, showing a gradual, though less spectacular advance.[227] For Germany the increase between 1939 and 1943 has been estimated at 140 per cent, to be explained by the wartime enlargement of German territory and changes in the methods of dealing with offenders.[228]

E. DIFFERENTIAL ASSOCIATION AND SIMILAR THEORIES[229]

1. *Differential Association*

Reference has already been made before to Sutherland's theory of differential association, and there is no need now for more than a few concluding remarks. It is a theory based on the learning process, i.e. maintaining that criminal behaviour is learned behaviour. This is true for many cases, but it is certainly not true for all. The theory might have been useful and gained an honourable place in the history of criminological thought had it not been artificially inflated by some of its adherents who tried to establish it at any cost as the 'one and only' explanation of criminal behaviour. Such claims have been refuted so often and so drastically that it is difficult to understand how they can still be upheld. Even some of its most devoted supporters have been forced to admit that the idea that criminality depends on the frequency and intimacy of contacts with other criminals cannot be empirically verified.[230] Moreover, there are the obvious criticisms that the theory can explain neither the origin of criminality, which 'has to exist before it can be learned by someone else' (Jeffery), nor the criminality of those without previous contacts with criminals or that it fails to distinguish between criminal and non-criminal behaviour, which latter can also be learned. Neither these nor other similarly cogent criticisms have so far persuaded some of Sutherland's followers to abandon their exaggerated claims. Apparently not only criminality but criminological theorizing, too, is learned behaviour. As Vold has said, the theory has promised 'much more than it has been able to deliver', and it is high time that it should cut its losses. It should also acknowledge far more clearly than has so far been done its indebtedness to Tarde's theory of imitation (see above, Chapter 20, I(3)) which, in its first—not class-oriented—law, stated that men imitate others in proportion to the closeness of their contacts, whereas according to its second law, with which we were previously concerned, the waves of imitation go from the lower to the higher social classes. While any attempt to verify this first 'law' statistically would end in failure daily experience shows that imitation is in fact a powerful force in the commission of crime. In particular sensational and widely publicized murder cases are occasionally copied soon afterwards, even after the execution of the first murderer, which shows by the way the deterrent effect of the death penalty to be less strong than the force of imitation. This happened, for example, in the notorious 'Blazing Car' cases where the victim was burned to death in his car in order to obtain the insurance money. Although the inventor of this technique, one Tetzner in Germany, was executed in 1929, this did not deter his English imitator, Rouse, from trying it again in 1931 with the same result.[231] There were other imitators as well in Germany and Switzerland, and it was proved that all of them had acted in the knowledge of the first case. This failure of the death penalty to deter certain persons from imitating crimes for which the perpetrators had been hanged was used already 130 years ago by E. G. Wakefield as an abolitionist argument when he related the story of a man who, after reading newspaper reports of the execution of somebody for killing a boy to sell his body for dissection, committed a similar crime.[232] Arson is another type of offence where imitation can often be observed. The sensational cases of multiple arson committed by part-time fire-fighters, referred to above in Chapter 16, occurred in fairly quick succession after the first reports had appeared in the papers. This seems to show that the reading of press reports may sometimes take the place of those frequent and intimate contacts which Sutherland had in mind. Sexual crimes, too, are liable to be copied. In 1927 a twelve-year-old girl was killed and dismembered in the U.S.A. The story made big headlines and was dramatized in parts of the American press, and the murderer became some sort of a public hero. Shortly after the trial a number of similar crimes were committed throughout the U.S.A. by individuals who confessed that they had tried to copy the first killer.[233] Such confessions, of course, are not always true, but the mere fact of repetition in such circumstances may create a presumption in their favour. Finally, the publicity often given to suicides has been deplored by Coroners as encouraging imitation, if only by individuals already inclined that way.[234] The latter reservation should not be ignored; it applies to imitation in general.

2. *The Influence of Techniques of Mass-Communication*[235]

The all-pervasive and persuasive effect of the press, the cinema, radio and television has made itself felt in the field of crime as much as elsewhere, especially with reference to juvenile delinquency, but not exclusively so. Most of the older literature on the subject was concerned with the movies and crime stories, notably 'horror comics'; more recently, radio and television have been added. Their criminological assessment has gone through three stages: in the first, which prevailed in the earlier decades of the century, most writers unhesitatingly and indiscriminately blamed the comics, the press and the cinema for a great deal of juvenile delinquency; children, it was believed, copied the crimes they read about or watched on the screen. It was mainly under the influence of the pioneers of a more scientific psychological approach to the subject after the First World War, especially of William Healy and Cyril Burt, that the theory of imitation was replaced by the more sophisticated idea of the 'healthy outlet', the 'safety valve' or 'vicarious enjoyment'. According to it, the reader or watcher of brutal acts of violence, of sex orgies, or whatever outrageous material press and cinema may choose to place before them, far from wishing to do the same would rather lean back happily and passively and let those actively engaged take his place. Looked at in this way, horror tales and crime films were not only not dangerous but positively useful as crime-preventing agencies. Of course, this theory was hardly ever stated so crudely by the psychologists. Take, for example, the finely balanced discussion by Burt who, while admitting the deep and often haunting impressions created on children, asks: 'Yet, of the ensuing acts, how much is crime? . . . The direct reproduction of serious film-crimes is, in my experience, exceedingly uncommon: and even then, it is usually the criminal's method rather than the criminal's aim that is borrowed; the nefarious impulses themselves have been demonstrably in existence beforehand' (pp. 144–5). This was to become the fairly generally accepted formula: it is not the motives but merely the methods of the gangster that are copied from the movies; the criminal disposition was already there before, and the film has merely provided the external stimulus.[236] Burt found only four or five cases in his material where the crime seemed to be directly inspired by the cinema, and they were mostly cases of dull or defective youngsters. In short, the criminogenic emphasis was shifted from the imitative to other, it was thought less sinister, aspects, mainly to the obvious incentive provided by the movie craze to steal the money needed for the ticket. In addition, it was stressed, however, that even if no straightforward copying could be discovered there might well exist far more subtle side- or after-effects, again well described by Burt: the distorted view of life in society which is presented to the young cinema-goer, with its entirely wrong scale of values which might exert its evil influence later in life. In any case, it is encouraging to see that leading child psychiatrists such as the late Lucien Bovet[237] object to the all too complacent views propagated by some of the adherents of the theory of the safety valve which, he writes, has in the light of present-day knowledge as much scientific backing as the equally uncritical theory of imitation.

A few interesting case histories have been given by psychiatrists, for example by Frederic Wertham in his *Dark Legend*.[238] His young Italian-American hero Gino had, on the night before killing his mother, seen a film containing several elements which seemed to him to reflect his own problems. Wertham, reflecting on certain famous instances in world literature such as Orestes hearing the Greek Chorus recite the story of his father's death and his mother's re-marriage, concludes that, while anti-social impulses do not originate in this way, once they exist they may receive an added impetus by way of identification with the hero of a film or novel or press report.

These quotations show that there is no clear-cut line of transition from the second to the third stage, which latter is characterized by the appearance on the scene of the sociologists and social psychologists on the theoretical and of television on the practical side. Statisticians and sociologists have analysed the contents of films and also compared the interest shown by delinquents and non-delinquents in the movies and television. It was found, for example, that out of 500 motion pictures analysed in the years 1920, 1925 and 1930 about 25–30 per cent had crime as their major theme[239] and also that delinquents exhibited a far greater interest in the movies and went to the cinema far more often than non-delinquents.[240] With regard to the first, the film industry replied that, as crime played such a dominant role in our society, they as faithful and impartial recorders of modern life had the moral and social duty to give it its proper share in the contents of the movies. To this it might be retorted that if it should be found that boredom, hanging about and doing nothing was an important feature of society—as they actually are—the film makers would be most reluctant to give them their true share as doing so might be bad business. It is similar with the time-worn argument that the industry has to give people the kind of entertainment they want; here as so often it is doubtful which came first, the wish or its alleged fulfilment. With regard to the more frequent cinema attendance of delinquents two doubts have to be stressed: first, as far as statistics are based on the delinquents' and non-delinquents' own stories the latter may, as Grygier has convincingly shown (Note 235), easily be falsified by bad memory and possibly also by the wish of non-delinquents to conceal the truth if they believe it to be unwelcome to the interviewer.

The principal objections to crime pictures, as seen from a point of view which tries to do justice to both, the theory of imitation and that of the healthy outlet, are thus in brief these:

(a) There is far too much crime on the screen, and in particular too much violence, which goes against even the present statistical proportion of such crimes;

(b) the actual psychological and sociological factors behind crime are often distorted in favour of cheap sensationalism or entirely ignored;

(*c*) the criminal is often pictured too attractively and as a hero;

(*d*) the crime-fighting agencies, on the other hand, are often shown to be weak, stupid or brutal, although in this respect there have been some improvements of late and in particular the police have been given a fairer chance now to become slightly less unpopular and prove themselves to be less inefficient than before ('Z Cars' and 'Dixon of Dock Green');

(*e*) even so, the final outcome of the crime films is often—though possibly not more often than in real life—too favourable to the criminal; crime still pays too well. Where punishment does follow it is often brutal and not in conformity with modern ideas, but it has to be admitted that the reformative elements in a modern penal system —whatever they may be—are much more difficult to present on the screen than old-fashioned brutality.

Already 20 or 25 years ago it was claimed that the Hollywood gangster film was dead, that the gangster had been replaced by the 'G' man as the hero of the film.[241] In 1947 the American Motion Picture Association decided to prohibit the production and exhibition of films picturing the lives and exploits of notorious underworld figures, 'unless the character shown in the picture is punished for the crimes shown in the film as committed by him'.[242] It may be doubtful how far this ruling has been effective. Moreover, it has been argued that especially younger children are unable to take in the story of a picture as a whole; what impresses and influences them is rather an isolated episode, and if this is bad its effect cannot be eliminated or toned down by a moral outcome artificially tacked on to satisfy the critics.[243] It is of course true that careful distinctions have to be made between the potential effects of a crime picture on younger and on older children, on boys and girls, on stable and on constitutionally unstable persons. But more or less for all of them the following words seem to be true: 'Our social life is . . . full of problems of the most serious and urgent nature, social and personal; why is it necessary that we create artifically nightmares and cruel psychological refinements? Where does this constant drugging lead us? It must naturally make us unfit to master our lives as they are.'[244] However, these are unpopular words.

With the coming of the television age the whole story of the crime film seems to be repeating itself, with the difference of course that children can now watch day after day for hours without having to worry about the entrance money. Research on the subject has already been done and more is on the way.[245] Dr. Hilde Himmelweit, whose Nuffield Foundation study has broken fresh ground, has been reported as stating that psychological tests had shown that scenes of violence on television did no good in spite of the moral which might be intended by the producer and that they did not help young audiences to get rid of violent tendencies; on the other hand, in the absence of control groups it could not be positively said that they did harm. There might, however, be a trigger action on a psychologically disturbed child.[246] Less cautiously, the National Association of Probation Officers criticizes the 'continuous display of violence' which, they believe, tempts 'the less responsible members of society of all ages to follow an easy lead into anti-social behaviour'.[247] The General Secretary of the Council for Children's Welfare stresses that the subject of violence cannot be separated from the general problem of quality and that it is the 'depressing lack of vision' in some television programmes that leads to the introduction of violence 'to give it spice'.[248]

An interesting discussion was carried on in *The Times* of August 1964, under the heading 'Blind Eye on Murder', where watching television was held responsible for the behaviour of a crowd of onlookers watching a murder committed before their eyes without any of them making the slightest attempt to assist the victim. Not without good reason it was contended that the constant watching of scenes of violence makes adults and children indifferent (e.g. *The Times*, 18.8.1964). While television is certainly not solely responsible it bears a great deal of responsibility in such matters. Perhaps more important than such views of laymen, which are all too often cast aside as immaterial, is the fact that professional psychologists seem to be more and more turning away from the soothing theory of catharsis. Professor Franco Ferracuti, in a paper presented to the Forty-first Annual Meeting of the American Orthopsychiatric Association, March 1964, refers to several recent American investigations in which that hypothesis was not confirmed. 'It seems', he writes, 'that portrayed violence is not as innocuous, or even beneficial, as the proponents of the catharsis hypothesis maintained.'[249] All these are under- rather than over-statements of a truly deplorable situation.

Legislative action was taken in 1955 against 'horror comics' to make it an offence to print, publish or sell 'pictorial publications harmful to children and young persons'. Under the Children and Young Persons (Harmful Publications) Act, 1955, the maximum penalty is four months' imprisonment or a fine of £100 or both.

The quite excessive amount of space devoted to crime stories in certain sections of the press and the glamorization of crime which goes with it are too well-known to require any further comments. Clinard, whose book was published as recently as 1957, has still a high opinion of the factual, verifiable manner in which crime reporting is generally done in Britain which he compares favourably with the press of his own country,[250] and for the majority of British newspapers this is true even today. What has recently incensed responsible public opinion more than anything else against the less scrupulous exceptions is the way in which they have handled the Profumo–Ward case in 1963 and its ramifications. In particular the payment of exorbitant sums of money to criminals or other socially not very desirable elements for their 'confessions' or memoirs, an evil practised of course also long before that case, has been one of the most deplorable features of the present scene. Not without justification, Lord Shawcross, while protesting against any form of press censorship, has written:

The subsequent advertisement, photographs and general glamorization of the women involved (without which they would be less likely to reap a rich financial harvest) must cause millions of good and honest, and one may add, often more beautiful young women who daily work for modest wages in our offices, shops and factories to wonder what sort of moral values it is that all this publicity is intended to support.[251]

The criminogenic, as distinct from the moral, effect of all this lowering of values is of course even more difficult to assess, but in the long run it is unlikely to be negligible. With such reflections we are returning to one of the main topics of Chapter 19.

Chapter 24

GROUPS AS FACTORS IN CRIME I
A. PRIMARY GROUPS: FAMILY AND SCHOOL

Introductory Remarks

The social group is one of the most important sociological concepts affecting criminology, but there is no need here to go more fully into the details of its very comprehensive literature.[1] There are many definitions of the group, for example 'a plurality of persons who interact with one another in a given context more than they interact with anyone else'.[2] In Merton's definition (p. 285) this element of the comparative frequency of the interaction is not present. While every individual is born into a group, the number of groups, to which an individual may belong, will differ greatly according to his status and functions in society and also in accordance with his personal inclinations. Groups are not identical with classes, as they may consist of members belonging to very different social classes, but the latter may be regarded as 'quasi-groups' (see above, Chapter 20). Groups are either primary or secondary ones. The former, corresponding to the German *Gemeinschaft*, are small, intimate, face-to-face associations such as the family, the small school class, the small gang, or a small peasant community, whereas secondary groups are larger and more impersonal, such as the nation, the army, church, trade union, large town; it is the German *Gesellschaft*, to use the two terms made famous by the German sociologist Ferdinand Toennies.[3]

In recent years, research on small groups has become highly popular, especially in the U.S.A.,[4] and criminology and penology have benefited from it. In particular the dynamics and problems of the behaviour of inmates of penal and reformatory institutions are now better understood as the result of these researches.[5] It is here that sociometric studies can also be of great value,[6] as can psycho-analytic studies or group psycho-therapy.[7] In the present chapter we shall be concerned with a few of the most important primary groups, notably the family, whereas gangs, though usually also small primary groups, will be dealt with in the following chapter together with secondary groups such as the crowd.

Another distinction frequently made by sociologists is that between in-groups and out-groups, i.e. inside each group there is a feeling of cohesion and of hostility towards non-members and particularly members of other groups, the outsiders, a distinction the utility of which has been questioned by Merton.[8]

A concept closely connected with this and even more popular in modern sociology and so thoroughly dissected that it is in danger of becoming meaningless is the concept of the reference group. Such groups are, as Merton writes,[9] in principle almost innumerable, as not only those groups of which the individual is a member but also those to which he does not belong can serve as 'points of reference for shaping one's attitudes, evaluations and behaviour'. In other words, the existence of groups of any kind will, regardless of the nature of their relationship to the individual, influence his behaviour. It can be argued that there is nothing very new in all this, to which Merton replies that such a negative view ignores 'the *distinctive* ideas in this developing theory' (pp. 282–3). We are inclined to agree with him, hoping that future criminologists will be able to make better use of this concept than has so far been done. According to Sherif[10] the need for it arose from the wish exactly to pinpoint those groups which supply the 'main anchorage for experience and behaviour', a desire no less strong in criminology than in other social sciences.

The existence of a multiplicity of social groups with a corresponding variety of standards of values, attitudes and conduct is of the greatest criminological significance on account of the likelihood of conflicts arising from such a variety. One has to conclude that groups may have a protective, crime-preventing, as well as a crime-producing effect. This will become clearer from the following discussion of the role played by a number of groups. On the whole, primary groups arouse stronger feelings of loyalty than secondary ones, but this is not invariably so as has sometimes been experienced in conflicts between the family and the state or the church.

I. THE FAMILY[11]

The family has been called many things by many people: a 'transmission belt for the diffusion of cultural standards to the oncoming generation' (Merton), the 'psychological agent of society' (Fromm), the 'shock-absorber of society' (Aichhorn), thus mainly stressing its valuable, constructive qualities.[12] The criminologist, while fully aware of the latter, has also to take account of certain less desirable elements of family life.

In common with other observers he will be aware of the dangers easily created, for example, by the sometimes extreme and one-sided solicitude of parents for their offspring at the expense of the interests of society at large. In such cases, offences against the latter are regarded as justifiable if committed for the sake of the family, just as international crimes are glorified if they seem to be required for the benefit of one's own nation. For too many people, charity not only begins, it also ends at home. The consequence is that conflicting views have emerged, depending on whether the main emphasis is on the constructive or on the destructive side of the subject. Such differences of emphasis cannot, however, detract from the overwhelming importance of the family as a unique force in the life of the individual, potentially determining the course of his whole life for good or evil.

As pointed out above, in spite of the considerable progress made in recent years in reaching a closer understanding between the psychological and sociological ways of approaching family problems, an unresolved residue will inevitably remain, the psychologist being inclined to place the emphasis mainly on the static and immutable nature of family life and the sociologist stressing rather its dynamic, changing aspects.

Moreover, even apart from such basic differences in approach, it is clear that the family does not play the same role in different types of cultures, periods or social classes. Family structures and situations which produce conflicts in one cultural setting may not do so in another. Even in our western civilization of today illegitimate birth is no longer as stigmatizing as it used to be a hundred or fifty years ago, and in the West Indies it has apparently never been regarded as a misfortune. 'The prevailing type of West Indian family', writes Simey, who has made a first-hand study of the subject, 'is very loose in organization. It is rarely founded on the ceremony of marriage . . . illegitimacy rates vary from 60–75 per cent of total births', but this is to some extent counterbalanced by the institution of 'faithful concubinage'.[13]

Anthropologists have collected masses of material to demonstrate the differences in family structure and relations existing in various parts of the globe, and as one of them has said, they have occasionally 'tended to overemphasize the differences at the expense of the similarities'.[14] Granting this tendency, it cannot be denied, however, that the variations may often be very striking at one time or another, even in European societies. One has only to refer to the many changes in the Soviet Russian attitude towards the family or to the attempts of the Nazi regime to subordinate the family and its values unconditionally to the demands of the totalitarian state.[15] The Hindu 'joint-family' is one of the most striking examples of a family organization fundamentally different from the European family structure,[16] and the case of Khuman Singh, the Indian fratricide, shows how its peculiar features can occasionally play their part in the interpretation of crime.[17]

For the normal family in a normal democratic western society it is true to say that the child learns to behave socially not so much out of respect for the abstract, at best only theoretically understood, state code of conduct, but out of love for his parents, and if this latter incentive should not prove strong enough the other is almost certain to break down.[18] Therefore, according to this view the whole, slow and often painful, process of the child's socialization depends on his early relationship to his parents. In an American investigation of the 'correlation between the moral judgments of children and their associates' it was found that these judgments were derived from those of the parents far more than from anybody else.[19] The absorbing interest in family matters, natural in children, whether it indicates dependence, loyalty, acceptance or criticism and antagonism, is very often carried over into adolescence, though with growing age feelings are bound to become more strained and complex,[20] until in middle age they tend to be more detached. The dominant place held by the family in working-class life has been described in many books; its core 'is embodied in the idea of, first, the family and, second, the neighbourhood'.[21] While the social training of the child begins within the family it is dangerous to limit it to the narrow family circle for too long instead of allowing the child to try himself and the code of values implanted by his parents in the life of wider and more diversified groups.[22] The 'peer-group' in particular is, and should be, a powerful competitor to the family. Even so, however, it is often striking to observe how, especially in the case of delinquents, right up to adult life their whole being is, for good or ill, centred round the family. When talking to boys in Approved Schools and Borstals the present writer was often struck by their excessive and almost exclusive interest in matters concerning their families, and similar observations were made by Kate Friedlander,[23] Stott,[24] and others.

In the following a survey will be made of the principal facets of family life and structure which have been regarded as potentially criminogenic. It has become customary to distinguish criminogenic factors present in families which are structurally normal from those present in families whose structure deviates from the norm.

While accepting this distinction we have to make it clear that our growing awareness of the preponderance of psychological over purely structural, i.e. basically external, factors is increasingly leading to a state of affairs where this latter category becomes rather empty and meaningless.

1. *Structurally Normal Families*

Here both parents are alive and live together with their offspring. Difficulties potentially leading to delinquency may here arise from faults in the roles played by the individual members of the family, from the nature of their relations to one another, and from the size of the family. Barbara Wootton, in her examination of what she calls 'twelve criminological hypotheses',[25] deals with a few of these factors in her analysis of twenty-one studies spread over a period of forty years. One of these twelve factors is:

(a) *The Size of the Family*. Here Wootton finds that, in spite of a certain vagueness in the definitions of 'size' used in these investigations—does it include only those children who are still alive? does it exclude half- or step-siblings? and so on—the total picture shows fairly clearly that the delinquents come from larger families than the non-delinquents. Information on the latter has usually been derived from matched control groups. There is no need to go into details, especially as the same result has throughout been reached in studies not mentioned by Wootton, whether they refer to English or foreign, old or recent material.[26] More difficult, however, than to establish the facts is to interpret their meaning. First, could we simply dismiss those findings on the ground that as most delinquents come from the lowest and poorest classes of the population who are also known to have the largest families we have merely been repeating what had already been established before? This way of reasoning would indeed be justified with regard to studies using no control groups or control groups not matched for social class and economic conditions, but it is not justified for studies with properly matched controls. If the control cases come from such groups the large family may represent an additional criminogenic element, and it will have to be considered in particular in connection with the overcrowding factor with which it is closely associated. The same may apply to the intelligence factor, although the evidence is not particularly strong. The *Report on Sterilisation* of 1934,[27] for example, reproduced some figures showing slightly larger numbers of children in families with one or more mentally defective children than in families of normal children, but concluded that 'the supposed abnormal fertility of defectives is, in our view, largely mythical.' Cyril Burt, whose material dated from the years immediately after the First World War, found that 'children from the poorest social classes not only have an intelligence that is nearly two years below that of the children from the better social classes, but are drawn from families that are nearly twice as large'.[28] But he thought that with improved living conditions this difference would grow smaller; how far this has actually materialized we do not know. What could, however, be maintained with some justification is that parents of low mental capacity are intellectually and emotionally less able to provide all the care and affection, material resources and discipline needed for more than a limited number of children. Even normal families living near the poverty line will often be defeated by an over-large offspring, and children's allowances are usually far too small to restore the balance.

Characteristic is this sentence in a probation officer's report: 'The parents—decent enough in a way—seem bewildered at the fact that there are seven children and spend their energies wondering what to do instead of doing it', or the following written by a Borstal medical officer: 'Parents are apparently too much occupied with reproduction to give much—if any—attention to moulding and shaping the material they had already produced. The boy had to gain his character in the streets and not in the home.'

On the other hand, it will be comforting to harassed parents of large families to know that according to Durkheim the suicide rate declines as the size of the family increases; therefore, 'it is the worst of investments to substitute wealth for a portion of one's offspring'.[29]

Szabo distinguishes between two types of large families: those which are large because of parental improvidence and others large because birth control is prohibited on religious grounds; only the first category is likely to be criminogenic.[30] This is a distinction which, if placed on a broader than the religious basis, might well be used to deal with the whole subject of family size in a more comprehensive way, to understand that numbers as such mean very little here unless they are symptoms of an attitude to life.

The fact that of a sample of, say, 100 offenders more are likely to come from large families than of a matched control group of 100 non-offenders should not be confused with the obvious fact that in a large family the chances that some of them may be delinquent are higher than in a small family.

(b) Sibling Position and Only Children. Delinquent Sibs.[31] Here we are concerned with the question of whether the position which the individual child occupies in the order of sibs, i.e. whether he or she is the oldest or youngest or the second or third born, etc., or the position as an only child may have any significance for his chances of becoming a delinquent. This has attracted some attention from statisticians, social anthropologists, and psychiatrists. Emanuel Miller, who made a survey of the English and American literature up to 1944, concluded that the available information was 'singularly poor and contradictory', and of the many variables involved in juvenile delinquency none seemed to be especially related to the birth order. Nevertheless, there are a few writers, especially Charles Goring, Karl Pearson and the anthropologist M. Fortes, who have claimed that their statistical investigations had shown a definite excess of first-born children in their samples of adult criminals or juvenile delinquents,[32] and according to Goring and Pearson this applied to second-born ones, too. Moreover, a few forms of mental abnormality which could have some bearing on delinquency were thought to be more frequent among children holding a certain rank in the order of birth: mongolism among late and last-born and imbecility among first-born. Alfred Adler, applying his concept of the inferiority complex (see above, Chapter 17), maintained that second-born children always found themselves in a position inferior to their first-born sibs and had to fight for recognition, becoming hostile and aggressive in the process.[33]

Plausible as this is, it would seem to apply not only to second, but to later children as well. Actually too much depends on individual personalities to establish hard-and-fast rules on such matters. The Gluecks maintain, on the strength of their statistical findings, that 'middle' children are more likely to become delinquents if this sibling position occurs in combination with certain traits, for example lack of common sense.[34] Whether this is more than a chance correlation is not yet clear, but generally speaking one has to agree with Murphy and Newcomb that psychological factors are here probably more important than the 'objective fact of ordinal position'.[35] In support of the findings of Goring and Pearson it can also be argued that first-born children are often saddled by their parents with responsibilities far too heavy for their age, which may lead them to delinquent acts.

In the Cambridge-Somerville material analysed by the McCords (Note 11 above) the middle children had the highest percentage convicted of crime (p. 118), which they think is due to the fact that such children arrive at a time when the family's burden is most pressing. This, however, may apply even more to the youngest child. Cyril Burt (p. 95) found only children surprisingly often among his delinquents, but he included in this category children who, while not actually only ones, had been in the same psychological position for several years, i.e. in cases where the age difference between them and their older or younger sibs was unusually large. One of the most recent investigations was carried out by Lees and Newson on two samples of juvenile probationers in the Midlands with, briefly, the following results: relatively more youngest and only children come from disturbed homes; the eldest and only ones were more inclined towards individual delinquencies, the intermediates more towards group delinquencies, as 'drifters'; the eldest and youngest tended more to be serious and recurrent offenders. The explanation given by the authors is that the eldest and only children, having nobody to imitate, learn to face up alone to the adult world and therefore tend to be 'lone wolfs' in their delinquent activities, too.

Occasionally the position of being the only girl in a family of several boys has also been regarded as criminogenic, probably on the ground that such girls may be infected with the delinquency bacillus by their brothers.[36]

Obviously, the characteristics and attitudes of other siblings, while less crucial than those of the parents, can be very influential, and it is here that the presence of other delinquents in the family plays its part. Wootton has examined the material offered on this point by the twenty-one studies selected by her (pp. 87–90). Her conclusion is that 'not infrequently (according to some investigators very frequently) other members of the delinquents' . . . families have also been in trouble with the law' (p. 134). Shaw and McKay (see above, Chapter 23, Note 1) found that while of the boys who had no brothers with official delinquency records 56·5 per cent continued as adults to commit crime, 72 per cent of the boys with delinquent brothers did so (pp. 176–7). And more clearly than in these figures is the criminogenic influence of older brothers on the younger ones demonstrated in Shaw's story of *Brothers in Crime*.[37] On the other hand, according to West, most of the preventive detainees in his sample were the only offenders in their families.[38]

(*c*) *Parental Attitudes*. We are now approaching what are the really crucial points of this discussion. It is here that we can hope to get some satisfactory answers to the age-old question: why is it that of several children of the same parents the one becomes a criminal and the other not? In the present context we are looking for the right answer not in the physiological field, i.e. we take the fact here for granted that even the same couple of parents may be not in exactly the same physiological condition when producing their various children and that important individual differences may result from this. Nobody who looks at families with several children with a critical eye will doubt this. Here we are trying to find the answer in terms of socio-psychological differences in attitudes and responses. Surprisingly, this factor was not included in Lady Wootton's list although several of the studies which she used provided information on it. The following survey, too, does not pretend to cover the whole or even most of the available material—repetitions and platitudes have been all too prominent in the literature—but at least some of the more important recent studies will be referred to, a few of them published too late to be available to Wootton: Burt, Healy and Bronner, Carr-Saunders *et al.* (*Young Offenders*), Stott, Andry, Glueck, McCord. No point-by-point analysis of these studies and comparison of their results will here be attempted; this would be largely futile because of the great differences in case material, approach, and techniques— differences only to be expected from studies scattered over a period of close to forty years. What they all have in common is that they stress the crucial significance of parental attitudes, affection and discipline. Cyril Burt finds defective discipline, defined as too strict, too lenient, or virtually non-existent, five times as often with his delinquents as with his non-delinquents, a coefficient of association as high as 0·55.[39] Less striking, but still highly significant are the differences given in *Young Offenders* (p. 67), where the percentages of London parents whose attitudes to the child could be regarded as normal were found to be 83·7 for the controls and 54·6 for the delinquents. Particular emphasis is placed on this subject of discipline by the Gluecks and the McCords. In their previous study *Unraveling Juvenile Delinquency* the former had found the usual striking contrast in matters of parental discipline[40] in favour of the non-delinquents. In their more recent *Family Environment* this has been taken a few steps further. It is one of the primary objects of that study to see how a given social factor influences boys possessing different traits. Consequently, matters of discipline are now no longer treated in isolation, but correlated to certain features in the boy's personality to ascertain the effect of certain kinds of discipline on certain personality types. It is in fact no longer a single tune, discipline, that is played in splendid isolation by a solo violin; a whole orchestra is let loose with a long succession of variations on that apparently so simple theme. Is faulty discipline, these authors ask, 'a direct influence on delinquency, or does it operate, in part at least, through the development in a child of certain traits which are, in turn, more characteristic of delinquents than of non-delinquents?' (p. 133). As throughout the volume, the answers are only tentative, but even so they have their value in helping to produce pictures of various personality types in which faulty parental discipline plays its part in a highly selective manner. Making use of the correlations presented in their Appendices they assert, for example, that overstrictness on the part of the mother makes for the development of hostility, whereas her permissiveness contributes to the child's feeling of isolation and resentment, and erratic discipline is associated with such traits as impracticality and lack of conscientiousness—all of them traits already found to be more frequent in delinquents than non-delinquents. Similarly, correlations are believed to exist between defective discipline on the part of the father and other traits previously found to be characteristic of delinquents. Some of these correlations may be said to be borne out by common sense, others not; for example why should a permissive discipline contribute to a child's feeling of isolation and resentment? Perhaps because certain children require firm handling and may feel that they do not receive their due without it?

Parental discipline is also treated very fully in the McCord follow-up analysis of the Cambridge-Somerville case material. These authors try to work out a typology consisting of six types of discipline: love-oriented, punitive, lax as the three main categories, with three combinations of erratic discipline, i.e. love-oriented and lax (A), love-oriented, lax and punitive (B), punitive and lax (C). It was found that children whose discipline had been consistent, whether love-oriented or punitive, or even a mixture of love-oriented and lax methods, had a significantly lower rate of subsequent sentences to penal institutions than the others (p. 77). There was, surprisingly perhaps, no evidence that consistently punitive discipline was a criminogenic factor; on the contrary. Consistency was more important than the choice between punitive and love-oriented methods. Notwithstanding such occasional observations, however, it is generally agreed that wrong methods of punishing used by parents, especially arbitrary or excessive punishment, or punishment meted out without an explanation which the child can understand, will make it bitter and resentful and prepare the ground for delinquency as an act of revenge.

Further material on the subject of inconsistent discipline is given by Kate Friedlander, who states: 'I have never found the same degree of inconsistency in the handling of primitive instinctive drives in the history of neurotic patients as I invariably find in the histories of delinquents.'[41]

This whole matter of parental discipline has, of course, to be seen against the background of country, social class, and the period of time we have in mind. Scores of psychologists and sociologists have stressed the fundamental differences existing between the different social classes in techniques of child rearing and disciplining, with higher-class parents preferring the technique of withdrawal of love, lower-class parents that of physical threats and penalties.[42] There are, however, similar differences between countries and periods, although in the course of the present century a general trend can be observed towards more lenient, indirect and subtle techniques. Was it not the twentieth century that started in the grand manner as the *Jahrhundert des Kindes*, the century of the child? Much has been accomplished under this slogan, but its beneficial results have been at least equalled by the mistakes and exaggerations which it has produced. Not least among them is the senseless spoiling of children, which parents usually excuse by explaining that since they had been so badly treated by their own parents they want their offspring to have a happier childhood; moreover, as they will anyhow, sooner or later, be the victims of a nuclear war or another world catastrophe why not have a good

615

time at least as long as the going is good? This attitude of mind has produced the faulty and inconsistent or completely lacking parental discipline which is by fairly common consent one of the root causes of juvenile and adolescent delinquency. 'Many children ... have done from childhood *what* they wanted to do *when* they wanted to do it. At times they have been reprimanded or punished for acts which are passed over unnoticed on the next occasion ... One parent may permit what another forbids ...'[43] Coupled with this are our corresponding inconsistencies, our 'sloppiness',[44] in our official dealings with delinquent children and adolescents—this, however, would require another book. According to Sellin, 'in one of the oldest known documents of ancient Egypt an unknown writer complains that the world is "going to the dogs" for children disobey their parents'.[45] What has changed since that complaint was made is that we possess a somewhat clearer understanding now of the factors behind such disobedience.

Consistency of treatment is required not only from both parents towards one individual child, but just as much in their dealings with their whole family. Discrimination against one, preferential treatment of another are, rightly or wrongly, among the most frequent complaints made by juvenile delinquents as well as adult criminals when trying to justify their conduct. Some of these complaints may be irrational, others only too well founded. Healy and Bronner call it 'most enlightening' to observe the great differences shown by the parents of their samples in feelings and behaviour towards different children,[46] and Eissler reports similar acts of injustice.[47] It would indeed be surprising if this feeling of injustice, to which attention has already been drawn in other connections, should fail to be a criminogenic factor in parent-child relations.

There may be cultures where consistency of treatment is not regarded as equally essential as it is in western society. In a thought-provoking, though perhaps not throughout convincing, comparison of adolescent values and behaviour among the Chinese population of Hawaii and those of white 'Chicagoans' the Chicago anthropologist Francis L. K. Hsu points out that the Chinese child has, as a matter of course and apparently without harmful effects, to experience a good deal of inconsistency in his social relationships.[48] This will be so partly because 'Chinese, especially the mothers, are not too concerned about consistency in discipline', and partly because there are always many other relatives present who will interfere with the efforts of the parents. Nor, by the way, do Chinese parents worry too much about frustration or security for their children; questions of 'social and ritual propriety' are much more important. The most striking difference between these Chinese-American adolescents in Hawaii and white American adolescents is, according to Hsu, the absence of rebellion against parental authority. 'The "big fight" with parents is lacking' (p. 43), because with the Chinese their initiation into the wider society has begun much earlier in life and because the parents, notwithstanding their very close relationship to their children, do not wish to retain their power over them for too long. This absence of frustration and rebellion makes for less adolescent crime.

In western society the overprotective and possessive type of mother has been held responsible for certain forms of delinquency. According to the description given by an English psychiatrist, P. D. Scott, the 'spiv' of the early post-war years, whether delinquent or not:

has typically been a timid, well-behaved uncomfortably mother-attached child who then at puberty or soon after begins to become restless, uneasy at home and rebellious and resentful of parental control . . . Typically the father has either been absent (and this I believe is one of the ways in which the influence of wars declares itself . . .) or is frightening, or has been forced into or kept in an inferior, deflated position by his wife . . . The mother, on the other hand . . . is possessive and keeps the child anxiously dependent upon her. . . .[49]

The unwanted child also has its secure place in criminological literature as being a serious risk, be it the accidental offspring of parents who did not want to have any more children or children at all or of parents who wanted a boy instead of a girl or vice versa. This may lead either to complete deprivation of parental love or to the wrong kind of affection and upbringing, if, for example, the mother who had been hoping for a girl treats the boy as if he were a girl and tries to suppress his masculine instincts, thereby unwittingly encouraging homosexual tendencies.[50]

It would be futile to attempt to draw up a list of inimical situations and parental mistakes which, even in structurally normal families, may produce the risk of delinquency; no such list could ever be complete. To the investigator, whether practical social worker or research criminologist, the difficulty of getting at the roots of such family troubles is immense as even in a seriously disturbed family atmosphere most members will usually, at least at the beginning, try to present a common front against the intruder and hide their real problems from him. On the other hand, surprisingly often interviewers of delinquents and their parents, in Britain as well as in the United States, rightly or wrongly believe they have been given a true picture of the family situation.[51] This naturally applies in particular to those who had been in closer touch with the delinquent and his family over a period of time. This difficulty of how to unearth the truth about the family relationships of delinquents has been systematically tackled in R. G. Andry's research incorporated in his *Delinquency and Parental athology*. In his interviews he put the same questions, 'suitably re-phrased', to the boys, delinquents and non-delinquents, and their parents and placed the main emphasis not on the actual facts but on the subjective perceptions of his interviewees of the affective roles played by parents and boys respectively (p. 9). By asking the boys, for example, 'Which parent do you think loves you most—or you feel is a little closer to you?' he found that 69 per cent of the delinquents felt more loved by their mothers than by their fathers, against 14 per cent of the non-delinquents, or that 62 per cent of the delinquents felt that 'the right amount of love was given by both parents', against 93 per cent of the non-delinquents (p. 30). Similarly, there was a far greater tendency among the delinquents than among the non-delinquents to feel parental hostility towards themselves (pp. 34–5). The correspond-ing interviews with the parents showed complete agreement with the assessments given by the boys in 73 per cent of the delinquents and 87 per cent of the non-delinquents (p. 38), which, together with the answers elicited on several similar questions, seemed to indicate that a true picture of the family atmosphere had been produced by these interviews.

The decisive influence of the home atmosphere is perhaps nowhere brought out more strongly than in D. H. Stott's already repeatedly quoted study of 102 Approved School boys. It has often been pointed out that such a sample is bound to contain an exceptionally high pro-portion of children from unhappy homes since this is one of the criteria which determine the juvenile courts to make an Approved School instead of a Probation Order, a factor of which Stott was of course fully aware. In the circumstances, it is hardly surprising that all the five principal sources of 'delinquent breakdown' in Stott's typology, i.e. avoidance excitement, spite and resentment against the parents, the need to test the parents' loyalty, withdrawal reaction, and inferiority compensation, had their roots in a feeling of insecurity, anxiety, fear created by a, to them, intolerable family situation.

2. *Broken Homes*

No other term in the history of criminological thought has been so much overworked (Glover), misused, and discredited as this. For many years universally proclaimed as the most obvious explanation of both juvenile delinquency and adult crime, it is now often regarded as the 'black sheep' in the otherwise respectable family of crimino-logical theories, and most writers shamefacedly turn their backs to it. The reasons for this volte-face are only too clear. Already in 1949 the present writer complained about 'the use of unscientific conceptions, unscientific because much too broad and inadequately subdivided.

Essentially different situations are lumped together without discrimination. One "broken" home is often treated in our statistics exactly like another, regardless of the fact that the break may have been due to death in the one and to desertion in the other case; regardless of the age of the child at the time when the break occurred.'[52] Barbara Wootton, who included the 'broken home' in her list of twelve factors, made a careful survey of the methods used and the results obtained in the twenty-one investigations on which her analysis was based and concluded that the material was 'quite exceptionally difficult to sort out'.[53] In our present survey the term will be used to refer to external breaks only, to the exclusion of homes which, though structurally intact, suffer from a bad psychological atmosphere and whose problems have been discussed under 1. However, even within such limits it is essential for a meaningful analysis of the significance of such external breaks that investigators should carefully distinguish, and make their system of classification clear, between the various types of break, such as death, desertion, separation, divorce, prolonged absence of one parent, etc., with the possible addition of step-parents and step-sibs.[54] Illegitimate children, who have not been subsequently legitimated in accordance with the Legitimacy Acts, 1926 and 1959, and whose home has never been structurally complete, have also to be included. Clearly, the social and psychological problems may be very different for each of these categories of 'broken homes'. A home broken by death of one parent may be far more harmonious than one that is broken by divorce or separation or one that is complete but torn by violent quarrels.

There would be little point in reproducing the comprehensive statistical material collected by large numbers of investigators in many countries on the incidence of the various kinds of broken homes among delinquents. As Wootton, whose analysis covers only a very small section of this material, has shown, they are hardly comparable, and many of them suffer from vagueness of definitions and weaknesses of execution. They all agree that a high proportion of delinquents, on an average perhaps one-third, come from broken homes. Very few of the writers, however, present any control group material to show the difference in this respect between delinquents and non-delinquents. Exceptions are, the Gluecks (whose figures show no striking contrasts),[55] Carr-Saunders *et al.* where the contrasts are slightly more pronounced (e.g. in 33 per cent of the delinquents against 20 per cent of the non-delinquents the parents were living apart),[56] and the Borstal Prediction Study. In the latter a comparison was made not between the Borstal boys and a matched sample of non-delinquents, but between the former and the general population, with the result that in the Borstal sample the 'normal' home, i.e. mother, father and siblings, accounted for 45 per cent, in the general population for 62 per cent.[57] It is interesting to remember in this connection that for a period approximately sixty years earlier the Rev. W. D. Morrison had quoted the figure of 51 per cent of the Industrial Schools population as coming from a broken home.[58] For Germany Exner mentions an estimate of 62 per cent of wayward youngsters in a sample of 2,000 as coming from incomplete homes (in 1934) against 31 per cent in the general population, a difference significantly greater than the English.[59] For post-war France, Szabo found one of the highest coefficients of correlation, i.e. 0·63, between criminality and divorce.[60]

Step-parents are in a difficult position generally and they have their niche in the criminological literature, too; not because they are all bad—many of them are kind and try conscientiously to replace the missing parent. But they have to fight against a natural prejudice and the traditional reputation of the wicked step-mother, and the bringing together of two or even three categories of children into one home often makes it impossible for them to distribute love and justice impartially.[61] Sexual offences committed by step-fathers against their step-daughters are not rare; there is here hardly the same psychological incest barrier which, though often enough ineffectively, exists towards own children; moreover, the age difference may be smaller than in the real father-daughter relationship. Clifford Shaw's 'Jack Roller' described himself as the victim of a bad step-mother. What C. G. Jung writes about foster-parents also applies to step-parents: 'Many children can adapt themselves to foster-parents, but not all; and those who cannot develop a most self-centred and ruthlessly egotistical attitude, with the unconscious purpose of getting some sort of satisfaction through themselves in place of that which real parents might have given them.'[62]

An extreme case, where a young man of 22 was charged with the murder of his step-mother by strangulation, came before the Central Criminal Court in London in 1937. In his statement to the police the accused maintained that 'trouble began as soon as the step-brother was born'; his own brother and sister left home because they could not get on with his step-mother, and the father agreed with counsel for the defence that 'on the whole the accused had had a rather unhappy life and did not get on very well with his step-mother' (*The Times*, 30.4.1937). The step-mother's story was not available.

For the past twenty years, ever since the first publication of John Bowlby's remarkable study *Forty-four Juvenile Thieves*, the issue of *maternal deprivation* in the sense of prolonged physical separation of a child from his mother during the first five years of life has been in the foreground of interest among criminologists, child psychologists and psychiatrists, and social workers of all shades.[63] It probably owed its origin to the psycho-social climate of the Second World War with its large-scale evacuations and prolonged separations of young children from their parents. According to Bowlby, his co-workers and other followers, such prolonged separation from the mother or mother substitute 'stands foremost among the causes of delinquent character development'. In his typological analysis of the forty-four delinquent children from a Child Guidance Clinic, compared with a non-delinquent group of the same size, also from a Child Guidance Clinic, Bowlby found that seventeen had suffered such separation against only two of the controls. Moreover, of the psychologically most remarkable sub-group of fourteen young thieves whom he labelled 'affectionless characters' twelve had been separated against only five in the remaining group of thirty, and these twelve children were 'significantly more delinquent than the other thieves', in that they included more than half of all the more serious and chronic offenders of the group. These 'affectionless' children showed no feelings towards other people and defied any efforts to treat them. From all this Bowlby concluded that separation of the kind described was one of the most important causes of serious and persistent criminal tendencies. Bowlby's thesis has been not merely of great theoretical interest; its practical impact on the whole social philosophy of the treatment and prevention of juvenile delinquency has been even more profound. If prolonged separation could have such unfortunate results, clearly it had to be avoided at almost any price, and the slogan had to be: 'The worst home is better than the best institution.' As far as this tendency has induced juvenile courts and others responsible for the sending of children away from their homes to think at least twice before taking this fateful decision the work of Bowlby and his associates has been most valuable, but where his ideas have been mis-used for futile attempts to keep children in intolerable family situations beyond breaking point it has been harmful. Which of these two alternatives has been more frequently applied cannot be said.

In the intervening twenty years Bowlby's work, though still widely and rightly admired, has met with increasingly strong criticism. Barbara Wootton has attacked its logical foundations[64] and maintained that what remains as the result of his work is nothing but the obvious truth that children 'need to be dependably loved'. R. G. Andry has, first, vigorously and successfully protested against the one-sided emphasis on separation from the mother and re-established the position of the father as an equally important figure. Secondly, he stresses the need to distinguish between the various possible types of separation: (*a*) psychological without physical—a possibility which

621

can be ignored in the present context, (b) psychological as a concomitant of physical separation, (c) physical without concomitant
psychological separation (p. 100). He then goes on to study the incidence of physical separation with special reference to some of the
criteria used by Bowlby, for example age of the child when separation
occurred, its length and frequency, with the result that the findings
neither validated nor invalidated the Bowlby theory (p. 113).[65]
Another attempt to validate or disprove the theory was made by the
Norwegian psychologist Siri Naess in two consecutive pieces of research,[66] also with inconclusive results, although the latter were more
favourable to Bowlby in the second than in the first investigation.
Naess sums up that mother-child separation as such is only a 'minor
criminogenetic factor which has to be conceived as part of the picture
of an unstable family life'. Similarly, Mary D. Ainsworth, in a very
detailed review of the whole literature on the effects of maternal
deprivation, not restricted to its delinquency aspects,[67] can say nothing more but that the matter 'remains problematic' and that it should
be seen in relation to some 'special form of distortion in early parent-
child relations'. In short, it has been demoted from one of the all-
important to one among many contributory factors.

One of the most recent studies has been made by Field[68] who,
applying a rather unusual criterion, obtained results incompatible
with Bowlby's theory.

There is one specific aspect of family life that has increasingly been
blamed for juvenile delinquency in recent years, absence of the
mother from home to work in factories, offices, or shops. Below in
Chapter 26, p. 705, figures are given to show the great war-time and
post-war increase in female employment, and there has been abundant
speculation on its responsibility for delinquency. The Gluecks have
tried to replace mere speculation by statistical evidence, especially by
correlating the factor 'housewife regularly or occasionally employed'
to a number of factors concerning the boys on whom information
had been previously collected in Unraveling Juvenile Delinquency.[69]
Factors such as 'deep-seated hostility' or 'emotional conflict' were in
this way correlated to the 'working mother' factor. The conclusion is
that especially the factor of the mother's irregular, sporadic work
outside the home had a deleterious influence on family life and was
contributing to delinquency, This finding was, however, regarded as
merely tentative, and at the same time the Glueck research makes it
clear that this factor is only one among many. One has only to ask
whether mothers may not occasionally go out to work because of
their own psychological instability and irritability or of a similar lack
of emotional balance on the part of their husbands. In such cases,
their temporary absence may rather be an advantage to the home.

Moreover, as Mays has recently stressed,[70] since the economy of many countries could not be maintained at its present level of affluence it is futile to complain about the criminogenic effects of female labour.

In particular: Illegitimacy and Delinquency

Bertrand Russell once maintained that illegitimate birth was an advantage in stirring the child to quite exceptional efforts to compensate for the blot.[71] This may happen in a minority of cases, but for the majority the outcome is more likely to be the opposite. Cyril Burt's story of 'Jerry', with which he opens his book,[72] is far more representative, or at least it was so forty years ago. In the meantime, with our changing views on many sexual matters and with new legislation[73]— the Legitimacy Acts of 1926 and 1959, which introduced the possibility of legitimation of children through subsequent marriage of the parents[74]—the stigma and other social, economic, and psychological handicaps of illegitimate birth have been lessened, but certainly not eliminated. A former Metropolitan Magistrate of great experience, Claud Mullins, writing in 1945, more than twenty years after Burt and, therefore, giving a more up-to-date assessment of the situation, concluded in his realistic and well-informed survey of the matter as he had seen it in court that 'all is far from being well with illegitimate children, and unfortunately public opinion is not alive to the fact'.[75] Besides many other important points, he regards illegitimate pregnancy or birth as a frequent cause of offences on the part of the mother: concealment of birth, abandonment or even murder or infanticide, abortion, and prostitution offences (pp. 121–2).

The statistical assessment of the frequency of crime among illegitimate as compared with other children is difficult. The matter can, as so often, be tackled from either of both ends: First, we can examine the incidence of crime in a group of illegitimate and a matched control group of legitimate children. Or, secondly, we can study the incidence of illegitimacy in a group of delinquents against its incidence in a matched control group of non-delinquents or in the general population. The second method has been more frequently used than the first. It is fairly reliable if the control group is well matched; where this is not the case and, in particular, where the comparison is made with the incidence of illegitimacy in the general population, the results will be unreliable since the incidence of illegitimacy in the general population is not known. We know only the frequency of illegitimate births, but on account of the higher mortality rate of the latter[76] we cannot say how many illegitimate children of a certain age are still alive in the general population at any given time.

623

The statistical material available shows throughout a preponderance of illegitimates in the delinquent as against the control groups,[77] or against the general population.[78] More impressive still are the case histories, of which that of 'Jerry' is probably the best known.[79] The absence of a father figure, with which the boy could identify himself, the resulting sense of insecurity and inferiority, coupled with hostility towards the mother, are very prominent features in many of these cases, which often defy the devoted efforts of probation officers.

3. *Social Problem Families*[80]

Much has been written in recent years about a special category of families which, for want of a better name, are called 'Problem Families'. The definition of this term is difficult. Most writers are content to include all families showing features generally regarded as undesirable from the point of view of an ordered society and belonging to its lowest strata: low intelligence, immaturity, self-centredness, poor health, very low and irregular incomes, bad and overcrowded housing; inability to look after their children, of whom there are usually far too many, and to spend their money wisely; drink, and so on. It is also agreed that very few such families possess all these characteristics, but most possess a fair collection of them. Occasionally another feature, almost inevitably arising from the usual ones, is added: making constant demands on the social agencies without profiting from the help given by them.[81] Similar is Wootton's definition as a family 'whose consumption of social workers' time greatly exceeds the average of the local community'. The question which is of a special interest to us is whether it has been proved that these families are a serious source of crime and juvenile delinquency. Wootton thinks this is not the case, but her own references cast at least some doubts on this conclusion (p. 58). The Cardiff study by Harriett Wilson, for example, which is one of the comparatively few criminological investigations of the matter, shows that the 52 problem families examined had a delinquency rate eight times as high as the general rate for Cardiff and well over twice as high as the rate for non-problem families living in the closest vicinity to them. Moreover, the problem families living in low-delinquency areas of Cardiff showed a delinquency rate similar to that of those residing in high-delinquency areas. From this, Wilson concludes that 'juvenile delinquency is home-centred and not area-centred', which, considering the small number of her cases, may seem to be somewhat too sweeping. Why not admit that juvenile delinquency is often home- *and* area-centred, although the bad influence of the area may be more easily offset by a good home than vice versa? What might possibly be conceded to

Wootton is that the worst types of problem families do not very often produce the most serious types of criminals.

After this section had been written a *Review and Annotated Bibliography* on the 'Multi-Problem Family' was published in Canada. Apart from a detailed Bibliography its most important contribution to the subject is an article by John C. Spencer who, in an international historical survey, stresses that the 'multi-problem family' becomes more noticeable as the general standard of the community concerned rises. He summarizes the various typologies employed in the definition and the most important experiments in treatment and prevention.[82]

A particularly perceptive analysis of the family problems of two groups of young inmates of two Belgian correctional institutions, one prison and one reformatory, has been given by Christian Debuyst in his *Criminels et valeurs vécues*, soon to be available in an Engiish translation.[83]

Looking back at the total picture of the family as a criminogenic factor our impression (see above, Chapter 22, 2(*c*)) seems to have been confirmed that the strength of those 'intergenerational' tensions, while still a serious source of adolescent delinquency, is gradually weakening because of the slow retreat on the part of the parents. On the other hand, class conflicts in the broadest sense of the word are, in spite of the changing pattern of our class structure, if anything becoming more tense. However, for the time being this has to remain mere conjecture.

4. *The Criminological Significance of Marriage*[84]

The criminological role of the family has to be considered not merely, as so far done in this chapter, in relation to the children, but also with regard to the adult persons concerned. Two inter-related questions arise: first, is marital status as such a crime-preventing or a crime-promoting factor in adult life, and, secondly, is there a difference in this respect between men and women?

Statistical material on the subject is provided in the volumes of official criminal statistics of many countries, not however in those of Britain. It is not easy to obtain reliable information of this kind without probing deeply into the family affairs of offenders, many of whom are inclined to give a wrong picture of their marital status, to pretend to be married when they are only co-habiting, to suppress information on desertion or separation, or illegitimacy, and so on. Characteristic in this respect is the experience of T. and P. Morris in their census of the Pentonville population (p. 68). Without thorough social case studies such official statistics may be valueless. Moreover, even as far as their facts may be reliable, statistical investigations into marital status are misleading unless careful distinctions are made according to age groups and the various possible types of marital relationships. Single persons have to be distinguished not only from married but also from divorced or widowed ones, separately for each sex. In the past, many investigators have failed to do so, with unfortunate results. If, for example, no distinctions are made according to age, the obvious fact that the most criminal age groups among adult males, i.e. those of 17–21, include a larger proportion of single individuals than older male age groups is ignored and the conclusion is easily drawn that single males are throughout more criminal than married ones, whereas the figures may merely prove that there are age differences in criminal propensities which may have but little to do with marriage. The beginnings of more careful classifications in researches on the subject are usually dated back to the work of the German medical statistician F. Prinzing, whose various papers on this and allied matters were published around 1900.[85] His and several subsequent investigations present roughly the following picture: for men up to the age of 25 the criminality rates are higher for married than for single ones, whereas the opposite is true for those over 25. This can easily be explained by the probability that for young men marriage often means financial and moral responsibilities with which they cannot well cope, especially as very early marriages are more frequent among the poorer classes.[86] To gain a reliable picture one would have to compare samples of married and unmarried men matched not only for age but also for social and economic class. The other fairly universally accepted fact is that, generally speaking, unmarried women have lower crime rates than married ones in all age groups alike, but for the most serious crimes against the person this is different.[87] If criminality is weighed, not merely counted, married women are therefore in a more favourable position than single ones. Widowed and especially divorced and separated persons have, for obvious reasons, throughout higher crime rates than the others, with differences according to age groups.[88]

Turning now from such large over-all statistical data to a few small groups, we find that unfavourable marital relationships are particularly frequent among criminals, especially persistent offenders, although comparisons with non-criminal groups are usually missing. There are occasional comments on the fortunate, crime-preventing, effect of happy marriages. D. J. West, who recently examined the circumstances of 'habitual prisoners' who were 'intermittent' recidivists, i.e. had gaps of 'at least four years at liberty and free from convictions', as distinguished from those recidivists who had no such gaps, found markedly better marital records among the first of these groups, and he comments: 'marriage or cohabitation played an important part in many genuine gaps, especially in the cases of those prisoners who allowed their women to assume a motherly, protective role....'[89]

Norval Morris, in his analysis of thirty-two preventive detainees and two hundred and seventy other 'confirmed recidivists', described the marital position of the first sample with the words 'It would be hard to find a more lamentable pattern of misdirected sexual energy and marital discord' and that of the second sample as, while not as bad as that of the first, 'an abnormally confused' pattern; the aetiological significance of these disturbed marital relationships, he adds, 'can only be surmised', but many cases were found where, he thinks, the death of a wife or other breaks in the cohesion of the marriage were a precipitating cause of relapse into crime.[90]

The Gluecks, in their follow-up study of *Later Criminal Careers*, had cases in their sample where a happy marriage had facilitated the 'natural process of maturation', but there was also evidence that in some cases, despite a happy marriage, the offender had failed to settle down.[91] Norval Morris draws attention to a number of cases where the prisoners were happily married to women who were active criminals, too, which he regards as evidence of complete 'professionality'; such women are usually perfect prisoner's wives and stick to them through long sentences.[92] A German investigation of the Nazi period found that in a sample of recidivists 45 per cent of their wives had also been convicted, whereas the figure for occasional offenders was only 1·3 per cent. The author regards this as evidence of a 'biological law' of choosing the marriage partner, but another German criminologist, Exner, while admitting the likelihood of a natural selection on such lines, quotes the example of identical twins whose conduct had in some cases been entirely different, depending on the different character of their wives.[93] The choice of the marriage partner can indeed turn out to be just as well a crime-preventing as a crime-promoting factor, and the outcome will depend on chance or personality in the broadest sense rather than on strictly biological affinity. It can here often be observed that the extremes possess a peculiarly attracting force in this respect. Howard Jones has a psychologically interesting chapter on the wives of alcoholics and the contributory part which they may play by, at least subconsciously, encouraging the drinking habits of their husbands.[94] While his observations may not throughout be applicable to the wives of criminals, at least for some such cases they may provide valuable clues.

II. THE SCHOOL AND EDUCATION[95]

In Chapter 20 this subject was dealt with in relation to social mobility; now it has to be seen in a wider setting as a potential factor in juvenile delinquency and adult crime. There are two main aspects of it, both of which have been discussed in the literature for many years: First, the relatively short-term aspect of the delinquent child at school and the role of the latter as a delinquency preventing or provoking agency, with special emphasis on the issue of truancy. Secondly, there is the much wider aspect of education as a continuing and, ideally at least, life-long process and the part which it plays in the anti-social behaviour of adults. It is strictly speaking only the first aspect which can be accommodated under the heading of 'primary group' problems with which the present chapter is concerned—and even here it may be doubtful whether the school is in fact a primary group—but it would in any case be cumbersome to allocate the second aspect, which is so closely related to the first, to a different chapter.

1. *The Short-term Aspect*

Next to the family, the school is the most important social group which the child enters, but unlike the family it is one which invariably makes immediate demands on him. Here the child learns that there is a world in which he can no longer take a privileged position for granted and expect maternal indulgence in case of misbehaviour. Here he may encounter a code of values different and occasionally even diametrically opposed to that of his parents. He observes his mother defending his misdeeds and lying to the teacher about his truancy, instigating or at least condoning his pilfering from outsiders, which is so strongly frowned upon by his teachers. He has to mix with children from other homes, some better and some worse than his own, with a variety of customs and class characteristics, and he may find that in the homes of certain of his new friends he is not welcome. The teacher, too, may prefer other pupils for reasons not yet clear to the child. In short, he receives the first glimpse of a world infinitely more complex and cruel than the one to which he had so far been accustomed. While this applies to the child from a reasonably good home, his fellows from very bad ones, though perhaps vaguely appreciating the better standards met at the school, will often be unable to benefit from them as the contrast with home conditions goes too deep to be overcome unaided. In any case, his ability to adjust himself to the complexity arising from the difference in standards and to get along with other people with different backgrounds will be severely tested. It is this capacity for social adjustment more than his scholastic ability that may be decisive for his behaviour and his attitude towards delinquency. When discussing the impact of the school on delinquency many points besides the mere effect of acquiring, or failing to acquire, knowledge as taught in school should therefore be considered. Only a few of them can here be taken up.

Already in the *Report of the Committee for Investigating the Causes of the Alarming Increase of Juvenile Delinquency in the Metropolis*, published in 1816, the 'want of education' is mentioned as one of the principal causes,[96] and ever since the same view has been taken by a number of official and private publications in various countries, until Lombroso raised some doubts with his view that better education merely meant better equipment for criminal exploits, a view to be dealt with more fully below in Section 2.

The 'uncongenial' school was listed by Cyril Burt in 7 per cent of his delinquent cases against 0·5 of the controls;[97] and he asked why the school was not blamed for a child's delinquency more often than his home. His answer was, first, that the school's material equipment was far superior to that of the average worker's home and, secondly, that there was a popular, in Burt's view mistaken, assumption that the home, not the school, was principally responsible for the child's morality. It should be the duty of the state, he suggested, to supplement through the schools the disciplinary shortcomings of the home (pp. 185–6). In the forty years since Burt expressed this view much has been written for and against, and it would be inappropriate for the present writer who has no intimate knowledge of the modern school system to take sides in the many controversies existing in this field and to pass judgment on the work of the schools in providing social education for citizenship unless he could call to his aid writers better equipped than himself. In one of the best-informed recent books, however, which, though limited to a survey of some working-class districts of Liverpool, provides a well-balanced and sympathetic picture of the whole subject, John B. Mays states that 'the Crown Street schools are failing to fulfil their functions in certain respects and that they are producing many young people who are technically and intellectually ill-equipped to find a satisfactory niche for themselves in the economic and commercial life of the city'.[98] And Professor T. S. Simey, in his Preface to Mays's book, sums up to the effect that 'to some extent, the Crown Street schools are alien institutions in a world which they seek to change. Their task is to redeem the society in which they are placed rather than to perpetuate it', a theme which Mays takes up again in the words: 'in the down-town neighbourhoods, education is increasingly an introduction of an alien culture, and in so far as this is true, a source of potential conflict' (p. 8). He finds hardly any relationship between the cultural contents of the teaching in these schools and the sordid environment in which the children actually have to spend their lives (p. 90).

With regard to delinquency, he stresses the class bias in dealing with delinquent school children (p. 17, fn. 4), but also shows in detail how much the general atmosphere and the behaviour of the children attending schools in this slum district have improved in recent years through the combined efforts of the schools, the police liaison officers and social workers.[99]

Turning now to a few studies comparing the attainment and conduct of delinquent with those of non-delinquent school children, reference may be made to one English and one American investigation. In this country, in *Young Offenders* school conduct and attainment were examined with the result that for both factors, particularly the first, the position was less favourable for the delinquents than for the controls (pp. 85–6). It should be borne in mind, however, that these assessments were made by the teachers, whose views may, unconsciously, have been occasionally influenced by the fact of delinquency which often means annoyance to the teacher and to the school as a whole.[100] On the other hand, one remembers the important part played in the American Cambridge-Somerville Study by the teachers in selecting the 'pre-delinquent' boys and their initial reluctance to 'point a finger at a child and say "This boy will be a criminal"'.[101]

More detailed comparisons were made by the Gluecks in *Unraveling Juvenile Delinquency*,[102] showing a similar inferiority on all points of the delinquents in spite of the fact that the two samples were matched for intelligence. Moreover, in addition to various other differences, there was a striking contrast in the percentages of those who had truanted at one time or another in the course of their schooling (94·8 per cent of the delinquents, 10·8 per cent of the non-delinquents) and of those who expressed a violent dislike of the school (61·5 per cent of the delinquents, 10·3 per cent of the non-delinquents). It might be argued that some of these findings were coloured by the fact that the delinquent boys were taken from a correctional school and that, although much of the comparative material referred to the school careers of the boys before entering that institution, nevertheless at least some of the information, notably the material collected by the research psychiatrist in his interviews with the boys, reflects their views as inmates of a correctional school. It is after all only natural that some of the boys in such a school, even if it is a model of its kind, may become prejudiced in their whole attitude towards schooling and education. However, attitude surveys such as that conducted by Reckless in English institutions show how complex the whole matter is.[103]

For young adults, much material on the educational position and problems of British army offenders sent to one of the Special Training Units is presented in Joseph Trenaman's *Out of Step*.[104] He asks how it was possible for so many of these young soldiers to pass through nine years of schooling without learning the elements of their own language (3 to 5 per cent were 'gross illiterates' and some 10 per cent semi-illiterate), and he regards as the causes dullness and very poor and often illiterate homes and as the main obstacles to education 'the twin feelings of frustration and inadequacy'. In 20 per cent of the cases he regards illiteracy as a possible or probable contributory factor in the men's misconduct (pp. 195, 199).

In the Belgian study by Debuyst (see above, I, 3) of two samples of young prisoners, some of them sent to a *Prison-Centrale* for serious crimes, the others to a *Prison-École* for less serious offences, detailed attention is also paid to their *milieu scholaire*.[105] In the first sample, 23 out of 33 are described as 'maladjusted to school life', and in the second the position was not much different. The author regards as the main cause of this maladjustment the failure to acquire the intellectual equipment needed for a normal participation in the life of the school, a failure not necessarily due to subnormal intelligence, and also the inability to take the normal part in the life of the school community, and to make friends on the basis of the reciprocity of give and take. His observations, similarly to those of Trenaman, show that the educational failure of delinquents is often due not to weaknesses in the school but to the personal, familial and cultural heritage which they take with them when entering school. This does, however, not necessarily absolve the educational system from its co-responsibility in these hard cases. Whether the primary and secondary modern schools in this country are at present in a position effectively to discharge this co-responsibility may appear doubtful from the details given in Mays's Liverpool study and also when we read in the reply given by a head teacher to a questionnaire sent out by the National Union of Teachers: 'We teach in corridors, cupboards, coaches, cloakrooms . . .' or when the general secretary of the N.U.T. states that 21 per cent of the primary schools were overcrowded even according to the low standard of 40 pupils per class laid down by the Ministry of Education. In the secondary modern schools, for which the official maximum was 30, two-thirds of the classes were overcrowded.[106] Surely, very little attention can be given in such conditions to the special intellectual, emotional and moral problems of delinquent or pre-delinquent pupils, and it is unlikely that the schools can act as delinquency preventive agencies in the sense so often envisaged. One of the many preconditions of such preventive work would be the ability to spot likely delinquents at an early stage. Are the schools equipped to do this? From talks which the present writer occasionally had with head teachers of primary schools it appeared that, considering the means at their disposal, they regarded this as entirely impossible.

Certain attempts made in the United States seem to show that in more favourable conditions it can be done. In the Cambridge-Somerville Study predictions of future delinquency of boys of school age were made by specially selected experts as well as by teachers with the result that both predictors 'succeeded above chance in predicting delinquency', but tended to over-predict it, partly because of unforeseeable events (p. 290). There was hardly any difference in the accuracy of the predictions between the two groups. The Gluecks, in their *Unraveling Juvenile Delinquency* (Chapter 20), produced a Prediction Table for children at the point of school entrance, based on social background and character structure, but there was naturally no place in it for predictive material derived from the school, which these children had not yet entered; the authors suggest, however, that in cases where maladjustment shows itself subsequently in school the information gained through the Prediction Table might be used by the education authorities to consider whether the child in question might be a potential delinquent (p. 269). This would, of course, require much better understanding on the part of the average teacher of the potential causes of delinquency than his present training enables him to acquire, but it may be worth while to arrange for some small-scale experiments in selected areas in Britain. As conditions are now the part played by the educational system in the prevention and prediction of delinquency does not do full justice to the possibilities within potential reach of the schools as the agencies through which the whole child population has to pass during some of the most crucial periods of life. In the words of Reckless, the school is 'strategically situated to deal with problem behaviour of youth',[107] but if we should have to accept the highly damning verdict of Clinard the general position in the United States is, in spite of this 'strategic position', very unsatisfactory in this field.[108] Some of the experimental work done in the sphere of prevention by a few selected American schools was impressively presented nearly thirty years ago in a symposium on *Preventing Crime*;[109] it might well be brought up-to-date now to examine the progress made in the meantime. Moreover, a similar symposium on corresponding pioneer work in Britain and other countries would be useful. In the otherwise very informative report written by Middendorff for the Second United Nations Congress of 1960[110] the emphasis is on special institutions for delinquent or maladjusted children, and the same naturally applies to the admirable books published in Britain by A. S. Neill, M. Burn, David Wills and Howard Jones.[111] In the present connection, however, we are rather concerned with the preventive work done, or often not done, in ordinary schools.

Truancy, labelled by William Healy as the 'Kindergarten' of juvenile delinquency, is frequently regarded as the yardstick of the failure on the part of the schools to prevent delinquency or to deal effectively with the actual delinquent. It is not necessarily a very accurate yardstick. First, we have to distinguish between truancy in the narrower sense of staying away from school without parental knowledge or approval and an absence which, though unjustified, occurs with such approval and is covered up by the parents.[112] In the available statistics these two forms of truancy, although basically different in their psychological background, are sometimes confused. Equally confusing are some of the views on the causal relationship between truancy and delinquency, which may in fact involve three different possibilities: (*a*) truancy may lead to delinquency since the truanting child, with idle time on his hands, little or no money and afraid of showing himself at home, has to roam the streets in search of food and entertainment and is likely to get into mischief; (*b*) in the opposite direction, the child who has committed an offence may be afraid of going to school where his misbehaviour may already be known; (*c*) what is probably most important, truancy and delinquency may both be symptoms of some deeper maladjustment which manifests itself in producing behaviour problems at home and in school.

There is a neurotic type of truant with a veritable 'school phobia' who is, however, not likely to become a delinquent,[113] but Stott noted persistent truancy 'as the counterpart in the schoolboy of those symptoms of avoidance in older boys which consist in their inability to tolerate steady activity . . . and their hankering after a change of scene' (p. 48). This seems to be a very apposite parallel and explains many cases of truancy in the younger and delinquency in the older boys. Already before Stott, another writer, Kvaraceus, had described truancy as an 'escape from conflict and failure'; in fact, 34 per cent of his sample had become truant to make an end to an unbearable situation (Note 95 above, p. 144). The administrative procedure available in cases of truancy has been described by Mays for Liverpool (pp. 77–81) and more fully by Croft in a very valuable, but unfortunately unpublished, historical study of the area of the London County Council (L.C.C.), enriched by a small number of characteristic case studies.[114]

2. *The Long-term Aspect*

The second aspect, education as a process continuing into adulthood and influencing, positively or negatively, the whole life of an individual, can here be treated only very briefly under the well-worn formula: Is education likely to prevent or to provoke crime? It was not difficult for Lombroso to take the pessimistic line. There are various types of crime which require a certain degree of general and especially technical education, and the modern criminal has often to be highly expert in his chosen branch if he is to succeed. Complicated financial transactions, ordinary and art forgeries, spying, and most other forms of white collar crime require not only above average intelligence but also specialized knowledge far superior to that of the ordinary law-abiding citizen, or the average house-breaker, pick-pocket, confidence trickster, shoplifter or similar small fry. 'Any police museum is a silent witness to the improvement of criminal technique in the modern world.' [115] The need to protect unsealed private writings by a special criminal statute arose comparatively late as so few people possessed the skill needed for forgeries.[116] Nowadays, much of this skill and knowledge will be acquired by the offender in any case, whether the community likes it or not, but apart from this can one really wish to deprive the great majority of those who might wish to use it for lawful purposes of their opportunities merely to prevent possible misuse on the part of the few? One has only to pose this question to realize its absurdity. It is certainly true and has been stressed over and over again in the present book that ability and education for which there are no legitimate outlets may in suitable cases produce a criminogenic disposition, but the remedy is not to cut off education but to provide the lawful outlets.

It is, of course, very important to distinguish, as many writers have done, between the two kinds of education, the one meaning nothing but the acquisition of—mainly technical—skill needed to practise a profession or occupation, and the other leading to a broad, liberal and sympathetic understanding of the world in which we live. It is not easy, however, to draw the line between these two types; moreover, we cannot even claim that the broadest and most sophisticated kind of education means a completely foolproof insurance against criminal tendencies. Serious crimes have been committed by highly educated persons, and Baschwitz has reminded us that the medieval witch-hunts were mostly arranged by scholars.[117] On the other hand, we cannot reasonably condemn the narrower, purely technical kind of education as potentially criminogenic, realizing that it is given to only very few human beings to achieve the other and that even the propor-tion of those who are capable of becoming 'educated' in the first, narrower, sense of the term is depressingly small. It is pathetic to read the reply of 'Robert Allerton', the intelligent professional criminal, to his interviewer's question whether he had any regrets: there were only two things he regretted in his life story, first, that as a boy he had stolen 2 shillings from his mother who could ill afford the loss, and, secondly, that 'I haven't ever given myself an education'. But, after consideration, he adds: 'Education needs hard work, concentration, determination . . . all the points I'm weakest on . . .',[118] which shows that what he had in mind may have been something more than a narrow technical education merely to enable him to become a more proficient safe-breaker. And if he, a man of obvious ability and fairly wide reading tastes, had such doubts, what can one expect from his weaker brethren? In spite of such handicaps determined efforts are now made by the Prison Administrations of several countries to bring the possibility of a modicum of education, in both senses of the word, to many prisoners and other inmates of penal and correctional institutions.[119] Even if their success as a crime-preventing factor cannot be statistically proved, such efforts are worth while for their own sake. They need not necessarily stand in the way of sterner measures against serious professional and organized criminals (Chapter 25 below).

Chapter 25

GROUPS AS FACTORS IN CRIME II
B. ASSOCIATIONS IN CRIME: OCCASIONAL CO-OPERATION OF A FEW. THE CROWD. ORGANIZED CRIME: ADULT AND ADOLESCENT GANGS. THE VICTIM OF CRIME

I. INTRODUCTORY[1]

The participation of two or more persons in the commission of crime is as old as crime itself. Even if we should not accept Freud's theory of the murder of the primal father by his sons as one of the earliest crimes known to mankind, standing at the beginning of human morality (see above, Chapter 17), such joining of forces for criminal purposes must be of very ancient origin. Cain, it is true, appears as a lonely slayer, but if we regard the killings done in the pursuit of blood vengeance as crimes, we find here an institution which, by imposing on the whole tribe the duty to execute an act of collective blood vengeance, was likely to foster co-operation between individual members of the tribe. In modern society the need for co-operation in crime has other roots. It is the growing complexity of modern life which makes such arrangements essential not only in ordinary business pursuits, but equally in criminal activities which differ from lawful ones mainly in the fact that the latter are permitted and the former proscribed. With only very slight exaggeration we can say that whatever is produced in our society—with the exception of highly individual works of art—is the product of the combined activities of a number of human beings. If in the field of crime this is true only to a somewhat lesser degree the reason for the difference lies in the natural reluctance of offenders to run the risks involved in collaboration; but even so the practical significance of associations in crime is very great and still growing. The subject under discussion in the present chapter has of course to be distinguished from the kindred one where crime is the outcome of the atmosphere prevailing in certain sections or sub-sections of our society without actual collaboration of several of its members. To this latter aspect attention has been drawn above in Chapter 21.

There are many potential shades of criminal association, and various typologies could be produced. It is here proposed to distinguish four principal types: first, two types showing no or only a very loose form of organization and cohesion, i.e. (1) the occasional getting together of a small number of persons for the commission of offences; (2) at the other extreme, the crowd which, though also of an occasional, transitory, character, consists of a large number of individuals; secondly, two types possessing a more or less tight form of organization and cohesion, i.e. (3) the gang, juvenile or adult, and similar forms of organized crime; (4) the corporation which, though usually established with lawful objectives in mind and throughout its existence mainly pursuing such objectives, nevertheless does not refrain from legally proscribed practices if they are deemed necessary in the interest of profit-making. With this last type, which has been dealt with in connection with white collar crime (Chapter 21 above), we are not concerned here.

Comparing our typology of collective behaviour with that used by some present-day sociologists we find that theirs is, quite naturally, much more comprehensive. Smelser, for example, whose valuable monograph contains one of the most recent treatments of the subject (see Note 1), covers the following types: '(1) the panic-response; (2) the craze response . . .; (3) the hostile outburst; (4) the norm-oriented movement, including the social reform movement; (5) the value-oriented movement, including the political and religious revolution . . .' (p. 2). As will be seen at once, this covers criminal and non-criminal forms of collective behaviour alike, and it is difficult to understand why Smelser wishes to exclude the criminal association from his scheme.

Some sociologists are also inclined to exclude the 'small group' from the term 'collective behaviour',[2] and it should be made clear that we also disagree with this view.[3]

II. THE OCCASIONAL CRIMINAL CO-OPERATION OF A SMALL NUMBER OF PERSONS[4]

1. *Legal Points*

This is the most frequent and most natural form of co-operation in crime in both primitive and highly developed societies. It is significant that the criminal law, true to its individualistic character, has devoted most of its energies to the working out of concepts dealing with this form of association, at the expense of the development of provisions designed to cope with those forms where larger numbers of participants are concerned. At the same time, in spite of this abundance of legal sophistry and casuistry, no system of criminal law and jurisprudence has so far succeeded in producing a satisfactory solution of the criminological problems of complicity. Pure legal dogmatism has all too often been the deadly enemy of common sense and criminological experience. Vouin and Léauté[5] call the French theory of complicity archaic, though to some extent modernized by legislation and jurisprudence. In English law, which is hardly more advanced, there are four main degrees of criminal participation in felonies: principal in the first degree, principal in the second degree, accessory before the fact, accessory after the fact. In most other legal systems corresponding classifications can be found. The practical significance of these legal distinctions varies; in some countries it is considerable, which may provoke much legal hair-splitting on the part of the courts and commentators; in other countries the distinctions are of little importance, and a great deal of discretion is left to the courts. The Soviet Penal Code of 1926, § 18, chose the second way, leaving it to the courts to impose penalties on each participant 'with due regard to the extent of his participation in the crime and to the extent of the danger which he or the crime constitutes'. The 'Basic Principles' of 1958[6] add definitions of the various forms of participation which do not fundamentally deviate from the traditional ones, but leave the distinctions regarding penalties again entirely to the courts. And, after all, what else can the legislator do in the face of the endless variety of human entanglements which constitute what we, in grotesque over-simplification, call 'association in crime'?

One has only to read the carefully reasoned analysis of the English law on the subject by Glanville Williams to realize how many dogmatic pitfalls may stand in the way of criminologically acceptable solutions.[7] To give two or three examples, the rule that a person can be guilty of 'aiding and abetting' the actual perpetrator (principal in the first degree) and be punished as a 'principal in the second degree' only if he knowingly assists or encourages at the time of the crime, whether present or not, or if he is present at the time of the crime, whether or not he in fact assists (except by acquiescence), has given rise to very subtle and often unrealistic distinctions as to the meaning of 'presence' and 'time of the crime' (pp. 181–3). Or, 'one who does not counsel any crime does not become guilty as accessory merely because the crime was a probable result of his conduct'; therefore, if 'D sells counterfeit notes to E, and E sells them to F, all three parties knowing they are counterfeit', and F passes the notes, D is not an accessory to the uttering by F (p. 189); nor of course do the producers of a film stimulating the viewers to break the law commit an offence in the absence of criminal intent (p. 188). This leads to the equally vexed question of 'supply of materials and information' (pp. 190–203), where the legitimate, and occasionally even the illegitimate, needs of the trade have enforced a very restrictive application of the criminal law. Glanville Williams suggests the creation of a special statute to punish the suppliers of material who know that it is intended for criminal purposes. Von Hentig, who in several monographs has produced a wealth of case material on various aspects of complicity for the crimes of murder, false pretences, larceny, burglary, robbery, and blackmail (see Note 4), has unceasingly poured scorn on the rigidity and narrowness of the relevant legal provisions and the unreality of their distinctions. Subjective elements play no doubt an important role in determining whether a person is guilty of complicity—'the accessory must intend the crime' (Glanville Williams, p. 188). Nevertheless, the emphasis on subjective elements can be overdone,[8] and Hentig may not be wrong when he tries to show that the rather clumsy ways in which law and courts handle these very subtle subjective factors may do no justice to the essential features of a case.[9] This all the more so as law and courts usually have to concentrate too much on the particular crime which is brought before the court, at the expense of the interpretation of the whole background and the total personalities of those involved and their relationship. Glanville Williams rightly stresses that 'the crime instigated must have an element of particularity' (p. 190), i.e. the instigator must have one particular crime in mind, although he need not know all its details beforehand,[10] but whether this legal restriction can do justice to the psychological impact of the personality of the instigator on that of the actual perpetrator is another question. The need for legal safeguards often clashes with psychological and sociological facts. Occasionally, these legal provisions may lead to absurd decisions, as, for example in the notorious Croydon case of 1952, when two youths, after an act of house-breaking, were chased by the police over a rooftop and one of them shot and killed a policeman. Being only 16 years old, he was sent to prison for an indefinite period. The other, Derek Bentley, aged 19, was sentenced to death and hanged, although he had no gun in his possession, because he had called out to the other 'Let them have it, Chris'. At the time of the killing Bentley had already been under arrest for 15 minutes, and he was regarded as a borderline mental defective.[11]

In the field of criminal procedure, too, the association of several persons can lead to technical difficulties, for example when it has to be decided whether there should be a joint trial for all of them or whether each or some of them should stand trial separately. This is not the place, however, to go into these intricate procedural matters, some of which are closely connected with the special needs of trial by jury.[12]

2. *Criminological Aspects*

The psychological entanglements of personalities which, to the great embarrassment of the law, can so often be found at the root of cases where two or three persons are somehow involved are of course of far greater interest to the criminologist than the legal categories of principal in the first or second degree, or instigator, or accessory before or after the fact. Particularly illuminating is in this respect Sir James Fitzjames Stephens' view referred to by Glanville Williams, that Iago could not have been convicted as 'accessory before the fact' to Desdemona's murder but for his remark: 'Do it not with poison, strangle her in her bed', a view with which Williams does not entirely agree (p. 189). Would the criminologists have shared Stephen's doubt? He would be interested in such chance remarks mainly as far as they reveal the state of mind of the person; he would use them to hang a person only if they are in keeping with the whole role the latter has been playing throughout the various stages of the drama which eventually led to the crime. The psychological guilt of the instigator is often much stronger than that of the actual killer—especially of course in the case where he makes use of a so-called 'innocent agent' (Williams, p. 178, in German law *mittelbarer Täter*). In other cases, however, the opposite is true, and there may be all the difference between one who, perhaps without much thought and in a moment of great emotion, rather carelessly put the idea into the associate's head and the latter who executes the killing in circumstances quite different and far more brutally than envisaged by the instigator. The court may not always be able to give sufficient weight to such differences.

Notwithstanding the infinite variety of possible combinations certain main patterns emerge fairly distinctly. Pinatel, Hentig and Trottier have, each in his own way, successfully attempted to bring something of a system into the seemingly baffling diversity of cases. Pinatel is mainly interested in the *maître-esclave* relationship, where one of the two partners commands and the other obeys, in the *couples amoureux et conjugal*, and in the parent-child relationship. He draws special attention to the attraction which often exists between persons of opposite physical and psychological characteristics—*les extrêmes se touchent*—and the ensuing state of love-hate. The relationship between a couple of lovers may not only lead to crimes against one of them and third persons, husbands, wives, parents, or outsiders, who in whatever form stand in their way (Macbeth!), but also more specifically to abortion and infanticide, with the man here usually acting as instigator. The parent-child relationship is equally replete with criminogenic situations, notably the mother-son relationship as potentially leading to parricide and the father-daughter relationship with its risk of incest. Cases have been reported of mothers inciting their grown-up sons to prolonged incestual relations, in order to prevent them from going to prostitutes.[13] An excellent survey of the various types of incestuous relationships has recently been given by Irving R. Weiner.[14]

In a short but important paper the French-Canadian Michel Trottier (see Note 4) presents three cases of partnership in crime to show that, while the role of each partner in these small groups of two to four people reflects his individual personality, nevertheless the collective decision may differ from that which each member would have taken if he had been acting in isolation; in other words, the group may commit crimes from which each member alone would have refrained. In one of the cases, two latecomers to crime plan a robbery but cannot muster the courage to carry it out until they succeed in finding a third man, a recidivist, under whose direction the crime is jointly completed; the individual consciences are temporarily stifled and supplanted by the criminal super-ego of the habitual criminal. After arrest and punishment, however, the two beginners regain their true personalities and shake off any relationship with the third man. In another case of a group consisting only of two lovers, the man, a frustrated spoilt child, meets a girl with a criminal past who makes excessive financial demands on him which he can satisfy only by crime. Their personalities are similar in that they have been used to exploit others for their selfish purposes, but in their relationship each of them uses the other for different objects, and they are not real partners in crime; the girl exploits the man in the same way as he used to exploit his parents, they 'operate separately but as a function of each other'. Particularly dangerous are such small associations when one of the members is a mentally deranged person. In July 1963 two Liverpool girls, aged 16 and 17, went on a hitch-hiking holiday to the South-West. They were given a lift by three young men passing them in a van who, after a while, drove into a side lane where one of them attacked the girls, killing one of them and severely injuring the other, while another of the men covered the girls and the third man with a gun. The latter, the driver of the van, who unsuccessfully and feebly tried to restrain his companions from assaulting the girls, was discharged.[15] This case is also instructive as showing that in small-size associations individual responsibility can be distinctly assessed for each member. If the principle of English law (s. 1 above) that mere presence plus acquiescence may be sufficient to establish co-responsibility should be taken too literally the driver of the van might have been a principal in the second degree, but as he protested and was himself threatened by the gunman he could be discharged, although without the assistance of his van the crime would probably not have been committed. If the association is very large, as in the case of crowds, such individual assessment of responsibility usually becomes highly superficial.

v. Hentig's writings on the subject, supported by ample case material, have the special merit that, as already mentioned, they are classified according to the various types of crime with which he is concerned: murder; theft, burglary, robbery; false pretences; blackmail. Naturally, the characteristics of the associations described often vary in accordance with those of the crimes; in cases of murder the association is likely to be more emotional than in crimes against property. There is, moreover, the fear aroused by the heavier penalties. Accordingly, the 'battle between the associates', after detection and arrest, their mutual hatreds and incriminations, are usually more bitter and vehement here than those between unsuccessful thieves or swindlers. This is particularly so where two lovers who have jointly killed the wife's husband accuse each other of having been the driving force. Often enough the partner becomes a victim, too, in order to avoid such risks. Family groups, in particular those of brothers, are usually more reliable and stand together right to the end, whereas associations of two lovers are more likely to collapse under the strain of the trial, which may lead to a mental breakdown, confession and attempted suicide of one partner.

There are persons who are destined to be instigators and others destined to be perpetrators; physical and psychological characteristics are here decisive.[16] Usually, the female sex is more suitable for the roles of instigator, for aiding and abetting, the male more for the actual physical execution of the plot as a 'principal in the first degree' (see also below, Chapter 26).[17]

Murder can be, and usually is, committed by one person; the risk of betrayal is too great to make associations here very popular, but for physical or emotional reasons the burden may be too great for one person to bear or the decisive stimulus may have to come from a third person. Criminal statistics give only very rudimentary information on the proportion of 'murder by association'.[18] False pretences, confidence tricks, and the like are probably more often dependent on the carefully planned collaboration of a few tricksters. The prospective victim is more easily reassured and persuaded to part with his, or her, money if the principal actor can, at the critical moment, produce an apparent outsider to confirm his story. Each of the players may have to represent a different type in his external appearance as well as in his specific gifts, educational equipment and manners; each of them in short has to play a different role. If the plot is too complicated and requires more than two or three roles, the organization may exceed the resources and the usual personnel of the small group with which we are at present concerned and may become a 'gang' (s. IV below). In this connection, Hentig refers to the analysis given by Würtenberger[19] of the various forms of collaboration needed by art forgers and the sellers of faked works of art: agents, middlemen, minor painters, occasionally real experts who have become financially all-too dependent on the criminals.

For burglaries v. Hentig thinks that modern techniques of safe-breaking, etc., have reduced the number of persons required for an expert job,[20] and this may be true for the highly skilled men who are real masters of their craft and will limit the number of their associates, if any, to the barest minimum. Amateurs and especially young beginners will be careless in the selection of their helpers and they will also far more easily succumb to the danger of committing an incidental act of homicide whenever meeting an unexpected obstacle. In this way, mere bank hold-ups and similar armed robberies may end in murder trials. The Worthing bank hold-up of 1961 is a case in point,[21] but in the superficially similar case of the armed raid on the Royal Arsenal Co-operative Society at Mitcham, Surrey, in November 1963 a far more experienced adult gang made the same blunder.[22]

In most cases of professional larcenies, burglaries, and robberies, whether committed by small groups or by larger gangs, the relationship between them and the receiver is of crucial importance. Receiving has been made a separate offence in the criminal law,[23] but the legal line between being a receiver and being an accessory to the crime is not always easy to draw.[24] To the criminologist, the receiver, while one of the most important figures in the rogues' gallery, appears to be part of an organized gang rather than of a small group of thieves, but whether he stands behind a large gang or a small, unorganized group, he can hardly ever be regarded as one of its members.

Certain types of blackmail, too, are based on the collaboration of two or three persons. For example there is the typical case of the woman, who leads a wealthy married man into an awkward sexual situation in which they are 'surprised' by somebody posing as her outraged husband who has then to be bought off by interminable payments of money. The same trick can be played against a wealthy lady where the 'wife' of the seducer enters the scene.[25]

III. THE CROWD[26]

1. Definition
The crowd has this in common with the small association dealt with in Section II that its organization, if any, is only rudimentary and that

it usually lasts for a short period only. In fact, continuity is even rarer here than in the case of small associations of two or three who, if successful, may remain together for a whole series of exploits. While this will not happen in cases of murder, burglars, swindlers and blackmailers may, without having any formal organizational links, collaborate for years or return to their old small cliques again and again after serving their prison sentences. Clemmer refers to the 'complete clique man' in and out of prison.[27] In fact, this common habit of the habitual criminal after discharge to rejoin their former associates is generally regarded as one of the major obstacles to reform.

On the other hand, the crowd differs from the small association in that it is far more numerous. Here as throughout in such questions of definition no absolute figures can be quoted to decide the minimum required to make a crowd, but it will probably have to be at least a dozen. This question of numbers, however, is not the only definitional difficulty. Not every agglomeration of considerable numbers of individuals constitutes a crowd; there must, in addition, be an environmental and a mental 'something' which transforms the purely factual agglomeration into a crowd in the psychological sense. This 'something' may be called 'a centre or point of common attention' (Sprott); it may be a sudden happening which attracts the interest of the individuals present. McDougall[28] gives the example of the 'dense gathering of several hundred individuals at the Mansion House crossing at noon of every weekday'; they do not yet form a psychological crowd because they have no common interests to bind them together, however temporarily. But if a fire-engine should come along galloping through the traffic or the Lord Mayor's state coach arrives these happenings produce a common link between those present which transforms them into a psychological crowd. It is this 'something' which produces many of the characteristics which, as will be shown below, may make the crowd potentially dangerous.

2. The Characteristics of the Crowd

It is a matter of great interest to observe that scientific attitudes to the problems of the crowd have, in the past seventy or eighty years, undergone changes similar to those which were described above (Chapter 23) with regard to the film and other media of mass entertainment, with the difference perhaps that the literature on crowds began somewhat earlier than that on films because the latter, for technical reasons, made their appearance at a later stage, whereas there have been crowds already in olden times. However, as the earliest critics of the film were over-inclined to concentrate on its dangers, so we find in the writings of the late nineteenth-century pioneers of crowd research, the Italian Scipio Sighele and the Frenchmen Tarde and Le Bon, a similar over-emphasis on the anti-social tendencies of crowd behaviour. In both cases there is further-more the same undue simplification and an exaggerated belief in the strength of suggestion, hypnosis, and imitation, although it has to be stressed that even those older writers were by no means quite as one-sided in their condemnation of crowd behaviour as is often believed.

The reaction came soon after the First World War. While Freud accepted many of Le Bon's views as supporting his own theory of the unconscious and of identification, most early twentieth-century psychologists and sociologists opposed them very sharply, and it was only natural that in the course of this process occasionally a picture of the crowd emerged which was as over-sympathetic as that of previous writers had been over-critical. It has been the task of present-day social scientists to restore the balance, a task which is still far from being completed.

Which are the main characteristics ascribed to the crowd by Le Bon and his school and of what kind are the main criticisms directed against their theory? Apart from the quantitative aspect and the psychological 'something' which are essential to the definition of the crowd (s. 1 above) these characteristics are according to Le Bon as follows:[29]

(a) Through joining a crowd, the individual members undergo profound psychological and moral changes in their personalities and their ways of thinking, feeling and acting.

(b) These changes involve a wholesale intellectual and moral de-gradation and a loss of previously cherished values. In fact, the in-dividual member suddenly climbs down to the level of the lowest components of the crowd and adopts their ways of thought and feeling.

(c) This leads to a complete loss of the sense of personal respon-sibility for one's own actions and, on the other hand, to the acquisi-tion of an uncritical belief in the invincible power and the justice of the cause of the crowd, coupled with an equally uncritical conviction of the worthlessness of the opposing forces. 'Fifty thousand French-men can't be wrong'—even if they should do the most outrageous things. In a crowd, men are over-credulous, apt to exaggerate, and to believe even the silliest rumours.

(d) There is therefore a feeling of security and a unity of purpose among the crowd to a degree not normally achieved outside a crowd by a number of individuals acting together, and its actions are subject to sudden, illogical and unexpected changes of direction, which make them unpredictable and dangerous.

(e) All this has to be explained as the outcome of the psychological forces of suggestion, contagion, imitation, and hypnosis.

Le Bon went so far as to postulate the existence of the crowd as a separate entity with its own group mind and to formulate his psychological *loi de l'unité mentale des foules* (Part I, Chapter 1), the law of the psychological unity of the crowd.

As already indicated, while the main emphasis of the Le Bon school of thought is on the degrading and criminogenic effects of the crowd, they were also willing to admit its potentially valuable and heroic moral qualities. Le Bon even takes the view that crowds rarely act out of selfish motives and he refers to the Crusades and the enthusiasm and the unselfish deeds of the volunteers in the wars of the French Revolution;[30] it is doubtful, however, whether these are not rather examples of more or less organized groups. Here as in many other ways it becomes clear that Le Bon (1871–1931), who was a medical man by profession, and perhaps also Sighele and Tarde, although no contemporaries of the French Revolution, were still spiritually much under the influence of the events of that period. Among his books was a work on the French Revolution, and again and again he refers to those years to demonstrate the criminogenic characteristics of the crowd, while on the other hand trying to excuse its outrages as manifestations of political and religious fervour.[31] For outrages such as those committed by the French Revolutionaries the actors can, he thinks, be held responsible only in a legal, not however in a psychological sense. He could not foresee that, barely half a century after he wrote this, crimes at least as outrageous but on a vastly larger scale were committed by men who could be, and were actually, held responsible in every sense of the word.

There is a fair amount of agreement that, whatever psychological effects membership of a crowd may have, they will differ according to national temperament and political conditions. As a rule, a crowd will behave differently in southern Mediterranean and in northern countries, in a country with a long-established democratic tradition and in one ruled by a rigid totalitarian regime. 'Even in civilized countries a crowd can become dangerous and uncontrollable', wrote Herbert Agar in a little wartime book which is still worth reading,[32] but once the tumult is over those who were in the crowd usually return to their normal peaceful occupations. 'In a tyrant state, however, *the crowd never breaks up*. It has no groups to return to, nothing to re-introduce sanity and order and discipline into its over-excited mind.' Or, as Drucker expresses it, in a totalitarian state the members of the crowd 'must convince themselves collectively that theirs is the right society',[33] and this has to be achieved through ever-increasing violence and brutality against outsiders.

There are still occasional voices reminiscent of the Le Bon doctrine,[34] but they are becoming rarer and less extreme under the impact of the criticisms directed against it. What are the main arguments of the critics? Let us make it clear at once that, except for Le Bon's now universally rejected concept of the group mind, most of the differences between the Le Bon school and their modern opponents are of degree only. There is hardly any quarrel with the view that human beings in a crowd are likely to behave differently from the way they would behave in isolation. This is in no way limited to crowds whose actions result in criminal outrages; it is also true of crowds in a state of panic injuring only their own members. To illustrate this two examples taken from the English war and post-war years may suffice: the events at a London tube station shelter on the 3rd March 1943, where 173 persons were crushed to death and nearly a hundred injured, and the happenings at the Bolton Wanderers' football ground on the 9th March 1946, when 33 persons died and hundreds were injured, 'the first example in the history of football of serious casualties inflicted by a crowd upon itself'.[35]

However, whereas according to Le Bon the individual by joining a crowd underwent a process of wholesale degradation, suddenly tumbling down the whole of the moral and intellectual ladder on which he stands, we nowadays believe that he falls no more than a mere one or two rungs. Whereas to Le Bon individual differences between crowd members hardly mattered, their importance is now duly emphasized, and it is also admitted that there are people who are altogether immune from the impact of the crowd.[36] Even among the others the feeling of personal responsibility is not entirely stifled as soon as they enter the crowd, except perhaps for those few hardboiled evil-doers who exploit the chaotic situation created by it for their own sinister purposes; they, however, do not really belong to the crowd although they move in the midst of it.[37]

Other critics have pointed out that Le Bon apparently took it for granted that the individual, left to himself, was good and reasonable and incapable of crimes as revolting as those sometimes committed by crowds—an assumption which the history of crime has shown to be wrong. 'One is always inclined to lay the blame on external circumstances, but nothing could explode in us if it had not been there.'[38] Le Bon, it has been said, was so successful because he flattered the individual.[39] In fact, 'the tendency to lose one's head is a normal part of the situation' when people are confronted by immediate danger.[40]

In short, Le Bon's radical, qualitative, distinction between individual and crowd behaviour has been replaced by a purely quantitative one, succinctly expressed in F. H. Allport's formula that the individual in the crowd behaves as he would behave if alone, 'only more so'.[41] Or should we perhaps rather say '*much* more so'? One has only to compare Le Bon's views even in his own special field, the French Revolution, with the work of modern historians such as Rudé and others to appreciate the progress made in these past seventy years from what was after all not much more than a kind of popular, at best semi-scientific, writing to the highly specialized historical and sociological studies of the present time. Nevertheless, Le Bon and Sighele should be given credit for the stimulus and the challenge they have provided to their successors.

Modern social psychologists have tried more objectively to define the various factors required to produce mass violence. Miller and Dollard distinguish three variables: the drive stimulus, which would operate in the individual when alone; the crowd stimulus; and the strength of response under the impact of these two stimuli.[42] Robin M. Williams lists the following conditions as most likely to provoke mass violence, in particular race riots: prolonged frustration causing high tension, the presence of elements anyhow inclined towards violence, marked changes in intergroup relations, and a precipitating incident.[43] The latter may be a gun shot or a blow,[44] but it may also be a rumour that something outrageous had been done by members of the opposite camp, for example, a white woman raped by a Negro. Smelser refers to Allport and Postman's 'law of social psychology' that no riot ever arose without rumour.[45] It has to be borne in mind, of course, that precipitating events play their fateful part not only in crowd outrages but also in most individual crimes of violence. Here, too, one provocative word may decide the issue; 'I might not have done what I did if she had remained silent', says Pozdnishev in Tolstoy's *Kreutzer Sonata*.

3. *The Different Components of the Crowd*

Within the crowd we have to distinguish three parts: (*a*) the active minority, of which the most important elements are (*b*) the leaders; at the other extreme there is (*c*) the passive majority, the followers. The existence of these three components is one of the factors which are peculiar to the crowd in the psychological sense as distinct from the mere agglomeration (s. 1 above), which is unclassified and may have no leader. The phenomenon of leadership is one of the fundamental elements and one of the great themes of history, politics, religion, and social psychology; it has been studied in all conceivable contexts from Max Weber's charismatic leader to that of a criminal or juvenile gang. It has been discredited by Hitler, Mussolini, and Stalin, but it is still indispensable for an understanding of human groups. Freud regarded it as a case of projection of the super-egos of the members on to the person of the leader as a father-figure, a theory which may be true but does not help us very much. Le Bon is particularly weak on the subject. His leaders are mostly political or religious figures, some of them men of action, nervous, irritable, half-mad, skilful orators who only pursue their own personal interests; others may be men of deep convictions and belief in the sacredness of their cause, such as Peter of Amiens, Luther, Savonarola. Apart from the role played by the French revolutionaries, there is nothing in Le Bon's book on the leader of criminal crowds. It might possibly be doubted whether a crowd in the sense of our present discussion can have a leader at all, i.e. whether the existence of such a figure does not run contrary to the character of a crowd as a short-lived agglomeration of people with only the barest minimum of organization. However, considering the additional 'something' needed to produce a psychological crowd (s. 1 above) it is clear that in its formation, direction, domination, and exploitation a leader figure, while not essential, can play an all-important role. It is a very temporary role only, executive rather than organizational.[46] Nevertheless, it is going too far when some writers[47] regard the leader as nothing but the personification of the emotional drives of the crowd, entirely dependent upon its whims and, without any will of his own, merely giving expression to its fleeting impulses. It is only consequent that according to this view the leader of a criminal crowd is neither legally nor morally responsible for its actions. To us this seems an undue generalization of a highly complex phenomenon. It has to be borne in mind that there is a mutual, not a one-sided, relationship between a crowd and its leaders, each of the two sectors influencing the other and being influenced by it. The leader is not immune to the atmosphere and the stimulus emanating from his followers; he is susceptible to their presence and their actions. Which of the two is the stronger depends on their personalities and the specific situation. We have only to consider the extreme case of what is probably the most famous poetical presentation of the leader-crowd relationship, Mark Antony's funeral oration in Shakespeare's *Julius Caesar*, to become aware of the potential impact of a leader of genius and to realize his responsibility for the actions of the crowd. The recent political history of Europe has done nothing to prove Shakespeare's imagination to be unrealistic. A considerable literature exists on the great diversity of the roles played by leaders in hostile outbursts. 'On some occasions,' writes Smelser,[48] 'a highly motivated, daring, psychopathic, etc., individual will deliberately harangue a group to action.' Rudé, who of course deals only with the crowds of the French Revolution, gives many interesting details to show how important it is to avoid generalizations on the lines of Le Bon. There were during that period instances of crowds whose members had, already before the crowd came into existence, been won over individually to the objects of the demonstration and whose mentality corresponded closely to that of the crowd; here the transformation into a crowd was effected not by anything the leaders had done, and its coming into existence was rather due to such objective events as a sudden rise in the price of bread and the fear of starvation.[49] Nor could the outrages committed by these revolutionary crowds always be ascribed to criminal elements drawn from the dregs of the city. In Britain, too, the rural riots of the eighteenth century originated in the high price of corn; they, and the Gordon riots, were rather movements of social protest. Towards the end of the eighteenth century these food riots were, according to Rudé, more and more replaced by strikes,[50] a statement which is of course also something of an over-generalization. It is true however that the strike, with the exception of unexpected and unorganized wild-cat strikes, is a planned movement quite different from a food riot.

Illuminating on this subject, the role of the crowd leader, is the detailed description given by Christopher Hibbert in his *King Mob* of the behaviour of Lord George Gordon during the various stages of his riots. As the leader of the crowd of 'Petitioners' he constantly moved about 'inside and outside the House of Commons' to keep his people informed about what was being said inside, 'extravagantly agitated . . . (and) so intoxicated by the sound of the hundreds of voices shouting his name that he was unaware that most of the reasonable petitioners had gone home, leaving behind them a mischief-making and violence-hungry rabble . . . yet on occasions he seemed to realize, despite his hysteria, . . . that he had started something dangerous which was now beyond his power to stop' (p. 44). Similar observations could probably be made with regard to the activities of modern leaders of crowds committing outrages in the course of race riots, political or religious demonstrations, and unorganized strikes.

No less diversified than the character and role of the leaders are the other components of the crowd and the numerical proportion between its active minority and the passive majority. In other words, how many of those who join a crowd will remain passive and how many will actively participate in hostile or even criminal action may depend on their backgrounds, personalities, and the national temperament, on the issues involved, on the ability of the leaders to arouse their passions, perhaps on the weather, and so on.

Apart from the literature already quoted, we find interesting material on the leadership and other problems of the crowd in Günther Kaiser's monograph on the German *Halbstarken-Krawalle* of the 1950's. He stresses the unorganized nature of these groups of youngsters which possessed none of the characteristics of the gang; anything involving a tie, a commitment, in short any kind of organization, was shunned by these boys.[51] Therefore no real leaders could be found, only spokesmen or *Hauptschläger*, i.e. boys who are stronger, more violent and reckless and commit worse excesses than the others and egg them on to further outrages. Consequently, very few of those brought before the courts in connection with such riots could be convicted as 'leaders' (*Rädelsführer* according to §§ 115 and 125 of the German Code, which provide heavier penalties for the leaders).

With regard to the proportion of the various components of these crowds, Kaiser has observed that in the German 'rock-and-roll' meetings which were often the starting points of serious riots, there were usually 5–15 young people to be found in the centre of events, performing grotesque contortions, with about 20–60 others standing around shouting and applauding, whereas a crowd of a hundred or more was watching approvingly from a distance. For such occasions, Kaiser regards this as the typical distribution of the forces.[52] In the Chicago race riots of 1919, the mob, though 'one in spirit', was 'divided in performance into a small active nucleus and a large proportion of spectators', with the nucleus consisting of perhaps 4 to 25 or 50 and the spectators numbering 250–300.[53]

Kaiser and, at some greater detail, Fyvel[54] review the international phenomenon of these mass outbreaks of adolescent lawlessness caused, to stress his point again, not by gangs but by casually assembled crowds of youths, from Sweden to Germany, France, Britain, Italy, Austria, and even Switzerland. Everywhere the underlying causes of the malaise seem to go down very deep to the roots of our affluent society, although at least in Fyvel's view in most Continental countries the 'traditional bourgeois standards' have survived and been capable of fighting back more effectively than in Britain and the United States.

4. *Some Special Types of Crowd Rioting*

(*a*) Riots in prisons and similar institutions are, strictly speaking, not committed by crowds as the term is here used because they are not the work of people suddenly flocking together without any previous organizational connections behind them. Nevertheless, such riots have much in common with crowd rioting in its narrow sense and are often discussed together with it.[55] The literature on the subject contains valuable material on mass crime and on leadership; references were given by the present writer in an earlier book,[56] and not very much has been added since then, as the worst period in American prison rioting seems to be over. On the special aspect of leadership in prison riots Negley K. Teeters probably voices the prevailing opinion when he writes: 'To blame a few disgruntled, hard-boiled criminals for a riot is naïve and unrealistic although popular.'[57] It may be more realistic to blame a few psychopaths for it.

As in the case of the mass movements, peasants' riots and others referred to before, one of the strongest underlying causes of many institutional disturbances is the desire to obtain redress for real or imaginary grievances. The report on the disturbances at the Carlton Approved School for senior boys in Bedfordshire, in August 1959,[58] provides an excellent illustration of how the various factors combine to produce an institutional riot. To put the findings of the report in a nutshell: 'two main underlying causes . . . first, the insufficient development of the personal relations' between staff and boys, which involved among other weaknesses 'the inadequacy of positive arrangements for the airing and clearing of boys' grievances', depriving the school of a most essential safety valve; and, secondly, the deterioration in the type of boy: 'Anti-social and anti-authority characteristics among boys committed for training over the last two years have increased and worsened in that period . . . Boys having the right qualities for choice as house captains and leaders are now difficult to find at Carlton School.' There was a hard core of trouble-makers, and no machinery to remove them in time; nor had the school the services of a psychiatrist, although a number of boys who had been the subjects of psychiatric reports had been received from the classifying school. Moreover, the boys had harboured a number of grievances, some real, some imaginary; and finally, the publicity given to the initial disorders in certain parts of the press 'heightened the attitude of bravado' and encouraged a repetition.

(b) Race riots are more frequent and of greater practical importance than institutional riots. They are also more typical products of crowds in the narrower sense, with usually little organization behind, or if organizations should be involved, many of the actual participants may not actually belong to them. While the classic countries of race riots have so far been the United States and the Indian peninsula, several others have followed suit in the course of this century, for example South Africa,[59] Egypt,[60] British Guiana,[61] and Britain, to mention only a few of them. Some of these riots were mainly political and economic in origin, but racial factors were hardly ever absent. Naturally, there is more information available on events in Britain than on those abroad, and reference was already made to them above (Chapter 23). While we were there approaching the crime problem from the racial angle, especially from the point of view of crime among racial minorities, we are now concerned more specifically with the impact of race on crowd rioting. Racial antagonism provides an ideal background for such riots: ready-made mistrust, jealousy, hatred, lack of understanding of the other person's way of life, problems, and reactions to stress, the easy spreading of rumours— all these factors make it only natural that at the slightest provocation —real or imaginary—hostile crowds may gather and riot against racial minorities. With the increasing influx of coloured immigrants after the Second World War the wave of such riots was bound to spread to Britain, culminating in the outbreaks at the Notting Hill area of London, and in Nottingham in August–September, 1958. It has occasionally been maintained that these outbreaks were essentially non-racial since various other factors such as overcrowding 'lowering the standard of the district', and many others mentioned above (Chapter 23) played an important part in them.[62] The presence of such other factors, however, quite inevitable in accordance with the multi-factor theory of crime causation, does not detract from the racial character of these outbreaks, which would probably not have occurred if racial antagonism had not provided the obvious direction and the driving force. Other writers have pointed out that as for many young people senseless violence has become an end in itself, there is no need to invoke the racial issue.[63] While this, too, is unfortunately true, it has to be repeated that the presence of coloured minorities provides a standing invitation and determines the choice of victims.

This is not the place to go into the details of the riots of 1958, they can be found in the columns of the serious daily papers of that period, but attention may be drawn to the following technical aspects: First, more than 400 people were stated to be involved in the disturbances at Notting Hill, of whom twelve were detained. Nine youths, aged between 17 and 20 and without previous convictions, were sentenced to four years' imprisonment each on charges of wounding with intent to cause grievous bodily harm.[64] There was general approval of these unusually heavy sentences as a necessary deterrent and also to show the coloured minority that they were afforded adequate protection by the courts. To a considerable extent these objects seem to have been achieved,[65] but it is generally realized that much more is required not only to prevent further race riots and individual outrages[66] but also to improve the relations between the British majority and the coloured immigrants in a more general sense. As far as mere numbers are concerned, the Commonwealth Immigration Act, 1962, has been successful in stemming the influx of immigrants from over 136,000 in 1961 to over 34,000,[67] but improved social services, better liaison, perhaps on the lines of the 'Nottingham experiment',[68] and a radical change in housing conditions and legislation and much else will be needed to soften the present bitterness. The Nuffield Foundation has taken an important step in allocating a research grant of £70,000 to the Institute of Race Relations in London for a survey of all aspects of the problem,[69] but such research notoriously takes a very long time to produce practical results.

5. *Legal Aspects of Crowd Crimes*

Crimes emanating from crowd behaviour present very special practical and legal difficulties to criminal law and procedure. First, there is the, often insuperable, difficulty of establishing who was actually in the crowd at the critical moment and who took part in the crimes committed, of distinguishing between the participants according to the degree of guilt, of sorting out leaders and followers. The German Penal Code (§ 125) makes it unnecessary to prove the actual participation in violence of each accused; evidence of conscious attendance at the tumultuous gathering of a crowd where violence is committed is sufficient for a conviction, but the penalties are of course less severe for mere members. There is further the question of whether the criminal law should treat the crowd factor as an aggravating or a mitigating circumstance, and, finally, the procedural difficulties of conducting a mass trial.[70]

Mass trials are not necessarily the outcome of crimes committed by crowds; one of the most notorious exceptions in recent history was the South African so-called Treason Trial, which began in December 1956 with the arrest and indictment of 156 persons who had certainly committed no crowd crimes.[71] In the words of Dean Griswold, 'Though a conspiracy lasting for four years is charged in the indictment, not a single act of violence is alleged.'

In English law the most characteristic offence dealing with crowd crime is the common law misdemeanour of riot which requires at least three persons acting with a common purpose and the intent to help one another against their opponents, if necessary by force; moreover, there has to be force or violence displayed in such a manner as to 'alarm at least one person of reasonable firmness and courage'.[72] Added to this, the famous Riot Act of 1714 makes it a felony for an unlawful assembly of twelve or more persons not to disperse within an hour after a justice of the peace has read, or endeavoured to read, a proclamation calling upon them to disperse. It was owing to a strange misinterpretation of this Act that in 1780 'London was abandoned to pillage for three days during the disturbances initiated by Lord George Gordon' as nobody dared to fire upon the plundering crowds because no magistrate was present to "read the Riot Act" '.[73] A similar common law offence is unlawful assembly, which can be committed whenever three or more persons meet together 'to support each other . . . in carrying out a purpose which is likely to involve violence . . .', even if no violence is actually committed. Herein lies the difference to rioting, where violence must actually occur.[74]

In a recent case of a London gang fight, in which a police constable was killed, eleven young men were charged with 'unlawfully making an affray', a common law offence so unknown that there are no references to it in modern text-books and that the Court of Criminal Appeal had to complain about the lack of authority in older writings.[75] It is, however, an offence which does not require the participation of more than two persons fighting each other and therefore not typical of crowd crime.

As mentioned above, in some Penal Codes more serious penalties are provided against leaders; moreover, directions are given to the courts as to whether the fact that a crime was committed by a crowd should be regarded as a mitigating or aggravating circumstance for the individual accused. In the Soviet 'Principles', for example, commission of a crime 'by an organized group' is an aggravating factor (§ 34, No. 2) but this does not, of course, refer to crowds. Under the Cuban Penal Code however, similarly to the Italian Penal Code of 1930 (art. 62, No. 3), it is a mitigating factor that the offender has acted 'under the influence of a mass suggestion or a general riot, unless he has provoked the latter himself or has been one of its leaders' (art. 37). In this connection it is also interesting that in a Polish mass trial the court granted the request of the defence to hear experts in sociology and psychology to explain the effect of the crowd atmosphere on an accused charged with murder.[76]

IV. ORGANIZED CRIME: ADULT AND ADOLESCENT GANGS[77]

1. *Adult Gangs*

We can now pass on to the more or less tightly organized forms of criminal association, the adult and adolescent gang. While much has been written on the latter, the adult species of organized crime is one of the subjects most conspicuously neglected in British and Continental criminology, perhaps even more than white collar crime with which it has certain features in common. This neglect is of course largely due to the fact that neither the gangster nor the white collar criminal are easy types to reach and to study in the quiet atmosphere of the prison psychologist's or probation officer's interviewing rooms, for which they have but little use. Some American gangsters are said to employ their private psycho-analysts from whom, however, not much information is likely to be forthcoming. Consequently, we know a great deal about petty recidivists and habitual prisoners, about the various types of inadequates and other comparatively minor nuisances who are the most frequent recipients of long sentences of preventive detention,[78] but we also realize that preventive detention, under the Criminal Justice Act, 1948, no less than under its predecessor of 1908, has failed to catch the really dangerous members of organized gangs of bank or train robbers, the men who specialize in wage hold-ups, thefts of lorries in transit, etc., and more often than not get away with it. Existing legislation and court practice on measures of preventive detention have, however, been unable to deal effectively with dangerous organized gang crime in other countries, too. Joachim Hellmer, for example, who made a special study in Germany of the files of 200 persons sentenced to the German equivalent of preventive detention[79] admits that there is no trace in his material of what he calls 'the intelligent large-scale criminal' who, he surmises, is probably clever enough to retire from the business in his own good time. There is no doubt a very considerable amount of relevant information in the hands of Scotland Yard and corresponding Continental organizations, but it has, apparently, not been placed at the disposal of criminologists, not even official ones, for purposes of research. The material now being collected in Scotland under the direction of John A. Mack, though on a small scale, is however likely to lead eventually to a more realistic approach to the subject.[80] While so far only the outlines of his investigation have been published, his tentative conclusions show a remarkable insight into this so far badly neglected problem. His starting point is the distinction between 'habitual prisoners'—the term used by D. J. West in his recent book[81] —i.e. those who tend to be psychologically maladjusted and spend most of their time in prison, and 'habitual criminals', who are psychologically normal, are the driving forces behind most organized crime and are but rarely caught. 'The Worktown study' (Worktown being an 'urban territory of 100,000 people') 'suggests that there are as many full-time criminals as there are full-time prisoners.' As Mack rightly stresses, 'the main work of delineating the criminal sub-culture, the system of organized criminal relationships which exists in any big industrial region, must so far begin with such information as emerged when the curtain is lifted by a spectacular High Court trial' (p. 46). To the recent Scottish trials of this kind, referred to by Mack, the English Mail Train Robbery case of 1963 should now be added (see below).

Shortly after the last war it was maintained by the authorities and part of the press that the rise in serious crime was largely the work of wartime deserters, whose number was estimated at 20,000 and who had become outcasts and been forced to form gangs and live by criminal exploits.[82] This explanation may have been correct at the time, but for the far more serious position which has arisen in Britain in the past five or ten years other factors have to be considered. The present wave of large-scale, well-planned and usually highly successful hold-ups by gangs armed with coshes or even fire-arms does not seem to be due to the activities of desperate outcasts deprived of ration books, which have long ceased to exist; it is more likely to be the inevitable result of deep-seated frustration coupled with the existence of good opportunities for easy get-away and disposal. 'Organized crime on a commercial scale', the chief security officer of a firm which moves loads of tobacco worth £300,000 each night is reported to have said.[83] According to the *Report of the Commissioner of Police of the Metropolis* for 1962 the number of robberies and assaults with intent to rob in the London area had risen from 162 in 1938 to 1,017 in 1962, of which 999 fell under s. 23 (1) of the Larceny Act, 1916, i.e. they were offences where the person or persons involved were armed with offensive weapons or instruments or were acting in company or used violence. Unfortunately, there are no separate figures to show the percentage of such robberies committed 'in company', but it is likely to be substantial. The percentage of robberies cleared up fell from a pre-war (1934–8) average of 54 to 32·6 in 1962, which is a disastrous decline. Even the Cambridge Institute of Criminology, sometimes inclined to take a slightly too rosy view of developments, began to realize the seriousness of the matter, but their long-drawn-out researches, while faithfully presenting the statistical picture, have so far failed to produce the all-important details on the men and the organizations behind these crimes. Moreover, in their *Robbery in London*[84] they still maintain that 'while all those changes are consistent with a tendency for robbery to become more organized, too much emphasis should not be placed on this' (!). The puzzled reader will ask himself in vain for the reasoning behind this astonishing statement or the subsequent one that 'it is probably still true that this type of organized crime is relatively infrequent'. It all depends on the meaning of relativity.

The activities of these gangs culminated in the great rail robbery near Aylesbury, Buckinghamshire, on the 8th August 1963, where the robbers got away with more than two and a half million pounds in banknotes of which only about one-tenth was recovered by the police.

Interesting and in many ways valuable as the extensive press reports of the main trial held in Aylesbury in April 1964 were, they could of course give only a minimum amount of information on the structure of the elaborate organization and the psychological make-up of the individual criminals who had built it up (see *The Times*, 17.4.1964). Twelve men were found guilty on the 16th April, of whom seven received sentences of thirty years' imprisonment each, sentences of a length imposed only in very exceptional cases by British courts. Two more of the men received 25 years each, one 24, another 20, and a third (on a less serious charge) 3 years. With two exceptions, they gave notice of appeal against conviction. In addition, a few men received minor sentences for receiving. In spite of the length and, we have to assume, thoroughness of the preliminary proceedings and the trial itself, the presiding judge, Mr. Justice Edmund Davies, had to admit at the end that the scanty nature of the evidence in this direction made it impossible for him to determine exactly what part had been played by each of the 11 convicted of the larger conspiracy or the eight convicted of the actual robbery; therefore, he proposed to treat them all, with two exceptions, in the same way (*The Times*, 16.4.1964). In view of this confession of, at least partial, failure on the part of the presiding judge to penetrate beneath the surface—a failure for which, of course, under the accusatorial system of an English criminal trial he was in no way to blame—it is hardly possible for the outside observer to gain a picture of the real inside story of the plot and its execution. One might perhaps venture to guess that at least five categories of people were here involved: first, the planners, those whom Mays calls the 'Top Villains' (p. 177); secondly, those who carried out the actual robbery; thirdly, the receivers who had to distribute and hide the stolen money, which owing to its sheer bulk was no easy task; fourthly, those who bought and equipped the near-by farm where much of the preparatory work was done and some of the loot hidden away; and, lastly, the hangers-on required for a multitude of minor jobs. According to the police, no real 'master-mind' was behind the plot, but whether or not this is correct will as usual depend on the definition of this term. The judge seemed to have a different view. In any case, the fact that even now only a small fraction of the loot has been discovered seems to show that in some ways at least this crime did pay, and it remains uncertain whether the men who received the heaviest sentences were actually the principal organizers of the plot or whether the latter may not have remained unknown and will, after a suitable interval, enjoy the profits and proceed to other, equally daring, exploits. However, according to the testimony of the presiding judge, even some of those actually sentenced were men of considerable ability. The lists of previous convictions showed remarkable differences, some of them being fairly long and serious, others negligible. One of them had received 12 strokes of the birch for robbery with violence. Their occupations, too, showed a great variety. Most of them lived in or near London. Their ages were mostly in the 30 to 40 range, but a few were between 40 and 50 and a few slightly below 30; none of them were under 25.

One of the lessons to be learnt even from the incomplete information so far available is that there was co-operation between fairly mixed strata of society, ranging from bookmakers, racing motorists, carpenters, to solicitors and their clerks, and including strongly active anti-social elements with heavy previous convictions as well as passively asocial elements who had before managed to remain, however uneasily, within the sphere of outward respectability. Modern large-scale crime needs a careful mixture of people of different talents and inclinations. The factors explaining the unusual severity of the sentences were obviously the exceptionally large amount stolen, the heavy coshing of the engine driver, whom the judge described as 'nerve-shattered', the refusal of the accused to give any helpful information, and what was described by the press as their lack of 'emotion' or repentance—as if anything of the kind could be expected from the principal figures in this trial.

The sensational success of this crime should, however, not detract our attention from the more modest ones reported almost daily in monotonous succession. On the 23rd February 1963 *The Times* commented on the yield of one single week: a £30,000 raid on wages from a Gas Board office, an attack on the Irish Mail train, the capture of a £43,000 load of cigarettes from a British Road Services lorry. The value of the property obtained by robbery in the London area in 1962 was £799,117, of which only £70,202 (8·8 per cent) was recovered (*Metropolitan Police Report* for 1962, p. 55). There were 40 wage robberies in London in the 16 weeks August–November 1962 (*Sunday Times*, 2.12.1962), and according to *The Times* of the 19th March 1963 a very active gang of safe-breakers was operating in the Chelmsford area of Essex with large quantities of explosives. In a B.B.C. television 'Panorama' programme (18.3.1963) the annual losses inflicted by organized 'hi-jackers' were estimated at £6 million.

Organized crime is not necessarily concerned with robbery and similar forms of violence; there are many other profitable outlets for its enterprise. As recent trials have shown, the doping of racehorses or dogs is one of them. At Sussex Assizes, six men and one woman were found guilty on the 30th October 1963 of conspiring to defraud, at various places in England between April 1957 and May 1963, the owners and trainers of racehorses, bookmakers and others by means of the administration of drugs to racehorses in order to affect their performances. One of the men was regarded as the brains behind the plot and as having corrupted a very large number of people.[85]

Looking at the history of this phenomenon we find gangs of adult criminals active particularly at times of political and social upheavals, such as the robber-knights (*Raubritter*) of the German Middle Ages with their counterparts, the *Vitalienbrüder* and many other gangs of pirates, professional beggars, and vagrants.[86] The seventeenth century saw the growth of gangs of coiners (*Kipper and Wipper*); in the eighteenth century the secret societies flourished as centres of large-scale frauds, and gangs of robbers terrorized the population of Germany and other Continental countries.[87]

For France, it has been pointed out by Vouin and Léauté[88] that adult gangs flourished there at the time of the great revolution, but disappeared slowly in the course of the nineteenth century which was 'as individualistic in this respect as in so many others'. It was also thanks to certain drastic provisions of French criminal law that banditism has practically ceased to exist in France since 1953, in which connection those authors mention the establishment of a special service charged with the repression of banditry in the *Direction générale de la Sureté nationale* and an Act of the 23rd November 1950 which imposes the death penalty not only for armed robbery but also for theft without the use of arms if one of the participants kept a weapon in the car used for the commission of the crime.

For England, some material on gangs can be found in the histories of criminal law by Pike and Radzinowicz, and particularly in Fuller's *The Beggars' Brotherhood*. The case of Jonathan Wild, the subject of Henry Fielding's famous novel, is interesting for the light it sheds not only on matters of eighteenth-century criminal law and procedure, but also on the activities of London gangs of thieves and robbers. Fuller reports that, according to Defoe, Wild at one time controlled an organization of more than seven thousand thieves, which if this was true meant that it could not have been a gang in our sense of the word. However, he divided his men into districts, which made them easier to control.[89] With his execution the Brotherhood came to an end (pp. 234–8). Fuller has some interesting details on the earlier history of the medieval gangs of tramps; the first occasion on which the beggars formed anything like an organized association with a common purpose was, he thinks, the peasants' rising of 1481 in Kent connected with the name of Wat Tyler,[90] but this was a political and socio-economic movement rather than a criminal organization. Medieval tramps were isolated and never formed gangs, but in the middle of the fifteenth century there were already bands of outlaws attacking and robbing travellers (Fuller, pp. 20–36).

The classic countries of present-day organized crime are the U.S.A. and Italy, and it is widely believed that it has been imported to the U.S.A. from Sicily through immigrant members of the Mafia.[91] The Kefauver Committee presented some evidence of this connection, but other American writers such as Bell as well as the Italian authorities declare it to be unconvincing.[92] The wisest course for us would be to leave the question 'wide open'. What cannot be doubted is that many members of the Mafia actually emigrated to the U.S.A. from the eighteen eighties on; that many notorious American gangsters have been of Sicilian origin, and that certain criminal techniques characteristic of Mafia methods are now, *mutatis mutandis*, conspicuously present in American crime. To understand these characteristics we should not exclusively rely on the views of American criminologists, but supplement them by the more first-hand accounts of such experts as the distinguished Anglo-Sicilian author Francis M. Guercio with his experience of nearly twenty years spent in Sicily.[93] According to him, the Mafia is not a secret society, but rather 'a habit of tackling all enterprises, great or small, in an indirect and underhand manner, by mediation, by recommendation, and other dubious forms of "influence"' (p. 65). While providing redress against evil-doers, it also protects criminals against the law and encourages their crimes. Its origins lie in the resistance of Sicilians against oppression and corruption right from the days of the Sicilian Vesper of 1282, but the organization itself seems to date from the time of the widely hated Bourbonic regime which was brought to an end by Garibaldi in 1860. Glimpses of this atmosphere can be caught from Guiseppe di Lampedusa's famous novel *The Leopard*. Guercio distinguishes two forms of Mafia, the lower, concerned with large-scale crimes against property, with blackmail, kidnapping, and murder as weapons to obtain its objects, and the higher, controlling politics, law, relations between landlords and tenants, with the aristocrats of the Mafia frequently being prominent pillars of society. All this resembles the position in some parts of the United States, with the difference that there the power of gangsterdom was built on bootlegging, drug traffic and gambling, whereas in Sicily its foundation was control of the land (p. 66). Guercio also shows that the Mafia was in fact able to safeguard the interests of the common people more effectively than the government, which latter, it has to be remembered, has often been regarded by Sicilians as a foreign body.[94] The First World War led to a clash between the older and the younger generation of *mafiosi*, on account of their different experiences during the war, followed by a temporary decline of their power. Interest in football replaced the attraction of the Mafia, but the demoralization of the Second World War with its economic and social chaos after the breakdown of Fascist rule led to its revival (pp. 78–83). According to Danilo Dolci, whose campaign for social reform in Western Sicily is one of the most promising features of the present situation, the Mafia have killed 39 trade union leaders and nearly 600 other persons in that area.[95] The effect of the recently organized large-scale police war against the Mafia remains to be seen.[96]

Even from this greatly condensed account the similarities and dissimilarities between the Sicilian and the American scene will become fairly clear. The latter, with its vastly larger, diversified, and intensely industrialized economy, offers a correspondingly greater variety of opportunities for organized gang activities. Moreover, the presence of many different races of immigrants, each with its own peculiar history of oppression and rebellion in their homelands—Hans v. Hentig[97] stresses the predominance of Irish, Italian, and Jewish immigrants in American gangsterdom—adds an element of racial rivalry to the existing competition between gangs, which is absent in the more homogeneous homeland of the Mafia. In fact, publications such as the Kefauver Report show an abundance of names belonging to those three national groups, but on the other hand Edgar Hoover claims that his files contain the best American names and only occasionally a foreign-sounding one.[98]

Equally conspicuous, however, are the parallels between the Mafia and its American counterpart. There is in particular that peculiar interplay of underworld big business and politics that strikes the observer. What American writers such as Merton, Daniel Bell, and William F. Whyte have told us about the services which the political machine, the racket, performs in the, real or alleged, interest of ordinary people is, though on a far greater scale, clearly reminiscent of Mafia techniques.[99] Nevertheless, we have to bear in mind that very similar techniques have also been developed in other parts of the globe, for example by the Chinese secret societies, the 'black society' which has 'always to be placated' by the ordinary business man and householder.[100] The practice of extracting 'protection money' from business people, one of the most familiar forms of racketeering, is even said to go back to the pre-Indian days of Lord Clive of India in the middle of the eighteenth century.[101] Even the notorious institution of 'Omertà', unconditional solidarity, loyalty, and conspiracy of silence (Guercio, p. 67), is not confined to the Mafia, but a characteristic of many criminal organizations. And with regard to the conspicuous role played by Italians in the American underworld, Bell has pleaded in their favour that, being the last on the scene, they found themselves at a considerable disadvantage against the Irish and Jews and had to use any means open to them to make up for this. With regard to the alleged Mafia influence, it has been suggested by Earl Johnson, the author of one of the most up-to-date and detailed studies of American organized crime, that this belief may be due to the fact that the traffic in narcotics, one of the most profitable activities of the gangs, requires close connections with Mediterranean and Far Eastern countries, for which Sicilians are particularly well located.[102]

In a recent book by Norman Lewis[103] some interesting information is given on the collaboration between U.S. officials in Sicily and the Mafia at the time of the invasion towards the end of the last world war, collaboration which, he thinks, has greatly strengthened the weakening power of the Mafia in its homeland. Moreover, the

Sicilian psychiatrist Carmelo Nobile has drawn attention to the need to destroy not merely the Mafia as a criminal organization but also the 'spirit', the whole 'mentality and customs uniting its active members with their protectors and their victims'.[104]

So far, no definition of the term 'organized crime' has been given, but it is clear that many different variants of it have to be distinguished. Johnson defines it as 'a group of considerable size which engages in continuous criminal activity over a long, usually indefinite, period of time' and he regards this element of long duration as the most essential one.[105] While this may be true of some of the very large and elaborate organizations established in the U.S.A. it hardly applies to the smaller organizations found elsewhere which may be formed for the commission of a few criminal exploits only and dissolve themselves afterwards. Among the other characteristics often mentioned are also some which seem to be peculiar to American conditions rather than to other countries. This is the case especially with the political domination of law-enforcement agencies by criminal organizations as we know it from many American studies.[106] While corrupt political contacts with police, lawyers, and even judges do exist elsewhere they are usually less close and on a smaller scale. On the other hand, it cannot be denied that in the long run organized crime can usually flourish only with the 'active and conscious co-operation of a number of elements of respectable society'.[107] It is not much different here from the position existing with regard to white collar crime, although the support given to the latter will be more open, unashamed, and unfettered by considerations of social propriety since there is not the same social distance between white collar criminals and their supporters as does often, though by no means always, exist between organized crime and its bourgeois supporters.

The more we study the very extensive, brutally frank and competent American literature on the subject, culminating for the time being in the symposium on 'Combating Organized Crime' published by the *Annals of the American Academy of Political and Social Science* (vol. 347, May 1963), the clearer will it become that in the U.S.A. the term 'organized crime' means in fact something far more specific than it does elsewhere and that in general definitions such as that of Johnson this specific element, though implied, is perhaps not brought out with sufficient clarity: it is the fact that in the U.S.A. the term is no longer primarily aimed at such comparatively small affairs as bank or train robberies, even if they should occasionally yield hauls of a few million pounds (or dollars as in the 1950 Boston case, *Annals*, p. 44). Its essence lies not in such passing exploits but rather in its country-wide operations in the fields of gambling, prostitution, drug traffic, liquor trade, protection rackets, and so on, where the profits are vastly greater and, what is more, can be relied upon as being fairly regular. To make the operation of these country-wide concerns possible they have to be organized in the same workmanlike manner as legal enterprises of corresponding size, in the words of Sellin (*Annals*, p. 12) 'they must have capital, physical plant, managerial personnel, and employees of various kinds'. And they need the political machine to support them. Looked at in this way, the Buckinghamshire train robbery was small and amateurish although the beginnings of something more professional can already be discovered, as for example the 'physical plant'. Its main weakness was, however, that seen in the light of American achievements this whole type of crime is hopelessly out of date.

With regard to the membership of criminal organizations, it may consist of very different categories, not all of them necessarily professionals of a high order. As pointed out above in connection with the great train robbery case there is need for the co-operation of people of higher and lower status in the criminal hierarchy. Moreover, habitual offenders are not necessarily members of an organization; there are also lone wolves among them, and, though to a much lesser extent, this applies to professional criminals, too. Reckless is also inclined to differentiate the degree of organization according to the various main types of criminal activity.[108]

Turning now once more to the present position in Britain and its more recent history, since the days of Jonathan Wild, we are immediately reminded of the white slave traffic, closely associated with the drug traffic—the existence of which is established not least firmly by the frequency with which it has been publicly denied—and also of the race-dopers—already mentioned before—and the race-course gangs.[109] With regard to the latter, it has been claimed that in the course of this century the racecourse had been 'purged of gangsterdom' and 'terrorization and blackmail ... had been effectively crushed' by the formation of 'Bookmakers' Protection Associations'.[110] Nevertheless, certain trials at the Old Bailey followed by questions in the House of Commons make it appear doubtful, to say the least, whether such gangs and gang warfare have been extinguished in London. Mr. Justice Donovan, sentencing two men to seven years' imprisonment each, is reported to have said in his summing up that 'the facts of this case sounded more like Chicago and the worst days of prohibition than London in 1956',[111] and in the House of Commons Mr. Peter Rawlinson, subsequently Solicitor-General in the Macmillan and Home Governments, stated: 'There certainly appeared to be gangs ... and there certainly were protection rackets in existence in Soho where wretched shopkeepers for fear of having their windows broken were paying protection money to persons who were in control of the gangs. If it was not gang warfare that was going on at present he would like to know what it was.'[112] It is interesting that one of the men closely connected with this gang warfare has recently maintained that in Britain too, organized crime was now controlled by the Mafia.[113] The evidence for this extraordinary contention has still to be awaited. If it were correct it would mean a step backward in the evolution of organized crime in Britain, which should be expected to move from the more primitive techniques employed by the Mafia to more refined ones. Not long ago, the leader of one of Glasgow's largest gangs of the period of the local razor battles in the nineteen twenties, was given an 'ostentatious funeral . . . with solemnity and floral grandeur'.[114] Today, the time for such battles, although they still happen, should be passing, and organized crime should acquire a new look. In particular, actual violence against victims is used by real professionals only where it is absolutely necessary, not because they are sentimental about the sanctity of human life, but simply because of the heavier sentences to be expected.[115] 'Robert Allerton' displays a very businesslike attitude towards the subject in *The Courage of his Convictions*. There is no hesitation among gangsters, however, to use extreme violence as a punishment for disloyal members and undesirable witnesses.[116]

The greatest need for future criminological research in Britain in this field is to face the facts of the situation more realistically than has so far been done by resolutely tackling at least one of the potential operating and recruiting grounds of organized crime and studying its structure and possible connections with police, business, and politics. The recent revelations about the so-called 'Rachmanism' might provide a possible starting point. However, if such research is undertaken not in earnest, but with lack of courage and inadequate funds and personnel, it is wiser not to try at all.

2. *The Adolescent Gang*

Some of the socio-psychological factors behind these gangs have been discussed above (Chapter 22) in connection with our review of the work of Cohen, Cloward, and Ohlin, and others. Here we have only to fill in certain gaps and draw attention to very recent happenings and interpretations. In the period of approximately 38 years which have elapsed since the classic study of Frederick Thrasher was first published many changes have occurred in the practice and theory of adolescent gangs, notably in the U.S.A., changes which, as far as the theoretical side is concerned, may even remind us of the ones which have occurred in our interpretation of crowd behaviour in the past 70 years but the trend is in the opposite direction. From Thrasher's book the following basic elements of adolescent gang formation emerged:[117] it was chiefly a phenomenon arising from the specific needs of under-privileged youths living in 'interstitial' areas of big cities, of spontaneous, unplanned origin, 'the natural outgrowth of a crowd of boys meeting on a street corner', slowly developing a common awareness and tradition, attached to a certain territory, and soon meeting some hostile elements, in particular rival gangs, which leads to conflict and through it to closer integration, solidarity, and loyalty to its chosen leaders. In their characteristics and their needs—which are basically identical with those four wishes of W. I. Thomas (Chapter 16)—the gang members are not much different from other boys, neither more nor less emotionally unstable, victims of an unsatisfactory environment, simply trying, in Thrasher's words, 'to create a society for themselves where none adequate to their needs exists'. While many of their activities are not, or not seriously, delinquent, they are often driven towards anti-social behaviour through lack of response on the part of the community and conflict with neighbouring gangs. In the words of Bordua, 'Thrasher describes an age of innocence indeed', although even from his description certain elements of less innocent malice and fundamentally anti-social trends already seem to emerge. These latter occupy the centre of the picture in Cohen's and Cloward–Ohlin's writings of more than a quarter of a century after Thrasher with their emphasis on the status problems of gang members (Chapter 22 above).

The most recent stage in this development is represented by Lewis Yablonsky's *The Violent Gang*, which, like Thrasher's book is based on the author's first-hand acquaintance with delinquent gangs, though not in Chicago but in New York. This is so far the most up-to-date analysis of the problem, and its findings are far from 'innocent' or reassuring. Apart from the bad taste it leaves in the mouth of the reader it shatters some of the traditional concepts of the American adolescent gang, being highly critical of the picture presented by Thrasher as well as by his successors. There is in fact very little left of the more positive, constructive, redeeming aspects of gang life as seen by Thrasher, and their place is taken by a senseless resort to brutal violence, brutality for its own sake or in order to prove to themselves, 'as a kind of existential validation', that they are alive (p. 8). Thrasher's emphasis on the need for a territory of its own is still true (p. 31), but there is no organization left worth speaking of, no element of friendship and loyalty towards a leader. Thrasher, too, had stressed the potentially close affinities between a gang and a mob, but Yablonsky's gangs are hardly more than an unorganized mob, and most of their own talk about size, leaders, and organization turned out to be nothing but empty bragging. Likewise, Cloward's and Ohlin's threefold classification and their description of the 'criminal' gang as an apprenticeship for a subsequent stable career in adult crime, which might have been true for the Chicago gangs of the twenties and thirties, no longer apply to the 'disorganized slum' of present-day gangland (p. 147). Even so, from Yablonsky's own classification it appears that there are two types, which he calls the 'socially-dominated' and the 'delinquency-dominated' gangs, that have still much in common with the ones described by previous writers. It is only the third type, the 'violence-dominated' gang, which presents a more radical break with the past. Altogether, it would seem to be likely that the contrasts discovered by Yablonsky are more of degree than of kind and perhaps also more due to the different racial composition of the gangs described by him, and to their special environmental stresses, some of which may have been only temporary. It was not race as such: as he stresses, the extraordinarily high delinquency rate of the Puerto Rican youths in New York appeared to be the result of their move from stable to disorganized slums, from a poor community to a 'non-community' (p. 173), from rural areas to a metropolis.

In a recent paper another American sociologist, Nathan L. Gerrard,[118] deals especially with what he calls the 'core member' of the gang. By this he means neither the average member nor the leader but rather the 'totally committed' member, whose personality is marked by 'response-insecurity', i.e. a 'generalized feeling that others are hostile or indifferent to one's welfare', coupled with inferiority feelings (weak self-esteem) and the resulting conviction that 'interests and self-esteem can be realized only through acts of aggression'. Such core members are, according to Gerrard, likely to pursue adult criminal careers long after their former partners have abandoned their delinquent ways in favour of conventional occupational and family roles.

As compared with the work done in the U.S.A. Britain lags greatly behind in research on adolescent gangs. This has been largely due to lack of financial resources and, closely connected with it, of well-trained workers who are suitable for this particular kind of work and willing to face the risks which it may involve. One of the few small-scale attempts to tackle it, undertaken in 1951–2 in the notorious Hoxton district of London, has been briefly described by M. L. Turner and John C. Spencer in *Spontaneous Youth Groups* (Note 77 above). It was a sequel to the better known 'Barge Club' experiment, also described by Turner and Spencer.[119] Its first stages of locating one of the gangs and making contact with it occupied the field worker for more than a year, after which the project had to be abandoned because of lack of further funds. 'The problems it had set out to answer were still unsolved', but it had at least become clear that delinquent gangs, whose very existence had often been denied by the authorities, were in fact active, making themselves a considerable nuisance to people living in the district. Even so, it is the prevailing view that adolescent gangs in this country, as compared with the U.S.A., are much rarer, less purposeful and dangerous.[120] In one of the most careful and detailed discussions of the subject the London psychiatrist Peter Scott divides his material, derived from juvenile courts, remand homes, psychiatric clinics, a residential school and a boys' club, into three categories: adolescent street groups, structured gangs, and loosely structured (diffuse) groups, the latter again falling under three sub-headings: the fleeting, casual groups; the groups of customary friends and siblings; the loose anti-social groups. Of the total sample of 151 associations, 17 were proper gangs and 43 loose anti-social groups; the other types are of no direct interest in the present connection. Scott, commenting on the small number of proper gangs in his sample, rules out the possible explanation that they may be too clever or well-organized to get caught, or, if caught, their loyalty may prevent them from disclosing information. Considering the difficulties, encountered in the previously mentioned Turner-Spencer study, of establishing contact with adolescent criminal gangs, it may seem doubtful whether in Scott's sample the proper gangs are in fact not greatly under-represented; it is a long way—not easily and willingly undertaken—from Hoxton to the juvenile court and the psychiatric clinic. Even so, it is interesting to note that the human material in Scott's collection did in his view not conform to the 'picture of healthy devilment, adventurousness, pride of leadership or loyal lieutenancy that is often painted'. His gang-members usually showed 'gross anti-social character defect' and came from homes with a disturbed and detrimental atmosphere.

One final remark may not be out of place to illustrate the progress made in the post-war period with regard to the definition of a 'gang'. While in 1949 the present author could still complain[121] that to many writers ' "gang" means "gang", although it may be nothing but a chance encounter, a casual collaboration in the commission of one isolated offence', there is now very little danger of this confusion happening again. Most present-day investigators are careful to make clear what their statistical figures of 'gang' crime are intended to cover.[122] There would be little point in reciting the percentages of gang delinquency found by different investigators, as their comparability may be questionable. It is perhaps more important to refer to the attempts to discover psychological and social differences between those who offend in company with others and those who offend alone. It has been suggested that the latter are more likely to be individuals of a more complicated psychological make-up and less amenable to treatment, especially in institutions. The Gluecks, for example, found a higher percentage of institutional success for those juveniles who had committed their offences in company, which, they suggest, may show that 'lone wolves' are less influenced by others and less adaptable to group life in institutions.[123] However, we have to bear in mind the great variety of types among gang members and also among lone offenders, which makes any clear-cut distinctions of this kind hazardous. Peter Scott discovered no striking contrasts between the groups. On the other hand, the treatment may have to be on very different lines for lone offenders and for gang members, since the very fact of such membership produces additional problems not present in other cases. The age-old questions arise of 'breaking up' the whole gang, removing the worst elements, treating individual members, or trying to transform the whole gang into a constructive, no longer anti-social, unit, but this cannot here be dealt with. Most of the publications quoted in Note 77 provide valuable material on the matter. It will be clear, moreover, that the phenomenon of the gang, at least where it possesses some permanence and organization, poses questions of treatment fundamentally different from those arising in cases of crowd hooliganism. where no permanent unit exists as a potential object of treatment. There are, however, certain well-known, more or less permanent, social constellations particularly likely to create outbreaks of hooliganism, such as football matches which attract very large crowds of supporters of each of the teams, with intense hostility between them, going back occasionally over periods of half a century.[124] Here at least measures of preventive treatment such as licensing football grounds, limiting the numbers of spectators, coupled with heavy penalties after the event, have to take the place of the more individual and constructive steps needed for gangs.

After this had been written, a great deal of public anxiety was caused in spring 1964, by the outrageous conduct of adolescent gangs who had flocked in large numbers to popular seaside resorts such as Clacton-on-Sea in Essex, Brighton in Sussex, and Margate in Kent, all of them situated within a range of 50 to 70 miles from London. Fairly large-scale battles were fought between the 'Mods' and the 'Rockers' in the streets and on the beaches, and damage was done to public and private property, accompanied by assaults on the police. In the discussions, a great variety of factors were held responsible, ranging from boredom, lack of constructive leisure-time activities and of reasonable prospects of promotion open to these adolescents, to the popular 'just for a laugh' (see the daily papers for April 1964, and the Sunday papers for the 5.4.1964). A sociologist,

David Downes, who had just completed a two years' study of adolescent delinquency in the East End of London (see above, Chapter 22, Note 38), is inclined to interpret the matter in accordance with Merton's theory (Chapter 22, s. 1), stressing at the same time that the situation in Britain was far less dangerous than in the U.S.A. He adds, however, that it might well become explosive in the future. (*Observer*, 5.4.1964.) How far these 'gangs' were real gangs or rather a mixture of gangs and crowd is difficult to decide from the material available. One characteristic feature was the importance of the contributions to the disturbances made by the girls by encouraging the boys to violence and rowdyism. Another regrettable feature was the exaggerated publicity given to the offenders by television and some sections of the press. The penalties imposed included some short prison sentences and heavy fines.

V. VICTIMOLOGY[125]

To include in a chapter on 'Associations in Crime' a section on the relationships between the criminal and his victim may seem to be a far-fetched interpretation of the subject. And indeed, so far we have been dealing only with associations consisting of criminals, although the degree of their participation may have differed greatly. There can, however, be a strong element of association in the criminal-victim relationship, with the two parties—so it seems at least—not working together, but in opposite directions. Actually, as will be shown below, this working in opposite directions may apply only to some part of the way, while the other, perhaps far longer, stretch shows collaboration.

The importance of the role of the victim has occasionally been acknowledged even by the criminal law in various provisions, although its general trend has been different. It is the modern view that the reaction to crime on the part of the state should not be solely determined by the interests and needs of the victim and his desire for vengeance. From this it does not follow that the role of the victim should be altogether ignored by the law. In fact, provocation on the part of the victim has been treated, for many centuries, as a mitigating factor in English law[126] as in other legal systems (e.g. § 213 of the German Penal Code), in particular in cases of homicide, but occasionally also in a more general way (e.g. Swiss Penal Code, art. 64, Cuban Penal Code, art. 38, where, moreover, the 'obvious abuse of authority' on the part of the victim is mentioned as a mitigating circumstance). The consent of the victim may also act as a mitigating factor in cases of homicide (e.g. § 216, German Penal Code), but the widespread demands for the legalization of acts of euthanasia have not yet been successful.[127] In cases of wounding the legal effect of the victim's consent is one of the most difficult and controversial questions of the criminal law; it has been very widely discussed in particular with reference to injuries received in boxing and other sports, through surgical operations, sterilization, castration, and artificial insemination. It depends on the seriousness of the consent, on the victim's mental and legal capacity to give a valid consent, on the object of the act to which he consents, and other factors, whether the consent has any legal force, and it fails to have such force if there are public grounds against its recognition[128]. In the case of false pretences, the folly and credulity of the victim of fraud have been used by the law in former centuries as a welcome excuse for doing nothing to protect him against swindlers.[129] These few examples may show that the law has treated the problem in casual and not always reasonable ways. Criminology was not much more successful until the study of the matter was taken up after the First World War and, more systematically, after the Second World War as part of the more socio-psychologically oriented approach to crime. Slowly it was realized that as crime always requires an object, personal or impersonal, the role played by this object, be it active or passive, should be submitted to closer examination as an essential part of our efforts to understand the criminal and the manner in which he should be treated. The poet Franz Werfel expressed these ideas very pointedly in his novel 'Not the murderer, the victim is guilty' (*Nicht der Mörder, der Ermordete ist schuldig*, 1920), and shortly afterwards Shostakovitch's opera *Lady Macbeth of Mtsensk* tried to show the heroine, Katerina Ismailova, as a murderess deserving more our sympathy than our condemnation. The psychologist Henri Ellenberger, in a fine essay on the psychological relationships between the two parties, drew attention to the pantheistic metaphysics of Brahman philosophy and to Schopenhauer's identification of the hater and the hated. The latter's moral philosophy of compassion was particularly congenial to such attempts to bridge the gulf between the two parties. In our time, the work of the late Belgian psychiatrist and criminologist Etienne de Greeff had already—in the words of Professor Paul Cornil—'been imbued with the importance and complexity of the criminal-victim relationship, especially in crimes of passion'.

The first criminologist who tried to produce a comprehensive analysis of the subject was v. Hentig in his famous monograph *The Criminal and his Victim*, which he followed up by several contributions in German on the role of the victim in such types of crime as murder, false pretences, blackmail. In the meantime, a pioneering study was made by the Langley Porter Clinic in San Francisco on a limited, but particularly intricate aspect, the different types of child victims of sexual offences.

The manifold interest thus shown in the role of the victim encouraged an Israeli lawyer, B. Mendelsohn, to put forward a very ambitious scheme for the foundation of a new and independent scientific discipline, victimology, with its own institutes, cliniques, international society, congress, and chair. As already mentioned (Chapter 1), there is no reason, however, why the study of the victim should not be left to criminology which, after all, includes not only the study of the criminal, but also that of crime in all its aspects. It is the fundamental error of the victimology-enthusiasts that they arbitrarily confine criminology to the study of the criminal. The position of criminology is still precarious enough and should not be rendered unnecessarily more perilous by making exaggerated claims on behalf of a potential sister discipline which would deprive it of some of its own territory. Criminology would be incomplete without the proper study of the victim. Moreover, although it has often been done in an unsystematic manner, criminological research has already achieved much to clarify the role of the victim. This is also the view held by Professor Paul Cornil in his valuable contribution.

In addition to the material collected on the role of the victim in specific categories of offences, certain general points have so far emerged in the literature. It may be useful to mention the following:

(a) The distinction between criminal and victim, which in former days appeared as clear-cut as that of black and white, actually often becomes vague and blurred in individual cases. The longer and the more deeply the actions of the persons involved are scrutinized, the more doubtful will it occasionally be who is to blame for the tragic outcome.[130] This is especially so in certain cases of homicide, where attention was already drawn before (Chapter 16) to the intricate nature of the relationships between the 'penal couple', to use a term coined by Mendelsohn. He distinguishes five types of victims according to their degree of guilt, ranging from the completely innocent to the 'victim due to ignorance', the equally guilty, the one who is more guilty than the offender, either as deliberate provocateur or through lack of self-control, and finally to the 'only guilty' victim, where the accused is acquitted as having acted in legitimate self-defence. Sometimes it is a matter of mere chance who becomes the criminal and who the victim. As Pinatel points out, the two roles may be exchanged either successively or simultaneously, i.e. one of the parties may be first the criminal and afterwards the victim, as in the case of a swindler who is killed by his angry victim, or of two swindlers who cheat each other at the same game. Vittorio de Sica's film *Bicycle Thieves* shows in a very simple and human fashion how an ordinary theft of a bicycle can plunge its victim into utter despair and lead him to crime. It is a fairly common attitude that the victim of such an offence is entitled to help himself to another bicycle.

(b) There are certain individuals who, either because of their personal characteristics or as members of certain occupations, can be described as 'latent victims', i.e. they are more prone than others to become the objects of crimes. This corresponds to the categoric risks to commit crime[131] or to be involved in traffic accidents. Obvious examples of such victim proneness are comparatively defenceless persons such as the young, the old, females, the drunks (Clifford Shaw's *The Jack-Roller*), the feeble-minded, the illiterate, the members of minority groups. Among members of victim-prone occupations are taxi-drivers, prostitutes, and all persons who have to handle large sums of money.[132] In London, for example, the naked bodies of four prostitutes were found in the same area between November 1963 and April 1964 (for the details see the *Sunday Times*, 26.4.1964); and in a recent study of the Chicago Skid Row district Donald J. Bogue (see above, Note 82 to Chapter 23) reports that criminals frequent such districts in order to rob the residents who are defenceless on account of age, infirmity, or drink. All this is common-sense experience, and no new discipline is needed to fill in the details. There are, however, also more complex psychological possibilities, as in the case of masochists who deliberately provoke physical or spiritual aggression to satisfy their own wishes. Moreover, there are those victims who are tired of life and provide the killer with every opportunity. According to Sueton and Plutarch, Julius Caesar belonged to this category.[133] v. Hentig has produced a comprehensive psychological typology of victims.[134]

(c) The victim is not necessarily an individual, it may also be a collective entity, a firm or a whole race or nation. The provisions of the substantive criminal law will usually indicate whom they are intended to protect. For example in cases of genocide victims are not only those individual members of the national, racial, or religious groups whose destruction had been the object of the crime, but also the groups as such.[135]

The details of the victim-offender relationship have been studied in particular for those types of crime where personal factors are most likely to play an important part, i.e. homicide and sex offences, but to some extent also for offences of an economic character. While the *Report of the Royal Commission on Capital Punishment* of 1953 presented nothing but a few statistical tables to show the bare outlines of the victim-murderer relationship (Appendix 3, Tables 4 and 5, similarly *Criminal Statistics for 1962*, p. xxxiv), Wolfgang in his Philadelphia study produced an all-round picture not only of offenders and victims as separate units but also with special emphasis on the frequency of primary group relationships existing between the two parties. To mention only one aspect of his study, in accordance with Durkheim's thesis that males participate more than females in collective life, he found primary group relationships far more frequent in the case of female than of male victims, i.e. women were more often than men the victims of men standing very close to them (p. 204). Attention was also paid to the frequency of victim-precipitated homicides, which term Wolfgang defined as cases where the victim was 'the first to commence the interplay of resort to physical violence' (p. 252). One could, of course, also use the term in a far wider sense as including the cases where the victim precipitated the crime in other ways. In view of his narrower use of the term it is not surprising that Wolfgang found an extraordinarily high rate of precipitating victims with police records; in fact, a significantly higher proportion of them had such records than had the offenders (p. 262).

Homosexuals are occasionally killed by their partners, whereby their indecent approaches are used as a pretext for violence, sometimes coupled with robbery.[136] Such cases are illustrations of what Sykes and Matza have called 'denial of the victim'.[137]

In the study of sexual crimes against children the distinction between participating and accidental victims has become generally accepted. The work of the Langley Porter Clinic has produced ample evidence for the existence of these two categories. Participant victims, as compared with the others, were found usually to be girls who had known the offender for some time, had had more than one sexual experience with him, had received some form of remuneration from him and kept the relationship secret from their parents. All of them showed considerable emotional disturbance and various other personality traits which distinguished them from the accidental victims, such as much stronger needs for security and love; a number of them were severely neurotic, felt rejected by their parents and had considerable anxiety about sex. In many cases, their parents too had sexual conflicts and marital difficulties. A sub-group of them had been molested by their stepfathers. The offenders also were examined and were found not to fit 'the popular stereotype of the sex maniac', but to be rather immature and incapable of developing satisfactory relationships with adults.

In a more recent British study, Gibbens and Prince[138] also stress the importance of the role played by the parents, especially of conflicts in attitudes within the mother or sexually stimulating behaviour by the parents towards the child or, in extreme cases, incest. Within the 'participating' group they believe that the majority of these victims show no widespread maladjustment, but are simply submissive and seductive girls, ready to establish immediate, superficial relationships. In a case from Lincolnshire where 18 young girls and 40 male persons were said to have been involved, the probation officer stated that all these girls had been willing participants acting from boredom and the desperate need for some form of excitement and that sexual adventure had become the vogue among them (*The Times*, 3.12.1963, Court of Criminal Appeal).

With regard to adult women who are victims of the white slave traffic, it has been maintained that 99 per cent of them are aware that they are taking a risk, although they may not fully realize its seriousness, and that most of them are 'neo-prostitutes'.[139]

In the field of economic crime we have to refer to our previous discussion of the distinction made by many offenders according to the type of property which they violate: if the victim is rich, or a big firm, or the 'Government' or an insurance company, scruples of any kind are entirely unknown, whereas the property of the small man is usually respected (see pp. 583–4 above). The many ways in which property owners, especially when insured, facilitate the work of thieves and burglars are a well-known source of concern to the police, and the often indifferent attitude of large stores to shoplifting has already been commented upon (Chapter 23).[140] Art forgeries have become the flourishing business which they are at present largely through the ignorance, snobbery, and speculative habits of certain well-to-do 'patrons' (see above, p. 464).

This leads to the part played by the victim in cases of false pretences. It has been examined in recent years by v. Hentig and Lenz, the former, as usual, basing himself on individual cases taken from American and German publications, the latter presenting the results of a questionnaire enquiry and personal interviews with a considerable number of victims. Lenz distinguishes 'active' victims, who 'approach' the swindler, and 'passive' ones who have to be approached by him, which is similar to the distinction between participant and accidental victims. Here, too, it is the first type who is in greater danger. For reasons of space, no further details can here be given.

In a brilliant chapter v. Hentig deals with the victims of blackmail. It is here, he points out, that the relationship between criminal and victim has to be particularly close since the former can operate only if he knows a secret of the victim. This, however, is a rule with at least two exceptions: first, the criminal may have obtained possession of the secret by mere chance without having established any relationship with the victim; and, secondly, he may be successful, even without knowing any secrets at all, provided his victim is in a position where he has to fear even the most groundless accusations. We are here reminded of Voltaire's famous dictum: 'If I were accused of having stolen the towers of Notre Dame I would immediately go into exile.'

Reference should be made to the attempts, made in the past decade in this country, to introduce legislation for compensating the victims of crimes of violence. Not surprisingly, in the report of the Working Party set up a few years ago by the Government to study the practical problems involved in the matter,[141] attention was drawn to the fact that not all victims of crimes of violence are deserving of our sympathy to the extent that public money should be spent on their behalf. Clearly, further research in the field of victimology should be of practical assistance to clarify the distinction between 'deserving' and 'undeserving' victims.

Chapter 26

AGE AND SEX FACTORS IN CRIME

I. THE AGE FACTOR[1]

The purpose of this section is not to deal with the subject of juvenile and adolescent delinquency as compared with that of adult crime in its various aspects from the point of view of age. It is the far more modest one to present some statistical figures to show how criminality is spread over the different age groups, coupled with a few allied questions arising from the age distribution.

This is a matter which has often attracted the interest of scholars, and speculative theories have occasionally been produced, built on statistical and other material of doubtful value. There can of course be no objections to serious attempts of the kind discussed below to use the statistical data available to explain the role of the age factor in criminality and possibly even to draw conclusions of a causal nature, provided we bear in mind their often all-too slender statistical basis and the risks attached to any causal speculations. The main points to be discussed are the following: First, the age curve itself, i.e. the comparative frequency of crime in the different age groups and changes in the types of crime with advancing age. Secondly, the question at which age most offenders commit their first offence and when they usually discontinue their criminal careers. Thirdly, are members of certain age groups particularly likely to commit crime if subjected to certain environmental experiences, or, to put it more clearly, are there any 'delinquent generations'? Fourthly, the special problems of the elderly offender.

1. *The Age Curve*

Even this apparently simple subject can lead to certain very puzzling questions when studied comparatively for a number of countries. In English *Criminal Statistics* it is presented more clearly than in most others, related to 100,000 of the age or age group (see next pages).

A few comments on these figures may be helpful. First, while there have been all-round increases between 1938 and 1962, they have been

TABLE SHOWING THE NUMBER OF PERSONS OF DIFFERENT AGES FOUND GUILTY OF INDICTABLE OFFENCES

MALES

Age or age group	Number of persons found guilty per 100,000 of population of the age or age group	
	1962	1938
8	294	220
9	633	451
10	1,073	703
11	1,500	931
12	2,107	1,111
13	2,700	1,315
14	3,139	1,141
15	2,254	1,145
16	2,448	1,110
17	2,673	867
18	2,492	740
19	2,397	766
20	2,230	665
21 and under 25	1,930	559
25 and under 30	1,280	431
30 and under 40	749	307
40 and under 50	395	182
50 and under 60	183	101
60 and over	67	51
Total	895	393

particularly striking for the age groups 14 to 30. Secondly, the peak age has shifted from 13 to 14 for males and from 18/19 to 14 for females. Thirdly, while the youngest age groups of males have throughout shown far higher crime rates than the ones over 50, this is not so for the females where, except for those aged 60 and over, the older women can well compete with the girls up to 10.

Those of us who may have been content to study these English figures are inclined to take this early peak age and the far lower criminality of older people for granted and regard them almost as a law of nature. It is only when we look at them in the light of comparative material that we begin to ask a few more searching questions. Such material from abroad, it is true, is not very comprehensive. For some countries, especially the U.S.A., the figures are not representative; for others, for example Israel, they are not very revealing since they are not related to the population figures. Moreover, as in most

FEMALES

Age or age group	Number of persons found guilty per 100,000 of population of the age or age group	
	1962	1938
8	12	9
9	44	27
10	74	37
11	151	62
12	252	66
13	355	73
14	405	84
15	293	97
16	311	91
17	328	99
18	275	106
19	267	108
20	232	94
21 and under 25	207	77
25 and under 30	163	62
30 and under 40	141	61
40 and under 50	126	50
50 and under 60	89	30
60 and over	33	10
Total	131	51

NOTE: Reprinted by permission of H.M.S.O., London, from *Criminal Statistics for England and Wales 1962* (Cmd. 2120, Sept. 1963), p. xlviii. For Vol. I of the present book the corresponding information (for the years 1938 and 1959) has been provided on p. 107.

countries there is no criminal responsibility below the ages of 13 or 14 these youngest groups, whatever their behaviour may be, are not included in their criminal statistics and therefore we have hardly any basis for treating one of the most striking features of English criminal statistics comparatively. There are, however, a few exceptions. In Japan, for example, although criminal responsibility begins at 14, 'offences' committed by younger children are shown in statistical investigations,[2] which will of course lead to doubts regarding the reliability of these figures. Nevertheless, the following numbers of arrests for 1955 may be of interest (omitting decimals): related to 100,000 of population—males under 14: 153; under 16: 1,043; under 18: 1,567; under 20: 2,463; 20–25: 3,286; 25–30: 2,546; 30–40: 1,780; 40–50: 1,159; 50–60: 600; 60 and over: 258; Total 1,182. Always bearing in mind that these are figures of arrests, not as the English ones of findings of guilt, we see that, while the Japanese totals are about 25 per cent higher, the figures for the younger age groups up to 18 are lower, for the youngest even much lower, but those for the age groups over 20 are much higher, for the oldest even very much higher. For females the total is lower, 87 against 131, and the peak occurs at 20–25 instead of 14, the rates for the older ones being not much higher than in this country. No explanation of the strikingly high rate for the oldest age groups of males (258 against 67) has been given, and one wonders whether it may be due to differences in the social services for old people. Equally striking is of course the fact that the peak occurs at 20–25 instead of 14.

For West Germany[3] the following figures, also related to 100,000 of population, are available, which however cover both males and females and lump together all age groups from 25 on; while therefore not strictly comparable with the English figures they will nevertheless illustrate a few differences (for 1958): 14–18: 993; 18–21: 1,543; 21–25: 1,683; 25 and over: 474; total 677. The fact that the total is lower than the English might well be explained by the omission of those under 14 and the inclusion of females. The rate for those between 14 and 18 is much lower, that for those between 18 and 21 still considerably lower; the peak, occurring at 21–25, is also still lower than the English, and for those of 25 and above it cannot be said whether the figures are distributed similarly to the English ones, but they do seem altogether lower. As these German figures cover all offences punishable under the Federal Penal Code, their coverage is at least as wide as, probably even wider than, the English figures which refer only to indictable offences. It may be added that the figures for 1954–7, although generally lower than those for 1958, show exactly the same trends, and it can therefore be concluded that the distribution just shown is not due to mere chance.

For France, Vouin and Léauté[4] present figures per 100,000 for 1954 which show a rise between 13 and 18: from 308 for those between 13 and 16 to 619 for those between 16 and 18. Selosse[5] gives the following data, per 1,000, for 1958 (males): 3·60 for 13, 5·12 for 14, 7·95 for 15, 12·05 for 16, 18·67 for 19, which is the peak age, and 11·18 for 20, 17·59 for the 21–30 group, 15·86 for 30–40. After the age of 40, the figure drops to 9·20, which still far exceeds the English rates. Here again we see, therefore, that the adolescent and young adults have a lower and the older men a far higher rate than in England. The rate for the 20-year-old ones is low because, as Selosse points out, their military service gives them but little time for offending. For women the peak lies much later than in England at 30–40, with 2·75, whereas the English peak age of 14 has in France only 0·88 per 1,000.

The Italian figures for the period 1950–56 show, for both sexes together, also per 1,000 of population, an even sharper rise from 0·71 for the 14–18 group to the peak of 4·61 for the 18–21 group and a decline to 3·43 for the 21–25, rising again to 4·07 for the 25–30 group, and thereafter a slow, but persistent decline to 2·87 for 40–50, 1·96 for 50–60, 1·09 for 60–70, and 0·45 afterwards.[6]

Without attempting to compare the total volume of crime in the Continental countries so far mentioned—which would obviously be futile—we note the tendency for the 14–18 group to have much lower crime rates than in England and for the peak to be several years later.

The weak points in U.S.A. criminal statistics are too well-known to require any further comments in the present context (see above, Chapter 5, s. 6c). For juvenile delinquency they are particularly obvious. 'There are at present no collections of data in this field that even begin to compile comparable information', wrote the Chief of the Californian Bureau of Criminal Statistics not long ago.[7] We have to be content with whatever data are available. In his painstaking study of pre-war data Thorsten Sellin came to the conclusion that the American peak age was at about 19,[8] and Reckless reported at the same time that the maximum was reached somewhere between 19 and 24.[9]

For Soviet Russia, Callcott[10] gives the peak age before the last war as at about 20–24 years for both sexes, with a sharp decline from then up to 40 and a less marked one from 40 to 60.

It might be tempting further to compare the age curves for different types of offences and for different periods of time, but this would require far more space than we can reasonably be expected to give to this subject. What cannot well be ignored, however, is the contrast between England and Wales and practically all other countries regarding the peak age of crime, which has often aroused the interest of foreign observers. Already Reckless, a quarter of a century ago, commented on it and suggested two possible explanations: either the administrative policy of the police and courts or the social order of England which induces crime in young people at an earlier age. However, he wisely recommended the greatest caution in accepting any of these statistics and explanations, and so did v. Hentig who pointed out that one should not try to compare figures which were not comparable.[11] Other writers have drawn attention to the fact that the male peak age was 13 when the school leaving age was 14, but moved to 14 when the school leaving age was advanced to 15, posing the question whether getting tired of school at a time when one feels ready for something more adult and, in particular, more profitable may towards the end of the waiting period lead to increased delinquency, especially if an overcrowded school class has but little to offer to the restless youth. The subsequent decline in the crime rate would then prove the beneficial effect of gainful employment. This is an argument which can easily be used against the Crowther Report of 1959 in its struggle for the raising of the school-leaving age to 16, after many years of delay now finally approved but not yet carried through, and it has therefore to be taken very seriously.[12] Again other writers have referred to the biological changes occurring at certain ages, in particular to the unsettling effect of puberty and pre-puberty.[13] Here, however, the fact would have to be considered that there are important differences in this respect between the various constitutional types. According to Ernst Kretschmer, for example, the leptosomes reach the peak age of their criminal activities much earlier than the pyknics, whose peak lies at 40–50 which is the lowest point for the leptosomes.[14] Moreover, the claim, which has recently been made so strongly, that puberty is now reached one or even several years earlier than, say, fifty years ago[15] seems to make the biological interpretation difficult to reconcile with the moving of the peak age of delinquency in the opposite direction.

The present writer is still inclined to attach very little significance to these 'peak age' figures. He still adheres to his earlier view, re-peated above, Chapter 5, s. 5(a), that statistics of juvenile delinquency merely indicate 'the varying degree of willingness on the part of the public and the police to bring this category of delinquents before the juvenile courts'.[16] The differences which have occurred in the figures for the age groups 13 and 14 are not striking enough to require any far-reaching explanations; they may simply be due to chance factors. More important is the fact that the English peaks occur so much earlier than in other countries; and here we may indeed be faced partly with an earlier onset of delinquency, possibly due to parental indifference, and partly to the earlier beginning of legal responsibility for crime, which may create in some quarters an atmosphere favour-able to court action with regard to younger age groups. All this, how-ever, remains mere speculation, and it would require a wholesale assimilation of the present English system to Continental standards to see whether this would be followed by drastic changes in the age curve of crime.

The very high share of the younger age groups in the country's total volume of crime can also be seen in the following percentage figures of indictable offences for males (1962):[17] out of a male total of 86·4 per cent those between 8 and 14 produced 14·2 per cent, those between 14 and 17: 15 per cent, 17 to 21: 15·6 per cent, together 44·8, against 20·4 per cent for those 21 to 30 and 21·2 per cent for those 30 and over. For females those between 8 and 21 had only 5 per cent out of a total of 13·6 per cent. Females of 30 and over committed nearly one half of the offences, males of that age less than one quarter.

Turning now to the changes in the type of crime which occur with advancing age, the younger age groups are, roughly speaking, predominant in larceny and breakings, the older in receiving, frauds and false pretences, white collar offences, and sexual offences. In Germany, Hellmer found that thieves committed their first offences when they were twelve years younger than sex offenders committing their first sex offence.[18] The peak group for violence against the person is that between 21 and 30, with 33·3 per cent, but those between 17 and 21 have increased their share from 10·3 per cent in 1938 to 27·5 per cent in 1962.[19] These figures, which, by the way, refer only to Magistrates' Courts, are misleading, however, as they are not related to the population figures which are much higher, of course, for the far more comprehensive age group of '30 and over' than for those comprising only the ten years 21 to 30 or the five years 17 to 21. Nevertheless, they are in accordance with common experience and the results of studies made of special samples. There is general agreement, for example, that sexual offenders, as a group, are older than other categories of offenders, although this is not true of certain types of sex offence such as indecent exposure.[20] In the Cambridge sample the proportion of those between 21 and 40 was 51 per cent, of those 50 and over 15 per cent, together 66 per cent against 41·6 per cent in our general figures above. Fitch gives the mean age of his group of sex offenders as 35–36, which is also considerably higher than the general mean age for prisoners in this country.

Of particular interest in this connection is the question whether recidivists change the type of their criminal activities with advancing age. In our study of the files of 1,274 recidivists appearing before the London Central Criminal Court comparatively little evidence was found of such changes in a specific direction, although it did happen that after a particularly heavy sentence men turned to less exhausting crimes, such as coining or false pretences in the place of breaking in.[21] Hammond, who examined the offences committed by preventive detainees after discharge, noticed slight changes in the type of offence committed, notably from breaking to larceny.[22] The Gluecks, too, found only comparatively insignificant changes in type of offence with advancing age, notably a drift into 'milder, less aggressive and less daring forms of misconduct'.[23] There is but little evidence for the popular assumption that criminals proceed with advancing age to more and more serious types of crime; this is, in particular, untrue of sexual offenders. An entirely different question is whether certain types of crime are more frequent in certain age groups than in others; here available statistics show quite clearly that there is a high correlation between age and type of offence, with violence more prominent in the adolescent and young adult groups, fraud, receiving, and sex offences, as already shown, more in the middle age groups.[24]

2. *Various Specific Aspects of Age*

Special attention was paid by the Gluecks in their follow-up studies to the effect of ageing on type of offence as well as on abstaining from further lawbreaking. With regard to the latter, they had first developed the theory that reformation was due mainly to the fact of reaching a certain chronological age, i.e. that of approximately thirty-five. Those who had not reformed by then were less likely to do so afterwards.[25] A few years later, however, when analysing the results of a ten-years follow-up of another group, they came to the conclusion, in some ways already foreshadowed in their earlier work, that the crucial factor was not arrival at a chronological age *per se*, but rather in conjunction with 'the achievement of adequate maturation', which can of course be greatly delayed by certain counteracting factors, especially mental abnormalities.[26] This seems to be only common sense, but coupled with it was the suggestion that the abandonment of a criminal career seems to occur 'rather after the passage of a certain length of time from the point of first expression of definite delinquent trends'.[27] In other words, if the juvenile who first embarks on a criminal career at the age of twelve may abandon it at, say, thirty, his brother, who started at seventeen, was more likely to reform at thirty-five. Those who have entered the field of crime in their youth require a certain length of time to get criminality out of their systems, regardless of their ages at the start. This suggestion has been criticized,[28] especially as it contradicts another generally held belief that those whose offences begin early in life are more likely to become dangerous and persistent adult criminals than are those who start late. This is the theory propagated in the important, but controversial work of the Swiss criminologist Erwin Frey, who made the reservation, however, that an early start of criminality was predictive of adult recidivism only when accompanied by early *Verwahrlosung*, a term so vague that it can cover almost any form of unmanageable and deviant behaviour.[29] Frey found that in his sample the percentage of adult recidivists among those who had been juvenile delinquents was about seven times as high as among those who had not been delinquents in their youth. The development of adult recidivism, he concluded, is in nearly all cases foreshadowed by juvenile delinquency. Obviously, this is a matter of considerable importance for the understanding and prediction of persistent adult crime. Research on it is often made difficult or impossible through absence of reliable data on early offences of juveniles,[30] but a limited amount of information is available. In the Borstal Prediction Study it was found that those Borstal boys who had been first found guilty at the age of 11 or under had a failure rate after discharge of 65 per cent, whereas for those with the first finding of guilt at ages 12–15 it was 54 per cent and for those with the first finding of guilt at 16–21 it was only 46 per cent.[31] The Gluecks, too, predicted a higher failure rate in prisons for offenders who had first been arrested under the age of 11 than for those aged 11 or older,[32] and Hammond also regards the age at first offence as prognostic of the likelihood of committing a further offence.[33] Of the 1,274 recidivists on whom information was presented in *Social Aspects of Crime*, 13·6 per cent had been found guilty before the age of 14, and only 51 after reaching the age of 40 (p. 358). Benson, Taylor, West, and Norval Morris all report that in their respective samples the mean ages at first conviction were later than expected, i.e. roughly between 18 and 20, but they are equally sceptical about the reliability of their results since, as Benson puts it, '50 years ago country police forces were very haphazard in reporting juvenile offences to C.R.O.'[34] In view of what has been said before, the present writer need hardly add that he is even less impressed by these figures. To complete this brief survey of the evidence we turn to Japan, where an investigation was made in 1950 of the ages of recidivists aged over 40 committed to Fuchu Prison, with the result that recidivism was far more serious in the case of those who had committed their first offences between 14 and 17 than of those who had started later in life.[35] Moreover, in Austria too Roland Grassberger, in a particularly careful investigation, showed that the likelihood and speed of recidivism was closely related to the age at first conviction.[36] Thorsten Sellin (see Note 36) quotes Quetelet's dictum that 'among all the causes that influence the growth and abatement of the penchant for crime, age is without question the most energetic' (*Recherches sur le penchant au crime aux different ages*, 2nd ed., Bruxelles, 1833, pp. 63–4).

Summing up this part of our discussion we might make the following points: First, the popular view that those who begin to offend very early in life are destined to carry on a criminal career of increasing gravity is true, but only in a limited sense. The mere fact that the crime rate declines very sharply, whether as in England after 14 or as in most other countries after young adult age, already shows that only a small proportion of juvenile delinquents ever become persistent adult criminals. While it is true that those who start early and have an unfavourable childhood are more likely to carry on than those who start later, this tendency should therefore not be over-estimated. Secondly, for those who continue their criminal activities in adult life, the question arises at what later stage they are likely to discontinue them. The finding of the Gluecks that the age of 35 is the crucial watershed has so far not been confirmed by English statistics.

According to Benson's material, drawn from Dartmoor and Park-hurst Prisons, 'between the ages of 30 and 55 there is not much to choose. Nor do the records of the failures suggest a gradual diminu-tion of criminality after 35. Indeed the number now serving long sentences of imprisonment and preventive detention is depressing.' Nevertheless, Benson concludes, it would be wrong to abandon hope for the middle-aged criminal. In particular, we may add, the slender hope of redemption through a happy marriage or constructive train-ing always exists. Between the ages of 30 and 60, Benson calculates, something like 80 per cent, or allowing for the death rate, 70 per cent 'disappear from the ken of the police by ceasing to recidivate or by death', while 'of 100 aged 55 we can expect 27 to cease before the age of 60'. The possibility of police failure to detect new offences is dis-carded by Benson as negligible in cases of men already known as recidivists.

There are still two more specific points to be dealt with. First, the question of 'delinquent generations'. Whereas we have so far been concerned with the crime rates of individuals on reaching certain ages, we are now faced with the problem of the criminality of whole generations, whole cohorts born within a certain period and under-going certain common experiences such as war. Can it be proved that children born between 1935 and 1942 have developed stronger delin-quent tendencies than those born in other seven-year periods? As mentioned above (Chapter 23, text to Note 222), this question has been fully examined by ingenious statistical techniques and answered in the affirmative by Leslie T. Wilkins. In his own words, 'the greatest "crime-proneness" is thus found to be associated with that birth group who passed through their fifth year during the war . . . There appears to be something particularly significant in social disturbances occurring in the fourth and fifth year of a child's life.' Without wish-ing here to speculate about possible explanations of this phenomenon —of which a few are tentatively presented by Wilkins—we have to say that it is only natural to expect delinquency to march, so to speak, in whole battalions or generations. If we accept the idea that, in spite of all individual differences, human beings as a mass tend to react to similar environmental stimuli in roughly similar ways and that this tendency is even stronger in the case of individuals having certain im-portant biological or psychological factors in common, it is clear that individuals of the same age undergoing similar disruptive influences such as war will be more likely to show similar responses than in-dividuals of different ages. One important statistical exception to the 'general rule of birth group effects' was noted by Wilkins: the crime rate among young males between 17 and 21 years of age greatly exceeded the expected rate; for them, 'some increase in criminality might have been expected, but not to the extent found to occur'. Wilkins's main thesis has been sharply criticized on statistical grounds by both G. Prys Williams and A. A. Walters (Note 1). It is not within the competence of a non-statistician to take sides in this argument, but it might well be argued that, while refined statistical techniques of the kind here used by the contestants can well produce interesting conclusions based on the available figures, they can never be a substitute for reliable basic material. As we regard the available statistics of juvenile offences as singularly unreliable we are unable to subscribe to any results based on statistical manipulation, however brilliant, of such statistics. Wilkins himself admits the many pitfalls of criminal statistics in his *Social Deviance*, esp. pp. 145 ff. Of course the fact that similar investigations in Denmark and New Zealand have confirmed Wilkins' findings is an important factor in their favour, unless we assume that they all suffer from the same weaknesses of their basic material.

The second subject to which attention might here be drawn is the criminality of those who enter the field of crime at an unusually late age. Unless we extend the term 'latecomer', as Cormier does, to all those first convicted after reaching the age of 20, they are comparatively few in numbers; but nevertheless they form an important group. Benson calculated that about 4 per cent of his sample had commenced their criminal careers after 30, Norval Morris about 5 per cent; in *Social Aspects of Crime* the present writer's figure was 8 per cent of the men and 11 per cent of the women, for those over 40 it was 4 per cent of men and less than 3 per cent of women (p. 358). To a considerable extent, these low figures are of course merely due to failure to detect earlier delinquency. In most life histories of criminals we find references to unreported juvenile offences, mostly not very serious ones, but offences nevertheless which if recorded would upset the official picture. 'Charlie Smith', the 'unknown citizen', is a typical example: officially, he had no record until the age of 30, but actually, his sister reports, already at the orphanage 'he was always getting into trouble for stealing and lying', and later in the Army 'he was always in trouble there too, for the same kind of thing'.[37] While the responsibility for these statements has of course to be left to his sister, it is unlikely that she should have been untruthful in this respect. Generally speaking, all one can say is that the actual proportion of late starters is probably much smaller than appears from the official figures, and that in such cases where detection and punishment were delayed until manhood the absence of any such official 'warning' may have acted as an encouragement to continue on the path of crime. Nevertheless, there can be no doubt that late recruits to crime do exist in far from negligible numbers, and with

687

the growing interest in gerontology and the psychiatric and social problems connected with ageing its criminological repercussions have been repeatedly studied in the last decades, though of course to a smaller extent than the far more important subject of juvenile delinquency. Three principal types of latecomers to crime can be distinguished: the first, smallest, group consists of those rare idealists who, on reaching middle age with an unblemished and in some cases even highly distinguished record, are suddenly faced with a problem, political or social, occasionally also a personal one, which threatens to undermine their whole *Weltanschauung*, the very foundation on which their moral existence has so far firmly rested. Consequently, for the first time in their lives seriously beginning to doubt the justice of the established order of things they eventually become rebels and lawbreakers. Such figures play a prominent part in world literature;[38] they are probably rarer in real life, except for the history of revolutions. Political assassins are usually youngish men, but the leaders often belong to more mature age groups.

Entirely different are the other two categories of latecomers; their motives do not spring from their strong moral, political or religious convictions, but are those of the ordinary offender, with the difference that only in mid-life do they encounter financial or sexual difficulties with which they cannot cope by lawful means. After committing their first crime, however, these two categories part company; while the members of the one group abstain from further lawbreaking, the others continue and often become persistent criminals. In *Social Aspects* it was found that many of those who started after the age of 40 became habituals with twenty or more convictions.

Among those who do not become recidivists are of course particularly prominent the elderly jealousy murderers with definite psychiatric symptoms such as mentioned above in Chapter 14, although the case histories published by Shepherd include also many men in their mid-thirties. In the case of many normal offenders of maturer age, too, the shock of detection and punishment, with accompanying publicity, is often enough to keep them straight, especially if their family links remain intact and they can find employment.

Among those of the last category, who become habitual criminals at a mature age, are some truly tragic cases. There is, for example, a man of 71, educated at a public school and a graduate of Cambridge, who was deprived of his assets and means of livelihood as a result of the Second World War, when some of his property was lost in Paris where he had worked and the rest was bombed in London. This led to a number of offences since 1949 and, eventually in 1962, to a sentence of five years' preventive detention, changed by the Court of Criminal Appeal to one of five years' imprisonment, for stealing valuable books from the Bodleian Library, Oxford.[39] On the other hand, there is some evidence that among these latecomers are many who commit their offences not because of a breakdown of their financial existence or their family bonds, but rather on account of, sometimes prematurely occurring, symptoms of psycho-physiological senility (Chapter 14, I (d) aggravating their social inadequacy.[40]

A valuable attempt has been made by the Canadian psychiatrist Bruno M. Cormier and his co-workers[41] to summarize the characteristics of latecomers, classified according to decades, beginning with those in their twenties—which seems to be rather early for the concept of 'latecomer'—and ending with those in their fifties, which seems to leave out the very small but not unimportant group who start after 60. His observations are derived from the personal study of 318 inmates of the Canadian Federal St. Vincent de Paul Penitentiary, first offenders aged 20 years or more and serving sentences of at least two years. Although we cannot accept the labelling of offenders under 30 as 'latecomers' and although some of his views may appear to be based on too narrow a factual basis, his work contains much of general interest, and our brief summary does not pretend to do justice to it. For example, among those in their twenties he found only rarely the 'lone operator'; most of them, while not like the adolescents members of gangs, tended to associate with a few criminal partners. Some of them had been protected by their families up to manhood and broke down as soon as they lost this protection. Many cases showed serious personal and social problems and an anti-social attitude, committing crime as an act of retaliation against society. As compared with them, those who became first offenders in their thirties were but rarely rebels with basic anti-social attitudes; their problems were more personal, often connected with unhappy marriages or with sexual disappointments in originally sound marriages, looking for new experiences or taking to drink. Recidivism is less frequent here than among those in their twenties. All these disappointments appear in even more intense forms in those who start when in their forties; many of them are seriously depressed, and in Cormier's pregnant phrase crime represents for them 'a last attempt at youth. Many men in this group come to the penitentiary because in their 40's for the first time in their lives they begin to act as if they were in their 20's.' Needless to say, such men are miles apart from the late rebels of our first category. Loneliness, physical and emotional deterioration are the chief characteristics of those who become first offenders in their fifties or still later. The probability of recidivism declines fairly steadily from about 65 or 75 per cent for those in their twenties to about 45 to 50 per cent for the older groups.

II. THE SEX FACTOR: FEMALE DELINQUENCY[42]

1. *Introductory Remarks*

Before going into the details of this fascinating subject, the following general points have to be made.

(*a*) While there is no doubt that according to official statistics and our general impressions the total female crime rate is much lower everywhere than that of males we should avoid the frequent mistake of studying the subject solely under such comparative aspects. This one-sided approach inevitably induces the observer to search for nothing but plausible explanations of the differential crime rate and unwittingly to limit his attention to those factors which are likely to furnish good reasons why females should commit less crime than males. An objective and scientific approach should try to treat female crime as a topic in its own right, which does not, of course, make frequent comparisons with its male counterpart unnecessary. Nor does it mean that we should try to understand female criminality exclusively from the sexual angle.

(*b*) Another mistake often found in statistical comparisons of the sex rates is to ignore the striking differences between the various categories of offences and between the various age groups. For the latter, reference can be made to the statistical tables above in section I, which show that the contrast between the overall male and female crime rates varies considerably according to age; while, for example, the 1962 ratio for the eight-year-old ones was 24 males to one female, for those 60 and over it was only two males to one female. The position when compared with pre-war figures has, on the whole, changed to the advantage of women, especially in the older age groups. A striking contrast between male and female crime rates, as also shown in our tables, lies in the far smaller variations in the female rates, the male peak age figures being about 46 times higher than the lowest ones, whereas for females the peak age figures are only about 12 times higher than the lowest. In pre-war years the contrast was, as far as the male figures were concerned, less striking.[43]

The sex differences for individual offences will be discussed below.

(*c*) Criminologists have occasionally been criticized for paying but scant attention to the subject of female crime. Lady Wootton in particular has accused them of being prejudiced and 'curiously blind to the obvious'; 'hardly anyone seems to have thought it worthwhile to try to find out' why there was such a difference in the respective crime rates.[44] If this were true we might well ask why this distinguished author, with her exceptionally favourable equipment both as a scholar and as a female protagonist, did not make use of her opportunities to fill the gap. In fact, the accusation is not altogether well-founded. It is certainly true that much less research has so far been done on the characteristics and possible explanations of female than on those of male crime, but this is largely due not to 'blindness' but to the comparative scarcity of case material and the greater difficulty of access to it; to the smaller numbers of female research workers who would be particularly interested in the subject and qualified to do research on it; and to the difficulties presented to statistical enquiries by the small numbers of cases. In any case, it is a distortion of the truth to maintain that the subject has been entirely ignored. Female scholars such as Pauline Tarnowsky, the Russian student of Lombroso, the Dutch lawyer Johanna C. Hudig, the American sociologist Mabel A. Elliott, the English psychiatrists Grace W. Pailthorpe, Hedwig Schwarz and Phyllis Epps, and the psychiatric social worker Moya Woodside—a list which is by no means complete—have made valuable contributions to it, and a not inconsiderable literature has also been produced by several male authors.

(d) There is, however, another point of fundamental importance which has not often received in criminological literature the attention due to it, i.e. the fact that hitherto female crime has, for all practical purposes, been dealt with almost exclusively by men in their various capacities as legislators, judges, policemen; and at least up to the end of the last century the same was true of the theoretical treatment of the subject not only by scholars but also by poets and novelists. This could not fail to create a one-sided picture. It has been said, not without justification, that what human beings think of members of the opposite sex is usually the result of their personal disappointments and therefore distorted. This centuries-old male predominance in theory and practice and the consequent distortions have, however, not throughout worked in the expected direction, i.e. to the disadvantage of females, but may indeed rather have favoured them in various ways. Men seem to have made penal laws mainly to prevent and punish actions which they thought endangered their personal interests, whereas certain specifically female forms of misconduct were often regarded as not serious enough or too pleasant or indispensable to them to warrant penal measures. The legislators, being males, may unwittingly have moulded the whole system of criminal law in such a way as to turn a blind eye to some of those anti-social actions most frequently committed by women, such as prostitution—which, unless accompanied by certain other activities, is not an offence in most countries—or lesbianism, lying or quarrelling. However, as the example of witchcraft shows, this hypothesis should not be stretched too far. Nevertheless, there have been occasional traces of what might be regarded as a guilty conscience in this man-made criminal law, showing that male legislators, aware of the under-privileged position of women in pre-twentieth-century society, have made special efforts to protect them against some of the consequences of that lack of equality. In this connection the English common law presumption has to be mentioned that a woman who committed a felony (except murder or treason) in the presence of her husband had committed it under compulsion and was therefore entitled to an acquittal, but this presumption was abolished by the Criminal Justice Act, 1925, s. 47, because of the improved social position and consequent greater independence of women.[45] A statutory provision in favour of women, but limited to one crime, infanticide, is contained in the Infanticide Act, 1938. On a far broader basis rests art. 37L of the Cuban Penal Code of 1936, which accords the benefit of mitigating circumstances to a woman who has committed a crime when under the influence of a mental disturbance due to climacterium, pregnancy, menstruation or the abnormal effect of childbirth.[46] On the other hand in a few countries adultery is a punishable offence only for women or at least punished more severely and in a more general fashion in the case of women than of men.[47]

The fact that homosexual acts between women are in most countries exempt from punishment—one of the few exceptions is Austria—has not entirely escaped criticism and has also occasionally been used as an argument against the penalization of male homosexuality. The West German Constitutional Court had to deal in 1957 with the case of two men found guilty of homosexual offences who claimed that the legal provisions under which they had been punished were against the principle of equality before the law, anchored in the West German Constitution, and therefore null and void. Art. 3 of the Constitution provides that men and women enjoy equal rights and that nobody should be treated better or worse for reasons of his or her sex only. The Court rejected this argument because equality before the law did not exclude differential legal treatment justified by fundamental biological differences; because of the existence of such differences female homosexuality, the Court held, was a phenomenon quantitatively and qualitatively not comparable to its male counterpart. The experts whose opinions were decisive for this judgment included the psychiatrist Ernst Kretschmer and the Austrian criminologist Grassberger, the latter pointing out that in Austria in the period 1946–53 the number of women sentenced for homosexual offences was less than 4 per cent of the men sentenced for such offences, a difference which he thought could not be explained by a larger hidden number of undetected or at least not prosecuted female offences. The German Draft Penal Code of 1962 accepts the view of the Constitutional

Court and limits the penalization of homosexual acts as before to males.[48]

In addition to such legal distinctions made in favour of the female sex there is further the inequality observed in detection and the practice of prosecution and sentencing. It has been argued by several investigators that women tend to commit mainly such offences which, by their very nature, can be detected only with special difficulties and are, even if detected, only rarely reported and prosecuted. Pollak mentions in particular non-professional shoplifting, thefts by prostitutes and domestic servants, abortions, perjury and indecent exposure.[49] To some extent this argument is probably correct, but exact proof is obviously impossible to obtain, and it can also be maintained that there are certain specifically male offences which show very low rates of detection too, such as burglary and housebreaking. While many of Pollak's points may be valid, one gets the impression that in his efforts to show that the sex difference in crime rates is actually much smaller than generally assumed he goes too much to the other extreme and tends to under-rate the size of the dark numbers in male criminality. As far as pilfering from employers is concerned, for example, male workers have probably the same opportunities as their female colleagues, and the proportion of those who use these opportunities is probably not lower than in the case of women, but all this is hardly more than mere conjecture. For blackmail v. Hentig offers some interesting observations to show that men are more vulnerable and open to exploitation by female secretaries, chambermaids or prostitutes, and that such acts of blackmail committed by women will very rarely reach the courts.[50] This, too, is very likely correct, but no exact proof is possible.

It is, however, not only the type of offence but also their manner of participating in it which reduces the official crime rate of women as they are more likely to play the role of instigator, aider and abetter than that of the actual doer, and it is usually more difficult to detect the former than the latter.[51] Our criminal law and, we might add, our administration of criminal justice are 'almost exclusively doer-centred' (Reckless).[52] As criminal statistics do not distinguish according to differences in participation it cannot be proved statistically, however, that there is such a sex difference in the kind of participation, and we are mainly dependent on the observation of individual cases.

Closely connected with the form of participation is the sex difference concerning acquittal: as those who take part in crime in less direct ways than as actual doers are more difficult to track down they stand a better chance of being acquitted in case of prosecution. To take, for example, a few post-war years at random, in 1954 of 17,806 males and

930 females brought before Assizes and Quarter Sessions, which is a ratio of 19:1, 1,739 males and 141 females were acquitted, i.e. 12:1. In 1961, 33,040 males and 1,284 females were brought to trial before Assizes and Quarter Sessions, i.e. a ratio of 25:1, whereas acquittals numbered 2,784 males against 163 females, i.e. a ratio of 17:1.[53] That members of the public are far more reluctant to take action against girls than against boys is common knowledge and accounts, at least to some extent, for the disparity of cases brought before the juvenile courts. Where proceedings are taken they are more often for being in need of care and protection or beyond parental control than for criminal offences, even in cases where the latter have actually been committed.

Moreover, when charged and found guilty women are more leniently treated by the courts than men,[54] but this does not of course affect the crime rate with which we are here primarily concerned. In many cases this greater leniency is probably justified, but in some others it is entirely misplaced.

On the other hand, the treatment facilities available for female offenders are usually even less adequate and up-to-date than those for males, mainly because their smaller numbers make it more difficult to classify, staff and equip institutions. The story of women in English prisons has been told in detail in Ann D. Smith's monograph (see Note 42); with a few exceptions, such as the open prisons, it is a rather dismal story, culminating in the sentence that 'in 1961 the shadow of Holloway still hangs over the prison system for women in Britain' (p. 324). Holloway, however, is by no means the only blot on this system; another is the presence there of large numbers of female 'drunks' for whom no constructive alternative methods of treatment have ever been consistently tried, whereas special training courses have been established for the increasing number of women sent to prison for cruelty to or neglect of children.[55] Actually, while the institutional treatment of delinquent women is, in some ways, even more difficult than that of men, there are also reasons why it could be made more progressive than the latter. The security aspect is less intricate as public opinion is less insistent here on maximum security than in the case of male prisoners, and the smaller numbers involved should make individual case work more easy to practise. On the other hand, the recruitment of suitable staff presents additional problems. A particularly intractable subject has always been the institutional treatment of adolescent girls. In a report by a Joint Committee of the British Medical Association and the Magistrates' Association on the problem of the unstable adolescent girl the conclusion was reached that 'not only are facilities for dealing with these girls inadequate, but those that are available are often of the wrong kind'.[56] This was written soon after the last war, and the position has improved since then; nevertheless, even the—certainly not over-critical—Ingleby Report of 1960 refers to the need for more varied vocational training schemes and the difficulty of recruiting senior staff of suitable quality in girls' approved schools, and reports that only twelve out of the thirty-three existing schools had psychiatrists to visit them for regular sessions.[57] Detention centres (Criminal Justice Act, 1948, s. 18) have for many years been regarded, on psychological grounds, as an unsuitable form of training for girls and it was only in 1962 that the objections have been over-ruled and the first centre has been opened; no results are so far available. These few scattered observations are not intended to provide a picture of the whole complex subject of the penal and correctional treatment of female offenders, but merely to show some of the many problems peculiar to this side of the system.

2. *Historical Sketch of Female Delinquency*

Historically seen, the crimes in which women were mostly involved in former ages used to be adultery and incest, witchcraft, poisoning and infanticide. Penologists and legal historians have collected much material to show how in ancient society, before the coming into existence of a state penal system, women caught in adultery were punished by their husbands exercising their right as heads of the family.[58] Penologists have also studied the medieval differences in penal methods as applied to the two sexes; drowning, burning or burying alive were regarded as particularly appropriate forms of execution for women in the Middle Ages.[59] In the medieval witch-craft trials women had to bear the brunt of the prosecutions because they were believed to be more likely to enter into sexual relations with the devil.[60] A fascinating international history of the witchcraft trials has recently been published in German by Kurt Baschwitz. He shows that most of the accused were elderly women and poor specimens. Jeanne d'Arc was one of the exceptions, but according to Baschwitz she was tried not for witchcraft but for heresy; although the original indictment had been for witchcraft, too, this point was dropped in the course of the proceedings.[61] The great astronomer Johann Kepler succeeded in 1621, after a struggle lasting six years, to rescue his mother from the stake. In some cases, in Sweden, for example, the authorities used children as witnesses against women accused of witchcraft (p. 318), and the same happened in the famous trial at Salem, Massachusetts (Baschwitz, Chapter 9). The last of these trials took place in the middle or towards the end of the eighteenth century.

695

According to Pike, women were continually mentioned in the fourteenth century not only as receivers of stolen property but also in connection with brigandage and other crimes of violence; they were, he writes, often 'almost as brutal as their husbands or paramours',[62] and among the masses of vagrants women, too, played a prominent part not only as companions of the males but often without them as prostitutes and beggars.[63] Later, in the eighteenth century, the type of female crime which attracted most of the attention of criminal law reformers and poets was infanticide; Radbruch and Gwinner call it 'the key offence of all eighteenth-century efforts to modernize the medieval criminal law'.[64] The tragic story of Gretchen in Goethe's *Faust* has, as these authors remind us, at least in part to be traced back to the execution of a Frankfurt woman for infanticide; and other great contemporary German poets, such as Schiller and Bürger, made effective propaganda in their works for the abolition of the death penalty for this crime. That the French Revolution should greatly stimulate such efforts was only natural, and it is not surprising that a prize-competition held in 1780 in Germany on the question 'Which are the most practicable means to prevent infanticide?' elicited nearly four hundred replies, among them Pestalozzi's book on the subject. Infanticide came to be regarded as one of the crimes symptomatic of the callous exploitation by the aristocracy of women belonging to the lower social classes.

At the same time, however, women who were themselves members of the French aristocracy took a prominent part in crimes of an entirely different kind. In the sensational 'Affair of the Queen's [i.e. Marie Antoinette's] Necklace', which was widely believed to bear some of the responsibility for the downfall of Louis XVI and his dynasty, the Comtesse de la Motte played the leading part, and the Marquise de Brinvilliers[65] had already made criminal history in the seventeenth century by using for the first time arsenic on a large scale to poison first some hospital patients, whom she used for experimental purposes, and afterwards several members of her own family.

There has been much less glamour in female crime since those romantic happenings, and the scene has been largely dominated by such more prosaic offences as drunkenness, prostitution, cruelty to children, shoplifting, and, of late, motoring offences.

3. *The Statistical Sex Ratio for Different Countries and Individual Offences*

International comparisons are as hazardous in this field as in all others. Since we dealt with them a quarter of a century ago in *Social Aspects of Crime* (pp. 334–5) work has been done on the subject mainly by Pollak, who has made a gallant attempt to use international statistics to answer the question whether the 'progressing social equalization between the sexes and particularly the entrance of women into ever wider fields of economic pursuits' has led to an increase in the volume of female crime and thereby reduced the gap in the sex ratio (Pollak, Chapter 4). He stresses, besides other difficulties, that international comparisons can make sense only if they relate to periods showing roughly the same stage of social and economic development. The periods of the two world wars, by producing similar problems and upheavals in belligerent and to a lesser degree also in neutral countries, provide, Pollak suggests, the best basis for comparisons obtainable in the circumstances (see also above, Chapter 23 D). The conclusion he draws from his fairly detailed studies is that in all those countries the social emancipation of women has produced increases in female crimes against property. This corroborates our findings in Britain in *War and Crime*[66] for the early stages of the Second World War, where it was pointed out, however, that the widening of their sphere of activities and the disturbance of family life had produced an increase not only in female delinquency but also in crimes committed against women.

It is in line with these observations that the total sex ratio of crime should be more unfavourable for women in highly industrialized and densely populated than in agricultural countries. Ignoring the war and immediate post-war years the figures reproduced in *Social Aspects* (p. 335) from Hacker's computation do not seem to have considerably changed. In a so far unpublished study of crime in Lusaka, the capital of Northern Rhodesia (now Zambia), William Clifford found a very low proportion of female offenders (in 1958–9 only 62 out of 3,127 cases). There are, however, a few striking exceptions. In France, for example, the proportion of female offenders has gone down from about 15 per cent to 5 per cent or, excluding the North-African prisoners, to 6·6 per cent. Pinatel, from whom these figures are taken, stresses, however, the great gap between the official and the actual rate of female delinquency and the important role played by women behind the scene.[67] For the U.S.A., where Hacker's figure for 1923 was 1:11·06, Reckless quotes for 1955 a ratio of 1:8 arrests.[68] Needless to say, the rate of females in prison is, here as everywhere else, much lower, 1:18. In Hacker's computation Belgium, one of the most highly industrialized and most densely populated of all countries, had the highest female crime rate, 1:3 against, for example, Finland's 1:22 and Sweden's 1:18. For England and Wales the rate has slightly deteriorated from 1:7·4 to 1:6 (persons found guilty of indictable offences). At the time when official criminal statistics began to be regularly published in this country the rate was even more unfavourable for women. As quoted above (Chapter 5, s. 2), in 1805 slightly under one-third of all those convicted at Assizes and Quarter Sessions were women.

All these figures for crime as a whole are of little significance, however; what really matters are the rates for individual offences. Already in *Social Aspects* (p. 335) attention was drawn to the possibility that the total female crime picture of a given country may be wholly dominated by one particular offence which may be of very little importance elsewhere, partly because of different climatic, social or economic conditions and partly because of the state of the criminal law. This was the case with drunkenness in Sweden and libel in Germany. How enormous the differences for specific offences in fact are has been shown in *Social Aspects* for England in the period 1932-6 (pp. 338-40), ranging from those for offences where the female rate is higher than the male, such as concealment of birth or abortion, to those where it is only slightly lower, such as bigamy, attempted murder, larceny by a servant and from shops and stalls, and attempted suicide, and finally to those where the female rate is almost insignificant as compared with the male (e.g. shopbreaking 1:243, larceny of pedal cycles 1:164, or takings and thefts of motor vehicles 1:121 for Assizes and Quarter Sessions and 1:157 for Courts of Summary Jurisdiction). In more recent years the proportion has for many offences changed in favour of women. For 1961, for example, the following figures of persons convicted by Assizes and Quarter Sessions may be quoted (from *Criminal Statistics England and Wales 1961*, Table III): capital murder 0:9, non-capital murder 1:20, attempted murder 1:5·5, manslaughter under s. 2, Homicide Act, 1957 (i.e. with diminished responsibility), 1:2, other manslaughter 1:10, felonious wounding 1:37·7, incest 1:14, burglary 1:42, housebreaking 1:17, shopbreaking 1:80 (the last three being more unfavourable to women than the pre-war rates), larceny by servant 1:9. The number of persons aged 21 and over convicted of larceny from shops and stalls by Magistrates' Courts was 3,667 males and 7,319 females; of those between 17 and 21 it was 789 males and 811 females, whereas for those between 14 and 17 found guilty of such offences it was 2,014 males and 1,372 females and for those under 14 it was 3,598 male and 1,299 females. For the non-indictable offences against the intoxicating liquor laws the rates (of persons proceeded against, *Criminal Statistics 1961*, Table II) are 1:12.8 for simple and 1:17·6 for aggravated drunkeness, which means a considerable improvement against pre-war years. For motoring offences the following rates may be quoted: reckless or dangerous driving 1:58, driving while under the influence of drink or a drug 1:57.5, which is even far more favourable than the rates for non-motorized drunks. Does this mean that women who can afford to drive a car while drunk are better treated than those who are content to lie on the pavement in an intoxicated condition? Or are they really less given to drink?

4. *Possible Explanations of the Differential Sex Rate*

Notwithstanding the existence of many strong arguments which make it likely that the 'masked' sector of female crime is much larger proportionally than its male counterpart and that the actual difference between the male and female sex rates is therefore considerably smaller than shown in official statistics, it is nevertheless almost universally agreed that such a difference does in fact exist in favour of the female sex. The exact extent of this difference is likely to vary greatly between different countries and civilizations, offences, and age groups. We have now to ask for possible explanations of this phenomenon and also, as pointed out before, try to understand the factors behind female crime regardless of its numerical relations to the male crime rate.

Naturally, most of the attempts so far made follow the traditional pattern by dividing their explanations into physical, psychological, and sociological ones and trying to combine them in an eclectic manner. We are not in a position radically to break with this pattern which is, after all, in line with our general approach. Pollak's suggestion that on close analysis the tripartition could be replaced by a bipartition, omitting the psychological section (p. 121), does not seem to be acceptable. As pointed out above, physical and social or economic factors can become operative only by going through the 'transformator' of a psychological or psychiatric factor.[69]

(*a*) *Physical Factors.* As above in Chapters 11–13, a distinction has to be made between physical factors of whatever kind which might possibly affect criminal behaviour, on the one hand, and definite physical types, on the other. The evidence presented in Chapter 11 on the prevalence of physical defects and illnesses among juvenile offenders was not regarded as particularly strong, especially not for more recent periods in prosperous countries where such offenders were on an average found to be as healthy as non-offenders. In the case of girl delinquents, physical over-development is often blamed for sexual misbehaviour, and it is only natural that where their physical precocity greatly outstrips their intellectual and emotional maturity violations of the social and legal norms of conduct are likely to happen. The frequency of 'care and protection' cases coming before the juvenile courts, most of which are, in fact, cases of sexual irregularity, often coupled with petty criminal offences, bears witness to this.[70] While some American writers lay special stress on the physical over-development of such girls,[71] this point is less conspicuous in the scanty English material available.[72] Dr. Epps, in her survey of a sample of Borstal girls, made between 1948 and 1950, received the general impression of a 'group of well-developed and physically healthy girls'.[73] In any case, this factor seems to be less strongly related to crime than to sexual irregularity. For women who have passed the stage of adolescence the menstruation factor, pregnancy and later the menopause, play a more important part. Their potential connection with so-called kleptomania and pyromania has been discussed above (Chapter 15, I(c)), but Gibbens, to whose study of shop-lifting we have already referred and who found that 31 per cent of his psychiatric shoplifters had what he terms gynaecological conditions, points out that the latter 'were not limited to severe menopausal symptoms, but were distributed throughout the generative cycle'.[74]

Lack of physical strength has often been quoted as explaining the lower female rate of offences against the person, but Pollak argues against this that in the present age technological inventions enable the weaker sex to be physically aggressive without possessing manual strength, and if women are strong enough to do comparatively heavy work in factories, shops and households, why should they not be capable of physical aggression, too? (p. 123). It is, he concludes, the 'cultural stereotype', the 'assignment of certain social roles' rather than their physique that reduces their use of violent methods. To some extent this is true, but one has to bear in mind that, as Pollak shows himself aware in other parts of his book, the average physical inferiority of women which can hardly be denied has inevitable psychological consequences favouring non-violent techniques. This in conjunction with their actual lack of physical strength explains why women prefer poisoning to other techniques of killing, or at least try to dope the victim before resorting to violence.

Some years ago, two young London women described as 'housewives' were sentenced to 12 months' imprisonment each at the Old Bailey. Armed with a pad soaked in ether and a knife, they had tried to rob a chauffeur who had given them a lift, by pressing the pad over his face (*The Times*, 20.1.1959). As the knife shows, they were quite prepared to kill or at least seriously injure him after overcoming his resistance by means of ether.

Lombroso and, following him, Sighele[75] speak of the greater 'ferocity' of women criminals, the latter explaining it as a consequence of their weakness, whereas the former believes at least the 'born criminal' variety to be less sensitive to pain and therefore devoid of compassion. The superintendent of a remand home in this country, too, finds girls just as much inclined to physical violence as boys and just as ready to use flick-knives, for which he blames the 'overdose of free discipline' in modern education (*The Times*, 21.10.1959).

Turning now to the typological side of the matter, we have, first of all, further to consider Lombroso's views on female offenders, to which no special reference was made above in Chapter 12 in connection with our general survey of his theory. In his monograph on the subject,[76] written jointly with his son-in-law G. Ferrero, Lombroso stressed the comparative rarity of the born criminal type among female offenders, only 14 per cent against 31 per cent among males. Prostitutes, on the other hand, he believed to belong far more frequently (about 38 per cent) to this type. Female offenders were mostly occasional lawbreakers, presenting only a few characteristics of degeneration and deviation from the biological norm. Psychologically, Lombroso thought, women are by nature more conservative in all matters affecting the social order, a trait which he thought to be due to the 'immobility of the ovule compared with the zoosperm'. To this we shall have to return later on. Primitive woman, according to Lombroso, was rarely a murderess, but she was always a prostitute, and from all this he developed his theory that prostitution was the female substitute for crime. Even without accepting these out-dated anthropological and typological speculations we can find a great deal of truth in his prostitution thesis. The latter does not mean that prostitution is 'the sum and substance of all female criminality'[77] in the sense that all female crime is caused and dominated by sexual factors—although much of it is—it merely means that in situations which make a man turn to crime, a woman can often find another alternative in prostitution, semi-prostitution, or at least in sexual behaviour such as a financially dictated marriage and similarly lucrative affairs. While all these alternatives open to women undoubtedly help them as a rule to keep out of clearly criminal entanglements, in some cases the opposite happens. To mention only one recent instance, the Ward case, with all its ramifications, shows how certain female actors in this political and social tragi-comedy, after successfully evading some of the pitfalls created by the criminal law, were eventually caught in others.

(*b*) *Psychological and Sociological Factors.* The material presented under (*a*) on the effect of physical factors has again clearly shown their close connection with the psychological and sociological side of the problem. Starting with biological characteristics Lombroso and his followers have inevitably been driven to the discussion of psychological traits and sociological differences. The list of such traits and differences used in the literature on female crime is impressive perhaps more through its length than its persuasiveness; nevertheless, a number of points have been made which are worth mentioning, if only to see whether a coherent picture emerges from them.

It is, generally speaking, easier to produce lists of personality differences allegedly existing between the sexes than to prove that such differences are responsible for a higher or lower crime rate. Nevertheless, as will be shown below, several such personality differences have been quoted in the literature as having some effect on crime.

Lombroso wrote of the greater, biologically conditioned, conservatism of women, which makes it easier for them to accept the existing social order even where it is to their disadvantage. On the other hand, he had to admit that their sense of property was not very strong; in Paris, he reports, lost property was almost invariably brought to the office by men, and shoplifting was already at that time regarded as a typically feminine occupation, a view confirmed by the figures for 1961 quoted above. It has to be borne in mind, however, that shopping, too, is a typically feminine occupation, and something is therefore to be said for the view of Gibbens and Prince that in proportion to the total numbers of shoppers there are even more male than female shoplifters.[78] A similar point was made by the present writer in *Social Aspects of Crime* with regard to larceny by servants, where it was pointed out that the official figures, apparently so unfavourable to women, should be interpreted in the light of the numbers of existing servants of either sex, which at the time showed a considerable predominance of females, (p. 341). Roughly at the time when Lombroso made his point on the greater conservatism of women the fight for their emancipation and equal rights was already on. Alexandre Dumas junior had published his *Les femmes qui tuent et les femmes qui votent*,[79] where he tried to show that women, deprived of any legal opportunities to air their grievances, had to resort to crime of violence, and Gunnar Myrdal draws a parallel between the Negro struggle for equal rights and that of women.[80] In both instances resort to violence proved to be unavoidable; for the English Suffragettes movement before the First World War a few figures have been given in *Social Aspects of Crime* (p. 347) to show its impact on criminal statistics. Another famous figure in the movement for women's emancipation, not less important than the real ones, Ibsen's Nora, committed no crime of violence but forgery in the interest of her family. 'It appears that a woman has no right to spare her dying father, or to save her husband's life! I do not believe that . . . I believe that before all else I am a human being.' Apparently, the conservatism of women allows for certain exceptions not only in favour of their struggle for equality but also for the sake of their families. Women can become rebels against established authority just as well as men and commit crimes for the sake of the values in which they believe.

A married woman with eleven children living with her real and a bigamous husband in the same house, was sentenced to four months' imprisonment at Birmingham Assizes. When the Judge told her: 'You have set the marriage laws of the country at complete defiance, you have made a mockery of the whole thing,' the woman replied: 'Did I do wrong in doing this for my children? The children are happy.' (*The Times*, 8.7.1939.) Apparently, according to her interpretation of the marriage laws at least two husbands were required to help her to feed eleven children.

Similarly, Mary Stevenson Callcott[81] tells us that in the earlier days of the Soviet regime the male peasants, seeing that opposition was useless, did not resist collectivization as fiercely as was done by their womenfolk who used to poison their cows or pigs before they were taken from them; no vision of the perfect communist society of the future could compensate them for the immediate loss of their property. In short, political ideals, whether conservative or communist, have to take second place in the female mind; the immediate needs of her own family come first and have to be protected if necessary by criminal action. This more individualistic approach to life also colours the female selection of property offences: for example women prefer shoplifting to looting, where individual choice of the articles is difficult, or to stealing money. Their lack of respect for abstract ideas such as the state and its system of justice shows itself in the greater ease with which they commit perjury. Admittedly, this is difficult to prove statistically (sex ratio for 1961, 1:6·8), but practical court experience leaves no doubt that it is true.[82]

Whether there is a wider variety in the male than in the female personality is a controversial issue;[83] men have probably produced more extreme types than women, i.e. more geniuses, saints and leaders, but possibly also more subnormal persons, although the latter is far from certain (see also below). For example Murphy and Newcomb report that as a rule sex differences in intelligence have not been found[84] and Cyril Burt does not even mention the matter as a general problem except for the statement that among his samples of girls, particularly the older ones inclined towards sex delinquency, the proportion of defectives was perceptibly higher than among the boys.[85] On the other hand, most writers agree that there are distinct sex differences in certain special aptitudes, attitudes and temperamental traits.

Burt[86] distinguishes in his scheme of temperamental conditions the strong or 'sthenic' instincts, such as anger, acquisitiveness, self-assertiveness and sex, and the weak or 'asthenic' instincts, such as tenderness, submissiveness, grief and fear, and maintains that the first are more pronounced in males, the second more pronounced in females, and as he regards the 'sthenic' instincts as chiefly responsible for crime such differences explain in his view the lower female crime rate. This is, however, only in part confirmed by his list in Table XVII which shows the incidence of such instincts and emotions as major or minor factors in his samples. The sex factor, for example, although one of his 'sthenic' instincts, is far more prominent in the girls of his delinquent sample. Whether such emotions as gregariousness or self-assertiveness belong to the sthenic or to the asthenic instincts, there is no doubt, however, that they are more prominent in males than in females (see again Burt's Table XVII). Girls do not form gangs, although they may occasionally join them for the sake of sexual adventures, nor do they often commit their offences in company with other females. With regard to self-assertiveness—a trait which the Gluecks distinguish from self-assertion, whereas Burt makes no such distinction[87]—this appears as a (minor) factor in Burt's table far more frequently among delinquent boys than among delinquent girls and leads among the former to 'feats of rivalry, daring and defiance', among the girls, however, to 'vain and romantic lying' and at a later age to theft and immorality to obtain gay clothes, jewellery, etc. Lying and cheating in school was observed by Hartshorne more often in girls than in boys, but mainly because of their higher ambitions.[88] The greater deceitfulness of women is also used by Pollak to explain their greater success in 'masking' their crimes; his explanation of the prevalence of this trait is partly a biological, partly a sociological one. Women are forced by the sex mores of our society every four weeks to conceal their period of menstruation and to misrepresent the 'facts of life' to their children; they are also forced to suppress their natural aggressive instincts—all of which is bound to make them deceitful.[89]

William Healy, who also found among his cases more female than male liars, is inclined to blame largely the social environment for it.[90]

We might add that the male-dominated character of the criminal law, to which we referred before, has made women, except for the natural 'rebels', accustomed to get 'around' rather than act against the law; one might therefore even venture the paradox that in a female-dominated legal system their crime rate would increase. Closely connected with this, the greater capacity of women to adapt themselves to reality and their greater elasticity and resourcefulness have been stressed. Men trained for a specific calling find it more difficult to adapt themselves to another occupation than their wives who, mostly possessing no such training, are usually elastic enough to change their life pattern.[91] Johanna C. Hudig, too, speaks of the greater adaptability of women who resign themselves more readily to the inevitable, who possess 'greater pliancy and tact'.[92] Added to this, men are at a further disadvantage in having to bear heavier responsibilities towards their families and the sometimes excessive financial demands of their wives. East quotes in this connection the observation of a bank employee that in nine out of ten cases bank clerks went wrong because of such demands,[93] but figures of this kind have invariably to be treated with the greatest caution. Moreover, criminologists have been aware of the profound changes in the social and occupational status of women in the course of the present century. Reference has already been made to the criminological impact of the political movements which helped to produce these changes; now we have to consider the impact of these developments on the female crime rate. Since Bonger, nearly fifty years ago, expressed the view that women were like hothouse plants, sheltered from the icy blasts of life and therefore less criminal,[94] women have assumed new roles in the economic and occupational life of society. The present century is not the first period of upheaval in the occupational lives of women.[95] The Industrial Revolution, too, deprived many of them of their previous work in the home and forced them to enter the factory. In the twentieth century it was first the two world wars that not only added greatly to their domestic responsibilities but also turned millions of married women into industrial workers or shop assistants, etc., and some of them even into managers and company directors. In the United States, with its female labour force of over 21 million in 1957, the proportion of married women in employment increased from 30 per cent in 1940 to 54 per cent in 1957. In Britain, 'between 1946 and May 1955 the number of married women in gainful employment rose by two and a quarter million to three and three quarter million or 48 per cent of all women at work'.[96]

While the number of domestic servants has greatly declined, that of female factory workers, office employees, etc., has greatly increased. Has this led to a corresponding increase in the female crime rate for offences connected with their employment? English official figures again show no coherent picture. For embezzlement, where the rate for 1932–6 was 1:46 (Assizes and Quarter Sessions) and 1:34·4 for Magistrates' Courts, it was, in 1961, 1:8·8 and 1:6 (age 21 and over) or 1:2·2 (age 17 and under 21), which would indicate a big increase. For false pretences and frauds (Nos. 50–3 of *Criminal Statistics*), where it was 1:12 and 1:7·8 respectively before the war, it was, in 1961, 1:16 and 1:5 (21 and over) or 1:2·7 (17 and under 21). For receiving, where it was 1:10·5 and 1:5·4 respectively, it was, in 1961, 1:9·7 and 1:7·8 or 8·7. There is, therefore, no uniform increase, and we should avoid hasty conclusions.

In certain other ways, however, the changed social and occupational position of women shows itself occasionally in the nature of the criminal situations in which they are caught. In former days it was one of the familiar patterns of spy trials to see more or less beautiful women being used as baits to extract military or political secrets from middle-aged men in high positions. Now we find a middle-aged woman holding an influential job in a government department, drawing a salary of £3,800, pleading guilty to eight counts of 'unlawfully communicating documents contrary to s. 2(1) of the Official Secrets Act, 1911' to an official of a foreign Embassy, to whom she had formed an attachment. She was sentenced to two years' imprisonment, and the Court of Criminal Appeal, stressing in particular the obligations of her high position, refused her application for permission to appeal against this sentence, in spite of the presence of a number of mitigating circumstances.[97] In another, less sensational, recent case a married woman bank clerk, again of middle age, was sentenced to 12 months' imprisonment for stealing foreign currency and obtaining money by forgery from her employers under pressure from her lover (*The Times*, 5.9.1963.) Extra-marital associations may, criminologically speaking, cut both ways: women may be persuaded or even forced by their lovers to steal, embezzle, defraud, receive or kill, or they may use them to commit such offences or crimes of violence for them. Their fairly high rate for receiving is, as Pollak rightly says (p. 87), largely due to their traditional role in the family as being given money for house-keeping, but also as receivers of presents. Not surprisingly, some small sums of the money stolen in the great train robbery of August 1963 (Chapter 25) were found in the possession of a few women who were however found not guilty of receiving.

Albert K. Cohen (Chapter 22 above) has tried to explain the lower female crime rate by suggesting that women may have their own brand of subculture which approves or disapproves conduct in ways fundamentally different from their male counterparts, with ideals and solutions entirely their own.[98] Their social status is largely determined by that of their husbands, whereas the opposite is not true to the same degree (with some notable exceptions, we might add). Consequently, Cohen argues, their behaviour is also less determined by opposition to the middle-class norms, with all the criminogenic dangers which such opposition implies. He admits the so far rudimentary and over-simplified character of his arguments which may not do full justice to the fact that in our society women are actually among the worst victims of the 'status-seeking' mania (Chapter 22 above).

Attempts, occasionally made by older writers, to use the lower crime rate of women to prove their higher moral standards or greater religiosity, have now been abandoned. Already Quetelet was rather sceptical, and later on von Oettingen derided the view expressed by a

French writer that because women went to church five times as often as men it was only natural that their crime rate should be only one-fifth of the male.[99]

Of greater significance may be the references to the high proportion of women in mental hospitals. Already in *Social Aspects* (p. 343, fn. 3) a pre-war article by Professor Penrose was mentioned, who pointed out that in Britain, France and Germany the population of these hospitals was rather more than half composed of females.[100] More recently, in the *Report of the Royal Commission on the Law relating to Mental Illness and Mental Deficiency 1954–7*[101] the following figures are given: Admissions to mental hospitals per 100,000 population in 1954: men, first admissions 86, second or subsequent admissions 54. For women the corresponding figures are 108 and 74. For mental deficiency hospitals, however, the position is reversed, men 7 and 0·8, women 5 and 0·7. These figures do not necessarily prove the higher incidence of mental disorders among women, but they do show that mentally disordered women stand a better chance than men to be admitted to mental hospitals and thereby to some greater extent to be deprived of opportunities to commit crimes.

While women are often labelled as hysterics, there is in the psychiatric literature a comparative scarcity of material on women psychopaths, although the descriptions given of many delinquent girls contain some of the characteristic features of the psychopathic personality. There are, however, some notable exceptions. William Healy has published several case histories of female pathological liars and swindlers,[102] and D. K. Henderson has also produced some material.[103] Dr. Grace W. Pailthorpe, in her pioneer study of women prisoners at Holloway and Birmingham, has a substantial chapter on a 'psychopathic group', but it seems doubtful how many of her cases are really psychopaths and how many psychotics or neurotics.[104]

Gibbens refers briefly to some cases of psychopathy among his sample of women shoplifters,[105] and Glover, in his penetrating study of prostitution, expresses the view that many psychopaths are prostitutes and that 'close observation of many apparently "normal" prostitutes uncovers the existence of a number of psychopathic traits'.[106] Might the fact of their being prostitutes perhaps often 'mask' the criminal activities of these psychopathic women and thereby also help to reduce the official female crime rate?

Better material on psychopathic women offenders than in the published case studies of psychiatrists will probably be found in world literature. It might be interesting to analyse, for example, Ibsen's Hedda Gabler from this angle: is she a tragic, suffering heroine or simply a blasée youngish society woman, empty and bored with life, looking desperately for distractions such as horses, butlers, fine dresses and 'interesting' lovers, a female psychopath, in law guilty of incitement to suicide and of wantonly destroying another person's property?

Lombroso's view that women offenders are but rarely habituals is not borne out by the facts. Even ignoring the leaders in this field, the 'drunks', the available English statistics give the following picture: in the period 1952–61, the percentage of women received in prison having six or more previous offences was between 30 and 48, while the corresponding proportion of men was between 39 and 47. The proportions of women entrants who were known to have served previous institutional sentences was also very high and not much lower than that of men.[107] In accordance with the general experience, however, that the more severe a form of punishment is the less likely is it to be used for women, the numbers of them sentenced to preventive detention are very small, between 1950 and 1961 altogether only 68 against 2,525 men, i.e. 1:38.[108] Their treatment in prison has been described by Ann D. Smith, who concludes that 'by 1961 enlightened opinion had come to believe that the "nuisance value" of a woman habitual criminal was not an adequate justification for society to detain her in prison for a period which might extend to fourteen years' (p. 204). In fact, public opinion has not to be very enlightened to realize this simple truth, but the pen pictures given by Tony Parker on the B.B.C. Home Service (17.1.1963) of five such women detainees recently discharged from Holloway may have helped to hasten the process.

The influence of marriage on female delinquency has been briefly discussed above in Chapter 24. Here it may merely be said that criminal associations between husband and wife may continue for many years. In one such case the association began when the man was 31 and the woman 17 years of age; it covered six joint convictions for stealing, etc., over 17 years. Although the husband's sentences were always considerably longer, the wife was never reconvicted during his absence, but soon after his discharge they both reappeared in court.

Selected Reading Lists

(see Note on p. 351)

CHAPTER 19

In addition to the appropriate chapters in the American textbooks listed in Note 1:

Lord Radcliffe, *The Problem of Power*, London, 1958 (Paperback).

Thorsten Sellin, *Culture Conflict and Crime*, New York, 1938.

T. S. Eliot, *Notes towards the Definition of Culture*, London, 1948 (also in Paperback).

Richard Wollheim, *Socialism and Culture*, London, Fabian Tract, 1961.

Gunnar Myrdal, *Values in Social Theory*, London, 1958.

H. Bianchi, *Position and Subject-Matter of Criminology*, Amsterdam, 1956.

Michael Shanks, *The Stagnant Society*, Harmondsworth, 1961.

T. R. Fyvel, *The Insecure Offenders*, London, 1961 (also in Paperback).

J. K. Galbraith, *The Affluent Society*, London, 6th imp. 1960 (also in Paperback).

Hermann Mannheim, *Social Aspects of Crime in England between the Wars*, London, 1940, Part 2.

Hermann Mannheim, *Criminal Justice and Social Reconstruction*, 2nd imp., London, 1949.

Richard M. Titmuss, *Essays on 'The Welfare State'*, London, 1958, Chs. 8–10.

Home Office White Paper *Penal Practice in a Changing Society*, H.M.S.O. 1959.

Home Office White Paper *The War against Crime in England and Wales*, H.M.S.O. 1964.

CHAPTER 20

On Class in general:

Ralf Dahrendorf, *Class and Class Conflict in an Industrial Society*, London 1959.

D. V. Glass (ed.), *Social Mobility in Britain*, 2nd ed., London, 1964.

T. H. Marshall, *Citizenship and Social Class*, Cambridge, 1950.

T. H. Marshall, *Class, Citizenship and Social Development*, New York, 1964.

Leonard Reissman, *Class in American Society*, London, 1960.

Vance Packard, *The Status Seekers*, London, 1960 (Paperback 1961).

Ferdynand Zweig, *The Worker in an Affluent Society*, London, 1962.

709

Brian Jackson and Dennis Marsden, *Education and the Working Class*, London, 1962.

On Imitation:

Margaret S. Wilson Vine in *Pioneers in Criminology*, ed. by H. Mannheim, London, 1960, Ch. 10 on Tarde.

O. H. Mowrer, *Learning Theory and Personality Dynamics*, New York, 1960.

Neal E. Miller and John Dollard, *Social Learning and Imitation*, London, 1945.

Vance Packard, *The Hidden Persuaders*, London, 1957 (Paperback 1960).

On Rebels:

Albert Camus, *The Rebel*, London, 1953 (Paperback 1962).

Robert K. Merton, *Social Theory and Social Structure*, rev. ed. 1957, Glencoe, Ill., Chs. 4–5.

Tony Parker and Robert Allerton, *The Courage of his Convictions*, London, 1962.

On the Criminological Implications of Class:

Preben Wolf, 'Crime and Social Class in Denmark', *Brit. J. Crim.*, Vol. 3, No. 1, July 1962.

Donald R. Cressey, *Other People's Money*, Glencoe, Ill., 1953.

Jerome Hall, *Theft, Law and Society*, 2nd. ed., Indianapolis, 1952, Ch. 7.

Thomas Würtenberger in *Symposium on Aspects of Art Forgery*, The Hague, 1962.

T. C. Willett, *Criminal on the Road*, London, 1964, Ch. 8.

CHAPTER 21

Edwin H. Sutherland, *White Collar Crime*, New York, 1949; new ed. 1961.

Edwin H. Sutherland, in *The Sutherland Papers*, ed. by Albert Cohen, Alfred Lindesmith, Karl Schuessler, Bloomington, 1956, Part 2.

Marshall B. Clinard, *The Black Market*, New York, 1952.

Herbert A. Bloch and Gilbert Geis, *Man, Crime and Society*, New York, 1962, Ch. 14.

Hermann Mannheim, *Social Aspects of Crime in England between the Wars*, London, 1940, Ch. 7.

Hermann Mannheim, *Criminal Justice and Social Reconstruction*, 2nd imp. 1949, London, Ch. 7.

John C. Spencer in *Criminology in Transition*, ed. by T. Grygier, Howard Jones and John C. Spencer, London, 1965.

George B. Vold, *Theoretical Criminology*, New York, 1958, Ch. 13.

Paul W. Tappan, 'Who is the Criminal?', *Amer. Sociol. Rev.*, Vol. 12, Feb. 1947.

Symposium on 'The Ethics of Business Enterprise', *Ann. Amer. Acad. Polit. Soc. Sci.*, Vol. 343, Sept. 1962.

CHAPTER 22

On Anomie:

Robert K. Merton, *Social Theory and Social Structure*, rev. ed. 1957, Chs. 4 and 5.

Emile Durkheim, *Suicide*, Eng. ed. London, 1952, Chs. 5 and 6.

Paul W. Tappan, *Crime, Justice, and Correction*, New York, 1960.

Burkart Holzner, 'The Problem of Anomie and Normative Change', *Arch. f. Rechts- u. Sozialphilos.*, Vol. L/1, 1964, pp. 57–86.

Bernard Lander, *Towards an Understanding of Juvenile Delinquency*, New York, 1954, pp. 55 ff.

Richard A. Cloward and Lloyd E. Ohlin, *Delinquency and Opportunity*, Glencoe, Ill., 1960, pp. 78 ff.

On Criminal Subculture:

Albert K. Cohen, *Delinquent Boys: The Culture of the Gang*, Glencoe, Ill., 1955, London, 1956.

William Foote Whyte, *Street Corner Society*, 2nd ed., Chicago, 1955.

Cloward and Ohlin (see above).

Hermann Mannheim, *Criminal Justice and Social Reconstruction*, Part 3.

Gresham M. Sykes and David Matza, 'Techniques of Neutralization', *Amer. Sociol. Rev.*, Vol. 22, Dec. 1957.

John B. Mays, *Education and the Urban Child*, Liverpool, 1962.

A. P. Jephcott and M. P. Carter, *The Social Background of Delinquency*, 1954 (Univ. of Nottingham, unpubl.).

T. R. Fyvel, *The Insecure Offenders*, London, 1961.

D. M. Downes, *Delinquent Subcultures in East London*, London, 1965.

John B. Mays, *Growing up in the City*, Liverpool, 1954.

John B. Mays, *Crime and the Social Structure*, London, 1963.

CHAPTER 23

On the Ecological Theory:

T. P. Morris, *The Criminal Area*, London, 1958.

Clifford R. Shaw, *Delinquency Areas*, Chicago, 1929.

Clifford R. Shaw and Henry McKay *et al.*, *Juvenile Delinquency and Urban Areas*, Chicago, 1942.

Howard Jones, 'Approaches to an Ecological Study', *Brit. J. Delinq.*, Vol. 8, No. 4, April 1958.

Hermann Mannheim, *Juvenile Delinquency in an English Middletown*, London, 1948.

On Mobility, Immigration, Urbanization and Urbanism:

Marshall B. Clinard, *Sociology of Deviant Behavior*, New York, 1957, Chs. 3, 16, 17.

Marshall B. Clinard, 'A Cross-Cultural Replication of the Relation of Urbanism to Criminal Behavior', *Amer. Sociol. Rev.*, Vol. 25, No. 2, April 1960.

Donald R. Taft, *Criminology*, 3rd ed., New York, 1956, Ch. 8.
Thorsten Sellin, *Culture Conflict and Crime*, New York, 1938.
Ruth Glass in *Society: Problems and Methods of Study*, London, 1962, Ch. 26.

On Delinquency Areas:

Clifford R. Shaw, T. P. Morris, H. Mannheim (see books quoted above).
John C. Spencer *et al.*, *Stress and Release in an Urban Estate*, London, 1964, Ch. 14.
'Symposium on Delinquency Areas' in *Brit. J. Delinq.*, Vol. 7, No. 2, Oct. 1956.

On Culture Conflict and Minorities:

Thorsten Sellin (see above).
Arthur Lewis Wood, 'Crime and Aggression in Changing Ceylon', *Trans. Amer. Philosoph. Soc.*, New Series, Vol. 51, Part 8, Philadelphia, Dec. 1961.
Arthur Lewis Wood, 'Minority-Group Criminality and Cultural Integration', *J. crim. Law, Criminol. Police Sci.*, Vol. 37, No. 6, March–April, 1947.
Hermann Mannheim, *Group Problems in Crime and Punishment*, London, 1955, Ch. 8.
Hans v. Hentig, *Crime: Causes and Conditions*, New York, 1947, Ch. 7.
W. A. Bonger, *Race and Crime*, New York, 1943.
Shlomo Shoham, 'The Application of the "Culture Conflict" Hypothesis to the Criminality of Immigrants in Israel', *J. crim. Law Criminol. Police Sci.*, Vol. 53, No. 2, June 1962.

On Religion:

H. Bianchi, 'Crime and Religious Profession', Amsterdam, *Free Univ, Quarterly*, Vol. 5, No. 1, Nov. 1957.
W. H. Nagel, 'Criminality and Religion', *Tijdschrift voor Strafrecht*, Vol. 69, No. 5, 1960.

On Economic Factors:

W. A. Bonger, *Criminality and Economic Conditions*, Boston, 1916.
Thorsten Sellin, *Research Memorandum on Crime in the Depression*, Soc. Sci. Res. Council Bull. 27, New York, 1937.
Hermann Mannheim, *Social Aspects of Crime in England between the Wars*, London, 1940, Chs. 4, 5, 7, 9, 10.
Hermann Mannheim, *Criminal Justice and Social Reconstruction*, Chs. 6–9.
George B. Vold, *Theoretical Criminology*, New York, 1958, Ch. 9.
Cyril Burt, *The Young Delinquent*, 4th ed., 1944, Ch. 3.
Dorothy S. Thomas, *Social Aspects of the Business Cycle*, London, 1925.

On War:

Hermann Mannheim, *War and Crime*, London, 1941.
The Effect of the War on Criminality, Bull. Int. Penal and Penitent. Comm.

(I.P.P.C.), Vol. 15, No. 4/II of the Select Papers on Penal and Penit. Affairs, Berne, 1951.

Marshall B. Clinard, *Sociology of Deviant Behavior*, New York, 1957, Ch. 20.

Hermann Mannheim, *Group Problems in Crime and Punishment*, Ch. 5.

Leslie T. Wilkins, *Delinquent Generations*, a Home Office Research Unit Report, London, 1960.

A. A. Walters, 'Delinquent Generations', *Brit. J. Crim.*, Vol. 3, No. 4, April 1963.

On Differential Association:

Edwin H. Sutherland and Donald R. Cressey, *Principles of Criminology*, 6th ed., Philadelphia, 1960, pp. 68–9.

Donald R. Cressey, *Delinquency, Crime and Differential Association*, The Hague, 1964.

Sheldon Glueck in S. and E. Glueck, *Ventures in Criminology*, London, 1964, Ch. 16.

George B. Vold, *Theoretical Criminology* (see above), Ch. 10.

On Mass Communications:

Kimball Young, *Handbook of Social Psychology*, 2nd ed., London, 1957, Chs. 15–17.

CHAPTER 24

On Groups in General:

Harry M. Johnson, *Sociology*, London, 1961, Ch. 1.

W. J. H. Sprott, *Human Groups*, Harmondsworth, 1958.

On Penal Institutions:

Gresham M. Sykes, *The Society of Captives*, Princeton, 1958.

Hugh J. Klare, *Anatomy of Prison*, London, 1960 (also in Paperback).

T. and P. Morris, *Pentonville*, London, 1963.

John James, 'The Application of the Small Group Concept in the Study of the Prison Community', *Brit. J. Delinq.*, Vol. 5, No. 4, April 1955.

On the Family:

S. and E. Glueck, *Unraveling Juvenile Delinquency*, New York, 1950.

S. and E. Glueck, *Family Environment and Delinquency*, London, 1962.

Barbara Wootton, *Social Science and Social Pathology*, London, 1959, Ch. 3.

G. R. Andry, *Delinquency and Parental Pathology*, London, 1960.

William and Joan McCord, *The Origins of Crime*, New York, 1959.

D. H. Stott, *Delinquency and Human Nature*, Dunfermline, 1950.

On 'Problem Families':

Harriett C. Wilson, *Delinquency and Child Neglect*, London, 1962.

John C. Spencer in Benjamin Schlesinger (ed.), *The Multi-Problem Family*, Toronto, 1963.

On Marriage:

Hans v. Hentig, *Crime: Causes and Conditions*, New York, 1947, Ch. 11 (13).

On Schools:

Sheldon Glueck, *The Problem of Delinquency*, Boston, 1959, Ch. 7.
Cyril Burt, *The Young Delinquent*, 4th ed. 1944, Ch. 4.
I. Roger Yoshino, *Juvenile Delinquency and the School, in Sociology of Crime*, ed. by Joseph S. Roucek, London, 1962.
John B. Mays, *Education and the Urban Child*, Liverpool, 1962.

CHAPTER 25

General and Legal:

George C. Homans, *The Human Group*, New York and London, 1951.
W. J. H. Sprott, *Human Groups*, Harmondsworth, 1958, Ch. 10.
R. T. La Piere, *Collective Behavior*, New York, 1938.
Glanville Williams, *The Criminal Law. General Part*, London, 1953, Ch. 6.

On Crowds:

Gustave Le Bon, *The Crowd*, London, 1952.
Lionel Penrose, *On the Objective Study of Crowd Behaviour*, London, 1952.
William F. Ogburn and Meyer F. Nimkoff, *A Handbook of Sociology*, London, 4th ed. 1960, Ch. 10.

On Adult Gangs and Organized Crime:

Herbert A. Bloch and Gilbert Geis, *Man, Crime and Society*, New York, 1962, Ch. 9.
Walter C. Reckless, *The Crime Problem*, 3rd. ed., New York, 1961, Chs. 9, 10.
John B. Mays, *Crime and the Social Structure*, London, 1963, Ch. 12.
'Combatting Organized Crime', ed. by Gus Tyler, *Ann. Amer. Acad. Pol. Soc. Sci.*, Vol. 347, May 1963.

On Adolescent Gangs:

Frederick Thrasher, *The Gang*, Chicago, 2nd ed., 1936.
William F. White, *Street Corner Society*, 2nd ed., Chicago, 1955.
Cloward–Ohlin and Albert K. Cohen (see above, Ch. 22).
Lewis Yablonsky, *The Violent Gang*, New York, 1962.
Peter Scott, 'Gangs and Delinquent Groups in London', *Brit. J. Delinq.*, Vol. 7, No. 1, July 1956.

On Victimology:

Hans v. Hentig, *The Criminal and his Victim*, New Haven, 1948.
Terence Morris and Louis Blom-Cooper, *A Calendar of Murder*, London, 1964, Ch. 7.

Marvin E. Wolfgang, *Patterns of Homicide*, Philadelphia, 1958, Parts 2 and 3.

CHAPTER 26

On Age:

Criminal Statistics England and Wales for 1963, London, 1964.

Howard Jones, *Crime and the Penal System*, 2nd ed., London, 1962, Ch. 9.

Barbara Wootton, *Social Science and Social Pathology*, London, 1959, Ch. 5.

Leslie T. Wilkins, *Delinquent Generations*, London, H.M.S.O., 1960. ✓

Thorsten Sellin, *The Criminality of Youth*, Philadelphia, 1940.

S. and E. Glueck, *Later Criminal Careers*, New York, 1937, Ch. 10.

Thorsten Sellin and Marvin E. Wolfgang, *The Measurement of Delinquency*, New York, 1964.

Sir George Benson, *Brit. J. Delinq.*, Vol. 3, No. 3, Jan. 1953, and Vol. 5, ✓ No. 2, Oct. 1954.

Hermann Mannheim, *Social Aspects of Crime in England*, London, 1940, Chs. 3, 9, 10.

On Sex:

Mabel Elliott, *Crime in Modern Society*, New York, 1952, Chs. 8 and 9.

Otto Pollak, *The Criminality of Women*, Philadelphia, 1950.

Ann D. Smith, *Women in Prison*, London, 1962, Chs. 1 and 2.

T. C. N. Gibbens and Joyce Prince, *Shoplifting*, London, 1962.

Cyril Burt, *The Young Delinquent*, Ch. 9. ✓

Ruth R. Morris, *Brit. J. Crim.*, Vol. 5, 1965.

Moya Woodside, 'Women Drinkers in Holloway Prison', *Brit. J. Crim.*, Vol. 1, 1961.

Hermann Mannheim, *Social Aspects of Crime in England*, London, 1940, Ch. 11.

Notes

CHAPTER 19

¹ On the sociology of crime in general see most American textbooks, notably Taft, Sutherland–Cressey, and Mabel Elliott. Also Marshall B. Clinard, *Sociology of Deviant Behavior*; Herbert A. Bloch and Gilbert Geis, *Man, Crime and Society*, New York, 1962; Joseph S. Roucek (ed.), *Sociology of Crime*, London, 1962, New York, 1961. Moreover, Wolf Middendorff, *Soziologie des Verbrechens*, Düsseldorf–Köln, 1959.

² Ogburn and Nimkoff, *Handbook of Sociology*, Ch. 24. The literature on 'culture' is very extensive, and reference may be made to the well-known texts on social anthropology, sociology, and social psychology. A brief and useful discussion is given, e.g., by Joseph Gittler, *Social Dynamics*, New York, 1952, Part 6.

³ London, 1958, Paperback ed., Harmondsworth, 1961, pp. 16 and *passim*.

⁴ London, 1948.

⁵ See, e.g., recently Kathleen Nott, 'Whose Culture?' the *Listener*, 12.4.1962, pp. 631–2.

⁶ Fabian Tract, 331, May 1961, pp. 16–17. See also the various comments on it in the *New Statesman*, 2.6.1961.

⁷ On this see B. M. Spinley, *The Deprived and the Privileged*, London, 1953, pp. 3 ff., referring to A. Kardiner's *The Psychological Frontiers of Society*.

⁸ Donald R. Taft, *Criminology*, 3rd ed., p. 28.

⁹ Quoted from Bonger, *Introduction to Criminology*, in the Eng. trans. by van Loo, London, 1936, pp. 78–9. Lacassagne used these words on the occasion of the First International Anthropological Congress in Rome in 1885 (see Bonger). J. M. van Bemmelen, *Criminologie*, 3rd. ed., Zwolle, 1952, p. 53 fn. 3, rightly stresses the priority of Quetelet.

¹⁰ Jacob Burckhardt's great book was first published in 1860. Here the 12th German edition, Leipzig, 1919, is referred to, where the material on crime in the Italian Renaissance appears in Section 6.

¹¹ London, 2 vols, 1873–6.

¹² London, 4 vols., 1861 ff.

¹³ F. C. Avé-Lallement, *Das deutsche Gaunertum in seiner sozialpolitischen, literarischen und linguistischen Ausbildung zu seinem heutigen Bestand*, 3 vols., 1858–62.

¹⁴ Stuttgart, 1951.

¹⁵ On the interesting subject of the *Gaunersprache* see, in addition to Avé-Lallemant, Hans Gross, *Handbuch für Untersuchungsrichter*, 7th ed., 1922, Part 1, Section 8; Jean Graven, *L'Argot et le Tatouage des Criminels. Etude de Criminologie sociale*, Neuchatel, 1962; on modern American Prison slang Donald Clemmer, *The Prison Community*, App. B, and Gresham M. Sykes, *The Society of Captives*, Princeton, 1958, Ch. 5.

¹⁶ Walter Goldschmidt, *Understanding Human Society*, London, 1959, p. 73.

¹⁷ Gordon Trasler, *The Explanation of Criminality*, p. 65.

716

[18] Harry M. Johnson, *Sociology*, New York–London, 1961, pp. 50, 87.

[19] Murphy and Newcomb, *Experimental Social Psychology*, p. 199.

[20] Gunnar Myrdal, *Value in Social Theory*, p. 77.

[21] H. Bianchi, *Position and Subject-Matter of Criminology*, Amsterdam, 1956, pp. 129 ff.

[22] Thorsten Sellin, *Culture Conflict and Crime*, pp. 28-9.

[23] Gordon Trasler, *op. cit.*, p. 66. On attitudes see also Muzafer and Carolyn W. Sherif, *Outline of Social Psychology*, rev. ed., New York, 1956, Ch. 15 and pp. 173 ff.; D. R. Price-Williams, *Introductory Psychology*, London, 1958, pp. 60 ff.; Murphy and Newcomb, *Experimental Social Psychology*, esp. Ch. 13.

[24] See, e.g., Murphy and Newcomb, *op. cit.*, p. 936.

[25] *Ibid.*, pp. 946 ff.

[26] Trasler, *op. cit.*, p. 103. On the whole subject of changing attitudes see also *Group Problems*, p. 17.

[27] R. B. Cattell, *Introduction to Personality Study*, London, 1950, p. 20.

[28] Tawney, *op. cit.*, London, 1921, also available in Paperback ed.; Galbraith, *op. cit.*, 6th imp. London, 1960; Titmuss: Fabian Tract 323; Shanks, *The Stagnant Society*; Fyvel, *The Insecure Offenders*, London, 1961. More recently Nicholas Davenport, *The Split Society*, London, 1964.

[29] David C. McClelland, *The Achieving Society*, Princeton, 1961.

[30] Lord Radcliffe, *The Problem of Power*, London, 1958, pp. 118 ff. 'The Postscript' was separately reprinted in *The Times*.

[31] See my contribution in *Law and Opinion in England in the Twentieth Century*, ed. by Morris Ginsberg, London, 1959, pp. 264 ff.

[32] On these developments see Richard M. Titmuss, *Essays on 'The Welfare State'*, London, 1958, Ch. 8-10; the same, in *Law and Opinion in England in the Twentieth Century*, pp. 299 ff.

[33] *Evening Standard*, 12.4.1960.

[34] Titmuss, *Essays*, Ch. 2, and now in greater detail in *Income Distribution and Social Change*, London, 1962.

[35] Durkheim, *Division of Labour*.

[36] Audrey Harvey, *Casualties of the Welfare State*, London, Fabian Tract 321, Feb. 1960; Peter Townsend, 'The Meaning of Poverty', *New Statesman*, 20.4.1962, pp. 553-4. Also Shanks, *The Stagnant Society*, p. 184: 'The British Welfare State tends to spread its benefits too widely and too thinly, so that not enough is available to help those whose need is greatest.' 'Our Welfare Services', he thinks, 'have begun to fall disturbingly behind those in many countries on the Continent and elsewhere.'

[37] J. K. Galbraith, *The Affluent Society*, London, 6th imp. 1960 (also Paperback), Ch. 23.

[38] See my *Criminal Justice*, p. 101, fn. 2, and Samuel Brittan in the *Observer*, 8.4.1962.

[39] See also Richard A. Cloward and Lloyd E. Ohlin, *Delinquency and Opportunity*, Glencoe, Ill., 1960, and London, 1962, pp. 84-5.

[40] *Social Aspects of Crime*, p. 125.

[41] *Report of a Committee to Inquire into the Operation of the Dock Workers (Regulation of Employment) Scheme*, 1947, H.M.S.O., July 1956, Cmd. 9813, pp. 15 ff. Meanwhile the trouble at the Docks has apparently become even worse, and another Devlin Report is eagerly awaited.

[42] London, 1961.

[43] See *Criminal Justice and Social Reconstruction*, pp. 152 ff., for the time up to the end of the Second World War; Wolfgang Friedmann, *Law in a Changing Society*, London, 1959, Ch. 8.

[44] On the issues involved in one of these battles see *Hansard* of the 14.2.1962, cols. 1329–1448.

[45] Sir Norman Angell, *The Unseen Assassins*, London, p. 176, fn. 1.

[46] Shanks, *op. cit.*, pp. 155 ff.; Titmuss, *Essays*, Ch. 6, esp. pp. 110 ff.

[47] See, e.g., John H. Goldthorpe, 'Organization and Supervisor-Worker Conflict', *Brit. J. Sociol.*, Vol. 10, No. 3, Sept. 1959, pp. 213 ff. (referring to the Mining Industry); J. A. C. Brown, *Industrial Psychology*, Harmondsworth, 1954.

[48] The *Listener*, 5.7.1962 and subsequent weeks; *The Times*, 17.7.1962 and subsequently.

CHAPTER 20

[1] On social class and class conflict the following non-criminological works may be consulted: Ralf Dahrendorf, *Class and Class Conflict in an Industrial Society*, London, 1959 (with comprehensive bibliog.). To this important book the present writer is particularly indebted, although he is not in complete agreement with some of the author's views. Moreover: L. A. Coser, *The Functions of Social Conflict*, London, 1956; D. V. Glass (ed.), *Social Mobility in Britain*, London, 1954, 2nd ed. 1964; T. H. Marshall, *Citizenship and Social Class*, Cambridge, 1950; H. M. Johnson (*op. cit.* above at Ch. 19, N. 18); David Riesman *et al.*, *The Lonely Crowd*, New Haven, 1950, and abridged by the authors, New York, 1953; Leonard Reissman, *Class in American Society*, London, 1960; Vance Packard, *The Status Seekers*, London, 1960, Harmondsworth, 1961; C. Wright Mills, *White Collar*, New York, 1956; Andrew Grant, *Socialism and the Middle Classes*, London, 1954; T. S. Simey, 'Class Conflict and Social Mobility', *J. roy. Soc. Arts*, Vol. 104, No. 4987, 28.9.1956, pp. 839 ff.; Richard Centers, *The Psychology of Social Class*, Princeton, 1949; H. J. Eysenck, *The Psychology of Politics*, London, 1954; Richard Hoggart, *The Uses of Literacy*, London, 1957, and Harmondsworth, 1958; Ferdynand Zweig, *The Worker in an Affluent Society*, London, 1962; Peter Collison, *The Cutteslowe Walls, A Study in Social Class*, London, 1963.

Popular: John Coleman, 'Class and the English', *Sunday Times*, 9.7.1961; Peter Laslett, 'Social Change in England 1901–51', the *Listener*, 4.1 and 11.1.1962.

[2] On the following see esp. Dahrendorf, *op. cit.*, *passim*.

[3] Sir Isaiah Berlin, *Historical Inevitability*, London, 1954.

[4] Dahrendorf, *op. cit.*, pp. 41 ff., who partly accepts, partly supplements and partly rejects and refute's Marx's theory of class.

[5] Pp. 48 ff.

[6] See, e.g., Preben Wolf, 'Crime and Social Class in Denmark', *Brit. J. Crim.*, Vol. 3, No. 1, July 1962, pp. 5 ff., referring to Svalastoga.

[7] *Status Seekers*, pp. 41 ff.

[8] See the valuable contributions by Basil Bernstein on language and class in *Brit. J. Sociol.*, Vol. 9, 1958, pp. 159–74, Vol. 10, 1959, pp. 311–26, Vol. 11, 1960, pp. 271 ff. Adherence to a certain political party is no longer a safe guide to social class in Britain as many working-class people vote Conservative and many middle-class people vote Labour; see the statistics given by Richard Rose, *The Times*, 12.10.1964.

[9] Trasler, *The Explanation of Criminality*, pp. 75 ff.

[10] Murray A. Straus, 'Deferred Gratification, Social Class, and the Achievement Syndrome', *Amer. Sociol. Rev.*, Vol. 27, No. 3, June 1962, pp. 326 ff., with many references.

[11] Straus, e.g., concludes that, although his research in Wisconsin had provided some evidence for a general pattern of this kind, it seemed 'one of the personality requisites for achievement roles in contemporary American society' rather than a peculiar middle-class pattern.

[12] 'The Social Background of Delinquency', The University of Nottingham, 1954 (unpublished), pp. 153, 275 ff.

[13] See also Zweig, *op. cit.*, pp. 104, 108.

[14] *The New Society*, No. 3, 18.10.1962, pp. 18–19.

[15] Eysenck, *op. cit.*, p. 14.

[16] Zweig, *op. cit.*, Part 6.

[17] *Brit. J. Sociol.*, Vol. 5, No. 4, Dec. 1954, p. 371.

[18] Packard, *op. cit.*, p. 286.

[19] *Ibid.*, Ch. 20.

[20] London, 1957.

[21] A survey by the Institute of Community Studies, London, 1962.

[22] Paperback ed., pp. 241 ff.

[23] In the meantime, the *Report on Higher Education* (Robbins Report), H.M.S.O., London, Oct. 1963, Cmd. 2154, has added some further information on the subject. Its table 21 (p. 5) shows the 'Percentage of Children born in 1940–1 reaching by 1960/1 full time Higher Education', by father's occupation (Great Britain). From the figures presented the Report concludes: 'Our survey confirmed that the association with parental occupation is, if anything, still closer (than according to the Crowther Report) where higher education is concerned', and (p. 52) 'There is impressive evidence that large numbers of able young people do not at present enter higher education'. Moreover, 'Children of manual workers are on average much less successful than children of the same ability in other social groups . . .'

[24] *Report of the Central Advisory Council for Education (England): 15–18*, Vol. 1, H.M.S.O., London, 1959, Vol. 2, 1960.

[25] See, e.g., the letters in the *New Statesman* following the review of the book in the issue of 12.2.1962.

[26] *Social Aspects of Crime*, pp. 153 ff.

[27] On imitation in general see, e.g., Murphy and Newcomb, *Experimental Social Psychology*, pp. 180 ff.; O. H. Mowrer, *Learning Theory and Personality Dynamics*, New York, 1950, pp. 573 ff.; Gordon W. Allport, *Personality*, New York, 1937; William McDougall, *Introduction to Social Psychology*, 29th ed., pp. 87, 280 ff.; Neal E. Miller and John Dollard, *Social Learning and Imitation*, London, 1945.

[28] Gabriel Tarde, *Les lois d'imitation*, Eng. trans. by E. Parsons, New York, 1903. On Tarde see Margaret S. Wilson Vine in *Pioneers in Criminology*, Ch. 10, esp. p. 231.

[29] Allport, *op. cit.*, p. 155.

[30] On identification from the psychoanalytical point of view see Glover, *Psychoanalysis*, p. 86; from the sociological point of view Merton, *Social Theory and Social Structure*, p. 302.

[31] Vance Packard, *The Hidden Persuaders*, Paperback ed., pp. 105, 115.

[32] Tony Parker and Robert Allerton, *The Courage of his Convictions*, London, 1962.

[33] Eng. trans., *The Rebel*, London, 1953, here quoted from Paperback ed. (trans. by Anthony Bower), Harmondsworth.

[34] See, e.g., Walter Reckless, *The Crime Problem*, Ch. 18; Clinard, *The Sociology of Deviant Behavior*, pp. 98–9; A. Vexliard, *Le Clochard*, Paris, 1957, with comprehensive bibliog.

[35] Richard Hare, *Maxim Gorki*, London, 1962, Ch. 3.

[36] Typical of this is Francis Williams's (now Lord Francis Williams) *The American Invasion*, London, 1962, and the discussion in the *Sunday Times*, 8.4.1962, Colour Section.

[37] Daniel J. Boorstin, *The Image—or What Happened to the American Dream*, London, 1962, Harmondsworth, 1963.

[38] Clancy Sigal, the *Listener*, 10.5.1962, p. 822.

[39] See my Preface to *Pioneers in Criminology* and Ch. 8 of *Group Problems in Crime and Punishment*.

[40] Quoted by A. Schönke, *Strafgesetzbuch Kommentar*, 4th ed., München–Berlin, 1949, § 130 II.

[41] So one of the leading commentators of the Penal Code, Eduard Dreher, in Schwarz–Dreher, Note 3 A to § 130. Also the *Official Motives of the Draft Code of 1960*, § 298, Bonn, 1960, p. 435.

[42] Kenny–Turner, *Outlines of Criminal Law*, 1952 ed., § 426.

[43] See the table in *Handwörterbuch der Kriminologie*, Vol. 2, pp. 48–9, which is now probably somewhat out of date.

[44] See Note 6 above.

[45] On this see also my *Criminal Justice and Social Reconstruction*, Ch. 6 ff.

[46] Marshall B. Clinard, *Sociology of Deviant Behavior*, pp. 23–4.

[47] William M. Kephart, *Amer. Soc. Rev.*, Vol. 19, August 1954, pp. 462 ff.

[48] See, e.g., the case of a former M.P. sentenced to four years' imprisonment for homosexual offences as reported in *The Times*, 18.7.1962.

[49] Roger G. Hood, *Sentencing in Magistrates' Courts*, The Library of Criminology, Vol. 7, London, 1962, Ch. 5, esp. pp. 81, 89, 92.

[50] Terence Morris, *The Criminal Area*, London, 1957, Ch. 10.

[51] Austin L. Porterfield, *Youth in Trouble*, Fort Worth, 1946.

[52] G. M. Trevelyan, *English Social History*, London, 1942, pp. 22 ff.

[53] *Geschichte des Verbrechens*, Ch. 18.

[54] *Sexual Offenders*, Eng. Stud. crim. Sci., Vol. 9, London, 1957, pp. 122 ff.

[55] J. H. Fitch, *Brit. J. Crim.*, Vol. 3, No. 1, July 1962, pp. 18–37.

[56] From the large literature on changes in attitudes towards sex and on the influence of class see, e.g., Packard, *The Status Seekers*, Ch. 11; Richard Hoggart, *The Uses of Literacy*, Chs. 2, 3.

[57] Some of these questions are discussed by Albert J. Reiss in the symposium on *Sex Offences, Law and Contemporary Problems*, Vol. 25, No. 2, Spring 1960, pp. 309 ff.

[58] Thomas Würtenberger, *Das Kunstfälschertum*, Weimar, 1940; *Der Kampf gegen das Kunstfälschertum in der deutschen und schweizerischen Strafrechtspflege*, Wiesbaden, 1951; *Symposium on Aspects of Art Forgery*, The Hague, 1962.

[59] Würtenberger (1951), pp. 32 ff.

[60] On defalcation by solicitors see *Social Aspects of Crime*, p. 209.

[61] *Other People's Money*, 1953. Sutherland also regards embezzlement as 'white collar crime'; *White Collar Crime*, New York, 1949, p. 231.

[62] *Theft, Law and Society*, 2nd ed., Indianapolis, 1952, Ch. 7.

[63] T. C. N. Gibbens and Joyce Prince, *Shoplifting*, London, 1962, p. 116.

[64] On this and on motor car stealing in general see T. C. N. Gibbens, *Brit. J. Delinq.*, Vol. 8, No. 4, April 1958, pp. 257 ff.; W. W. Wattenberg and J. Balistieri, *Amer. J. Sociol.*, Vol. 57, No. 5, May 1952, pp. 575–9; Leonard D. Savitz, *J. crim. law, Criminol. Police Sci.*, Vol. 50, No. 2, July–August 1959, pp. 132 ff. (with bibliog.); Bloch and Geis, *Man, Crime and Society*, pp. 332–5.

[65] *Social Science and Social Pathology*, London, 1959, p. 26.

[66] *Criminal Justice and Social Reconstruction*, 1946, p. 57.

[67] See, e.g., the references in my contribution to *Society*, ed. by A. T. Welford *et al.*, London, 1962, pp. 293–4.

[68] London, 1964, International Library of Criminology, Vol. 12.

[69] Ferdynand Zweig, *The Worker in an Affluent Society*, London, 1961, p. 104.

[70] Wolf Middendorff, *Soziologie des Verbrechens*, Düsseldorf–Köln, 1959, p. 161; the same, *600 Alkoholtäter*, Hamburg, 1961, pp. 25–6.

CHAPTER 21

[1] *Literature on White Collar Crime:* Edwin H. Sutherland, *White Collar Crime*, New York, 1949; new ed. 1961; the same in *The Sutherland Papers*, ed. by Albert Cohen, Alfred Lindesmith, Karl Schuessler, Bloomington, 1956, Part 2; the same in *Ann. Amer. Acad. Polit. Soc. Sci.*, Vol. 217, Sept. 1941, pp. 112 ff.; Marshall B. Clinard, *The Black Market*, New York, 1952; Herbert A. Bloch and Gilbert Geis, *Man, Crime and Society*, New York, 1962, Ch. 14; Gilbert Geis, 'Towards a Delineation of White Collar Offences', *Sociol. Inquiry*, Vol. 32, No. 2, Spring 1962, pp. 160–71; Hermann Mannheim, *Social Aspects of Crime*, London, 1940, Ch. 7; the same, *Criminal Justice and Social Reconstruction*, London, 1946, Ch. 7; the same, *War and Crime*, London, 1941, pp. 42 ff.; Howard Jones, *Crime and the Penal System*, London, 1956, 2nd ed., 1962, pp. 6–9; Paul W. Tappan, 'Who is the Criminal?' *Amer. Sociol. Rev.*, Vol. 12, Feb. 1947, pp. 96–102; John C. Spencer, 'White Collar Crime', in *Criminology in Transition*, ed. by T. Grygier, H. Jones, and John Spencer, International Library of Criminology, Vol. 14, London, 1965; Donald J. Newman, 'White Collar Crime', *Crime and Correction, Law and Contemporary Problems*, Vol. 23, No. 4, Autumn 1958, pp. 635–753; Frank E. Hartung, the same number, pp. 722 ff.; George B. Vold, *Theoretical Criminology*, New York, 1958, Ch. 13; Robert G. Caldwell, *Federal Probation*, March 1958, pp. 30–6. Of considerable interest are also the various contributions to the symposium on 'The Ethics of Business Enterprise', *Ann. Amer. Acad. Polit. Soc. Sci.*, Vol. 343, Sept. 1962. Of contributions written in a foreign language see the outstanding contribution by O. Terstegen in the symposium *Strafrechtspflege und Strafrechtsreform*, Bundeskriminalamt Wiesbaden, 1961, pp. 81–118 (with full Bibliog.), and W. Zirpins and O. Terstegen, *Wirtschaftskriminalität*, Lübeck, 1963; also Wolf Middendorff, *Soziologie des Verbrechens* (cited at Ch. 20, note 70), pp. 51 ff.

[2] This is not the place to embark on a discussion of the legal concept of political crime which has been very controversial in Continental literature. According to the prevailing objective theory it depends on the nature of the values attacked by the offender; according to the subjective theory on his motives. In the above-mentioned case the value attacked was the existing class structure of the society in which the offender lived. It is doubtful whether this would satisfy the objective theory.

[3] Robert K. Merton, *Social Theory and Social Structure*, 1957 ed., pp. 142–4.

[4] On these cases see *Ann. Amer. Acad. Polit. Soc. Sci.*, Sept. 1962, pp. 77 ff., 115; Geis–Bloch, *op. cit.*, p. 390; Geis, *op. cit.*, pp. 166 ff.

[5] *White Collar Crime*, p. 9.

[6] Roger Wilson, *Difficult Housing Estates*, London, 1963, p. 18, now makes the same point.

[7] Tappan (*loc. cit.* at note 1).

[8] *Group Problems*, p. 193.

[9] See esp. *Criminal Justice and Social Reconstruction*, Sects. III and IV.

[10] L. C. B. Gower in *Law and Opinion in England*, ed. by Morris Ginsberg, London, 1959, p. 145.

[11] *White Collar Crime*, pp. 10–11.

[12] C. Wright Mills, *White Collar*, New York, 1951, also in Paperback ed., New York, 1956, pp. ix–x and *passim*.

[13] See also Terstegen, *op. cit.*, p. 82.

[14] *White Collar Crime*, Ch. 9.

[15] Frederick K. Beutel, *Some Potentialities of Experimental Jurisprudence as a New Branch of Social Science*, Lincoln, 1957, pp. 257 ff.

[16] Wolfgang Friedmann, *Law in a Changing Society*, p. 263.

[17] *White Collar Crime*, p. 6.

[18] *The Sutherland Papers*, p. 96 (from an unpublished paper of 1948 on 'Crime of Corporations').

[19] See my *War and Crime*, p. 44.

[20] Donald R. Cressey, *Pacific Sociol. Rev.*, Vol. 3, No. 2, Autumn 1960, pp. 52–3.

[21] Ernest W. Burgess, *Amer. J. Sociol.*, Vol. 56, July 1950, pp. 32–4.

[22] Vold, *Theoretical Criminology* (cited at note 1), pp. 283 ff.

[23] 'Criminal Law and Penology', in *Law and Public Opinion in England in the Twentieth Century*, p. 283.

[24] Bloch and Geis, *op. cit.*, p. 385; Geis, *op. cit.*, pp. 160 ff.

[25] On this see Glanville Williams, *Criminal Law, The General Part*, Ch. 22; Wolfgang Friedmann, *op. cit.*, pp. 192 ff.

[26] See Williams, *op. cit.*, pp. 217–18; Friedmann, *op. cit.*, pp. 194–5, quoting the Tentative Draft No. 4 (1955) of the Model Penal Code of the American Law Institute.

[27] Editorial in *J. Business Law*, Oct. 1959, p. 309.

[28] See, e.g., *The Times* of 15.6., 16.6., 28.6., and July 6, 7, 8, 9, 12, 14, 15, 19, 20, 21, 22, 23, 1960. Also the 'Proceedings at the Registrar's Court of the City of London Magistrates', *The Times*, 2.2 and 2.4.1960. Moreover Spencer, *loc. cit.*, p. 250, and the official report by Neville Faulks, Q.C. *Investigation into the Affairs of H. Jasper and Co., Ltd.*, Board of Trade, H.M.S.O., London, 1961.

[29] According to press reports the shareholders of the State Building Society have now received full capital repayments, and it is hoped to repay also full interest.

[30] Cairns, 'Monopolies and Restrictive Practices', in *Law and Opinion in England* (cited at note 23), pp. 173–92; Spencer (*op. cit.* at note 1); Clay, 'The Problem of Monopoly, *The Times*, 19 and 20.1.1951; Wragg, 'The Work of the British Restrictive Practices Court since 1958', *Amer. J. comp. Law*, Vol. 10. No. 4, Autumn 1961, pp. 393 ff.

[31] *Report of the Monopolies and Restrictive Practices Commission*, H.M.S.O., June, 1955, Cmd. 9504.

[32] Abe Fortas, 'America's Electrical Price Conspiracy', *The Oxford Lawyer*, Vol. 5, No. 3, Michaelmas 1962, pp. 29–32; R. A. Smith in Wolfgang, Savitz and Johnston, *The Sociology of Crime*, New York, 1962, pp. 357 ff. (reprinted from *Fortune*).

[33] £10m. damages were awarded in June 1964 (*The Times*, 3.6.1964).

[34] Richard Titmuss in the *New Statesman*, 31.8.1962, and in his book *Income Distribution and Social Change*, London, 1962.

[35] London, 1961, and Paperback ed. Harmondsworth, 1963.

[36] On this see my *Social Aspects of Crime*, pp. 201 ff.

[37] Sherman Adams, *First-Hand Report*, New York, 1961, pp. 439 ff.

[38] J. Hall and D. Caradog Jones, *Brit. J. Sociol.*, Vol. 1, 1950, pp. 31–55.

[39] R. Beermann, 'The Parasite Law in the Soviet Union', *Brit. J. Crim.*, Vol. 3, No. 1, July 1962, pp. 71 ff.

CHAPTER 22

[1] Morris Ginsberg, *Studies in Sociology*, London, 1932, see also Dahrendofr (*op. cit.* at note 1 to Ch. 20), p. 180.

[2] See the quotation in my *Criminal Justice and Social Reconstruction*, p. 107, and Ch. 2, above.

[3] See Thorsten Sellin, in *Pioneers in Criminology*, pp. 289–90.

[4] *Social Theory and Social Structure*, rev. ed., Glencoe, Ill., 1957, p. 135, fn. 6.

[5] Emile Durkheim, *Suicide*, Eng. ed., London, 1952, pp. 246 ff. (trans. by John A. Spaulding and George Simpson).

[6] *Suicide*, p. 246.

[7] *Suicide*, pp. 355 ff. On the relationship between homicide and suicide, see also Ch. 16 under 4.

[8] Chs. 4 and 5.

[9] Deryck Cooke, *Mahler 1860–1911*, London, 1960, p. 13.

[10] This contrast between Durkheim's and Merton's theory of anomie is also stressed by Ohlin and Cloward (*op. cit.* at note 22 below), pp. 78 ff.

[11] On the concept of values or valuations and their relationship to the norms of society, see above, Ch. 19.

[12] Paul W. Tappan, *Crime, Justice, and Correction*, New York, 1960, pp. 169 ff.

[13] See Ch. 8 on Gambling in the author's *Social Aspects of Crime in England between the Wars*, esp. pp. 216 ff.

[14] Herbert A. Bloch and Gilbert Geis, *Man, Crime and Society*, New York, 1962, pp. 133–4.

[15] Bernhard Lander, *Towards an Understanding of Juvenile Delinquency*, New York, 1954, esp. Ch. 5.

[16] Glencoe, Ill., 1955; Eng. ed., London, 1956.

[17] Hermann Mannheim, 'Juvenile Delinquency', *Brit. J. Sociol.*, Vol. 7, No. 2, June 1956, pp. 148 ff.; Merton, *op. cit.*, p. 178.

[18] William Foote Whyte, *Street Corner Society*, 2nd ed., Chicago, 1955. Cohen had to use the first edition of 1943.

[19] See, e.g., William F. Ogburn and Meyer F. Nimkoff, *A Handbook of Sociology*, 1st ed., London, 1947, p. 139; Joseph B. Gittler, *Social Dynamics*, New York, 1952, pp. 237 ff.; Marshall B. Clinard, *Sociology of Deviant Behavior*, New York, 1957, pp. 9–10.

[20] Gordon Trasler, 'Strategic Problems in the Study of Criminal Behavior', *Brit. J. Crim.*, Vol. 4, No. 5, July 1964, pp. 422–42.

[21] On this see John I. Kitsuse and D. C. Dietrick, *Amer. Sociol. Rev.*, Vol. 24, No. 2, April 1959, pp. 208 ff.

[22] Richard A. Cloward and Lloyd E. Ohlin, *Delinquency and Opportunity*, Glencoe, Ill., 1960, Eng. ed., London, 1961. See Toby in *Brit. J. Sociol.*, Vol. 12, 1961, pp. 282 ff., and my review, *Brit. J. Crim.*, Vol. 3, No. 1, July 1962, pp. 91–3.

[23] Herbert Bloch and Arthur Niederhoffer, *The Gang: A Study of Adolescent Behavior*, New York, 1958. Against them Cloward and Ohlin, *op. cit.*, pp. 54 ff.

[24] *Ann. Amer. Acad. Pol. Soc. Sci.*, Vol. 347, May 1963, pp. 20–9.

[25] Dahrendorf (*op. cit.* above, at Ch. 20, note 1), pp. 280; Hoggart, *op. cit.* at Ch. 20, note 1), Ch. 3.

[26] *Criminal Justice and Social Reconstruction*, § 3.

[27] *Group Problems in Crime and Punishment*, p. 21, and above, Ch. 8, text to note 40.

[28] Gresham M. Sykes and David Matza, 'Techniques of Neutralization: A Theory of Delinquency', *Amer. Sociol. Rev.*, Vol. 22, Dec. 1957, pp. 664–70.

[29] John Barron Mays, *Education and the Urban Child*, Liverpool, 1962, p. 89.

[30] David J. Bordua, 'Delinquent Subcultures: Sociological Interpretations of Gang Delinquency', *Ann. Amer. Acad. Pol. Soc. Sci.*, Vol. 338, Nov. 1961, pp. 120 ff.

[31] Merton, *op. cit.*, pp. 72–81, 194–4; Daniel Bell, 'Crime as an American Way of Life', *Antioch Rev.*, Vol. 13, 1953, pp. 131–54 (reprinted in *The Sociology of Crime and Delinquency*, ed. by Wolfgang, Savitz and Johnston, New York–London, 1962, pp. 213–25); W. F. Whyte (*op. cit.* at note 18), esp. Part 3.

[32] Talcott Parsons, *Psychiatry*, Vol. 10, May 1947, pp. 167–81; *Essays in Sociological Theory*, 1954 ed., Glencoe, Ill., pp. 304–5; *Amer. Sociol. Rev.*, Vol. 7, 1942, pp. 604–16; Cohen, *op. cit.*, pp. 162 ff.; Cloward–Ohlin, *op. cit.*, pp. 48 ff.

[33] Parsons uses a rather narrow concept of aggression.

[34] Sheldon and Eleanor Glueck, *Unraveling Juvenile Delinquency*, p. 30; R. G. Andry, *Delinquency and Parental Pathology*, London, 1960, pp. 12–13.

[35] Shlomo Shoham, 'Conflict Situations and Delinquent Solutions', *J. soc. Psychol.*, 1964, pp. 185–215; David Matza and Gresham M. Sykes, *Amer. Sociol. Rev.*, Vol. 26, 1967, pp. 217 ff.

[36] Ralph W. England, Jr., 'Middle-Class Juvenile Delinquency', *J. crim. Law Criminol. Police Sci.*, Vol. 50, March–April 1960, pp. 535–40.

[37] Walter B. Miller, 'Lower Class Culture as a Generating Milieu of Gang Delinquency', *J. soc. Issues*, Vol. 14, 1958, pp. 5–19, reprinted in Wolfgang *et al.* (cited at note 31), pp 267–76. On this see also Martin Gold, *Status Forces in Del. Boys*, Ann Arbor, Michigan, 1963.

[38] See the details in *Brit. J. Crim.*, Vol. 1, April 1961, p. 376, Vol. 3, Jan. 1963, p. 283; and in particular, Wolfgang and Ferracuti, Vol. 3, April 1963, pp. 377–88.

[39] Planned by Shlomo Shoham.

[40] A. P. Jephcott and M. P. Carter (under the direction of Prof. W. J. H. Sprott, University of Nottingham, Rockefeller Research), 'The Social Background of Delinquency' (privately circulated, 1954, unpublished); J. B. Mays, *Growing up in the City*, 1954; the same, *On the Threshold of Delinquency*, 1959; the same, *Education and the Urban Child*, 1962 (all three published in Liverpool); the same, *Brit. J. Crim.*, Vol. 3, Jan. 1963, pp. 216–30; T. P. Morris (*op. cit.* at note 50 to Ch. 20); T. R. Fyvel (*op. cit.* at note 28 to Ch. 19).

[41] See my review in *Brit. J. Delinq.*, Vol. 5, No. 4, April 1955, pp. 307–8.

[42] See, however, Morris, *op. cit.*, pp. 104–5.

[43] *The Uses of Literacy*, p. 62.

[44] *Howard J.*, Vol. 8, No. 4, 1953, pp. 167 ff.

[45] See the quotation above text to note 29.

[46] 'Delinquency Areas—A Re-assessment' in *Brit. J. Crim.*, Vol. 3, No. 3, Jan. 1963, pp. 216–30.

[47] John B. Mays, *Crime and the Social Structure*, London, 1963.

[48] E.g., *Growing up in the City*, p. 91; *On the Threshold*, p. 165.

CHAPTER 23

[1] On human ecology in general: see Amos H. Hawley, *Human Ecology*, New York, 1950. On social ecology: M. A. Alihan, *Social Ecology*, New York, 1938; Radhakamal Mukerjee, *Social Ecology*, London, 1942 or 1944?

On the ecological theory of crime and delinquency: see in particular T. P. Morris, *The Criminal Area* (cited at note 50 to Ch. 20); Clifford R. Shaw, *Delinquency Areas*, Chicago, 1929; Clifford R. Shaw and Henry McKay *et al.*, *Juvenile Delinquency and Urban Areas*, Chicago, 1942; Walter C. Reckless, *Criminal Behavior*, New York, 1940, Ch. 4, 5; Pitirim A. Sorokin, Carle C. Zimmermann and Charles J. Galpin, *A Systematic Source Book in Rural Sociology*, Vol. 2, Minneapolis, 1931, pp. 266 ff.; also Sorokin and Zimmermann, *Principles of Rural–Urban Sociology*, New York, 1929; Barnes and Teeters, *New Horizons in Criminology*, Ch. 7; Cyril Burt, *The Young Delinquent*, pp. 70–8; Howard

Jones, *Crime and the Penal System*, pp. 79–86; the same, 'Approaches to an Ecological Study', *Brit. J. Delinq.*, Vol. 8, No. 4, April 1958, pp. 277–93 (on Leicester); Hermann Mannheim, *Juvenile Delinquency in an English Middletown*, London, 1948 (on Cambridge); 'Delinquency Areas: A symposium', *Brit. J. Delinq.*, Vol. 7, No. 2, Oct. 1956, pp. 137–48; Solomon Kobrin, 'The Conflict of Values in Delinquency Areas', *Amer. Sociol. Rev.*, Vol. 16, Oct. 1951, pp. 653–61; the same, 'The Chicago Area Project—a 25-year Assessment', *Ann. Amer. Pol. Soc. Sci.*, Vol. 322, March 1959, pp. 19–29; Calvin F. Schmid, 'Urban Crime Areas', *Amer. Sociol. Rev.*, Vol. 25, 1960, pp. 527 ff., 655 ff. (on Seattle); W. H. Nagel, *De Criminaliteit van Oss*, The Hague, 1949 (in Dutch, with English summary); Hassan El-Saaty, 'Juvenile Delinquency in Egypt' (unpublished, London, Ph.D. Thesis, 1946); *Sozialgeographische Karten*. Herausgegeben vom Hauptamt für Gesamtplanung. Magistrat von Gross-Berlin, 1950; H. van Rooy, *Criminologische Contrasten tussen stad en land*, Nijmegen, 1947; van Bemmelen, *Kriminologie*, Ch. 7. The University of Utrecht, under the leadership of W. P. J. Pompe, has in the past 25 years produced a considerable number of monographs on the criminality of various Dutch cities and provinces. The first of them was G. Th. Kempe and J. Vermaat, *Criminaliteit in Drenthe*, Utrecht, 1938. See also Kempe in Bonger, *Inleiding*, 3rd ed., p. 19. Irving Spergel, *Racketvill, Slumtown, Haulburg*, Chicago, 1963.

On Urbanization and Urbanism as Criminogenic Factors: Marshall B. Clinard, *Sociology of Deviant Behavior*, New York, 1957, Ch. 3; also in several papers, esp. 'A Cross-Cultural Replication of the Relation of Urbanism to Criminal Behavior', *Amer. Sociol. Rev.*, Vol. 25, No. 2, April 1960, pp. 253–7; Bloch and Geis, *op. cit.*, pp. 183–5; Howard Jones, 'The Rural Offender in England', *Bull. Soc. int. Criminol.*, 1959, 1er Semestre, pp. 23–32; George B. Vold, 'Crime in City and Country Areas', *Ann. Amer. Acad. Pol. Soc. Sci.*, Vol. 217, Sept. 1941, pp. 38–45; Donald R. Taft, *Criminology*, 3rd ed., 1956, Ch. 11; *Prevention of Types of Criminality Resulting from Social Changes and Accompanying Economic Development in Less Developed Countries*: General Reports by J. J. Panakal and A. M. Khalifa, Second United Nations Congress on the Prevention of Crime and the Treatment of Offenders, London, 1960; Hans Hermann Burchardt, *Kriminalität in Stadt und Land*, Berlin–Leipzig, 1936; Denis Szabo, *Crimes et Villes*, Paris, 1960; W. Gierlichs and H. H. Burchardt, 'Stadt und Land', in *Handwörterbuch der Kriminologie*, Vol. 2, Berlin–Leipzig, 1935, pp. 654–75; E. C. Rhodes, *J. roy. Statis. Soc.*, Vol. 102, Part 3, 1939, pp. 384 ff.; Carr-Saunders, Mannheim, and Rhodes, *Young Offenders*, London, 1944, pp. 46–50. On the history of ecological studies in England: Yale Levin and Alfred Lindesmith, 'English Ecology and Criminology', *J. crim. Law, Criminol. Police Sci.*, Vol. 27, 1936–7, pp. 801–16.

[2] Tappan, *Crime, Justice and Correction*, New York, 1960, pp. 205–7; Vold, *Theoretical Criminology*, pp. 189–90.

[3] J. M. van Bemmelen, *Criminologie*, 3rd ed., Zwolle, 1952, Ch. 7, very detailed; Franz Exner, *Kriminologie*, 3rd ed., 1949, pp. 234 ff.; Stephan Hurwitz, *Criminology*, London–Copenhagen, 1952, pp. 252 ff.; *Handwörterbuch der Kriminologie*, Vol. 2, 654 ff.

[4] T. P. Morris, *op. cit.*, p. 7.

[5] Franz Exner, *Kriminalbiologie*, 1st ed., Hamburg, 1939, pp. 57 ff.

[6] Reckless, *Criminal Behavior*, pp. 59 ff.

[7] Morris, *op. cit.*, pp. 48 ff.

[8] *J. roy. Statis. Soc.*, Vol. 43, 1880, pp. 423 ff., 434.

[9] Willem Adriaan Bonger, *Criminality and Economic Conditions* (Eng. ed. Boston, 1916), pp. 529 ff.

[10] On this see Ch. 5 on 'Unemployment' in my *Social Aspects* and the present Chapter under CII/3(g).

[11] Denis Szabo (*op. cit.* at note 1), p. 79.

[12] *Group Problems*, pp. 169–70.

[13] Mabel A. Elliott and Francis E. Merrill, *Social Disorganization*, 4th ed., New York, 1960, p. 565.

[14] *Group Problems*, pp. 86 ff., and earlier already in *War and Crime*, p. 136.

[15] Cyril Burt, *The Young Delinquent*, p. 77, found in Shoreditch a delinquency rate of 0·28 against 0·14 in Bethnal Green, but he gives no figures to show the rate of mobility. He shows, however, a poor relief rate of 51·2 for Shoreditch against one of 24·8 for Bethnal Green.

[16] Gianfranco Garavaglia e Gianluigi Ponti, 'Immigrazione e Criminalità', *Quad. Criminol. Clin.*, Anno 5, No. 3, July–Sept. 1963, pp. 347–58. Also Clinard, *Sociology of Deviant Behavior*, pp. 71–3.

[17] Leonard Savitz, *Delinquency and Migration*; a report prepared for the Commission on Human Relations, Philadelphia, 1960; reprinted in Wolfgang *et al.*, *The Sociology of Crime and Delinquency*, pp. 199–205.

[18] See *Group Problems*, p. 198.

[19] Mannheim and Wilkins, *Prediction Methods in relation to Borstal Training*, pp. 88–9.

[20] *Group Problems*, pp. 86 ff.

[21] See for U.S.A., *Group Problems*, pp. 194–5; Thorsten Sellin, *Culture Conflict and Crime*, Soc. Sci. Res. Counc. Bull. 41, New York, 1938, pp. 63–116; Samuel Koenig, 'The Immigrant and Crime', in Joseph S. Roucek, *Sociology of Crime*, London, 1961, pp. 138–59; Donald R. Taft, *Criminology*, Ch. 8; E. H. Stofflet, 'The European Immigrant and his Children', *Ann. Amer. Acad. Pol. Soc. Sci.*, Vol. 217, Sept. 1941, pp. 84–92; Mabel A. Elliott, *Crime in Modern Society*, New York, 1952, pp. 288–97; W. I. Thomas and F. Znaniecki, *The Polish Peasant in Europe and America*, New York, 1927, Vol. 2.

[22] Lloyd P. Gartner, *The Jewish Immigrant in England 1870–1914*, London, 1960, pp. 183–6.

[23] See Taft, *op. cit.*, pp. 153–4; Elliott, *op. cit.*, pp. 288–9.

[24] See the interesting and fully documented article by A. G. Mezey, 'Psychiatric Aspects of Human Migrations', *Int. J. soc. Psychiat.*, Vol. 5, No. 4, Spring 1960, pp. 245–60. Also Clinard, *Sociology of Deviant Behavior*, pp. 71–3.

[25] See *Handwörterbuch der Kriminologie*, Vol. 1, p. 91, and on the excess of adolescents and young adults among the migrant population in general D. S. Thomas, *Research Memorandum on Migration Differentials*, Soc. Sci. Res. Counc. Bull., 1938, p. 43.

[26] Stofflet, *op. cit.*, p. 84.

[27] See, e.g., the tables in Elliott, *op. cit.*, pp. 290–2, and Sellin, *op. cit.*, pp. 75–7.

[28] Taft, *op. cit.*, p. 155; Sellin, *op. cit.*, pp. 78–82.

[29] Frederick M. Thrasher, *The Gang*, 1st ed., Chicago, 1927, pp. 191 ff.

[30] 'Culture Conflict and Delinquency', *Mental Hygiene*, Vol. 21, No. 1, Jan. 1937, pp. 46–66.

[31] A. L. Wood, *J. crim. Law Criminol. Police Sci.*, Vol. 37, No. 6, 1947, p. 504.

[32] Stofflet, *op. cit.*, p. 85.

[33] Thomas and Znaniecki, *op. cit.*, Vol. 2, p. 1756.

[34] E. D. Beynon, *J. crim. Law Criminol.*, Vol. 25, 1935, pp. 755 ff.

[35] See also Walter C. Reckless, *The Crime Problem*, New York, 1940, pp. 111–112.

[36] Gabriel Tarde, *Philosophie pénale*, 4th ed., Paris, 1895, p. 343. See also Henri Joly, *La France criminelle*, Paris, 1889, p. 61.

[37] Denis Szabo, *Crime et Villes*, pp. 130-1.

[38] *Social Survey of Merseyside*, Vol. 1, ed. by D. Caradog Jones, Liverpool–London, 1934, Ch. 3.

[39] See the figures in *Social Aspects of Crime in England between the Wars*, p. 139, but also the explanation given on pp. 38, 74, 140.

[40] According to the (unpublished) 'Home Office Supplementary Statistics relating to Crime and Criminal Proceedings in the year 1961', Table 4, the figures of indictable offences known to the Police were for Liverpool 20,909, for Manchester 24,804, for Birmingham 25,498.

[41] F. H. McClintock and Evelyn Gibson, *Robbery in London*, London 1961, pp. 51, 65.

[42] It was perhaps somewhat unfortunate that *The Times* of 12.3.1962, while also scrupulously fair in its extracts from the study, should have headed its report, 'High proportion of Irishmen and West Indians convicted'.

[43] See in particular Ruth Glass, *Newcomers, The West Indians in London*, Centre for Urban Studies, Report No. 1, London, 1960; K. L. Little, *Negroes in Britain*, London, 1948; Anthony H. Richmond, *Colour Prejudice in Britain*, 1954 (now in a revised Paperback ed., 1960), and the material quoted in these books.

[44] Michael Banton estimated the number of persons of Negro descent in Britain in 1954 at about 35,000 and of coloured residents of all nationalities at about 75,000 (*The Times*, 31.5.1954). In recent years these numbers will have considerably increased. In a letter to *The Times*, 12.10.1964, Ruth Glass quotes the following net annual intake by Britain from Asian, African, Caribbean countries of the Commonwealth: 1961: 125,400; 1963: 53,350; 1964, first half: 28,250. As the control of immigration started in July 1962 these figures show an increase before and immediately after the institution of control, with a subsequent decline.

[45] Ruth Glass, *op. cit.*, Chs. 2-5. See now also the careful study of a particularly difficult area of London by Pearl Jephcott, *A Troubled Area. Notes on Notting Hill*, London, 1964.

[46] T. C. N. Gibbens and Joyce Prince, *Shoplifting*, London, I.S.T.D., 1962, Ch. 4.

[47] *Hansard*, 4.4.1963.

[48] See the literature in note 1.

[49] See *Items*, published by the Social Science Research Council, New York, Vol. 13, No. 4, Dec. 1959, pp. 40-3.

[50] Ruth Glass, Ch. 26 in *Society, Problems and Methods of Study*, ed. by A. T. Welford, Michael Argyle, D. V. Glass, J. N. Morris, London, 1962, pp. 481-97. Also Ch. 27 on 'Rural Society' by V. G. Pons in the same volume.

[51] Quoted from the Rev. W. D. Morrison, *Young Offenders*, London, 1896, pp. 30-1.

[52] Quoted from Roger Wilson, *Difficult Housing Estates*, London, 1963, pp. 9-10.

[53] Robert Sinclair, *Metropolitan Man*, London, 1937, p. 133.

[54] David Riesman *et al.*, *The Lonely Crowd*, pp. 34 and *passim*.

[55] Clifford R. Shaw, *The Natural History of a Delinquent*.

[56] Vold in *Annals* (see note 1), pp. 42-3.

[57] See, e.g., Clinard, *op. cit.*, pp. 69, 88, against the hypothesis of selective migration of deviants; Otto Klineberg, *Race and Psychology*, UNESCO, 1951, p. 18, similarly against the theory of selective migration of more intelligent individuals.

[58] In Sidney and Beatrice Webb, *English Prisons under Local Government*, London, 1922, p. xxvi.

[59] *Social Aspects of Crime*, pp. 115–17.

[60] P. 117.

[61] John A. Mack, *Brit. J. Sociol.*, Vol. 15, No. 1, March 1964, p. 43.

[62] See note 41 above.

[63] Clinard, *Sociology of Deviant Behavior*, p. 69.

[64] See note 1 above.

[65] Note 1 above.

[66] Now Pinatel also in his *Criminologie*, Paris, 1963, p. 93.

[67] *Archivum Kriminologii*, Vol. 1, Warsaw, 1960, pp, 364–6.

[68] Bombay, 1959, pp. 43 ff., 113 ff.

[69] S. Venugopala Rao, *Facets of Crime in India*, New Delhi–London, 1963, p. 57. See also the case of homicide discussed by G. M. Carstairs, *Brit. J. Delinq.*, Vol. 4, No. 1, July 1953, pp. 14 ff., also referred to above, p. 608.

[70] E. C. Rhodes, *J. roy. Statis. Soc.*, Vol. 102, Part 3, 1939, pp. 384 ff.

[71] *Prediction Methods* (cited at note 19), p. 95.

[72] See note 1 above.

[73] Clinard, *Amer. Sociol. Rev.*, Vol. 25, No. 2, April 1960.

[74] See the literature cited at note 1 and on one specific aspect Donald J. Bogue, *Skid Row in American Cities*, Chicago, 1963.

[75] Quoted in A. M. Carr-Saunders *et al.*, *Young Offenders*, my Ch. 1, p. 7.

[76] *The Young Delinquent*, pp. 70–8.

[77] See note 1 above.

[78] See in particular the relevant Chapters in T. P. Morris's book.

[79] For the details see T. P. Morris, *op. cit.*, and the relevant chapter in such American textbooks as Barnes and Teeters, *op. cit.*; Taft, *op. cit.*; Reckless, *Criminal Behavior*; and also Ogburn–Nimkoff, *Handbook of Sociology*, Ch. 14.

[80] R. E. Park, E. W. Burgess and R. D. McKenzie, *The City*, Chicago, 1925, p. 55. This design is reproduced in Ogburn–Nimkoff, *op. cit.*, Fig. 11.

[81] Kobrin, *Conflict of Values* (cited at note 1).

[82] According to Bogue the residents of the Skid Row areas of the big American cities are social outcasts, drunkards, and misfits rather than criminals, but such districts attract criminals, especially 'jackrollers' and pickpockets, who find easy victims among the residents.

[83] See, e.g., the data given in Shaw, *The Jack Roller* (cited at Ch. 8, note 18), p. 35, which are a good illustration of the national and racial changes between 1900–26.

[84] Lander, *op. cit.*, p. 84.

[85] Jonasson, *Amer. Sociol. Rev.*, Vol. 14, 1949, pp. 614 ff.

[86] C. R. Shaw and H. D. McKay, *Juvenile Delinquency and Urban Areas*, 1942. On this see Morris, *op. cit.*, p. 80.

[87] *Juvenile Delinquency in an English Middletown*, pp. 34–5.

[88] Morris, *op. cit.*, p. 23.

[89] Tony Parker and Robert Allerton, *The Courage of his Convictions*, London, 1962, Ch. 1.

[90] J. W. M. Thompson, the *Evening Standard*, 9.5.1963. In May 1963 several men were sent to prison at the Central Criminal Court in London for operating a 'protection racket' among Chinese restaurant owners in Soho (*The Times*, 17.5.1963). Another expert on Soho, Mark Benney, described it as a district of 'inexhaustible interest' to children on account of the innumerable opportunities for pilfering and gambling which it offered; see his *Low Company*, London, 1936, pp. 49–50. The evidence given to the Challenor Tribunal in 1964 has thrown further light on conditions in Soho; see, e.g., the summing up in the *Sunday Times* of the 20.11.1964.

[91] *Middletown*, pp. 31–37, and the map, pp. 60–1.

[92] Roger Wilson, *Difficult Housing Estates*, London, 1963. The first part of the report of the Bristol team has been published under the title *Stress and Release in an Urban Estate*, by John C. Spencer *et al.*, London, 1964.

[93] Spencer, *Brit. J. Delinq.*, Vol. 7, p. 146.

[94] Howard Jones, *Brit. J. Delinq.*, Vol. 8, 1958, pp. 277–93.

[95] *Middletown*, p. 32.

[96] Thomas Ferguson, *The Young Delinquent in his Social Setting*, London, 1952, p. 18.

[97] Tadashi Uematsu, 'The Delinquency Area in Tokyo', *Int. Ann. Criminol.*, 1962, pp. 357–9.

[98] Solomon Kobrin, *Annals* (see note 1), p. 19.

[99] On this see also Merton, *op. cit.*, above, Ch. 22.

[100] Unpublished Annual Report, issued by the Chicago Area Project, 907 South Wolcott Avenue, Chicago 12. On the Project see also Clinard, *op. cit.*, pp. 526–8.

[101] Cyril Burt, *The Young Delinquent*, p. 87.

[102] Carr-Saunders, Mannheim, Rhodes, *Young Offenders*, London, 1942, pp. 77–83.

[103] *Middletown*, pp. 30–1.

[104] See, e.g., Clinard, *op. cit.*, pp. 110–12.

[105] Lander (*op. cit.*, at Ch. 22, note 15), pp. 73 ff.

[106] *Ibid.*, pp. 55–6, 71, 88.

[107] *Social Aspects of Crime*, pp. 350–1.

[108] Sellin, *Culture Conflict and Crime*, p. 58, fn. 1.

[109] The Doukhobors are called 'a unique and baffling criminological problem' by W. T. McGrath, Executive Secretary of the Canadian Corrections Associations, *Int. Ann. Criminol.* 1963, p. 610.

[110] Rao (*op. cit.* at note 69), pp. 54–7.

[111] Arthur Lewis Wood, 'Crime and Aggression in Changing Ceylon', *Trans. Amer. Philosoph. Soc.*, New Series, Vol. 51, Part 8, Philadelphia, Dec. 1961; the same, 'Minority-Group Criminality and Cultural Integration', *J. crim. Law Criminol. Police Sci.*, Vol. 37, No. 6, March–April 1947, pp. 498–510.

[112] *Sessional Paper XIV—1959*, Government Publication Bureau, Colombo, pp. 19 ff., 27.

[113] Barnes and Teeters, *New Horizons in Criminology*, 1st ed., pp. 198–202. See also *Group Problems in Crime and Punishment*, p. 201; Arthur Raper, *The Tragedy of Lynching*, Chapel Hill, N.C., 1933; T. Grygier, *Oppression*, p. 173 with bibliog.

[114] See, e.g., the important discussion of this question by Herbert Jäger, 'Betrachtungen zum Eichmann-Prozess', *Mschr. Kriminol. Strafrechtsreform*, Vol. 45, No. 3–4, Aug. 1962, pp. 73–83.

[115] W. A. Bonger, *Race and Crime*, trans. from the Dutch by Margaret Mathew Hordyk, New York, 1943; Hans von Hentig, *Crime Causes and Conditions*, New York, 1947, Ch. 7; Franz Exner, *Kriminalbiologie*, 1st ed., Hamburg, 1939, Ch. 5: 'Volkscharakter und Verbrechen'; also Ch. 6 of the 3rd ed., which appeared in 1949 under the title *Kriminologie*, Berlin-Göttingen-Heidelberg.

[116] In addition to the literature in note 115 see Hans von Hentig, *J. crim. Law Criminol. Police Sci.*, Vol. 31, 1940, pp. 662–80; my *Group Problems*, pp. 196–205, with many further references.

[117] *The Negro in the United States*, revised ed. 1957, New York, Ch. 25.

[118] *Democracy in America*, 1945 ed., New York, Vol. 1, p. 362.

[119] Joseph S. Roucek, 'The Sociological Framework of the Negro Problem', *Indian J. Soc. Res.*, Vol. 2, No. 1, Jan. 1961, p. 13.

[120] The table by Roesner in *Handwörterbuch der Kriminologie*, 1st ed., 1933, Vol. 2, pp. 48-9, may be out of date, but no major additions are likely to have been made to the few countries listed, all non-European except Czechoslovakia. The Netherlands should also have been included, however.

[121] A case of this kind is reported by Cloward and Ohlin, *Delinquency and Opportunity*, p. 200.

[122] *Crime: Causes and Conditions*, p. 159.

[123] H. A. Bullock, *J. crim. Law Criminol. Police Sci.*, Vol. 52, No. 4, Nov.-Dec. 1961, pp. 411-17.

[124] Quoted from Bloch and Geis (*op. cit.* at Ch. 21, note 1), pp. 180-1.

[125] See the references in *Group Problems*, pp. 198-9.

[126] Bonger (*op. cit.* at note 115), pp. 51-66.

[127] *Op. cit.* at note 115, pp. 67-71.

[128] Hagemann, *Handwörterbuch der Kriminologie*, 1st ed. 1934, Vol. 2, p. 457.

[129] E. Mezger, *Kriminalpolitik auf kriminologischer Grundlage*, Stuttgart, 1934, p. 144, and fn. 3.

[130] Radbruch and Gwinner, *Geschichte des Verbrechens*, pp. 109 ff., Ch. 14.

[131] On the historical background of this process see, e.g., Morris Ginsberg, *Reason and Unreason in Society*, pp. 204-5; Gerhard Masur, *Friedrich Julius Stahl*, Berlin, 1930, pp. 4 ff. (in German); *Encyclopedia Britannica*, art. Jews.

[132] Werner Sombart, *Die Juden im Wirtschaftsleben*, Leipzig, 1911, Eng. trans. by M. Epstein, London, 1913, esp. pp. 130 ff., 153, 169 ff.

[133] On the following text see Shlomo Shoham, 'The Application of the "Culture Conflict" Hypothesis to the Criminality of Immigrants in Israel', *J. crim. Law Criminol. Police Sci.*, Vol. 53, No. 2, June 1962, pp. 207-14. Also Eisenstadt, 'The Oriental Jews in Israel', *Jewish Soc. Studies*, Vol. 12, No. 3, 1950.

[134] Shoham, *op. cit.*, p. 211. Bonger, *Geloof en Misdaad*, 1913.

[135] Publications of the Institute of Criminology, No. 1, Jerusalem, 1962, Table 47.

[136] G. Th. Kempe, *Criminaliteit en Kerkenootschap*, Utrecht, 1938; the same in the 3rd ed. of Bonger's *Inleiding tot de Criminologie*, Haarlem, 1954, pp. 175 ff.; G. H. A. Feber, *De criminaliteit der Katholieken in Nederland*, 1933; J. M. van Bemmelen, *Kriminologie*, 3rd ed. Zwolle, 1952, pp. 298 ff.; H. Bianchi, *Crime and Religious Profession* (in English), Amsterdam, *Free Univ. Quart.*, Vol. 5, No. 1, Nov. 1957, pp. 24-42. For a very popular discussion of the subject see J. Arthur Hoyles, *Religion in Prison*, New York, 1955.

[137] E.g., Taft, *Criminology*, Ch. 15; Barnes and Teeters, *New Horizons in Criminology*, Ch. 11; Mabel Elliott, *op. cit.*, pp. 834-6; Ernst Seelig, *Lehrbuch der Kriminologie*, pp. 189-91; Exner, *Kriminalbiologie*, pp. 118-21; Erwin Hacker, *Der Einfluss der Konfession auf die Kriminalität in Ungarn*, Miscolc, 1930.

[138] See also T. P. and P. Morris, *Pentonville*, pp. 39, 297.

[139] See on this my *Juvenile Delinquency in an English Middletown*, pp. 27-8.

[140] M. J. Moroney, *Facts from Figures*, Harmondsworth, 1951, p. 303.

[141] Max Weber, 'Die Protestantische Ethik und der Geist des Kapitalismus' *Gesammelte Aufsätze*, Vol. 1, 1921.

[142] Tawney, *op. cit.*, Paperback ed., Harmondsworth, 1938, p. 284.

[143] Walter Mannzen, *Mschr. Kriminalpsychol. Strafrechtsreform*, Vol. 23, 1932, pp. 365-71. Also Ernst Seelig, *Kriminologie*, pp. 189-91.

[144] W. H. Nagel, 'Criminality and Religion' (in Eng.), *Tijdschrift voor Strafrecht*, Vol. 69, No. 5, 1960 (special Congress number), pp. 236-91.

[145] Wood (*op. cit.* at note 111), pp. 34-6.

[146] The literature on economic factors in crime is very extensive, especially on the Continent. Only the following publications can here be mentioned: J. van

Kan, *Les causes économiques de la criminalité*, Paris–Lyon, 1903; W. A. Bonger, *Criminalité et Conditions économiques*, Amsterdam, 1905, Amer. ed.: *Criminality and Economic Conditions*, Boston, 1916; Karl Roesner, art. 'Wirtschaftslage und Straffälligkeit' in *Handwörterbuch der Kriminologie*, Vol. 2, 1936, pp. 1079–1116; Thorsten Sellin, *Research Memorandum on Crime in the Depression*, Soc. Sci. Res. Counc. Bull. 27, New York, 1937; Hermann Mannheim, *Social Aspects of Crime in England between the Wars*, Ch. 4, 5, 7; the same, *Group Problems*, Ch. 5; the same, *Criminal Justice and Social Reconstruction*, Ch. 6–9; the same, *War and Crime*; van Bemmelen, *Kriminologie*, Ch. 2; Exner, *Kriminalbiologie*, Ch. 8; Taft, *Criminology*, Ch. 9; Bonger, *Introduction*, pp. 26 ff., 90 ff.; George B. Vold, *Theoretical Criminology*, Ch. 9; Dorothy S. Thomas, *Social Aspects of the Business Cycle*, London, 1925.

[147] Aristotle, *Politics*, II, 7, 11, 13 (B. Jowett's trans., Oxford, 1885, vol. 1). See also my *War and Crime*, p. 40.

[148] Sir Thomas More, *Utopia*, Everyman's ed., London, 1951, pp. 21 ff.; G. M. Trevelyan, *English Social History*, 1st ed., London, 1944, pp. 109 ff., has surprisingly little to say on More's *Utopia* and the social evils which he attacked. Only some forms of enclosure, he thinks, defrauded the poor, but he had to admit that no doubt a certain proportion lost their places and swelled the ranks of the 'sturdy beggars'.

[149] Edouard Ducpétiaux, *Mémoire sur le pauperisme dans les Flandres*, Bruxelles, 1850.

[150] Some details are given by Sellin, *op. cit.*, pp. 20–1.

[151] T. P. Morris, *The Criminal Area*, pp. 60–1.

[152] Cesare Lombroso, *Crime: Causes and Remedies*, Chs. 6, 9.

[153] Enrico Ferri, 'Studi sulla criminalità in Francia del 1826 al 1878', *Annali di statistica serl. 2*, Vol. 21, 1881, reprinted in his *Studi sulla criminalità ed altri saggi*, Turin, 1901, pp. 17–97. See on this Sellin in *Pioneers in Criminology*, p. 283.

[154] Georg von Mayr, 'Statistik der gerichtlichen Polizei im Königreiche Bayern, etc.' in *Beiträge zur Statistik im Königreiche Bayern*, München, 1867.

[155] See, e.g., Bonger, *Introduction*, p. 54; Roesner, *Handwörterbuch*, p. 1089; van Bemmelen, *Kriminologie*, p. 171; Exner, *op. cit.*, 1st ed., p. 94.

[156] For the details see Bonger's exhaustive book.

[157] Widely quoted in this connection has been W. Woytinski's paper 'Kriminalität und Lebensmittelpreise', *Z. ges. Strafrechtwiss*, Vol. 49, 1929, pp. 647–75.

[158] Even in Dagenham Peter Willmott found that the Ford Company did not dominate the estate, and the community was by no means merely a 'company town', *Dagenham*, 1963, pp. 16–7.

[159] Useful critical discussions of Thomas's work can be found in Sellin's *Crime in the Depression*, pp. 33–8, and Vold, *Theoretical Criminology*, pp. 178–81.

[160] The question has been very fully discussed by Sellin, *op. cit.*, Ch. 4.

[161] See my *Social Aspects of Crime*, p. 125.

[162] Vold, *op. cit.*, pp. 177–8.

[163] *The Young Delinquent*, 1st ed., 1925, pp. 66 ff.

[164] Charles Booth *Life and Labour of the People in London*, London, 1892–7; Seebohm Rowntree, *Poverty*, 4th ed., London, 1902; the same, *Poverty: A Second Social Survey of York*, London, 1941; S. Rowntree and G. R. Lavers, *Poverty and the Welfare State: a Third Social Survey of York*, London, 1951.

[165] A. M. Carr-Saunders, Hermann Mannheim and E. C. Rhodes, *Young Offenders*, London, 1942, pp. 72 ff.

[166] Ewald Renger, *Kriminalität, Preis und Lohn*, Leipzig, 1933; on it also Exner, *op. cit.*, 1st ed., pp. 99–101.

[167] See, e.g., Peter Townsend, 'Measuring Poverty', *Brit. J. Sociol.*, Vol. 5, No.

2, June 1954, pp. 130–7; also, *New Statesman*, 20.4.1962, pp. 552–4; Brian Abel-Smith, *ibid.*, 28.2.1963; Dorothy Wedderburn, *Sociol. Rev.*, Vol. 10, No. 3.

[168] See also Vold, *op. cit.*, pp. 99 ff.

[169] Reprinted in *Group Problems*, p. 105.

[170] London, 1961, pp. 145, 163.

[171] See my article 'Rechtsgefühl und Dichtung' (see above, end of Chapter 2, and note 7 to Ch. 16).

[172] *Criminal Justice and Social Reconstruction*, pp. 102–8; *Group Problems*, pp. 20–4; and the literature quoted.

[173] See above, Ch. 10, II, 1.

[174] See, e.g., an interview published in the *Kentish Times*, 24.5.1963.

[175] See *Social Aspects of Crime*, pp. 188–97.

[176] See *Juvenile Delinquency in an English Middletown*, pp. 66–7, *Group Problems*, p. 90, and the *Report of the (Curtis) Committee on the Care of Children*, London, H.M.S.O., Cmd. 6922, 1946, paras. 206 ff.

[177] On the methods of coping with stealing and destructiveness in Children's Homes see Howard Jones, *Reluctant Rebels*, London, 1960, pp. 121–3. On vandalism by young people see the symposium in *Fed. Prob.*, Vol. 18, March 1954, pp. 3–16.

[178] *The Insecure Offenders*, pp. 126–8.

[179] *The Times*, 13.12.1962.

[180] *The Times*, 17.12.1962.

[181] *The Times*, 23.10.1962.

[182] *Group Problems*, pp. 102–4.

[183] See, e.g., Kerawalla, *op. cit.*, pp. 58–9; Rao (*op. cit.* at note 69), pp. 33–5.

[184] *The Times*, 24.5.1963; 'Requiem for a Missing Smuggler'.

[185] Danilo Dolci, *The Outlaws of Particino*, London, 1960. (Eng. trans. of *Banditi a Particino*); Carlo Levi, *Christ Stopped at Eboli*, London, 1954; the same, *Words are Stones*, London, 1959, pp. 169–70 and *passim*.

[186] Exner, *Kriminologie*, 1st ed., pp. 110–13; 2nd ed., pp. 82–4.

[187] *Group Problems*, *op. cit.*, p. 102.

[188] Hans von Hentig, *Crime: Causes and Conditions*, pp. 209–19; Hermann Mannheim, *Social Aspects of Crime*, Ch. 5; Howard Jones, *Crime and the Penal System*, pp. 64–7.

[189] Cloward and Ohlin, *Delinquency and Opportunity* (above, Ch. 22), p. 84, fn. 6; also Daniel Glaser and Kent Rice, *Amer. Sociol. Rev.*, Vol. 24, 1959, pp. 679–86.

[190] John Morgan, 'The Other Face of America', *New Statesman*, 5.7.1963, p. 6.

[191] On the various aspects of the relationship between occupation and crime, in particular juvenile delinquency, see: Norwood East, *The Adolescent Criminal*, Ch. 6; Hermann Mannheim, *Social Aspects of Crime*, Chs. 9–10; Joseph Trenaman, *Out of Step*, London, 1952, Ch. 16; Mannheim and Wilkins, *Prediction Methods in Relation to Borstal Training*, Ch. 5, pp. 102–8, 165–9; Carr-Saunders, Mannheim, Rhodes, *Young Offenders*, pp. 100–4; Paul Reiwald in *Die Prophylaxe des Verbrechen*, ed. by Heinrich Meng, Basle, 1948, pp. 173–80; Max Hagemann, art. 'Beruf' in *Handwörterbuch der Kriminologie*, 1st ed. 1932, Vol. 1, pp. 113–26; Franz Exner, *Kriminalbiologie*, 1st ed., pp. 294–9; Donald R. Cressey, *Other People's Money*, Glencoe, Ill., 1953, pp. 84–5; Mabel Elliott, *Crime in Modern Society*, New York, 1952, pp. 354–5; Clifford Shaw, *The Jack Roller*, Chicago, 1930, p. 166; Mark Benney, *Charity Main*, London, 1946, pp. 168 ff.; *Reports of the Advisory Council on the Employment of Prisoners*, (1) on 'Work for Prisoners', H.M.S.O., 1961, (2) on 'Work and Vocational Training in Borstals', H.M.S.O., 1962.

[192] See on the pre-war position Roesner in *Handwörterbuch der Kriminologie*, Vol. 1, p. 48.

[193] Pacifist writers describe militarism as 'une véritable école du crime' (see *War and Crime*, p. 80).

[194] A. J. Loughborough Ball, *Trial and Error. The Fire Conspiracy and After*, London, 1936, p. 17.

[195] Hans Walder, *Triebstruktur und Kriminalität*, Bern–Stuttgart, 1952, pp. 46–7.

[196] Mark Benney, *Charity Main*, pp. 168–70.

[197] For interesting examples of this kind see H. E. Burtt, *Psychology and Industrial Efficiency*, New York–London, 1929, pp. 195 ff. Recently T. Grygier has stressed the dangers arising from discrepancies between intelligence and occupation: in *Criminology in Transition*, ed. by him, Howard Jones, and John Spencer, London, 1965, p. 164.

[198] C. Wright Mills, *White Collar*, Paperback ed., New York, 1956, p. 229.

[199] *Young Offenders*, p. 103; Trenaman (*op. cit.* at note 191), p. 138.

[200] See the author's *War and Crime*, London, 1941; *Social Aspects of Crime*, Ch. 4; *Group Problems*, Ch. 5; Walter A. Lunden, 'War and Delinquency', U.N.O., 1960 (stencilled); Hans von Hentig, *Crime: Causes and Conditions*, Ch. 13; Franz Exner, *Krieg und Kriminalität in Österreich*, Vienna, 1927; Moritz Liepmann, *Krieg und Kriminalität in Deutschland*, Stuttgart–Berlin–Leipzig, and New Haven 1930; 'The Effect of the War on Criminality', Bull. int. Penal Penitent. Comm. (I.P.P.C.), Vol. 15, No. 4/II, of the *Select Papers on Penal and Penitentiary Affairs*, Berne, 1951 (in English and French, also published as a separate volume; in the present book the page references are to the separate volume); *La délinquance juvenile en Belgique de 1939 à 1957*, par Aimée Racine, Centre d'Etude de la Delinquance Juvenile, Publication No. 2, Bruxelles, 1959; Marshall B. Clinard, *Sociology of Deviant Behavior*, Ch. 20; the same, *The Black Market*, New York, 1952; Karl S. Bader, *Soziologie der deutschen Nachkriegs-Kriminalität*, Tübingen, 1949.

[201] *War and Crime* (cited at note 200), pp. 72 ff.

[202] Ernst Seelig, *Kriminologie*, p. 182; Exner, *op. cit.*, 3rd ed., p. 102.

[203] Stephen Hurwitz, *Criminology*, London–Copenhagen, 1952, p. 298. This seems to be a reference to Liepmann's remarks (see note 200), pp. 164–5.

[204] *War and Crime*, pp. 65–6.

[205] E.g., Exner, *Kriminologie*, 3rd ed., p. 99; Seelig, *Lehrbuch der Kriminologie*, Graz, 1951, p. 179; Wolf Middendorff, *Soziologie des Verbrechens*, Düsseldorf–Köln, 1959, pp. 244–5; H. Mannheim, *War and Crime*, pp. 75–6, 108; I.P.P.C. symposium, pp. 86 (England), 160, 246 (Sweden).

[206] *War and Crime*, p. 65.

[207] Hans von Hentig, *Crime*, pp. 341–2; Renger (*op. cit.* at note 166), p. 60.

[208] This is also stressed with regard to revolutions by Lyford P. Edwards, *The Natural History of Revolution*, Chicago Univ. Sociol. Ser. 1927, p. 136. See further Edward Glover, *War, Sadism and Pacifism*, London, 1933, p. 127.

[209] E.g., I.P.P.C. symposium, p. 7 (Belgium).

[210] This is emphasized by Exner, *op. cit.*, pp. 101–2.

[211] Bader, *op. cit.*, pp. 74 ff., 84, 124, 129; Exner, *op. cit.*, pp. 100 ff.

[212] *War and Crime*, pp. 98–9, 134; *Group Problems*, pp. 94, 102.

[213] Norval Morris, *The Habitual Criminal*, London, 1951, p. 26. Also I.P.P.C. symposium, p. 95.

[214] I.P.P.C. symposium, pp. 76, 143.

[215] *Ibid.*, pp. 214, 263.

[216] *Ibid.*, pp. 37, 141, 161 ff.

[217] Bader, *op. cit.*, pp. 154 ff.

[218] See, e.g., *War and Crime*, pp. 108–9, *Group Problems*, p. 94.

[219] *War and Crime*, pp. 101 ff.

[220] *Group Problems*, pp. 88 ff.

[221] D. H. Stott, *Delinquency and Human Nature*, p. 365.

[222] A Home Office Research Unit Report, H.M.S.O., London, 1960.

[223] Notably by A. A. Walters, *Brit. J. Crim.*, Vol. 3, No. 4, April 1963, pp. 391–5.

[224] *War and Crime*, p. 71.

[225] Lunden, *op. cit.*, p. 25; I.P.P.C., pp. 58, 79, gives different figures, but the trend is the same.

[226] Lunden, *op. cit.*, p. 33, 41; similarly I.P.P.C., pp. 12, 205; Racine, *op. cit.*, p. 24.

[227] Lunden, *op. cit.*, p. 35; I.P.P.C., p. 141.

[228] Wolf Middendorff, *Jugendkriminologie*, Ratingen, 1956, p. 26; Blau, *Z. ges. Strafrechtwiss.*, Vol. 64, pp. 1 ff.

[229] Sutherland–Cressey, *Principles of Criminology*, 5th ed., 1955, pp. 77–9; *The Sutherland Papers*, Part 1; Donald R. Cressey, 'The Differential Association Theory and Compulsive Crime', *J. crim. Law Criminol. Police Science*, Vol. 45, No. 1, May–June 1954, pp. 29–40; the same, 'Application and Verification of the Differential Theory', the same Journal, Vol. 43, No. 1, May–June 1952, pp. 43–52; the same, 'Epidemiology and Individual Conduct: A Case from Criminology', *Pacific Sociol. Rev.*, Vol. 3, No. 2, Autumn 1960, pp. 47–58.

Critical: Sheldon Glueck, 'Theory and Fact in Criminology: A Criticism of Differential Association', *Brit. J. Delinq.*, Vol. 7, No. 2, Oct. 1956, pp. 92–8; George B. Vold, *Theoretical Criminology*, pp. 192–8; Clarence Ray Jeffery, 'An Integrated Theory of Crime and Criminal Behavior', *J. crim. Law, Criminol. Police Sci.*, Vol. 49, No. 6, March–April 1959, pp. 537–8. See also several contributions to *Crime and Correction in Law and Contemporary Problems*, Vol. 23, No. 4, Autumn 1958.

In recent years Walter C. Reckless has tried to establish a 'Containment' or 'Norm Containment Theory', see his *The Crime Problem*, 3rd ed., New York, 1961, pp. 335–60, and *Exc. Crim.*, Vol. 3, No. 6, 1963, with further references; also *Mschr. Kriminol. Strafrechtsreform*, Vol. 44, June 1961.

[230] Cressey, *Other People's Money*, pp. 27, 147–8; the same, *Epidemiology*, p. 53.

[231] Helena Normanton, *The Trial of Alfred Arthur Rouse*, Edinburgh, 1931; see also *Social Aspects of Crime*, p. 188; *Handwörterbuch der Kriminologie*, 1st ed., Vol. 2, p. 955.

[232] E. G. Wakefield, *Facts relating to the Punishment of Death in the Metropolis*, London, 1832, App. p. 205.

[233] John Newton Baker, 'The Press and Crime', *J. crim. Law Criminol. Police Sci.*, Vol. 33, March–April 1943, p. 463.

[234] *The Times*, 29.6.1948.

[235] See Cyril Burt, *The Young Delinquent*, pp. 143–50; the same, *The Subnormal Mind*, p. 173; Negley K. Teeters and John Otto Reinemann, *The Challenge of Delinquency*, New York, 1950, pp. 177–91; Herbert S. Blumer and Philip M. Hauser, *Movies, Delinquency and Crime*, New York, 1933; Richard Ford, *Children in the Cinema*, London, 1939; Kimball Young, *Handbook of Social Psychology*, 2nd ed., London, 1957 (2nd impr. 1960), Ch. 16; J. P. Mayer, *Sociology of Film*, London, 1947; Edgar Dale, *The Contents of Motion Pictures*, London, 1936, Ch. 8; The British Film Institute. *Report of the Conference on Films for Children*, 20 and 21.11.1936: Emanuel Miller, *The Psychology of Children in Relation to Film-going*; C. Stanford Read, 'Children at the Cinema',

the *Nineteenth Century*, Dec. 1935, pp. 750 ff.; Frederic Wertham, *Seduction of the Innocent*, New York, 1953 (on 'Comics'); Marshall B. Clinard, *Sociology of Deviant Behavior*, pp. 163–7. On Television: Hilde B. Himmelweit *et al.*, *Television and the Child*, London, 1958; F. E. Emery, 'Psychological Effects of the Western Film', *Human Relations*, Vol. 12, No. 3, 1959, pp. 195–232. On the methodological issues involved: T. Grygier, 'Leisure Pursuits of Juvenile Delinquents: A Study in Methodology', *Brit. J. Delinq.*, Vol. 5, No. 3, Jan. 1955, pp. 210–228.

[236] See, e.g., Miller and Read as child psychiatrists (*op. cit.* at note 235).

[237] Lucien Bovet, 'Psychiatric Aspects of Juvenile Delinquency', W.H.O., Geneva, 1951, p. 38.

[238] *Dark Legend*, London, 1947, pp. 87–90.

[239] Dale (*op. cit.* at note 235), pp. 13, 123.

[240] S. and E. Glueck, *Unraveling Juvenile Delinquency*, p. 161; Maud A. Merrill, *Problems of Child Delinquency*, London, 1947, pp. 257–8.

[241] *The Times*, 4.8.1937, 3.12.1937, 29.1.1943.

[242] *Ibid.*, 5.12.1947.

[243] J. P. Mayer, *op. cit.* (note 235), pp. 140 ff.

[244] *Ibid.*, p. 279.

[245] A committee has been set up to organize research on the subject, *The Times*, 11.7.1963.

[246] *The Magistrate*, March 1962, p. 38. See in particular, Nuffield Foundation Study, *Television and the Child* (cited at note 235).

[247] *The Times*, 22.7.1960.

[248] *Ibid.*, Sept. 1962.

[249] See, L. Berkowitz, *Scientific American*, 1964, pp. 2, 35–41, 210.

[250] Marshall B. Clinard (*op. cit.* at note 235), p. 174.

[251] *The Times*, 8.7.1963.

CHAPTER 24

[1] On Groups see Harry M. Johnson, *Sociology*, London, 1961, Ch. 1; George C. Homans, *The Human Group*, London, 1951; Robert K. Merton, *Social Theory and Social Structure*. Chs. 8, 9; W. J. H. Sprott, *Human Groups*, Harmondsworth, 1958; *Social Behavior and Personality: Contributions of W. I. Thomas to Theory and Social Research*, ed. by Edmund H. Volkart, New York, 1951; Josephine Klein, *The Study of Human Groups*, London, 1956; Peter R. Hofstätter, *Gruppendynamik*, Hamburg, 1957.

[2] Sprott, *op. cit.*, p. 9.

[3] See the references in Merton, *op. cit.*, p. 393, fn. 7.

[4] Some of the general literature is listed in Michael Argyle's chapter on 'Experimental Studies of Small Social Groups' in *Society: Problems and Methods of Study*, London, 1962.

[5] On this special aspect of small group research see, e.g., *Theoretical Studies in Social Organization of the Prison*, Soc. Res. Counc. Pamph., No. 15, New York, March 1960; John James, 'The Application of the Small Group Concept in the the Study of the Prison Community', *Brit. J. Delinq.*, Vol. 5, No. 4, April 1955, pp. 269–80; Gresham M. Sykes, *The Society of Captives*, Princeton, 1958; Terence and Pauline Morris, *Pentonville*, London, 1963.

[6] J. L. Moreno, *Who shall survive?* Washington, 1934; Gordon Rose, *Brit. J. Delinq.*, Vol. 6, Nos. 3, 4, Jan. and April 1956, Vol. 9, No. 4, April 1959.

[7] S. H. Foulkes and E. J. Anthony, *Group Psychotherapy*, Harmondsworth, 1957.

[8] Merton, *op. cit.*, pp. 297–8.

[9] Merton, *op. cit.*, p. 233. See the whole of his Ch. 8.

[10] Muzafer and Carolyn W. Sherif, *An Outline of Social Psychology*, rev. ed. 1956, New York, pp. 175 ff.

[11] On the Family see:

(a) *In general:*

O. R. McGregor and Griselda Rowntree, Ch. 21 in *Society* (cited at note 4), with full Bibliog.

(b) *In relation to crime and delinquency:*

Sheldon and Eleanor Glueck, *Unraveling Juvenile Delinquency*; the same, *Family Environment and Delinquency*, London, 1962; Barbara Wootton, *Social Science and Social Pathology*, Chs. 3, 4; Carr-Saunders, Mannheim, Rhodes, *Young Offenders*; William Healy and Augusta Bronner, *New Light on Delinquency*, New Haven, 1936; G. R. Andry, *Delinquency and Parental Pathology*, London, 1960; William McCord and Joan McCord, *Origins of Crime*, New York and Oxford, 1959; Cyril Burt, *The Young Delinquent*, pp. 93–101; F. Ivan Nye, *Family Relationships and Delinquent Behavior*, New York, 1959; Hermann Mannheim, *The Criminological Significance of the Family*, Bull. int. Soc. Criminol., Vol. 1, 1960, pp. 1–11; Joseph Trenaman, *Out of Step*, London, 1952, Ch. 21; Christian Debuyst, *Criminels et valeurs vécues*, 2nd ed., Louvain, 1960, Eng. trans. *Criminals and Their World of Values* by Nancy Ralli, London, 1965.

[12] Merton, *op. cit.*, p. 159 (similarly T. S. Eliot, *Notes towards the Definition of Culture*, p. 43); Erich Fromm, *The Fear of Freedom*, London, 8th imp. 1960, p. 245; August Aichhorn, *Wayward Youth*, Eng. ed., New York, 1935, p. 159.

[13] T. S. Simey, *Welfare and Planning in the West Indies*, Oxford, 1946, p. 15.

[14] Clyde Kluckhohn, 'Variations in the Human Family', in *The Family in a Democratic Society*, New York, 1949, p. 3. On the details of these variations see the relevant chapters in the anthropological and sociological textbooks. On the legal side W. Friedmann, *Law in a Changing Society*, London, 1959, Ch. 7.

[15] Friedmann, *op. cit.*, p. 206.

[16] See, e.g., *The Changing Pattern of Family in India*, ed. by P. D. Devanandan and M. M. Thomas, Bangalore, 1960.

[17] G. M. Carstairs, *Brit. J. Delinq.*, Vol. 4, No. 1, July 1953, pp. 14 ff.

[18] See also above, Chapter 17 on Freud.

[19] See the figures quoted by Ogburn and Nimkoff, *A Handbook of Sociology*, 1st ed., p. 120.

[20] See, e.g., the American questionnaire enquiry reported in *Adolescent Development and Adjustment* by Lester D. Crow and Alice Crow, New York, 1956, pp. 387 ff.

[21] Richard Hoggart, *The Uses of Literacy*, p. 20.

[22] George C. Homans, *The Human Group*, pp. 314–15.

[23] Kate Friedlander, *The Psycho-Analytical Approach to Juvenile Delinquency*, p. 202.

[24] D. H. Stott, *Delinquency and Human Nature*, p. 376.

[25] Barbara Wootton, *op. cit.*, Ch. 3.

[26] See, e.g., Olof Kinberg, *Basic Problems of Criminology*, Copenhagen, 1935, pp. 188, 412; Magri, *Arch. di Psichiatria*, 1896, quoted by Havelock Ellis, *A Study of British Genius*, London, 1904, p. 110; Jean Pinatel, *Criminologie*, 1963, p. 249; Ruth Durant, *Watling*, London, 1939, p. 72.

[27] *Report of the Departmental Committee on Sterilisation*, H.M.S.O., 1934, Cmd. 4485, pp. 18, 96.

[28] *Intelligence and Fertility*, London, 1946, p. 15.

[29] Emile Durkheim, *Suicide*, Eng. ed., London, 1952, p. 201.

[30] Denis Szabo, *Crimes et villes* (cited at Ch. 23, note 1), p. 82.

[31] See M. Fortes, 'The Influence of Position in Sibship on Juvenile Delinquency', *Economica*, August 1933, pp. 301 ff.; Emanuel Miller, *The Problem of Birth-Order and Delinquency*, in *Mental Abnormality and Crime*, pp. 227-39; Raymond F. Sletto, *Amer. J. Sociol.*, Vol. 39, 1934, pp. 665 ff.; Walter C. Reckless, *Criminal Behavior*, pp. 224-6; Cyril Burt, *The Young Delinquent*, p. 95; J. P. Lees and L. J. Newson, 'Family or Sibling Position and Some Aspects of Juvenile Delinquency', *Brit. J. Delinq.*, Vol. 5, No. 1, July 1954, pp. 46-65; J. Asa Shield and Austin E. Grigg, 'Extreme Ordinal Position and Criminal Behavior', *J. crim. Law Criminol. Police Sci.*, Sept.-Oct. 1944, pp. 169-73; Jean Pinatel, *Criminologie*, p. 248. On the special difficulties of the only child, see also Christian Debuyst, *Criminels et valeurs vécues*, Part 2, Ch. 3, with interesting case material.

[32] See the references in *Young Offenders*, p. 27.

[33] Alfred Adler, *Individual Psychology*, p. 201.

[34] *Family Environment and Delinquency*, p. 127.

[35] Gardner Murphy, L. B. Murphy and Theodore M. Newcomb, *Experimental Social Psychology*, New York, 1937, pp. 348 ff., 362.

[36] Sletto, *op. cit.*, p. 666.

[37] Clifford Shaw, *Brothers in Crime*, Chicago, 1938, p. 48. Some interesting observations on the effect of the sibling position are also made by Burgess in Shaw's *Natural History of a Criminal Career*, p. 245 ff.

[38] D. J. West, *The Habitual Prisoner*, London, 1963, p. 91.

[39] See, however, the critical remarks on Burt's findings and the whole concept of defective discipline by D. H. Stott (*op. cit.* at note 24), pp. 368 ff.

[40] *Unraveling Juvenile Delinquency*, pp. 130-3; *Family Environment and Delinquency*, pp. 132 ff., 154 and *passim*; definition, p. 220.

[41] *The Psycho-Analytical Approach to Juvenile Delinquency*, p. 101.

[42] For a popular discussion of the matter from an American angle see, e.g., Vance Packard, *The Status Seekers*, Harmondsworth, 1961, p. 200.

[43] *The Adolescent Boy*. A Report of the Joint Committee on Psychiatry and the Law appointed by the British Medical Association and the Magistrates' Association, published by the B.M.A., London, 1951, p. 6.

[44] See the recent remarks of an English High Court Judge, Mr. Justice Lawton, *The Times*, 23.5.1964.

[45] Thorsten Sellin, *The Criminality of Youth*, Philadelphia, 1940, p. 12.

[46] *New Light on Delinquency*, p. 9.

[47] *Searchlights on Delinquency*, ed. by K. R. Eissler, London, 1949, p. 15.

[48] Francis L. K. Hsu, Blanche G. Watrous and Edith M. Lord, 'Culture Pattern and Adolescent Behavior', *Int. J. Soc. Psychiat.*, Vol. 7, No. 1, Winter 1960-1, pp. 33-53 on p. 45. With the conclusions of this paper might be compared Norman S. Hayner, 'Social Factors in Oriental Crime', *Amer. J. Sociol.*, Vol. 43, May 1938, pp. 908 ff.

[49] P. D. Scott, 'The Natural History of the Spiv', in *Biology and Human Affairs*, Vol. 20, No. 3, June 1955, pp. 1-7.

[50] Edward Glover, *The Roots of Crime*, p. 227.

[51] See, e.g., Edwin Powers and Helen Witmer, *An Experiment in the Prevention of Delinquency*, New York, 1951, pp. 38 ff.; D. H. Stott (*op. cit.* at note 24), p. 5.

[52] Reproduced in *Group Problems in Crime and Punishment*, p. 135.

[53] *Social Science and Social Pathology*, p. 118.

[54] See, e.g., the definition in Glueck, *Family Environment and Delinquency*, p. 219.

[55] Glueck, *Unraveling Juvenile Delinquency*, pp. 89-90.

[56] Carr-Saunders, Mannheim, Rhodes, *Young Offenders*, pp. 109–10.

[57] Mannheim and Wilkins, *Prediction Methods in relation to Borstal Training*, p. 86.

[58] W. D. Morrison, *Juvenile Offenders*, New York, 1898, p. 136.

[59] Franz Exner, *Kriminalbiologie*, 1st ed., pp. 276–7.

[60] Denis Szabo, *Crimes et Villes*, pp. 80–1; see also Jean Pinatel, *Criminologie*, p. 103.

[61] On this problem see M. Fortes, *Soc. Rev.*, Vol. 25, 1933, p. 158; *Social Aspects of Crime*, pp. 273–4; T. Earl Sullenger, *Social Determinants in Juvenile Delinquency*, New York, 1936, p. 28, who regards the stepfather as a stronger factor in delinquency than the stepmother; similarly Exner, *Kriminologie*, p. 227.

[62] C. G. Jung, *Contributions to Analytical Psychology*, London, 1928, p. 335.

[63] John Bowlby, *Int. J. Psycho-Anal.*, Vol. 25, 1944; also separately, London, 1946. See further his *Maternal Care and Mental Health*, Wld Hlth. Org. Monogr. Ser., Geneva, 1951. On Bowlby's work see also Howard Jones, *Crime and The Penal System*, 2nd ed., pp. 54–7.

[64] *Social Science and Social Pathology*, Ch. 4.

[65] Andry's Study has been widely accepted, but criticized by Mary D. Ainsworth in *Deprivation of Maternal Care*, Wld. Hlth. Org. Pub. Health Papers, No. 14, Geneva, 1962, p. 116.

[66] Siri Naess, *Brit. J. Delinq.*, Vol. 10, No. 1, July 1959, pp. 22–35, and *Brit. J. Crim.*, Vol. 2, No. 4, April 1962, pp. 361–74.

[67] See note 70 above.

[68] Jack G. Field, *Brit. J. Crim.*, Vol. 2, No. 4, April 1962, pp. 377–81.

[69] S. and E. Glueck, *Ventures in Criminology*, Ch. 3, London, 1964.

[70] John B. Mays, *Crime and the Social Structure*, London, 1963, p. 79.

[71] Bertrand Russell, *Education and the Social Order*, London, 1956.

[72] *The Young Delinquent*, pp. 1, 507.

[73] *The Law in relation to the Illegitimate Child*. A Report of the Joint Committee on Psychiatry and the Law appointed by the British Medical Association and The Magistrates' Association. Published by the B.M.A., London, 1952. The section on delinquency was contributed by the present writer.

[74] McGregor and Rowntree (*op. cit.* at note 11), pp. 423–4.

[75] Claud Mullins, *Why Crime?* London, 1945, Ch. 4.

[76] See *The League of Nations* study quoted by Mullins, p. 107. Also Exner, *Kriminalbiologie*, p. 280.

[77] Burt, *op. cit.*, p. 64; *Young Offenders*, p. 97; Glueck, *Unraveling Juvenile Delinquency*, pp. 117–18. For the nineteenth century Morrison (*op. cit.* at note 58), pp. 119 ff.

[78] For Germany Wolf Middendorff, *Jugendkriminologie*, Ratingen, 1956, pp. 113–14; Exner, *op. cit.*, p. 280. For Sweden Sven Ahnsjö, *Delinquency in Girls and Its Prognosis*, 1941, pp. 207 ff.

[79] See also Claud Mullins (*op. cit.* at note 75); *Social Aspects of Crime*, pp. 276–9; Stott, *op. cit.*, Ch. 13.

[80] On 'Problem Families' see: *The Problem Family*, an I.S.T.D. Publication, London, 1958; Barbara Wootton, *Social Science and Social Pathology*, pp. 54–62; Harriett C. Wilson, 'Juvenile Delinquency in Problem Families in Cardiff', *Brit. J. Delinq.*, Vol. 9, No. 2, Oct. 1958, pp. 94–105; the same, *Delinquency and Child Neglect*, London, 1962; A. F. Philps and N. Timms, *The Problem of the Problem Family*, London, 1957, with extensive bibliog.

[81] Dr. T. A. Ratcliffe in I.S.T.D. Publication, p. 11. Critical, T. G. Rankin, pp. 20 ff.; A. F. Philps, pp. 330 ff.

[82] Benjamin Schlesinger (ed.), *The Multi-Problem Family*, Toronto, 1963.

[83] See above, note 11 (b).

[84] See Hans von Hentig, *Crime: Causes and Conditions*, pp. 269–83; Ernst Roesner, art., 'Familienstand' in *Handwörterbuch der Kriminologie*, Vol. 1, pp. 398–414; Stephen Hurwitz, *Criminology*, 1952, pp. 347–56; Franz Exner, *Kriminologie*, pp. 244–9; on marital adjustment in general: Marshall B. Clinard, *Sociology of Deviant Behavior*, Ch. 14.

[85] See the details in Roesner, *op. cit.*, pp. 399, 414; Hurwitz, *op. cit.*, p. 348.

[86] McGregor and Rowntree in *Society*, p. 399.

[87] Roesner, *op. cit.*, p. 405; Exner, *op. cit.*, p. 248.

[88] Hurwitz, *op. cit.*, p. 350; Exner, *op. cit.*, p. 248; Roesner, p. 404; von Hentig, pp. 280–3.

[89] D. J. West, *The Habitual Prisoner*, London, 1963, pp. 20, 45.

[90] Norval Morris, *The Habitual Criminal*, London, 1951, pp. 309, 351.

[91] S. and E. Glueck, *Later Criminal Careers*, New York–London, 1937, pp. 151, 205–6.

[92] Norval Morris, *op. cit.*, pp. 352–3.

[93] Franz Exner, *Kriminologie*, p. 245. Against the over-emphasis on 'biological selection' see also Hurwitz, *op. cit.*, p. 354.

[94] Howard Jones, *Alcoholic Addiction*, London, 1963, Ch. 5.

[95] On the role of the School see, e.g., William C. Kvaraceus, *Juvenile Delinquency and the School*, New York–London, 1945; John B. Mays, *Education and the Urban Child*, Liverpool, 1962; Sheldon Glueck, *The Problem of Delinquency*, Boston, 1959, Ch. 7; Jean Pinatel, *Criminologie*, Paris, 1963, pp. 98–100; Wolf Middendorff, *Jugendkriminologie*, Düsseldorf–Köln, 1956, Ch. 8; Barbara Wootton, *op. cit.*, pp. 128–35; Hermann Mannheim, *Juvenile Delinquency in an English Middletown*, pp. 45–8; Powers and Witmer, *Prevention of Delinquency*, Ch. 8; I. Roger Yoshino, 'Juvenile Delinquency and the School', in *Sociology of Crime*, ed. by Joseph S. Roucek, London, 1962, pp. 217–38.

[96] Carr-Saunders *et al.*, *Young Offenders*, p. 2.

[97] *The Young Delinquent*, pp. 130–82.

[98] Mays, *op. cit.*, p. 89.

[99] The same, pp. 70–3. For a detailed critical analysis of 'Police Juvenile Liaison Schemes' see J. A. Mack, *Brit. J. Crim.*, Vol. 3, No. 4, April 1963, pp. 361–75.

[100] See also Wootton, *op. cit.*, p. 311.

[101] Edwin Powers and Helen Witmer, *Prevention of Delinquency*, p. 33.

[102] Ch. 12 and p. 277.

[103] Walter C. Reckless and P. P. Shervington, *Brit. J. Crim.*, Vol. 4, No. 1, July 1963, pp. 7–23.

[104] Trenaman (*op. cit.* at note 11b), Chs. 12, 13, 20.

[105] Christian Debuyst, *Criminels et valeurs vécues*, 2nd ed., Louvain, 1960, Part 3, Ch. 1; Eng. trans. by Nancy Ralli, London, 1965.

[106] *The Times*, 14.1.1963. The figures given by Mays, *op. cit.*, p. 25, for Liverpool are still worse.

[107] Walter C. Reckless, *The Crime Problem*, 2nd ed., New York, 1955, p. 684.

[108] Marshall B. Clinard, *Ann. Amer. Acad. Pol. Soc. Sci.*, Vol. 261, Jan. 1949, pp. 44–5.

[109] *Preventing Crime*, ed. by Sheldon and Eleanor Glueck, New York–London, 1936, Part 2: School Programmes. Sections on the role of the School in preventive programmes are contained in most American textbooks on criminology and juvenile delinquency.

[110] Wolf Middendorff, *New Forms of Juvenile Delinquency, their Origin, Prevention and Treatment*, U.N.O., New York, 1960, § 4.

[111] See, e.g., W. David Wills, *The Hawkspur Experiment*, London, 1941, and *The Barns Experiment*, London, 1945; the same, *Throw away thy Rod*, London, 1960; Howard Jones, *Reluctant Rebels*, London, 1960, with many references.

[112] Mays, *op. cit.*, p. 77.

[113] T. C. N. Gibbens, *Trends in Juvenile Delinquency*, Wld. Hlth. Org. Pub. Health Papers, No. 5, Geneva, 1961, p. 47.

[114] J. J. Croft, 'Juvenile Delinquency and the School', London University M.A. (Soc.), Thesis, 1953.

[115] Henry T. F. Rhodes, *The Criminals We Deserve*, London, 1937, p. 231.

[116] Kenny–Turner, *Outlines of Criminal Law*, 16th ed., London, 1952, p. 289; Herbert A. Bloch and Gilbert Geis, *Man, Crime and Society*, pp. 202–4.

[117] Kurt Baschwitz, *Du und die Masse*, Amsterdam, 1938, p. 87. See also Radbruch and Gwinner, *op. cit.* above, Ch. 16, Ch. 13.

[118] Tony Parker and Robert Allerton, *The Courage of his Convictions*, pp. 187–8.

[119] On this subject see, e.g., Max Grünhut, *Penal Reform*, Oxford, 1948, pp. 231–42; D. L. Howard, *The English Prisons*, London, 1960. Karl Peters, *Grundprobleme der Kriminalpädagogik*, Berlin, 1960, gives a searching and comprehensive discussion of the relevant questions within a wider framework.

CHAPTER 25

[1] General sociological and psychological literature on collective behaviour: *Older*: Gustave Le Bon, *Psychologie des foules*, 1st ed., Paris, 1895, Eng. ed., *The Crowd*, London, 1952; Gabriel Tarde, *L'Opinion et la foule*, Paris, 1901; Wilfred Trotter, *Instincts of the Herd in Peace and War*, London, 1922; Sigmund Freud, 'Group Psychology and the Analysis of the Ego', *Collected Works*, Vol. 18, London, 1955 (2nd German ed. 1923); W. McDougall, *The Group Mind*, New York, 1920.

More recent: R. T. La Piere, *Collective Behavior*, New York, 1938; Ogburn–Nimkoff, *A Handbook of Sociology*, Ch. 10; Kimball Young, *Handbook of Social Psychology*, London, 2nd ed. 1957, 2nd impr. 1960, Ch. 12; H. Cantril, *The Psychology of Social Movements*, New York, 1951; Neil J. Smelser, *Theory of Collective Behavior*, London, 1962 (with comprehensive bibliog.); J. C. Flugel, *Man, Morals and Society*, London, 1945, Ch. 13; Joseph B. Gittler, *Social Dynamics*, New York, 1952, pp. 84–100; W. J. H. Sprott, *Human Groups*, Harmondsworth, 1948, Ch. 10; George C. Homans, *The Human Group*, New York–London, 1951; Peter R. Hofstätter, *Gruppendynamik*, Hamburg, 1957; Theodor Geiger, *Die Masse und ihre Aktion*, Stuttgart, 1926; Arnold M. Rose, *Theory and Method in the Social Sciences*, Minneapolis, 1954, Chs. 2, 6, 12 (on the 'hiatus' between sociologists and psychologists in their attitudes to group problems).

[2] See Smelser, *op. cit.*, p. 6, on the views of Herbert Blumer.

[3] See also *Group Problems in Crime and Punishment*, pp. 19–27.

[4] On this see Michel Trottier, 'La Complicité criminelle', *Canad. J. Corrections*, Vol. 1, No. 4, July 1959, pp. 56–61; Jean Pinatel, *Criminologie*, pp. 358–63; H. v. Hentig, *Zur Psychologie der Einzeldelikte*, Tübingen, Vol. 1, 'Diebstahl, Einbruch, Raub', 1954, pp. 156–9; Vol. 2, 'Mord', 1956, Ch. 7; Vol. 3, 'Betrug' 1957, Ch. 7; Vol. 4, 'Erpressung', 1959, Ch. 8.

[5] Robert Vouin et Jacques Léauté, *Droit Pénal et Criminologie*, Paris, 1956, p. 282. Also Léauté in *Revue Pénale Suisse*, Vol. 72, 1957, pp. 1–19.

[6] *Law in Eastern Europe No. 3: Federal Criminal Law of the Soviet Union*. Russian Text with an English translation by F. J. Feldbrugge, Introduction by J. M. van Bemmelen, Leyden, 1959, pp. 10–12, 46–7.

[7] Glanville Williams, *Criminal Law, The General Part*, 1st ed., London, 1953, Ch. 6. Also Kenny–Turner, *Outlines of Criminal Law*, Ch. 5.

[8] This was often the case in the decisions of the German Supreme Court, see, e.g., Schwarz-Dreher, *Strafgesetzbuch*, 25th ed., München–Berlin, 1963, p. 161.

[9] v. Hentig, *Der Mord*, pp. 250–2.

[10] This is also true in German law, see Schwarz-Dreher, *op. cit.*, p. 169.

[11] See James B. Christoph, *Capital Punishment and British Politics*, Chicago, 1962, pp. 98–100. Christoph does not mention the crucial words 'Let them have it, Chris', which were apparently vital to the decision of the Court.

[12] See, e.g., Glanville Williams, *The Proof of Guilt*, 1st ed., London, 1955, pp. 183–9; Hermann Mannheim, *Group Problems in Crime and Punishment*, p. 281.

[13] v. Hentig, *Mschr. Kriminol. Strafrechtsreform*, Dec. 1962, pp. 193–202, produces similar case material.

[14] Irving R. Weiner, *Excerpta criminologica*, Vol. 4, No. 2, March–April 1964, pp. 137–55. See also Denis Szabo, 'L'Inceste en milieu urbain', *L'Année sociologique*, vol. 1957–8, pp. 29–93.

[15] *The Times*, 11 and 12.9.1963.

[16] v. Hentig, *Der Mord*, pp. 257 ff.

[17] See, e.g., the 'Cleft Chin' murder case, where an American Army deserter killed a London taxi driver in the presence of his girl friend who, he alleged, had told him she wanted to do something exciting, to become a Chicago 'gun moll' (*The Times*, 17–24.1.1945).

[18] See, e.g., *Criminal Statistics—England and Wales for 1961*, p. xxxiii.

[19] Thomas Würtenberger, *Der Kampf gegen das Kunstfälschertum in der deutschen und schweizerischen Strafrechtspflege*, Wiesbaden, 1951, pp. 36–8.

[20] v. Hentig, *Diebstahl*, p. 156.

[21] *The Times*, 29.3.1961.

[22] *The Times*, 14.3.1963.

[23] For English law see the Larceny Act, 1916, s. 33 (1).

[24] Glanville Williams, *Criminal Law*, 1st ed., p. 224; for French law, Vouin–Léauté (*op. cit.* at note 5), p. 189.

[25] See the cases in v. Hentig, *Erpressung*, p. 281.

[26] *Literature on the Crowd:* In addition to the books quoted in note 1 see: Scipio Sighele, *La Foule criminelle*, Paris, Bibliothèque de philosophie contemporaine, 1901; Paul Reiwald, *Vom Geist der Massen*, Zurich, 1946 (Fr. trans. *De l'ésprit des masses*, Neufchatel–Paris, 1949); Lionel Penrose, *On the Objective Study of Crowd Behaviour*, London, 1952; Neal E. Miller and John Dollard, *Social Learning and Imitation*, New Haven, 1945, Chs. 14, 15; E. D. Martin, *The Behavior of Crowds*, New York, 1920; George Rudé, *The Crowd in the French Revolution*, Oxford, 1959; Günther Kaiser, *Randalierende Jugend*, Heidelberg, 1959.

[27] Donald Clemmer, *The Prison Community*, Boston, 1940, pp. 118, 327; also p. 120 on the size of the primary groups existing in the prison community.

[28] *The Group Mind*, p. 22.

[29] See in particular Le Bon, *op. cit.*, Part 1, Chs. 1–3, Part 3, Ch. 2.

[30] *Ibid.*, Part 1, Ch. 2.

[31] *Ibid.*, Part 1, Ch. 4.

[32] Herbert Agar, *A Time for Greatness*, London, 1943, p. 61.

[33] Peter F. Drucker, *The End of Economic Man*, London, 1939, p. 214.

[34] E.g., Martin Buber, *Between Man and Man*, Paperback ed., London, 1961, p. 87.

[35] See the *Report on an Inquiry into the Accident at Bethnal Green Tube Station Shelter on the 3rd March, 1943*, by Laurence R. Dunne (one of the Metropolitan

Magistrates), London, H.M.S.O., 1945, Cmd. 6583, and the *Report into the Disaster at the Bolton Wanderers' Football Gound on the 9th March, 1946*, by R. Moelwyn Hughes, K.C., London, H.M.S.O., 1946, Cmd. 6846.

[36] Pinatel, *op. cit.*, pp. 371–2; Ogburn–Nimkoff, *op. cit.*, p. 187; Miller and Dollard, *op. cit.*, p. 191.

[37] Geiger, *op. cit.*, p. 136.

[38] C. G. Jung, *Essays on Contemporary Events*, London, 1947, p. 77.

[39] Hofstaetter, *op. cit.*, pp. 13, 17.

[40] Murphy and Newcomb, *Experimental Social Psychology*, rev. ed., New York, 1937, p. 700, fn. 1.

[41] F. H. Allport, *Social Psychology*, Boston, 1924.

[42] Miller and Dollard, *op. cit.*, p. 184.

[43] Robin M. Williams, *Reduction of Intergroup Tensions*, Soc. Sci. Res. Counc. Bull. 57, 1947, p. 60.

[44] See, e.g., the case in Allport, *Social Psychology*, pp. 309–12.

[45] Smelser, *op. cit.*, pp. 10, 249–53.

[46] Geiger, *op. cit.*, pp. 147 ff. Against him Reiwald, *op. cit.*

[47] Geiger, *op. cit.*, p. 150.

[48] Smelser, *op. cit.*, p. 254.

[49] Rudé, *op. cit.*, pp. 219–21.

[50] *Ibid.*, pp. 235–7.

[51] Kaiser, *op. cit.*, pp. 60 ff.

[52] *Ibid.*, pp. 72, 172 ff.

[53] *Chicago Commission on Race Relations: The Negro in Chicago*, Chicago, 1922, pp. 22–5.

[54] Fyvel, *The Insecure Offenders*, pp. 242 ff.

[55] Smelser, *op. cit.*, pp. 236–7, deals with them briefly, but his book is concerned not only with crowds, but with collective behaviour in general.

[56] *Group Problems in Crime and Punishment*, pp. 183–5.

[57] *Prison J. (Amer.)*, Vol. 33, No. 1, April 1953, p. 17.

[58] *Report on Disturbances at the Carlton Approved School on 28th and 30th August, 1959* by Mr. Victor Durand, Q.C., London, H.M.S.O., 1960, Cmd. 937.

[59] See, e.g., *The Times*, 18.1, 19.2.1949 (Durban riots between Africans and Indians); *New Statesman*, 29.1.1949.

[60] See, e.g., *The Times*, 28.7.1948 (Alexandria riots).

[61] *Report of a Commission of Inquiry into Disturbances in British Guiana in February, 1962*, Colonial Office No. 354; *The Times*, 4.10.1962.

[62] E.g., by a Labour M.P., J. P. W. Mallalieu, Q.C., in the *New Statesman*, 11.7.1959.

[63] Letters in *The Times*, 4.9.1958.

[64] *Ibid.*, 16.9.1958.

[65] *Ibid.*, 20, 21.5.1959. Nevertheless occasional riots did occur in other towns a few years after the passing of those sentences, e.g. in Dudley, see *The Times*, 1, 13.8.1962, but firm police action prevented large-scale injuries and damage.

[66] E.g., *The Times*, 5.9.1958.

[67] Home Office White Papers, *Commonwealth Immigrants Act, 1962*, Cmd. 2151, October, 1963, and *Report of Commonwealth Immigrants Advisory Council*, Cmd. 2119, July 1963. See also *The Times*, 5.10.1963.

[68] *The Times*, 5.6.1959.

[69] See the article by Philip Mason, the Director of the Institute, in *The Times*, 27.9.1963.

[70] In his important article in *Temple Law Quart.*, Vol. 19, No. 4, April 1946,

pp. 371-89, Robert H. Jackson, the chief American Prosecutor at the Nuremberg Trial, wrote: 'No system of jurisprudence has yet evolved any satisfactory technique for handling a great multitude of common charges against a multitude of accused persons.'

[71] On this trial there is a considerable literature; here it will suffice to refer to the article by Dean Erwin Griswold of the Harvard Law School, *The Times*, 25.9.1958, and to *The Times* of the 20, 21, 22.12.1956.

[72] Kenny-Turner, *Outlines of Criminal Law*, 16th ed., Cambridge, 1952, §§ 437-41.

[73] Kenny-Turner, *op. cit.*, § 439. On the Gordon Riots see further, Leon Radzinowicz, *History of English Criminal Law*, Vol. 3, London, 1956, p. 89, and especially Christopher Hibbert, *King Mob*, London, 1958. According to Radzinowicz, 134 persons were charged (out of a crowd of many thousands), of whom 58 were found guilty and 25 executed; among those found guilty may have been some mere spectators; see also Radzinowicz, *op. cit.*, Vol. 1, p. 170, fn. 25.

[74] Kenny-Turner, *op. cit.*, § 430.

[75] *The Times*, 16.2.1957, 29.12.1958, 8.1.1959.

[76] *The Times*, 28.9.1956. For further details of that interesting trial see *The Times*, 6.8, 10.10, 11.10.1956.

[77] *Literature on Organized Crime.*

(1) *Mainly on Adult Gangs*

(a) *Historical:* Gustav Radbruch und Heinrich Gwinner, *Geschichte des Verbrechens*, Stuttgart, 1951; Luke Owen Pike, *A History of Crime in England* (see Ch. 19, note 11); Ronald Fuller, *The Beggar's Brotherhood*, London, 1936.

(b) *Contemporary:* Herbert A. Bloch and Gilbert Geis, *Man, Crime and Society*, New York, 1962, Ch. 9; Alfred R. Lindesmith in *Ann. Amer. Acad. Polit. Soc. Sci.*, Vol. 217, Sept. 1941, pp. 119-27; Estes Kefauver, *Crime in America*, London, 1952; Donald R. Taft, *Criminology*, Ch. 13; George B. Vold, *Theoretical Criminology*, 1958, Ch. 12; Earl Johnson, 'Organized Crime: Challenge to the American Legal System', *J. crim. Law Criminol Police Sci.*, Vol. 53, No. 4, Dec. 1962, Vol. 54, Nos. 1 and 2, March and June 1963 (with excellent bibliographical notes); Daniel Bell, 'Crime as an American Way of Life', *Antioch Rev.*, Vol. 13, June 1953, reprinted in Wolfgang, Savitz, Johnston, *The Sociology of Crime and Delinquency*, New York, 1962, Ch. 29; Walter C. Reckless, *The Crime Problem*, 3rd ed., New York, 1960, Chs. 9, 10; Hans v. Hentig, *Der Gangster*, Berlin-Göttingen-Heidelberg, 1959; W. Naucke, 'Methodenfragen zum "Typ" des Gewohnheitsverbrechers', *Mschr. Kriminol. Strafrechtsreform*, Vol. 45, Nos. 3-4, Aug. 1962, pp. 84-97; John B. Mays, *Crime and the Social Structure*, London, 1963, Ch. 12; Jean Pinatel, *Criminologie*, Paris, 1963, pp. 296-302. Now in particular the excellent American symposium, 'Combatting Organized Crime', ed. by Gus Tyler, *Ann. Amer. Acad. Pol. Soc. Sci.*, Vol. 347, May 1963. In the *Sunday Times* of the 14.2.1965 an analysis of the Great Train Robbery of August, 1963, is given. Also Peta Fordham, *The Robbers' Tale*, London, 1965.

(c) *On the Mafia:* Frederick Sondern, *Brotherhood of Evil: The Mafia*, New York, 1959; Francis M. Guercio, *Sicily*, 2nd ed., London, 1954, Ch. 5; E. J. Hobsbawm, *Social Bandits and Primitive Rebels*, Glencoe, Ill., and Manchester, 1959, Ch. 3; Giovanni Lo Schiavo, *The Truth about the Mafia*, New York, 1962, and notes 103 and 104 below.

(2) *Mainly on Adolescent Gangs*

Frederick Thrasher, *The Gang*, Chicago, 1st ed., 1927, 2nd ed., 1936; William F. Whyte, *Street Corner Society*, 2nd ed., Chicago, 1955; Cloward and Ohlin, *Delinquency and Opportunity*, and Albert K. Cohen, *Delinquent Boys* (see above, Ch. 22, note 16); David J. Bordua, 'A Critique of Sociological Interpretation of

Gang Delinquency', *Ann. Amer. Acad. Pol. Soc. Sci.*, Vol. 338, Nov. 1961, pp. 120–36 (reprinted in Wolfgang *et al.*, Ch. 39); Harrison E. Salisbury. *The Shook-Up Generation*, London, 1959; Lewis Yablonsky, *The Violent Gang*, New York, 1962; *Reaching the Fighting Gang*, New York City Youth Board, New York, 1960; Peter Scott, 'Gangs and Delinquent Groups in London', *Brit. J. Delinq.*, Vol. 7, No. 1, July 1956, pp. 4–26 (with bibliog.); M. L. Turner and J. C. Spencer, 'Spontaneous Youth Groups and Gangs', in *Spontaneous Youth Groups*, ed. by P. H. K. Kuenstler, London, 1955; Lloyd T. Delany, *Brit. J. Delinq.*, Vol. 5, No. 1, July 1954, pp. 34 ff., with Commentary by John Spencer; *La délinquance des jeunes en groupe*, Centre de Formation et de Recherche de l'Education Surveillée, Vaucresson, Paris, 1963.

[78] See *Preventive Detention: Report of the Home Office Advisory Council on the Treatment of Offenders*, H.M.S.O., 1963, pp. 26–7; W. H. Hammond and Edna Chayen, *Persistent Criminals*, H.M.S.O., 1963; D. J. West, *The Habitual Prisoner*, London, 1963. See also the reviews of these publications in *Brit. J. Crim.*, Vol. 4, No. 1, Oct. 1963, pp. 181 ff.

[79] § 20a of the German Penal Code and § 85 of the Draft Code of 1962; Joachim Hellmer, *Mschr. Kriminol. Strafrechtsreform*, Vol. 43, No. 5–6, Nov. 1960, pp. 145–6, and more fully in *Der Gewohnheitsverbrecher und die Sicherungsverwahrung, 1934–45*, Berlin, 1961.

[80] John A. Mack, 'Full-time Miscreants, Delinquent Neighbourhoods and Criminal Networks', *Brit. J. Sociol.*, Vol. 15, No. 1, March 1964, pp. 38–53.

[81] D. J. West, *The Habitual Prisoner*, London, 1962.

[82] See *Group Problems in Crime and Punishment*, pp. 113–14.

[83] 'London Lorry Gangs Moving Out', *The Times*, 2.2.1963.

[84] F. H. McClintock and Evelyn Gibson, *Robbery in London*, London, 1961, pp. 107 ff.

[85] *The Times*, 31.10.1963.

[86] Radbruch-Gwinner, *op. cit.*, Chs. 6, 7, 9.

[87] *Ibid.*, Chs. 19, 24, 27.

[88] *Droit pénal et criminologie*, p. 291.

[89] Jerome Hall, *Theft, Law and Society*, 2nd ed., Indianapolis, 1952, p. 72.

[90] On Wat Tyler, see also John Richard Green, *A Short History of the English People*, 1929 ed., London, pp. 252–3.

[91] Kefauver (*op. cit.* above at note 77), pp. 24, 27 ff.

[92] Bloch and Geis, *op. cit.*, pp. 247–8; also Walter C. Reckless, *The Crime Problem*, p. 201.

[93] Guercio (*op. cit.* at note 77), p. 15.

[94] *The Times*, 29.7.1957, and also *The Leopard*, Ch. 4.

[95] *The Times*, 13.3.1963, and Danilo Dolci, *op. cit.*

[96] See, e.g., the *Observer*, 6.10.1963.

[97] v. Hentig, *Der Gangster*, p. 4.

[98] v. Hentig, *op. cit.*, p. 7, referring to J. Edgar Hoover, *Persons in Hiding*, Boston, 1938, pp. 94 ff.

[99] On Merton see above, Ch. 22, s. 1. William F. Whyte, *Street Corner Society*, 2nd ed. 1953, Chs. 4, 5, 6.

[100] *The Times*, 18.11.1957.

[101] Johnson (*op. cit.* at note 77), Vol. 53, p. 403.

[102] *Ibid.*, p. 402.

[103] Norman Lewis, *The Honoured Society*, London, 1964.

[104] Carmelo Nobile, 'Su talune esigenze psicho-igieniche della lotta contro la mafia', *Quad. Criminol. clin.*, Anno 5, No. 4, Oct. 1963, pp. 461–74.

[105] *Ibid.*, p. 401.

[106] E.g., Lindesmith (*op. cit.* at note 77), p. 120; Johnson, *op. cit.*, pp. 412 ff.; Kefauver Report throughout.

[107] Lindesmith, *op. cit.*, p. 119.

[108] Reckless, *The Crime Problem*, p. 179.

[109] For a popular account of the work of those organizations see Henry T. F. Rhodes, *The Criminals We Deserve*, London, 1937, pp. 57, 237, and Chs. 8, 11.

[110] Letter to *The Times*, 4.7.1956.

[111] *Ibid.*, 21.6.1956.

[112] *Ibid.*, 3.7.1956.

[113] Jack 'Spot' Comer, the *Sunday Times*, 6.10.1963.

[114] *The Times*, 26.7.1962.

[115] Johnson, *op. cit.*, Vol. 53, pp. 407–8, explains the decrease in violence as a consequence of the decline in inter-gang warfare and the consolidation of power in the hands of a few large criminal organizations.

[116] C. H. Rolph, 'London's New Gangsters', the *New Statesman*, 21.5.1960.

[117] Thrasher, *op. cit.*, Ch. 3.

[118] Gerrard, 'The Core Member of the Gang', *Brit. J. Crim.*, Vol. 4, No. 4, April 1964, pp. 361–71.

[119] M. L. Turner, *Ship Without Sails*, London, 1953; John C. Spencer, 'The Unclubbable Adolescent', *Brit. J. Delinq.*, Vol. 1, 1950, pp. 113–24.

[120] Anthony Forder, review of Cloward and Ohlin, *Case Conference*, May 1962.

[121] *Group Problems in Crime and Punishment*, p. 135.

[122] See, e.g., S. and E. Glueck, *Unraveling Juvenile Delinquency*, p. 164. No distinction as yet in *Young Offenders*, 1944, p. 110, but in *Juvenile Delinquency in an English Middletown*, London, 1948, pp. 39–40, 'real gangs' are distinguished from 'gangs' in the traditional sense.

[123] *Juvenile Delinquents Grown Up*, New York, 1940, p. 181. See also Ruth Topping in S. Glueck, *The Problem of Delinquency*, Boston, 1959, pp. 844–9.

[124] See, e.g., *The Times*, 9.9.1958, on the position in Glasgow, where Protestant and Roman Catholic factions were involved. Similar scenes were reported from Belfast on the occasion of a match between an Irish and an Italian team, *The Times*, 5.12.1957.

[125] *Literature on Victimology*. Hans v. Hentig, *The Criminal and his Victim*, Part 4, New Haven, 1949; the same in *Der Mord*, Ch. 8; *Der Betrug*, Ch. 8; *Die Erpressung*, Ch. 9; Marvin E. Wolfgang, *Patterns in Criminal Homicide*, Philadelphia, 1958, Parts 2 and 3; J. P. Morris and Louis Blom-Cooper, *A Calendar of Murder*, London, 1964, Ch. 7; Jean Pinatel, *Criminologie*, pp. 345–50; Edgar Lenz, *Der Betrogene*, Hamburg, 1961; Paul Cornil, 'Contribution de la "Victimologie" aux sciences criminologiques', *Rev. Droit pén. Criminol.*, April 1959; B. Mendelsohn, 'Victimologie', *Rev. int. Criminol. Police Tech.*, Vol. 10, No. 2, April–June 1956; the same, 'The Victimology', *Etud. int. Psycho-Soc. crim.*, No. 1, July–Sept. 1956, pp. 23–36; Henri Ellenberger, 'Psychological Relationships between Criminal and Victim', *Arch. crim. Psychodyn.*, Vol. 1, No. 2, Spring 1955, pp. 257–90; California Sexual Deviation Research, State of California Department of Mental Hygiene and Langley Porter Clinic: *Study of Sex Crimes against Children*, Report of Jan. 1953, pp. 47–84, Final Report, March 1954, Summary, pp. 59–63; H. Schultz, *Rev. pén. suisse*, 1958, Vol. 71, pp. 171–91; *Cambridge Report on Sexual Offences*, London, 1957, Ch. 6; W. H. Nagel, 'Victimologie', *T. Strafr.*, Vol. 68, 1959, pp. 1–26.

[126] Kenny-Turner, *Outlines of Criminal Law*, § 117.

[127] See *Criminal Justice and Social Reconstruction*, pp. 13–17.

[128] Kenny-Turner, *op. cit.*, §§ 130, 156. The German Penal Code, § 226a, now

contains a special provision to this effect; see the commentary by Dreher on this provision, which has also been taken over by the new German Draft Code of 1962 (see its § 152 and the detailed discussion, pp. 286-88).

[129] *Criminal Justice*, p. 121.

[130] If we should accept the rather tortuous arguments of Hannah Arendt, *Eichmann in Jerusalem*, London, 1964, the Jewish leaders would be almost as guilty as Eichmann of the destruction of European Jewry. Against her arguments see, in particular, the unsigned review in *The Times Literary Supplement*, 30.4.1964.

[131] Walter C. Reckless, *The Crime Problem*, Ch. 3.

[132] See also *Social Aspects of Crime in England*, p. 194.

[133] See v. Hentig, *Der Mord*, p. 277.

[134] *The Criminal and His Victim*, pp. 419-50.

[135] A provision of this kind is contained, e.g., in 220a of the German Penal Code, which was added to the Code in 1954 in conformity with the Genocide Convention of 1948 (reproduced in Donnelly, Goldstein and Schwartz, *Criminal Law*, p. 965).

[136] For a case of this kind see *The Times*, 22.1.1963.

[137] 'Techniques of Neutralization', *Amer. Sociol. Rev.*, Vol. 22, Dec. 1957, pp. 664-70 (reprinted in Wolfgang-Savitz-Johnston, *The Sociology of Crime and Delinquency*, No. 34).

[138] T. C. N. Gibbens and Joyce Prince, *Child Victims of Sex Offences*, London, 1963.

[139] Henry T. F. Rhodes, *The Criminals We Deserve*, p. 209.

[140] See *Social Aspects of Crime*, pp. 191 ff.

[141] *Compensation for Victims of Crimes of Violence*, London, H.M.S.O., June 1961, Cmd. 1406, p. 11; *Compensation for Victims of Crimes of Violence*. A Report by 'Justice', London, 1962; Gordon Rose, *Brit. J. Crim.*, Vol. 3, No. 4, April 1963, pp. 396-7. Another Home Office White Paper (Cmd. 2323) on the subject was published in Spring, 1964, and at the time of writing an 'experimental Scheme' is in operation, under which a considerable number of small awards, totalling over £11,000 in the first six months, have been made by the recently established 'Criminal Injuries Compensation Board' (see *The Times*, 7.2.1965 and on the whole scheme Bernard W. M. Downey, 'Compensating Victims of Violent Crime' *Brit. J. Crim.*, Vol. 5, No. 1, Jan. 1965, pp. 92 ff.).

CHAPTER 26

[1] On the age factor: *Criminal Statistics England and Wales*; Howard Jones, *Crime and the Penal System*, 2nd ed., London, 1962, pp. 123-7; A. Besson et al., *Seuils d'Age et Legislation pénale*, Paris, 1961; Ernst Roesner, *Handwörterbuch der Kriminologie*, Vol. 1, pp. 23-35; Alfred-Johannes Rangol, 'Die Straffälligkeit nach Hauptdeliktsgruppen und Altersklassen, 1884-1948', *Mschr. Kriminol. Strafrechtsreform*, Vol. 45, Nos. 5-6, Oct. 1962, pp. 158 ff.; Gianluigi Ponti, 'Studio statistico sulla Criminalità senile', *Quad. Criminol. clin.*, Vol. 4, No. 2, April-June 1962, pp. 145-78; H. Bürger-Prinz and H. Lewrenz, *Die Alterskriminalität*, Stuttgart, 1961; C. Amelunxen, *Die Alterskriminalität*, Hamburg, 1960; Bruno M. Cormier et al., *Canad. J. Corrections*, Vol. 3, No. 1, Jan. 1961, pp. 2 ff., 51 ff.; Barbara Wootton, *Social Science and Social Pathology*, Ch. 5; *Social Problems of Post War Youth*, Econ. Res. Counc., London, Jan. 1956; Leslie T. Wilkins, *Delinquent Generations*, Home Office Studies in the Causes of Delinquency and the Treatment of Offenders, No. 3, London, H.M.S.O., 1960; G. Prys Williams, *Patterns of Teenage Delinquency England and Wales, 1946-61*,

Christ. Econ. Soc. Res. Found., London, Oct. 1962; A. A. Walters (review of Wilkins), *Brit. J. Crim.*, Vol. 3, No. 4, April 1963, pp. 391–5, and Wilkins's rejoinder in Vol. 4, No. 3, Jan. 1964, pp. 264–8.

[2] Tadashi Uematsu, 'Criminality in Japan Observed from the Points of Age and Sex', *Ann. Hitotsubashi Acad.*, Vol. 9, No. 1, Oct. 1958, p. 79.

[3] Rangol, *op. cit.*, pp. 159–60.

[4] Vouin–Léauté, *op. cit.*, p. 301.

[5] Selosse in Besson, *op. cit.*, p. 111, and the table, pp. 116–17.

[6] Ponti, *op. cit.*, p. 150; and now *The Measurement of Delinquency* (see above, Ch. 5, note 1).

[7] Ronald H. Beattie, *J. crim. Law Criminol. Police Sci.*, Vol. 51, No. 1, May–June 1960, p. 64. Also Sellin, *Ann. Amer. Acad. Pol. Soc. Sci.*, Jan. 1962, pp. 11–24; Negley K. Teeters and John Otto Reinemann, *The Challenge of Delinquency*, New York, 1950, pp. 15–16. The newly founded 'Center of Criminological Research' of the University of Pennsylvania is making special efforts to establish a reliable 'index of delinquency'; see *Constructing an Index of Delinquency. A Manual*, published by the Center, Oct. 1963, and now Thorsten Sellin and Marvin E. Wolfgang, *The Measurement of Delinquency*, New York, 1964.

[8] Thorsten Sellin, *The Criminality of Youth*, Philadelphia, 1940, pp. 50–1, 67.

[9] Walter C. Reckless, *Criminal Behavior*, p. 103.

[10] Mary Stevenson Callcott, *Russian Justice*, New York, 1935, p. 62.

[11] H. v. Hentig, *Crime: Its Causes and Conditions*, p. 130.

[12] See, e.g., the correspondence in *The Times*, 30.10, 2.11, 13.11.1962.

[13] Norwood East, *The Adolescent Criminal*, London, 1942, p. 15.

[14] Ernst Kretschmer, *Physique and Character*, 21st/22nd. ed., London, 1955, pp. 340–1.

[15] Some writers take it for granted that, with improved health and nutrition, the age of the onset of puberty has steadily declined; the mean onset of menstruation for girls, a century ago at 17, is now given as $13\frac{1}{2}$; see G. M. Carstairs, *This Island Now*, London, 1963, pp. 49–50; Gerald Gardiner, *The Times*, 12.9.1963. This view has, however, been strongly contested by other authorities.

[16] *Social Aspects of Crime in England*, p. 80.

[17] *Criminal Statistics England and Wales*, 1962, p. xi.

[18] Joachim Hellmer, *Der Gewohnheitsverbrecher und die Sicherungsverwahrung 1934–1945*, Berlin, 1961, p. 116.

[19] *Criminal Statistics*, 1962, pp. xv–xix. See also F. H. McClintock, *Crimes of Violence*, London, 1963, pp. 98–9 and App. XI.

[20] *Sexual Offences: Report of the Cambridge Department of Criminal Science*, London, 1957, pp. 113–15; J. H. Fitch, *Brit. J. Crim.*, Vol. 3, No. 1, July 1962, p. 19; *Prison Commissioners' Report for 1959*, pp. 178–9.

[21] *Social Aspects*, p. 371.

[22] W. H. Hammond and Edna Chayen, *Persistent Criminals*, H.M.S.O., London, 1963, p. 111.

[23] See note 26 below.

[24] See, e.g., McClintock and Gibson, *Robbery in London*, p. 46.

[25] S. and E. Glueck, *Later Criminal Careers*, New York, 1937, Ch. 10.

[26] S. and E. Glueck, *Juvenile Delinquents Grown Up*, New York, 1940, Ch. 8, and *After-Conduct of Discharged Offenders*, London, 1945, pp. 80 ff.

[27] *After-Conduct*, p. 84; *Juvenile Delinquents Grown Up*, p. 97.

[28] E.g., by Howard Jones, *Crime and the Penal System*, 2nd ed., p. 126.

[29] Erwin Frey, *Der Frühkriminelle Rückfallsverbrecher* (*Criminalité précoce et Recidivisme*), Basel, 1951, pp. 62 ff., 72 ff. See also my review of this book in

Group Problems, pp. 139–46, and on the whole question Barbara Wootton, *Social Science and Social Pathology*, London, 1959, pp. 165 ff.

[30] See, e.g., *Juvenile Delinquency in an English Middletown*, p. 81; *Social Aspects of Crime*, pp. 80–1.

[31] Mannheim and Wilkins, *Prediction Methods in relation to Borstal Training*, p. 65.

[32] *Juvenile Delinquents Grown Up*, p. 211.

[33] Hammond and Chayen (*op. cit.* at note 22), p. 28.

[34] Sir George Benson, *Brit. J. Delinq.*, Vol. 3, No. 3, Jan. 1953, pp. 198–202, Vol. 5, No. 2, Oct. 1954, pp. 138–43; R. S. Taylor, *Brit. J. Crim.*, Vol. 1, No. 1, July 1960, pp. 22–3; D. J. West, *The Habitual Prisoner*, Cambridge, 1963, pp. 84, 96; Norval Morris, *The Habitual Criminal*, London, 1961, pp. 301, 339; Barbara Wootton, *op. cit.*, pp. 159 ff.

[35] Yoshitsugu Baba and Tsugio Nakano, *Some Observation of Recidivism in Japan*, (no year), p. 21.

[36] Roland Grassberger, *Die Lösung kriminalpolitischer Probleme durch die mechanische Statistik*, Vienna, 1946, esp. p. 83. This part of Grassberger's important work has been well summarized in English by Thorsten Sellin, 'Recidivism and Maturation', *Nat. Probat. Parole Assoc. J.*, July 1958, pp. 241–50, where he also reproduces the findings of several Swedish studies, which all confirm the close relationship between age at first conviction and likelihood and speed of relapse.

[37] Tony Parker, *The Unknown Citizen*, London, 1963, pp. 66, 129.

[38] Some of them were discussed 45 years ago in the present writer's paper *Rechtsgefühl und Dichtung* (see above, note 7, Ch. 16).

[39] *The Times*, 13.1.1962.

[40] This is stressed by Bürger-Prinz and Lewrenz, *op. cit.*, Ch. 5.

[41] See note 1 above.

[42] On the Sex Factor: Cesare Lombroso and G. Ferrero, *La donna delinquente, la prostituta e la donna normale*, Torino, 1893, Eng. ed. *The Female Offender*, London, 1895; Pauline Tarnowsky, *Etude anthropometrique sur les prostituées et les voleuses*, Paris, 1889; also *Les femmes homicides*, Paris, 1908; Johanna C. Hudig, *De Criminaliteit der Vrouw*, Utrecht–Nijmegen, 1940; Hermann Mannheim, *Social Aspects of Crime in England between the Wars*, London, 1940, Ch. 11; Stephan Hurwitz, *Criminology*, pp. 269–79; Mabel E. Elliott, *Crime in Modern Society*, New York, 1952, Chs. 8, 9; Otto Pollak, *The Criminality of Women*, Philadelphia, 1950; Hans v. Hentig, *Crime: Its Causes and Condition*, New York, 1947, Ch. 5; J. M. van Bemmelen, *Kriminologie*, 3rd ed., Zwolle, 1952, Ch. 11; Wolf Middendorff, *Soziologie des Verbrechens*, Düsseldorf–Köln, 1959, pp. 248–256; 'The Female Offender', *N.P.P.A. Journal*, Vol. 3, No. 1, Jan. 1957; S. and E. Glueck, *Five Hundred Delinquent Women*, New York, 1934; Ernst Roesner and Max Hagemann in *Handwörterbuch der Kriminologie*, Vol. 1, 1933, pp. 574–95, and Vol. 2, 1936, pp. 1049–63; Jean Pinatel, *Criminologie*, Paris, 1963, pp. 154 ff.; Sebastian von Koppenfels, *Die Kriminalität der Frau im Kriege*, Leipzig, 1926; Leon Radzinowicz, 'Sex Rates of Criminality', *Sociol. Rev.*, Vol. 29, Jan. 1937 (Polish material); Grace W. Pailthorpe, *Studies in the Psychology of Delinquency*, Medical Research Council, H.M.S.O., London, 1932; Hedwig Schwarz, 'The Psycho-Analysis of a Case of Stealing, *Brit. J. Delinq.*, Vol. 1, No. 1, July 1950, pp. 29–44; Phyllis Epps, 'A Preliminary Survey of 300 Female Delinquents in Borstal Institutions', *Brit. J. Delinq.*, Vol. 1, No. 3, Jan. 1951, pp. 187–97; the same, 'A Further Survey of Female Delinquents Undergoing Borstal Training', *Brit. J. Delinq.*, Vol. 4, No. 4, April 1954, pp. 265–71; the same, 'Women Shoplifters in Holloway Prison', in T. C. N. Gibbens and Joyce Prince, *Shoplifting*,

Ch. 14, London, 1962, I.S.T.D.; Moya Woodside, 'Women Drinkers in Holloway Prison', *Brit. J. Crim.*, Vol. 1, No. 3, Jan. 1961, pp. 221-35; Ann D. Smith, *Women in Prison*, London, 1962, Chs. 1, 2.

[43] See *Social Aspects of Crime*, pp. 336-7.

[44] Barbara Wootton, *op. cit.*, pp. 31-2, 318.

[45] Freud, in *Totem and Taboo*, p. 21, quotes from Sir James Frazer an instance of the same presumption of coercion in a New South Wales tribe.

[46] On this and similar provisions in other foreign codes see H. H. Heldmann, *Mschr. Kriminol. Strafrechtsreform*, Vol. 40, Nos. 3-4, June 1957, pp. 86-104.

[47] See *Criminal Justice and Social Reconstruction*, p. 77.

[48] § 376 of the Draft Code.

[49] Pollak, *op. cit.*, Ch. 1: 'The Masked Character of Female Crime'.

[50] v. Hentig, *Zur Psychologie der Einzeldelikte*, Vol. 4: 'Die Erpressung', Tübingen, 1949, pp. 220 ff.

[51] *Social Aspects of Crime*, p. 344.

[52] Reckless in N.P.P.A. *Journal*, p. 1.

[53] *Criminal Statistics for 1961*, p. 32.

[54] See, e.g., *Social Aspects of Crime*, pp. 342-4; *Criminal Statistics for 1961*, pp. 40-1; Pollak, *op. cit.*, pp. 3-5.

[55] Ann D. Smith, *op. cit.*, pp. 188, 194; Moya Woodside, *op. cit.*, p. 235.

[56] B.M.A., London, 1946, p. 10.

[57] *Report of the Committee on Children and Young Persons*, H.M.S.O., London, Oct. 1960, Cmd., 1191, pp. 130-2.

[58] See, e.g., H. von Hentig, *Die Strafe*, Vol. 1, Berlin, 1954, pp. 122 ff.

[59] Ann D. Smith, *op. cit.*, p. 57.

[60] Radbruch-Gwinner, *Geschichte des Verbrechens*, Ch. 15, esp. p. 158; Wallace Notestein, *A History of Witchcraft in England 1558-1718*, Washington, 1911.

[61] Kurt Baschwitz, *Hexen und Hexenprozesse*, München, 1963.

[62] L. O. Pike, *A History of Crime in England*, London, 1873-6, Vol. 1, pp. 255-6.

[63] Radbruch-Gwinner, *op. cit.*, Ch. 9, esp. p. 94.

[64] On this and the following text see Radbruch-Gwinner, *op. cit.*, Ch. 22.

[65] See Frances Mossiker, *The Queen's Necklace*, London, 1961, and on this and the case of the Marquise de Brinvilliers Henri Robert, *Les grands procès d'histoire*, Paris, 1923-35.

[66] *War and Crime*, London, 1941, pp. 116-20.

[67] Jean Pinatel, *Criminologie*, p. 155.

[68] Reckless in N.P.P.A. *Journal*, p. 2.

[69] See above, Preliminary Observations to Part 3.

[70] Report of the Children's Department, Home Office, H.M.S.O., 1964,

[71] E.g., Pollak, *op. cit.*, pp. 123-5.

[72] E.g., Gibbens, *Brit. J. Delinq.*, Vol. 10, No. 2, Oct. 1959, pp. 81-103.

[73] Epps, *Brit. J. Delinq.*, Vol. 1, p. 150.

[74] T. C. N. Gibbens and Joyce Prince, *Shoplifting*, p. 66.

[75] Scipio Sighele, *La foule criminelle*, 2nd ed., Paris, 1901, pp. 97-8.

[76] C. Lombroso and G. Ferrero, *La donna delinquente, la prostituta e la donna normale*, Torino, 1893, Eng. ed. *The Female Offender*, London, 1895. On this work see Marvin E. Wolfgang in *Pioneers in Criminology*, pp. 190-2, 202.

[77] Against this view rightly S. and E. Glueck, *Five Hundred Delinquent Women*, New York, 1934, p. 307.

[78] Gibbens and Prince, *op. cit.*, p. 126.

[79] Alexandre Dumas, *op. cit.*

[80] Gunnar Myrdal, *An American Dilemma*, New York–London, 1944, pp. 237–62.

[81] Mary Stevenson Callcott (*op. cit.* at note 10), p. 62.

[82] See also Middendorff, *op. cit.*, p. 251, who gives the sex ratio for perjury in Germany as 1 : 3.

[83] See, e.g., F. H. Allport, *Institutional Behavior*, Ch. 18.

[84] Murphy–Murphy–Newcomb, *Experimental Social Psychology*, New York–London, p. 71.

[85] *The Young Delinquent*, pp. 299–300.

[86] *Ibid.*, Ch. 2, esp. Table 17 and pp. 491–2.

[87] Burt, *op. cit.*, pp. 470, 491; S. and E. Glueck, *Family Environment and Delinquency*, p. 207.

[88] Hugh Hartshorne and Mark A. May, *Studies in Deceit*, New York, 1930, Vol. 1, p. 177. On this study see also *Group Problems in Crime and Punishment*, p. 21.

[89] Pollak, *op. cit.*, pp. 9–12.

[90] W. and M. T. Healy, 'Pathological Lying, Accusation and Swindling', Crim. Sci. Monogr. No. 1 (Supplement to *J. Amer. Inst. crim. Law Criminol.*), London, 1915.

[91] Karl Mannheim, *Man and Society in an Age of Reconstruction*, London, 1940, p. 156.

[92] Johanna C. Hudig (*op. cit.* at note 42), p. 257.

[93] W. Norwood East, *The Adolescent Criminal*, London, 1942, p. 300.

[94] Willem A. Bonger, *Criminality and Economic Conditions*, Boston, 1916.

[95] For the following see Mabel A. Elliott and Francis E. Merrill, *Social Disorganization*, 4th ed., New York, 1961, Ch. 9.

[96] Richard M. Titmuss, *Essays on 'The Welfare State'*, London, 1958, p. 102.

[97] See *The Times*, 29.11, 8.12.1962, 22.1.1963 (Court of Criminal Appeal).

[98] Albert K. Cohen, *Delinquent Boys*, pp. 44, 137 ff. In a small but useful piece of research Ruth R. Morris, *Brit. J. Crim.*, Vol. 5, 1965, has undertaken to prove that the differential sex rate is due to the 'different sex role objectives for boys and girls . . . Society provides more cultural and sub-cultural support for male than female delinquency.' There is more tolerance for male than for female delinquency. It may be doubted whether this is generally true. One can often observe a greater reluctance on the part of representatives of society to charge girls before a juvenile court than there would be in the case of boys.

[99] A. Quetelet, *Recherches sur le penchant au crime*, 1838, p. 38; A. v. Oettingen, *Die Moralstatistik in ihrer Bedeutung für eine Sozialethik*, 3rd ed., Erlangen, 1882, p. 526, fn. 2. Also Gabriel Tarde, *Philosophie pénale*, 4th ed., 1895, p. 379, fn. 1.

[100] L. S. Penrose, *Brit. J. med. Psychol.* 1939, vol. 18, p. 9. A. F. Tredgold, *Mental Deficiency*, 9th ed., London, 1956, p. 18, reproduces material from the Report of the Committee of 1924, showing that at the time the proportion of mental defective males was 9·21 per 1,000 against 7·97 of females.

[101] London, H.M.S.O., 1957, Cmd. 169, p. 310.

[102] W. and M. T. Healy, 'Pathological Lying, Accusation and Swindling' (cited at note 90 above).

[103] D. K. Henderson, *Mental Abnormality and Crime*, English Studies in Crime Science, ed. by L. Radzinowicz and J. W. C. Turner, London, 1944, p. 116.

[104] *Op. cit.* at note 34 above.

[105] T. C. N. Gibbens and Joyce Prince, *op. cit.*, pp. 63–4.

[106] Edward Glover, *The Roots of Crime*, p. 261.

[107] *Annual Report of the Prison Commissioners for 1961*, pp. 144–5.

[108] *Preventive Detention: Report of Home Office Advisory Council on the Treatment of Offenders*, 1963, pp. 34–5.

Appendix

I. SOCIETIES

The Howard League for Penal Reform, 6 Endsleigh St., London, W.C.1.
The British Society of Criminology, c/o The I.S.T.D., 8 Bourdon St., Davies St., W.1.
The British Sociological Association, 13 Endsleigh St., W.C.1.
The National Association of Probation Officers, 6 Endsleigh St., W.C.1.
Union nationale des Associations pour la Sauvegarde de l'Enfance et de l'Adolescence, 28 Place St. Georges, Paris 9.
The International Society of Criminology, 28 Avenue de Friedland, Paris, VIIIe.
The International Society of Social Defence, c/o Count Filippo Gramatica, Genoa, Italy.
Deutsche Kriminologische Gesellschaft, c/o Kriminalistik, Hamburg 1, Schopenstehl 15, West Germany.
Deutsche Vereinigung für Jugendgerichte und Jugendgerichtshilfen, Hamburg 13, Moorweiden Str. 18.
Kriminalbiologische Gesellschaft, c/o Professor Thomas Würtenberger, University of Freiburg i. Br., Günterstal Str. 70, West Germany.
Svenska Kriminalistföreningen, Riddarhuskaien 1, 1 Stockholm St.
Association of Scandinavian Criminologists: Dr. Carl Holmberg, Secretary, The Northern Association of Criminalists, Justitie departementet, Stockholm 2.
Schweizer Kriminologische Gesellschaft, c/o Professor Erwin Frey, University of Zürich, Faculty of Law, Zürich, Switzerland.
Canadian Corrections Association, 55 Parkdale Avenue, Ottawa 3, Ontario.
National Council on Crime and Delinquency, 44 East 23 Street, New York, 10010.
American Society of Criminology, 115–17 West 42nd Street, New York 36, N.Y.
Japanese Association of Criminology, Tokyo Medical and Dental University, 3-Chome, Yushima, Bunkyo-Ku, Tokyo.

The International Penal and Penitentiary Commission (I.P.P.C.) was the body which organized the International Penal and Penitentiary Congresses held between 1872 and 1950 at intervals of five years (with the exception of the years 1915 and 1920). Their Proceedings were published in French as *Actes des Congrès Pénitentiaires Internationaux*. Brief but adequate English summaries of these Congresses, with the answers, are to

751

be found in Negley K. Teeters, *Deliberations of the International Penal and Penitentiary Congresses 1877 to 1935* (Temple University Book Store, Philadelphia, Pa., 1949). The I.P.P.C. also published from time to time a *Recueil de Documents en matière pénale et pénitentiare*, a series not only of penological, but also of criminological interest (see e.g. *The Effect of the War on Criminality* referred to in Chapter 23 above). After the 1950 Congress the work of the I.P.P.C. was taken over by the United Nations Department of Social Affairs which held the Congresses in 1955 (at the Hague) and in 1960 (in London) and is organizing the Third Congress for 1965 (Stockholm).

Some of the activities of the I.P.P.C. are at present carried on by the International Penal and Penitentiary Foundation.

The International Society of Criminology has so far held Congresses in Rome (1938), Paris (1950), London (1955) and at The Hague (1960) and is preparing its Fifth Congress for 1965 in Montreal. The Proceedings have been published by the national Organizing Committees. In addition, the Society has been responsible for annual international courses in criminology, held in different countries, the proceedings of which have in some cases also been published by the national Organizing Committees. The last three of these courses were held in Jerusalem (1962), Cairo (1963) and Lyons (1964). National and regional Congresses and courses in criminology have been held in several countries since the Second World War.

II. INSTITUTES

Britain

Institute of Criminology, Cambridge University, 7 West Road, Cambridge.

Institute for the Study and Treatment of Delinquency (I.S.T.D.), 8 Bourdon St., Davies St., London, W.1.

West Germany

Institut für Kriminologie und Strafvollzugskunde, Universität Freiburg i. Br., Günterstal Str. 70.

Institut für ausländisches und internationales Strafrecht, Universität Freiburg i. Br., Günterstal Str.

Kriminalwissenschaftliches Institut, Universität Köln, Köln.

Seminar für Strafrecht und Kriminalpolitik, Universität Hamburg, 2 Hamburg 13, Schlüter Str. 28.

Kriminalwissenschaftliches Institut, Freie Universität, West Berlin.

Moreover, Institutes of Criminology have recently been established at the Universities of Heidelberg, Munich and Tubingen.

Austria

Kriminologisches Institut, Universität Wien, Liebiggasse 5, Vienna.

Kriminalistisches Institut, Universität Graz.

Switzerland

Kriminologisches Institut, Universität Zürich.

Belgium

Centre d'Etude de la Delinquance juvenile, 49 rue du Chatelain, Brussels 5.

L'Ecole des Sciences criminologiques, Brussels, University.

L'Ecole de Criminologie, Louvain, University.

L'Ecole de Criminologie, Ghent, University.

L'Ecole de Criminologie, Liège, University.

France

Centre d'Etudes de Defense Sociale de L'Institut de Droit Comparé de l'Université de Paris.

Institut de Criminologie, Faculté de Droit, Université de Paris.

Institut Universitaire de Médicine Légale et de Criminologie Clinique de Lyon, 12 avenue Rockefeller, Lyon.

Institut des Sciences Criminelles et Pénitentiaires, Université de Strasbourg, Strasbourg.

U.S.S.R.

Federal Institute for the Study of the Causes of Crime and of the Means of Prevention, Moscow.

Italy

Centro Studi Penitenziari, Ministero di Grazia e Giustizia, Rome.

Scuola di diritto penale con Annesso, Istituto di Criminologia, University of Rome.

Instituto di osservazione, Roma-Rebibbia, via R. Majetti 162, Rome.

Instituto di Antropologia criminale, University of Rome.

Holland

Criminological Institute, University of Utrecht, Koningslaan 10, Utrecht.

Institute of Criminal Law and Criminology, University of Leiden, Rapenburg 38, Leiden.

Institute of Criminology, University of Groningen.

Poland

Institute of Criminology, University of Warsaw, Warsaw.

Canada

Institute of Criminology, University of Montreal, Montreal, P.O. 6128.

Centre of Criminology, University of Toronto, Toronto 5.

Israel

Institute of Criminology, Hebrew University of Jerusalem.

Institute of Criminology, Bar-Ilan University, Ramat-Gan, Tel-Aviv.

Norway

Institute of Criminology and Criminal Law, Oslo, Karl Johans Gt. 47.

APPENDIX

Sweden

Karolinska Institut of Forensic Psychiatry, Stockholm.
Kriminologiska Insitutet, Västmannagatan 27, Stockholm.

Denmark

Institute of Criminology, University of Copenhagen, Studiestraede 10, Copenhagen.

Finland

Institute of Criminology, University of Helsinki.
For all Scandinavian countries together there is the Scandinavian Research Council of Criminology.

U.S.A.

School of Criminology, University of California at Berkeley.
Center of Criminological Research, University of Pennsylvania, Philadelphia 4, Pa.
A Centre for Studies in Criminal Justice is being established at the University of Chicago Law School.
American Society of Criminology, 115–7 West 42nd St., New York 36.
Centro de Investigaciones Sociales, Universidad de Puerto Rico, Rio Piedras, P.R.

United Nations

United Nations Asia and Far East Institute for the Prevention of Crime and Treatment of Offenders (UNAFEI), 26–1 Harumicho, Fuchu, Tokyo, Japan.

Chile

Instituto de Ciencies Penales, Santiago, Chile.

Ecuador

Instituto de Criminologia, Quito.
(Other South American criminological Institutes are listed in Negley K. Teeters, *Penology from Panama to Cape Horn*, Univ. of Pennsylvania Press, Philadelphia, 1946.)
Information on Institutes of Criminology is also given in the UNESCO 'Report on The University Teaching of Social Sciences', *Criminology*, 1957, 19 Avenue Kleber, Paris 16, especially in the General Survey, pp. 19–21, and in the national reports. Some of this information is, however, already out of date.

III. JOURNALS

Great Britain

(a) Criminological Journals

The British Journal of Criminology, published under the auspices of the I.S.T.D., 8 Bourdon St., Davies St., London, W.1.
The Howard Journal, 6 Endsleigh St., London, W.C.1.

Probation, c/o National Association of Probation Officers, 6 Endsleigh St., London W.C.1.

Prison Service Journal, H.M. Prison Service Staff College, Love Lane, Wakefield.

(*b*) *Other Journals which publish material of criminological interest from time to time.*

The British Journal of Sociology, The London School of Economics, Houghton St., London, W.C.2.

The British Journal of Psychiatry (formerly *The Journal of Mental Science*), c/o R.M.P.A., 11 Chandos St., Cavendish Square, London, W.1.

The Sociological Review, University of Keele, Keele, Staffordshire.

The Criminal Law Review, Stevens & Sons, 11 New Fetter Lane, London, E.C.4.

The Modern Law Review, Stevens & Sons, 11 New Fetter Lane, London, E.C.4.

The Law Quarterly Journal, Stevens & Sons, 11 New Fetter Lane, London, E.C.4.

The Juridical Review, W. Green and Son, Ltd., St. Giles' St., Edinburgh 1.

The Justice of the Peace and Local Government, Little London, Chichester, Sussex.

The Magistrate, c/o The Magistrates' Association, Tavistock House South, Tavistock Square, London, W.C.1.

The Medico-legal Journal, published for the Medico-legal Society by W. Heffer, Cambridge.

Medicine, Science and the Law, Official Journal of the British Academy of Forensic Sciences, Sweet & Maxwell, 11 New Fetter Lane, London, E.C.4.

Case Conference, published by the Association of Social Workers, etc., 60 Denison House, 296 Vauxhall Bridge Rd., London, S.W.1.

Social Science Quarterly, published by the National Council of Social Service, 26 Bedford Square, London, W.C.1.

The Lancet, 7 Adam St., London, W.C.2.

British Medical Journal, Official Organ of the British Medical Association, B.M.A. House, Tavistock Square, London, W.C.1.

Human Relations, Tavistock Publications Ltd., 11 New Fetter Lane, London, E.C.4.

British Journal of Medical Psychology, Cambridge Univ. Press, Cambridge.

British Journal of Social and Clinical Psychology, published by the British Psychological Society, Tavistock House South, Tavistock Square, London, W.C.1.

Germany

(*a*) *Monatsschrift für Kriminologie und Strafrechtsreform,* 2 Hamburg 13, Schlüter Str. 28.

Zeitschrift für die gesamte Strafrechtswissenschaft, W. de Gruyter, 1 Berlin 30, Genthiner Str. 13.

Bewährungshilfe, 532 Bad Godesberg, Friedrich Ebert Str. 11.

Zeitschrift für Strafvollzug, c/o Prof. Albert Krebs, Wilhelm Str. 24, Wiesbaden.

(b) *Recht der Jugend,* 545 Neuwied, Heddersdorfer Str. 31.

Goltdammers Archiv für Strafrecht, 2 Hamburg 13, Heimhuder Str. 53.

Kölner Zeitschrift für Soziologie und Sozialpsychologie, Westdeutscher Verlag, Köln and Opladen, 567 Opladen, Ophovener Str. 1–3.

Juristenzeitung, Verlag J. C. B. Mohr (Paul Siebeck), 74 Tübingen, Wilhelm Str. 18.

France

(a) *Revue de Science criminelle et de Droit pénal comparé,* 31 Rue Saint-Guillaume, Paris VIIe.

(b) *Sauvegarde de l'Enfance,* U.N.A.R., 28 Place St. Georges, Paris, IXme.

Switzerland

(a) *Revue internationale de Criminologie et de Police technique,* Case Postale 129, Geneva 4. Chief Ed. Prof. Jean Graven, Geneva.

(b) *Schweizerische Zeitschrift für Strafrecht* (Revue Pénale Suisse), c/o Prof. H. Schultz, Thun, Pappelweg 11.

Belgium

(a) *Revue de Droit pénal et de Criminologie,* Ministère de la Justice, Palais de Justice, Brussels.

(b) *Revue de Sociologie,* Institut de Sociologie (Ernest Solvay), Université Libre de Bruxelles.

Holland

Tijdschrift voor Strafrecht, E. J. Brill, Leiden.

Scandinavian countries

Nordisk Tidskrift for Kriminalvidenskab, Dalsvinget 7, Hellerup, Copenhagen.

Italy

(a) *Quaderni di Criminologia clinica,* Ministero di Grazia e Giustizia, Via Arenula 71, Rome.

La Scuola Positiva, Dott. A. Giuffre Editore, Foro Buonaparte 24, Milan.

Rassegna di Studi Penitenziari, Ministero di Grazia e Giustizia, Via Arenula 71, Rome.

(b) *La Giustizia Penale,* Via Giovanni Nicotera 10, Rome.

Austria

Zeitschrift für Rechtsvergleichung, Institut für Rechtsvergleichung der Universität, Vienna.

APPENDIX

Several South American criminological journals are listed in Negley K. Teeters (see above under Institutes).

U.S.A.

(a) *The Journal of Criminal Law, Criminology, and Police Science,* published for Northwestern University School of Law, Chicago, by The Williams & Wilkins Co., 428 East Preston St., Baltimore 2, U.S.A.
The Journal of Research in Crime and Delinquency, National Council on Crime and Delinquency, 44 East 23 St., New York 10.
Crime and Delinquency, National Council on Crime and Delinquency, 44 East 23rd St., New York 10.
Federal Probation, Supreme Court Building, Washington, D.C. 20544.
American Journal of Correction, American Correctional Association. 2642 University Avenue, St. Paul, Minnesota.
Corrective Psychiatry, Medical Correctional Association, 927 Fifth Ave., New York 21.
The Prison Journal, published by the Pennsylvanian Prison Society, 311 South Juniper St., Philadelphia 7.
Archives of Criminal Psychodynamics, Station L, Washington 20, D.C.

(b) *Mental Hygiene,* Official Organ of the National Association for Mental Hygiene Inc., 10 Columbia Circle, New York 19.
American Journal of Orthopsychiatry, 1790 Broadway, New York 19.
American Journal of Sociology, Univ. of Chicago Press, 5750 Ellis Ave., Chicago 37.
American Sociological Review, 49 Sheridan Ave., Albany, N.Y.
Social Problems, Northeastern University, Boston, Mass.
American Journal of Psychotherapy, 15 West 81st St., New York 24.
Social Forces, Univ. of North Carolina Press, Chapel Hill, N. Carolina,
American Journal of Psychiatry, published by The American Psychiatric Association, 1500 Greenmount Ave., Baltimore 2.
The Pacific Sociological Review, Department of Sociology, University of Oregon, Eugene, Oregon.
The Social Service Review, Univ. of Chicago Press, 5750 Ellis Avenue, Chicago 37.
The Annals of The American Academy of Political and Social Science, 3937 Chestnut St., Philadelphia 4, Pa.
Law and Contemporary Problems, School of Law, Duke University, Durham, North Carolina.
Journal of Social Issues, published for the Society for the Psychological Study of Social Issues, Univ. of Michigan, Ann Arbor, Mich.

Japan

(a) *Acta Criminologiae et Medicinae Legalis Japonica,* published by the Japanese Association of Criminology, Department of Legal Medicine, Tokyo Medical and Dental University, 3-Chome, Yushima, Bunkyo-Ku, Tokyo.

Journal of Correctional Medicine, Japanese Correctional Association, Ministry of Justice, Tokyo.

(b) *Annals of the Hitotsubashi* Academy, Hitotsubashi University, Kunitachi, Tokyo.

Canada

The *Canadian Journal of Corrections* (La Revue Canadienne de Criminologie), Canadian Corrections Association, 55 Parkdale Ave., Ottawa 3, Ontario.

India

Journal of Correctional Work, Government Jail Training School, Lucknow, Uttar Pradesh, India.

International

(a) *International Review of Criminal Policy*, United Nations Publication, United Nations, Section Social Defence, New York.

Annales Internationales de Criminologie (International Annals of Criminology), published by the International Society of Criminology, 28 Avenue de Friedland, Paris VIIIe.

Excerpta Criminologica, published by the Excerpta Criminologica Foundation, 119–123 Herengracht, Amsterdam-C., Holland.

The *International Criminal Police Review* (Revue internationale de Police Criminelle), Interpol, 37 bis Rue Paul Valery, Paris XVIe.

Etudes Internationales de Psycho-Sociologie Criminelle, 56 Boulevard Raspeil, Paris VIe.

(b) The *International Journal of Social Psychiatry*, 7 Hollycroft Ave., London, N.W.3.

The *International Journal of Psycho-Analysis*, published for the Institute of Psycho-Analysis, Baillière, Tindall & Cox, 7–8 Henrietta St., London, W.C.2.

Revue internationale de Droit Pénal, Recueil Sirey, 22 rue Soufflot, Paris Ve.

Government and University Departments and other official or private bodies occasionally or regularly publishing the results of criminological research (excluding regular annual publications of criminal statistics, etc.)

Britain. Home Office Research Unit, Home Office, London, S.W.1: Studies in the Causes of Delinquency and the Treatment of Offenders (H.M.S.O.).

West Germany. Bundeskriminalamt Wiesbaden: Schriftenreihe des Bundeskriminalamtes, Wiesbaden, Tränkweg.

World Health Organization, Geneva: Public Health Papers (Cahiers de Santé publique), Geneva.

United Nations, Department of Social Affairs, New York.

Council of Europe, Department of Criminology, Strasbourg.

Ministry of Housing and Social Development, Northern Rhodesia, Lusaka: Social Welfare Research Monographs, The Government Printer, Lusaka.

University of Cambridge, Institute of Criminology: Cambridge Studies in Criminology, Macmillan & Son Ltd., St. Martin's St., London, W.C.2.

Institute for the Study and Treatment of Delinquency (I.S.T.D.), Bourdon St., London, W1.: International Library of Criminology, Tavistock Publications, 11 New Fetter Lane, E.C.4.

Research and Training Institute, Ministry of Justice, Tokyo.

NOTE: None of the above lists can claim to be exhaustive. Our object was merely to include the most important and/or most widely known bodies and periodicals in the fields of criminology and penology and those other disciplines which contribute to the study of crime and its treatment.

IV. BIBLIOGRAPHIES

1. *Exclusively Criminological*

D. C. Culver (later Tompkins), *Bibliography of Crime and Criminal Justice,* Wilson, New York, 1927–31, 1932–37, 1934–39.

D. C. Culver, *Administration of Criminal Justice 1949–56,* California State Board of Corrections, 1956.

Sir John Cumming, *A Contribution towards a Bibliography dealing with Crime and Cognate Subjects,* 3rd ed., London, 1935.

P. S. de Q. Cabot, *Juvenile Delinquency: A Critical Annotated Bibliography,* New York, 1946.

Thorsten Sellin and L. D. Savitz, 'A Bibliographic Manual for the Student of Criminology'. In: *International Bibliography on Crime and Delinquency* (National Council on Crime and Delinquency, NCCD, New York, 10010, 44 East 23 Street, see also below under 'Continuing Publications'), 1964, 1(3). Earlier ed. published separately by the University of Pennsylvania 1959.

D. C. Tompkins (formerly Culver), *The Offender: A Bibliography,* Institute of Governmental Studies, Berkeley, Calif., 1963.

D. C. Tompkins, *Probation since World War II: A Bibliography,* Berkeley, 1964.

Continuing Publications

International Bibliography on Crime and Delinquency, NCCD (see above).

International Review of Criminal Policy, published by United Nations, New York, in English, French, and Spanish: The bibliography, which had previously appeared in every other issue of this periodical, has since 1963 been presented 'separately from, and as a supplement to, the Review'.

International Annals of Criminology, the Bulletin of the International Society of Criminology, 28 Avenue de Friedland, Paris VIIIe, also published in French, English, and Spanish. It now contains in every issue a substantial bibliography on selected aspects of criminology.

Excerpta criminologica. An international abstracting service in the field of causation, prevention, treatment and control of offenders, criminal procedure and the administration of justice. Excerpta Criminologica Foundation, 119–123 Herengracht, Amsterdam-C., The Netherlands.

Bibliografia sui criminali anormali, published by Centro Nazionale di Prevenzione e Difesa Sociale, Sezione Criminologica, prepared by F. Ferracuti, M. Fontanesi, I. Melup, G. Minervini, Palazzo di Giustizia, Rome, 1965.

U.S. Children's Bureau: Juvenile Delinquency references, Washington, 1961.

Correctional Research, published irregularly by the United Prison Association of Massachusetts, 33 Mt. Vernon Street, Boston 8, Mass., contains bibliographies on specific subjects.

2. *Bibliographies dealing with Criminology and Other Disciplines*

P. R. Lewis, *The Literature of the Social Sciences*, Library Association, London, 1960.

Continuing Publications

Mental Health Book Review Index, sponsored by the World Federation for Mental Health and other bodies, published annually, with references to signed book reviews in the English language, located at the Research Center for Mental Health, New York University, New York 10003.

Current Sociology (La Sociologie contemporaine). An International Bibliography of Sociology, published by UNESCO, 19 Avenue Kleber, Paris XVIe, in English and French, prepared by the International Sociological Association with the support of the International Committee for Social Sciences Documentation.

Psychological Abstracts. Section 'Crime and Delinquency'. Published bimonthly by the American Psychological Association, 1233 Sixteenth Street, New York.

Sociological Abstracts. Section 'Crime and Delinquency'. Published by the International Sociological Association, Midwestern Sociological Society and the Eastern Sociological Society, 2315 Broadway, New York 24.

A London Bibliography of the Social Sciences, The London School of Economics and Political Science, ed. by the Director of the School, 11 vols., 1931–55.

(For assistance in the compilation of this list I am obliged to Professor Franco Ferracuti, Rome and Puerto Rico, lately of United Nations; to Mr. Hugh Klare of The Howard League for Penal Reform; and to the Librarian of the Cambridge University Institute of Criminology.)

V. TEXTBOOKS*

United States of America

(a) *General*

Edwin H. Sutherland and Donald R. Cressey, *Principles of Criminology*, 6th ed., Lippincott, Philadelphia, 1960.

Walter C. Reckless, *The Crime Problem*, 3rd ed., Appleton-Century-Crofts, New York, 1961.

Donald R. Taft, *Criminology*, 4th ed., Macmillan, New York, 1961.

Harry Elmer Barnes and Negley K. Teeters, *New Horizons in Criminology*, 3rd ed., Prentice-Hall, Englewood Cliffs, N.J., 1959.

Mabel A. Elliott, *Crime in Modern Society*, Harper, New York, 1952.

Robert G. Caldwell, *Criminology*, Ronald Press, New York, 1956.

Paul W. Tappan, *Crime, Justice and Correction*, McGraw-Hill, New York, 1960.

Herbert A. Bloch and Gilbert Geis, *Man, Crime and Society*, Random House, New York, 1962.

Richard Korn and Lloyd W. McCorkle, *Criminology and Penology*, Holt, Rinehart & Winston, New York, 1960.

George B. Vold, *Theoretical Criminology*, Oxford University Press, New York, 1958.

Hans von Hentig, *Crime: Causes and Conditions*, McGraw-Hill, New York, 1947.

Ruth S. Cavan, *Criminology*, 2nd ed., Crowell, New York, 1955.

Marshall B. Clinard, *Sociology of Deviant Behavior*, 2nd ed., Holt, Rinehart & Winston, New York, 1964 (dealing with crime only as one aspect of 'deviant' behaviour).

(b) *Especially on Juvenile Delinquency*

Negley K. Teeters and John Otto Reinemann, *The Challenge of Delinquency*, Prentice-Hall, New York, 1950.

Paul W. Tappan, *Juvenile Delinquency*, McGraw-Hill, New York, 1949.

Sheldon Glueck (ed.), *The Problem of Delinquency*, Houghton Mifflin, Boston, 1959.

Herbert A. Bloch and Frank T. Flynn, *Delinquency. The Juvenile Offender in America Today*, Random House, New York, 1956.

Sophia M. Robison, *Juvenile Delinquency. Its Nature and Control*, Holt, New York, 1960.

Martin H. Neumeyer, *Juvenile Delinquency in Modern Society*, 3rd ed., Van Nostrand, New York, 1961.

Harry M. Shulman, *Juvenile Delinquency in American Society*, Harper, New York, 1961.

---

* Only the most important textbooks have here been included. For some further data, especially on works written in Spanish, see Jean Pinatel, *Criminologie*, pp. 16–29. Also Leon Radzinowicz, *In Search of Criminology*, Harvard University Press, Cambridge, 1962, pp. 223–46.

Milton L. Barron, *The Juvenile in Delinquent Society*, Knopf, New York, 1959.

Clyde B. Vedder, *The Juvenile Offender*, Random House, New York, 1954.

W. C. Kvaraceus, *et al.*, *Delinquent Behavior*, National Educational Association, Washington, 1960.

Great Britain

Howard Jones, *Crime and the Penal System*, 1st. ed. 1956, 2nd ed. 1962, University Tutorial Press, London.

Nigel Walker, *Crime and Punishment in Britain*, Edinburgh University Press, 1965

Historical: Pioneers in Criminology, ed. by H. Mannheim, Stevens, London, 1960.

Austria

Ernst Seelig, *Lehrbuch der Kriminologie*, 1st ed., Jos. A. Kienreich, Graz, 1951. French trans., Presses Universitaires de France, Paris, 1956.

Belgium

Etienne de Greeff, *Introduction à la Criminologie*, Vanden Plas, Brussels, 1946.

Brazil

Leonidio Ribeiro, *Criminologia*, Sudamericana, Rio de Janeiro, 1957.

Denmark

Stephan Hurwitz, *Criminology*, Allen & Unwin, and G. E. C. Gad, Publishers, London and Copenhagen, 1952.

France

Robert Vouin et Jacques Léauté, *Droit Pénal et Criminologie*, Presses Universitaires de France, Paris, 1956.

Jean Pinatel, *Criminologie*, Librairie Dalloz, Paris, 1963.

German Federal Republic

Franz Exner, *Kriminalbiologie*. 1st ed., 1939, Hanseatische Verlagsanstalt, Hamburg. 3rd revised ed. *Kriminologie*, Springer, Berlin–Göttingen–Heidelberg, 1949.

Hans von Hentig, *Das Verbrechen*. Vol. I: *Der kriminelle Mensch im Kräftespiel von Zeit und Raum*, 1961. Vol. II: *Der Delinquent im Griff der Umweltkräfte*, 1962. Vol. III: *Anlage-Komponents im Getriebe des Delikts*, 1963. All 3 vols. Springer, Berlin.

Eduard Mezger, *Kriminologie*, Beck, Munich, 1951.

Armand Mergen, *Die Wissenschaft vom Verbrechen*. Kriminalistik, Hamburg, 1961. This book is not intended to be a 'textbook' in the technical sense.

Wilhelm Sauer, *Kriminologie als Reine und Angewandte Wissenschaft*, De Gruyter, Berlin, 1950.

Wolf Middendorff, *Soziologie des Verbrechens*, Eugen Diederichs, Düsseldorf–Köln, 1959. This is, as the title implies, limited to the Sociology of Crime.

Fritz Bauer, *Das Verbrechen und die Gesellschaft*, Reinhardt, Munich and Basel, 1957.
(On Juvenile Delinquency) Wolf Middendorff, *Jugendkriminologie*, Aloys Henn, Ratingen, 1956.

Holland

J. M. van Bemmelen, *Criminologie*. 4th ed., W. E. J. Tjeenk Willink, Zwolle, 1958.
W. A. Bonger, *An Introduction to Criminology*, transl. by Emil van Loo, Methuen, London, 1936. The same in Dutch: *Inleiding tot de Criminologie*, 3rd ed. by G. Th. Kempe, De Erven F. Boon, Haarlem, 1954.

India

S. Venugopala Rao, *Facets of Crime in India*, Allied Publishers, New Delhi and London, 1963.

Italy

Benigno di Tullio, *Principi di criminologia clinica e psichiatria forense*, 2nd ed., Istituto di Medicine Sociale, Rome, 1960.
Alfredo Niceforo, *Criminologia*, 6 vols., 1941–52.

Sweden

Olof Kinberg, *Basic Principles of Criminology*, Munksgaard, Copenhagen, and Heinemann, London, 1935.
Ivar Agge *et al.*, *Kriminologi*, Wahlstrom och Widstrand, Stockholm, 1955.

Soviet Russia

A. B. Sacharow, *Die Persönlichkeit des Täters und die Ursachen der Kriminalität in der UdSSR*, Staatsverlag der Deutschen Demokratischen Republik, 1962.

International Surveys of specific aspects of Criminology, in particular teaching and research

UNESCO, *The University Teaching of Social Sciences: Criminology*, Paris, 1957.
Leon Radzinowicz, *In Search of Criminology*, Harvard University Press, Cambridge, 1962.

VI. ENCYCLOPAEDIAS

Handwörterbuch der Kriminologie, 2 vols., Berlin und Leipzig, Walter de Gruyter, 1932–36. (2nd ed. in preparation.)
Encyclopedia of Criminology, ed. by Vernon C. Branham and Samuel B. Kutash, Philosophical Library, New York, 1949.
Elsevier's Dictionary of Criminal Science, ed. by J. A. Adler, 1960. In eight languages. Distributed by D. van Nostrand Company Ltd., London, for Elsevier Publishing Company, Amsterdam.

VII. READINGS

Marvin E. Wolfgang, Leonard Savitz, and Norman Johnston, *The Sociology of Crime and Delinquency*, John Wiley, London and New York, 1962.

Clyde B. Vedder, Samuel Koenig, and Robert E. Clark, *Criminology. A Book of Readings*, The Dryden Press, New York, 1953.

Index of Subjects

765

their role in crimino-sociological studies, 196-8

Resistance movements in war, 593

Responsibility; see Criminal responsibility

Retreatist type, 504, 518-20

Right and wrong test; see McNaghten Rules

Riots, special types of, 651-4

Roman law
and the law of nature, 43
and the law of insanity, 338

Rorschach test, 289, 292

Royal Commissions as potential agencies of criminological research, 80-4; see also Royal Commissions on specific subjects

Royal Commission on the Care and Control of the Feeble-minded, 1908, 270-1

Royal Commission on Capital Punishment, 1949-1953, 81, 340-2, 344

Royal Commission on the Law relating to Mental Illness and Mental Deficiency, 1954-7, 242-3, 269, 271, 274

Samples, their use in criminological research, 124-7, 377

Schizoid type, 238

Schizophrenia, 252-3
its relation to physical types, 237
legal position, 340

Schizothyme type, 238

School, Chapter 24, II; see also Education

Senile dementia, 244

Sentencing policy of magistrates' courts, 461

Sex factor in crime, Chapter 26, II; see also Female criminality, Sex offenders

Sex offenders
books written by, 160

hormone treatment of, 236
their feelings of guilt, 323

Sex ratio of crime, 596-7, 697-8; see also Female criminality

Shoplifting, 465, 700, 702
by foreigners, 543

Short-circuit crimes, 300-2

Short-term imprisonment, research on alternatives to, 82-3

Siblings; see Family

Sicily, poverty and crime in, 585-6; see also Mafia

Sin; see Religion

Social class; see Class

Social mobility, 449-53
and education, 450-2

Social problem families; see Family

Social Sciences, Committee of Inquiry into Research in the, 83

Society, our criminogenic, Chapters 19-21

Sociology, research in, 75, 77, 80
sociological methods in criminology, Chapter 10, II
sociology of crime, Part IV

Sociometric techniques in criminological research, 195

Soho, crime in, 555, 728

Somatotypes of Sheldon, 240-1

Soviet Russia
its anti-parasite laws, 497-8
age distribution of crime, 681
female criminality, 703

Specificity of character and conduct; see Generality

Spivs, 617

Statistical research in criminology, Chapters 5 and 6; see also Criminal statistics

Statistical correlations do not prove causal nexus, 10 ff., 124, 361

'Statistician-sociologists', 222

Statistics; see Criminal statistics, Statistical research in criminology, Statistical correlations

Statutes; see Criminal statutes, British and foreign, Foreign penal codes

List of Statutes and Bills cited

List of Cases cited

(in alphabetical order)

Index of Names

779

Lander, Bernard, 506–7, 711, 728–9
Lange, Johannes, 231–3, 252, 268, 301, 357, 393, 398, 401, 407
LaPiere, R. T., 714, 740
Laubscher, B. J. F., 413
Laune, Ferris F., 185, 388
Lavater, J. K., 212
Léauté, Jacques, 379
Le Bon, Gustave, 645–9, 714, 740
Lecky, W. E. H., 422
Ledig, Gerhard, 404
Lees, J. P., and Newson, L. J., 612, 737
Leferenz, H., 401
Lejins, Peter, 360–1
Lejour, G., and Racine, A., 400
Lenz, Adolf, 239, 407
Lenz, Edgar, 745
Leopold, Nathan, 160, 194, 354, 383, 389, 407
Leppmann, Friedrich, 395–6
Levi, Carlo, 586, 732
Levi, Leone, 535
Levin, Yale, 725
Levit, S. G., 393
Lewis, Sir Aubrey, 73, 89–90, 244, 252, 358, 371, 373, 399
Lewis, E. O., 402
Lewis, Norman, 744
Liepmann, Moritz, 595, 733
Lindesmith, Alfred R., 8, 167, 351, 357, 361, 365, 385, 399, 710, 725, 743, 745
Lindner, Robert M., 359, 407, 409
Lindzey, Gardner, 412
Lippmann, Werner O., 409
Little, Alan, 332, 412
Little, K. L., 727
Llewellyn, K. N., and Hoebel, E. Adamson, 366
Locke, John, 46, 62, 370
Lockwood, David, 363, 448
Lodge, T. S., 375–6
Lombroso, Cesare, 8, 79, 85, 156, 164, 203, 213–29, 236, 238, 245, 279–80, 283, 317–18, 391, 393, 403, 405, 575, 633, 700–2, 708, 731, 748

Lorand, Sandor, 409–10
Lundberg, George A., 355, 386–8
Lunden, Walter A., 369, 733
Lunt, Paul S., 376
Luther, Martin, 64
Lynch, G. W., 192, 583

MacCalman, D. R., 358, 400
Maclay, David T., 358, 400
McClelland, David C., 717
McClintock, F. H., 727, 744, 747
Mack, J. A., 739
McCord, William and Joan, 133, 210, 275, 353, 358, 378–9, 391, 400–1, 403, 612, 615, 713, 736
McCorkle, Lloyd, et al., 355, 386
McCormick, Thomas C., and Francis, Roy G., 380, 382–3
Macdonnell, Sir John, 375
McDougall, William, 303, 407–9, 644, 719, 740
McGrath, W. T., 729
McGregor, O. R., 372, 736, 738; and Rowntree, Griselda, 738–9
MacIntyre, A. C., 409–10
McIver, R. M., 9–10, 351, 361, 388
Mackay, G. W., 402
McKay, Henry, 711, 724; see also Shaw, Clifford R.
McKenzie, G., 411
McKinney, John C., 355, 387–8
McNiven, Angus, 357, 396–8
McRae, Donald G., 371
Mack, John A., 656, 728, 744
Maconochie, Alexander, 85
Madge, John, 354–5, 371, 377–8, 382, 386–7, 389, 395
Maine, Sir Henry, 35, 365
Maitland, J., 387
Malinowski, Bronislaw, 20, 352, 363, 366
Mannheim, Hermann, 12, 18–19, 25, 55, 61, 67, 86, 115, 132, 222, 335, 351, 353, 355–7, 359–67, 369, 371–82, 384–7, 389–95, 397, 401–4, 406, 408, 411–15, 470, 513, 683, 697–8, 709–13, 715, 717, 721–6, 731–3, 738–9, 748–9